The Diary of
Catherine Ann Devereux Edmondston

Catherine Ann Devereux Edmondston (1823–1875)

"Journal of a Secesh Lady"

The Diary of
Catherine Ann Devereux Edmondston
1860-1866

Edited by
Beth G. Crabtree and James W. Patton

Raleigh
Division of Archives and History
Department of Cultural Resources
1979

Third Printing
1995

CONTENTS

LIST OF ILLUSTRATIONS

FOREWORD TO 1995 PRINTING

In 1979 the Division of Archives and History published one thousand copies of *"Journal of a Secesh Lady": The Diary of Catherine Ann Devereux Edmondston, 1860–1866*. It immediately went out of print. A second printing of one thousand copies kept the diary in print for more than another decade. It finally went out of print again in 1991.

This third printing of the diary comes at a time when interest in women's history has never been higher. During the past two decades the study of race, class, and gender has revolutionized historians' understanding of the past. Numerous women's diaries have been published, but none has surpassed *"Journal of a Secesh Lady"* in capturing the mood and day-to-day drama of the southern home front during the Civil War. C. Vann Woodward's revelation in *Mary Chesnut's Civil War* (New Haven: Yale University Press, 1981) that Chesnut wrote most of her acclaimed journal during the 1880s underscores the significance of the Edmondston diary as a primary source. It remains a document of endless fascination and insight as readers witness the demise of the southern aristocracy through the eyes of a sharp-tongued, opinionated, and astute planter woman.

Reprinting *"Journal of a Secesh Lady"* also permits Kate Edmondston's likeness to appear for the first time in her diary. In the 1979 printings a four-color picture of Hascosea, the Edmondstons' summer home, appeared on the dust jacket and as the frontispiece. In 1993 John Sykes, a researcher in the Division of Archives and History's Historic Sites Section, brought to the attention of the State Archives the existence of a photograph album held by the Mordecai House in Raleigh. Sykes and Stephen E. Massengill, iconographic archivist, inspected the album and obtained permission to make copies of twenty-two images, including a carte de visite labeled "Kate Devereux." Rudolph Turk donated the album to the Mordecai House in 1977. It is believed that the album belonged to Ellen Mordecai, who was the sister of Margaret Mordecai, who married John Devereux Jr., Kate Edmondston's brother. In her diary Kate spoke warmly of her brother's family (see the entry for July 25, 1860). A Richmond, Virginia, photographer named Anderson made the photograph. Based on the image's placement in the album and the dates of other photographs, the picture of Kate Edmondston probably was made in the late 1860s.

Students of the Civil War, women's history, and North Carolina history will welcome once again the availability of the Edmondston diary.

Jeffrey J. Crow

Historical Publications Administrator

March 1995

FOREWORD

The diary of Catherine Ann Devereux (Mrs. Patrick Muir) Edmondston was placed on loan with the North Carolina Historical Commission on May 1, 1921. Subsequently, on July 1, 1959, all rights to the journal, including rights of publication, were sold to the commission's successor agency, the State Department of Archives and History, by Margaret Mackay (Mrs. George Lyle) Jones of Alamance County. In the meantime, Mrs. Jones had published excerpts from the journal in a privately printed, limited edition of 500 copies.

The original four-volume journal is now preserved in the North Carolina State Archives. Plans for publication of an edited edition of the complete diary were considered years ago. Miss Beth Crabtree, longtime member of the Archives and History staff, transcribed the diary and did a tremendous amount of research and preliminary editing. She was later joined in her endeavor by the late James W. Patton, for many years director of the Southern Historical Collection at the University of North Carolina at Chapel Hill. After his death on May 17, 1973, Miss Crabtree continued working on the diary as time permitted. Though she retired at the end of 1975, she maintained her interest in the diary and was most helpful during the months others spent doing last checks and carrying through with final preparation of the diary for the press. She was particularly cooperative in working with the staff in getting illustrations for the diary, and she proofread and indexed the volume.

Many delays prevented earlier publication of the diary, among them lack of funds for printing and a saturation of the market with Civil War materials during the centennial observance of the war. At long last, however, a special bill introduced by Rep. J. Guy Revelle, Sr., of Northampton County, provided $5,000 to help pay the costs of typesetting. This money, coupled with funds from the regular budget of the Historical Publications Section, made possible the publication of this book.

Members of the staff of the Historical Publications Section assisted in many ways in the production of this book. Though Miss Crabtree had done a great deal of work on the appendix of military leaders, Dr. Jeffrey J. Crow, head of the section's General Publications Branch, completed the job; and he and Miss Marie Moore helped check footnotes. Particular recognition and thanks should go to Terrell L. Armistead, who reviewed the manuscript before it went to the printer, verified footnotes, and proofread the volume in galley and page proof. Her predecessors in the position of proofreader, Robert G. Anthony, Jr., and Nancy Pentecost, began the work completed by Ms. Armistead. Mrs. Henri T. Dawkins, Mrs. Rose P. Ennemoser, and Mrs. Cora B. Sherron contributed their typing skills. In the last weeks the book was in preparation, members of the Historical Publications staff mentioned above were aided by Mrs. Ruth C. Langston, Mrs. Mary Reynolds Peacock, Ms. Jo

Ann Williford, Mr. Robert M. Topkins, and Mrs. Elizabeth Morgan in completing the index and in final checking. J. Arthur Parker Edwards's photographs of Conneconara, taken years ago, were used. JoAnn Sieberg-Baker photographed several portraits reproduced in this volume, and she and her colleagues in the Division of Archives and History processed pictures. Appreciation is hereby expressed to each of these individuals for the work they did on Mrs. Edmondston's diary.

Without the assistance of Mrs. Graham A. Barden, Jr., of New Bern, members of the Devereux, Clarke, Pollock, and related families would not have been properly identified. Mrs. Barden, a great-granddaughter of Mary Bayard Clarke, was most generous in making available information from family records in her possession, in reading and helping prepare introductory biographical sketches, in verifying genealogical information, and in reviewing footnotes. It was she who wrote the epilogue, which gives an account of the family after the period covered by the diary.

Other Devereux descendants were helpful in supplying photographs and information. Their names are noted in cutlines, but mention should be made here of Mrs. S. H. Millender of Mebane, Mrs. J. D. Eudy of Kinston, and William and Devereux Joslin of Raleigh. Mrs. Julian D. Bobbitt of Rocky Mount supplied information on the Skinner family. Misses Eleanor and Elizabeth Simons of Charleston, South Carolina, great-granddaughters of Henry Edmondston, the youngest of Charles Edmondston's children, contributed pictures from the Edmondston family.

The generosity of Dr. Claiborne T. Smith of Philadelphia made possible the use of a frontispiece and jacket picture of Hascosea in color. Dr. Smith's grant also provided funds for the use of more photographs throughout the book than would otherwise have been possible. Dr. Smith, who is now part owner of the Looking Glass property, supplied information which was invaluable in writing cutlines.

Memory F. Mitchell

Historical Publications Administrator

July 1, 1978

EDITORIAL PROCEDURE

In editing the diary of Catherine Ann Devereux Edmondston, several decisions with regard to editorial methods and procedures had to be made. Mrs. Edmondston's handwriting, though clear, is interspersed with dashes, and punctuation and spelling are not always either consistent or accurate. Her use of capital letters, style of giving dates, and use of quotation marks is also inconsistent.

The editors made certain decisions to assure consistency of style and form but made only minimum changes so as to preserve the flavor of Mrs. Edmondston's words. The following rules were established:

Some words incorrectly capitalized were transcribed in the lower case.

Commas were added as needed for clarity. Some exclamations were replaced with periods or commas; others were omitted; a few were retained.

In most cases dashes were replaced with commas or semicolons or were omitted. Question marks were substituted for dashes when required by the context.

For consistency, dates were put in the same form throughout; i.e., June 1, 1860, rather than Friday, June 1st 1860, or 1st June, 1860, or simply 1st as was done in the diary itself.

The use of the word "and" and the use of ampersands were preserved as in the original manuscript.

Misspellings were retained; confusion was common in spelling words containing the letters "e" and "i" in conjunction one with the other.

Misspelled proper names were correctly spelled in brackets when there was doubt as to the name intended by Mrs. Edmondston. In all cases, however, the original spelling was retained.

The surname of Catherine Edmondston's forebears was spelled both Pollock and Pollok, and the name of the same individual can be found spelled each way. Earliest extant records use the "c" in the name, but in the nineteenth century several members of the family began spelling the name Pollok. It is thought that this spelling stemmed from a theory that the use of Pollok instead of Pollock was the purist Scottish form, and the use of this spelling became quite prevalent in the 1800s. There is evidence that Mrs. Edmondston's father spelled his name without the "c," but his signature on innumerable deeds, letters, and in his will is simply Thomas P. Devereux or T. P. Devereux. For purposes of clarity and consistency, the name has been spelled Pollock.

It should also be realized that John Devereux, Jr., was the grandson, not the son, of John Devereux, Sr. The former, a brother of Mrs. Edmondston, was the son of Thomas P. Devereux. The use of "Jr." to differentiate two individuals with the same name was also used by Thomas P. Devereux, Jr., the son of John Devereux, Jr.; he was named for his grandfather, Thomas P. Devereux.

To prevent long, unbroken passages, the narrative was broken into paragraphs; the original diary contains few divisions.

Every effort was made to identify individuals mentioned in the text, but it was impossible to locate information on a number of obscure persons. Slaves were not footnoted unless additional information about them was available. Military people were footnoted only when they were introduced in the journal for some reason other than their military service; prominent military people were briefly identified in an appendix.

Explanation of events, correction of misinformation concerning battles and other Civil War happenings, and correction of incorrect or incomplete first impressions were not generally included in footnotes. Inclusion of material of this sort would have almost resulted in a Civil War history in the footnotes.

The source of quotations and the translation of foreign phrases were given insofar as possible. Where there were quotations from the Bible, reference was made to the King James version.

Many footnotes were researched prior to the death of James W. Patton. In reviewing the manuscript for the press, it was impossible to locate the source for some of the information given by Dr. Patton; though every effort was made to document all footnote material, success was not realized in all cases.

Work was under way on the second printing when a letter came from Elizabeth D. Rivers (Mrs. C. Ford Rivers, Jr.) of Charleston, South Carolina, dated August 1, 1979. At the request of her cousin, Eleanor Simons, she forwarded a number of corrections in the Edmondston genealogy, based on family records. Henry Edmondston was the grandfather, not great-grandfather as stated on page viii, of Eleanor B. and her sister, the late Elizabeth D. Simons.

Though it was too late to incorporate the genealogical changes in the second printing, persons interested in the Edmondston family may obtain a copy of Mrs. Rivers's information by writing to the Historical Publications Section, Division of Archives and History, 109 East Jones Street, Raleigh, N.C. 27611. Corrections will be made if and when there are future printings.

INTRODUCTION

The diary of Catherine Ann Devereux Edmondston is full of references to individuals, many of whom were members of the Devereux and Edmondston families. Though identifications are given in footnotes, the relationships can be clearly understood by a review of genealogical charts and by brief histories of various branches of the family groups. The following short family histories give information about individuals, providing insight into their relationships. Genealogical facts are also included.

There are two brief sketches, entitled "Plantations" and "Roanoke River and Halifax County." These serve to acquaint the reader with the territory so familiar to Mrs. Edmondston and to make her environment known to those who read her journal.

Patrick Muir and Catherine Ann Devereux Edmondston

Reading her diary reveals far more of Catherine Ann Devereux Edmondston than any other record available. Comments in family letters provide a glimpse of her, but in her journal she becomes a definite and interesting personality. The diary not only brings her to life, but also animates the people with whom she was associated, as well as those whom she read about or discussed. It reveals a wide background of knowledge and indicates that she shared in the extensive private education attributed by biographers to her sister, Mary Bayard Clarke. It also reveals deep-seated prejudices, at times in sharp contrast to those held by other members of her family, which probably reflected some of her husband's sentiments. But at all times it reveals an individual capable of forming her own opinions, quick to express herself, interested in domestic life, but even more absorbed by events related to the war.

Catherine Ann Devereux was born October 10, 1823. On February 19, 1846, she married Patrick Muir Edmondston of Charleston, South Carolina, at Conneconara, "the seat of Thomas P. Devereux." The Reverend Dr. Richard Sharpe Mason, rector of Christ Church in Raleigh, performed the ceremony. Notations relative to Charles Edmondston of Charleston in the entries and accounts of Devereux, Chester, and Orme, merchants in New Bern, indicate that the Devereuxs and Edmondstons were acquainted in 1819 and possibly before that date.

Patrick Edmondston, a younger son of Charles and Mary Pratt Edmondston, was born August 1, 1819. He briefly attended the South Carolina College and entered West Point in 1837, but he did not graduate. At some time before permanently moving to North Carolina, the Patrick Edmondstons lived in Charleston. Thomas Pollock Devereux, Catherine's father, later rented one of his plantations to them but financial reverses forced them to seek other arrangements. Devereux then offered them Looking Glass, which adjoined Conneconara, plus a smaller plantation the Edmondstons called Hascosea. These two plantations comprised the final execution of a $10,000 marriage settlement Devereux had promised the Edmondstons but had only partially paid. The 1850 census listed the Edmondstons as residents of Halifax County with a 1,200 acre estate; the 1860 census recorded 1,894 acres valued at $19,600, plus eighty-eight slaves.

Edmondston was active in county affairs before and after the war. The Scotland Neck Mounted Riflemen, which he was instrumental in organizing, was one of the first North Carolina cavalry troops to volunteer its services to the governor at the start of the war. Edmondston served as a county justice of the peace, and he was also active in the Home Guard and in construction of defenses on the Roanoke River. After the war, in 1869, he was a vice-president and member of the executive committee of the Scotland Neck Agricultural Society. He died August 19, 1871.

Mrs. Edmondston died in Raleigh on January 3, 1875, in her fifty-first year, at the home of her sister Mrs. Henry W. Miller. The Edmondstons were buried in the cemetery at Trinity Church in Scotland Neck.

Catherine Edmondston's will, dated October 11, 1874, and two codicils dated December 14 and 17, 1874, appointed John Devereux as executor. With the exception of certain bequests he inherited the whole of her estate. She bequeathed to her niece Rachel Jones the annual interest on $4,000, and she also provided for two former slaves, Owen and Dolly Richardson. They were granted during their natural lives one acre of land, a house, and an annual allotment of 200 pounds of pork, five barrels of corn, and $10.00 each.

The first codicil to the will changed the Rachel Jones bequest to a single gift of $4,000 and also provided $1,000 each for three of her sisters, Frances Miller, Elizabeth Jones, and Nora Cannon. The second codicil revised her bequest to John Devereux so that her real estate would in no way be liable for any of his debts. To avoid this she granted all her land and other real estate to his son, Thomas Pollock Devereux, in trust for his mother during the life of his father, and to him and his heirs in fee simple after that time. The monetary legacies Catherine Edmondston bequeathed to her family, totaling $7,000, exceeded the value of her personal estate. The matter was taken to the North Carolina Supreme Court, which determined that the proceeds from her real estate should be used to complete payment of those legacies.

The Edmondston Family

The earliest record of an Edmondston in the Shetland Islands, "Andrew Edmestowne, Minister of Yell (1599)," appeared in a copy of a deed in the clerk's office of the Antiquarian Department of the Register House, Edinburgh. A Protestant clergyman, Edmestowne acquired property in Yell and Hascossay during the reign of the Scottish Queen Mary.

Edmestowne's descendants included three grandsons: John, skilled in medicine and botany; Jasper, who apparently immigrated to Holland; and Lawrence of Hascossay, who married the daughter of Sir Andrew Mitchell of West Shore. This marriage produced three sons—Charles, William, and Arthur. Arthur's son married Mary Sanderson of Buness and they had four sons, Arthur, Henry, Charles, and Thomas, and three daughters, Ursula, Jessie, and Mary. Arthur and Henry became doctors; Charles became a merchant in Charleston, South Carolina; and Thomas became a well-known naturalist who served as a professor of botany at the University of Glasgow when he was only twenty years old. As naturalist on the expedition of H.M.S. *Herald*, Thomas was commissioned to investigate and collect specimens "at the express desire of the Prince (consort)" and orders were sent to the governor of the Falklands and various British consuls to cooperate with him. Prince Albert also presented him with a pair of binoculars. Thomas wrote the *Flora of Shetland* which was published in 1845. In 1868 his life and letters were edited by his mother and published under the title *The Young Shetlander or Shadow Over the Sunshine*.

Charles and Mary Pratt Edmondston

Charles Edmondston, born June 20, 1782, in Lerwick, Shetland Islands, immigrated to Charleston, South Carolina, and became a merchant there in the early 1800s. He married Elizabeth Church of Wilmington and following her death married Mary Pratt, daughter of Capt. John Pratt of Chestertown, Massachusetts.

Edmondston developed an extensive business as a factory and wharf owner. Charleston directories from 1809 to 1841 list his various businesses and residences on Church, Meeting, Laurens, Eastbay, and Legare streets, and on the Battery.

He entered into many other business and civic activities. In 1819 he was listed as a director of the Bank of South Carolina, a position he apparently held until 1831. He was one of the "assistants to the Com. and Trustees of Shirras' Dispensary Ward No. 1." He was the fifth president of the Charleston Chamber of Commerce, and in 1828 was a member of a special committee of ten appointed from the chamber to consider and report on the building of a railroad to Augusta, Georgia. The proposition was reported favorably and adopted, a charter was secured, and the first railroad was subsequently organized in March of the same year. Edmondston appears in 1829 as a "commissioner of appeals."

Mary Pratt (Mrs. Charles) and Charles Edmondston were the parents of Patrick Muir Edmondston, who married Catherine Ann Devereux. The Charles Edmondstons lived in Charleston and Aiken, South Carolina. (Photographs from files of Beth Crabtree.)

Other offices Edmondston held were in the Charleston Port Society and Saint Andrew's Society. The Charleston Port Society for Promoting the Gospel Among Seamen had as its aim the protection of sailors on shore. Annual collections were taken in the city churches and the most efficient and prominent members were designated trustees of the Mariner's Church. Charles Edmondston represented St. Peter's Church and was president of the Port Society in 1851.

The Saint Andrew's Society of the City of Charleston was founded in 1729 and incorporated in 1798 for the purpose of cultivating and maintaining a "good understanding, and acquaintance with one another . . ." and "any man of honor and integrity, of what nation, degree or profession soever" was eligible for membership in the society. Before the Revolution it planned to sponsor an institution for clothing and educating poor and orphaned children, but the war caused a suspension of the society and prevented execution of the plan. With the conclusion of hostilities the society established a school for the education of children of indigent parents which continued in successful operation until the state began to support free schools. Charles Edmondston's name was included in the list of members for 1809, and it appeared on membership lists for the next fifty-two years.

The Edmondstons moved to Aiken, South Carolina, before the Civil War and Charles died there, June 15, 1861, in his seventy-eighth year. The notice of his death in the *Charleston Mercury* stated he had been a prominent merchant in the city and was "one of those of whom our community has a right to be proud . . . his unchangeable probity as a merchant, made him an exemplar, among his brethren. . . ." The Charleston Port Society passed a resolution eulogizing Edmondston as an "honest, upright and intelligent merchant, a warm friend, a useful citizen and sincere Christian. . . ."

By his will, dated April 17, 1850, Edmondston provided that any property which he possessed, real or personal, was left to his wife Mary Pratt, and she was appointed executrix. The will was probated July 25, 1861, and Mary Edmondston, widow, qualified as executrix. Mrs. Edmondston died at the age of eighty-three at the home of her son, Patrick Edmondston, on April 18, 1872.

Thomas and Martha Cullen West Pollock

Thomas Pollock, born in Glasgow, Scotland, in May, 1654, immigrated to the Carolina colony in 1683. Pollock practiced law and was active in the government of the colony as a member of the governor's council and as deputy and agent to Lords Proprietors Carteret and Beaufort. He was elected governor pro tem on the death of Gov. Edward Hyde in 1712 and remained in office about two years. For some thirty years he held both civil and military positions. As major general of colonial forces he was active in suppressing dissident colonists and in ending the Indian war which had disturbed the colony for a number of years.

Pollock married twice. By his first marriage to Martha Cullen West, daughter of Thomas Cullen of Dover and widow of Robert West, two sets of twins were born who died in infancy. One daughter, Martha, and three sons, Thomas, Cullen, and George, reached maturity. He married his second wife, Esther Wilkinson, the widow of Col. William Wilkinson, fairly late in life and they had no children.

He was a member of the first vestry of St. Paul's Parish in Edenton (Queen's Creek) in 1701 contributed money towards a new church building completed in 1705. Successor to Gov. Charles Eden, who died in 1722, Thomas Pollock was the first governor to serve a second time. His term was brief, however, as he died a few months after election to office.

From the time of his arrival in 1683 until his death in 1722, he accumulated large tracts of land on the Chowan, Roanoke, Neuse, and Trent rivers, and lots in the towns of Bath and New Bern. Pollock's residences included his Balgra plantation near Queen Anne's Creek and a plantation on Salmon Creek. He was buried at Balgra but was later moved to St. Paul's Church in Edenton.

Edmondston Genealogy

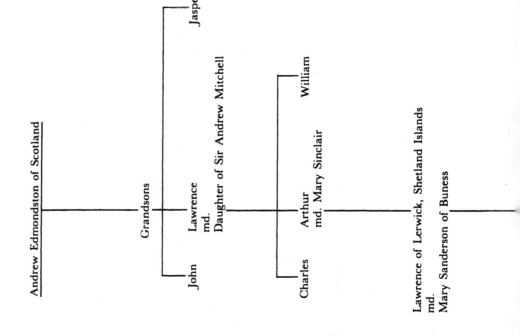

Andrew Edmondston of Scotland

Grandsons

John

Lawrence
md.
Daughter of Sir Andrew Mitchell

Jasper

Charles

Arthur
md. Mary Sinclair

William

Lawrence of Lerwick, Shetland Islands
md.
Mary Sanderson of Buness

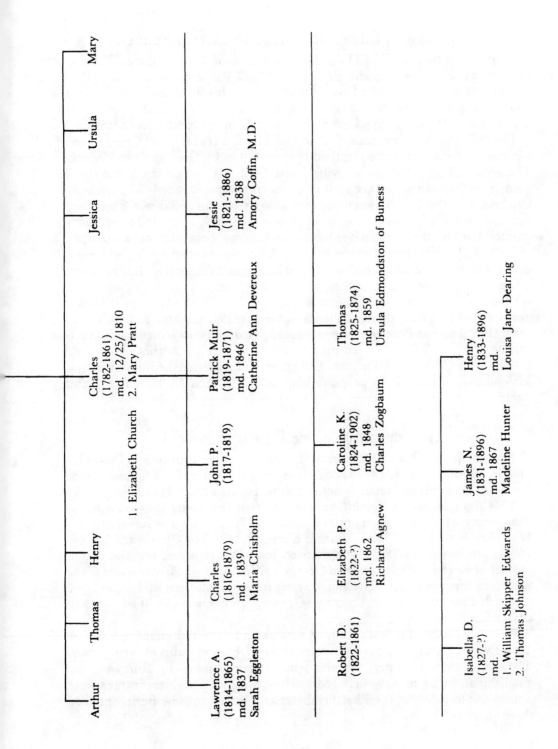

Thomas and Elizabeth Sanderson Crisp Pollock

Thomas Pollock (1695-1733), the eldest son of Gov. Thomas Pollock, married Elizabeth Sanderson, daughter of Col. Richard Sanderson of Pasquotank at whose home the first assembly met. This Thomas Pollock was a colonel in the colonial forces, surveyor general, and chief justice of North Carolina in 1724. Catherine Devereux Edmondston descended from this line.

The Pollocks had three sons, Cullen and Thomas (twins), and George, who inherited the vast estate bequeathed to their father by Gov. Thomas Pollock. The second Thomas Pollock's will, dated 1732, left Cullen the Black Rock plantation after his mother's death, the plantation called Manuel's or Crickets, and the land between the easternmost swamp of Salmon Creek and the Chowan River, amounting to approximately 8,900 acres. Thomas was granted land on the Trent River in Craven County, consisting of two patents of 8,500 and 1,500 acres. George received 2,560 acres called Springfield, land at "Unaroye" (Runiroi) Meadows, two tracts near "Tuskarora" Indian town, 300 acres on the southside of the "Moratock" (Roanoke) River, another 235 acres on the Moratock, and four tracts on Fishing Creek. Thomas Pollock's executors were his brothers, Cullen and George Pollock, and Robert West.

Of Gov. Thomas Pollock's three sons, only George Pollock died without offspring. His will (1736) divided his property between his brother Cullen and his nephews Cullen and Thomas. Cullen and Thomas reached maturity and left children to inherit the property bequeathed to them by their father and uncle.

Thomas and Eunice Edwards Pollock

The third generation of Thomas Pollocks in North Carolina (1731-1777) married Eunice Edwards (1743-1822), seventh daughter of the famous divine Jonathan Edwards of Massachusetts. Following their marriage in New Jersey in 1764, they settled in North Carolina; but two years later they returned to New Jersey where they lived until his death in 1777, during the Revolutionary War. The Pollocks had four children: Elizabeth (1765-1800); Thomas (1769-1803); Frances (1771-1849) who married John Devereux and was the grandmother of Kate Edmondston; and George (1772-1836) who became one of the wealthiest men in North Carolina, owning many plantations and some 1,500 slaves before his death. Thomas, George, and Elizabeth died without descendants.

After her husband's death, Eunice Pollock and her children moved to New Bern, North Carolina, where she later married Robert Hunt of New Jersey. They had one daughter, Sarah, who married John F. Burgwyn, an Englishman living in New Bern. Mrs. Hunt and her daughter Frances were among the founders of the First Presbyterian Church in New Bern. She died there in 1822.

The Devereux and Pollock coats of arms. The name Pollock was spelled Pollok by many members of the family. (Photographs courtesy of Mrs. Graham A. Barden, Jr., of New Bern, a descendant of Mary Bayard Clarke, sister of Mrs. Edmondston.)

Thomas Pollock's will gave instructions for an equal division of all slaves, stock, and personal estate in North Carolina. To his wife he bequeathed his dwelling house, lands, and other property in Elizabethtown, New Jersey, and an annual income of 500 Spanish milled pieces of eight. Daughters Elizabeth and Frances were granted, after their mother's death, the property in Elizabethtown and 7,500 Spanish milled pieces of eight when they married or reached the age of twenty-one.

John and Frances Pollock Devereux, Sr.

The Devereux family, according to family sources, originated in Evereux, Normandy, from which they got their name. They immigrated to England after the Norman invasion, and a branch of the family eventually settled in County Wexford in southern Ireland. John Devereux, a descendant of this family, was born in Ireland in 1761. As a younger son destined for the priesthood, John was sent to be educated at the monastery in St. Omer's,

John Devereux, Sr., 1761-1844, was born in Ireland. His wife, Frances Pollock Devereux, right, was born in 1771. They were the grandparents of Mrs. Edmondston. The portraits are now owned by Devereux Joslin of Raleigh. (Photographed from portraits courtesy of Mr. Joslin.)

France. Nearing the completion of his education, he decided that he could not take his vows as a priest. With a companion he left the monastery and sailed for England. One family tradition maintains that they were captured by a British man-of-war and were pressed into service to fight against the rebelling American colonies. According to another descendant Devereux's commission in the navy was purchased by his family. In any event, Devereux entered the British navy as a midshipman and served as a captain's clerk. By the end of the war he had earned the rank of first lieutenant.

Following the war Devereux returned to Ireland but was rejected by his family because he had turned his back on the priesthood. He never again visited Ireland and in later years would not allow his children to do so, saying they would not be welcomed. Devereux rejoined the British navy but on one voyage reportedly quarreled with his superior officer after being insulted by him. Upon reaching British soil Devereux resigned his commission and challenged the officer to a duel. His opponent refused to fight and Devereux found himself without money, job, or friends. Devereux later made his way to America and entered the mercantile business of a Mr. Fitzsimmons in Charleston, South Carolina. They soon had a successful trade with northern cities and the West Indies, and Devereux put his navigational skill to use as captain of one of his trading vessels. On a voyage to the West Indies he was shipwrecked off the coast of North Carolina. He went to New Bern, intending to go on to New York as soon as his financial affairs were settled. While waiting he met Frances Pollock, a wealthy heiress whom a descendant described as inheriting "great beauty from her mother, and so large a share of her father's wealth that she was nicknamed 'The Spanish Galleon.'" Devereux sold his business in Charleston and returned to New Bern to marry her in 1790. He remained in the mercantile business but did not again go to sea.

John Devereux was a refined and cultivated gentleman and was considered a financial wizard in business circles. He managed his wife's fortune to good advantage while amassing a sizable estate of his own. Mrs. Devereux was recognized as a woman of remarkable intellect, well known in the Presbyterian church for her piety and liberality in giving. The Devereuxs had three children, Thomas P., George P., and Frances Ann Devereux.

The Devereuxs moved to Raleigh in the 1820s and lived in a house "situate near and adjoining the city of Raleigh in the north . . . containing by estimation 2 acres." An interest in education, so apparent in the Devereux descendants, is found in a deed conveying John Devereux's law library and other volumes to his son Thomas, and in his promotion of the University of North Carolina at Chapel Hill through a subscription to the South Building fund. Devereux died at his Raleigh residence in July, 1844, and was buried in City Cemetery. A local newspaper observed that he was one of the oldest citizens of the state. Frances Pollock Devereux died on June 3, 1849, and was buried beside her husband.

Thomas Pollock and Catherine Ann Johnson Devereux

Thomas Pollock Devereux, born in New Bern, November 17, 1793, was graduated from Yale in 1813 and received an honorary M.A. degree from the University of North Carolina at Chapel Hill in 1818. Devereux continued his connection with the university as a trustee from 1820 until 1827, as a member of the land committee in 1825, and as an attorney for the institution in 1832. Well known and respected as a lawyer, he was a United States district attorney and reporter for the state supreme court (1826-1839). Devereux resigned these positions in 1839 following the death of his uncle, George Pollock, who bequeathed the majority of his estate to Frances Pollock Devereux, Thomas P. Devereux's mother. Devereux felt that he was the only member of the family capable, from age and experience, of managing the property and thus abandoned his professional career for the management of the estate. His name appears on several maps of Raleigh in the 1830s as the owner or partial

The portrait of Thomas Pollock Devereux, Mrs. Edmondston's father, is owned by William Joslin of Raleigh. (Photographed from portrait courtesy of Mr. Joslin.)

owner of lots on the corner of Person and Martin streets, on the corner of Edenton and Wilmington streets to New Bern Avenue, and on the south corner of Edenton and McDowell streets, east of the Methodist church.

Despite his involvement in family business, Devereux continued his interest in politics. A Federalist, he advocated a strong Union and opposed the states' rights doctrine represented in nullification and later in secession. His political views are found in his correspondence and in letters to various newspapers. From his student days at Yale he was a close friend of George Badger, Whig leader in state and national politics. As an active member of the party Devereux represented his district in the reception for Henry Clay during his visit to North Carolina in 1844, and Devereux championed William A. Graham as a candidate for governor. Through the war years Devereux gradually abandoned this political philosophy; but at the war's conclusion he petitioned Congress, in an effort to receive remuneration for his confiscated cotton, using his lifelong devotion to the Union as the basis of his argument.

Devereux married Catherine Ann Johnson of Connecticut, a descendant of a long line of distinguished English and American clergymen, educators, and jurists. They had one son and six daughters who survived to maturity. Catherine Ann Devereux, described by Henry King Burgwyn as "one of the purest, loveliest, best of women," died of tuberculosis at Sulphur Springs, Greenbrier County, Virginia, on July 18, 1836. Devereux later married Ann

Mary Maitland, a daughter of the successful New York merchant Robert Maitland, and they had one daughter, Susan.

Thomas Pollock Devereux died at his Conneconara plantation in Halifax County, March 7, 1869. A Raleigh newspaper described him following his death: "In private life he was sincere, kind, courteous, generous and hospitable. As a lawyer he was learned and able, and in equity practice, he had but few equals and no superior in the State. As a public officer, he was diligent, faithful and always equal to the demands upon him."

Reverses from the Civil War were clearly reflected in the condition of Devereux's estate. He commented in his will, dated 1867, on a new disposal of his property because the emancipation of slaves, "at least on paper," greatly reduced his estate. Devereux left his land to his executors (George W. Mordecai and John Devereux, Jr.) with certain trusts and some statements describing the proper management of it. The executors were free to exercise their judgment relative to selling, leasing, or farming the land, but Devereux hoped that the land would be retained and cultivated or leased for an annual rent paid in money or crops. After payment of his debts, the next charge upon his estate was an annual sum for the "proper and consistent" support of his wife and unmarried daughter, including a home for them. Devereux wished his wife to give up her residence at Conneconara, but she was to have her choice of the china and furniture moved at the expense of the estate. He bequeathed his daughters Susan Devereux and Sophia Turner $10,000 and $7,500, respectively, to be paid only after his debts and his wife's legacy were paid. He felt the best solution would be for his son John Devereux to work the estate out of debt.

After an evaluation of his estate, Devereux declared his son should inherit three tenths in full for all charges for management of his affairs. The other heirs, Frances Miller, Elizabeth Jones, Catherine Edmondston, Mary Bayard Clarke, Honoria Cannon, Sophia Turner, and Susan H. Devereux, were each to inherit a tenth. If John Devereux elected to work the estate clear of debt, his sisters were not to call on him for their inheritance so long as he paid them interest on the net income of the estate after payment of expenses. If John did not choose to work the estate clear of debt, the residue was to be divided equally among all the children, taking notice of a $3,000 charge against Catherine Edmondston and a $1,000 charge against Mary Bayard Clarke.

Bankruptcy proceedings were brought against Thomas P. Devereux before his death. A meeting of his creditors, called by the court to prove the debts and to choose assignees of the estate, was held in Raleigh, September 21 and 22, 1868. The court ordered Devereux's estate settled and distribution made among the creditors by trustees under the direction of a committee of the creditors. George W. Mordecai and Dr. William J. Hawkins of Raleigh served as the trustees charged with the distribution of the estate. William H. Smith of

Norfolk, Virginia, Collin M. Clark of Halifax County, and Richard C. Badger of Raleigh formed the committee of creditors to whom the trustees were responsible. From a list of creditors and amounts owed, the debts apparently amounted to well over $290,000. By a deed dated October 20, 1868, Thomas P. Devereux conveyed his estate and effects to George W. Mordecai and Dr. William J. Hawkins.

Devereux's will came up for probate on March 19, 1869, at which time Mordecai appeared in court and renounced his right to qualify as an executor or trustee and Ann Mary Devereux, widow of Thomas P. Devereux, entered a dissent to the 1867 will which was allowed. The economic plight of Devereux's heirs and creditors was deepened further by a bill of equity filed against the estate by Devereux's two nieces living in New York. The case, formally initiated in 1859, concerned the disposition of Frances Pollock Devereux's estate and dragged on over thirty years. It was finally settled in 1883 by the United States Supreme Court which ruled in favor of the nieces who eventually collected over $33,900 from the estate. The staggering debts charged against Devereux and his heirs sealed the family's financial ruin.

George Pollock and Sarah Elizabeth Johnson Devereux

George Pollock Devereux, the brother of Thomas P. Devereux, was Mrs. Edmondston's uncle. Some twelve years after his graduation from Yale in 1815, he married his New England cousin Sarah Elizabeth Johnson of Stratford, Connecticut. The couple, childhood friends, became engaged at his commencement dance but the marriage was delayed by parental dissent. They moved south after the wedding, living at Runiroi plantation from 1827 until 1837. The plantation, in a "rich, low savanna, lying on the Roanoke River not far from the Great Dismal Swamp," was George's inheritance from the Pollock estate. Summers were spent in the North away from the less healthy swamplands of eastern North Carolina. The Devereuxs had two daughters, Elizabeth and Georgina, the latter born after her father's death. Elizabeth (Lillie) was born at the home of her grandparents (John and Frances Devereux) in Raleigh in the "large, cool mansion, shaded by tall trees."

George Devereux's health, always delicate, declined in middle age and he died in the spring of 1837 at the age of forty-two. His death occurred in Suffolk, Virginia, during a family trip to Connecticut. The second daughter, named Georgina for her father and great-uncle, was born the following August. The birth of a daughter was a blow to the family fortune. Devereux's uncle George Pollock, the brother of Frances Pollock Devereux, was extremely wealthy and George P. Devereux had hoped to inherit most of his property if he had a son. Disappointed by the birth of another niece, George Pollock delayed making a will; and when he died unexpectedly in 1839 without one the North Carolina courts awarded the major portion of the estate to his sister

Frances Devereux. Each of George Pollock Devereux's daughters received $50,000 from the Devereux estate, however.

In making his will George P. Devereux stated that his wife would probably prefer to live in New England, and she was accordingly empowered to sell her slaves and land in North Carolina. She sold Runiroi and the plantation's slaves to the John Devereuxs, Sr., and returned north to live. Thomas P. Devereux, answering a complaint filed by George's daughters in later years in an effort to get more of the Pollock estate, declared he had done all in his power to help their mother, but she had sold a large part of her land in North Carolina and made other investments.

The family remained in the North, making occasional visits to relatives in North Carolina and Louisiana. Lillie Devereux married Frank Geoffrey Quay Umstead of Philadelphia and after his death married Grinfill Blake. She became a successful writer and one of the leaders in the women's suffragist movement in the two decades prior to 1900. In 1861 Georgina Devereux married the Reverend John Townsend of Albany, New York, who initially served as rector of St. Paul's Episcopal Church in Wallingford, Connecticut, and later as rector of Trinity Church in Troy, New York.

Leonidas and Frances Ann Devereux Polk

Frances (Fanny) Devereux, the only daughter among John and Frances Pollock Devereux's three children, married her childhood friend Leonidas Polk. Polk, the second son by the second marriage of Col. William Polk, was born in Raleigh on April 10, 1806. He studied at the Raleigh Academy, the University of North Carolina at Chapel Hill, and was graduated from West Point before entering the Virginia Theological Seminary. Frances and Leonidas were engaged in 1828 and married at Easter two years later. Following his ordination in Richmond in 1830, the Polks settled there; and he served as assistant to Bishop Richard Channing Moore at the Monumental Church. Later they lived with John Devereux, Sr., in Raleigh.

After serving as bishop to the Southwest, Polk was ordained bishop of Louisiana in 1841 and moved to Leighton, Bayou Fourche, about sixty miles from New Orleans. He owned a large sugar plantation where the slaves were taught in Sunday school and treated in a "most enlightened manner." The duties of planter and bishop were a source of conflict to Polk, however, and Polk finally decided to abandon his plantation interests and concentrate on his bishopric. In this capacity he supported the establishment of a university in the South with one of its goals being the education of planters to the idea of slave emancipation. Funds exceeding $500,000 were raised and land was donated enabling Bishop Polk to lay the cornerstone of the University of the South in Sewanee, Tennessee, on October 9, 1860.

Polk entered the Confederate army at the outbreak of the Civil War. He was commissioned major general in 1861 and was promoted to lieutenant general the following year. Assigned to the defense of Mississippi, Polk fought at the battles of Perryville and Murfreesboro. He was killed at Pine Mountain near Marietta, Georgia, in June, 1864.

A niece recalled that Frances Devereux Polk lived a long, eventful life "in fullest sympathy with her husband." She was for months at a time in charge of the plantation and was "always ready and competent to meet any exigencies that might arise. . . . She never assumed responsibilities, but never shrank from bearing any that her position imposed upon her. . . . She had a clear business head, great executive ability. . . . She was well read in the literature of the day, and always had some book on her work table, which she picked up at spare moments."

After the war Frances Devereux Polk, "without visible means of support," accepted a position as teacher of English literature at Columbia Institute. She later established her own school in New Orleans. The Polks had eight children: Hamilton, who married a Miss Buck; Katherine, who married William Gale; Frances, who married P. Skipwith; Lily, who married William Huger; William Mecklenburg, who married a Miss Lyon; Lucia, who married Edward Chapman; Sally, who married "a Blake of South Carolina"; and Susan, who married Dr. Joseph Jones.

John, Jr., and Margaret Devereux

John Devereux, Jr., the son of Thomas P. and Catherine Ann Johnson Devereux, was born in Raleigh in 1819. He graduated with distinction from Yale in 1840 and two years later married Margaret Mordecai, the daughter of Moses and Ann Lane Mordecai.

Margaret and John Devereux lived at Runiroi Meadows, a plantation in Bertie County, during the winter months. John Devereux, Sr., lived there at infrequent intervals until his death, using the house as a "camping-out" shelter. A few months before his marriage to Margaret, the younger Devereux wrote that his grandfather was planning his annual "hegira" out of the lowlands. John, Jr., managed the plantation after the death of his grandfather in 1844, and in 1846 his father deeded the land to him. During the summer the Devereux family resided in Raleigh at Wills Forest, a former Lane family home Margaret Devereux had inherited from her mother.

Plantation dwellers on the Roanoke were dependent upon the river for the transportation of many of their supplies. Its vagaries in flooding and drought caused irritation, if not hardship. The yearly moves to and from their plantation in Bertie to Raleigh became tiresome to the Devereuxs and early in 1851 John seriously considered selling his property in Bertie. During the war they lived exclusively at Wills Forest.

Henry King Burgwyn wrote in his diary in May, 1855, of meeting John Devereux and his family on their way to Raleigh. He described Mrs. Devereux as "a sweet lovely looking person, charming expression, and very young for a mother of six children. . . ." The Devereuxs eventually had eight children— Thomas Pollock, Jr., Annie Lane, Catherine, Margaret (Meta), John III, Laura, Mary, and Ellen.

In August, 1861, John Devereux carried an advertisement in the *Raleigh Register* which urged those patriots willing to aid in procuring volunteers for a company of infantry to organize for immediate service. In the meantime, Devereux had received a commission in May, 1861, as an assistant commissary agent with the rank of captain. In September of the same year he was appointed chief quartermaster for the state with the rank of major. Under his guidance the quartermaster department in North Carolina successfully supplied the clothing and equipment needs of North Carolina troops. When the Confederate government appointed a tithingman for the state in 1863, John Devereux was selected although he refused to accept the commission. The *North Carolina Standard* (Raleigh) approved the appointment and lauded Devereux as a man "thoroughly identified with the cause of the South and a gentleman of first-rate business qualifications."

John Devereux, Jr., followed the pattern of his father's life in abandoning a career in law for the management of a large estate. He became a planter and slaveowner but remained vitally interested in the development of North Carolina. A detailed description by a contemporary mentioned his "short stature, which nevertheless never gave the impression of a small man; the careless but scrupulously neat dress, the fine, manly sun-burned face; the clear, truthful kindly eye; the quiet speech whose pure English was never marred by slang or vulgarity. His predominant trait was a genuine love of books, and his wide acquaintance with them, especially with Classic English prose and poetry, his fine discriminating taste and apt power of quotation made him a most delightful companion; the more charming that he seemed unconscious of his own powers, using them only in his family circle for the amusement and instruction of his children and grandchildren, or in good fellowship with his friends. His knowledge of a wider range of subjects, with which men are seldom acquainted except as specialists, was so remarkable as to justify the observation of one of his friends that if he wanted information upon any subject, Major Devereux could either supply it or tell him where it could be found."

John Devereux died in Raleigh on April 10, 1893, after a long illness. The family fortune had dissipated with the South's defeat in the Civil War, and Devereux died in debt. His wife, forced to sell Wills Forest to settle her husband's estate, continued to live in Raleigh with her eldest daughter until her own death in 1910. Both were buried in Oakwood Cemetery.

William John and Mary Bayard Devereux Clarke

Mary Bayard Devereux Clarke, born in Raleigh on May 13, 1827, was the fourth daughter of Thomas P. Devereux. Her education and that of her sisters followed a curriculum similar to their brother's at Yale University, the girls probably receiving their instruction from governesses. Mary Bayard's later accomplishments were based on more than natural ability and reflected a background of knowledge unusual for women of her day.

In 1847 Mary Bayard spent the year at La Fourche, Louisiana, at the home of her aunt, Mrs. Fanny Polk. She was married there April 6, 1848, by her uncle, Bishop Leonidas Polk, to Maj. William J. Clarke who had just returned from the Mexican War. Clarke, who graduated from the University of North Carolina with an A.B. degree in 1841 and an A.M. degree in 1844, had interrupted his law practice to fight in the Mexican War. Captain of an infantry company, he was wounded at the battle of National Bridge and promoted to major for bravery exhibited at Cerro Gordo.

The couple returned to North Carolina where Clarke resumed his law practice and in 1851 was appointed state auditor by the legislature. During this period Mary Bayard, using the nom de plume "Tenella," published a two-volume work entitled *Wood Notes or Carolina Carols* in 1853. This was the first anthology of poems written by North Carolina poets and it established Mary Bayard Clarke among the literary people of the state. From this time on she wrote and published poems and stories in various newspapers and magazines.

Because of Mary Bayard's poor health, the Clarkes traveled to Cuba in the winter of 1854-1855 where Mary Bayard's "easy and graceful manners" and "delicate and fragile beauty" enhanced their popularity. Her adventures there are delightfully told in a series of articles, "Reminiscences of Cuba," written for the *Southern Literary Messenger* in 1855.

Still seeking a climate beneficial to Mary Bayard's chronic lung condition, the Clarkes moved to San Antonio, Texas, in 1856 where they remained until the outbreak of the Civil War. Clarke practiced law and served as president of the San Antonio and Mexican Gulf Railroad. When the war began in 1860 Clarke volunteered in the Confederate army and was commissioned colonel of the Twenty-fourth North Carolina Regiment in 1861. He was severely wounded in the battle of Drewry's Bluff in 1864 and in 1865 was captured and imprisoned in Fort Delaware.

Mary Bayard Clarke returned to North Carolina with her children in June, 1861, and immediately plunged into various war relief efforts which included composing patriotic poems for the Confederacy. Much of this time she lived with her father at Conneconara; but by the end of the war she was living in Raleigh and supporting her family with her writings while her husband was in the Union prison.

For a short time in 1865 she was assistant editor of *Southern Field and Fireside*, a magazine "entirely devoted to Polite Literature, gem for the fireside, an ornament for the parlor, and an indispensable companion to the housewife and agriculturist." In 1866 Mrs. Clarke published a collection of poems called *Mosses from a Rolling Stone*, contributed to *The Old Guard* and the *Land We Love*, and wrote book reviews for Harper, Appleton, and Scribner and novelettes for *Peterson's Magazine*. She also served as private secretary to Judge E. G. Reade of the North Carolina Supreme Court.

When William Clarke moved to New Bern in 1868, to serve as principal of the New Bern Academy, Mary Bayard continued her literary life and recorded that she was "busy editing my paper, the *Literary Pastime*; corresponding with two others; contributing to two magazines; and translating a French novel; added to which I am composing the libretto for an opera, and writing Sunday school hymns at five dollars apiece." Although some of her work was regarded as "romantic and imitative," the majority of critics viewed her writing favorably. *Southland Writers* described her as "one of the sweetest poets and truest women of America."

The period following the war was not one of complete success for the Clarke family. William Clarke's diary, written in New Bern, describes his financial and political struggles. He became a Republican, much to the distress of other members of the Devereux family, and was later affiliated with William Woods Holden. Clarke participated in the Kirk-Holden War and commanded the second regiment furnished Governor Holden by the federal government when Holden requested troops to suppress riots and uprisings. Clarke was also appointed judge of the superior court of New Bern from 1871 through 1874. With a Conservative party victory, however, Clarke's political fortunes quickly declined, and in 1874 he was defeated as an independent candidate for superior court judge of the third district. Clarke returned to his private law practice but found it difficult to collect his fees, and the family suffered from poverty. In 1879 Clarke, with his wife's help, launched the *Signal*, a newspaper in Raleigh which served as the official voice of the Republican party; but the venture was not a monetary success.

William J. Clarke died January 23, 1886, at his home in New Bern after a long illness. Mary Bayard Devereux Clarke died later that same year on March 30, 1886. They were buried in Cedar Grove Cemetery in New Bern.

Thomas Francis and Elizabeth Devereux Jones

The second daughter of Thomas P. Devereux, Elizabeth P. (Betsey) Devereux, married Thomas F. Jones of Perquimans County on July 29, 1836. Jones was graduated from the University of North Carolina at Chapel Hill in 1832 and apparently studied law afterward, as he was listed as a lawyer and a farmer in the 1850 census for Perquimans County. His name appears frequently in the county court records in guardian and estate accounts. In 1852 Jones served as a senator for Perquimans County in the state legislature. Jones achieved brief notoriety in 1846, as well, when he fought a duel with Dr. Daniel Johnson, also of Perquimans County, and killed him. The cause of the duel was the alleged infidelity of Elizabeth Devereux Jones with Johnson.

Following Jones's death on April 7, 1857, in Hertford, the *Raleigh Register* described him as an "estimable gentleman and an able lawyer" and stated that despite his loss of eyesight and generally delicate health, he followed his profession with ability and success. Jones's estate consisted of forty-nine Negroes and miscellaneous farming equipment and stock, in addition to outstanding notes in his favor.

The widowed Elizabeth Jones moved to Owego, New York, where she remained until the Civil War. During the war she lived with her sister Frances Miller in Raleigh most of the time. Shortly after the war's conclusion Elizabeth Jones moved to Baltimore to live with her daughter Rachel. The couple's other three children were Thomas Devereux, William Francis, and Elizabeth Jones. Guardianship papers, filed by Elizabeth D. Jones, listed the expenditures made for private schooling of the girls and the two boys. William worked in Baltimore prior to the war and served as second assistant engineer on the ironclad *Chicora* during the war. Thomas, a captain in the Confederate army, was mortally wounded in the battle at Bristoe Station. He died at a hospital in Richmond on November 6, 1863, shortly after his marriage to Pattie Skinner. Rachel never married; Elizabeth married a northerner in Owego during the war, upsetting her relatives greatly.

Henry Watkins and Frances Devereux Miller

Frances Johnson Devereux, the eldest child of Thomas P. Devereux, married Henry Watkins Miller in Raleigh on June 15, 1837. Miller was born in Buckingham County, Virginia, but was a resident of Raleigh from his twelfth year. He was graduated from the University of North Carolina at Chapel Hill in 1834. Miller studied law, practicing in county and superior courts, the state supreme court, and the United States Circuit Court in Raleigh. He was an active Whig politician in the state with a reputation as orator, statesman, and newspaper writer of "unusual force, clearness, and ability."

In 1860 he joined the Democrats and was appointed a member of the executive committee of the national Democratic party. Before the pressure of events necessitated a choice between the Union or the Confederacy, mass meetings were held in many sections of the state in an effort to save the Union, and Miller was in frequent demand for such occasions. However, as war seemed imminent, the attitudes of many staunch Unionists changed. The *Hillsborough Recorder*, May 1, 1861, carried notice of the withdrawal of Miller and James T. Littlejohn of Oxford as candidates for Congress from that district. The April 16, 1861, *State Journal* (Raleigh) printed Miller's statement relative to his withdrawal which declared Lincoln's call for troops tantamount to a declaration of war against the South. He urged all men to stand together, regardless of former political affiliations, to create a united South.

In the 1862 elections Miller was a conservative candidate for the Confederate House of Commons. He was elected in August but died in September before he could serve. The Wake County bar, meeting in November, passed a resolution giving "public expression of our feelings, regarding the loss of a man whose kindliness and generosity of temper won the affection of his associates." Following her husband's death Mrs. Miller opened a boarding house in Raleigh where many legislators and judicial men frequently stayed.

The Millers had three children living in 1860: Henry, twenty; Kate, eighteen; and George, sixteen. Henry married Lizzie Collins of Granville County, May 21, 1861, and Kate married Capt. George B. Baker, April 15, 1863.

Robert Hines and Honoria Devereux Cannon

The fifth daughter of Thomas P. and Catherine Ann Johnson Devereux, born May 15, 1829, was named Honoria for her grandfather's sister, the only one of his family to welcome him back to Ireland after he left St. Omer's monastery without taking his vows. She was always called Nora by her family. Her husband, Dr. Robert Cannon of Raleigh, was the son of Robert Cannon of Pitt County and Anne Hill of Franklin County. He was born December 20, 1824. Soon after their marriage the young couple followed Robert's brother, Henry Jordan Cannon, to Tennessee and made their home in Somerville, near Memphis, where Dr. Cannon practiced medicine.

As the war progressed into Fayette County, the Cannons found themselves "living within Federal lines." Their home was raided and ransacked on numerous occasions by Kansas Jayhawkers and other Union troops. Nora endured personal threats and insults, lost slaves, horses, wagons, silver, clothes, and provisions, and lived with the constant fear of having her home burned. Dr. Cannon's medical instruments were destroyed, and he was briefly jailed and threatened with imprisonment for refusing to take the Oath of Allegiance to the Union. Robert Cannon died about 1867 and soon afterward Nora and her young daughters Katie, Nonie, and Sadie, and her baby Mattie returned to North Carolina. By 1868 they were making their home with Kate Edmondston at Hascosea. There Nora was busy supervising her children's lessons and giving what help she could with the running of the household. In 1872 she taught at St. Mary's School in Raleigh where she lived with her three younger daughters until her return to Somerville three or four years later.

Nora Cannon blazed a trail for women's rights and as an educator by her election to the post of superintendent of public instruction for Fayette County,

Pollock-Devereux Genealogy

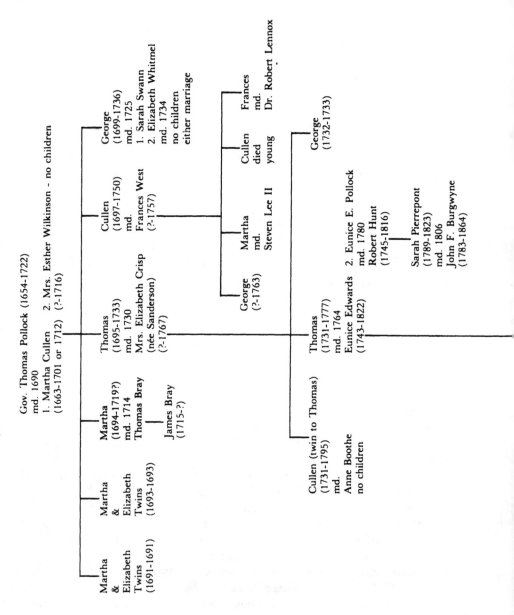

Gov. Thomas Pollock (1654-1722)
md. 1690
1. Martha Cullen   2. Mrs. Esther Wilkinson - no children
(1663-1701 or 1712)   (?-1716)

Martha
&
Elizabeth
Twins
(1691-1691)

Martha
&
Elizabeth
Twins
(1693-1693)

Martha
(1694-1719?)
md. 1714
Thomas Bray

James Bray
(1715-?)

Thomas
(1695-1733)
md. 1730
Mrs. Elizabeth Crisp
(née Sanderson)
(?-1767)

Cullen
(1697-1750)
md.
Frances West
(?-1757)

George
(1699-1736)
md. 1725
1. Sarah Swann
2. Elizabeth Whitmel
md. 1734
no children
either marriage

George
(?-1763)

Martha
md.
Steven Lee II

Cullen
died
young

Frances
md.
Dr. Robert Lennox

Thomas
(1731-1777)
md. 1764
Eunice Edwards
(1743-1822)

George
(1732-1733)

Cullen (twin to Thomas)
(1731-1795)
md.
Anne Boothe
no children

2. Eunice E. Pollock
md. 1780
Robert Hunt
(1745-1816)

Sarah Pierrepont
(1789-1823)
md. 1806
John F. Burgwyne
(1783-1864)

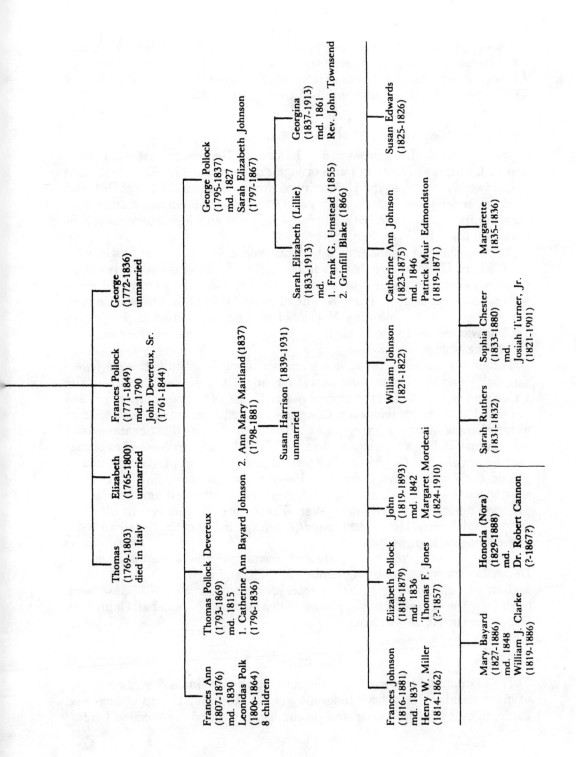

Tennessee, in 1881. She served for two years and was reelected to the office in 1886. At that time she supervised fifty-five schools for whites and seventy-nine for Negroes with an enrollment of nearly 5,000 pupils and received a salary of $300 per year for her work. She died in August, 1888.

Josiah, Jr., and Sophia Devereux Turner

Josiah Turner, Jr., husband of Thomas P. Devereux's sixth daughter, Sophia Chester, was born in Hillsborough on December 27, 1821. He studied at Caldwell Institute, at the University of North Carolina at Chapel Hill, and read law under Judge John L. Bailey and Chief Justice Frederick Nash, securing a license to practice in 1845. Turner served as a state legislator almost continuously from 1852 through 1860.

Although he was at one time a Unionist and a Whig, Turner fought with the Guilford Grays at Fort Macon in the early months of the war. He subsequently raised a company of cavalry and was elected captain and commissioned in September, 1861. Wounded in April, 1862, in Onslow County, Turner resigned the following November and became active in politics. In 1862 he was elected to the Confederate Congress and remained there until the end of the war.

Turner maintained a conservative and antagonistic attitude toward Jefferson Davis and the Democratic party. He advocated an early return to the Union and was elected to the United States House of Representatives in 1865 but failed to attain his seat when Congress adopted a resolution denying seats to members of insurrectionary states. His election to the state Senate in 1868 was disqualified by a legislature filled with Republicans. In November of that year he bought the *Daily Sentinel* (Raleigh) and thereafter persistently championed the Conservative party over Holden and the Republicans. He was spectacularly successful, although his press was dynamited and he was imprisoned during the Kirk-Holden War. Turner later turned against the Conservatives, however, lost his newspaper, was expelled from the Senate in 1880, and dropped out of politics.

Sophia Chester, the youngest and seemingly the unhappiest of the Devereux sisters, was born September 9, 1833, and died in a Raleigh insane asylum on September 25, 1880. Turner died October 26, 1901. Both were buried in the Turner family plot at St. Matthew's Episcopal Church in Hillsborough, North Carolina.

Plantations

The plantation life of the first Pollock in North Carolina is described by one of his descendants in a brief biography of the governor. Droves of hogs and cattle, foraging in the forests and on the higher grounds or "second lands," were the main source of wealth for early planters. The stock required no shelter in the mild climate. Ownership was determined by cutting the ears at stated intervals with each planter's distinctive mark. The Pollock brand, "a swallow fork and keel (notch and crescent)" continued in use until after the Civil War. Corn, which grew in the "wonderfully productive" soil of the river bottom or low grounds, also proved profitable.

Transportation by water, rather than by land, necessitated wharves and landings on each plantation. Planters owned canoes and other vessels. These were used locally and larger ships were used to make the passage to Boston and the West Indies and occasionally across the ocean.

With no towns of any consequence commerce was principally in the hands of New England traders. They visited the plantations "bringing their cargoes almost to the doors of the planters." Coins were few and exchange chiefly by barter. Merchants traded imported wares for "skins, salt beef and pork, tallow, staves and tar." The Assembly established a money value on rated commodities. Negro and Indian slaves were sold and Gov. Thomas Pollock's heirs owned "many descendants of Narraganset Indians bought from these traders."

Of the 55,000 acres Gov. Thomas Pollock left his sons Thomas, Cullen, and George, eight plantations descended to John and Frances Pollock Devereux, and through them to their children Thomas P., Frances Ann, and George P. Devereux. The descent is indicated in the various deeds and wills made to different members of the family: father to son, brother to brother, brother to sister, and uncle to nephew or niece. Included was land in the rich Roanoke River bottom in Halifax, Northampton, and Bertie counties, land in Hyde, Jones, and Craven counties, and land in the present city of New Bern.

In her *Plantation Sketches* Margaret Mordecai Devereux enumerated the plantations inherited by the Devereuxs—Runiroi, Feltons, Looking Glass, Montrose, Polenta, Lower Plantation, Barrows, and Conneconara. These names appeared frequently in the estate papers of the Devereux and Pollock families.

Margaret and her husband John lived on Runiroi. She described this plantation in some detail in *Plantation Sketches*. The house was a "comfortable, old rambling structure, quite innocent of any pretence at comeliness." Typically, according to her account, there was an overseer's house, ginhouse, screw, barn, stable, pork house, smokehouse, carpenter's shop, blacksmith's shop, and loomhouse. Slave dwellings were in two or more long rows with a street between and at some distance from the "great house." Each house had a front and back porch and a garden with peach and apple trees. A chaplain was employed to conduct services at Runiroi every other Sunday; a bell hung in the branches of a giant oak summoned the slaves to worship. For their further religious instruction, Frances Pollock Devereux designated $140 per annum, if her son thought it proper, for the employment of a teacher to instruct the slaves living on the Roanoke, particularly those in the possession of her descendants. Halifax served as the trading post for the Devereux slaves at Feltons, Conneconara, and Montrose. Coins made specifically for barter were used by them and were of value only to the merchants with whom the slaves were allowed to trade.

The Devereux-Pollock slaves, numbering over one thousand, were divided into two classes, hands and idlers, for the purpose of feeding. During the year the hands received 156 pounds of meat and 52 pecks of meal, and the idlers were rationed according to their eating capacities. At Christmas the Negroes received clothes, shoes, high waterproof boots for the ditchers, and similar articles.

Crops of corn and cotton and droves of hogs were shipped down the river by scow to Plymouth and from there to Southampton, Virginia. Later, freight steamers took produce directly to Norfolk and brought back merchandise. At the beginning of the year crops were housed and sale corn stored in barns or cribs on the river bank; the cotton was sold or held for better prices. Planting began about the middle of March and crops were harvested in August, followed by a three-day midsummer holiday with the slaughter of pigs and beef for the annual dinner. Then came the fodder-pulling and cotton-picking. With the arrival of frost, wagons were sent into the fields for the harvested corn; as the fields were stripped the stock was turned in to feast on the stubble.

Thomas P. Devereux, his second wife Ann Mary Maitland, and their daughter Susan lived at Conneconara while Catherine and Patrick Edmondston lived at Looking Glass. The original Conneconara patent, granted by Lord Carteret in August, 1720, contained approximately 2,560 acres on the Roanoke River and Conneconara Swamp. "Conneconara" was used in colonial times to designate that section of Halifax County. The house stood on a bluff overlooking the river where the "pretty house of the overseer, small church and other minor buildings, looked like a small village." Nearby was Pollock's Ferry, owned by Thomas P. Devereux, and the old post road running south from Philadelphia.

Looking Glass plantation was managed by Patrick Edmondston for his father-in-law. An agreement between Thomas P. Devereux and Edmondston, dated August 31, 1865, located the plantation in the upper fork of Looking Glass Creek and the Roanoke River. The line began at a point on the Roanoke River known as the division line between Conneconara and Looking Glass plantations, the latter consisting of some 1,365 acres of lowgrounds and uplands. By the indenture Edmondston agreed to farm the land upon an improvement system, give it his personal attention, procure the necessary labor, and cultivate the property as would a "discreet owner." The books and accounts of the plantation were to be presented to Devereux at the end of the year, and he was to receive one half of the net profit. The indenture also stated that upon Thomas P. Devereux's death the Looking Glass plantation was to become the sole property of Patrick and Catherine Edmondston. Because of Thomas Devereux's subsequent bankruptcy, however, the Looking Glass tract was auctioned at a public sale in December, 1874, the proceeds going to Thomas P. Devereux's creditors. Catherine Edmondston, widowed and only one month away from her own death, made the highest bid at $6,000 and thereby managed to retain possession of her home. She died before final payment on the land was made, and her heir, Thomas P. Devereux, Jr., paid the residue. He subsequently sold part of the land to a Halifax County farmer.

Hascosea, which the Edmondstons used as a summer home, was described as typical of the homes of the old South, situated in a grove of oaks with a wealth of beautiful flowers including "the never-to-be-forgotten dahlias and hyacinths." This property, also inherited by Thomas P. Devereux, Jr., was later sold as well.

Roanoke River and Halifax County

The Roanoke River is as much a part of Mrs. Edmondston's diary as any of the individuals mentioned. The river played an important part in the daily lives of the people living in its valley and had been a determining factor in the selection of a place to settle in colonial times. The Indian name for the Roanoke, "Moratuck" or "Morattock," appeared in the descriptions of land in the wills of the early settlers who explored the Roanoke from the coastal sounds to the falls, a distance of about a hundred miles of navigable but difficult water; beyond that, passage was by canoe or other small vessels.

The first settlements on Conneconara Swamp and Quanky Creek were made about 1723. The previous year a colony of Scottish Highlanders crossed the Roanoke from Virginia and settled along a great bend in the river, giving the name of Scotland Neck to their settlement. The exact locality of the settlement is unknown, but it was in the fertile land between the present-day Caledonia farms and Palmyra. The first appearance of the name in the records was in 1740 when Lord Nairn, a Scottish nobleman, settled there and sold to Marmaduke Norfleet land which he described as "my Scotland Neck Plantation." After they had built their homes and raised crops a tremendous freshet washed away everything they had accumulated. The settlers became discouraged and moved from that area, settling in the Cape Fear region.

Other settlers, chiefly of English descent, moved into the area in small groups from Pennsylvania and New Jersey and in greater numbers from Virginia. The towns of Halifax, Enfield, Weldon, Littleton, Brinkleyville, Palmyra, and Crowell's Crossroads developed. Before the Revolution, slaveholding was widespread with the cultivation of cotton, corn, wheat, and tobacco. Tobacco, lumber, and staves were exported. Revolutionary leadership centered in the more settled towns of Halifax and Enfield.

"Scotland Neck" apparently covered an indefinite area rather than any particular center and the land so designated was owned principally by the Smiths and Clarks prior to the Civil War. The present town of Scotland Neck is an outgrowth of the villages of Clarksville and Greenwood. In 1860 Clarksville had a general store run by Higgs and Pittman, a drugstore, and a blacksmith shop. Greenwood had one or two saloons, a buggy shop, and two general stores, one run by Buck Biggs and the other by John Speed and James Lawrence. One of the stores also served as the post office for Scotland Neck. In 1867 John Hyman of Greenwood bought the land between the two villages and began the project of surveying and grading.

In 1829 the first steamboat on the Roanoke arrived at Halifax, passed on to Weldon, and returned the next day. From that time on Weldon, Halifax, Palmyra, and other places on the Roanoke were accessible by steamboat and the river became the transportation system for the farms of that section in their trade with Norfolk.

About seven miles south of the present town of Scotland Neck was Hill's Ferry, at Palmyra, the shipping point for plantation owners along the river in Halifax, Martin, and Bertie counties. A few planters owned brigs and schooners while others used those of their neighbors. Peter E. Smith, W. H. Smith, James N. Smith, R. H. Smith, W. R. Smith, and Gilbert Elliott owned an iron barge, a vessel without engines or machinery, employed solely for freighting produce. The Smiths also owned a steamer, the *Cotton Plant*, which plied between Norfolk and Halifax. Numerous invoices from J. M. Smith and Brother of Norfolk to Thomas P. Devereux indicate the extent of the Devereuxs' use of these transportation facilities.

[Among the sources used for the preceding biographical sketches were: *Blake and others v. Hawkins and others*, 19 Fed. 204 (1884); *Blake v. Hawkins*, 98 U.S. 315 (1878); John Devereux Papers, State Archives, Raleigh; *Thomas P. Devereux, Trustee v. John Devereux, Executor, et al.*, 78 N.C. 386 (1878), 81 N.C. 12 (1879); Edmondston family records in possession of the Misses Eleanor and Elizabeth Simons, Charleston, South Carolina; Margaret Engelhard and Katherine Devereux Mackay (comps.), "Hinsdale Genealogy," Genealogical Section, State Library; family correspondence and records of the Devereux, Clarke, Cannon, Turner, and Miller families in possession of Mrs. Graham A. Barden, Jr., New Bern, North Carolina; Halifax and Wake County census records, wills, deeds, marriage bonds, and bankruptcy proceedings; *Hawkins and Another, Assignees, et al. v. Blake and Another*, 108 U.S. 422 (1883); Stuart H. Hill Collection, State Archives; Mrs. John W. Hinsdale, "Governor Thomas Pollok," *North Carolina Booklet*, V (April, 1906), 219-231; information from Charleston Chamber of Commerce and St. Andrew's Society, Charleston; George Mordecai Papers, Southern Historical Collection, Chapel Hill; *Margaret B. Mordecai et al. v. John Devereux, et al.*, original North Carolina Supreme Court Records (1876), State Archives; Pollock-Devereux Papers, State Archives; Josiah Turner Papers, Southern Historical Collection; James G. Wilson and John Fiske (eds.), *Appleton's Cyclopaedia of American Biography* (New York: D. Appleton and Co., 7 volumes, 1887-1900), II, 156.]

1860

I have many times in my life commenced a journal, faithfully kept it for a few months and then gradually left it off, perhaps from weariness, perhaps from an absolute dearth of events; for a journal to be readable ought to have plenty of Plums in it! None of your Milestone puddings but a real Christmas Pie, wherein no "Jack Horner" can "put in his thumb" without "pulling out" a juicy sugar of "plum"! Now however in these troublous times a lack of incident can be no excuse for dullness, & perhaps I may be enabled to carry this one on with greater profit & pleasure than I have hitherto done. To this end I have thrown together one or two little Diaries, skeletons as it were that I have kept at intervals for the past three years, & connected the lapses with narative so as to impress on my memory the antecedents of the stirring events through which we are now passing so as to ensure my pleasure in their perusal in future years. I am the more impelled to this as I find that from preoccupation I suppose things make less impression on me than they formally did; or it may be that from the rapidity with which we pass from event to event—the last more startling than the first—the past is obliterated by the deeper impression made by the present & like writing on sand swept by the passing breeze its character is lost so soon as received!

I commence in the midst of a journal I was keeping in the month of June 1860, as Mr. Edmondston's absence just after that time in attendance on the Military Convention held in Goldsboro[1] seems a sort of crisis in our lives, the time when that great change took place & we who had never been parted but once or twice before & then for a short time were forced to experience the loneliness of absence. Altho the absence did not commence until the spring after—still this was the commencement—little did I then dream however how pregnant it was for the future, or that we stood as it were on the brink of a precipice! But to have done with introduction!

June 1, 1860

Moved from Looking Glass[2] to Hascosea[3] for the summer.

---

[1] This convention of 125 delegates representing twenty-seven militia companies met July 11, 1860, to consider the efficiency of the militia law and to recommend measures for promoting the volunteer system in North Carolina. Capt. Patrick M. Edmondston was elected president of the convention and a committee, composed of two members from each congressional district, was appointed to draft a military code for presentation to the legislature. *North Carolina Standard* (Raleigh), July 21, 1860, hereinafter cited as *North Carolina Standard*. The title of the newspaper varies, depending on its publication on a weekly, semiweekly, or triweekly basis; for clarity it is simply referred to as the *North Carolina Standard*.

[2] Looking Glass was one of the Devereux plantations in Halifax County. See Introduction.

[3] Hascosea, the summer home of the Edmondstons, stood in Halifax County. See Introduction.

The house pictured above, with its gambrel roof and double-shouldered chimneys, was one of the out-
buildings at Looking Glass. It was used as an overseer's house and, on occasion, as a guest house. A small
porch extended across the front at one time, and the smokehouse and dairy house were to the right of this
structure. For a side view, see page 656. There was an identical house for the overseer at Conneconara,
Mrs. Edmondston's father's plantation. Looking Glass derived its name from the creek which began near
Spring Hill and which formed the southern border of the Looking Glass Plantation. (Information and picture courtesy of Dr. Claiborne T. Smith of Philadelphia, who is now part owner of Looking Glass. The picture was made in September, 1958; the structure was burned in 1965.)

JUNE 6, 1860

Mama and Susan[4] came out to spend the time with us until they should
leave for the Va Springs,[5] Father being absent in Raleigh & Fayetteville and
their house having been invaded by plasterers & carpenters. Mama, poor

---

[4] Ann Mary Maitland Devereux was the second wife of Thomas Pollock Devereux. Their only child was
Susan Harrison Devereux. See Introduction.

[5] Thomas Pollock Devereux and his family were regular summer visitors at the Salt Sulphur Springs in
Monroe County, Virginia (now West Virginia). Devereux entered an agreement with William Erskine,
owner of the springs, whereby Erskine "doth hereby assign and set over to the said Thomas P. Devereux
and wife Ann or the survivor of them three rooms in the new brick cottage . . . next to the large stone
building and now designated as Cottage No 1 . . . and doth hereby agree that the said Thomas P. Devereux

lady, still suffers severely with her foot; she is unable to walk without pain. With much difficulty we induced her to occupy our bed chamber down stairs. With many protests she at last consented, but it seems a real affliction to her!

JUNE 9, 1860

Mr. E. all day drilling his troop[6]—hot work. Pray God it may not give him a fever. So much for John Brown[7] and Northern philanthropy! I am the mark. Father arrived from Fayetteville where he had been to make his friend Mr. Haigh[8] a visit.

JUNE 15, 1860

Made some Blackberry wine by a receipt given Mr. E. by Mrs. Haigh. Opened a barrel of Flour.

JUNE 20, 1860

Mr. E. went to Enfield with his Troop, by invitation of the Enfield Blues,[9] to be present at the presentation of a flag given by the ladies to that company. It is fearfully hot! Poor fellow—I pity him. Got home, however, less wearied than I had feared. The Lady presenting made a speech. She attempted to deliver it extempore as it were, but unfortunately broke down & after some

---

and his family or his appointee shall at all times during the season at the said Springs have the full occupation thereof as a Sitting Room and two Bedrooms. . . ." This agreement, dated September 15, 1858, is found in miscellaneous items in the John Devereux Papers, State Archives, Division of Archives and History, Raleigh, hereinafter cited as Devereux Papers.

[6]The Scotland Neck Mounted Riflemen (S.N.M.R.) was organized in November, 1859, as an independent volunteer company armed and equipped by its members. Edmondston was elected captain. The troop, mustered into Confederate service in August, 1861, was sent to Wilmington and later to Wrightsville for picket and guard duty along the coast from Fort Fisher to Masonboro Sound. Reorganized under a new set of officers and attached to the Forty-first North Carolina (Third Cavalry) Regiment as Company G, the unit served at various places in North Carolina and Virginia until its surrender on April 9, 1865. Walter Clark (ed.), *Histories of the Several Regiments and Battalions from North Carolina in the Great War, 1861-'65* (Raleigh and Goldsboro: State of North Carolina, 5 volumes, 1901), II, 771-773, hereinafter cited as Clark, *Histories of the North Carolina Regiments*; Louis H. Manarin and Weymouth T. Jordan, Jr. (eds.), *North Carolina Troops, 1861-1865: A Roster* (Raleigh: Division of Archives and History [projected multivolume series, 1966—]), II, 178-180, 227, hereinafter cited as Manarin and Jordan, *North Carolina Troops*.

[7]John Brown (1800-1859), a fanatic abolitionist, believed slavery should be ended by force. In 1859 he led a band of men who seized the United States Armory at Harper's Ferry, Virginia, as the prelude to setting up a free state for fugitive slaves from which attacks could be launched against slave owners. Brown and his men were quickly captured by United States troops, and Brown was convicted of treason and hanged. Many local militia groups, such as the Scotland Neck Mounted Riflemen, subsequently began drilling throughout the South in order to prepare a defense against any similar attacks in the future. Joseph G. E. Hopkins and others (eds.), *Concise Dictionary of American Biography* (New York: Charles Scribner's Sons, 1964), 169, hereinafter cited as *Concise Dictionary of American Biography*.

[8]Charles T. Haigh was the president of the Fayetteville branch of the Bank of Cape Fear. *State Journal* (Raleigh), May 29, 1861, hereinafter cited as *State Journal*.

[9]The Enfield Blues (Co. I, First North Carolina Regiment) was organized in Halifax County in the fall of 1859. The unit enrolled for active service on April 17, 1861, and was mustered into state service May 13, 1861. Manarin and Jordan, *North Carolina Troops*, III, 45-46.

fumbling the M S was produced out of Dr. Joyner's[10] pocket. Her place being found she proceeded to read the rest. It proved to be only twenty pages long! There was a Fair and a dinner & speeches—hot work. Mr. E. brought home presents for Sue & I—"fairings"[11] in fact. Does it not sound English and rural!

JULY 4, 1860

Father & Susan left for Norfolk, she on shopping bent. Father will leave her with her relatives in Va & return here for Mama & take her up as they go to the Springs.

Mr. E. out with his Troop—intensely hot all day; in the afternoon a thunder storm accompanied with much wind. A tree on the road in front of the house struck. Mama poor lady suffered terribly from fright. What a blessing not to live in such terror. Is it constitutional or educational—I mean the exemption from such fears. Educational I fancy. Mr. E. came in late detained by the storm. Well that he was as a tree was blown across the road about the time he would have been at the point. Politics ran high he tells me between the Douglas & Bell men. How can men of sense advocate the claims of such a drunken demagogue as Douglas?[12] I am sure that I cannot see, but "party" is everything with some men—the greater pity!

On the first of this month, July, I commenced with a new account book. I am determined to try and keep this regularly & correctly so as to know how much of the "vile dross" we actually spend in one year. I headed it with the same old mottoe—John Randolph's[13] famous "Philosopher's Stone." "Pay as you go!"—an excellent one truly with more sense in it than many better known and oftener quoted aphorisms! Would that we could practice it!

JULY 13, 1860

Today father signed the deed settling Looking Glass upon Patrick & I. How glad I am that he has done it! for ever since he was broken up at

---

[10] Dr. Henry Joyner was listed as a forty-year-old physician in Halifax County in 1860. Eighth Census of the United States, 1860: Halifax County, North Carolina, Population Schedule, 83, State Archives, Division of Archives and History, Raleigh, hereinafter cited as Eighth Census, 1860, with appropriate schedule, county, and page number.

[11] Fairings are presents given or bought at a fair.

[12] John Bell (1797-1869) and Stephen A. Douglas (1813-1861) were the presidential nominees of the Constitutional Union and Democratic parties respectively, in 1860. Douglas, indifferent in personal habits, was noted for being "convivial beyond even the custom of the day." Allen Johnson, Dumas Malone, and others (eds.), *Dictionary of American Biography* (New York: Charles Scribner's Sons, 20 volumes, 1928; index and updating supplements), V, 399, 401, hereinafter cited as *Dictionary of American Biography*.

[13] John Randolph (1773-1833), a statesman and brilliant orator from Virginia, served in the United States Congress almost continuously from 1799 through 1829 and as minister to Russia in 1830. *Dictionary of American Biography*, XV, 363-367.

Barrows[14] he has not taken half the interest in life as when he felt that his labours were all directed to securing a competency for our old age. True many years have been lost & the deed is by no means so advantageous a one as we at one time hoped for. Property has risen in the mean time so greatly that if the same thing had been done when we first took Looking Glass as has been done today, we would pecuniarily have been much better off. But I am too thankful to have even the semblance of a complaint. The lines are cast to us in pleasant places[15] & it needs now but energy and self denial & a strict attention to detail to master this debt which otherwise will consume us.

JULY 15, 1860

Father and Mama left for the Springs & we are alone once more! I am hospitable and it is a great pleasure to have my friends with me, so to my own diary I can express the happiness of the life I lead alone with Patrick. What more do I want? Our independance is now I hope secured. We have the same tastes, the same pleasures. He reads to me & gardens with me. We do not miss *Society* yet are happy when our friends come to see us. Everything is a source of pleasure. I walk with him & enter into all his business as keenly as tho I were a farmer too. We are never long apart & our religious life is so bound up each in the other that I sometimes doubt whether he is not more to me than he should be there—whether my prayers may not turn to sin because there is an Idol there! God keep me from such a state!

JULY 16, 1860

Finished making Blackberry wine. Made in all 28 1/2 gal exclusive of one Demijohn which from being I suppose accidentally corked burst. I am told however that a Demijohn will burst even when uncorked if it is filled into the neck. I do not understand it—I should think it would run over & thus releive itself, & even unless corked uncommonly tight, why does not the pressure rather drive out the cork than burst the vessel? Questions for Sir Humphrey Davy to answer or rather Sir Isaac Newton[16]—seeming not more simple than "why does an Apple fall to the earth?"

Mr. E. went to Goldsboro to attend a Military Convention, its object being to draw up a Code for the organization of the Militia & to petition the Legislature to that effect. God be with him & make him useful in this new sphere of duty! Father seems to think it all useless & descants upon the folly

---

[14] See "Plantations" in the Introduction.

[15] Psalms 16:6. "The lines are fallen unto me in pleasant places. . . ."

[16] Sir Humphrey Davy (1778-1829) was an English chemist and author noted for his studies of gases and acids. Sir Isaac Newton (1642-1727) was the renowned English philosopher and mathematician best known for developing the idea of universal gravitation. *Webster's Biographical Dictionary* (Springfield, Mass.: G. & C. Merriam Co., Publishers, 1966), 396, 1095, hereinafter cited as *Webster's Biographical Dictionary*.

of Gen Wm Augustus Blount[17] who some years ago made a great fool of himself with his Military aspirations. Because Gen Blount's a fool & did not know how to go to work, is no reason that these gentlemen now in Goldsboro should also decorate themselves with ears. I think they are right, tho I wish they had taken cooler weather for it!

Heard today on Mr. E's return that they had made him President of the Convention! How shall I behave? I feel like the Militia Colonel's wife who when her husband was made Colonel, kept exhorting her daughters to "sit up & behave like Cunnel's daughters"! He says the crowd was terrible, the weather intensely hot, the Military generally well represented by delegates from almost the whole State. A Committee whereof he is Chairman is appointed to draft a Militia Law—the Convention to reassemble in the fall at Salisbury at his call.

I wish father was more sympathizing! He does not conceal that he thinks it all folly, childs play, no need of preparation for war; & always winds up with an abuse of S Carolina for her extreme views. Wonder if he takes S C as an exemplar, & by a reverse of the usual figure wherein one stands for many, he makes the many stand for one viz Mr E. I do not see how in the present attitude of the North, sample they have given us in the John Brown Raid, he can be so indifferent to our preparation for a future one. Peter,[18] however, is on the other extreme; he is like the War Horse in the Bible who "sniffs it afar." He almost says with Patrick Henry that "the next breeze that sweeps from the North will bear with it the resounding clash of arms."[19] He is sure that Abraham Lincoln will be elected & we plunged into a civil war before the year is ended! God avert it!—and keep him from being a veritable Cassandra![20] He is one only in prediction now; may he never be so in fulfilment.

---

[17] William Augustus Blount (1792-1867) was a younger son of John Gray Blount, Sr. He served with the North Carolina troops during the War of 1812, obtaining the rank of captain, but never participated in actual combat. Blount was discharged from regular service June 15, 1815, but in November of that year he was elected commander of the Sixth Division of the North Carolina militia and was addressed as General Blount thereafter. Blount also was a member of the state legislature, served on the State Board of Internal Improvements, and was a trustee of the University of North Carolina from 1826 until his death. Samuel A. Ashe and others (eds.), *Biographical History of North Carolina: From Colonial Times to the Present* (Greensboro: Charles L. Van Noppen, 8 volumes, 1905-1917), I, 164-166, hereinafter cited as Ashe, *Biographical History*.

[18] Another name the diarist occasionally called her husband.

[19] This statement was delivered by Patrick Henry (1736-1799) at a meeting in Richmond, Virginia, on March 23, 1775. Henry, by challenging British power and authority, sought to compel his fellow colonists into recognizing the deterioration of British influence and prestige in America. John Bartlett, *Familiar Quotations: A collection of passages, phrases and proverbs traced to their sources in ancient and modern literature*, edited by Emily Morison Beck (Boston, Toronto: Little, Brown and Co., Fourteenth Edition, Revised and Enlarged, 1968), 465, hereinafter cited as Bartlett, *Familiar Quotations*; *Concise Dictionary of American Biography*, 427-428.

[20] Cassandra was the daughter of Priam, ruler of Troy, and an accurate prophetess of impending disasters doomed to have her predictions ignored. William Rose Benét (ed.), *The Reader's Encyclopedia* (New York: Thomas Y. Crowell Company, 1948), 185, hereinafter cited as Benét, *Reader's Encyclopedia*.

JULY 20, 1860

My Dahlias are magnificent! Malakoff is worthy of its name; Glory is gorgeous indeed; & Cheltenham Queen is indeed a Queen for delicacy and purity! My garden is beautiful—how I love it!

JULY 25, 1860

Came brother John[21] & persuaded us to go with him the next day & make him a visit in Raleigh. So calling Fanny and Vinyard,[22] I hastily packed our trunk, we gave the necessary orders and were off by sunrise on the 26th on our way to Weldon. We are "Light Cavalry" indeed, tho he is Captain of Mounted Riflemen! Met brother at Weldon & got to Raleigh to dinner taking Margaret[23] quite by surprise. How pretty she is! What a gift beauty is! Perhaps I prize it too much as it has been denied me; not so much however as Mad de Stael[24] did, but then it has not been denied me to the degree that it was to her. Neither has its absence been made up by corresponding gifts. There is a system of *Compensation* in this world. N'importe I am content. I have beauty enough to please Patrick & sense enough "to keep out of the fire."

Margaret's children[25] are delightful. I am very fond of them; they are so pretty, so good, & so engaging. Do I wish for any of my own? No, I beleive not. I am contented and thankful I can enjoy neices and nephews without a pang—tho' sometimes a helpless little baby excites. But no matter for that.

Laura is a beautiful child & so intelligent & has such pretty little wilful ways. I heard such a good thing of Meta's saying that I must put it down. They are much annoyed by little boys from town coming out & shooting & fishing in the Grove & branch & Margaret has given orders that when they meet them they (the little girls) should instantly return to the house. Meta's liberty being thus circumscribed & her manorial and seignorial rights infringed, she resents it accordingly. So she came to her Mother & with great earnestness asked her "to do one thing" for her—viz—"Please Mother buy me a Cuthing Parrot!" As she lisps she had often to repeat the "cuthing parrot" before she was understood, which she did with great vehemence. "Meta my love! What do you want of a "cursing parrot!?" "Mother! I want

[21] John Devereux, Mrs. Edmondston's only brother, was a wealthy planter and nonpracticing lawyer who visited the Edmondstons frequently. See Introduction.

[22] These were house slaves. Though no attempt has been made to identify slaves, it should be noted that Patrick M. Edmondston was listed as the owner of eighty-eight slaves in 1860. Eighth Census, 1860, Slave Schedule, Halifax County, 48-49.

[23] Margaret Devereux was the wife of John Devereux and the daughter of Moses and Ann Willis Lane Mordecai of Raleigh. See Introduction.

[24] Anne Louise Germaine Necker, Baronne de Staël-Holstein (1766-1817) was a French authoress who exerted tremendous influence on the development of romanticism through her writings and literary salons. She was described as being very plain in appearance. Benét, *Reader's Encyclopedia*, 1061.

[25] John and Margaret Devereux's children were Thomas Pollock, Jr., Annie, Katherine, Meta, John III, Laura, Mary, and Ellen. See Introduction; Devereux Papers.

to keep it in the Grove to *Cuth* them town boys." How many of us would be thankful for a "Cuthing Parrot" to express our feelings sometimes when politeness, good taste, or *expediency* seal our lips. Give me a Cuthing Parrot!

JULY 28, 1860

Dined with Sister Frances. Mr. Miller[26] is very provoking! He abuses South Carolina until it is almost unbearable! He is a Douglass Elector & is sure that his man will be elected & talks already as tho he had the world in a sling.

AUGUST 1, 1860

Got home to Hascosea! Ah it is sweet to be here once more & to forget Politics!

AUGUST 2, 1860

Went to the Plantation with Mr E. The crop looks finely. Got home very tired. Played chess for the first time since Father left—played often enough then. Found my Pigeons doing finely. Rabbits not so well. One pr of Fantails hatched just before we left seem determined to enter life as Sydney Smith[27] said he had done on a hot day—"taken off his flesh and sat in his bones." They have not a feather on them—a little down only on the head and down the back and some sticks on the pinions where the pin feathers ought to be; But it is too hot for clothes they think, yet they are fat & hearty & run after their parents squeaking & flapping their skeleton wings in a manner ludicrous to behold.

AUGUST 19, 1860

Mr Hill[28] sent us some splendid Pears! When will our trees bear such! How we have laboured over our trees—Peach, Apple, & Pear, & with how little reward!

AUGUST 21, 1860

Bessie & James[29] arrived to make us a visit on their way home from their Northern tour. They seem to have enjoyed it greatly, the only draw back to

---

[26] Frances Devereux Miller, Mrs. Edmondston's sister, was married to Henry Watkins Miller, a prominent state politician. See Introduction.

[27] Sydney Smith (1771-1845) was an English clergyman, essayist, and wit. Benét, *Reader's Encyclopedia*, 1043. Mrs. Edmondston's reference to Smith and to other authors, books, and literary characters reveal the nature and breadth of her reading. For further discussion of the subject see James W. Patton, "Serious Reading in Halifax County, 1860-1865," *North Carolina Historical Review*, XLII (April, 1965), 169-179.

[28] This reference was probably to Whitmel John Hill (1804-1872), a farmer who lived at Kenmore, Hill's Crossroads, near the Edmondston plantation. He was the son of Rebecca Norfleet and Thomas Blount Hill. Pardon of Whitmel John Hill, 1865, Stuart H. Hill Collection, State Archives.

[29] Elizabeth Pratt Edmondston and James Nicolson Edmondston were Patrick's sister and brother. See Introduction.

Bessie poor thing being the fear she is under lest James should become a Roman Catholic. She distresses herself unnecessarily I think; a young man like him depends generally for his religion upon the wife he marries! It is some years since we have seen James, & we find him much improved both in body & mind. He is handsomer, more self reliant, & seems to take much juster & more rational views of men & things than formerly. He has led a life of great adventure in New Mexico & has often been in great personal danger, & that, I suppose, develops character more rapidly than aught else.

August 25, 1860

Making Brandy Peaches & Preserves. James read to me in the back Piazza an essay of Wilson's,[30] I the while with an eye in the kettle. Patrick is used to this mixture of house keeping cares & literature, but it must have seemed odd to James. I remember one summer he read to me Bulwer's[31] King Arthur whilst I was thus employed, & to this day I have an association of Blackberry Jam with that highly romantic Poem! Ah happy days! In those times I could not make bread, & yeast was the greatest mystery to me in life! Everything was an event! The shooting of the corn, the blossoming of the Peas were recorded as fully as tho it was an unusual occurrence. I am sorry now I destroyed the Diary I then kept; it would be amusing now to see the change in myself and my notions. Even yeast has lost its mystery & is merely an adjunct to bread. In fact since I have learned that it is only a cryptogamous plant allied to *mould* my respect has wonderfully diminished for it!

August 28, 1860

Made some Brandy Peaches & put up some in their own juice to send to Ursula & Tom.[32] Poor Shetlanders. They never taste any thing of that sort from their native land. A greasy pudding with currants in it, & that fried, is their greatest native luxury. I ought to beware! The taste of these Peaches may give Tom nostalgia even as the sound of the "Rantz des Vaches"[33] & "Lochaber"[34] make the Swiss and Highland soldiers desert by Companies.

---

[30] John Wilson (1785-1854) was a Scottish author who wrote for *Blackwood's Magazine* under the pseudonym of Christopher North. Benét, *Reader's Encyclopedia*, 1216.

[31] Edward George Earle Lytton Bulwer-Lytton (1803-1873) was a prolific English writer and a minor politician. His *King Arthur*, an epic poem, was published in 1848. Sidney Lee (ed.), *Dictionary of National Biography* (New York: Macmillan and Company, 63 volumes, 1893; index and updating supplements), XXXIV, 380-387, hereinafter cited as *Dictionary of National Biography*.

[32] Thomas Edmondston (1825-1874), Patrick's brother, married his cousin Ursula Edmondston and moved to the Island of Unst in the Shetland Islands. See Introduction.

[33] "Ranz des Vaches" (chime of the cows) is a melody sung by Swiss herdsmen or played on the alpenhorn to call cattle. Benét, *Reader's Encyclopedia*, 907.

[34] "Lochaber No More" is an air attributed to the Scottish poet Allan Ramsay (1686-1758) of which some two or three versions are extant. David Patrick (ed.), *Chambers's Cyclopaedia of English Literature* (Philadelphia: J. B. Lippincott Co., 3 volumes, 1902), II, 312-316, hereinafter cited as *Chambers's Cyclopaedia of English Literature*.

Ursula will not thank me for awakening association of home & native land in Tom's bosom.

SEPTEMBER 5, 1860

Bessie and James left after a fortnights visit which we enjoyed greatly. James gives us gloomy news of the antagonistic temper of the North; Abolitionism rampant! It will go almost a unit for Lincoln whilst we it is feared will be divided between Bell & that demagogue Douglas, but I cannot beleive that we will ever have such a man as Abraham Lincoln President of the U S. No! It cannot be tho' Patrick says it will!

SEPTEMBER 6, 1860

Patrick went to work in earnest on his Military Code, "the Code Patrick," as I call it. He has got it all arranged in his head & has principally manual labour now to do.

SEPTEMBER 10, 1860

Commenced copying the Code Patrick. Went to the Plantation.

SEPTEMBER 15, 1860

All day making Tomato Paste & putting up fresh Tomatoes.

OCTOBER 6, 1860

Father, Mama & Sue arrived from the Va Springs—all in good health & spirits. Father is sure of Bell's election and oh! how he abuses that fellow Douglas. I for my part think Douglas as bad as Lincoln, & I beleive he will do just as much as Lincoln to undermine the South & Slavery! This wretched Missouri Compromise! I cannot see why Clay[35] ever made it, & I am beginning to lose my early admiration for him. He was not so far seeing as he was supposed to be.

OCTOBER 8, 1860

Sue left for Raleigh.

OCTOBER 10, 1860

A slight Frost; not enough to kill the Dahlias however—they continue splendid!

---

[35] Henry Clay (1777-1852) was an American lawyer and statesman who served in the United States Senate and House of Representatives and as secretary of state under the Adams administration. A strong nationalist, he was the principal author and sponsor of the controversial Missouri Compromise which passed the United States Congress in 1820. The bill ended slavery north of the Missouri boundary (36°30') but guaranteed its existence south of the line. Missouri was admitted to the Union as a slave state while Maine entered as a free state, thus preserving the balance between the free and slave states in the Union. *Concise Dictionary of American Biography*, 169-170.

OCTOBER 25, 1860

Brother came.

OCTOBER 26, 1860

Mama & himself got into an argument about the Puritans or rather he fired the Petard & left & Mama got Patrick in the Drawing Room & kept him three quarters of an hour telling him what she would have told John Devereux! I shocked her terribly by saying that if S C did secede & there was any attempt made to coerce her, I would go to South Carolina & load guns for her men to shoot! She thinks me a terrible traitor. I wish she would tell me what are "the principles that placed the House of Brunswick[36] on the throne"!? It is a clap trap expression which may mean any thing or nothing, & it is astonishing how wise these old saws & party cries sound when uttered with emphasis! What has the House of Brunswick to do with us or Northern encroachments!?

Poor Franky died last night. She has been a great sufferer & has borne it with great patience poor old thing! I hope I did all I could for her. She seemed so grateful for my reading & praying with her that I felt reproached that I had not commenced sooner!

OCTOBER 29, 1860

Thos Jones[37] came to spend a few days bringing with him one of his friends Mr. Jos White.[38] Their arrival is most opportune as tomorrow the ladies of Scotland Neck present to the Scotland Neck Mounted Riflemen a Flag & thus celebrate their 1st anniversary the 30th of Oct. The Edgecombe Guards,[39] the Enfield Blues, the Halifax Light Infantry[40] are invited to be present, and at night they give a grand ball to the Ladies & their guests in honour of the occasion.

---

[36] Seemingly, this allusion refers to the accession of the Hanoverian line to the English throne in the eighteenth century. The relation between this incident and the southern states in 1860 is obscure.

[37] Thomas Devereux Jones was Mrs. Edmondston's nephew, the son of Elizabeth Devereux and Thomas Francis Jones of Perquimans County. See Introduction.

[38] This reference was probably to Joshua Warren White of Perquimans County, the son of Joshua White III and Emily White. Mrs. Watson Winslow, *History of Perquimans County* (Raleigh: Edwards & Broughton Co., 1931), 429.

[39] The Edgecombe Guards, organized shortly after the American Revolution, was reorganized in 1857. It became Company A of the First North Carolina Regiment in May, 1861. J. Kelly Turner and John L. Bridgers, Jr., *History of Edgecombe County* (Raleigh: Edwards & Broughton Co., 1920), 196-197, hereinafter cited as Turner, *History of Edgecombe County*; Clark, *Histories of the North Carolina Regiments*, I, 125; Manarin and Jordan, *North Carolina Troops*, III, 1, 4.

[40] The Halifax Light Infantry, raised in Halifax County, enlisted on April 25, 1861. It served as Co. G, Twelfth North Carolina (Second Volunteers) Regiment. Manarin and Jordan, *North Carolina Troops*, V, 195.

OCTOBER 30, 1860

Father & Mama insisted on leaving for Conneconara,[41] altho it was raining & as damp as it could well be. We represented the house, now undergoing a painting inside & out, the smell of paint, the weather, etc., to no purpose. They were bent on going. Ah! if I did so, what an obstinate woman I would be! Why is it that some people never have their own way? It is a curious problem; some others always do as seems right in their own eyes i.e. as they choose. I beleive I will take a way, tho I know I shall never hold it in Peace!

Went in the carriage with Thomas & his friend to Clarks store to see the presentation of the Flag, Patrick having preceeded us on horseback. Cloudy lowering & misty—a real Scotch mist! We hoped against hope that the rain would keep off, but no! Down it came in a determined steady obstinate drip drip just at the critical moment, whilst Mr. Smith[42] was making his speech prior to the presentation on behalf of the ladies. They fortunate in being women, occupied the balcony of the Store to the exclusion of the masculine gender who stood without. It would never do for soldiers to mind weather. O! No! It invited people to call them "fair weather soldiers"! "Carpet Knights"[43] & such pleasant epithets! So there they stood taking it manfully. Their horses heads & tails hung meekly down, water dripping from every hair. Their beautiful new Rifle Uniforms, Blue faced with green getting soaked, & their sabres scabbards actually tarnishing as you looked at them. Won't Fanny have a time cleaning her master's!? Then when it became the Captain's turn to speak, how well he did it! As he took the Flag from Mr. Smith's hand, & tho his horse started as he did so, with admirable skill he controuled him. Then grasping the Flag staff with one hand whilst with the other he managed his horse he made a handsome and appropriate speech to the ladies, thanking them for their beautiful gift & pledging himself & his men to defend it with their lives. Then turning towards his men his voice rang like a clarion as he held up to them the painted bauble which is identified with a soldiers honour & exhorted them to "rally under its folds," & delivering it to the Cornet, ordered a salute! The band played "Star Spangled Banner." The parade was dismissed & all was over!

The Flag is a beautiful one of Blue Silk with heavy Bullion fringe & tassels. On one side is the Coat of Arms of N C surrounded with gold stars, one for each State; on the other a wreath of Corn in the Silk & ripe Ear, Cotton in

---

[41] See "Plantations" in Introductio...

[42] This reference was probably to Richard H. Smith, Sr., of Scotland Neck, who graduated from the University of North Carolina at Chapel Hill in 1832 and studied law in Warrenton with Judge John Hall. He served in the state legislature in 1848, 1852, and 1854. William C. Allen, *History of Halifax County* (Boston: Cornhill Co., 1918), 209-212, hereinafter cited as Allen, *History of Halifax County.*

[43] This derogatory expression refers to political appointees in the military who have not earned their rank by service in the field. Benét, *Reader's Encyclopedia,* 182.

blossom & bole, & wheat encircling the words Scotland Neck Mounted Riflemen—Organized Nov 30th 1859, & on the Ribbon which ties the wreath the words "Pro aris et focis."[44] The staff represents a Corn Stalk surmounted by a Battle Axe—Peace and War in juxtaposition! The ladies all adjourned to the School House to finish the preparations for the evening. How it rained! The dinner al fresco had to be given up, & the long tables in the grove stood dripping wet, looking like anything but *"Hospitable Boards."* The Ladies dinner was sent in trays to the school House, but as the managers forgot the Knives and Forks & it consisted of Barbecue & Ham, the dear creatures were some what puzzled to reconcile elegance with good appetites. Fancy a delicate lady tearing the limbs of a Barbecued Shoat apart! The fear of spotting my drab silk gown "put a knife to my throat" (would that it had placed one in my hands!) so I made out badly enough!

Mrs. Smith & I dressed the Pyramid of Flowers which were really beautiful! My Dahlias made a most magnificent show & won universal admiration. My cakes too, ornamented with sugar plums in devices—one on a chocolate, the other on a white ground, the date of the Company's organization on one, its Initials on the other—mounted on stands & surrounded with wreaths of delicate flowers were quite an addition to the table. In fact, Mrs Edmondston is a wonderful woman, & all her sayings, doing, & even her thoughts ought to be faithfully chronicled here. After all, what is the use of a Diary if one cannot be egotistical in it?! I admire Pepys[45] for his perfect self candour! His failings, his vanities, nay even his pettinesses & his deceits are set down in so ludicrously earnest a manner, & whilst I respect Evelyn[46] I had far rather *read* Pepys. But deliver me from other eyes seeing how like Pepys I can be! Did I write for them Evelyn himself should not be more reticent. But to go on—Rain! rain! rain! so much so that I went to Julia Smith's[47] to dress for the evening, Patrick going home & sending my wardrobe to me.

We came in upon Mr. Norfleet[48] & his wife newly married tete a tete, he as devoted and as Honeymoon fashion as though he had not seven or eight children at home! What a blessing that youth renovates itself as it were. Doubtless he is as happy as in his first Honeymoon. As for Louisa, it is her

---

[44]"For altars and hearths, for home and religion."

[45]Samuel Pepys (1632-1703), an English author and politician, gained renown for his *Diary*, written in shorthand and not deciphered until 1825. Benét, *Reader's Encyclopedia*, 839.

[46]John Evelyn (1620-1706) was an English diarist and contemporary of Pepys. His *Diary* is quite valuable historically due to his strong royalist sympathies. Benét, *Reader's Encyclopedia*, 356.

[47]Julia A. Smith was the wife of William H. Smith and the daughter of Mr. and Mrs. George Evans Spruill. Stuart Hall Smith and Claiborne T. Smith, Jr., *The History of Trinity Parish, Scotland Neck, Edgecombe Parish, Halifax County* (Scotland Neck, N. C.: Privately printed [by Christian Printing Co., Durham], 1955), 114, hereinafter cited as Smith and Smith, *History of Trinity Parish.*

[48]Stephen Andrews Norfleet was a Bertie County planter. His second wife was Louisa Spruill, the daughter of George E. and Mary Louisa Spruill. Interview of James W. Patton with Thomas Figures, Jr., Roxobel, N.C., undated, hereinafter cited as Figures interview.

first; she is gathering spring flowers at midsummer, so she has a right to enjoy them!

Patrick found on his return that Father & Mama had on experiment thought better of it & concluded to return to Hascosea, the smell of Paint being too strong for them in a close house. How glad I am that I left the keys where they could get them & had their room undisturbed. Went to the Ball & found it as all Balls are to me now-a-days, only bearable in seeing the young folks enjoy themselves. Got home worn out about daybreak, as Patrick being the Captain could not leave until the last & then was detained by having to "pay the Piper," the music bill being presented to him & a little Draft to the tune of $120 having to be drawn. I wonder if the Company will ever think of refunding it?

OCTOBER 31, 1860

Wearied to death all day from the late hours & fatigue of yesterday. Pleasure is like the Measles in that its dregs are to be dreaded!

NOVEMBER 2, 1860

Thomas and his friend left. Went to the Plantation with Mr. E. The cotton crop looks finely; the fields are "white to the Harvest." Played Chess with father all the afternoon.

NOVEMBER 5, 1860

Finished copying the "Code Patrick"!

NOVEMBER 6, 1860

Election day. No fears in my mind that Lincoln & that half blooded Hanibal Hamlin[49] will be elected, tho' Patrick feels gloomy about it. Brother John is enough to depress anyone he talks so gloomily about debts, politics, etc—"*ruin*" is a house hold word with him. I have no patience with him. If we are to die, let it be but once, not daily! As to Politics, Peter is worse than brother. He thinks us on the eve of Civil War. Father hoots at it and so abuses S C for her ultra views, & particularly for sending commissioners to Va after the John Brown Raid last fall to consult about a uniform policy for the South, that I dread to hear him!

NOVEMBER 22, 1860

We got home.

---

[49] Hannibal Hamlin (1809-1891), a lawyer and politician from Maine, served as vice-president during Lincoln's first term in office. Hamlin was described as having such a dark complexion that the story of his being of Negro blood was circulated and believed by the more credulous in the South. *Dictionary of American Biography*, VIII, 196-198.

NOVEMBER 25, 1860

Sunday, I left off on Election day when I could not be persuaded that Lincoln would be elected, but how greviously was I disappointed. He is our President Elect, having received every Northern vote but three of New Jersey's, but not one single Southern one. We were divided between Bell, Breckenridge[50] & Douglas. Ah! would that we as a people had studied old Esop to better purpose! But the lesson in the fable of the old man & the bundle of sticks has been lost to us.[51] A sectional President! Pray God his Administration may not be so also.

Father & Mama left Hascosea on the 11th, Sunday. On the 12th we also left, Mr. E. leaving me in Hillsboro whilst he goes over to the Military Convention in Salisbury[52] which he has convened for the 14th. I hope the Convention first & the Legislature next will take the same view that I do of the "Code Patrick" which he carried with him. I think it an excellent one, & ought not I to know? Am not I a judge? At any rate "I made the saddles," i.e. copied it.

Sophia[53] has fine children. Her boys are hardy & promising & her infant named after my Mother Katherine Johnson is a sweet little creature. It was christened whilst I was there, I being one of its sponsors.

Mr. Turner[54] amuses rather than provokes me. He assumes so indulgent an air of superior wisdom, looks at Patrick's sabre as a man might at a childs pop gun. "It would hurt a fellow if you were to stick him with this!" Talks about the Military Convention & its object as tho' it was merely one of the asides of life, a something which a few idle spirits had taken to amuse themselves with which would do no harm & perhaps keep them quiet. But when he gets on South Carolina he is laughable in his patriarchism. One would think that the Shade of the old humbug Benjamin Franklin had revisited the earth & taken up its abode in the body of the "Senator from Orange" for he is now in the

[50] After the southern delegates left the Democratic Convention at Charleston in 1860, due to differences over the extension of slavery, they held their own convention at Baltimore and nominated John Cabell Breckinridge (1821-1875), then vice-president under Buchanan, as their candidate for the presidency. *Concise Dictionary of American Biography*, 104-105.

[51] Fables written in Greek prose traditionally have been attributed to Aesop (6th century, B.C.). The fable to which Mrs. Edmondston referred, "a Bundle of Sticks," concerns a father's lesson to his sons that strength depends upon unity. Thomas James and George Tyler Townsend (trans.), *Aesop's Fables* (Philadelphia: J. B. Lippincott, 1949), 20.

[52] The Military Convention, convened by order of the earlier session, met in Goldsboro on July 11, 1860. The convention received a report on the military code drafted in its name, approved the final version, and submitted the code to the legislature for adoption. Probably as a result of these recommendations, "An Act to Amend the 70th Chapter of the Revised Code, 'Militia'" was ratified by the General Assembly, February 20, 1861. *North Carolina Standard*, October 31, 1860; *Western Democrat* (Charlotte), November 21, 1860, hereinafter cited as *Western Democrat*; *Public Laws of the State of North Carolina Passed by the General Assembly at its Session of 1860-'61* (Raleigh: John Spelman, Printer to the State, 1861), c. 24, hereinafter cited as *Public Laws*, with appropriate date.

[53] This is a reference to Mrs. Edmondston's sister Sophia Chester Devereux who married Josiah Turner, Jr., of Hillsborough. See Introduction; Ashe, *Biographical History*, III, 415-426.

[54] Josiah Turner, Jr.

Legislature. I did not think it the *best* breeding in the world however for him to volunteer the information that he should not vote for the Bill presented by the Convention. Nobody asked him & nobody cared, but as he had not *seen* the bill, nor even heard what it was to be, his premature announcement made his impartiality a little questionable. He might have waited & not have volunteered a disagreeable speech unnecessarily [under his] own roof!

Patrick got back to Hillsboro on the 16th with a severe cold, having worked very hard—day & night—revising & altering the codes presented. There were but two, his own & Capt. De Rossett's; they were combined I think to the injury of Patrick's, tho' his was the ground work. But I dare say Mrs De Rossett thinks her husband's was the injured one. So much for different stand points!

On the 18th we went to Raleigh, where brother amused us not a little by the way in which he was "reading up" on the Puritan question. He had armed himself with a few pleasant facts about John Knox,[55] such as his witnessing the martydom of [George Wishart] from a window with which he intended making a keen defence when the tilt between himself & Mama should really come off. He rather posed me with some of the questions he put to me as to the responsibilities I had assumed with the Sponsorship of Sophia's child. I am afraid I have not thought sufficiently about it. I must study the point before I again accept the position.

Found all well in Raleigh and as happy as possible. Brother dreadfully gloomy about the future, but Patrick is worse than he is about that. Annie is at a grand finishing school in N Y & he is beginning to be uneasy lest he should be forced to go on & bring her home. Margaret & I are more hopeful however, & think Politics will hardly run so high. He fears bread riots so soon as the water courses close at the North which will now be soon.

It is disagreeable to be with Mr. Miller. He is disappointed because Douglas was not elected & vents his spleen upon the South generally. He has not the true *Southern* feeling, the true Patriot's heart! He mourns over the defeat of that wretch Douglas who is at heart not one whit better than Lincoln. A vulgar whisky drinker, he is for any policy by which himself Stephen A. Douglas is to be benefitted. I am glad he at least is beaten.

Mr. Miller seems to have an especial spite against Slave holders; asks in a tone of acrimony and bitterness if "we expect the West and the white population who have none, to fight for our negroes?" "Certainly I do." "Well that's cool!" "Cool! I call it patriotism, for I should like to know what is to become of the country when our slaves are free. How will the West like such a neighbor? Or the white folks who have none to be governed by them. Fine patriotism that." Then he croaks so abominably, has such a gloomy budget,

---

[55] John Knox (1505-1572) was a prominent Scottish religious reformer and historian who formulated and propounded the doctrines of the Presbyterian church in opposition to the Catholic church. *Webster's Biographical Dictionary*, 830; *Dictionary of National Biography*, XXXI, 308-328.

that one cannot help thinking that if Henry W. Miller Esq. had a nice office or was U S Senator all these evils would be averted. I wish he would take a blue pill before I see him again.

Sister Frances is no better—says "*you* slave holders have lived so long on your plantations with no one to gain say or contradict you & the negroes only to look up and worship you, that you expect to govern every body & have it all your own way. I can see it in Father, in brother John, in brother Patrick, & in you too"! A pleasant way to spend the half hour before dinner in truly! But let it pass. I do not think every body estimates the force of *words*. Words are things. She does not realize that she is calling her kindred domineering, unjust, arbitary & insolent; yet so it is.

NOVEMBER 25, 1860

Have been very busy, packing up Dahlia Roots, decanting Wine, my own Blackberry Vintage, overlooking Pantry. Went to Church today & heard the new assistant.[56] Mr Cheshire[57] has read the service. Certainly he is not bonnie to look upon!

NOVEMBER 27, 1860

Rev. Mr. Benton the new clergyman called. He stayed to dinner—seems pleasant, well read and agreeable. I hope he is not High Church but I doubt. Mr. E lent him Sartor Resartus.[58]

NOVEMBER 29, 1860

Packed up a keg of Dahlia's for Margaret. They have been so beautiful the past summer & have given me so much pleasure that I am grateful to them & show the Roots the best possible care.

Mr. E. has been so busy with his Troop, Company meeting, drill, officers drill & what not that I have seen little of him comparatively. He deserves success he is so earnest, but then he says he is preparing for War! I cant

---

[56] The Reverend Angelo Ames Benton assisted Joseph Blount Cheshire, Sr., at the Trinity Parish Episcopal Church in 1861 and later officiated at St. Timothy's Church in Wilson in 1869. He served from 1871 until 1874 as rector of St. Paul's Church in Edenton, and became a professor of theology at the University of the South in Sewanee, Tennessee. Smith and Smith, *History of Trinity Parish*, 39, 56; George Blake Holmes (comp.), *History of Saint Paul's Episcopal Church in Edenton, North Carolina*, (N.p.: Privately printed, n.d., unpaged [copy in State Archives]), unnumbered photograph facing 25, 37.

[57] Joseph Blount Cheshire, Sr. (1814-1899) studied law under Thomas Pollock Devereux and set up practice from 1836 to 1838 before entering the ministry in 1838. His first work after being ordained was as an Episcopal missionary in Bertie and Halifax counties. Later he served as Episcopal priest at Trinity Church in Scotland Neck, and at Calvary Church in Tarboro, Edgecombe County. Lawrence Foushee London, *Bishop Joseph Blount Cheshire: His Life and Work* (Chapel Hill: University of North Carolina Press, 1941), 2-3, 124-125; Smith and Smith, *History of Trinity Parish*, 75-76, 78-79.

[58] *Sartor Resartus* is a philosophical satire written by Thomas Carlyle and first published in 1833 and 1834. Benét, *Reader's Encyclopedia*, 991.

beleive it; but as the "price of Liberty is eternal vigilance," maybe he is only laying down his purchase money!

DECEMBER 1, 1860

Saturday—Moved down to Looking Glass for the winter. Mr E joined me at night having been out all day with that wearisome Troop. They ought to be fine swordsmen. Ah! little did I think when I used to read that Broadsword Exercise to him so constantly just after we were married. "Cut one" "Cut two" "St. George" et[c] that he would ever be practising it in earnest! But they have changed the manual since then. "Cut one" "Parry" are not what they used to be & as for "Moulinet"—I doubt whether the Pole with the unpronounceable name who used to drill him ever heard of it.[59]

DECEMBER 3, 1860

Unpacking my years supply of groceries from New York[60]—excellent they seem and very grateful am I that God has blessed us with means of getting them. Truly the lines are cast to us in pleasant places. We have an abundant heritage.

DECEMBER 4, 1860

Was terrible shocked this morning by a note from Mr Speed telling Mr Edmondston that Mr. Spier Pittman had killed Mr Riddick![61] Shot him in his own store! Ah—this whisky! What does it not do? Poor Riddick lived in great pain until about 9 o clock; he was shot at 2 in the afternoon. This comes of drink and concealed weapons!

DECEMBER 6, 1860

Went with Mr. E. to poor Mr. Riddick's funeral, the first member of the Scotland Neck Mounted Rifles who has ever died. A large crowd. The sad circumstances of the death & the Military funeral brought many out. The people were all deeply affected. Spier Pitman would have been in great danger could they then have arrested him. He poor fellow must be in the agonies of remorse.

---

[59] The editors have been unable to determine the author or title of the manual of swordsmanship referred to, nor the identity of Edmondston's instructor. Edmondston attended West Point from 1837 to 1839 when broadsword exercise was part of the training in the course on Practical Military Instruction. The position of Sword Master at this time was held by Ferdinand Dupare, which does not sound like a "Pole with an unpronounceable name." Information furnished to James W. Patton by Kenneth W. Rapp, archivist, United States Military Academy, February, 1963.

[60] The Devereux and Edmondston families ordered goods from Baltimore, Norfolk, and New York regularly, including edible delicacies such as mushroom catsup, essence of lemon, jars of limes, bleached Jamaica ginger, East India ginger, and vanilla beans. Bill of sale, September, 1860, in miscellaneous papers, Devereux Papers.

[61] John H. Speed (1826-1874), Spier Pittman (1824-1869), and A. M. Riddick (1834-1860) were all Halifax County merchants. Eighth Census, 1860, Population Schedule, Halifax County, 66, 82.

Not one of Riddicks kindred could get here, so he was buried by strangers to his blood. How sad!

DECEMBER 8, 1860

Patrick out with his troop all day. I hard at work icing a marvellous cake which I intend to carry to Papa & Mama[62] for their anniversary, their golden wedding, on the 25th of Dec—50 years married! think of it! But to my cake—it has some of all the good things I got from N Y in it, as rich as all my cookery books can make it. But the icing is the point on which I rest my fame! Pure white—on the top Papa's and Mama's Monogram—"C M E"—surrounded with the words "25th Dec 1810–25th Dec 1860" done in pure white comfits. Then beading of white sugar plums, festoons, etc., on the side of the first tier. The second is divided by sugar plums into eleven medalions, each medalion containing the Initials of one of their children beginning with Lawrence & ending with Henry.[63] I have succeeded in keeping the icing smooth & white & am more proud of my chef d'oevre than was ever Eude or Soyer.[64]

DECEMBER 10, 1860

Rode with Patrick through the Corn in the Low grounds, to my eyes a magnificent crop, & reminded me of the Psalmist's words, "the valleys shall stand so thick with corn that they shall laugh & sing,"[65] & it seemed literally true. Cut after cut, each seeming to surpass the last, running over, smiling, yes laughing with plenty!

Ned led the 'Shuckers.' I asked him how much he thought we would make this year. "I don'no Miss, I reckon we will push 10,000 barrels." Patrick only hopes for 3,000! I wish they would count three bushels to a barrel of corn, as they do to a barrel of flour. 5 bushels to a barrel always confuses me. For instance, 3000 barrels is 15000 bushels, but as a barrel is to me, it is only 9,000. Counting it in bushels it makes it much more "soundable" as Dolly says. The corn in the crib was beautiful but talk as you will about the market value, showing no stain etc of yellow corn, I prefer white. Saphires, no, Topaz I mean are beautiful but I prefer pearls. White was the corn of my childhood.

---

[62] Charles and Mary Pratt Edmondston were Patrick's parents. At this time they were living in Aiken, South Carolina. See Introduction.

[63] Lawrence Augustus was the eldest of the Edmondston children and Henry was the youngest. See Introduction.

[64] Louis Eustache Ude was a famous London chef who at one time served as chef to Louis XVI of France. He wrote *The French Cook; or The art of cookery developed in all its various branches* (London: Privately printed [by Cox and Baylis], 1813). Alexis Soyer (1809-1858), a French chef and successful dietary reformer who fled to England in 1830 to avoid political troubles in France, wrote *A Shilling Cookery for the People; Embracing an Entirely New System of Cookery and Domestic Economy* (London: Privately printed [by G. Routledge and Company], 1855). Esther B. Aresty, *The Delectable Past* (New York: Simon and Schuster, Inc., 1964), 125, 174, 237, hereinafter cited as Aresty, *Delectable Past; Dictionary of National Biography*, LIII, 308-309.

[65] Psalms 65:13. "The valleys also are covered over with corn; they shout for joy, they also sing."

White is the only corn fit for bread, & as you look at a pile of it—white plenty & I will say pearly—an unconfessed association of snowy hominy & white crumbling bread comes over you, & you already smell & taste the appetizing "pone." No! White corn for me tho' the price current does quote it a few cents below yellow.

Viney was sorting seed corn, under heavy complaint as usual. I wish I could for once see a hearty negro woman who admitted herself to be such over 40, one who was not "poorly, Thank God!" To be "poorly" is their aim & object, as it ends in the house & spinning. Viney I know has real cause for complaint, but she makes the best of it!

Zeke had his "ditcher's boots" on & after due reprimand was ordered to grease them & carry to the overseer to keep for him until he was ordered into the ditch, much to Zeke's discomfiture & the merriment of his compeers.

Came home by the River. What a beautiful country we have. There were the Lowgrounds loaded down with bending corn whose Russet hue, even tho gilded by the setting sun, was but a foil to the brilliant blaze of colour showed on the river & creek banks—Red Orange, Scarlet, flame colour, the deep copper & bronze of the Gum relieved by the vivid brown of the Cypress if I may apply vivid to a neutral tint all sparkling & shining in the setting sun light. God be praised that he has given us an eye to see & a heart to feel his beautiful creation!

December 11, 1860

Dined at Father's. Owen's[66] harness broke, & to think of it, he had no knife to punch a hole in the leather. I do not know what we should have done had not the steel stiletto Frank Jones[67] made me been fortunately in my basket. With this & a string which the careless fellow produced from some where about his own person we managed by slow & careful driving to get home. I was so late that I found Patrick quite uneasy about me.

December 12, 1860

The first sound I heard this morning was "Miss! Aunt Dolly say she give out"—a knell to all future peaceful slumbers. I tried to induce Peter to take another nap but failed. So with visions of burnt hominy & all sorts of mishaps I went to table & found that none of my anticipations were groundless. Fanny & Owen, separately by their accounts, jointly in effect, had spoiled the breakfast. Sent for Becky & gave her orders for dinner & winding up with an

[66] Owen Richardson, one of the Edmondston house slaves and the family coachman, lived with the family after he was freed. He and his wife Dolly, in accordance with the terms of Mrs. Edmondston's will, were given the use of a house and annual provisions during the course of their natural lives. Halifax County Probate Court, 1875, Book 6, 128. See Introduction.

[67] William Francis Jones was Mrs. Edmondston's nephew, the son of Elizabeth Devereux and Thomas Francis Jones. See Introduction.

exordium not to let Dolly "counterfeit" her, hoped for better things from the dinner.

Went to the Nursery. Gatty seems to take excellent care of the children & they are all fond of her—an excellent sign. She was taking potatoes out of the ashes for them, & the little monkeys all knew their own & claimed them. Delia had a terrapin which she had roasted in its shell & was picking the flesh out & eating it with as much gout as an Alderman. I asked her how she had killed him. "I put him in the ashes & kivvered him up & kilt him with the fire stick"! Think of the poor wretch's torment.

I heard all that Gatty calls the "sponsible ones" say their catechism, but I do not hope for much from it. It is up hill work and ought to be done more regularly than I do it. Bishop Ives[68] catechism I do not like at all; the repetition is tiresome. Dr. Watts[69] combined with the Church Catechism is the best I can do.

I wonder how Mr Collins[70] manages. Tho' he is no test for his negroes are said to be the worst any where to be found. This teaching of negroes is a sore problem to me. It ought to be done & I ought to do it. I am afraid I magnify the Lions in the Path because it is disagreeable. They learn nothing from me but the mere rudimants of Christianity—who made them, who Redeemed them, with the certainty of a future of reward or punishment, the Creed, the ten Commandments, & exhortations against lying & stealing—and only the little ones get that. They will not come to church even when Patrick has it for them. He has never yet determined whether it is right to carry the doctrine of their unaccountability, the "child like" theory so far as to make them. As to a Clergyman resident on the plantation even could we afford it it would be at too heavy a sacrifice to our selves. We could not have him in our small family stuck like the ham in a Sandwich between Patrick & I the whole time. It would be intolerable. A separate residence could not be well managed. So I do not know what we could do, even as I said before could we afford it![71]

---

[68] Levi Silliman Ives (1797-1867) served as the bishop of the Episcopal Diocese of North Carolina from 1831 until 1852, when he resigned his Episcopal office and entered the Catholic church. *Dictionary of American Biography*, IX, 521-522.

[69] Isaac Watts (1674-1748) was an English clergyman, hymn writer, and author of numerous works, including catechisms. *Webster's Biographical Dictionary*, 1551.

[70] Josiah Collins III, owner of one of the largest estates in North Carolina, had a chapel built for his family and slaves near Somerset Plantation and employed a resident clergyman to conduct regular services and to give instructions in the Bible, catechism, and prayer book. Josiah Collins Family Papers, 1761-1892, State Archives, hereinafter cited as Collins Family Papers.

[71] Thomas Pollock and John Devereux employed a chaplain who held services at the Runiroi plantation every other Sunday. A bell hung in the branches of a giant oak summoned the people to worship. Thomas Pollock Devereux's mother willed $140 annually to her son for support of a teacher (if he thought it proper to employ one) to give religious instruction to the slaves on the Roanoke, particularly those in the possession of her descendants. Margaret Mordecai Devereux, *Plantation Sketches* (Cambridge, Mass.: Riverside Press, 1906), 12, 22-26; Devereux Papers. See Introduction.

My difficulties I am convinced beset many a well intentioned misstress who like me because she cannot do what she feels she *ought* does *nothing*. It is not right. I ought to do something, but I do not know what; nor can I ask Patrick's assistance, which I know he would give me cheerfully & gladly unless I had a feasible plan to suggest to him. I will try and find out more about Mr Collins system, but that I think consists wholly in having a resident clergyman, daily prayers, responses etc.—& I hear it whispered that the "*system*" works badly—mere lip service & that they are just as profligate, lie & steal as much as their neighbors. God help. We are put here with a heavy responsibility on our shoulders which we do not discharge aright. One duty I am sure of—I am put here to be Patrick's companion & help meet, & I cannot spend all Sunday preaching, teaching, & "missionizing" without an evident neglect of that my plain duty. (Yes Madam well argued—but then you might give them a regular *part* of the day which you know you do not!)

Gatty gave the children their dinner by my orders whilst I was there. She "trayed" up two trays of Dumplins & greens with plenty of "sop" & gave every child a peice of meat in its hand. They needed no further orders, but to use Dr Salmond's[72] word they "*dashed in*"! When she thought the rage of hunger was partially appeased, she called out "mind them babies now you nusses!" So the "nusses" each lugged a baby to the tray & commenced feeding it. The look of sleepy contentment that gradually came over their faces was most ludicrous. Gatty kept up a running fire of exhortation or reproof the whole time which like a symphony "filled up the intervals between" "You Miriam! mind you stuff dat chile's trote too ful! you choke 'um presently!" "You Ailsie stop gieing that chile so much greens! give it bread and sop!" "You Nias (Annanias) feed that chile better. You aint gie it nuff. It stretch out its hands, & you wont gie it no more! You too lazy! Done got your own belly full & wont gie the chile belly full too"—and so on, her eye and tongue both busy.

She had some loaves of Persimmon bread standing on edge in the fire place. I asked what they were for. "Simmon Beer Missus. De ole man Dick gwine make him some beer. He axed overseer for a keg last lowance day & the chilluns is picked up Honey shucks & he gwine put it to work tonight. I allows its mighty healthy & the Lord knows its pretty drinking."

I left Gatty to the anticipated enjoyments of her "Simmon Beer" & walked off thinking of the misplaced philanthropy which would take these fat, healthy, well fed, greasy little wretches & throw them on the care & kind attentions of their parents. They show a vast improvement since the plan of

---

[72] Two Salmond brothers, Edward A. and Thomas W., were residents of Camden. Both Edward and Thomas were physicians. A third brother, Burwell Boykin, lived in Camden until 1855, when he moved to Alabama. Thomas J. Kirkland and Robert M. Kennedy, *Historic Camden, Part II: Nineteenth Century* (Columbia: State Company, 1926), 259, 427-428.

feeding them at the nursery independent of their Mamy's and Daddies household arrangements—and that too when the food was regularly put in abundant quantity for them in their parents' hands. What would it be when they had to work for perhaps scanty, certainly a precarious livelihood.

Ah! Mrs Stow![73] Ah! Madame la Duchesse de Southerland.[74] You have much yet to learn. Gatty evidently does not beleive in the power of self government as possessed by Cuffee.[75] In her eyes their manifest destiny is to wait upon white folks, for as she called up all hands to make their manners & tell Missus thanky for their dinner. She drew a harrowing picture as to what they would [be] if they didnt have no Master & Missus to give it to them. She knowed their daddies would not have it to give them. Gatty understands talking to Buncombe[76] too it would appear.

After dinner hurried on my skirt & out to ride with Patrick. It was too wet either for houseing corn or picking cotton, so all hands were in the New grounds. Just commenced, it will take many a vigorous blow with axe & grubbing hoe before the plough can run through the woods we rode through this afternoon. Went to the ditches. Patrick is getting insane upon secret ditching; gets off his horse, which he gives me to hold, & peers into a damp, black looking burrow which looks as if it might be the work of an industrious mole or ground puppy, & exclaims in triumph "its running! just look how it runs!" & sure enough there does trickle out a few spoonsful of water—just enough to swear by!

DECEMBER 14, 1860

Busy preparing things to take to Aiken to the Golden Wedding—Collared Beef, Hunter's Round, Pickles, Sausage meat etc. I hope they will be nice when they get there, tho' the baggage is something to carry.

---

[73] Harriet Beecher Stowe (1811-1876) was the author of *Uncle Tom's Cabin, or Life Among the Lowly* (first published serially in 1851-1852) and other antislavery works which were bitterly resented by many people in the South. *Webster's Biographical Dictionary,* 1419.

[74] Harriet Elizabeth Georgiana Leveson-Gower (1806-1868), duchess of Sutherland, whose London residence at Stafford House was often the headquarters for various philanthropic enterprises, including a written protest (1853) against American slavery, entertained Harriet Beecher Stowe there in 1853. The duchess presented a gold bracelet in the form of a slave chain to Mrs. Stowe as a token of her admiration. Forrest Wilson, *Crusader in Crinoline: The Life of Harriet Beecher Stowe* (Philadelphia: J. B. Lippincott Co., 1941), 375-377, hereinafter cited as Wilson, *Crusader in Crinoline; Dictionary of National Biography,* XXXIII, 152-153.

[75] "Cuffee" was a patronizing term for a Negro, denoting familiarity or humor.

[76] "Talking for Buncombe," meaning to talk or do something for show or applause, sprang from a statement by Felix Walker (1753-1828) during a debate in the Sixteenth Congress (1819-1821). Walker, a congressman from western North Carolina, delayed a vote on the Missouri Compromise by making a long speech "for Buncombe," part of his constituency. John Preston Arthur, *Western North Carolina: A History (From 1730 to 1913)* (Raleigh: Edward Buncombe Chapter of the Daughters of the American Revolution, 1914), 643-644.

December 15, 1860

The South Carolina Convention[77] is in Session at Columbia. We conclude to go the upper route & see it.

December 16, 1860

Sunday. Am ready to leave in the morning. Why is it that I always hate to leave home so? Here I am going to see friends whom I am anxious to see & dreading the journey—the leaving home—as tho' it was something terrible. Tying up parcels to be sent to different children before Christmass, as from Santa Claus. Santa Claus!—how much happiness does he bring with him!

December 17, 1860

Father's birthday. We left home for Aiken via Raleigh where Patrick had business connected with bringing the Military Code before the Legislature. Found all well at Brother's. Wavering however about sending for Annie, Brother advocating, Margaret armed with Uncle George's[78] advice opposed to it. Brother yields most reluctantly to her—is sure there will soon be bread riots in New York. Southerners already are insulted and find it unpleasant being there.

December 21, 1860

Left Raleigh via Wilmington having changed our route on account of Small Pox prevailing in Columbia. The Convention has also adjourned to Charleston.

December 22, 1860

Between Wilmington & Florence met Dr Tennant[79] & Mr Gregg who told us of the Secession of South Carolina. The Ordinance was signed upon the 20th of December. So South Carolina is no longer one of the United States! One link is missing! One pearl lost from the glorious string! Pray God that it be not the beginning of Evils as Patrick predicts. As the cars started he heaved a sigh and said it is the begining of the end.

---

[77] The South Carolina Convention, called to consider secession from the Union following the election of Abraham Lincoln, convened in Columbia but, after an outbreak of smallpox in the city, adjourned to Charleston. Mary Boykin Chesnut, *A Diary from Dixie*, edited by Ben Ames Williams (Boston: Houghton Mifflin Co., 1949), 3, hereinafter cited as Chesnut, *Diary from Dixie*.

[78] George Washington Mordecai (1801-1871), one of the large and prominent Mordecai family of Warren County, became an outstanding lawyer in Raleigh and president of the Raleigh and Gaston Railroad. Mordecai was the uncle of Margaret Mordecai Devereux. For further information see the George W. Mordecai Papers, Southern Historical Collection, University of North Carolina Library, Chapel Hill, hereinafter cited as George W. Mordecai Papers; Pattie Mordecai Collection, State Archives.

[79] Dr. Edward Smith Tennent, son of Charles and Anne Martha Smith Tennent, was a grandson of Rev. William Tennent, for many years pastor of the Independent Church in Charleston. Newton B. Jones (ed.), "The Writings of the Reverend William Tennent, 1740-1777," *South Carolina Historical Magazine*, LXI (July, 1960), 129-133. Dr. Tennent's wife was Harriette Taylor of Wilmington.

CHARLESTON

MERCURY

EXTRA:

Passed unanimously at 1.15 o'clock, P. M. December
20th, 1860.

AN ORDINANCE

To dissolve the Union between the State of South Carolina and
other States united with her under the compact entitled "The
Constitution of the United States of America."

We, the People of the State of South Carolina, in Convention assembled, do declare and ordain, and
it is hereby declared and ordained,

That the Ordinance adopted by us in Convention, on the twenty-third day of May, in the
year of our Lord one thousand seven hundred and eighty eight, whereby the Constitution of the
United States of America was ratified, and also all Acts and parts of Acts of the General
Assembly of this State, ratifying amendments of the said Constitution, are hereby repealed;
and that the union now subsisting between South Carolina and other States, under the name of
"The United States of America," is hereby dissolved.

THE

UNION

IS

DISSOLVED!

The Edmondstons learned of the secession of South Carolina as they traveled between Wilmington and Florence. This extra edition of the *Charleston Mercury* announced the South Carolina action. (Photograph from files of Beth Crabtree.)

At Florence we unexpectedly met our friends Mr & Mrs John Wither-spoon[80] of Society Hill. They gave us an account of their adventures on the night when the news of the Secession of S.C. reached their village, which to show the bitterness of party politics I will set down here. In the dead hour of the night they heard guns, first at one neighbors then at another. Whilst they were speculating as to the cause, came a message from Mrs. W's father Col Williams[81] who was alone in his own house, that persons were firing around his house, that he had returned it & desired their immediate presence. They sprang out of bed, Mr Witherspoon taking his gun, Mrs W her pistol, whilst their servant Stephen brought up the rear with the carving knife. On the way Mrs Witherspoon stumbled &, not having stayed to put on her Hoop, became entangled in her skirts & rolled over with the loaded Pistol in her hand! Fortunately it did not explode!

Col Williams is violently opposed to the Secession of SC, & when the firing commenced at his door, he took what was intended for a harmless Salute, for a personal insult to & triumph over himself & seizing the only loaded gun in the house fired at random in the direction where the saluters stood! Most fortunately it was only a fowling peice loaded with small shot, and the Saluters interpreting it as a friendly response retired before he could load his Musket & Rifles; which he immediately did placing some of them in the hands of his servants! They found him in a state of terrible excitement, chasing up & down with a loaded musket in his hand.

Is it not terrible!? Here is gall & wormwood infused into a hitherto peaceful community. Bitterness & strife are the fruits of this political difference, for Col W next day went into the village & informed his visitors what he had done, what were his intentions—a death blow to all future pleasant intercourse! God in his mercy only averted an awful scene of bloodshed & murder! Such scenes however will be rare in S Carolina for she is a Unit on this point. Col Williams & Mr James L Pettigru,[82] the eminent Lawyer in Charleston are said to be the only Union men in the state.

Parted from Mr & Mrs Witherspoon at the Camden station & reached Aiken about 10 o clock at night Sat the 22d. Found Papa & Ma quite well & delighted to see us. They seem very happy in their new house & were looking forward with great pleasure to a re-union of the family on the 25th. Papa is a wonderful man, so clear a head, so excellent a memory, so affectionate a

---

[80] John and Serena Chesnut (Williams) Witherspoon lived in Society Hill, South Carolina. She was the daughter of John Nicholas Williams (1797-1861). J. S. Ames, *The Williams Family of Society Hill* (Columbia: State Company, 1910), 18-19, hereinafter cited as Ames, *The Williams Family*.

[81] John Nicholas Williams (1797-1861) was the son of a former governor of South Carolina, David Rogerson Williams (1776-1830). Ames, *The Williams Family*, 18-19.

[82] James Louis Petigru (1789-1863), a prominent South Carolina lawyer and political leader, adamantly opposed secession. He remained in South Carolina until his death but never ceased to regret the dissolution of the Union. W. A. Swanberg, *First Blood: The Story of Fort Sumter* (New York: Charles Scribner's Sons, 1957), 23, 80, 93, 191-192, 249-250, 278, 324, hereinafter cited as Swanberg, *First Blood*.

friend, so judicious an adviser is seldom seen—whilst the brightness of his Christian character, shining like pure metal the more it is in the fire of affliction, is an example to us all. Jessie[83] & her little folks were well and as usual devoted to Uncle & Aunt Kate.

DECEMBER 25, 1860

On their 50th wedding day, we had everything arranged for a series of surprises to our dear old people. There was present Lawrence, Sarah[84] & their son Willie; Charles,[85] Patrick & myself; Jessie, her husband & children; Bessie; Isabella[86] & her two children; James & Henry. Poor Carrie[87] was prevented by her situation from taking the journey; indeed we afterwards heard that her daughter was born on the 24th! She was the only member of the family on this Continent who was absent—Tom in Shetland, Rob[88] at sea, completes the circle.

Besides presents from their children many of their friends & persons whom Papa had befriended took the opportunity of testifying their gratitude or affection. Before they were out in the morning the Drawing room carpet was taken up & replaced by a new one sent by Mr Whilden[89] a Charleston young man whose father dying in Papa's employment had been befriended by him & placed in a situation to secure a handsome independance for himself. Then a pair of Arm Chairs from Patrick & I ordered from NY & whose ponderous box had exercised Papa's curiosity the day before, but which the family had sternly refused to gratify were ready for their occupation. On the breakfast table new cups from Charles' children, a Silver Egg Stand from James, spoons, salt cellars, butter dishes and in short I cannot enumerate everything.

Then a table was laid out in her chamber—holding the Bridal gifts. New Toilet appurtenances, such as Mama delights in—Caps, Elegant Lace Collars & sleeves, Vases, china, ornaments, slippers, Cologne, scents of all kinds & bottles to hold them, trifles from the grandchildren, and an elegant bouquet containing a white Camellia sent by a young lady in the vicinity, embroidered handkercheifs, stockings, Knick nacks for Papa from the children, more than I can enumerate, more than they could possibly want or use. Amongst other things a bill of exchange for $50 sent by a former Governess, who had married at their house & now resides in Liverpool, & a note saying

---

[83] Jessie Edmondston, Patrick's sister, married Dr. Amory Coffin from Aiken, South Carolina, in 1838. See Introduction.

[84] Lawrence Edmondston married Sarah Eggleston in 1837. See Introduction.

[85] Charles Edmondston, Jr., Patrick's brother. See Introduction.

[86] Isabella Donaldson Edmondston, Patrick's sister. See Introduction.

[87] Carolina Kirkpatrick Edmondston, Patrick's sister. See Introduction.

[88] Robert Donaldson Edmondston, Patrick's brother. See Introduction.

[89] Mrs. Edmondston possibly referred to W. G. Whilden of the firm of Hayden and Whilden, dealers in watches, clocks, and house furnishings, at the corner of King and Hasell streets in Charleston.

that she had heard of their celebration too late to send a present but begged Mama to lay out that in a gift in token of her gratitude for past kindness!

They seemed at the acme of human happiness. Indeed Papa frequently said it was the happiest day of his life. We all treated & addressed Mama as a bride, & she sat up with her Bridesmaid her sister Mrs Matheson[90] who came from Charleston to be present in State. In the afternoon we were all busy in laying out the supper table. The children had provided the supper & an elegant & bountiful one it was. We sorted out all the relics of Mama's former grandeur—the elegant Buff China, the Glass, & the table fairly groaned with her Silver! Then the good things heaped upon it & abundant Light, which I insisted on made truly an elegant display. In the centre was my cake! & very much delighted was my dear Papa with both the design & execution. He was never weary of admiring it & was much opposed to cutting it. We however over ruled him.

Then at night when all was ready we put on our best apparel & assembled in the Drawing Room. Papa entered dressed in a suit of clothes woven for this very occasion in his own native land, of his own Shetland wool, upon his Grandfather['s] estate (now Tom's), leading Mama, elegantly dressed in a rich brocaded black silk dress & lace Cap, collar & Sleeves to match. The clergyman Mr Cornish[91] made a handsome & appropriate address, altering the marriage Service, making the ring an evidence of past happiness & a pledge for future; then a prayer and congratulations & felicitations from all the children & grandchildren. The Bridesmaid entered behind the bride, led by the eldest son Lawrence. Then came an old fashioned "Contre Danse,"[92] headed by Papa & Ma, Mrs Matheson & Lawrence, & filled up in regular gradation with sons & their wives, daughters & their husbands, & grandchildren down to Jessie's youngest, a little two year old. It was astonishing to see how Mama danced! how she took her steps & enjoyed it! Amory Coffin,[93] the eldest grandson, read a piece of poetry composed by himself on the occasion & the evening was filled up with music & dancing. Papa danced a Highland Fling with Isabella to the tune of the Fisher's hornpipe. He had a Scotch bonnet on his head, & he took the steps as well as a man of thirty could have done, throwing out his legs from the knees as the true Horn Pipe ought to be danced but rarely is, & snapping his fingers at the right moment in unison with the music, as not one man in fifty could do now.

---

[90] This reference was probably to Mrs. Elizabeth Matheson who was living at 9 Laurens Street, Charleston, in 1861. *Census of Charleston, South Carolina, for 1861* (Charleston: Evans and Cogswell, 1861), 129.

[91] John Hamilton Cornish (1815-1878) was the rector of St. Thaddeus Episcopal Church in Aiken, South Carolina, from 1846 until 1848. See also Diary of James Hamilton Cornish, December 25, 1860, in the Southern Historical Collection for another account of the Edmondston golden wedding.

[92] *Contredanse* is the French term for an English country-dance. Benét, *Reader's Encyclopedia*, 247.

[93] Amory Coffin, Jr., Mrs. Edmondston's nephew, the son of Jessie Edmondston and Amory Coffin, Sr. Mrs. Edmondston occasionally referred to him as Amo.

Then came supper. The only persons present beside the family were Rev Mr & Mrs Cornish & Mr Cameron, a friend of Jessie's. Papa gave health after health, toast after toast calling on each member of the family in turn to respond, which they all did in the happiest manner. At last came the crowning act, the cutting of the Cake! Lawrence as eldest son & groomsman officiated. Paper & Ribbon had been provided & first severing the upper Cake intact for the Bride and Bridegroom the lower one was divided according to the Medalions, each child receiving his own peice. Mama took in charge Rob's, Tom's, and Carrie's they being the only absentees. Patrick most gallantly passed his over to Mrs Cornish, & James not to be out done in politeness handed his over to Mr Cameron—the first time that ever I heard of sons giving away their parents' wedding cake, tho it was most happily & handsomely conceived & executed by them. At last worn out with happiness the dear old lady & gentleman retired, Papa repeating that it was the happiest day of his Life. Long may they be spared the centre & head of a united family!

DECEMBER 26, 1860

In the morning we had a terrible revulsion of feeling which seemed to plunge us at once from the most profound peace into almost War! Major Anderson, the U S Commander of Forts Moultrie, Sumter, & Pinckney,[94] in the night suddenly evacuated Moultrie & Pinckney after spiking the Guns, burning the carriages, and cutting down the Flag staff, and retreated with his whole command into Sumter! Most remarkable conduct & well calculated to bring on the attack which he seems to dread, but of which, beyond a few idle threats there has as yet been no evidence. We heard it on the morning of the 26th, & it seemed to plunge us into a sea of care after basking in the sunshine of happiness.

DECEMBER 27, 1860

On the 27th the Government of SC took possession of the vacant forts Moultrie & Pinckney & hoisted the Palmetto Flag[95] in defiance as it were to the US. Preparations were hastily made to put them in a defencible position. Troops were ordered from the interior, & batteries commenced on the channel with a view to prevent the re-inforcement of Sumter. Thus has one ill advised act thrown down the gauntlet as it were, which SC is not slow to accept!

We had a delightful visit in Aiken disturbed only by exciting news from Charleston and the passage of Troops, which was so new to us that it excited the liveliest forebodings. The Ladies of SC displayed an enthusiasm & earnestness in their preparations for War that was almost sublime in its unity &

---

[94] Fort Moultrie, Fort Sumter, and Castle Pinckney were defensive works guarding the Charleston harbor. Mark M. Boatner III, *The Civil War Dictionary* (New York: David McKay Company, Inc., 1959), 131, 299, hereinafter cited as Boatner, *Civil War Dictionary*.

[95] The Palmetto Flag served as the official flag of South Carolina.

self devotion. They spent their whole time scraping lint, making bandages, & even learned to make Cartridges. One lady in Aiken made 500 with her own hands. Never was known such unanimity of action amongst all classes.

South Carolina having seceded from the US, amidst the jeers & laughter of the whole country calmly organized her own government & prepared for War singly and alone. It at first made one smile to see the news from Washington put under the head of "Foreign News," but all disposition to it was soon taken away by the sight of the terribly earnest way in which all looked at & spoke of it. I often thought, "Have we indeed come to this?" Pray God that Mr. Buchanan[96] would quietly withdraw the troops from Sumter. Let SC peaceably go her own way. Perhaps after a little, when she sees that Mr Lincoln does not meddle with Slavery, she may return & this threatened dismemberment of our country may be prevented. But God ordained otherwise. Papa entered most keenly into it, regretted that he was not a son of her soil, & was as enthused about the attitude adopted by SC as the youngest man in the State.

On the 3d of Jan Georgia seized Fort Pulaski,[97] & Alabama, the arsenal at Mt Vernon[98] with 20,000 stand of arms.

Whilst in Aiken we went over to Augusta to see Henry's wife[99] who was not able to come over to the wedding. I was too unwell suffering with a severe cough to remain longer than to dine. She seems a nice domestic little woman & Henry very fond of her.

We also took the children & Bessie & went over to the China Factory at Kaolin[100] a visit which interested us greatly. I was much struck with the "Potter's Wheel" the same which has been used since remote Antiquity, the similitude of the Prophet, "Like clay upon the Potter's Wheel" and the text,

---

[96] James Buchanan (1791-1868), the fifteenth president of the United States, assumed an indecisive stance during the last months of his term in office. He denied the right of secession but felt he had no authority to force the seceded states back into the Union. He believed he had a responsibility to try to hold on to Fort Sumter and other federal military outposts in the South, however. *Dictionary of American Biography,* III, 212-214.

[97] Fort Pulaski, a United States fort located on Cockspur Island, Georgia, guarded the sea approach to Savannah via the Savannah River. Boatner, *Civil War Dictionary,* 296-297; R. N. Scott and others (eds.), *The War of the Rebellion: A Compilation of the Official Records of the Union and Confederate Armies* (Washington: Government Printing Office, 70 volumes, 1880-1901), Series I, VI, 148, hereinafter cited as *Official Records (Army).*

[98] Mount Vernon was a United States arsenal in Alabama located thirty miles from Mobile. On January 4, 1861, Gov. Andrew B. Moore ordered Alabama troops to seize Mount Vernon and other federal forts in the state. Walter L. Fleming, *Civil War and Reconstruction in Alabama* (New York: Columbia University Press, 1905), 61.

[99] Henry Edmondston was married to the former Louisa Jane Dearing. See Introduction.

[100] There were several kaolin deposits being worked in the Aiken-Augusta area. The one visited by Mrs. Edmondston and her party was near the present town of Langley in Aiken County, South Carolina. Writers Program, Work Projects Administration (comp.), *South Carolina: A Guide to the Palmetto State* (New York: Oxford University Press, 1941), 14, 67, 119, 161, 178.

"Hath not the Potter power"[101] arose upon my mind with more of a personal application than I ever before felt. Who indeed hath made me to differ? Why was not I an outcast & forlorn—a slave to my own passions! To Thee O Lord is my praise & gratitude due!

Papa enjoyed our visit greatly. I never saw him take more pleasure in anything than he did in Patrick's society. His reminiscences of the past were so bright, his reccollections so graphic, that I longed to be able to take them down. His hearty "God bless you my children," as he parted from us at the Depot, is in my ear still.

---

[101] Romans 9:21. "Hath not the potter power over the clay, of the same lump to make the vessel unto honour, and another unto dishonour?"

1861

JANUARY 7, 1861

We left Aiken for Charleston taking little Frank Coffin[1] with us. Found all well at Charles['s] where we stayed one night.

JANUARY 8, 1861

Went to Lawrence at Mt Pleasant in the afternoon of the 8th. We had a most hearty welcome from Lawrence who seems really fond of Patrick.

JANUARY 9, 1861

On the morning of the 9th as we were dressing we suddenly heard the report of a heavy gun! followed by another! and another! A few moments sufficed to collect us all out in the front of the house where we had a fine view of Sumter, Moultrie & the Channel, and there sad to relate, steaming up the channel was a vessel with the US Flag flying at her peak![2] The expected re-inforcements for Sumter doubtless! Boom! Another cannon from the shore Batteries on Morris Island.[3] "Is she struck?" No! On she comes! Another! and another, whilst Sumter opens her Port Holes and slowly runs out her cannon, prepared for instant action. Now a heavy gun from Fort Moultrie! Will Sumter respond? No! Not yet! Another from Moultrie! How with Sumter now? Still silent! The vessel turns slowly. Is she struck? No one can tell, but slowly, reluctantly as it were, almost with a baffled look, the Steamer retreats down the channel.

Thank God! Every one ejaculates! But what think we of the treacherous Government who whilst pretending to treat, assuring its own Cabinet & the nation that no re-inforcements should be sent, deliberately breaks faith and attempts it? I blush for my country! Would that the North was not our exponent! Eleven guns in all were fired. Good God! Is this true? Is this the beginning of the Civil War of which we have heard so much, was the thought which sprung into my mind. And as I afterwards sat at Lawrence's breakfast table and looked from the luxurious & peaceful family scene in doors, across the still smooth water smiling in the beauty of the crisp morning air, to Sumter, standing stern, silent, sullen, defiant as it were, bristling with cannon, whilst a light smoke stealing up from her Battlements told that they were heating shot, ready for instant action, & thought how in an instant it could all be changed, that horror & ruin might take the place of peace and comfort, never did I feel so vividly the full force & beauty of the Collect for Peace in our Prayer book. Never did I utter it so fervently, never desire it so earnestly!

---

[1] Frank Coffin was Mrs. Edmondston's nephew, the son of Jessie and Amory Coffin, Sr.

[2] The *Star of the West* was a United States steamer dispatched by President Buchanan to take reinforcements and supplies to besieged Fort Sumter. Boatner, *Civil War Dictionary*, 793.

[3] Morris Island was located at the entrance of Charleston Harbor. Boatner, *Civil War Dictionary*, 299.

The same day we went back to the city & found it full of flying rumours.
Men in Uniform filling the streets, singly and in squads, all wending their way
to East Bay where steamers were firing up & leaving with re-inforcements,
munitions of War & supplies for Pinckney, Moultrie & the Batteries below on
Morris Island. Left on the same day for Raleigh.

JANUARY 10, 1861

Arrived [at Raleigh] on the morning of the 10th carrying with us the news
of the repulse of the "Star of the West"—for so was the steamer called—& Mr
Buchanan's treachery. Every where it was received with surprised dismay, the
feeling almost universally being to leave SC to herself, give her her Fort if she
required it, but deny her all the benefits of the Government, refuse her all
Postal intercourse etc. Predictions were freely made that in that event, in a
year at most she would if Mr Lincoln's government should be an impartial
one, petition to return into the Union. She met but few sympathizers, but Mr
Miller is the only man whom I have yet seen who upholds the action of the
Government. Margaret's exclamation when she heard it was "Why Kate, you
have been seeing History!"

Found Annie D at home, her Mother having become uneasy at last begged
her father to go for her. I am glad of it, as a grave cause of uneasiness is thus
removed from their minds. Frank Coffin and John Devereux struck up a
friendship to which David's & Jonathan's was but a joke. The other children
all well and already inflamed against the Yankees & "old Lincoln." The
North is sowing the wind; see that ere the next generation she does not reap
the Whirlwind!

JANUARY 13, 1861

Got home safely to Looking Glass on Sunday the 13th. My cough much
better, from a practice reccommended me by Dr Coffin[4] of "swabbing out"
my throat with a spunge and a weak solution of Caustic. Saw Mrs Mills at Mt
Pleasant—told me she had been cured of her Asthma by Iodide of Potassa.
Made a note for Dolly's benefit.

Found Father much excited against SC—cannot say enough of the folly of
her conduct. It almost frightened me to hear him. I hope he will not say so
much to Mr Edmondston. I do not think he does her full justice. For instance
he thinks it beneath their pretentions to chivalry, ungenerous & unhandsome
in fact, that they fired one shot at the Star of the West after she turned to
retreat! I do not agree with him, & tho' this "Gentlemen of the English
Guards fire . . . we never fire first!"[5] may be very grand—yet it is too high

[4] Dr. Amory Coffin, Sr. With William H. Geddings he wrote *Aiken; or, Climatic Cure*, later entitled *Aiken and its Climate* (Charleston: Walker, Evans and Cogswell, 1872). See Introduction.

[5] At the Battle of Fontenoy in 1745, Lord Charles Hay, commander of the First Grenadier Guards, was said to have requested the opposing French forces to fire. The French commander politely refused, saying "that the French guard never fired first." *Dictionary of National Biography*, XXV, 253.

strung for me! I never before heard of an action in which the firing ceased until the Flag was hauled down.

We went on as usual all the month of Jan. Killed Hogs, attended to house hold matters, Planted garden seed, Rode, walked, went to Hascosea, wrote letters, Read my new books—in short enjoyed ourselves in our usual way, the only draw back being the difference of feeling on Political matters between ourselves & father. As for Mama & Susan they are really bitter in their expressions, & Susan talked more nonsense about her "devotion to the Flag" than I ever thought I should hear a sensible woman like her utter! Altogether it was rather uncomfortable at times being with them.

Brother had a hearty laugh on me. He declared that he thought that the war would begin then & there between Mama & myself, because when I said that SC & Va had both a right to their Forts Sumter & Monro,[6] & that when they reclaimed them the Government ought to restore them, she became personal, called me "Catherine Edmondston!" told me that I had been brought up by honest people, & that she was surprised that I should be guilty of uttering such dishonourable & dishonest sentiments, & more to the same purpose. I made some retort & was going on when fortunately I remembered my Mother's last injunction & checked myself. But I was very indignant! What a pity that politics will intrude into private life!

January 28, 1861

Fanny['s] child was born—which in compliment to the centre upon which all eyes are fixed, I called Sumter. A few days after my Diary recommences.

February 6, 1861

Yesterday the dam just above the Looking Glass line broke. Our people had worked like beavers day & night below, but all to no purpose as it broke above them.[7] Owen went with the carriage to Weldon to bring Sister Frances to pay us a visit, but he cannot get back, & today Mr Edmondston has gone in a canoe to meet her & bring her here in that to her novel conveyance. I wander about on the edge of the water with Frank, put down sticks to measure how rapidly it falls or rises, & am unsettled generally.

---

[6] Fortress Monroe, completed in 1834, was located on the tip of Virginia's peninsula, commanding the entrance to Hampton Roads and the entire Chesapeake Bay. The fortress remained under Federal control throughout the Civil War. James T. Adams and others (eds.), *Dictionary of American History* (New York: Charles Scribner's Sons, 5 volumes, 1940; index and updating supplements), IV, 12-13, hereinafter cited as *Dictionary of American History*.

[7] Beginning about 1830 a system of building dams or dikes against the annual overflow became general along this section of the Roanoke River. For an illustration showing the present appearance of one of these dikes (at Ventosa Plantation), built over 100 years ago by slaves, see Aubrey Lee Brooks and Hugh Talmage Lefler (eds.), *The Papers of Walter Clark* (Chapel Hill: University of North Carolina Press, 2 volumes, 1948), I, 193.

I read an Essay in a book I bought in Charleston, "Recreations of a Country Parson"[8] which I like very much on Gidiness. I wish I could write like that man. What an endless source of happiness it must be. Commenced Robertson's Sermons;[9] will try & read one every day. I like what we have read of them greatly.

FEBRUARY 10, 1861

Sunday. Sister Frances is a terrible Unionist! Right or wrong, this "Glorious Union" is every thing. Now it is no longer glorious—when it ceases to be voluntary, it degenerates into a hideous oppression. Regret it heartily, mourn over it as for a lost friend, but do not seek to enforce it; it is like galvanizing a dead body! Mr Edmondston['s] arguments with her would be amusing were they not both so vehement & decided in their expressions; one is on thorns lest they should become personal. She mourns the defeat of Douglas, whilst she admits that he is "a vulgar drunkard," which I cannot understand. However if "Self the wavering balance shake—'tis rarely right adjusted."[10] Mr Miller was to have had an appointment probably a Cabinet one under him. For my part I execrate him even more than I do Lincoln; he is the cause of all this.

President Buchanon who could do much now, does nothing from a desire to keep Peace during the short remnant of his Administration. "Apres nous le Deluge!"[11] is I beleive his mottoe. He cares not for the future. It is "Gentlemen for God sake, wait until after the 4th of March, then fight as much as you please!" So he lies to both sides & keeps Faith with neither! He promised that Sumter should not be re-inforced without due notice—actually passed his word to Mr Thompson,[12] Sec of the Interior to that effect—& yet sends on to NY & hurries on the preparations & dispatches the "Star of the West." Mr Thompson discovers it, taxes him with his bad faith, Telegraphs to the authorities of SC, & resigns.

---

[8] *Recreations of a Country Parson*, written by Andrew Kennedy Hutchison Boyd (1825-1899), was published in three series in 1859, 1861, and 1878. *Dictionary of National Biography, Supplement*, I, 244-245.

[9] Frederick William Robertson (1816-1853) was an English clergyman and pulpit orator. His *Sermons*, in separate series, were published in 1855, 1857, 1859, and 1890. *Dictionary of National Biography*, XLVIII, 404-407.

[10] Robert Burns, "Epistle to a Young Friend," stanza 3.

[11] "After us the deluge"—a statement attributed to Louis XV of France. Bartlett, *Familiar Quotations*, 443.

[12] Jacob Thompson (1810-1885), originally from Caswell County, North Carolina, moved to Mississippi in 1835 and began a political career. He was appointed secretary of the interior in 1857 by Buchanan but resigned at the beginning of the Civil War to work for the Confederacy in various capacities. *Dictionary of American Biography*, XVIII, 459-460.

During the past month Florida, Mississippi, Alabama, Georgia & Louisianna have all passed Ordinances of Secession, seized the Forts & Arsenals within their borders & besieged Fort Pickens.[13] So now we are in a distracted state of affairs, seven States out of the Union & the US Flag beseiged in two places for on the 1st of this month Texas went out also. The Southern States I see take the name of Confederate States, & have assembled in Congress at Montgomery to form a provisional government. This Humbug of a "Peace Convention"[14] now assembled at Washington will do nothing. It is not equal to the emergencies of the times.

FEBRUARY 13, 1861

Mr E went to Halifax. Fanny's child reported quite sick. Sister F & I went to see it & prescribed amongst other things a warm bath as it was greased & *tarred*, actually tarred all over. I planted some Fruit trees we brought from Aiken in the Fowl Yard, Dick in Owen's absence playing the part of Adam. I teach Frank to read but it is slow work. "Reading without tears" has already cost him a flood!

FEBRUARY 14, 1861

Valentine's Day. Went to Hascosea. Sister F went with me. Began to plant my Fruit trees from Augusta, but was interrupted by a visit from Nannie & Mr Tom Hill[15] who spent the morning. They must have thought it a pursuit of pleasure under difficulties. Valentine's used to be thought the commencement of Spring. It does not feel much like it now however.

FEBRUARY 16, 1861

Sister F left. I have not enjoyed her visit as I should have done were she less violent & bitter against SC & the South generally. This glorious Union,

---

[13] Fort Pickens was located on the western extremity of Santa Rosa Island in Pensacola Bay. It remained under Union control throughout the war. Boatner, *Civil War Dictionary*, 641.

[14] The Washington Peace Conference met February 4-27, 1861, on call by the Virginia legislature, in an effort to preserve peace through compromise. The delegates from twenty-one states were hampered in their efforts at accommodation by extremists in Congress on both sides of the question who dismissed the convention's seven proposals on March 2, 1861. The convention's recommendations, essentially the same as the Crittenden Compromise attempt to guarantee the existence of slavery as a palliative for the South, failed to appease either faction, and their rejection was a source of satisfaction to partisans in the North and in the South. James G. Randall and David Donald, *The Civil War and Reconstruction* (Lexington, Mass.: D. C. Heath and Co., 1969), 151-152, hereinafter cited as Randall and Donald, *Civil War and Reconstruction*; Hugh Talmage Lefler and Albert Ray Newsome, *North Carolina: The History of a Southern State* (Chapel Hill: University of North Carolina Press, Third Edition, 1973), 449, hereinafter cited as Lefler and Newsome, *North Carolina*.

[15] Thomas Norfleet Hill (1838-1904) and Lucy Anne Hill were the son and daughter of Whitmel John and Lavinia Dorothy Barnes Hill. Thomas N. Hill was a lawyer in Halifax County before and after the Civil War, and from 1862 through 1866 he served as solicitor for Halifax County. Lucy Anne Hill married Gilbert Elliott of Elizabeth City, who performed construction work on the C.S.S. *Albemarle*. Pardon of Whitmel John Hill, 1865, Stuart H. Hill Collection; Smith and Smith, *History of Trinity Parish*, 85.

broken up for the sake of a few negroes! Rather let them go than destroy the Union. This is to me treason against Liberty. In the first place, it is not a "few negroes." It is the country, for I should like to know who could live here were they freed?—& then the principle involved! I *yeild nothing*—no compromise— where my *liberty*, my *honour*, dearer than life is concerned!

She knows too no more about the proper management of negroes than a child, tho' she has had them under her since she came to woman's estate. She thinks all discipline *severity*, *yet* complains if they are not perfect & makes them ten times more unhappy by her want of government than severe masters do by their excess of it. Vinyard was married whilst she was here & tho she had what to her was a splendid supper & was as happy & contented with it as tho it was a feast & desired nothing more, she took her for the object of her especial sympathy.

Planted Beets, Carrots, Spinach, Parsnips and Salsafy.

FEBRUARY 18, 1861

Finished planting fruit trees at Hascosea. Planted 2 doz Albany Strawberry plants bought in Augusta at Looking Glass. Walked with Frank.

Today was inaugurated at Montgomery Jefferson Davis,[16] President of the Confederate States of America, consisting of the states of South Carolina, Georgia, Florida, Alabama, Mississippi, Louisiana & Texas. O that North Carolina would join with her Southern sisters—sisters in blood, in soil, in climate & in institution. Would that these vile party politicians had no part or lot in her. For their own selfish agrandizement they hold her in a state almost of supplication to the North & make her seem deficient in spirit and in affection to the South! Virginia is jealous because she "the Mother of States" did not lead the movement. She will be the fag end of the Dis united States ere long.

All eyes on Fort Sumter, all tongues ask will Buchanon reinforce? Much sympathy is felt for Maj Anderson, even tho' many blame him for his hasty evacuation of Pinckney & Moultrie, his defiance as it were of SC, which did so much to bring things to a crisis, but all consider him a brave & Christian Gentlemen—"a foe man worthy of their steel."[17] He is treated by the authorities of SC with the most romantic & chivalric courtesy, allowed full access to the market of Charleston, nay supplied with all its delicacies, his mails uninterrupted & untampered with. In place of simply feeding her Enemy, South Carolina "brings forth butter in a Lordly dish," tho in better

---

[16] Jefferson Davis (1808-1889) was chosen by the provisional congress as president of the Confederacy on February 18, 1861. He was later elected by popular vote to the same office for a term of six years and was inaugurated at Richmond, Virginia, on February 22, 1862. *Webster's Biographical Dictionary*, 395.

[17] Sir Walter Scott, *The Lady of the Lake*, canto 5, stanza 10, line 239, hereinafter cited as Scott, *Lady of the Lake*.

faith than did Jael;[18] & whilst she goes to an enormous expense to beleaguer an enemy who must ultimately fall by the want of stores, she allows him to husband them by daily supplies of fresh rations. If that is not high toned courtesy I know not what it is. But they are a nation of Gentlemen.

Patrick with his Troop all day.

It gets almost painful to go to Father's we differ so widely. He it is true says nothing personal or unhandsome, but he censures so sweepingly every thing that SC does. Mama & Susan do go on so about the "*Flag.*" Who cares for the old striped rag now that the principle it represented is gone? It is but an emblem of a past glory. How can it be upheld when the spirit—nay even the body—that gave it value is lost?

That hateful National Intelligencer[19] is a fruitful bone of contention between us. A vile unjust deceitful sheet, it has the effrontery too to pretend to impartiality and under that flimsy mask stabs the South, decries her conduct, ridicules her position, digs out every improbable slander it can hunt up from the obscurity into which good taste, to say nothing of justice, would consign it, blazons it to the world with a manifest gout & says "See how just I am; even the faults of my own side I will not stoop to conceal, painful as it is to me to admit them"! My beleive is that it is as much a Northern—Abolition anti Southern sheet as the Tribune[20] only in a more Machiavelli like manner. Impartial indeed! & yet at Father's it is a text book, a political Koran, which can say no wrong, "so gentlemanly"! "so dignified"! "no personalities here"! "Old Federalist"! Had I patience to study its editorials perhaps I might find out what are "the principles which placed the house of Brunswick on the throne," but I have not.

Father actually beleives that this generous patriotism of the gentlemen of SC which leads them to make such munificent donations to the State Treasury is the result of compulsion, a sort of "Vehmgericht"[21] I suppose who informs them that so much is expected from them, "that they are marked men"! It is worse than the torture of the Inquisition,[22] for with the thumb of the victim in the screws they never expected them to say that it was pleasant,

---

[18] Judges 5:24-27.

[19] The *National Intelligencer* was a Washington, D.C., newspaper established in 1800 and edited at this time by William Winston Seaton (1785-1866), a staunch Unionist. Clarence S. Brigham, *History and Bibliography of American Newspapers, 1690-1820* (Hamden, Conn.: American Antiquarian Society, 2 volumes, 1947), I, 103-104; *Dictionary of American Biography*, XVI, 541-542. Mrs. Edmondston sometimes refers to the newspaper as the "Nat Int."

[20] Horace Greeley (1811-1872), a noted antislavery leader and staunch Unionist, edited the *New York Tribune* and was vociferous in his radical views. *Concise Dictionary of American Biography*, 366-367.

[21] The Vehmgericht was one of the various criminal tribunals which flourished in Germany during the late medieval period. It met in secret and usurped many of the functions of government. *Encyclopedia Americana*, XXVII, "Vehmgericht," 720-721.

[22] The Inquisition was a court, noted for its use of torture to extract information, instituted to inquire into offenses against the Roman Catholic church. Benét, *Reader's Encyclopedia*, 541.

tho they did sometimes make them declare that a confession was voluntary tho rung from them by torture. I did not think he would give credit to so glaring a falsehood, even tho endorsed by the Nat Intelligencer. Then the amount of taxation he sums up which the poor South Carolinians are forced to pay casts Sidney Smith's taxed Englishmen in the shade altogether. He is the mettled steed caracoling gaily along, whilst the Carolinian is the over borne pack horse hardly able to hobble.

FEBRUARY 19, 1861

Our Wedding Day! fifteen years married! fifteen years of happiness! Had our usual celebration & the servants their plum pudding & Glass of Wine. Grant that the next fifteen may find us as united and happy. Walked with Patrick to the Ploughs. Another mule sick. I suppose he will die too.

FEBRUARY 21, 1861

Planted the Apple trees we brought from Augusta. Peach trees begining to bloom. From my record I see that in 1851 they first bloomed on Feb 25th; in 52 on March 6th; in 56 on April 6th—56 was a most backward spring, for on the 1st of April I see "not a leaf has expanded not a green thing to be seen." In 1860, the Peach bloomed here about the 1st of March, as we saw them first between Society Hill & Florence on the 29th of Feb. Patrick out with his Troop.

FEBRUARY 28, 1861

Election by the people of NC as to whether they will call a Convention and if so, what course it shall adopt in these troublous times.[23]

MARCH 1, 1861

Planted at Looking Glass more Salsafy, Celery, Leeks, Vic Cabbage, Lettuce of Kinds, Radish for brother's children. In hot bed sowed Egg Plant & Tomatoes. Saw the first strawberry blossom.

MARCH 2, 1861

First Shad caught. Planted Tom Thumb & Aults Extra Early Peas, Sage, & Onion setts. Plum trees in blossom. Peaches bloom scatteringly.

MARCH 4, 1861

Today was inaugurated that wretch Abraham Lincoln President of the US. We are told not to speak evil of Dignities, but it is hard to realize he is a

---

[23] North Carolinians voted, February 28, 1861, on whether to hold a convention to consider secession; 47,323 votes were cast against the convention resolution, while 46,672 votes supported it. Lefler and Newsome, *North Carolina*, 448-449.

Dignity. Ah! would that Jefferson Davis was our President. He is a man to whom a gentleman could look at without mortification as cheif of his nation. "How glorious was the" President elect on his tour, asking at Railway Stations for impudent girls who had written him about his whiskers & rewarding their impudence with a kiss! Faugh! Sweet Republican simplicity how charming thou art, when the future head of a great nation, a man upon whom all eyes are bent measures his august person inch by inch with a visitor whom he fears is taller than himself & chuckles to find himself mistaken. But then Saul was a head & shoulders higher than the multitude—why should not Abraham rest his importance on his stature? How dignified was his entrance in disguise into his future Capital. How grateful should we be to the long cloak & Scotch Cap which saved him from the bloody designs of his Southern enemies.[24] Well, we have a Rail Splitter and a tall man at the head of our affairs! Ned Bartley is both & perhaps excels Mr Lincoln in one or both points, but then he is not of Anglo Saxon blood. Neither is the Vice President Mr Hannibal Hamlin. Gentlemen we can match you on all points to a nicety. Ah my country! God keep you when such hands hold the helm!

Went to the nursery. Noticed an Aldermanic development about one or two of the children & called Gatty's attention to it. She said, "Miss, I'se give them chillun worm seed fried & worm seed biled & it dont do em no good. I have laid off to ax Master for some worm draps." I taxed Dicy with dirt eating[25] which she vehemently denied until most traiterously Ailsie stepped in & said, "Now Dicey you know you does." "& how do you know Ailsie?" "I seed her when we went to the spring & she give me some"! So Dicey & Ailsie were put on a course of rusty nails & Vinegar, with severe threats for the future if they continued it.

MARCH 5, 1861

Went to Hascosea. Straightened Asparagus beds. Sowed Beets, Carrots, Salsafy, Onions, Leeks, & turnips. Mr. Edmondston & I set out 22 Dwarf Pears from Philadelphia & 4 Dwarf Apples. Brought 2 pears & 2 Apples to Looking Glass.

Patrick is dreadfully despondant and enough to take the heart out of one. Whilst we were planting the Trees—I holding it & he throwing in the Earth— he suddenly stopped & said "where is the use? We may be doing this for the Yankees! Before this tree bears fruit the Yankees may have over run our whole country." On my remonstrating he continued, "Yes before a year has

---

[24] Due to reports of assassination plots in Washington, Lincoln chose to change his original schedule and arrive by night. The report of his disguise in a "Scotch Cap" was false. Carl Sandburg, *Abraham Lincoln: The Prairie Years and The War Years* (New York: Harcourt, Brace and Co., 1-volume edition, 1954), 203-207.

[25] Dirt- or clay-eating, apparently the result of a dietary deficiency, existed among Negroes and some of the poorer rural whites in the South. Clement Eaton, *A History of the Old South: The Emergence of a Reluctant Nation* (New York: Macmillan Publishing Co., Inc., Third Edition, 1975), 282-283.

gone over our heads a rascally Yankee may pull this identical tree up." It cast a damper upon me & I said, "O Patrick, dont talk so; you distress me." "Well" he said as he resumed his spade, "I wont! But depend on it before this tree bears fruit—we shall be in the midst of the most desperate War the world ever saw!" Pray God he prove a false prophet.

MARCH 6, 1861

Came Mr Lincoln's Inaugral. I scarcely know which to dwell most on, its wickedness or its weakness! The cloven foot is there & an attempt made to draw a drapery around it—an attempt which fails so signally as to excite ones contempt.

Rode with Patrick. Had a long & gloomy talk about the state of our country. I hope no one will say any thing more about SC to him. It needs but the spark to fall upon the carded flax. Went to the Ploughs & the Ditchers.

At Father's. Could I have beleived that any Southern person could find any thing to commend in Lincoln's message? But so it is. Mama & Sue both think "he means well"! Heaven save the mark! Father does not like it & looks gloomy. Lincoln's intense vulgarity disgusts him, his talk about "running the Machine as he finds it" revolts every sentiment of good taste. Rather say he will drive in his wedge where he finds the split & that Mr Lincoln will be Mason & Dixon's line.[26] Virginia surely cannot stand every thing, nor can this so called "Peace Congress" long throw sand in her eye. Should she secede, what an odd position N Carolina would occupy, fairly "squeezed" out of the Union. Mrs Lincoln's invitation to Mr Buchanon to stay with them when he came to Washington must have made him wince, for he at least understands how gentle folks ought to behave.

Heard Frank's lessons. He begins to think that Mrs Devereux "dont like South Carolina at all"!

MARCH 7, 1861

Rode with Patrick all over the Plantation & wound up at the Log Bridge where the hands are making a water fence; thence down the line of new fence in the woods on the outside of the Brown Swamp to a point opposite the Fox field where there is to be another Water fence. Such sudden ascents & descents, such gullies & such Ravines I had no idea were to be found in our flat country. Judas Tree in bloom.

Heard today that on the 5th of this month Major Beauregard, an officer of the old US Army, a native of Louisiana, had been placed in command of the forces beseiging Fort Sumter. The first order he issued was to stop the supplies of Tallow candles, which until then were regularly admitted. Patrick

---

[26] A symbolic border between the North and South that originated as a line surveyed to settle a border dispute, the Mason-Dixon Line served to divide slave territory from free territory during the antebellum period. Boatner, *Civil War Dictionary*, 516.

says that Grease of some sort—& tallow is best—is almost a necessity in handling case mated Guns, & so Tallow is in fact a munition of War! It shows the importance of having a regular Army officer at the head of affairs!

All the negotiations, the messages to & from Washington & Sumter which have kept us on the qui vive [27] for weeks, seem to come to nothing! I have said nothing of them for many of them were mere rumours waiting for the result which seems destined never to come. This wretched farce of a "Peace Congress" held at Washington to which N C must disgrace herself by sending Commissioners[28] will soon end in smoke. I would not have such a Peace as they are negotiating, rather patching up.

Poor old Mr Crittenden! [29] the best thing his new wife can do for him is to take him home to Kentucky & hide him. He drivels so about this "Glorious Union," as though it were not already broken. He must be in his dotage. I say roll him in a US Flag & put him in a Museum as an speciman of an extinct species of the genus "old Fogy." "Let me not live after my flame lacks oil to be the snuff of younger spirits"[30] and his flame lacks it most essentially.

After being doubtful for some days it is now pretty well satisfied that this other bit of fine Adamite earth, North Carolina, is satisfied with things as they are & does not want a Convention. Well is she named Rip Van Winkle! [31]

MARCH 9, 1861

Opened a new barrel of Flour from Richmond. This year I hope we shall be able to get our own Wheat Ground. Our "Biscuit Patch" looks finely now. Patrick with his Troop.

MARCH 10, 1861

Sunday. Mr Benton came & preached for us. A well educated, cultivated, & excellent young man, but I cannot tell what it is—he has too much of the young Clergy man about him! I have been trying to read "Ruskin,"[32] which he lent me, but get on slowly The truth is I am interested in nothing now but

---

[27] *Qui vive* is a French expression meaning "who lives, who goes there?"

[28] North Carolina's delegates to the Peace Convention were Thomas Ruffin, Daniel Moreau Barringer, David S. Reid, John Motley Morehead, and George Davis. Ashe, *Biographical History*, II, 75-76, 257.

[29] John Jordan Crittenden (1787-1863), a nationally prominent politician from Kentucky, was the author of the Crittenden Compromise of 1860. This proposal sought to avert open conflict between the North and South by restoring the status quo of the Missouri Compromise and guaranteeing the protection of slavery in Washington, D.C. It also formed the basis of discussion at the Washington Peace Conference. *Dictionary of American Biography*, IV, 546-549.

[30] William Shakespeare, *All's Well that Ends Well*, act 1, sc. 2, lines 58-62, hereinafter cited as Shakespeare, *All's Well that Ends Well*.

[31] During the early nineteenth century North Carolina, underdeveloped, backward, and indifferent, was often characterized as the "Rip Van Winkle state." Lefler and Newsome, *North Carolina*, 314.

[32] John Ruskin (1819-1900) was an English painter, art critic, and essayist. Benét, *Reader's Encyclopedia*, 958.

the State of the country & the aesthetics of painting fall dead on my ear, tho
there are some fine thoughts & fine writing in what I have read. He gave me
some lines of Carlyle which struck me so much that I will transcribe them
here:

> Lo here hath been dawning
> Another—blue day!
> Think wilt thou let it
> Slip useless away?
>
> Out of Eternity
> This new day is born
> Into Eternity
> At night doth return!
>
> Behold it aforetime
> No eye ever did—
> So soon it forever
> From all eyes is hid!
>
> Here hath been dawning
> Another blue day!
> Think wilt thou let it
> Slip useless away?![33]

MARCH 11, 1861

Patrick with his Troop. Went to walk with my little attendant Frank Coffin
& his sable attendant Sharper. It was a lovely afternoon, the grass a "living
green," Peach & Plum trees in full blossom, & the air filled with the delicate
fragrance of the latter. The sheep were in the Lot & the lambs amusing themselves like children by running around in a circle & jumping one after the
other over some Logs which lay in front of the Gin House. I stopped & called
Frank's attention to them when Sharper with a look of undisguised astonishment on his broad features said, "Why! Miss! aint you ever seed 'em afore!
I've seed 'em jump a many o' times!" Poor Sharper!

> "A primrose on the River brim!
> A simple primrose that to him
> And it was nothing more!"[34]

---

[33]Thomas Carlyle (1795-1881) was a Scottish essayist and historian. Mrs. Edmondston's quotation,
"Today," has some inaccuracies in it. See Burton Egbert Stevenson, *The Home Book of Verse, American and
English, 1580-1920* (New York: Henry Holt and Co., Fifth Edition, 1922), 2920.

[34]William Wordsworth, "Peter Bell," part 1, stanza 12.

March 14, 1861

I used to take delight in the French proverb "Heureux les peuple dont la vive ennui."[35] It was to me a picture of calm quiet domestic life & content, and I often made a personal application of it; it applies now no longer! For tho my life would in its repetition weary one to the full extent demanded by happiness, by its lack of stirring incident, it is not happy. I look outwards with a feverish anxiety, a longing. "What next?" I wait on the mail with an eagerness almost inexpressible; a foreboding for the future weighs on me all the time, & I look to Fort Sumter as a mine which may in a moment explode.

March 15, 1861

Snowing almost all day heavily. Peach Trees covered with blossoms & light fleecy snow. It is difficult to imagine anything prettier than the tender green of the lilac & syringa Foliage flecked with snow! A winding sheet I fear, tho it is not cold & no freeze.

March 17, 1861

St Patrick's day in the morning. Walked with Patrick. Talked of Fort Sumter & the state of the country all day. Ah! would that father & ourselves agreed better in our political notions. Thank God for the unity of spirit & feeling which exists between Patrick & myself. I do not beleive I could live had I not him to lean on & confide in. He is the only person to whom I ever talk *out*, that is unburden myself fully & fairly, feel perfectly at home, & say all I think. Some others I fear tiring, others again I know do not agree with & would not enter with my feelings. He gives me credit for all the best qualities of my nature & so fosters them that with him I am really better, more sensible, more entertaining than I am to any other mortal besides. He draws me out & makes me by his sympathy more of a companion & friend than I otherwise would be. Some people shut me up as it were. Being with them is like being plunged into an astringent bath, whilst with others I expand & become more genial, more communicative, brighter & more brilliant than I ever thought I could be. Is it sympathy? Mesmerism the fanatics at the North would call it, but I avoid even a word that they use if I can.

March 18, 1861

Another and this time a real wintry snow storm! Very cold & occasionally sleeting. This is certainly the death blow to the fruit & we shall pay in the loss our sense of *taste* will suffer this summer—for the gratification our sixth, our aesthetic sense now enjoys! The snow on the leaves & flowers is beautiful!

---

[35]"Happy are the people whose lives are boring."

MARCH 19, 1861

Had an amusing illustration of the value in which Cuffee holds himself to-day. Sharper & Frank were playing in the Lot when little George came up with the sheep. Sharper began to banter him about his size & among other things wound up the climax by telling him he "warnt worth a hundred dollars." "How much are you worth?" said Frank. "Me I am worth 500 dollars!" "And such an one?" "200 dollars," & so on until Frank, not wishing to be out done, said "And me! How much am I worth?" "Lord Marse Frank," said Sharper in a tone of ineffable disdain "You's white! You aint worth nothing!" Frank accepted his Anglo Saxon lot with an air & tone I thought of mortification!

MARCH 20, 1861

At the Nursery found Gatty under heavy complaint because Henry "had took Dicey & Ailsie & Mauzy & Mary & Dick & some others & give up a pair of shoes & turned 'em loose amongst the others!" "Why Gatty are they not old enough to work out?" "Yes Miss I spose they is, but its powerful hard on me. Just look at them babies. They was just getting sponsible and trustable to take care of them." So goes it Cuffy. Your aim & I suppose the aim of the whole world is to keep things from getting "powerful on yourself"! Patrick with his Troop.

MARCH 23, 1861

A little snow still left. We have had hard frosts since the 18th. Even the Apples will fail us & for the first time in my reccollection we shall not have a Lilac Blossom. Walked with Patrick—a regular tramp—all over the Plantation.

MARCH 24, 1861

Rode with Patrick. Went to the new dam which is slowly rising again under the hands of Father's Free negro gang. I do not like employing them however. Patrick does not like the Wheel barrow work. He says it will not stand like cart work; the packing of the hoofs & wheels consolidate it.

MARCH 25, 1861

Planted Potatoes at Hascosea later than we have ever before done so, Bishop's Dwarf & Champion of England Peas.

MARCH 26, 1861

Resowed all my garden seeds at Looking Glass, the frost & sleet having destroyed the whole of them. Mr E planted some Horse tooth corn. I wonder if it is called so from its shape or because it is particularly "toothsome" to the Equine species? Swallows arrived! Welcome to the little merry light hearted creatures. I see by my record that in 51 they came on the 24th of March; in 52 on the 30th; in 56 on the 23d & this year it is the 26th. Resowed Hot bed, Egg Plant & perfected Tomatoes in boxes.

Fort Sumter occupies all our thoughts. It is said that Beauregard has ordered the supplies from the Market to be cut off & that Maj Anderson has given the Government notice that he has provisions for only fifteen days! What will be the end, the wisest cannot conjecture.

MARCH 27, 1861

Dined at Father's. Mr E drilling his troop. Mama & Sue more enthusiastic than ever about the "Flag," what is, now that the Spirit which it represented is gone but a striped Rag! "The Flag under which we gained our Liberties"? No such thing. It was adopted after, or about the time of the last war in 1812 but the devotion Sue expresses for it is appalling. "We should get on very well were it not for the Cotton states." Well do it, for they are out of the Union. "Virginia is the Old Dominion—that's enough." "Where M' Gregor sits is the head of the table,"[36] I suppose, so we must be content!

Heard a good joke on the Va Convention[37]—an applicant for office said he wanted a good comfortable berth for life. A seat in the Va Convention would suit him!

I wish that the Post Masters would seize the Nat Int—as it passes through the office. I consider it an incendiary publication!

Commenced using 5 gals of Kerosene from Halifax.

APRIL 2, 1861

At Hascosea. Stayed all night. Dressed Flower garden. Found Asparagus coming up.

APRIL 3, 1861

Planted at Hascosea Snaps, Parsley, Vic Cabbage & Lettuce, Cabbage of kinds, cress, Lettuce of kinds, Pepper, Tomatoes, Celery, Leeks, Corn, Musk melons, cucumbers, Parsnips, & set out onion sets. Came home to Looking Glass in the evening. Found Aspargus coming up. Walked with Patrick to the Ditchers & the "Trash gang." No news from Fort Sumter.

APRIL 5, 1861

Replanted Beets; resowed Carrots & Salsafy.

---

[36]This quotation was first associated with Sir Walter Scott's *Rob Roy* (1817), a novel based on the life of the Scottish outlaw Robert MacGregor (1671-1734) who was called "Rob Roy" because of his red hair. Ralph Waldo Emerson used the same quote in *The American Scholar* (1837) with the substitution of "MacDonald" for "MacGregor." Alfred R. Ferguson (ed.), *Nature, Addresses, and Lectures*, Volume I of *The Collected Works of Ralph Waldo Emerson* (Cambridge, Mass.: Belknap Press of Harvard University Press [projected multivolume series, 1971—], 1971), 64; Benét, *Reader's Encyclopedia*, 936.

[37]Mrs. Edmondston was again referring to the Washington Peace Conference, also called the Virginia Convention.

APRIL 6, 1861

1st Rock Fish.

APRIL 7, 1861

Dog wood in blossom. In 51 it bloomed March 28th; 52, March 30th; 56, April 16th.

APRIL 8, 1861

Transplanted Cabbages sowed on the 28th of Jan viz. E Battersea, Ox heart, E. York. Planted Bush Squash & orange Melon.

APRIL 9, 1861

Sowed 6 weeks beans. Intense anxiety about Sumter. The S C. & Georgia troops concentrating there. Rumours of a reinforcing fleet being fitted out in N Y. Supplies from Charleston Market certainly stopped.

APRIL 12, 1861

Planted one Peach Stone Emilia and 5 concord grape seed sent me by Mrs Coffin.

APRIL 13, 1861

Dined with father. Mr Dunlop[38] of Petersburg there. Talked of nothing but Fort Sumter & the country until the mail came in, when every one drew a sigh of releif as there was no news. Great sympathy felt for Maj Anderson & his wife.[39] Poor Cousin Eliza, I should not wonder if it cost her her reason, tho I can not beleive that on the 1st of Jan she had her infant little Robert dressed in a Major's Uniform & made him receive visits at the Brevoort house as his father's representative. It cannot be true.*

* Yes, it is too true. I have seen his picture, which she sent her & my friend Ellen Mordecai,[40] dressed in Regimental. He looked like "Dandy Jack."

---

[38] This reference was probably to James Dunlop (1805-1870), whose wife Isabella Lenox Maitland (1811-1880) was a sister of Mrs. Edmondston's stepmother.

[39] Eliza Clinch Anderson was Mrs. Edmondston's cousin on her mother's side. Both Mrs. Anderson and Mrs. Edmondston were granddaughters of Nicholas Bayard (1736-1775) of New York. The New Year's reception discussed here is briefly mentioned in Swanberg, *First Blood*, 141. See Introduction.

[40] Ellen Mordecai (1790-1884) was the eldest daughter of Jacob Mordecai of Warrenton and the aunt of Margaret Mordecai Devereux, John Devereux's wife. She taught in her father's school in Warrenton and wrote an unpublished sketch of that town entitled "A History of Hastings." After the Warrenton Academy closed in 1819 she lived in Richmond and in New York as governess to various families. At the time of her death at the age of ninety-four she was living in Raleigh with her brother George Mordecai. For further information on the Mordecais, see George W. Mordecai Papers; Pattie Mordecai Collection; James A. Padgett (ed.), "The Life of Alfred Mordecai as Related by Himself," *North Carolina Historical Review*, XXII (January, 1945), 58-108; Lizzie Wilson Montgomery, *Sketches of Old Warrenton, North Carolina* (Raleigh: Edwards & Broughton Company, 1924), 13, 16-17, 138-139, hereinafter cited as Montgomery, *Sketches of Old Warrenton*.

Maj Anderson is a good officer & I suppose doing his duty, as those who know say he cannot resign. I do not see why, but I suppose that is because I dont know; tho I should think he could without charge of cowardice refuse to fight his brothers-in-Law & a country which holds all his property & where he is Administrator to so large an Estate as his Father-in-Law's was & request to be superceded & retire. Tho' if he is attacked he must I admit, do his best even against his own brother. That "noblisse oblige" & he must remain true to his trust. I am sorry for him but I cannot make a Hero of him.

On our way home Patrick left me to look after some plantation matters & Frank & I came in alone. On the table lay our mail from Scotland Neck. I idled about for some time, thinking all news from that quarter was forestalled by that from Halifax, when conceive my horror as I leisurely opened the Dispatch at seeing in large Capitals "Bombardment of Fort Sumter!" I burst into tears & Patrick entering at the moment I threw myself into his arms & wept like a child! Yes, it is done! The beginning of the end! Who can tell what will be?

APRIL 14, 1861

Sunday. Sent to Halifax for the news, which came in the form of a Telegram—Fort Sumter surrendered on Sat after 36 hours heavy bombardment. No lives lost on either side. God be praised! But what a miracle.

APRIL 15, 1861

Got full accounts of the Bombardment of Sumter. The authorities of South Carolina having positive information that the fleet in N Y was fitting out & was ready to leave for the re-inforcement of Sumter, Telegraphed to Mongomery & received positive instructions from the War Department to attack it. Accordingly, after due summons & notice given on the morning of the 12th, Friday, very early, the canonading began. Sumter was silent until after breakfast when she responded east & west to Moultrie, the Floating Battery, & the Batteries on Morris Island. Steadily the Bombardment continued all day and all night, without a casualty on either side.

On Saturday the U S fleet with the expected reinforcements arrived off the harbour. Then was the firing redoubled! Sumter signaled violently to her friends for aid, fought with her colours at half mast, yet no aid came. Sumter took fire. Gallantly she fought enveloped in smoke & flame, yet still lay [the] U S navy, "as idle as a painted ship upon a painted ocean"![41] Cowards! to stand at a distance & see a brave comrade perish! Her flag is down! Has she surrendered? No, shot down by one of the Batteries, see it streaming from her Battlements. Again she signals for assistance. Shame on the dastard Navy outside! So wore on the day.

---

[41] Samuel Taylor Coleridge, *The Rime of the Ancient Mariner*, part 2, stanza 8, lines 117-118.

One chivalrous act I must mention When the Flag was shot down, admidst the thickest of the fight, through the smoke of battle went a little boat with another U S Flag for their enemy to fight under. Was ever anything handsomer? Worthy of Bayard![42] After thirty four hours heavy bombardment, everything that could burn in the Fort being destroyed, Major Anderson in despair of releif from the Fleet outside struck his Flag & hung out a white one. Articles of capitulation were agreed on by which it was stipulated that the Garrison should march out with all the honours of War & salute their Flag & then have the option of Chartering a vessel or of returning in one outside to N Y.

Now comes the strangest part that during all this heavy canonade, kept up for so long not one man was hurt on either side, yet when the U S troops came to salute their Flag, their own canon burst, killing two & wounding three men, two of whom have since died.[43] Does it not seem wonderful? Truly as tho' the hand of Providence had been interposed, as tho God himself had said "Ye shall not shed thy brother's blood." Thank God for it. The breach not being yet stained with blood we may separate in Peace. The Union is gone, but it may fall apart from its own want of cohesion & we be spared a protracted civil struggle.

The conduct of the Fleet is inexplicable & so it appears thought Maj Anderson, as he refused their Commander——his hand when he went on board his ship which was to convey him to N Y. Major A has behaved well & gallantly. Let him now go North, resign his Command, & return. He will find a nation of friends and admirers. Beauregard has distinguished himself; would that we as a nation had the right to join in the ovation he deserves! But alas, we are not of the Southern Confederacy!

April 15, 1861

All hands hard at work on the Dam above the Looking Glass line. It is nearly completed & the River is rising so steadily & bearing upon it that we fear it must go. Walked there with Frank & Sharper. Found Mr E hard at work. Met Sue & Mr John Whitaker[44] there. Hurried home to have a supper cooked for the hands. Had a bushel of Beans made into soup & five or six quarts of Coffee parched & a large wash pot of Coffee made, besides bacon, Potatoes etc, & bread of course.

---

[42] This name is associated with extreme bravery and courage after the French national hero Pierre du Terrail Chevalier de Bayard (1475-1524). Benét, *Reader's Encyclopedia*, 84.

[43] Mrs. Edmondston's figures are slightly in error. One man was killed instantly and five others were wounded, only one of whom died. Swanberg, *First Blood*, 328.

[44] John H. Whitaker, plantation owner in Northampton County, was captain (later major) of Co. B, Ninth North Carolina (First Cavalry) Regiment. He died at Fairfax Station, Virginia, June 29, 1863. Manarin and Jordan, *North Carolina Troops*, II, 7, 19.

APRIL 16, 1861

All of no avail. The dam gave way about daylight this morning. We lost all the work; the Low grounds are just ploughed & planted with corn, besides fencing & ditching. But outside matters occupy us so that tho' it is a heavy blow in both money & work & entails strict economy on us for the rest of the year, we do not regard it as ordinarily we should. Public affairs absorb all our interest; the desire to know what next Mr Lincoln will do!

APRIL 17, 1861

Heard last night that Lincoln had issued his Proclamation calling for 75,000 troops to compel South Carolina to obedience. Set to the Gov of N C. for [———] that being the quota required from N Carolina. Thank God! that we had a governor[45] who had spirit to refuse, which he did most decidedly & firmly. Think of the insult the man puts on us!—call upon us to subdue our Sister! The Proclamation was dated the very day of the Evacuation of Sumter! So he must have had an agent to Telegraph to him, when lo! out rumbles his thunder!

Am sorry to hear that Mr Walker, the Sec of War,[46] on the news of the surrender of Sumter's reaching Mongomery, made a speech & pointed to the Confederate Flag & said "On to Washington & plant this there"! We do not intend to go & it seems an idle threat.

Here my journal stops for a short time, for events flowed so thickly one on the other, that I thought only of the present & never recorded anything but a bare skeleton of dates and a few notes to assist my memory, land marks as it were but the events are so recent that I remember them quite well.

Never was known such excitement as was caused by Mr Lincoln's proclamation. The whole South flew to arms. On the day the Gov. refused N Carolina's quota, Forts Caswell & Macon & the Arsenal at Fayetteville were seized by volunteer troops without waiting for orders.[47] On the 18th in

---

[45] The governor of North Carolina at this time was John Willis Ellis (1820-1861) of Rowan County. North Carolina's quota consisted of two regiments with a total complement of seventy-four officers and 1,486 men. *Official Records (Army)*, Series III, I, 68-69.

[46] Leroy Pope Walker was named secretary of war for the Confederate government on February 21, 1861. For reasons of health, he resigned on September 16, 1861, but continued to serve in various capacities throughout the war. Boatner, *Civil War Dictionary*, 885.

[47] Fort Caswell, a bastioned masonry structure of great strength, was located about 30 miles south of Wilmington on the west bank of the Cape Fear, where it controlled the river's main entrance. Fort Macon, located on the eastern extremity of Bogue Banks on a narrow strip of sand with ocean on one side and the sound on the other, guarded the harbor at Beaufort. Early in 1861 these forts and the Fayetteville Arsenal were occupied by ordnance sergeants. When Governor Ellis refused to order their seizure, a group of Wilmington citizens calling themselves the "Cape Fear Minute Men" took possession of Fort Caswell and Fort Johnston (at Southport, formerly Smithville). Ellis ordered the forts evacuated, but in April he ordered in troops and in June the forts were ceded to the Confederate government. Daniel Harvey Hill, *A History of North Carolina in the War Between the States: Bethel to Sharpsburg* (Raleigh: Edwards and Broughton, 2 volumes, 1926), I, 27-28, 155-156, 247, hereinafter cited as Hill, *Bethel to Sharpsburg*.

secret session Va signed her Ordinance of Secession. She had sent on a commission composed of three of her most dignified Citizens,[48] asking Mr Lincoln in her name what course he intended to pursue in relation to the coercion of the South. What does the underbred boor do but ask in an excited tone, "Did you read my inaugral? Read that. I shall stick to that." Some persons even say that he rushed out of the East Room & returned in a few moments with some copies of it which he thrust into their hands. Polished diplomacy that!

Before the Commissioners reached Richmond with their answer the call for troops was made. The Ordinance was signed in secret session to enable Virginia to resume her sovereignty over the Navy Yard, but Lincoln had his spies in the convention itself. One member, Carlyle,[49] first telegraphed & then immediately left himself for Washington. The traitor! Orders were immediately issued by the government at Washington to Commodore Rogers & Pendergrast to repair to the Navy Yard, bring off what property he could, burn, blow up, and destroy the rest. The first thing the citizens of Norfolk knew was the commencement of this wholesale act of treachery & destruction.

Gov Wise[50] who happened to be in the city sent and remonstrated. The only answer the Commodore gave was to point to a line of loaded mortars commanding Norfolk & say that if molested he should instantly shell the town! There being no force to resist, there was nothing to be done but to sit passive whilst this act of Vandalism was going on.

All night long did the gallant U S sailors labour on their work of destruction, spiked canon, broke & threw into the Dock ton after ton of small & side arms from the Armory, removed the muskets from the fire proof building that held them & stacked them in the Sail lofts & other wooden buildings which when they left they set on fire! They loaded what ships that were ready for sea with powder, canon, arms etc. The others, the Merrimac, the old Pensylvania, & two more they first scuttled & then set on fire; but the water gaining on the fire, they sunk comparatively uninjured, & when they were afterwards raised, betrayed an act of treacherous cruelty which if anything could make them blush would do so. The guns were found all shotted & placed at such an angle as to command Norfolk, with the horrible design that

---

[48] The committee consisted of Alexander H. H. Stuart, George W. Randolph, and William Ballard Preston. Randall and Donald, *Civil War and Reconstruction*, 181-182.

[49] John Snyder Carlile (1817-1878) was a member of Congress from Virginia from 1855 through 1857. A strong Unionist, he was determined (following passage of the Virginia Ordinance of Secession) to create the new state of West Virginia and keep it in the Union. Carlile secured the support of the United States Congress in his endeavor to secure passage of a bill establishing a new state. His attempts to include portions of Virginia loyal to the Confederacy in West Virginia's borders, however, were disavowed by the West Virginia legislature; and he never held public office again. *Dictionary of American Biography*, III, 493-494; Henry T. Shanks, *The Secession Movement in Virginia, 1847-1861* (Richmond: Garrett and Massie, 1934), 212.

[50] Henry Alexander Wise (1806-1876) served as governor of Virginia from 1856 to 1860. He aided in the suppression of the John Brown raid and was a strong advocate of states' rights during the Virginia Convention in 1861. He was appointed brigadier general in 1861 and was promoted to major general in 1865. *Dictionary of American Biography*, XX, 423-425; see Appendix.

as the fire reached them they would go off & rake the wharves & shipping then crowded with men, women & children all anxious to see what was going on! But a Merciful God averted this calamity, by causing one element to gain upon the other, & the vessels sunk before the fire reached the guns. Upon the Germantown they cut down the large Shears used in putting in masts & sunk her as she lay at the wharf.

They were greatly hurried in their work of devastation by the device of the President of the Norfolk road, who caused an Engine & a train of cars to run out & in again at short intervals as the troops were arriving in large numbers, and as they were not strong enough to resist a large force they feared being overpowered. At length they set sail, with the Pawnee, The Cumberland, the Richmond & some other vessels loaded as full as they could get them in the short space of time. But the authorities had outwitted them, for when they came to the passage from the Elizabeth River into Hampton Roads, they found the channel obstructed with sunken vessels & in order to get over had to throw overboard a large quantity of their ill gotten plunder. They left every thing in the Navy Yard that could burn blazing behind them! They even at great labour undermined the magnificent dry dock & placed about twenty kegs of powder under it. This they fired as they left by a slow match, but a little boy from Portsmouth, who had hid himself under a pile of timber from childish curiosity to see what they were about, understood their intention & when they had lighted their fuse & departed he emerged from his conceal-ment, & kicking the planks over upon which the train was laid, saved that magnificent work to the country. His name was [———].[51]

The scene is described as awful & grand in the extreme—the tall ship houses, the sail lofts, the vessels upon the stocks, everything in short that would burn, being at the same time wrapped in flame, whilst at intervals the heavy explosion of some mine which they had left behind told how complete was the work of destruction! In fact that anything was spared is owing to the fire proof nature of the work shops of the Armories etc. & their want of time to under mine & blow them up.

We heard all this the day after it happened on our way to Clarksville where Mr E was going to drill his troop. He instantly called a meeting of them, & they authorized him to tender their services to the Gov of N C. This he did in-stantly & was accepted with the information that they were the first Cavalry Co. & the second of any kind who had come forward.

---

[51] The commandant of the Gosport Navy Yard reported that on April 20, 1861, he was unable to get the *Merrimack, Germantown,* and *Plymouth* to a place of safety and decided to destroy them. The guns on board were spiked, and anything which could not be put on the *Cumberland* was thrown overboard or destroyed. Capt. H. G. Wright, United States Engineer Corps, and Comdr. John Rodgers of the navy were assigned the duty of blowing up the drydock, "a massive structure of granite masonry" for which a platform was constructed on the gallery, and 2,000 pounds of powder were laid. Richard Rush and others (eds.), *Official Records of the Union and Confederate Navies in the War of the Rebellion* (Washington: Government Printing Office, 30 volumes, 1894-1914), Series I, IV, 288-291, 297, hereinafter cited as *Official Records (Navy).*

On the same day, the 20th of April, Va also seized the Arsenal at Harper's Ferry which was evacuated by the U S after an attempt to burn it in which they signally failed. Then was raised the furious cry of the "Capital in danger," in consequence of Mr Walker's ill considered speech of "on to Washington," & tho Washington was not menaced, nor was there a single body of armed men nearer than Charleston, troops were massed in large numbers from Pensylvania, New York & Massachusetts to resist its seizure. Lincoln & the leaders knew there was no danger, no intention of an attack, but used this cry to inflame the masses.

On the 19th, tho we heard it on the 20th, a Massachusetts Regiment on its passage through Baltimore was hissed & a few stones thrown by the mob, where upon the gallant soldiers discharged their peices at random, most of the shot striking innocent spectators in the secon & third story windows, where upon the mob exasperated, charged them pell mell with bricks, paving stones & missiles of all kinds & fairly routed the gallant Massachusets men, hunted them through the streets insomuch that their officers could never re-assemble them all again. Only one was killed, but many innocent Baltimorians perished by their random shot.[52] Baltimore became immediately the scene of terrible excitement. The Mayor protested against the passage of any more troops, but the citizens took that into their own hands & burned the Bridges & tore up the R R track on both sides even so far as the Pensylvania line.

Mr Lincoln is waited on by Baltimore Commissioners. They find him in terrible excitement—"must have troops!"—takes them to the window & points over to Arlington Heights, tells them "of the danger to Washington"! "The Rebels can command the city! They can throw a shell in here sir, here where we stand!" However he promises that nothing more shall be done to exasperate Baltimore, that his troops shall pass through Anapolis; so to prevent that road being torn up he lines it with troops. The North seizes the cry of the "Capital in danger," rushes to arms, takes great credit to itself for Loyalty & is violent in its abuse of the Rebels! The miserable sham of a Peace Convention breaks up without doing anything. Mr Crittenden cries & gets insulted by the Northern Abolitionists but does not seem to be aware of it. But I resume my journal which I fortunately find has not all been destroyed as I thought.

---

[52] When about 1,800 Massachusetts and Pennsylvania militiamen arrived in Baltimore on April 19, 1861, the police force was alerted and requested to maintain order during their passage through the city. Before all the men could be transported by cars to the Washington depot, obstructions were thrown up and the remaining men were forced to march through the city. The mayor put himself at their head; nevertheless, missiles were thrown at the men and some were injured. Col. Edward F. Jones of the Massachusetts Volunteers, on learning that passage of the troops would be resisted, issued ammunition but ordered the troops to shoot only if they were fired on and anyone was hit and then to shoot only at those people firing upon them. When some of the mob fired on the soldiers, the fire was returned and several were killed on both sides. *Official Records (Army)*, Series I, II, 7-11.

April 20, 1861

Went to Father's & found every one in intense excitement about the news of yesterday. Had not seen Mama since the fall of Sumter & almost dreaded to meet her. Mr Edmondston feels so keenly about it, his own flesh & blood having been concerned in it—actually under fire—that I fear neither of us will bear as patiently as perhaps we ought the strictures on South Carolina! But fortunately Virginia, "the old Dominion" having herself seceeded, the outrages at the Navy Yard, & the outbreak in Baltimore formed the principal indeed the engrossing topic to us all.

Father looks grave & unhappy, but I am delighted to see that all uphold the action of the Gov of N C in denying troops. This difference of opinion with Father has been very sad to me, for I think I can honestly say that it is the first time in my life that my judgment & feelings did not yeild to him. Ah! my love for him has been a sentiment with me all my life. The admiration, the pride, the earnest warm affection of my heart have all been concentrated on him since my childhood & to differ from him now in so vital a point has been unhappy indeed to me. I cannot enter into Sue's enthusiasm about the Flag. I consider it disgraced, disgraced by the cowardly conduct of the Fleet off Charleston & by the acts of Vandalism perpetrated under its folds at Portsmouth, but we cannot all think exactly alike.

April 22, 1861

Mama & Sue left for Petersburg on a shopping expedition. Father for Halifax Court & Patrick, Frank & I for Home. We all left the house on foot owing to the freshet, they up the river to the carriage, we down to where we had a canoe in waiting for us. The scene was beautiful & peaceful in the extreme, drifting along over the still, placid water through a wall of living green, for we went through the Swamp. The bright sunshine, the tender foliage, the graceful canoe—all made a picture which could we have banished the thought that the water covered our best land & that our corn was ten feet beneath its surface, we would have enjoyed exceedingly! I do not think that "utility" is always one of the elements of the beautiful, but true it is that we cannot enjoy this scene to the full of our aesthetic sense.

April 23, 1861

Came brother John, full of news about the action of the State & preparations for war; told of us a shocking thing that himself & another gentleman, a slaveholder, had the greatest difficulty in preventing yesterday at Weldon. The actual hanging of a man by the mob, for the suspicion even of Abolitionism. Mama & Sue were in the cars, & he had to use every endeavour to keep concealed from them the actual state of affairs. He intends to join the SNMR. So Patrick will have some one he can confide in with him in case of

The description of the Roanoke River in the entry for April 22 is verified by this picture. (Photograph from files of Beth Crabtree.)

actual War. With him came Mr John Whitaker, & they had a long & earnest conversation with Mr E which resulted in his determining to go to Raleigh with Brother tomorrow. Ah this absence—how hard it will be to bear, but courage! "As thy days—so shall thy Strength be"![53]

APRIL 24, 1861

Mr E. left for Raleigh. Frank & I went to Hascosea on a gardening expedition. How lonely it is without Mr Edmondston! Gardening is no longer the same occupation. Planted my Dahlia Roots. As I worked Mrs Hemans[54] Lines "Bring Flowers to strew in the Conquerer's path" recurred again &

[53] Deuteronomy 33:25. "Thy shoes shall be iron and brass; and as thy days, so shall thy strength be."

[54] Felicia Dorothea Hemans (1793-1835) was an English writer best known for her lyrics. This quotation is from "Bring Flowers," stanza 2. [Felicia Dorothea Hemans], *The Complete Works of Mrs. Hemans, Edited by Her Sister* (New York: D. Appleton and Company, 2 volumes, 1866), I, 543; Benét, *Reader's Encyclopedia*, 493.

again to me. Yes! I will plant flowers for the Conquerer's—for our own path! A short time of conflict & the day is ours—ours for Freedom, for Right, for Self Government! They can never overcome, never conquer us, for we fight for our Birthright—Freedom! Let them try their boasted *Blockade*! *Who cares?* Who will be most hurt—us? themselves? or England? Not us, for we make the necessaries of Life. But what will England do for Cotton when her looms are idle? what her starving population for bread? King Cotton will raise his own blockade in his own time in spite of the Yankee vessels.

A heavy & sudden thunderstorm came up about dark. As I sat in the still silent house alone with little Frank, almost in utter darkness, as the storm caught the servants out of the house, & I could not find a match, he asked me if I was afraid. I said "No! my child, God will take care of us, even tho Uncle is gone. Are you afraid?" "No Aunt Kate not with you," & then waxing bold he continued "I am not afraid of Thunder, and I know I am not of old Lincoln & the Yankees. I hate Yankees!" I could feel his little fist clench in my hand & his pulses quicken as he said it! Can they nourish so insane an idea as reconstruction when the very children feel it so? And as for subjugation, annihilation first!

April 25, 1861

Up early and to work in the garden. I missed "the grand old gardener" awfully all day. Planted all my Flower Seed, Ochra, Nasturtium, Lima Beans, Squash; re-planted Snaps, Musk melons, & Sage—generally delightful work to me, but woe is me, gardening is not what it used to be—Patrick from home! I alone preoccupied & heavy hearted. Went to Father's in the afternoon intending to remain with him whilst Patrick is absent. Mama & Sue both in Petersburg. Mr John Whitaker came in. Father & himself had a long discussion as to the Election or Appointment of officers. We are really at war! Troops are concentrating in Raleigh, not to assist but to resist Mr Lincoln, & that too before North Carolina has resumed her own sovereignty or renounced that of the US. The catastrophy foreseen by those who wanted a Convention has arisen, & the NC Troops fight with a halter around their necks. However an Election for Convention has been ordered, & that will I suppose put things right.[55]

April 26, 1861

Just as we had done breakfast came brother as hungry as a hunter having traveled all night & in the haste of an Express. He is acting Commissary & has been ordered by the Gov to go down into the Eastern Counties & make

---

[55] Following the attack on Fort Sumter and Lincoln's call for troops to suppress the southern "insurrection," Governor Ellis summoned a special session of the legislature which met on May 1, 1861. The legislature called for an election two weeks later of delegates to a convention to meet in Raleigh on May 20. It was this convention that adopted North Carolina's ordinance of secession. Lefler and Newsome, *North Carolina*, 450-451.

contracts for Bacon & Fish for the troops. He tells me that the Gov is opposed to Cavalry & is trying to force the Cavalry Companies tendered to him to dismount. Charged me not to express my hastily conceived opinions to Patrick but to keep them to myself. He set me at sea & I hardly know this moment what I think Patrick ought to do.

Knit on a little sock & played chess all day, & at night went to a sleepless bed, for I tossed & turned & do what I would could not compose myself.

APRIL 27, 1861

Patrick returned from Raleigh. I do not know what I wish him to do—propose to his Company to dismount in accordance with the Gov's wishes or to hold his Commission as Captain of the SNMR & wait until Cavalry shall be needed. For if the war continues, needed they will be & greatly too. I incline to holding on to the Cavalry I think, & I beleive it the course of true Patriotism.

Whilst in Raleigh he was requested by some gentlemen to wait upon his friend Major Hill & induce him to accept the post of Col of a Regiment of Volunteers whom he has been drilling. He did so & by his representations I hope convinced that it was his duty, even tho' an unpleasant one, as the troops are not what he wishes. Thrown together as they are at random, they are discontented, ignorant & raw of course. However some changes being made in the Companies, & greater harmony prevailing, he accepted the post.

APRIL 29, 1861

Came home to Looking Glass. Found the Strawberries begining to ripen. Went out in the Buggy with Patrick to Scotland Neck to meet the Ladies of the Neighborhood about making up a fatigue Uniform for our Troop, Tents, etc. Waited almost all day at the Store for Patrick & got home about Sun down worn out, without dinner &, fatigued to death! However I must not complain. That is a trifle to what I may be called on to endure, but this waiting. Ah! it tries one's patience.

APRIL 30, 1861

Went in the Carriage to Scotland Neck. Brought home a peice of grey woolen cloth to be cut into Uniforms & a Tent, which I immediately put the negro women to work on in the Piazza—Mary, Phoebe, Catey, Angeline, besides my own force Dolly, Fanny, & Vinyard. Great cry & little Wool!

MAY 1, 1861

Hard at work all day cutting fatigue Jackets. Had the women at work in the Piazza & through the open window could hear their comments on the "War" & the "*Cloth house*" they were making for their Master to sleep under.

"Yankees?" said one. "What are Yankees Sister?" "Yankees, why that's them rampaging folks that cum a cussin & a swearin to Mount Roe![56] Done like they was gwin to take the Plantation. I heard overseer call um Yankees."

"No," said another, "Yankees is them folks that does mean work. Them Axes that broke fust pop, I heard Mr Fields say was Yankee, & I heard Henry say that that Cotton planter that rolls around & mashes the cotton in the ground & forever a breaking was a Yankee"!

As for Dolly, she fairly broke down, blubbered out right when she heard that some new tin Cups that came home were for her master's use. "My master to drink out 'n this," she said with a gesture of contempt to the offending article, "when he's got so many nice ones & particular as *he* is about his chany ones"!

May 2, 1861

Mr Edmondston went to Raleigh. One of the horses being sick, Dolly drove Frank & I in the buggy to Mr W R Smith's[57] where I went to work with the Ladies on the Uniforms. But not liking to trust myself to her guidance so far from home, I made Owen come as outrider. But the horse, either owing to unskillful driving or to the desire to see who was behind him, twisting about the road in a most uncomfortable fashion, I was fain to order him to ride *before*, when we got on very nicely but after rather a ludicrous fashion. Owen going before acted like the bundle of oats to Sidney Smith's horse & sure of a companion he trotted pleasantly on. Sent Owen to work the Hascosea garden whilst I remained at Mr Smiths & sewed steadily all day.

Mr Benton came in & read Poetry to us all the afternoon. My mind was far away, and when he appealed to me for an opinion, or asked if I had read such & such a thing, I could not for my life collect either my thoughts or my memory sufficiently to give him an intelligible answer. In fact it comes to me as strange that I have ever taken any interest in anything but the War & the state of the country. Ages seem to have past over me & all my senses been so long absorbed in one thing that I have forgotten aught else. God help me! Here I am sewing on Uniforms which may ere long be drenched in Blood, the blood of my neighbors, yes perhaps of my own husband, & yet I am petty enough to be provoked at this well meant but ill timed Poetry! Away with it! It no longer interests me! The time for it is past! I feel as tho' I could *live* poetry, poetry of the sternest & most heroic cast. Sue came in the afternoon & stayed all night with me, most kind affectionate & considerate; wishes me to get some work for her to do on the Uniforms.

---

[56] Montrose was one of the Devereux plantations in Northampton County. See "Plantations" in Introduction.

[57] William Ruffin Smith was a wealthy Halifax County planter. Eighth Census, 1860, Population Schedule, Halifax County, 71.

Mrs. Edmondston refers a number of times to sewing for the military forces. On October 24, 1862, she discusses caps. The sketches show a variety of forage caps used by Confederate forces. (Sketches from W.N. Hedges's letter containing pen and ink sketches, Miscellaneous Records, Civil War Collection, Military Collection, State Archives.)

May 3, 1861

Sewed all day on Patrick's fatigue Uniform, Grey trimmed with Green. The change in Sue is most delightful & pleasant to me. She is really a pleasant companion now, & one does not feel obliged to keep continually "turning corners" to prevent discussions. Her Southern feelings are thoroughly aroused, and she is as warm & patriotic as one could wish. Beyond a few regrets for the "Flag," in which I cannot join, she is not the same person she was! "The guns of Fortress Monroe being now turned inwards upon the bosom of Virginia," Mama no longer thinks it "dishonest" or "dishonourable" to expect the US "to surrender to Virginia her own Fort which she originally ceded for her own defence." Well so the world goes! We change, don't realize it ourselves & would be angry were we reminded of it. It is human Nature!

Brought home yesterday another tent on which my forces are busily engaged. The Cloth for these Uniforms & Tents is purchased by individual subscription, not waiting for the State to equip its men, & this thing is going on all over the whole South. Thousands of Ladies who never worked before are hard at work on coarse sewing all over our whole country.

May 3, 1861

Just after breakfast to my great surprise Charlie Coffin[58] arrived. I had not certainly expected him, tho' Patrick in view of his prolonged absence had written & requested Dr Coffin to let him spend some time with us. The Drs answer was to send him on immediately with most kind and affectionate letters indicative of true & deep friendship. I must exert myself & not let this be lost time to him. It will be good for me to have something which will make me forget myself & Patrick's absence if possible. I must try & keep up a few lessons & regular reading at all events. Put thirty Hams in Bags. At night after I had given him up, Patrick arrived. God be thanked.

May 4, 1861

Sunday—Went to church[59] with Patrick tho it was cold & drizzling, thinking it might perhaps be the last time for some time to come. Communion Sunday. Ah, what a blessed privilege to cast our cares upon Him

> —"who feels my greifs—he sees my fears
> And counts and treasures up my tears—"

Grant me, O Lord, a cheerful spirit—under whatsoever burden Thou layest upon me.

As we passed Mr Smith's we saw the White Tents pitched—ready for service. Mr E brought orders from the Gov to take his men into Camp should he

---

[58]Charles Coffin was Mrs. Edmondston's nephew, the son of Jessie and Amory Coffin, Sr.

[59]The Edmondstons were communicants of old Trinity Episcopal Church. Smith and Smith, *History of Trinity Parish*, 103-104; see Introduction.

think it necessary for their drill, and this week I beleive he intends doing so. Nothing gives me any pleasure. I feel like one in a feverish dream and often ask myself: Can all this be true? Shall I not awake and find it a night-mare? Even Frank's and Charlie's lessons are irksome to me & this journal disgusts me. I feel so much more than I ever think of putting on paper. How is it—do I feel too deeply to write? to analyze it?

MAY 10, 1861

Have been very busy for some days past getting Mr Edmondston ready to go into Camp. Today he went. O! how sorrowful! What with the confusion, the bustle, the real work I have had to do, I have scarcly realized it; but tonight as I sit in my lonely room it presses fully upon me. O! my God! give me strength to bear what Thou imposest upon me.

MAY 11, 1861

Yesterday before breakfast came Frank Jones. He has some idea of joining his Uncle & has gone into Camp with him to try it. He is just from Owego[60] & Baltimore; was on a visit to his mother in Owego when the Baltimore outbreak occurred & was advised by some friends there to leave, as the exasperation against the South & Southerns was very great. On reaching [———] he was arrested as a Southern man & carried before a Committee who asked him many questions, some of which he answered & others he refused to reply to. At length they told him to stand aside, that in an hour they would be ready to attend to him. A Sentinel stood at the door of the room in which he with some others was ordered to wait. But Frank observing that the man was negligent and allowed many to pass in and out unchalenged, mingled with the crowd & passed him unmolested! He went immediately to the Depot but found a guard posted at the door of the cars. So in this emergence he went up to the Conductor, told him that he was in the employ of the Balt & Ohio road & was anxious to get on. The man's esprit de corps being thus appealed to, he directed him to go over the bridge & stand close to the track & that as the Engine left he would take him up on the tender. He sauntered leisurely across the bridge, past an armed guard, & his friend proving faithful, when the hour designated by the Committee arrived he was at [———]. He fortunately found the conductor quite warm in his Southern feelings.

He walked through the encampment of the Pennsylvania troops & describes them as filthy, ragged & ignorant to the last degree. All the whole North animated with one idea the "defence of Washington," which is not even threatened! So much for Mr Walker's foolish speech. When he reached Baltimore he was advised by his Employers that, as his Southern feelings were

---

[60] Elizabeth Devereux Jones, Mrs. Edmondston's sister, moved with her daughters Rachel and Elizabeth to Owego, New York, following the death of her husband in 1857. Devereux Papers; see Introduction.

warm & he a member of the Maryland Guard, he had better return home, as Baltimore would surely be over run by the Northern army. In fact preparations are making for an armed occupation of it, and Southerns will be in danger there.

MAY 17, 1861

Every day have I paid a visit to Patrick in Camp. Short, unsatisfactory & tantalizing they are, but I prize them greatly for think how soon and I will not be able to see him at all! Where he will be ordered none can tell, probably to Va, but where ever it may be, may I have strength cheerfully to bid him go. I would not have him stay when he can strike one blow for our Freedom, our honour, our native Land! Tomorrow he comes out of the Camp of Instruction & will be a short time at home with me again. Diamond dust will the moments be. Ah! how I shall prize them?

During the past week the threat of a Blockade has been put in execution. Charleston, Norfolk, & New Orleans all have a fleet of War vessels off their harbours.

There has been a terrible & uncalled for massacre of innocent citizens at St Louis, the soldiers firing upon an unarmed crowd killing women & children. At the accidental discharge of a Pistol, which hurt no one, they pretended to think they were to be attacked. Shame on their commander, Capt Lyon![61]

MAY 18, 1861

Went for Mr Edmondston & brought him home in the carriage. How happy I was when the door shut on us & I seemed to have him at home once more! I have not been like myself this past week. I have cared for nothing but the Camp & news from it. My sole pleasure has been to send things to Mr Edmondston. Strawberries in profusion, enough to feast a Regiment, have we & my delight has been to gather & send them there. I have done much work in the garden but I do not care for it. I begin to think I do not like gardening, that it is only Patrick's presence with me that interests me so. As for reading, I have long given that up. I do not remember when I turn the page what was on the other side. I force myself to an interest in Charlie's reading & his notes, for that is a duty, but the Lessons are not much. How delightful was the walk with Patrick when we got home. The trees seemed greener, the flowers more beautiful, and Ah! what a welcome the Mocking Bird sang us! The servants all came with their greeting & congratulations, & I forgot the country, the War, everything but the pleasure of having him at home once more!

---

[61] Lyon's report of May 11, 1861, from St. Louis to the adjutant general in Washington stated: "... I left to Captain Callender and Lieutenant Saxton the duty of receiving and arming about 1,200 men from the northern portion of the city, who on returning to their station were fired upon by a mob, which fire was returned by the troops, from which, all told on both sides, about twelve persons were killed, two of whom, so far as I am informed, were of the United States troops;..." *Official Records (Army),* Series I, III, 9.

MAY 21, 1861

Came back to Looking Glass. Heard that an attack had been made on our Batteries at Sewell's Point by the Minnesota, the Harriet Lane, & the Monticello. Was repulsed without loss to us but great damage to the enemy, particularly the Harriet Lane.

Preserved a large quantity of Strawberries yesterday. Sugar will be scarce but Patrick likes them and they will be excellent for him in Camp. Found the Stores which Patrick ordered in anticipation of the Blockade had arrived— Salt, Iron, Cotton Bagging, Rope, Coffee, Sugar, & I know not what. I think I have household supplies sufficient to last for some months & before the Fall the Blockade must be raised. England & the Dis US herself cannot do without our cotton. Once let us have a supply & say to England, come & get it & the Navies of Mr Lincoln will be swept away like dust!

MAY 22, 1861

Heard today that on the 20th, it being the anniversary of the Signature of the Mecklenburg Dec of Independance, the Convention of NC signed the ordinance of Secession. The scene is said to have beggared description. So soon as the Ordinance had been signed & the Speaker had announced that North Carolina "abjured her allegiance to the U S" & solemnly "assumed her own Sovereignty," Ramseur's Battery[62] stationed outside fired a Salute of a hundred Guns! This seemed a signal for men, women & children to flock to the State House. The men shook hands, the women rushed into each other's arms, every body congratulated every body else. Persons who had not spoken for years exchanged the most cordial & fraternal greeting. When quiet was restored after a brief interval, the President put the Question as to whether North Carolina should join the Southern Confederacy, which was carried by acclaim first, then by individual vote without one dissentient! So now we are under Mr Davis rule! "Hurrah for Jeff Davis!" On that day we good people of N C were under three distinct Governments. We woke up members of the U S; then having resumed our own sovreignty North Carolina claimed our allegiance. But she like a wise and careful custodian deposited the jewel in the Casket by the side of her Southern Sisters & gave the Key to President Davis!

MAY 25, 1861

Heard of the invasion of Va by the Federal troops; 5000 of them occupied Alexandria yesterday! Col Elsworth of the Elsworth Zouaves entered the house of one Jackson a Hotel keeper & tore down a Secession Flag, which he

[62]The name "Ramseur's Battery" was briefly used by Co. A, Tenth Regiment (First Artillery) North Carolina State Troops in April, 1861, in honor of their commander Stephen D. Ramseur. When Ramseur was promoted and transferred from the company it assumed the name "Manly's Battery" after its new captain, Basil C. Manly. Manarin and Jordan, *North Carolina Troops*, I, 40-41; Clark, *Histories of the North Carolina Regiments*, I, 551-552.

had raised from the Cupola of his house. As he was descending the Stairs, Jackson stepped from his bed chamber (it was very early in the morning) & shot him dead on the Stair landing. His companions instantly returned the fire, & Jackson fell peirced with many bullets. Not content with this, they mangled his dead body before the eyes of his wife![63] My God! Can these things be? Grant that every house they enter may contain another Jackson.

MAY 27, 1861

Charlie's Lessons drag so heavily that I am a great mind to intermit them entirely. He dislikes study so much that I will make myself hateful to him by enforcing it & we look at "study" in the abstract from such a different stand point that we never shall agree as to the manner in which it should be executed!

MAY 28, 1861

What a true observation that is of women in "Respectability A Dialogue,"[64] that ideas in some Women's heads are like old nails in a beam—break them off, drive them in, you can; but pull them out, never! When you think you have disposed of them, there they are as obstinate & rusty as ever.

Went to Father's and stayed all night. In the morning Mr Edmondston went to Raleigh again. I came home to Looking Glass. I have got to be like the Ephesians always looking "to hear & tell some new thing"![65] I take no interest in any thing but War news & preparations for War.

Sewed on Mr E's outfit. Charlie read his History of England to me.

Got excited over the outrages committed at Hampton by the Federals under the Guns of Fortress Monro! Poor people, they have my earnest & true sympathy, driven from their homes by a horde of vile leveling Yankees who exalt the negro & debase the white man. What must their feelings be when they think of the occupants of their houses, the enjoyers of their property. Hampton is said to be a refuge for run-a-way negroes of the lowest stamp. The scenes enacted there make ones blood curdle. Their own letter writers describing President Tyler's house between Hampton & Old Point make it a Pandemonium! Deliver us from such rioters. Baltimore is being gradually over run. It is dangerous to express an opinion there. Habeas Corpus denied there. Judge Tany[66] has given his opinion of their oppressions, but little good

[63] James W. Jackson mortally wounded Ellsworth on May 24, 1861, as he attempted to remove a Confederate flag from the Marshall House in Alexandria, Virginia, where Jackson was proprietor. Jackson was immediately killed by one of Ellsworth's escorts. *Official Records (Army)*, Series I, II, 41-42; *Dictionary of American Biography*, VI, 109-110.

[64] "Respectability.—A Dialogue" appeared in *Blackwood's Magazine*, LXXX (December, 1856), 678-693.

[65] Acts 17:21. Mrs. Edmondston meant the Athenians rather than the Ephesians.

[66] Roger Brooke Taney (1777-1864) was chief justice of the United States Supreme Court from 1836 until 1864 and is best remembered for the *Dred Scott* v. *Sandford* case he presided over. The Dred Scott decision of

will it do. Fort Henry [67] is full of political prisoners, confined without knowing their cause of offence.

MAY 30, 1861

Mr Edmondston got home. He brought news that Mr Davis had gone to Richmond, removed the government in fact as the Heads of Departments accompany him. I wonder whether James will come too. He seems so dissatisfied with a clerks life that I should not be surprised to hear of his resignation at any moment!

Butler of Mass has been ordered to Fortress Monro. It is for his ingenuity to discover a new word for the Negro. The vexed question is no longer "a Nigger," "a Darkie," or even a "Colored Person"; Cuffee is "a Contraband" [68] and as a "Contraband" is to be forfeited! He does not entice "Slaves" from their masters; does not contravene the Fugitive Slave Law. [69] O no! He seizes "Contrabands." Faugh! on such Puritanic, fanatical lies!

JUNE 1, 1861

Patrick with his troop all day. I preparing for one summer more. It is very hot. I hope the Yankees feel it! I forgot to mention that when Patrick went into camp he sent me a present, his last present, a Colts Pistol! & now he is teaching me to shoot it! What more significant fact of the change in our country, when a husband gives his wife a parting present of a Pistol! Yes, I will learn to use it & should the occasion arise God will give me strength & nerve to use it aright!

JUNE 2, 1861

Frank Coffin woke up quite sick. He played out in the sun yesterday & has got fever in consequence. I fear a Bilius attack or it may be measles which are very prevalent.

Walked with Mr Edmondston. Ah these walks will soon be put a stop to, tho' I did not enjoy this as I otherwise would have done being uneasy about

---

1857, in which slaves, for the first time, were legally defined as property by the United States Supreme Court with none of the rights guaranteed United States citizens, was a landmark case in the slavery issue. The court also denied that Congress could constitutionally exclude slavery from the territories. Randall and Donald, *Civil War and Reconstruction*, 108-114; *Concise Dictionary of American Biography*, 1042-1043.

[67] Fort McHenry was a fortification defending the Baltimore Harbor. Wayne Andrews (ed.), *Concise Dictionary of American History* (New York: Charles Scribner's Sons, 1961), 597, hereinafter cited as *Concise Dictionary of American History*.

[68] In May, 1861, Benjamin F. Butler, in command at Fortress Monroe, declared that slaves fleeing from Confederate owners to Union lines were "contraband," although the term "contraband" did not appear in official correspondence. The term clung to escaping slaves throughout the war. Hans L. Trefousse, *Ben Butler, The South Called Him Beast* (New York: Twayne Publishers, 1957), 79, hereinafter cited as Trefousse, *Ben Butler*; Boatner, *Civil War Dictionary*, 172; Randall and Donald, *Civil War and Reconstruction*, 371.

[69] The Fugitive Slave Law of 1850, passed as part of the Compromise of 1850, provided for stricter enforcement in the return of escaped slaves to their owners. *Dictionary of American History*, II, 354-355.

Frank. I was much struck by a remark Mr E made in the carriage the other
day. He said were he "Autocrat he could put a stop & restore peace to the
land by *one single order*." "Certainly" I said! "I suppose you would order every
body, every where to lay down their arms & go home." "No!" he said, "I
would stop *all News* Papers! This is in its incipiency a News paper War. It is
now fed & fanned by News papers & their total suppression would give us
Peace in thirty days! But it is passing rapidly beyond the control of editors &
demagogues. They have lighted the fire, but they cannot controul the Con-
flagration." There is much truth in what he says.

I wish we would cease this lamentation first & abuse now of General Scott.
A hoary headed old Traitor, they make too much fuss over him. His pay as
Liut General & his hatred to Mr Davis will keep him at the North & for my
part let him stay! I do not value the old vain, inflated bag of Wind! Half the
ability he plumes himself so on showing in Mexico was the result of Southern
minds & Southern skill, good officers & soldiers whose laurels old Fuss &
Feathers was not slow to reap. See how he will do with the South opposed to
him!

JUNE 3, 1861

Frank still sick. I feel so uneasy about him that tho against his wishes I have
got Mr E to consent to move out to Hascosea. If it is measles I wish him in a
larger house where I can keep him cooler & be nearer the Dr, reasons which
are of double force should it be Bilius. So Patrick out with his Troop all day, I
moved the invalid & he joined me at Hascosea at night. Sue came out to see
me hearing of Frank's sickness. She is most kind & it is a real pleasure for me
to have her with me now. She is so true & so sympathizing.

JUNE 4, 1861

Frank much better! I am greatly releived for I was really unhappy about
him. I think I will never again take a child from its Parents—the responsibility
is too great. Here have I been miserable for three days over what is perhaps
only a severe fit of indigestion brought on by eating Mulberries!

JUNE 5, 1861

Heard of the battle, or rather I think we should call it the Skirmish at
Phillippa on the 3d. Our Commander Col Porterfield does not appear to have
showed the requisite energy & promptitude. The night before he was ap-
prized of the approach of the enemy in force by two Ladies, ——— who, after
escaping through the enemies lines rode thirty miles alone on horseback to
give him the information, & yet in the morning, instead of being on the qui
vive or in fact working all night, the enemy found his waggons, some of them
only half loaded, none with the teams attached, standing in the streets of
Philippa about sun rise, the troops themselves being still in their quarters.

Hascosea was the summer home of Patrick and Kate Edmondston. The house was built by Whitmel Hill Anthony soon after he married Charity Barnes in August, 1831. She had inherited the land from her grandfather James Barnes. Whitmel Anthony sold the place to the Edmondstons in 1851 through the auspices of Thomas Pollock Devereux, who paid for the house as part of a marriage settlement he previously had offered the Edmondstons. The architectural features of the house can be discerned by studying the photographs, which were taken from all four sides. A porch extended across the front façade at the time the house was occupied by the Edmondstons. (Photographs from files of Beth Crabtree.)

The alarm was sounded & they flew to arms, formed outside the town but were repulsed by the Yankees under Col Kelly who was severely if not mortally wounded. The conduct of the Ladies of Philippa is beyond all praise! They rushed into the streets, aided in packing the waggons, & with their own hands assisted to harness the horses. That anything was saved is in great measure owing to them. As it was, we lost several boxes of muskets unpacked which we could ill spare! Our men were completely routed & several killed on both sides, including Capt Porterfield.

JUNE 11, 1861

On the 8th of this month as Mr E was preparing to drill his Troop a Telegraphic Dispatch was put into his hands. Thinking it an order from the Governor he opened it at once, when to his horror he read that his brother Robert had died suddenly in Charleston on the 5![70]

Think what a shock to hear such news at such a time & place. He gave the Co up to his 1st Lieut & came home, but only to hear by mail from Bessie that his father was "seriously" but not dangerously ill in Aiken! The letter was written on the very day & before they had heard of it of Poor Rob's death. Pray God the effect of it may not be what we dread upon him! But we hope for the best.

The next day Sunday the 9th whilst he was wavering whether he could go to his father or not, came his 1st Lieut Mr W H Smith with a letter from his Uncle, Mr Smith[71] who is in the Convention to him, telling him that it was the Governor's wish that he, Patrick should wait on him immediately!

Of course there was but one thing to do, so the next day he went to Raleigh accompanied by Lieut Smith. Mrs Smith (Julia) & child came to remain with me during the Lieuts absence & we have been hard at work today & yesterday, covering Canteens for the Company. Poor fellows I hope they will never be polluted by whiskey. But why should I wish that? Whiskey in moderation is a good thing & on a march may be necessary.

As I sit tonight alone in my own room the remembrance of Rob comes over me in overpowering vividness. So young, so strong, capable of so much. How sudden & awful is his summons. We have but the bare Telegraphic announcement that he is dead. How and under what circumstances we are left to conjecture. Last winter when he received a Commission as Midshipman in the service of his native State, how proud we all were & what a brilliant future did we see opening before him. Even when he resigned we hoped for a better

---

[70]On June 7, 1861, the *Charleston Mercury* carried the notice: "Relatives Friends and Acquaintances of Mr. and Mrs. Chas. Edmondston, are requested to attend the Funeral Services of their son, Robert D. at the residence of Chas. Edmondston, Jr., No. 20 Savage Street...." See Introduction.

[71]William Henry Smith was a farmer in Halifax County. A member of the Scotland Neck Mounted Riflemen, Smith enlisted with that company on April 23, 1861, for twelve months. He was appointed first lieutenant to rank from his date of enlistment. Smith was present or accounted for through August 31, 1861. Eighth Census, 1860, Population Schedule, Halifax County, 81; Manarin and Jordan, *North Carolina Troops*, II, 228. Richard Henry Smith (1812-1893), William H. Smith's uncle, served as a delegate at the North Carolina secession convention held in Raleigh in 1861. Claiborne Thweatt Smith, Jr., *Smith of Scotland Neck: Planters on the Roanoke* (Baltimore: Gateway Press, Inc., 1976), 123-128.

time & that he would yet become a useful & a happy man. Now all hope is gone and we are left to cruel uneasiness as to the effect his death will have on Papa already seriously sick. God help us. Our troubles as a family seem beginning when we already have as much National anxiety as we can well sustain. What can the Gov want with Patrick but to order him into active service? Then shall I be desolate indeed! But God will be with me.

JUNE 18, 1861

Patrick is gone, and I am alone, for how long God only can tell. On the 12th he got home from Raleigh bringing with him the Gov's orders to repair with his troop at once to Wilmington. As he came out of the Commissary's office with orders for supplies etc a messenger met him and placed in his hand a Telegram saying that his father was desparately ill and desired at once to see him. What could he do? In one hand he held the Gov's orders to repair with all speed to Wilmington where an attack was anticipated; in the other a summons to perhaps his father's death bed!

One course alone was open to him as a soldier, a patriot or a man of honour, to stifle the impulses of his heart and go on with his public duty. He did so. Came home on the 12th, sent out the summons for his troop to assemble on the 13th. They live over an area of thirty miles. On the 14th came an Officer of the Confederate States, who happened to be my brother in Law Maj Clark[72] & mustered them into the service. Received the valuation of their horses etc and administered the oath of allegiance to the Confederate States to them. This was on Friday.

Sat & Sunday were incessantly occupied with preparations for departure. He had scarcely a moment to think. Every day came these dreadful heart rending Telegrams! "Your Father weaker!" "Your Father worse!" "Come at once if you would see him!" But how could he? So with a heart torn with anxiety he was forced to keep a calm clear head to give & see that the necessary orders were obeyed. For not an officer or man knew any thing about his duty or had even seen a camp. So every order had to emanate from him, every direction no matter how trifling. At last every thing was ready & yesterday, Monday the 17th, marshaling them into line, he gave the order & they marched for Wilmington!

The women many of them wept, sobbed, nay even shreiked aloud, but I had no tears to shed then. With a calm, stern, determined feeling I saw them depart. The sentiment of exalted Patriotism which filled my heart found no echo in Lamentations, no vent in tears. He is gone, gone in the exercise of man's highest & holiest duty! And tho' now as I sit in the silence & solitude of this lonely house and take the fact of his absence home to myself, tho it seems

---

[72]William J. Clarke was the husband of Mrs. Edmondston's sister Mary Bayard Devereux. See Introduction.

to me a tangible thing, a thing I can take into my hand & look at so vividly does it press upon me. Yet I would not have him here, would not have him fail in one duty, falter in one step. "As thy days so shall thy strength be," and blessed be God the promise still sustains me.

I have been very busy packing his trunk & Camp Chest with every thing I can conceive he will want to go down with the baggage & tents, for they took nothing but what their horses could carry. Amunition & provisions of course excepted. They marched on the anniversary of the Battle of Bunker's Hill. Let those who are fond of omens read one in this!

Ah! poor Papa, God grant that you may be better tonight.

June 23, 1861

On the 19th as I was busy packing Patrick's trunk came a Telegram telling us of Papa's death.[73] He died in Aiken on the 15th & was buried on the 17th, the very day that Patrick marched! Heavy news to meet him poor fellow on the road where he must hear it, for never was there a more affectionate & dutiful son. Never did filial affection burn brighter than in his bosom, and never did father better deserve all the love, reverence & pride of a son's heart than did Papa. Few men have had greater trials, fewer still have come through them as unscathed as he did. When I think of him as we last saw him, hale, hearty, vigorous, exemplifying the beauty of old age more than almost any man I have ever seen, I cannot credit the fact of his death, cannot realize that we shall never see him more, that we have lost our stay, our support, our centre, the judicious adviser, the sympathizing friend, the one to whom we could always turn for aid & counsel. It seems impossible. My own individual loss has been heavy. I have few such friends left, few who judge me so leniently, look so tenderly upon me, or find something right in almost all I do or say. The day after I heard of his death, I heard also that Sophia had lost her little girl, Katherine Johnson, to whom I was sponsor last fall. She was a lovely child & my heart bleeds for Sophia. She cannot now realize that she is taken from sin, from cares, & she must mourn for it is her first affliction. Poor thing!

Susy came yesterday to spend the summer with me & father & Mama will soon follow. I find great pleasure in Sue's society. She is sympathizing & kind. But there is a want I cannot express. Is it Patrick I want? Seeking vainly for something not to be found in any other human being? Would that I could hear from him. How he has borne this hot dusty ride & that dreadful news which met him in Goldsboro, but I must be patient.

June 27, 1861

Letters from Patrick! He has reached Wilmington safely after a terrible ride

---

[73] The *Charleston Mercury* carried an obituary notice and resolutions eulogizing Charles Edmondston, Sr., on June 17, June 22, and June 24. See Introduction.

in the heat & dust. Thank God! for that he says little about his father, in fact has no time for thought. His men are quartered near the Toll gate in a warehouse, the officers with Mr Green,[74] Mrs John Haigh's father whom he describes as a kind gentlemanly old man.

I shall not attempt to keep up this journal. It will be if honest but a record of lonely days & sleepless nights, of stern resolves against repining, & determination to be cheerful! The spirit is gone! Of what use to record the body only of my daily life? I seem to live only to read & write letters & my diary will be found in them. They at least shall be cheerful. Patrick shall hear no murmuring from me.

I find on looking back that I have not even mentioned the Battle of Bethel Church which took place on the 10th between Hampton & Yorktown, the news of which Patrick brought when he came home from Raleigh. If I could omit this important & stirring as it is and in which our own State people, our neighbors even were engaged what will not pre-occupation make me omit?

We had but 1100 men mostly North Carolinians under Gen Magruder & Col Hill, whilst the enemy were 4,500 strong, yet we repulsed them with the loss of only one man killed & four wounded whilst their dead are reckoned by hundreds. Col Hill is glad that he took Patrick's advice, as he has had an opportunity of greatly distinguishing himself. The Enfield Blues & the Edgecombe Guards were in action & Capt Bridgers of the latter Co. has been promoted.

Major Winthrop a son of a cousin of my Grandmother's (the identical "Laura W." to whom Willis[75] wrote those pretty lines is his sister & he is a nephew of Uncle Charles' wife, Aunt Sarah), is among the killed. He is said to have behaved with gallantry, but I have not a regret for him. From his birth, his education and his breeding he had opportunities to have known better than to be there & I am less sorry for him than I am for the ignorant multitude who compose the bulk of their armies. Poor Wyatt's[76] fate touches me much more. He died in defence of his native land, having volunteered to burn a house which stood in the way of our guns & behind which the enemy

---

[74] This reference was to James Severin Green (1792-1862) of Wilmington, whose daughter Caroline Cochran Green married John C. Haigh, a Fayetteville merchant. Gilbert Cope (comp.), *Genealogy of the Sharpless Family* (Philadelphia: Privately printed, 1887), 495, 954.

[75] Maj. Theodore Winthrop, son of Francis Bayard Winthrop of Connecticut, served under Butler as acting military secretary and was killed at the Battle of Bethel. Nathaniel Parker Willis (1806-1867), journalist, poet, and dramatist, wrote the poem "To Laura W–, Two Years of Age," addressed to Theodore Winthrop's sister and future biographer. See Willis, *Poems, Sacred, Passionate, and Humorous* (New York: Clark and Austin, 1845), 216-218; Laura W. Johnson, *The Life and Poems of Theodore Winthrop* (New York: Henry Holt and Co., 1884); Clark, *Histories of the North Carolina Regiments*, I, 96-97.

[76] Henry Lawson Wyatt of Edgecombe County, an enlisted man in Co. A, First North Carolina (Bethel) Regiment, was the first North Carolina soldier killed in a Civil War battle. *Official Records (Army)*, Series I, II, 92, 96; Manarin and Jordan, *North Carolina Troops*, III, 8; Clark, *Histories of the North Carolina Regiments*, I, 100-102.

sheltered themselves. I am much more sorry for his mother than I am for "poor Elizabeth," as father calls Mrs. Winthrop.[77]

One amusing incident I must record. Gen Butler, the Commandant at Fortress Monro rode out in his carriage to see how his subordinate Gen Peirce was getting on "whipping the Rebels" for such they now call us. Suddenly he was astonished by the sight of a rabble route in full flight without guns, coats—in fact any thing that could impede them. Standing up in his carriage he demanded authoritively of the fugitives "What was the matter"? "O! Sir!" was the disconsolate answer as they still ran, "there is a whole lot of Virginia gentlemen on horse back coming right after us"—and on they ran! Shortly Gen Butler thought it best to retire also & the glorious conquerer returned full speed through Hampton to the Fort, where the valliant Knight consoled himself by personal abuse of his poor subordinate Pierce who could not face the "Va gentlemen"! That is just the difference between us. Our army is composed mainly of gentlemen, the best blood of the South, which will be poured out like water 'ere that rabble shall conquer us! Theirs is the riff raff, the off scouring of their cities! I take this anecdote about the Va gentlemen from one of their own papers, as none of our side were there to hear it!

Father & Mama came out for the summer. I received a letter from Henry Miller inviting me to his wedding[78] which took place last week, but I alaas! am "no wedding guest," & tho I received it in ample time & would have gone had I been under different circumstances, I wrote offering him my best wishes.

We hear daily of skirmishes in the West of Va, in Missouri, but nothing of much importance. The worst for us is the Evacuation of Harper's Ferry, but as the Machinery has all been removed to Fayetteville in this State & it is said to be of no strategtic importance now, I think the out cry against general Jos Johnston rather excessive.[79]

Tennessee has joined the Southern Confederacy, whilst Kentucky has issued a proclamation announcing her neutrality! Warns off both North & South from her soil, says she will maintain an "armed neutrality"! An anomolous position but not one which will effect her object, I fancy—the non payment of the expenses of the War. O! Kentucky! Kentucky! how art thou fallen!

---

[77] Elizabeth Woolsey Winthrop was Theodore Winthrop's mother. Elbridge Colby, *Theodore Winthrop* (New York: Twayne Publishers, Inc., 1965), 18.

[78] Henry M. Miller, Mrs. Edmondston's nephew, married Lizzie Collins of Granville County, May 21, 1861. *Raleigh Register*, July 10, 1861.

[79] Gen. Joseph E. Johnston was in command at Harpers Ferry in June, 1861. His troops were disabled by measles and mumps; lacking in arms, munitions, and transportation, they quietly withdrew when confronted by a superior Federal force under Gen. Robert Patterson. Boatner, *Civil War Dictionary*, 441; *Official Records (Army)*, Series I, II, 470-472.

June 30, 1861

Sunday. Have been all this week in a sad task making up my mourning for my dear Papa & today for the first time put it on. The sight of this black dress brings the cause why I wear it more fully to my mind, if possible brings him more vividly before me, dear old gentlemen! I never realized how dear you were to me until now I have lost you. The loss of your letters is a sad blank to me & when I suddenly come across any little peice of his personal property which he left here I start to find how little I realize that I shall never see him more. His Hat hangs in the passage, his cane in the corner & at every turn I come upon something he prized, something he commended. His hearty "Aye! Aye!—that's right!" is in my ear & I cannot beleive I shall never hear it again!

This past week came in a letter to Charlie from his Mother a little printed slip which tells us that Isabella was married at Lawrence's house in Mt Pleasant on the [———]![80] We have had no notice of it & it is all a mystery to us. Why is she there instead of with her Mother in Aiken? Another proof that our dear Papa is indeed gone! He would not have left us in ignorance of such an event, not allowed us to learn it through the public prints!

Letters from Patrick tell me that he has been ordered to the sea shore, at a point about eight miles from Wilmington near Wrightsville, where the Wilmingtonians spend the hot months in sea bathing & fishing—a rural Newport I suppose!

July 8, 1861

Today—O! day of days! Patrick came home, having requested a furlough to go & see his Mother and attend to his father's estate. They granted him a fortnight & he came home for me, so that I have now twelve days of his society before me as he takes me to South Carolina with him.

Here my Diary does indeed end for some time so in accordance with my plan I fill up the chasm with a narrative. The dates I am enable[d] to give correctly from a little hand book, a vade mecum[81] which I always keep & my memory supplies the incident.

On looking back over my Journal I find that for some time back it has gradually ceased to be an echo of my own doings, for I have made no mention of Plantation matters & the thousand and one little things which in Patrick's absence devolved upon me. In fact the sorrow I was under & the great loneliness I felt absorbed all other feeling & tho I went through my daily duties, housekeeping, gardening, sewing, playing chess etc., it was almost mechanically. My Diary was but a meagre account of anything I either did, felt or said & it would have been irksome in the extreme to me to have been forced to record it.

---

[80] Isabella Donaldson Edmondston married Thomas Nightingale Johnson. See Introduction.

[81] A manual.

The servants, both house & plantation, behaved themselves extremely well & showed an amount of affection for & consideration to me that I had not beleived them capable! I remember one of Dolly's attempts at consolation which in its simplicity & faith evinced such child like confidence in her Master & contempt for his enemies that I must preserve it.

"Never mind Mistress," she said to me one morning when perhaps I looked more depressed than usual; "Never mind. Master will not be gone long, for them folks won't have the impudence to stand up now that Master himself is gone out again 'em"!

Even little Frank felt the change, for he told me "that now that Uncle was gone & Grandpapa was dead, I was'nt funny—that he wished I was like I used to be, for now I did'nt talk much." He wrote a letter to his Mother telling her of all he was doing & amongst other things said that "Aunt Susan" as he called Sue, "read him a story about a little boy named Frank. He wished he had him here to play with, but Aunt Sue said he was dead! He beleived almost every body was dead: Grandpapa & Uncle Bobbie & Aunt Kate's little neice & one of Mr Hills servants, & now this little Frank! He wondered if it was the Yankees"?!

On the 10th of July Patrick and I left for Charleston where we heard Mama was, taking Charlie & Frank Coffin with us. We got there on the morning of the 11th & for the first time in our lives stopped at an Hotel in Charleston— the Charleston Hotel.[82] We found Mama & Bessie staying with Isabella & Mr Johnson, who had just been married & gone to house keeping in a nicely furnished house in [———] St.

Mama was much more composed than we had expected. Unfortunately they had mislaid Papa's will & Bessie was forced to go the next day to Aiken in search of it. Charlie & Frank went with her. That day, the 12th, we dined with Isabella & Mr Johnson. They seemed happy & as was natural much absorbed with each other. In the afternoon Isabella being much engaged dressing her children for a Party & Mama having visitors, we left & went to see Mr Edmondston Aunts. His Aunt Mrs Kirkpatrick was very ill & I felt as we left her that we should never see her more & so it proved for in less than a fortnight we heard of her death.[83]

We heard that Lawrence was quite sick confined to his bed with a low fever so we went over to Mt Pleasant to see him. We left the city very early on Sunday morning and as we steamed out through the quiet Harbour could but contrast it with the different aspect it held when we last saw it, the morning after the firing upon the Star of the West! The shadows lay long & cool upon

---

[82] The Charleston Hotel was located on the corner of Meeting and Pinckney streets. Swanberg, *First Blood*, 1.

[83] Mrs. John Kirkpatrick's death was reported in the *Charleston Courier*, August 17, 1861, slightly more than "less than a fortnight" after the Edmondstons were there.

Patrick's father, Charles Edmondston, built the house shown above, left, in 1828. He was a merchant and wharf owner, and the house faced the Charleston harbor. In 1838 Col. William Alston purchased the house for his son, who redecorated it in the Greek Revival style. The Edmondston-Alston House, 21 East Battery Street, Charleston, is now owned by the Historic Charleston Foundation which operates it as a house museum. (Photograph from files of Beth Crabtree.) Above, right, an interior view of the house. (Photograph courtesy of Historic Charleston Foundation.)

Left, a piece of Edmondston china. (Photograph from files of Beth Crabtree.)

the water. The shipping, the docks, the wharves so still and quiet all impressed a Sabbath peacefulness upon us, whilst the chimes of the Church Bells calling their Congregations to the early morning service—which they have in some of the Churches in Charleston during the hot weather—came mellowed over the water. Everything combined to attune our hearts to thankfulness & Peace.

Suddenly, on rounding a point where we could look past Sumter down the channel, out to sea, a black object struck our eyes in the dim distance. "What is that?" I inquired, whilst Patrick got up to fetch the Glass. "The Blockading Squadron, Madam!" said a passenger. I cannot describe the rage which instantly seized me. The revulsion of feeling was greater than I ever reccollect to have undergone. I felt strong enough in my own single person to head the boat sea-wards, & seize, grapple, & sink them! There they lay, three vessels, insolently barring our way from the great God-given highway! O! for a navy that could cope with them! That banner should not long flaunt in our sight, over our soil! At any rate they robbed me of my Sabbath peace & quietness for that day, tho they do not so effectually shut us out as they suppose, for Privateermen slip past them every dark night both to & from the West Indies.

We found Lawrence much depressed & needing something to arouse him. His greif was very great & had something sincere & touching in it. Preparations were going on for the marriage of his daughter Laura,[84] but he took no interest, in fact seemed scarcely aware of them. We induced him to get out of bed & take a ride with us & the exertion was of manifest service to him.

As we went back to the city which we were forced to do at mid-day as there is no afternoon boat on Sunday, it was intensely hot! We sat under the awning on Deck in a dreamy listless state. Everything seemed half asleep. The boat hands moved idly about & the steam as it feebly escaped from the pipe seemed to mingle with its kindred element. The sun light shimmered in a white dazzling glare over the face of the water. The white houses fairly glistened amidst the dark sombre green of the live oaks, whilst the few passengers who moved slowly down the long hot wharf added to the dreaminess of the scene.

Suddenly every one was aroused by the quick sharp report of a gun! Every one started & looked around. There was the white smoke curling lazily around the sides of Sumter. "What is that for?" exclaimed every body; but we were soon answered by the sight of a Steamer, which we had scarcely noticed before so closely had she hugged the shore of Sullivan's Island, head directly across the channel towards the Fort. "That," said Patrick, "was to order that Steamer to heave to & report. Had she disregarded it the next would have been a shotted gun which would probably have sunk her"!—& so it was. It was a little steamer which from her light draught can elude the Squadron by running into the shallows out of range of the guns & who thus is enabled to keep up a water communication with a point some where on the coast, Georgetown I beleive; but Sumter stands a vigilant sentinel & whenever she passes she has to "heave to" & be examined lest she should prove an enemy in disguise.

Charles was absent in Georgia, but I went to see Maria[85] & she gave me a full account of poor Rob's death. He had been on shore as we knew since Jan,

---

[84] Lawrence Edmondston's daughter, Laura Augusta Edmondston, married Richard S. Venning.
[85] Maria Chisolm Edmondston was married to Charles Edmondston, Jr. See Introduction.

when his vessel came in, leading a comparatively idle life & of course from the change of diet etc had made blood more rapidly than usual & had grown quite stout & fleshy.

One week before his death he came down from Aiken in high health & joined the Privateer Sumter[86] as second mate—then fitting for sea. He went immediately to hard work in the sun, in the hot decks, & was perhaps imprudent in his diet & mode of life. On the morning of the 5th of June he came to his brother's house saying that the ship was ready for sea & would sail the next day but that he could not enjoy his last day on shore as he had a wretched headache. He would eat no breakfast but said he would go up stairs & lie down.

As he passed the table where she sat he took up a phial of Laudanum, which was accidentaly there, & banteringly raised it to his lips saying "how much of this would it take to kill a fellow?" She is confident he swallowed but a few drops, as there was but little in it, & the quantity taken was so slight that she on examination afterwards could not miss it. She replied jestingly & he went on up stairs telling the children as he went not to make too much noise & awaken him. She thinking Sleep was the best thing for him left him undisturbed all day. Late in the afternoon the servant going into the room found him breathing strangely & called her mistress who to her horror found him insensible! Physicians were instantly summoned but as they reached him he died! They gave it as their opinion that his death was the result of Congestion of the Brain, brought on by a sudden change of life & exposure when in high health to the sun & did not think the Laudanum had any thing to do with it, the quantity being manifestly too small to effect a man so vigorous as he was.

Charles was in Aiken & was instantly telegraphed for. When the dispatch arrived Bessie & himself were out walking. Mama sat in Papa's room who was sleeping & as Bessie had that day written her brother, sick tho' not seriously. The Telegram was handed to Mama who not seeing or not heeding the "junr" upon the address opened it & by the failing light spelt out, "Your Brother Robert is lying dead in your house—Come down at once!" She awoke Papa with a shreik, telling him the contents. He never rallied again & when the Dr saw him the next morning the change was so great that he gave up all hope & tho he lingered for a week he never left his bed, never recovered from the shock! All of his children who were at his Golden Wedding in Dec were at his bed side but Patrick, who poor fellow was kept by the sternest duty

---

[86] The privateer *Sumter* should not be confused with the C.S.S. *Sumter* which Raphael Semmes was fitting out in New Orleans during May and June, 1861. The vessel alluded to possibly was the steamer *Sumter* which began operations in 1863. Naval History Division of the Navy Department (comp.), *Civil War Naval Chronology, 1861-1865* (Washington, D.C.: U.S. Government Printing Office, 1971), VI, 307-308, hereinafter cited as *Civil War Naval Chronology*; See also Raphael Semmes, *Memoirs of Service Afloat During the War Between the States* (Baltimore: Kelly, Piet & Company, 1869), 97-104.

away from him. At first Papa constantly asked for him, but when he learned that he was under orders he acquiesced at once & accepted the impossi[bility] of his leaving. He left his blessing for "his own his dear Patrick" & lay quietly with the greatest patience tho' in severe pain until death released him. "Let me die the death of the righteous—& let my last end be like his"![87] We gathered these last particulars when in Aiken from Jessie, but I put them here from their connection with Poor Rob.

On the 15th we left Charleston for Aiken. We left Mama sooner than we had intended, but Patrick after his month in Camp longed for quiet & solitude. Isabella was just married & no one can tell how the necessary company (for Mr Johnson had to be considered & his friends constantly received at *his* house) & the inevitable return to daily life & daily cares grated upon us! At Lawrence's they were preparing for a wedding & the quiet Patrick needed could not be found there. Hotel life, always irksome to him was doubly so in Charleston where he had never been before without his father & where every thing brought him vividly before him. So after getting Mama to promise to put her business in the hands of Mr Pettigru we went up to Aiken & spent the remmant of the furlough with Dr Coffin & Jessie.

We had a quiet & happy visit to Aiken. Jessie had so much to tell us of Papa; her greif was so deep, so sincere, & so chastened that it accorded delightfully with our own feelings. We were never weary of talking of & about our dear Papa. We went over to his house & sitting there, Patrick in his own chair & surrounded by things that he most valued, Jessie gave us an account of his last sickness & death. Everything which he had said during his sickness had been treasured up by her & was carefully repeated to us to be laid up in the store house of our precious memories!

Whilst in Aiken we heard of the defeat of our forces under Gen Pegram in Western Va by Gen M'Clellan. We lost 500 taken prisoner & in the retreat Gen Garnett was killed. The Battle is know as Rich Mountain. Gen. Garnett was a fine officer & one whose loss we shall find it difficult to replace. He was an early friend of Mr E's. They were at West Point together.

We heard too some amusing anecdotes of the seige & taking of Fort Sumter, the by-paths of History as it were; amongst others that Mrs Young, the widow of the clergyman, in the exercise of that missionary spirit which burns so fiercely in her bosom, after the order of Beauregard prohibiting the admission of Tallow Candles into the Fort, visited her friend & protege Major Anderson with rows of them tied all around her to the tiers in her Hoop, tier above tier. Of course she could not sit down but made the voyage from Charleston to Sumter standing.[88] & this reminds me that I said nothing of the

---

[87] Numbers 23:10b.

[88] This reference was probably to Anna R. Young (1805-1881), the widow of the Reverend Thomas J. Young (1803-1852), who served as the assistant minister of St. Michael's Church in Charleston. Clare Jervey (comp.), *Inscriptions on the Tablets and Gravestones in St. Michael's Church and Churchyard, Charleston, South*

hero of a day, the Commander of Fort Sumter, after he ascended the vessel which was to take him to N Y. Well he went North & tho he had expressed himself when at the South in the greatest admiration for the gallantry & true chivalry shown him by the Conquerers, yet when he got [to] Philadelphia he allowed some one, I forget who now, to make a public speech in his presence at a reception held in his honour, wherein he gave a most false, outrageous & garbled account of the affair, he Maj A standing by & by his silence tacitly assenting to it. Then the speeches he made, the reflections he cast on SC, the stuff he talked about "the Flag," completely weaned the southern people from him. Lincoln gave him employment in his native state Kentucky, but she proclaiming her neutrality gave him leave to withdraw. He was promoted to Brig Gen by Lincoln & now is reported as out of health recruiting in the mountains of Penn. But never was there such an opportunity for distinction for firing the Southern heart thrown away so completely as was his!

James came to Aiken whilst we were there. He had resigned his office in Montgomery & stopped to see Patrick & consult with him as to the best way of getting into active service & concluded to come on & join his fortunes with him.

After a short but quiet & refreshing visit to Aiken we left it on the 19th, Patrick's furlough expiring on the 21st. He had brought me an invitation from Mrs W H Lippitt,[89] whom I had known when a tiny interesting child at her father's house as Alice Haigh, to spend some little time with her at Wrightsville, Mr E's camp being about a mile & half from her house—an invitation which I most gladly accepted.

The excitement all on the line of RR was intense as to an impending battle expected at Manassas junction, a point between Richmond & Washington held by our forces under Beauregard. The grand army which Seward & Lincoln had been at vast expense collecting at Washington ostensibly for the defence of the Capitol, had now thrown off the mask, & "On to Richmond" was the gathering cry of the whole North! The cars were filled with people who had friends at Manassas & our hearts bled for many of them from the cruel suspense they were in, for rumours of a great battle—vague & contradictory—filled the hearts of wives & children with agony. Surgeons going on to volunteer their services in view of immediate & pressing neccessity, cars filled with troops, every thing bespoke a conflict at hand. But tho we saw many excited, I do not think we met one dispondent person!

Carolina (Columbia: State Company, Publishers, 1906), 31, 304. The incident mentioned is not in eyewitness accounts of Abner Doubleday in *Reminiscences of Forts Sumter and Moultrie in 1860-'61* (New York: Harper and Brothers, 1876) or in Samuel Wylie Crawford, *The Genesis of the Civil War: The Story of Fort Sumter, 1860-1861* (New York: C. L. Webster and Company, 1887), hereinafter cited as Crawford, *Genesis of the Civil War.* Nor does it appear in the more recent study by Swanberg, *First Blood.*

[89] Alice Haigh Lippitt was the wife of W. H. Lippitt, a Wilmington druggist. Eighth Census, 1860, Population Schedule, New Hanover County, 97.

We reached Wilmington on the 20th & heard that on the 18th at Bull Run we had signally defeated the advance of the "Grand Army" & driven it back to Centreville, tho the main body under McDowell was still to be met. The Yankees call this "the Battle of Stone Bridge," we "Bull Run."

Col Kershaw of SC, our old neighbor, remarking upon the homely name to Gen Beauregard, he replied, "I do not know sir—is it not as good as Cow Pens? & will stand well by its side"!

On the 21st—Sunday—the very day we got to Wrightsville occurred the "Battle of Manassas," by the Yankees called Bull Run, the bloodiest battle ever fought on this continent, a battle which filled our hearts with thankful exultation & correspondingly depressed the spirits of our enemies!

Gen Joe Johnston had been for some time marching & counter marching in the neighborhood of Winchester, now seeming to offer Battle to Gen Patterson, then unaccountably declining. These manoevres had excited the animadversion of the Press & the whole country who, because they could not understand, took the liberty of condemning him, but the sequel showed that he knew well what he was about & was in fact a master of strategy! For suddenly after completely bewildering Patterson he withdrew from Winchester & with great rapidity & with forced marches joined Beauregard at Manassas. And well was it that he did so, for the Federals under McDowell advancing with high hopes of success, beleiving him far off at Winchester, met their combined forces & to their amazement suffered a complete defeat, a defeat which degenerated into a rout, the most disgraceful ever known in the annals of war! Everything was thrown away in their flight by the frightened multitude. Arms, accoutrements, guns, ammunition, provisions, clothing, every thing which makes the personel of an Army, all fell into our hands!

Their baggage on being ransacked afforded a most remarkable evidence of their intentions towards us—thousands of pairs of Handcuffs, some of them marked "for Officers"! Handcuffs for the wrists of Southern gentlemen! Packages of printed invitations to a Ball to be given by them in Richmond in honour of their expected triumph. A number of trunks containing Ladies wearing apparel, Ball dresses, etc. As for the Ladies themselves who accompanied the march of the Army, they made their escape as best they could. Miss Weed, the daughter of the infamous politician Thurlow Weed,[90] is said to have made her entry into Washington on a mule riding Portugese fashion!

Our forces were estimated at 28,000, theirs at 55,000 men. Our's were worse armed & we had but little Artillery & no men skilled in the handling of it. T⌐ were armed & equipped in the most splendid style, had Battery after

---

⌐ed (1797-1882) was an American journalist and politician who vigorously supported Lin-⌐ policies. *Webster's Biographical Dictionary*, 1554. The episode referred to by Mrs. Ed-ing Weed's daughter is not recorded in Weed's autobiography. Harriet A. Weed (ed.), *Including His Autobiography and a Memoir* (Boston: Houghton, Mifflin and Co., 2 volumes,

THE EDMONDSTON DIARY 81

Battery of the best Field peices served by experienced & well-trained Gunners of the old US Army. Sherman's, said to be among the most effective Batteries in the world fell into our hands.

At our first discharge, Capt Ricketts, (my Kin), who was wounded & a prisoner, said "more than half his horses were killed." "Talk who will of a panic," said the candid officer, "we were beaten, beaten because their men shot better than ours. No troops can stand before such markmen. Before I could unlimber half my horses were dead." Our loss in killed & wounded 1600 (sixteen hundred); theirs killed, wounded, & missing, & Prisoners— 15,000 (fifteen thousand)!

President Davis himself came out to the field of Battle & riding along cheered & thanked the men. They say that even our enemies were affected to tears as they saw him, cheered as he rode along by the wounded lying as they were on the ground helpless & dying! But as the details of this battle are matters of History I will not dwell on them.

President Davis ordered that the next Sunday thanks be offered in all the Churches to Almighty God for the signal deliverance He had wrought for us; and as I sat in the little sea side Church at Wrightsville & heard the Anthems which rose from the hearts of a grateful people, never did I so desire the gift of Song, that I too, in the words of Deborah the Prophetess, might "sing unto the Lord"! Non nobis Domine, non nobis Domine, but unto Thy name be the praise! [91]

Could we have followed up the Victory by an immediate march on to Washington it is the opinion of almost all now that we could have dictated terms of Peace—from our own captured Congress Halls—but our troops were greatly exhausted & it did not enter into the heart of man to conceive the extent of their panic. The "grand Army" was thoroughly disorganized, demoralized & destroyed, many of the troops not stopping until they reached their homes in the different distant States.

The disappointment to the hoary heady old traitor Scot delighted the whole nation. He said to a Lady in Va on the day of the march, "Madam, I now have the rebels so," extending his open palm "Tomorrow I shall have them so," & suiting the action to the word, clenched his fist with vehemence!

But he was mistaken for once & then had the unmanliness to set up a horrible driveling complaint, abuse himself, & tell Mr Lincoln that he ought to be broken, for against his own better judgement he had yeilded to popular clamour & the newspaper cry "on to Richmond" & marched before he was ready. He forgot the "closed fist."

However Lincoln & the Congress took him at his word & virtually deposed him by the promotion of Gen M Clellan who had distinguished himself in Western Va, & then adding insult to insult—tho his averice made him pocket

---

[91] Judges 5:3 and Psalms 115:1.

it cheerfully—Congress passed an order saying that "When Lieut Gen Scott *should* retire his full pay should be continued to him." This tho took place later, but here on the field of Manassas he lost his prestige & his precious popularity!

McDowell was made the scape goat & McClellan appointed over the heads of all the older officer of the Army & Gen Wool was so disgusted that he did not play cards for a week!

On the 21st as I said before we got to Wrightsville where I was most hospitably received by Mr & Mrs Lippitt. The same afternoon Mr Edmondston left me and returned to his camp. My intention had been to remain but a few days, see Mr E.'s encampment, how he was occupied, stationed & then to return home. But Mrs Lippit was so kind & so pressing in her entreaties to me to remain longer under her roof that I nothing loth to be persuaded to remain near Patrick gradually lengthed my stay until from days my visit stretched into weeks! I found the camp on the sea shore commanding a view of the coast for miles, & the duty of the Company was to act as Picket Guards & give notice should an attempt at landing be made by the enemy. Mr Lippitt went every morning up to his business in Wilmington, & I remained either quietly with Alice or, when Mr E's duty permitted it, went over & spent the day & dined with him in Camp.

The only thing that occurred to break the monotony of the continued drill—drill twice every day—was the occasional passage of a Lincoln War Steamer, which would steam slowly by spying & sounding as she went. From without we hear of continual skirmishing in which neither side gained much advantage, particularly in the West of Va where Wise & Floyd carried on a warfare rather against the elements than the Yankees, & the same may be said of them.

In the Peninsula Gen McGruder held his own & prevented the advance of the enemy from Fortress Monro. On the 7 of Aug he made a descent upon Hampton—which had become a den of run, a way negroes who stole & destroyed every thing within their reach & decoyed the negroes from the adjacent country—& set it on fire. Many of the houses were fired by the owners themselves who preferred destroying their homes with their own hand to seeing them poluted with such inhabitants. This act annoyed Gen Wool at Fortress Monro greatly as he was forced to find shelter for the "Contrabands" nearer the fort.

About that time occurred the entire cessation by letters with the North. Up to that time we had occasionally heard from Sister Betsy & her daughters via Kentucky, the mails being still sent there & the PM at Louisville forwarding the letters. Now however this was forbidded by both governments.

An immense amount of Money was made in Kentucky as all our supplies, since the seizure of Baltimore, were got from there. Medicine, Leather, groceries, in fact all the neccessaries of life which we had been accustomed to buy at the North, were sent there by Speculators & bought by Southern merchants at fabulous prices. This was now however put a stop to & Kentucky assured by the Dis U S that her neutrality would not be respected. In Sep they made preparations for an armed occupation of Paducah, & we did the same thing by Columbus, Gen Polk commanding our forces. I omitted to mention his commission given him which we heard of in June, the week after Papa's death. At first we could not credit that it was really the Bishop, but letters from Aunt Fanny soon convinced us that he it was who was Maj Gen Polk. How little did any one think when Rev Mr Polk married Aunt Fanny, first that he would ever be Bishop, still less that he would return to his Military life & yet be Major General. Hamilton is as his Father's aid.[92]

This matter of trade in Kentucky it is supposed made her adopt the neutral line of policy which she found signally fail her. Her Patriotism could not resist the temptation of the "Almighty Dollar," the Yankee's God!

Maryland was kept in a most arbitrary & cruel despotism. The Baltimore Police Commissioners were seized & without trial imprisoned in Fort Warren, Habeas Corpus denied. Everything Red, White & Blue the Confederate colours seized & confiscated. Even children's socks of the obnoxious colours & ladies bonnets were seized in the windows of the shops & in some instances off the heads of Ladies in the streets & carried to the new Military Police station.

Yet the ladies managed with invincible spirit to defy them all & tormented General Dix in every way that the female mind could devise. Deputations of them relieved each other at Head Quarters asking permission to do & to wear all manner of frivolus things. They stung the officers with their sarcasm, refused to acknowledge or receive them as acquaintance, returned their Cards, openly evinced their sympathy for the prisoners they captured, & supplied them liberally with money; when passing them, the federal officers, in the streets kept their dresses carefully drawn in, as tho contact was pollution, & worse than all, maintained in spite of their utmost endeavour a correspondance with the South & transmitted information & aid to their Southern friends.

Mr Seward[93] seized some of the ladies in Washington, imprisoned them & subjected them to the grossest indignities, Mrs Greenhow,[94] Mrs Phillips, &

---

[92] Leonidas Polk, Episcopal bishop and Confederate general, married Frances Devereux, Mrs. Edmondston's aunt. His son was Alexander Hamilton Polk. See Introduction.

[93] William Henry Seward (1801-1872) was an American statesman from New York who uncompromisingly opposed slavery yet sought to avert civil war during the first months of the secession crisis. He served capably as secretary of state through the Civil War until 1869. *Dictionary of American Biography*, XVI, 615-621.

[94] Rose O'Neal Greenhow, a Washington society leader, informed Beauregard of McDowell's plans for the first Bull Run campaign. She was put under house arrest and later confined in Old Capital Prison with her small daughter. Following her release, she was sent south where she continued to support the Confederacy. Ishbel Ross, *Rebel Rose, Life of Rose O'Neal Greenhow, Confederate Spy* (New York: Harper & Brothers, 1954), 113-116, 141-149, 192-193, 250-265.

her sister, our old friend Miss Martha Levy,[95] being of the number. These last were soon liberated, but Mrs Greenhow remains now in custody. His treatment of them comes nearer to that of the wretch Haynau[96] to the Hungarian Ladies than aught else we ever hard or read of choking one by the throat to compel her to give up a paper which she had swallowed, keeping a sentinel always in their bed chambers, and other vile treatment. I think I mentioned the fact that medicine was pronounced Contraband—thus making war upon the sick & wounded.

Galveston in Texas was shelled without notice, & that but one man was killed was owing rather to their bad aim than to any goodness in their hearts! In Missouri the civil war raged with intense fury. Price & McCullock kept their head way against Lyon's & his marauding crew & finally McCullock on the 10th of Aug defeated & killed Lyons at the Battle of Oak Ridge. Fremont was put in charge & his first official act was on Sep. 2d to Issue a proclamation Confiscating the Slaves of all in Arms in the Southern Cause.

In the Territory of Arizona we gained a signal victory, nearly expelling them from the Territory.

Aug. 25th & 6th we signalized by a general advance on the line of the Potomac & occupied Mason's and Munson's Hill near Alexandria in the hope of drawing McClellan out of his intrenchments, but he declined the gage. We succeeded in blocking up the Potomac with our Batteries, thus forcing them to bring all their supplies for the armies in and about Washington at a heavy expense by the Land route.

The Blockade of our coast continued & the vessels occasionally "ran it" & brought in a few arms, etc., yet the fear of a dearth of them & of Powder caused us serious uneasiness. Their Blockade was by no means an effective one, & we looking in good faith to Europe that she would insist on the observation of the treaty of Paris, which declares that a Blockade to be binding shall, be effective had a right to expect her intervention; but though the magic "*three* vessels" were multiplied again & again out of every Southern Port but Norfolk, still they held aloof & plumed themselves on "*impartiality.*"[97]

---

[95] Eugenia Levy Phillips (1819-1901), wife of Alabama congressman Philip Phillips, was accused in 1861 of abetting the southern cause. With her sister Martha Sarah Levy and other family members, she was confined under guard for a short time. In 1862 Mrs. Phillips became the subject of international comment when she clashed with General Butler in New Orleans and was imprisoned by him on Ship Island. See Eugenia Phillips Journal (written during her imprisonment in Washington) and her diary recording her confinement on Ship Island. Phillips-Myers Papers, Southern Historical Collection.

[96] Baron Julius von Haynau (1786-1853), an Austrian general, was notorious for his cruelty. *Webster's Biographical Dictionary*, 682.

[97] Lincoln issued three blockade proclamations aimed at crippling southern trade. Lincoln stopped overland trade with the South on April 16, 1861, and on April 19 he ordered a naval blockade of all ports from South Carolina to Texas. The ports of North Carolina and Virginia were added on April 27. Confederate authorities protested constantly against the Union's "paper" blockade, insisting that the large amount of blockade running proved the blockade ineffective and therefore illegal. Frank L. Owsley, *King Cotton Diplomacy* (Chicago: University of Chicago Press, Second Edition, 1959), 229-234; Boatner, *Civil War Dictionary*, 70; *Civil War Naval Chronology*, II, 50.

I omitted to mention that Mary had come in from Texas early in June.[98] Her husband was elected Col of one of the Volunteer Regts & was ordered to report to Gen Lee in Western Va. Sister Betsy declined coming South when she could, giving as a reason, that she was not willing to expose her daughters to the horrors of a servile War & so now she was cut off from all intercourse with her family & sons—in a hostile country!

Sophia's husband Mr Turner received from the Gov the appointment of Captain in the 2d Regt N C Cavalry. Brother John had done most efficient service all the summer as Ass Quarter Master on Gen Martin's staff, at first with the rank of Captain, but was afterwards promoted to that of Major. Thomas Jones was a Lieut in Captain Nixon's Co of foot, [27th] Regt, whilst Frank was a private in the same Company.[99]

I beleive I have now brought up all the different threads of my narrative up to Aug 28th when occurred the Bombardment of Fort Hatteras. This was but a Land Fort, hastily thrown up at the commencement of the War to defend Hatteras Inlet, which tho by no means an important one in time of Peace was, from the impossibility of blockading it by vessels stationed outside, most valuable to us in time of war as vessels running the Blockade found a safe harbour and a secure entrance into Pamlico & Albemarle Sounds in defiance of their pursuers. It ought by all means to have been well defended, which unfortunately however was not done. As this was the beginning of our troubles in this State, I ought to be particular in mentioning it.

It was attacked by a powerful fleet under command of Com Stringham, the Land forces being under Gen Butler commonly known as "Picayune."[100] After some hours heavy Bombardment with but little damage, night coming on with a heavy wind on shore the fleet was compelled to draw off & beat out to sea. They had landed a force of 300 men whom they were compelled to leave unsupported on the Sands. These our men in the Fort left unmolested, tho' they could easily have overpowered them, conduct considered inexplicable then & which has never yet been satisfactorily explained. The next day exposed not only to a terrific Bombardment from the Fleet but to a land attack from these men, they capitulated, Commodore Barron being in command. We lost but few men either killed or wounded in the engagement. Our loss was wholly in prisoners, as they captured 691 men & sent them to N Y.

---

[98] Mrs. Edmondston's sister Mary Bayard Clarke had been living in San Antonio with her husband seeking a climate agreeable to her health. See Introduction.

[99] William Nixon was the captain of Co. F, Twenty-seventh North Carolina Regiment. Thomas Devereux Jones served as a lieutenant in this company, and William Francis Jones served as a first sergeant. Clark, *Histories of the North Carolina Regiments*, II, 426; files and records of the Civil War Roster Branch, Historical Publications Section, Division of Archives and History, Raleigh.

[100] "Picayune," a name given to General Butler, came from a popular song about a barber:
"Picayune Butler's coming, coming
Picayune Butler's come to town
Ahoo! Ahoo! Ahoo!"
Trefousse, *Ben Butler*, 107, 283.

The excitement was tremendus throughout the State. Censure was unsparingly heaped upon the officers in command, the men, & the State authorities. Two heavy Columbiads sent weeks before by Government for the protection of the Inlet—were found by the enemy lying unmounted on the beach.[101] Why? The officer responsible would find it hard to tell.

Mr Warren Winslow[102] had been a sort of Secretary of War to the State before its military affairs passed into the hands of the Confederate Government & an Adviser in cheif to the late Gov, for I omitted to mention in its place that early in July Gov Ellis died at the Va Springs of Consumption. He had been succeeded by the Speaker of the Senate Mr Henry T Clark.[103] Upon Mr Winslow however the wrath of the whole State seemed justly to fall, he having dissuaded Gov Ellis, who for weeks was so feeble as to be scarcely able to speak, far less to discharge the duties which devolved upon him, "that the navies of the world could make no impression on the coast of N C, so well had nature defended it with shoals & sand bars"—an impression which they found an egregiously false one!

Immediately upon the news of its fall Mr Edmondston volunteered the services of his Co to the Gov to assist in retaking it, an offer which was secconded by Mr Flanner[104] of Wilmington by the tender of his Steamboat gratis to transport the troops. Both offers were accepted but never alaas, acted on, for no attempt was made either to disloge them from their quiet possession or to prevent their spies and scouts ranging at will through our whole interior navigation, tampering with the negroes & fisherman who in that region are mere nomads owing allegiance to Neptune & Boreas[105] only & selling their

[101] Major General Butler reported on August 30, 1861: "Upon taking possession of Fort Hatteras I found that it mounted ten guns, with four yet unmounted, and one large 10-inch columbiad all ready for mounting...." Fort Clark he described as "a square redoubt, mounting five guns and two 6-pounders." The guns were spiked "in a very inefficient manner" upon abandonment the previous day. *Official Records (Army)*, Series I, IV, 584.

[102] Warren Winslow (1810-1862) of Cumberland County was speaker of the North Carolina Senate from 1854 until 1855 and governor from December, 1854, until January, 1855. He served in the United States House of Representatives from 1855 until 1861. When Governor Ellis became ill in 1860, Winslow was one of three people chosen to serve on a board to advise Ellis concerning military affairs. *Biographical Directory of the American Congress, September 5, 1774, to October 21, 1788, and the Congress of the United States from the First to the Eighty-sixth Congress, March 4, 1789, to January 3, 1961, Inclusive* (Washington, D.C.: Government Printing Office, 1961), 1837, hereinafter cited as *Biographical Directory of Congress*; John G. Barrett, *The Civil War in North Carolina* (Chapel Hill: University of North Carolina Press, 1963), 32, hereinafter cited as Barrett, *Civil War in North Carolina*; Hill, *Bethel to Sharpsburg*, I, 155.

[103] Henry Toole Clark (1808-1874), a prominent planter from Edgecombe County, became speaker of the North Carolina Senate in 1858. He succeeded John W. Ellis as governor of North Carolina upon Ellis's death on July 7, 1861, although he had been acting governor since June 27. Samuel A. Ashe, *History of North Carolina* (Vol. I, Greensboro: Charles L. Van Noppen, 1908, and Spartanburg, S.C.: The Reprint Co., 1971; Vol. II, Raleigh: Edwards & Broughton Printing Co., 1925, and Spartanburg, S.C.: The Reprint Co., 1971), II, 520, 634, 651, hereinafter cited as Ashe, *History of North Carolina*.

[104] William Flanner was a Wilmington merchant. Eighth Census, 1860, Population Schedule, New Hanover County, 37.

[105] Neptune was the Roman god of the sea. Boreas, in Greek mythology, was the god of the north wind. Benét, *Reader's Encyclopedia*, 764, 130.

services to the highest bidder. Had they been vigorously attacked before they had time to strengthen themselves, many of the ill consequences which flowed from the first neglect & consequent loss might have been averted!

A thousand rumours, the last wilder than the first, were put in circulation throughout the State. Now this town was reported burned, now that. Troops were hurried to Edenton, to Washington & to Roanoke Island, but to no place in sufficient numbers to make an effectual resistance. If one half the misdirected energy now used in vain endeavours to "shut" the stable Door had been expended in preventing its being opened, the horse would never have been stolen, & we all spared months of anxiety & a vast expense.

One thing struck me throughout the whole progress of the summer; the universality & the eagerness with which the women entered into the struggle! They worked as many of them had never worked before, steadily & faithfully, to supply the soldiers with clothing & the Hospitals with comforts of various kinds. "*The Soldiers*" excited an enthusiasm in the bosoms of all! Every thing must be given to them, every thing done *for* them. James soon joined his brother in Camp & was not long after followed by Amo who came to spend his summer vacation where he hoped to encounter an enemy.

Patrick was ordered by Gen Gatlin, his superior in Command, to lay out & construct a Military Road from Confederate Point to the Plank Road to Wilmington. In this work which kept him some weeks in constant employment he was much assisted by Amo, whose civil Engineering was in great requisition.

I went over to camp whenever his avocations would permit him to receive a visit from me and spent many delightful days in his tent. I had many different ways of going over. Sometimes he sent a boat for me, & I sailed across the Sound; at others James or Amo brought a buggy & drove me over; & very often I walked, never however unless he sent for me. One great pleasure we had which, however, we could not often enjoy, as it interfered with Patrick's drill was to sail across the shallow Sound to the Banks which separated it from the Ocean & to wander up & down the hard level beach & watch the incoming tide! I could have sat for hours & watched it. I never tired of it, and those beautiful lines of Wildes'—

> My Life is like the tracks, which feet
> Have left on Tampa's desert strand!-
> Soon as the rising tide shall beat-
> All trace shall vanish from the sand!-
> Yet as if greiving to efface-
> All vestige of the human race-
> On that lone shore loud moans the sea-
> Yet none shall thus lament for me!-[106]

[106] Richard Henry Wilde (1789-1847) was a Georgia lawyer, politician, and poet who moved to New Orleans in 1843 where he taught constitutional law at the University of Louisiana. Mrs. Edmondston's

became more beautiful to me as I felt the strength & beauty of the comparison. Every time I repeated them however, I felt in my inmost heart that *my* life was *not* thus, that there was *one* whose heart like the moaning sea would refuse all comfort were I to be taken; & such is the contradiction of human nature that whilst magnifying the *unselfishness* of my love, I felt a secret satisfaction in the beleif of an undying greif for me!

I received much kindness & attention from the hands of all the inhabitants of Wilmington & Wrightsville with whom I was thrown. Mrs Lippitt never wearied in her hospitality & kindness & made my stay in her house so pleasant that it was with many regrets that I bid her adieu, which however after a long visit took place on the 10th of Sept. Patrick's Military business calling him to Raleigh, he took me with him, Amo Coffin accompanying us. We found Brother immersed in the business of the Qr Master's office & as James had long been in that Department & understood it perfectly well & as he was seeking employment in the service of the Country, we both—each unknown to the other—spoke of his high qualifications to him & besought him to call him into the service of the State.

Everybody was knitting "socks for the soldier." Ladies & children, all seemed absorbed in it. Young Ladies took their knitting in their carriages as they rode out & knit in the intervals and indeed *during* their visit. Children left their play & voluntarily sat for hours steadily occupied. Every family was coming forward at the call of the Gov & giving what Blankets they could spare to the Army, the Blockade putting an embargo upon the importation of any from abroad. The Ladies all over the country had formed themselves into Hospital associations & were at work on quilted comfortatables, shirts, drawers, etc. for the sick & wounded. The hearts of the whole population was fired—& could Lincoln & Seward have seen with what unanimity & self abnegation they acted they must have been shaken at least in their ideas of conquest!

They were reported to be collecting an immense army in Washington for another march "On to Richmond" and a second superior in size at Cairo & Paducah for a march down the Mississippi. We were preparing to oppose them, but feebly I fear as our eyes were bent on England in anticipation of the day when her want of Cotton would cause her to insist on our Ports being opened. But she husbanded her resources, worked her factories on short time, & the little Cotton she had seemed like the widow's cruse[107] never to fail!

---

quotation is from the third and last stanza of "My life is like a summer rose," which was composed about 1815. Mrs. Edmondston's version of the poem is not exact. *Dictionary of American Biography*, XX, 206-207; Anthony Barclay, *Wilde's Summer Rose; or the Lament of the Captive* (Savannah, Ga.: Georgia Historical Society, 1871), 17-19.

[107]"The widow's cruse" refers to a small supply of anything that is made to go a long way by good management, the supply seeming inexhaustible. The source for the tale is II Kings 4. Benét, *Reader's Encyclopedia*, 1208.

Seward promised her she should have a Cotton Port open in sixty days & she relied upon his promisise & his ability to "crush the Rebellion out."

The Gov was pleased to compliment Patrick greatly, saying that he "was on the look out for an appointment where he could have a wider field for his exertions, that he would have given him the Majority of Spruill's Regt—(2d N C Cavalry) then thus vacant, but that he did not think either officers or men were such as it would be pleasant for him to be associated with"!

Patrick having finished his business carried me home which we reached on Sunday the 15th. We left Amo in Raleigh, the young folks having some gaiety on foot into which he wished to enter. We found all well at home, Father & Mama having occupied our house all the summer. Susan had gone to pay Kate Miller[108] a visit in Raleigh. The servants had all conducted themselves well & we found everything flourishing both at Hascosea & the Plantation, tho' the crop did not promise the yeild we had hoped for. Patrick remained at home until the 20th when he returned to his command at Wrightsville the same day we gained a signal victory at Lexington, Missouri. Our forces under Gen Price forced the enemy under Col Mulligan to surrender. He took a large no of prisonners, besides amunition stores, horses, arms, etc. & recovered the great Seal of the State, the public Records & nine hundred thousand dollars which Mulligan had stolen from the Banks a few days only before, but which we however promptly restored to the rightful owners—!

On the 15th of this month was killed whilst on a scout in Western Va Col John A Washington the great grand Nephew & representative of Gen George Washington. His wife my old friend & schoolmate, Ellen Seldon[109]—had died the year before, & he now left a family of small helpless children almost without protector. One would have thought that when they learned that their fratercidal hands had killed one of the blood & lineage of their great Benefactor, whom they profess to revere, it would have made them at least pause! But no! they seemed to exult over it! Little did I think when I saw him a young man in the heyday of youth, proud of his name, his blood, his proprietorship of Mt Vernon, that he would ever fill a bloody grave!

On the 24th Amo Coffin got down from Raleigh. On the 28th I do not think a bombshell crashing through the roof would have startled us much more than the announcement of Sister Betsy's arrival in Raleigh with Rachel, Betty having been married & left behind in Owego. Married! & so young! and to a Yankee!—a man with whom her country was at War, against whom her brothers might perhaps be arrayed! It was terrible to think of!

---

[108] Kate Miller was Mrs. Edmondston's niece, the daughter of Frances Devereux and Henry Watkins Miller of Raleigh. See Introduction.

[109] John Augustine Washington, Jr. (1820-1861), the last owner of Mount Vernon in the Washington succession, was married to Eleanor Love Seldon. They had seven children at the time of his death. Minnie Kendall Lowther, *Mount Vernon: Its Children, Its Romances, Its Allied Families and Mansions* (Chicago, Philadelphia, Toronto: John C. Winston, Co., 1932), 66-68.

On the 2d of Oct during a heavy shower as Amo & I sat in the piazza at Hascosea we saw a man walking up to the house with a valise in his hand. The rain was so heavy that he was close upon us before we could make out who it was when Amo exclaimed, "I declare, it is the Captain." And so it was. Patrick had come home having resigned the Captaincy of the Scotland Neck Mounted Riflemen! His reasons were more than I can well set down here, the main, however, being the discontent engendered in the Company by the tender of the Co to the Gov to assist in the recapture of Hatteras, which discontent being as I fully beleive exagerated & mis-represented to him by "that gallant Militarist who had the whole theorick of War in the Knot of his scarf & the practice of it in the chape of his dagger,"[110] his 1st Lieut Mr W H Smith, so chafed his spirit and irritated his pride, wounded his Esprit de Corps to that degree, that rather than command a Company who had so low an estimate of the tie between a Captain & his command he resigned it promptly.

As he said in his letter to the Gov, "he was convinced that it was more conducive to the good of the service & consulting the best interests of the country that he should do so." Another man who they understood better & who understood them better than he did would he thought be more useful." Mr Smith went so far as to tell him that the men said they would refuse to follow him, that he had too high an opinion of Cavalry, & what it could effect, & when he gave the word 'Charge!' he would find himself at the head of a mob rather than a discipline[d] Phalanx." Tho they did not use the word *Phalanx* perhaps. The rest is quotation.

It is useless now to recall all I felt or said. Suffice it that the mortification was keen for I had thought that they prized him & were personally attached to him. I am sure he was to them, but it is over now, tho' I am sometimes annoyed that another should reap the fruits of so much toil & labour as he had taken with that Company. But it is all for the best! He did his duty whilst at the head of it, & one day they will feel it! It was the best drilled & most efficient Cavalry corps in the service of the State of N C.

The day after he got home on the 3d Father left for Tennessee, taking Mama to Raleigh with him. On the 4th Patrick left for Raleigh & Amo Coffin to return home to Aiken. Patrick left to see the Governor about a new field of service, for he could not bear the idea of inaction. I was left at Hascosea entirely alone! Patrick saw the Governor who gave him, so far as he had the power to bestow it, the appointment of Lieut Col & placed him in charge of the remnant of the Hatteras Regt[111] not captured when the Fort was, but as

---

[110] Shakespeare, *All's Well that Ends Well*, act 4, sc. 3, lines 34-37.

[111] This reference was probably to the Seventh North Carolina Volunteers, commanded by Col. William F. Martin, the principal body of Confederate troops at Hatteras, although some detachments from the Tenth North Carolina Artillery, under Maj. W. S. G. Andrews, and a few smaller organizations were also

this appointment had to be confirmed by the Sec of War, he advised him to go home & await the action of the great man Mr Benjamin.[112]

In accordance with Patrick's wishes that I should not remain at Hascosea alone I sent for Samantha Currie to bring her children & stay with me, but she was unable to comply with my request before Monday, so I passed the interval alone in the house—a longer time than I had ever been alone before. The sensation of having no one to speak to was so new, so odd, so curious to me, that I do not think I felt lonely. From Thursday morning until Monday night I saw but one white face & that was one of Mr E's men who came on business to him.

He seemed so much affected when he spoke of his resignation, seemed to have so exalted an opinion of the Captain & his deserts, that I was confirmed in my opinion of the misrepresentation, & it required all my prudence, & fears of the consequences of a personal accountability on Mr Smith's part to some member of the Co, to prevent me from telling him what had been said to Patrick of them—but I forebore.

On the 1st of Oct we met with our first naval success in the capture of the Steamship Fanny in Albemarle Sound by our little boats the Curlew & the Raleigh. We took, beside the boat, $100,000 worth of stores of various kinds & forty five prisoners.

On the 3d Gen Jackson gained another success over the enemy at Green briar.[113] His cognomen of Stone Wall was gained at Manassas—when one of our Col's encouraging his men said "There stands Jackson—like a Stone Wall—receiving the full shock of the enemy." Since then he has been known as "Stone Wall Jackson."

On the 6th the Northern papers claim a magnificent victory which on the contrary we call the "Chiccomiocomic Races." Their victory was in this wise: Col Wright of a Georgia Regt chased an Indianna Regt 20 miles down the sands towards Hatteras, taking 32 Prisonners their munitions of War & part of their camp equipage, losing one Georgian who fell exhausted from the chase & died! Had not our Steamer misunderstood the signals he would have captured them all as they forded a shallow where fortunately for them the tide was low. Had it been six hours sooner or later they would all have fallen into

present. Only a small portion of the defenders of Hatteras escaped capture. Those who surrendered were later exchanged and formed the Seventeenth North Carolina Regiment. Hill, *Bethel to Sharpsburg*, I, 152-170.

[112] Judah Philip Benjamin (1811-1884) represented Louisiana in the United States Senate from 1852 until 1861 when he resigned as an early advocate of secession. Three weeks after his resignation he was appointed attorney general of the Confederacy; and in September, 1861, he became secretary of war. Benjamin was not popular in this position due to various military defeats. Davis appointed him secretary of state in March, 1862, in order to keep him in the government. Benjamin held this post until the end of the war. *Concise Dictionary of American Biography*, 66-67; Boatner, *Civil War Dictionary*, 59.

[113] The Confederate commander of Camp Bartow on the Greenbriar River was Gen. Henry Rootes Jackson of Georgia, not Stonewall Jackson as stated by Mrs. Edmondston. *Official Records (Army)*, Series I, V, 224.

his hands. This was their magnificent victory & to such shallow artifices is Seward forced to resort to keep up the war fever with the masses!

On the 9th we beat up their quarters on Santa Rosa Island & drove them into Fort Pickens with considerable loss. The famous, or infamous "Billy Wilson" Col of Zouaves made his escape by runing in his shirt only into the friendly shelter.

On the 9th Patrick returned from Raleigh bringing Sister Betsy & Rachel with him. It is worse than useless to relate all I felt about Bettie & her marriage with one of our enemies. I fear my feelings are not yet sufficiently chastened to bear repetition, so prudently forbear deepening them by recording them. Suffice it to say that the difference of opinion the entire different stand point from which Sister Betsy & myself viewed the matter cast a shadow over the freedom & pleasure of our intercourse which neither party could cast off. Rachel I found much grown & improved & warmly southern at heart.

On the 15th Mama returned from Raleigh Sue remaining behind to finish her visit. On the same day our forces having vainly attempted to draw the Northern army from its entrenchments in and about Washington fell back from Mason's & Munson's Hills which they had occupied for seven weeks. On the 20th James Edmondston came down from Raleigh to make his brother a little visit. Brother John had taken our suggestion about James & had got him as his assistant in the Qr Master's office, an appointment which a little later resulted in a Staff appointment on Gen Martin's staff with the rank of Captain of Ordonance.

He gave me more particulars with regard to his brother's resignation, which confirmed me in my opinions of Lieut Smith's conduct. It seems that he was very unpopular with the Company & wanted an excuse to resign, but having none desired company. So he deepened the misunderstanding between the Co and the Captain in order that the Capt's might cover the 1st Lieut's resignation & that it might be supposed that they had common cause against the men. James remained but two days when he returned to Raleigh.

On the 21st occurred the brilliant victory of Leesburg or Ball's Bluff, as the enemy call it, when the enemy with twelve Regts crossed the Potomac at Leesburg & attacked three Regts under Gen Evans stationed there. We repulsed them killing 500, wounding as many, & taking 600 Prisonners. We drove them over a steep Bluff into the River & scores of them were drowned in their retreat by the sinking the Flat boats they were escaping on by our Artillery.

Gen Baker was killed. He was the California Representative a native of England, who before the War made such violent speeches in Congress against us. Col Stone James old friend, was severely censured for his conduct by his Government & some say broken but I beleive that is a mistake—only passed over in the giving of appointments. Belmont [114] the place where I was at school used as a hospital & Goose Creek the scene of our daily walks was the theatre of a bloody fight—

> "Alaas! thou lovely lake—that ere
> Thy Banks should echo sounds of fear"—
> The woods, the bosky thickets sleep—
> So stilly on thy bosom deep—
> The lark's blythe carol from the cloud—
> Seems for the scene too gaily loud" [115]

Think of our school room & our dormitories echoing as they did to the groans of the wounded & dying!

We almost fell into our usual habits of life, disturbed only by an expectation that Patrick's orders would come from the Department. I got his equipments & winter outfit ready. We sauntered in the garden & Cotton field after our usual dolce far niente[116] manner, gathered Dahlias, pruned fruit trees, read nothing however but newspapers. Even the English Reviews which Mrs Jones brought us fell upon an indifferent circle, tho we long had been debarred from their perusal.

Went to the plantation, & had it not been for Patrick's annoyance at the delay of his orders—for he longed for active service—we would actually have enjoyed ourselves. A strange inaction seemed to take place in the head of our affairs. Mr Benjamin, whether he was expecting the enemy to go into winter quarters or built too confidently on the hope of English intervention, none can tell; but the formation of new troops almost ceased, & volunteering was actually discouraged. We paid for it afterwards, however. On the 27th Father returned from Tennessee bringing us news of the birth of Nora's[117] son, her first one & of a great improvement in her health, for which God be praised!

About this time we were made very unhappy by father's requesting our renunciation of the Deed he had given us for the Looking Glass Plantation & negroes. He gave as a reason that he wished to avoid the payment of a double tax on it—a tax on the property & one on the deed—but as we paid one & he the other, I did not think it so very hard. Mr Whitaker was in the same position, & he did not have to renounce his. Father gave us a codicil to his Will which he said would have the same effect, but besides hating anything about Wills & especially father's, it unsettled us, & made all our plans which we had for the future like Chateaux en Espagne—so airy did they seem.

---

[114] Belmont, the home of Ludwell Lee (1760-1836) in Loudoun County, Virginia, was sold after his death, and the house was converted into a school for young women. Writers Program, Work Projects Administration (comp.), *Virginia: A Guide to the Old Dominion* (New York: Oxford University Press, 1940), 526.

[115] Scott, *Lady of the Lake*, canto 3, stanza 14, lines 340-345.

[116] *Dolce far niente* is an Italian phrase meaning "sweet idleness."

[117] Honoria (Nora) Devereux, Mrs. Edmondston's sister, married Dr. Robert H. Cannon. They were living in Fayette County, Tennessee, during the war. See Introduction.

Mr Edmondston said we could not in honour & respect to Father refuse it, so we acquiesced; but it made me very unhappy & unsettled, tho perhaps I was unreasonable, & I tried very hard to conquer it. But we were much happier & more hopeful before. Nothing seemed *ours* now. He says after Peace, when the War tax is paid he will restore it. So we have an additional motive were any needed to pray for Peace.

On the 31st Gen Scott resigned & retired to private life, having been virtually superceeded by McClellan. Some time before, his pay had been secured by Congress "when he should desire to retire," a broad hint & one which he took. I wonder if he retains the previlege of wearing his Epaullettes & Cocked Hat? It would be a sore blow to him to be forced to forego them! He announced his intention of going to Europe & have something done for his "back and legs" in a public speech, in answer to one of fare well. "Horrors! The Queen of Spain has Legs! ["] Where was his gentleman usher that he did not restrain him from so undignified an admission!

On the 31st we were walking out & were hastily summoned to the house to see the Misses Hill who had ridden over to tell Mr E that an attack was momentarily expected at Wilmington. All furloughs were withdrawn & their brother[118] who had been elected Captain of Mr E's old Company hastily recalled to his command. Everything seemed to indicate that the magnificent Armada, which had long been fitting out in New York, was intended for our Coast. Accordingly very early next morning he left for Wilmington intending in the event of an attack to volunteer on Brig. Gen Anderson's, his old Commander's, staff.

On the 1st of November Father & Mama left for Conneconara. On the 2d, 3d and 4th occurred a great storm on our Coast for which we were heartily thankful to Almighty God, as it scattered the Armada Lincoln had fitted out with so much secresy & expense, driving some of it far out to sea, others back to the shelter of Hampton Roads, & wrecking five or six large transports on our coast—loaded some with provisions, one with horses, & the rest with men. We captured the entire crew of one. Others were all drowned & for miles the shore was strewn with coffee, stores, potatoes, & about six hundred horses were in one place washed ashore. Nov 6th was the battle of Belmont in Missouri. Pillow was being beaten, but happily was re-inforced just in time by Uncle, I should say Gen Polk, & together they routed the Federals in fine style.[119]

---

[118] Atherton Barnes Hill, the son of Lavinia Dorothy Barnes and Whitmel John Hill, was the brother of Lucy Anne and Louisa Catherine Hill. He initially served as the second lieutenant of the Scotland Neck Mounted Riflemen but was promoted on October 9, 1861, to captain. Eighth Census, 1860, Population Schedule, Halifax County, 83; Manarin and Jordan, *North Carolina Troops*, II, 227.

[119] Mrs. Edmondston is referring to the defeat of Gen. Ulysses S. Grant at Belmont, Missouri, by Gen. Gideon Joseph Pillow with reinforcement from Gen. Leonidas Polk. See Appendix; Boatner, *Civil War Dictionary*, 57-58, 653-654, 657-658.

Nov 7th Mr Edmondston came home very early in the morning from Wilmington via Raleigh. Early as it was he found me up & in the garden looking for the Diamond Pin he had given me, which to my great sorrow I had lost the night before. He brought letters from Gens Gatlin and Anderson & from the Gov for the Secretary of War urging him to combine some independant Companies in & about Wilmington with a Battalion & to give the command of it to him. This neccessitated his going on to Richmond & he would not have stopped at home but that he had been taken so unwell on his journey that he feared he would not be able to proceed. He allowed me to nurse & Doctor him to my heart's content, which I did to such good purpose that the next day he was able to proceed on his journey. On the 7th he went to Richmond taking Rachel Jones with him, Father having determined to send her to Mr Le Fabre's school.[120] I stayed at home & spent the week with all hands looking diligently for my Pin but to my great sorrow to no purpose; however, I have not yet despaired!

On the 7th fell the long expected blow. The Armada upon which our eyes had been so long fixed & of whom news had been so eagerly demanded had, it appeared, orders to rendezvous in the harbour of Port Royal, South Carolina, and on that day commenced the Bombardment of two Sand Forts which the authorities had thrown up at the mouth of the harbour.[121] Pity it was that they were ever put there, as they were too small & insignificant to afford either protection or great resistance. Not so much, however, as to prevent the self-glorification & rejoicing which filled the whole north on their fall. The flourish of trumpets which they sounded over the magnificent triumph of the Union Arm reverberated across the Atlantic & confirmed Lord John Russel[122] in his non intervention policy by strengthening his beleif in Seward's promise of soon opening a Cotton Port.

The evolutions of the Yankee Fleet were said to be magnificent. Riding at will at the mouth of that splendid harbour, they steamed slowly in line of Battle, discharging a Broadside at one fort, rounding too & passing the other, they did the same to it. Then standing out to sea, they tacked; headed in land again & performed the same manovre again. This they did in such quick succession, pouring volley after volley into the forts, that our men had not time to reload between them & the forts so called (a misnomer, however, for they were mere sand Batteries without casemates) soon having their guns dismounted, it was determined by the troops in them to evacuate them. This

---

[120] M. Hubert Pierre Lefebvre's boarding school, located at Grace and Foushee streets in Richmond, was attended by "types of girls from the higher classes of society all over the South. . . ." Constance Cary (Mrs. Burton) Harrison, *Recollections Grave and Gay* (New York: Charles Scribner's Sons, 1911), 41-42.

[121] Forts Walker and Beauregard, located on opposite sides of the entrance to Port Royal, South Carolina, were occupied by Union soldiers on November 7, 1861. Boatner, *Civil War Dictionary*, 663.

[122] John Russell (1792-1878) was an English statesman who took a leading role in the disputes between the United States and England over neutrality during the Civil War. *Webster's Biographical Dictionary*, 1294.

they did along a narrow causeway of two miles in length, exposed to a terrific shower of grape, canister & shell, carrying off all their wounded & leaving but few dead behind them for the enemy to exult over.

One sad case I must mention. Lieut [———] received a terrible wound in the side which broke his sword. Feeling that he was mortally wounded, he called the surgeon & unbuckling the broken sword & drawing a ring from his finger, requested him to convey them to a lady to whom he was affianced & to say to her that his last thought was of her—& died! Think of the distress into which she was plunged by the receipt of so sad a token.

Our troops made good their retreat & made a stand on the mainland where being re-inforced they kept the enemy at Bay, but they seized the whole of those magnificent Islands on the coast known as Sea Islands, where the Sea Island Cotton is made. Indeed without a fleet as we were, it was impossible to hold them. Their Gun boats commanded every inlet and Bayou; but they did not venture beyond their protection & dared not attempt the mainland.

Then commenced a wholesale system of plundering such as we never dreamed civilized nations could be guilty of. The fields were white to the harvest & seizing the negroes they compelled them to go on with their daily task, in some instances at the point of the bayonnet, in others by the hope of reward which they paid them in counterfeit money. They picked the cotton but either the gins having been burned or being deceived by the negroes into the beleif that their task was done, packed it in the seed in bags of different sizes & loading a vessel with it sent it to N Y where it was heralded in flaming capitals as 30,000 bales of cotton seized from the rebels. Some of it heated from being packed in the seed, but after all their expense in transporting the seed & all to Market there was so small a quantity of merchantable cotton that even they were ashamed of it. Thus did Mr Seward keep his promise to the British government!

Before escaping some of the gentlemen of the Islands with their own hands burned the cotton which had already been gathered, either baled or in bulk, & set fire also to their residences & out houses, choosing rather to offer them a sacrifice on the altar of Liberty than leave them to the occupancy of their enemies. Owing, howeve[r], to the profound security into which they had been lulled since the defeat at Manassas, the Yankees became possessed of much valuable property in household furniture, books, plate, wine, etc. which they most unscrupulously appropriated, in many instances loading vessels with private property and shipping it to N Y!

On the Island of St Helena is situated the estates of the Coffin family,[123] a share in which was owned by Mr E's brother-in law. These were seized &

---

[123] Coffin's Point, the plantation of Thomas Alston Coffin, was at the eastern end of St. Helena Island. The library was "sufficiently large to attract the attention and admiration of the conquering army officers in 1861." Guion Griffis Johnson, *A Social History of the Sea Islands* (Chapel Hill: University of North Carolina Press, 1930), 103, 114.

here unfortunately they got the crop on hand. Negroes, stock, everything, was lost and they even had the audacity to mention it as the splendid Estates formerly belonging to "the Coffin family." Dr Coffin lost everything & with his little family we feel most deeply for him; & never felt the burden of debt as we have done since we find ourselves unable to give anything but our sympathy.

We were inexpressibly startled & shocked by the news that in one night eight of the bridges on the Va and Tenn had been burned, the work of traitors in East Tennessee. At one of them there was a desperate conflict between the guard & fifteen men. He succeeded *alone* in beating them off & saving the bridge but with a loss of both hands in the struggle.[124]

On the 12th Mr Edmondston returned from Richmond, the Secretary of War refusing to unite the Companies into a Battalion on the ground that one of them was for Local defence only. As to the Hatteras Regt, he said it was not worth while to appoint an officer to command it as negotiations were on foot for an exchange of prisoners & the captured officers would soon be released. Everyone was loud in condemning him for the coolness & supineness he showed as to the increased organization of our Army. He in common with the whole nation was looking abroad to see what England & France will do.

The news from England was looked for with feverish anxiety, for from her was confidently expected a deliverance from the inconveniences we now began to suffer from the Blockade. The price of Salt, of Leather, & in consequence shoes now became alarming. Coffee, Sugar & luxuries of various kinds had long been enormously high; but provisions being plenty, there had been no suffering. But now with salt at 10, 15 and in some instances $28 a sack, negro shoes—brogans—at 4, 5 and $6 per pair, things began to look serious.

Now was exemplified the parable of the wise & the foolish Virgins, for thanks to Patrick's foresight, with the single exception of negro shoes, we wanted for nothing either in the clothing, the housekeeping, or the Plantation line. Blankets we found the negroes could well do without one year, their stock being so abundant. Indeed I was occupied all the Fall making Comfortable for myself so as to be enabled to give my blankets to the government to supply the Army. Nails went up enormously & the want of Cotton Bagging & rope was a serious one to many. A large quantity of Cotton was put up in thin boards, slabs bound around with white oak-splits & pressed in the screw in the ordinary way from the absolute inability to get Bagging & Rope; but we, so far from wanting, were enabled to supply some of our neighbors.

On the 18th Patrick went up to Halifax Court & I well remember I took that day for digging up my Dahlia Roots which had blossomed splendidly all the Fall & had been a source of great pleasure to me; but I had not been called to "strew them in the Conquerer's path" nor to "deck the Halls where

---

[124] While defending the railroad bridge at Strawberry Plains in eastern Tennessee, James Keelan lost his left hand and was severely wounded. Bromfield L. Ridley, *Battles and Sketches of the Army in Tennessee* (Mexico, Missouri: Missouri Printing and Publishing Co., 1906), 29-31.

the bright wine flows" in honour of Peace as I had fondly thought when I planted them.

When he came back he brought the news that Messrs Mason & Slidell,[125] our commissioners to France & England, had been forcibly taken from the deck of an English Mail Steamer by an armed U. S vessel against the protest of the English Captain & the Mail Agent, who being an employee of Government represents it on the English Mail Packets. Messrs Mason & Slidell with their families & suites had succeeded in running the Blockade & reaching the West Indies in safety. There they took passage on the English packet & were proceeding prosperously on their voyage when overhauled by Commodore Wilkes & forced via arms on board his Frigate & brought with their suite's into Fortress Monro. Their wives & families they left in the steamer.

The North was in a blaze of exultation, jubilant and defiant. Congress passed a vote of thanks to Com Wilkes. The press exhausted itself in boasts of what they would do should England *dare* to complain. Ambassadors were pronounced "*Contraband*," their favourite word when they wanted anything, precedents hunted up, the act proved by authorities on international Law to be perfectly allowable; indeed, they cited England's own conduct to convince themselves that she had no right to remonstrate even. They boasted of how they would take Canada—should she make it a cause of war & were altogether as insolent, defiant & boastful as the Yankee nation knows how to be, & that is saying a great deal.

On the other hand, we saw in it a presage of Peace. England would not suffer such an insult to her Flag. She would re-demand then. The Dis U S could not give them up or apologise after the vote of thanks to Com Wilkes & the enthusiasm of the whole nation. When they went to War the Blockade must be raised, our trade reopened, & a sale for our cotton—& we could carry on the war for almost an indefinite period. The sentiment was universal that Mason & Slidell in Fort Warren were doing more for their country than they could do were they where they were accredited at the Courts of St James & St Cloud, respectively; and all eyes were eagerly bent on the Foreign news to see what England would do & say.

On the 19th Mrs Jones left our house for Raleigh, and we on the same day made our semi-annual move—from Hascosea to Looking Glass. Scarcely were we settled when we were startled by the arrival of an Envoy sent express to summon Patrick to Wilmington, but it proved to be only to attend a Court Martial at which he was needed as a Witness.

He left home on the 25th. In the afternoon of the same day I went upon horseback to father's to remain there during his absence. On the way I met

---

[125]James Murray Mason (1798-1871) of Virginia and John Slidell (1793-1871) of Louisiana were Confederate diplomatic commissioners bound for England and France respectively, seeking diplomatic recognition of the Confederacy. Randall and Donald, *Civil War and Reconstruction*, 360-362.

the mail & opening it read, as I walked my horse, the account of the Bombardment of Fort Pickens. It continued furiously for two days, during which time they fired Warrington with their shells whilst we damaged their vessels badly. Col Brown, the Commandant, reported to his Government the loss of one man killed & six wounded. Our loss was also one killed & several wounded, I do not remember the no. After two days, finding they inflicted no damage upon us, they ceased & as Gen Bragg found we also were wasting powder, he ceased also & the two combattants returned to their normal quiescent state. We have been before it since April & the only good we do is to make them keep a powerful armament in the bay & put them to enormous expense transporting provisions from N Y & prevent their occupation of the Navy Yard at Pensacola & occupation of the country. It has proved an excellent school in which to drill our men. As fast as they are drilled they are sent to other fields & their places supplied with raw troops.

On the 24th they occupied Tybee Island at the mouth of the Savannah & threaten the city itself.

Nothing was being done by us in the way of raising new troops. We seemed to have fallen into a state of masterly inactivity, Mr Benjamin watching England. So Mr Edmondston's friends advised him to remain quietly at home & see what would be done when the New Year opened & what would then be the chance of getting into active service. The Gov with many regrets said that he had nothing to give him to do. No State troops were being organized, so that he had no Commissions to issue. The Department was raising none, in fact it looked for Peace, so tho' he chafed terribly at the inactivity, Patrick was forced to remain at home. Home life & home pleasures seemed to have lost their charm for him & I am sure he grumbled more about having to sleep comfortably *in* his bed than any soldier, be he ever so discontented, did at sleeping *out* of his.

Skirmishes constantly took place with varying success, but one at Dranesville resulted in our serious discomfiture and heavy loss. Gen Stuart was said not to have sent out an advanced guard & in consequence we came near losing our forage waggons, but happily our troops were enabled to stand against a superior foe until they, the waggons, had retreated.

Gen Jackson (Stone Wall) made a terrible march in the severest kind of weather over frozen roads & succeeded in cutting Dam No 5,[126] an important point on the Chesapeake and Ohio Canal, thus cutting off one of the arms of supply to Washington and their Grand Army. Our Batteries below blockaded the Potomac & everything had to be brought by R R & waggons, so living

---

[126] Dam No. 5, on the Potomac seven miles above Williamsport, Maryland, supplied water for a long section of the Chesapeake and Ohio Canal, providing the Federals with an east-west artery by which coal, grains, and other bulk cargoes poured eastward. Jackson's heroic efforts to cut the dam in December, 1861, were only partially successful and stopped operation of the canal only temporarily. Lenoir Chambers, *Stonewall Jackson* (New York: William Morrow, 2 volumes, 1959), I, 412-413.

went up in Washington & Coal was in proportion there as high as salt was here!

And the mention of Salt reminds me that I have not mentioned father's conduct with regard to it. When the Blockade was declared he had on hand a quantity of Salt which he had bought & was in the act of using for Agricultural purposes. This he instantly stopped & reserved it, well knowing that by the fall it would be greatly needed. And so in fact it turned out. The poorer classes throughout the country, those people who had from three to eight or ten Hogs—& who had been in the habit of supplying themselves from the neighboring merchants with the few bushels they needed, were terribly ground & imposed upon by Speculators who in some instances had the face to ask 25 and $28 per sack. In this state of things he gave notice that he would distribute in parcels not exceeding 5 bu all he could spare & as money was scarce he would take his payment in *socks* which he intended to bestow upon the Government. He accordingly did so & gave his salt at the rate of 2 pr of yarn or four pair of cotton socks per bushel, thus bringing the Salt to about eighty cents. He gave away in this manner about 800 bushels of salt. The socks which he received he forwarded to the Qr Master & they were given to the soldiers, they costing the Government nothing. In this way he prevented an amount of suffering which it is difficult to estimate & became a benefactor to the poorer class throughout this whole region!

On the [11th] and [12th] of December occurred the most disastrous fire that had ever visited Charleston.[127] Many persons are convinced that it was the work of Yankee emisaries, whilst others contend that being accidental in commencement it was fanned by the wind & the sparks flying in great profusion & carried to some distance by the wind, gave it the appearance of being set in different places at once. I know not which are right, but certain it is that the Blockading squadron fired a Salute, a feu de joie,[128] in the morning when the extent of the damage became known to them.

The fire originated in a sash & blind factory on Cooper River & sweeping diagonally across the best built & oldest part of the city was not arrested until it had burnt itself out & there was nothing left for it to consume on the banks of the Ashley. Churches, the Theatre, the Institute Hall, & what would have greived our dear Papa more than I can express, St Andrew's Hall, together with a vast number of splendid old houses, many of them built before the Revolution, one of them the actual residence of the Colonial Governors, were all burned. Mr Edmondston's brother Charles lost house, furniture & almost all his own children's clothing. The distress was very great but was alleviated in a great measure by the liberality of the citizens of the Confederacy generally, who made large contributions for their releif.

---

[127] For accounts of this fire which consumed two thirds of Charleston and destroyed 576 buildings, see the *Charleston Courier*, December 12, 13, and 14, 1861, and the weekly *Raleigh Register*, December 18, 1861.

[128] French, "bonfire in celebration."

About the same time came the anxiously expected news from England. They had heard of the arrest of Messrs Mason & Slidell and England was in a blaze of indignation. Troops were ordered in hot haste to Canada, the exportation of Salt Petre & Gun Powder forbidden. The Dock yards exhibited signs of instant & lively preparation for War. The heart of the whole people was deeply stirred at the insult to their Flag.

Lord Lyons,[129] the British envoy at Washington, was ordered to demand the instant rendition of Messrs Mason & Slidell to him as the representative of an outraged nation. Seward attempted, it was said, to reply, but was answered by a premonitory roar from the British Lion, Lord Lyons, saying that his orders were to demand the Commissioners & to treat after their surrender into his hands. Whereupon Mr Seward produced a State paper which for meanness, craft & low cunning distinguished itself beyond all other State papers ever published. He began by defending the act, gradually came to excuses, & wound up by saying that an order to the Commandant of Fort Warren had been issued directing him to surrender Messrs Mason, Slidell & suites to any one empowered by Lord Lyon's to receive them.

Our hopes were high at the reception of the news from England. Few persons beleived that the U S government had sunk so low as after committing itself by thanking Commodore Wilkes by a vote of Congress, after boasting & bullying, talking great swelling words as to what they would do should England *dare* to demand the rendition, as at the first word, the first growl from the British Lion to back down from its lofty pretensions and with a hang-dog dreprecating look give up the whole bone of contention! No one I say beleived, first that the Government would do so, secondly that the people would sustain it. The least we *looked* for was a change in the Cabinet; but neither contingency happened. The Government meekly gave up! & the people as meekly sustained it. "O Lucifer—son of the morning how art thou fallen"![130]

Our disappointment was keen as we saw our Commissioners peaceably depart on board the British ship Rinaldo without their having effected for us that good which we so confidently hoped for. They were surrendered on the 26th of December & so closed the year for us. Disappointed in our hopes of Foreign aid, the Coast of S C ravaged & destroyed, its garden spot in the hands of a ruthless invader, Savannah threatened, Charleston in ashes, an immense fleet of Mortar boats & gunboats backed by an enormous army preparing to descend the Mississippi & seize its fertile valley, another army ready to march through Kentucky and Tennessee, Norfolk beleagured and blockaded, Fortress Monro where we had spent our money like water, with its impregnable position and complete armament in the hands of our enemies—a

---

[129] Richard Bickerton Pemell Lyons (1817-1887) was the British minister at Washington from 1858 until 1865. He was responsible for conducting negotiations during the Mason-Slidell affair. *Webster's Biographical Dictionary*, 933.

[130] Isaiah 13:12. "How art thou fallen from Heaven, O Lucifer, son of the morning."

thorn in our sides to vex and destroy us, an army equal to our own fronting us on the Potomac, ready at any moment to fall upon Richmond and rumours, nay authentic accounts, that another immense Armada was being fitted out for the coast of N. Carolina, whilst preparations were actively making for the Bombardment of N Orleans—the hearts of our people might well—"fail—for fear"—& we shrink before the inevitable fate which our conquest involved. But it did not! Men & women looked the alternative sternly in the face and prefered death, extermination, anything to being conquered, subjugated, our God given Blessing of self Government infringed or even tampered with, and determined to resist to the last, to be free!

My diary begins again in Jan in Raleigh, so here I end the narative which connects the two—fragments—shall I call them?

1862

Raleigh

I am sorry that I intermitted the practice of keeping a Diary! This year of all the years of my past life I ought to have been most faithful in keeping my Record, for it is not, I hope, probable that I shall ever pass through so stirring a time again; and so I who have all my life been sighing for something to write about and who have burnt up so many Diaries, because on a re perusal I have found them hopelessly inane & insipid, have like the woman in the Fairy tale who lost her chance of Wealth & honour by an indiscreet wish for a "yard of Black Pudding,"[1] lost the desire of my heart not by a silly gratification of my palate but from mere inattention to my own wishes. There is the less excuse for me too, for if I remember rightly I left off in July not long before the Battle of Manassas when life was as full of incident as a pudding of Plums. Heigh ho! it is no use lamenting it, but as we are just entering on a New Year I will try & be more punctual and as I faithfully recorded the gradual steps by which we were led into War I will now, I hope, have the agreeable task of tracing our way out to the glorious goal Peace, even tho I lost a portion—may it be a large one—of the progress of the War itself. I am in Raleigh, but I had better retrace a little so as to commence with the first of the year.

The 1st of Jan found us with War staring us directly in the face! War, obstinate, bloody & cruel, brought to our very hearthstones! But blessed be God, our hearts are still strong and we shall yet prevail, even tho all hopes of Foreign aid are put to an end by the rendition of Messrs Mason & Slidell. Patrick and I lived almost as usual, as "in piping times of Peace,"[2] disturbed, however, with a terrible sense of insecurity on my part as to how long it would last, he chafing terribly at inaction and mentally turning over every stone by which he thought he possibly could get into active service, but as the Secretary was organizing no more troops, acting in fact as tho Peace was a "fait accompli," there was nothing for it but "to bide his time" with what patience he might.

Since the middle of Dec we had heard continual rumours, in fact read in the papers minute accounts of a magnificent Armada which was being fitted out in the Northern cities, destined for some point on the Southern Coast. It was to rendezvous at Fortress Monro under the command of Gen Burnside. Some maintained that it was to reinforce Gen Sherman at Port Royal, others that it was aimed at Savannah. Others again sent it to N O or Mobile, but the best informed & sagacious contended that it was destined for the Coast of

---

[1] Blood pudding.

[2] Shakespeare, *King Richard III*, act 1, sc. 1, line 24.

Above is a page from Mrs. Edmondston's journal. (Photographs from Division of Archives and History unless otherwise noted.)

N Carolina with the intention of taking Norfolk in the rear. Where the blow was to fall none knew, but all sat expectant.[3]

We had, as I said before, fallen into our usual habits—we read, rode, talked & walked together as usual—when on the night of the 17th of Jan, on coming in from a visit to Hascosea, Mr E found a letter from brother awaiting him, telling him that authentic information had been received in Raleigh telling the Governor that the Fleet was intended to attack Roanoke Island; that in the event of its landing the Governor would order out the militia, 10,000 strong under the command of Gen Martin; that he (Brother) had volunteered Mr E's services on Gen Martin's Staff (Brother himself, already being a member of it with the rank & pay of major); that he must come up without delay and tender his services in person and winding up by urging him to bring me up with him to remain with Margaret during their joint absences.

Mr E. lost not a moment, but hastily making his preparations for an indefinite absence from home, the next afternoon saw us on our road to Raleigh, where we arrived on Sunday the 19th of January.

We found all well & much surprised at the rapidity of our motions. Margaret had a sweet little infant about a fortnight old, the rest of the children as lovely and as attractive as ever. Nelly, the most delightful little girl I have ever seen—that child always seems so happy to see one—has so affectionate and child like way of evincing her pleasure in your society that she goes direct to your heart.

On Monday Mr E waited on Gen Martin & renewed the offer of his services which were accepted.

The weather which had been for some days bad, foggy and disagreeable, now to our great thankfulness became worse, terrible in fact—Rain, Wind, & Fog, by turns & sometimes all three together. Earnestly did we wish that Gen Burnside might have the full benefit of it, & no one remarked on it without an expression of thankfulness, but still no authentic accounts of him save that he was supposed to be at Hatteras Inlet.

On Wednesday I went up to Hillsboro to see Sophia & found her fairly taken to her bed, having fretted herself almost sick with the thousand rumours which represented Burnside as landing at New Berne where her husband was stationed with his Company. Sister Frances & I cheered her up as we best could & next day came down again in spite of the weather which was desperate. It rained, snowed, sleeted, hailed & blew by turns & sometimes did all together, but as Burnside was getting it, we took it with greater equanimity.

---

[3] A Union naval and army expedition of overwhelming force captured Roanoke Island on February 8, 1862, after two days of heavy fighting. The victory enabled Union forces to occupy Elizabeth City, terminus of the Dismal Swamp Canal, and overrun many North Carolina counties bordering on the Albemarle Sound. Robert U. Johnson and Clarence C. Buel (eds.), *Battles and Leaders of the Civil War* (New York: T. Yoseloff [Second Edition], 4 volumes, 1956; originally published 1887-1888), Volume I: *From Sumter to Shiloh*, 640-645, 666-668, 670, hereinafter cited as Johnson and Buel, *Battles and Leaders*, I.

Mrs. Edmondston went to Raleigh to stay with her sister-in-law Margaret Mordecai Devereux while John Devereux and Patrick were absent with the militia. The Devereux home, Wills Forest, was located just off present-day Glenwood Avenue, the vicinity of what is now the Methodist Home. Two streets west of Glenwood Avenue are called Wills Forest and Devereux streets. Above are two views of Wills Forest; below, left, is the "forest." The girl dressed in black, standing on the porch, is Katherine Devereux Mackay, niece of Mrs. Edmondston and daughter of John Devereux. The journal was willed to her. At the foot of the steps, left, is Margaret Devereux. (Photographs courtesy of Mrs. S. H. Millender, Mebane, N.C.)

Sophia is much afflicted at the death of her little girl & her husband being absent she broods over her greif too much. She will I hope be more cheerful soon.

Friday the weather was but little better. "No news," was the answer to our anxious inquiries each day. It even began to be douted that the fleet seen at Hatteras was Burnside's at all, many contending that it was only transient vessels put in for shelter, that Burnside had passed down the Coast, treated us in fact as the Ghost that frequented Lincoln's Inn did that dingy abode when reminded by the student that he was free to roam at will & inhabit King's Palaces if it so pleased him whereupon the Ghost made a polite bow, thanked him for the suggestion, & was never afterwards seen in that locality. Ah Mr Burnside, we like well to be treated with the same neglect. Go to the orange groves of the South, where cotton & Contrabands abound; and, if you can, revel in their abundance. That sounds selfish, tho I do not mean it so, for they are better prepared than are we to give him a warm reception.

So passed the week. Rain, fog and "No News" until Saturday when Patrick received a letter from the Hon Mr Davis[4] our Senator in Congress in reply to one which he had addressed the President through him—laying before him some ideas which he had of the most efficient manner of arming a body of Cavalry & asking his authority to raise one. The President in reply stated through Senator Davis, that he desired "a personal interview" with Mr Edmondston. So, in accordance with that desire, this morning before daylight Patrick set off for Richmond. He wished me to accompany him, but I thinking only of the expense, like a good for nothing long-headed calculating creature, did not think best to go. I never repented anything so heartily in all my life, but I must say in my own defence that I did not know how much he was bent on my going until it was too late to recall my decision & so this morning in the cold, cheerless, grey light of the early dawn, & that damp foggy & disagreeable, he set off alone for Richmond leaving me here with Brother.

Margaret is still confined to her Chamber, and as brother is kept all day closely at his business in the Qr Masters office, the children at school, Nannie on household thoughts intent, Margaret & I have nice long mornings together & sit & talk as we have not had the opportunity of doing for some years. The baby, Laura, John & Meta divide our attention & cause an agreeable diversion with their childish wants & pleasant prattle.

I have been reading to her some of the "Recreations of a Country Parson," and she is as much pleased with them as I am. I read today the one on "Giving up and Coming Down" & take home some of its lessons to myself. How many of my youthful aspirations have I "come down" from & yet never "given up" my endeavours after something yet in the future. Like a child who when crying for one object is directed by the nurse to another perhaps equally unattainable, but which serves the purpose of quieting it for the moment. Blessed Hope which has never yet deserted me. The strongest desire of my heart when I first began to reason on life, to aim at anything, was to be a companion, help, a friend to my father. For how many years was it the dream, the hope, the main stay of my life, & when I gradually found out that I was not & never could be what I desired and hoped to be to him, how for a time utterly wretched & unhappy I was! Then came [_____], but what is the use of retrospect? I am lonely enough without Patrick not to encourage sad thoughts this gloomy day. So a truce to moralizing.

The household is divided about a name for the baby & Grandmothers are sought out & their names brought down from the dim past & every thing ever

---

[4] George Davis (1820-1896) of Wilmington, Whig and Unionist, was appointed to the Peace Conference held in Washington in February, 1861. He was elected to the Confederate Congress in 1862 and in 1864 was appointed attorney general. He accompanied Jefferson Davis on his flight at the war's end, was arrested and released on parole. Ashe, *Biographical History*, II, 75-78.

heard of them, every anecdote handed down by tradition, retold—their names, their descent, discussed in the hope of finding an euphonious & family name for the little Lady. Martha Cullen, Mary Livingstone, Mary Bayard, Rosamond Bouchier, Sarah Sanderson, Frances Pollock, Sarah Pierrepont, & more than I can enumerate here, are conned over; but as the father seems to prefer Mary Livingstone, Mary I suppose it will be.

I dined today with Ellen Mordecai. How tenderly time touches her, how like herself she is, how gentle, how earnest, how true. Mr Rayner and Susan were there.[5] Susan does not give one the idea of a happy woman. She before whom life was spread out all bright, all prosperous, who had her own way in every thing, despite her property, her position, her children, seems to have some thing which one cannot define present with her. Is it greif for the sad death of her eldest son? I think not, for she spoke with a sad chastened feeling of afflictions & loss of relatives which, tho she made no personal allusion to her own sorrow, yet it was easy to see that they were present with her & her greif was that of a Christian. What it is one cannot define, but there is a shadow there. Mr. Rayner is one of the Croakers about the war, abuses every body from the impersonal "Government" down to the private soldiers, stopping to have an especial fling at Gov Clark & Gen Martin. He sees all manner of ill in Burnside's expedition, thinks he certainly will ascend the Roanoke & seize our Cotton & Corn—in short "we are kilt intirely." I am glad I do not live with such a Raven! But it is bed time, near the "wee sma hours ayout the twal."[6]

Patrick makes me keep better hours than this, but I am always better with him. So to dream of him.

JANUARY 28, 1862

Brother came in, in a great hurry & excitement today, swallowed a hasty dinner and was off to the Roanoke to carry orders to Col David Clark (Militia) about defending the River.

The fleet at Hatteras is certainly Burnsides & he intends an advance somewhere, as he is lightening his transports over the Bar. The Gale has been

---

[5]Kenneth Rayner (ca. 1810-1884), a planter born in Bertie County, was the youngest member of the state constitutional convention of 1835. He was elected to the House of Commons as a state representative in 1836, 1838, and for three successive terms beginning in 1846. From 1839 until 1845 he served as a United States congressman and returned to the General Assembly as a senator in 1854. A strong advocate of states' rights, Rayner distrusted the Confederate government under Davis. In 1863 he secretly joined Holden's peace movement and returned to some of his former Whig principles. Rayner served as a judge on the *Alabama* claims commission from 1874 through 1876, when he resigned to become the solicitor for the United States Treasury. His wife was Susan Spratt Polk Rayner (1822-1909), the daughter of Col. William Polk and the sister of Bishop Leonidas Polk. Archibald Henderson, *North Carolina: The Old North State and the New* (Chicago: Lewis Publishing Company, 2 volumes, 1941), II, 85, 185, 207, 211, 223, 248, 319; *Biographical Directory of Congress*, 1501; *Dictionary of American Biography*, XV, 416-417.

[6]Robert Burns, "Death and Dr. Hornbook," stanza 31.

Maj. John Devereux was the brother of Mrs. Edmondston. On September 20, 1861, he was appointed chief quartermaster of North Carolina, a position he held until the end of the war. He married Margaret Mordecai, daughter of Moses Mordecai and his wife Ann Willis Lane Mordecai, of Raleigh. (Photograph of John Devereux is from a portrait owned by and photographed courtesy of Devereux Joslin of Raleigh; that of Margaret Devereux courtesy of Mr. John Burgwyn Baker of Richmond, Virginia, and Mrs. Graham A. Barden, Jr., of New Bern.)

a most terrific one to him. Several of his vessels are complete wrecks. We have news of him via Fortress Monro, telling of their sufferings for want of water during the storm, etc., etc. One letter writer in a fit of adulatory bombast says that during the heaviest of the storm "Gen Burnside stood like a Sea God, distinguished by his yellow belt," giving orders for the releif of the stranded vessels. At present he is lying quietly in the Sound, inside of Hatteras Inlet, another proof if any were wanting of the folly of letting the Yankees hold quiet possession of it for so long.

I followed Brother out as he left to tell him where he would find Mr E's pistol & some other munitions of War which his foresight has provided in case he should need them, which he thinks he will. We are a lonely & dejected family tonight—Brother gone, Margaret thinks into active service, Mr E in Richmond, the weather, now that Burnside is in safety, depressing in the last degree, for now we suffer with no compensating advantage. I wavering whether or not I shall Telegraph Patrick, but as he is at Head Quarters I think not. Had he been here, he would have gone instead of brother, which would have been greatly to Margaret's releif.

JANUARY 29, 1862

No more news from Burnside. Confined close prisoners to the house by the weather. Amused myself by finishing some conundrums which I commenced long ago & which for want of something better to write I will transcribe here—

Conundrum

In Babylon proud Persia's king
His royal revels high doth hold.
The perfumed Camps their lustre fling.
Blazes that princely Hall with gold.
Belshazza, King of Persia crowned,
   His noble lords feast high tonight.
Sparkling the Ruby wine goes round
   In golden goblets blushing bright.
Why starts the King? His Satraps stand
   In serried ranks around the Hall!
Does treason lurk within their bands?
   No: see my First upon the Wall!—

Thick, thick the fog, the murky air
   Hides like a pall the beacon light.
In vain the pilot's anxious care;
   No friendly signal greets his sight.
Heave forth the Lead! What water Ho!
   One fathom! One?! Then help us God.
Hark! hark! the breakers sullen roar!
   Sudden my Second's warning sound
Port! Port your helm—back from the shore!
   We're saved—we're saved!—the danger's o'er!

Name ye my whole, my tiny call
   Ends Betty's gossip in the hall.
I watch the bed of pain & care.
   Muezzin like I call to prayer.
E'en Time acknoledges my sway;
   I end the longest hour of day.
See yon Cathedral's crowded aisle—
   The giddy throng now talk, now smile,

But silenced by my silver call;
   Repentant all they prostrate fall.
Nay more than this myself a host
   I aid the Priest to lay a ghost!

Conundrum

Enveloped with jewels rich & rare
   Enclosed in casket quaint & old
The cloistered monk's peculiar care
   My first was valued more than gold.
Now Sheperd's cot & lordly hall
   Alike my varied love can gain.
E'en Poverty frequents my stall
   Nepenthe like I ease its pain.
In leathern vest or gorgeous dye
   Maid, Monk, & Matron I allure.
No monarch better paged than I.
   No Dean hath Chapter more secure!

Seek ye my second? Look but near
   Thou'lt find it in the rosebud's heart.
Hear how his accents, stern and drear,
   Fall on the ear like poisoned dart.
Nay haughty beauty! nor turn thy head
   Nor shuddering view my loathed form.
Know that with me thou'lt make thy bed;
   With me take refuge from Life's storm
That beauty decked with price & care
   That cheek where Paestum's roses glow—
That graceful shape, that braided hair,
   Is mine! a victim sure tho slow!

Pale, thin, & haggard; see my whole
   His careless dress & absent tone
Bespeak a mind, a heart, a soul
   Absorbed in thought & thought alone!
What boots it that the stocks are down
   The Army routed, burned the town.
He cons his Elzivirs all o'er
   And turns to Aldus all the more!
And if we judge him by his looks,
   He feeds on dainties bred in books!

The answers I suppose need not be given, as my labour is well lost if a child
cannot read them.

JANUARY 30, 1862

Walked all the afternoon in Brother's grounds watching for the cars[7] to pass in hopes of a signal from Patrick. Was disappointed in that but, however, the exercise & the fresh air, damp tho' it was, invigorated & brightened me up greatly. On my way back to the house stopped in at the Office where the remnant of Father's library is—Books that I was familiar with when I was a child—opened some of them & became so interested in reading over what I read with relish & profit when I was a girl of eighteen or nineteen that I forgot how time passed & stood up until I was exhausted & found the family wondering what had become of me. Margaret declared that no one but Undine[8] could stay out, but as Dr Breckenridge says—"I am tough."

JANUARY 31, 1862

Dined with Sister Frances. All well & as usual, she busy making Haversacks and Flags for the Regiments to take the field in the Spring. Went visiting in the morning. Susan Rayner carried me into the Ladies Soldiers Aid Society, the same one to whom I gave my wool Mattrass in the Fall to be knit into socks. Ellen Mordecai is the President and Susan the Treasurer. We found about a dozen ladies all hard at work on Hospital shirts & drawers. Ellen & Susan had their Sewing Machines & all were as busy as possible. The work they have done is wonderful, indeed the Ladies all through the country have been heart & soul in the cause. Never was there such universal enthusiasm, enthusias too which does not evaporate in words but shows itself in *work*, real hard work, steady and constant. These Ladies have spent three days of the week at this Society room since Sept & show no signs of flagging. Promised Ellen & Susan some Dahlia Roots & some Tube Roses in the spring when I plant mine out. The first sunshiny day we have had in weeks! I hope it crippled Burnside.

FEBRUARY 1, 1862

Walked with John & Meta to the Rail Road, ostensibly to allow him to flatten some pins on the track by letting the engine run over them, but really with the unconfessed hope that I might see Patrick in the Cars, in which hope, however, I was disappointed, he not being there. We walked on over to see Ellen, but she being out we returned as the cars backed down from the Depot. John & Meta had supplied themselves with another store of Pins at their Aunts which they wished to make "old bulls" and "great bears" of, so we

---

[7] John Devereux's home, Wills Forest, was located on a knoll above a meadow where the Raleigh and Gaston Railroad tracks ran. It was in the vicinity of the present-day Methodist Home, west of Raleigh's Glenwood Avenue. See Shaffer Map of Raleigh, 1881 and 1888, State Archives.

[8] Undine, a water-sylph, appeared in a story written by De La Motte Fouqué published in 1814. Benét, *Reader's Encyclopedia*, 1155.

stopped to place them. As the cars passed & the Engine reversed to return to the Depot, a gentleman jumped from the platform. Was it Patrick? No! only Mr Richard Mason.[9] He joined me & walked home with me, I making up in politeness what I suffered in disappointment.

As we sat in the Library, he just entering on an abstraction, in came the children shouting, "Aunt Kate, Uncle Edmondston's come!" & so it proved. He had come by the N C Road when I had been looking for him in the R and G. He saw the President & was much struck with the kindness & firmness of his tone & manner. The President sent him to Mr Benjamin, telling him if he had any difficulty to recur to him. Mr. Benjamin gave him not what he wanted, a *Commission,* but an Appointment to Raise a Battalion of Cavalry for the service of the Confederate States. He did not much fancy Mr Benjamin, tho this is by no means the first time he has seen him. Perhaps had he handed him a Commission as Lieut Col the old gentleman might have been more impressed with him!

FEBRUARY 3, 1862

Rain! Rain! Rain! again Sunday & today. Went in the pouring rain to dine with Mrs Mordecai,[10] or rather I should say Mr and Mrs George Mordecai. Burnside the engrossing topic, what we will do should he come. As to his ever reaching Raleigh, the idea is simply ridiculous. He may make a foray up our river & burn or destroy all he can lay his hands on, but that he will ever make a permanent lodgement even there I doubt. But so the world goes. Mrs Mordecai thinks of her mirrors, I of my books; & I suppose every one has some little ewe lamb, some particular hobby that they think he will destroy.

FEBRUARY 7, 1862

Reached home yesterday, Thursday, having left Raleigh on Tuesday afternoon, Kate Miller with us, coming down to pay a visit to Susan. Slept at Goldsboro & next morning when at Enfield 10 miles from the end of our Rail Road journey we met with an accident to the Engine, which it was God's mercy only which prevented from being a most serious one! The driving wheels were bent & twisted entirely off and had it not occurred just as the train was stopping none can tell what might have been the Consequences. As it was, we were detained all day, waiting for another Engine, & had no other amusement than to watch the peculiarities of the different passengers.

---

[9]Richard Sharpe Mason (1795-1874) was the Episcopal rector of Christ Church in Raleigh from 1840 until 1874. John Devereux and his family were communicants of this church. For Mason's obituary, see *Daily Sentinel* (Raleigh), February 22, 1874, hereinafter cited as *Daily Sentinel; Centennial Ceremonies Held in Christ Church Parish, Raleigh, North Carolina, A.D. 1921, Including Historical Addresses* (Raleigh: Christ Church Vestry, 1922), 15-17, 27, 34.

[10]Margaret Bennehan Cameron Mordecai (1810-1886) was the wife of George Washington Mordecai and the daughter of Judge Duncan Cameron of Stagville in Orange (later Durham) County. For further information see the George W. Mordecai Papers.

One, an old priest, Kate decided, took the whole thing as a pennance & bore it as tho it were a part of his cross, resignedly and stoically. One lady from Baltimore, Mrs Norris, pleased us much with an account of how the Baltimore Ladies teased the U S officials, & she also gave to her friend in our hearing a minute account of the late attempt of Com. Tatnal to victual fort Pulaski. She has a son on Tatnal's vessel. She was going to try & get to Baltimore via the Flag of Truce & intends coming back.

A little before dark we got off & reached Halifax in good time for tea but found no carriage in waiting there. Next morning—it was raining again steadily—about twelve o'clock Patrick succeeded in hiring one & in the rain we set off. Just at father's we met our carriage, which he had detained because he wanted something about Mr Smith, so sending Kate up to the house in the hired vehicle we got in our own & came home.

Rain again today, but father & Mr Smith came down to see Patrick. The Misses Smith[11] are there and I am invited to dine with them tomorrow.

FEBRUARY 9, 1862

Sunday—Dined at father's yesterday & was persuaded to remain all night and to dinner today. The Misses S—nice lady like girls; the young folks seem to enjoy themselves greatly together. Talked of Burnside & wondered what he intends to do. Mr Smith is sure Norfolk is the point of attack, says he learns that we are well prepared for him at Roanoke Island, that Wise is in command. We heard the reverse in Raleigh, that Cols Shaw & Wright did nothing all the Fall but wrangle about the command: in one case one Regt leveling the entrenchments thrown up by the others, each claiming to rank the other; that Wise was building a bridge from the Island to Nag's Head for the men to retreat on, which I do not beleive and much more to the same purpose.

FEBRUARY 10, 1862

Tonight's mail brought the news of the attack & fall of Roanoke Island! It has fallen to our horror & dismay, for we were led to expect some fighting at least there. I fairly burst into tears as I read it. Capt O Jenning Wise is mortally wounded & a prisoner. Gen Wise sick with Pneumonia at Nags Head, the command devolved on the senior Colonel, Shaw. After a short fight with the boats they, being out of ammunition, retreated to Elizabeth City for some. Burnside threw out a large force which landed & walked over a Swamp—which our engineers had pronounced *impassable!*—flanked our men who, some of them fought well when the order for surrender was given.[12] O why did not

---

[11] Mrs. Edmondston was probably referring to the daughters of Richard H. Smith, Nannie E. and Sallie H. Eighth Census, 1860, Population Schedule, Halifax County, 80.

[12] Although Gen. D. H. Hill ordered a line of defensive works built through the swamps to the sounds, his successors failed to carry out the order, leaving the Confederate forces open to a flanking movement by the Union troops. A committee appointed by the Confederate Congress to investigate the defeat found that

our men have a leader worthy of them! When will our rulers begin to think that we have a deadly & determined foe to conquer. Roanoke Island is now called the back door key to Norfolk. Why did they not find that out before putting it in the hands of our enemies! Albemarle Sound & its tributaries are now open to inroads & incursions of all kinds. Wherever their Gun boats can go they will be masters.

FEBRUARY 11, 1862

The Misses Smith, Sue & Kate, dined with us. We thought of little else save Roanoke Island & tho' I made an effort to throw off the gloom & talk of other things yet it all seemed hollow & artificial & I could not enter into the merriment of Kate & Sue as I wished. At night came the news of the Bombardment and burning of Elizabeth City. The whole of our vessels with the exception of two *only* has fallen into their hands or been burned by us to prevent it. The Yankees landed and put out the fire in Elizabeth, but the inhabitants fled in great confusion. We have no particulars.

Mr E. was at Clarksville and heard [said] that the Militia were ordered out, that every one was at Hamilton devising ways to blockade the River, & has concluded to go down & see what aid he can render.

FEBRUARY 12, 1862

Mr E. was off this morning. Before he left he had the negroes summoned & told them of the enemy below & gave them orders that when the Plantation Bell should ring & the Horn blow at the same time, every one of them should assemble in the lot and accompany me to Hascosea. The team is to be driven out & all the wheels on the plantation, lest they should be able to haul supplies to their boats. The work of moving the Cotton, Meat, etc. is to go steadily on & he charged them in his absence to remember their duty to me and to give me no trouble. They were much affected and poor things in much fright, for they know that they are the objects sought after by these miscalled Philanthropist. They entreated me not to leave them & I have promised to remain at home & take what care I can of them.

Commenced packing up the most valuable things in the house preparatory to removing them to a place of safety, comparative safety I mean, for our population is too thin to make much of a resistance should they come in force. Fortunately we have sold some of our Cotton, so every mule & cart & waggon on the plantation was in requisition to haul it part of the way to Halifax, & when we get it all moved so far & the car is ready for it, it will be carried the rest of the way & shipped instantly to the Factory. Sent my horse up to father's for Kate Miller who had promised to come down & remain with me during Mr E's absence.

Gen. Benjamin Huger and Secretary of War J. P. Benjamin were culpable for the island's inadequate defense, despite repeated requests for more troops and munitions. Hill, *Bethel to Sharpsburg*, I, 205-206.

February 13, 1862

Early in the morning the overseer sent me a requisition from the Qr Master of the 34th Regt calling for all our team & waggons to move the baggage & equipage of the Regt down from the R R to Hamilton.[13] Of course they must go, but it is a sore draw back to the moving our Cotton & valuables. The height of the water too inconveniences us greatly. Owing to the incessant rains Hill's Mill is impassable & every thing is forced to go through the most circuitous route, through the woods & swamps, & over the worst roads ever seen even in this muddy country. Ah! what trouble that neglect of the defences at Roanoke Island has cost us! Would that the Gov had taken Patrick's suggestion & reconquered Hatteras before they had secured themselves in the position, but regrets are useless. We have the *stern present* & the uncertain future before us. God grant us strength to meet them with a determined will and a cheerful spirit.

Kate Miller is a great amusement to me. Her spirits are naturally high & she is a girl of stirling principles, as truthful as the day, and her original observations & strong good sense entertain me greatly. I do not think I will tell even my Diary all the things I move or where I put them. In these days of treachery even this dumb friend may fail me. Kate & I watch the mail with a most feverish interest, but we do not see much to console us for the Roanoke island disaster. The management there was worse than bad. How can troops fight under such leaders? Capt Wise is since dead of his wounds. They would not even let him die in peace, but his last moments were disturbed by their cant about the Flag & the indissoluble Union. Faugh! They have neither the courtesy of gentlemen nor the sense of boors, for the one would teach them how to treat a vanquished & dying enemy, the other would show them the impossibility of their Utopian *Union. Union* now means Conquest—and Conquest, Confiscation. So we go!

February 14, 1862

The mail tonight brought Mr Edmondston a Commission as Lieut Col of Cavalry in the service of the Confederate States! Ah! me, I ought to be happier than I am but the prospect of long and uncertain separation eclipses for the present the glory & honour of serving his country. After all I am but an "Earthen vessel," but Courage! I will be a vessel made to honnour! Courage! I will be worthy of my blood, of my husband. Yes, I am glad, glad that he can serve that land to which we owe so much, our home, our native-land. The

---

[13] The Thirty-fourth North Carolina Regiment, under the command of Col. Collett Leventhorpe, was stationed at Hamilton in the spring of 1862 to challenge enemy gunboats that tried to come up the Roanoke River. Companies A and B of the Ninth North Carolina (First Cavalry) Regiment also guarded the river. Clark, *Histories of the North Carolina Regiments,* I, 445-448; II, 582; Manarin and Jordan, *North Carolina Troops,* II, 1.

Cotton creeps slowly away. I go out & count the bales & do numberless sums in addition & substraction, calculating how long ere it be all gone!

Susan came down today & made a strong appeal to Kate Miller to go up with her. The Misses Smith being gone, she feels lonely, but Kate was stanch & steadily refused to leave me. Then came the resort to me, backed by a message from Father that he had sent the carriage and expected me, but I declined & to Sue's chagrin wrote and gave my reasons, in which McCullamore fully sustained me.

Young Selden[14] of Norfolk, nephew of my friend Mrs Henry Selden, had his head blown entirely off by a shell at Roanoke Island! What sorrow for his family!

How differently has this Valentine's Day been passed from the last! Then I was peacefully planting fruit trees at Hascosea. Today, in the face of a stern reality am I packing up my household goods to remove them from the enemy. Ah, this water and these roads!

FEBRUARY 15, 1862

Kate & I went up to Father's to dinner. As we stopped at the door we were surprised to see the windows of the Dining Room crowded with little faces watching our descent from the carriage. On entering the Drawing Room two strange ladies sprang up & met us with the exclamation—"Where did you come from!?" We soon found that they were Refugees & thought that we were in the same sad situation! Poor people, they have been driven from their homes by the advance of the enemy and are now seeking an asylum, a shelter for their heads—Mr & Mrs Leary,[15] his sister, Mrs. Charlton, his daughter, Mrs Skinner, & children & Grandchildren, to the number of nineteen whites and seventy negroes, all homeless & houseless. The day was a terrible one, rain & fog, but Mr L had gone out to Scotland Neck to endeavor to rent a place where he could put his negroes in safety & they were awaiting his return.

They brought sad accounts from below. The inhabitants of Edenton were leaving panic stricken to avoid the alternative of the oath of allegiance to the U S or a residence in Fort Warren.[16] The Gun boats came up to Edenton & issued Burnside's proclamation, assuring the people he was civilized & a Christian, that he came to restore order & bring them back to the bosom of

---

[14] During the battle at Roanoke Island, Lt. William B. Selden of the Engineer Department "received a rifle ball in his head and fell without a groan. . . ." *Official Records (Army)*, Series I, IX, 170.

[15] Mrs. Edmondston possibly was referring to Thomas H. Leary, a sixty-two-year-old planter who lived with his wife Parthinia in Chowan County in 1860. The census records of the county contain the names of several Leary families. Eighth Census, 1860, Population Schedule, Chowan County, 3.

[16] Fort Warren, located in Boston Harbor, housed Confederate prisoners during the Civil War. Boatner, *Civil War Dictionary*, 673.

their Mother, that he did not intend to molest private citizens in the enjoyment of their rights but to protect them in it. On the wharf was five bales of Cotton which the retreating steamer had not been able to carry with it up the River & whilst the commander of the Boats was expatiating on the respect he should pay to private property his men were busy rolling the cotton into their vessels. Seeing this the Major stepped up & assured him that that cotton was "private property"—it belonged to one individual. "Oh! Cotton!" said the crafty Yankee, shrugging his shoulders, "Cotton is contraband!"—and so is everything "Contraband" that they want—the scoundrels!

Mr Fearing[17] of Elizabeth [City], after starting his wife & children to a place of safety, remained behind to fire his dwelling. As he left his own door he was shot by a file of Yankee soldiers & fell dead on his own threshold! But I have not time for half these poor people told me—how some of their negroes had refused to come with them, how their Coachman stole their best horse & started to run away in the night but fortunately was overtaken & sent back in irons to them. My heart bled for them, helpless women & little children under the convoy of one feeble old man, but a day of Vengeance will yet come!

Poor Mama, I was truly sorry for her. She had commenced packing her linen & valuables & sending them off when this influx of people came upon her. She could not be persuaded quietly to accept it, to go on with her preparations & give them what was most easily obtained—Bacon, Ham, Corn bread, etc. No, she worried herself to prepare a handsome dinner & an elaborate desert & whilst actually threatened with invasion & loss of almost every thing. I beleive Pherebe's carelessness in spilling water in some Apple jelly she was making in the Pantry & Mary Clark[e's][18] mischeif in pulling the furniture of her room out of place & leaving her Aunt Susan's door open worried her more than Burnside and his host, not that she was not frightened, for she was & thoroughly. Her Linen & her Wine—the first, the thing of all else but her Silver, that she prizes—was in danger; but the little present worry, that one unboiled pea in her shoe, caused her as much affliction as the prospect of the amputation of the whole foot!

Is this a blessing or otherwise? It may be a blessing to the person concerned by distracting their attention from the real to the imaginary trial, but is by no means one to the persons around, when every nerve & fibre seems strung to its utmost tension; to be compelled to listen to a long history of spoilt jelly, disorderly children, no wheat bread, etc., etc., all of which are but trifles at the best, is no ordinary trial of patience & yet sympathy, true Christian sympathy

---

[17] An Isaiah Fearing, twenty-six, merchant, a Submit W. Fearing, fifty-six, druggist, and a J. B. Fearing, thirty-five, merchant, lived in Pasquotank County in 1860. Eighth Census, 1860, Population Schedule, Pasquotank County, 9, 10, 15.

[18] Mary Clarke, Mrs. Edmondston's niece, was the daughter of William J. and Mary Bayard Devereux Clarke. See Introduction.

demands it. For as a man thinketh, so is he,[19] and if those trials distress her so much, I ought to listen to them patiently & kindly & congratulate myself on the fact that the deeper one is not correspondingly felt.

Came home in the pouring Rain & ordered four loaves of bread to be set for her, which I hope will releive some of her cares; but it is really most sorrowful to see the passage filled with boxes, bales, & baskets packed ready for a move, whilst the choice old Wine & Brandy, carefully boxed, creeps in ox carts to a temporary place of safety. When the roads improve its travels will recommence—the books, the pictures, the linen, the silver are all such cares now that one is tempted to exclaim "Blessed be nothing."

FEBRUARY 16, 1862

Sunday. Dick brought me a letter from Mr Edmondston[20]—to whom I had sent his Commission. He writes me that matters are in terrible confusion at Hamilton—Conflict of authority between the Militia Cols, Orders and counter orders from Raleigh, no one knowing his duty, nor how to fulfil it when he finds it out. They are endeavoring to construct a raft, a Fire Raft, to be turned loose when the Gun boats approach in the hope of destroying them or at least arresting their passage up the River. He tells me it is pitiable to see the fright of the inhabitants. The roads are crowded with Refugees in vehicles of every description, endeavoring to move what of their property they can to save it from the grasp of the invader. He gives a grave account of the disaffected state of feeling in Washington and Beaufort counties. Even Bertie is thought to be unsound, so greatly does fear affect principle!

Raining all day, yet nevertheless the work of moving goes steadily on, terrible work it is too, with the roads in the state they are & the ordinary road impassable from high water & with only the Oxen to do everything. Sent out what books I had down here to Hascosea & moved my household stores, blankets & linen. My household all day baking biscuit for the Refugees at father's. After we left yesterday afternoon another party came up, Mr Mixon & family & some young ladies entrusted to his care. They brought news of the arrest of Mr James C Johnston.[21] The oath of Allegiance to the U S was tendered to him which he refused to take. They then threatened to shoot him—the Cowards! he an old man of seventy & upwards—when he calmly replied,

---

[19] Proverbs 23:7a. "For as he thinketh in his heart, so is he. . . ."

[20] Patrick had been sent to Hamilton to aid in blockade preparations of the river as part of a statewide defense network ordered established by Gov. Henry T. Clark. Governor Clark to the Hon. Weldon N. Edwards, February, 1862, Letter Books of Governor Henry T. Clark, 1861-1862, 253-254, State Archives.

[21] This was probably a reference to James Cathcart Johnston (1782-1865) of Chowan County, who owned Hayes Plantation located near Edenton on the Albemarle Sound. Johnston, the son of former Gov. Samuel Johnston, remained loyal to the United States during the Civil War and disinherited most of his relatives who supported secession. J. G. de Roulhac Hamilton and Max R. Williams (eds.), *The Papers of William Alexander Graham* (Raleigh: North Carolina Department of Archives and History, [projected multivolume series, 1957—]), II, 229, hereinafter cited as Hamilton and Williams, *Graham Papers*.

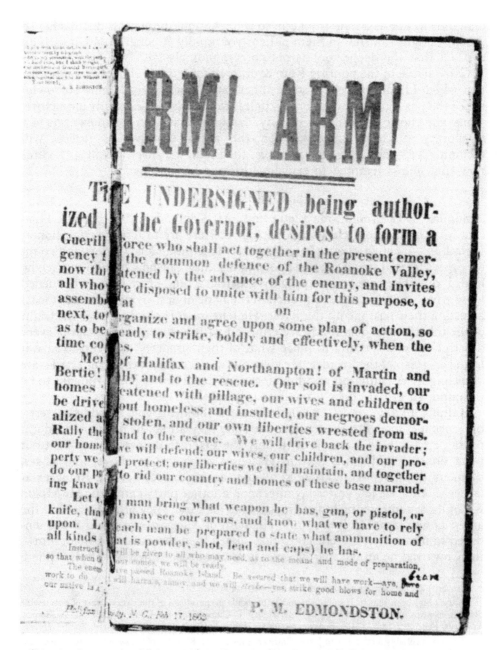

This advertisement, dated February 17, 1862, was a call by Patrick Edmondston for men to join him in planning a defense of the Roanoke Valley. The notice had been clipped and pasted into the diary by Kate Edmondston.

"If you do, you cannot cheat me out of much of life." When they left he was a prisoner in his own house.

FEBRUARY 17, 1862

Came a requisition for one fourth the able bodied men on the Plantation with Spades, Axes, grubbing Hoes, & all the large Augers that can be found & one weeks provision. Prayerfully do I send them, hoping that their labour *there* may protect us *here*. Rain still! The memory of man runs not back to such combined high water in the River, which is all in their favour & greatly against us, as the current is so rapid & the river so wide that our endeavors to blockade it are almost useless. Moved the Salt, the Gin, and a Loom. What shall we do for cotton cards? They are $8 a pair in Halifax.[22]

FEBRUARY 18, 1862

The negroes ordered out came back bringing word that the military were going away. Just after came our waggons & team, who have been absent more than a week hauling their baggage & camp equipage down. Nelson is full of them, says they are "valliant men & certainly can shoot." They brought letters from Mr E telling me it is doubtful whether or not he can come home on the 19th, our Wedding Day, but he will do his best.

We learn that Suffolk is to be the point of attack, that Troops are being massed there in large numbers. They have found out now that Roanoke Island is the "back door to Norfolk." Would that they had taken better care of the "*Key*" then, for it would have saved us a world of anxiety & unhappiness, to say nothing of the labour. All hands hauling away the Plantation supplies. My arithmetical calculations about the cotton are all over now, however, as the last Bale is gone, some of it in the Factory by this time. The roads worse than ever and the weather not much better.

Authentic news of the Fall of Fort Henry[23] and the capture of our forces there. High Water occasioned it. Our troops outside could not operate at all & the gun Boats had it all their own way. They were enabled to steam close up & throw their shells into the fort where they pleased. There were no casemates, in fact the so called "Fort" was simply a Redoubt of mud & earth.

---

[22] The scarcity of cotton and wool cards became a severe hardship for southerners during the Civil War. In an effort to alleviate the problem the North Carolina State Convention, in March, 1862, passed an ordinance authorizing a loan of up to $10,000 to anyone who would erect buildings and construct machinery for the manufacture of cards. The state's blockade runners included cotton and wool cards in their cargoes as well. *North Carolina Standard*, March 19, 1862; *Daily Sentinel*, May 27 and June 10, 1863; Hill, *Bethel to Sharpsburg*, I, 339-340, 372-376; Elizabeth Yates Webb, "Cotton Manufacturing in North Carolina, 1861-'65," *North Carolina Historical Review*, IX (April, 1932), 117-137.

[23] Fort Henry, located on the east bank of the Tennessee River, stood a short distance south of the Tennessee-Kentucky line. Forts Henry and Donelson, key Confederate positions on the Tennessee and Cumberland rivers, were strategic targets in the Union's efforts to split the Confederacy. Boatner, *Civil War Dictionary*, 394-395.

No wonder our men could not operate. This involves the evacuation of Columbus & Bowling Green, Ky to Nashville, Tenn., the latter being out Flanked by the possession of Fort Henry by the enemy. The next point of attack is Donaldson,[24] where we are said to have a strong force under Gens Floyd & Pillow. Beauregard it is rumoured has been ordered out there. Our Army on the Potomac will miss him greatly. Gen A S Johnston falling back from Bowling Green to Nashville, Tenn.

FEBRUARY 19, 1862

Our Wedding Day! The first we have ever been parted—sixteen years— sixteen years of happiness & youth! I cannot add that last "youth" much longer, but God grant that the first "happiness" may end but in our graves. I waited dinner until nearly dark for Patrick, but at last with a heavy heart ordered it in. I was almost overcome as the anniversary Plum pudding was placed before me & thought of the different days on which we had eaten it together. Had in the servants as usual & divided it & in addition to their regular toast Dolly gave a special one for Master, with a wish that he would soon come home for good. God grant it!

Long after dark came Patrick, having come up over these terrible roads just to keep tryst with me. Ah! the happiness of seeing him once more! Can I ever get accustomed to his absence? He has been placed in command of the Special Defences of Roanoke River by Col Leventhorpe (Confederate) and Clark (Militia) with authority to call out every body & every thing he needs to aid him in constructing his Fire Rafts—men, team, oxen, and for ought I know "women" also. One thing is sure. They have spirit & enthusiasm enough to answer the call if he makes it!

Came a commission from the Gov as captain of a guerilla force for the defence of the Roanoke Valley for Patrick. For his address see the end of this Vol marked

FEBRUARY 20, 1862

Patrick returned early to Hamilton. Sue came just after breakfast & told us that a detachment of Wise's Legion had been quartered at Montrose last night. The officers were entertained at Father's house. The Officer in command, Capt Rosser married an old schoolmate of mine, Mary Armistead— since dead—poor Mary![25] She invited me to be her bridesmaid and well do I remember the disappointment I felt when months after the letter came out of

---

[24]Fort Donelson was located on the west bank of the Cumberland River near Dover, Tennessee. Boatner, *Civil War Dictionary*, 395-397.

[25]J. Travis Rosser, major of the Tenth Virginia Cavalry in 1862, married Mary Walker Armistead (1821-1857), daughter of Gen. Walker Keith Armistead (1783-1845) of Upperville, Virginia. Virginia Armistead Garber, *The Armistead Family, 1635-1910* (Richmond: Whittet & Shepperson, 1910), 66, hereinafter cited as Garber, *The Armistead Family*; *Official Records (Army)*, Series I, XIX, Part II, 57.

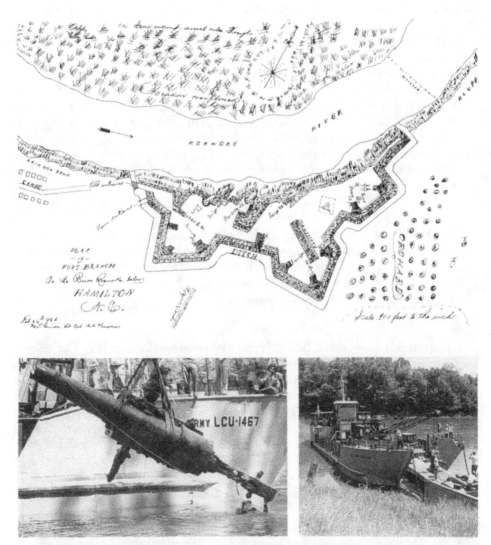

On February 16, 1862, Mrs. Edmondston had recorded in her journal Patrick's message "that matters are in terrible confusion at Hamilton. . . . They are endeavoring to construct a raft, a Fire Raft, to be turned loose when the Gun boats approach in the hope of destroying them or at least arresting their passage up the River." Patrick visited home briefly on February 19, saying he had been placed in command of the Roanoke River defenses, and then he returned to Hamilton the next day. The map, above, shows the plan of Fort Branch on the Roanoke River at Hamilton. More than a hundred years later, archaeologists raised cannon from the river at Fort Branch, below, left, and loaded them onto a truck, right.

Grandpapa's little letter drawer where he had placed it in my absence & forgotten it.

Kate went up with Sue, it being time for her to pay her visit to her Grandfather's, & all the portable plantation valuables being in a place of safety for the present, I after remaining at home to do some writing for Mr E, followed on horse back in the afternoon. I sent out his advertisements[26] for the Battalion of Light Horse he is authorized to raise, copied letters, had the Silver & munitions of War packed up & with many charges to Dolly & promises to the negroes to return at the first danger went up to Fathers where I heard, alaas! that it was too true that Fort Donaldson had indeed fallen on the 15th & that Gen Johnston was in retreat from Nashville! Heavy news, but we have no particulars.

FEBRUARY 21, 1862

Mr Daughtrey,[27] the overseer at fathers, whom we met in our afternoon walk, tells us he heard heavy cannonading for some time this morning about breakfast time. I hope it is only the Batteries at Craney Island & Seawell's Point discharging their guns after the recent rain & damp weather. They have often excited us before to no purpose.

FEBRUARY 22, 1862

The guns Mr Daughtrey heard yesterday are explained today. The enemy bombarded the town of Winton[28] and without notice burned it to ashes! Think of the wretches! The unfortunate inhabitants were at breakfast when without a moments notice a shower of Bomb Shells fell into their midst. The boats were concealed by the high Bluff on which the town is built, & they had no warning even of their approach. From the angle at which they were forced to sit their Mortars in order to throw the shells over the Bluff they found that they were not doing the execution they expected, so they landed in force. The

---

[26] An extract of Patrick's advertisement in the *North Carolina Standard*, March 22, 1862, reads: "... $146 will be paid for each horse in battalion, in 2 months installments. They will be fed and cared for at the expense of the government, and if killed in action, the value of the animal will be paid. Equipments for the men will be furnished but each man must bring his rifle, gun, pistol and knife or such arms as he has which will answer until a uniform weapon can be furnished by the government. Action—energy of action—is what the country needs now—and the men of the country must show by their readiness to come forward, their determination never to be conquered.

The battalion will consist of six companies of sixty men each.
$100 bounty will be paid to each man upon being mustered in."

[27] George L. Daughtrey was a farm overseer who owned 200 acres of land. Eighth Census, 1860, Population Schedule, Halifax County, 79.

[28] The burning of Winton, February 20, 1862, was ordered by Col. Rush C. Hawkins of the Ninth Regiment New York Infantry Volunteers. He reported that Confederate soldiers led his men into a trap there and that the buildings burned had housed enemy soldiers and army supplies. *Official Records (Army)*, Series I, IX, 195-196; Thomas C. Parramore, "The Burning of Winton in 1862," *North Carolina Historical Review*, XXXIX (January, 1962), 18-31.

affrighted inhabitants fled in terror when the invaders after helping themselves to what they wanted, amongst others to a valuable Library belonging to Dr Sheilds,[29] deliberately applied the torch & burnt the whole village. Our troops under Lt Col Williams seem to have given a lame account of themselves, for we hear of their doing nothing but falling back & burning a bridge over a creek to prevent the Yankees from following them on the road to Murfreesboro. But "falling back" is the order of the day with us!

Today was Inaugrated, amidst rain & clouds, at Richmond our first President Jefferson Davis! God grant him a prosperous & *peaceful* Administration! He is to be our Ruler for six years. May we be a *united* people. May our sentiment, a sentiment of determined and vigorous resistance, animate the hearts and minds of us all. God be with you Mr Davis. God guide and inspire you with His own Spirit, that forgetting self and selfish aims, you may look only to the best interests of your country & in her happiness & prosperity find your reward. May the mantle of Washington, whose birthday we have chosen for the natal day of our nation, fall upon you. May his spirit animate you!

Came Mr Peter Smith[30] to Fathers to have the Steamer under his command repaired at the Blacksmith's, which Mack effected to the satisfaction of all parties & to the gratification of his own especial vanity!

Details of the fall of Fort Donaldson begin to come in. They seem sorrowful in the extreme. Our troops fought three days in the snow, sleet and ice, whilst the enemy were constantly re-inforced with fresh troops. At first we were victorious & repulsed them with terrible slaughter. Whole Regiments would be driven back, when their place would be promptly filled by fresh troops and another attack made upon our wearied but gallant soldiers until from mere exhaustion they were compelled to surrender. We had about 14,000 men, they 40,000; and yet the whole North has been as jubilant as tho they had gained a victory by outfighting, instead of outnumbering, us. But the accounts are as yet imperfect. Only we know we have lost many taken prisoners including Gen Buckner, but that Gens Floyd & Pillow escaped in the night. Why the rest did not is not known. Johnston was at Nashville directing the falling back from Bowling Green, made a military neccessity by the fall of Fort Henry. Immediately on the defeat at Donaldson he withdrew his troops & marched southward to the great disgust of the whole nation. Such a storm of abuse has rarely been heaped on any man.

---

[29] R. H. Shields was a physician living in Hertford County in 1860. Eighth Census, 1860, Population Schedule, Hertford County, 45.

[30] Peter Evans Smith (1829-1905), who lived at Sunnyside in Halifax County, was a farmer and a civil and mechanical engineer. He handled the actual construction work on the C.S.S. *Albemarle*, under the initial supervision of its designer John L. Porter, chief constructor of the Confederate navy. Smith also owned the steamer *Cotton Plant* which patrolled the Roanoke River until its capture by Union forces on May 22, 1865. Allen, *History of Halifax County*, 218; Clark, *Histories of the North Carolina Regiments*, V, 315-323; Barrett, *Civil War in North Carolina*, 214-215; *Civil War Naval Chronology*, IV, 46, 54; V, 100.

FEBRUARY 23, 1862

Sunday—Last night after I had gone to bed came a letter from Patrick telling me to our dismay that the Regt under Col Leventhorpe had been ordered to Garysburg and that the Steam boat was wanted to convey their baggage up the River! Did any one ever hear of "Move House" being played on so stupendus a scale? The very day our waggons returned from moving them down we heard they were ordered up again. This was countermanded, however, & not five days after reordered, and they go now positively to Garysburg. This leaves nothing but the Militia, & they ill armed, between ourselves and Burnside; but there is a system of compensation in most matters in this world—so perhaps our crooked river with its terrible reputation for sudden rises and falls, which ordinarily is such a draw back to us, may now be the best bulwark we could have.

Walked with Father in the afternoon. As the sun went down we distinctly heard the booming of a Canon in the distance, probably the "Evening Gun" of the Enemy now in the Chowan River. It sent a thrill, by no means of pleasure, through us. It was a solemn sound that still Sunday evening. That sudden & heavy report, it brought the War to our doors & hearth stones. Alaas—for our poor houseless neighbors in Winton! How soon your fate may be ours none of us can tell!

FEBRUARY 24, 1862

More details of the disaster at Donaldson. Up to the night of the 14th our men held their own, sent messages announcing their ability to hold out, & cheered the nation with the hope of Victory. That night the enemy was again heavily reinforced & our men, wearied out, could fight no more. A council of War was called & surrender, to save the useless effusion of blood, agreed on. Floyd in command, he immediately transferred it to Pillow who as promptly passed it to Buckner & upon him the junior Gen devolved the odious task of surrender. Floyd & part of his Brigade & Pillow being nearest to the river made their escape in the steamboats which had brought supplies to the forces. Buckner [———] and 6000 wearied & exhausted men, our wounded, arms and munitions of War fell into the hands of the enemy. Their loss in killed & wounded was greater than ours—had there been anything like equality of force we would have beaten them terribly, even tho' the most of our men were Militia. The President has ordered a court of Inquiry & in the mean time releived Gens Floyd & Pillow of their commands.

Johnston's conduct in giving up Nashville without a blow is much criticised; indeed the Tennessee Delegation in Congress has waited on the President & requested him to supercede Gen A S Johnston & send another & more competent Gen in his place. Mr Davis reply was "Gentlemen, if Albert Sydney Johnston is not a *General*, I have no General"! Nashville is occupied by the Federal troops, the inhabitants "sullenly and sulkily," they say, but "firmly & patriotically," we call it, refusing to hold any communication with them. The Ladies behave with great dignity & one of them, a former Belle in Washington City, on receiving the card of Gen McCook, a former acquaintance, "begged that he would excuse her—she saw no one, was in mourning for her country"!

Col Shaw of Roanoke Island memory has been ordered to Richmond to attend a Court of Inquiry summoned by the President to determine who is to blame for that deplorable affair. "Disgraceful," Mr Davis terms it, and disgraceful it is—only I hope the disgrace will fall on the right person. At night most unexpectedly came Patrick from Hamilton, the Military all gone & the Militia even disbanded, but he has been left in command of the Defences projected to stop the ascent of the enemy up the River. He has progressed well so far with it. It consists of a number of condemned vessels firmly bolted together & loaded with Turpentine, Tar, Rosin and other combustible. This is anchored at Rainbow Bend where the River makes a sudden turn. This is to be cut loose on the aproach of the enemy & drifting slowly with the current & extending entirely across the River it will, it is hoped, carry fire & distruction in its path. The River is narrow just there & in the turns or the backing down in haste it is hardly possible but that they will run into each other. So I hope that Rainbow Bend will be no Bow of promise to them—a sign of speedy destruction. The River is very high & rising rapidly, which is a great draw back to his labours.

FEBRUARY 25, 1862

Just after breakfast came Ben with the alarming intelligence that the new dam just above our line was giving way. All hands were immediately called out & Father and Mr E hurried down, I having persuaded him to remain one day & help father. God grant that their efforts may be successful, but as I sit here & from time to time lay down my knitting, & go out and measure the marks I put down to note the rapidity of the rise, my heart fails me. A bulletin from Mr E however says he has some hope. At dark came father, exhausted but still more hopeful, & "is sure of ultimate success—all hands were there & working like beavers." But at ten came Patrick. It is gone. All hope is over. It broke suddenly from the base, so suddenly that every one had to run for their lives, some on one side some on the other. Patrick was fortunately above it. His horse had a most narrow escape, so rapid was the flow of water. This is a heavy blow, especially to Father. Keep us O Lord from repining!

FEBRUARY 26, 1862

On coming down this morning was met with the news that Timothy the carpenter came near being drowned last night. He was on the lower side of the break & instead of walking down to Looking Glass with his compeers & sleeping at his brother's & coming home this morning in a canoe, he must attempt "to head" the water, run around the break and get to the upper side. The first thing he knew he was up to his arm pits in a raging torrent which nearly swept him off his feet! Fortunately he was not far from a Mulberry tree in the Hedge Row, into which he succeeded in climbing, & there chilled & benumbed he sat throughout the whole of the long, dark, cold night! He was taken off this morning insensible but fortunately he had passed his arm around a limb of the tree & then put his hand in his pocket. This little support kept him balanced after he became insensible & so his life was saved. It was a most wonderful escape, but poor Tim, now that he is out of danger, gets but little sympathy from anyone, his folly being on every one's tongue. Ah! Tim— had you fallen you would have been a martyr, a faithful negro falling in the pursuit of your duty, but as you survived to tell the tale, Tim, you are only a "*stupid fool.*" So goes the world. On such slight things hang the judgement of men!

Water every where, a muddy lake whereever we turn our eyes save on the River side, & there for a change we have a muddy torrent! Walked with Mr E. on the Dam; met the mail & found he had a handful of letters on his Battalion business. Noticed Plum trees in blossom. Ah, to what peaceful time does their scent carry us!

FEBRUARY 27, 1862

Mr E. returned to Hamilton. Burnside seems inclined, or is perforce made, to give us a little rest. He has possession of the Sound & his Gun boats steam about to show their power, but beyond enticing negros he does little else. It is said he is refitting.

FEBRUARY 28, 1862

Patrick got back from Hamilton. He found that the Government had sent an officer of Engineers, one Capt Meade,[31] to construct scientific Defences; so being thus relieved from further duty, he came home to attend to his own matters which greatly need him. Col Leventhorpe is ordered back to Hamilton! I was not born a Brigadier Gen and perhaps Gen Huger was, so I suppose it is all right.

---

[31] Mrs. Edmondston possibly meant Richard Kidder Meade, Jr., of Virginia, who aided in the construction of Fort Fisher. Meade, a former lieutenant in the United States Army's Corps of Engineers, served under Major Anderson at Fort Sumter. He resigned his commission on May 1, 1861, however, and was assigned to the Confederate Corps of Engineers. He participated in the skirmishes at Williamsburg and McDowellville, obtaining the rank of major before his death in Virginia in July, 1862. There is some confusion as to the actual date of his death—the *Official Records* record him as participating in the Battle of Cedar Mountain in August, 1862. Ellsworth Eliot, Jr., *West Point in the Confederacy* (New York: G. A. Baker & Company, Inc., 1941), 980; Clark, *Histories of the North Carolina Regiments*, IV, 419, 422.

MARCH 1, 1862

Got home to Looking Glass—came in a canoe down the River, Mr Edmondston shooting as we came. Many a "Chicken Pie" do I owe him, for I am sure he put several Hawks "hors de combat." Home is charming! One feels such a sense of ease, such a belong-a-tive-ness. You get up when you please, go to bed when you like. There is no one to give a short dry cough and expatiate on the injury to your particular health in keeping late house & remark en passant, "you must have been up *very* late last night," & you know like a flash that they have been looking at your candle! Ah! would that we were never *forced* to go from home. Sat up until "wee sma hours," Mr E. having some important letters to write, amongst others to Col Riddick who cooly wishes him to sink his Batalion & join him in a Regt of which Riddick is to be Col!

MARCH 3, 1862

Yesterday, Sunday, all the morning copying Mr E's Report to Col Leventhorpe respecting the work he did at Rainbow Bend. In the evening took canoe & came up to father's. It was a sad scene. A dull cold grey sky seemed almost to close down upon a world of dark turbid water. The very birds had a melancholy fly & the wind soughing & sweeping in an unsatisfied restless way, "ever seeking & never finding," made leaving home seem sadder than ever.

After we ladies had retired a stranger, one Mr Rockwell[32] from Columbus, arrived to see Mr E on Military business. He had reached our house just after we left & knowing that Mr Edmondston would be off early this morning had trusted himself to Aaron's guidance & followed. Bitterly must he have repented of his "act of faith," for Aaron got lost in the swamp & after paddling about in the dark for hours finally drew up at the Rain house with announcement that he was "afeard" to go further. Fortunately he was rescued by Ned who on going home after carrying us up answered their "halloo" & piloted him here to father's house.

Mr E left early this morning for Wilmington on business connected with his Batalion. How long he will be gone he cannot tell. I spent the morning making two copies of his report, one for David Clark, the other for Gen Gatlin.

MARCH 4, 1862

Was much amused today with Mary Clark's spelling. It seems Mama's maids, fired with a desire to emulate their mistress, wished to embroider their

---

[32]This reference was probably to Capt. Henry C. Rockwell, the assistant quartermaster of the Fifty-first North Carolina Regiment. John W.Moore, *Roster of North Carolina Troops in the War Between the States* (Raleigh: [State of North Carolina], 4 volumes, 1882), III, 447, hereinafter cited as Moore, *Roster of North Carolina Troops*; Clark, *Histories of North Carolina Regiments*, III, 205.

names upon their P K H Fs & Mary was to draw the pattern for them. She in the true Phonetic spirit spelled one "Enuk" (Enoch), the other Caraty (Charity). The ludicrous look of the handkercheif can be better imagined than described.

Read an Article in a Review today on "Things Slowly Learnt," which tho I read it last fall I have been so slow in learning that I deemed a revision necessary to quicken me. I am sure it is by the author of "Recreations of a Country Parson." Would that I could accept the fact once for all that my servants are careless & negligent, as it advises, and have *one worry* at it and not let each successive instance fret me any more—take them only as proof of a known fact. But I cannot. Each successive proof only brings the fact home to me & I am fretted all the same. If I could, as he says, admit that some people are dull, unamiable & obstinate & never look for any thing but distress, ill temper, & obstinacy from them, it would perhaps be better. In one noted instance where I know the person is selfish & thinks of no one in comparison with herself, I wish I could accept her selfishness & henceforward when I come in contact with it I should be spared the feeling as tho' I had been rubbed with a mullen leaf.

Kate Miller is an amusing girl. She says whatever comes uppermost in her mind & is withal so down right & sincere that she attracts one greatly. She strips off many a false gloss by a single straight forward question or a quiet assertion that it is difficult for her opponent to meet. She has just told me that when she is angry she goes up stairs, cleans her teeth with prepared Chalk, & then sits down & sings "Days of Absence"! & by that time she is composed once more & in an equable frame of mind. Ah! Kitty! it takes more than Chalk or Song to bring most people to their equanimity when once it has been ruffled.

Knit little fancy Socks for Sophia in fancy stitches. Dull prosy work it is, but it suits the dull prosy woman I am in Patrick's absence. Ah! that I could see him tonight. Copied letters for him until it is now so late that I must creep into bed. Enclosed a pleasant note to him from Mr Shaw,[33] telling me that Austin's house was burned this afternoon and that he lost every thing he had, poor fellow, Blankets, Clothes, beds, everything in short. Where more are to come from to supply that large family I am sure I cannot tell, but that does not distress Cuffy. Master must build him a house & give him the where-with-all to make himself comfortable. Ah! Mrs Stowe when you drew your picture you should have put some of the lights of Cuffy's life in it—not all shadow—but you made your money & Madam, that is all you cared for. What boots it to you that you have aided to plunge your country into the most terrible war ever waged, that tens of thousands of your country men are dead, & your

---

[33] Rufus H. Shaw was employed by Patrick Edmondston as a farm overseer. Eighth Census, 1860, Population Schedule, Halifax County, 82.

country women plunged into poverty and greif, an amount of human suffering undergone that the world rarely ever saw before? Your Dividend at the Bank is greater & *part* of the world calls you a woman of Genius. *We* call you *murderess*, and a murderess for *gain*!

MARCH 5, 1862

Sat up so late copying letters to send to Patrick that I am half asleep & whole stupid! Rumours today of an intended evacuation of our lines on the Potomac, a falling back, from Manassas and Centreville. We outsiders do not understand it but Gen Joe Johnston does. The President says we have undertaken more than we can accomplish—viz to defend so long a line and they must know. Every one blames Gen A S Johnston for not defending Nashville. The President, however, is his firm friend, says if he is not a General he has none! The Nashville people continue stanch. Refuse to hold intercourse or to buy any of the wares which the Yankees carried in the wake of the Army, so the baffled Pedlars—for Pedlars they are on a large scale—were forced to carry them back to St Louis.

Read in Robertson's Sermons today—"These moments of profound Faith do not come once for all; they vary with the degree and habit of obedience. There is a plant which blossoms once in a hundred years. Like it the soul blossoms only now & then in a space of years; but these moments are the glory and the heavenly glimpses of our purest humanity." Grant unto me O Lord these heavenly blossomings. Plant me in Thy garden and teach me to grow—to grow in grace and the knoledge of our Lord Jesus Christ.

MARCH 6, 1862

Went out to Hascosea & dined there. Kate, Sue, Mary Clark went with me. Found all well tho' Hascosea I think looks more cold & forlorn this Spring than usual, even in cold weather, for it to do. The Spring is a very backward one. The Peach trees are only straggling into bloom, tho the first bloomed on the 28th of Feb. No signs of my Diamond Pin which I have not yet given up. Planted a Magnolia which I bought in Raleigh—my only horticultural purchase this year being two Magnolia's, one for Looking Glass & one for Hascosea. When did that ever happen before? Copied Battalion letters & sent them off to Patrick—God bless him!

MARCH 9, 1862

Whilst in Church, Mr Bartley preaching, came in Mr Jack Wheeler[34] of Murfreesboro. He has an order from Government to buy teams & waggons

---

[34] The identity of Bartley was not determined by the editors. The "Jack Wheeler" Mrs. Edmondston mentioned possibly referred to either Samuel Jordan Wheeler, a physician in Murfreesboro, or to his brother John Hill Wheeler. John Hill Wheeler (1806-1882) served in the state legislature from 1827 until

for the army at Suffolk where a large number of troops are being massed. Father refused to sell saying that we could do more for the Government by raising corn to supply the Army than in aught else we could do. He is a terrible bag of wind—that same Mr Wheeler—a broken down politician too. I wonder the Government employs such Agents.

MARCH 10, 1862

Went to Looking Glass to give poor Austin & family some more clothes. Blankets not being possible to get, I was forced to give them some of my own & a comfortable or two, with which they must make out this summer. With those that their kins folk have lent them they will do very well. I fear I shall need the bed tick I gave them; but the poor creatures have none, so my feathers must stay in bags another summer. Had a terribly round about road through the woods on account of the water in the Low Grounds. Was almost all day going & coming. Went by the "Quarters" of more people than I thought lived in that Pocosin.

Got back to father's about five & shortly after he came in from Halifax Hurrah!-ing, actually Hurrahing at the top of his voice! We all ran down for we knew there must be some good news & glorious news it is! Our single iron clad vessel—the Virginia—has at last gone out from the Navy Yard & attacked the Federal Fleet lying in Hampton Roads. She sunk the Cumberland, burned the Congress, crippled the Minnesota, repulsed the Roanoke & the St Lawrence, and drove all the other vessels under the shelter of the guns of Fortress Monroe, besides shelling Newport News. The two Gunboats lying up the James, the Patrick Henry and the Jamestown, on hearing the firing, came down & assisted in the latter part of the fight, taking the attention of the Gunboats off the Virginia. With this exception she was unaided. The Yankee loss is terrible; ours, four men scalded by steam on board the Patrick Henry, Frank Jones ship. Pray God he may have escaped! The only lives we lost in the fight, except those scalded, were some of our men & an officer who, after the Congress held out a flag of Truce, boarded her & were rendering assistance to the wounded on her decks when they were basely fired upon from the shore by men with long range guns—an act of treachery of which even a Savage would feel ashamed. This is glorious news & will cheer the heart of the nation now cast down with the reverses in Tennessee. The fight was renewed on Sunday but authentic details are wanting.

1830, became the superintendent of the Charlotte branch of the United States Mint in 1837, served as the state's treasurer from 1842 until 1844, and was appointed minister to Nicaragua by Pres. Franklin Pierce in 1853. With the start of the Civil War Wheeler returned to North Carolina although he was too old to participate in combat. Eighth Census, 1860, Population Schedule, Hertford County, 7; Ashe, *Biographical History*, VII, 472-478.

MARCH 11, 1862

The Virginia is the old Merrimac which the Yankees sunk at the Navy Yard last April & which when raised was found to have her guns pointed so as to command Norfolk in the hope that the fire would discharge them! She has been refitted & iron clad after a plan of our own, & gloriously has she distinguished herself! On Sunday she was met by the Iron clad boat the Monitor, or the Erickson Battery as she is sometimes called, which fortunately for the Yankees arrived at Fortress Monroe on Sat night. Then ensued a battle such as was never seen before. The balls bounded off the sides & roofs of the vessels, for the Va has a sloping roof, like hail stones from a shed! making no mark where they struck. Neither side injured the other but the tide being on the turn the Virginia drew off & the Monitor was only too glad to escape with the loss of the eyes only of her commander Lieut Worden![35] Commodore Buchanon[36] our Commander was the only man injured on board & he was wounded in the thigh by a Minie ball. To God alone be the praise. "He giveth not the Victory to the strong." Ah! for our brave men wounded at Donaldson.

MARCH 12, 1862

Capt John Whitaker came to dinner. He is full of detail about the Army of the Potomac & its Commander Gen Joe Johnston—he gave high praise to him—but said "Gen Beauregard possesses the *enthusiasm* of the troops." He tells us that we are falling back from the line of the Potomac, a move being executed with great silence & celerity in the face of the enemy. What will we do when we get where we can no longer "*fall back*"? The case of the White Man & the Indian is fast getting to be ours—we can "move further" not much longer.

Kate Miller left for home, Sue accompanying her as far as Weldon. I knit on a little sock, played chess, read newspapers and copied letters for Patrick. He gets a vast number of them. If one half the men that *wish* "go into Cavalry" he will have no difficulty in raising a Regt, but he says we must not count on them until they are sworn. They do not know what they want, nor what influences will be brought to bear on them.

MARCH 13, 1862

Came an order last night for one fourth our men hands to work on entrenchments for Col Leventhorpe's Regt at Hamilton, he having been ordered

---

[35] Lt. John Lorimer Worden (1818-1897), commander of the U.S.S. *Monitor*, was injured and almost blinded by a shell exploding against the pilothouse. *Dictionary of American Biography*, XX, 531.

[36] Capt. Franklin Buchanan, commanding the C.S.S. *Virginia* and the James River Squadron, was wounded by a minie ball from shore batteries in the engagement at Hampton Roads, March 8, 1862. *Official Records (Navy)*, Series I, VII, 41-42.

back there. He will know the road well I think! This victory of the Va will unsettle Burnside's plans greatly. Wool & himself were to have made a joint attack on Norfolk, he by land, Wool on Seawell's point. Wool's part is now impossible, but what Burnside will do none can tell. Perhaps ravage the country! If so, then God help us. Father received a letter from Frank Jones giving an account of the fight in Hampton Roads & as I would like to keep it I transcribe part of it here:

Dear Grandpapa:
    I should have written you to inform you that I am unhurt by our recent engagement but that I was so tired & worn out that I could not. I had no sleep & did not eat a single meal from Sat morning until Sun. night, so you can imagine what condition I was in for writing. I will endeavour to give you as good a description of the fight as I can. We left Mulberry Island at ½ past 2 o clock on Friday morning with the expectation of meeting the Va at Newport News, but the wind blew so hard & the tide was so low that she could not have worked to advantage in the Roads & therefore did not come out at all. So we stopped off Dey's Point & lay there until Sat afternoon 2½ o clock when we saw the smoke of the Va's guns as she was engaging the ships & batteries off Newport News. We weighed anchor & steamed down as quickly as possible, but before we got down the Cumberland was sunk. We ran past the batteries receiving only three shot in doing so, none of them doing any material damage. We ran in very near them going within 800 yds of the Batteries. After we had passed them we backed up to them and commenced shelling the men out of their quarters. We made them scamper in all directions. It was whilst we were engaged protecting the Raleigh & Beaufort whilst they were removing the wounded from the Congress that we received a shot in our boiler. I was in the fire room at the time having gone down there a minute before to give some directions about the fires. As soon as the shot struck us the steam rushed out of the boilers & everything was enveloped in coal dust & Vapour. I made my way up the ladder and just managed to reach the top round when I should have fallen back & been killed but that some one caught me by the collar and pulled me out. I was very nearly suffocated as it was, but in half an hour I was all right. We lost four men by that one shot. They were scalded to death by the steam. I was in the same room with them when the shot struck us; there were six of us down there & only two escaped & one of them is scalded internally. I escaped entirely unhurt. After we received that shot we were disabled for a short time on account of all the Steam blowing off out of both boilers & whilst we were in this position the enemy piled shot and shell into us tremendously. But wonderful to say, they did not hurt us at all, nearly all of them being intended to sink us & consequently were fired at our bottom, but that being heavily plated with Iron was proof against their shot. We fought on until it got so dark that we could not see to aim & then withdrew and anchored under the guns of Seawell's Point Battery. I was on watch that night from 12 until 4. About ½ past 12 I thought that I would go up & look at the Congress burning and I was just in time to see her blow up. I never saw such a splendid sight in my life! She threw her shell in all directions. One of them passed away over us & fell some where near the Rip Raps. I could see them bursting in the air almost every where it seemed to me.

At ½ 8 oclock on Sunday morning we commenced the action again, but on the appearance of the Monitor (Ericckson's Battery) we came to the conclusion that it was best for us not to meddle with her, so we lay off in order to render any assistance which the Virginia might need & then these two went at it in fine style, lying right along side of each other & hammering away at each other—neither of them being in the least hurt by the other's shot! The Virginia, after tearing the Minnesota all to peices nearly, withdrew & we all came up here to the Gosport Navy Yard where we will lay until we can get sufficiently repaired to justify us in trying them again.

I did not feel so much excited during the engagement as I anticipated, though when I would hear a shell whistle pretty near us I could not help ducking down my head. I must close now as it is getting pretty late. Give my love to all and write soon to your affectionate

Grandson,
W F Jones

Heard today of the threatened attack by Burnside on New Berne. He is in force at the mouth of the River. Pray God he may be repulsed. What a hero Gen Branch will be. Am too dull to write more but must close with a wish that Tom Jones may distinguish himself & come off unhurt.

MARCH 14, 1862

No mail! We are all in a state of cruel suspense about New Bern. God protect Tom Jones.

MARCH 15, 1862

No mail again! It is terrible! Mr McMahon writes that the trains rush past the Depot without stopping, carrying troops to reinforce Gen Gatlin at New Berne most likely. Ah! poor Sophia! My heart bleeds for you!

MARCH 16, 1862

Sunday—All day in great anxiety & suspense. Mama allowed Isham to go to Halifax & I beleive her anxiety lest he should abuse the liberty and come home drunk is almost as great as that about New Berne!

At night when Hope had worn itself out came Mr Edmondston, to our great delight & releif. He brought news of the disgraceful retreat from Newberne, but as he charges us not to beleive all he tells us he has heard, for that the rumours are too many & too contradictory to be trusted, I will tonight say nothing more than that we are beaten! Our troops have made a most inglorious retreat to Kinston.[37] The enemy have possession of the town. Our loss

---

[37] Operating against Burnside's greatly superior forces and handicapped by inadequate equipment and fortifications, General Branch was unsuccessful in his defense of New Bern. On March 14, 1862, he withdrew and concentrated his troops at Kinston. Barrett, *Civil War in North Carolina*, 95-107; Manarin and Jordan, *North Carolina Troops*, IV, 394-395.

small, but we burnt the bridge & the naval stores. Gen. Gatlin was not there & the command devolved on Branch—a political General.

MARCH 17, 1862

"St Patrick's Day in the morning." Came home to Looking Glass, partly on horse back, partly in the canoe, & partly on foot—on account of the water. Father rode with us to the place where we took canoe. Dear old gentleman, I am greived to see him so despondant & low spirited. It is so unusual for him that it is doubly distressing. God send us good news to lighten his heart. Found the Hyacinths in most beautiful bloom! They are truly exquisite & as we came into the gate & their fragrance stole over us, the charm of a quiet home never seemed greater. As they looked up to us in their peaceful beauty, smiling in the midst of these War's alarms, it made us prize our seclusion the more. Ah! Lord Falkland[38] I could emulate you in the ingemination of Peace! Peace!

All the afternoon preparing a basket of eatables of divers kinds for Patrick to send to Col Leventhorpe at Hamilton. I omitted to mention last night, not I am sure from want of thankfulness, that Thomas Jones was safe and that Mr Turner was absent on leave when the attack on New Berne occurred. Happily for Sophia, as her baby was born on the day of the fight in Hampton Roads— the 8th—rather more than 9 days before the Newberne disaster.

MARCH 18, 1862

Rode out to Hascosea on horseback with Mr E after dispatching two baskets full of supplies for Col Leventhorpe. Poor man, he is in a place to make him relish them. Talked of the Batalion and its prospects. Patrick is never sanguin, but now he is almost sure of success. God grant that he may be useful to our Country! Our road lay through the woods, on account of the water, a large portion of it through old fields. How melancholy they seem, the hands that cultivated, the heads that planed their cultivation now all mouldering in the grave; yet still the furrow remains, a monument of former industry. How true are the words of the Psalmist: "they call the lands after their own name,"[39] for many of these overgrown fields are known by names extinct amongst the living here. Perchance their owners may have died in the South and South West. The memory of man runneth not back to the time of their proprietorship—for "Never the less, man will not abide in honour."[40]

---

[38] Lucius Cary (ca. 1610-1643), second viscount of Falkland, English politician and writer, was killed fighting on the Royalist side. In his history of the rebellion in England the Earl of Clarendon states that Falkland, "sitting among his friends, after a deep silence and frequent sighs, would, with a shrill and sad accent, ingeminate the word *Peace, Peace*." Edward Hyde Clarendon, *History of the Rebellion and Civil Wars in England* (Oxford: University Press, 7 volumes, 1849), III, 197.

[39] Psalms 49:11. "Their inward thought is, that their houses shall continue for ever, and their dwelling places to all generations; they call their lands after their own names."

[40] Psalms 49:12. "Nevertheless man being in honour abideth not: he is like the beasts that perish."

This is the way of them. Ah how sad to think that these fields which we now cultivate with so much pleasure, this property we now view with so much pride may some day be like these fields—a place for the "bittern and stork"[41] to congregate.

Authentic details of the New Berne fight take some what away from the bitterness of the disgrace, but it is bad at best. The Cavalry did *not* run as at first reported, they having been dismounted & placed in the trenches, but the militia in their panic seized the horses of the Cavalry & never stopped until they reached Kinston, thereby riding forty of the horses to death. Sinclair's regiment which was placed in the post of honour, I suppose on account of the Laurels he won as chaplin at Manassas, took a panic & ran, even consulted about surrendering, the Col at the head![42] They gave up the most important landing place with scarcely a blow in its defence. Vance's regt behaved *well*, Avery's nobly. The Yankees themselves say that if we had fought ten minutes longer they would have been forced to retire. But our men, as Tom Jones of Martin says, can't stand "Bumbing" (he was describing the Roanoke Island disaster) "they just stand off and 'Bumb' our men & they cannot stand it." But treachery too was at work. Imbecility & bad management is not enough for us but there must be traitors in our midst who avail themselves of it. The River obstructions were not complete, a passage having been left open for our own boats. This passage on the approach of the enemy was to have been closed, but it was not and the Yankee boats sailed or rather steamed in as easily and safely as our own have done—piloted by a traiterous negro who ought never to have been trusted with the knoledge.[43] Then the entrenchments at the R R had never been completed. The cannon lay on the ground & have lain there for weeks—that were intended to defend it. Through this opening swarmed the Yankee soldiers out flanking our men & attacking the trenches in the rear. Here was the most desperate fighting. Would that we could have sustained it, but the Militia took panic first & fled & the soldiers were not long after them. The Bridge was burned before all our men had passed & two Regts & some companies were compelled to make a large detour, which led to the impression that they had been cut off.

Our loss in killed, wounded & prisoners is not as great as the enemy's killed & wounded, however, but we took but one prisoner, who calls himself a Lieut. He says he has been in the camp in disguise & what he says is upheld by the fact that when taken he was mounted on a Col's horse & seemed to be piloting

---

[41] References to bittern, translated as meaning a porcupine or stork, are found sporadically in the Old Testament.

[42] At the battle of New Bern the Reverend James Sinclair, colonel of the Thirty-fifth North Carolina Regiment and former chaplain of the Fifth Regiment, was ordered to leave the trenches and "charge bayonets upon advancing columns." He failed to do so and "left the field in confusion." Clark, *Histories of the North Carolina Regiments*, II, 313, 592, 595; Manarin and Jordan, *North Carolina Troops*, IV, 128, 394-395.

[43] The Union ships were "piloted by a man named Westervelt, who had commanded a vessel plying between New Bern and New York" before the war. Hill, *Bethel to Sharpsburg*, I, 232.

the others and he knew Sloan, Vance, Avery & some other of our Cols by name & sight & mentioned how they stood with their commands. He says Burnside paid $5000 for the attempt (frustrated) to burn the Bridge a few nights since & 5000 for the same thing in Washington Co. The loss of the New Berne bridge would have caused the destruction or capture of our whole command unless they had fought better than they did.

Beverhout Thompson the Engineer is blamed for purposely constructing the defences so that they were useless against a water attack, but I cannot beleive it. I think the fault must have been in the defenders. Political generals have a hard time should disaster overtake them & poor Gen Branch is the object of universal animadversion. He is the best abused man in N C just now. Gen Gatlin too has his full share. "Incompetent" & "inefficent" are the mildest terms he gets, but we must have a "Scape Goat." It is a want of human nature—Adam's sin—"the woman Thou gavest me." "The Government" is too impersonal to meet every requisition; we demand a human victim! The town was fired by the retreating troops, as were the naval stores, but unfortunately the advancing Yankees extinguished the one & rescued much of the other. Thomas Jones Regt was not engaged. He remained behind until the last to fire a cannon and blow up the Regimental ammunition. So we go! "Fall back" to Kinston. The rears of our two armies may yet meet if they fall back far enough!

MARCH 19, 1862

Remained all last night at Hascosea & came back this afternoon. No news by mail except that Johnston's retrograde movement has been entirely successful—a most masterly executed manoevre performed in the very face of the enemy without his knoledge or suspicion, one of the most skilful peices of Generalship on record. McClellan is completely outwitted & must make an entirely new disposition before he can enter on his summer Campaign. The North is in a storm of indignation against him & unless he does something to regain his lost prestige will soon dethrone their Idol. But perhaps he can "lie" himself out of it, tho' I do not think he can be as good at that as one of the Yankee Charivari's[44] represents Seward to be. Lincoln in a eulogy of Seward says "Sir! he is the only man I ever knew who could tell you a thing, which you knew to be a lie, sir, & which he knew to be a lie & which he knew that you knew to be a lie & yet, sir, you would beleive him! He is a great man, Sir!, a live man." Certainly he must be a favourite son of the father of such commodities as he deals in.

---

[44] A charivari usually refers to a mock serenade of discordant noise. Benét, *Reader's Encyclopedia*, 198.

MARCH 20, 1862

Contradiction innumerable, criminations and recriminations about the New Berne fight, but I have done with it. It would take Seward himself to white wash it and to hear them all makes one heartily assent to Sir Robert Walpole's—"Read no history to me my daughter, read no History to me, for I know how it is made."[45] It strikes at the root of ones faith in all things human to hear what is strongly affirmed one day as gravely denied the next upon authority equally as reliable. One would like to take refuge with Arch Bishop Whately & entertain "Historic doubts on the being & existence of Napoleon Buonaparte"![46]

Peach Trees in splendid blossom & the promise for fruit fine.

Finished Mrs. Hutcheson's Memoirs[47] for the second or third time! What a picture of Domestic love & Happiness does it present & how sad to think that their descendants fell from the state & in all probability from the *cultivation* of their parents. Ah Poverty! thy worse evil is the debasing intercourse you force upon your subjects! I doubt whether Col Hutchinson's lineal descendants know now that they had such an ancestor. He is lost to them, & his example & influence which, where the chain of descent is known, is all powerful—is to them only as it is to others who have no claim on his blood. Think you that the blood of the noble house of Stanley does not run quicker through their veins as they read the "Defence of Lathom House" than it does in those of other people, enthusiastic tho they be, who cannot say as a Stanley can "Charlotte de la Tremouille[48] was my Grandmother! Shall I prove recreant to the blood she has given me? Can I ever disgrace it? Never!" There is the true ennobling influence of ancestry, the exalting effect of an honourable descent. Mrs Hutchinson loved as few women can love, and her character of her husband, so exalted, so tender, so free from "spot or speck or stain," is beautiful & yet she is humble where she speaks of herself; & when she describes her own virtures as but the mirror of his, the graces which are but the result of his cultivation, she presents to my mind one of the finest exhibitions of true noble love in the language.

---

[45] This quotation by Sir Robert Walpole has appeared in several versions. One source cites Walpole's remark to his son Horace as "O! do not read history, for that I know must be false." William Coxe, *Memoirs of the Life and Administration of Sir Robert Walpole* (London: T. Cadell and W. Davis, 3 volumes, 1800), III, 356.

[46] Richard Whately (1787-1863), English logician, author, and the archbishop of Dublin, wrote a clever essay directed against the excessive skepticism applied to biblical history, which was entitled *Historic Doubts relative to Napoleon Buonaparte* (1819). *Dictionary of National Biography*, LX, 423-429.

[47] Lucy Hutchinson (1620-1675) wrote *Memoirs of the Life of Colonel Hutchinson*, which traced the life and career of her husband and his support of Cromwell. Benét, *Reader's Encyclopedia*, 529.

[48] Charlotte de la Trémoille (1599-1664), the daughter of Claude, duc de Thouars, and the granddaughter of William the Silent, Prince of Orange, was the wife of James Stanley (1607-1651), seventh earl of Derby. She successfully defended Lathom House, seat of the earls of Derby, against Parliamentary forces in 1644. *Dictionary of National Biography*, LIV, 48-49.

March 22, 1862

First swallow came! Welcome little messenger! May you bring Peace to this war-tost land! May your merry laughing note be a harbinger of that harmony which we hope will soon bless us all!

March 23, 1862

I have waited long for authentic details of the battle of Sugar Creek in Arkansas. It seems to have been a drawn one. Price's retreat was a most masterly one. Of one thing however I fear we must be certain. Gen MCullough is killed. He was a useful man in his way, gallant & intrepid & he is a great loss to us.

In Tennessee things continue much the same. Nashville is defiant still & the North much exercised to find a Union feeling, which they maintain however exists. Gen Johnston falling back to the Mississippi line. It is said he intends making a stand at Corinth. Andy Johnson made Military Govorner of Tennessee, an insult to the people! Did my old Grandfather when he sent his Coachman to whip him & his cousins, altogether known as "Jesse Johnson's[49] boys," back to their cabin because they had a fancy to run naked on the road, ever think he would reach such a height as that? So we go.

March 24, 1862

Commenced planting corn at Looking Glass. If Patrick goes on cutting down his cotton crop much more we will not make seed for another year.

March 25, 1862

Went to Hascosea & found them planting corn there. The long mooted point is decided. We plant only 40 acres of Cotton. Last year we planted 300. Ah! Mother England! You little know the misery in store for you! You think you can raise the Blockade when you will & releive your suffering children, but Mistress of the Seas tho you are, what will you do when there is no cotton for your ships to carry your idle factories, when your children cry for bread & you have not the wherewithal to feed them, & all because you resolutely closed your eyes to an injustice you profess to disallow—to an oppression you affect to abhor? Mr Seward & Lord Russel, you have the heaviest accountibility that human shoulders ever before bore, except perhaps Buonaparte's, that is of *misery* and *blood*. The misery and blood of your brethren which you could prevent weighs in the eyes of a Mighty & Divine Judge!

Col Leventhorpe moved again, this time to Goldsboro. I suppose we will mass an army there, dig trenches, throw up redoubts, & fall back—those

---

[49] Mrs. Edmondston's "old grandfather" was John Devereux (1761-1844). Andrew Johnson's father was Jacob Johnson, a sexton and bank and tavern porter in Raleigh "esteemed for his honesty, sobriety, industry, and his humane, friendly disposition." Ashe, *Biographical History*, IV, 228; Eric L. McKitrick (ed.), *Andrew Johnson: A Profile* (New York: Hill and Wang, 1969), 1-5.

seem our tactics. Zeke, when he came back from Hamilton, described their work, the intrenchment the negroes threw up, as a "Canal a mile long in the wild woods"—much good will it do!

Our people suffer terribly from extortioners & Speculators, the Army Worm as they are called. Salt $28 a sack, sugar 25 cts, coffee 80 cts, and $1.00, butter 75 cts, beef 30 cts, Shoes & Leather almost fabulous. But this must have an end.[50] The people will take it into their own hands—& yet our privations cannot be what our fore fathers endured in the Revolution! We have not yet dreampt of them. True, our wants are greater & "as a man thinketh so is he," but we must curb our wants.

Our Grandmothers for seven years had no pins, actually dressed with thorns. I remember that my Grandmother used to tell us when we were children, by way of exciting our thankfulness, that in the village in which she lived there was but *one* needle; this one needle sewed everything! & went the rounds of the village, being lent from house to house. But we being by no means willing disciples of Arachne,[51] I fear did not estimate the blessing of needles as we ought, for in our childish confidences we came to the conclusion that that *one* needle was too precious ever to be trusted to the hands of the children & that they therefore enjoyed an immunity from sewing and particularly "stocking darning" which excited our envy.

MARCH 26, 1862

A furor of marriage seems to possess the plantation. On Thursday, the 20th, Fanny after bustling aimlessly about the room came out with "Master, Joe, Joe Axe from the ferry wants to see you. He wants to axe you & Miss to let him marry me." So Joe was admitted into the dining room, the preliminaries settled & they left with the permission to fix their own time. This was of the shortest for the next day, Sat the 22d, I was called on for the materials for the wedding supper & then on Sunday came Dempsey with a request for Rachel, on Wednesday Lorenzo Dow to marry Mela, & on Thursday Hercules with a similar request for Chloe! So Cupid gave place to Hymen[52] in a shorter time than usual—primitive customs one will say, but Cuffee strips off the elegancies & refinements of civilization with great ease. White people would have been months in accomplishing what they have been days about!

---

[50]To combat the evil of widespread speculation, Governor Vance in 1863 issued a proclamation prohibiting the exportation of bacon, lard, pork, beef, corn, meal, flour, wheat, potatoes, shoes, leather, hides, cotton cloth, yarn, and woolen cloth. *North Carolina Standard*, October 8, 1862; May 13, 1863.

[51]According to Roman mythology, Arachne was a Lydian maiden who challenged Minerva, the Roman goddess of wisdom and patroness of the arts and trades, to compete with her in needle tapestry. As punishment for her presumption Arachne was changed into a spider. Benét, *Reader's Encyclopedia*, 43.

[52]Hymen was a Greek wedding song later personified as the god of marriage, while Cupid was the Roman god of love. Benét, *Reader's Encyclopedia*, 263, 530.

MARCH 28, 1862

Came up yesterday to father's. Mr E went off this morning to Goldsboro on Batalion business, and I went out to Scotland Neck to see Rebecca Spruill—poor thing! what a sufferer she has been & how patient an one! When I think of her Youth, her bright anticipations for the future, the pleasure that life—daily life—was to her & remember the disappointments, the sorrows, the trials and suffering she has been called upon to undergo & look at her now shattered in health, weakened it may be in mind, with little hope for the future—nothing which we call *happiness* to look forward to—and as it appears no hope but in the Grave, I pause in wonder at her patience, her cheerfulness & ask myself could I thus be interested in the pleasures of others, in the trifles of daily life, so pleased with a book, made so happy with flowers? Ah! she is an hourly reproach to me, so charitable in her judgment, so kind in her estimate of men & motives, so patient in suffering! "God tempers the wind to the shorn lamb," said that hateful moralist Sterne;[53] surely it must be tempered to her or she would fold her hands in helpless despondancy. I must do all I can to alleviate what she is called to bear & amuse if possible the ennui which might posses her. Julia is a delightful woman, so pretty, so cheerful, so considerate of others; & as to Louisa, she is a gem, one of the most original children I ever saw. I wish she looked less like her father.[54]

MARCH 30, 1862

Sunday—Mr E came home. Says he must soon go to Richmond & wishes me to go with him. I do not think it best on some accounts, but I remember how I regretted not having gone with him last Jan. So drown all prudential motives & resolve to enjoy myself. Separation will come soon enough & then I can economize & make up the expense of the trip. Father when out walking heard heavy canonading in the direction of Norfolk. Perhaps the Virginia is out again!

MARCH 31, 1862

Came home to Looking Glass. Few people I beleive love their homes as I do. It is exquisite happiness to return to it. The flowers seem to welcome me. Would that I never had to leave it! These constant absences, too, are telling on the servants; they are getting so awkward, inefficient & even lazy! I must put a stop to them & if Mr E's absences from home are to be continued I must get a "Refugee" of my own—some nice lady to live with and give me her

---

[53] Laurence Sterne, *A Sentimental Journey Through France and Italy*, edited by Wilbur L. Cross (New York: Liveright, 1926), 158.

[54] Rebecca, Julia, and Louisa Spruill were the daughters of George Evans Spruill of Warren County. In 1845 Spruill, his son Thomas, several other whites, and slaves died from drinking water from a well that had been poisoned by seepage from a compost pile. Rebecca Spruill was an invalid and spent much of her time in rest and in reading to her sisters. Montgomery, *Sketches of Old Warrenton*, 378-380.

society in return for the comforts of a home. But who will it be? I am particular as to *"quality"* and perhaps expect an impossibility. Ah! Home! to
your full enjoyment once more!

APRIL 1, 1862

Went to Hascosea with Patrick in the carriage.

Chatted most delightfully all the way about the Battalion, the War,
Politics, etc. Walked around to all the covered drains, saw them running
steadily; sat down at length on the bank of the Canal & watched the pure
water running underneath. Patrick amused himself, dropping straws, sticks,
etc. into the water two at a time saying that they were emblems of two people
starting out in life together—one dallied, caught in an eddy sailing slowly
round and round, whilst the other, borne on the bosom of the current, floated
swiftly away. "See the man of energy & decision how he distances the other!
see! see! how steadily on he goes! how he succeeds in life! how he leaves his
companion far behind! He does nothing but go round and round aimlessly!"

"No," said I, "*this* is the man occupied at *home* by a round of *home* duties.
See how faithfully he performs them all, not so brilliant as the first but more
useful and to my mind happier." Just then the whirl of the eddy carried it to
its outer edge and it was caught by the current in its strongest and swiftest
part and swept rapidly on. It gained steadily on the first, which had reached a
slacker part of the stream and threatened to stop every moment.

"Yes," he continued, "so it is you are right. See how he rises with the
emergence. Forced out of his little sphere he shows equal energy & determination with the first & gains upon those who in the outset had distanced
him." In fact at this point the laggard stick passed the fleet one & driving
swiftly on was soon out of sight! I thought within my heart that it was an apt
emblem of himself, for how many years have we lived here alone almost, "the
world forgetting," certainly "by the world forgot," in a little circle of home
duties and home pleasures. But called forth by the force of circumstances, see
how already his worth is acknoledged, his energy yielded to by those who
have lived for & in the world! Ah! me! how happy was that home life! I fear
me never to be so fully enjoyed again as it was of old, but Courage! it is for our
Country!

The farm is in beautiful order, but I looked at it with a sad eye as I feared
he would not be with me to envy it in its beauty & greenery. Found the first
Asparagus shoot & ordered Allen to plant some Stowels Corn. Came home to
Looking Glass to Dinner.

No news of importance by mail except the commencement of the Bombardment of Island No 10[55] in the Mississippi River. We have heavy defences there
& hope to repulse them and prevent the descent of their Gun boats.

---

[55] Island No. 10, situated 60 miles below Columbus, Kentucky, and fortified with land and floating
batteries, was designed to obstruct Federal forces on the Mississippi River. When the fortification fell on

APRIL 2, 1862

Rode with Patrick to the Ploughs in the Sheep Pasture—bad ploughing & slovenly work. The overseer was there. Mr E asked him why he ploughed around the old trash heaps instead of burning them. "I dont know, Sir," came in a most nonchalent drawl—as tho' it was none of his business. Were I Patrick, I would not make myself a "Barber's block" in my absence at least for these young overseers to learn to shave on. This young man has not the begining of the root of the matter in him, as indifferent as tho' he was not taking "Master's money" & doing nothing to earn it.

Thence to the covered ditches. It is astonishing how well they dry the land. Before long father's plantation will be so thoroughly under drained that it will resemble a Beef steak on a Gridiron! Patrick's remark upon the pleasure an English farmer must have when he drains with tiles for posterity put me in a train of thought upon the effect that a consideration for posterity must have upon the character. The Irish are said to "live on the past." I do not know any nation who live on the future, except perhaps the Yankees. They Gasconade[56] enough, but it has not had a very ennobling effect on them.

Then to the Corn Planters. It makes one sad to see these beautiful uplands in such order as they are too going into corn & remember too that it will tell in the next year's cotton crop. But it is all right so long as England admits the Blockade. Cotton is too troublesome a peice of property to encumber ones self with. "What will we do with it," vexed us enough last winter without encountering it again; & now as we have no prospect of bagging & rope it would be madness in the extreme.

Good news—the enemy after Bombarding Island No 10 for fifteen days have made no impression whatever upon it. Killed only one man and wounded a few others. Our batteries intact. Pray God it may continue.

APRIL 3, 1862

Went to Fathers on Horseback to dine, as Sue & Father leave for Raleigh in the afternoon, Sue going to R to go to the Communion. Whilst we were there the disabled horses of the 1st N Carolina Cavalry passed, coming down into our plentiful country to recruit. Such a set of Rosinante's[57] I never before saw, galled, sore backed, poor, lame—some of them with scarcely a hair upon them—Patrick said occasioned by vermin! I did not think 280 such jades could be found. The Lieut in charge, Lieut Andrews,[58] came to dinner. He

---

April 7, Federal troops had effectively cleared the upper Mississippi of Confederate strongholds as far south as Fort Pillow, Tennessee. *Official Records (Army)*, Series I, VIII, 78; Boatner, *Civil War Dictionary*, 587-588, 756.

[56] An archaic verb meaning to boast or brag excessively.

[57] Rosinante, Don Quixote's horse in the novel of the same name, represented excellence and honor. Benét, *Reader's Encyclopedia*, 948.

[58] Alexander Boyd Andrews (1841-1915) was lieutenant and later captain of Co. B, Ninth North Carolina (First Cavalry) Regiment until he was wounded and disabled on September 22, 1863. After the war he

gave a terrible & heart rending account of the state of the country in Va outside our lines now given up to the enemy by the contraction of our line of defence. Loyal to the South to the hearts core, wealthy & independant heretofore, they are left to the tender mercies of the enemy. A terrible fate, but a day of retribution will come, a day when we shall enjoy our own again & the cruel oppressors driven back to their homes again & we once more free!

Came a letter by mail from Gen Anderson enclosing one from Gen French, in which he says, "If Lieut Col Edmondston will report to him he thinks he can assign him to duty." Weighed the pro's & cons as to whether under the appointment to Raise a Bat he could do so with propriety & concluded finally that it was best to go to Head Quarters, to the Sec of War, & get him to order him to Gen French. So putting my wardrobe into Vinyard's hands & her master's into Fanny's & revising their labour closely, in half an hour we were ready. Who will say we are not light Cavalry, for tea was over before we even discussed the point & we are off to Richmond by sunrise tomorrow.

Riding out of Father's yard I saw a *Rose*!—the first of the season, in bloom, so I went back and announced its advent to Mama & she kindly came out & gathered it for me. Bright little visitant! I accept you as an augery of happier days to come!

APRIL 8, 1862

At home once more, for which thank God! Got to Richmond safe & without adventure on the evening of the 4th, the trains crowded with soldiers returning from furlough, rough and weather beaten indeed they look, & I am sorry to say, tho' coming *from* home, *dirty*. Just from Camp, one readily excuses it, but going in so dirty does not raise ones ideas of their refinement.

On Sat the 5th Mr E took me first to Mr Le Febvre's to see Rachel & leaving me there went about his military business. Took R with me to the Hotel & thence for a walk in Main St. where I could find nothing of the very few things I wanted. "The best we can do," "none in town," "just out," were the answers I got to all my queries—. Letter paper—ordinary—a dollar a quire, $9 by the ream. Such is the success of the Blockade that it will go far to teach us economy & self denial!

Mr E joined us before dinner—had had good success with the Sec. The N C troops will be accredited to the State. Has received authority to contract for any arms or equipments he wishes, is allowed to name his own place of rendezvous & empowered to muster in the troops himself & received what he did not expect, the first instalment of his pay as Lieut Col, $236—a happy augury!

---

became a railroad promoter and was first vice-president of Southern Railway from 1894 until 1915. Clark, *Histories of the North Carolina Regiments*, I, 445-446; Manarin and Jordan, *North Carolina Troops*, II, 19, 44; Ashe, *Biographical History*, I, 46-57.

The City filled with the most exciting rumours of an advance in the Peninsula, the enemy threatening Yorktown. Reinforcements ordered from Gordonsville. Ah, Magruder! how much depends on you? God grant you a clear head, a calm judgement & a sound body.

Knots of people were collected throughout the streets & crowds at the Telegraph & Newspaper offices. On Sunday, the 6th, went to the Monumental Church & heard Cousin Woodbridge.[59] It was in this Church that Bishop, now Gen., Polk commenced his ministerial career. He was pastor of this church when he married Aunt Fanny. Who could have predicted his career? When they saw him a young soldier of the Cross donning the surplice for the first time, who could have foreseen that he would one day rise so high in the ranks of earthly warriors? We stayed to Communion. It is long since Patrick & I partook of it together & it may be longer before we join in it again!

Just before us sat Mr Edward Barnwell,[60] who was the President of the S C College when Patrick was a student there (idle & wild he says but I do not beleive him; his was never a wasted youth—the fruit is too abundant now). It seems strange that they should meet thus at the Table of their Lord in a strange city & join in so solemn a feast in such exciting times, drums beating, the heavy tramp of passing troops filling the air, for owing to a collision on the R R the reinforcements had been detained—some killed & many wounded & ten thousand men were actually on their passage through the streets of the city.

We met an Alabama Regt as we came out of Church, travel stained & war worn indeed they looked, and as I gazed on their resolute determined air & thought of the aching hearts in their distant Southern homes & of the change that another Sunday might see in them, on the eve as they are of a great battle, my heart melted within me, & with Lord Falkland I could only ingeminate the word Peace! Peace!

Walked in the afternoon past the President's house in hopes of seeing him but in that was disappointed, he having gone on an errand of mercy to the poor soldiers wounded in last night's collision. We saw at a distance, however, the Presidential baby! & verily beleive if it had had a respectable black "Maumer," as the child of a Southern President ought to have, I should have called her, kissed the baby & made her a present for its father's sake; but the white Nurse over awed & restrained me. God help and keep our President! Give Wisdom to his councils, victory to his arms, and unity to his government.

---

[59] George Woodbridge was the rector of Monumental Church in Richmond. William B. Sprague, *Annals of the American Pulpit* (New York: Arno Press & the New York Times, 5 volumes, 1969; originally published 1861), 370.

[60] Robert Woodward Barnwell (1801-1882) was the president of South Carolina College (now the state university) from 1835 until 1841. He was a member of the South Carolina legislature in 1826, a member of Congress from 1829 until 1833, the successor of Calhoun in the Senate in 1850, a delegate to the Confederate Congress in Montgomery in 1861, and a Confederate senator. *Dictionary of American Biography*, I, 640-641.

Went to bed early quite unwell, having taken a sudden & severe cold. It does seem to be my fate to get sick at Hotels! I hate them!

Woke up on Monday suffering severely, headache & fever, with pain in all my limbs. Poor Rachel had a dull day of it. Patrick was busy & I too unwell to talk much. In the afternoon Mr E took her out & had her ambrotype & his Photograph taken for me. I was sorry I was too unwell to have mine taken for him as I had promised.

When he came here he brought news of the Victory at Corinth fought on Sunday the 6th. A dear bought victory—be the result what it will—for it has cost us Gen A S Johnston, the ablest and best general we have. He was wounded whilst gallantly leading his men to a charge with a Minie Ball which cut an artery in his thigh. He said nothing of it for fear of dispiriting his men, but after the charge retired to the rear & was taken dying from his horse, having literally bled to death! His life might have been saved had he stopped sooner. I wonder what family he leaves. God be with his wife, if he has one. He was just sixty years old, & died in the height of his usefulness, in the maturity of his judgement, before age had dulled his brain, rich with the stores of experience. Beauregard succeeds him in command. Be Thou his Shield and Buckler, O Lord!

Tossed all night on the hard bed with a high fever & heard the heavy measured tramp of troops at intervals as they marched from Depot to Steamboat on their way to the Peninsula. As each successive detachment would arrive & they heard the news from Corinth, their shouts of triumph filled the still air. Grant O! Lord that we may soon have another & more glorious victory to commemorate.

Found it hard work getting up sick, sore & feverish, to take the train before four o clock in the morning. Patrick urged that it was imprudent in me to leave in such a state, especially as it rained heavily, but the goal—home—was too tempting to be resisted, & if I am to be sick let it never be in a Hotel again. So I over persuaded him & we started. Truly a wretched morning. Such a getting & showing of passports, both in Richmond & Petersburg; such a passing between sentinels with crossed Muskets looked like any thing but a free country, but both cities are under Martial Law.

At Petersburg we came upon the gentleman who had amused me so at table with his baldhead which looked as tho it had just received a coat of Zinc paint! & the pompous air with which he surveyed every thing. He proved to be a Dr West, a New Yorker, now in the confederate Service. He had married in N C, so Hon Mr Bridgers[61] told us.

----

[61] Mrs. Edmondston was evidently referring to Robert R. Bridgers (1819-1888) of Edgecombe County. Bridgers was a lawyer, state legislator (1844, 1858-1861), and a member of the Confederate Congress (1861-1865). He was also prominent in educational and agricultural development in his county and was president of the Wilmington and Weldon Railroad after the Civil War. Ashe, *Biographical History*, I, 171-180.

Passed on the Road between Petersburg & Weldon five long trains loaded with soldiers and their equipage on their way to the Peninsula. Cobb Legion (Georgian) was on one, a full Battery on another, and a sixth was loaded with what may be called the sinews of War, viz, "provisions." The men on the open cars were most picturesquely huddled, some in groups, some singly, under any temporary shelter they could rig up, the corner of a tent, the body of a baggáge waggon, whilst their baggage in its diversity & arrangement was really artistic. Cooking utensils, camp furniture, trunks, muskets, stools, waggons, cannon, tents, caissons, beds, blankets, and wheels and men thrown together at random would have delighted the heart of a Wilkie.[62] Very anxious were they for news & eagerly held out their hands for the morning papers which we brought from Richmond.

Got home safely but in the rain & found a cold welcome, for Madame Dolly, not thinking we were coming, tho Owen had gone for us, had the key of the house in her pocket some where off in the New Grounds. We got a fire in the kitchen & before she got home, being fairly warmed and wholly grateful for being at home, she did not get the amout of "blowing up" she deserved. Got a hasty dinner & O how I relished *my own tea.*

After Patrick went out I fell into a train of thought suggested by Gen A S Johnston's noble letter[63] to the President which had been published in the morning papers giving the reasons of his falling back from Nashville & explaining to the satisfaction of every one the neccessity of the step & the noble motive which had enabled him to bear the censure & obloquy unsparingly heaped upon him—a splendid vindication & which I paste in the end of my book to preserve it (Mark A). Patrick had been expressing his admiration of him & the regret he felt for ever having even blamed him in thought, tho he never joined in the out cry against him, in the carriage as we came down; so, as I felt in the humour, I wrote a few lines which I think worth keeping.

Lines on the Death of Gen A S Johnston
Respectfully Inscribed
To
President Davis
by a Lady

Mourn in the midst of triumph! mourn for the slandered
    dead!
Mourn for the heart ye thoughtless broke! the shaft
    ye thoughtless sped!
Ye called him laggard. Read on Corinth's bloody field
The calm stern answer which his blood hath sealed!

---

[62]Sir David Wilkie (1785-1841) was a prolific and successful Scottish genre and portrait painter. *Dictionary of National Biography*, LXI, 253-258.

[63]This letter, dated March 18, 1862, was clipped from a newspaper and pasted on the verso of the last leaf in the first volume of the diary. The letter also appears in *Official Records (Army)*, Series I, VII, 258-261.

Think ye that rankling stab his brethren gave,
His ingrate brethren whom he died to save,
More bitter was than Death—more cruel than the
Grave!
Yes! Yes! "without an argument" indeed ye speechless
stand!
Ye thoughtless host whose hero must by fav'ring breeze
be fanned!

Apply your own base test "success"; see Shiloh's serried
ranks!
From Mississippi to the sea list to a nation's thanks!
See how from edge of Southern steel the Northern squad-
ron's fly.
See how on edge of Southern steel the base invaders die!
Swift thro the plains of Tennessee they sweep in hideous
wrack!
The avenging Southron thundering close, close on their
glory track!

Yet one there was who knew him! One who could read
aright
That warrior head, that patriot heart, that faith,
that diamond bright!
His friend the generous Davis; he who our helm of State
Grasped firmly with a giant's hand throughout our
darkest fate.
His is the clarion voice which flings defiance to
our foes!
He the calm centre whence our hopes, our fate, our
future flows.

He never wavered, never swerved, that friendship yields
to none.
"No general have I, if indeed great Johnston be not
one."
True to its friendship! to itself how true! Ah!
now that noble heart
Mourns in the misjudged Patriot its own bright
counterpart!
He mourns his General, mourns his friend, whilst on
the hero's bier
Amidst the hymns of victory falls a nation's
grateful tear.

I was never before under the rule of Martial Law & but for the armed guard, the sentinels at the Depot, and the demand for passports, I should not have known the difference between it & civil law; but I was assured that had I been there a few weeks ago I should have most gratefully recognised it, for then it was unsafe for a Lady to go out alone, the streets were so much crowded with drunken insolent soldiers. Now, tho' there was no lack of them, it would be impossible to find a better behaved or more orderly set any where. They say that "Uniforms" have greatly diminished in the streets of Richmond latterly but it is difficult to realize it, such a numbers are left.

Found vegetation coming out finely. The few days of our absence had made a great difference in it. Asparagus begining to shoot, Red Bud in blossom, Peach trees still looking splendidly & promising an abundant Harvest, corn & Irish Potatoes coming up, and every thing grown as tho there was no war to depress us. Who would not be a vegetable? No care. Ah! yes but we would have periodical enemies of our own—snails, worms, Guerilla like Sparrows, & worse than all, "Cooks." War is to us an occasion evil, but "Cooks" are to them a perpetual foe!

APRIL 10, 1862

This morning Mr E went to Hascosea preparatory for leaving the afternoon for Wilmington, but "L'homme propose[.]" He came back chilly & creepy & in a short time, to use his own words, his head was as hot as the Crater of Vesuvious and his back like an Iceberg in the open sea! So instead of leaving home he is at this moment quietly in bed with a schorching fever. I have been quite unwell with fever & sore throat since my return home so there is now a pair of us invalids.

The mail tonight brought news that Grant had been reinforced by Buel after the battle of Shiloh. On Monday Buel & Grant on one side, Beauregard on the other, fought desperately for seven hours, when both parties simultaneous fell back, a drawn battle, after terrible slaughter. This, to us, untimely reinforcement deprived us of the full fruits of our victory on Sunday, the day before, as we could not bring off all the guns then captured. We however burnt their tents & camp equipage & tho we were forced to abandon large quantities for the want of transportation, we brought off large quantities of small arms, & our men generally exchanged their inferior for the enemies superior muskets & long range Rifles. Indeed had it not been for the dispersion of our men, bent on plunder & ransacking the Yankee stores, we would have given a better account of ourselves even than we did on Monday, badly as we worsted them. Even as it was, the slaughter was tremendus—more on their side than on ours—& yet with true Yankee effrontery they have thanked the army & ordered a national Thanksgiving for the magnificent Victory gained by them on Sunday & Monday, the 6th and 7th of April, when the truth is we beat them on Sunday & had a drawn battle on Monday! We slept in their tents on Sunday night & had not Buel come up their army would have been annihilated!

April 11, 1862

All night both of us quite sick & unable to sleep, I coughing most distressingly the whole time. I must have annoyed Patrick greatly, but no sound of impatience did he utter. This morning as we lay in bed discussing our ability to get up, we looked so ludicrously like the "sick parents" in the pictures in the "Babes in the Wood"[64] that it gave me a hearty laugh! The children only were wanting to complete the resemblance. We have managed to creep about all day, each of us too sick to do more than comfort the other.

Father came down & cheered us up. He gave us an account of his trip to Raleigh where he had been to take Susan to the Communion. In the afternoon came Susan herself. She had been mistaken in the day for the communion & was consequently disappointed. From what different Standpoints do we view each the other's conduct. Father & Mama look upon Susan's trip to Raleigh as an evidence of deep christian piety, earnest self abnegation; I am afraid that the selfishness shown in being willing to leave her mother alone for so many days at such a time as this & taking father [on] a journey manifestly to his great reluctance strikes our minds with more force than aught else. Poor Mama, I was really sorry for her. She seemed to dread their going, so uneasy for them & for herself & to father his repugnance to the journey was most evident, but neither of them seemed to think of themselves at all in the matter.

For the first time since we have been keeping house there was no table set, on account of the sickness of both of us. Mr E had his bowl of chicken water on one side & I my cup of tea on the other side of the fire, & that was our dinner. The Mail brought news of the Bombardment of Fort Pulaski. I suppose its fall is a question only of time!

Had the Sweet Potatoes bedded in the afternoon. Copied my lines on the death of Gen A S Johnston & with Patrick's consent sent them to the President. I wrote a letter with them which, however, Patrick thought unnecessary, so with a sigh I relinquished it. Ah! Mrs Edmondston, I fear me you are a vain woman & have a hankering after dignities, for even tho' your name was not to be sighned to the letter, you wished to write to the President! Well, to gratify you, I will allow you to copy the letter here & tho the President's eyes will never rest upon it, your own shall & you may have the fond conceit that once you wrote to President Davis, even tho the letter was never sent.

To President Davis—
> Sir
>
> I offer no apology for the sentiment of earnest & affectionate sympathy which prompts the enclosed lines. I send them to you simply because I think

---

[64]"Babes in the Wood" is an old English ballad and nursery tale. Benet, *Reader's Encyclopedia*, 62.

they will give you pleasure. Perhaps it would have been better to have sent them through the public prints, but never having filled, and having no ambition ever to fill the "Poet's corner," I prefer a direct address to yourself. As this is the first letter I have ever written to one in so exalted a station, so it is the first which has ever left my hand without a signature; but being like most country people troubled with a peculiarly terrible "Mrs Grundy"[65] (tho Mr Yancy[66] I see dignifies the feeling as "Southern individuality," still an old enemy under a new name is none the less formidable) & as my "Mrs Grundy" has no idea that I ever even write a line of poetry and still less that I have the boldness to send it to the President, so I simply subscribe myself,

A Lady.

There! Now Mrs Edmondston I hope you feel better, but, Madam, let me tell you that those lines which you took such pleasure in sending will hardly reach your hero'[s] eyes. The letter will be opened by a Clerk, fancy it, who when he sees poetry, "faugh! trash!" pop they go into the waste paper basket! Come try the homopathic plan! Cure vanity with vanity. Do you think yourself the boldest & silliest woman in the Confederacy? "Certainly not!"—that is you think yourself a sensible woman? Well if a "sensible woman" like you intrudes herself thus on the President, what do you *think the fools do*? I warrant scarcly a mail passes but that some woman sends something to him, so what can the poor clerk do but fill the waste paper basket with their lucubrations? Are you sorry now that you asked your husband to let you send them? No? Then you are not so wise as I thought you were! It would serve you just right to see them attributed to some one else, tho you will be spared that for you will never hear of them more!

APRIL 12, 1862

Quite sick all day. Patrick better but still not in a state to travel, so we stayed at home instead of going up to fathers as we had proposed, especially as the river is "up" & we should be forced to go in a Canoe. I have not been so sick in a long time as I have been these past three days.

Tonight's mail, brought news that the Virginia had been "*out*" again but found no enemy, the ships all retreating under the guns of Fortress Monroe, the Monitor amongst the number, which is a clear admission of defeat & that too before the eyes of the French & English Men of War lying in the Roads!

---

[65] Mrs. Grundy, a character in Thomas Morton's play *Speed the Plough* (1798), became synonymous with conventional propriety and morality. Benét, *Reader's Encyclopedia*, 463.

[66] William Lowndes Yancey (1814-1863), newspaper editor, lawyer, and politician, served as a representative from Alabama in the United States Congress (1844-1846), as a delegate to the Alabama secession convention, and in the Confederate Senate (1862-1863). He was also the Confederate commissioner to England and France from 1861 until 1862. *Biographical Directory of Congress*, 1855; *Dictionary of American Biography*, XX, 592-595.

She captured, under the eyes & guns of the Monitor, two brigs loaded with hay, an empty Schooner & 13 men, she calmly allowing it.

An article from the English papers is scathing in the contrast drawn between the North & the South, as regards *veracity*; says that both are pure Democracies but governed the one by the *tail*, the other by the head. The Northern Government can *lie* with impunity, the Southern cannot, for the intelligence & integrity of the gentlemen who compose it would instantly detect & expose it.

The Bombardment of Fort Pulaski goes on. No result as yet, tho it must fall. The Bombardment of Island No 10 has been kept up for more than a fortnight with the loss to us of only one man. The Bombardment is terrific & constant. We have sunk one Gunboat, disabled one, & silenced one Battery. I see the withdrawal of the commander & his farewell to his command. What it means we cannot imagine, as he seems to have done well. Pray God that this change of commanders under the fire of an enemy may not result in disaster.

Heavy frost this morning & one also yesterday. I hope the fruit will escape but I fear me.

Patrick gave me a conundrum—"What is that which down faces you always without ever once offending you?" I gave it up. "*A Clock!*" Then encouraged he went on with "What servant is least of an eye servant?" I guessed a "*watch*" & then gave him—"What servant is the greatest of all eye servants?" This posed him and I had to tell him—"A pair of Spectacles!" None of these, however, are as good as his—"What is the difference between a Newberne fight & a Newberne flight?" "An l-(ell) of a difference!"

Heard that the Yankees had landed near Elizabeth City & captured some Militia stationed there, so that it would appear that Burnside is coming back this way again. Both better tonight. "With sweet sleep our eyelids close."

APRIL 13, 1862

Sunday. Patrick had all the children on the plantation up & vaccinated them—26 in all. The mingled look of terror & curiosity with which they regard the operation before their turns come, & the intense & eager interest with which they examine their arms after it is over, is most ludicrous. There they stand, their arms extended like St Simon Stylites,[67] wondering what it is all about & why it hurts no more; but the Sugar afterwards ends all speculation & heals all wounds, either of flesh or spirit.

Came to Fathers partly in his carriage, partly in a canoe. This water is a sad draw back to us. I am by no means well tho Patrick is better.

Heard of the Surrender of Fort Pulaski one day before the anniversary of the fall of Sumter! How much has happened since then! The walls were

---

[67] Simeon Stylites belonged to a medieval ascetic group, prevalent in Syria and Palestine, known as the Pillar Saints. These ascetics practiced their faith from the fifth century to the twelfth by living on the summits of pinnacles or natural stone pillars to receive redemption. Benét, *Reader's Encyclopedia*, 1080.

breached through & through & the whole interior of the Fort commanded. Four shot in the magazine! We knew they had not ammunition sufficient to defend it long but hoped for better than this. The wounded only are to be delivered under a flag of truce, otherwise the surrender is unconditional!

APRIL 14, 1862

Patrick left for Wilmington leaving me at Father's. He goes to see Gen French & tell him that the Sec thinks he cannot report to him for duty consistently with the raising this Battalion which he was appointed to do & to see something about his companies there. I quite sick all day. What weak helpless creatures we are! Here am I sighing, unsettled, unable to do any thing, scarcly to think after a few days indisposition. What would it be were I to have a severe fit of illness? God grant that to a death bed sickness may not be added a death bed remorse.

A note from Patrick tells me that on his way to Halifax he heard of the death of Mr Elias Hines,[68] Peggie Norfleets husband. He died last night at Mr W R Smith's. Poor thing! Poor thing! Would that I could go & see her & give her at least my sympathy, but this I am unable to do. I have not seen her since her marriage, now four years since. The force of circumstances has kept us apart, but I have thought often of her. She has two children whom I have never seen, I who was so fond of her. Poor thing! How desolate she must be! A widow & homeless! God help her!

APRIL 15, 1862

Father gone to Mr Hines funeral. I unable to go. Poor Peggie! I can think of naught but her & her sorrows!

Reading one of Robertson's Sermons today, came to a fine comparison speaking of the Roman Empire:

"The Roman Empire crumbled into fragments; but every fragment was found pregnant with life. It broke, not as some ancient temple might break; its broken peices lying in lifeless ruin overgrown with weeds; rather as one of those mysterious animals break—of which if you rend them assunder—every separate portion forms itself into a new and complete existence. Rome gave way, but every portion became a Christian Kingdom—alive with the mind of Christ & developing the Christian idea after its own peculiar nature"!

That is fine—what happiness to be able to write thus!

Congress has passed a vote of thanks to the women of the South—"for their ardent & cheerful patriotism"; and well do they deserve, for they have indeed

---

[68] Elias Carr Hines of Edenton married Margaret A. Norfleet of Bertie County on January 19, 1859. He served in Co. M, First North Carolina (Bethel) Regiment and died of disease on March 23, 1862. *Raleigh Register*, February 2, 1859; Manarin and Jordan, *North Carolina Troops*, III, 63.

done nobly & upheld the hands & strengthened the hearts of the soldiers.[69] A Yankee account of some of their letters captured by them expresses the greatest surprise that throughout the whole number written, too, by all classes & degrees of women there is not the slightest approach to repining or even a desire for their friends return. It is all, "Fight John—let me hear of you in the front ranks." Such a people he fears are unconquerable, & well he may fear it!

Beauregard's call for Plantation Bells to be cast into canon is most cheerfully responded to by every one. Church bells are freely & gladly tendered by the congregations throughout the land. Preserving Kettles are joyfully given to the government to make into Caps & all the old copper is eargly sought after & rumaged out by the housewifes all over the country. One little child asked plaintively as she saw the Preserving Kettle going, "but what shall we do for preserves?" "My child," said the father, "we think now only of preserving our country." When she at once assented, I wonder what her idea of a "Preserved Country" is? Some thing like Rachels about "Washington's being the 'father' of his; I reckon he laid an egg." I warrant she thinks it a large peach! Father's & our Bells have gone & henceforth the negroes must return to the primitive "Horn"—more musical and more poetic, by the way, so I shall not regret it.

Heard a rumour of the fall of Island No 10. Pray God it be not so. The Northern accounts admit a loss of 23,000 men killed, wounded, & prisoners and 100 cannon, some of which they regained at Shiloh.

Yesterday passed both Houses of Congress the Conscription Bill, giving the President controul of all the men between 18 & 35 in the Confederacy, in fact considering them in the Army. Father thinks we shall see trouble from it, it conflicting with the State sovreignties, in fact unconstitutional.[70] I wonder what effect it will have on Mr E's Battalion, for it is thought that it will put a stop to Volunteering and all change of service for men now in the field; &

---

[69] A newspaper clipping containing this item was pasted on the last page of the first volume of the diary. The text of the resolution, adopted April 11, 1862, may also be found in James D. Richardson, *A Compilation of the Messages and Papers of the Confederacy* (Nashville: United States Publishing Company, 2 volumes, 1905), I, 230-231.

[70] The Confederate conscription act of April 16, 1862, and subsequent conscription acts providing for the enrollment of all able-bodied white males between the ages of eighteen and thirty-five (later extended to seventeen and fifty), were extremely unpopular in North Carolina. Some of the state's ablest lawyers, including Chief Justice Richmond Pearson, considered the conscript acts unconstitutional. The conscription debate precipitated a long controversy between Governor Vance and the Confederate authorities in Richmond. R. D. W. Connor, *North Carolina: Rebuilding an Ancient Commonwealth* (Chicago and New York: American Historical Society, 4 volumes, 1929), II, 188-192; J. G. de Roulhac Hamilton, "The North Carolina Courts and the Confederacy," *North Carolina Historical Review*, IV (October, 1927), 366-372. See also Memory F. Mitchell, *Legal Aspects of Conscription and Exemption in North Carolina, 1861-1865* (Chapel Hill: University of North Carolina Press [James Sprunt Studies in History and Political Science, Vol. 47], 1965).

three of his companies, four in fact, are enlisted men, but as they were re-enlisted under the direct authority of the Sec of War he ought to make an exception. Or he will be an "Indian giver." What a term of reproach that used to be to our youthful minds!

April 17, 1862

A letter from Patrick—God bless him! He is not well, has not yet seen Gen French, so does not know whether or not he will assign him the Co's about Wilmington, is despondant about the Conscript Law.

Count Mercier, the French Minister to the Dis U S, has arrived in Richmond. Expectation is on tip toe as to his errand. Some think it means Recognition, others Mediation & others again "Tobacco."[71] At any rate he can tell his government that he finds a *determined* people who will *die* rather than live conquered! The Yankees claim a Victory at Shiloh, & Lincoln has ordered a general Thanksgiving! We know what that means well enough. The regular Steamer sails for Europe before it can be contradicted. Buel is reported mortally wounded, Halleck ordered to Corinth. All eyes and hopes bent on the Peninsula. They cannot long be without a battle, indeed the 'Examiner'[72] thinks *today* is the eventful one. McClellan in command.

Copied circulars for Patrick & wrote the gentleman himself & sent copies of his letters. So now for bed. I get "no better" fast. I verily beleive I have "Broken Bone Fever."[73] Ah! for Patrick & home.

April 18, 1862

No news worth recording. Two great armies face each other on the Peninsula. An instant may bring on the conflict, but as both armies have taken to the "Spade" it may be postponed for weeks. Terrible it will be, however, when it does come. God grant us the Victory!

A letter from Mr E. Has seen Gen French who, tho anxious to do so, thinks that under the Appointment he holds from the Department he has no right to assign him to the command of the Co's in and about Wilmington. I was not

---

[71] Mercier made an offer of mediation on February 3, 1863, to the authorities in Washington urging the necessity of Federal and Confederate authorities meeting on neutral ground to discuss peace terms. The United States government quickly rejected any form of mediation initiated by a foreign power, however, insisting that any such conference implicitly recognized the legitimacy of the Confederacy and that foreign interference such as Mercier's only served to prolong Confederate hopes of eventual recognition by foreign governments. The mission is dealt with at some length in Ephraim D. Adams, *Great Britain and the American Civil War* (New York: Longmans, Green and Company, 2 volumes, 1925), I, 279-300, hereinafter cited as Adams, *Great Britain and the American Civil War*. See also Randall and Donald, *Civil War and Reconstruction*, 509.

[72] The *Daily Richmond Examiner*, edited by Edward Alfred Pollard (1831-1872), was a "caustic critic and bitter enemy" of President Davis. Pollard believed that Davis was incapable of leading the Confederacy to victory or to a stable government. *Dictionary of American Biography*, XV, 47-48.

[73] Breakbone fever or dengue, a tropical epidemic disease, is attended with eruptions and severe pains.

anxious for it, for they are ill drilled & worse disciplined and are in the very face of the enemy. I prefer his having troops of his own, who will not have so much to *unlearn* & who know & have been drilled by himself in person. I know not the effect of the Conscript Law on the Bat, but if the Sec should refuse to transfer the troops I fear will put an end to it.

The enemy are said to be steadily advancing on Wilmington. Their pickets are within 20 miles of it. A skirmish below in which Lt Col Robinson[74] of the 2d Cavalry is reported killed.

Went to Hascosea, Sue with me. I fear I was but a dull companion. My cold depresses me & makes it difficult for me to talk. Gave her some old papers to amuse herself with whilst I directed the gardening. Planted Ochra, Muskmelon, Corn, 2d crop squashes of kinds, Beans of kinds—Lima & Snap, Tomatoes, Thyme, Pepper, Lettuce, Rice, Corn, Black Hamburg Grapes given me last summer by Amo, Celery & mustard & marked places for Dahlias & water melons.

Sec Stanton,[75] in his orders thanking the troops for their Victory at Shiloh—save the mark—mixes up Pea Ridge & Island No 10 in such a manner that plain people cannot but suppose all three are triumphs; now we know Pea Ridge was a drawn battle, Shiloh a defeat, tho partially retrieved the next day, & as to Island No 10 we are yet in the dark. The last accounts represent a furious canonading but without result. What are we to think of a Government which is forced to bolster itself up thus? I think that the whole Dis United States ought to be invited out to dine & be seated before innumerable boiled tongues & solemnly told as children, poor things, often are, "This is a tongue which never told a Lie." I remember once retorting, my pride resenting the insinuation, & saying, "No, & it never told the Truth either!" & being called by the powers that were—"Very Pert!" So perhaps I ought not to wish others to be led into the same temptation that I yeilded to!

My cold *intense* & my cough incessant.

APRIL 19, 1862

Heard today that Mr Turner was wounded in the skirmish near Gilletts (in which Lt Col Robinson was reported killed, but he was not, only wounded

---

[74] Lt. Col. William G. Robinson of the Nineteenth North Carolina (Second Cavalry) Regiment was captured in the skirmish at Gillett's Farm in Jones County, April 13, 1862, by Baron Egloffstein, colonel of the Seward Infantry, One Hundred and Third Regiment New York State Volunteers. *Official Records (Army)*, Series I, IX, 297-298; Clark, *Histories of the North Carolina Regiments*, II, 82; Manarin and Jordan, *North Carolina Troops*, II, 104.

[75] Edwin McMasters Stanton (1814-1869), an able lawyer and attorney general of the United States under Buchanan in 1860, served as United States secretary of war from 1862 until 1868. He extended the thanks of his department "to Generals Curtis and Sigel, and the officers and soldiers of their commands, for matchless gallantry at the bloody battle of Pea Ridge; and Major Generals Grant and Buell, and their forces, for the glorious repulse at Pittsburg [Landing], Tennessee; to Major General Pope, his officers and soldiers, for the bravery and skill manifested against the rebels and traitors intrenched at Island No. 10. . . ." *Official Records (Army)*, Series I, X, 381; *Dictionary of American Biography*, XVII, 517-521.

and taken prisoner) severely, but not dangerously, in the head by a Minie ball. Poor Sophia, what must she suffer. His men brought him off & Lt Graham,[76] his 1st Lieut, writes Sophia to say that he will be at home on Thursday, the day Dr Hooker's letter was written. Poor Sophia, my heart bleeds for her.

An attack has commenced on the Forts below N Orleans—Jackson & St Philip.[77] The bombardment is furious, as yet harmless to us. We fear that Island No 10 is taken but we have only Northern accounts & they have not taken my advice as regards a diet on innocent guiltless of lies. A skirmish in the Peninsula. The enemy forded Warwick Creek and attacked our men but were repulsed with heavy loss. The [Fifteenth] N C bore the brunt of the battle & conducted themselves well, losing their Col McKinney.[78] We killed two entire Companies of their men, four only escaping.

Fort Macon is attacked. It must soon fall. Cut off as they are, the want of ammunition alone will soon force it to surrender, even if not breached as was Pulaski.

A letter from Capt Ward[79] Mr E's future Major, now in front of the enemy in Onslow, says that a marauding party swept through their county last week stealing what they wanted & arresting & taking off in Irons several of the most prominent men. They actually went so far as to whip two & paddle one, their offence being that they had hired free negroes to work for them. The vile hypocrites! To pretend to be so shocked at the whipping of a negro & yet to inflict it on a free man! My blood boils as I write it!

Sue read me a letter from her friend Miss Seabrook of S C. She has been driven from her home in Edisto by the Yankees & is a refugee in Yorkville, where the College[80] is crowded with unfortunates in the same sad situation.

---

[76] First Lt. William A. Graham, Jr., of Orange County, was a member of Co. K, Nineteenth North Carolina (Second Cavalry) Regiment. He later resigned his commission to become assistant adjutant general for the state of North Carolina. Clark, *Histories of the North Carolina Regiments*, II, 89; Manarin and Jordan, *North Carolina Troops*, II, 170; Hamilton and Williams, *Graham Papers*, VI, 11n-12n.

[77] Forts Jackson and St. Philip, the former on the west bank and the latter on the east bank of the Mississippi River 75 miles below New Orleans, guarded the approach to New Orleans and other cities along the river. Johnson and Buel, *Battles and Leaders*, Volume II: *North to Antietam*, 22, 25, 30, 71-73, hereinafter cited as Johnson and Buel, *Battles and Leaders*, II.

[78] Col. Robert M. McKinney of the Fifteenth North Carolina Regiment, former commandant and a professor of tactics at the North Carolina Military Institute in Charlotte, was killed at Lee's Farm near Yorktown, Virginia, on April 16, 1862. Hill, *Bethel to Sharpsburg*, II, 15; Clark, *Histories of the North Carolina Regiments*, I, 295; Manarin and Jordan, *North Carolina Troops*, IV, 270; V, 494-495, 502.

[79] The reference was probably to Capt. Edward W. Ward of Onslow County, who was a member of Co. B, Forty-first North Carolina (Third Cavalry) Regiment. Captain Ward and his company were active in the defense of eastern North Carolina during the spring of 1862. Ward resigned his position in November, 1863, because of ill health. Manarin and Jordan, *North Carolina Troops*, II, 190.

[80] The Yorkville Female College in Yorkville, South Carolina, originally called the Bethel Female Institute, was opened in 1853 by the Presbyterian church. It prospered until the Civil War when the school was closed and the college buildings were rented to refugees from the Low Country. After the war the school struggled to reopen, but debts forced it into bankruptcy in 1875. Frank D. Jones and William H.

She describes the theiving carried on by wholesale which almost passes beleif. Her Uncle, Dr Seabrook, stood on the beach at North Edisto & saw the contents of a stranded vessel, bound North, wash on shore—furniture marked with his brother's name, his own books, a most valuable library which he being unable to remove thought he had concealed, & other things which he recognized as the property of his neighbors & friends!

She describes the delightful residences the Yankees now occupy, the early fruit, strawberries, etc. they enjoy &, contrasting it with the situation of the rightful owners, hints a wish that it may make *them* sick. I more than hint it, I ardently desire it. For I am not so Christian like as Mrs McPheeters,[81] good lady, who when she heard a rumour of Gen Lyons death (he had persecuted her children terribly in St Louis) half expressed a hope that it was true, but checking herself, said, "But no! It is not right to wish any human being's death." But suddenly, nature asserting her rights & her mother's feelings getting the better of her, she exclaimed "Well, yes! I will be wicked for once. I do wish it may be true. I hope he is dead."

I fear I am wicked all the time, for besides confusion & ruin, I wish to punish them well for daring to come & invade our land. They occupy the river opposite Fredericksburg in force, owing to the falling back of our troops on the Potomac. Affairs cannot long stand as they are in the Peninsula; something must soon be done.

No letter from Patrick. I fear he is doomed to disappointment about his Battalion, but I hope for the best & yet why should I hope. If the conscrip law gives troops enough to the country, why not let him stay at home & grow food for those who fight? At any rate I wish him to do something for the Cause— something for our country in this hour of her need. God has greatly blessed us and given us a "fair land." I wish him to do *something* to show his love for that land, his gratitude to God for his past freedom by his determination not tamely to give it up.

I am quite sick & were I at home I beleive I should take to my bed. So it is best perhaps to have a motive to keep me stirring. I long for home & home cares & it amuses me to see the pleasure that I take in making myself a cup of tea occasionally in the Etna I brought with me from Hascosea. I verily beleive half of it arises from the fact that it is a "household care," a sort of play

---

Mills (eds.), *History of the Presbyterian Church in South Carolina Since 1850* (Columbia: Synod of South Carolina, 1926), 358-359.

[81] Margaret Ann Curry McDaniel, from Washington in Beaufort County, was the third wife of William McPheeters, principal of the Raleigh Academy from 1810 until 1826 and pastor of the First Presbyterian Church of Raleigh. Their son, Samuel Brown McPheeters (1819-1870), was the pastor of Pine Street Presbyterian Church in St. Louis, Missouri. In 1862 he was suspended from his pulpit by military authority and threatened with banishment for alleged disloyalty to the United States. John S. Grasty, *Memoir of Rev. Samuel B. McPheeters* (St. Louis: Southwestern Book and Publishing Company, 1871), 28-29, 141-154. See also McPheeters Family Papers, State Archives.

"Housekeeping"! Ah! woman, what a curious mixture you are! Do you know yourself?" I do not beleive you do.

APRIL 21, 1862

Have just been reading the accounts of the outrages of the Yankees about Elizabeth City and am at fever heat. Their conduct to that old man & his daughter exceeds all human beleif—worse than that of Indian Sepoys, for these men call themselves "*Christians*," nay more, Gen Burnside him self has assured us of the fact! But what can we expect of the soldier of a nation who first makes medicine "*Contraband*" & then when it supposes that the stock on hand is exhausted "*poisons*" & allows it to be smuggled, mixes strychnine with Quinine & Morphine & then winks at its introduction! Can any thing be too base after that?

Skirmishing of out posts going on at Yorktown but nothing more. Island No 10 has we fear surrendered; but, from what we hear, the credit is due rather to the rise in the waters of the Mississippi than to Yankee prowess, but we have no details from our own side. New Recruits offering for the Batalion. Wrote to Patrick 2 letters, one to Yanceyville & one to Richmond.

APRIL 23, 1862

No news from Patrick since he started to Yanceyville to muster Capt Reinhart's[82] Company into his Batalion.

Mr Turner has got home. Sophia writes she fears lest he may have received an internal wound by the fall from his horse, as he has been raising blood ever since. The ball, a Minie one, was fired from above (they were attacking Gillet's house) & struck where the hair is parted & glanced around the head. The physician fears a Compound fracture of the Skull but says he will recover. Truly he had a most marvellous escape!

The Bombardment of the Forts below N Orleans goes on furiously as yet with the loss of only 5 men—tho' they have shot off 100 tons of Iron & I cannot repeat the quantity of powder. Island No 10 is doubtless evacuated, tho' we have no particulars, as the bombardment of Fort Pillow[83] below has commenced.

Count Mercier, the French Minister, has left Richmond & "made no sign" that we are permitted to see. Expectation has been on tip toe to know what

---

[82] Hannon W. Reinhardt of Caswell County was the captain of the "Caswell Rangers," Co. C, Forty-first North Carolina (Third Cavalry) Regiment. He resigned in 1864 because of poor health. Manarin and Jordan, *North Carolina Troops*, II, 198.

[83] Fort Pillow was located on the Tennessee side of the Mississippi River approximately forty miles above Memphis. Its capture figured prominently in the Federal strategy designed to split the Confederacy in half along the Mississippi River. Boatner, *Civil War Dictionary*, 752-755; *Official Records (Army)*, Series I, X, Part I, 902.

Above, left, Sophia Chester Devereux Turner, sister of Kate Edmondston; right, her husband Josiah, editor of the Raleigh *Sentinel* during the period of Reconstruction. Turner was a champion of the Conservative party and a bitter opponent of the Republicans after the Civil War, and his editorials were full of attacks on them. Sophia, addicted to morphine in the 1870s, spent her last years in the hospital for the insane in Raleigh in an effort to overcome her dependency on the drug. (Photograph of Sophia Turner courtesy of Mr. J. C. Woodall of Hillsborough and Mrs. Graham A. Barden, Jr., of New Bern.)

brought him here, but she may now stand on the flat of her foot, for she will not be gratified.

The lies told are terrible. I fear the moral sense of the nation will be injured by the reckless lies the news papers indulge in. We have but one comfort—that we do not lie like the Yankees. Burnsides official Report is out. Says he had hard fighting. Ah! that we had held out a little longer, he might have told a different tale.

Troops are concentrating at Fredericksburg. The wise ones predict that the March to Richmond will be made from that quarter now that McClellan finds that we are prepared for him in the Peninsula. Spade work still goes on there. A trench has been cut by them from River to River. The York & the James can mingle, if it be deep enough.

Lincoln has signed the Bill abolishing Slavery in the Dist[84] & allowing the testimony of negroes to be taken in Court against Whites, "a sop for

[84] Congress passed an act on April 16, 1862, emancipating slaves in the District of Columbia, paying the owners an average of $300 for each freed slave. Ashe, *History of North Carolina*, II, 751; *Dictionary of American History*, II, 204-205.

Cerberus."[85] The Abolitionist have their wedge now entered & the first fruits of it is to revolutionize Kentucky. For on the reception of his message reccommending Congress to make provision to pay for the slaves in the Border States with a view to their gradual emancipation, a Kentucky Regt mutinied, fired into & killed 200 Illinoisans—& then dispersed to their homes.

Nashville gives them more trouble than Baltimore even & they begin to talk of arresting & trying the most prominent men for *Treason*. Andy Johnson has been fired at in the streets & goes out only with an armed guard to protect his august person. They are sending their supplies to Bowling Green for safety. Would that Kentucky would rise in their rear. Who would have thought years ago when "Jesse Johnson's boys" was a name of such terror to our youthful ears that one of them would have ridden in such state. Military Gov of Tennessee and yet your Excellency I can remember when my Grand father sent his coach man to whip you home to your uncle's shanty because yourself and cousins had a fancy to run naked through the fields and along the path that ran between father's and his house. What changes we see! His father fills a felon's grave in Raleigh, whilst the son ruffles it perhaps over the children of him who allowed his Uncle "Jesse" with whom he lived to occupy a cabin on his estate. I mean Col William Polk[86]—of Revolutionary Memory, father of the Bishop and over whose descendants you now lord it! Fremont, another upstart, who has not even a felon father's grave to point to, has been ordered from Eastern Kentucky with his whole force, 20,000 men, to Corinth to reinforce Buel, Halleck or Grant, whoever is Commander, for it is hard to tell which. Johnson and Fremont—fit instruments for an upstart tryanny—to endeavor to forge fetters for the wrists of freemen!

April 25, 1862

Letter from Patrick at Yanceyville; may be at home tomorrow; has mustered Capt Reinhart's Co for "Edmondston's Batalion of Light Horse."

---

[85] In Roman mythology the three-headed dog Cerberus guarded the entrance to the underworld and was appeased by the passing dead with a cake (sop) seasoned with poppies and honey. Benét, *Reader's Encyclopedia*, 193. Mrs. Edmondston was implying that the United States government used such a sop as bribery to "quiet a troublesome customer."

[86] William Polk, native of Mecklenburg County (1758-1834), the father of Leonidas Polk, served during the Revolutionary War as a major in the Ninth North Carolina Continental Regiment, as lieutenant colonel of the Fourth South Carolina Regiment, and later as colonel of the Third South Carolina Regiment. After the Revolution he served in the North Carolina House of Commons for three terms. He moved to Raleigh in 1800. Polk helped found the North Carolina Society of the Cincinnati and supervised the collection of internal revenue in the state for seventeen years. He was an ardent champion of education in the state as well and served on the Board of Trustees of the University of North Carolina from 1792 until his death. *Roster of Soldiers from North Carolina in the American Revolution* (Baltimore: Genealogical Publishing Company, 1967), 44; Lefler and Newsome, *North Carolina*, 300; Ashe, *Biographical History*, II, 361-368; Paul H. Bergeron (ed.), "My Brother's Keeper: William H. Polk Goes to School," *North Carolina Historical Review*, XLIV (April, 1967), 190n.

He goes to Richmond to see the Sec of War, thence home. Would that I were well to welcome him.

The smoke of Battle has cleared up from the field of Corinth & seems now settled that on Monday we had a splendid Victory equal to Manassas, dimmed only by the loss of Gen A S Johnson; but the enemy during the night being reinforced by Buel snatched its fruits from the grasp of our jaded troops & retook much of their field artillery which we had captured the day before, but we burnt their tents & camp equipage, inflicting a heavy loss on them besides sleeping Sunday night in their encampment. Monday's battle was a drawn one, both sides falling back.

Island No 10 was taken by a feat of the most remarkable Engineering skill ever displayed & for which the enemy deserve the greatest credit for their energy & perseverance, being nothing less than the sawing out a passage through a swamp, capable of passing their gun boats around the Island & thus flanking & attacking it on the undefended side. They took advantage of a swamp called the "Earthquake seam," it having been the effect of a supposed Earthquake years ago & now grown up into a thick & impassable swamp. At high water their boats can readily float but trees, some of them three feet through, fill the whole space. Nothing daunted, the engineers went to work & sawed a passage three feet under water the whole distance. The branches interlock, so that it was necessary to use ladders of rope for the men to ascend them & cut off the branches which interfered with their smoke stacks. The details are so marvelous that, as our Northern brethern are given to lying, we must be excused beleiving them all. The fact that they passed is wonderful enough. Ah! that the Mississippi had fallen to its usual level suddenly & impaled their gun boats upon the snags & stumps they had just sawed off with such labour! Our men being thus out flanked, spiked their guns, sunk their gunboats, destroyed what of the provisions & ammunition they could & then all who were able made their escape. Our sick of course were forced to remain & a number who could not get over the River. The adventures of those who did escape are thrilling!

Bad news from New Orleans. Two steamers have succeeded in passing the Forts and are on their way to the city. We have some Iron boats above them however which they will have to pass. I hope they will give a good account of themselves.

The finding of the Court of Inquiry appointed to investigate the causes of the Roanoke Island disaster is that Maj Gen Huger & the late Sec of War Mr J B Benjamin are to blame for the whole affair. The situation of the defences were repeatedly represented to them by Gen Wise & Col Shaw. A deputation of gentlemen from the neighboring Counties waited on the Sec & offered to send their negroes there to complete the fortification but to no purpose. If their consciences have not already done so, the Court has now planted a thorn in their pillows for them.

The affair at South Mills in Pasquotank County grows in importance. Col Wright's Georgia Regt repulsed three Yankee ones under Gen Reno, captured their canon, & the powder they had provided to blow up the Locks of the Canal, besides killing & wounding many. Our loss slight.

April 27, 1862

Sunday. Yesterday came Patrick bringing Rachel with him from Richmond. Mr Le Febvre having every thing ready for a hasty flight in case of an advance on Richmond which is now imminent, he thought it best to bring her home. Patrick feels discouraged about his Batalion. The Sec says that those Companies re-enlisted, which were already organized before the passage of the Conscript Act, can, on proof being given & consent of the Col's commanding, be transferred to his Battalion. He hopes this is the case with three—Holmes, Huggins, and Stephens—but as the Conscript act deprives him of one month & the Sec says he has no power to give it to him, tho it is his right as shown on the face of his Commission, & there will be much to do before the 17th when the Conscript Law goes into effect, he fears he will fail. Reinharts Co is already mustered in. He has the promise of two others & the Sec held out hopes that he would fill up the Battalion with Independant Co now in the service, but he did not promise. At any rate he has worked hard & done his whole duty & his failure will be entirely owing to the Conscript Law, which human foresight could not fore see.

He brought news of the fall of New Orleans which, however, no one beleives. One of the freaks of Dame Rumour.

The enemy are concentrating troops behind the Rappahanock, whilst fresh troops are constantly thrown by them into the Peninsula. Patrick thinks that McClellan is withdrawing his old well drilled Army from the latter place & throwing it upon the Rappahanock, whilst its place is being filled with raw recruits & infers that the real battle will be fought between Fredericksburg & Richmond.

Gen Joe Johnson it is rumoured is "falling back" to the line of the Chickahominy. We always "fall back."

Walked with Patrick in the afternoon, the first time I have been out since he went away. It is wonderful how his presence brings me back to my old habits & old ways of thought—my normal state as it were. I feel more like myself than I have done for days. Like a spring, when the pressure of his absence is removed, I bound back to my original position. Ah! what a rejuvenator Happines is!

April 30, 1862

Came home on Monday afternoon in a Canoe with Patrick & Rachel. Just as we left came the mail. New Orleans had indeed fallen, fallen, and to two Gun boats! We came home deeply dejected, nay humiliated, at the news.

Lovel,[87] the General in command, is a Yankee! & one too who remained at the North until after the battle of Manassas. Whispers not loud but deep of treachery & cowardice! The last telegram was to the effect that the Forts held out well, the men in fine spirits expecting a victory. We have a fleet of Gunboats—one the Louisiana, equal to the Va. The batteries on the Lake were dismounted but the Guns not spiked & a precipitate retreat made where there was no foe. The Military, 15,000 strong, have abandoned the city & retreated thirty miles off. It is said the cotton was fired & the steamboats burnt, but why were they not sent up the River we cannot understand it. Gen Johnston's sad fate ought to give us warning against a precipitate censure; but we cannot but blame the Government & Gen Lovel, the one for placing such a man in command, the other for not being prepared & making some resistance. The loss of N O cuts off our supply of Beef from Texas, the great stay & support of our army, & thus may cripple us more than any thing else. The supply of sugar & molasses there is immense, & hitherto our men have had it in abundance. Now that will be cut off from their rations.

God help us we seem to be at the darkest now, but we will never give up. He will help. He will deliver us, if we are but true to ourselves & quit ourselves like men!

Whilst we were sitting despondantly in the dusk of the evening, discussing our state & the effect the capture of New Orleans would have on us, came (unusual sound) a knock at the door, the *Adjutant* to be of the Battalion. He cheered us up with the assurance that Commodore Hollins,[88] with whom he came down in the train, had said in his hearing that it was simply absurd! New Orleans was *not* captured—he was just from there & it was all a traiterous lie. So we went to bed much consoled but not reassured.

On Tuesday went to Hascosea & dined there. I commenced planting my Dahlia Roots but it was dull work. Patrick had gone to Clarksville about his Taxes & I so much distressed about the news from New Orleans & at sea about the Batalion that I did not feel like singing "Bring flowers to strew in the Conquerer's path!" as I did last year. One comfort we have: we may be beaten, lose all our cities, our whole seaboard even, but conquered! subjugated! never! Death first!

Patrick and Amo came to dinner. Had a merry time with the young folks, but the fall of New Orleans hung like a pall over us & in the midst of laughter, I would catch myself sighing.

---

[87] Sharp criticism of Gen. Mansfield Lovell's failure to prevent the capture of New Orleans, as well as political pressure on authorities in Richmond, resulted in his being relieved from command in December, 1862. Despite subsequent skillfully managed skirmishes against Federal forces in Mississippi, he received no further major assignments. Boatner, *Civil War Dictionary*, 494.

[88] Commo. George Nichols Hollins returned from the upper Mississippi to defend New Orleans when Farragut threatened the city in April, 1862. He left before the city was captured to serve on a court of inquiry in Richmond. Boatner, *Civil War Dictionary*, 405.

Came home in the Rain to Looking Glass where the Mail which we found awaiting us did not cheer us up. More gloomy & disgraceful accounts of the neglect of government to fortify New Orleans & of the falling back of our troops. The city has not yet surrendered & our Flag still floats. The two gun boats lay there short of men & ammunition, and Lovel has actually the face to telegraph it to the Government and leave them there in *peace*. Grant me patience!—30,000 men in & about the city tamely submitting to be held at bay by two Yankee Gun boats! Gen Bragg, it is said, has been ordered there. I hope he will be able to retreive Lovel's misconduct. I do not wish to be harsh in my censure, but I cannot help with the light before me condemning him most bitterly.

Patrick much discouraged about his Batalion, fears he will not succeed. It takes more interest to get into the army in this country than it does to get out in others, and yet we are fighting for life, for freedom.

May 2, 1862

This is sad work, this continued leaving & coming back home restless, unsatisfied. I feel as tho I held in my hands only broken threads, thwarted plans. I care not to begin anything, as I may leave home at any moment & be disappointed in finishing it. My time seems like the fragments of a broken mirror; it reflects nothing perfectly. The servants feel the same. They get out of the way of their duties, neglect, forget them. This causes me to carry a double portion of that "Jacob" Ladder by which Jean Paul says "men ascend to heaven," i.e., Household cares. I thank you Richter[89] for the word. I thank you for the perception which enabled you to see what a drag it sometimes is on woman to "lug about" the ladder upon which man plants his foot & ascends to the intellectual heaven of peace in ignorance of the machinery which feeds his daily life—& yet it is not always so. Rightly managed, prayerfully taken, women also may ascend, using each of their petty cares as an advance toward that "heaven" which is gained by *self conquest*, self abnegation.

Patrick feels so uncertain about his Battalion, fearful that the Conscript Act will render useless the labour of the past two monts, yet hoping that the Sec will be regulated by the principles of justice & fair dealing & transfer those Companies which he gave him leave to re-enlist into the Cavalry service.

This Conscript Act is a hard one. It breaks faith with the twelve months men, which I suppose was in a measure neccessary, but surely not in so odious a way as this law does. It commences too young too. The President himself has said that it is like "grinding seed corn" to allow boys to enter the army & yet he calls for all over eighteen. From 20 to 40 would I think have

---

[89]Johann Paul Friedrich Richter (1763-1825), usually called Jean Paul, was a German novelist of the Romantic Period. Mrs. Edmondston was probably acquainted with this writer through Thomas Carlyle whose translations, published in 1827, included some of Richter's works. Benét, *Reader's Encyclopedia*, 926; *Dictionary of National Biography*, IX, 111-116, 126.

been a better limitation, but then Mrs Edmondston you are not of the Cabinet. Well, it is unsettled & uncertain business & this terrible fall of New Orleans—coming so unexpectedly as it does—makes it the harder to bear.

What a blow it is to us, Sugar gone, Texas Beef & wool for the food & clothing of the Army, leather, Horses! all lost to us by criminal conduct somewhere.

Now indeed begins the war of "Endurance"—a war in which we women must show the men that we are their equals—nay their superiors! "Endurance." Let me write the name of my commander. Endurance! Patience! Cheerfulness! Faith!—these be the Captains under whose banners I enlist! God grant that under them my country men may all be united into a glorious band, a band which can Die but be disgraced never! Then shall we never be conquered, never be subdued.

May 5, 1862

I have been sick in bed for the last two days—how unusual a thing for me. I cannot remember the last day I spent in bed. Grant me, O' Lord, a renewed spirit of thankfulness for the health with which Thou hast so abundantly blessed me. May these two days of pain & fever be to me a reminder of how long I have been exempt from them & show me upon how frail a tenure I hold this activity which I prize so dearly & which forms so large a portion of my enjoyment of life! May I use it to renewed usefulness with renewed cheerfulness & renewed energy in the earnest employment of my time & talents & may no such week as the last idle ennuyee listless blot the record against me.

Patrick too is quite sick. The fact is we have neither of us been quite well since that terrible cold & fever we took in Richmond & I hope this is the winding up, the last muttering of the storm. We both suffer from sore throat, fever, intense pain in the limbs, back, and in short all the many ills which go to make up the "Break Bone Fever." We are both so weak as scarcly to be able to help each other. Father calls it the "Grippe." It must then be the New Orleans Grippe, as that is the heaviest blow we have had during the War.

The U S Flag floats over the Custom House & nine steamers have gone up the river to reduce the remaining towns & I suppose, if possible, to effect a junction with Com' Foot, so all hope in that quarter seems to be over for the present. As the night falls darker we seem to cling the closer to the hope of European Intervention. I wish our Rulers would dismiss the idea. I am sure it weakens, it enervates us. "He who would be Free, Himself must strike the blow."[90] We have men, enough determined men, and a goodly heritage to defend. Give us *Leaders*! Leaders that can fire the Southern heart by *Action, hearty*

---

[90] Lord Byron, *Childe Harold's Pilgrimage*, canto 2, part 76, lines 1-2:
"Hereditary bondsmen! Know ye not
Who would be free themselves
must strike the blow?"

action! & not depress it with a heavy dull defensive policy. Such a policy would suit the plegmatic Dutchman, the calculating Scot, not the impulsive warm blooded Southron!

Patrick sits opposite to me & read a line from Shakespeare, Timon of Athens, "Here's that, which is too weak to be a sinner, Honest water,"[91]—the same idea which that wretched woman, Mad Malibran,[92] uttered when, after drinking a glass of cold water, she wished it was "a sin to give it a zest." Of all speeches, to me one of the saddest on record! What a blasé ennuyee' burnt out life does it disclose! Hope turned to ashes; faith, trust, every high & holy aspiration Dead! "would that it were a sin to give it a Zest." Ah! unhappy woman! how unhappy may it never be my fate to realize & yet who hath made me to differ? Who hath delivered me from Temptation & sheilded my Youth, my whole life, from snares which beset hers? To Thee, O Lord, be the glory. To Thee let my heart arise in grateful adoration!

Slavery in the Dist of Columbia has been abolished by Congress & approved by Lincoln. So the life long effort of the Abolition party has been finally crowned with success, for it is the entering wedge to anarchy & confusion. Mr Vallandigham[93] made a splendid effort to arouse Congress to reason, to justice, to a respect for their boasted "Constitution," but failed. What a heroic spectacle he presents! One man alone doing battle for Truth, for Right, against a whole Nation! "*Courage! Courage*"! was the Key note he attempted to strike in their hearts, to induce them to be consistant & refuse the rendition of Mason & Slidell, but alas, he met no response. "Courage"! it is indeed his key note! Justice & Courage. He is the only Northern man I ever desire to see during the whole remnant of my natural life & I would go far to see & thank him!

Came a letter from Lt Wren, who is recruiting for the Battalion. Thinks he has a company.

---

[91] Shakespeare, *Timon of Athens*, act 1, sc. 2, lines 60-61.

[92] María Felicita García Malibran (1808-1836), an outstanding Parisian opera singer, married "Monsieur Malibran," a French banker living in New York. She divorced him when he went bankrupt and in 1836 married a Belgian violinist, De Beriot, with whom she had been living for several years. *Webster's Biographical Dictionary*, 958; Rupert Hughes (comp.), *Music Lovers' Encyclopedia*, edited by Deems Taylor and Russell Kerr (New York: Doubleday & Company, Inc., 1954; originally published 1903), 274.

[93] Clement Laird Vallandigham (1820-1871), an Ohio lawyer and politician of southern ancestry, disapproved of slavery but was an opponent of the radical abolitionists. Outspoken in his championship of compromise and freedom of speech, both before and during the Civil War, Vallandigham served as the leader of the peace Democrats. He continued his criticism of the Lincoln government despite General Burnside's warning that expression of sympathy toward the Confederacy would not be tolerated in the Military District of Ohio. Consequently Vallandigham was arrested, tried for treasonable sympathy, and sentenced to imprisonment in Fort Warren. Lincoln commuted the sentence and banished him to the Confederacy from whence he ran the blockade and escaped to Canada to continue agitating for peace. *Dictionary of American Biography*, XIX, 143-145. For a complete discussion of Vallandigham's role in the peace movement, see Frank L. Klement, *The Limits of Dissent: Clement L. Vallandigham and the Civil War* (Lexington: University Press of Kentucky, 1970). The Copperhead movement is ably treated by Wood Gray in *The Hidden Civil War: The Story of the Copperheads* (New York: Viking Press, 1942).

MAY 6, 1862

Mr E. really sick. He has been very unwell since Thursday. Indeed he has not been himself since he came home & the miserable uncertainty he is under about his Battalion agravates it. Today he is really sick & suffering and I only able to creep about. So there is a pair of us!

Neither health or spirits were improved by a Bomb Shell which Sue threw into our midst, viz., that preparations to evacuate Norfolk were going on! It seemed madness. Are we never to cease retiring? Are we to give up undisturbed possesion of the water to our enemies? For with the loss of the Navy Yard all hopes of a Navy are forever lost to us. Of what use will breaking of the Blockade be to us when we have no longer a Port to unlock? And the Virginia? What of her? Is she too to be sacrificed? For with no place to fall back upon, what will be her fate, it will not be difficult to guess—captured or blown up to avoid capture as the Louisannia[94] was by her commander. What can Mr Davis mean? I fear me Gen Lee is at the bottom of all this. He is too timid, beleives too much in masterly inactivity, finds "his strength" too much in "sitting still."

Our Army is falling back from Yorktown away from these dreaded Gunboats, leaving their intrenchments & I suppose abandoning their Cannon after attempting to spike them. The Gunboats of the enemy have advanced up the York River to West Point & thus compelled the destruction by our own hands of five gun boats which we had there in process of building. We, of course, "fell back"! Perhaps the notion may be to wear out the U S Government, crush them with a debt too heavy for them to bear. It may be so, but in the mean time they try a most dangerous experiment with our own people. But I remember Gen A S Johnston & try to be content & think Gen Joe Johnson and Mr Davis know best. But it is hard work. He (Gen Johnson) is falling back to the line of the Chickahominy, where I suppose he means to make a final stand & a desperate defence for Richmond.

Rumours of an impending fight at Corinth yesterday or today. Grant us, O Lord, the Victory!

Amo Coffin left for Raleigh today. Things begin to look brighter for the Battalion.

Ah! if Dr Ward had done his duty & either been Major or declined it & let Patrick choose another who would have been an assistant to him, what a world of trouble he would have been spared! Burnside is moving—but where, it is for the future to disclose.

Came a letter from Mr Hall saying that he goes into Camp today & will report to Patrick tomorrow.

Oh! for health & strength once more!

---

[94] The C.S.S. *Louisiana*, an unfinished Confederate ironclad, mounted sixteen guns. The vessel was blown up on April 28, 1862, by its commander, C. F. McIntosh, after the New Orleans river defenses fell to Farragut's fleet. *Civil War Naval Chronology*, II, 50, 54, 57; VI, 263-264.

May 7, 1862

Patrick still quite sick, suffering terribly with his hip joint. What can be the matter with him? It worries him the more as the 17th is near at hand & his Battalion business needs him.

Mary & Sue came to dinner. Mary looks better than I ever saw her before. A winter in N C has not killed her, it seems. We are evacuating the Peninsula as rapidly as we can; and McCellan, it is said, is doing the same and intends making his approach via West Point. He is pledged to his government to push us to the wall.

The number of sick & wounded soldiers in Richmond is incredible, the Hospitals over flowing & the Ladies earnestly requested by the authorities to assist in preparing nutriment for them. The suffering there is terrible. Would that it were over!

Emancipation proclaimed to all Slaves who come within the enemy's lines. The next step will be to extend it over the whole South, what our far seeing ones have long predicted.

No news from Corinth.

Came a letter from Dr Shaw[95] tendering his Company. So if the Sec will release Huggins there will be five Companies to begin with. This will not entitle him to a Major, but the disappointment to Dr Ward who has done nothing at all to aid Patrick will almost reconcile me to the additional duty he will have to perform.

May 8, 1862

Patrick better. We are both similarly affected with constant & severe pain in the limbs & muscles. With such a total loss of strength & such serious throat affections, we are both of us more sick than we care to admit. Father too is affected much as we are. Pray God that it be not an epidemic! Think of our Camps! What destruction it would work there!

A severe & brilliant skirmish on Monday between our rear guard and the advance of the enemy near Williamsburg—killed & wounded on our side 200, which had to be left on the field of battle. We gained a complete victory & our wounded were only abandoned in consequence of the neccessity under which Gen Johnson thought he was to avoid a general engagement. The enemy were driven back three miles & lost 600 prisonners; their killed & wounded not known, as we resigned the field to them after checking their advance. We took eleven peices of Cannon.

---

[95] Elias F. Shaw, a farmer and practicing physician from Sampson County, enlisted at the age of forty as captain of Co. C, Sixty-third North Carolina (Fifth Cavalry) Regiment. In March, 1865, he was appointed lieutenant colonel and was transferred to the Field and Staff of the same regiment. Shaw was killed at Chamberlain Run, Virginia, on March 31, 1865. Manarin and Jordan, *North Carolina Troops*, II, 372, 389; Clark, *Histories of the North Carolina Regiments*, III, 529, 541.

The people of New Orleans occupy a proud & defiant position. They refuse to surrender the town or take down the Confederate flag. They have burnt all the Cotton, 20,000 bales, in the city and for days the gutters of the streets ran with Molasses whilst large quantities of sugar was thrown into the Mississippi. The U S. Flag was hoisted on the Custom House but torn down the first day & torn into shreds by an indignant crowd of citizens. The Gunboats opened fire upon them but without effect. The bearer of the demand for the surrender said that Com Farragut was much annoyed at the burning of the Cotton, to which the Mayor replied that "as it was our own property he did not see that any one had a right to be annoyed by what we did with our own." The officer added that it "was like biting off ones nose to spite the face" when the Mayor said, "We have judged differently."

Perhaps after all our distress this capture of N O may be a good thing for us, for it must open the eyes of the World to the impossibility of ever subjugating us & this burning Cotton on so large a scale will touch England in a tender place.

Even Lincoln & Seward must in their hearts admit the impossibility of Union now, & the war must be maintained wholly with a view to our conquest. Ah! gentlemen—Messrs Lincoln & Seward— I would not have such a pillow of thorns where on to rest my head as you are laying up for your future slumbers! Conscience must at some time awake & "thy brothers blood cryeth from the ground."[96] Misery & suffering! A wail goes up from ten thousand times ten thousand hearths and *you*—*you* are the cause of it all.

Despairing of being strong enough in time I sent Owen out to Hascosea to plant my Dahlia & Tube Rose roots, the first time it has ever been entrusted to other hands than my own! The high water in the River has been a sore draw back to me this winter & spring, for before I was sick I was a prisoner.

This War has developed one bad phase of human nature, "*Extortion.*" The prices charged for the very neccessaries of life are enormous & out of all reason but that of a haste to be rich. Salt at 25 or 28 dollars a sack, shoes, Bacon, leather, sugar, Coffee in proportion. The worst thing to be dreaded by the government is that the necessities of the people, the want of *salt* particularly, will force them into trading with the Yankee invaders, or rather the pedlars who follow in their wake; that trade once opened cannot be controuled. Well is the army of Extortioners named "the Army Worm." The Battalion is looking up. Patrick hopes to take the field against the enemy & to do good work.

MAY 10, 1862

"Prisoners of Hope"! yes we are indeed prisoners but to a most delightful tho delusive jailor. We have become quid nuncs & watch the papers to see what more we can find to feed our hopes on, that is to rivit our chains with.

---

[96]Genesis 4:10b.

The skirmish near Williamsburg was a most brilliant one. The enemy admit a loss of 600 prisoners, killed wounded & yet claim a victory because they held the field which we did not want & were retreating from when they attempted to arrest us. Between West Point and New Kent Court House at Barhamsville in another skirmish we repulsed them three times & finally drove them to their gun boats, but the evacuation of Norfolk is more than we can understand. It seems to us madness & folly. The Captain of a Steamer sent from Norfolk to Seawell's Point to bring off a Columbiad there, a Yankee named Byers, instead of obeying orders, turned traitor & steamed down to Fortress Monroe & gave information to Gen Wool of our intended &, in fact, half executed evacuation. In consequence two Frigates, two Iron Clads, & some Gun boats came up and made an attack on the Batteries at Seawell's Point; but the Merrimac, getting up steam, came out of the Harbour, but no sooner was she seen rounding the Point off Craney Island than Hey! Presto!—the Yankee ships vanished & left her without an opponent.

Burnside it is rumoured is aiming at the R R at Wilson. The Cotton in that section is fortunately all burnt and if Gen Holmes uses his troops well—we have nothing to fear in that quarter.

Intimations of recognition from France. Suffering great in England for the want of Cotton. Reversing the Divine will of one suffering for many, there many suffer for the fault of *one*! Yours, my Lord Russel!

The [Thirteenth] N C Regt was terribly cut up at Williamsburg. This is the Regt which thought of running Patrick for its Col on the Promotion of Pender & with whom he would not electioneer, despite his being urged to it, thinking it out of a Soldiers duty to be running after promotion. How much suffering & anxiety have I been spared!—& this is not the only instance, for had the Sec of War placed him, as the Gov requested, in command of the remnant of the Hatteras Regt, he would have been in the disastrous fight at Roanoke Island. And again, had the Governor's wishes been carried out he would have been placed in command of Fort Macon on Bridgers retirement & the gallant & hopeless task of its defence would have fallen upon him & he now be, if he had escaped, chafing on his parole. What short sighted mortals we are! Can we never learn that God ordains every thing and that He alone knows what is best for us? Let me learn the lesson now before the disappointment about the battalion comes and know that after he has done his utmost there should be no repining because God brings it to naught.

I went yesterday to see Mrs Hines—Peggie Norfleet. I have not seen her since her marriage, and now she is a widow! with two children. Poor thing—my heart bled for her! Her desolation and isolation of heart is terrible, & were it not for her children to absorb & occupy her, draw her out of her greif as it were, I know not what would become of her. So affectionate & capable of loving as she is, homeless, a widow, and a Refugee. And all because of these wicked Yankees!—for Mr Hines met his death at their hands as surely as tho they had shot him, for his sickness was the result of exposure in the Peninsula. She has many friends & kind friends, but what are they when one suffers from loneliness of heart? She tells me that Alethea Collins[97] servants whom she left in charge of her house have plundered her shamefully—old servants, too, in whom she had every confidence. They have taken what they wanted. Miss Blount's[98] new servants have gone to the Yankees. Alethea's are riding in Edenton. The low white population, wonderful to say, commit few excesses even in the presence of the enemy, upon whom they could lay the blame, but the indulged negroes, servants of widows & single Ladies who have not been kept in proper subordination, are terribly insolent. As a general rule the "*favourite*" servants, who have had more liberty than their fellows, are worse. Where ever the Yankees are they encourage the negroes to join them & tell them they are free, but they are beginning to be disgusted with them themselves. The negro thinks he is as good as a Yankee & is insolent in proportion.

About Fortress Monroe they have proclaimed Emancipation & allowed the negro to appropriate the houses & property of their masters. Near Hampton an officer entering one of the houses was, to his great indignation, asked for "his *pass*" by the negro occupant. So we go. I wish they would give them even more trouble than they do. Mrs Daves[99] servant walks about New Berne with a *Lease* of his mistress' house in his pocket! He has actually *leased* it to a Yankee official; & yet our government releases negroes taken prisoners, gives to what is our own property the priveleges of prisoners of War! I suppose it is done for fear of retaliation on our own men in their hands, but I think they surrender a principle when it does so.

The attitude of New Orleans is a noble one. Left defenceless by the withdrawal of the troops they yet offer a proud & defiant aspect to the enemy & refuse all intercourse with them or even to lower their Flag. I append the correspondance of the Mayor and Com Farragut on the subject.[100] The Mayor's letter is written in a noble spirit of patriotic defiance. Gallant New Orleans, persevere in your tacit resistance; the day of your deliverance will yet come. In Nashville, too, they meet with a dignified yet manifest repugnance from all classes, from the ladies particularly. So will it be with us all! We will

---

[97] Elizabeth Alethea Collins, the daughter of Josiah Collins, Jr., lived on Somerset Plantation in Washington and Tyrrell counties. She married Dr. Thomas Davis Warren on January 12, 1863. Collins Family Papers.

[98] Mrs. Edmondston probably meant Anne Collins Blount (b. 1789), an unmarried daughter of Ann Collins (sister of Josiah Collins, Jr.) and Jacob Blount. Miss Blount was living at the Collins's "Old Homestead" at the outbreak of the war. Collins Family Papers.

[99] Mrs. Elizabeth Batchelor Graham Daves was the third wife of John Pugh Daves (1789-1838) and the mother of Graham Daves (1836-1902), the adjutant of the Twenty-second North Carolina Regiment. Ashe, *Biographical History*, VI, 183-187.

[100] This correspondence was clipped from a newspaper by Mrs. Edmondston and pasted on the back of the front cover of the first volume of her diary. The correspondence was later published in *Official Records* (*Navy*), Series I, XVIII, 232-235.

never hold intercourse with you more, ye vile money worshipers! You understand neither the instincts of a gentleman nor the impulses of a freeman.

May 11, 1862

Do I indeed go through life whining after sympathy, unattainable because unreasonable in its requirements? Am I a "femme incomprise"? No, I am not, for I am contented, nay happy, with the sympathy I get from *one* person! Is it vanity that makes me expect or desire that others should be interested in me & my belongings? I hope not. Prone as I am to view my own failings leniently, I hope I am not so blinded as this. Those were hard words I heard this morning, but are they not wholesome ones? Teach me O Lord to examine myself and to weed out all vanity, all undue opinion of myself, to be humble because *Thou* art humble, because it is pleasing in Thy eyes; & instead of sitting here mortified and low spirited, let me think on my blessings, spared as I am from the heart crushing anxiety of those whose husbands are at this moment exposed to the bullets of the enemy. I was not expecting sympathy for myself—it was for him & his disappointments. I was not even thinking of how little I get outside of him. The sympathy I get from him is sufficient for my happiness and tho' the want of it in others annoys, it does not distress me. I was not prepared for the turn the conversation took, this personal application of my words, but if I have not sense enough to tell the difference between flattery & sympathy, I am indeed in a pitiable state & the sooner I know it the better for me. I may expect too much from friends, but from him my highest aspirations, my warmest expectation are fulfiled. He is everything to me. Keep me, O God, from Idols!

May 12, 1862

The spirit of Lies seems indeed to be abroad. We can truly say with the Scotch Clergyman in his comment on the text, "I said in my haste all men are Liars," "Ah, David, my mon gin you were in this parish ye might say it at your Leisure"! There has been no fight at Barhamville & no Yankees at Greenville, consequently we did not drive them three times to their Gun boats, nor are they threatening the R R at Wilson.

A great battle is imminent at Corinth & in Va. Two such armies cannot long face each other thus. How much hangs on the event! Gun boats are going up James River. Where is the Va that she allows it, protecting the Evacuation of Norfolk, I suppose. Ah! what a blunder is there!

On coming home from my visit to Mrs. Hines, I finished some lines which I had commenced years ago. Something said in our conversation reminded me of & put me in a frame of mind for them. Ah my God! make us indeed feel that "as our days, so shall our Strength be," now in the time of this our Country's darkest gloom!

As Thy Days, So Shall Thy Strength Be

When the whirlwind of passion has swept o'er my soul
And left it all blasted, to spurn at controul
When faithless & feeble, no prayer can I raise
No thought can I lift in petition or praise
Then strengthen my soul with Divine grace from Thee
And say "As thy days are, so shall thy strength be!"

When stunned by the shock in the battle of life
And wearied & care worn I shrink from the strife
When the world loses brightness & Despair's heavy cloud
Like a pall my dead heart & my spirit enshroud,
Then whisper O! sad one "Cast thy whole care on me!
For know as thy days are, so shall thy strength be."

When Death like a Tyrant my friend shall enfold,
And from life I turn murmuring like a tale that is told,
When the Past has its sting & the present is Drear
And I look to the Future less with hope than with fear
Say "I am thy friend; lean thou wholly on me,
And know as thy days are so shall thy strength be!"

And O when this mortal corruption shall see,
And struggling with Death all my proud thoughts shall flee
When I shrink from the touch of the worm & the grave
And despairing cry out for thy mercy to save,
Be then Thou my Refuge! my sole Hope be in Thee!
For I know as my days are so shall my strength be.

MAY 13, 1862

Went to Fathers. Found him better & heard the sad sad news that the Va had been blown up.[101] It came in this wise: In consequence of the information given by that traitor Byers, Gen Wool instantly dispatched some Gun boats up James River & threw a column 12,000 strong upon Seawell's Point which was almost deserted by our men. They pressed upon our retiring troops & would have followed them into Norfolk but for the destruction of a bridge & the position of our artillery. This hurried the evacuation of Norfolk. Com Tatnall, the Commander of the Va, was uninformed of it until late in the afternoon. He immediately commenced lightning the ship so as to bring her

---

[101] The Confederate ironclad C.S.S. *Virginia*, formerly the United States steamer *Merrimac*, fought the famous naval duel with the U.S.S. *Monitor* in Hampton Roads on March 9, 1862. After Norfolk's evacuation the crew of the *Virginia* destroyed the ironclad, under the orders of Flag Officer Josiah Tattnall, because she drew too much water to ascend the James River. A naval court of inquiry, which met in July, 1862, to determine if the *Virginia's* destruction was necessary, acquitted Tattnall with honor and agreed the ship's destruction was unavoidable. *Civil War Naval Chronology*, II, 62-63, 85.

draught to 18 ft water, which the Pilots said would enable her to get up James River. This exposed her Rudder, Propeller, etc., leaving her in no state to fight, or resist the attack which would most probably be made upon her with day light, so in Commodore Tatnalls mind the best course was to destroy her & with her one of the safeguards to Richmond & the James River. We unlearned disagree with him, for to our "foolish thinking" had he gone into the mouth of the James River, she would not only have been safe herself but in all probability have captured the Gun boats already in the River. Tatnall blames the Pilots & the Pilots ask a suspension of public judgment, but some body is woefully to blame; she was run ashore on Craney Island & set on fire. About day light she blew up & with her 3,500 lbs of powder—a shame, a burning shame to some one. Who, it is not just yet to decide, but it seems our fate to make blunders & in a Ruler "a blunder," Tallyrand tells us, is worse than "a crime"! What would he have thought of the Evacuation of Norfolk?

Another blunder is that Mrs Davis has left Richmond and gone to Raleigh, fairly deserted her colours.[102] I fear me she is not a woman of the true stamp. I fear she does not strengthen her husband, or she would never have abandoned her post & set such an example to the rest of the women of the Confederacy.

On coming home found Dr Shaw, who is raising a troop for Patrick's Battalion, at the house.

Was much shocked & greived by a note from Sou Hill telling me of Rebecca Spruill's death! Poor thing! few have suffered as she has & fewer still have led a life of such simple faith, such reliance upon her Saviour as she has done.

May 14, 1862

Went out to see Mrs Spruill and the girls. Found them composed & resigned. Poor Rebecca, as I sat by her dead body & thought of her past life, of all she had suffered mentally & bodily, I could not mourn for her. Yet I felt her death greatly. She was a tie to my youth & tho I have been unable to see much of her latterly yet she was one of those upon whom I rested, to whom I spoke unreservedly, & who reposed in me. Few people look on me with the eyes of favour that she did, few judge me so leniently, & to fewer still does my society & presence give the pleasure that it did to her.

May 15, 1862

Mr Edmondston left early in the morning to go down to Sampson County to muster in Dr Shaw's Company, thence to Wilmington, and I went out to Rebecca's funeral. They were unable to procure a clergyman, so Mr James

---

[102] Varina Howell Davis (1826-1906) went to Raleigh at the express insistence of the president, who feared for the safety of his wife and children in Richmond. Eron Rowland, *Varina Howell, Wife of Jefferson Davis* (New York: Macmillan Company, 2 volumes, 1931), II, 269. The *North Carolina Standard*, May 14, 1862, reported that "The President's lady, Mrs. Davis, accompanied by her family and friends, arrived in this city on Sunday morning last, and has taken lodgings at the Yarborough House."

Smith[103] read the funeral service, simple & solemn. They buried her where she would have wished to have been buried, near the Chancel of the Church where the solemn tones of the Organ, the words of thanksgiving, & praise, will float sweetly over her last resting place. The wreaths of white flowers twined by the hand of affection on her coffin seemed, as they were lowered into the grave, to smile as in promise of a glorious resurrection! & I thought of her favourite verse in Mrs Hemans song, "Bring flowers," with a sigh but not of regret:

> Bring Flowers, pale flowers, o'er the bier to shed,
> A crown for the brow of the early dead!
> Though they smile in vain on what once was ours,
> They are love's last gift. Bring flowers, pale
>   flowers!
>
> For this in the woods was the Violet nursed!
> For this through its leaves hath the white rose
>   burst,
> They speak of Peace to the fainting heart,
> With a Voice of promise they come & part,
> They sleep in dust through the wintry hours,
> They break forth in glory. Bring Flowers, bright
>   flowers!

Ah how often have we sung it together!

In the evening to our great surprise came Patrick. He got on the train at Halifax but before it had gone 200 yds a collision occurred and it was God's mercy alone which prevented them from all being killed! As it was, one poor man—a soldier, had his leg broken. As both engines were badly broken & there was no getting on he returned in the carriage, which fortunately had not left. May God make me truly thankful for the Life He has thus spared me!

He brought news of the capture of the Steamer Alice[104]—loaded with Bacon in our river—by the enemy who have five Gun boats lying at Plymouth. Twelve hundred cavalry are at Blackwater threatening, it is thought, the R R at Weldon. God help us if they do, for then our section will be overrun & they may sweep down upon us like a tornado—carrying fire & destruction in their course.

---

[103] James N. Smith was a forty-three-year-old Halifax County planter. Eighth Census, 1860, Population Schedule, Halifax County, 81.

[104] The *Alice*, carrying a cargo of bacon for the Confederate army and church bells from Plymouth for casting into cannon, was overtaken and captured by Lt. Charles W. Flusser, aboard the U.S.S. *Perry*, and two other ships patrolling the Roanoke River, May 14, 1862. *Official Records (Navy)*, Series I, VII, 374-375.

MAY 16, 1862

Sent what Bacon we had left here to a place of safety & commenced packing up our valuables. In the afternoon came Sue bringing Patrick a letter containing the news brought by the Courier from Plymouth. Eleven Gun boats are lying there, but whether meant for Roanoke or Chowan Rivers we cannot tell. Ah that our River would *fall*, but instead of that it is rising! We have repulsed the Gun boats in the James at Drury's Bluff,[105] fairly driven them back, the Galena, Iron clad, riddled with shot. Loss on our side two only whilst they are known to have buried 70 men at Bermuda's Hundred. We are busy doing what we ought to have done before Norfolk was evacuated, viz., blockading the River.

We see that the U S have ceased enlisting their own citizens in their army but have sent out emissaries to induce the very scum of Europe to emigrate, and on their arrival here they are met on board ship & held out great promise of pay & a grant of land at the South if they will enter the army. They are the very offscouring of Europe, principally Dutch & Italian, and the North is actually savage enough to exult in the fact that when one of their army falls, he simply leaves more room behind him for "others as useless as himself, but that when a Southerner meets the same fate, his death carries distress & sorrow into loving hearts at home & cuts off a useful citizen from the service of his country." How diabolical!

Johnson & McClellan still face each other & a battle is thought to be imminent & may take place at any moment.

Mrs Spruill tells me that a letter from her boys[106] now on their retreat from Norfolk tells her that with the rest of Huger's Division they are ordered to reinforce Stonewall Jackson who, it is supposed, is to lead an invading army into Maryland! I hope it may be so and that his presence there may create a diversion here.

MAY 17, 1862

The "advantages of a state of expectation" are not I fear properly appreciated by us, for we have lived in a Micawber like frame of mind—looking "for something to turn up" for weeks now & we do not find it pleasant. First about the Battalion, the 17th it was supposed would settle that, as after that

---

[105] Drewry's Bluff, a strategic point on the James River seven miles below Richmond, defended by the Confederate battery at Fort Darling, served as a refugee and military camp during the war. The Confederates prevented naval attacks on Richmond by successfully defending that part of the river until the end of the war. Boatner, *Civil War Dictionary*, 247-249, 292; *Sentinel* (Raleigh), July 29 and September 28, 1863, hereinafter cited as *Sentinel*.

[106] Mrs. George Evans Spruill had two sons in the Confederate army. Charles W. Spruill (1838-1873), a lawyer, was a private in Second Co. C, Twelfth North Carolina Regiment. Peter Evans Spruill (1836-1862), also a lawyer, served in Co. F of the same regiment until his death in Richmond from disease. Montgomery, *Sketches of Old Warrenton*, 378; Manarin and Jordan, *North Carolina Troops*, V, 155, 193.

day the Government takes all the organization of troops into its own hands by the operation of the Conscript Act. But that day has arrived but with it no end to our expectant state. For Patrick now waits for letters which come not & upon which hangs its fate. Then Burnside keeps us with the sword of Damocles[107] over our heads. We know not what moment may see us over run by a horde of Yankee savages. Then in a national point of view, we are still more "expectant," for all eyes are turned both to Corinth & Richmond, daily expecting "sounds as of an army joined." God be with us & grant us nationally and personally a deliverance from all our troubles, or the strength to bear them.

MAY 20, 1862

At Hascosea. Came out yesterday to get things in order for the summer & to remain whilst Mr E is absent in Richmond. River up as usual. Moved most of our clothes, silver, etc., in case of a surprise by the enemy during our absence. Found things terribly out of order here, for we have been so much absent & so harried by other things that they have not had the usual attention. The Garden, however, is in magnificent bloom, tho' it wants work sadly. Mr Edmondston tho far from well left this morning for Richmond to report to the Sec of War & get his final decision respecting the transfer of the Infantry Companies; should he consent the Battalion is made up.

The Yankees at N Orleans—are endeavoring to open trade by kindly allowing supplies to be brought in for the use of the city—use the pretence of feeding the city as a cloke for the admission of "food, Cotton, Sugar & Molasses only." I wonder what else ever goes there by R R or Steamboat. For the three last, the staples, he offers "cash." But crafty as you are Maj. Gen Butler, I hope you will be outwitted & that not a single pound of either Cotton or sugar will reach your insatiable clutches. Supplies for the city, I suppose, must be allowed by us to pass even tho that should insure supplies for the Federal Army. The Mayor still continues the civil government of the City, but the inhabitants are kept down only by the presence of an armed force, Gun boats being kept in position to shell the city should an outbreak take place.

Skirmishing at Corinth. The ineffectual Bombardment of Fort Pillow still goes on.

No news from the Army north of Richmond, tho a battle must soon take place at both points. The repulse of the Gun boats at Drury's Bluff more important than we had first thought. The North is much cast down by it. "Iron clads" have lost their prestige and we, I hope, our fear of Gun Boats. An attack on Fort Caswell by two vessels. I suppose only a recconnoisance and to get the range & calibre of her Guns. Next will come an attack in force.

---

[107] The "Sword of Damocles," from Greek mythology, refers to a sense of foreboding or a dread of evil. Benét, *Reader's Encyclopedia*, 270.

Mrs Davis is, I hear, a Philadelphia woman! That accounts for her white nurse & her flight from Richmond. I fear she is not worthy of her husband, for I learn that she is neither neat or Ladylike in her dress, travels in old finery with bare arms covered with bracelets. Would that our President, God bless him, had a truehearted Southern woman for a wife. She would never have deserted him!

Put the Hams out here into bags. I have 50 all told, 15 old ones, 29 sides, 15 shoulders, Joles [illegible]. Make me thankful O God—that Thou hast placed me beyond want & made an abundant provision for me!

Between Tatnal & the Pilots, we cannot tell who is to blame about the Va. The Pilots give the Com' some hard nuts to crack & ask most pertinently why he lightened the ship when he knew if he could succeed in getting her into James River that she would have to fight the Gun boats sent by Mr Lincoln up to Richmond, & accuse him of a disobedience of orders in not lying in the mouth of James River, & deny that they ever said that if she was lightened to 18 ft that she could ascend the River. A Court of Inquiry has been ordered, but I fear me that it is composed entirely of the Com's friends.

MAY 22, 1862

I have just read Butler's infamous proclamation[108] about the ladies of New Orleans, and cannot finds words to express my horror and indignation. Was such cold blooded barbarity ever before conceived? Can he have a gentleman under his command? If so we shall soon see, for no man with one spark of honour or humanity will serve under such a cheif! If the U S Government does not at once disavow this brutal order, it will be stamped with infamy deeper even than Austria's! And yet is it worse than the order of Gen Hunter emancipating the slaves of Florida, Georgia & S Carolina,[109] which appears in the same paper? Coarser and more brutal in words, more directly insulting, but in spirit is it less infamous? Are its intended consequences (which God in his mercy avert) less horrible? Good God! Have we come to this? To *insult*, to threatened disgrace and infamy? No! Even tho' our foes should be those of our own households, we have a spirit unconquerable, invincible! We have

---

[108] Gen. Benjamin F. Butler's "Woman Order," issued May 15, 1862, stated: "As the officers and soldiers of the United States have been subject to repeated insults from the women (calling themselves ladies) of New Orleans in return for the most scrupulous non-interference and courtesy on our part, it is ordered that hereafter when any female shall by word, gesture, or movement insult or show contempt for any officer or soldier of the United States, she shall be regarded and held liable to be treated as a woman of the town plying her avocation." *Official Records (Army)*, Series I, XV, 426. Mrs. Edmondston clipped the order from a newspaper and pasted it in her diary. Her comments were typical of the resentment which Butler's action aroused in the South.

[109] Gen. David Hunter (1802-1886), commanding the Department of the South, issued an order on April 12, 1862, emancipating the slaves actually in Federal hands. On May 9 he expanded the order by freeing all slaves within his department. Lincoln annulled the last order on May 18, 1862, stating that Hunter had exceeded his authority. *Dictionary of American Biography*, IX, 400-401.

Gen. Benjamin Franklin Butler was perhaps the most hated by Mrs. Edmondston of all the Union generals. In August, 1861, he captured Forts Hatteras and Clark in North Carolina, and the next year he occupied New Orleans. In 1863 he took command of the Department of Virginia and North Carolina but was relieved of command after his failure at Fort Fisher in December, 1864. Mrs. Edmondston refers often to "Beast" Butler.

severed all bonds. We no longer will hold any intercourse with you, ye puritanical, deceitful race, ye descendants of the Pilgrims, of the hypocrites who came over in the Mayflower. Plume yourselve on your *piety*, your civilization. Wrap yourselves in your own fancied superiority. We are none of you, desire naught from you. We detest you!

MAY 23, 1862

Came Patrick home from Richmond. He saw the Sec of War who told him that holding as he did a Commission, the Conscript Law does not put an end to his efforts but that he could still muster in Companies already organized & could also attach any Independant Companies now in service to his command who wished to join him. As to the transfer of the Infantry Companies, as the papers have not yet come before him, he could give no decision—so he is to go on for a month more. I had hoped that the matter would now be decided, the suspense now be over, & that we could settle down to one thing or the other, but it appears not. Before Butler's order, I had cooled greatly about the Battalion, and my desire for Patrick to go into active service, thinking that the Conscript Law called out men enough without him and younger & stronger men; but that infamous order has roused me to that degree that I wish every man in the country to rise & drive out this dreadful crew.

Just before dinner came father. He looks very badly; this severe cold has made him really sick. Patrick suffers still with his knee & I from loss of strength, but I call myself well. Transplanted Tomatoes & set out Dahlia offsets. Sent to Looking Glass for the rest of my Egg plants, but they are far from promising, for which I am sorry as Mama is so fond of them.

A letter from Frank Jones tells us that he was in the fight at Drury's Bluff where the Gunboats were repulsed. It was a gun from his ship, the Patrick Henry, which first disabled the Galena. We had but two guns mounted & yet see the execution they did!

Pickets from a Cavalry force station above us have been posted at Montrose & Polenta[110] immediately opposite us to give warning of the approach of the enemy up the River. War is indeed brought to our very doors. The first victims to it, however, will be the young Spring chickens. No flag of Truce on their behalf. I must see to that.

Tallyrand's saying that in public matters a blunder was worse than a crime seems true about the surrender of Norfolk, for few crimes could have spread the distress that that has entailed on this whole section of country. Most of the money in circulation was Norfolk money. All our crops are sold there & it is our general Exchange. The money now is not current—& many have their all—of ready funds—lying in the hands of some Norfolk merchant, not only unavailable but in great danger of total loss. God help the poor. We can wear

---

[110] Polenta was one of the Devereux plantations in Northampton County. See Introduction.

old clothes and live off the plantation for years without suffering if we can only get salt, but what is to become of those who have no such resource?

McClellan sent a Flag of Truce to our army on the Peninsula to inquire into the fate of 200 men who crossed Warwick Swamp & made an attack upon us. Gen Johnson's answer was, "we had two left to send to Richmond—the rest we buried." Terrible! This was the skirmish in which Col McKenny of the [Fifteenth] N C was killed. That unfortunate Regt has since lost a second Col who was killed two days after he took command.[111]

MAY 29, 1862

During the night of Friday the 23d Mr Edmondston was taken quite sick with fever & increased pain in his knee, so that in the morning he was unable to leave his bed & indeed scarcely able to turn over without assistance. The Dr pronounced it Inflamatory Rhumatism. He has suffered terribly all the week but is now, I hope, a little better tho' still confined to his bed. He is so patient that it is difficult to tell what his sufferings are, but the knee is still so stiff & swollen that he can neither straighten or put it to the ground.

Frank Jones arrived on Sunday & has been with us until yesterday, he having received permission from the Sec of the Navy to volunteer in the army whilst his ship is inactive. He gave us a stirring account of the affair at Drury's Bluff & thinks he killed the Pilot of the Galena himself; says that unless a strong force is landed & our battery flanked & taken it will be impossible for the enemy to get to Richmond by the River. He brought me a Bayonette taken from the decks of the Congress during the fight in Hampton Roads on the 8th of March, which I shall prize highly as a relic & place by the side of our Revolutionary Swords.

The daily news from Richmond keeps us almost breathless with anxiety, a fight being momentarily expected. Johnson has fallen back until his rear rests *upon Richmond*, McClellan steadily advancing, entrenching as he comes. We have deserted the West Point R R, which they have seized, & can run a train from their boats to within 15 miles of Richmond, a great advantage to them & to us civilians a terrible blunder in us. Two heavy skirmishes have taken place, in one of which we were driven back, but in the other were signally victorious. Yesterday Johnson was reported to be crossing Chickahominy Swamp to give them battle, but I do not beleive it. Anderson's and Branch's Brigades of the Army of the Rappahannock were at Hanover Court House when the enemy made a dash & seized the Central Road, thus cutting them off. We attacked them front and rear, when a terrible fight took place. Our

---

[111]The number of this regiment was left blank by Mrs. Edmondston. If it was the regiment commanded by Robert M. McKinney it would have been the Fifteenth, but no other colonel of that regiment was killed during the war. Henry A. Dowd, elected colonel of the Fifteenth on April 20, 1862, was wounded at Malvern Hill, July 1, 1862. *Official Records (Army)*, Series I, XI, Part I, 407; Clark, *Histories of the North Carolina Regiments*, I, 733; Manarin and Jordan, *North Carolina Troops*, V, 502.

loss was fearful, especially amongst Branch's N C Division, but as we took 55 prisoners & regained the position I hope communication was reestablished. How much hangs on the events of the next few days; for should we be beaten and a victorious army, flushed with victory & animated with such passion as theirs is, pursue our troops into Richmond, imagination shrinks in terror from the scenes that will be enacted there. For even if the city be not given up to pillage the officers will be unable, even if willing, to restrain the men; but what confidence can we have in them, that they will not be our worst enemies? I remember Butler's order and shudder.

Johnson is a master of strategy & he ought to know, but to us it seems madness to allow the enemy to entrench themselves as they have done & are even now doing on the north bank of the Chickahominy; but we were not born Brigadier Generals.

Jackson has had another splendid success in the Valley & has completely routed Banks at Front Royal & driven him into and through Winchester which we now hold. He peirced his column, one part of which fell back to Strasburg, the other fled in panic to Winchester. He sent 5000 men after the Strasburg fugitives, whilst he himself followed the Winchester portion. We took all their cannon, camp equipage, Baggage & Hospital stores, which are most valuable, destroyed their waggons & took an immense amount of supplies & a large quantity of ammunition—in short the rout is complete and we are encumbered with 4000 prisoners! This victory has cheered our army before Richmond greatly. God grant that it may have correspondingly depressed our enemies. It is whispered confidently that the next news we will hear of him is that he has led his victorious column into Maryland, so we shall see whether or not "there is life in the old Land yet," or whether the "Despot's Heel" has crushed it entirely out of "Maryland, My Maryland"!

June 1, 1862

Mr Edmondston well enough to leave his room today for which I thank God most fervently. He has suffered much & so patiently that he has excited the sympathy of all who have seen him. Ah! that his recovery may be rapid & that I may soon see him in full health & vigour. His thin pale face & sad eyes go to my heart & then he is so weak that it is sad to look at him! It frets him the more as he is absolutely unable to attend to any business what ever & his Battalion needs him as his time for raising it is short, and it will be a sore disappointment to him to fail in it. First the Conscript Act & the liberty allowed to Ranger Companies & now his sickness gives another heavy blow to it.

No public news. The army still has its rear on Richmond & the enemy advancing & entrenching. Skirmishes & serious ones constantly occurring, but in view of the great conflict now close at hand we over look their importance. An article in Friday Dispatch announced that the enemy were in full retreat in consequence of Jackson's victory & the danger to the Capitol and that

Gustavus Smith, the second in comman[d], was pressing upon them, but the unblushing Editor after sounding a flourish over the news, singing an "O be joyful" & saying that it would henceforth be a day sacred in Richmond on Friday, on Sat, congratulates his readers that the "bad news" of the enemy's retreat without a fight is not so & tho' he assured us one day that he had it from the highest authority & that it had been known to our generals for three days, on the next he gravely tells us that it had no foundation in fact.* Truth, blessed angel, why have you deserted this Earth?

At Corinth matters stand as they have done since the battle of Shiloh, skirmishing but nothing important. The Bombardment of Fort Pillow still goes on furiously but ineffectually. At Vicksburg the inhabitants have defied the Enemy, despite his threat of shelling the town & determine on a bloody resistance, so he is still far from the possession of the Father of Waters.

The eyes of the nation are fixed on Richmond & Corinth where desperate battles must soon ensue. God defend the right!

Brother John has gone down as temporary Aid without pay to General Martin who, shorn of his glory as Major General of the forces of N C by the Conscript act, has accepted a Brigadiership in the C S A. I hope Master Johnnie will not stay long there. It is a post not worthy of him. James E has received the appointment of Quarter Master C S A and has been assigned to duty to the 3d Brigade, Col Daniel acting Brigadier & stationed at Weldon.

Two years ago today the first entry in this book is dated & what a change has come over the country since then! This was then but a record of domestic incidents, trifling in themselves, but interesting to us, because they made up our lives. Now how different! My garden, that great source of interest, passes unnoticed by & my housekeeping, which absorbed so large a portion, is now not deemed worthy of a single entry; but battles and seiges, bloodshed, and the suffering of a mighty country occupy every thought. For once I will recur to my former simple home tastes & for auld lang syne give them a casual notice.

I have had a grand house cleaning this week. Every thing has on its summer garb & is as clean as Cuffee can make it. I might, were the times better, say with Mrs Nicely in the School for Reform, "Ah! a clean house & a clean conscience will make any one merry,"[112] so neat is it.

I am amusing myself in the manufacture of Fly brushes of my Peacocks feathers & have just completed one for Mrs Lippitt that I consider a marvel of beauty.

As to the Garden, it is particularly backward. We have but few of the vegetables which it ought to give us at this season. As regards Peas, I excuse it,

*Richmond Dispatch—we ceased taking the paper in consequence of.

---

[112] Thomas Morton, *The School of Reform; or How to Rule a Husband*, act 4, sc. 2, lines 46-47.

for during our continued absences this spring the pigeons & birds took them under their care & tho often replanted they never failed in their attentions! But for Beets, Lettuce, Snaps, Squashes, etc., Garden! I fear I must pronounce you ungrateful, for you had every appliance to enable you to perform your duty. Strawberries we have & have had in abundance for a month past. Our Quinces are for the first time in their lives loaded with fruit & as I walk past them, both themselves & the Strawberries seem to look at me saucily & defiantly, as tho' they would say "*Preserve* me if you dare!" for they must know that I have not sugar to spare for such luxuries. The Apples, even my young trees, are most promising, the peaches abundant. The old Pears are loaded with fruit, whilst a few are even to be seen on some of the Dwarf Pears in the garden for the first time. The flower Garden has been magnificent, "The Gardens of Gul[illegible] in their bloom,"[113] Paestum, or any other garden either of poetry or antiquity never surpassed it! I trace an outline of a bud of Isabella Grey which has not yet commenced to expand, the green calyx barely beginning to turn back in proof of it. It has been five days gathered & has shrunk. Sir Joseph Paxton has been a blaze of beauty & the blooms on Fellenburg & Beauty of Greenmount are literaly countless; but I feel in enumerating them as a General might who cannot name all the soldiers who distinguish themselves & when he once commences does not know where to stop, for Woodland Margaret looks at me reproachfully, whils "Thad Trotter," "Rivers," "Alex Backmetoff" & Giant of Battles seem to glow redder with indignation at being passed over and Alpha grows more saffron with mortification. So I desist. The Dahlias are growing fine and have increased greatly so that I look for a harvest of beauty from them.

All here is peaceful & happy—a bright contrast to some portions of our desolated country. Teach me to estimate the blessing as I ought! Give me, O God, a grateful heart and to our country the blessing of Peace! One thing reminds me of war, a trifle it is too, but still a change in my domestic economy: I have come to the manufacture of Tallow Candles! Fanny & I worry over the wicks & Patrick over the light, whilst Vinyard is kept on the qui vive about grease on the floor. Some people have not the tallow to make candles of, so I have another cause of gratitude.

JUNE 2, 1862

Frank Jones left. Today for the first time in my life I weighed out the plantation Allowance. The Conscript having taken the overseer, Patrick has concluded, as we have only a Corn crop, to manage it with Henry. So the task devolves upon us, half a pound a day for every one above ten years, those younger being fed at the Nursery & with the children who work out, and their portion is weighed together & apportioned according to age & requirements

---

[113] Lord Byron, *The Bride of Abydos: A Turkish Tale*, canto 1, stanza 1.

by the old woman presiding. It is said to be more than any other labouring class on the globe gets regularly. Think what the Irish get—"*Potatoes & porid,*" the French—"bread & grapes," Italians—Maccaroni & olive oil, the Spanish—Black bread & Garlic, the Sweedes—but it is useless to go through the catalogue. The object of their misplaced sympathy, the poor negro, fares better than any of them & has as much freedom. The *name* only is wanting & there is much to superficial thinkers in a "name," Juliet to the contrary notwithstanding.

A few words on the back of an express notice from Halifax excited us greatly—"Fighting at Richmond yet," but as there was no mail we were left to conjecture & found it most agreeable to place an omitted negative before "*fighting*," & there was none to contradict us! So we had it all our own way.

JUNE 3, 1862

Came Father & Mary to dinner. They brought the missing news from Richmond, the want of which left us so wide a field for speculation yesterday. On Sat, the 31st, our scouts reported that a portion of the enemy having crossed the Chickahominy the night before & the terrible rains of Friday night & Saturday morning having raised the swamp so that they were cut off, it was determined at once to attack them & the last account was that a terrific fight was raging, we being in the ascendant, but as the mail has failed every day since, we know nothing more.

Waited in painful suspense for the mail which in part confirmed the above, but the enemy does not seem to have been cut off, for he was constantly re-inforced during the fight. We were Victorious, driving them from their position & Camp which we captured & held, taking also some of the finest peices of Artillery known in scientific warfare, three entire batteries & some single peices, but at a terrible loss to us both in men & officers. We drove the enemy three miles from his camp. He then made a detour & attacked us in the Flank, but here again he was repulsed & he spent the night in the wet swamps without food or shelter, we occupying his tents.* Our Commander Gen Joe Johnson was wounded in the groin & the command now devolves upon Gen Gustavus Smith a native of Va and said to be an able general, which God grant he may prove himself. Amongst the killed is Gen Johnston Pettigrew, a native of our State but now hailing from S Carolina. A young man of high attainments & great Ambition, he was destined to have made himself a name in the world. God be with his poor sisters. Mary I know was much devoted to him. One Louisiana Regt charged shouting, "Butler!" "Butler!" & carried every thing before them! Ah! if mens blood can be stirred the conduct of that infamous villain should do it! I hope when he hears it that his coward heart

*Seven Pines

will sink beneath the fear it will excite in him. The other particulars are not authentic, so I will wait for further news.

The last accounts were that Stonewall Jackson was at Martinsburg in Maryland,[114] had destroyed a portion of the Baltimore & Ohio RR & threatened Washington or Baltimore. Lincoln was in a panic, calling loudly for the "Loyal men of the North to defend the Capitol," whilst volunteers & recruits were pressing there with all expedition. The Rout of Banks was complete; 4000 prisoners, & an immense quantity of stores of all kinds, baggage, tents, arms, ammunition, horses, etc., have fallen into our hands. The next account will be I hope that Jackson has taken Washington, blown up the White House & the Capitol, scattered Congress, & driven Lincoln to the disguise of the long Cloak & Scotch cap once more.

June 6, 1862

No mail until last night & even now we are one behind hand. The fighting of Sat was desperate beyond description. North Carolina distinguished herself, several of her Regts being on the field, but the heart sickens at the slaughter and at the sufferings of the wounded now in the hospitals at Richmond. The city is crowded to overflowing with them & there are neither nurses or beds sufficient for them all. Ah! that we could do something, but the transportation on the R R is so uncertain & difficult that it amounts to an embargo almost. Still we must try; it is a releif to us to be able to act!

Gen Lee has issued an order to the army in which he tells them that "there will be no more retreating." The watch word is "Victory or Death." As he is accused of being the principal cause of our continued "falling back," it seems that now we may begin to drive the enemy "back" in earnest.

The condition of N Orleans is terrible. No people ever were more oppressed or insulted. Mayor Munro was, we learned, sent to Fort Jackson. I now preserve the letter which gave offence to the tyrant Butler, and caused his arrest.[115] Humanity sickens at the thought of the barbarity, the groveling cowardly cruelty of the wretch Butler! He has forbidden the issue or circulation of Confederate money in the city & the suffering consequent upon it is dreadful. The letter of Monro previous to the surrender of the city I preserve in the beginning of this book. It is a noble one and the author of it could not be marked out for vengeance by such a coward as Butler. He must admire, envy

---

[114] Martinsburg is located in present-day West Virginia.

[115] John T. Monroe, mayor of New Orleans, wrote an indignant letter addressed to Butler, protesting Butler's "Woman Order" and stating ". . . I will never undertake to be responsible for the peace of New Orleans while such an edict . . . remains in force. . . ." Butler promptly relieved Monroe of his mayorial duties and arrested him for the "offensive" tone of his letter. Monroe vacillated between standing by his letter or withdrawing it with an apology, but eventually resubmitted his letter to Butler and was subsequently imprisoned. *Official Records (Army)*, Series I, LIII, 526; James Parton, *General Butler in New Orleans* (New York: Mason Brothers, 1864), 88-90.

& hate a man so different from himself. Ah, that some one would shoot him as he rides through the city he has insulted and oppressed!

JUNE 7, 1862

Rain again yesterday & the night before. During the hardest of it came a squad of the 1st Cavalry on foot seeking shelter, very miserable, cold & wet did they look.[116] Had a fire kindled in the Work Room for them & set all hands to work to get them some dinner. Gave them what I am sure the poor fellows have not had for some time—a good hot & strong cup of Coffee. I dare say they would have preferred whiskey but they were not asked! All day they straggled past in two's & threes & altho it was rainy & cold, they were uncommonly thirsty. I suppose to keep up the character of the month—for tho it is June—fires are comfortable & more rain has fallen during the past few days than was ever known to fall before, the River rising furiously altho all the Low Grounds are under water already.

Finished another Fly brush, this one for myself.

JUNE 8, 1862

Last night during a severe thunder storm came James, dripping wet. He is stationed at Garysburg & ran down for a night only to see his brother. He gave us the sad news, kept however a secret from the Army, that Gen Joe Johnston is supposed to be mortally wounded! The ball (a Minnie) entered at the point of the shoulder, he standing sideways, & ranged diagonally through, coming out through the Chest. Should he recover, which will be almost miraculous, it will be months before he is fit for duty. A heavy loss to us! He has proved himself a master of strategy, tho' we civilians do not like his allowing the enemy to entrench themselves, but then we ought not to judge for we do not know the circumstances. But he is an able & prudent general & his experience will be greatly needed. Gen Lee takes the command in person. I do not much like him, he "falls back" too much. He failed in Western Va owing, it was said, to the weather, has done little in the eyes of outsiders in S C. His nick name last summer was "*old-stick-in-the-mud.*" There is mud enough now in and about our lines, but pray God he may not fulfil the whole of his name.

Gen Pettigrew's obituary is in the paper but happily for him he will be able to read and comment on it himself, as instead of being killed he is severely wounded & a prisoner. And yet the papers announced that his friends had taken charge of his body in Richmond, a mistake which might have occurred to any officer or man under his command but not, I should think, with the

---

[116]The Ninth North Carolina (First Cavalry) Regiment was recalled from Virginia and stationed near Kinston from March until May, 1862, after Burnside captured Roanoke Island and threatened the rest of the state. Companies A and B of the regiment remained in North Carolina when the main body of the regiment returned to Virginia. Clark, *Histories of the North Carolina Regiments*, I, 420, 445-448; Manarin and Jordan, *North Carolina Troops*, II, 1.

Brigadier. His Uniform would at once stamp him. News has been brought by a Flag of Truce that he is doing well & will in all probability recover. So much for the news! Our loss is heavy—2500 killed & wounded. The battle is known as "The Seven Pines" & was a terrific one. McClellan, tho repulsed with the loss of his Camp & stores, claims a victory and so telegraphs to Washington.

Lincoln repudiates Gen Hunter's order emancipating the slaves & preaches us a sermon on our delinquencies intended to be touching but simply ridiculous. How about Butler's infamous order? As mercy is the order of the day, he having also rescinded Wool's prohibition of trade & the entrance of provisions into Norfolk, issued with the avowed intention of "starving" the inhabitants into "taking the oath," saying that the "Flag shall carry its blessings & benefits whereever it goes" & confined Wool's jurisdiction to Fortress Munro—perhaps he will try the same policy on the New Orleanians. But tell it not in Gath! This mercy is owing to the seizure by the English Consul of a vessel belonging to a Yankee & refusing to allow the hatches to be opened, saying that as trade with one part of the world was winked at by them the Blockade was null and void, & that in the name of his Government he protested. The French war steamer did the same. So now the people of Norfolk have trade with all the world & can buy French & English goods & provisions to the exclusion of Yankee notions. I hope that they may soon be able to show their preference. So thank you for nothing, Mr Lincoln!

A tremendous, or as father calls it, a "ferocious freshet," in the River yesterday—22 ft & rising 2 inches an hour—the water on his doorstep. He writes that so soon as they can get out they will all come out here for the summer. The whole Conneconarra crop is, of course, lost. Our Lowgrounds fortunately were not planted. We never knew a June freshet before, but the measure is now full. The lunar cycle is complete.

JUNE 9, 1862

Mary's boys came out saying that their mother & Grandfather would follow before very long. Father had a most narrow escape on Saturday night. He went upon the steps to mark the rate of the rise in the river when they, being improperly fastened, or rather not fastened at all, floated up & he was thrown backwards, striking the back of his head against the Piazza floor. He received a severe blow on the back & went down under the water. Mary, thinking he was stunned, jumped off the piazza & seized him by the shoulders & attempted to raise his head, but fortunately it was not the case & beyond a thorough wetting they both escaped unhurt. It is the highest freshet ever before known, being 20 inches beyond the highest water mark, full [———] ft.

JUNE 10, 1862

Mary & Sue came out wet to the skin having performed the first half of their journey in an open canoe & it raining. In a short time father & Mama

Mary Bayard Devereux Clarke, sister of Kate, was a well-known writer who contributed to leading periodicals of the South. Her long hair was re-painted by a later artist to make her appearance conform to then-current styles; the shadow in the photograph of the portrait indicates the original painting of her hair. (Photograph courtesy of Mrs. J. D. Eudy of Kinston, owner of the portrait.)

followed they having stopped at Feltons to wait for the carriage & succeeded in drying themselves there.

Andy Johnson in Tenn & the infamous Butler at N O. are reported as having been shot, but we do not credit it, the wish perhaps being "father to the thought."

JUNE 11, 1862

Went with Mr E to Looking Glass for the first time since we moved out. The last part of our trip was taken by me in a cart, Mr E on Horseback, such an inconvenience is the River. Our Dams are torn to peices, but in this we have fared no worse than our neighbors, as the whole valley has been swept from the source of the river to the mouth. The loss of property, stock, fencing, corn, wheat & Labour is immense. In our immediate section 1,000,000 bushels would not cover it. One of our neighbors lost two negroes drowned. We, thank God, escaped that distress. It is a serious question with father & Mr E whether they will put back the Looking Glass dams or not. I hope not. Make what corn we can & pasture the rest & by raising stock for the future fill up our income. The risk and loss is too great & our force too weak to put back the work.

Jackson has gained another victory in the Valley of Va. He has beaten Shields & holds Fremont in check, who fears to attack him singly. No particulars as yet. He is the only one of our generals who gives the enemy no rest,

Col. William J. Clarke, a Republican judge after the war, is shown in his Civil War uniform. He was the husband of Mary Bayard Devereux Clarke. (Photograph courtesy of Mrs. Graham A. Barden, Jr., of New Bern.)

no time to entrench themselves. Matters before Richmond look gloomy to us out siders. McClellan advances, entrenching as he comes. Why do we allow it? Richmond must fall after a time if he is allowed to go on. The loss of life was terrific on Sat & Sunday. The enemy admits a loss of 5,000 killed & wounded, we 2,500 on our side, & both of course are under the mark—& yet to us it seems a useless bloodshed, as after removing their Camp & stores we "fell back" and allowed them to occupy the entrenchments from which we had driven them. It is more than we plain people can understand & *faith* was never so much needed as now, earnest unquestioning faith!

Never was known such a summer for wet & cold. We have had a fire all day & a good one too ever since the 1st of June. Verily it is no "summer at all, but a winter painted green," as are the Sweedish summers; and as for rain, never did so much & so violent & heavy rains fall before. It is more than a week since a plough has been put in the ground & from present prospects it will be a week longer & that near the summer solstice!

JUNE 12, 1862

Mr Edmondston left for Wilmington tho scarcely able to travel, but he is so much interested in his Battalion that he will leave no stone unturned to get into Service. His knee still very painful.

In the afternoon came brother. Being a volunteer aid without pay, he can leave when he pleases & so came home to see what was best to be done after the freshet. He feels gloomy about Richmond & in fact about the cause generally, as he has seen so much of the inefficiency of our officers. Huger, he tells us, has been suspended for not bringing up his reserve on Sunday & cutting the enemy off. Had he done so, the loss of life would have been much less & the whole of the Yankees on the South side of the Chickahominy would have fallen into our hands! "Thy sin shall find thee out"[117] comes true with nations as well as men, for had they superceeded him as they ought to have done, after the finding of the Court of Inquiry after the Roanoke Island disaster, this would never have happened now & indeed the Va might have been still spared to us.

Stanley[118] the *renegade*, the traitor Governor, appointed by Mr Lincoln to rule his native State, finds the way of the transgressor hard. He has stopped the negro schools as being contrary to the Statute Law of N C, by which he has offended his Northern masters, but with a strange inconsistency he ignores the fact (of which Mr Badger[119] has reminded him however) that his being here, as Gov, is as much an infringement of our rights, for the Laws of N C provide for an election of the Gov by the people. He said that if there was one man in N C whom he regarded more than another, *one man* whom he *loved*,

---

[117] Numbers 32:23b.

[118] Edward Stanly (1810-1872), a former native of New Bern living in California who adamantly opposed secession, was commissioned military governor of North Carolina by Lincoln in May, 1862. Stanly had hoped to find most North Carolinians willing to return to the Union if their property was guaranteed. Consequently, upon his arrival in New Bern, Stanly ordered that a semiofficial school for Negroes operated by Vincent Colyer, an abolitionist minister acting as superintendent of the poor under Burnside, should be gradually closed so as not to harm the Union cause. Colyer, angered by Stanly's policy, immediately closed the school in protest over Stanly's interference with his teaching and went to Washington, where his complaints eventually led to the school's reestablishment later that year. Stanly resigned his office in January, 1863, after the publication of Lincoln's Emancipation Proclamation, which he felt ended any hope of reconciliation between North Carolina and the Union. Stanly also opposed plans to recruit blacks into the Union army, fearing it would encourage servile war. *Dictionary of American Biography*, XVII, 515-516; Barrett, *Civil War in North Carolina*, 127-128; Norman D. Brown, "A Union Election in Civil War North Carolina," *North Carolina Historical Review*, XLIII (October, 1966), 381-400. See also Norman D. Brown, *Edward Stanly: Whiggery's Tarheel "Conqueror"* (University, Ala.: University of Alabama Press [Southern Historical Publications No. 18], 1974).

[119] George Edmund Badger (1795-1866), North Carolina statesman, lawyer, and superior court judge, served as secretary of the navy for six months in 1841 under Pres. Benjamin Harrison and as a United States senator from 1846 until 1855. A strong Unionist, Badger personally rejected the validity of secession and deplored the South's withdrawal from the Union, but he remained in North Carolina and acquiesced in the decision to secede. Ashe, *Biographical History*, VII, 35-44; *Dictionary of American Biography*, I, 485-486.

that man was Richard S Donnel,[120] & yet the first sight which greeted him on stepping ashore at New Berne was the coffin of Mr Donnell's *mother* with her name & the date of her birth & death cut on it waiting shipment to N Y, her remains having been thrown out to give place to the body of a Yankee officer! Such is our foe.

I sympathize deeply with the Donnells & hope that poor Fanny was buried in Raleigh where she died & that her remains are not exposed to the insult that her Mother's & Grandfather's have been—for it is said that the skull of Gov Richard Dobbs Speight[121] was stuck upon a pole & that Stanley was forced to look at it as he landed! Meet & right it is that his father's foe should rise from his grave to exult over Stanley's infamy, for know that Gov Speight was killed in a duel by Stanley's father now fifty years ago at least. I fear me the "false Stanley" as he is still called in England is "false" still, even tho' represented now by Lord Derby, false to his master at Bosworth field.[122] Now this one of the same name, tho I doubt not the same blood, is false to his country, to his name, & to his fame. Let him go down to the "vile dust" "unwept" & "unhonoured."

The Yankees have in and about New Berne more than 6,000 negroes who work when they please & if they do not please they draw their rations from the Q Master. This cannot last. No government can stand it. The end must soon come. Burnside is arming & drilling the negroes & expects when the fate of Richmond is decided to commence active operations. God be with us & vain will be the rage of men.

JUNE 14, 1862

Came Patrick home sick. I fear he left too soon. Gen French is to take the matter of the Independant Companies into consideration. That means that he is not going to do it, Patrick says. Well, he has nothing to reproach himself

---

[120] Richard Spaight Donnell (1820-1867) of New Bern was a United States congressman from North Carolina from 1847 until 1849, a delegate to the state secession convention, and speaker of the North Carolina House of Commons in 1862 and 1864. He was the son of Margaret Spaight and John R. Donnell. Daniel Lindsay Grant, *Alumni History of the University of North Carolina* (Chapel Hill: [General Alumni Association], 1924), 167, hereinafter cited as *Alumni History; Biographical Directory of Congress,* 821.

[121] Richard Dobbs Spaight, Sr. (1758-1802), the maternal grandfather of Richard Spaight Donnell, fought in the Revolution, represented Craven County for several terms in the state legislature, and served in the Continental Congress from 1782 through 1785. A delegate to the constitutional convention held in Philadelphia, he was one of the signers of the Constitution. He served as governor of North Carolina from 1792 until 1795, and from 1798 through 1801 he was a member of the United States Congress. Spaight was mortally wounded in a duel with John Stanly, Edward Stanly's father, in September, 1802. Although Stanly has usually been represented as the aggressor and Spaight the martyr, the correspondence between them clearly shows Spaight forced the duel. *Raleigh Register,* September 14, 1802; Ashe, *Biographical History,* IV, 397-402; *Dictionary of American Biography,* XVII, 419-420; *Biographical Directory of Congress,* 1633.

[122] Thomas Stanley (ca. 1435-1504), first earl of Derby, holding high office under Richard III, made excuses for not joining Richard at Bosworth Field in 1485 to help repel the attack of Henry Tudor, earl of Richmond. After the battle Stanley was one of the first to salute the new king, Henry VII. *Dictionary of National Biography,* LIV, 76-78.

with; actuated by a feeling of pure patriotism, he is anxious to do something for the country in this her hour of need, but so many obstacles are thrown in the way of the Cavalry that he has been unable to raise his corps and no infantry is now being organized. It is a sore disappointment to him, but he bears it manfully & cheerfully. God knows what is best for us & he must be content with the consciousness of having striven to place himself in active service, having done everything in his power consistantly with his principles to effect it. He has still to go to the Secretary of War to report & then I suppose all will be over. Lieut Col Edmondston will be a thing of the past.

At night came brother. He tells us that the damage from the freshet is terrific, the most destructive ever known. The loss to the army of our supplies will be severely felt & not only on our river but all the Rivers in the country have overflowed & the Low-ground crops are lost. I hope our armies will not feel it.

Jackson's victory over Banks & Shields has developed a more enormous capacity for lying than the father of lies himself even possesses. Altho we have 3,000 men now prisoners in Lynchburg, in his official report Banks acknoledges the loss of only 85, says he had but 3,000 men & out of 500 waggons he lost only 50. As to the stores at Front Royal & Winchester, he knew nothing of their being there until he came upon them during his orderly retreat when he burnt them. Liars ought to have long memories, for by his own showing he had a waggon to every six men in his army & was so supremely indifferent to all sublunary things that he did not know with what or how his men were fed. But this seems the vice of the age—lying. To "lie like a Greek" has been proverbial; we ought hence forth to say lie like a Yankee!

JUNE 16, 1862

Yesterday James came in whilst we were at dinner, hot, dusty & tired. He brought us the rumour that our army of the west, now that Corinth has been evacuated, is to be with drawn entirely & thrown before Richmond. Fort Pillow has at length fallen, having been flanked by a land force, & Memphis is in the hands of the enemy. No cotton found there, however, it all having been burned. Our Cotton clad fleet under Jeff Thompson[123] is destroyed & Vicksburg alone remains to make any opposition to the navigation of the Mississippi.

Yesterday was the anniversary of our dear Papa's death. Ah! what a loss to us. He was the bond that kept us united into one family & now that he is gone how separated are we all. We have not heard even from any of the family for two months. Children are born to them & we hear it accidentally only. A severance seems to have taken place & we are no longer one family but

---

[123] M. Jeff Thompson, former mayor of St. Joseph, Missouri, and a partisan fighter in that state, led the "Swamp Rats." He directed the Confederate rams at Fort Pillow and fought in the western theater of the war until his surrender in May, 1865. Boatner, *Civil War Dictionary*, 837-838.

several; each son is the head of his own circle & now that the central head is gone around which all revolved each goes on in his own eccentric orbit without heed to the other—the course of nature, I suppose, but it seems very sad.

A brilliant exploit has enlivened our Army before Richmond. Gen Stuart with a strong force of Cavalry left Richmond on a reconnoissance and made a circuit of the entire lines of the enemy, burning three transports loaded with supplies, overthrowing a force of Cavalry sent to oppose him, & taking many prisoners and 300 mules & horses besides destroying a number of army waggons & a warehouse filled with Coffee. He left Richmond on Thursday, went by Hanover Court House around to the Pamuncky where he burned the vessels, & returned by the Charles City road. He reached the Chicahominy during the night of Friday & found the stream swollen & the bridge destroyed. What was to be done? The cavalry could cross at some risk by swimming, but what of the prisoners & mules?

During the conference a friendly voice whispered in the darkness, "The old bridge can be repaired. The sleepers are standing. It is but a little way up the stream." Placing a guard over the prisoners with directions to shoot them if they made a noise, to work they went & before the following foe could overtake them in the darkness the bridge was repaired. Men & horses crossed over & as day dawned on them they could see the Yankees mustering on the other side; but in vain!—their escape was made and they entered Richmond in triumph! Truly a brilliant episode.

Went to the plantation with Mr E & commenced digging up my Hyacinth roots. To my sorrow I found some of the finest of them rotted. So much, Mrs Edmondston, for procrastination or over particularity in wishing to see it done yourself.

June 17, 1862

The Psalms for today[124] reminded me of a hymn which I wrote years ago, before I was married, so I looked it up from some old papers & transcribe it here to see how I stand in an intellectual point of view. Have I improved? Candidly, which are the best, these or the lines I wrote Mrs Hines? Neither have any great claims. Both lack originality, but am I making as much of my material now as I did then? I hope so, for I can conceive no more sorrowful or humiliating thought than for one honestly to be convinced that he is not the man he was, that age or neglect has dimmed the force of his intellect, the brilliancy of his imagination. "Let me not live after my flame lacks oil, to be the snuff of younger spirits," says Shakespeare—a wise wish—and one which I hope will be granted me. But to the lines:

---

[124] Psalm 87 was a portion of the Psalter read at morning prayer in the Protestant Episcopal church on the seventeenth day of the month.

PSALMS 87:7th

All My Fresh Springs Shall Be in Thee!

When fainting in this strife I thirst
For living water from on high
O help my struggling soul to burst
From earthly cares & find Thee nigh
O let me find my strength in Thee
In Thee may all my "fresh springs be."

When in temptation's trying hour
I feel my weakening spirit yield
Then send Thy Word—Almighty Power
To be my strengthner & my shield
O! give me then Thy Spirit free
And make my fresh springs flow from Thee.

When 'neath thy rod I murmuring lie
Rebellious at thy chastening hand
Then Lord my soul with grace supply
Meekly to bend at Thy command
O then in mercy make me see
That all my fresh Springs are in Thee.

When earthly joys grow dim in death
And like a dream my life appears
Then Lord receive my latest breath
And shield my soul from Earth born fears
O then my Refuge make me know
That from Thee all my fresh springs flow!

Raleigh   June 17, 1842

No mail today, which disappoints us all sadly but especially father who is quite sick.

JUNE 18, 1862

The Yankee loss seems from their own accounts to be a terrible one at Chickahominy, now called indifferently Seven Pines & "Fair Oaks." They admit eight thousand killed, wounded & missing. The hospitals in Washington, Baltimore, Phil & New York are filled, whilst New Haven & Boston are receiving their quota. Ours is nothing like so heavy, though they insist that it is much worse; but it seems a fact that had our reserves been brought forward on Sunday, we would have annihilated them.

Rumours reach us of a French intervention & that sixteen war vessels, French & English, are lying in Hampton Roads, refusing to allow any American vessel to enter until those of foreign nations are received on equal terms. This coupled with the fact that Lord Lyons has left the country, actually sailed in the last Steamer, looks significant tho the Northern papers maintain that "he has gone by request of Mr Seward to represent to his Government how nearly the Rebellion is crushed out." But they are great at lying.

No more news from Jackson, but that he is being heavily reinforced.

An attack has been made near Charleston in which we were victorious, repulsing the enemy with the loss of 500 men. Sad to relate, Mr Henry King,[125] Patrick's old friend & compeer, was killed at the head of his company, the Sumter Guards. This is the corps in which Patrick volunteered in Jan last before the receipt of his Commission, when Charleston was threatened by Butler. Lieut Edwards,[126] Isabella's brother-in-law, also fell. He is the Uncle of our little neices and tho no connection of ours, his death brings the war home to us. Dr Tennant, another friend, was wounded but we hope not seriously. He has just had a son[127] born to him in Wilmington, his first child, for he married late in life. Ah, how many hearts are desolate now, how many weep for friends killed in this terrible war.

June 19, 1862

Father quite sick and has sent for the Dr. Went to see Mrs Spruill & her daughters. It is sad when one feels how soon one is forgotten. How true it is that "their place shall know them no more."[128] Poor Rebecca but for the mourning dresses one would not have known that she was no more & yet they are not heartless people. O far from it, none more so, & yet there we sat, her most intimate friend & her family, & tho she was in all our thoughts not an allusion was made to her. The way of the world I know, but is it a good way? Is it a way that we ourselves like? and yet from fear of "a *scene*" all repress the natural expression of the heart & pass as it were an act of oblivion upon the dead. It is not right! It is over cultivation—unnatural & injurious. I will no longer accede to it, but speak freely & sorrowfully & as my heart prompts of those who have gone before me.

---

[125] Capt. Henry C. King of the Charleston Battery, First South Carolina Battalion, was killed at Secessionville on James Island near Charleston, June 16, 1862. *Official Records (Army)*, Series I, XIV, 87, 90.

[126] Third Lt. J. J. Edwards was the brother of Isabella Donaldson Edmondston's first husband, William Shipper Edwards. *Charleston Courier*, June 17, 1862.

[127] The infant son here mentioned, Edward Smith Tennett, Jr. (1862-1938), was born in Marion, South Carolina, where his mother was a refugee, and not in Wilmington as stated by Mrs. Edmondston. He grew up in Wilmington but later lived and died in Spartanburg, South Carolina.

[128] Job 7:10.

Went to see Samantha & carried her some little rarities and delicacies proper for her situation. They were just in time for I found her with an Infant, a daughter, not two hours old! So I made but a short stay promising to come again soon. Read L Allegro, Penserosa, and Comus to the girls.[129] They had never read them before & were surprised to find how many quotations constantly on their lips were to be found in them. Read also the contrast between Melancholy & Pleasure in Burton's Anatomy of Melancholy,[130] thought by many to have given Milton the idea of L Allegro & Penseroso. What a wonderful book, that. Burton is such a mine of thoughts, such a quarry of quotations, but the trouble with me now is that I cannot remember them as I once could. Is it the war and its consequent preoccupation or is my memory less pliant than formerly? I fear the latter, which is most mournful, as I have hitherto been gifted with a most excellent one, but nonsense, I talk like an old woman! and I am not yet a middle aged one. I am still young and my *memory shall not fail.*

Tied my Grape Vines to their new trelisses. It ought to have been done before. They would have thriven better. They were given me by my dear Papa, and I prize them the more on that account. He wrote me that he could never expect to sit under them but wished me many happy years under "my own Vine & my own Fig tree."[131] Dear old gentleman, he has left few behind him like himself, but he has been taken from the evil to come. So we must not mourn for him, yet I miss him sadly.

JUNE 20, 1862

It is years since I had so many children in the house at a time & tho' these are good & by no means troublesome, still I find it pleasant to escape from their noise once in a while. Children make a vast difference in people's character. I feel they would have changed me greatly. When I look at a helpless little one now, my heart yearns to it, and a boy or girl old enough for companionship draws me strongly to them, but I beleive children between four & sixteen have lost their charm to me. I no longer devote myself to them because they are *children.* I like them for a while, but I tire of them; yet I have a strong attraction about me for them. They are almost always fond of me & I can teach them with great ease to myself & pleasure to them. I have what is called the "gift of teaching" but I do not prize it as I ought nor practise it when I can, perhaps because I am not thrown much with children of whom I am very

---

[129] *L'Allegro* (1632), *Il Penseroso* (1632), and *Comus* (1634), all works of John Milton (1608-1674). Benét, *Reader's Encyclopedia*, 233, 536, 604, 725.

[130] *The Anatomy of Melancholy* (1621) by Robert Burton (1577-1640), an English churchman and prose-writer, discussed melancholy through illustrative examples from classical sources. Benét, *Reader's Encyclopedia*, 33, 157-158.

[131] Micah 4:4a. "But they shall sit every man under his vine and under his fig tree. . . ."

fond & perhaps, Mrs Edmondston, you fear being used as a convenience & have a dread of having some neglected little child put off on you to dry nurse! Fie, Madam, you shrink from being useful. "Bear ye one another's burdens."[182] Why will not you who have no burden of that kind take one from your over burdenened sister or brother? Simply because I wont!

June 21, 1862

My dear Patrick's birthday "God bless" and keep him, and may we spend many more together as happily as we have spent the last few. He has been much depressed latterly, thinking of his father, & tho he bears it well & manfully, this disappointment about his Battalion weighs upon him and his health is far from good. Would that he were well once more!

June 22, 1862

We hear that Lincoln has recalled Stanley from the Governorship of N Carolina. How true it is that it is hard to serve two masters! In both attempts he has signally failed. The shallow artifice by which he attempted to throw dust in to our eyes by professing to govern us by the Statute Laws of N C displeased his Northern masters, whilst his being here at all is such an infringement of our rights that no plausibility could even gild the pill. I have written some lines which I would greatly like to fall into his hands, but as I see no possibility of that I will 'een confide them to my journal, that it at least may see how I loathe the Traitor!

Lines

Richard Dobbs Speight, Gov of N C, was killed in a duel by Edward Stanley's father many years ago. His grave was violated by the Yankees when they had possession of New Berne, and his skull stuck upon a pole was one of the first objects which met Stanley's eyes when he landed in New berne as Lincoln's Governor, appointed to subjugate his native State.

————

> Room for the Traitor! room! Lo thy father's sins
>   rise from the grave to greet thee!
> Look on me thou false Stanley! look on me and shuddering
>   hear thy welcome!
> By thy father's hand—untimely nipped my days were
>   ended—my budding fame cut down
> And to dust my name was given! Yet revenge like
>   this I had not dared to picture!
> Thanks! to the impious hand which rudely burst
>   My coffined cerements and brought me forth

————

[182] Galatians 6:2a.

To greet thee! thanks! tho unwilling all! for that
    base act of sacralegious violence
Has filled my cup of Vengeance!
I see that name—that name of Stanley which thy father
    bore—proudly and purely!
('Een tho' I hated him—yet this he forced me to accord
    him)
I see that once revered name I say—discrowned!
    dishonoured a by word! and a hissing!
Babes shall lisp it out with scorn! Woman shall forget
    her gentleness and learn
To curse it!—And Stanley the Statesman!
    Stanley the patriot shall be by men—
Forgot—in Stanley—the Traitor!

Thy foul presence doth eclipse his greatness! doth blot
    out his nobleness!
And with the noisome stench of Treason! thou has drowned
    the perfume of his memory!
Welcome thou traitor! welcome here to infamy! hug thou
    the chains of Life
Until thou loathest them—and then thou false one—
    doubly dyed in Treason!
Welcome to the feast where Arnold's self awaits thee!

JUNE 26, 1862

Journals are not correct exponents of peoples thoughts, wishes or feelings. Why it is I cannot say, but it is certainly the fact. I have no fear of any one ever reading this, so that cannot be the reason; but I think it is partly the habit of reticence which from long use I have acquired & partly mortification at the exceeding pettiness of some of the causes of annoyance which however small as they are do not the less make up my happiness or unhappiness.

For instance this week I have been on tenter hooks respecting the future disposition of our property & prospects which were all unsettled by the renunciation of the deed for Looking Glass last fall. Am to have a conversation with father & I turn & revolve what I am to say, ceaselessly in my mind, to no purpose as yet, so tho' I say nothing of it yet it does not the less affect me. Then Mary's eldest children are sick, the cause being variously stated according to the different bias of the various members of the family as "Green Apples," "miasma in this Low Country," "going fishing in the sun,"—or "sleeping with the window on their bed raised one damp night"—& tho these points are matters of grave discussion, yet no word of them have I recorded. Then the state of anxiety in which we are as regards our army before Richmond, the feverish restless desire for news, the looking for the Mail, the disappointment when "no news" is uttered by the first opener of the newspaper, the sorrow when it is discouraging, the eager delight that shines in every face when it is the reverse—are matters of such daily occurrence now that a recital of them here would be tiresome & yet they are neither tiresome in their repetition nor does their effect diminish in the slightest. It makes up the sum, the whole of our existence. Just now it is most keen, most intense.

Mr Hill came over this morning and told us that his son is just from Richmond, that the battle must take place this week, that Jackson is there ready to fall upon the enemy at Hanover Court house whilst we make an attack in front, that our generals have made all their dispositions, & that our long suspense must consequently soon be terminated. God grant that it may be a splendid and decisive victory! Evans Spruill, poor fellow, is he tells us very ill at a Hospital in Richmond, his life despaired of. His poor Mother, God be with her!

June 27, 1862

The battle has commenced. Our wing is engaged, with a prospect of the engagement becoming general. Jackson is really there, but the papers went to press before there was anything decisive.

Col Clark was ordered to leave Petersburg with four days rations, for what point he knew not when he wrote but Mary has since heard that the 24th Regt, his, is in Richmond. So, poor thing, her anxiety is intense. Thank God that I am spared the cruel suspense in which I would be plunged were Patrick there. God would give me strength to bear it, but I thank his merciful Providence which lays no such burden upon me.

Evan Spruill is dead,[133] died of Camp fever, another martyr to our liberty. His poor Mother, her presentiments are realized, for when Rebecca died she was sure that she should soon lose another child. Her grief she said always came doubled. George will reach here with the body today. Never was there a more afflicted family. This is the fifth child she has lost, four of them of mature age.

Just as we were going to bed came a note from Sou Hill with the news which George & Charles Spruill brought from Richmond. The battle "began" at six and continued until nine when we had taken all the batteries on the River (this the papers told us, with the addition that we had turned them on the enemy), driven the enemy across, taken possession of all the bridges, & run the Yankees three miles. Gen Branch led the attack, was in the thickest of the fight, & covered himself with glory. They are still fighting.

George saw the flashing of the canon at Petersburg, glorious news. God grant that it may be all true. Ah! for our wounded! Think of the poor fellows lying out all this night, bleeding, dying, with no one to minister to or raise

---

[133] Peter Evans Spruill died of typhoid fever or chronic diarrhea in Richmond on June 25, 1862. *Raleigh Register*, September 10, 1862; Manarin and Jordan, *North Carolina Troops*, V, 193.

them from the ground, whilst we can go peacefully & quietly to bed, to sleep and forget them. They suffer that we may be spared. God preserve our liberty, for it is dearly bought! The best blood of the country is flowing for it.

Poor Mary, I sympathize deeply with her, for her husband is there & who can tell what may be his fate, what he may be enduring now this very moment. Tom Jones & himself are in the same Brigade, Ransoms. God watch over & preserve them! We cannot wait the slow progress of Nathan & his mule with the mail tomorrow, so sent Owen on one of the best horses with charges not to dally. Our suspense is keen. God give us the victory! The attack was delayed on our side in order to hear from Jackson. At six, nothing having been heard from him, the attack was made. God grant that he may come up in time.

June 28, 1862

Went to Evans Spruill's funeral, the first victim to the war whose funeral I have attended. His poor Mother, the accounts of her greif are terrible; her friends fear for her reason. She does nothing but walk up & down & repeat his last letter. It seems, poor lady, that she thought him recovering and was expecting him home when she received the telegram announcing his death.

The excitement about the battle is tremendous; it was on every tongue & in every heart. The news of today is still encouraging, yet we almost fear to hope. They are falling back in good order, carrying their dead & wounded & burning their stores. We have captured their siege Guns. Jackson is reported in their rear, but of that there is no certainty. They have left their rifle pits filled with sharp shooters who pick off our officers & who immediately as we advance on them throw down their guns & surrender; but our men are directed, in order to put a stop to such cold blooded deliberate murder, to tell them that [it] is too late, they deserve no quarter, & dispatch them immediately. Gen Lee has issued an order commanding our officers to take off their uniforms and fight without any badge by which they can be distinguished, a wise and proper precaution.[134] The 18th N C. and a Georgia Regt have suffered severely. The carnage is reported as terrible, exceeding anything ever before seen on this Continent. God be with our unfortunate wounded!

June 29, 1862

Sunday—Went to Church, but there was no service, Mr Cheshire having been sent for to bury a young man, one of his Tarboro congregation, whose body was brought from the battle field yesterday—another house plunged into greif & mourning by this needless cruel war![135]

---

[134] The editors have been unable to locate such an order by General Lee.

[135] Second Lt. Francis D. Foxhall of Co. B, Thirty-third North Carolina Regiment, was killed at Mechanicsville, Virginia, on June 26, 1862. Moore, *Roster of North Carolina Troops*, II, 606; Parish Records, Calvary Church, Tarboro, North Carolina; Clark, *Histories of the North Carolina Regiments*, II, 538.

Sent up to Weldon for news & after waiting with feverish impatience all day for it received only rumours brought by passengers—so good, however, that we fear to trust them. According to them, Jackson is certainly in their rear, between them & their Gun boats, has captured their main depot of supplies; our men steadily advancing, driving them with the bayonnette. Gen Whiting has driven in their front & we have out flanked them—the carnage terrific. Major Trim Skinner,[136] 1st Regt, killed on Friday; Capt Wright[137] of Wilmington certainly dead. We have captured two Brigadiers & a brig of 5000 men who have laid down their arms. Rumour even gives us McClellan & the forty Congressmen who chartered a vessel & engaged a band of music & came down to see us vanquished; but this is too much, it cannot all be true, so we must wait with what patience we can until the mail tomorrow.

Sue & Rachel left us yesterday for Raleigh. We miss the young folks greatly. Father much better. Willie Clark, Mary's second child, quite sick.

JUNE 30, 1862

Continued successes of our army. We are so excited that we think of little else. Huger was ordered to watch the passes of the Chickahominy so as to prevent McClelan forming a junction with his force in the South side of that river, but he stole a march on him & when morning dawned he had twelve miles the start of our troops. Huger always does contrive to make blunders & fail at the critical moment. Our troops at the last accounts were pressing on M'Clellan, he in apparent retreat to the James where his transports lie. Our loss is heavy both in officers & men—the sufferings of the wounded terrible!

Tristram Skinner, whom I knew in former days, & Duncan Haywood[138] are among the killed. God be with their families! The Yankees have destroyed an enormous quantity of stores. At one place we came to a pile 30 ft high by 60 in base of the most valuable articles—Bacon, Coffee, Clothes, sugar, shoes, etc., all burning. Acres of Pontoon bridges were found, the bare Iron skeletons only, they having been subjected to the flames. We have captured an immense quantity of small arm, only eighty guns, he carrying off the rest. He retreats—slowly and in good order, we pressing him close!

---

[136] Tristram Lowther Skinner (1820-1862) of Chowan County, a major in the First North Carolina Regiment, was killed at Ellerson's Mill, Virginia, on June 26, 1862. Clark, *Histories of the North Carolina Regiments*, I, 135-136, 139; Manarin and Jordan, *North Carolina Troops*, III, 141, 144.

[137] James A. Wright of New Hanover County, captain of Co. E, First North Carolina Regiment, was killed at Ellerson's Mill on June 26, 1862. Clark, *Histories of the North Carolina Regiments*, I, 137-139; Manarin and Jordan, *North Carolina Troops*, III, 191.

[138] Duncan Cameron Haywood (1840-1862) of Wake County was first lieutenant of Co. E, Seventh North Carolina Regiment. He was killed while commanding his company at Gaines's Mill on June 27, 1862. According to Clark, Haywood "seized the flag, and in the effort to bear it forward, he in turn lost his life...." Clark, *Histories of the North Carolina Regiments*, I, 368-369; Manarin and Jordan, *North Carolina Troops*, IV, 396, 453.

Went to see poor Mrs Spruill. She exclaimed constantly, "Catherine is it not dreadful?" She read me some lines which her son wrote on the death of one of his young companions last winter to a plantive little air, "The Dying Volunteer"—touching in themselves, but doubly so as they foreshadow exactly his own fate. Poor woman, she is bereaved indeed & the fate of her son cut down in the midst of his usefulness & activity seems indeed inscrutable—the second son who had attained manhood that she has been called to part with.

JULY 1, 1862

The battle still rages. McClellan certainly in retreat to the James, Jackson on one flank, Longstreet on the other & Magruder & Hill pressing him in front. God be with our poor wounded! The sight is pitiable in the extreme. Every house is shattered with shot or shell, yet amids the ruins are huddled our own & the enemy's wounded, for they no longer attempt to carry them with them but are forced by our advance to abandon them. God help them. Dispatched all the Hospital stores I have, Linen, Cotton, Wine, Cordial, etc., to Richmond, praying that they might alleviate some poor fellow's sufferings. Our anxiety intense.

JULY 2, 1862

The fight of Monday night, of which we have details today, was terrific. Hill, Gen A P, in command of his own & Longstreets Divisions fought for five hours without reinforcements against tremendous odds, driving the enemy at the point of the Bayonette one & a half miles & occupying the battle field. The conflict at one time was carried on in the dark, illuminated only by the flashing of the Muskets. He went in 14,000 & came out 6,000 strong—that tells its own tale! The enemy still retreating, stopping at intervals & making desperate stands, which our men overcome at the expense of a heavy loss in lives. It seems as tho we could not wait for the mail. Henry Miller has been in action in the midst of a heavy fire. William Clark's Regt was engaged, lost 7 killed, but is Ordered on the Reserve—a great blessing to Mary. Transports with re-inforcements are in the River but they do not seem to be landing them. I wonder how the North will take this. "On to Richmond" & the fourth to be celebrated there in the Rebel Capitol is harder than they had thought!

JULY 3, 1862

Still undecided. The country is so favourable for concealment, so overgrown with bushes & undergrowth that it is hard to find them. They are still in retreat to Curl's Neck[139] on the James a little above City Point, but we

---

[139] Curles Neck is located along a deep bend of the James River in Henrico County about 40 miles upriver from Jamestown. It stood in close proximity to several of the battles fought during the Union army's various

have a Division between them and the River & hope yet to make them surrender. They must be short of provisions & ere long their ammunition must
fail, for they cannot carry both for such a host. We have captured so enormous
a number of Army Waggons & Mules that they cannot have many more. The
Gun boats in the James are shelling our troops but they do little damage; as
many of their shells fall in the Yankee army as do in ours. Tomorrow will
bring us the decisive news, and the 4th of July will, we hope, be celebrated as
being the era of our second Independance. Late Northern papers tell us the
excitement & anxiety there is intense.

McClellan on Thursday & Friday Telegraphed that he was doing all he
wished, his success complete, when hey, Presto, Jackson cut his wire! The
Lincoln Government refuse to communicate any news at all, saying the result
is unknown, the communication cut off, etc. In consequence the public are
terribly exasperated. Good! I hope they will be more so when autocrat Lincoln removes the seal of secresy from his defeat, or rather has it done for him
by the fugitives. Out of 1500 wounded Yankees in one Hospital, one third are
wounded in the back! There is valour for you. They fight well, however, as
our dead testify. We have captured their Balloon & fixtures & can spy in our
turn.[140] It is said that some of the Transports have dropped down the River,
heavily laded with men, but that lacks confirmation. O! for tomorrow's news.

July 4, 1862

No connection with the mail train at Weldon which cruelly disappoints us.
Mary had an old letter from Col Clark written on Sat. He had been engaged
the evening before & escaped unhurt. Thank God that Patrick, my hope, my
stay, my all, is not exposed to these murderous bullets! The loss fearful. God
help the wounded & dying. Father sent back to Halifax to see if it was not possible to get a paper by the evening train & happily succeeded. Late at night
came Philip with two & we sat up until long after twelve poring over their bad
print & half effaced type.

We are still victorious. The retreat goes steadily on. Squads of stragglers fill
the whole country & even swim the James when our Pickets capture & carry
them to the Army at Drury's Bluff. At one place we came to several tons of Ice
abandoned by them—think of their being able to carry such a Luxury when
we fancied they were suffering for the neccessaries of life! Thousands of
Waggons are collected at Berkeley; it is supposed to be protected by the Shells

---

campaigns against Richmond and the surrounding vicinity. Johnson and Buel, *Battles and Leaders*, II, 167,
384.

[140] An aeronautic corps, organized and headed by Thaddeus S. C. Lowe (1832-1913), constructed and
used balloons in reconnaissance for the Army of the Potomac at Bull Run, the Peninsular Campaign, Gettysburg, and Chancellorsville. *Dictionary of American Biography*, XI, 452-453.

of the Gun boats in the river. Thirty transports are there, whether to reinforce or to carry off McClellan's army, we cannot tell. Thousands of his wounded are left behind him, he commending them to the kindness of Gen Lee. The barbarities they commit are enormous. At one place we found three Georgians hanging & the bodies of several Alabamians horribly mutilated. The small arms captured are innumerable, besides a large quantity of Ammunition both fixed & loose.

Mr James Bruce, poor man, has lost a son.[141] He has already been so very unfortunate, in losing three children within the past few years by disease, that I hoped War might spare him. Col Gaston Meares killed & Major De Rosset, Mr E's rival in the militia Law, reported among the missing. Poor fellows, how I sympathize with their families. Col Mat Ransome, our neighbor, made a brilliant charge on an entrenched Battery & took it in the handsomest style, getting, however, two severe wounds. Col Clarke was engaged on Tuesday at the same time, his regt being in the same Brigade as Col Mat Ransom's and Col Ramsour's—& as their wounds are reported and no mention made of Clark—we suppose he escaped.

The enemy are crowded upon the James between City Point and Berkely[142] Curl's Neck, Mr Allen[s] estate, and Shirley,[143] Mr Hill Carter's, have been over run with the enemy; Curl's Neck the scene of desperate fighting, but they have been driven beyond it. The prisoners, of whom 7,000 were brought in in one day, represent their suffering as extreme. They say that were they not surrounded by water & hemmed in by our troops McClellan could not keep them together, they would disband with a "sauve qui peut"[144] and return home. The famous 7th Regt New Yorkers has been, to our delight, engaged & worsted, as we learn from some prisoners taken from it. They will now see Richmond in another phase. To the *Hospitable*, one in which she scarce two years ago entertained them, it is now the *Hosital* phase. Would that they could all be confined in the hall where they were feasted! & left to a calm comparison of *then* & *now*. Today is the 9th since the first battle was fought. Never

---

[141] Capt. Charles Bruce of the Fourteenth Infantry Regiment, Virginia Volunteers, was killed at Malvern Hill on July 1, 1862. He was the son of James C. Bruce of Berry Hill in Halifax County, Virginia. *Official Records (Army)*, Series I, XI, Part II, 821, 991; "Trustees of Hampden-Sidney College," *Virginia Magazine of History and Biography*, VI (October, 1898), 180.

[142] Berkeley, built in Charles City County, Virginia, in 1726, was the home of Benjamin Harrison (1726-1791), a signer of the Declaration of Independence and governor of Virginia. His son William Henry Harrison (1773-1841), president of the United States, was born there. Thomas Tileston Waterman, *The Mansions of Virginia, 1706-1776* (Chapel Hill: University of North Carolina Press, 1945), 163-164, 413, hereinafter cited as Waterman, *Mansions of Virginia*.

[143] Shirley, an estate on the James River, was the girlhood home of Ann Hill Carter, daughter of Charles Carter and the mother of Robert E. Lee. Hill Carter, colonel of the Fifty-second Regiment, Virginia Militia, inherited Shirley. *Official Records (Army)*, Series I, IV, 636; Waterman, *Mansions of Virginia*, 358, 422-423; Blair Niles, *The James* (New York: Farrar & Rinehart, Inc., 1939), 189, hereinafter cited as Niles, *The James*.

[144] French, meaning every man for himself, or a disorderly retreat.

was there such a series of severe combats, each a bloody battle; never such a retreat, never such an attack. What a scene for the Majesty of Heaven to look down upon! Man whom he created "in His own Image," to be happy, tearing, rending, destroying one the other.

There is news from Vicksburg & N O, but I have no heart for it. Fighting at Vickburg, but nothing decisive as yet, & that brute Butler embroiling himself with the foreign Consuel.[145] His day is almost run. Now that the English papers & Parliament itself denounces him as a disgrace to the Anglo Saxon blood, the North feebly follow in their wake and deprecate his Infamous Order; but it is too late—we see the reason.

July 5, 1862

Our excitement and anxiety increase I beleive every day. Nothing definite is known of McClellan's whereabouts but that he has succeeded in reaching the River at Shirley, Mr Hill Carter's magnificent place on the James. What a waste he will leave it! He is under cover of his Gun boats, his force unknown, even the fact of his having been reinforced resting on rumour.

Went to call on Mrs Baker, my old school mate Nannie Johnson. She has been desperately ill & now looks terribly. Heard of the death of our young neighbor John Anthony.[146] He was shot in the charge of Tuesday, that useless charge, which cost so many lives, as the Battery could as well have been taken in the rear by Jackson, as was proved in an hour's time! We have captured one Major and five Brigadier Generals, and the other commissioned officers mount up to 128 already. The privates are at least 10,000. All their wounded are in our hands & the suffering amongst them has been & is terrific. Altho they burnt quantities of stores at the very doors of their Hospitals, but one of them was supplied with food, and the first request that they all make is for "Bread! bread!"

July 6, 1862

Came brother & brought some rumours, but as today being Sunday & we have no papers, nothing is known of the enemy. James River is crowded with transports & Gun boats, but whether the enemy is disbarking or embarking, no one knows. They have left Shirley & gone further down the River. All our

---

[145]One of Butler's controversial actions in New Orleans was the seizure of $800,000 in bullion held by the French consul on behalf of southern owners. Protests by governments throughout Europe and by United States officials followed. Butler ignored the protests and assumed financial control of his military department, collecting taxes and making expenditures on his own authority. *Dictionary of American Biography*, III, 357-359.

[146]John Hill Anthony (1836-1862), the son of Whitmel Hill and Charity Barnes Anthony of Halifax County, was a corporal in Co. G, Twelfth North Carolina Regiment. He was killed at Malvern Hill on July 1, 1862. Moore, *Roster of North Carolina Troops*, I, 459; Stuart H. Hill Collection; Manarin and Jordan, *North Carolina Troops*, V, 196.

friends are so far safe. Brother & Mr E both despondent. Brother looks on it as but an episode in the Seige of Richmond, that McClellan will entrench & await reinforcements & begin again to make regular approaches. I doubt it. I do not think he will ever again have such an army under his command.

July 7, 1862

The enemy in the fork of Chickahominy & James, a strong natural position, which he is strengthning. We must either attack at great disadvantage or fall back. Westover[147] and Berkeley are the scene of their ravages now. Their tents dot the river for miles & there is a desolate wilderness behind them. How I pity the families in that garden spot of Va! Hitherto War has not come near them. One week ago and their crops were smiling with plenteousness, the Wheat Harvest had commenced & secure in their remote situation with impassible swamps, without roads, too, between them and the enemy, they dwelt at home & viewed from far the horrors of war. Suddenly with one swoop they found themselves environed with blood & carnage, their houses pillaged, their crops destroyed, their stock killed, their fences gone, & they driven outcasts from their happy homes. God be with them & support them in this time of trial! Ah! for the Virginia. Were she still afloat McClellan would have capitulated in the Swamp of the Chickahominy instead of entrenching himself, a new thorn in our side.

The N Y Herald admits the fact of Intervention, but that is such a lying sheet that we do not trust it. Probably he has some stocks which he either wishes to raise or depreciate & hence his admission. Vicksburg still holds out, but our eyes are so bent on Richmond that we see scarcely anything else. The enemy have abandoned James Island, it is supposed to reinforce McClellan, so Charleston feels the first good effect of the repulse we have given him at Richmond. Lincoln calls for 300,000 more troops. Will he get them?

July 9, 1862

Last night came brother with his son Thomas. He is more despondant than ever. It greives one to hear him. He made father really low spirited. He (Father) improves very slowly and we are all discussing some pleasant place up the country where he can have a change of air.

Patrick left for Richmond early this morning to make a report to the Sec of War & make a final effort to get into the service. I shall not greive much if he fails. Since the Conscript Act has gone into force there are so many younger men called into the field that I do not think there is the same necessity there

---

[147] Westover, standing in Charles City County near Berkeley and Shirley, was built by William Byrd (1674-1744) around 1730. A magnificent colonial home which features some of the finest woodwork and architectural design in America, Westover suffered some damage during the Civil War, and the east wing of the house burned. Waterman, *Mansions of Virginia*, 146-163, 423.

was either for his example in Volunteering or for his personal services. His health is far from good and as father's has failed latterly, I think both brother & Patrick will find their paths of duty at home.

Just at sunset came George Daughtry and brought father the unlooked for intelligence that the Yankees were shelling Hamilton! at two P M today.[148] Whitaker's company have been engaged, with what effect he knew not. He was terribly excited & had ridden his horse until it was a lather of sweat, but I am not so much alarmed. I do not think that the Gunboats will come above Rocky Bar & consider it only a feint to draw some portion of our troops from Richmond. Three Gun boats are at Hamilton & the community beleive he has many more behind, which do not I, for I fancy M Clellan needs all the boats he can command in James River at this present writing. The Militia are all ordered out, but I do not think they will do very efficient service armed, or rather unarmed, as they are.

Altho I see no need for it, yet in event of alarm sent Henry word to come out here—all hands—& bring the team. Unhappily Patrick is from home. I wish it could have happened otherwise, but I hope all things will remain quiet until his return. No mail connection today, caused by the breaking down of the Northern train of Cars. I hope that there was no wounded on board, as their sufferings must have been terrible. Sent by Patrick almost the last of my stock of old Linen & cotton for the Hospitals. It is the third installment, so my fourth will be but a small one as I must keep some, least I have a wounded soldier here to nurse, and as they are being distributed through the country it is not at all improbable. Tom George Arrington[149] was killed in that useless charge on Tuesday. Magruder is said to have been drunk when he ordered it but I am loathe to beleive it.

Mary has announced her intention of leaving on Sunday with her children.

Rumours only of mediation; we had better not beleive or trust in them. Vicksburg still holds out. Weather intensely hot, a great contrast to last week when we had fire every day & all day long. Father better.

JULY 10, 1862

About sunrise this morning was awakened by Fanny with the agreeable intelligence that one of the horses was sick. Why is it that our Equine friends

---

[148] Three gunboats commanded by Lieutenant Flusser of the United States Navy proceeded to Hamilton from Plymouth on July 9, 1862. A detachment of the Ninth North Carolina (First Cavalry) Regiment under Lt. A. B. Andrews fired on them at Rainbow Banks two miles below Hamilton, killing two soldiers and wounding nine others, but failed to stop them. Ten men of the Ninth New York Zouaves and twelve seamen landed and captured a Confederate steamer. They returned down the river to Plymouth without encountering any gunfire. *Official Records (Navy)*, Series I, VII, 519, 557; Clark, *Histories of the North Carolina Regiments*, I, 445-448; Manarin and Jordan, *North Carolina Troops*, II, 1-2; Barrett, *Civil War in North Carolina*, 131-132.

[149] Mrs. Edmondston probably meant Capt. William T. Arrington of Nash County, a member of Co. I, Thirtieth North Carolina Regiment. He was killed at Malvern Hill on July 1, 1862. Arrington formerly served as assistant commissary of subsistence to the Twelfth North Carolina Regiment. Clark, *Histories of the North Carolina Regiments*, II, 496, 498; V, 667; Manarin and Jordan, *North Carolina Troops*, V, 115.

always select the time that their master is from home for their indispositions? Felt much releived when I heard that Grachus was the sufferer and commenced the administration of "a whole pharmacopeia," which excited Mr Higgs[150] admiration so much, by mixing two tablespoonsful of Laudanum, 3 of Spt of Turpentine, & a pint nearly of Apple Brandy which I sent to Allen with orders at once to give it to him & tried to take another nap but failed. The mental exercise I had undergone banished sleep, so lay. Speculated upon the probable doings of the Yankees until I heard father come down stairs, then dressed at double quick so as to attend to breakfast. I would not have "dawdled" half so much had Peter been at home, but so it is—I miss him in all things. After breakfast to Chess as usual until we were interrupted by brother, who came out on receipt of the news from Hamilton. Shortly after came a note from Nannie Hill kindly telling us the news.

In all probability the Yankees came up to seize a steamer which was there loading with Corn for Weldon. It seems Mr George Smith[151] had what he considered reliable information that there were no Gun boats at Plymouth & ventured down so low hoping to secure at least one cargo, but he was mistaken or rather purposely misled it is thought through their agency. Three Gun boats suddenly made their appearance & commenced an indiscriminate shelling in which however they succeeded in killing only one poor harmless little child! Mr Smith & crew jumped overboard and escaped by swimming. Capt Whitaker's company under command of his Lieut fired upon them & with such success that five of them were killed and seven wounded. This we know to be a fact, for they landed in Hamilton, seized a physician who chanced to be there, carried him on board, & made him dress the wounded; & he saw the dead men, after which they released him, remarking that they had paid "dear for the whistle," i.e., the little steamer which they captured. Nannie wound up her note with the information that "the Yankees had taken Richmond," that is, Mr Smith's negro of the name of Richmond who remained on board when they all left, whether voluntarily or not I cannot tell. We could not learn the name of the child who was killed. Poor little thing, a gallant acheivement truly for men to be engaged in. It is great cause of thankfulness to us that they have suffered so severely. Capt Coles[152] Company repulsed them recently at

---

[150] Mrs. Edmondston probably was referring to Jacob Higgs, a prosperous fifty-two-year-old farmer living in Halifax County. The 1860 Halifax County census also recorded a George A. Higgs, however, as a merchant in the county. Eighth Census, 1860, Population Schedule, Halifax County, 72, 80.

[151] George A. Smith was listed in the 1860 census as a twenty-five-year-old farmer with forty slaves and eleven slave houses. Eighth Census, 1860, Population Schedule, Halifax County, 81; Slave Schedule, Halifax County, 59.

[152] W. H. H. Cowles of Yadkin County served as lieutenant and later as captain of Co. A, Ninth North Carolina (First Cavalry) Regiment. In October, 1863, Cowles was promoted to major and transferred to the Field and Staff of the same regiment. Promoted to lieutenant-colonel in 1865, to rank from June 1, 1864, Cowles was wounded at Chamberlain Run and hospitalized in Petersburg where he was captured on April 1, 1865. Clark, *Histories of the North Carolina Regiments*, I, 428, 430, 441, 775, 782; V, 673; Manarin and Jordan, *North Carolina Troops*, II, 7, 10.

Winton & now this second repulse at Hamilton will make them dread our crooked narrow River more than ever!

No mail again today, which we think strange. We are impatient for news, news of McClelland, will he retreat or entrench? Entrench say I and wait reinforcements & then advance up the River to Drury's Bluff, perhaps on the South side under cover of his gun boats.

Brother left after dinner. I think he seems more hopeful. Father better. So to bed, wondering where Mr E is and whether he will get home tomorrow.

Poor old Phoebe died yesterday. It is wonderful that she has lived so long. She has been sick since April & seriously so, too, & she must have been a very old woman from her appearance and infirmities.

The Militia all ordered to Enfield which we do not understand. Probably
. . . "An order came"—
"Someone had blundered!"[153]
Not however with the serious consequences which followed the blunder at Balaclava.

This charge of MaGruders to capture the battery in front when it could have been in half an hour more taken in the rear is a similar one to that celebrated, "c'est magnifique!—mais ce n'est pas la Guerre"[154] one of Lords Lucan or Cardigan, I forget which, at Balaklava.[155] The loss of life is tremendus and the wounded are counted by scores—all North Carolina troops. She had thirty three Regts in the battles before Richmond. One *fourth* the troops on the field were furnished by her.[156] This charge is pronounced "not one of the ills necessary to War" and yet I fear if many more such blunders are made by ignorant or *temporarily* incompetent Generals, as ours have latterly shown themselves, it will not long be the case. Mistakes of officers & neglect of duty by them have cost us rivers of blood.

Ah! Gen Huger, I wish you would retire to private life. But for you, McClellan would never have joined forces & ere this one half of his army

---

[153] Tennyson, "The Charge of the Light Brigade," stanza 2:
"Not tho' the soldier knew
Some one had blunder'd."

[154] The observation "c'est magnifique, mais ce n'est pas la guerre" attributed to Pierre Jean Francois Bosquet (1810-1861), a French army officer who served in the Crimean War and later became a marshal of France, referred to the charge of the Light Brigade at Balaklava in 1854. *Webster's Biographical Dictionary*, 175; Bartlett, *Familiar Quotations*, 655.

[155] George Charles Bingham (1800-1888), third earl of Lucan, was in command of the cavalry division during the Crimean War which contained the light cavalry brigade made famous by the charge of October 25, 1854. The Light Brigade, under James Thomas Brudenell (1797-1868), seventh earl of Cardigan, executed the order to charge which Lucan had received from his superior officer although both Lucan and Cardigan realized the futility and costliness of the charge. After the battle both officers received some criticism for following orders at all costs. *Dictionary of National Biography*, VII, 136-138; *Supplement*, I, 196-198.

[156] North Carolina furnished thirty-five and a half regiments, a little more than one fifth of the 181 regiments engaged in the Seven Days' battle. Hill, *Bethel to Sharpsburg*, II, 172.

would have been routed & the other either annihilated or forced to surrender. All this lost by your negligence! Commodore Tatnal's blunders cost
us the Merrimac: you dashed the cup of full success from our lips as we were
about to drain it to the dregs.

July 11, 1862

No news of Patrick tho' I sent to Halifax yesterday for him a letter, however, from Gen Gatlin reccommending him most highly to Gen Holmes. Had
he received it I doubt not that his Commission would have been confirmed &
he placed in command of the unattached Companies as he desires. Accustomed as I am to wishing him success in all he desires I cannot find it in
my heart to regret that he did not get this, for I am convinced that he is better
off at home. His health is by no means good enough to take the field.

July 13, 1862

Sunday—Yesterday came home Patrick & to my great sorrow quite sick.
He gives a most moving account of the suffering in Richmond. He says it is
fearful—the hot weather, the crowded Hospitals, the stench, the want of attendance, the filthy muddy James River water, tepid at that, the actual want
of proper food—altogether make an amount of human suffering difficult to
conceive of & then add to that the desolation of heart, the anguish endured by
those who have lost friends, or have them suffering unable to alleviate their
pain, and it makes a picture of War from which one turns appalled! Twice
since he has been gone did he see Ladies going on to nurse their husbands,
one of whom heard of the death of hers in the Cars & the other saw a Coffin
marked with the name of hers carried past her as she sat by the window! My
God! I thank Thee that thou hast saved me this suffering, this anguish!

The Secretary directed him to reduce his Bossiness to writing & lay it
before him, saying he could not remember all the cases brought before him &
must have time to consider and reccollect. So the matter is no nearer settled
now than it was when he went & he has had his journey & consequent sickness for nothing. All night & today he has a scorching fever and I feel uneasy
about him.

About eleven came Jacob Higgs bringing news that there is a Regt of
Yankees at Plymouth and ten Gunboats.[157] He is in a terrible "*swivet*" (mem
look out that word & see whether it be slang or not) for fear that his Cotton
will be burned. I do not beleive the news, & am thus saved much distress &
anxiety.

Brother came to dinner, if possible more despondant than ever. I would not
have such a disposition to look on the dark side for millions, for I never could

---

[157] In June, 1862, Col. Rush C. Hawkins was authorized "to place a company in Plymouth as a nucleus
around which the Union men can rally under the protection of the gunboats." *Official Records (Navy)*, Series
I, VII, 476; Barrett, *Civil War in North Carolina*, 124.

enjoy them & therefore would be better off without them. Mary & her children left us today. She takes the boys to school & goes herself to spend the summer in Clarksville near them. Children are blessings I suppose. I know that they are sore trials and a great trouble & anxiety. "Sour grapes" perhaps, Mrs E, but who want grapes at all?

Mr E brought us a map picked up on the battlefield. I wish it could tell its tale! It is on an Extra Herald & is a map of the South Western States & of the seat of the War about Corinth. True it might say with the "Knife Grinder"

"Story!? God bless you!
I've none to tell."[158]

but I would like to hear even that.

Jackson's Division have marched North, it is supposed to invade Maryland. Vicksburg holds out nobly, but the enemy have seized 250 negroes & put them to work digging a canal which they intend to make so large that they can pass their ships through it & thus avoid Vicksburg altogether, make an island of it as it were. Matters look well for us in Arkansas, & Missouri is preparing to rise.

JULY 14, 1862

Father & Mama went to Conneconara today leaving Patrick and I alone in the house. On looking back I find it is nearly two years since we have been in this house alone! Everything is so still and quiet that it presents a strange contrast to the noise & confusion of last week. A dreamy idleness seems to over take me, & Patrick being in bed to keep off his chill makes the silence & quiet more felt. I beleive I love quiet. I thoroughly enjoy this day. Not that I am inhospitable or annoyed by children, but they are not part and parcel of my enjoyment. They are a thing aside, as it were, to me & when they leave I fly back at once like a spring bent out of place & resume old habits & old modes of thought without once missing them; & yet I do thoroughly enjoy their prattle when I have it & never mind any trouble they give me or the servants. The continued noise some times wearies me, but I always make allowance for that. Certain it is, however, with Patrick at home I never suffer with ennui & long

---

[158] George Canning (1770-1827) was a major political leader in England from the Napoleonic era until his death. Strongly royalist in sentiment, he supported William Pitt's ministry and served as undersecretary of state for foreign affairs (1796-1801), treasurer of the navy (1804-1806), and secretary of the Foreign Office (1807-1810). Pitt died in 1806, and Canning's political fortunes waned until 1822, when he again ran the Foreign Office. In 1827 he served as prime minister and chancellor of the exchequer. During the brief period between September, 1797, and July, 1798, Canning and several associates published the political newspaper *Anti-Jacobin; or Weekly Examiner* in support of Pitt and the Tory administration. Satirical and witty, the newspaper featured poetry by supposedly anonymous authors which ridiculed liberal philosophy and its proponents. The above poem, written for the November 27, 1797, edition of the *Anti-Jacobin* and attributed to Canning and John Hookham Frere, satirized "*Republican enthusiasm and universal philanthropy*" for failure to correct those evils in the world which were incessantly denounced. *Dictionary of National Biography*, VIII, 420-431; L. Rice-Oxley (ed.), *Poetry of the Anti-Jacobin* (Oxford: Basil Blackwell, 1924), xx-xxii, 6-9.

Conneconara, the home of Kate's mother and father, stood on the west bank of the Roanoke River where the swamp and river meet. Though situated on a high bluff on the river, the property was subject to frequent flooding, and there is discussion in the diary of problems caused by "freshets." The shell of the house still stands and is used as a hunting lodge. The porch is not original, and there have been exterior alterations. A large tree fell during an ice storm in February, 1978, causing heavy damage to the back and left side of the house. Conneconara as it appeared in 1967 is shown above.

for no other human companionship except father's & brother's. I am afraid I do not *love* many people; they are not neccessary to me.

Have just been overlooking the work on the Flax, having the seed stripped off. We have a good crop and the fibres seems strong. I will get a wheel & learn to spin it & at least spin some towels & gloves for Patrick & father. Patrick, God bless him, is better today but far from well. If his fever does not fall tonight I must send for the Dr.

Above is an interior view of Conneconara, showing the original stairs. (The railing is a replacement.) The interior of the house was redone around 1870 in a Victorian style, but remnants of earlier woodwork remain.

JULY 15, 1862

Patrick better today. Whilst we were at tea came news that the Yankees have occupied Williamston in force, that they have arrested the magistrates at Hamilton, & hold them personally responsible for their repulse by Capt Whitaker's Co last week.[159] They demand to know who fired upon them. The cowards, to come & take peaceful unarmed men, who had nothing in the world to do with the action, & hold them responsible for the conduct of a body of regular Confederate soldiers! Who fired upon them? Why the

[159]Three gunboats came up and landed about 250 men and two pieces of artillery at Williamston. The men requested the mayor to call the commissioners together, demanded all government stores, and ordered citizens who were in the fight at Rainbow Banks to give themselves up. *State Journal*, July 23, 1862.

Southern Confederacy, which they have come to invade, represented by a company in the 1st N C Cavalry. Who fired upon them? What a question, when you came here to be fired upon? Ah! the rascals. They are uncomfortably near us tho, and I trust that the Government will send troops down to keep them in check.

A Steamer has got in from Liverpool & brings as a present from the Liverpool merchants to the Confederate States thirteen Batteries of Light Artillery, 78 guns in all, Rifles, carriage, harness, & every thing complete—a magnificent present and one for which Liverpool has my warmest thanks. We will not forget her when trade opens & Liverpool shall have the precedence of all other goods in my estimation. The first real act of kindness which we have received from any nation in the world.

Johnson has thrown into the Pententiary at Nashville all the clergyman of what denomination soever who refuse to take the oath and to pray for the President of the U S. Where is your boasted liberty, your boasted *Religious* freedom, when a man cannot even *pray* as he wishes but must stain his soul with a lying lip prayer? Truly, he tries to make us realize one of the curses in the Psalms—"their prayers were turned into sin."[160]

Vicksburg holds out gallantly & there are rumours that in Arkansas we have captured Curtis and 5,000 men, but it wants confirmation. Major Gen Liar Halleck, as the English papers call him, claims a victory for the Feds at Richmond, says Richmond has fallen & that 15,000 Confederates are captured. Shame where is thy blush? Indeed, the Northern Journals generally claim that McClellan has only changed front and in fact made a magnificent strategetic movement & that too in the face of an enemy, that he is nearer Richmond than he was at the commencement of the Battle. Truth surely has left this earth.

As I walk in the garden this morning and look at my young Pear trees bending with fruit, Patrick's prophecy about the Yankees being here before they ripened fruit, uttered when he planted them two years since, comes over me like a chill. True, Doyenne d Ete has done its best to falsify his Cassandra-like anticipations, but the Vicar of Waikfield & Bon Chetien look as tho months of sun were needed to soften them and the close vicinity of the marauders at Williamston not twenty five miles off may well make us tremble, but God knows best and He will direct everything in His own way.

July 17, 1862

Father left us yesterday for a jaunt up the country & to Kittrells & the Catawba White Sulphur Sprs in hopes the change would be of service to his health.[161]

---

[160] Psalms 109:7. "When he shall be judged, let him be condemned: and let his prayer become sin."

[161] Kittrell's Springs was located on the Raleigh and Gaston Railroad about eight miles from Henderson and was described as being safe from the invading enemy in 1862. Catawba Springs, a popular pre-Civil

Patrick is very weak & feeble but more bent than ever on getting into active service. He was all day drawing up a Memorial to the Sec of War & had to pause and rest many times.

The papers tell us that our Government have demanded Butler from the U S Government to be hung for hanging Mumford![162] Failing him, it declares its intention of hanging Maj Gen McCall, the only Maj Gen in our possession. It may be right & may save hundreds from the fate of poor Mumford, but it seems hard and almost blood thirsty! But this law of Retaliation is so opposed to all Christian ethics that I know not how to judge it! It may be but the beginning, as brother says, and inaugrate a scene of bloodshed & deliberate murder from which we turn with horror. Yet Mumford's death was an outrage, a crime against humanity, a cold blooded murder, from a repetition of which our citizens should be protected. Butler has imprisoned a Mrs Philips for laughing on her Balcony, at what is not stated, when a Yankee funeral was passing. Was ever such tyranny heard of before? He deserves death. Would that his nation would give him up.

The enemy have, we learn, left Williamston & returned to Plymouth. What was the fate of the unfortunate magistrates we have not heard. I hope they resisted & refused to take the oath. I hope so for the honour of N C.

JULY 18, 1862

A great triumph in the Mississippi—the Steam Ram Arkansas, which was being built at Memphis, but which was towed in an unfinished state when Memphis was evacuated up the Yazoo River, has been quietly finished. Suddenly she emerged from the mouth of the Yazoo and fell upon the fleet before Vicksburg. She sank two, crippled two, blew up one, drove one ashore, & damaged others & in spite of a shower of shell & ball more terrific than can be conceived of, entered Vicksburg in triumph and now lies under our guns. She would have effected more but her smoke stack, the only damage she received, was so riddled with shot that she lost steam. She lost 9 killed & 11 wounded by a shell which entered a port hole which most imprudently was opened for air. The defence before Vicksburg is most heroic. The town has been bombarded for days. Scarcely a house remains which is not perforated with shot or shell. The liquid fire shells carry ruin & destruction where ever they burst, yet the town still holds out. The shelling commenced without notice at day light in the morning when the city was full of women & children. Would that

War resort, was in eastern Lincoln County. The North Carolina White Sulphur Springs was 56 miles west of Salisbury, near the Western North Carolina Railroad, and was advertised as being "far removed from the invading vandals." *North Carolina Standard*, May 21, 1862; *Raleigh Register*, June 11, 1862; *Daily Progress* (Raleigh), June 18, 1864.

[162]William B. Mumford, a forty-two-year-old professional gambler originally from Onslow County, North Carolina, was hanged by General Butler in New Orleans on June 7, 1862, for pulling down a United States flag that had been raised over the Mint after Farragut's capture of the city. *Raleigh Register*, July 16, 1862; *Official Records (Army)*, Series II, III, 645, 673; Series II, IV, 134-135, 170.

the like resolution had been showed at New Orleans. How different would be its fate now.

I append the orders relating to Mrs Phillips,[163] for in the space of a few years it will be difficult to convince one self even of the petty tyranny & monstrous injustice, the unrestrained temper & cruelty of the man—well is he called "Butler the Beast." Poor woman! How I sympathize with her under this foul wrong. Every drop of blood in my veins boils as I think of the insult to which she is exposed, the horrible outrage which can with impunity be perpetrated upon her, for has not Butler himself given his brutal soldiery license for anything? Her poor parents, Mr and Mrs Levy, how little did they think that such sorrow would fall upon them in their old age. I should like to hear Phoebe[164] speak of it; how she would scorch them! I must think there is some private pique, some personal feeling which he thus abuses his power to revenge. Her tongue is a sharp one, her influence in society large, & she may have put some slight upon Butler or his wife which he now has it in hands to avenge. The Infamous Judge Jeffries[165] himself was but little worse & when one considers the different ages in which they lived, not so bad as this blot on the nineteenth Century—"this canker worm"—"this Butler"!

Grant is emulating him at Memphis, for he has issued an order[166] ordering all families who have any member of it, directly or indirectly, in the service of the Confederate Government, all state or municipal officers, to leave the city in five days. Unheard of tyrrany! No wonder Vicksburg holds out with such examples before them.

We succeed in annoying the transports & even the Gun boats in James River. On Monday we disabled their Mail boat, running her aground. Mr Lincoln has been to pay McClellan a visit, see for himself the condition of the Army, & will it be beleived that he the President of a great nation actually with his suite undressed and "took a swim and a bath" in the waters of the Potomac on their way back to Washington? Thank God! he is not our President! We have no part or lot in him, the vulgar flat boats man! With strange inconsistency the Northern papers claim both the triumph of a victory & the sympathy of being out numbered after fighting with desperate valor before Richmond.

---

[163] This newspaper clipping is pasted in the diary at the entry for July 18, 1862. The orders are published in *Official Records (Army)*, Series I, XV, 510-511.

[164] Phoebe Yates Pember (1823-1913), a sister of Mrs. Phillips, served as matron of the Chimborazo Hospital in Richmond from 1862 until 1865. She later recorded her experiences in *A Southern Woman's Story: Life in Confederate Richmond* (Jackson, Tenn.: McCowat-Mercer Press, Inc., 1959; originally published 1879).

[165] George Jeffreys (1644-1689), successively lord chief justice, privy councillor, and lord chancellor of England and a staunch supporter of the crown, was notorious for the flagrant injustice and brutality which he displayed on the bench, especially during the trials of participants in Monmouth's rebellion of 1685. *Webster's Biographical Dictionary*, 777.

[166] This order, issued by General Grant on July 10, 1862, was later modified. *Official Records (Army)*, Series I, XVII, Part II, 88, 98-99.

July 21, 1862

Aniversary of the Battle of Manassas. Who would have thought one year ago that this war would still be raging and the Blockade unraised? With the exception of salt & shoes I think we suffer less from the Blockade than we did; our people having determined to do without many things which formerly they thought to be neccessaries cease to feel the want of them as they did at first. The want of coffee is a sore discomfort, but it is astonishing how cheerfully it is borne. Thanks to Patrick's far seeing I suffer less than my neighbors; indeed I have not yet felt the want of a single thing, a blessing vouchsafed to few. Shoes for the servants I need most, but the weather is warm & they can go bare foot tho' I do not like it.

Went with Mr E. to the Plantation. An effort had been made to break into our Pork House. The rogues got nothing, but Mr E took most summary & immediate measures to repress the spirit of disorganization & theft before it should become prevalent amongst our people. He summoned all the men, told them such a thing must be known to some of them, it could not occur without the cognizance of somebody, & gave them half an hour to bring him the guilty person, but that two people in the throng were to be whipped for the offence. At the end of the time, they being unable to agree in a verdict, he had twenty or more straws of different lengths thrown into a basin and the lots drawn. Upon those two who had the shortest straw the punishment was to fall. Hogfeeder Solomon and Ishmael were the unfortunate ones & were without more delay made to suffer the penalty. This plan seems hard, but he says it is the only one to prevent theives being as rampant here as they are at Conneconara. It makes it the duty of the whole plantation to detect offenders. This must be one of the fruits of the War, as we never had such a thing before.

In the afternoon came Mr Shaw for a nights lodging & shelter from a coming shower & well for him, good man, that he reached one in time, for a harder, longer, more uninterrupted rain was never before seen. It cannot be general. The quantity of water which fell we have no means of estimating, but the whole yard & lot were afloat. Tho well drained with large ditches, the bridge in the road in front of the house was washed up and the water almost deep enough to swim a horse there, where there is never a drop in ordinary times. If, however, it should be general we have a terrible freshet before us, so goodbye to the young corn.

Mr Shaw is on his way to join the Scotland Neck Mounted Rifles. He joins to avoid the Conscription. He brought us an idle rumour of seven hundred Conscripts having rebelled in Raleigh & having been fired upon, but I do not beleive a word of it.

July 22, 1862

The mail yesterday brought Patrick letters from James to the effect that Gen Holmes has been transferred from this Department to the Trans

Mississippi—just as Patrick had presented his credentials & Statement to him requesting to be placed in command of the Cav Companies in this State. He seems unfortunate, but I am not inconsolable under it, as I see the hand of God in thus directing him. Gen Holmes successor is to be Gen D H Hill, his old friend but some time must elapse before he could know enough of the Companies to be able to reccommend the Sec to throw them into a Regt & in the mean time his Commission will expire. So he has only to look to the result of his application to the Sec, which is but a faint hope; but as I said before I am content.

Walked with Patrick through the grove & orchard. Had some trees cut out & must speedily mark more so as to give it a good thinning. Found the apples on Woolman's Harvest ripe & most beautiful, perfect in form and with an exquisite waxen look & what is better, as pleasant to the taste as beautiful to the eye. Amused myself with my note book much to Patrick's merriment. He says not one fact I have recorded is of any practical use, but I boldly answer Mr Utilitarian that the amusement that compiling it affords me is use enough. It keeps me from ennuie & rubs up my education, besides fostering the taste for Literature & Belles Lettre which with some persons flag as they grow old— may it never be so with me.

Looked out "*swivet*," could only find it in the Provincial Dictionary where, quite in opposition to the sense in which I used it, it means "a deep sleep." So it is "slang," & therefore Mrs Edmondston you owe your journal a humble apology for having used it, for tho' it does not aspire to be "a well of pure English undefiled"[167] yet it scorns modern innovations & slang disgusts it outright. What is slang, however? "Rennible" is in no dict that ever I could discover & yet it is a good old English word, crowded out of the language by more modern "fluent" altho they do not express exactly the same thing & tho obsolete still it is not "*slang*." Quiz was slang, but it has been adopted into good society & tho it has not yet found its way into the Dict, has not yet that certificate of right, yet no one would venture to accuse another of inelegance in its use. But a little good sense & good taste I suppose determine the matter for every one. This Yankee habit of coining new words when they have old ones which express their meaning perfectly is abominable. "*Skedaddle*" is their elegant word to express a precipitate retreat. They make the "rebels *skedaddle*" very often in imagination and sometimes they "*skedaddle*" themselves. I hope that this will be one point of difference between us in future. They may be as careless in their language as they choose; we, I hope, will preserve our noble gift with jealous care & make our spoken conform to our written language.

Vicksburg still holds out whilst we are making advances in Tennessee, even beating up their quarters at the gates of Nashville. Andy Johnson, a wretch,

---

[167] Edmund Spenser, *The Faerie Queene*, bk. 4, canto 2, stanza 32.

has resigned & gone to Washington after oppressing his native state as much as he could & heaping up for himself a future of infamy.

McClellan lies quietly on the James awaiting re-inforcements. His army is represented as being prostrated with sickness. Burnside with the most of his force has gone to him & the rumour goes that he is to march up the South side of James River, take Petersburg, & then co operate with McClellan in an attack on Drury's Bluff to open the River to the Gun boats when all three, McClellan, Burnside, and the Gun boats, will advance on Richmond. Conscripts are being hurried on to fill up our broken ranks & we are preparing to give them a warm reception on their next "On to Richmond" movement.

Pope is at the head of a Column which menaces the Valley, but Jackson I hope will soon manage him. Huger is releived of his command and placed at the head of the Ordnance Department—a place he is fitted for & would that he had occupied it instead of the passes of the Chickahominy. Had he been alert every thing goes to prove that the whole northern army would have fallen into our hands.

A cartel for the exchange of prisoners has been concluded, but we hear nothing more of the demand for Butler. Neither do we of the present said to have been sent by the merchants of Liverpool, so I fear it was a false statement. Truth pure maiden where art Thou? Certainly not abroad in this Country!

Letters from father. He has left Kittrells & is in Raleigh on his way to the Catawba White Sulphur—in some respects better, in others not so well.

July 25, 1862

The last & most petty act of tyranny that I hear of the Northern Government's committing is holding the Rev Samuel McPheeters, the "Sam" of our childhood, son of my old teacher Dr McPheeters, to a rigid account and threatening him with imprisonment for having baptized a child whose parents gave it the name of "Sterling Price." Think of it! Was ever cause so weak before that the name of a poor little six weeks baby could effect it? This is liberty? Well might Madame Roland exclaim "O liberty what crimes are committed in thy name"?[168]

Gen Pope has issued an order which I append.[169] It is monstrous in its cruelty and contrary to the practices of all civilized warfare, but this is not civilized warfare, nor do our enemies show either the genius of Christianity or the spirit of Civilization.

---

[168] This quotation has been attributed to Jeanne Manon Roland (1754-1793), the wife of Jean Marie Roland de La Platière (1734-1793), a French revolutionary. *Webster's Biographical Dictionary*, 1276.

[169] Mrs. Edmondston pasted a newspaper clipping dated July 18, 1862, in her diary opposite the entry for July 25, 1862. The article contains General Pope's orders instructing his troops to subsist upon the country and warning the inhabitants of the Shenandoah Valley that they would be held responsible for any injuries to the railroad or attacks upon trains or straggling soldiers by bands of guerrillas.

A cartel for the exchange of prisoners has been agreed on, so at last we have forced them to recognise us as beligerants.

Read McCauley's masterly review of Warren Hastings life.[170] What a writer he is! How he puts the scene, the people, even their motives & springs of action, before you! His description of Westminster Abbey at the time of the trial is the finest peice of word painting I ever—to carry out the metaphor—I ought to say "*saw*." Warren Hasting was a great man, great in his retirement, great in his fall. How few would have taken refuge as he did, from the stings of disappointed ambition, from a cutting sense of ingratitude, from the consciousness of great administrative powers, unjustly cooped up—in short taken refuge from *self* in the pleasures of planting, in the satisfaction felt at the daily production of a copy of verses. Weak they may be, deficient in poetic fire certainly they were, a mild, very mild, and much diluted draught from the Castalia fount,[171] yet in their end strong—their attained object, happiness, satisfaction, peace, high and noble.

We are told to admire Diocletian[172] cultivating his Cabbages. Were his Cabbages the best brought to Rome? did they possess an exemption from the inroads of the worm, from drought? Is that the ground of our admiration? No, we admire not the thing produced but the mind capable of finding happiness in its production, after relinquishing the cares of an empire. Why then call Warren Hastings a poetaster? Consign him to the society of Miss Seward[173] and a provincial Blue Stocking clique? Reverence rather the energy of mind, the buoyancy, the vigor, the strength which could turn from objects such as had engrossed his past & manfully & bravely keep himself from soured dejection, hopeless repining, endless complaining of injustice & unappreciated merit, by forcing itself to an interest in a thing so pure, so harmless, so refining, as writing verses, weak tho' they be.

Today my handmaidens made their advent into the house barefooted! to their infinite delight, the price of shoes being such as to prohibit us from indulging in the luxury of waiting maids tramping about, actually trampling, under foot from ten to fifteen dollars; for that is now the price of negro shoes. The commonest pair to be had, & very inferior ones at that, cost in Petersburg ten dollars!

Walked in the Orchard & picked up apples until I was all in a heat, but they are so beautiful, so abundant, that I am led from tree to tree in search of new beauties. Red Astrachan bore off the palm until Summer Rose stepped in

---

[170] Mrs. Edmondston is referring to Thomas Babington Macaulay's review of the *Memoirs of the Life of Warren Hastings*, by the Reverend G. R. Gleig, in the *Edinburgh Review*, LXXIV (October, 1841), 81-133.

[171] The mythical Castalia fountain supposedly inspired the gift of poetry in those who drank its waters. Benét, *Reader's Encyclopedia*, 186.

[172] Gaius Aurelius Valerius Diocletian (245-313) was the emperor of Rome from 284 until 305. Benét, *Reader's Encyclopedia*, 298.

[173] Anna Seward (1747-1809), a minor English poet, was known as "the Swan of Lichfield." Benét, *Reader's Encyclopedia*, 1016.

& bore off its *"blushing honors."* Summer Pearmain has a fine aromatic flavor but the Woodpeckers and Jays have as nice a discrimination as man in the choice of fruit & few perfectly ripened ones fall to our lot without having first been tasted by them.

That vile insect the Apple tree borer eludes my sagacity. Knife in hand I probe, cut, & pare the little excrescences which betray his presence, but beyond a bright crimson spot in the centre, which even under a powerful microscope reveals nothing, I cannot detect the intruder. I find occasionally at the junction of the branches, just under the bark, a repulsive looking white grub, but they are not plentiful enough to account for all the Knobs which seem to sprout out on the trunk & branches. I am experimenting on the virtue of Sulphur & Lard upon Northern Spy & thus far with much success. Busy packing a barrel of good things & vegetable for James. Poor fellow, he has a hard time of it in that crowded Camp—few things to be got at best, & where there are so many competitors fewer still fall to the lot of one.

July 30, 1862

The Sec of War still delays answering Mr E.'s application to fill out his Battalion. It is annoying on his own account & doubly so on that of Capt Reinhart, the Yanceyville Co., which was mustered into Edmondston's Battalion & is encamped awaiting orders which seem indefinitely delayed. Went yesterday to the Plantation with Mr E. Very busy sowing turnips both there & here. The seed are put in good order. God grant the increase!

News by the mail indicates that McClellan having strengthened himself on the James by entrenchments is sending part of his men down the river, with what object it is not certainly known, but it would appear to join Pope at Fredericksburg, I suppose to try "On to Richmond" by another route. Pope's army are committing the most horrible excesses in the Valley and about Fredericksburg. His order which I append is, I think, the most oppressive which has yet appeared. To expatriate a whole country & then to treat as spies those whom the care of their families, the protection of all man holds dear, may cause to linger round their homesteads is cruelty which no despot yet has surpassed. The atrocious order will not be beleived in future times. True is it that no war is so savage as a civil one!

A cartel for the exchange of prisoners has been signed, we having greatly the advantage in both numbers & rank. The seige of Vicksburg has been, after weeks of Bombardment, for the present abandoned, the enemy admitting a defeat. They have damaged the town to the amount of $80,000 to effect which they threw shells. Our loss is thirty killed & wounded, theirs unknown. Truly these Yankees are savage and unchristian enemies. Even the sanctity of the grave is not respected by them! The body of Gen A S Johnston was deposited temporarily, subject to the orders of his wife now in California, in the vault of Mayor Monro in New Orleans. This they have sacraleigiously invaded, taken the coffin out & removed the outer case, with what object does not appear & this too by order of Butler.[174] Was ever such warfare waged by Christian before, a warfare upon women & dead bodies? Cromwell's was the last grave outraged by authority by the Anglo Saxon race[175] & that has always been considered a blot upon Charles 2d's administration & that the civilization of the 19th Century should now revive it seems incredible!

In Kentucky Morgan carries all before him. He has even threatened Cincinnati & thrown the whole south of Ohio into a terrible panic. In Cincinnati it was terrible & had he troops enough to protect his rear, he would have been able to shell it from Covington.

Negroes are admitted to testify in the Courts of the District of Columbia. Lincoln is making a desperate effort "to run with the hare & hunt with the hounds,"[176] i.e., to please both Abolitionists & Democrats. He has signed the bill confiscating the slaves of all engaged in active "rebellion," as he terms it, has had the members from the border States at the White House, & made a most piteous appeal to them "to releive him from the pressure upon him" by assenting to the proposition made some time since to pay them for the slaves in their respective States—to consent to the gradual abolition of Slavery, but for the credit of humanity, be it said, very few of them yielded to his overtures. The minority report is most Uriah Heap-ish, but the Majority speak out & throw the blame of the war back on Mr Lincoln's shoulders in defiance of the attempt he makes to fix it on them. Recruiting goes on slowly at the North, not a moiety of his 300,000 men being forth coming & no enthusiasm exhibited at the cry of To Arms.

How comes it that I can be so happy in the midst of such wide spread distress? Is it that I do not see & thus do not realize it? It must be so for I am neither selfish nor callous. God has mercifully protected me so far from it & I hear of it only through the papers or from the report of others, & here I live quietly amid my groves & gardens, wandering from tree to tree to see how the apples ripen, the peaches blush, peep at the Figs, bring in baskets of choice Dahlias, red, write, make Lavender baskets & Flybrushes—in short lead so delightful a "dolce par niente" life that I could almost forget there was a war. No I could not do that. The sufferings of the wounded, the sick, rouse & stir

---

[174] The story of Johnston's body being molested by Butler in New Orleans appears to have no foundation in fact. The alleged incident was not mentioned in a biography written by Johnston's son, who was quite sensitive to any form of "Yankee atrocity." See William Preston Johnston, *The Life of Albert Sidney Johnston* (New York: D. Appleton and Company, 1878).

[175] Oliver Cromwell's bones and those of his mother were disinterred and thrown into a lime pit. Cromwell's head was placed on a pole over Westminster Hall where it remained for twenty years. Theodore Roosevelt, *Oliver Cromwell* (New York: Charles Scribner's Sons, 1923; originally published 1900), 233.

[176] The proverb "To hold with the hare and run with the hound" has been attributed to Humphrey Robert, who included it in his book *Complaint for Reformation*, published in 1572. Bergen Evans (comp.), *Dictionary of Quotations* (New York: Delacorte Press, 1968), 302.

my heart of hearts & the most serious employment of my time is I beleive devoted to them. God, I thank Thee that Thou hast thus blessed me, I thank Thee for the contentment which enables me thankfully to enjoy the blessings which Thou has sent me.

Amused myself for the past few days writing some Lines on the Mosque of St Sophia.[177] It has long been a favourite notion of mine & I had some ideas at one time sending it to Longfellow & asking him to elaborate & adorn it, but this War has taken all relish from his productions. Poet tho he is, I never care to read again either of his past or of his future writing. So I concluded to try what I could do myself. I am not exactly pleased with them. They lack fire, viz., Life, energy. The fact is, Mrs Edmondston, they lack the poetic inspiration! The lines are good, smooth, pretty, *very neat* in short, but they do not stir the blood or make one pulse beat quicker. Shall I insult you by calling them "*Hemanic*"? They are better than the "*tolerable.*" They mount even to fine in some lines, very well for an amateur & better than much of the published poetry one reads, but still, Madam, so far below your own standard that, honestly put, I do not think you take unalloyed pleasure in them. There is a something which you wish to say, something you *feel*, something which these lines do not say & which, Madam, in short, I fear you are not capable of saying! At any rate then I am thankful for the capacity of *feeling*, thankful that I can *feel* a grand idea, an exquisite beauty, even if the expression of it has been denied me. With the German poet, translated for me years ago by own dear brother, I will say

      "Beloved! if thou has not fame thou hast
      happiness."

But it is too late to copy the lines today, so I leave them for a leisure moment.

Patrick thinks he hears Guns all the morning. I sharpen my ears but can hear nothing. They are in a North Easterly direction, so they may be at Drury's Bluff or in the James River. It is a solemn sound, that of a heavy booming Gun here in the stillness & solitude of the country & the thought that it may be an announcement of the death of some loved one in our army of patriots may well depress one.

Throughout the North Negro Regts are being raised, equipped, & drilled as soldiers, Lincoln in this having yeilded to the popular cry. Hunter in S C has a Regt of them which he styles the 1st S C Volunteers. Amo writes me that he has seen two men who were taken prisoners at Port Royal guarded by negroes in the U S uniform. Cuffee did not do his duty, as they escaped! In this State they are doing the same thing. Some of them marched from

---

[177] Saint Sophia, a Christian cathedral founded in 325-326 by Constantine, was rebuilt by Justinian in 538. When Constantinople was conquered by Turks in 1453, the building was converted into a mosque. It remains a brilliant example of Byzantine architecture. "Saint Sophia," *Encyclopedia Americana* (New York: Americana Corporation, 30 volumes, 1952), XXIV, 169-170, hereinafter cited as *Encyclopedia Americana*.

Washington to Plymouth last week. Col Williams hung two sent out as emissaries to induce others to run away & enlist. They had U S. money & enlistment papers with them![178]

AUGUST 1, 1862

St Sophia

The Mosque of St Sophia was built in part from the remains of the Grecian temples. The Emperor Justinian laid the world under contribution for it's erection. Greece, Egypt, and Rome all sent their tribute. I have combined with this fact the well known legend that at the moment of our Saviours death a voice swept over the Egean & announced that "Pan is dead," whereupon the Oracle of Delphi instantly ceased.

Within this dome for Christian worship reared, stand
Mute witnesses, the treasured trophies of all Heathendom!
And in the dusky twilight as they rear their huge collossal columns
A whisper—such as erst with might voice the Egean swept—
Floats up the footworn aisle; breathes round each chis'led capitol
And with mysterious cadence—thrills through the mighty Dome!
    "Great Pan is Dead"!!
Where is thy Oracle O Delphi?! mute!—Great Goddess Dian!
Queen of the night! Chaste huntress—where is thy greatness?!
    gone!
Thy thunderbolts O Jupiter are powerless! Thy mysteries Eleusis
    vanished
No gratitude we pay—to thee O teeming Mother Ceres! Phoebus thy
    fiery Car
Is empty! Minerva offspring of Intellect,—Queen of the mind thy
    sceptre
Has departed! Myths of a past—whose dust the world admires
    ye all pay tribute—here!!—
This glorious Dome uprears its vaulted space upon the porphry columns
Which upbore the Roman temple of the Sun! Here stands the pride of
    Isis & Osiris"!—
Those chisled capitals—have seen the homage paid in Athens to
    Minerva!
Torn—from thy shrine at Cyzicus, these O Ceres once were thine!
Yon long line of granite pillars have adorned the boast of Ephesus!
    the temple of Diana!—
That mysterious Sphinx—hiding her Lion's paws—beneath a woman's
    drapery—
Those Lotus crowned shafts—Egypts unsmiling offering—from Memphis
    came!
A stately Pantheon! meet for the worship of the One Almighty Purity!

---

[178] For a thorough discussion of the roles Negroes played in the Union army and the northern war effort, see Benjamin Quarles, *The Negro in the Civil War* (Boston: Little, Brown Co., 1953), and Dudley T. Cornish, *The Sable Arm: Negro Troops in the Union Army, 1861-1865* (New York: Longmans, Green and Co., 1956).

Here, in one universal strain converging—the separate worship of
    the Past—is blended!
Dian's purity, Minerva's wisdom, Apollo's prescience Phoebus' glory—
    Jove's and Osiris power—
Types which the heathen mind—too weak to grasp in one combined
    whole!—
Worshiped as separate—& oft opposing Deities—the diamond dust
    of Truth!
Meet in a Diamond blaze of Glory! the worship of the One God given—
    Unity!
"Great Pan is Dead!—silenced was thy Oracle O Delphi—when a
    far mightier voice
Than that which spoke thy requiem—proclaimed in tones
Which sweep through Time!—that—"It is finished"!
The worship of the unknown God is o'er!—the worship of the many
    gone!
God in man!—the all glorious One—the High Preist of humanity!
Now reigns supreme! He the collected sins of all Past—all future
    ages bore—
And in one vast sacrifice forever ended the feeble offerings—
Which these human shrines oft witnessed!—
"Great Pan is dead"! dead with his pomps—his pageants
    with his restless longings—
For the unattained—the unattainable—the infinite—the perfect
    mortal happiness!
God in man!—for gloomy mysteries shrouded in terror and by the
    hand of preistly tyrants
Wrapt in the mists of darkest superstition—for bloody human
    sacrifices—
Shreiking victims—! offered up in secret midst the awful silence
    of their sacred groves—
Gives Light! gives Life! gives human sympathy—a heart which can
    be touched—
With human fraility! human to feel! God like to pardon!
"Great Pan is dead! he sought a heaven without—find heaven
    within!
A heaven of Love—of perfect & unblemished purity—a Heaven
    to do—
To feel—to *be* like God—as God was man!—
Therefore rejoice ye relics of a buried age! Rejoice that here
The pious hand of that most Christian Emperor Justinian
Snatched from decay—thy sculptured treasures, and in one grand
    galaxy of beauty
Framed of thy separate gems—a temple to Eternal Truth
Where in thy stern majestic silence thou shalt stand
Perpetual witness to all time—that "Pan is dead"!!

AUGUST 2, 1862

Sad news reached us last night, sad news indeed, of the death of Mr Edmondston's old friend Dr Tennant. He was wounded but slightly it was thought at the battle on James Island before Charleston & was carried up to his young wife at Walterboro, to die of Erysipilis induced by his wound. Poor fellow. With domestic happiness just opening upon him, for he barely saw his infant son, his young wife, not two years married, looking forward to a happy country home, to be cut off thus suddenly and sadly is hard indeed. I thank Thee O my God that my husband is still spared to me.

Peace! Peace! Grant us Peace! Dr Tennant was in Camden on a visit to Dr Salmond when Mr Edmondston carried me there a bride of a fortnight. Little did I think when I opened the ball given us by Dr S with Dr T that both my host & my partner would fill bloody graves! One died for his country, died for my freedom, died in the discharge of the highest duty man knows, the defence of his fireside. He fell wounded in sight almost of St Michel's spire, in sound of the chimes which had quickened his loitering foot when a schoolboy, in sight of his Mother's grave, of his Grandfather's pulpit. Out on this cruel war which sows broadcast the blood of our best & noblest, gives it in exchange for the scum of Europe, the outcasts of the Northern cities. Dr Tennant it was who first told us of the Secession of S C when in that misty raw December morning we met him on the W. & Manchester road, he on his way to see the woman he afterward's married, we to attend Papa's golden wedding—eighteen short months ago & what changes we have seen! Death thou hast had a noble harvest since then! Patrick is much cast down, as well he may be, poor fellow. He has recently seen his domestic happiness, seen him with his young wife & child, and the thought of them saddens him greatly!

Today came a letter from the Sec. of War telling Mr E. that he was "requested to designate such unattached Companies as he thought could conveniently be assembled to complete a Battalion & then if the Gen Comdg, Maj Gen Hill, approves, the Department will organize the Battalion." It came like a thunder clap upon me for I had brought myself to suppose that nought would come of his application & that after a reasonable time of suspense & waiting the whole thing would fall to the ground & we be allowed to go on as usual. Now it all depends upon the view that Maj Gen Hill will take of it & as he has heretofore expressed himself in the most friendly way & thought or seemed to think highly of Patrick's Military qualifications, he may think it will conduce to the good of the service to have him in the field. If so, then fare well to domestic happiness for a time.

In the afternoon came brother on his way to Raleigh. Was very busy getting up things to send to his children & to Sophia: Dresses to make her little one some clothes, Turnip seed, & nice things for the little ones.

We attacked the enemy lying in James River yesterday morning about 2 A M, brought our heavy guns to bear upon their Gun boats. Instantly every light was extinguished, & a terrible crashing & splashing heard on the river. At Daylight not a boat was in sight; all had fled precipitately, & McClellan's camp was observed to be in great commotion, but we had no means of ascertaining the amount of damage inflicted by us. An accident to one of our guns killed one & wounded more of our men which were the only casualties on our side. The orders issued by the Heads of the Army & the President are so infamous that I make a collection of them & paste them in the end of this book where they may hereafter be referred to—an infamous record which should die the face of Civilization with a crimson blush.[179]

The seige of Vicksburg has recommenced. Nobly has she hitherto held out! Pray God she may be enabled to continue. They say that their canal is finished & that the first rise in the river will cut it out so deep that their gun boats will securely pass & avoid the batteries that frown from the heights of Vicksburg. We maintain that it must be a failure & that time will prove it. I hope we are right.

AUGUST 3, 1862

Sunday—brother left very early this morning in our Carriage for Weldon & I occupied myself in writing letters. I dispatched five & then rested! I wrote Alethea Collins yesterday, which completes the task of six that I set myself.

Mama heard from her sister[180] in Petersburg that we fired some small guns about two o clock, sufficient to annoy the enemy who came over to the south side & responded. Suddenly we opened upon them with Long Tom & Big Charles, Parrot guns captured at Manassas, when a terrible crashing & splashing, as the newspapers told us, ensued & in the morning their fleet was like the host of Senacharib![181]

"By their fruits ye shall know them"![182] I am more forcibly struck with the force & beauty of this comparison this summer than I ever was. Our young orchard is bearing for the first time & as I wander through it the feeling with which I look upon the different trees is almost a personal one. I have a different feeling for each: Red Astrachan, Summer Rose, Summer Pearmain, there is a shade of sentiment towards each of you which varies in kind & as contrasted with those that are yet to be proved the difference is immense. Domine, Roman Stem, Mattamuskeet, etc., I look to you with hope, but

---

[179] This collection of clippings on the second and third pages from the end of the first volume contained about a dozen orders issued by Lincoln, Pope, Halleck, and other Federal commanders in July, 1862, delineating methods of control over civilian populations in areas of the South under Federal authority.

[180] This could have been any one of Mrs. Thomas P. Devereux's three living sisters, Jane Catherine (Mrs. A. T.) Van Courtlandt, Sarah MacKenzie (Mrs. W. M.) Osborne, or Isabella Lenox (Mrs. James) Dunlop.

[181] Sennacherib was the Assyrian king who besieged Jerusalem. This incident was described in II Kings and used by Lord Byron in his lyric poem "The Destruction of Sennacherib." Benét, *Reader's Encyclopedia*, 1010.

[182] Matthew 7:20.

rather with indifference as yet; but to Astrachan & Pearmain I mentally nod my head as to old friends—say "well done, I know you now, feel intimate with you, know what you can do and how you do it"! "By their fruits ye shall know them"! How vividly do these Bible similies taken from the world about us, the Vegetable and farming world, come home to the heart of one intimate with them & how strong is the impress which the "grand old garderner Adam has left on us all"!

Am making some experiments on my peach trees with boiling water poured around & upon the collar. I find that it does not kill the tree but the question is does it the borer? Will go on & try the experiment thoroughly to try & rid our trees of this pest.

AUGUST 4, 1862

A note from poor Samantha this morning tells Mama that her husband is ordered off with the Conscripts. Poor thing, she is in deep distress, with three little children. I know not what is to become of her! She seems resigned & thankful that she can trust in God. How much better off am I, for no fear of personal bodily suffering enters into my anxieties, & she has serious ones!

AUGUST 6, 1862

A letter from James yesterday tells me that he was in the nocturnal attack on the fleet in James River, had a terribly fatiguing time, but escaped unhurt. He thinks the damage we inflicted on them must have been severe, as when the guns were trailed the lights on board the transports were burning brightly. I am afraid they shot too high or there would have been some evidence of the damage in the morning. An adventurous party of our men dashed into McClellan's lines & captured 200 beeves, which were at least a mile within them. We will make him repent his "brilliant strategetic movement" yet. The day after the night attack a force estimated at 10,000 strong landed on the south side of James River, supposed to reconnoitre. The cowardly scoundrels sent over a detachment of men & burned the residence of Mrs Cole, a widow lady living nearly opposite Berkeley, because one of the Batteries had taken position in her Grounds & fired at them opposite, as if she, even had she the inclination, could have helped it. She with her children were at the house of a neighbor when they landed & fired every building on the premises. I warrant they plundered the house, which is a very fine one, first.

Seventeen years ago yesterday Mr Edmondston first told me that he loved me and asked me to marry him. Seventeen happy years—no not seventeen, for the year of my engagement was not a happy one; it was a severe struggle to break off old ties & it cost me much but after that was over I was as happy as it was possible for mortal to be. No, I was not, for I am happier *now* than I was then. I know him better & have a feeling of more entire friendship for him which grows stronger the longer I live. I had a little superstitious feeling yesterday, lest the anniversary of the day which gave him to me might take him away, i.e., order came ordering him into active service, but I was agreeably disappointed. I have at least two days respite, for we do not send to the mail before Thursday again.

Night before the last came Dr Alston, a son in Law of Mrs Joiner's,[183] seeking shelter & a nights' lodging. He had with him four of Mrs Joiner's men servants who had been hired out about Hamilton & whom she had sent for to remove them from the vicinity of the Yankees. An incessant tiresome talker, what did his wife see to fancy in him! One of the negroes he told us had been with the Yankee's & had expressed the intention of joining them "when they were ready for him." Pleasant news that when one reflected that he was at that moment "cheek by jowl" with your own servants & as he was going to bed he sent for one of them to see how he was, as he had symptoms of typhoid fever—bodily as well as moral pestilence. I beleive I prefer the first, the neither are pleasant guests!

We (I mean the whole estate—Father, brother, & Mr E) have sustained a heavy loss in the damage to our cotton from exposure to the weather. We were ordered to move it twenty miles from the river under the penalty of having it burned when Burnside threatened an advance. This it was impossible to do, so the next best thing was to secrete it where the marauding Yankees should never find it. This was done & temporary shelters erected over it, but owing to the incessant & heavy rains which have beaten under & through them it has rotted the bagging, stained, & mildewed the cotton to an extent which we dreamed not of. Brother, out of a hundred & ninety bales, thinks he will save ninety & that slightly damaged. Ours has not yet been overhaul owing to the want of a shelter in which to do it—it having been for greater security moved out here.

Mrs John Anthony's[184] estate loses almost all theirs. The damage through the county & consequent loss will be heavy, as all the cotton on the navigable water courses which was not burned has been subjected to the same treatment. We lost at ordinary prices at least $12,000 & at the present high ones of course it is much greater. (We are offered 16 cts as it lies in the woods is undamaged)—& in New York & Phila it is now 55 cts per lb!

On Tuesday last was published our President's order for retaliation on the Officers of the commands of Pope & Steinweyr for their treatment of our citizens within their lines—a dignified and a noble paper which I append at the end of this book in connection with the brutal orders which gave rise to

---

[183]Archibald Alexander Austin married Temperance Williams Joyner, who was the daughter of Col. and Mrs. Andrew Joyner.

[184]Mrs. John Hill Anthony's maiden name was Lucy Tunstall. Smith and Smith, *History of Trinity Parish,* 103.

it.[185] Some persons complain that it does not go far enough; others that it responds to their inhumanity & will embitter and ensanguin the war. It is impossible to please every one, especially people of such diverse ways of thinking, so I suppose Mr Davis' "Via Media" between bloodthirstyness and maudlin sentimentality is the best—in fact the only true course.

AUGUST 10, 1862

Yesterday came an order from Lieut Col Morehead,[186] by authority of Maj Gen Hill, ordering under pain of impressment 500 negroes from this section to work on some defences or other, the officer beleived about Petersburg. It is most rash, ill considered, and, as it is arranged, oppressive & unequal. There are negroes enough on James River whom their owners would be glad to employ & keep from the domination of the Yankees—negroes whom they fear will go over to them. Thousands below us in Martin and Bertie are in the same condition. Why not then take them & leave these here in this comparative peaceful country alone until their crops are laid by & a provision for the future ensured. To remove forty hands now from Father's and Mr E's crops is to destroy it, for in consequence of the Freshet it is late this year. I know not what we shall do.

Bad news from the South West. The Steam Ram Arkansas[187] came out from Vicksburg to assist in an attack on Baton Rouge, but a peice of timber becoming entangled in her propeller, she was disabled and in this state was attacked by five Federal Gun boats. After an unequal contest, the Lieut in command seeing that her capture was inevitable, she being unable either to escape or to attack them, lying helpless in the water, blew her up, the crew escaping to the shore. For want of her we were unable to take Baton Rouge, tho we drove the enemy into the citadel & swept the streets but for want of water

---

[185]General Order No. 54, dated August 1, 1862, was issued by Davis in response to orders by Pope and other officers of his command which, in Davis's view, allowed "the murder of our peaceful inhabitants" by holding them "as hostages to the end that they may be murdered in cold blood if any of his soldiers are killed by some unknown persons whom he designates 'bushwackers.' " Accordingly, Davis decreed that Pope and his officers, if captured, were not to be considered as prisoners of war but as murderers to be executed in retaliation for the deaths of any noncombatants killed by Federal troops following Pope's orders. *Official Records (Army)*, Series II, IV, 830-831, 836-837.

[186]Mrs. Edmondston was probably referring to either James Turner Morehead, Jr. (1838-1919), lieutenant colonel and later colonel of the Fifty-third North Carolina Regiment; or John Henry Morehead (1833-1863), lieutenant colonel and later colonel of the Forty-fifth North Carolina Regiment. Both Moreheads were from Guilford County. Clark, *Histories of the North Carolina Regiments*, I, 160-161; III, 35-37, 52, 255, 259-260, 264; Manarin and Jordan, *North Carolina Troops*, III, 421; Ashe, *Biographical History*, II, 272-277.

[187]The C.S.S. *Arkansas*, under the command of Lt. Isaac N. Brown, successfully terrorized Union ships on the Mississippi River in July, 1862. Badly damaged in these encounters, the *Arkansas* had sought refuge under Vicksburg's guns until repairs were effected; but Gen. Earl Van Dorn ordered the ship to join the Baton Rouge campaign before the repairs were completed. During the battle the *Arkansas*, under the temporary command of Lt. Henry Stevens, suffered engine failure and was destroyed on August 6, 1862, to prevent its capture. *Official Records (Navy)*, Series I, XIX, 132-136; *Raleigh Register*, August 10, 13, 1862; *Civil War Naval Chronology*, II, 56, 81, 83, 85-86, 89.

were compelled to retire one and a half miles. A renewal of the attack expected—loss of life great on both sides. *No officers* were taken prisoners now. All dressed as privates with nothing to mark their rank. A Yankee trick to prevent the execution of Mr Davis scheme of retaliation upon the officers of Pope's command. He will be forced to extend it.

Skirmishing at Malvern Hill which has been alternately for the last few days in ours & the enemy possession, both parties having retired and again advanced. The weather intensely hot. For five days now the heat has been excessive. Our army must suffer terribly. I hope the Yankees will have the full benefit of it. Our prisoners lately in the enemies hands are arriving. Their suffering has been great. We have released many thousand of theirs, but in all negotiations they will be sure to get the better of us. Punic faith may henceforth give way to Yankee craft as a by word for deceit. They retain about four hundred of our men on the pretense that they have taken the oath of Allegiance to their Government. I hope that we will keep the same number.

On Friday came Mr Ed Hill to see whether Mr E would take Command of a Battalion of Partisan Rangers to be organized. Of course pending Gen Hill's answer he can say nothing. Decided he would not object if the first should fail.

AUGUST 13, 1862

Yesterday to my great surprise as I was standing in the Store Room a finely dressed Military looking old gentleman, tho in citizen's clothes, with beard & moustache as white as snow, came walking across the back yard having driven in to the back gate in a most familiar style, who on coming near enough for my blind eyes to recognize proved to be Charles! Great was my surprise at first to see him and next at his altered appearance. His hair & beard have become grey since we last saw him & it gives him really a *venerable aspect*. He is in the Medical Purveyor's office in Savannah, & being in Richmond on business stopped for a day to see us. He is in fine health, has his family in Laurens safe from the Yankees. He is getting a good salary. Passing through Petersburg last night he heard the roll of musketry & the roar of canon distinctly & was told by the Conductor that it was on the River five or six miles below, but whether we attacked or the enemy is making an advance no one could learn.

Jackson has attacked & beaten the advance of Pope's army, driving them back with heavy loss & capturing 300 prisoners, amongst whom is one Brigadier, Gen Prince & twenty seven commissioned officer. Much to their apparent surprise they learned that they were not to be treated as prisoners of War, in accordance with Mr Davis' expressed determination to retaliate upon them the outrages and oppressions to which Pope's command have subjected the people of the Valley of Va, a determination which he expressed to their President some ten days since. I hardly think he would be so cruel as to leave them ignorant of it, but they profess to be so & demand to be treated as the other officers taken by us have heretofore been; but for answer they have been placed in solitary confinement & notified that they are to be answerable for the future oppressions of Pope & Steinweyhr.

Our returned prisoners give a terrible account of the sufferings they have undergone. One of them brought home a ration as it was issued to them. The meat weighed one ounce, the bread 3½ ounces, & this was all they were allowed per diem. Some of them were manacled before their wounds were healed. Gen Pettigrew was taken from his relatives house in Baltimore where he was on parole under the care of Dr Buckler & confined in solitary confinement without even a servant to attend on him, at a time when he could not walk from a wound in the thigh from a Minie ball nor use his arms well from one in the shoulder and chest from a peice of shell, & fed on soldier's diet, salt pork & bread, altho his physician protested against it—& all because the ladies of Baltimore sympathized with & showed him every care and attention in their power. It is infamous!

To my great dismay I find that my hams & bacon are spoiling, owing I suppose to the barrels of Pork which Burnside forced us to store in the Smoke House. I have been overhauling both the shoulders & the sides & to my horror find skippers in them! I had Dolly & Vinyard scalding & picking them yesterday, Harry in the Store Room heading up this years supply of flour, & Angeline boiling down the old Pickle to save the salt & finding it tiresome waiting on them, & my bodily presence being needed when so many valuables as I have there were exposed, I sat down in the store room and sent for my book, "Literature du Midi,"[188] & when Charles came upon me I had a hearty laugh at myself and the situation in which he caught me: Harry pounding the flour into the Barrels with a heavy pestle, Dolly & Vinyard with a pot of boiling water & all the sides spread out on the grass, peeping into, scalding & examining them, whilst further on Angeline with a cauldron like the witches in Macbeth, which with "double double, toil & trouble" she was making "boil & bubble," whilst Mistress sat composedly on the step, deep in the Chansons & Tensons of Troubadours & Trouvareres, occasionally lending an eye or an admonition to each. Such is life, such is Southern Life. What would an English lady have thought of my situation & occupation? Would the ridiculous or the sympathetic have predominated as she looked at me? And yet I was in happy unconsciousness of exciting either. The occupation was not distasteful to me, for it was a necessary & ordinary duty, & I enjoyed my book none the less for my surroundings.

---

[188] *De la litterature du midi de l'Europe* by Leónard Simonde de Sismondi (1773-1842) is a four-volume work published in 1813 containing expanded versions of lectures delivered at Geneva in 1811. Sir Paul Harvey and J. E. Heseltine (eds.), *The Oxford Companion to French Literature* (Oxford: Clarendon Press, 1959), 677.

AUGUST 14, 1862

The news from Jackson's army confirmed. The Commissioned officers are in close confinement in Richmond, the common soldiers treated as formerly. On our side Brig Gen Winder is killed together with some others, but our loss is comparatively slight.

Lincoln has ordered a draft if the ranks are not filled up by today, the 14th, for the War for 300,000 men & an immediate draft for nine months for 300,000 more—600,000 which he intends to "hurl down upon" us & "*crush out the Rebellion.*" He has issued a most preemtory & oppressive order, refusing to allow any one liable to be drafted to leave the country, stopping all travelers or would be travelers, and if need be imprisoning them and suspending the writ of Habeas corpus to all arrested on account of the draft on the militia. I do not know what he is coming to. Russia does but little more. The next thing I suppose will be to order the return of all subject to draft who may be absent in foreign countries. The Czar of Russia does so when he wishes his subjects. Why should not the Czar of the U S, the Czar Lincoln? I append the order[189] with the others at the end of the book.

This order to draft will, it is supposed, put Kentucky, Missouri, & Maryland in a blaze, but I dare say they will submit. The Spirit of freedom seems to have deserted them. In Tennessee Gen McCook has been killed whilst riding in an Ambulance by Guerrillas, and a most savage retribution has been taken upon the innocent inhabitants. Every house in the circuit of miles has been burned & indiscriminate hanging ordered to all the males captured. God help the poor women! And this in a thickly settled country neighborhood not far from Nashville by people who call themselves Christians and in the nineteenth century.[190]

Charles left this morning for Savannah. I sent off a barrel of vegetables yesterday to James. I hope they will not be so long on the road as the last. Brother was here to dinner but left with the negroes for Petersburg, to see where and under whose supervision they were to work & make all proper arrangements for them. I hope they will all come home, but I doubt it!

AUGUST 17, 1862

Yesterday came father from his up country jaunt looking thin but improved in health, I think, and seemingly in better spirits. He will be here for a few days & then go on to the Roanoke Red Sulphur[191] for a short time taking

---

[189]A copy of this order by Lincoln does not appear in the diary.

[190]Brig. Gen. Robert Latimer McCook (1827-1862), wounded and forced to direct the Ninth Ohio Regiment from an ambulance, was mortally wounded by Confederate guerrillas near Decherd, Tennessee, on August 5, 1862. The Ninth Ohio sacked houses in the vicinity and shot at least one suspected guerrilla in revenge. *Official Records (Army)*, Series I, XVI, Part I, 838-841; Boatner, *Civil War Dictionary*, 528-529.

[191]The Roanoke Red Sulphur Springs, located in Monroe County, Virginia (later West Virginia), were approximately 42 miles west of the White Sulphur Springs in Virginia. Peregrine Prolix, *Letters De-*

Mama with him. He brought a letter from Maj Gen Hill to Mr E, which though it was directed to Halifax yet by some means found its way to Raleigh to Brother's house. It was post marked the 7th, and is the very letter whose arrival Patrick has been so anxiously expecting. It was very short, telling him to come on immediately, that he had no doubt but that his matters could be speedily arranged & that he wished to consult him as to a field of operations. So this morning bright & early he left.

Ah, me I feel sad at heart. Today is the anniversary of the severest affliction which ever befel me—the death of my mother and I cannot raise my hopes, cannot look forth with confidence to the future. Twenty times did I resolve to try & persuade Mr E not to go on this of all other days & firmly had I to close my lips & resolutely determine that I would not be governed by so superstitious a feeling. Would that I could also prevent its making me unhappy! It seems that the day which took my Mother is to take my husband also, for I suppose there is little doubt but that he will be called into active service, but I will try & not despond, call upon Thee O my God for grace & strength to meet this trial. Thou wilt never fail me! It is strange how strength does come to us to meet sorrow and trouble such as we think at one time we would sink under. Here have I been talking with brother, hearing him pour forth such a Jeremiad, such terrible forebodings for the future as would one year ago have plunged me into profound greif, made me feel as though a grasp of ice had seized my heart & I rise from it calm & self sustained with no greater despondancy than the anticipation of evils far less has often thrown me into. "As thy days so shall thy strength be"! We ask only for our Daily bread. Then why anticipate evils? I will go out & walk, dawdle round the Orchard, & see if *Nature* cannot make me more cheerful & hopeful.

AUGUST 18, 1862

How foolish, nay how wicked are presentiments and omens! How weak to indulge in superstitious forebodings. I made myself actually miserable yesterday, had to exert a strong and determined *will* to keep myself from persuading Mr E [not] to leave home because it was the anniversary of my Mother's death and I thought that the day which took my Mother was also to take my husband, when Lo, talking last night with father I found that both brother and myself had by some most unaccountable confusion of mind mistaken the day, and that she died in July! I immediately referred to some old letters, letters from her and from Grandpapa which gave me a pang to look at, far more to read, & found that he was right & for years I have been under the mistake. I was too young at the time to take much note of dates & so as I rarely speak of her I suppose that I fell into the error from miscounting & the 17th of

---

scriptive of the Virginia Springs; the Roads Leading Thereto, and the Doings Thereat, With a Map of Virginia (Philadelphia: H. S. Tanner, 1835), 24, 39, 52-55.

August has by me been kept as a sorrowful sacred memory when in fact it is as any other day in the year to me. So as I have caught myself in such foolish presentiments on such causeless ground as I yesterday indulged let me be careful how I look forth gloomily to the future again.

Father & Mama have gone down to Conneconara today, and I am neither sad nor lonely. I have been since breakfast on my knees at the shrine of Pomona & it is now twelve o'clock. That is, I have been examining our young Peach Trees & cutting the borer out, & a tiresome job it is. I have had all of them scalded with boiling water at the collar & then well rubbed with sulphur & Lard, a process which I hope will destroy the eggs & make the tree so distasteful to the fly that she will deposite no more there. I must go at the Peach orchard tomorrow. There the trees being older the work will be more difficult, but none the less neccessary, for there I think is the nursery from whence they all proceed. I had no idea that the grub was so large. Some of them are as long as a joint and a half of my little finger.

AUGUST 20, 1862

News yesterday from Mr Edmondston. He has seen General Hill & has by him been reccommended to the Secretary of War as Colonel of the Regt of Cavalry to be formed of the unattached Companies in the State.[192] They have been ordered to rendezvous at Goldsboro today. Gen Hill has written to the Sec & sent Mr E. to Richmond with the letter reccomending him for Col, Faribault[193] for Lieut Col, & Brother for Major, but the Sec may see fit to order an Election instead of appointing the Field Officers. In this case Mr E says he has "no chance" & I can well beleive it, for he would not Electioneer to be made President, and without electioneering there is no office to be had in the gift of our gentlemen volunteers. Every Captain in the Regt would immediately rush into the Arena as a candidate himself, but we shall see what his fate is to be.

The President's message announces that it will be neccessary to give him the power of calling out all the men between thirty five & forty five to meet the

---

[192] The Forty-first North Carolina (Third Cavalry) Regiment was mustered into Confederate service on September 3, 1862. Company C of the regiment, originally the "Caswell Rangers," was previously mustered into Confederate service on March 14, 1862, as "Captain H. W. Reinhardt's Company in the Edmondston's Battalion of Cavalry of North Carolina Volunteers." Patrick Edmondston never completed his battalion, however, and Confederate officials refused to recognize the companies in it as being part of a battalion. When the "Caswell Rangers" were reassigned as Company C in the Forty-first, the command went to John A. Baker, not to Edmondston. Ironically, Company G of the same regiment, originally the "Scotland Neck Mounted Riflemen," was mustered into Confederate service by Edmondston as well. Edmondston had resigned this position in 1861 in anticipation of securing a better position in the army, but this resignation essentially finished his military career in Confederate service. Manarin and Jordan, *North Carolina Troops*, II, 178, 180, 198, 227.

[193] George H. Faribault of Wake County served as lieutenant colonel and later as colonel of the Forty-seventh North Carolina Regiment until his resignation in January, 1865. Moore, *Roster of North Carolina Troops*, III, 325; Clark, *Histories of the North Carolina Regiments*, III, 83.

additional 600,000 called for by Mr Lincoln. In this case both brother & Mr E. will be subject to conscript, so I ought to hope that they will get Commissions as officers before they are forced into the field.

Congress met on Monday and one of the first bills introduced was an amendment to the Conscript Act authorizing the President to call out all under forty five. They had better enforce the first Conscript Act before they pass another & do away with all the excuses of clerks, deputies, P Masters, Mail Contractors, Justices of the Peace, County Soliciters, etc., which are now so rife—have *no* exemptions but from bodily disability.

News from the James River. McClellan is really gone! Evacuated his Camp & steamed down the River to re-inforce Pope! Not a tent or a transport in sight! Where were we that we allowed him to do it without molestation? What were our Generals about that they allowed him to slip through their fingers so easily? A battle with Pope on the line of the Rapid Ann imminent. Lee has reinforced Jackson & taken the command.

In Tennessee Morgan is carrying all before him. He insults the Federals at the very gates of Nashville, has blown up the Railway tunnel & burnt three millions dollars worth of Commissary store within sixteen miles of the town. The Yankee Generals there deny the obligation of a Parole given to Guerrillas & have ordered three thousand men paroled by him during his late expedition into Kentucky into service. So it goes! He will next have to shoot all he takes. The U S Government refuses to answer Mr Davis' demand as to whether they sanction the acts of Butler, saying that it is an insult to their Government. How, no one can comprehend, as they still keep him in command. They have already disregarded the Cartel of Exchange by ordering their paroled prisoners to guard ours at Sandusky, or is it at Chicago, where they are confined—some where in Ohio? Was ever seen so faithless a nation? Missouri is in a blaze with Guerillas. From Maryland the male population is flocking into Va to avoid the draft and the organization of Maryland Regts & Battalions is going on rapidly in Richmond. On Sat they seized two U S. Steamers in the Potomac in which they crossed the river & then burned them. Burnside has drawn all the men he could spare from N C & is at Fredericksburg. Now is the time for us to make a vigorous effort here & recover what we have lost.

Brother came last night but left this morning for Raleigh. Father left also. He goes to Petersburg to look after our negroes. I suppose the evacuation of the James ought to release them, for where is the need of fortifying Petersburg when there is no enemy?

AUGUST 21, 1862

I stopped writing yesterday morning to look after Mr Edmondston's cotton and was all day closely attending to it. They finished hauling it up in the afternoon & then I had all the force out here engaged in sorting it. It is pitiable to see it, and the want of room to store it will be a sore drawback soon. They opened & assorted eleven bales. The dairy and wash kitchen are filled with it, & what to do with it when the Crib loft is also full I know not. What is wet & stained is spread out on the grass, a sorrowful sight indeed! It needs the closest attention. I find if I leave them a half hour they neglect it and either throw quantities of prime cotton with the wet or mix the stained with the good. I wish Mr E was at home. Master's eye & voice are more potent than Mistress's. I am looking for him home today, but I fear he will not be able to stay—but God's will be done!

Harry and Mr Eaton Powel's[194] carpenter, whom Mr E sent here the day he went away, have been engaged shingling the new stable in order to store the Cotton in it, but this morning Mr P's man left saying it was his Master's orders. Fortunately among the hands I ordered from the plantation was old Aaron who knows something about the work, so I sent him to Harry and quickened them all I could. The work seems fearful, 103 bales all to be sorted out by hand and then repacked and stored—a Legacy left by Burnside. It was moved from the plantation in the wettest kind of weather, piled in the woods, to keep our authorities from burning it, & to hide it from the Yankees should they occupy the country. Mr E. was away & Mr Shaw, a careless, negligent overseer, did not shelter it properly. Hence when these two last severe rains came it got wet & rotted the bagging and some of the ropes. Our loss will be a heavy one as cotton is now twenty cts a pound, but with care we will save much of it yet and that care, please God, I will give it. How thankful I am that we sold some of it in the winter. I wish it had been more.

August 23, 1862

Yesterday came Mr Edmondston home. Upon what trifles turn our success or failure in our undertakings! Had that letter summoning him to Gen Hill arrived only a *day sooner* he would now have been Colonel of a Regt of Cavalry in the Confederate service! He found Gen Hill all that he could wish, most kind, friendly, and desirious to do every thing for him. The plan of action was agreed on. The Regt was to be formed, Mr E Col, Mr Causey,[195] Lieut Col, and Brother, Major & their field of operations was to be between Roanoke & Chowan Rivers. Mr E went to Richmond with the letter to ascertain whether there was to be an election or appointment; could not see the Sec, so soon as he got there. When he did get an audience received a letter to Gen Hill telling

---

[194] An E. T. Powell farmed in Halifax County in 1860 and owned eleven slaves. Eighth Census, 1860, Population Schedule, Halifax County, 36; Slave Schedule, 21. Harry was one of the Edmondston slaves.

[195] Mrs. Edmondston possibly referred to either H. C. Causey of Randolph County, a first lieutenant in Co. F, Seventieth North Carolina Regiment, or to Pvt. S. H. Causey of Co. C, Nineteenth North Carolina (Second Cavalry) Regiment. Clark, *Histories of the North Carolina Regiments*, IV, 13; Manarin and Jordan, *North Carolina Troops*, II, 123.

him to have the companies inspected, formed into Battalion & Regts & the Gen to name the field officers. He went back to Petersburg & found Gen Hill had with the consent of the Department turned his command here in N C to Gen French & he was packing up to join the army on the Rappahanock. Gen H gave him a letter to French stating the facts & the endorsed letter of the Sec of War. He waited on French & was received almost brusquely. He ordered him at first to go to Goldsboro & report every day to him. Then on Mr E's going back to the office for his overcoat, he countermanded the order. Said he would get Col Bradfoot[196] to inspect the companies. Mr E then told him that if he had any communications to make to him, his office was Halifax and left him. So the whole matter depends upon his caprice. If he acts as a gentleman would under the circumstances feel bound to do, Mr E will get the appointment, but he is said not to be a gentleman nor to understand the instincts of one, so there is no calculating on his course. He refused to place Mr E in command once & he may do so again from peak despite the reccommendations he has & the claims he has to the appointment, having worked so hard on the Battalion & been promised to have it filled up for him—all this caused by the delay of a mail, for had there been one day longer to spare, it would have been arranged before French took command.

Mr E is well but harassed & worried and the sight which met him of stained & rotted cotton spread out on the grass to bleach was not an enlivening one. Disappointment seems written on everything this year. I feel the disappointment in Military matters only through him, as unless the Conscript law is extended I shall have him at home—no hardship to me if in the line of his duty, but God will direct all things for the best.

AUGUST 24, 1862

Today came a letter from Mr Haxall[197] of Richmond, one of the gentleman reccommended for Lieut Col. He has seen the Sec for the purpose of knowing whether Gen Hill's reccommendation will not stand, it having been made before French took command. He gives however for answer that "if Maj. Gen Hill has turned the matter over to Gen French, he, the Sec, is bound to pay Gen F reccommendation the same respect as he did to Gen Hill's." So there the matter ends. It all depends upon Gen French's ipse dixit.[198] Damp, Cold, rainy weather—bad for the cotton on the grass & feels very like August Freshet weather.

---

[196] Lt. Col. Charles W. Broadfoot was head of the First North Carolina Reserves in the Second Military District of the Department of North Carolina and Southern Virginia. *Official Records (Army)*, Series I, XLII, Part II, 1224-1226.

[197] Capt. Philip Haxall was the assistant adjutant general under Brig. Gen. Beverly H. Robertson in the Second Military District of South Carolina in 1864. *Official Records (Army)*, Series I, XXXV, Part I, 550, 553.

[198] Latin, meaning he himself said so.

August 26, 1862

Yesterday Vinyard's child was born, a boy. I was very uneasy for a time as there was no nurse here, but by God's blessing she did very well; if the child lives I intend to bring him up as a table servant, have him in by the time he can talk & walk & never let him be rusty—some time to look forward to, but I have a stout heart & am hopeful.

Last night came Frank Jones in search of a horse & a Cavalry outfit, as he thinks of joining the Partisan Rangers. Father gave him a horse, but Patrick has no Sabre to spare & he wants also a military saddle, which Mr E has not.

This morning Patrick left again for Petersburg to see Gen French about giving him the appointment of Col or filling up his Battalion—he cares not which. Employment in his country's service is what he wishes. I am going on with the Cotton, a tedious job, & one which demands great care & circumspection. Ah Burnside you little wot of the legacy you left us. How you would exult if you knew it!

Pope's army is in full retreat, but for what purpose we know not, so we fear to rejoice. It may be draw us on in hot pursuit with the hope of turning suddenly, whilst we are in the disorder of a hasty advance; it may be to join McClellan who has gone to Fredericksburg; others again think that he wishes to draw us on & leave McClellan to fall in our rear by a hasty march & thus annihilate us between two armies; whilst some opine that he cannot trust his own men, so demoralized are they by the license to plunder he has given them that he fears to bring them in face of an enemy. Whatever it is, I hope our Generals will be wary & in place of being entrapped, entrap him. Certain it is, we have captured two hundred men & a train of cars & two engines left behind to burn the bridge over the Rappahanock, but we were too quick for them, seized them before they had materially injured the bridge. All our troops have been pressed on to Lee & Jackson. There is hardly a Corporal's guard at Richmond.

Frank gives me a terrible account of the Yankees in the Northern Counties stealing negroes & property of every description. They have a Steamboat the [————] which is not under Military rule, in fact a private speculation, a band of *pirates* which they allow to cruise through the waters of the Albemarle & help themselves to whatever they desire. Unmolested by any military authority whatever, they rob, plunder, and arrest by the wholesale.[199] He tells me that the people are *true* & this company of Union men which they boast so

---

[199] One such incident occurred on August 4, 1862, and involved C. W. Flusser, commander of the U.S.S. *Commodore Perry*. Flusser reported he had sent the *Putnam*, *Shawsheen*, and *Brinker* up the Chowan River "to frighten the rebels and to pick up any conscripts who might wish to enlist in the Army or ship in the Navy." He also stated his intention of seizing some cotton in the vicinity until he discovered it was owned by Union men "who write by this opportunity to Governor Stanly for a permit to ship." Corn and wheat taken from the farm of Josiah Collins, "a wealthy secessionist absentee," was turned over to the superintendent of the poor at Plymouth for distribution. *Official Records (Navy)*, Series I, VII, 622-623.

of raising in Chowan & Gates is composed of the offscouring of the people & foreigners, people who can neither read or write & who never had a decent suit of clothes until they gave it to them, poor ignorant wretches who cannot resist a fine uniform and the choice of the horses in the country & liberty to help themselves without check to their rich neighbors belongings. We should judge them leniently, but justice to ourselves demands that we shoot them down like wolves on sight. The Messrs Nixon have lost all their men. His cousin Miss Gordon, his Aunt Mrs Gordon, Tom's lady love Miss Skinner,[200] & scores of others have been equally unfortunate. Poor people, when will it end! Your fate may soon be ours. God avert it! But to go from modern to ancient wars, am amusing myself greatly with the History of King Arthur & the Knights of the Round Table, the Mort d Arthur, the delights of Lords and Ladies in the olden time when Gestes and Chansons were sung by Troubadour's and Trouvaries in Ladies bower & Lordly Hall. The world of Literature has improved greatly since then, greatly in decency, the actual world in comfort, in all that goes to make life desirable, & yet the glow of Romance thrown by these old Chevaliers upon their age, the Knightly Courtesy, the mixture of the impossible, the incomprehensible, with the daily life is very attractive & fascinating & we exclaim with Bulwer as we read it,

"If the old beauty from our paths has fled
"Is it that Truth or that Beleif is dead?"

Ah! for "Excalibur," sword of magic power, for Lieut Col Edmondston to charge home upon our enemies with! Ah! for the wondrous scabbard which prevented the flowing of its wearers blood to gird him withall! Arm him, O Lord with Thy Spirit! Go Thou forth with him. Be Thou his shield and buckler!

AUGUST 28, 1862

This morning Father & Mama left for the Springs, Frank Jones for his Camp, brother for his plantation, so I am left entirely alone. My solitude will however I hope be of short duration, as I am expecting Patrick to dinner. It is the Negroes Midsummer holiday, and as all of them but Fanny & Dolly have gone down to the Plantation dinner, the premises are deserted & as silent as "Tara's Hall." The "Harvest home" of England is I suppose the antetype of this annual three days holiday. True the labour of gathering our crop is not yet begun, but that of cultivation is over. There remains now nothing to do

---

[200] "The Messrs Nixon" possibly were Francis Nixon and/or his sons William and Thomas, all of whom had Negroes who left the Nixon property. "Miss Gordon" was probably Sarah Gordon, and "Mrs. Gordon" her mother, Elizabeth Jones Gordon. Mrs. Gordon was the wife of George B. Gordon and half-sister of Thomas Francis Jones, the father of Frank and Thomas Devereux Jones. "Miss Skinner," later the wife of Thomas Devereux Jones, was Martha Blount (Pattie) Skinner, daughter of Benjamin and Elizabeth Leigh Skinner. Information from records furnished by Granberry Tucker, Edenton, North Carolina, hereinafter cited as Granberry Tucker Records.

but to wait for its maturity, when the ripe shock shall be gathered in to the garner. There is something inexpressibly touching to me in this waiting time of the year, this golden autumn, when corn stands with bended head, its work accomplished, its growth over, in meek expectation of the hour—when ripened by Time the whole purpose of its creation shall have been fulfilled and it ready for the food of man! It reminds me of that autumn of life into which I will soon enter when, maturity reached, there is no more intellectual improvement but a ripening in all the Christian virtues & graces, a waiting time for Death. Grant us, O Lord, a peaceful, happy waiting time & after that a Glorious re-awakening in Thy garden.

The news yesterday is good, if true, but the facilities for its transmission are meager indeed. Pope is still in retreat, we closely pursuing. We have crossed the Rappahanock and occupy Warrenton. We pressed him so closely that his private baggage, his papers, plans, & even his overcoat have fallen into our hands. It is now thought that he cannot trust his army & that he designs to fall back to Washington & avoid a battle until a fresh element from the 600,000 new recruits shall have been infused into it.

McClellan it is reported is with his whole force in Washington & that he has tendered his resignation, but this is doubtful.

At Norfolk the enemy have a large force of negroes busily at work tearing up the Rail Road & relaying it with an altered guage. This is to prevent our using it with the engines & rolling stock which we now have, so that in their present enfeebled state we cannot pour fresh troops upon them but must make our approach in the manner of olden times by marching—a Yankee trick.

Pope has in consequence of our retaliatory order issued a second, an adenda, as it were, to his first, quartering his army upon the country, which he says has been misunderstood, explaining and doing away with its obnoxious features. I append it with the others to show how he eats his own words.[201] The English papers have dubbed him the "Sir John *Falstaff*[202] of the American war," say that he captured 10,000 men in Buckram, etc. Halleck they named the "Major General Liar of the Western Army" sometime since. They see through them.

The house is too still. I will go & commune with my Pears & Peaches, gather some Dahlias, & peep at the ripening Grapes. We have splendid Cantalopes this summer in spite of the wet weather.

At night—Mr Edmondston did not come today but in place of him a letter in which he tells me that Gen French offered to reccommend him for the "Lieut Colonelcy of the Regt of Cavalry." He reminded him that he had

---

[201] A copy of this order does not appear in the diary.

[202] The Shakespearean character Sir John Falstaff, a comical figure who appeared in *The Merry Wives of Windsor* and *Henry IV*, boasted of his strength and bravery but in reality was a coward and a thief. Benét, *Reader's Encyclopedia*, 364.

"already been reccommended for the Colonelcy," at which he hummed &
hawed & finally wrote a letter to the Sec of War in which he say[s] "I (Mr E)
has been reccommended for the Colonelcy of Cav, but as I (Gen French) does
not personally know my (his) qualifications for the office, leaves the matter for
selection to you (The Sec of War)." This letter Mr E has taken on to Richmond, so he cannot get here until tomorrow if then. Patrick winds up his letter with a query, If Gen French was willing to reccommend him for the lieut
colonelcy, why could he not do it for the Colonelcy? & answers it in a manner
by no means complimentary to Gen F, "because he is one mean man." And
he must be.

I am alone with only Cuffee to speak to. The house seems very still and a little eerie, so I will go to bed & write the news, the capture of Gen Pope's grand
dress parade coat tomorrow. Goodnight Journal!

AUGUST 29, 1862

Being alone in the house—I am reminded of a subject for a Magazine article on the subject which Mr E & myself talked over last winter—"Alone in the
House." It was to be the husband who was left, the wife having gone off on a
visit somewhere, and we settled the touches of sentiment, which the sight of
her work basket & little personal belongings should excite in him, and to my
amusement Mr E particularly ennumerated her "*shoes*"! He says the sight of
my *shoes* give him a more lively sense of my absence than aught else. They
bring me more to him & he quarreled more vehemently with Fanny for
moving *my shoes* from the place where I had changed them than for anything
else whilst I was gone! Why is it? There is nothing sentimental or individual
in a *pair* of walking shoes, unless it is that they can be used by no one else. I
will go and look at his boots & see whether they excite the same feeling in me!

I have been!, but I cannot say that they excite any particular emotion in
me. The cap he wears in the garden & here about the orchard & fields
touches me far more. As to the boots, I cannot individualize them. They are
boots & nothing more. Perhaps it is because he has so many that the sentiment
is frittered, trodden out as it were! To go back to my article, I dwelt on the little housekeeping difficulties, the leathery toast, the smoky tea which would
assail a man, but to me the trouble is to get *little* enough. My appetite is taken
away by the profusion I see before me & I shrink from attacking it alone.
Yesterday at dinner I might have fared sumptuously, Ochra Soup, a leg of
Mutton, a Ham, Vegetables & fruit in profusion, but I made my dinner on
Soup and a Roasting ear & sent a magnificent dish of Peaches & cream to
Emma Higgs. (Be it known to you, O Journal, that I would not have ordered
that dinner had I not expected Patrick to eat it)—& so the harvest home feast
went untasted from the table. Cuffee however profited by Mistress' delicacy.
Are farm labourers so well treated any where as here? I doubt it.

Now for the news which, Journal, I promised to give you last night. The tidings of Pope's retreat are fully confirmed. We pressed him so closely that we seized two millions of dollars worth of stores which however Gen *Stuart* burned, as our advance was not, he feared, strong enough to hold the post.[203] Pope's dress Coat, his Uniform as Major General with his name on the collar, his plans & paper, copies of his dispatches, etc., also fell into our hands as did his two horses, his body servant, & the cheif of his Staff, & what was better than all, his sword & a mail bag made up for Washington containing most valuable information. This latter is in Gen Lee's hands & the possession of it by us will involve a change in their plans, if our pressing on them has not already done so.

I see that these trophies were brought to Richmond by Mr Walker Keith Armistead.[204] I wonder if it is the son of Gen Walker Keith Armistead whom I knew when a girl of fifteen. I spent a part of a school vacation with his sisters at his father's house near Upperville. He was then a fine boy about twelve years old & together we rambled over the mountains in which his father's house was embosomed & gathered crystals & flowers, as I well remember, to the detriment of my school wardrobe. I wonder if it can be the same? How changed are the times! His father's house was within twelve miles of the Warrenton Springs where Pope has had his headquarters for so long & from whence he has been so rudely driven. If so, the seat of the war is in his own land, almost in his play ground. Well may he strike, for it is in defence of his home, his sisters, his parents graves! What a blessing that the future is veiled from our eyes! How life would have been poisoned could we have known that those hills, those peaceful valleys, smiling in their luxuriance, would so soon have echoed to the horrid tramp of War! We captured many prisoners, losing but two men killed & three wounded. As yet Pope's men will not fight & seem to have no aversion to being taken, as their short imprisonment & the chance they have of being paroled instead of exchanged gives them a hope of a furlough. They may make a stand yet however to our cost. Pray God our men press not on too eagerly or in disorder. James Edmondston's Brigade has, we hear, been ordered on. If so, his hands as Quarter Master are full. No time to write, poor fellow!

---

[203] Thomas J. (Stonewall) Jackson's cavalry, together with two regiments of infantry, captured Manassas Junction in order to seize Pope's supplies and to cut his communication with Washington. The Confederates retained a portion of the captured stores and burned the surplus before leaving the town. Geer, *Campaigns of the Civil War*, 132; Johnson and Buel, *Battles and Leaders*, II, 501-505, 516-517.

[204] Walker Keith Armistead, Jr. (1835-1904), serving in the Sixth Virginia Cavalry, was the son of Gen. Walker Keith Armistead, Sr., and the brother of Confederate Brig. Gen. Lewis Addison Armistead who died at Gettysburg. The capture of Pope's coat was described in the *Richmond Enquirer*, August 27 and 28, 1862. See also Garber, *The Armistead Family*, 69; *Dictionary of American Biography*, I, 347; Douglas Southall Freeman, *Lee's Lieutenants* (New York: Charles Scribner's Sons, 3 volumes, 1942-1944), II, 72, hereinafter cited as Freeman, *Lee's Lieutenants*.

At night—Disappointed again. No husband & no letter even! Patience, he may come tomorrow! Waited dinner until five o'clock, the train having been detained Owen tells me. Then took a walk with Rondo & home to my solitary cup of Tea. Amused myself with my "Index Rerum" I suppose I might call it, writing down some facts & derivations which I have latterly found in my reading. Read 120 pages of "Literatur du Midi," rather dull work, tracing the downward course of the Italian muse just now. From Tasso to Goldoni and Gozzoli.[205] What a fall!

No news by mail. Papers filled with rumours only. In the West all goes well for us. Morgan has captured his captors or rather his would be captors.

SEPTEMBER 2, 1862

On Sat came Patrick wearied & worn out with the deceit & selfishness, the management, & the petty artifices exhibited by those who want position & the delay and uncertainity, the meanness of those who have the disposal of places. As he wrote me, Gen French sent him over to Richmond with a letter to the Sec of War saying that Gen Hill had reccommended him to the Colonelcy of the Regt of unattached Companies but that as he knew nothing personally of his qualifications for the office he left the appointment to the Sec himself. Accordingly Mr E took the letter the same afternoon. In the train with him was Mr Baker[206] of Wilmington, a member of Gen French's staff. He saw the Sec and our Representatives in Congress,[207] got them to do what they could for him, referred to Gens Hill, Gatlin, and Anderson's reccommendations—in short did all that remained for him to do in order to bring himself to the Sec reccollection & present his claim in a favourable light.

The next day he met Mr Baker in the street. He (Mr Baker) took him aside & addressed him thus, "Col E, I fear we are coming in competition" & went on to state in answer to Patrick's query as to what office he was seeking that he was "seeking none," that Gen French had tendered to him the afternoon before the Colonelcy of the unattached Regt of Cavalry and sent him over with

---

[205] Carlo Goldoni (1707-1793) was an Italian playwright noted for his comedies; Benozzo Gozzoli (1420-1498) was a Florentine painter and goldsmith; and Torquato Tasso (1544-1595) was known chiefly for the epic poem *Jerusalem Delivered*. Benét, *Reader's Encyclopedia*, 444, 450, 1102.

[206] John A. Baker previously served in Co. E, Tenth North Carolina (First Artillery) Regiment, and on the staff of Gen. Samuel G. French when French was in command of the Department of North Carolina. Baker resigned this position when he was commissioned colonel of the Forty-first North Carolina (Third Cavalry) Regiment on November 17, 1862, to date from September, 1862. He was taken prisoner near Petersburg, Virginia, by Union forces on June 21, 1864, and remained a captive until he took the Oath of Allegiance on March 6, 1865. Clark, *Histories of the North Carolina Regiments*, II, 769; Manarin and Jordan, *North Carolina Troops*, II, 178-180.

[207] North Carolina's representatives in the Confederate Congress were William N. H. Smith, Robert R. Bridgers, Owen R. Kenan, Thomas D. S. McDowell, Archibald H. Arrington, James R. McLean, Thomas Samuel Ashe, William Lander, Burgess Sidney Gaither, and Allen T. Davidson. The state's senators were William Theophilus Dortch and William Alexander Graham. Wilfred B. Yearns, Jr., "North Carolina in the Confederate Congress," *North Carolina Historical Review*, XXIX (July, 1952), 361, 364-366.

strong reccommendations to the Sec of War! Mr E. bowed & they parted, but think of French's meanness & duplicity, to lead Patrick in the morning to think that he had left the matter to the Sec & send him on a fool's journey & within a few hours to press the same post on another person & do his utmost to get him the appointment! & then have the face to meet him & ask how the business was progressing! I am only sorry that Patrick did not answer him that he did not know which of his suggestions the Sec would respect, but the matter has a further complication. When Patrick was in Gen Hill's office & when Hill reccommend himself & brother for the posts of Colonel & Major, the Major General of many offices, Martin, was in the room. He remarked that he thought an Election was the proper course. Mr E differed. Hill did not know but wrote to the Sec to decide. He, as I before stated, said the Department claimed the right to appoint & yet Gen Martin posts off home & without authority, he not being in command, orders an election & takes most excellent care that Patrick shall know nothing of it. So an election is held at which Captain Humphrey is elected Colonel, Captain Newkirk, Lieut Col, & Mr Ed Hill, Major.[208] This the Sec or Gen French, I forget which, pronounced illegal & ordered the Regt to the command of the senior Captain. So there the matter stands. Whether the Sec will respect the Election & appoint the officers elected which, unless there are grave faults in the officers themselves, Mr E thinks the best, or whether he will act on Gen French's first or second reccommendation, remains to be seen.

As to Major General of Militia Martin, Adjutant Gen Martin, Commissary Gen Martin, Quarter Master Gen Martin, in the service of the State of N C, Brigadier Gen Martin C S A, by whichever of his many titles he chooses to be called—I have not enumerated them all—as to his conduct, I say it arose either from a personal animosity against Mr E or from a fear that brother would be appointed Major & accept & that thus he would lose his services, which he needs to bolster him up under the weight of the many offices which he absorbs. Perhaps from both as he has shown himself inimical to Mr E before, but to have done with the whole of it. I am weary of the pettinesses, the deceits, the littleness of the whole transaction, & this election has taken from me all the desire I had that Mr E should have the appointment, for it has rendered the situation of the appointee an exceedingly unpleasant one. I feel more settled than I have done for months & was it not for the probability of the extension of the Conscript age to all under forty five (in which case Patrick

---

[208] Lott Williams Humphrey, formerly a first lieutenant in Co. B, Forty-first North Carolina (Third Cavalry) Regiment, served as captain of Co. H of the same regiment from May, 1862, until October of that year. Abram Francis Newkirk was captain of "Newkirk's Coast Guard," Co. A of the Forty-first regiment, until September, 1863. Atherton B. Hill, originally a lieutenant in Patrick Edmondston's "Scotland Neck Mounted Riflemen" and then in Co. G of the Forty-first, became captain of the company when Patrick resigned in October, 1861. Hill resigned the position in 1862 and later served as captain of Co. B, McRae's Battalion North Carolina Cavalry. Manarin and Jordan, *North Carolina Troops*, II, 190, 236-237, 182, 227, 699; Clark, *Histories of the North Carolina Regiments*, II, 770-771.

says he is going as a private; that he is sick of this management & manovering & hanging up by the eyelids for the pleasure of these little great men), I think I could sit down content with my husband at home & forget that he ever attempted to raise this unlucky Battalion. Let's forget it now!

Went down to the plantation & dined there yesterday for the first time in more than a year, nearly two I beleive. Felt a weight of ennui & expectation which I could not account for. I beleive it is a want to regular occupation. I have been in a state of expectancy for so long that I have lost my regular habits & the war having broken up sewing & work of that sort, for we have no cloth to sew, I beleive I am getting idle, which will never do. I will, so far as I can, return to my former life.

We did not hear from the mail today, but brother came at night & told us that there had been a battle between our troops under Gen Lee & Pope's army in which we gained a Victory &, what is strange enough, on the old battle field of Manassas, we occupying the position the Yankees did at Bull Run. But we shall hear the particulars tomorrow.

SEPTEMBER 4, 1862

Such a disappointment last night! We sent to Feltons for our mail where brother promised to send it by his carriage & found that Moses had not brought it. It is too bad! I had been counting the hours the whole day, actually checking them off as they passed, & could scarce await the slow motion of the carriage as we came home from the plantation, & then to be put off for another twenty four hours! But so it is & we must bear it. I am lazy and that is the fact. I have become a "*Quid Nunc*," & the sooner I get out of this frame of mind the better for my happiness. It is partly chess playing, for when father is with me I can do nothing else & that tends to a dissipation of mind, a frittering away of the moments, which is not conducive to a well regulated, well balanced employment of my time—partly the state of unsettlement in which I have lived since Feb & partly the war, which keeps me always on the qui vive. I must end it, or it will be the worse for me, by some regular steady occupation.

My third day Ague, Mrs Barnes, has been here all morning & now, twelve o'clock, has just left, so here is this morning gone, for I do not beleive I can do anything until Alsbrook comes from the Post Office. Dined again yesterday at the Plantation. Mr E sent Henry to see if he could buy some leather to make our house servants some shoes. He was unsuccessful, but the Quaker who had the leather showed him a side of upper leather from which the "uppers" for one pair of shoes had been cut. For this single pair of uppers only he had received three dollars—almost incredible, & yet twelve barrels of Copperas brought last week in Wilmington $5000. It is three dollars a pound at retail! Cotton is however selling at 20 cts in Petersburg. In Nashville it is 30 cts for gold, 42 cts. U S treasury notes, and 55 cts for Confederate money.

SEPTEMBER 5, 1862

News of a victory at Manassas! Few details, enough only to show us what we have won. McClellan & Burnside effected a junction with Pope & we beat them all. Jackson by forced marches outflanked Pope, got between him & Washington, but I will wait for details until they are fuller. To God alone be the praise! He giveth us the Victory! As yet we have an unclouded picture of success, a Queen Elizabeth picture without a shade in it! That is yet to come with the list of our killed and wounded. God be with our wounded! I fear their sufferings are terrible, so far from transportation, from help, even such feeble help as we are able to give them. Be with them O Lord and give them strength to bear their suffering like men & Christian Patriots. O that I could do something for them instead of sitting down in ease & comfort at home and giving them wishes which cost me nothing. Were I only near them or near the Rail Road, I would not have a vacant bed in the house!

SEPTEMBER 9, 1862

Details of the late great battle come in so slowly that the heart sickens at the delay! God help those who have friends, husbands, sons in the army. Their suspense must be cruel! We fought on three successive days, Thursday, Friday, & Saturday, the 28th, 29th, and 30th of Aug. On Friday night the enemy acknoledged a loss of 17,000 & several entire batteries of cannon & yet that shameless liar Gen Pope, altho in full retreat, sent a dispatch to his Government claiming a victory and at the same time wrote to Gen Lee requesting a suspension of hostilities & leave for his ambulances to pass through our lines to attend his wounded. We have killed & taken many officers, several Generals amongst them.

The battle was fought precisely on the battlefield on Manassas & we captured some batteries in precisely the same spots as those then taken. Where Rickets battery stood, in particular, we took another. The bayonnette charge of our men was splendid in the extreme. We have only our enemies account of it & they admit it to have been beyond praise. Gen Kearney was killed in a most disgraceful & inglorious manner, so as to deprive him of all claims to a heroes Laurel crown. He rode up to one of our Regts, the 49th Georgia, by mistake, during the fight. Instantly a hundred muskets were presented to him, when he called out—"I surrender! I surrender!"; but no sooner were the guns withdrawn than lying down on his horse he started off at full speed! Before he was out of range however he fell peirced with innumerable bullets. The scoundrel! I suppose he will be deified & made a martyr of by his countrymen who do not understand the point of honor & who will affirm that he was shot after having surrendered!—& what is stranger than all, he belonged to the old army & has had an opportunity of knowing better by an association with the *Southern* gentlemen! *Officers in the old U S A!* But some people can never learn.

The Northern Army has fallen back to the lines about Washington and Alexandria. They have burnt the long bridge (we hear) over the Potomac & destroyed the Aqueduct. A panic pervades Washington. McClellan has been placed in command again & his own, Pope's, and Burnsides armies massed for the defence of Washington. Jackson is said to have crossed the Potomac at Leesburg, or Edwards Ferry, on Friday & three Divisions of our army are said to be there now menacing the Relay House. It now remains for "Maryland my Maryland" to prove her patriotism & devotion to the Southern cause. Whether she is really down trodden or a willing slave, opinions are diverse about her, but she must now show her hand. Pray God it be for us, for if against us we shall be compelled to retreat I fear.

The sufferings of the Yankee wounded are terrible. Days after the battle they lay there unheeded & uncared for. We had our hands full with our own & were utterly unable to attend to them. A corps of citizens from Washington City came out with ambulances & vehicles to assist in gathering them up so as not to weaken Pope's force (which he represented as in active pursuit of us) by detailing men for the duty. They were overcome at their number & the utter inability to obtain food for them, as well as thunderstruck at finding Pope the pursued instead of the pursuer.

Since writing the above I see that Gen Kearney's body, instead of being struck by "innumerable bullets" as I stated, was at first supposed to be unwounded & his death to have ensued from heart disease but on being placed in the hands of the embalmers they discovered that he had been wounded in the back near the lower portion of the spine & the ball had ranged *longitudinally* through the body lodging in the chest. So much for lying down on his horse! His horse was riddled with bullets.

The Yankees propose to make hospitals of the Capitol, the Patent office, the White House, & the other Public building in Washington, so that by hoisting the Yellow Flag over them they will be protected from our shells. I hope we will show them a trick worth two of that, viz.—that we will take the city & make them remove their wounded to a place of safety & then burn or blow up every public building in the place, make it "*a heap of stones.*" We paid for more than half of it, & we do not want their corrupt Capitol so near our border &, if we get Maryland, actually within it. Our army must have suffered for food severely but they bear it bravely and cheerfully with stout hearts like men fighting for all that men hold dear.

On Monday Gen A P Hill succeeded in capturing a long train of waggons at Germantown. The enemy disposed themself in order of battle to receive the shock of our troops, but before we came close enough to charge they broke and ran in inextricable confusion! They are said to be completely demoralized & represent themselves as sick of fighting & desirous only to go home. But we must not be too confidant. They are terribly afraid of Jackson

& cannot comprehend his rapid movements & unexpected assaults. One of our men who was taken prisoner was carried before their Dutch General Seigle. So soon as he entered his presence he demanded with great vehemence, "Vere is he?" "Vere is he?" For some moments the southerner could not understand his broken *Yankee* (for their language is not English) at last, however, he took it in & asked "Who?—who do you mean?" "Why Shackson! Vere is *he*?! Vere is Shackson?"

Our wounded are cared for principally at Aldie, Aldie the county seat of the late venerable Charles Fenton Mercer[209] who, when I was a schoolgirl, I revered and admired so as a gentleman of the olden time. Jackson crossed the river at Edwards ferry near Leesburg. His army must have passed by Belmont where I was at school. Wool it is said in the Northern papers has 70,000 men for the defence of the Relay House where it is supposed Jackson will swoop down upon the Railroad between Baltimore & Washington & cut the arteries which connect Washington with the West & North. The Road via Annapolis will be open it is true, but that is not only round-a-bout but runs through a hostile (to them) country. Ah for the news! *Glorious* news! News which will lead to Peace!

SEPTEMBER 11, 1862

Patrick left home this morning for Garysburg to see Capt Reinhart, the sole Capt left in Edmondston's Battalion. He has been ordered there & knows not what to do. This delay of the War Department in a matter seemingly so simple seems very strange! Why can't Mr Randolph[210] say, "No Col E, I cannot fill your Battalion" & order Capt Reinhart elsewhere, or "Yes, Col E., take such & such Companies & take the field at once." But no it requires as much management as an affair of State.

I was shocked & distressed greatly yesterday by hearing of the death of my young neighbor, Mrs Sheilds (Susan Whitemore).[211] I saw her on Sat &

---

[209] Charles Fenton Mercer (1778-1858) was a lawyer, state legislator, United States congressman, and brigadier general in the War of 1812. Mercer strongly supported internal improvements, public education, termination of the slave trade, and colonization of free Negroes in Africa. He resided at Aldie, an estate from which the town of Aldie, Virginia, took its name. *Dictionary of American Biography*, XII, 539.

[210] George Wythe Randolph (1818-1867) was secretary of war for the Confederacy from March until November, 1862. Before his appointment as secretary of war he was a lawyer and a Confederate brigadier general. He resigned his political post in the Confederacy because of ill health and friction with Davis over the administration of his office. *Concise Dictionary of American Biography*, 841; Freeman, *Lee's Lieutenants*, I, 145.

[211] Susan J. Whitemore, a twenty-year-old schoolteacher, lived with her father H. B. Whitemore, a Halifax County farmer, in 1860. Charles C. Shields, listed as a twenty-five-year-old farmer in the 1860 census, served in Co. G, Forty-first North Carolina (Third Cavalry) Regiment as a private from April 23, 1861, until December 31, 1861. He was discharged because of an unspecified disability. Eighth Census, 1860, Population Schedule, Halifax County, 53, 63; Manarin and Jordan, *North Carolina Troops*, II, 234.

thought her quite sick, but I have had daily messages from her (she sending to me only the day before for some crackers & some Cordial & Wine), & each time they have said she was improving; & when the servant came with my empty baskets, so sure was I that she wanted something from me that I met her with the query—"how or now, what can I do for Miss Susan today?" and to my horror heard she had died about an hour before. Her infant was born on Wednesday & she, poor thing, taken with dysentery the night after. She lived just a week & sunk suddenly, I suppose, for Dr Hall[212] could not be summoned to her, as he had gone to visit a distant patient.

After Patrick left this morning I made a beautiful Chaplet of White and delicate Lilac, Dahlias, Evergreens, Feverfew, Citarena, etc., & sent it over to be laid on the coffin, being unable to go myself as Patrick went in the carriage. Poor Mrs Whitmore! when I saw her on Sat, in all the importance of a Grandmother, & noticed the change which the possession of a little property has wrought in her (for I have not seen her since her husband left father's employment), the glories of her new front & stylish cape, the De Dage dress, the tone in which she spoke of "Mr Moore's orchard," "our niggers," etc., & thought how much happiness the possession of a little money can give & what changes it brings in the manners & conduct of its possessors, I little thought so heavy a cloud was hanging over & ready to burst upon her! Poor woman, she must be crushed to the earth. I will go & see her, fifteen miles tho it is to her house, in a few days & at least assure her of my sympathy & kindly interest.

Worked steadily all day on my large flat fan fly brush. It is a beautiful peice of work but very troublesome. I will never undertake another so large. However, it amuses me & it is employment. Read Sismondi.[213] I have got to Calderon[214] in the Spanish Literature. I am sorry that Nannie wanted to begin the book before I had finished it, for I feel impelled as it were to read on steadily so as not to keep her waiting & I wished when I got to a review of those books to which I have access to run through them myself in connection with Sismondi, Cervantes,[215] The Spanish Ballads, particularly those of the Cid,[216] & now Calderon, but I must trust my memory. I have only Leigh

---

[212] A.S. Hall was a physician living in Halifax County in 1860. Eighth Census, 1860, Population Schedule, Halifax County, 80.

[213] Jean Charles Léonard Simondé de Sismondi was a Swiss historian and economist. *Webster's Biographical Dictionary*, 1368. See footnote 188, 1862.

[214] Pedro Calderón de la Barca (1600-1681), a Spanish author and playwright, influenced the work of Dryden and Shelley. Benét, *Reader's Encyclopedia*, 165.

[215] Miguel de Cervantes Saavedra (1547-1616), author of *Don Quixote*, was a Spanish novelist and playwright. Benét, *Reader's Encyclopedia*, 193.

[216] Cid was an honorary name given to Roderigo or Ruy Diaz de Bivar (ca. 1040-1099), national hero of Spain. His exploits were the basis of Corneille's *Le Cid*, published in 1636. Benét, *Reader's Encyclopedia*, 212.

Hunt's Italian Poets[217] & Boiardo,[218] Pulci,[219] Ariosto,[220] Tasso, Dante[221] even, etc., are run through by him almost as expeditiously as Sismondi dispatches them, so there is not much to be gained there. "Beware of the man of one book,"[222] it is said, & I beleive it to be true, for I fancy I read too much. My mind is I fear like a Kaleidiscope, one picture effaces the other before it is fixed, and I am too old now to remedy it. Ah! that we could be wise on the experiance of others! My Grandmother often told me the time would come when I would not remember what I read, & I used to listen to her with a respectful wondering *unbeleif*, but I find it is so. Ah, she was a remarkable woman, my Grandmother, how few we see like her, and yet with all her cultivation, with all the true piety I beleive she possessed, her vigorous mind even, I am glad I am not. For to me to be *loved* is greater happiness than to be either *revered* or *admired* & we all stood too much in awe of her to dare to pour out the full feelings of our hearts before her & that I would not like.

It is lonely here tonight, so Journal, as you are my only companion, I feel like having a long chat with you. Let me see, there are many topics which fill my heart & thoughts. We will discuss them. First the Conscript Act & Mr E's plans—but no! I want a relaxation & that I have thought over so often & looked at in so many lights that my mind turns from it as from a sorrowful remembrance. It awakens an *ache* of anxiety at the bare mention. Then Bessie's matters, but Journal, that is not my own secret. "Noblesse oblige," that I confide it not even to you. Then anxieties about Raleigh people, but I have no business to express them either. Cant I find one topic, pleasant, and at the same time open, which I can freely talk over with you, Journal? No not one! *Literature* is the only perfectly unfettered and at the same time cheerful subject left to me & to dwell long on that changes you, Journal, from your legitamate & proper sphere to a mere Composition or Essay. So Journal, I will first express my fears for our Army in Maryland & then—

---

[217] James Henry Leigh Hunt (1784-1859) was a prolific English poet, essayist, and editor who occasionally worked with Byron and Shelley. His *Stories from the Italian Poets, with Lives of the Writers*, published in 1846, analyzed the work of Dante, Pulci, Boiardo, Ariosto, and Tasso. *Dictionary of National Biography*, XXVIII, 267-271.

[218] Matteo Maria Boiardo (1434-1494) was an Italian poet noted for the epic *Orlando Innamorato*. Benét, *Reader's Encyclopedia*, 125.

[219] Luigi Pulci (1432-1484) of Florence was the author of *Morgante Maggiore*, a "serio-comic romance in verse." Benét, *Reader's Encyclopedia*, 741, 890.

[220] Ariosto (1474-1533), author of *Orlando Furioso*, was a prominent Italian poet. *Orlando Furioso* continued the adventures and characters of Boiardo's *Orlando Imnamorato*. Benét, *Reader's Encyclopedia*, 46.

[221] Dante Alighieri (1265-1321), best known for *The Divine Comedy* (ca. 1300), has been considered as possibly the greatest poet "known in the history of the human mind." Benét, *Reader's Encyclopedia*, 272-273.

[222] This quotation by St. Thomas Aquinas (1227-1274) was included in Isaac D'Israili's (1766-1848) *Curiosities of Literature*, published in six volumes from 1791 through 1834. Bartlett, *Familiar Quotations*, 158; Benét, *Reader's Encyclopedia*, 300.

September 12, 1862

I had written thus far last night when a heavy step in the back Piazza arrested me. Who could it be? Owen was with his Master and none of the other servants had shoes but Dolly & it was too heavy for her. My speculations were cut short by the entrance of "Master" himself. He got through his business sooner than he expected & was enabled to return home. I soon had his tea ready & instead of disquisitions in my journal I chatted with him until bed time. He brought the papers, but there is no news except that Gen Lee's headquarters are at Fredericktown in Maryland. Our troops have been well received by the inhabitants so far. Rumours of a rising in Baltimore & that the U S Provost Marshal had been hung by the mob, but this is by no means authentic.

Our Cavalry made a brilliant dash into Williamsburg last Tuesday, captured the commander & Military Governor, Col [———], burnt the camp & stores of the enemy, destroyed a large amount of U S Government property, but hearing of the advance of the enemy in force from Fortress Monroe, retired with the loss of three men only & one of them was killed accidentally by his comrade.

Gen Martin made a demonstration on Washington in this state which was not so successful. He had a large force (comparatively), took the town & held it three hours, when the advance of the Gun boats drove him back with the loss of—but the accounts conflict so, that for the honor of Maj Gen Martin, I will delay recording it. He took three peices of artillery, a few prisoners, but rumour says he was forced to leave twenty of our wounded behind him! Maj Gen Martin himself is said to have remained at a safe distance, three miles from the conflict, but that I cannot yet credit. Nothing was gained, & for aught I can see nothing was to be gained but the capture perhaps of a few negroes & a reputation for Maj Gen pluralist Martin.

Vance[223] was inaugurated on the eighth of this month as gov of the State, & as Maj Gen Martin expects a lively time with him as Adjutant Gen of the State of N C & Brig Gen of the Confederate states, it was as well to have a little military reputation on hand to begin with. If the Brig could distinguish himself, the Gov would find it more difficult to attack the Adgt Gen. So I fear those men lost their lives for the advancement of Gen Martin's schemes, for why he should go there when he *knew* the Gun boats would shell him out is more than I can see. One of the Gun boats took fire, from no action of ours, however, & was burned until she blew up, killing many of her crew, so it is

---

[223] Zebulon Baird Vance (1830-1894), prior to his governorship of North Carolina (1862-1865 and 1877-1879), had enlisted as captain of the "Rough and Ready Guards" from Buncombe County at the start of the war. Subsequently commissioned colonel of the Twenty-sixth North Carolina Regiment on April 27, 1861, Vance held the position until his election as governor. Clark, *Histories of the North Carolina Regiments*, II, 81, 306.

said, but I will record no more rumours. Wait until they have settled into consistency.

SEPTEMBER 14, 1862

This Conscript extension Act hangs like the sword of Damocles over my head. They are still debating it in Congress & we cannot tell which side will get the Victory. A letter yesterday from Mr E's friend Mr Haxall tells him that it is in contemplation to send Brig Gen Beverly Robinson [Robertson], the successor of the lamented and gallant Ashby, out here to organize the North Carolina Cavalry. It seems an odd movement to take him from the face of the enemy for such a purpose, but we have many things now beyond our comprehension & which call for the exercise of simple, unquestioning *Faith*. Be that as it may, I suppose the organization of the Regt ordered by Maj Gen Martin will go for nothing & new appointments or Elections will take place. Capt Haxall has received a Commission as Lieut & is detailed to act as drill master with the prospect of a field office in the distance. I do not know how it will be & have been so worried by the whole of it that—but *that* is not true, I do care & deeply, for beyond my interest for Mr E they are my countrymen, my country's defenders, & I *care* for every one & all of them & wish them to have the best officers in the country, & I know they will distinguish themselves. Gen French is made a Major General, I suppose because he is a Northern man, for no one can see any other earthly claim he has. On dit that his wife was a sister of Mrs Davis.[224] If so, that accounts for it! Curtain influence!

No news by mail, but the Yankee press continues to distinguish itself by lying. On Tuesday, five days after Jackson crossed the Potomac, the Washington papers persistently denied that there was a Rebel soldier in Maryland. One of them, the Star I beleive, with some little compunction, some weak aspiration after Truth, modestly asserted that the Rebel Jackson had crossed the Potomac, but in a few hours judiciously fell back & re-crossed into Virginia. News from the West tell us that we are having it all our own way in Kentucky. Lexington is taken & the Kentuckians flocking to our Standard. The enemy are evacuating Corinth & have burned every house in the Village! They are retreating northward & are removing their stores preparatory to an evacuation, it is supposed, of Nashville. The whole country is filled with guerrillas who annoy the Yankees terribly. The war has assumed such giant proportions that I cannot take it all in; so, many things in Tennessee, Kentucky, Missouri, & Arkansas are omitted by me, not because they are not of great importance but because the nearer object of interest eclipses them.

---

[224]The source of this rumor has not been determined. General French's first wife, Matilda Roberts French, died in June, 1857. In January, 1865, French married Mary F. Abercrombie of Russell County, Alabama. Samuel G. French, *Two Wars: An Autobiography* (Nashville: Confederate Veteran, 1901), 132-133, 304-305.

Bragg is in command in the South west & censured for inactivity, but I remember Sidney Johnston & am silent. Beauregard has reported for duty & been assigned to South Carolina & Georgia. Joe Johnson has also recovered from his wound & been placed in command of the trans Mississippi. Yellow fever said to have broken out in New Orleans & the Yankees dying like sheep, but not authentic.

September 18, 1862

The news from our Army in Maryland is so unsatisfactory that there is little to record. They took possession of Fredericktown and were well received by the inhabitants. A part of our Cavalry were reported at Hagerstown and another part at Emmetsburg, threatening an advance into Pensylvania. The papers are full of rumours brought by "reliable gentlemen" & "passengers," and we are kept in a state of most cruel excitement & suspense.

Jackson has marched south from Hagerstown & suddenly thrown himself over the Potomac again above Harpers Ferry & attacked & routed the enemy at that point, capturing five thousand prisoners. This is the Southern account. The Northern on the contrary maintains that they opened fire upon Jackson as he was crossing the Potomac *at* Harper's Ferry & drove him back with heavy loss. We cannot tell which is true. Certain there was a fight on Saturday last. Beyond that all is in mystery. Gen Loring detached Gen Jenkins who captured the enemy's stores & provisions at Buchanon, drove him west, skirmishing & capturing detached Regiments, to the Ohio which he crossed & advanced twenty miles into the interior. Then suddenly wheeling, he recrossed the Ohio and advanced up the Kanhawa. Loring in the mean time attacked the enemy at Fayette Court House & after a hard fight drove him from his entrenchments, capturing his stores & supplies, followed him to Gauley & Cotton Hill where there were sharp skirmishes, thence to Charleston, Kanhawa County, were a battle was fought with great loss to them; drove them from that point down the Kanhawa, Jenkins being between them & the Ohio, & Loring pressing on in front, so the next news will we hope be of their utter annihilation.

In Kentucky Kirby Smith is carrying everything before him, calls for twenty thousand stand of arms for the Kentuckians who have joined him. He has captured Frankfort & the Confederate Flag now floats from the Capitol! The Unionists are flying to Ohio & he menaces Covington & Newport & even Cincinnati itself. In Tennessee the Federal forces are concentrating at Nashville & intrenching themselves, having stolen 12 000 negroes who they have put to work on their fortifications. They feed them badly, however, & they are running off in scores to their masters. Cumberland Gap still holds out against us. Pope has been sent to Minnesota to try his tactics against the Indians! His country men cannot say enough against him for his want of sense & hardheaded obstinacy[.] He has left a sting behind him, however, in charges against several of his Generals. The investigation of these has, however, at the representation of Gen M Clellan been postponed owing to the urgency of the case & they ordered to their several commands. In his report he is particularly severe upon Gen Fitz John Porter[225] whose brigade was old U S regulars & charges him with dilatoriness & disobedience of orders. The great cry of the North is for a General! They admit that they have been out Generaled, out manoevered, flanked whenever the Rebels chose, utterly routed and defeated, & all they maintain for the want of a General. They praise & admire Jackson & Lee & confess their combinations are masterly. They are finding us out now it would appear! Human nature to value a thing after they have lost it! They think now that [the] South has a genius for military manuvres & that there are no such troops in the world as compose Jackson's Division! They are in a state of terrible panic as to what we will do when we cross the Pensylvania line. *Now* the Rebels are orderly & respect private property for they claim Maryland as a part of the Confederacy, but then, in an enemy's country, there is no end to the atrocities they will commit. I trust that they will find themselves mistaken & that our Army will remember that it is composed of Southern gentlemen, whose hearts are too enlarged, whose refinement is too pure & exalted to take pleasure in a retaliation upon their innocent women & children—what they have made ours suffer. Above all they a[re] Christians & brave men, men who fight *men*, not women, as Butler, Pope, & their compeers do.

Today is the Thanksgiving ordered by President Davis for the second Victory of Manassas. "Lord with glowing heart I do praise Thee." Thou only has given us the Victory! Thou hast preserved us from the power of the enemy! To Thee be our praise & gratitude due! May our lives show forth Thy praise! May each soldier in our army realize that he is Thy servant, bound to Thee by ties of gratitude & obedience & may he never soil his sword by or commit an act upon which he would shrink to ask Thy blessing! May he remember that "Thou O God see'st him."

Yellow Fever reported in Wilmington. It rages at Key West. God help our soldiers in the Sea ports; unacclimated as they are, it will make fearful ravages amongst them.

---

[225] Gen. Fitz-John Porter (1822-1901), in command of the Union V Corps during the second battle at Manassas, was ordered to strike Jackson while he was separated from Longstreet and crush him. Porter failed to do so and in November, 1862, was relieved of command because of this blunder. A court-martial was convened to consider the case, and Porter was found guilty of "disobedience, disloyalty, and misconduct in the face of the enemy" and cashiered out of the army on January 21, 1863. Porter immediately began efforts to clear his name, claiming that his battle orders had been vague, conflicting, and obsolete; by the time he received them, Jackson and Longstreet were already united. Finally, in 1879, Porter secured a review of his case; in 1882 the review board cleared him, and the president remitted the part of his sentence disqualifying him from office. In 1886 Porter was reappointed to the army as colonel, retired. *Dictionary of American Biography*, XV, 90-91; Boatner, *Civil War Dictionary*, 661.

Our Army occupy the Sugar Loaf[226] mountain as a Telegraph & look out station and well is [it] adapted for the purpose. How well I remember it! How it was the first object which met my gaze as I looked out in the morning, the last upon which the Sun seemed to love to linger at night, & that one white spot—half way up—which used to excite our curiosity & interest so! Was it a house? If so it was an enormous one. Or was it a "cliff of shadowy tint"? How we longed to be able to fly that we might see the view from its summit! Little did it enter into our girlish heads—that it would ever be of such use to us; that from it the issues of life & death perhaps to our nearest & dearest friends would be viewed. The Yankees say that from it all movements of troops from Washington, Baltimore, Harpers Ferry, etc., can be viewed and that is of immense advantage to us. I hope it is with all my heart.

Heard from Sue that Frank Jones has an appointment as 3d Ass. Engineer on board the C S Steamer Chicora & has gone to Charleston to join her. I hope he will be satisfied now & not resign again, especially as he has seen how difficult it is to get a Commission.

Kate Miller has gone to Augusta to pay a visit to Miss Eves. Mr John Dunlop[227] was wounded in the thigh at Manassas, slightly only, she writes me, but he cannot get home nor his friends get to him. She goes to Petersburg soon.

Father & Mama well & at the Salt Sulphur Springs. Mama indignant at Gen Loring's long inactivity which she hears attributed to a desire to pay his addresses to Mr Beirne's daughter,[228] whilst one of his Staff, Butler King's[229] son, had like aspirations as regards Miss Caperton. She ought now to forgive him & the ladies to smile on him, as—

"None but the brave!—
"None but the brave!—
"None but the brave!—deserve the fair!"[230]

[226] Sugarloaf Mountain is located in Frederick County, Maryland, across the Potomac River from Loudoun County, Virginia, where Mrs. Edmondston went to school.

[227] Lt. John Dunlop, the son of James and Isabella Lenox Maitland Dunlop, was a staff officer with Brig. Gen. Lewis A. Armistead. *Official Records (Army)*, Series I, XI, Part II, 819.

[228] Mrs. Edmondston probably was referring to either Oliver Beirne, a rich Virginia and Louisiana planter whose daughter Betty married William Porcher Miles of South Carolina in 1863, or to his brother Andrew Beirne, a prominent planter and politician of Monroe County, Virginia (now West Virginia), whose daughter Rosalie married Col. Garnett Andrews of Tennessee in 1867. General Loring never married. *Biographical Directory of Congress*, 536, 1328; *Concise Dictionary of American Biography*, 23; *Dictionary of American Biography*, I, 291.

[229] Thomas Butler King (1800-1864) was a lawyer, planter, and United States congressman from Georgia. His son, John Floyd King (1842-1915), worked on General Loring's staff, obtained the rank of colonel, practiced law in Louisiana after the war, and served in the United States Congress from 1879 until 1887. In 1862 John F. King wrote love letters to a Miss Sue Caperton. Thomas Butler King Papers, Southern Historical Collection; *Biographical Directory of Congress*, 1166, 1168; *Concise Dictionary of American Biography*, 527.

[230] John Dryden, *Alexander's Feast or the Power of Musique*, stanza 1, lines 12-14.

In this case we must add the successful brave. I fear Sydney Johnston was right when he said that the test of military actions in most minds was "*success.*" It is a "base test" but one which influences the many. Few can see the merit which *only deserves* success & fewer still are contented with it.

SEPTEMBER 22, 1862

Much has happened since I last discoursed with you, Journal, & something which I cannot even tell you as it is not my secret. Last Friday as we were at tea one of father's servants from Tom's came out with our mail, which Mr Hill had left there to be sent to us, & a verbal message to the effect that my brother-in-law, Mr Miller, was dead! We were terribly shocked, but that was all & could not but wonder at Mr Hill's want of consideration in sending such a message in the manner he did. It might be a mistake. How & when did he die & how did Mr Hill hear of it? & a thousand more questions, all of which were without a solution. A letter from Rachel, when we opened the mail, told us that he had had an apopleptic fit on Tuesday but on Wednesday was thought to be better. Not one of her children was at home, the sons in the Army & Kate on a visit to a friend in Augusta. Next day brother came out & confirmed it. He was indeed dead!

Thus has perished one of the finest minds & the most finished scholars in our country. As a Lawyer he had few equals, as an orator perhaps fewer. His conversational powers were fine & showed in every turn the man of learning, cultivation & refinement. His writings evinced a thorough acquaintance with the power & genius of the English Language, forcible, elegant, & dignified; & with all he was singularly modest. His faults, perhaps I should say (humanly speaking) his sole fault, the sole bar to his distinction, will be buried with him.[231] Let us not lose sight of his many virtues.

My poor sister! I greive for her. She will feel his loss terribly in more respects than one. The loss of such society, intellectually is a sore one. Add then the care she has taken of him, the position & political importance she derived from him & in which she took such pride—make the bereavement all the more severe. It adds greatly to father's cares & expenses, as he was not one to lay by anything & henceforward Kate and herself must look to him for everything.

The public news is most inspiriting. Jackson's victory at Harper's Ferry is officially confirmed. We have taken an immense amount of Ammunition but few other stores, for it seems they were expecting re-inforcements of both men

---

[231] Henry Watkins Miller died from injuries sustained when he stumbled on a staircase, "lost his ballance & fell *over* the railing clear down to the floor below!" The doctor handling the case was not "satisfied that it was apoplexy" but eventually agreed to list it as the cause of death. Intimations by Mrs. Edmondston and other family members that Miller's death was caused by "Some thing we will scarce say to any, . . ." and that his "sole fault . . . will be buried with him . . ." suggest that Miller's fall was caused by something other than apoplexy. Elizabeth Devereux Jones to Mary Bayard Devereux Clarke, September 26, 1862, letter in the possession of Mrs. Graham A. Barden, Jr., of New Bern, North Carolina.

& provisions. We have taken from 8 to 10,00 prisoners with but slight loss to ourselves. They capitulated at discretion (Gen Miles[232] in command), the Officers being allowed to retain their side arms, but we have captured an immense amount of small arms & muskets which are much needed to arm the Marylanders & Kentuckians with, who are flocking to our Standard.

But there is better news even than this, tho' not as this official but still "reliable." M Clellan fell with his whole army upon our rear under Gen D H Hill who, tho terrible outnumbered, managed with fearful loss, however, to maintain himself until Longstreet's division came to his assistance. United they drove the enemy back five miles with terrific slaughter. M Clellan it is supposed went to the releif of Harper's Ferry & intended to capture Jackson but found Hill & the N C Brigade too much for him. Jackson is said to be crossing the Potomac again with the design to fall on his rear & crush him between his own and Longstreet's division. This is conjecture, however. We have no lists of killed or wounded, no estimate even of our loss, but it must be heavy!

This battle occured beyond Frederick town but as the locality is disputed I will wait for the official dispatches. One thing I must not omit to tell you, Journal—brother who got here at dinner time Sat & left the next morning tells us that Gen Martin did not order the election of Field officers in the Regt of Cavalry. That was a blunder of Brig Gen Clingman, who it seems misunderstood the orders of the Department. So I have done Martin great injustice. To no one, however, Journal, but to you & to Amo & I write to correct the false impression I have made on him, so no harm will be done. The other thing which occupies me I said before was a secret &, Journal, as you are a Journal of honour, I know you will not importune me to betray it. "Noblesse oblige." You I am sure recognise that law; otherwise I should not recognise you, Journal.

Went today to Samantha Curries. Poor thing, it is well to know something of other people's trials. It makes our own lighter. She told me that Mr Currie had sent three dollars to Wilmington to buy her some sugar & got for it four pounds only! She got a pair of cards at the same time for which he paid eight. Think of it, a pair of cards & four lbs of sugar for twelve dollars!

SEPTEMBER 25, 1862

I have waited for time to clear the mists that lie around our recent actions on the Potomac, but even now I cannot tell if what I record is correct. As I mentioned Gen D H Hill repulsed the enemy at one of the passes of the Blue Ridge beyond Frederick on Sunday. Hill & Longstreet after repulsing the

---

[232] Col. Dixon S. Miles was mortally wounded at Harpers Ferry, and Brig. Gen. Julius White (1816-1890) assumed responsibility for arranging terms of surrender. *Official Records (Army)*, Series I, XIX, Part I, 546-548.

enemy fell back to the main body of our army which Gen Lee had marshalled in battle array in front of Sharpsburg. On Tuesday evening M Clellan in force attacked him. The battle raged all through Wednesday 17th with terrific slaughter, we driving back the enemy & retaining possession of the field which we held until Friday, removing our wounded. When a corps d armee was thrown across the Potomac to Shepherdstown under the command of Jackson to intercept a body of the enemy, who had crossed below & were endeavouring to flank us & regain Harper's Ferry under the command of Gen Pleasanton, this body he entirely routed & put to flight. Then turning suddenly, he attacked a corps coming to their assistance in the act of crossing the Potomac & in the river repulsed them with terrific carnage. Our guns mowed them down by columns & the River was filled with dead, wounded, and drowning men! It's heart rending to read it. All this we claim to be authentic. Our loss said to be heavy in the battle of Sharpsburg, slight in the subsequent engagements. Then come a rumour of another Victory at Sharpsburg but not reliable. The only loss mentioned in our Dispatches is that of Gen Starke of Mississippi & Gen Branch of this state.

Now per contra the Yankees publish the most flaming accounts of a victory over Hill & Longstreet at the passes of the Blue Ridge on Sunday; another the same day at Crampton's pass a little lower down—that their whole army moved in pursuit of the flying Rebels who rallied & made a desperate stand in front of Sharpsburg but were completely routed & disorganized on Wednesday & Thursday & driven towards the Potomac in fearful disorder—whole batteries captured, Longstreet wounded & captured, Hill killed—all wound up with the announcement that "the Rebellion is virtually subdued"! McClellan's dispatches to his Government claim at one time a brilliant Victory, at another that "he thinks he can claim" one; says "*it is reported*" that Gen Lee admits that they (the rebels) were terribly whipped, Pleasanton in full pursuit, the Rebels driven across the Potomac & more to the same purpose. At the news Stocks in New York have gone up, the people jubilant & defiant, rejoicings every where!

Our means of communication are so deficient & so slow that we cannot trust them entirely & consequently these Yankee lies give us some uneasiness, but the general beleif is that M Clellan was attempting the releif of Harper's Ferry, that Lee wished to avoid a general engagement until that place was taken & Jackson had rejoined him & therefore posted Hill & Longstreet on the Blue Ridge to dispute the passage & delay M Clellan. This being accomplished they fell back to the main body at Sharpsburg, Jackson re-crossing the Potomac & together received the shock of battles they repulsed the enemy, removed our wounded, & held the field until Sat when a large portion of our army crossed back into Va to protect Harper's Ferry & save themselves from being out flanked & have done so by the repulse or annihilation of Pleasanton. Thus matters stand. Every mail is looked for with the most eager impatience

& I trust that re-inforcements are being hurried to Lee. There are said to be thirty thousand stragglers betwen Gordonsville & the Potomac, an army in itself. Alas, for General Branch! alas, for his poor wife![233] It seems but yesterday when they were married, when I met them during their Honeymoon, so devoted & so full of each other! How little could any one have predicted that he would die such a death? Mr E too met them on their way to Richmond last Nov when he went to solicit the post of Brigadier Gen, which he got through his political influence. Poor woman, bitterly does she now regret it, for what is distinction under such greif as hers?

But the news from Kentucky, I must not omit that. Bragg has captured 5 000 Federals at Mumfordsville & destroyed the splendid bridge over the [Green River] at that place & thus cut Louisville off from assistance from its Yankee friends. Kirby Smith is making forced marches from Frankfort and the country in front of Cincinnatti to join him, and then it is thought he will offer battle to Buel. Memphis has long since been evacuated & all things point to an abandonment of Nashville likewise.

SEPTEMBER 26, 1862

Yesterday came Mr Ed Hill from Petersburg & brought Mr E the news about the N C Cavalry. The Sec of War unable or unwilling to decide between the opposing Candidates presented by the different Generals Hill & French, referred the matter to the Gov of N C & he without a thought as to fitness, I hear, took the opportunity of advancing some of his old associates in the [———] Regt;[234] made one of the Captains Col & I forget who Lt Col, but *Tucker*[235]—*Tucker* the dry goods merchant of Raleigh—Maj, a man who hardly knows how to *ride* & who has got rich by charging enormous prices for luxuries in peace & extortionate ones for neccessaries in *war*, a man whose name has become a synonyme for extortion, *"to Tucker"* being well understood in Raleigh, & what seems more unjust still he has taken Mr E's two companies

---

[233]Brig. Gen. Lawrence O'Bryan Branch (1820-1862) was married to Nancy Haywood Blount, the daughter of Gen. William Augustus Blount of Washington, North Carolina. Ashe, *Biographical History*, VII, 56.

[234]Governor Vance commissioned John A. Baker as colonel of the regiment to rank from September 3, 1862. Alfred Moore Waddell served as lieutenant colonel to rank from August 18, 1863, and Roger Moore received the appointment as major on the same date. Moore, after Baker's capture and Waddell's resignation in August, 1864, became colonel of the regiment. Manarin and Jordan, *North Carolina Troops*, II, 178, 180.

[235]W. H. Tucker and his brother Rufus Sylvester Tucker were merchants in Raleigh whose store was located at 8 Fayetteville Street. Rufus S. Tucker (1829-1894) served as captain of the "Wake Rangers," an independent cavalry company, and retained his captaincy when the unit was assigned to the Forty-first North Carolina (Third Cavalry) Regiment in September, 1862. He resigned his captaincy in December of the same year "by reason of his desire to remove his Negro property to a plantation in Georgia. . . ." On January 24, 1863, Tucker was promoted to major and appointed "Governor's Aide-de-Camp" and assistant adjutant general on assignment in Raleigh. During the war he also acted as director of the North Carolina Railroad Company. Manarin and Jordan, *North Carolina Troops*, II, 245; Clark, *Histories of the North Carolina Regiments*, I, 50; II, 771; V, 651; Ashe, *Biographical History*, VII, 454-461.

& given them one to the Regt & the other to a Battalion & appointed to the Bat Maj Peter Evans.[236] He has given him *seven companies*, whereas he is entitled as a Major to but three or four & yet Mr E. was the only officer Commissioned under Act [———] & a Lieut Col at that.

It seems unjust, but I suppose amongst so many applicants, those who are most pressing or who have political influence are successful & Gov Morehead is a tower of strength to his son in Law, Peter Evans.[237] Well, it seems & is hard, after working so hard as Patrick has done, to be thus ignored, but we must bear it with the best grace we can. Were it not for the Conscript act, now in the act of passing, I could take it most philosophically, but courage, God will provide! I have endeavored for months to divest myself of all uneasiness about it, knowing that He knows what is best for us & now is the time to put my faith in exercise. I hope & beleive that we are both actuated solely by desire to serve our country, to do our whole duty & no wish for Military distinction or rank dazzels us. Just listen to yourself Mrs Edmondston! You talk as tho' your Husband & yourself were Siamese twins & that when he charged at the head of his Regt, you would be there & charge with him. Well, so I would in spirit!—& I should like to know if in giving him up & condemning myself to a life of loneliness & heart sickness, if I do not do something for the cause? Hey, you critical, Journal?! But to have done with the whole, I will not be "over anxious to cast the fashion of uncertain evil"! Before the Conscript extension goes into execution some post will be found for Patrick. A man of his abilities will not be forced into the ranks. Besides he is physically unable to do the duty, so peace, dull care, & heavy foreboding for the future.

No news from Aiken which surprises us. Three hundred paroled prisoners captured in arms have been sent to Richmond to be dealt with according to the Laws of War. 300! Jackson paroled them at Harper's Ferry on Monday & by the end of the week he re-captured them at Shepherdstown. He ought to have shot them immediately himself & not thrown the onus of it on the President. It will be more difficult to do & have less effect in cold blood than immediately after the action. "Burnside with the choicest troops of the army of N C," choicest marauders rather, made the attack on Jackson at Shepardstown & were so fearfully cut up. Jackson held the North bank of the Potomac at that point. They advanced upon the South side. He concealed his

---

[236] Peter G. Evans (1822-1863) of Chatham County, previously the captain of the "Macon Mounted Guards" (later Co. E, Forty-first North Carolina [Third Cavalry] Regiment), served as colonel of the Sixty-third North Carolina (Fifth Cavalry) Regiment, organized October 1, 1861. The regiment was assigned to Gen. Beverly H. Robertson's brigade, and Evans remained the regimental commander until his capture on June 21, 1863. He later died from wounds received at Middleburg, Virginia, on July 21, 1863. Clark, *Histories of the North Carolina Regiments*, III, 529, 551, 566, 587; Manarin and Jordan, *North Carolina Troops*, II, 212-213, 367, 372.

[237] Col. Peter G. Evans was married to Ann Eliza Morehead, the daughter of Gov. John Motley Morehead. Burton Alva Konkle, *John Motley Morehead and the Development of North Carolina, 1796-1866* (Philadelphia: William J. Campbell, 1922), 177, 399.

troops & left in view two batteries only which were ordered to fire two rounds & retreat. They did so, when the whole Yankee force, ten thousand strong, plunged into the river in order to capture them. At that moment Jackson's force opened fire & mowed them down in the bed of the River like ripened grain, "in the mowers vacant swathe" (to quote a line from our gifted poetess Mrs P M Edmondston)—(you did not quote it right tho'). The slaughter was terrific. The River was choked with the dead & wounded & scores of bodies floated down to tell the tale in Washington. Another battle at Sharpsburg is reported, but it lacks confirmation.

September 27, 1862

No news at all from any point, neither national or domestic. I do not like our army needing so much *rest* after a victory. I should think two days were sufficied. I fear our losses were heavier than we admit. No official report published either & it is quite time. Nothing about Boonsboro, Sharpsburg, or Shepherdstown. Col Tew[238] 2d N C has been killed! Poor fellow, not two years since he showed us with so much pride through his school at Hillsboro & drilled his boys for us. We thought little of war then, tho it was on our lips, for it was just after Lincoln's election; but to *talk of war* & to fight are different things. His poor little wife, what a blow to her! She is a Columbia woman & if I judge of her father from what I saw of him on the cars when on our way home from the Golden Wedding, he is but little fitted either to support her mentally or bodily. He, Col Tew, was a Mt Pleasant man & his father's house near L A E's. No news from Aiken!

SEPTEMBER 28, 1862

Sunday—Yesterday came the news of the passage of the Conscript Act, which puts all the men in the Confederacy under forty five at the command of the President. It is unjust in this point, that it provides for no new organization, but the oldest men are thrown without previous preparation into the ranks of the younger & more athletic who have the advantage of eighteen months or a years drill & inureance to the hardships of camp life, & virtually says "now keep up with them or be disgraced." It should in justice have consolidated the Regts now in the field, filled up the missing places with veterans, & then given the officers of the divided Regts a set of new men to drill & gradually harden to Camp life. Mr E is under forty five but I will not weaken myself by looking forward to his being placed in the Ranks. "As thy days—so

---

[238] Col. Charles Courtenay Tew, originally from South Carolina, founded the Hillsboro Military Academy in 1859 and served as colonel of the Second Regiment North Carolina State Troops beginning May 8, 1861. He tendered his resignation from the army in order to return to the school, but before it was accepted he was killed at Sharpsburg on September 17, 1862. His wife was Elizabeth Faust Tradewell. Clark, *Histories of the North Carolina Regiments*, V, 637-639, 641; Manarin and Jordan, *North Carolina Troops*, III, 379; Freeman, *Lee's Lieutenants*, II, 252.

shall thy strength be"! And tho' Mr Randolph has not treated him right in this matter of the Battalion, some door will yet be opened to prevent a man of his capacity & abilities, his age, & dignity being placed under the command of a young ignorant officer of yesterday, who perhaps could not read when he was at West Point! There is great excuse for Mr Randolph I know, for he has so much on his mind that he must forget & sometimes yeild to present & pressing applicants, & Mr Edmondston is too modest & conscientious to be either pushing or unscrupulous as many of those now in commission are. God will provide; come what may, may I see His hand in it all!

The same mail brought the announcement that Mr Lincoln has declared the slaves of all "*Rebels*" *free*, to take effect on the 1st of Jan. 1863! What unprincipled Villany! He does his best to inagurate a servile war & should it fail, it is from no lack of malice or diabolical hate & revenge in him. What a userpation too of power, for never yet did fanatic maintain that the right lay in the *President*. Even Beecher, Stowe, Greely,[239] & that set looked to Congress to fulfil their wicked designs!

John Quincy Adams, poor old man, you lived in an error all your life! You aided these unprincipaled fanatics by upholding their right of petition to Congress.[240] Rather ought you to have referred the matter to the Executive, instead of fighting in Congress to allow them the privilege of petitioning that body to do what you always knew it had no right to. You should quietly have sent them to the White House & let the President work their own sweet will for them. Ah! You old traitor! You & such as you brought these evils upon us. Upon your heads be the blood & misery of this wretched war! Lincoln & Seward are but traitors of your development. You entered the wedge, they drove it home. They are more to blame for they see the iniquity & misery which your beginnings lead to & which your blind folly or ambition hid from you, & still they do not stay their hand. God be with us! & keep us from internal as well as external foes! Give us brave hearts & united hands & in Thy own good time grant us the blessing of Peace!

SEPTEMBER 29, 1862

Above is the Proclamation of Mr Lincoln emancipating the slaves after the 1st of Jan 1863.[241]

---

[239] Horace Greeley (1811-1872), an influential journalist and political leader, founded the *New York Tribune* in 1841 as a Whig paper and served as its editor. He was a dedicated opponent of secession and slavery on moral and economic grounds, and he quickly joined the Republican party when the Union was threatened. He strongly advocated emancipation and complete Negro equality. *Concise Dictionary of American Biography*, 366-367.

[240] After one term as president of the United States, John Quincy Adams (1767-1848) served as congressman from Massachusetts for seventeen years. In that capacity he opposed and finally secured the defeat of the "gag" resolution which provided for the tabling of all petitions concerned with slavery. *Concise Dictionary of American History*, 2, 137, 726.

[241] A newspaper clipping of Lincoln's preliminary Emancipation Proclamation of September 22, 1862, was pasted on a page in the first volume of the diary.

"Whom the gods destroy they first make blind."[242] For to us it cannot be much more injurious when they are in possession than their conduct has already been to us, for practically emancipation has followed in their footsteps since Butler pronounced them "Contraband," and where they are not in possession the proclamation cannot do us much harm. Mere "brutem fulmen"[243] but to the border states Maryland & Kentucky. I should think it would speak in tones of thunder & if anything *can*, make them a unit against the North.

Good news yesterday from Aiken. We feel much releived on that score. No mail today, the schedule of the Wilmington & Weldon R. R. said to be changed on account of the prevalence of yellow fever in Wilmington. It has been pronounced epidemic.[244] Sad news in yesterday's papers from our dead at Sharpsburg. Besides Gen Branch & Col Tew, Capt Meares, & many officers of the 3d N C, the Col. of which Regt, Col De Rosset, is severely wounded. Capt Meares was engaged to be married to Miss Amouret Bradley of Wilmington, a lady whom I often met when at Wrightsville last summer. Poor thing, what a blow to her! Col De Rosset is the same gentleman, then Capt De Rosset, who I mentioned as writing a Military Code for the organization of the Militia at the time that Mr E wrote his "Code Patrick" & which I thought inferior to it, not two years since—& Ah! what changes! The other dead & wounded officers I do not know personally, but their names are of the best in the State.

Full accounts of our losses since the army left for Manassas have been received, but the authorities in Richmond do not think it best to publish them—a bad sign for us! The Northern papers recede somewhat from their arrogant claims of a victory at Sharpsburg. They now say that it was the bloodiest & most indecisive battle of the War—clearly a drawn battle tho we retained the field. We have, it appears, retired from Harpers Ferry, which they re-occupy in force—a bad omen for the Victory we claimed. The possession of Harpers Ferry was claimed by us as worth the advance into Maryland, & yet we cannot hold it. God be with us! Turn not away Thy face, O God, but be with our army a help in time of need.

OCTOBER 4, 1862

Yesterday went down to the plantation with Mr E & dined there. Everything is so peaceful & quiet that I long to forget the War and dream

---

[242] This statement was attributed in part to Euripides by James Boswell in his *The Life of Samuel Johnson L.L.D.* (New York: Modern Library, Random House, 1931), 1029.

[243] Latin, a futile threat or display of force.

[244] The fever was apparently brought into Wilmington by the crew of the *Kate*, a blockade-runner from Nassau. It was reported to have declined in late October. *North Carolina Standard*, September 17, and October 1, 8, 15, and 29, 1862; *Official Records (Navy)*, Series I, VIII, 82.

away these October days in our usual "dolce par niente" manner, but it is impossible! That dread shadow hangs over us & uncertainty & change is written upon every thing.

Patrick has since the freshet gone largely into the hay bussiness & has cut a quantity of Hay off the low grounds—& as I saw the huge stacks & the loaded waggons bringing more, where there already seemed an abundance, & heard his calculations as to its value & the relative yeild of the same land in corn & Hay, it came over me with horror that Yankee horses might feed on it & Yankees reap the fruit of our labour & care. The sword of Damocles is suspended over us & at any moment these marauding theives may be turned loose upon us to ravage & spoil us! They are increasing their forces at Suffolk, which looks like an occupation of this part of the country or an attack on Richmond from the South side of James River, & we learn are building boats for the ascent of all our rivers—Iron boats carrying one gun & drawing but two feet of water. However, in face of it all I planted my Hyacinth roots. I cannot tell who will enjoy their fragrance & beauty, but I plant in hope & with a strong faith in God's mercy.

I commenced on Thursday, the 25th, a large & heavy peice of work—no less than the knitting a set of undershirts for father. The War deprives him of his usual supply from Shetland so I have determined to do my utmost to prevent his feeling their loss. So I have carefully saved all the Lambs wool which we have had from our Lambs this summer & have made Becky spin it. She has done it very handsomely & tho not so soft as the Shetland, still the thought that it is our own will cover many defects. I have the needles made by Henry (to knit a peice on his shirts last winter—a long job which I accomplished to his comfort & which gave me the notion of this), so the shirts will be all together home grown, home spun, & home knit. I will get them done for his birthday & I know he will be pleased. I knit yesterday 15 000 some odd hundred stitches besides going to the plantation which is a great distraction.

Letters from Raleigh tell us that his Mother has received a letter from Tom Jones written on the field of Sharpsburg with the dead & the dying around him. It is terrible! He is the only officer in his company that escaped unhurt, tho none were killed. Eighteen out of twenty seven officers in his regt were killed! How thankful we should be for his escape! The Regt went into battle only 299 strong & came out 109 only. The carnage was terrific—the bloodiest battle of the war & a drawn one, for tho we retained the ground we were unable to follow up the advantage & when we retreated across the Potomac the enemy could not seriously molest us. Lee's headquarters are at Bunker Hill nine miles from Winchester, M Clellan's at Martinsburg only a few miles off, so that the fight may be renewed at any moment. We are stronger than we were at Sharpsburg, our stragglers having come in; 30,000 were said to be absent from the battle field. Had they been in place M Clellan would have been routed! There is one sign in our favour at the North, symptoms of disaffection amongst themselves. A Convention of sixteen governors has been held in Altoona[245] & incendiary, I might almost say, resolutions passed, requesting the President to declare *immediate* emancipation, to remove M Clellan, etc. They will soon get to quarreling amongst themselves.

OCTOBER 6, 1862

Saturday night came Brother, as usual, despondant! He tells us that the sufferings of our army have been incredible, that for days they had nothing to eat but green corn, that they straggled from mere exhaustion & in search of food, that in one instance a Brigade was turned into a corn field with orders to prepare three days rations. God help the poor fellows. What courage, what devotion, what *endurance* they show! God help and releive them & grant them the victory, so that they may rest from their labours!

He learned from an officer just from there, Engelhard[246]—who was aid to Gen Branch & brought his body home, that it is a mistake that we captured 300 paroled prisoners. We undoubtedly captured many, but twenty were all that could be indentified. The officer who paroled them at Harpers Ferry came to Jackson at Shepherd'stown & told him that he recognized them. Jackson replied that it was too serious a matter to hang a man on the reccollection only of an officer who had ten thousand pass before him & paroled them in the midst of such excitement. So he went himself & personally demanded of each man, as they stood in line, whether or not he had been paroled. They admitted it, saying "that they had no choice, as they were ordered to fall into the ranks or they would be shot." "Then my men," he answered, "the next of you who are placed in such a situation will likely prefer to be shot, for I shall hang every one of you," and he accordingly did so. Right & just, but it must have been a painful duty for him to execute. After that few will admit that they have been paroled & as it is not to rest on the memory of an officer, I do not know how we can detect them if they change their organization or they may when captured give us a false one, tho I suppose the letters & no's on their caps and knapsacks would prevent that.

---

[245]The Altoona, Pennsylvania, conference of Union governors was held on September 24, 1862. Organized to consider methods of urging Lincoln to adopt specific antislavery measures, the governors met on the day Lincoln issued his preliminary Emancipation Proclamation. Upon hearing this news, sixteen governors signed a letter pledging their loyalty to the Union, their support of Lincoln's emancipation policy, and requesting Lincoln to call for more troops. Carl Sandburg, *Lincoln: The War Years* (New York: Harcourt, Brace & Company, 1939), 585-586, hereinafter cited as Sandburg, *Lincoln: The War Years*.

[246]Joseph A. Engelhard, originally from Jackson, Mississippi, was graduated with honors from the University of North Carolina at Chapel Hill in 1854. During the war he served as both assistant quartermaster and quartermaster of the Thirty-third North Carolina Regiment before he was transferred to the Branch-Lane Brigade in 1862 as adjutant with the rank of major. After the war Engelhard resumed his law practice, served briefly as clerk of the state senate, and was elected secretary of state, serving from 1877 until 1879. Clark, *Histories of the North Carolina Regiments*, II, 537, 554; IV, 472, 474; Ashe, *History of North Carolina*, II, 1032, 1178-1180; Battle, *History of the University of North Carolina*, I, 641, 654, 805, 835.

Brother hears that Col De Rosset is dead! Poor fellow! Col Riddick, the gentleman who excited my wrath so, by attempting to get Patrick's Battalion attached to his command, is also dead. The yellow fever raging in Wilmington—30 deaths in one day last week & in the face of a thin population, as every one has gone who can leave. Wrote some days since, inviting Alice Lippitt to come & remain with me during the prevalence of the epidemic. No answer as yet.

The Conference of the Military committees of both Houses of Congress report in favour of the Senate Exemption bill.[247] This amongst other clauses exempts one white man as "owner, agent, or overseer to every plantation on which twenty or more slaves are worked." Should this pass and the President approve, Mr E will be exempted from the Conscript as we own more than eighty slaves & will only go if he gets an appointment, for he has not the health or strength for a common soldier & the change in his habits would be fatal to him. As an officer he can take care of himself, have a horse & a servant, & the exposure is not so great. His talents too & habit of command eminently fit him for such a position. His West Point education stands him in good stead & had he political influence to ensure him a position he would have been eminent, but it has not been God's will to call him into service, for he has done all that man could do to be there. Ten journeys has he made to Richmond, but for the want of a friend at Mr Randolph's ear to press his claims he has as yet been unsuccessful. Well, he has done his duty & if he is left at home to me, I am content. I do not find his *society oppressive*! Pray God the Exemption bill may pass & in face of Lincoln's Emancipation Act I think it will. For fifteen miles on both sides of the River, if it does not, father will be the only white male & that with a population of at least four thousand negroes! But we fear them little enough. It would astonish our "Northern brethren," save the mark, & England also, did they know how little we regard it.

At Catechism yesterday I asked: what did God do to Adam & Eve when they ate the fruit of the forbidden tree? Sharper answered up bold & bright. "*He whipped em*"! Poor Sharper, that is the greatest punishment he knows. He never felt want or pinching cold in his life, has always had plenty to eat & to wear & the idea of its being a punishment to be driven out & sin & death by sin being brought into the world is more than he can comprehend. "*He whipped em*" & that was the end of the matter. It is up hill work teaching them. I fear my heart is not enough in it. God forgive & enlighten me.

---

[247] The Confederate Congress passed a conscription bill which included an exemption of one slaveowner or overseer for every twenty slaves, a number later reduced to fifteen slaves. The exemption clause remained highly unpopular in the South, causing small farmers and nonslaveholding whites to level the criticism that it was a rich man's war but a poor man's fight. Much open resistance of the law ensued in North Carolina and other areas of the South. Randall and Donald, *Civil War and Reconstruction*, 264-265; *Official Records (Army)*, Series IV, I, 1081-1082.

We have some idea of going to Raleigh tomorrow. Mr E wishes to place himself in the Dentist's hands & has some other business there & go to see my sister Mrs Miller on account of the death of her husband. I wish to see & condole with her & learn if there is ought that I can do for her, but I have not yet decided to go, for ah! me I hate to leave home—this peaceful life has so many attractions for me and I have a superstitious fear of breaking the spell.

At night. Well! I have concluded to leave in the morning & my trunk stands ready packed. I went to ride with Mr E on horseback this afternoon, the first time I have been on horse back for several months. The evening was delightful & as we rode in the still evening, I could not but contrast our present with the scenes that would be around us tomorrow. What a difference! Ah! home— how many attractions you have!

We went to Mrs Barnes, a poor woman for whom Mr Edmondston is building a house. She lives on the boundary of our Land & Mr Edmondston in the kindness of his heart is so touched with the condition of the house she lives in that he is building her a new one from the foundation. I went into her present abode whilst he was doing some business relative to her new one, & I could not but contrast my own comfortable home, with rooms for all my wants, with the miserable hovel in which I sat—draughts & leaks—in fact it would be hard to find a dry spot in a shower judging from the looks of the roof. My God! who hath made me to differ! Thou hast filled my cup! Thou has blessed me beyond others perhaps more deserving. To Thee, O Lord, be my praise & gratitude due. Thou has "cast my lines in pleasant places."

OCTOBER 11, 1862

God be praised! We got back home last night from our visit to Raleigh. Ah! home! how delightful you are! Would that I were never compelled to leave you! Journal! I have come back so disgusted with the heartlessness & hollowness of the world & the human beings that compose it that I desire never to come in contact with them again but to live at home with my books & my garden & to see no one who will remind me that such a false, empty, tiresome, heartless world exists as lives outside the pales of Hascosea.

We left here before daylight on the seventh & went up to Weldon to take the cars. There we met brother &, when the Petersburg cars came in, Henry Miller. His first salutation to his Uncle was a congratulation on his appointment to the newly organized Regt of Cavalry, a report of which he said was prevalent in Richmond when he left. Gen Clingman having been informed of it and he telling his Staff, one of which Henry is, makes it the more probably. However we do not beleive it, as surely the War Department would have informed him if it were true. Henry says that Mr E is Colonel, Capt Haxall Lieut col, & Capt Tucker Major. We dismissed it from our minds & went on our journey with a determination not to be unsettled by it.

The papers we got in the Cars told us that the Exemption bill had passed, so that every one who works twenty negroes is exempt from the Conscript Act. One white man as "owner, agent, or overseer" on every plantation of that no of negroes is exempt from Conscript. I suppose we owe that to Mr Lincoln's Emancipation act. It will not do to remove all the owners from the plantations and leave the negroes to themselves or their overseers.

My heart was touched on my journey by the sight of the wounded soldiers on their way home! My heart goes forth to every soldier but doubly so to them, some on crutches, some with their arms in a sling or their heads bandaged, looking so pale & wan, so utterly unfit for locomotion, & yet so uncomfortable where they were, that I longed to do something for all of them. One fine looking man, a private but evidently a gentleman, occupied the seat in front of us. His wife seemed so devoted to him & there was an air of such refinement about him that I longed to know his name. I could only conjecture that it was Witherspoon. Had I been sure I would have asked him & entered into conversation with him, but I feared to intrude, for if I was traveling with my wounded husband, I know I would shrink from the interrogatories of strangers. So I could only look my sympathy & offer him newspapers, etc. I wish I was not so diffident. I would so like to have asked him where & how he was wounded.

Got to Raleigh on Tuesday the 7th. Found all well. Attempted but vainly to dissuade sister F from her wild scheme of opening a boarding house.[248] What infatuation it is! And so soon after her husband's death! I can neither comprehend or have any patience with it—this pretence of Independance—but, Journal, I will say more than I ought. Some thing we will scarce say "to any," and all I think of this matter comes under this class. Patrick alone knows all I do think & feel. So, Journal, dont you set yourself up by thinking you are my confidant. I do not tell you one half I feel. Some where in the Psalms I think it is there is a text about man's life being "like water spilled upon the ground."[249] And so it indeed seems.

Sophia & her children came down whilst we were there. Three fine boys she has! Her youngest is a splendid baby & right well he looks in his Aunt Kate's old clothes. The six little dresses I carried him fit him well, & sturdy & solid he looks in them. Mr Turner was to be down the next day to have his head put under medical advice. Sophia tells me he suffers terribly with it. Trepanning may be neccessary, but I hope not.

---

[248] Mrs. Henry W. Miller advertised in October, 1862, that she would be ready "on the first of next November to receive boarders, both with and without rooms." A notice in January, 1869, gave her boardinghouse location as the corner of New Bern Avenue and Person Street in Raleigh. As late as November, 1874, a notice appeared describing her "well known boarding house on New Bern Avenue" and stating that members of the General Assembly "wishing to secure rooms would do well to make early application." *Raleigh Register*, October 8, 1862; *Daily Sentinel*, January 1, 1869, November 19, 1874.

[249] II Samuel 14:14a. "For we must needs die, and are as water spilt on the ground. . . ."

Dined on Thursday at brothers. His children as attractive as usual. Kate is growing up a beauty. Pray God to have her in his Holy keeping. Saw James Edmondston most unexpectedly, he being there for clothing for his Brigade; says he likes his officers and is well & pleasantly situated. Poor fellow, I feel for him, so much alone does he seem to be. I wish he could have a furlough & spend it here with us. It would do him good. Mary Livingston, brother's youngest, is a nice little thing, not so pretty as Laura but better perhaps for it. Nelly is sweeter & more attractive than ever. I do love that child.

Saw but few of my Raleigh friends as our stay was so short. What few I did see were full of forebodings & warnings, urging us to remove all that we valued from this house, in short dear old home to break you up for fear of the enemy making an ascent of the river & harrying our whole country side. The negroes they were urgent for us to remove, but where to carry them?—that is the question. How to support them, how to house them, all questions easier put than answered. Saw Mr Cannon from Perquimans. He gives a deplorable account of the state of affairs in the Eastern Counties. At least ten thousand negroes have been stolen or enticed off from their owners since the fall of Roanoke Island. All our acquaintances have lost their men, many of them their negro women also. A gentleman, a friend of Mr Cannon, one whom he considers reliable, told him that in a ride from Sunbury to Suffolk, a distance of *twenty eight* miles, he counted on the side of the road the corpses of *fourteen* negro children left unburied for the fowls of the air to prey on. They had died from want or sickness, it may be deserted by their Mammies, & just left as they fell. Mr Bynum, of Winton, the same who kept that comfortable house where we were so kindly treated on our journey from Perquimans with sister Betsy after Mr Jones death, lost 97 negroes in one night! During the next week he found the bodies of five or six (Mr C did not remember which) of his little negroes in the swamp opposite his plantation (which lies on the Chowan) who had evidently died of starvation, their fingers being in their mouths and they in an evident state of emaciation & want, deserted probably by their parents in their flight. We must hope that they thought they would be retaken & cared for by their owner, otherwise their conduct is worse than that of "the brutes that perish."

The Yankees had two Camps in Gates county & received all that came to them & sent them to Suffolk where they are assorted, the able bodied sent to the army & the women & old ones with the children left literally to starve after they have stolen every thing that could support life. It is terrible. Ah! philanthropy! What a cheat! What a delusion you have been to the infatuated Abolitionists! Do they wear you as a cheat, a mask, or are they mistaken themselves? I fear the former. Ah Madam Stowe, I wish you could look on your own work; heartless and unprincipled as you are, it would make you shudder!

Mr Thomas Newby, now an old man, was left in one night without a servant to feed his horse, out of a large plantation! How soon may this fate be ours! We hurried home to enable Mr E. to attend a meeting of the neighborhood to represent to the Commanding Gen the importance of defending Roanoke River at Hamilton or Rainbow Bluffs instead of Bridgers ferry, as is at present proposed. I hope they may be successful.

Whilst we were in Raleigh Gov Vance arrived from Richmond & he also brought the news that Patrick was made Colonel, Captain Haxal Lieut Col, and Mr Tucker Major of the newly organized Regt of Cavalry, but he found no announcement of it from the Department. So we know not what to think. Just after Henry Miller told us of it we read of the passage of the Exemption Bill by which Mr E is exempt from the Conscript as we own far more than twenty negroes. I had lost all desire for the appointment after so many recommendation & cross purposes except to save him from the Conscript, so I care but little for the honour. If the country need him I wish him to go; otherwise I ardently desire him at home.

Journal, I brought you a present from Raleigh—a new blank book where in to extend yourself—so we will presently adjourn to it & I will give you the war news, which, alas, is not cheering!

[End of Vol. I, Original Manuscript Journal]

October 11, 1862 [continued]

I told you, my dear Journal, that I had a new book for you, not new exactly as it is an old account book of Mr Miller's given me by Sister Frances; but tho not gifted with personal pulcritude, you, Journal, must add value to it by the sincerity & delicacy of your record. Write only words of truth & they will be so rare that they will have a value of their own!

Van Dorn has been terribly repulsed at Corinth. He telegraphed a victory after the first two days, but the enemy being reinforced, a new face & one adverse to us, was put up on everything & he compelled to retreat with great loss. The enemy report a like loss, especially amongst their officers, but no particulars as yet. Lee's army is represented in fine condition & spirits, not known whether or not it is falling back or offering battle.

We had a brush at Franklin & drove back three Gunboats sent up to reconnoitre with heavy loss—from our sharp shooters on the banks. For that God be praised! The enemy has been heavily reinforced both at Suffolk & Newberne & all things point to an advance into N Carolina. Grant us strength to bear what Thou sendest O Lord.

We left Raleigh about day break without breakfast & had a most fatiguing ride home, which we reached about sun set. Ah! how I enjoyed my own tea! How long can I drink it—how long enjoy the blessed quiet which reigns around us? Journal! This book does not seem natural to me at all! It depresses me to write in it. I think of the hopes which clustered *around* the opening of a career so bright as that of the owner of this book & how they were clouded & the shipwreck of a life on the altar of ambition & politics & shrink more into myself & my home duties & associations than ever. I have not enough to tell you to make me shake off the feelings which oppress me. It is a dull gloomy afternoon. The rain falls, drip! drip drip! Mr E is gone to the meeting for the defence of our homes & I feel dispirited by my surrounding. So I will stop—so tais toi & au revoir!

OCTOBER 15, 1862

Last night came Father & Mama home from the Salt Sulphur Springs. Father looking rejuvenated and quite himself again. He saw a Richmond paper of yesterday. (Since the yellow fever at Wilmington we hear so irregularly from the Mails that it is next to not hearing at all) & by it he learned that Stewarts Cavalry, 3,000 strong, had made a dash into Pensylvania, captured three towns & were then in possession of Chambersburg. This was Northern news, not a word of it having transpired from our side. Extracts from Northern papers in the Monday issue admit that there has been a battle between Buel & Bragg in which the Confederate's kept the field. Gold went up in New York on the receipt of the news to 128, higher than it has yet been. Foreign Exchange 140! Can the war long continue in the face of this? No particulars of the fight. We must wait the slow course of our mail. Van Dorn was beaten at Corinth. This victory of Bragg's is most opportune for us.

Coffee is four dollars a pound! & very scarce, Calico 1.50 a yard, Salt at fabulous prices—$100 and $150 per sack has been paid for it!

Tom Jones had three bullets shot through his clothes at Sharpsburg but was unhurt. What an escape! On Monday Patrick & I walked through the upper part of our Grove and marked the trees which ought to come out. How they have grown! I could not but think of Dumbiedyke's[250] advice to his son, to be "ay slicking down a tree—it ill be growing whiles you are sleeping." Ours are literally so, for it seems but a few years since we thinned it out with grubbing hoes & now it takes a good axeman to cut one down!

Finished father's undershirt on Monday, so that he should have it when he came home. It is a large peice of work. As nearly as I can compute it, it has 111,626 stitches in it & this is only the first—two more are to come.

Made up a basket of stores for Capt Haxall, Mr E's friend in the Camp of Instruction at Garysburg,[251] bread, Crackers, butter, pickles, pepper, Ham, Catsup, Vinegar in one basket & Irish and Sweet Potatoes & Apples in the

[250] The old laird of Dumbiedikes, a character in Sir Walter Scott's *Heart of Midlothian*, was a demanding landlord who forced his tenants to improve his land. Benét, *Reader's Encyclopedia*, 322.

[251] Garysburg, Northampton County, was one of the numerous army camps established in 1861 for regimental organization and training. Hill, *Bethel to Sharpsburg*, I, 63.

other—a nice treat after the hardships of Camp life! Nothing more of Mr E's appointment, & I am not sorry for it. He has been quite unwell for the past few days & I think is better off at home in a hygeine point of view, but I would not keep him did my country need him.

My Dahlia's are exquisite. It is a treat to me to look at them! I thank God daily for the enjoyment I find in them. They are perfect. "Bethel"—my seed-ling named in honour of the battle—I shall divide with Mrs D H Hill[252] when I take it up. Her husband is the hero of Bethel & no one has a better right to it.

I saw Sophia in Raleigh. Her baby looks sweetly in the little frocks I carried him—one of my dresses made six for him. Brought down some Comfortables to make for Sister Frances. She gave her blankets to the soldiers last winter & has not bed clothing sufficient for the family she expects. I am delighted to hear through brother that she has given up her notion of taking boarders this winter. It is a wild scheme & instead of paying Mr Miller's debts she will have some of her own before Spring. It will not do, Journal, it will not do!

Marked A—I append to this, or rather I now prefix another infamous order issued by Major Gen Sherman.[253] How sad it seems—this covering peaceful accounts, written by a hand now cold in death at a time when we were one country, with the records of such brutality & cruelty from the hands of those who called themselves our brothers! Brothers! Heaven save the mark! I shall use the leaves in the beginning of this vol. for an olla pod of divers & heteregenous matter—Receipts, direction for Knitting, poetry, etc., etc., so I will place the fiery blood & thunder war orders next to you my peaceful, harmless journal. I shall begin next to you & go on with those of later date un-til they are crowned with that epitome of all happiness "the Declaration of Peace"!

October 17, 1862

Yesterday we were delighted with a slip of paper signed R H Smith—telling us that the President had received a Telegram from Gen Bragg—announcing a complete victory over Buel & that the enemy admitted a loss of 25,000 men. Today, however, our hopes are dashed by the papers which tell us that it is only a rumour brought by a passenger who has seen a Louisville Journal! A great disappointment & I wonder at Mr Smith for having circulated as cer-tainty news which he must have known to be doubtful, as he had the Rich-mond papers in which it was so stated—papers published the day he left

---

[252] Isabella Morrison, the daughter of the Reverend Robert Hall Morrison, first president of Davidson College, married Daniel Harvey Hill in 1852. Ashe, *Biographical History*, VII, 138, 144; William K. Boyd, *History of North Carolina*, Vol. II: *The Federal Period 1783-1860* (Chicago and New York: Lewis Publishing Co., 1919), 368-369; Ashe, *History of North Carolina*, II, 409; Freeman, *Lee's Lieutenants*, I, 21; II, 320.

[253] Special Order No. 254, dated September 27, 1862, threatened to remove families from Memphis in retaliation for firing upon gunboats. Mrs. Edmondston included it in a group of newspaper clippings marked "A" and pasted on page 45 of the second volume of the diary.

Richmond & which in consequence of the alteration in our mail we do not now get until the day after their issue. Gen Stuart has returned from his expedition unto Pensylvania after capturing many prisoners, horses, etc., & burned large quantities of army stores, besides throwing the North into a state of wild alarm & panic. He cut his way through a detachment of Federal Cavalry sent out to intercept him without the loss of a man, which seems almost miraculous, & recrossed the Potomac with his spoils & prisoners in safety! Accounts from the Army represent it as in good condition & spirits.

Went out on horseback with Mr E. Went to Tanners to see the girl Catherine Jackson of whom I told you, Journal, in the summer. I have found a home for her with Samantha Currie, who promises to teach her to read & write & endeavor to exalt her a little—poor thing, utterly friendless as she was when Tanner so kindly took her in. It seemed a struggle for her to leave them, so I told her to take until Saturday to decide & come to me then with her decision. Tanner, poor man, is in feeble health & then when he dies, which I fear will not be long, first his family will be left a charge upon their neighbors.[254] God help the poor, for they must suffer this winter—clothing not to be had & provisions & leather so high and that prime necessity *salt* of so difficult attainder & at fabulous prices!

OCTOBER 18, 1862

Saw so good & characteristic an anecdote of President Lincoln that I must record it. An office seeker waited on him in search of an appointment & in order to press his claims said that "he had made him President." "You made me President, did you," said Lincoln with a merry twinkle of his eye, "You made me President, then a precious mess you got me into"! The applicant left! Evidences of division at home appear in the Northern journals—the Emancipation Proclamation meets with some bitter opponents & M Clellan is like to have a fire in his rear.

Went out on horseback with Patrick to the house he is building for Mrs Barnes. Poor people, they seem truly grateful to him; their present residence is a mere hovel. Think of their being forced to sit up Sat, Sunday, & Monday nights last because their bed clothing & beds got so wet that during all those damp cold days they could not dry them & so slept by the fire! Nails are the great want in the building of the house. Some of them cost 25 cts per pound & those she got by way of favour. We have none to spare, as our new Stable this summer exhausted our store. Mr E. let her have what he could for the rafters & gable ends. Three & at times four of our hands have been at work there for a fortnight past & it is now nearly done. The roof was about two thirds finished but at a stand still for the want of nails which she had got a neighbor

---

[254] The Tanners and the Curries seem to have been less favorably situated neighbors of the Edmondstons. A number of families by one or the other of these names appear in the 1860 census of Halifax County.

to go to Enfield for. Father promised to see if he could spare some & if he can the house will soon be done—I hope before the next rain. How true it is that one half the world does not know how the other half lives! That comfortable double cabin, for it has two rooms, will be a palace to that poor widow & her crippled sister & little children. What would I think were I reduced to it! God grant me gratitude for all the mercies, the comforts & luxuries which he has given me! May I never again be guilty of the sin of repining!

Catherine Jackson has just gone. She assents to going to live with Samantha, which will be a great advantage to her & she may in time become a useful woman. She is as strong as an Amazon & tho only sixteen looks like a woman of twenty. She will be a great comfort to Samantha who, poor thing, is very feeble & unable to attend to her children.

No letters from anyone which seems strange as Mr E has many important matters in hand, but the mails are terribly out of joint. Yellow fever still virulent in Wilmington. Mr Joseph Lippitt, brother of the gentleman with whom I stayed last summer, is dead of it! His wife is a fine woman &, poor woman, has my deepest sympathy in this double bereavement, for she has just lost her father also. Would that I could do something for her. I hope her father left her independant, as otherwise she has, I know, nothing. Rev Dr Drane[255] also has the fever, but I hope so useful a life will be spared to his Congregation & the community at large.

Letters from Sister F tell us that it is a mistake about her giving up the taking of boarders, for which I am truly sorry. I hope it will end better than I fear.

Mr Dunlop writes that Longstreet's division is ordered South & is to be posted below Petersburg, between that point & Suffolk. The enemy are strengthing themselves greatly there & everything points to an advance into the country. Would that the Government would fortify Roanoke River below Hamilton; otherwise a successful dash may be made up the River to Weldon. The R R bridge there once destroyed, Richmond would be in great danger. Our fertile valley, too, has fed the Army there all the summer & if they resign it with the growing crops to the enemy they will, when too late, feel what a blow has been struck them. I say this, I think, without reference to our private losses which will be great in such an event.

OCTOBER 20, 1862

My birthday! Journal—I will not tell you how old I am! Tho past the age when "man suspects himself a fool,"[256] I have not yet arrived at that when he

---

[255] The Reverend Robert Brent Drane, a University of North Carolina graduate of 1844, served as rector of St. James Episcopal Church in Wilmington from 1844 until 1862. He died of yellow fever in October, 1862. Battle, *History of the University of North Carolina*, I, 485; James Sprunt, *Chronicles of the Cape Fear River* (Spartanburg, South Carolina: The Reprint Company, 1973; originally published 1916), 286, 609, 612.

[256] Edward Young, *Night Thoughts*, night 1, line 412, "At thirty man suspects himself a fool." Mrs. Edmondston, born in 1823, would have been thirty-nine in 1862.

"knows it & resolves reform." So know me as a sedate lady, who has survived some of the follies, none of the enjoyments, of youth. Many happy birthdays have I had, some of them happier or more quiet than this has been. Patrick is so kind so tender in his sympathies, has so much the manners & feelings of a bridegroom & expresses it with such genuine interest and affection that I would be insensible indeed did I want anything else to make me happy. I am happier than most of my fellow creatures & could I infuse a stronger element of *Faith* in my daily life, my hourly thoughts, I should be blest indeed. "Increase our Faith"!

Yesterday (Sunday) we sent to Halifax for Capt Haxall, the gentleman reccommended for the Lieut Colonelcy when Patrick was reccommended for Col & who is now engaged drilling the N C Cavalry at the Camp of Instruction at Garysburg. He came down & spent the day & night here, a pleasant, gentlemaly, young man whose heart & soul seems to be with the Cavalry. He told us of the death of several of our young Richmond acquaintances, amongst others of Clarence Warwick,[257] a fine lad whom we met a few years since with his sisters in the mountains of Va. Poor fellow—a bright career cut short by these wicked enemies of ours! "How long? O! Lord! how long?"

Brother came in & brought the rumour through Senator Davis—of Mr E's and Capt H's appointment, but it made no impression on either, for neither of them beleive it.

This afternoon gathered our winter Apples—not much of a labour, however, for the wet weather has played sad havock amongst them. They have rotted by the barrel full. What we have left I hope will keep. Father went to Raleigh leaving Mama with us. Capt Haxall said so many polite things about the supplies we sent up to him last week that I was quite inflated. "Woman's hand," "uncommon care," etc., etc. Mrs Edmondston, you will need "*a taking down*" soon. Brother as usual most despondant. Patrick will not admit our Victory in Kentucky, altho the papers go far to confirm it. Well, time will show & that "right speediely," I hope. Busy knitting on Father's undershirts. Handmaidens making comfortables for sister F.

OCTOBER 22, 1862

Went to the plantation yesterday with Patrick—a delightful day. Had our first frost the night before, the 20th, a white one, which, however, has done no damage to vegetation. Mr E longs for a few more such to check & mature the cotton before a killing one comes to "shut the gates of mercy" upon the hope of further yeild! Came home & found Mrs Hall & Mrs Clark here—pleasant visitors, but I was reminded of the Scotch proverb, "It is ill talking between a full man & a fasting," for we, having been detained by Solomons sickness later

---

[257] Clarence Warwick of Co. I, Fourth Virginia Cavalry, was killed near Cold Harbor on June 27, 1862. *Official Records (Army)*, Series I, XI, Part II, 528.

than usual, I was terribly hungry, whilst it was after dinner with them. Found the mail coming in the gate as we drove up.

Bad news from Kentucky—Bragg falling back towards Cumberland Gap, Buel pressing him & attempting to out flank him. It seems he gained a bloody but decisive victory at Perrysville on the [———], but Buel being immediately & heavily reinforced pressed on him in overwhelming numbers, threatening his supplies, hence his retreat. The War Department has received two letters from him which they decline making public—a fact from which we auger the worst. Sad indeed does it seem that even tho' we gain victory after victory they are barren of results! Mr E was right not to rejoice as he is saved the disappointment now. M Clellan too is advancing & Lee is making dispositions to meet him—so that every day we may expect tidings of a battle. The greatest hope we now have is from the divided state of the North—the Democratic & Republican parties are quarreling bitterly amongst themselves as to the conduct of the war. John Van Buren[258] has made a remarkable speech at a public meeting in N Y & read so remarkable a letter written by Gen Scot to the President at the time of his Inaugration that I preserve it in the first part of his book marked B.[259] It shows the deception of the Government & the rascality of Gen Scott in a light which neither of them can envy. So odd an exposition of the Southern character was made by one of our bitterest enemies that I preserve that also marked C.[260] It shows what they really think of us. Do they ever hope to conquer their superiors, as they admit us to be?

Some time ago, Journal, I wrote some lines on Butler's causing the Coffin of Gen A S Johnston to be opened & in order to get Mr E's unbiassed opinion of them sent them to the Enquirer unknown to him; but Alas, my friend, the Enquirer did not think them equal to the trash usually published in its columns & tho day after day I looked for them they have never appeared. So snubbed was I that at first I thought to burn them but plucked up heart of grace and as it was my birthday I thought I would venture to read them to Patrick. So with many misgivings I commenced &, watching his face as I went on, gathered courage to read with emphasis & most agreeably surprised was I, as I ended, to hear him say, "That is stirring, Katie." So, Journal, I will give them to you, hoping that you too will have better taste than the Enquirer.

---

[258] John Van Buren (1810-1866), son of Martin Van Buren (1782-1862), was a prominent Democratic politician who opposed slavery but did not want a war to develop between the North and South over the issue. He bitterly criticized Lincoln's call for troops and many of the Federal government's subsequent war measures, particularly the draft, the suspension of the writ of habeas corpus, and the use of black troops. During the presidential election of 1864, Van Buren supported McClellan against Lincoln and later rallied to the defense of Andrew Johnson during his clash with the Radical Republicans over Reconstruction. *Dictionary of American Biography*, XIX, 151.

[259] A newspaper clipping of the letter from General Scott to Secretary of State Seward, dated March 3, 1861, was affixed to page 47 of the second volume of the diary.

[260] A newspaper article entitled "Northern Opinion of Southern Society," based on the proceedings of the Unitarian Autumnal Convention meeting in New York, was pasted on page 47 of the second volume of the diary.

To Maj Gen Butler, U.S.A.

Upon hearing that he had caused the coffin containing
the body of Gen A S Johnston C. S. A. to be opened

Yes, gaze upon the dead hero's face which living dastard
    like ye feared!
Tear from that noble brow its cov'ring & read if thou
    canst the record written there!
Read if thou canst! thy guilty frame steeped to the lips
    in infamy.
Thy craven heart, thy grov'ling soul, nor reads nor
    understands
A patriot's faith, pure as unblemished crystal, a Warrior's
    soul
Firm as twice hardened adamant! exalted! pure untarnished
He died as heroes like to die, amidst victorious shouts!
This was his earthly fetter! calm & serene it lies
    in its stern dignity
To mock thy senseless rage, *thou Warrior on the Dead*!
Yet fear thee! for the blood doth burst forth from the
    insensate corse!
Murderer! his body calls for vengeance! from Mumford's
    bloody grave
Hark how the cry re-echoes! List how New Orleans crushed
    by thy despot heel
In one long lingering gasp sobs out her wrongs!
From every street, from every heath, goes up the cry
    against thee!
Insulted womanhood raises her pure front & unabashed
    calls on the world for Vengeance!
Eugenia's* tears fall on her country's heart & for every
    one base tyrant
Her countrymen demand of thee a stern Revenge!
    Revenge!
And they shall have it! pressed to their lips to thee they
    drain an overflowing cup!
Already does thy hated name urge on the fearful carnage!
Remember Butler & New Orleans! strike for our women!
    Strike! Remember Butler!
Is the cry that on Virginia's plains maddens the Southern
    blood!
Remember Butler! and at the shout! down goes the Northern
    ranks—thy countrymen,
Thou Tyrant, ('een as the ripened grain falls in the mower's
    vacant swathe!

*Mrs. Phillips

Remember Butler! Aye! thou blot upon thy country's scutcheon!
    Aye!
Remember Butler! It shall be a war cry to humanity!
Remember Butler & New Orleans! Aye! the world remember!
Him who wars on Woman and the Dead!

This faculty of writing rhymes amuses me & as I neglect no duty by it, I think it no harm to indulge it. Tho' the lines themselves are not found worthy of a place in the Poet's corner, still if mediocre poetry gives you any pleasure, Mrs Edmondston, by all means enjoy it. But beware. O! beware of stepping out of your sphere & publishing them. Then indeed you would forget a woman's first ornament, modesty. Women have no business to rush into print; so wide an arena does not become them.

Went with Mama to Samantha's & carried the girl Catherine Jackson with me & left her. If they both do their duty the association will be of mutual advantage to them. Went also to Mr William Smith's to call on Mrs Spruill. I do not like to go to a house for whose master I have so little respect! I like Julia, but our intercourse will henceforth be but limited, as I shall not continue to go there. I just checked myself in a significat "Oh!," when she told me some peice of news giving Mr George Smith as authority. I beleive neither of the brothers, & the memory of Mr W. Smith's conversation in the cars with James is not easily forgotten. So as the world is wide enough for both of us, I think henceforward I will avoid that part occupied by him.

OCTOBER 24, 1862

Yesterday came Amo on his way from Richmond where he has been to stand an examination for ordnance Officer. It will be three months before the decisions are published. In the mean time my young country men hang by the eyelids in expectation. You will prize it so much the more when you get it. It is a shame! Such circumlocution! Where is the patriotism, the energy of the country? Does it take three months to weigh the merits of a young man of twenty? One would think the memory of their examination would fade some what from their examiners' minds. Be it so. The *political* influence will weigh so much the heavier. Ah! my country! Ah! Mr Davis! Was it for this that I loved and revered you so? Yet I love and revere you still! Rouse to a sense of the injustice practised in your name, ignore politics & politicians, & be the exponent of a *free people*—a people free from the shackles of party.

Amo has been with James at Drury's Bluff. Left him well but very busy. The wants of our Army lie very near my heart. The thought of what I can do for them occupies me constantly. I can by using my table covers, scraps of flannel, etc., manage to peice out six flannel shirts. Patrick will give cotton cloth from the plantation supplies for six pr of drawers & woolen cloth for six pr of pantaloons & six pr of shoes, even if the old women who never go out but sit by the fire & burn wood all the winter go without. I can I think spare 2 Blankets more & will take my chintz coverlids & make four comfortables. So together we will fit out six soldiers. He thinks I can make caps. I will try but doubt if the material (plantation cloth) will answer. However, a will finds a way; our soldiers must not suffer if we can help it. Ah Peace! Peace! Our hope of you hangs on our Army. God grant the soldiers *endurance* & the Generals wisdom! Well, Journal, I have chatted with you under difficulty today. Mama keeps up an incessant talking to me & reads the newspaper, in spite of the fact that she sees me occupied with my pen even tho' I have just laid down the paper, yet the power of abstraction is not sufficiently mine to ignore the sound of her voice entirely so, Journal, you suffer for it.

McClellan who it was reported was advancing and crossing the Potomac has fallen back, his object being, prisoners say, merely a reconnoisance in force. Bragg still retreating before Buel, who does "not press" upon him. The Victory at Perrysville is a barren one. He is too weak to reap its fruits. The country rings with complaints of him but I remember A S Johnston & am silent. Would that Beauregard was in command however! A great naval expedition is ready to sail from the Northern ports, it's destination unknown— Charleston or Mobile, it is surmised. God grant that they be confounded, scattered, & dispersed before they reach "the haven where they would be." Commander Semmes C S A in command of the Confederate Steamer 290, or the Alabama, is striking terror into the Northern shippers. We have Northern accounts of the destruction by him of six of their first class trading vessels, three of them New Bedford Whalers.

Nashville, it is rumoured, is to be attacked soon by us, but I do not beleive it. We have not the force. Would that Bragg's army was strengthened instead of being weakened [by] these desultory expeditions. Gen Loring is suspended from command & ordered to Richmond to be Court Martialed for disobedience of orders. Gen [———] succeeds him.

The enrollment of all men between 35 & 40 is ordered, preparatory I suppose to their being ordered out. What distress it will cause, but it is necessary. Would that they had enforced the first Conscript Law better, this would not now be needed. Sent off six Comfortables to Sister F yesterday. Journal, I am sorry to tell you that that wild scheme of hers of taking boarders is not given up. She still insists on trying it. I disapprove but will do what I can to help her. Ah! this is a hard world to live in, but courage, Our Father guides it. He appoints our lot and apportions our trials.

October 28, 1862

Father & Mama left us for the winter yesterday, or until the Yankees drive them from home, in which case their first stop will be here until we can see how they, the Yankees, comport themselves. They have been here for some time & seem to enjoy themselves. I hope they will be allowed by a merciful Providence to remain in peace at home.

On Sat Patrick attended an adjourned meeting of the County people at Clarksville. Mr Hill in the chair to take under consideration the state of the Roanoke River defences. Resolutions were passed declaring that if the Government did not send an engineer here in a fortnight that the inhabitants themselves would engage one & commence the work of fortifying the river. Three weeks have now passed since one was promised & no steps have been as yet taken to fulfil their engagement. A committee of three, of which Patrick is one, was appointed to enrol all the men in the county over the Conscript age & the exempts in a voluntary association for home defence, under the Act of Congress authoring such associations for Local Defence & guaranteeing to the members the privileges & immunities of prisoners of war if captured. He immediately succeeded in enroling 34 names. Another Committee of three of which he was also a member was appointed to write an address to the people in the five counties bordering on the River, urging them to come forward with men & money for the defence of their homes. So perhaps Patrick's disappointment about the Colonelcy was for a wise end. He may be of more use here at home than in the Army.

The papers tell us that there has been an advance by the enemy in two columns upon the Charleston & Savannah R Road; in one they were instantly repulsed, in the second they were at first successful & tore up a portion of the track, but our men being re-inforced advanced & drove them back to their gunboats, they leaving their dead & wounded behind them. The damage to the track was instantly repaired and the telegraph in order again, so they have not much to boast of. No details of our loss, which is very slight. Beauregarde in command. Our men behaved well. The news from Kentucky is gloomy, Bragg still *"falling back."*

I was up until long after twelve last night, Owen having been taken much worse & his Master out with him & I spreading mustard plasters, etc., here in the house until he was releived—& rose before day break this morning to give Amo his breakfast & see him off. So Journal, if I am dull excuse me. Amo left us in fine spirits & today I miss his whistling about the house. He is a fine young man & bids fair to do us all credit. Ah! pity it is that metal such as his should be exposed to the bullets of Abolition hirelings—the off scouring of humanity. He is worth a thousand such, young, refined, cultivated, pure, upright, & withal a soldier of Christ. How many such lives can balance his! God be with & defend him!—be his sheild and buckler from all that would harm either body or mind. Good Lord, deliver him!

Was busy yesterday morning at Chess with father. In the afternoon packing a box for Amo. Fortunately we were enabled to give him a winter outfit, good warm comfortable clothes, which is much in this time of scarcity. Sent Lizzie one of my silk dresses & Frank a pair of his uncle's pantaloons. Had nothing

for Mary but one of my enameled studs & think of it, Patrick sent Dr Coffin a
bottle of Absinthe & a few pounds of Coffee! and a great present it is too, for
Absinthe is not to be had & coffee is four dollars a pound! But Salt, that is our
greatest want, the greatest suffering aside from the loss of friends which this
cruel war inflicts on our country. If it be not releived famine will cast his gaunt
shadow over our land before another summer; already can the far sighted see
it in the dim distance.

Uncle Polk had a narrow escape from capture at Perrysville. In the dusk of
the evening he thought he saw two of our own Regiments firing upon each
other. He rode rapidly up & seized the Colonel of one of them, exclaiming
"what are you firing upon your friends for," to which the Col replied, "I am
not! that is the enemy!" "Why what Regt is this?" "The [———] Illinois"!
"Well, sir, cease firing instantly," in an authorative tone, & clapping spurs to
his horse lost no time in leaving that part of the field! His presence of mind
only saved him from the snare into which the dusk led him.[261]

Busy making a comfortable for James, which Amo says he needs greatly.
Have my hands full, for Patrick wishes to move on Friday & my Dahlia roots
are not dry & Owen sick & Neptune gone with Amo, and he wishes all our
valuable books to be packed up & sent to a place of safety—a heavy job, but
any thing rather than allow the Yankees to get them.

OCTOBER 29, 1862

Am just leaving home for father's. We dine today at the plantation & sleep
at Conneconara. Home I hope tomorrow morning. Mr E. is to meet brother
there & consult as to the expediency of taking a Contract on the Coal Fields
R R, so as to place our men hands at least in safety.[262] O! the sword of Damocles hangs over our heads & it may fall at any moment. Sat up last night &
talked with Patrick. Counted & assorted the negroes, so many to go, so many
to stay, & as I looked around our comfortable sitting room & thought how
soon strangers feet might tread, stranger's eyes might pollute, & strangers
hand destroy this home so dear to us, whilst we would be eating the bitter
bread of exile & perhaps poverty, my heart seemed to die within me. But the
blessed thought, "as thy days so shall thy strength be," came to my mind &
like a cordial revived & strengthened me. Blessed be God for it! In His name

---

[261] This incident is fully recorded in William Mecklenburg Polk's, *Leonidas Polk: Bishop and General* (New
York: Longmans, Green and Company, 2 volumes, 1915), II, 155-156, hereinafter cited as Polk, *Leonidas
Polk: Bishop and General*.

[262] The Chatham Railroad Company was projecting a line from the Deep River coal region in Chatham
and Moore counties to Raleigh to ensure a supply of coal in the event fuel from the Virginia mines was cut
off. To provide labor for grading the roadbed, the proposal was made to bring slaves from the threatened
points nearer the coast. The arrival of Sherman's army stopped work on the road and prevented its completion during the war. Kemp Plummer Battle, *Memories of an Old-Time Tar Heel* (Chapel Hill: University of
North Carolina Press, 1945), 173, 175-177.

Mrs. Edmondston speaks often of dining at Conneconara, her father's home. The platter and soup tureen pictured above are from a set of Staffordshire ironstone made by Mason for Catherine Ann Johnson when she married Thomas Pollock Devereux. Originally there were three platters, the largest big enough to hold a small boar. The large set was blue and white, patterned after Chinese export-porcelain designs. The remaining pieces of the set were divided among descendants. (Photographs courtesy of Mrs. Graham A. Barden, Jr., owner of these pieces.)

do we fight & He will give us strength to bear what He in His Providence assigns to us. Our Lot has hitherto been cast in pleasant places. Should He ordain us a rugged path, His hand will lead us still. I feel almost as tho, like the Psalmist, I could sing, "Why do the heathen rage & the people imagine a vain thing? In God's name will I comfort me! He shall be my sheild and buckler"![263]

No news by yesterday's papers which Amo sent from Weldon except that Bragg's waggon train—40 miles long—was safe through Cumberland Gap with stores too numerous to mention, amongst others 100,000 yds of Kentucky jean for our Army. This will clothe 33,000 men. It seems very little when we think of the forces we have in the field. Cavalry horses, which are greatly needed, pork, beef, hogs, etc., which will keep the wolf from the door for some time—but alas! Kentucky's heart does not seem to be with us! That is one reason why Bragg could not maintain himself. He is in Richmond. Lieut Gen Polk in command of the Army of the West—what a change from the peaceful young clergyman who in my earliest childhood I saw married to my Aunt! It seems so far in the dim distance that I wonder if I can remember it! My new white dimity dress & pink sash of which I was so proud & my curosity to see the "Bride" & the disappointment I felt when I found that the much talked of "*Bride*" was only Aunt Fanny, looking just as she always did, & the shyness

---

[263] Psalms 2:1 and 91:4b.

with which I looked at him & wondered how "*Mr Polk*" could be my Uncle & how meekly & without question I accepted Susan Polk's claims to be my Aunt—she a little girl two years older than myself—it seems all a "myth of the past," to quote my own poetry!

OCTOBER 30, 1862

Got back from father's at one instead of ten o'clock, the harness breaking no less than five times on our route thanks to Owen's slack twistedness, he having it tied up with a peice of leather where the blacksmith could have mended it securely in five minutes. Ah! Cuffee! Cuffee! you are no manager, & yet I love you. Faults & all I accept you and prefer your carelessness & affection to the best groom that England ever sent forth!

Father, Brother, & Mr E in conference as to the Contract on the Coal Fields R R they propose taking. Mr E. advocates the removal of all the hands—women & children—leaving behind only the aged, the decrepid, and weakly. Father & brother oppose it—say the cost of feeding them is too great—impossible to build houses for them etc! etc. They have a menagerie of Lions, one of which they unloose upon him at every step. So far he is firm & heeds not their roaring, but they may yet vanquish him. Ah! sorrowful & heart breaking it is! Our country never looked more lovely, more brilliant in scarlet & crimson, than it now does, & it is hard to leave it. Patrick has cut all his young corn for fear of frost & has it shocked in the Low Grounds—very picturesque he tells me it looks. Father's looks forlorn; standing white and frostbitten it seems to shiver in every breeze. Commenced preparations for moving to Looking Glass. I shall take as few things as possible. I remember last Feb when the enemy was reported advancing up the river & what terrible times we then had! Beauregard I see suggests that we drop the terms Yankee, Northerner, Federalists, etc., & call them simply "Abolitionists," which they all are since Mr Lincoln's Emancipation Proclamation. A good idea & one which will I hope be generally adopted. Mr E gone this afternoon to Clarksville to see about his duties of enrolment and to present his address to the committee. A fine one it is, short, stirring, and to the point. Instead of 100,000 I learn we have captured 1,000,000 yds of Kentuck Jean. I hope it is true, but I doubt!

OCTOBER 31, 1862

Finished Father's second undershirt last night & as he does not immediately need them think I will, before knitting the third, knit some stockings & gloves for the soldiers. Have been all day rumaging my stores & devising ways to make a small peice of flannel do duty for a large one, & by peicing & putting collars & cuffs of different colours so as to look like Uniform or fancy trimming I find I can get out 8 flannel shirts. But all my table covers go

& bare mahogany is the order of the day henceforward, but that is better than bare soldiers. Anything but that. Finished James' Comfortable today & a nice warm one it is. Amo took little Catherine Edmondston's[264] dresses, so they are off my mind, & sister F's comfortables have arrived safely—so I am at leisure for the Army.

General Gwinn,[265] sent by Government to construct defences for Roanoke River, has decided on Rainbow Bend & has ordered out 500 negroes with a fortnight's provisions to begin work on Monday next. Col Leaventhorpe had them for ten days at the same place last Feb. I wonder what more they can find to do, but Patrick says a Government Engineer always makes it a rule to undo all that his predecessor had done, so as to monopolize the credit. So General Gwin is no exception to the universal practice. Capt Meade's[266] straight entrenchment, or as Zeke called it a "canal a mile long in the wild woods," has been greatly criticised. So perhaps he is right. He has a chain weighing *sixteen thousand* lbs, so *Mr Smith* says, to stretch across the River. (How did he ever get it there?) There is no water transportation, no machinery to lift it & it would not do to bring it in sections & depend upon welding the links together there. So Mr Smith I fear me you exagerate. At any rate he has a chain & the Government is to send troops, so we are to be defended at last. Mr E's address to the people of the four Counties lying on the River was accepted by the Committee & today it went to be printed.[267] I will prefix it when it comes and then Journal you shall read it.

All quiet along our lines & no prospects of an immediate fight. The victory in S. C. was a signal one, the enemy leaving their dead & wounded. Our loss small. The Abolitionists are strengthening themselves at Suffolk & two Regts left N. Y. last week for New Berne, so it would appear they intend an advance into N C & an attack of Richmond from the South. There was an accident on the R & Gaston R R[268] on Tuesday, the very day Amo went up. I hope most

---

[264] Catherine Edmondston was the young daughter of Patrick's brother Charles. See Introduction.

[265] Col. Walter Gwynn, a graduate of West Point, civil engineer, and commander of the Northern District of Coastal Defenses, was ordered to examine the Neuse, Tar, Roanoke, and Chowan rivers, and to build obstructions commanded by batteries in the channels of each. It was further recommended that the construction of special defenses at Rainbow Bend on the Roanoke and at Whitehall on the Neuse would provide protection for gunboats being built on the rivers. Clark, *Histories of the North Carolina Regiments*, IV, 415-416; Hill, *Bethel to Sharpsburg*, I, 155-156.

[266] An inspection of the Roanoke River was made by Lt. J. Innes Randolph of the Corps of Engineers to determine the best points of defense. He selected Rainbow Bend on the Martin County side, three miles below Hamilton, where a battery and rifle pits had already been established by Capt. Kidder Meade. *Official Records (Navy)*, Series I, VIII, 185.

[267] On October 25, 1862, a meeting of citizens from Martin, Halifax, Bertie, and Northampton counties ordered the printing and distribution of an act authorizing the formation of companies for local defense. Richard H. Smith, Patrick M. Edmondston, and Edward P. Conigland were selected to write an address urging support of the act. A copy of this communication was affixed to page 42 of the second volume of the diary.

[268] A train of cars going north collided with a southbound train about 15 miles from Raleigh. Three persons were killed and several were severely wounded. *Raleigh Register*, October 29, 1862.

earnestly that it was not to the train on which he was. He should have written, but young folks are never as considerate of anxiety as those who have felt it. So we must pardon him. He cannot have been hurt or we should have known it, but I wish they had published the names of the sufferers. Put up my Apples yesterday for winter use—only a barrel & a Champagne basket full of sound ones after all our magnificent promise—cause, incessant wet weather. So we must not complain.

NOVEMBER 1, 1862

Last night came a letter from Mr McMahon telling Mr E that he heard through Rumour (I hope she is a lying dame this time) that the Steamer Cotton Plant with all Mr G W Barry's hands on board had been captured somwhere about Hill's Ferry—a heavy loss to us & heavier to the Confederacy—for she was the only boat in the River, the only hope we had of getting our Corn to market, and the only way Government had of getting supplies for the Army from this country. Hauling over our roads in the winter is almost impossible, so we have only Pandora's comfort left to us. The enemy have never ventured so far up the River before—past Hamilton & Rainbow Bluffs—where Gen Gwin is or was & where we thought we had a Battery to dispute their passage. Truly it makes one shudder! The sword of Damocles seems about to fall! Ah! Gen French, Gen Smith, you both are in command, of what are you thinking that you neglect this granery of the Army for so long? How terrible to think that our corn, our hogs, our forage for which we have so laboured should go to feed Abolitionists & traitors, should nourish civil war such as they wage, should be swallowed into the maw of such voracious wild beasts as compose that army of villains & lost to our beloved country. There is a heavy accountability somewhere, an accountability sufficient to crush any one mortal on whose head it lies!

Halleck, we see, says that the disposition & care of the negro falls upon the civil authority. The military have nothing to do with him, simply to remove him from the "*Rebels*" and leave the provision for his future to the civil arm. That is to say, Gen Halleck, you are to *starve* the civillian or to bury him. You take him from comfort, ease, & plenty, put him where you know he cannot maintain himself, where he must perish, & wash your hands of the consequences. Yes, but does a just God view it in this light, & even tho' there stand none to say his blood be on us & our children, on whose head will the retaliation fall? On whose but the Government & its ready tools? Tools such as yourself, Maj Gen Halleck!

Merchandise of every description is falling. The mercantile pulse is a prophetic as well as a sensitive one, so we ought to feel encouraged by such a manifestation in it. It points to plenty and a consequent abolition of speculation & extortion. Have knit almost a whole sock today for James, so as Peter is out I will go and walk out alone & enjoy the brilliant spectacle spread out before me. Nature in her most gorgeous dies, crimson, orange, & yellow, contrasting finely with the olive & russet of the gum & oak & the sombre green of the Pine. Would, old friend, that you had "eyes to see."

NOVEMBER 2, 1862

Mr Edmondston left this morning at day light for Tarboro to meet a gentleman on business. Business, Journal, which is none of yours and which I once before told you that as you were a high spirited high toned Journal you had no curiosity about. Suffice it that the gentleman's name is Mr Josiah Collins.[269] He will not be back before tomorrow at dinner-time, so I am left to my own sweet will until then. It is not good for man to be alone was the verdict of an all wise all kind Father, a Father who knows our wants before we utter them. I have written three long letters & had a solitary walk, and as it is Sunday & the negroes having no work to do about the house are at their respective houses it is as still and quiet here as a La Trappist could desire. Journal, I must beware. I shall sign your Death warrant if get too chatty and discursive to you. Your elder sisters all died from that & inanition. Together they were hopelessly helplessly dull & withal knew too much of my inner woman. This War which is the death knell to so many others is your life, your vital breath. That alone & the record of it contained in you is your hold upon existence. Think how much poetry, how many thoughts have fed your devouring flame! Yet, Journal, I love you better than the others. It would pain me to lose you, so for your sake I will be more reticent & not fritter you away upon idle thoughts & ideas "long drawn out." You have eased my anxiety & soothed my pain many a time this past year, but I make too large demands on you!

Mr E heard last night to our great releif that the rumour of the capture of the Cotton Plant was an entire fabrication. Not even a mistake, as she went up the river in safety yesterday & had we been at Looking Glass we could have seen her. Truth is indeed dead. Galveston in Texas is captured by the enemy. I know not which behaved worse or with more pusillamnity, the captors or the captured, if the Newspaper record is the true one. Two Regts are below us at Hamilton. Tomorrow our hands are to go down to work on the entrenchments, 500 called out with a fortnight's provisions. I hope they will make it safe this time. We captured a company of "Buffalos,"[270] so we hear, about

---

[269] Patrick possibly met Josiah Collins to discuss the removal of their slaves from areas threatened with a Union invasion or to consider sending their slaves to Hamilton to work on the Confederate defenses being constructed there. Collins had transferred a number of his slaves from a Tyrrell County plantation to a plantation in Franklin County when Federal forces invaded eastern North Carolina.

[270] "Buffalo," a term broadly applied to deserters, thieves, and murderers who used the chaos of the Civil War to cover their lawlessness, eventually was applied specifically to the First and Second North Carolina (Union) Volunteers, commanded by Col. E. E. Potter and Lt. Col. C. H. Foster, respectively. The companies contained eighty-six members in November, 1862, but as Confederate conscription tightened, men unwilling to leave North Carolina and those who were Unionists enlisted in these regiments on the promise

Plymouth. What "Buffalos" are does not appear, but they are enemies. The traitor Col Jones[271] has been captured and is in Jail at Hamilton. If the State authorities do their duty they will hang him for treason. I hope earnestly that they will never release him whilst the War lasts, for with his grand airs & pretended intimacy with the best people in the land, which he will be anxious to exhibit to his Abolition friends, he would be a dangerous person to us. He would pilot the enemy all through our country. He has long been an admirer of our fair neighbor Nannie Hill & came up often to see her. I would be sorry for him, much as I despise him, should he ever again encounter her!

NOVEMBER 9, 1862

Sunday at Conneconara. It is a week since I opened this book & Ah! what a week of anxiety & care! Tonight a week ago I made my last entry, Mr Edmondston being absent in Tarboro. He is absent again tonight probably in the same place but on how different an errand! He came home on Monday to dinner & found me in gay spirits, looking for him, knitting a stocking for James & superintending the digging of my Dahlia roots. He seemed anxious & worried & so soon as he got warm & comfortably at home told me that the enemy was reported as advancing in force, having marched across the country from Washington, compelling Burgwin's, Ratcliff's, & Lamb's Regts to fall back & that Faison's[272] was on its way to join them having encamped at Tarboro the night before. They had had a skirmish in which some of our men were killed & more wounded. This came like a thunderclap upon me & we hastily concluded to go down to father's that night, not only to see him, but to stop the sending of our negroes to work at Rainbow Bend Hamilton, as they had been ordered to do in the morning. We went & carried our heavy news with us. Next morning came Mr Hill & brought more encouraging news to the effect that Gov Vance had gone to Tarboro to take command & that more troops were en route & that we had repulsed the advance. We returned home, dining at Looking Glass as we passed & making our arrangements to move in the morning from Hascosea. Went out in the afternoon and I attended to the housing of my Dahlias, dividing them so as to send a nice portion to Mrs.

---

of serving only within the state. By April, 1863, 561 men served in the regiments; most were able soldiers, although Confederate forces in the state bitterly resisted them and some Union officers despised them. Hill, *Bethel to Sharpsburg*, I, 293-294; Barrett, *Civil War in North Carolina*, 174-176.

[271] Mrs. Edmondston possibly meant Col. J. Richter Jones, commander of the Fifty-eighth Pennsylvania Regiment stationed in North Carolina. He fought in a skirmish at Gum Swamp and on May 23, 1863, was killed at Batchelder's Creek. Barrett, *Civil War in North Carolina*, 162-163; *Official Records (Army)*, Series I, XVIII, 363-364.

[272] Mrs. Edmondston was referring to Col. Harry K. Burgwyn, Jr., Col. James D. Radcliffe, Lt. Col. John C. Lamb, and Col. Paul F. Faison, commanding or serving in the Twenty-sixth, Sixty-first, Seventeenth (Second Organization), and the Fifty-sixth North Carolina regiments, respectively. Clark, *Histories of the North Carolina Regiments*, II, 337-338, 654; III, 318-320, 503; Manarin and Jordan, *North Carolina Troops*, IV, 201, 204, 207, 305; V, 394.

Rayner, Ellen Mordecai, Mrs Mordecai, Thos Hogg's children,[273] & Mrs James Smith.

No additional news at night, so we went to bed quite reassured. Scarcely were we asleep when we were aroused by a note from Mr Hill telling us that the Yankees had taken Hamilton—were advancing in force, 12000 strong with 1200 Cavalry, that our troops had fallen back toward Tarboro, & that they had killed Bennet Baker & some others! This struck horror into my heart, for but a few days before I had seen Bennet Baker, young, vigorous, & full of life & the thought of his bleeding corpse, which had been carried to his father's house, banished sleep from my eyes for the rest of the night. About three we heard the tread of a horse & this time it proved to be John Currie with a note from Mr Speed telling us that "times is serious," "the Yankees advancing," "Cavalry in pursuit of our men." We were soon dressed & down stairs—found Mr C. in a state of excitement and alarm scarcely to be described. He told us that our neighbors were all moving, or making preparations to move, that a heavy land force occupied the roads whilst five Gun boats were in the River, & much more to the same effect. My heart sickened within me. I felt weak & faint but, thank God, He gave me strength to subdue all manifestations of fear & in a short time by His support I rallied & was enabled to go calmly to my preparations for leaving home.

Our first destination was the plantation, there to attend to the welfare of our negroes, & next to father's to give what aid & assistance lay in our power. I packed up our clothing, books—that is our most valuable ones—& made such disposition of them as I deemed proper, getting some things ready to send to Raleigh & Hillsboro, others to remain with us. I was mortified to find that anxiety or sleeplessness had made me really sick, so that it was with difficulty I could eat. This I forced myself to do & with many reproaches to my own weakness went on with my packing. About eleven Mr E went to our neighbor's Mr Hill's & found that he had already sent off his family & servants & was preparing to leave for his plantation himself! I packed up Rachel's things & a bundle for James E, having a good opportunity of sending it on to him; & about two we left Hascosea perhaps forever—as being on the high road between Hill's Ferry & Weldon (their probable destination), there is little doubt that should they penetrate so far it will fall a victim to their love of plunder & destruction.

I do not tell all I did, for time would fail me, & besides I can never forget it, so will not need this to remind me. Suffice it to say that at Looking Glass we

---

[273] Thomas Devereux Hogg (1823-1904), a physician, commissioner of the state's lunatic asylum, and chief commissary in the state Subsistence Department during the war, with the rank of major, was Mrs. Edmondston's first cousin. The Hogg children were Sallie, Janet (Mrs. Colin M. Hawkins), and Lucy (Mrs. Isaac F. Dortch). Commission, Thomas D. Hogg Papers, State Archives; Clark, *Histories of the North Carolina Regiments*, I, 37, 48, 51.

made the best dispositions we could, telling the negroes how to comport themselves & what to do in case of the enemy's occupation, promising not to leave
them, & came here to father, who was most happy to see us.

This was on Wednesday the 5th. Our dispatches, of which we received two
every day, have varied from hopeful to despondant ever since. It is needless to
record them all. On Thursday Mr E went to Clarksville to attempt to organize
a Co for local defence but failed, there being but few there willing to join him.
Capt Clements[274] read him a letter from his sister, Mrs Kinchin Taylor, telling
him of the outrages they committed at her house. She said the Zouaves
swarmed in like Devils, yelling, whooping, & screaming. Her negro servant,
Ness, drew a knife & took his station by her telling them that he would kill the
first man who laid a finger upon her. Noble conduct, as all who know how
timid the race is generally will admit. They sacked the house, threw
everything out of it, breaking every thing that could break & chopping the furniture to peices! They built a fire out of doors, cut up the corn crop & threw it
on it, killed all the fattening Hogs, sheep, cattle, & cows & threw them also
into it. They took her carriage & every horse on the premises, telling her that
they would have burned the house but that she was in it. She went herself on
foot to their head quarters, saw General Foster, the officer in command, & requested that her horses might be returned to her. He looked & spoke so cross
that she feared him, but his Aid, to his praise be it spoken, Capt George Anderson of Boston interceeded & obtained one horse for her. Her carriage was
also returned with the harness cut into bits. He (Capt A), when he saw the
desolation & destruction wrought in her house, actually wept! His tears did
him credit. I did not think a Yankee capable of it! Let him now only resign the
service of such a Government & he may yet do well.

At Mr John Williams they burned his Gin, Screw, & all his cotton and
leather. Mr E had this from Mrs Williams herself. What fiends! & what
useless barbarity, a barbarity which God will punish! We have been thus anxious ever since, one account encouraging, the next discouraging us, accordingly as they reported favourably or otherwise of their advance.

On Friday the 7th we opened our eyes upon a heavy fall of snow!—the
earliest ever known in this climate. I could not enjoy the unusual & brilliant
spectacle of the autumn leaves, crimson, yellow, & orange covered with a
fleecy Veil. I was too uneasy & fearful lest the snow should raise the River &
allow the Gunboats which we heard were aground on Williams Bar to get off.
On Friday came brother, less despondant at first, it appeared, than usual, but
we soon found his calmness partook of the nature of despair. Mr E & himself
arranged to go & offer their services to the Comdg-Gen & the Gov as Volunteer Aids & today they left for the head quarters of our Army, now said to

---

[274]Lycurgus L. Clements of Martin County served as captain of Co. G, Seventeenth North Carolina
(First Organization) Regiment until it was disbanded on or about March 20, 1862.

number thirteen Regts, but we do not credit it. We suppose an advance is to be made simultaneously with this from Suffolk & look anxiously for news, but as yet none seems to be threatened. Brother has sent to Richmond for Annie, fearing our R R communication may be cut off. I am so sleepy that I will go to bed now & leave the outside news, i.e., news from all but this corner of the Confederacy until tomorrow. Mr E keeps me in better order when he is at home. Were he here I should have been asleep long ago. I am not half done yet.

November 11, 1862

Went yesterday to Hascosea to see how things get on there and attend to some matters that I had not time for when we left on Wednesday. Snow still lies on the ground in sheltered & Northern exposures & the severe frost has taken the beauty from the autumn leaves—another enjoyment we have lost this time by *Northern* weather. Whilst there three Companies of Cavalry passed going *up* towards Halifax—a favourable sign I hope of the departure of the enemy. Two men from one of them came in & politely requested me to give them some cold bread & meat. Having nothing but a cold Ham in the house, having just finished my lunch of Ham, bread, & *tea*, I invited them in, whilst Dolly should bake some bread & fry some potatoes—all I had to offer. They proved to be members of Dr Shaw's Company, which was raised for Edmondston's Battalion, so they seemed to have a claim on me. Mr E started down to muster them in last May but was detained by the collision of the Cars at Halifax. They were full of polite regrets at his & their disappointment at not having him for their Colonel & left messages for him. I filled their Haversacks with Ham & bread and wishing them good speed they left me with many thanks—their names Lieut Peterson and Mr Bunting.[275] Had they known that it was Mr E's house when they came in, the Capt would also have stopped. He was at our house on the plantation last spring. They told me that the Yankees had all left for Plymouth after attempting to burn Williamston, in which, however, they only partially succeeded. They left in a great fright thinking that our men were upon them, leaving some of their baggage & camp equipage. Mr Bunting showed me some tin plates on which they had been eating with the cold beef gravy still upon them! They left some waggons & a Jersey waggon & a lot of candles. Thirty of the company were left behind as pickets to guard us for the future & Lieut Peterson reported a strong force of Infantry below.

Came home & stopped at Looking Glass for some Black Pepper for Mama. Carried her three P's, not so famous as those needed in education, "Praise,

---

[275] Everett Peterson of Sampson County was a second lieutenant in Co. C, Sixty-third North Carolina (Fifth Cavalry) Regiment. Thomas Owen Bunting of Sampson County was a sergeant in the same company and regiment. Manarin and Jordan, *North Carolina Troops*, II, 389-390.

Punishment, & Physic" but almost as much used, viz., Pears, Pickles, & Pepper! At night came Mr E from Tarboro. He reports shameful mismanagement of our troops by the General in command. Had he had proper information which he could have got & advanced by one road, sending one Regt by another, it is the impression of everyone that we could have captured the whole force which was variously reported as from five to ten thousand strong & in a panic of fear all the time, dreading the woods for fear of ambush & the swamp for fear of guerillas. On Friday they were, some furiously and others helplessly, drunk, having taken Mr [———] Apple Brandy, drank as much as they liked & staved in the heads of twenty barrels—a heavy loss to him poor man for it now brings twenty dollars a gal! Had our men been near every man of the party would have been taken! Gen Martin reports that they have gone back to Plymouth & he has issued an order for one fifth of the road hands to be in readiness when called for to work on the fortifications at Rainbow Bend, promising a sufficient force to guard them whilst at work.

After breakfast today came Mr Leary, the old gentleman who was here with his family last winter—refugees from Chowan. His opinion of Gen Martin as a military man was so ludicrously expressed that I record it. On father's expressing his regret that the enemy had escaped, he said, "Well sir, as to that, from what I can learn, if the Gen in command, Martin, was in heaven the rest of mankind would be no worse off for anything he can do!" He is on his way to his own house in Chowan, intending to make his way through the enemies lines, in order to bring off his carpets which he secreted when he left to cut up for blankets for our soldiers and he an old man near seventy!

Have just come in from seeing Mr George Daughtry, the brother of fathers overseer, who is I fear in a dying state. He joined the Scotland Neck Rifles to avoid the Conscription in the summer. Has been sick in the Hospital at Wilmington & since in Camp. He was discharged from the service on account of his health & came up on Sat in the snow from Wilmington without an overcoat & in summer clothing. Got to his brother's on Sunday & has been unable to go further. Mr E was sent for before daybreak this morning & found him insensible & evidently dying. He lies now in a comitose state from which death only will release him. He dies a victim to bad management & want of energy, for had his friends made proper exertion to get his winter clothing to him, or even sent him his overcoat which they could have done, or had his Captain looked after his comfort at all & furloughed him so as to allow him to come home for it, he would in all probability be living & a healthy man now, for he has seen no service & had no exposure to hurt a well clad man. "But no," they said, "they would give him soldiers clothes." Who said does not appear & so as the Government could not do their duty from the want of material his friends have left his warm clothing & overcoat at home, for the moths to consume, from mere shiftlessness and want of consideration, for they appear deeply concerned about & attached to him. I have been thus minute in my account of him, for his case is a key to the mortality in our army & especially to that in Western Va where the 24th [and] Col Clark suffered so severely for want of clothing, it was said, and blankets & especially overcoats, within six weeks after they went into service. I remember I did not beleive there was a Regt of such improvident men in the country & blamed their officers, but I fear I was hasty. George Daughtry is well to do, has plenty of clothes, a mother & sister (who seems to be a sensible woman) & yet he dies a victim to carelessness, or rather thoughtlessness.

On the Potomac things seem serious. The Abolitionists are throwing themselves to the South of Lee & endeavoring to take possession of the Gaps in the Blue Ridge so as to confine him to the Valley west of it, whilst they propose an easy "On to Richmond" march of it. I have every confidence in our General & do not beleive that he will allow himself to be outmanovered thus. Still the position is a serious one & we may soon hear of a battle in that quarter. We have occasional skirmishes & some of them severe ones, capturing trains & detachments, etc., but nothing which bears on the general issue of the campaign. The Democrats have carried the N Y Elections by an overwhelming majority, defeating the Republicans in the city alone by 30,000. Many feel hopeful that this is an evidence of "Peace" but I do not. The only thing they seem agreed about is to fight the South, but the Democrats condemn Lincoln's proclamation & declare that they are tired of the "eternal negro" & cry "down with the Wooly Heads." So perhaps we will not lose so many under their regime. A more hopeful sign to me is the desire that the Government men evince to shake off the odium of causing the War. Gen Scott since the publication of his remarkable letter by Mr Van Buren is out with an article reflecting on Mr Buchanon who replies by delicately giving Maj Gen Scott the *lie*, not in words it is true but by a statement of facts. He has "Old Fuss and Feathers" in rather an unpleasant predicament. The Northern Papers are full of rumours of an Armistice, Intervention, & recognition, which Lord Lyons, they say, is directed to make, but we none of us beleive them or in fact attach any importance to them. We have to conquer a Peace with our own good swords & by God's help we will do so!

November 12, 1862

This morning before day light Mr E was sent for by Mr Daughtry, thinking his brother worse, but he was dead before he could get down to him! Poor fellow, but for this cruel war & Lincoln & Seward's want of principle, he might have lived to a good old age. Came home to Looking Glass to dinner, having sent our baggage before us, so we are I hope settled for the winter. God grant us an undisturbed possession of our home. Unpacked our trunks & reunited our scattered & divided wardrobes, for in prospect of the advance of the enemy last week and our uncertainty as to which was the safest, Hascosea or the River, I left a portion there, took a portion with me, & packed one large trunk to send up to Raleigh so as to be prepared for the worse. We enjoy the ease & independance of home, for tho' father and Mama are most kind & do all to make us comfortable & happy & are urgent with us to combine house holds & make one family until Peace, still *home* has so many attractions that we are loth to give it up. Mr E quaintly expressed it tonight, as sitting in his own chair he stretched out his feet with an air of proprietorship & said, "It is good to be here where one is Top Lawyer"—& so it is. That expresses it exactly, a sense of authority & power one never feels in any house save ones own. Grant that our lives this winter may be marked with a sense of deeper gratitude to God, the giver of all our blessings, than we have yet felt.

November 13, 1862

Succeeded yesterday in getting my tenth woolen shirt for our soldiers, tho the cover of my sofa pillow went to make out the sleeves! Busy with my knitting. Finished James stockings & commenced altering some which I had knit last winter but being too short did not send them. Left Vinyard at Hascosea on account of her child, there being so severe a cough epidemic amongst the children that I fear to bring Morgan into it. We think it the Hooping Cough. Went to the Nursery yesterday with Mr E. All the children have it & all look puny. Ailsie lost one last week from fits, brought on, Tatty thinks, by the cough. Poor thing, she lost her infant the week before also from convulsions. She is most unfortunate with her children. They all die in the same way. They seem radically diseased. We prescribed Cotton Seed tea, an old remedy for chills which the blockade & consequent scarcity of quinine has revived. Gen Jackson (Old Hickory) said it was a cure for Whooping Cough. Nitric Acid is the specific, but that we cannot get. Out on a nation who wars on the inoffensive and innocent! & makes children & invalids suffer for what, were they *men*, *men* worthy of the name, they would visit on the *men* of the country. None but cowards & scoundrels could act thus.

Went to Hascosea with Mr E to make some further arrangements about our move for the winter. Met Mrs Whitehead & her daughter. They told us that they had been amongst those who fled for fear of the Abolitionists. They got to Halifax & were detained by the Snow storm & when that was over found that they could return home. The killing of Bennet Baker struck the wildest alarm and horror into our scattered community. Each one thought that might be his or her fate & hence the panic. He was peaceful, inoffensive, & unarmed & there was no reason or excuse for his death. We hear so many exagerated accounts of the doings of the enemy that I will not record them. Only in one thing all agree in, viz., that they could have been captured. Gen Martin's ears must burn if there is anything in the old saying.

I append an extract from one of Mr Sewards diplomatic letters, marked H which I think stamps him.[276] Had he a single one of the instincts of a gentleman, Mr Lincoln's Proclamation of Emancipation would have been followed by his resignation.

NOVEMBER 14, 1862

Sue got home from Petersburg on Wednesday & came down to see me to-day. She tells me that Bishop Lay[277] is out with a publication signed by twelve other respectable gentlemen in which he says that Gen Mitchel, commanding the Abolitionist at North Alabama, said that the Northern army needed no pay; the possession of the Lands & women of the South was inducement sufficient for them. It had been used as an inducement to promote volunteering. It was enough! What an infamous wretch! Let his name go down to posterity by the side of Butler's, & speaking of him, Mayor Monroe of N Orleans has fallen a victim to his cruelty in imprisoning him at Ship Island for so long. He is dead! How long O Lord! how long! Brother has just gone; he tells me that Gen Martin is relieved of his command here by Gen Evans of S C—a good officer, but he likes whisky, in fact *drinks* very hard. I wonder if it can be true. People now-a-days cast about firebrands in the shape of allegations of drunkenness, incapacity, etc., with such recklessness that I hope brother has been mis-informed. Mr E is at Clarksville now to learn news from below & whether we are to fortify Rainbow Bend, so I will wait for his return for the news.

I write out a list of prices to let us see when peace comes what hardships must have been endured by those who had but little money.

Bacon	75 to 100
Pork	75 to 70
Leather	
Coarse cotton cloth	75 to $1.00
Wool—per lb—	75
Flannel—per yd—	$5
Shoes negro—	$10 to $18
Ladies Gaiters	$15
Spool Cotton—	$1.00
Coffee—	$2.75
Sugar—	$1.00
Factory Cotton per block	$8.50

[276] Seward's letter to the French government, dated April 22, 1861, is the subject of a newspaper article pasted on page 41 of the second volume of the diary.

[277] Henry Champlin Lay (1823-1885), an Episcopal clergyman in Huntsville, Alabama, served as the missionary bishop for Arkansas and the Indian Territory from 1859 through 1869. After the war he was the bishop of Easton, Maryland. *Concise Dictionary of American Biography*, 551.

Flour—per lb—	$30
Tea—per lb—	$9.00
Boots—per p	$30 to $35
Coarse Woolen cloth	$12
Country homespun	$ 1 to $2 p yd
Fodder Richmond market per cut	2.50
Apple Brandy—per gal—	$20
Black Alpacca—ordinary—	$5.00
Salt per bu—(thirty dollars)	$30
Tobacco—ord—	
Shuck—Richmond market—	2.25[278]

Patrick showed me a side of Leather which he had had tanned, which he told me would have cost him $50 & a small side at that.

Gen Mitchel, the Abolition commander at Port Royal S C, and most of his Staff are dead with a disease that their Doctors cannot tell which it is, Yellow, Billious, Country or Coast fever. Gen Hunter again in command.

From the West the news is discouraging. Bragg has campaigned himself out of Kentucky & a storm of abuse follows him. I append an order from the Yankee Gen at Suffolk which proves that the outrages we hear of are no fiction, marked D.[279] Mr Smith of Norfolk, our merchant Mr Marsden Smith, his brother tells my brother is kindly allowed by Gen Viele, the Abolitionist in command there, to leave Norfolk if he will give up the whole of his property to the U S, hand in a Schedule, resign all & depart. "The tender mercies of the wicked are cruel"[280] truly. A gentleman of Norfolk, name I did not hear, demeaned himself so far as to apply to Gen Viele a short time since to be allowed to punish his maid servant by whipping. Permission was readily granted with the addition, "but bear in mind that she may apply to me next week to have your wife whipped, in which case it will be my duty to grant it." Can one conceive of such an insult? Can one receive it and live? God keep me from a sight of them even.

November 17, 1862

Monday morning before daylight. I am up early this morning, I cannot say *bright* for I feel uncomonly stupid & were it not for very shame and a fear of oversleeping myself I would take immediate refuge in bed from this uncomfortable dark eerie seeming hour! We were up in order to enable Mr E. to take an early start for Raleigh, whither he has gone in accordance with the wishes

---

[278] Numerous invoices on J. M. Smith and Brother, Norfolk, found in the Devereux Papers, State Archives, listed these items and others.

[279] This order of Gen. John James Peck, Union commander at Suffolk, Virginia, is included in the second volume of the diary on page 43.

[280] Proverbs 12:10b.

of the gentlemen of the neighborhood to request Gov Vance to detail Mr Winder[281] from the State Adgt' Gen's Office to superintend the defences at Williams Bar, which we engage to put up if he will order out the Militia to protect the negroes whilst engaged in the work, leaving the Confederate Government the defences [at] Rainbow Bend to work its own sweet will upon, which from all present appearances will be a profound inactivity, they having ordered away all but one Regt of the Military, which is now all that lies between us & the enemy.

I have cut 4 doz candle wicks & put them to steep, one half in spt Turpentine, the other in Salt Petre & Lime Water, for be it known to you, O Journal, that I am becoming deeply versed in the *practical* manufacture of Tallow candles, the War having developed that necessity. Formerly we sold. all the Tallow & bought Stearine Candles, the difference in price being so little that it was well repaid in the additional comfort derived by it. That is now, however, impossible so we revert to first principles, principles practised "when Adam delved & Eve span,"[282] for I suppose Mother Eve must have lengthened out her day of labour by a farthing *dip*. I am better off, however, than she was, for thanks to pewter moulds I can make a very fair "*six*." Well I put out the candles which depress me with their sickly glare & look the day fairly in the face. Let me see, I have Candles to make, first the Tallow to purify, a Lye stand to have put up, six pr drawers for the soldiers to cut out & baste, a cart to send off to Samantha with a side of Bacon, some Potatoes & Beans, & meal, which Mr E in his kind thoughtfulness knows will be acceptable. I have Dolly's spinning work to arrange & superintend. She commences some yarn for me to knit for the soldiers & I have to go into the Pork house loft & select, or make her do it, such wool as I wish for my own work before the Plantation spinners commence on it. Fanny will make the candles but "Missus" must see her & arrange the wicks in the moulds. Cuffee is not up to that yet, tho she soon shall be for I am fully of the old opinion that there is no use in having a dog & barking for one's self—& then there is a glove to be knit for Mr E. The first one I knit on Sat, as I gave Amo when he left the memorable pair that I knit last Feb, when he was on the Roanoke River defences, the wool for which was clipped from a black sheep's back in tuffs so that she should not miss it; spun & commenced knitting the same day! Some

---

[281] Capt. John C. Winder, a North Carolinian formerly employed as an engineer on the Croton aqueduct in New York, returned to his native state at the outbreak of the war. He was appointed assistant adjutant general under Gen. James G. Martin in October, 1861, while serving in the North Carolina Corps of Engineers. He helped with the construction of Fort Fisher in 1861, and in November, 1862, he supervised the construction of batteries near Hill's Ferry on the Roanoke River. Winder later became a captain in the Confederate engineering department. Clark, *Histories of the North Carolina Regiments*, IV, 414, 416-417.

[282] Mrs. Edmondston was quoting a line used by John Ball in a speech to the men in Wat Tyler's Rebellion of 1381. Bartlett, *Familiar Quotations*, 1084.

of the yarn is fortunately left, so I will have a second edition. Then this afternoon Peter *advises* me to go to father's & remain until his return. Advises, mind, so I do not know whether or not I shall take it. There is not a white soul within five miles of me & eighty-eight negroes immediately around me! What becomes of the dread of a servile insurrection in view of the fact that I have not a sensation of fear? Well as I have gone through the enumeration of my work, like "the old woman who lived in the woods," I had better be up and at it, but first for the War news.

The last mail brot news of McClellan's having been relieved of his command & Burnside being assigned to his duty, an astonishing step, & one so directly in the face of the Democratic element at the North with whom McClellan is a favourite that it can be accounted for in two diametrically opposite ways—the first that it is a ruse to deceive us & that he will make his next appearance as commanding Gen in Halleck's place or at the head of a column advancing upon Richmond by the way of Suffolk (this would propitiate the army); the other is that Lincoln & his Cabinet are so disgusted with the recent elections & the majority against them that knowing they have the reins for a year longer, they are resolved to keep no terms with the Democrats but throw their favourite overboard without scruple, make him in fact the scape goat for their past blunders. Burnside is the valiant gentleman who came here to N C to subdue us last winter & who, during the storm off Cape Hatteras, stood like a sea god—distinguished by his yellow belt. He issued a proclamation to assure us he was "a Christian," but his after acts, like those of many who make the like profession, showed that he was either a hypcrite or a backslider. Witness the ravages & thefts of his command through the whole Eastern part of our State—"the most Christian Gen Burnside," we salute you! & hope that our Gen Lee will give you a reception worthy your merits and distinguished Christianity. Lee's position keeps us uneasy, but such confidence is felt in his generalship that we all beleive that he will extricate himself with safety & skill and inflict a blow on the enemy in doing so. An advance by Gun boats is threatened up the James River, another attack it is thought on Drury's Bluff. The S C reserves have been ordered to Charleston & ordered to report to Beauregard who expects and attack soon. In the West the news is discouraging. Bragg seems to have mismanaged shamefully & Buel to have got the better of him in all points but the battle of Perryville which was bloody & barren. Butler continues to distinguish himself by his brutality, has made all the inhabitants of N O take the oath or confiscated their property. So many assertions per & contra have been made about the force of the enemy that recently threatened our country that I paste a slip containing an account of their force taken from a Northern paper.[283] It

---

[283] This account appears in the second volume of the diary on a page containing a portion of the entry for November 17, 1862.

will be seen that there was cause for our aprehensions. To this we had a force of 5 000, & yet all agree such was their panic & ignorance of the country that Gen Martin had he had pickets out & made a proper division of his forces could have captured them all. But it is easy to *talk* & be a carpet general. It is one thing to manovre crumbs of bread & slips of paper, say *this* is Lamb's, *that* Faison's, & *there* Burgwin's regts, & to take the Regts themselves & order them into position. I prefix a list of Richmond prices marked G to show how the money of our soldiers goes in that Maelstroom of extortion. I also prefix Mr E's address to the counties marked F and an article on Diptheria marked E.[284] I put it here because my receipt book where I always preserve such things is out of my reach on account of the Abolitionists & I wish it for reference, that disease being so prevalent & fatal.

It is a fact that the vile wretches stole all Mrs Bell's bed clothing, cut open her feather beds & threw the feathers from the chamber windows & after they left one scoundrel ran back & took the covering from her cradle in which her infant was lying! The details of their enormities would fill a volume. They killed the stock, Hogs, sheep, milch cows, steers, etc., for mere wantonness, leaving them where they shot them.

Well I must to work. My house is in order & my handmaidens wait upon me & O! annoyance, here comes Mingo with a message from Patrick to the effect that I must go to fathers tonight. The crafty creature! He *advised* for fear that I should *coax* him. He knew he would meet Mingo on his way to his work here. Well obedience is a wife's first duty, so I must go, tho it cuts short my day & leaves me no time to wind the bobbin of yarn that I spun yesterday. I send a couple of lbs of Black Pepper each as a present to Margaret, Sister F, and Ellen Mordecai, there being none to be had in the country. Fortunately we have "a Pocket" of it—a comentary on the times. Surely this War is meant to check the profusion in which we have lived & to teach the rising generation economy & the employment of their resources.

NOVEMBER 21, 1862

Thursday night—At home again & again alone. On Monday I went up on horse back to Fathers & met Sue on the road coming to see me. Lee has crossed the Blue Ridge unmolested after all the vaunts of the Northern Press that McClellan had him cut off and held all the Gaps! They held no such thing. Snickers & other important ones were in our possession. Still his position was a dangerous one & we are doubly thankful that our headquarters are now at Culpepper Court House where we can watch & fall upon them when & where our General thinks best. McClellan was removed because he would not advance although *positively ordered to do so*. The Democratic party at the

---

[284] These clippings are pasted in the second volume of the diary on pages 42 and 43.

North are indignant & in fact say that it has made McClellan the next President. Burnside must advance or resign, as he was placed in command solely to do so. If he fails he is lost, but should he succeed! Ah! then what will be our fate? But my trust is in God! He giveth the Victory!

On Tuesday Sue & I rode over to Montrose to give brother a call. Found him in the field & as usual dolefully dismal. A wild rumour is running through the country to the effect that an order has been issued to burn all the Cotton in this section by the 25th, but I do not beleive it. If so it is a renunciation of this part of the country & I do not beleive the authorities insane as yet tho they do keep Gen French in command.

Came home & found the mail awaiting us. Mr Randolph, Sec of War, has resigned; cause said to be a disagreement with the President who wishes to curtail his power & make all the appointments himself. I do not beleive it. I think it is only one of the Examiner's slanders. I do not like that paper. It has not respect enough for "the powers that be,"—ignores the fact altogether that they are "ordained of God." There has been a dash of Cavalry into Fredericksburg capturing some woolen cloth manufactured there for the Army. Our Cavalry stationed there seemed to have behaved badly as they could have cut them off & captured the whole of them had they been on the alert & not *feared* they were the Vanguard of a host who followed at their heels.

On Wednesday came down here, weighed & marked 22 bales of Cotton, & sent them off to Halifax in obediance to orders from Mr E. I know he intended trying to sell them, so perhaps he has done so, or the order may be true. Sue was with me. We had lunch & chatted pleasantly together & got back just in time for dinner—found Mr E awaiting us. He brought Mary & her children down with him, much to the surprise of everyone, as we fear that our condition is not secure enough for father to undertake the care of another female & two children. In case of a Yankee raid he will have his hands full!

Mr Leary had been at father's during our absence & to our sorrow we learned that my nephew Thomas Jones had been captured by a Co of Buffalos whilst collecting clothing for his men. He had succeeded in getting a large quantity when they laid their hands upon him. I hope he will soon be released as we have a surplus of prisonners, but I fear these lawless unprincipled Buffalos; they are worse than the Yankees & under even less restraint. God be with & help him. Mr L gave us a hope that he would be retaken, as our men were after them, but it was only a hope, as our troops do not seem to be successful in that quarter. They want *leaders.* News from Fredericksburg that a few days after their cavalry expedition (which was but a handful & for the purpose of reconnoissance, which we should not have allowed & could have prevented) a large body of troops advanced & occupied Falmouth on the opposite side of the River. A brisk Artillery fight was going on, but without much effect on either side. It is surmised that Burnside intends his "On to Richmond" by that route.

Mr E was successful in his application to the Gov. He promised to send Maj Winder down to examine the River & to report on the possibility of its being obstructed, so the carriage went immediately back for him & we came home the next morning, Thursday, on horseback. In due time he arrived, a gentlemanly quiet person who made a most agreeable impression on me, & this morning early they were off, intending to go first to Hamilton & see what the Confederate authorities were doing & act accordingly, so as not to clash with them. Brother went down yesterday with a gang of free negroes, whom he called "Falstaff's ragged Regt," to report to the Engineer in command of the defences projected by Gen Gwynn. I hope they will be successful. That grounding of their Gun boats at Williams Bar was a most excellent thing for us & will I hope deter them from any future attempts this way. Mary met a Lady who had been detained some months in Maryland by the Abolition authorities & refused permission to come South to her husband, one Capt Kennedy. She gave her a most terrible picture of the oppression & tyranny exercised by the Northern Governt, spies everywhere, arrests, searching for clothing & supplies for the Confederate Army, insults to women, imprisonment without charges & the writ of Habeas Corpus suspended—seizure of private papers & all the machinery of a despotic governmen suddenly develloped full grown & in its most odious form!

One story I must insert. From the lower part of Maryland which is staunch to the South large quantities of clothing & particularly socks have been sent over into Va for the Confederate Army by the ladies acting on their own part & as their feelings dictated. This has excited the wrath of the Lincoln Governt and active measures have been taken to seize & confiscate them.

At one retired farm house to which they rode up in a hot Sept afternoon the young ladies of the family were taking their siesta, the father was out, & the only person visible on the premises was an old lady of nearly seventy who sat in the passage knitting & dozing. The soldiers came up unawares to her & the first thing she saw was a U S officer in full uniform coming into the door whilst his men filled the piazza. Rising up she immediately advanced to meet him, & he, it is supposed, thinking from her promptness & calmness that there were others to back her in order to strike terror into their hearts drew out his sword with a flourish & said, "By authority of the U S Government I come," when she cooly patted him on the shoulder & said, "Put up you sword honey! I *wouldn't hurt you for the world*"! He then seeing that she was alone proceeded with what face he could to explain that he was sent out to search for & seize socks which he heard were intended for the Confederate Army & observing her knitting said, "And what are you doing Madam?" "Knitting socks for the Confederate soldiers! Honey! Knitting socks for the Confederate soldiers." "Well, Madam it is my duty to seize all such." "Well, Honey! to be sure! I suppose you do not want the needles too" & suiting the action to the word she pulled out the needles deliberately one by one, stuck them into her cap, broke off the ball of yarn, rolled up the half knit sock, & politely handed it to him! That unfinished sock was all the gallant officer got for his afternoon's work.

At Mr Contee's the ladies seeing the soldiers approach bundled up their shirts & pantaloons, cleared up their work room, & calling a faithful negro gave them in charge to him and from being as busy as bees they were as idle as drones when the officer entered, & whilst he was searching the house the servant succeeded in getting the negroes dressed up in the clothes, some of them with 2 prs of pantaloons on! On returning from their fruitless expedition they remarked that "they had no where seen such well dressed well cared for slaves as Mr Contee's"! Ah, tyranny, you have need of Argus eyes[285] when it is the aim of so many to out wit you.

Well I will go to bed for it is late & I have been hard at work all day. Let me see, I got Mr E off, then prepared 6 doz candle wicks & attended to the moulding 2 doz candles. I lapped thread or yarn with my own hands for three yds of cloth for a pr of soldiers pants, hanked 6 broaches of cotton, knit two fingers & a thumb of a pr of *fine* white yarn gloves for dress parade for Col Clarke & then after dinner commenced a soldiers sock, read the paper, took a nap, drank tea, finished the sock to Dolly's delight & wonderment, wrote my journal, & now with a sense of "something accomplished—something done" think I have "earned a night's repose."[286]

The paper reports a large force supposed to be the whole of the Abolition Army lying before Fredericksburg. Lee, the Examiner says, is ready for them. A skirmish on the Blackwater on Tuesday the guns of which we heard, in which we repulsed them, supposed to be Foster & the troops he had here. No particulars of our losses. I will leave Mr Johnston's treatment of a Fed officer until tomorrow—so to bed, this time in earnest.

NOVEMBER 24, 1862

Sunday—Mr E still absent & not much public news of interest to report. At the last dates Lee's headquarter's were still at Culpepper. Prisoners taken at Fredericksburg report that Sumners corps occupy Falmouth & that the whole Abolition army are advancing in force. Our scouts report their Camp fires for a distance of twelve miles. At intervals they shell the town & our troops vigorously but make no further demonstration. Mr Seddon,[287] a lawyer of

---

[285] Mrs. Edmondston's use of the expression "argus eyes" denoted the need for jealous watchfulness on the part of Union soldiers. Benét, *Reader's Encyclopedia*, 45.

[286] Henry Wadsworth Longfellow, "The Village Blacksmith," stanza 7, lines 5-6.

[287] James Alexander Seddon (1815-1880), a former United States congressman and a successful lawyer, served as the Confederate secretary of war from November, 1862, until February, 1865. After the war he

Richmond, has been made Sec of War. I well remember when he married one of the great belles of the day, one of the Misses Bruce, sister of Mr James Bruce of Halifax. He was freely discussed then, but the lady had rejected so many suitors that they in themselves were numerous enough to create a public opinion! He is well spoken of as a lawyer & a man of sense, so I hope he will do well tho a change at this time is most unfortunate. Mr Randolph has worked wonders & deserves the thanks of the country.

Indignation at the North great and bitter at McClellan's disgrace, the population en masse seem striving to do him honor & already do they speak of him as their next President. But popular favour is like the patterns in a kaleidescope, at the next turn it has vanished forever. Let Burnside but succeed & then Maj Gen McCellan, you are forgotten as completely as last years snow.

Our army in the West is being concentrated. Gen Joe Johnson is to take command & Bragg I hope shelved. Lieut Gen Polk has just been in & with my Aunt was in Raleigh. She tells my sisters that the story of the wife of the Lieut Gov of La having been kissed in the street by one of Butler's beasts & shot by her & handed into a carriage by another Fed officer & passed beyond the lines in safety, is true, only it was not the wife of the Lieut Gov but a Mrs [———] & that instead of shooting she stabbed him in the throat & that the other Yankee officer, her rescuer, did not deliver himself to the nearest Confederate post but returned so soon that he was not missed & to this day Butler does not know which is his white amongst his flock of black sheep. The Gen left his youngest daughter[288] to go to school at St Mary's in Raleigh.

The sufferings of the poor negroes in the Yankee lines are said to be terrible. They themselves admit that they do not know what to do with them, that they are unfit for freedom, & show but little sense of all that has been done for them, looking to the future only with a hope of being returned once more to their masters plantations "& strange it is," they say, "they look back with longing & affection to their owners." Strange indeed!—Yankee impertinence & Yankee vanity—a wilful closing of their eyes & ears to Cuffee's real wants & position until Cuffee himself with his own hands pulls the one open & deafens the other by his cries for bread & "old master." Strange! Not so strange as your foolish wickedness, O ye nation of 'isms—Abolitionism & fanaticisms have long ago led you captive! Here have I been for three days & nights, the only white soul on a plantation of eigty odd negroes and not another white person within five miles of me & that a man of near seventy surrounded with 300 or more slaves as safe as tho' "an army with banners" encamped around me without even a fear for myself. A comentary truly on Lin-

---

retired to his farm in Goochland County, Virginia. Seddon married Sarah Bruce, daughter of James Bruce of Halifax County, Virginia, in 1845. *Dictionary of American Biography*, XVI, 545-546.

[288] Lucia Polk, born in Louisiana in 1848, was the youngest daughter of Leonidas and Frances Devereux Polk. See Introduction.

coln's Emancipation Proclamation! which lacks one short month only of going into execution.

The River was rising so rapidly last night that I directed Henry to go on
with his work of gathering corn in the Low Grounds, Sunday tho it be, to have
everything that could work out bright & early & had their dinner put on here
at the kitchen myself—6 gals and a half of white beans, 1/2 lb bacon for each,
& bread without limit & as I went out but now to see to it, it looked and smelt
so nice that I was fain to take a taste of it myself & capital good it is & this is
extra on account of Sunday work. What other labourers are so well treated?—
& yet "the poor negro" there is everything *in fashion*!

Mr Johnston, our neighbor, has continued at his house near Edenton
within the enemies lines the whole summer. He has lost many of his negroes,
more than 100, & been subject to many annoyances & thefts, but since their
failure to make him take the oath he has been personally unmolested by them.
A few days since the Yankee Col dressed in his full uniform went to call upon
& pay his respects to him. Mr J received him in his most formal & dignified
manner. After the first civilities were over & the official I suppose a little awed
by his venerable aspect & old school manners, Mr J remarked: "some of your
men passed by this morning Col, and they paid me a much higher compliment, treated me with more marked consideration than you have done."
"Ah!" said the officer, "I am glad to hear it. How was that?" "They passed
by without intruding their company upon me sir!" It is supposed the Col soon
found it pleasant to leave.

I did yesterday what I have often said I could do & been laughed at for my
boast. I knit a *pr* of medium fine socks. Commenced at 10 in the morning, did
not fatigue myself with work, went to walk, took a nap, attended to the clarify-
ing some Tallow, etc., & yet by fair bed time they were finished & ready for a
soldier to put on his feet. It is a great blessing to be able to work so, to see the
work grow under your hands. It is heartsome & encouraging, & it is all a matter of habit. After all any one can do it who gets in the way of moving her
fingers rapidly.

NOVEMBER 30, 1862

Have been from home almost all the week assisting to nurse Mama who,
poor Lady, has been quite sick with an attack of pleurisy or Pneumonia, the
Dr does not say exactly which. She was better yesterday, and I came home to
look after home matters a little but will go back tomorrow. Mr E & Capt Winder got home from Rainbow Bluff last Sunday, brother with them. The Confederate authorities are at work there & it is so much better a place than any
other on the River that Maj Winder thought the State had better not attempt
fortifying any other point. Mr E drew up a Remonstrance addressed to the
Gov of N C stating our resources & the madness of abandoning this portion of

the country to the enemy & winding up with a *protest* against "the novel manner" of defending a country adopted by Gen French, viz., destroying its product, which was signed by as many of the citizens of the county as could conveniently be got at & carried by brother to Gov Vance with a request that he would endorse it & forward to President Davis. I prefix a copy marked I.[289]

The enemy made a formal demand for the surrender of Fredericksburg, threatening to shell it within sixteen hours if not complied with. The Mayor represented that from 5 P M, the hour when he received the notice, to 9 the next morning gave but four hours of daylight in which to remove the women & children, when these gallant soldiers graciously extended the time, but will it be beleived that they in the face of that actually threw shells at a train filled with helpless women & little children who were flying from the certain death which awaited them. One poor lady had been confined only the day before & such was her terror at the shreiks of the frightened women & cries of the poor children that it agravated the already critical state in which she was & she was taken from the train it is feared in a dying state! Fortunately no one was hurt, but that does not lessen the fiendish act; it reflects only on the bad aim of their Gunners. Father's friend Mrs Fitzgerald, whose house occupies an exposed situation, finding that it was a target for their shells—they bursting in the yard & kitchen—walked out of it with some other ladies & little children in full view of the gunners, the gentlemen of the family remaining behind so as to leave no excuse for their being molested & yet tho there was no possibility of their being mistaken, after they left the house & were some little distance on the highway in plain and full view, women & children only, several shells were thrown at them, one bursting within a few feet of them. Was ever greater cowardice, more unmanly or baser conduct? They do indeed "war on woman & the dead." An agreement was afterwards entered into with the Mayor that if the Confederate army would not use it as a Depot from which to draw supplies that they, the Abolitionists, would refrain from the bombardment, but all the non combattants have left the place, so I suppose its fate will soon be sealed as they are no respecter of promises. Nothing else has been done this whole week.

Both armies have faced each the other on opposite sides of the River. Burnside cannot cross in the face of our army, as he would be cut to peices in doing so, so he too must "change his base." Many think that the next attempt will be by way of Suffolk, but it will take some time to transport such an army by water. We cannot tell but must await future developments. In the West things remain as they were, only we are concentrating our Army under Gen Joe Johnson, Bragg to be second in command. A storm of abuse is showered upon him for his conduct of the Campaign in Kentucky. Leading Kentuckians

---

[289]These articles appear in the second volume of the diary, pages 44-46.

denounce him in no measured terms. He is pronounced incapable of making the combinations necessary for the management of an Army—"a good Artillery officer but no general,"—& many other flattering speeches all of which are generally beleived to be *true*.

We had a visit from a Lieut with a squad of men to give us notice of Gen French's order to remove all the Cotton east of the R R by the 15th of Dec, as after that period it is to be burned. He named the 25th of Nov at first, but Mr Hill succeeded in lengthening the time to the 15th prox. This Lieut is to ride about through the country, find out where the cotton is, & make his report accordingly. He estimated ours unginned & in the field at 20 bales. Actually last week a Corporal of a Cav Company burned Mr Kearney Williams in his Gin House, Gin, seed, cotton, House & all, altho the overseer who was present with twenty or more hands begged him to wait until he could remove it. He refused & set the whole on fire & destroyed at the same time a lot of leather which Mr W had there—& this by Gen French's order! The country is roused with indignation against him & many do not hesitate to say that he is in collusion with the speculators who hope by this Order to force Cotton into Market, & in this connection they add that he is courting Miss Lucy Ragland, daughter of Ragland, the trader and Speculater in Petersburg, which he finds it pleasant to make his headquarters instead of a more central point where he would be nearer the enemy & could concentrate his troops against an advance with greater speed & readiness. So we go. A child ruled Rome through his mother, who ruled the Dictator! Miss Lucy Ragland carries our prosperity and our adversity, our weal or our woe, in her Vinaigrette, for I suppose she hardly owns a work basket. Les nouveau richesse rarely do. I wish she would make Petersburg a place of unpleasant remembrances to the gallant Gen. Let him feel "how hot her little foot is." May you go into partnership with Ragland & may the man of money make much out of you, is my kind wish for you, O Maj Gen French.

The first thing I have seen which even points to an end of the war is an article from the Herald which I prefix—marked J.[290] It does it but faintly; based, however, upon the depreciation of their currency & the stagnation of Trade consequent on the War tax, so as they have been two of our best hopes for the future it is encouring to see that they are beginning to act. He says Burnside must advance.

I sent up to the Qr Master at Raleigh by Maj Winder, who left us on Tuesday, 12 1/2 yds of double-lapped yarn cloth, 6 prs of homespun Drawers, 1 Woolen Shirt (fatigue), 1 blanket, 2 prs of socks. I am going on with my work & hope soon to have it done.

---

[290] The article was affixed to page 41 in the second volume of the journal.

DECEMBER 1, 1862

Walked with Patrick all through the town & saw the different plantation operations going on. The Tanning was the most important as Leather is an object now-a-days. Thanks to wooden soles we can comfortably shoe all our people without spending a cent beyond what they (the soles) cost us. Walked by the Hog-pen & saw in imagination my future Hams, which will some day grace our table. Very greedy are the present owners & any thing but tempting do they look at present. The Nursery children are better, but the Cough is a terrible one & they all are puny from it. Spinning, Weaving, & Shoemaking going on steadily. We are put to our trumps for cards & for Wool Cards have been forced to get Jim Crow's & combine two into one, Henry making a new frame for it. It does pretty well, a change from negro to sheeps wool.

In Onslow Capt New Kirk's Cavalry co (the same heavy looking man whom I used to see in Mr E's tent at Wrightsville & whose Company Patrick raised & organized as a Coast Guard) has Captured a Gun Boat, that is, the crew escaped after setting it on fire[291]—a blessing to us, for anything that destroys the prestige of these sheet anchors of the Abolitionists & brings the dangers of our narrow crooked Rivers home to them is a Godsend to us. Pray that many more may meet the same fate!

DECEMBER 2, 1862

Went to Fathers with Mr E on horseback & dined there. Mama better. Mary's boys are there for their Winter vacation. Tom Devereux came down also today. Not much news from the Army. Burnside has received some pontoon bridges with which assistance it is surmised he intends attempting a passage of the Rappahanock. Lee awaits him. An occasional shelling is the only break to the monotony on each side. We take many prisoners & if we beleived them would think badly of the Abolition Army, as all profess an intention to *desert* & say that they are sick of the War, but they are Cretans for lying.

The much talked of European Intervention is published at last & consists of a proposal from France that Russia & England should join her in a reccommendation to an *Armistice*. Russia opposes but says she will do as England decides, whilst that little man Lord Russel, with a pettiness almost incomprehensible even in him, declines & fills a sheet with his reasons which, Journal, I do not think enough of to record. The mountain has at last brought forth its mouse & a very small mouse it is!

---

[291]Capt. Abram F. Newkirk, commanding Co. A, Forty-first North Carolina (Third Cavalry) Regiment, and Capt. Zachariah T. Adams, commanding Second Co. G, Thirty-sixth North Carolina (Second Artillery) Regiment, captured the gunboat U.S.S. *Ellis* in the New River on November 24, 1862, after she had run aground. The crew escaped after removing "everything valuable from the vessel," but some of her arms were salvaged by the Confederates. Clark, *Histories of the North Carolina Regiments*, II, 770, 774; *Official Records (Navy)*, Series I, VIII, 233; Manarin and Jordan, *North Carolina Troops*, I, 272; II, 178, 181; Barrett, *Civil War in North Carolina*, 134-135.

Met brother on our way home, dismal as usual; is sure the cotton will be burned, "pack it instanter & sell it to the State at 16 1/2 cts," but how it is to be packed without bagging & why, if the State can *buy*, we cannot *hold*, passes my comprehension. I beleive it is all a game played for the Speculators & I fear the State is becoming one too, as if she can protect her own Cotton, why cannot she protect that of her sons also?—16 1/2 cts is too little for it, as it is 22 in Petersburg. The Col Comdg has issued an order directing the Cotton belonging to the State of N C to be exemped from the order. Now as the State desires & has sent out Agents to buy one million lbs of cotton, it seems to me that there is grave ground for aprehension, nay a firm beleif that we are sold to Speculation. If the State cotton is exempt, I do not see why that of Loyal citizens should be sacrificed. Brother is authorized to purchase one million pounds on State account & when I ask the reason he answers "because the State is more powerful than a single individual" and if that is not oppression and bad government, I do not know what is.[292] We have taken another Gun boat, in Craven County, captured the whole crew also—another lesson as to the perils of ascending our narrow crooked Rivers which will not I hope be lost upon the enemy.[293]

Thomas Jones has (Thomas Devereux brings the news) been paroled & is now in Raleigh, which is a great blessing. The villains went to Mr Newby's house in Perquimans a few days since with their faces blackened, shot Mr Newby's son dead, & then beat & abused the old gentleman terribly. Mrs Newby was so much alarmed that she fainted dead away. They then marched off one hundred negroes after helping themselves to what they wanted & left. Think of it. My blood boils! Mr. N. christian name is not given, but I greatly fear that it is Mr Frank Newby, the uncle of my late brother-in-law Mr Jones.[294] I have often in days gone by met him at his nephew's house. He was a wealthy, independant, & influential county gentleman, a dweller at home, and the thought of his being exposed to such outrages stirs every nerve and fibre in my body. How long—O Lord? How long?

---

[292] The Confederate government issued an order that in the event of Federal forces making raids in the interior of the South seeking cotton, tobacco, and naval stores, that these articles should be removed or burned to prevent their falling into Federal hands. Governor Vance instructed the state quartermaster, John Devereux, to buy 10,000 bales of cotton and store it as security for loans obtained abroad. In December, 1862, Devereux appointed agents in the biggest cotton-producing counties and instructed them to buy at a maximum price of 20 cents per pound until 10,000 bales of prime cotton were secured. Hill, *Bethel to Sharpsburg*, I, 351; Quartermaster Records, State Archives.

[293] A detachment of First Co. I, Tenth Regiment (First Artillery) North Carolina State Troops, commanded by Capt. John N. Whitford, captured a gunboat on Bay River in Craven County. *Raleigh Register*, December 3, 1862; Manarin and Jordan, *North Carolina Troops*, I, 137-138.

[294] Francis Newby's sister, Parthenia Newby, married William Jones and was the mother of Thomas F. Jones, Mrs. Edmondston's brother-in-law. Granberry Tucker Records.

December 3, 1862

Have nearly put my eyes out putting on a new black velvet collar to Mr E's coat, so I will try them no further than merely to say that Burnside does not yet attempt the passage of the Rappahanock & has not shelled Fredericksburg as he threatened. Continues to plant batteries and is strengthning himself at Port Royal, twenty miles lower down the River, where he has the unfailing Yankee adjunct to success—Gunboats! Rain all day.

December 4, 1862

Went to Hascosea with Mr E. A delightful day and I enjoyed walking about with him greatly. Walked through the New Grounds & down his secret ditch. It is wonderful how dry it has made the surface of the land. I walked dry shod where the water would even in ordinary times have been over my shoes—& yet it had rained all the day before! This drain is put down differently from the rest, a triangular peice being cut with a spade made for the purpose in the bottom of the ditch and simply covered with a slab or large chip like looking peice of pine, flat tile perhaps would be a better word, and the earth rammed upon it. The ditch is cut primarily deeper than ordinary. I fear it will fill up, but Mr E says not. It works beautifully now at any rate & does its task most effectually.

Came home to dinner & then packed some things to be sent to different friends, viz., three bags of hominy (2 bu in each) 1 do Navy Beans, and 2 of potatoes for Sister Frances; a basket with a round of spiced Beef, a ham, a bucket of Butter, a bottle of Cayenne Pepper, one do French Vinegar, some Apples, Navy Beans & Hominy, & a barrel of Sweet & Irish Potatoes & Turnips for Capt Haxall in camp at Garysburg; another a basket with a peice of collared Beef, some Sausage Meat, Cayenne Pepper, & Potatoes for Mr Charles T Haigh Jr,[295] son of our old friend of the same name, who is Sergeant Major of Evans Regt of Cavalry, also stationed at Garysburg; and a barrel of potatoes & one pr of socks for James at Drewry's Bluff—almost more than the waggon could carry. No news from the army but a rumour brought by some one who had seen a Northern paper that Burnside had been superceeded by Hooker. If so, most Christian Burnside, you must feel that a Democracy is a hard master but console yourself with the reflection that Republics are proverbially ungrateful & go and take a house opposite Maj Gen McClellan in N Y and near Gen Scot. Invite McDowell to join you & in a short time you may have a select circle of deposed Generals which "On to Richmond" has decapitated. Burnside cannot advance because the *mud* & roads prevent his receiving his supplies as rapidly as he needs them. We had a Cavalry Skirmish

---

[295] Charles T. Haigh, Jr., was sergeant major in the Sixty-third North Carolina (Fifth Cavalry) Regiment. Clark, *Histories of the North Carolina Regiments*, I, 119; Manarin and Jordan, *North Carolina Troops*, II, 373, 377.

near Snicker's Gap a few days since in which we were getting the worst of it when happily we were reinforced.

I prefix, marked L & K, an account of a horrible outrage on humanity perpetrated in Missouri by Gen McNeil—ten men for one is raising the Black Flag truly. I place next it, marked M, President Davis Retaliatory order to Gen Holmes, which will I hope put a stop to such conduct for the future. Then comes marked an account of the conduct of the Confederate soldier whilst in Maryland from the pen of one our enemies themselves & in juxtaposition the narration of an eye witness to the manner in which the Yankees comported themselves in N C during their recent foray into our country, marked N, which narrative is corroborated by one of the correspondants to the Boston press who accompanied the expedition, marked O. And finally Fernando Woods' summary of the causes of the present War, which acquits us I think thoroughly of all blame in the matter, marked P.[296]

DECEMBER 6, 1862

"All quiet on the Rappahanock." Burnside has put his Quarter Master & one other official under arrest for delaying his pontoon bridges and other means of transportation by which he says the difficulty of crossing the River is now increased ten fold! Mr Lincoln's Message[297] is published in our papers today and a weaker, worse written, bungling attempt at a State Paper never disgraced the archives. "Compensated Emancipation" is his Hobby, and he rides it John Gilpin[298] fashion—blindly, ignorantly. He proclaims it as ending the war, as the Chinese formally did their Lanterns in the face of an enemy, sounds it as they did their drums, Ging-Galls & Gongs, & expects, like them, that overcome by its sound of terror that the South will lay down their arms, return to the bosom of the Union, & permit themselves quietly to be despoiled of their property under the specious tittle of Compensated Emancipation. The logic by which he attempts to convince the Yankee mind that this hobby of his is to pay the war debt is particularly amusing. He gravely admits that "it is not so easy to pay *something* as it is to pay *nothing*" & then comforts them with the assurance that "it is easier to pay a *large* sum than it is to pay a *larger* one, and it is easier to pay any sum *when* we are able than it is *before* we are able." Most sapient, Mr Lincoln! We are, that is the "Loyal" portion of the South, to be paid in bonds for our slaves which are to be emancipated & live in Utopian felicity with their old masters. White labor is to rise, negro labor not to

---

[296] These articles can be found on pages 38 through 41 of the second volume of the diary.

[297] Mrs. Edmondston was referring to Lincoln's message to Congress on December 1, 1862, which prepared the way for his Emancipation Proclamation of 1863. Sandburg, *Lincoln: The War Years*, I, 618-623.

[298] *The Diverting History of John Gilpin, Showing How He Went further than He Intended and Came Safe Home Again*, a humorous ballad, was written by William Cowper in 1782. Gilpin, an inexpert equestrian, was trapped on a runaway horse which eventually circled back to where it had started. Benét, *Reader's Encyclopedia*, 564.

depreciate—in short we are all to live in the enjoyment of the most unbounded prosperity, North & South, pay our debts, especially the *War* debt of the North, if we will only accept Mr Lincoln's grand panacea, Compensated Emancipation. Were I a caricaturist, I would draw Mr Lincoln offering his bonds & promises to pay to the South, whilst she should stand off defiantly & ask with a significant gesture "Did you ever hear of *Repudiation*, Mr Lincoln?" Weather severe today. Would that our army was well provided against it. I knit a soldier's sock every day this week besides doing many other things such as dining out, going to Hascosea, putting a collar on Mr E's coat, making a night cap, etc.

DECEMBER 8, 1862

A sharp night & thick ice today. Went to Hascosea to put up my Dahlia Roots which have been delayed by other things. Put them all safely in barrels in the Potatoe house where all my demijohns & things that could freeze also found a refuge. Packed a keg of Dahlias & Tube Roses for Ellen Mordecai & Susan Rayner, a nail keg each for Thomas Hogg's children & Mrs G W Mordecai, sent a basket full to Mrs James Smith, & brought a basket full here to be sent to Mrs Dunlop in Petersburg. What a pleasure to have some thing to give!

DECEMBER 9, 1862

Went on Horseback to Father's & dined there. Went to see the Flax spinning & determined to have a wheel & spin our own myself. It is pretty work. No news from the army.

DECEMBER 11, 1862

No news from Va. Some successes in the West encourage us. Morgan is again at work, capturing & cutting off army and R R trains. Near Corinth also we seized a valuable army train. Butler growing more & more oppressive in New Orleans—has Regts of armed & uniformed negroes. Banks Expedition which has been so long fitting out in N Y has at length sailed, destination unknown, supposed to be James River & that Burnside waits for him when they will make a simultaneous attack.

DECEMBER 12, 1862

Went to Hascosea with Patrick. Walked all about & looked at his ditches, new grounds, and ash-burners. Transplanted some Grape vine cuttings but came home to dinner where presently to our great pleasure & surprise father joined us. He had been out to Scotland Neck where he learned that our troops under Lieut Col Lamb had marched down & captured Plymouth with forty of the enemy, killing & wounding thirty more. The town was partially burned[299] to prevent its affording shelter to the Abolitionists & run-away negroes in their train. I know not whether or not we can consider it good news or not, so much depends on the state of our defences at Rainbow Banks. If they are not mounted & suitably manned it may provoke Gen Foster into making another foray.

DECEMBER 14, 1862

Last night came the news of the commencement of the expected engagement at Fredericksburg. The battle of the Rappahanock, Lee reports, commenced at five o'clock a m on Thursday the 11th. The enemy attempted the passage of the River at three different points; at two they were repulsed, at the third under cover of their guns it is presumed they were successful as the Dispatch states that they could not be interrupted in their construction of a bridge. The carnage was frightful. We cut their pontoon bridge at one place & poured in grape & canister, & the air is described as being filled with "legs, arms, & disjointed members of the Yankees." Longstreet's Division it was which was principally engaged. No accounts of our loss. This from Friday's paper; Saturday's tells us that whether permitted or not by Gen Lee that the enemy crossed the River near the R R Bridge & marched into the town of Fredericksburg about seven o clock P M Thursday.

Sharp skirmishing in the streets for an hour or more when we relinquished the town. Many of the principal buildings in the town were fired & the place itself about half consumed. At dawn on Friday Gen Jackson moved forward from Guiney's Station towards Fredericksburg. The fire of musquetry was continuous throughout Friday, but the results were, when the paper went to press on Sat, unknown. It seems a fearful time to wait the slow moving hours until Monday night, as we can have no news until then, no paper being issued today (Sunday). It seems as tho I cannot bear the suspense. Mr E is downhearted & dejected at their occupation of Fredericksburg, but I hope for better things. I do not beleive in "a surprise." Lee has most probably allowed it, intending to cut them off in detail. I look with hope & confidence to the next news. I beleive it will tell a "flattering tale" but (an anomaly) a *true* one! God be with our soldiers, with our wounded, & our dying men. I could not sleep last night for thinking of them & as I listened to Mr E's regular breathing by my side my heart melted in grateful thankfulness that he was not exposed to the dangers and hardships of the battle field & that I was spared the torture of uncertainty & anxiety as to his fate which now agonizes the hearts of thousands of wives & mothers in this Confederacy. My God I thank

---

[299] On December 8, 1862, Lt. Col. John C. Lamb, commanding five companies of the Seventeenth North Carolina (Second Organization) Regiment, surprised the Federals at Plymouth, routed the garrison, and burned a portion of the town. *Official Records (Army)*, Series I, XVIII, 49; Manarin and Jordan, *North Carolina Troops*, VI, 201.

Thee! Be with our army, grant our soldiers *endurance*, & our Generals *wisdom*. May each man feel Thy presence, Thy aid, feel that he is indeed a soldier of the Cross, that under Thy banner he fights, fights for all that man holds dear.

Thomas Jones, who was whilst a prisoner carried to New Berne to be paroled, had an interview with Gov Stanly & was told by him that he intended imprisoning every man in N C who refused to take the oath so long as he had a place in which to imprison them. He represents the state of things in the North Eastern counties as dreadful in the extreme. Men are daily arrested & sent off, their families know not where, without any cause being assigned or charges preferred. The negroes are demoralized & have left their owners. One of his own, a boy by the name of Daniel who was given by my Grandfather to his Mother, came to see him & told him that the reason his negroes all left was that they were told that he was killed & that they were all to be sold. Just as he had done speaking, a Yankee came in & kicked him out of the room! Thomas comment to him was "There Daniel! you see what you are to expect." Daniel committed no offence to any one, but I suppose his crime lay in speaking to his master who was a prisoner and unable to protect him.

The affair at Plymouth was worse than we thought. Moore's Battery disabled a gun boat & sent it with what speed it could make in its crippled condition out of range—down the River.[300] The Yankees & negroes had taken shelter in the Custom House, a trick building, which they had pierced for musquetry & from which they fired upon our men. Capt Moore turned his attention upon it & in a few shot nearly battered it down over their heads. The loss of life was terrible, as several shells burst in the house. About fifty negroes were captured, amongst whom were four of Mr Urquehart's stolen in Fosters late raid upon us. Many negroes were killed. I hope their brethren will hear of it & that it will be a lesson to them how they leave home with their false friends.

The Small Pox I am sorry to say is spreading fearfully in Richmond.[301] It was introduced there from Fort Delaware by returned prisoners last Aug & has been silently spreading in our Hospital's ever since. The City Council of Richmond have made arrangements for compulsory vaccination & I wish the Government would issue like orders to every Colonel in the service—make each of them have a company per day vaccinated until it had gone through the army. Knit a pr of fancy Gloves for little Nelly this week. Have not been very industrious as I have not been well & was not at home the greater part of

---

[300] A segment of the Third Battalion North Carolina Light Artillery, "Moore's Battalion," helped disable the U.S.S. *Southfield* during the Confederate assault on Plymouth. *Official Records (Navy)*, Series I, XVIII, 275-282; Barrett, *Civil War in North Carolina*, 136.

[301] The *Richmond Examiner*, December 12, 14, and 22, 1862, described a smallpox epidemic as starting in the military hospitals and spreading to the civilian population. The issue of December 22 concluded the epidemic had reached a culminating point and was on the decline.

three days. No news of Banks Expedition as yet tho it has had time to reach James River, if that is its destination.

DECEMBER 16, 1862

No news last night to our infinite disappointment there being no mail. This suspense is most trying!, but *it must be borne*. One of our neighbors tells us too that he heard from Weldon that they were fighting at Kinston, & Samantha & her husband heard guns all Sunday. God give us the victory! We fight for home, for freedom, for independance; they for conquest & tyranny. The Raleigh papers tell us that an advance upon the Blackwater was threatened, 12 Yankee Regts having landed in Gates, supposed to intend a march across the country from Murfreesboro to Weldon, but that does not seem to tally with the advance from New Berne. Perhaps the Guns were at Wilmington. Banks Expedition may be destined for that point. This uncertainty is wearing; nothing, absolutely nothing, from the Rappahanock.

DECEMBER 17, 1862

Father's birthday—sixty nine today. Grant him many happy birthdays, O Lord, each more peaceful & calm than this, tho I was enabled to carry him good news as a birthday offering. We had no mail again last night, but this morning just after breakfast came Mr Price, a Government Agent who is buying supplies for the Army, for Patrick's Hay, & he told us that Capt Lucius Johnson[302] of the 17th Regt now stationed at Rainbow Banks came down on the train yesterday and says that there is no doubt that Lee has gained a victory on the Rappahanock, that Burnside advanced four times & was four times repulsed, & on the fourth driven back across the Rappahannock, and that Lee was in pursuit, Burnside killed & his body with us, but that must be a mistake, that Beauregard had telegraphed from Charleston that Banks expedition had sailed *North* from Port Royal supposed to be destined for a port in N C, that if they wanted 5,000 men he would send them on, that the advance upon Kinston was in force. Prisoners taken say they have 30,000 men. On our side we have 16,000. Gen Gustavus Smith in command, French, Pettigrew, Robinson, & Evans all under him. The prisoners above mentioned say that Foster thinks from the attack we made on Plymouth last week that we have a large force which he fears will out flank him if he marches on too rapidly, falling on his flank & rear from Washington, whilst he pushes on to Kinston. Blessed delusion!

I carried this good news, which after all is but rumour, up to father as a birthday offering & we waited in the most intense suspense for the mail to confirm it. Again to our infinite disappointment no mail came but a letter

---

[302] Lucius Junius Johnson of Perquimans County was captain of Co. I, Seventeenth North Carolina (First Organization) Regiment. Manarin and Jordan, *North Carolina Troops*, VI, 181.

from Mr McMahon containing what he was enabled to pick up from passengers on the train. They confirm the news of our victory—say that Burnside has been driven across the river and his troops entirely demoralized, for which O God we thank Thee! May our lives show forth Thy praise. Mr M also says that since Monday troops have been whirled by as fast as steam could carry them to Kinston, thirteen long trains heavily loaded having passed since then, that at one time the enemy had advanced to White Hall bridge within eight miles of Goldsboro on the Wilmington & Weldon R R, but that our troops being reinforced drove them back beyond Kinston which we retook & held, that it was beleived our force was sufficient to repulse and defeat them in that quarter. Again have we cause for thankfulness to God in thus bringing the plans of our enemies to confusion & rescuing us from a peril which seemed overwhelming. No mail again, Government having seized all the cars & the mail agents are willing I suppose to take a holiday. We must wait for details another day. One thing we may be sure of, that Lee must have greatly gained the better of Burnside or they would never send so many troops from Richmond & Petersburg. Daniel's Brigade from Drury's Bluff went down this morning, James I suppose with it.

DECEMBER 18, 1862

Today just before dinner came a brother of Capt Galloway[303] (who was wounded in the attack upon Plymouth) going down to see and care for him. I was glad I could give him some news of him, having inquired particularly of him from a member of Walker's Cavalry who staid here on Tuesday night. The poor man with a friend he had with him had lost his road and stopped here for "*rest & a guide.*" That, with "food & fire," he found & in return he gave us the news. He has *seen* Lee's dispatch announcing that he has driven the enemy across the River & that he has disappeared from his front. Says that Gens Maxy Gregg and St Georg Cook are killed. Gen Stuart has had a narrow escape, the ball grazing his neck. Gen T R Cobb who had been acting Maj Gen also killed. Jackson did his share of the fighting and was in the thick of it. No news from any of our N C troops. No more details—so it is true. Our suspense as to the fact is at an end & our hearts are filled with thankfulness!

Gave Mr Galloway some coffee for his brother, and Patrick invited him to bring him here for nursing until he should be well enough either to take the field again or to return home for entire convalescence. I hope he will come, for I long to do something for those who risked their lives in our defence & in that of our common sacred cause! He had no news from Kinston beyond what we had heard from Halifax, which he confirmed, & gave us the names of brigades

---

[303] John Marion Galloway, serving as captain of Co. D, Sixty-third North Carolina (Fifth Cavalry) Regiment, was seriously wounded during the attack on Plymouth in December, 1862. He later served as major of the regiment in 1865. Clark, *Histories of the North Carolina Regiments*, III, 529-531; Manarin and Jordan, *North Carolina Troops*, II, 372, 395.

which had gone down, viz., Robinson's (Cavalry), Pettigrew's, Daniel's, Evans's—besides troops from Wilmington & 5 000 from South Carolina—in all a stout force. I can scarcely write I am so anxious for the mail & to see the details of our successes & Ah! sad thought, the list of our wounded & our gallant dead!

DECEMBER 19, 1862

No mail again last night. Ah, this suspense is cruel. There must be papers, as Major Galloway & friend had both seen Wednesday's papers. Poor Mary, I do not know how she can stand it, for her husband is in Longstreet's Division which bore the brunt of the first day's engagement on Thursday, a week yesterday, & not a word from him. I should go on myself, "tho father & mother & all should go mad,"—for I know well that if I did not an Assylum would soon be my portion. I prefix an article on the "Cotton Burning Order of Maj Gen French" written by Patrick & which he published in the Standard.[304] He weilds a trenchant pen & the gallant Maj Gen if he has any sensibility will wince under censure so keenly expressed, satire so cutting. I mark it Q. On Sunday morning when our suspense was greatest and our anxiety for our Army well nigh overpowering, Patrick wrote a little prayer which we have since used in our family devotion. It expresses so entirely our wants & the one master wish of our hearts & minds that I copy it here in order to preserve it.

Prayer for our Army

O God, the Lord of Hosts, be with the Armies of our Confederacy, overshadow them with Thy Love, sheild them with Thy mercy, sustain them by Thy Power, succor the wounded, give deliverance to the prisoner, give Thy Peace to the dying, animate the souls of all with true courage, imbue them with Faith in their just Cause and a firm reliance upon Thee the God of Battles. Turn the hearts of our enemies from the lust of rapine & conquest and incline them to Peace & Justice or else enable us in Thy name & strength to drive the Invader & Spoiler from our Land. O! may Victory rest upon our Standards, and do Thou O Lord establish us firmly as a nation amongst the Kingdoms of the Earth in lasting Peace & Truth & Honour through Christ our Savior & Redeemer. Amen.

DECEMBER 20, 1862

No mail again today, but happily Father being in Halifax saw James Edmondston on the train & he gave him three papers of the day before. By them we learn that the Abolitionists have re-crossed the Rappahanock under cover

---

[304] This newspaper article signed "Roanoke Valley" appears in the second volume of the diary on page 37.

of their guns, unmolested by us. Where he will make his next appearance no one knows, probably at Suffolk via Fortress Monroe. The fighting has been severe about Kinston, the enemy repulsed & in retreat. A Cavalry force made a dash at the Wilmington & Weldon R R, tore up a few rails, cut the Telegraph wire, & attempted to fire the Depot but retreated without effecting it. The country is full of wild rumours about the burning of the R R bridge over the Neuse. I must beleive that it is the bridge at Kinston on the N C Road & not that at Goldsboro on the Wilmington & Weldon. The slaughter of the enemy at Fredericksburg is reported as terrible. They estimate it at 20,000 killed & wounded, so we hear via Norfolk. Ours is put down at 1200 (twelve hundred) & most of our wounded are slightly so, mostly in the limbs, many in the legs, which seems odd. Almost all their dead were struck in the head, which shows that our men are fine marksmen. Mary has received two letters from her husband. He is safe & the loss in his Regt small, which is a cause of great thankfulness to her. Her friend Mr Cook is wounded.

DECEMBER 21, 1862

The mail yesterday brought the Richmond papers from Monday to Thursday, the first mail we have had for a week! Details of the victory on Sunday. It is said by prisoners that Burnside ordered a renewal of the engagement, but it was met with such discontent by the men & remonstrances from the officers that he withdrew it & ordered instead a retreat across the River. Our loss is so small in comparison that we are ready for another attack at once. Gens Cobb & Gregg are killed, Cook wounded. Beyond these there seem few officers of any prominence, none published as yet that I know anything of. A Rumour reached Halifax on Friday that an attack had been made on Charleston, the battle commenced, but we do not credit it. The papers mention some shelling of our outposts on James Island & we beleive it to be a feint to draw off attention from the attack on Goldsboro & to prevent Beauregard's sending reinforcements to Evans. Another rumour has it that Banks is landing below Wilmington. We have no authentic news & are the prey to every wild report that runs like wild fire through the country. May God end this suspense in a glorious victory to us—every where!

DECEMBER 22, 1862

After writing yesterday came a note from Mama saying that father was too unwell to go to Halifax to attend to the weighing of his Cotton & wished Patrick to go for him. So we went up immediately & today Patrick went as father desired to Halifax whilst I came back home for a few hours to attend to some domestic matters which I had left unfinished. Saturday's paper gives but little news from the Rappahanock. The loss of the Abolitionists was terrible. They (non-officially) admit a loss of 20,000. Ours was very slight, both in dead and wounded, and most of our wounded are but slightly so, principally in the limbs. [———]covers our whole loss. The Northern papers raise a cry almost of despair, say "the best appointed army the world ever saw is reeling back from the Rappahanock, with the loss of 20,000 of its best soldiers." The enemy is in retreat from Goldsboro, committing the most terrible excesses. Their retreat is marked by a column of smoke rising from the houses and property they have destroyed. They burned the R R bridge on the Wilmington and Weldon R R and tore up the track for several miles and escaped without material loss towards New Berne. We claim to have had four engagements with them, but I do not think we could have inflicted much loss upon them. Mallett with 300 of the best troops we have was taken prisoner. Radcliff & a portion of his command also captured, whilst the injury to the road, tho not so great but that it can be soon repaired, puts us to serious inconvenience & loss. I think they had the best of it, but the published accounts are but meagre.

DECEMBER 28, 1862

Got home on Friday night from fathers where we spent our Christmas, a quiet time, no merry making or festivity, but a deep sense of thankfulness to Almighty God, for the deliverance he has wrought out for us pervades our hearts & gayety would be unfitting to the tone & temper of our minds.

The news of Burnsides repulse & retreat from Fredericksburg has fallen like an avalanch upon the North. "God help us" is the cry of the newspapers, "for vain is the help of man." They have found out that Lincoln "jests" have but little comfort in them, that their Secretary of War is a *"bungling Idiot,"* say that their President knows nothing of the state of feeling throughout the country & abuse their whole Cabinet, their Government, & their Generals in the most unmeasured terms. Burnside resigned his post as commander in Cheif of the Army of the Potomac & at one time it was rumoured in their papers that Fremont had been placed in command, but it was a mistake, as Mr Lincoln refused to accept Burnside's resignation and continued him in his position. A committee from a Caucus in the U S Congress waited on Mr Lincoln & demanded "a partial reconstruction of his Cabinet," whereupon Seward & his son, the Ass. Sec of State tendered their resignation, Seward refusing to stay in if Chase[305] and Stanton be kept in power. After a few days of imbroglio and discussion with the Committee & the Cabinet and a free expression of opinion all around which exemplified the old adage "when Rogues fall out Honest men get their deserts,"[306] Mr Lincoln once more "put his foot down

[305] Salmon Portland Chase (1808-1873), lawyer, United States senator from Ohio, governor of Ohio, and an outspoken opponent of slavery, became secretary of the treasury under Lincoln in 1861. He served in the cabinet until July, 1864, when he resigned, with Lincoln's concurrence, because of "mutual embarrassment in our official relations." When Roger B. Taney, chief justice of the Supreme Court, died in October, 1864, Lincoln chose Chase to replace him. *Dictionary of American Biography*, IV, 27-34.

[306] Sir Matthew Hale, "When rogues fall out, honest men get into their own." Kate Louise Roberts (comp.), *Hoyt's New Cyclopedia of Practical Quotations* (New York and London: Funk & Wagnalls Company, revised and enlarged, 1922), 371.

firmly" and declared that Congress should not dictate to him in the appointment of his Cabinet or His Generals, returned Seward & Son their portfolios saying that "it was compatible with the welfare of the public service that they should now resign." So the wheels of their Government turn on still, but the dissension & want of confidence disclosed & engendered make it sure that the reins cannot long continue in the same hands. Burnside writes a letter to the President taking upon himself the whole blame for the late disaster, exculpates Halleck, the President, & the Sec of War, dwells emphatically upon the fact (a new one to us that) "he came near success." Cold comfort & one to which he is always welcome from our hands. His official Report says his loss was 1152 killed & 9,000 wounded, considerably within the mark, my most Christian Maj Gen Burnside.

The thefts committed in the sack of Fredericksburg by persons who called themselves gentlemen are astonishing to us Southerns. Gen King, grandson of Rufus King & brother or cousin, we know not which, to Mrs Martin, boxed up a Lady's Piano & sent it home to his wife! Every thing they could carry off with them they took & what they had not transportation for they destroyed. Pictures, books, mirrors, china, furniture, everything in short, that could tempt cupidity or on which they could wreak their Vengeance. Nothing was spared. In order to conceal the number of their dead it said that they filled the Icehouses with them. Can it be true? One thing is certain—on their retreat they propped up their dead so as to make them look like sentinels & thus attempted to conceal the fact of their retreat. A party of Abolitionists landed last week in Gloucester county Va & insulted the Ladies, ordering them "to get their dinner, get them wine, etc., or they would blow their———rebel brains out." Here too they stole and destroyed indiscriminately.

At the West we have had a series of successess, small in themselves with one exception, but all tending to animate & cheer the spirits of our soldiers depressed by the retreat from Kentucky. Morgan has captured several government trains with supplies for the Army. Forrest & his Cavalry have not been idle, tearing up R R tracks, cutting Telegraph wires, seizing commissary supplies, & taking prisoners. Morgan has been captured himself, but by Hymen, as he was married recently by the "Rt Rev Lieut Gen Leonidas Polk to Miss Maggie E. Reedy."[307] A brilliant Honeymoon to him. Van Dorn has partially retrieved his losses at Corinth, for he made a dash at the Abolitionists at Holly Springs, killing and wounding many, taking fifteen hundred prisoners, bringing off as many stores as he could, and destroying provisions & forage collected for their use to the amount of one million dollars. We now hold Holly Springs.

---

[307] John Hunt Morgan (1825-1864), a widower, was married December 14, 1862, to Martha Ready, daughter of Charles Ready, at Murfreesboro, Tennessee, with Gen. (Bishop) Leonidas Polk officiating. The *North Carolina Standard*, December 31, 1862, observed: "Gen. J. H. Morgan, our noted Ranger, was married recently at Murfreesboro, Tenn., to Miss Mattie E. Reedy. Captured at last."

Leonidas Polk (1806-1864) was the son of Col. William Polk, a veteran of the Revolutionary War. He studied for the Episcopal ministry, was ordained a deacon in 1830, was named missionary bishop of the Southwest in 1838, and bishop of Louisiana in 1841. Polk was active in the establishment of the University of the South at Sewanee, Tennessee, in 1860. He was appointed major general in June, 1861, and was killed during the Atlanta campaign on June 14, 1864, at Pine Mountain. His death is discussed in the diary entry for June 17, 1864. Polk married Frances Devereux, sister of Mrs. Edmondston's father. (Photograph from Archives, Jessie Ball duPont Library, University of the South, Sewanee, Tennessee.)

In New Orleans under Butler's rule the state of things is most deplorable. Negroes rule the day & there is little more to be looked for when the 1st of January & its attendant emancipation day arrives. The Yankees themselves are ashamed of him. I prefix an extract, marked R,[308] from the World newspaper giving its opinion of him. Thus do they desert their heroes when they are no longer popular. A short time since, before the civilized world cried "shame" on him, who so great as Butler? He was held up as a model to their other *Union* generals! "The Loyal feeling" he elicited was quoted as an evidence that such conduct as his was the true way to restore their Vaunted Union & crush out the Rebellion. He was publicly applauded in their public

[308] The clipping appears in the second volume of the diary on page 36.

meetings amids groans for those of their Generals who had protected Southern property. But now that England, the mouth peice for humanity & refinement in the civilized world, has spoken—who so poor as to do him reverence? Out on such time serving hypocrites! Your condemnation now, O universal Yankee nation, cannot save you from a participation in his infamy. You are but the rogue who turns States Evidence against his accomplice. I also prefix, marked S, a statement of some of his acts of villany from the pen of one who has escaped from his reign, & lastly, the crowning act of all, I prefix, marked T, the Proclamation of our President declaring him a "Felon deserving of capital punishment" & ordering "that he be no longer considered or treated simply as a public enemy of the Confederate States of America but as an outlaw or public enemy of mankind & that in the event of his capture the officer in command of the capturing force do cause him to be immediately executed by hanging & further ordering that no commissioned officer of the U S—taken prisoner shall be released on parole before exchange until the said Butler shall have met with due punishment for his crimes."

This in Retaliation for the murder of Mumford & the other acts of oppression which President Davis most ably sums up. This is as it should be & the voice of the world will sustain Mr Davis in his action. The hanging of Mumford was a cold blooded deliberate murder and as such should be punished. The infamous Villain will not have, now it appears, the sympathy of his own nation. It is fashionable to abuse him, so now "Tray, Blanche, and Sweetheart bark at him." I beleive their meanness disgusts me as much as Butler's brutality!

The Northern papers now announce that Banks Expedition is intended for Texas & they are furious with Mr Chase for sending it there instead of to the James River. Some of them, however, contend that it is to rendezvous at Ship Island & is to attack Mobile, Banks superceeding Butler in New Orleans nous verrons. I hope that old Neptune will have somewhat to say to it & that Burnside will not be the only Yankee General who "stood like a Sea God, distinguished only by his Yellow Belt"!

Our President is still in the West cheering and animating our Army there, now under Gen Joe Johnston's command. He is said to be in fine health & spirits. God preserve & bless him. I wish I could see him, were it but for a moment.

Two years ago this week, for I think it was on the 21st, we heard on the cars between Wilmington & Florence of the secession of So Carolina! Two years ago only & what a life time has been compressed into them! What changes everywhere! Death, thou hast reaped a rich harvest since then! Dr Tennant, who told us of it, died by the hand of the invader and oppressor, died in defence of that land whose freedom he first announced to us. Papa, whose golden wedding we went to celebrate, was spared the anxieties & distress which this dreadful war would have brought on him, for he died when as yet but little blood had been shed, before we realized what oceans, what seas of it, were to deluge our land. Jessie this week writes me of the death of Mr Cameron the only guest present besides the Clergyman who was not our own family, a young man of excellent character and great usefulness. He will be much missed in Aiken. Dear Papa, I often think of him & how this war would have affected him. What an interest he would have taken in it! How keenly he would have felt for the wounded, how liberally would he have provided for their wants, & with what triumph he would have announced our successes, but God saw fit to take him from this world of strife & turmoil, to transplant him to a heavenly Kingdom where Wars & discord cease. He was gathered like a shock of corn when fully ripe into His own garner & tho' we feel the need of his support, the want of his society, we should not murmur or complain. "God will wipe all tears from their eyes,"[309] & he is spared ten thousand pangs which this inhuman war would have cost him.

The last news from the Abolition Army is that they were assembling in force at Bull Run. Whether they mean to try another advance into Va, or are on their way to Winter Quarters around Washington, as their papers advise, we are not informed; but as they are also at Dumfries, it seems to point to a retreat upon Washington. Gen Hampton captured an army train with Christmas delicacies for the officers of the Abolition Army. One case of choice Liquors was marked "A Christmas present for Gen Burnside." Our men enjoyed the good cheer & wished that many more such windfalls may be in store for them. A large quantity of stores were destroyed for the want of transportation which were in store at Dumfries when Lo, a few hours after he captured a long train of new & empty waggons on their way to be filled. Lemons, sugar, tea, coffee, choice wines, preserves & all the adjuncts of a Christmas dinner were for the time abundant in our camp.

In the Yazoo we have, by means of a newly invented Torpedo, blown up one of the best of the Abolition Steam Rams, the first authentic instance of the destruction of a vessel in that way.[310] The chamber is filled with shells which penetrate the bottom of the vessel & sink her immediately. We have seven soldiers here tonight on their way to join their commands below Williamston, 6 cavalry & an infantry soldier. My heart warms to them tho' I have not seen them. The overseer's house has been opened to them & Hopey gets their supper & breakfast, so they are as comfortable as if they were here at our house, & both parties like the separation, I warrant.

---

[309] Isaiah 25:8a. ". . . the Lord God will wipe away tears from all faces. . . ."

[310] The U.S.S. *Cairo* was blown up by a torpedo on December 12, 1862, while on a mission to discover and destroy torpedoes in the Yazoo River. Adm. David Porter, commanding the Mississippi Squadron, described the Yazoo as being full of torpedoes. In a letter to a subordinate, he emphasized his concern over the torpedo threat by warning that "No one must be allowed to handle these torpedoes or break them up until we know more about them." *Official Records (Navy)*, Series I, XXIII, 544-546, 567; *Civil War Naval Chronology*, II, 113.

Van Dorn's success at Holly Springs was greater than at first reported. He captured 1500 prisoners, killed & wounded four hundred, with a loss to him of *fifteen* men only. A large quantity of arms & ammunition were captured. Four Army trains with property to the amount of one million three hundred thousand dollars destroyed. Gen Grant the Abolition Commander made a narrow escape from capture! At Hartsville, too, the supplies & prisoners captured by Morgan are considerably more than that at first given. Eleven Commissioned officers taken by him have been placed in close confinement to be held so until the murder of citizens in cold blood by the Abolitionists is atoned for & the practice stopped. All things point to a system of Retaliation, neccessary it is true, but from which one turns in Horror.

The Abolitionists are concentrating their forces for an attack & we for the defence of Vicksburg. A bloody battle will soon take place there. Pray God give us the Victory.

December 31, 1862

The last day of the Year! An eventful one it has been. Pray God that the next may bring us Peace for a New Year offering! I have been busy finishing some little odds & ends of work which I had on hand, so as to commence afresh with the New Year, & beleive I have done. Let me see, I yesterday knit the last of thirteen prs of socks for the Qr Master at Raleigh, finished a pr of gloves for James Edmondston & another pr with fancy gauntlets for little Mary Coffin, and as I have a cold & troublesome cough think I will give myself a holiday, write in you, O Journal, bring up my correspondence, & only overlook the mending which I have going on in the next room, for tomorrow I am determined both my handmaidens shall set to work upon something *new*, if it is only for an augury!

The news from the West is stirring, a battle imminent at Murfreesboro. The Abolitionists advancing on our troops steadily & tho the Telegram makes a flourish about the spirits & confidence of our men, I do not like the aspect of matters. The name of our Commander is not given. I fear me it is *Bragg*. Our troops have been driven back with the loss of two guns. They were reinforced & ordered to occupy their first position at all hazards. This does not look like "*Victory*," but I wait in faith & hope. On Christmas Eve Gen Morgan captured Glasgow, Kentucky, drove out the Abolitionists with great slaughter, burned all the bridges between Mumfordsville & Elizabethtown, & destroyed fifteen Miles of the R R the next day, went on to Gallatin & again blew up the R R Tunnel which the enemy have been months in repairing. This will embarrass Buel & Grant & perhaps compel them to evacuate Nashville, for we can cut off their wagon trains. At Vicksburg the enemy landed 25,000 men about seven miles above the town and attempted to drive us from our position. We repulsed them three times with the loss to us of thirty six killed & wounded to three hundred & fifty on theirs, besides many prisoners. At the third repulse we left our position & drove them back to their Gun boats. Names of Commanders not given on either side. Not Lovel however. He at last accounts "awaiting orders." Long may he wait! & I only wish he had Pemberton to keep him company. A couple of fortune seeking Yankees, they have no business to be in command over Southern Gentlemen!

From Norfolk the accounts of Gen Dix's tyrany bids fair to rival Butler's. He has ordered an election for the U S Congress & says every one who is entitled to vote but who declines "performing their duty as citizens by voting under this Proclamation" were to be regarded & treated "as hostile to the Government & subject to all the penalties of disloyalty." He has also issued another Order which says that "provision has been made for the introduction into the District of such commodities as may be neccessary for the subsistence of the inhabitants. Any person attempting to smuggle any portion of those commodities into the Insurgent States shall be put to hard labour in Fort Norfolk." He goes on with a tissue of lies, alike insulting to the honour and commonsense of the people of the unfortunate counties under his controul.

On election day no returns were received from Isle of Wight, Windsor, or Smithfield. The ballot box was sent by Lieut Col B F Underwood of the N Y Mounted Rifles with a detachment of Cavalry to the "rebellious sections" before named (Isle of Wight, Windsor, & Smithfield). He had sent the precious ark of freedom as far as Smithfield & was about visiting other places when he was set upon by an overwhelming rebel force & had a hard race to Suffolk, so says the N Y Tribune's Suffolk correspondant. A few votes only were polled in Suffolk. They have not heard from Norfolk or Portsmouth, but I hope a like disappointment awaits them there. Gen Dix winds up with a solemn assurance "that the cities of Norfolk & Portsmouth will never be surrendered to the insurgents; that the Government of the U S will retain possession at all hazards"—etc., an assurance which when you wrote it you knew to be false, O most wily Yankee. Maj Gen Dix, you are a charlatan, a getter up of scenes, but you will never set the Elizabeth River on fire with your genius or gain the character of an honest man whilst you talk such empty balderdash!

The citizens of Norfolk have much to endure and after tomorrow much more is I fear in store for them. A lady of Norfolk recently sat on her piazza & observing an Abolition Officer with a female coming up the street she turned her parasol so as to shut herself off from their view, when instantly the woman ran up the steps of the Portico & slapped her on the face, thereby proving most conclusively to my mind that she was what I suppose the lady took her for when she interposed the parasol—*a woman without character*! But think of such outrages as that being borne! Gen Dix in his order says that "No person excepting those who have taken the oath of allegiance will be permitted to carry on any traffic within the Department." What a kind lenient fatherly Government it is! How it wins men back into its arms! "Come to me my children, come to me & be taxed, give me all you have, or stay away and be starved!' ''

The only news from the Rappahanock is that Stuart is absent on an important & secret business & that heavy firing of musquetry was heard for an hour the day before in the direction of Dumfries, followed by columns of dense smoke from which it was inferred that he had attacked & destroyed some of Burnside's Army trains. The Peace feeling gains ground at the North; even Greely cries out for it & says let the South go, but the extreme Abolition party in Congress, in the face of it, are attempting to pass a bill organizing ten Negro Regts for seven years, providing them with schoolmasters, chaplains, etc. A high compliment they pay their own troops truly. They admit that they cannot crush the rebellion, but they expect, it seems, Cuffee to do that for them which they confess is beyond their own power. Banks is to superceed Butler in N O. He commences by ordering disbandment of the Negro Regts. So much for Europe, or perhaps they have found out that Cuffee wont fight. He is afraid of cold iron & a shot terrifies him. Shame on such deceitful policy! All things to all men is the mottoe of Lincolndom. Shame! Shame!

I have been reading some of the first parts of my Journal today, and it comes over me with a sense of sadness to see how changed its tone is. How few are the records of my domestic, my daily life, in comparison now to what they were then! War! war! it absorbs all my thoughts my anxieties my interests! For instance this week Mr E has been most busy in the construction of an Ice House down here on the Plantation, the War having rendered ours at Hascosea useless. For even with Peace we will never care to fill it with Northern Ice & it is too remote from a pond to fill it in any other way. So we will try one here near Beaver Dam Swamp. Patrick has worked early & late upon it & tho all that concerns him interests me, not one word have I spoken of him. I do not deserve the nice Wild Ducks he has shot for my New Year's dinner!

I have not even told you, O my Journal, of them. He sent seven up to Raleigh last week to Margaret. She having a little dance for the young folks on Christmas Eve, he thought they would be a fine addition to their supper. We were invited to said dance & had a faint notion of going but expected company at home which this Yankee foray upon Goldsboro disappointed. But heigh ho! dances do not seem to suit us just now. Young folks ought to have their sugar plums when they can enjoy them & they ought not to be depressed & care worn with anxieties which they cannot lessen, suffering & pain which they cannot alleviate, but for older people who look life in the face, who cannot shrink from its responsibilities or throw off its duties & before whom the future stands in dread, stern earnestness, presenting a cup that they know they must drink, even though they take it in Faith & with a hopeful smile, trusting that a Father's hand will sweeten its bitterness. Still it is a solemn, an awful thing, this unknown *future*, when the *present* is so dark & dreary, dancing

& merry making jar on the heart & feelings & come as ill timed to ears which sympathize with the groans of the wounded & dying. And yet it is right! Far be it from me to blame my sister-in-law for the exertion, for I know it must be such to her thus to please her children, but I have no children & from the sacrifice is not demanded so I consult my own pleasure and stay at home.

I this week have commenced gardening for another year, sowed Early Hotspur Peas & Spinach. I never once told you, Journal, of the nice Princess Alice Strawberry & New Rochelle Blackberry Plants Mrs Dunlop sent me three weeks or more ago. That was crowded out by war's alarms. Neither have I told you of the new interest I am taking in my Dorking Fowls. How I have three in this Yard, Knickerbocker, Mrs Maitland, & her daughter, whom I have not yet found a name for, & their nice warm house heated by a pipe from the Kitchen chimney which I call Sleepy Hollow. Then in the upper fowl yard is the Patroon and his Hens, in the lower one "Joe Johnson" & his family, whilst at Hascosea I have Lord & Lady Baltimore & Miss Calvert in one family and Stonewall Jackson & his in another. I expect to do wonders in the Egg line but never to rival that never-to be forgotton Shanghai flock, Becky, Dame Durden, Uncle Ned, etc., who laid in six months (19 Hens) one hundred & ten dozen Eggs!

Well the year is at a close—full of blessings it has been to us. How many mourn the loss of near and dear friends, parting with whom has given them a taste of the bitterness of Death itself, whilst we in our persons & our friends have all been spared. How many are cast down from affluence to poverty, whilst as yet we are untouched by the hand of the spoiler. How many eat the bread of exile & dependance, whilst we dwell at home "under the shadow of our own Vine & our own Fig tree." My God, I thank Thee! May my life this year show forth Thy praise.

1863

New Years Day 1863

Sue came down and dined with us today, and we had a quiet chat over our glove knitting. I had long promised her a Goose, her favourite bird, & today I had one which had hung to a turn. Patricks Wild Ducks too came into play and it being New Year, I indulged in now the unwonted luxury of a Pudding, for with sugar at 87 1/2 to $100 a lb, and with so many calls upon us as we have, I do not think it right to visit the sugar barrel every day. A dinner of four courses is, as Sue remarked, a rarity now–a–days, but New Year must have a new face to welcome it.

The most important news last night was from Vicksburg, where we have again repulsed the enemy. At Murfresboro all things remain as they were, a battle imminent but as yet the opponents have not crossed swords. The Yankee rule is even more severe in Western than in Eastern Va. I prefix marked V[1] a number of orders from Milroy, the tyrant now reigning, and one of his German subordinates, one Keiffer which will show better than I can give the state of things there. I just remark en passant that Milroy, as usual with his nation, lies in his order most bare facedly. The U S Congress have not yet admitted the "State of Western Va" into the U S. A motion is before Congress to that effect but their Attorney Gen Bates[2] pronounces it *unconstitutional* & even Mr Lincoln has the grace to say that if they pass it he will not sign it. But with Gen Milroy the end, I suppose, justifies the means; so, after calmly assuming as fact what he knows to be fiction, we need not be astonished at the second Machiavalli-like falsehood which follows, viz., that North Western Va has sent 20,000 men to the service of the U S Government to assist in the suppression of the Rebellion. Truth! sweet maiden! where hast Thou fled?

One anecdote of Lincoln I must record, it is so intensely characteristic. The Marquis of Hartington,[3] eldest son of the Duke of Devonshire, at present in Richmond was recently in Washington & was presented by Mr Seward (who had been entertained by his father when in England) to the President. His Excellency, not catching his name, said "What name did you say Sir?" "The Marquis of Hartington," repeated Mr Seward. "Well I declare," said the polished Abraham, "Well I declare that rhymes with Mrs Partington." It is supposed that Mr Seward fainted at this brilliant & well bred speech of his "chef" and was carried out in a comitose state! What a blessing that our exponent, our head, is a *gentleman*, a man not only of good sense but of good

---

[1]These orders appear in the second volume of the diary on page 34.

[2]Edward Bates (1793-1869) of Missouri held numerous minor political offices as well as serving in his state legislature and the United States Congress. He was the attorney general of the United States from 1861 until 1864. Boatner, *Civil War Dictionary*, 50; *Dictionary of American Biography*, II, 48-49.

[3]Spencer Compton Cavendish (1833-1908), eighth duke of Devonshire, known until his father's death in 1891 by the courtesy title of Marquis of Hartington, visited the United States in 1862. "Devonshire, Spencer Compton Cavendish, 8th duke of," *Encyclopaedia Britannica* (Fifteenth Edition).

breeding. But Journal I will not begin the New Year by being to chatty to you. Suffice it to say that we wound up the old year with all the customary honours, had our Egg Nog and the attendant good wishes from the servants as they took it, with the additional one that before this year was out the war would be over. Mr E wished them Happy New Year, Good Luck, and death to the Yankees, which done they retired glass in hand. We drank ours & saw the last of 1862.

JANUARY 2, 1863

This morning before our breakfast came a note from Col Leventhorpe C S A, the Col who placed Mr E in command of the defences of the Roanoke River last winter, telling him that he (Col L) had been ordered by Gen French to look after the defences of the River & he very much wished that Patrick should join him and be with him tomorrow—that he should wait at Mr Tillery's for him this morning. The note closed with a most ominous sentence to the effect that all things indicated a speedy attack upon Weldon and that "in fact there was no time to lose"—a knell to our peace but our trust is in the Lord. He will not suffer "thy foot to be moved & He that keepeth Israel shall neither slumber nor sleep."[4]

JANUARY 3, 1863

Last night after tea as I sat reading the papers most unexpectedly I heard Patrick's foot on the door step, for I had not expected him before Sunday at the least. He found Col Leaventhorpe waiting for him at Mr Tillery's and together they proceeded to select such points of defence upon Tillery's and Haile's Millponds as Col L deemed it advisable to fortify in case of an advance upon Weldon via Tarrboro. Col L. requested him to lay off the defences but this he declined as not holding a commission whatever he should do would not only excite criticism but bad feeling in the Army, a feeling, too, which might reflect upon Col L, but proposed to him to send to Hamilton and obtain the services of Lieut Bender C S A[5] on duty at that point. Col L saw the force of his objection but assigned to him the superintendance & erection of the works after Lieut Bender should lay them off. He then went on to Halifax with him where he received the neccessary orders & they parted. Today he sent for Lieut Bender who may be here tonight. Col Leaventhorpe aprehends that the attack upon Weldon will be made from the Chowan across the country & is most desirous of having works constructed on Pottacasey Swamp in Northampton to intercept their advance. The last news is "that Albemarle Sound is filled with transports," where bound we cannot tell. The paper

[4]Psalms 121:3-4.

[5]Lt. W. G. Bender was under orders to aid Gen. Walter Gwynn in the construction of river defenses in eastern North Carolina. Clark, *Histories of the North Carolina Regiments*, IV, 415.

yesterday published an official dispatch from Gen Bragg dated Murfresboro Dec 31st. As it is short I will copy it.

> Murfresboro—Dec 31st 1862
> We assailed the enemy at seven o'clock this morning, & after ten hours hard fighting have driven him from every position except his extreme left where he has successfully resisted us. With the exception of this point we occupy the whole field. We captured four thousand prisoners (including two Brigadier Generals, thirty one peices of Artillery, & some two hundred waggons & teams. Our loss is heavy, but that of the enemy is much greater.
>
> Signed   Braxton Bragg
> Gen Comdg

There! That is the New Year's Gift presented by our brave soldiers to the country. We thank you, gallant men, thank you from the bottom of our hearts & a nation mourns for those sacrificed on their country's altar.

We await the next news most anxiously. If Rosencrans succeeds in rallying on his "extreme left," and if there are any reinforcements to strengthen him, he may pluck the victory from our grasp, for he outnumbers us greatly, but I hope for better things. Gen Joe Johnson has effected wonders already in the West by organizing & massing the troops in the field. The men were there with arms & munitions & well provided but they lacked a head, a leader able to combine, to manoevre an Army. Bragg is a good Division Commander, nothing more, & it is wrong to place him in a position for which he has not capacities. Van Dorn, a good Cavalry officer, but he needs a head to tell him what to execute. The same may be said of Stuart who is a brave & brilliant executive commander, but without Lee to plan his expeditions, make his combinations for him, & thus ensure his success we should often mourn over instead of triumphing in his acheivements. So say those who know the man and judge him from an impartial standpoint. News from the expedition in which he is now engaged tell us that he has been on the line of the enemies communications between Falmouth and Alexandria. From the neighborhood of Occoquan he has sent back three hundred prisoners, dispersed the enemy's cavalry, & was within twelve miles of Alexandria. He has cut off several wagon trains and destroyed Comissary stores to what amount does not as yet appear. The enemy have made a successful foray upon the Va and Tennessee R R; a body of Cavalry, about 4,000, made a rapid desent upon the Road between Jonesboro, Tennessee, & Bristol & burned the bridges over the Holston & Watauga rivers, tore the track up in many places burning the sills & iron. The inconvenience & loss to us will be very great as the distance between the two bridges is nine miles. So this much of our R R communication is cut off for some weeks. At Blountsville on the Holston the bridge was guarded by 200 of our Cavalry who were surprised & captured. Bad management or carelessness somewhere!

Our loss in the battle of Fredericksburg as official[ly] stated is 500 so slightly wounded that they are not in the Hospital, 500 prisoners, 400 killed, 2,600 wounded—total four thousand. Compare this with Burnsides official dispatch 1152 killed, 9000 wounded. He says nothing of his prisoners which were many, but I have mislaid the slip containing the no. Gen Bayard was of the no. killed, said to have been a good officer & he ought to have been a gentleman for he comes of gentle blood. We have in the dim distance a common ancestor, my Grandmother on my Mother's side being descended from one of two brothers who came to this country with the Knickerbocker's & patented a large part of the Island of Manhattan, whence my Mother derived her title to her New York City property and we our claim to the Corporation Cellars (much good will it do us!). The other brother went to Delaware & from him Senator Bayard & this General are descended.[6] They claim to be of the lineage of the Chevalier, tho how they prove it I am at a loss to tell. Perhaps by the coat of arms, "A Horse Rampant," or as we in our childhood's days used to call it on some old plate which my mother had inherited from our grt grandfather, a "Rearing" or a "Rear up Horse." Shade of Bayard! has it come to this, that that crest which you bore unstained through many a bloody field (if indeed it be thy crest) is soiled, stained, polluted by being displayed on such a field, in such a cause? Where is that chivalric devotion to woman? That knightly honour which gave thee thy tittle of "sans peur & sans reproche"[7] when he who claims to be thy descendant is found in the service of a nation who outrages woman & makes war upon children—the fellow soldier & comrade of a wretch like Butler.

I preserve some choice excerpts from the President of the U S's last message—in order that in future I may not convince myself that its folly and absurdity are myths, fictions with which we at one time amused ourselves.[8]

A few days since had a letter from Amo; he has, unsolicited by himself or his friends, been appointed Assistant Professer with the rank of 2d Lieut in the Military Acadamy of the State of South Carolina with a salary of $1,000, this a high honour for one so young barely twenty one and is a source of great pride & gratification to us. The pathway to honour & usefulness is now open

---

[6]Gen. George Dashiell Bayard (1835-1862), formerly an instructor of cavalry at West Point, enlisted in the Union army in 1861. His brother, Thomas Francis Bayard (1828-1898), was a noted lawyer and United States senator from Delaware from 1869 through 1885. He served as secretary of state under Grover Cleveland and from 1893 until 1897 was the ambassador to Great Britain. Their father, James Asheton Bayard (1799-1880), and their uncle, Richard Henry Bayard (1796-1868), were both lawyers and United States senators from Delaware, as well. Boatner, *Civil War Dictionary*, 52; *Concise Dictionary of American Biography*, 57.

[7]French, "without fear and without reproach."

[8]This clipping is in the second volume of the diary on page 38.

to him. God grant that he may have strength & endurance to march steadily on in it.[9]

I forgot to mention in its place, I see by looking back, that the appointment to the Colonelcy of the Regt of Unattached Companies of Cavalry had been given last month to Gen French's favourite Lieut Baker—a more rank peice of favouritism never disgraced any Administration, for putting Patrick's qualifications entirely aside, Mr Baker is notoriously unfit for it, so much so that Gen French has expressed a desire to find some good officer whom he could appoint Lieut Col to make up for Baker's deficiencies. The day after his Commission was issued came a Telegram from the War Department ordering its stoppage in the name of the President, but it was too late, he had already received it & it could not then be taken from him until he had proved his incompetency. Gen French offered Patrick the Lieut Colonelcy, but being in nomination by Gen D Hill for the Colonelcy he declined it. At any rate, poor fellow, he has paid for his honours dearly already, for in a skirmish below Kinston a few days after the Commission was bestowed on him he had the misfortune to lose one of his ears, whether by shot or sabre I did not hear. So Mrs Edmondston it is well for you that you did not repine when your husband was disappointed, for perhaps the aim of the Yankee might have been surer & the ball might have passed through your darling's head. We none of us know what is good for us. Why cannot we be always content to leave it to God without a murmur?

Oh! for news from Murfresboro, of the discomfiture of that obstinate (why not say gallant, Mrs Edmondston? You know that is the term you would apply to them were they Confederates!) left wing! How exacting we are! We treat our good fortune very much as a little boy I heard of recently treated his Grandmother. For being asked by a lady who had brought him a package of sweeties from her, "What shall I say to your good Grandmother for sending you such nice sugar plums?," answered with his mouth full of them, "Tell her to send me some more." Whilst one gift still lies untasted in our grasp we say "Send me some more." But it is *Peace* we want! Peace, that glorious goal, to attain which all our efforts are bent, & that only will satisfy us. News from Vicksburg to the 30th; the enemy had again attempted to storm our lines but were repulsed with heavy loss—no particulars beyond that our loss was fifty killed & wounded. Mr E considers that the most important point of the War. Grant that we may hold it.

JANUARY 4, 1863

News last night of a complete victory at Murfresboro. Gen Bragg says "the enemy has yeilded his strong point & is falling back. We occupy the whole

---

[9]Amory Coffin, Jr., graduated from the Citadel Academy in 1862 and was thereupon elected assistant professor of drawing with the rank of second lieutenant. John P. Thomas, *Historical Sketch of the South Carolina Military Academy* (Charleston: Walker, Evans and Cogswell, 1879), 42.

field & shall follow him. Gen Wheeler with his Cavalry has made a complete circuit of their army. He captured & destroyed 300 of their waggons loaded with baggage & commissary stores & paroled seven hundred prisoners. He is again behind them & has captured an ordnance train. Today we secured several thousand stand of small arms. The body of Brigadier Gen Sill was left on the field. Three others reported killed. God has granted us a happy new Year."

signed Braxton Bragg

The newspaper dispatches tell us in addition that we have captured four thousand prisoners including Gens Willing & Fry, thirty one peices of artillery, & two hundred waggons & teams. The loss is heavy on both sides, much heavier on theirs. We have lost Brigadier Gen Rains killed & Gen Chalmers wounded, Colonel Fry of Mississippi killed. The Yankee Generals Shradon [Sheridan] and Grierson reported killed & (good news) the wretch McCook wounded, but this lacks confirmation. I do not know any of the officers on our side who are reported killed, so I will not record them. Lieut Gen Polk was on the field & displayed, as did Gen Bragg also, great judgment and heroism. There is no doubt but that we have gained a splendid victory! Ah! that we now reap the fruits of it! How can we ever be grateful enough to our Almighty Father who has thus blessed & rescued us! For had we been beaten, Tennessee would have been lost to us as Kentucky is & the Mississippi Valley been open to them, for they could then have massed troops on Vicksburg & overwhelmed us.

Gen Stuart has returned safely from his expedition, but I have already given most of the fruits of it on another page. It is all confirmed with the addition of an immense amount of Army stores & waggon trains destroyed by him, especially at Anandale a point seven miles only from Alexandria where in addition was a Depot of Army & camp equipages. From thence he telegraphed to the U S Quartermaster at Washington "that if he did not furnish more transportation to the Army of the Potomac that Gen Stuart would cease to look after it"! Curses loud and deep followed that Telegram, I warrant.

The 290—Alabama—Captain Semmes has captured a California Steamer. Got no gold, however, only a small amount in silver & 300 in Treasury notes.[10] Instead of destroying her, however, he bonded her in the sum of $125,000 & her cargo & freight for $135,000 to be paid to the Confederate Authorities within thirty days after the establishment of the independance of the Confederate States. I fear me that bond will not be redeemed. The Punic faith of the Yankee is too notorious. He has recently burned two valuable

---

[10]The ship captured on December 7, 1862, was the *Ariel*, a vessel of the regular California line. *Richmond Examiner*, January 4, 1863; *Civil War Naval Chronology*, II, 112. A list of ships captured by the *Alabama*, totaling twenty-two, appeared in the *Raleigh Register*, November 15, 1862.

vessels & cargoes in addition to those I formerly mentioned, one an East Indian, the other a Whaler.

Last night after we had gone to bed came Dick home from his expedition after the Engineer & with letters from Col Martin for Col Leaventhorpe. Lieut Bender cannot come just now as the Fort he is constructing needs his presence, so after all it is not done & we are still open to the enemies' land attacks as well as to the River ones. Col Martin writes that he has just received news from Plymouth. The enemy strengthing both Gun boats & infantry there, five Gunboats being reported in the River, at Washington two Gunboats, & they have refused to buy any more produce from the country people which looks like an evacuation of the town, but of that nothing is known. The Yankee papers say that Gen Prince is assigned to an important command in N C. He has been a prisoner in our hands once. I hope he may soon meet the same fate again. The Examiner published yesterday a statemen signed by Bishop Lay of Arkansas & eleven others, citizens of Huntsville, Alabama, detailing the treatment they experienced at the hands of Gen Mitchel, late U S Commander of the district of North Alabama. It is too long to record here. Suffice it that it is a tale of oppression & outrage, now alaas so common under Abolition rule that I do not know that I should have alluded to it but for the closing sentence in which they say that this infamous Gen Mitchel "boasted to a Southern woman that the North could overwhelm us with 500,000 armed men, who would ask no other recompense than the privilege of occupying our lands & ruining our daughters." Civilization! where is thy blush! Can it be beleived? & yet Bishop Lay[11] is an ordained bishop of the P Episcopal Church & these others are said to be gentlemen of Huntsville. There is publised by the authority of the Government a tale of outrage & horror perpetrated here in N C by two Yankee troopers before which the atrocities of the Sepoys in India pale. Death to every woman at the South! Death! welcome Death! before such dishonour!

JANUARY 5, 1863

Walked yesterday with Mr E to see the Ice House & very promising does it look, dark & cool & gives one an anticipation of Ice creams & Sherbet in the hot days of July & Aug. Heard distinctly the report of two heavy guns in the direction of Weldon. The boom was unmistakeable. I hope it was but for practice to our gunners. They have "Long Tom" & "Laughing Charlie." There two notable guns captured from the enemy, the first at the first battle of Manassas, the second I beleive before Richmond. What a sad solemn sound it is! The deep toned roar! This note of horrid War which comes booming over the peaceful fields & through the still quiet swamps & woods, awakening

---

[11]This episode is described by Bishop Lay in his diary for 1862-1863. Henry Champlin Lay Papers, Southern Historical Collection.

echoes which until now have slept to all save peaceful sounds. It makes the blood tingle through ones veins & brings the war home to our very thresholds.

Went today with Patrick to Hascosea, he on farming bent, I on gardening. Commenced transplanting Grape Vine cuttings. Find that eight of the cuttings which Mr E brought from Wrightsville Sound, & which in honor of the State where they originated we call "The Old North State," have taken finely. This is a native Grape, said not to be inferior to Black Hamburg. If so it may yet make its name in the world. Coming back as we stopped to let the horses drink in the stream at the Mill, Mr E grew eloquent in the praise of Running Water, thought if he had his choice to be any one inanimate thing it would be a running stream, strong, swift, exhaustless, always in motion, an emblem and type of purity and energy, sweeping along through sunshine & shade until it loses itself in the ocean of eternity. I beleive I differ. I would be a tree, broad, umbrageous & lofty, anchored deep in the Earth, throwing my branches up to heaven, a refuge & a shelter to all who sought my shade. An Undine is too cold, too ethereal, too pulseless for me. I would be a Hamadriad, inhabiting one spot, a spot around which should cluster all the associations of home. But what folly to fill you O my Journal with the fancies & follies which amuse us for the passing moment. Have you forgotton, Madam, what is the price of paper, that there is a Blockade, & that a Yankee General taken prisoner by us said in derision of our home made letter paper, whity brown, or rather browny-white for the want of chlorine to bleach it, that "The Southern Confederacy had not yet arrived at the dignity of White paper," that you are thus discursive?

JANUARY 6, 1863

Went again to Hascosea, this time by myself. Finished my Grape cutting & attacked the Peach tree borer. Was hard at work following him up all the morning with pen Knife & boiling water. He is a sore pest. Would that I understood his habits, his likes & dislikes better. One thing is certain, that Sulphur does not revolt him, for I found him plentifully in the tree from whence I thought I had expelled him last summer, under bark which smells even now, after all the fall rains, like Pluto's dominions, he seemingly careless of his surroundings. I destroyed immense numbers of a small white thread like worm which filled the gum which has exuded from the trees. Whether it is my enemy under a new form or some other perhaps harmless grub I cannot say. If so they suffered for being in bad company. The trees are full of them (the borer) now. Perhaps by following him up with hot water every month in the year I may destroy him, but it is a ceaseless labour. The price of Peaches will be similar to that of Liberty at this rate, "Ceaseless vigilance."

Came home & found Mr Price here buying Mr E's forage for Government. He, Patrick, has had a quantity of Hay & Shucks baled, for which the Government gives him 1.50 a hundred. Mr P brought the rumour that

Nashville is in our possession. I cannot credit it. Troops are being stationed all along the Wilmington & Weldon R R, so as to be concentrated upon any point the enemy may attack. I hope it will not be at a point near us. What selfish creatures we are! Have been much interested trying to dye some yarn to knit Col Leventhorpe & Gen Hill some gloves, but mordants are so scarce that I find it hard to get the right colour. Sweet Gum & Cedar tops with Alum makes a greenish olive, unfit for gloves. Sweet gum & Sycamore bark, a light brown & even when set with Muriatic acid too yellow—so I added Logwood—then treated with the same acid, when Lo! I had a crimson! Sanguinary gloves those would be! I have had to fall back as time presses (for Patrick promised Col L the gloves) on white & black wool mixed before it is spun. It is a dark grey & one advantage is warranted not to fade. Met in my reading today a quotation from "Proctor" (tho who Proctor is & what he wrote my belles lettres lore does not inform me) which are so apropos that I requote them here

I Hate the Camp

I hate its noise & stiff parade, its blank
And empty forms and stately courtesy,
Where between bows & blows, a smile and stab
There's scarce a moment. Soldiers always live
In idleness or peril, both are bad.

"In idleness or peril"! What an alternative for a fond mother to send, perhaps the joy of her heart, the delight of her eyes into! Yet it is true— "Idleness or peril"! Sheild our army, the hope & stay of our country from both, O Lord! Came home in the rain & to bad news, for on opening the mail we found that so far from occupying Nashville our army in Tennessee was falling back. The Abolitionists now occupy Murfresboro when we confidently expected from Braggs dispatches to hear that we were pursuing them. Rosencrans must have been heavily reinforced and rallied whilst we perhaps pursued in disorder! The capture of the waggons & supplies by Gen Wheeler is confirmed by the Northern accounts. We cannot understand it, as our Cavalry was said to have made a circuit of their lines & should have known of the advance of reinforcements. The War Department is as much in the dark as we are & has telegraphed Gen Bragg preremtorily "for further information." So we must wait.

Mr Lincoln on New Year's day issued his Emancipation Proclamation which, however, our papers very properly do not publish. Some day we shall see it.

Wilmington is said to be the point of attack by the Abolitionists. We hear they have 42,000 men concentrated at New Berne for it. All the force from Suffolk marched last week through Gates County to Holly's landing about thirty miles or less from here where they embarked on transports and gun boats for that point. One peice of good news is that the Monitor on her passage from Fortress Munro to some point on the N C Coast foundered at sea off Cape Hatteras & all on board perished.[12] Her consort the Galena narrowly escaped the same fate & had to throw overboard all her Armament, Ammunition, & stores, so she is useless for the present. The Monitor it will be remembered is the same iron clad which fought the Merrimac in Hampton Roads last spring & saved the Yankee Navy there. Cape Hatteras is a tower of strength to us, for there too Burnside received a severe lesson. We might fancy the genius of North Carolina meeting her enemies there, as Camoëns[13] tells us the "Spirit of the Cape of Good Hope," or was it Neptune, met Lope de Vega off the Southern point of Africa & denounced Woe & curses upon all so venturous as to enter upon or search out her inmost recesses.

JANUARY 10, 1863

Have been very busy knitting gloves for Col Leventhorpe. Have knit a glove of the largest size each day for the last three days & the last day fringed cuffs for both. Col L is not *exactly* a Briareus[14] as my knitting *three* gloves for him would seem to import, Journal, but the first was badly proportioned. I not knowing the size of his hand until the thumb was knit & then attempting to enlarge it, the fingers did not accord, so I raveled out & commenced anew. Today Neptune took them up with some supplies for his table, viz., a round of spiced beef (Boeuf de la Chasse), a chine, some tongues, sausage meat & stuffed sausages, a bucket of butter, bread, biscuit, Coffee, Mustard, Pepper, Apples, and Sweet Potatoes—which we hope will be a pleasant addition to his Camp fare.

Dined at father's & came home in a cold steady rain which will we fear raise the River. There is but 2 1/2 ft of water on Rocky bar now, a *bar* indeed to the advance of the Abolitionists. They are reinforcing largely at Newberne for an advance, but upon what point we cannot tell. Pettigrew's Brigade is stationed at Rocky Mount, another force at Wilson, a strong one at Goldsboro, Col Leventhorpe at Weldon, & the redoubtable Gen French at Halifax. The line of the R R swarms with men but whether they will advance so far to the East as to defend our section should it be attacked, we cannot tell. Brother says not, in which case God help us. He will help us. He knows what is best for us.

---

[12]The *Monitor*, in tow of the U.S.S. *Rhode Island* bound for Beaufort, went down in a gale a few miles off Cape Hatteras on the night of December 31, 1862. Four officers and twelve seamen were drowned, but forty-nine men were saved by the boats of the *Rhode Island. Official Records (Navy)*, Series I, VIII, 346-354.

[13]Luis de Camoëns (1524-1579) was a celebrated Portuguese poet and the author of *The Lusiad* (1572), an epic poem of the Portuguese which revolved to a great extent around Vasco de Gama's voyages to India. Benét, *Reader's Encyclopedia*, 170, 659-660.

[14]Briareus, in Greek mythology the son of Heaven and Earth, was a monster with a hundred hands and fifty heads. Benét, *Reader's Encyclopedia*, 141.

Father is much depressed on account of his old friend Mr Badger's having had a stroke of Paralysis.[15] They were boys together and have had a life time of uninterrupted friendship, friendship too of no common kind & it is a blow of uncommon severity when a severance of such ties is threatened.

I am sure I do not undervalue "Ceremony." Selden that prince of Tabletalker[s], that prototype of the whole species, likens it to "a penny-glass to a rich wine—without it the wine were lost."[16] It keeps up things (or some such words for thanks to the Abolitionist I have not the book by me), and Chesterfield[17] calls it "the outworks of manners & decency," which would "be often broken in upon were it not for their defence." So with the man of intellect & the man of the world on its side—I would be presumptious and stupid indeed to take the converse, but I take it that they meant ceremony that *conveyed a meaning* or kept up a decorum of manner, a refinement of social & every day life. But this tiresome ceremony that Mama practices of setting at the table until every glass, spoon, nay even the tablecloth itself is removed and we see the bare mahogany, is more than I can either like or see the sense of. When there is a desert or even a simple glass of wine it is well enough to let the decanter revolve around the table in its silver coaster, but when there is neither & the only point gained seems to be to watch a parcel of awkward little servants blunder over the removal of the dinner whilst you shiver in the draught from the constantly opened & shut door & then whisk a napkin over a surface already polished & free from "spot or speck or stain" would be ludicrous did not the *tiresome* predominate. Give one order and the "rigour of the game," but let me see something gained, something accomplished by it.

JANUARY 11, 1863

Sunday—We saw on Friday that the Abolitionists claimed to have captured Vicksburg, but thinking it a Yankee lie I did not notice it, especially as we had advices to the 2d. Now, however, they maintain that Grant has telegraphed to Halleck that Sherman took it on the 3d. We feel a little uneasy but hope predominates. I prefix, marked W, Lincoln's infamous Emancipation Proclamation issued on the 1st of Jan.[18] Henceforward he stands forth a

---

[15]George Edmund Badger (1795-1866) suffered a stroke of paralysis in January, 1863, but recovered partially and lived for three years. *Raleigh Register*, January 7, 1863; Ashe, *Biographical History*, VII, 43-44.

[16]John Selden (1584-1654) was an English jurist, scholar, and author. The quotation from Selden's *Table Talk* (1689) should read, " 'Tis like a Penny-Glass to a rich Spirit, or some excellent Water; without it the Water were spilt, the Spirit lost." John Selden, *Table Talk* (London: John Russell Smith, 1856), 24, hereinafter cited as Selden, *Table Talk*; Benét, *Reader's Encyclopedia*, 1008; *Dictionary of National Biography*, LI, 212-224.

[17]Philip Dormer Stanhope (1694-1773), the fourth earl of Chesterfield and a prominent politician and author, wrote for the benefit of his son a series of letters delineating the proper conduct of a gentleman in society. Lord Chesterfield, *Works Including His Letters to His Son* (New York: Harper and Brothers [First American Edition], 1859), 635; *Dictionary of National Biography*, LIV, 24-36.

[18]This newspaper clipping is on page 38 of the second volume of the diary.

perjured man, false alike to oaths, to principles, to professions, deaf to the Instincts of humanity, the dictates of reason, or the promptings of Common Sense. Well has he said, "We cannot escape History," for he goes down marked with the finger of Scorn to the latest posterity for an act alike weak & wicked!

No news from the Rappahanock. McCellan it is said has been ordered to Fortress Monroe to organize an army to advance upon Richmond by the James River, his old base. The enemy daily strengthning themselves in N C but as yet no indications of an advance to any given point.

A most gallant & daring feat has been accomplished in Texas. Aout two o'clock on New Year's morning four small gunboats came down Buffalo Bayou into Galveston bay & running up to the U S Cutter Harriet Lane, two on each side, began deliberately to pick off her gunners. This they soon affected by means of the Texan sharp shooters, killing also Captain Wain [Wainwright] her Commander. They then boarded her & after a sharp conflict captured the vessel. The Texan boats were lined & fortified with cotton bales (I suppose as Gen Jeff Thompson's Cotton fleet was). This was not all, for the Westfield Commander Renshaw USN determined not to be taken, so after a consultation with both men & officers it was agreed to blow her up, which was done, eight only of the crew escaping.[19] This is the Northern account taken from their organ, the N O Delta. I do not beleive the latter part. The Yankee is too calculating to lose his life for mere honour. He wants "*a consideration.*"

JANUARY 15, 1863

Just at home from a few days visit to Father's. No news but a continued confirmation of the strenghtning of the Abolition force at New Berne for an advance into N C supposed Goldsboro, Wilmington, & Weldon sumultaneously. Troops are quartered all along the line of the R R where they can be readily concentrated at any point attacked. Butler has had a public reception in New York, some members of the Chamber of Commerce only protesting, a serenade & complimentary demonstration in Washington. The miserable wretches, were they worthy of the name of *men*, or had they one spark of national honour, they would blush at the thought of the outrages he has committed. Instead of that an oration! Mr Yeadon of the Charleston Courier offers ten thousand dollars for his capture or death, a bona fide offer for Mr Y. is a man of fortune & as he is outlawed there is no crime in killing him. I prefix the advertisement marked X.[20]

---

[19]On January 1, 1863, Confederate naval forces successfully drove the Union fleet out of Galveston, capturing the U.S.S. *Harriet Lane* and destroying the U.S.S. *Westfield*. Cdr. William B. Renshaw of the *Westfield* died when he blew up his ship to prevent its capture, while Jonathan M. Wainwright, commander of the *Harriet Lane*, was killed during the fight. *Civil War Naval Chronology*, III, 1, 3, 4.

[20]Richard Yeadon (1802-1870) was a lawyer, editor of the *Charleston Daily Courier* from 1832 until 1844, and a South Carolina legislator. *Concise Dictionary of American Biography*, 1264. A copy of his notice concerning Butler appears on page 37 in the second volume of the diary.

Had a letter yesterday from my nephew Thomas Devereux Jones announcing his marriage to Miss Skinner.[21] Quite a surprise, but as the young folks have been engaged two years I do not see why they should longer postpone it. I write wishing them all happiness & prosperity & inviting the bride here should she see fit to leave her Mother's house, now in the lines of the enemy. He also writes me that he has lost but two of his negroes, both of them girls. Some of his men left, but they returned after a short time saying that they had enough of the Yankees.

Came home on horseback with Mr E. Had a long ride through & over the Conneconara Plantation, a beautiful estate, but with one sad drawback—liable to inundation. There were but two steamboats which captured the Harriet Lane instead of four. Magruder ordered & planned the whole affair and much credit does he deserve for it.

JANUARY 16, 1863

Last night came our President Mr Davis' message to Congress, an able, dispassionate, & dignified document, I might almost say *perfect*. There is nothing either to be added to or taken from it. A perusal of it & a contrast between it & that of their exponent Mr Lincoln would, I should think, make the intelligent men at the North blush for shame. It must have a strong influence upon men of sense, both in the U S and Europe. So anxious am I to have it in extenso that tho it takes up much of my room I prefix it, marked Y.[22]

Northern dispatches dated the 11th admit a severe repulse at Vicksburg. They call it a second Fredericksburg affair. Their loss they say was "terrific" both in officers and men. That at Murfresboro was, they said, "heartrending," so perhaps they are coming to their senses. Some of the democratic party there are beginning to find out that the War was wrong in its inception, its cause, & its progress & to profess a desire to give us Constitutional provisions for & protection of Slavery, but it is too late for that. Had they seen & expressed themselves thus two years ago before their eyes were opened with the point of the bayonette, the War & its consequent misery & bloodshed would have been avoided. Now we have no faith either in them or their paper Constitutions, which can with impunity be violated "ere the ink wherewith was writ could dry." We want simply to be left alone & allowed to manage our own domestic institutions in our own way.

JANUARY 19, 1863

Dined at Father's. Rumours that the Abolition Army is advancing, making preparations to cross in two places above & below Fredericksburg. Some consider it only a feint to cover an advance into N C & to prevent Gen Lee from

---

[21]Martha Ann (Pattie) Skinner was the daughter of Benjamin and Elizabeth Leigh Skinner of Perquimans County. Eighth Census, 1860, Population Schedule, Perquimans County, 68-69.

[22]A newspaper article containing this address is in the second volume of the diary on pages 30-33.

detaching any men to support Gustavus Smith. We hear constantly of a projected advance upon Goldsboro & Wilmington & we are massing troops to meet them, but as yet there has been nothing done. Two of their Iron Clads are in Beaufort Harbour awaiting Ammunition & the arrival of two more Turret crowned monsters on the Monitor pattern. Then comes a sea & land attack on Wilmington, I suppose. Pray God that they may all join their prototype, the Monitor, six fathom deep off Cape Hatteras, where they will make cool grottoes for the Mermaids & Sea Nymphs to disport themselves within! Old Glaucus[23] could fold his whole flock in a fleet of them without causing us a pang of regret. The U S War Steamer Columbia went ashore off Masonboro Inlet a few miles from the point where Patrick was encamped in 61. The crew were captured & two blockaders who came to her releif driven off by Col Lamb. The vessel we were forced to burn. A valuable transport was also wrecked off Wrightsville sound, in full view of Mr Lippett's house, on the very bank which bounded my view as I every morning gazed through the telescope from his piazza watching for the blockading squadron as it steamed slowly by.

JANUARY 21, 1863

All day yesterday at Hascosea gardening until the rain drove me in. Transplanted & divided some of my choice Roses which last summer did not blossom as they ought, cause I think too deeply planted. I am much needed out there both in orchard & garden. Knife & saw must both be at work pruning. My out door occupation contrasted mournfully & even oddly with my in door, which was nothing less than making Fanny pack my largest trunk with Mr E's & my own summer wardrobe, so that if we should be driven from home they might be ready to accompany us. I feel the want of my books greatly. True I do not now read much but they stood silent monitors & a glance even at their covers refreshed me. I was not aware how much I used them in my daily life, as references I mean. My knoledge must be very superficial when I have need to turn so often to the fount. "*Beware of the man of one book.*" I fear I am a woman of too many for proper digestion & reflection. I beleive I will try & confine myself to *one* single one for a month, but the question is—which shall that be? Patrick tried for a time *Butler's Sermons*[24] but that is not a pabulum for my daily fare. I am not seeking to improve my style or even my depth of thought I fear. Mrs Edmondston, I fear me, you will have to take a lower flight. What say you to a volume of old Ballads, associate for a time with "fair Annet" & "the Nut brown mayde." "Take thy old cloke about

---

[23]In classical legend Glaucus, a fisherman from Boeotia, became a sea god blessed with the gift of prophecy. Benét, *Reader's Encyclopedia*, 438.

[24]Joseph Butler, an English divine, bishop of Durham, and a rector of St. Paul's Cathedral, published *Fifteen Sermons* in 1726. The sermons were a systematic account of the moral nature of man. *Dictionary of National Biography*, VIII, 67-72.

thee" in good earnest and "sayle" his "schip" with *"Sir Patrick Spens"*[25] &
(query—why did Coledrige call that the noblest ballad in the language? A
fine one it is indeed, but to me there are others of equal merit).

Took from my desk of private papers a book containing memoranda, I
might almost call them, of my religious & my mental state for some years immediately after my marriage. What a picture of myself do I there behold! I
have long ceased this practice of recording my own self examinations, ceased
it since father gave me my mother's papers & I read there much that I know
she did not intend any one to see. In fact one volume had inscribed on it a request which he had overlooked, asking him alone to peruse it. True to her request, I burned it unopened & the thought then entered my mind that should
I die, I left no child behind me to whom it would be a sacred filial duty to
destroy such memorials of me as I should not like to meet the eyes of those indifferent to me, that under the most favourable circumstances it would cost
Patrick a pang either to peruse or to destroy them, a pang which I could spare
him, so I destroyed all the notes, memoranda, journals, etc., which I had been
years in making, partly from that reason & partly that they were dull.

This by some means, some secret spring unknown to myself, escaped & as I
read it & look the Catherine Edmondston of twelve & even fifteen years back
fairly in the face, I declare I hardly know her! My religious life does not cost
me the struggles, the pangs, the unhappiness, it used. Is it that my conscience
is less tender? I am impatient often enough now & idle too often, but I do not
smite and accuse myself as I then did. I do not examine myself one half as often and as to reviewing my opinions & motives of action as I find I then did,
insensibly I have intermitted it altogether & am contented to take my opinions on matters religious mental & moral as they start unbidden in my brain.
The machinery that they result from does not cost me a thought. Why is it? I
read & studied more then, but I am a happier woman now. Am I happier
because I am more self satisfied? I hope not—indeed—I beleive it is because I
yeild myself up more to Patrick's guidance & regulation than I then did. My
housekeeping gives me but little trouble & that of a pleasurable nature. My
cares are few, my enjoyments many, but stupid that I am, blind, & unthankful
too. One great reason for my happiness now is my excellent health. I can do
more work in one day now than I could in three in those days, so I suppose
knowing what I ought to accomplish & then not doing it fretted me & I had
not so good servants then as I have now & so had more to see after. Now the
idea of sitting down & apportioning my time as I did in 1848 is not only horrible to me but simply impossible. *Then* I lived in a city, had feeble health, rarely
went out, & Patrick had regular office hours during which I never saw him.
Now this country life, the thousand & one calls on my time, the garden, the

---

[25]*Sir Patrick Spens*, a ballad by an unknown author, describes Sir Patrick's voyage to Norway to carry the
king's daughter home. On the return voyage the ship sank and Sir Patrick and his men drowned. Stevenson, *The Home Book of Verse*, 2685-2688.

orchard, the poultry yard, all interest me so that I verily beleive if I were to set myself such a portion to read, such to write, such to sew, etc., the temptation to leave it would be so irresistable that I would throw it all aside if I heard Mrs Maitland or Katrine Von Tassel cackle & go out to see if they had laid an egg! Patrick too is with me much more & at almost all hours & I go out with him so often that rules would be fetters which I would soon break did I attempt to wear them.

So Mrs Edmondston, if not so cultivated a woman as you then were, I think you can sum up an amount of usefulness now which will counterbalance it. You make your husband happier, if he has not a right to be so proud of you now. You are impatient now & Vinyard frets you as much or more than is good for you. I do not think you have improved much there. That you are not *so* impatient is, I fear, simply because you are not *so much tempted.* Dolly makes good bread, but if you wish fairly to try yourself, throw the yeast in the fire & forget how to make more & blunder over & heat yourself into a fever trying to learn as you then did. Fling your Papin's Digester[26] aside & try your hand on some of the insipid wishy washy greasy Soups you then used to have.

Do you remember, Madam, how you wept & cried the first year of your marriage when your husband said "that the first duty of woman was to attend to the cooking"? I do not mean to accuse you of neglecting it—that you had too high a sense of your duty as a wife ever to do. What pained & mortified you was the exaltation in which he placed it. He was not fault finding, simply expressing his sense of woman's mission. "Was it for *this* that you had been educated?" Was "it for *this* that such tastes had been cultivated in you?" You were willing enough and happy in attending to domestic duties. You were too well brought up by your mother either to undervalue or feel them a burden to you, but the pedestal on which he placed them debased all else. You could not worship at such a shrine! and yet, Madam, have you not long years ago seen and confessed that your husband was right?; that a well ordered table, well cooked, well prepared food was the keynote to health, happiness, and usefulness? Remember how you exulted in a passage in Plutarch's Paulus Emilius[27] that it required more genius to order a feast well than to marshal an Army! How much good it did you, but how long would I chatter on if the light did not fail and what paper I am wasting. Really I must be less discursive.

Last week an attack was made on Fort Caswell by five war Steamers. The Canonading was kept up for some hours without result on either side. It is

---

[26]In 1679 Denis Papin (1647-1712?), a French physicist, invented a digester which softened bones by raising the boiling point of water through increased steam pressure. *Webster's Biographical Dictionary,* 1144.

[27]The Dryden translation of Plutarch, corrected and revised by Arthur H. Clough, recorded that Aemilius Paulus stated that "there was the same spirit shown in marshalling a banquet as an army; in rendering the one formidable to the enemy, the other acceptable to the guests." John Dryden (trans.), *Plutarch: The Lives of the Noble Grecians and Romans,* revised by Arthur Hugh Clough (Chicago: Encyclopaedia Britannica, Inc., 1952; originally published 1864), 124.

supposed that it was a mere preliminary to the grand attempt soon to be made with a view to ascertain the range and calibre of the guns in the Fort. Rumours that the enemy were crossing the Rappahanock are contradicted in last night's paper & it asserted on the contrary that he was moving upon Warrenton. Wheeler's cavalry in Tennessee "after burning a bridge in the rear of the enemy pushed on to the Cumberland River when he intercepted & captured four large transports loaded with supplies, burning three & boarding the fourth to carry off 400 paroled prisoners; being hotly pursued by a gun[boat], he attacked, captured & destroyed her with her whole armament," so telegraphs Gen Braxton Bragg, but how a gunboat formidable as it is could pursue, & hotly pursue, a squad of Cavalry passes my comprehension! Perhaps she was of the class of those "amphibious animals who cant live on land & die in the water." At any rate she seems to have met her fate for venturing out of her element. The enemy have evacuated Island no 10 & concentrated at Fort Pillow; cause, guerillas. We captured & burned a gunboat between the points & Forest actually made a dash into Memphis, tore down the U S & hoisted the Confederate Flag and allowed the citizens to bring off & appropriate many supplies & stores accumulated there for the Abolitionists.

Patrick is very unhappy at a dispatch which reaches us through the Northern papers via Cairo to the effect that the combined Land & Naval force under Porter & McClernand had captured Arkansas Post, a fort about 70 miles from the mouth of the Arkansas—mounting 9 guns; killed 500 Confederates & captured from 5 to 7000 more with a loss to themselves of 200 only killed and wounded. It does not distress me for I do not beleive it. I fancy it is a Yankee lie, coined to freight the English Steamer which sailed on the 20th. It is by no means the first time that Bro Johnathan has tried in to pull wool over John Bull's eyes in this way.

January 22, 1863

That infamous villain Milroy has distinguished himself by being the first even of the Yankee Gen.'s who has attempted to enforce Lincoln's Emancipation Proclamation. In an order which I prefix, marked Z,[28] he affirms and endorses it, extends its operation over the county of Frederick & town of Winchester. He "admonishes" those who resist it that they will be held & treated as Traitors. To the negroes, his loving friends I suppose, he gives also an admonition to "abstain from violence and at once betake themselves to some useful occupation." Suppose they do, now what will you O wise & obedient Gen Milroy, do—close your eyes to the one & issue rations to your loving subjects to nulify the other? I paste also in the beginning of this book a prescription from Dr Buckler of Baltimore for dyspepsia. It seems an odd place to preserve it, but "the *War*" must be my excuse. My Receipt books

---

[28]Milroy's order can be found in the second volume of the diary in a newspaper clipping on page 30.

where such things are copied is in a place of security to save it from the enemy, so I put it here to have it for immediate reference. It is said to work wonders. I mark it A no 1.[29]

How true is Lord Byron's estimate of Military glory! To lose one's leg in an action & then see your name spelled wrong in the Dispatch! The Commander of the Harriet Lane could echo this were he alive to do so, for far & aside the Telegraph transfered him as Captain Wagneugth when in reality it was the essentially New York one of Wainwright. Well Wagenegth or Wainwright, it is all the same to us. The Texas sharp shooters did not ask for his card!

The Harriet Lane is gone to sea to join the Alabama, Capt Semmes, who by the way has again left his card with the Yankee nation by taking two more their first class clippers, one he burned, the other having an English cargo, he bonded. The howl that goes up from their shipping interest is amusing. Ere long they will have half their Navy engaged in pursuit of him. The San Jacinto has been playing bo peep with the Alabama since Sept & is always "just in her track."

Butler, "the Brute," is receiving an ovation in the Northern cities! They relish what revolts even the brewers of England & *ladies* (heaven save the mark), *Abolition Ladies*, magnificently attired, wait on and add lustre to his Levees! I fancy I can hear the nasal drawl with which they whine out, "Tell us of the *poor negroes* Gen Butler. Did you really arm them & are the poor things ready to strike for freedom?" Ah! Mrs E, you cannot forget your early prejudices nor how your childish blood boiled when you heard that Yankee protege of your Grandmother's, Mrs Dutton, call Ellen, a little negro whose office it was to brush flies, "a sweet child."

Speaking of brushing flies reminds me of a good story of a poor deluded negro who a short time since in exercise of her Yankee given right went in search of a mistress in Ilinois to keep her from starving. Said the Yankee woman of all work to her would be maid, "Well what you do? Can you cook?" "Naw Mme, Aunt Phyllis she always cooked." "Well can you wash?" "Naw Mme, Aunt Judy she always washed"! "Can you sew?" "Naw Mme, Aunt Mira she always sewed." "Can you set the table?" "Naw, Mme, Sam he always set the table." "Can you tend the baby?" "Naw, Mme Aunt Calline she always nussed." "Can you clean out the bedrooms?" "Naw Mme Aunt Sally she always put up the bedrooms." "Well, what *did you use to do*?" "I brushed flies off of *ole Miss! Mme.*" The Yankee woman is supposed to have fainted, if Yankee women ever do a thing so little strong minded!

There has been a great upturning of the Militia. What is left of them are ordered out for drill every Saturday. There is a reorganization, & confusion worse confounded prevails. Patrick's Commission as Adjutant Gen on Gen

---

[29]Thomas Hepburn Buckler (1812-1901), a physician in Baltimore, Maryland, actively studied epidemic diseases and the treatment of tuberculosis. *Concise Dictionary of American Biography*, 120. His prescription for dyspepsia is on page 34 of the second volume of the diary.

David Clark's (Militia) staff with the rank of major saves him from all annoyance on that score. The only good I knew before of the appointment was that it killed the *"Captain."* I cannot bear the title. If they wish to be polite why do not they say Col, as he held a Lieut Col's commission? Besides having once been aid to the Gov of S C he has right to that title for life. It is too much I fear in these days of military titles to expect him to be called what I always call and like to hear him called, *Mr Edmondston*, but "Captain" Edmondston always grates upon me. Besides reminding me of an unpleasant episode in his life, it sounds snobbish and common. I hope "the Major" will finally kill the "Captain." The Majority does him good service now however.

JANUARY 23, 1863

Last night Patrick made me a present of a nice new blank book in which to write my Journal. I am the more pleased at this, as he takes you, O my Journal, for an object of especial merriment—merriment at once good humoured and pungent. He cannot disapprove of you, or he would not aid and abet me thus in keeping you. I have been most especially fortunate since this year came in in getting little presents, tokens of affection & regard given me. It had been so long since I had received any that I thought my time for present getting was over & that I had reached the stage of life when present *making* was my role, & as "to give is more blessed than to receive" I accepted my part & endeavoured to fulfil it acceptably to the young folks. But I beleive I am mistaken, for let me see. I had a New Year's gift from Mama of a barrel of apples. Sue gave me two beautiful worked night caps, so pretty that I am tempted to play the invalid in order to show them. Mama a pretty dress collar & a few days since Patrick came home from Greenwood & bade me guess who had sent me a present. I began & almost ran through the list of my acquaintances there when it proved to be Mr Clark, the little English Taylor, & the gift a most characteristic one—spool of black glace thread! He took Patrick to his shop & shewed him his Rabbits, the progeny of those that I had given him, told him he had been enabled to sell twenty five dollars worth of them, & begged that he would allow him to offer Mrs E a small evidence of his respect & esteem, that it was not much he had to give, that things were very hard to get now, & if Mrs E would accept it he would like to offer her this, producing the Cotton. I was really touched. Gratitude is so rare & as I prize it greatly & most acceptable was it too for I was quite out & knew not where to get more.

My last letter from James E told us that the Brigade was under marching orders, to what point they did not know, but yesterday Patrick heard that they were at Kenansville in Duplin County, ready I suppose to intercept the land attack upon Wilmington from New Berne. Little but Pine Knots & gall berries in that section I fear. His commissariat will be of the plainest.

Yesterday I was employed in a work that brought the War forcibly before me, viz., cutting out some night Shirts for Mr E from some Cotton sheets

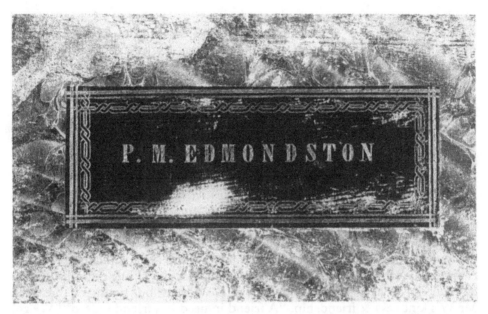

The front of the book given by Patrick to his wife to use for her journal had his name embossed thereon. This new book was begun with the entry for February 3, 1863.

which Mama was so kind as to give me. I have already mentioned my own under clothing from the same source & Fanny's amusing disgust at her "Missis" having clothes made "*out en sheets*," & now when *Master* is in the same category her cup will I fear be full. It is a reminiscence to look back to in plentiful & prosperous days "*when we wore clothes made from sheets.*" Our Lot has been truly blessed, for not only have we suffered *no* bodily privations as yet, but we have been enabled to give largely to our friends who were not so fortunate. Owing to the mourning which I put on for Papa in the early part of the war, I have had a well stocked wardrobe of coloured clothes to give to my neices & others who have needed them, theirs having been worn out. We had a good stock of groceries which Patrick's forethought increased & we have not wanted for a comfort, scarcely a luxury. Latterly in order to eke out our stock of Tea I have mixed it with dried Blackberry leaves which are both wholesome & pleasant. But with that exception & the cessation of all desserts but baked Apples we live as usual, & how few in our wide spread country can say so much?

Make us thankful O Lord! Hitherto the rude hand of War has not been laid upon us either in our persons or our home. We suffer only with our bleeding country. Look down upon the wide spread misery and anguish throughout the Land, upon the agonized hearts of those bereft by death of their husbands & children, upon the loneliness felt by thousands of hearthstones where the head, the stay, the support, is absent, exposed to the dangers & hardships of war, upon the sorrow of those driven from their comfortable & happy homes by the invader & spoiler, upon the pinching want felt by many who never felt want before & who are compelled to eat the bread of exile & perhaps dependance. Look down upon this O Lord & let their tears & their sorrows cry unto Thee. Stay Thine Hand & send Peace upon this afflicted, this bleeding country.

Patrick had yesterday a most kind & generous offer from Mr Witherspoon—a letter so kind, so considerate it is not often the lot of man to receive. He urges him in view of the danger to which our negroes are exposed in case of an advance of the enemy to remove them & offers him 300 Acres of Land *Rent Free*, a thousand bushels of corn which he can replace when he wishes, can supply him with forage & four empty houses, will vacate two more, & poles enough to build as many more as he needs, & all expressed in so handsome & friendly a manner as makes the offer doubly welcome. He has the matter under consideration. The transportation is the difficulty. We must carry tools, team, & meat & it is a long way to Society Hill & everything must be hauled over heavy roads & in inclement weather, but nothing can exceed Mr W's kindness & friendship. "A friend in need is a friend indeed"! We got no mail yesterday which leads Patrick to suppose that there has been a fight somewhere.

JANUARY 25, 1863

Three mails last night. Wheeler & his Cavalry continue to cut off Rosencrans supplies. Immediately after the exploits mentioned when "the Gunboat hotly pursued him," he proceeded down the Cumberland & destroyed a fleet of transports with supplies for Nashville. A bearer of Dispatches, Lt Sanders,[30] has been captured off Charleston with letters from our Government to its Agents in England. I do not beleive one half of that the Yankees profess to have found on him. He must be either a traitor or a fool not to have destroyed them when he saw his capture was inevitable. Amongst other probabilities is a design of Louis Napoleon to dismember our Confederacy by erecting Texas into an independant sovreignty in order to have a *weak* power between his Mexican conquest & a *strong* government such as the Southern Confederacy, proposals for contracts for Iron clad ships, the thanks of the President & Mr Benjamin to Mr Mason for consenting to be treated "with scant courtesy," etc., trash & balderdash of the flimsiest material.

Off Galveston the U S Iron clad Hatteras, observing a strange sail, got up steam & went to look after it. Heavy firing being shortly heard, the Brooklyn

---

[30]Maj. Reid Sanders, a Confederate agent, was captured while attempting to run the blockade disguised as a laborer. Despite his protests, he was searched and documents were found "secreted on his person" which confirmed suspicions that he was carrying rebel dispatches. He was then transported to Fort Lafayette. *Raleigh Register*, February 11, 1863.

followed to help her consort. She picked up the Launch of the Hatteras with a Lieut & five men who reported that on coming up to the "strange sail" she immediately opened a terrific fire upon them which in twenty minutes disabled the Hatteras. On cruising to look for her she was found in seven fathoms water! The Brooklyn could see nothing of the stranger which the Yankees say was the Alabama,[31] Capt Semmes. Great discontent reported in the Northern Democratic party as to the emancipation Proclamation, a discontent which extends to their Army who clamour for peace. Rumours of a mutiny at New Berne which has prevented the advance so long threatened into the interior of our State. I hope it is true, but it is negro news.

On coming down stairs found a note from James, brought by Lt Bond's[32] servant Hayne, telling me that he (Hayne) would bring anything I had to send & asking for a pr of flannel drawers and some Boeuf de Chasse. Sorry I have none of the latter prepared, but Sunday as it is, I went to work with my household & by four in the afternoon had a box containing a smoked & a Green ham & two chines all cooked, a pr of Wild Ducks ditto, a bottle of Cayenne & one of black pepper, one do Vinegar & one of made mustard, one do Tomato & one Walnut catsup, three long smoked Sausages, some coffee, several lbs of Butter, a pr of Flannel drawers & the "dunnage," as Papa used to call it, of Apples & a barrel of Sweet Potatoes & Turnips ready. Owen took them immediately out to Hayne & tomorrow at dinner I hope James will enjoy them.

JANUARY 27, 1863

Yesterday dined with Mr E at Father's. A requisition impressing one fourth of our hands to work on the fortifications about Weldon has been made on us by General Gwin. This father has declined to comply with, stating the manifest injustice of calling out our hands four times whilst others have not been once called on to contribute & offering to pay $225, the amount of wages offered us, rather than withdraw the labour from our farms just now. It seems hard too to make us defend a point above us, for before Weldon is reached we shall be over run by the enemy. Warren & Granville should do that & leave us free to work when required at Rainbow which protects us. James supplies cost us dear, for Owen not meeting Hayne went on to Enfield & not meeting him there brought them back to Hascosea. He makes a second attempt today, but two days ploughing with two mules is missed at this season.

The mail yesterday tells us that Burnside had everything ready for an advance on the 20th. Why he did not do so is not stated, but the army letter

---

[31]The *Hatteras* was sent in pursuit of a strange ship which turned out to be the *Alabama.* The *Alabama* opened fire and the *Hatteras,* "a frail iron shell, with her machinery all exposed," was sunk. *Official Records (Navy),* Series I, XIX, 582.

[32]William R. Bond of Halifax County, formerly a private in Co. G, Twelfth North Carolina Regiment, served as second lieutenant in Co. F, Forty-third North Carolina Regiment. Clark, *Histories of the North Carolina Regiments,* III, 3; Manarin and Jordan, *North Carolina Troops,* V, 197.

writers all thought a battle imminent on the 21st. The most christian & valliant Burnside issued an address telling his men that our army was diminished & dispirited by the recent brilliant actions in N C., Ten, & Ark, that now was the time to attack us & gain a victory due to the country. Whether he found out that we were not so weak as he had supposed or feared to trust his men or whether it was all a feint to deceive the North does not appear. Certain it is the attack was not made. Yesterday, however, it was reported that one division of his army had crossed the Rappahanock about twelve miles above Falmouth with a design to circumvent our position & attack us in the rear, so we may hear of a battle at any moment. All officers & men of our Army absent on leave have been in general orders recalled immediately to their respective commands. Longstreet's Division, or part of it, went South to Goldsboro on Friday, which looks as tho Gen Lee had not expected much of a battle then. The Abolition Army is said to be dispirited, discontented, & dejected & their leaders fear that another defeat will utterly demoralize & disperse them.

JANUARY 28, 1863

No mail today which looks badly as the weather is fine.

JANUARY 31, 1863

Have been quite sick for the last three days, one day, Thursday, confined to my bed & Friday to my room. No mail until Friday night when we heard that the Northern Army had as announced attempted an advance but became hopelessly and helplessly entangled in the mud. The accounts given by their letter writers are ludicrous in the extreme! Their lamentations rise into Bathos. Artillery horses mired up to their bellies, men sinking up their knees in the tenacious *"sacred soil,"* generals, teamsters, men, everybody in fact, bemired, cursing, swearing, floundering in the red Rappahanock mud! After hours of labour the valorous Yankee Army got back to their camp, muddy to their eye brows, tired, worn out, dispirited, & jaded, having encountered no enemy, but alone vanquished by mud and bad roads. Where now is the Yankee ingenuity, the Yankee mastery of difficulties? It seems they had to deceive us as to their place of crossing, at great labour cut many new roads at different points over which they hoped to transport their troops with ease & rapidity, but sadly were they disappointed. Their waggons & artillery sank to the hubs of their wheels & at every rise might be seen caissons, Guns, & camp equipage abandoned because their horses were unable to extricate them from the slough into which they had fallen. Their demoralization in consequence is represented as extreme, their disgust to their leaders almost overpowering. Letter writer after letter writer has been arrested for giving the details, but defeat like "murder" will *"out."*

At Galveston Gen Magruder has issued a Proclamation declaring the blockade of that Port raised & inviting neutral ships to enter. A discussion is raised as to whether the U S can renew it without giving the requisite 30 days notice to foreign powers.

Amo sent me a paper containing my lines on Butler which as it is the first time I have ever seen myself in print I think I will preserve in my repository. The same paper contained also an announcement which has given us deep pain and unfeigned sorrow—sorrow which it is needless here to express & pain too poignant for utterance. Bessie's marriage! May a good God over rule for her happiness a step to our eyes fraught with so much misery.[33]

We have had a sad blow in the loss of the Princess Royal[34] & her cargo off the harbour of Charleston, she having fallen into the hands of the Blockaders. She contained amongst other things five Whitworth Guns & machinery for several Gun boats now building by us, besides Arms, Ammunition, and several workmen well skilled in the manufacture of new projectiles. All these have fallen into the hands of our enemies & will doubtless be used against us. This goes far to confirm Patrick's notion that the running of the Blockade is winked at by the enemy. Winked at as a "sop for Cerberus"—first to keep up a semblance of trade & thus prevent England's breaking into open discontent, giving her a little cotton to keep her hopes up and a market for her manufacturers. For when a vessel sails from Nassau with a cargo particularly valuable to us, as was this, she is almost sure to be over hauled, but dry goods, merchandise, etc., pass every day unmolested. They have spies out to tell them what to capture.

[End of Volume II Original Manuscript Journal]

FEBRUARY 3, 1863

Thank God! I can begin my new book with a signal & glorious success to our arms! Thank God! For "He giveth not the race to the swift nor the battle to the strong."[35] On the morning of Sat the 31st of Jan the Gunboats Palmetto State & Chicora, accompanied by three small River Steamers, the Clinch, Etiwan, & Chesterfield, all under the command of Com Ingram[36] went out

---

[33]The marriage of Elizabeth Pratt Edmondston to Richard Agnew was strongly opposed by the Edmondston family.

[34]The *Princess Royal*, a British ship out of Glasgow which carried a cargo containing two engines intended for Confederate ironclads, guns, rifles, and powder, was captured by the U.S.S. *Unadilla* on January 29, 1863. Assorted Confederate dispatches referring to the cargo were also captured and sent north by the Union navy. *Official Records (Navy)*, Series I, XIII, 551-552; *Civil War Naval Chronology*, III, 18

[35]Ecclesiastes 9:11a.

[36]Duncan Nathaniel Ingraham, Confederate flag officer in charge of naval forces on the South Carolina coast, supervised the construction of the ram *Palmetto State*. On January 31, 1863, the *Palmetto State*, under Lt. John Rutledge, and the *Chicora*, under Cdr. John R. Tucker, attacked the Union blockaders outside Charleston harbor. The Confederate rams forced the U.S.S. *Mercedita* to surrender, crippled the *Memphis* and *Keystone State*, and damaged slightly the *Quaker City* and the *Augusta*. *Civil War Naval Chronology*, III, 18-20; IV, 3, 212, 279.

from the harbour of Charleston and boldly made an attack on the Blockading Squadron, succeeding in sinking two & crippling a third, besides putting the whole fleet, thirteen sail in all, (amongst them two first class Frigates, the Susquehanna and the Canandaigua) to an ignominious flight. The Palmetto State opened fire upon the Mercedita, 11 guns 158 men, which she soon sunk in five fathoms water. The officers & men were paroled, but it is feared that most of them were lost, as the Palmetto had no boats & besides was fighting and could not sucor them, & her own consorts all fled.

Captain Tucker of the Chicora, the official dispatch says, "thinks he sunk one vessel & set another on fire when she struck her flag." The published accounts say that this was the Quaker City who tho she had one wheel torn off & had struck her flag to us managed afterwards to escape. By all the laws of War she is clearly ours & I suppose owes her escape only to the fact of her surrender & our consequent inattention to her and the early dawn which favoured her ignominious and dishonorable conduct. We lost not a man nor did a single shot strike one of our boats! General Beauregard, the General Comdg, & Com Ingram, Flag Officer, issued a joint Proclamation "whereby" they "formally declare the Blockade by the U S of the said city of Charleston to be raised by a superior force of the Confederate States from & after this 31st day of Jan 1863."[37] General B put a Steamer at the disposal of the Foreign Consuls to see for themselves that no blockade existed. The French and Spanish consuls accepted the invitation, the British Consul, having previously gone on board the war Steamer Petrel five miles beyond the usual anchorage of the Squadron & reported that with a powerful glass not a vessel could be seen. The foreign Consuls then had a meeting & declared unanimously that in "their opinion the blockade had been legally raised." So now we shall see whether this boasted neutrality is to be exercised in our behalf or not, for by all the laws of Nations the U S cannot resume it without giving the world 30 days notice.

On the same day was brought into Charleston Harbour the Gunboat John P Smith, captured with her whole crew the day before in Stono River. She mounts one Parrot gun, ten 8 inch guns, & one 34 pounder, & she was almost entirely uninjured, will soon be ready for sea.

My nephew Frank Jones is Ass Engineer on board the Chicora, and was I suppose in the action. As we escaped without the loss of a man, we have an additional & personal reason for thankfulness.

Rumours reach us via Richmond that the Legislature of Kentucky has seceded from the U S & that her hitherto Union Governor has called for 60,000 men to resist Mr Lincoln's Emancipation Proclamation. They want

[37]A group of six officers commanding various vessels of the blockading squadron asserted that Beauregard's and Ingraham's proclamation was based on false information. They noted that no vessels were actually sunk, although they acknowledged that two were seriously injured. See footnote 36, 1863. *Official Records (Navy)*, Series I, XIII, 605-607.

confirmation, however, and we must not be too sanguin of a fire in Rosencranz's rear. Immense preparations are being made for a third Bombardment of Vicksburg, a point which the Abolitionists announce their determination to take. May disappointment be their portion! A second bombardment has taken place at Fort McAllister below Savannah without damage to the works.[38] The only loss is that of the Commander Major Gallec who was struck by a fragment of a shell on the head & instantly killed. In Tennessee Wheeler's Cavalry continue to harrass Rosencrans by cutting off his supplies & destroying both transports and RR cars. On Friday the 30th he destroyed 25 transports on the Cumberland & on his retreat on Sat cut off a Locomotive & five cars, taking the guard & passengers prisoners. On Sat the 31st Gen Prior—in command of our outposts on the Blackwater was attacked about seven miles from Suffolk by the Abolitionists 15,000 strong. After an obstinate engagement of three hours he repulsed them, holding the entire battle field, our loss not considerable being less than fifty, the enemy's supposed much greater.

Late arrivals from the North bring us Burnside's farewell address to the Army of the Potomac—a weaker tamer, humbler document it would be difficult to find in the annals of Military Literature! He tells them that the short time he has commanded them "has not been fruitful of Victory . . . but it has again demonstrated an amount of courage, patience, & endurance which under more favorable circumstances would have accomplished great results." He then exhorts them to a continuance of "those virtues," bespeaks for their new General their "full & cordial support," and winds up with the assurance that they will "deserve success." Not, my Grand Army, that you will get it, simply you will "*deserve*" it. The rebels under Lee may be so ungenerous as to snatch your well earned "success" from your hands. But be comforted. You have *deserved* it & the fault be theirs if you do not gain it! Such, my most Christian Burnside, is your exit from the scene of Military fame. You marked your entrance upon it by an assurance to the people of N C, over whom you came to trample, that it was a "Christian" foot which was to be placed upon their necks and you now take your farewell in a manner truly Pecksniffian.[39] Hooker, the Californian black-leg & gambler who denominates himself as "Fighting Joe," succeeds him. General Lee will scarcly need to take his gloves off to him, "*Card shuffler*" tho' he is. Sumner and Franklin comdg each an Army corps both retire with the Christian Burnside, whether voluntarily or not does not certainly appear. Sumner is said to be the ablest of their Generals, but not being an Abolitionist, the Government is blind to his merits.

---

[38]The battery at Fort McAllister, guarding Savannah at Genesis Point, resisted the attack of an ironclad monitor armed with 15- and 11-inch guns. Maj. John B. Gallie, commander of the post, was mortally wounded. *Official Records (Army)*, Series I, XIV, 212.

[39]Pecksniff, a character in Charles Dickens's *Martin Chuzzlewit*, preached the beauty of charity and forgiveness but lived a selfish, inconsiderate life. Benét, *Reader's Encyclopedia*, 832-833.

Fitz John Porter, Court-martialed upon charges preferred by Pope the braggert & whose trial was postponed by McClellan as he was neccessary to the service of the U S, has at length been brought to the bar & not fitting the Procrustian bed[40] of Abolitionism has been "dishonorably dismissed from the service." The city of New York registers its condemnation of the sentence & offers him the Governor's Room in the City Hall "in which to hold a Levee." Such are the beauties of Republicanism!

Mary & Sue came down yesterday and dined with us. I still far from well, confined in fact to the sofa with an obstinate billious attack. The day was mild, pleasant, & promising, so this morning we were doubly surprised to find on awakening that there had been a heavy fall of snow during the night. The high wind accompanying it caused it to drift as it rarely does with us & today the wind is keen & bitter & the driving blasts carrying the light snow before it makes it difficult to keep either warm or dry out of doors. God be with our poor soldiers exposed many of them without tents to the pittiless blast!

February 5, 1863

No mail last night in consequence of the snow. Just after dinner brother came in cold & hungry. He brought a budget of news from the outside world, the only thing of interest to you, my friend, being a confirmation that somewhat more than ordinary is amiss with the enemy about New Berne—72,000 men have been lying idle there since Christmas & all the rumours of their discontent & mutiny on account of the Emancipation Proclamation are not idle.

Stanley, the would be Governor of N C, has resigned on that account tho this is not certain. The traitor! His Mother Earth well might open her mouth & swallow him up "quick" when he poluted her soil bent upon the infamous errand which brought him here. He sees now I suppose that the proclamation is not popular. Hence his conscience! That wretch Hurlbut, too, a recreant son of S C whom I well remember being introduced to me in Charleston by Mr Edmondston before we were married, he too must now prate about his *conscience*. Well has he charmed it to sleep hithertoo, but "vox populi" cries louder than even it. "Murder" may "sleep" when the dear people will it, but when popularity is at stake then awakes his horror and with Macbeth he cries "*sleep no more.*" I remember I neither liked or trusted him when but a young girl. I am glad of it, shining as were his talents. Brother brought me a nice present of Apple, Pear, & Peach trees for my Orchard & garden & most kindly wishes me to go to Raleigh with him and make him a visit, but I cannot now go. Besides being quite unwell I am not settled enough to enjoy myself away

---

[40]Procrustes, a legendary robber of Attica, placed prisoners upon an iron bed and forced them to fit exactly by either cutting or stretching them. Thus, efforts to force uniformity in thinking or behavior in people is known as "placing them on Procrustes's bed." Benét, *Reader's Encyclopedia*, 882.

from home. I know not if the Abolitionists will let me return. He brought a rumour of the resignation of Maj Gen Hill, Bethel Hill, but as it wants confirmation I cannot credit it.

Patrick commenced yesterday filling the Ice House, a work which has gone on steadily all day in spite of the Rain. The snow thaws rapidly but as the ice is thick Patrick thinks if he can get it in the Ice House that it will create an atmosphere for itself & freeze again. It is a pity, however, that it is put in wet. A steady rain has set in & the snow is thawing under its influence. No military operations can take place for some days as the roads will be impassable. "Fighting Joe" must curb his martial ardour "will he nil he." Rappahanock mud will be worse now than when it mastered Burnside.

FEBRUARY 10, 1863

Not much news worth recording. Vicksburg is the point of interest. The most enormous preparations both for its attack & defence have been made. We are said to have 100,000 men in easy supporting distance of it, but that I beleive is a Yankee estimate. We have not half that number. One Gunboat has succeeded in running past our Batteries which is a bad omen for us. The reason why the attack is delayed is said by the Northern accounts to be the bad condition, the insubordination, & discontent of the men under Banks command. The Emancipation Proclamation is unpopular & many refuse to fight for the "*nigger*." Per contra, their Congress has passed a bill authorizing the raising & drilling of Negro regiments.[41] Think of it, armed negroes! Think what it means! And this is the nineteenth Century! and the proposers of this infernal act call themselves enlightened Christians. Northern accounts report the Brooklyn as sunk by three Confederate vessels, viz., the Alabama, the Florida, & the Harriet Lane. She was sent to recapture the latter, but we have heard nothing of her movements. We have had a success at Sabine Pass capturing 15 guns & munitions of War together with three hundred prisoners.

The Kentucky Legislature have passed a bill forbidding their soldiers from enforcing Mr Lincoln's Emancipation Proclamation & resolutions declaring that if it be not withdrawn in twenty days they will call a Convention to consider on the propriety of seceeding from the U S. A motion being then made to go into secret Session, the U S Commander posted a file of Michegan Soldiers at the door of the House and informed them that they must deliberate with *open doors*. If the blood of Kentucky submit to *that*, it is degenerate indeed.

Mr Benjamin, Sec of State, has issued a Pronunciamento declaring the Blockade of Charleston legally raised. What good will result from it we know not. We do not see with the spectacles of *Neutral Europe*! One thing seems to outsiders strange & may point to a pre-concerted action on our part with the

---

[41]This bill, calling for the enlistment of 150,000 "armed Negroes," including slaves from the southern states, passed the House of Representatives on February 2, 1863, but was not acted upon by the Senate. *Congressional Globe*, 37th Congress, 3rd session, 1862-1863, 33, pt. 1, 689-690.

privity of England. The day but one after the action arrived H M Ship of War Cadmus ordering the British consul Mr. Bunch[42] immediately to report to his own Government in person. They gave him no time to arrange his private affairs but taking him immediately on board steamed to the West Indies to meet the mail steamer. Hopeful persons see in the fact an intention on the part of the British Government to avail themselves of his personal testimony, he having gone out immediately after the action in the War steamer Petrel to ascertain for himself that the blockade was really raised; despondant ones on the contrary think it only a fatherly care on the part of England (tho I beleive she is of femine gender) of her son Mr Bunch, he being personally obnoxious to the Lincoln Government & in event of the impending attack on Charleston, antipathy to him might embroil her with the U S. These persons expect an immediate attack. The Yankees themselves admit that in the late action at Genesis Point below Savannah their Ironclad Montauk received a severe injury, her turret in consequence refusing to work. Anything is welcome which affects the prestige of their tower of strength—Gunboats.

Everything reported quiet here in N C. They have an immense force lying absolutely idle about New Berne. Hooker—"*Fighting Joe*"—is reorganizing his army & promises to do great things so soon as the roads "*harden.*" Guns & good ones too went down last week to Rainbow Bend & ere this are in all probability mounted. Heavy discharges of Artillery aroused the whole country last Saturday & speculation was rife as to whether they were in Roanoke or Tar River, but as nothing has been heard of the presence of an enemy in either place the hope has grown into conviction that it was our own gunners at Rainbow practicing & getting the range of their peices.

I have been quite sick now for some days, not confined to bed but ailing & puny so much so that at last Mr Edmondston becoming uneasy sent for the Doctor. He prescribed a blister on the pit of my stomach which confined me to my bed yesterday, & today I am feeble and far from well. I crept to the door just now and was saluted with so bright a smile from my crocuses on the sheltered border at the Piazza that I beleive it invigorated me!

I have written some lines which with, I hope, a pardonable partiality for my own bantling, I think good. I am going to send them to Amo to publish for me, so as to get Mr Edmondston's unbiased opinion of them, an experiment I tried once before but failed from the *want of appreciation* in the Richmond Enquirer. I will copy them when I feel stronger. I have also re-cast and re-modeled my Lines on St Sophia &, Mr E thinks, improved them. So I efface

---

[42]Robert Bunch was the British consul in Charleston. Bunch and the British consuls in other southern cities were originally appointed to posts in the United States. They continued their service within the seceded states, however, even though no official diplomatic relations existed between England and the Confederacy. England's refusal to recognize southern independence caused serious conflicts to develop between the consuls and Confederate authorities. Adams, *Great Britain and the American Civil War*, I, 43; Randall and Donald, *Civil War and Reconstruction*, 506-508.

the first copy in the 1st vol of this Journal & paste them in their new form over the old ones, a *domestic Pallimpsest.*[43]

Father has just been in to see me & brought me a letter from Frank Jones to his Aunt Susan giving her an account of the attack on the Blockading Squadron off Charleston. As I copied his containing an account of the Battle of Hampton Roads I can do no less by this.

C.S. Steamer Chicora—Feb 6th 1863

Dear Sue:

I think the people make too much fuss over our affair of the 31st for we did nothing more than we ought to have done. We had so much the advantage. On Friday night about 11 o'clock we cast loose from our moorings & got under way. We steamed slowly down the harbour. We could not cross the Bar until 1/2 past three on account of the tide. After we had crossed the Bar we were some two or three miles from the enemy. We started towards them or at least where they ought to be, for it was so dark that we could not see them. We moved along very slowly waiting for the moon to go down. About a 1/4 before 5 we made out two of them lying about half a mile apart. The Palmetto State moved off toward one & we took the other. We steamed along slowly without making the least noise. Presently the signal officer told us we were in about 100 yds of the ships. I thought it was still before but now it was more so than ever. I held my breath so fearful was I of making a noise. When we were within 50 ft of them we fired our bow gun (7 in Rifle) loaded with an incendiary shell. It exploded inside of her. Our men could hold in no longer but gave three cheers. We could hear the Yankees screaming with pain & fright too I suppose. In the mean time we had turned so as to bring our broadside to bear. That sent a 9 in shell crashing through him; we kept on turning and gave another incendiary shell from our stern Gun (7 in Rifle). That set him on fire we suppose for he commenced ringing his fire bell. We next gave him another shot from our other broadside gun & another 9 in shell went through him. He was now settling very fast. He had gotten under way just after our first shot & whilst we were firing into him we had been separating all the while. We lost sight of him just after the last shot was fired & as he was no where to be seen when day broke a few minutes afterwards we think he must have sunk. In the meantime our firing had aroused the whole Yankee fleet (about 20 vessels) and they thinking no doubt that it was some vessel trying to run the blockade came bearing down upon us; one very large ship came within about 100 yds of us when we gave him a shot from our broadside Gun & as he rounded to we gave him a shell from our bow gun. It entered just under his bow & in passing towards his stern broke one of his engines & when the shell burst a tremendus cloud of smoke arose from him. We then gave him

---

[43] Mrs. Edmondston's revised poems were not located in the diary.

a shot from one of our broadside guns which burst his boiler. He then hauled down his flag but kept his good engine at work trying to get away. The Captain would not fire upon him again, because he had no flag up. We put after him in hopes of catching him but could not do so as he was so much faster than we were. When about a mile off he hoisted his flag again and fired at us. There were at that time seven different ships around us but were firing at very long range & as it was broad daylight they could make out what we were & of course kept out of our way. We were then about fifteen miles from shore & out sight of Land. The Commodore who was on the Palmetto State then signaled us to stop firing & come in, which we did about 7 o'clock. We had to wait for the tide until about four o'clock in the afternoon before we could come up to the city. When the P S bore down upon the ship she started after she ran into & sunk her at her anchor after which the P S did not do much. She fired only 7 shots whilst we fired 27. The soldiers had the day before captured a ship in Stono River so I think the Yankees are some what sick of this place. Just imagine what an eye opener it must be to have a 7 inch rifle shell to come crashing through the side of a ship and then explode inside! Neither of our ships were struck the other morning so we do not know how they will resist shot. There are four or five iron clads on this coast at present. The authorities anticipate an attack here very soon. We are ready for them whenever they see fit to come. Write soon to your affectionate nephew.

Frank Jones

February 16, 1863

But little news worth writing about for some days past & I have been too unwell to make any extra exertion, so I have per force winnowed my chaff this last week. The Abolition army is reported to be almost entirely withdrawn from N C & is being concentrated at Port Royal for an attack either on Savannah or Charleston it will soon appear which. We hear that most of our troops have followed them. All accounts agree in stating that their army is in a terrible state of discontent on the negro question, officers resigning on account of the Emancipation Proclamation. The preparations at Vicksburg go on but as yet nothing has been done. The Florida, Capt Maffitt, is rivalling the Alabama, Capt. Semmes. The Brookly W S is reported sunk by her & she has captured many prizes in the West Indian Seas. Sue came down on Thursday & remained until Sunday with me & today hearing I was no better kindly returned and is with me now. The Abolitionists came up last week on Friday to Hamilton in three Gunboats, landed & burned the Hotel there & retired without doing further damage. This is supposed to be a peice of petty personal spite, unworthy the arms of a great nation. The building in question is the *private* property of Lieut Col Lamb who commanded the expedition which some weeks ago attacked Plymouth battering down the Custom House, retaking many negroes, & disabling one of their Gunboats. So like cowards they wreak their vengeance on Col Lamb instead of the country which directs him!

FEBRUARY 19, 1863

Our wedding Day! We were forced to do without our usual Plum Pudding but supplied the deficiency with a much more wholesome "Cottage Pudding." Mr E very busy packing a waggon to send to Petersburg, a return to primitve customs enforced by the War as there is no transportation by R R & he wishes not only to get some Ploughs but to send off his Lard which is now worth one and a quarter dollars per lb.!

"Fighting Joe's" Grand Army is represented to be retiring from Fredericksburg, part of it en route for Washington & part for Fortress Monroe to try an advance on Richmond from the South side of James River. Nous verrons the Emperor of the French has made overtures to the U S pointing to peace, has suggested an Armistice & that Commissioners from both sides meet in a neutral country, Canada or Mexico, and discuss the points at variance. To this Mr Seward has replied saying that it involves treating on the part of the U S with Rebels, that he is certain the South will accept no terms but those of separation from the North (in which, o wise Senator Seward, you are quite right), & to that dismemberment the North will never consent, & winds up with telling his Majesty that *Washington* is the place & *Congress* the body wherein to discuss these measures. Thus flippantly *"snubbed"* I think the consequence will be that the Emperor will acknoledge the Confederate States & that we may soon have a treaty with France in our separate and independent nationality. In this opinion, however, I am singular. Sue left us yesterday in the rain. She has been most kind & considerately affectionate in staying so long with me. I am much better & soon hope to be well again. The River rising rapidly in consequence of the late heavy and continuous rain.

FEBRUARY 20, 1863

Planted Irish potatoes here at Looking Glass. Walked for the first time in some weeks with Mr E. Went to the river. The Low grounds are full of water, in fact it is running out at the Lower breaks but still rising steadily. The land & negroes are soon to undergo a valuation by State Assessors for the purpose of Taxation. I wish they could see it now. It would convince them of its uncertainity in a manner not to be mistaken.

Am reading Bulwers new book "The Strange Story,"[44] very Strange indeed is it and to my mind even as a collection of horrors, unaccountable &

---

[44] Edward George Earle Lytton Bulwer-Lytton was exceedingly popular with contemporary audiences. He published *A Strange Story* in 1861, *What Will He Do With It?* in 1859, *The Caxtons* in 1849, and *My Novel,*

mysterious, unworthy of the mind which wrote "What will he do with it." He has united modern Mesmerism & clairvoyance with medieval necromancy & demoniacal domination in a manner at once clumsy & ridiculous—raises Ghosts & makes dogs howl in consequence in accordance with the most vulgar and uneducated superstitions. The character of "Margrave" is not even original—a combination of Donatella in the "Marble Faun" & "The Man with Two Lives" of some German enthusiast or other, I forget who. Lillian too is very like the "Sleep Walker" of Zachocce. In fact the book is neither original or forcible, sad to say, and I fear presages a sadder fact still, that that noble mind is wearing out! And yet it is deeply interesting & flashes of Bulwer's thought, Bulwer's mind, illumine it like the phosphorescent play upon the water in the wake of a vessel in a dark night. The last few pages where Fenwick acknoledges the immortality of the Soul & *prays* with his whole heart, feels the *need*, the longing for prayer, for communion with, submission to God, thrill & touch the heart strongly & deeply. The characters are all Bulwer's & brought before one with his life like touches, but the wand, the incantations, the magnetism, & Mesmerism jar. One does not beleive & not beleiving, feels *critical*. I wish I had another like "The Caxtons," "My Novel," or "What will he do with it" to read now. I feel in the need & the humour for it. I wish I could write a novel, a *good* novel. I am sure it would amuse & interest me.

FEBRUARY 21, 1863

News last night by mail most interesting from Europe. Mr. Davis Message is making a deep impression. Louis Napoleon expected the U S (so says the French press) to reject his offer; his next step will be recognition of the Southern Confederacy. He scarcly expected the "snub" Seward gives him, however, & will, I hope, resent it. River very high & still rising. Father came down in a canoe to see us—quite well & considering the Water in good spirits. Planted all of the Wood's Seedling Potato I could find left from the unfortunate experiment of summer planting. Sent a few to Mama to get her into the Seed. An attack on Charleston or Savannah considered imminent. We say we are all prepared but Gen Beauregard has issued a call for 3,000 negroes to work on defences, probably the land defences in view of a debarkation & also to defend Wappoo Cut.

FEBRUARY 23, 1863

Father sent us yesterday Seward's & Dayton's[45] correspondance with the French Government relative to a conference for Peace. A more rascally weak

---

or *Varieties of English Life* in 1853. See footnote 31, 1860. Frank N. Magill and others (eds.), *Cyclopedia of World Authors* (Englewood Cliffs, N. J.: Salem Press, Inc., revised edition in 3 volumes, 1974), I, 269-271.

[45]William Lewis Dayton (1807-1864), a lawyer and United States senator from New Jersey, served as minister to France from 1861 until 1864. *Concise Dictionary of American Biography*, 223.

flimsy pack of lies were never before penned, & that is saying much. I copy on the next page my lines on Peace—blessed Peace.

Peace!

Hark! there's a whisper abroad on the breeze! List to the musical
      mumur! Now it swells!
Now it dies! faint! faint! as an infant's first sigh!—'till the
      grand old Pines
Catching the soft inspiration breathe from their mighty Harps the
      full Eolian diapason—Peace!
And the swift rushing rivers murmuring to the sea swell the grand
      Anthem—Peace!
And the idle waves kissing the pebbly shore, with a sudden deep
      sonorous rush answer in chorus—Peace!
And the ancient hills with a deafening roar from their craggy
      fronts fling back the loud thunder—Peace!
Till the Earth, the sky, the very atmosphere of our broad land
      thrills with rejoicing! Nature's Te Deum! Peace!

Hark how the glad Echoes vexed no more by horrid War give back the
      welcome sounds of Peace.
The lowing herd, the distant horn, the mellowed music of the hounds,
      the woodman's axe upon the hill—soothe the pained ear,
Dulled with the clash of arms, the tramp of steeds, the deep mouthed
      boom of cannon and the fierce cries of furious men!
The mill resumes its busy clack & from the factory hear the whirr
      of its thousand spindles.

Forth to the dewey field goes the glad huntsmen, his questing dog,
      wide wandering o'er the plain
And as the ploughman turns his long furrow the grateful incense that
      goes up from the fresh Earth
Stirs at his heart the thought of Peace, smiling & with sturdy
      arm, deeper he presses the glittering share—
Assured that what he soweth *now*—no foeman's hand shall reap.

Oft doth the anxious housewife pause in her thrifty care, oft
      does her expectant gaze turn townward
Down the hot dusty road, for now that the War is o'er & Peace O
      blessed Peace has come, returns once more her absent spouse.
Hark! there's a footstep at the door! List to the house dog's
      welcome bark! Tis he!
Stronger & sturdier, sadder perhaps, sunbrowned by toil & seamed
      with scars, but 'tis he!

His children cluster round his knee. Scarce can their feeble
      memories link the long absent father with the soldier.

With frightened wonder now they gaze upon his half drawn sword,
     & with gentle fingers timidly & tenderly
As tho they feared to pain him trace they now his scars, hear
     how *this* came.
And with sparkling eye list how the man who gave him *that* n'eer
     spoke again.
Now comes the full fruition of his labours! the full enjoyment
     of the blessed Peace.

The cock hence forth shall sound his reveile!
No Bugle knows he save the huntsman's horn, the only "Charge" he
     heeds, the rush of hounds.
Slowly he loiters through the fragrant Orchard where the ripe
     Apples tempt the willing hand, his children gambol round him,
His wife is at his side, her small white hand close pressed within
     his stalwart one.
With moistened eye now hears he how she managed in his absences,
     draws from her reluctant lips
The cares & troubles which with tender love she still had failed
     to write him,
And then with many a loving kiss he vows that *she* henceforth shall
     be his General
And that her gentle sway, stronger than War's stern "Regulations,"
     henceforth alone shall be his guidance!
Together now the garden walks they tread—sure Roses such as *these*
     n'eer bloomed before. One Rose one single Rose
From out that charmed spot is worth whole groves of war won Laurels!
Reverently & with bated breath, lifting his cap the while, speaks
     he of his lost comrades,
Dwells on their many virtues, how like a living wall they stood
     betwixt their country & her foes;
Tells o'er their sufferings, their uncomplaining patience, their
     privations such as her gentle breast n'eer dreamed of.
Then as the theme swells his full heart, sudden he clears his
     laboured breast, turns to his children,
And with a father's pride notes how his boys have grown & in his
     daughter's gentle face traces her still youthful Mother.
Forth o'eer his fields he rambles, marks how *this* needs him, how
     that is in his absence altered
And with a smiling confidence to himself repeats that now that
     Peace has come he soon will bring all right.
Leaving their tasks, close round him press his servants, their
     earnest simple greeting, their hearty welcome home
Tug at his heartstrings. Loud they proclaim their infelt confidence
     that when *he* their Master, he *himself* went forth against them,
That those dread enemies, those loathed Yankees n'eer would have the
     front to stand against him.

So pass his days amidst the joys of Peace—Peace which his own
    right arm hath helped to win.

Turn we the picture. In yon silent house, pale, sad, & grief
    worn sits a lone mourner!
No expectant watcher she! The glad echo of a well known step
    quickens no more her pulse with sudden start
And as the sounds of mirth, the voice of those who with gay shout
    & song welcome the new born Peace,
Fills the soft summer air, closer she hugs her greif the while and
    shuddering thinks on *Sharpsburg*—
And the long trenches filled with mangled Dead!
Patience sad mourner, patience! Think on Him who with His blood
    forever placed on voluntary sacrifice,
A sacramental seal! Forth in the flush of manhood, at his country's
    call, forth went thy loved one.
Fame, health, happiness—yea *Life* itself freely he laid upon his
    Country's altar. Think not hard
That God with pitying eye accepts the voluntary offering,
    think not hard! He works by *means*,
Means to a glorious end. That grand vicarious sacrifice by which
    the *One* set free the Universe
Is to our mortal eyes inscrutable, unfathomable, but precious—
    precious as the price of our Eternal Freedom.
Thy loved one died, but still his *Cause*, his country, lives & by
    that act, that glorious act of self devotion
He helped to set that Country free. Fragrant his memory lies
    embalmed in thousand grateful hearts!
Long years hence, when with slow fingers time has traced his furrow
    on thy Cheek,
Busy men shall turn aside from the stern strife of life through
    thee to do him reverence.
Mothers with gentle eye & tender tone—shall to their little
    children tell thy sorrow
And in low whispers, as in presence of a holy thing shall say,
    "She wears those weeds for one who fell at Sharpsburg."

Feb 9th, 1863

FEBRUARY 24, 1863

Do you know Mrs. Edmondston why your own poetry does not give you
pleasure? I will tell you, Madam; it is because your mind is a *store house*, not a
mine. You take nothing from it but what you have formerly put there. Those
lines on the other page are very good, the best you ever wrote, but turn to the

bookcase, take down Tennyson or Bulwer's translation of Schiller,[46] read "In Memoriam" or "The Mystery of Reminiscence," & then re read your own! How do they sound? Fie, madam! you take pleasure in "a *tolerable egg*"? "Your standard is not so high" hey? "Is that what you say?" I might call your mind a crucible, so I might, madam, but a crucible it is not in the true Alchemist sense. It does not from simples transmute the pure virgin gold. I liken it rather to your own "Papin's Digester." You put in the ingredients one by one & simmer them slowly, for days perhaps years, but still, madam, after all your simmering you bring nothing out but a good broth, in which you can still detect the different ingredients. You make no new substance, nothing which defies a critic. Vattel[47] or Soyer would at first sip re-resolve your humble broth into its original elements, & that, Madam, is why your own poetry does not please you. You do yourself injustice. Your standard *is high* & you feel you do not attain to it. Is there one single original idea in those lines opposite? The nearest approach you make to it is calling the Pines "Eolian harps," but I doubt me you heard that somewhere. No Madam, the poet is "nascitur not fit"[48] & "nascitur" you are not. "Fit," I would not be. Say rather with the proud motto of the proudest family of France, " 'Rois ne puis Prince ne daigne—*Rohan Je suis.*' Poet you cannot, Imitator deign not; useful everyday sympathizing woman you are."

FEBRUARY 25, 1863

Dr Hall has just left me. He thinks I am suffering with a nervous affection of the stomach & has prescribed accordingly—a serious calamity if it be so & one which will call forth all my powers of endurance & patience to combat and meet as I ought.

No news from Charleston. Foster & Hunter the Abolition Generals it appears quarreled as to precedence & who had the right of command. Foster refused to disembark his troops from the transports & posted off to Washington for orders—hence the delay. Before Vicksburg all things remain quiet; the enemy seem to be making preparation for an attack but as yet have done nothing. We captured the Gunboat "Queen of the West" which ran the gaunlet past our batteries before Vicksburg in the Red River. It seems they had forced the Pilot, John Burke of the C S Steamer Eva which they had captured, to take the helm. He at first feigned fear but finally took the wheel un-

---

[46]Johann Christoph Friedrich von Schiller (1759-1805) was a German poet, philosopher, dramatist, and historian of the Romantic Period. His philosophical poems, ballads, and historical dramas brought him extensive critical acclaim. Benét, *Reader's Encyclopedia*, 998.

[47]Francois Vatel, a prominent French chef and a steward to the French finance minister Fouquet, was the famous maitre d'hotel to the Prince de Condé. He committed suicide in 1671 in despair over the late arrival of the fish course he had ordered for a dinner given by Condé in honor of Louis XIV. Aresty, *Delectable Past*, 72.

[48]"The poet is born, not made."

der a Yankee guard. On nearing our Batteries he told them that they were fifteen miles off & brought the vessel close in alongside. We instantly opened fire & the first shot broke the steam Pipe, disabling the boat. Burke jumped off & drifted safely to shore. The boat swung round to the other side of the river when her crew escaped on board their transport DeSoto, which we hear they afterward burned to prevent her from falling into our hands.[49] In the North West there is a great re-action taking place in favour of *Peace*. They pretend that it is on account of Lincoln's Emancipation Proclamation, but if so it is very strange that no symptom of it was manifested by them from Sept when he gave notice of his intentions until Feb a month after it had been actually issued. I doubt! It is the want of *success* in that said Emancipation Proclamation which now disatisfies them. So long as they *hoped* it would be effective they were as mute as fish. Now when they *see* it is "brutem fulmen," "O! it is outrageous! horrible! barbarous!" "We are their brethren!" "They cannot see a million half civilized blacks turned loose to prey on the innocent women and children of the South!" Fudge, they would be willing enough to see it!, but Cuffee is more contented & in better subjection than they thought. So now is the time to make "humanitarian capital." Fit descendants of the Puritans, you effect to abhor true disciples of Exeter Hall.[50] We scorn you and your newly developed philanthropy!

MARCH 2, 1863

We have captured another Gunboat in the Miss. River. The Indianola, sent out by the Abolitionists to retake the Queen of the West, was in her turn taken by would be prey assisted by the C S Steamer Webb. She sank, being much disabled, but it is thought we can raise & make her fit for service again. Things remain as they were before Vicksburg. Preparations for an attack still going on. Pope has been ordered there, it is said, to take command. Semmes & Maffit playing havoc with the Abolition shipping in the West Indian Seas. Every arrival brings news of some new capture. A conscript law similar to ours has passed the Abolition Senate. It remains to see how the House & the dear people will view it. Our country the past week filled with troops going to the Blackwater. A cavalry Regt encamped for some days at Halifax waiting

[49]The description of this incident is confused and oversimplified. The U.S.S. *Queen of the West*, under Col. Charles R. Ellet, had gone to Gordon's Landing on the Black River looking for Confederate ships, cotton, and slaves. Rebel shore batteries opened fire on the ship and, as the pilot attempted to back her down the river, she ran aground directly below the rebel batteries at Fort Taylor. The pilot had expressed disloyal sentiments earlier and Ellet, questioning his loyalty, placed him under arrest. The officers and the majority of the crew abandoned the *Queen of the West* and escaped on the *Era No. 5. Official Records (Navy)*, Series I, XXIV, 382-386; *Civil War Naval Chronology*, III, 29-31.

[50]Exeter Hall, the London headquarters of the Evangelical party in the Church of England from 1831 until 1907, and of other philanthropic groups, came to be equated with evangelical fervor. J. Holland Rose, A. P. Newton, and E. A. Benians (eds.), *The Cambridge History of the British Empire*, Volume II: *The Growth of the New Empire, 1783-1870* (Cambridge: University of Cambridge Press, 8 volumes, 1929-1959), 509, 659, 663; Wilson, *Crusader in Crinoline*, 374.

for the river to fall so that they could cross. All quiet as yet in S C. Our River rising again, & again is the plantation being filled with water.

March 5, 1863

Have been riding on horseback with Mr E. every afternoon for a week past & find much benefit from it. Yesterday saw the first Plumb blossom fully expanded. Spring will soon be upon us. We have planted a larger crop of Irish Potatoes than we ever did before, in view of the need of our Army & the high prices they command. We were fortunate in being able to buy good seed. A letter from brother to father yesterday fills us with alarm on account of the supplies of food for our Army in Va. He says the Sec of War has written to Gov Vance that unless supplies of provisions come in faster for the next five weeks than they have done for the past five that our *Army in Va will be out of food* & that in consequence Richmond must be abandoned and the Army fall back here into N C. Startling news! I hope exagerated in the hope of increasing the amount of corn sent on & to excuse the conduct of the Quartermasters. If *they* exerted themselves, however, more corn could be got. They stay at Weldon & content themselves with Agents who idle through the country. There is corn enough in the neighborhood to last them some time, in small lots it is true & requiring trouble to hunt it up, but I think we can rub on until the wheat Harvest. The want is not provisions but *management*. They do not feel uneasy about *meat*. It is bread. Government now pays $5 per bu in some sections. It offers us two & we have 800 bu waiting for the water to fall so that it can be shelled and shipped. Brother thinks the Army will be down upon us and urges that we plant 100 bu of Irish Potatoes & all the Sweet that can be bedded, as our corn for bread will in that case be seized. We will do it but I do not think we are in such danger as that; but what looks a little ominous, yesterday a C S Engineer deputed, to examine & make a report of the country between Roanoke & Tar Rivers a (Topographical Engineer), dined at father's, having got so far in the prosecution of his work. He sees our property just now, most of it under water, under most unfavorable auspices for military manoevres; all the better for us.

Below Savannah our Steamer Nashville coming up the Ogeechee got aground on a sand bar above Fort McAllister. The Abolition Iron Clads opened fire upon her across the Marsh & an Incendiary shell striking her she was soon a total loss. The fort attempted but vainly to protect her. Her captain, William McBlair, who when I was a girl I remember visited at our fathers house died the week before & was succeeded by Capt Sinclair[51] on a day or two before the accident.

---

[51]The loss of the *Nashville* occurred on February 28, 1863. Capt. William McBlair, who died on February 16, 1863, was succeeded by Arthur Sinclair, the commander of the C.S.S. *Atlanta*. *Official Records (Navy)*, Series I, XIII, 704-705, 820, 769.

The Abolition Congress has passed a Conscription Act, similar in some respects but better than ours. Any one can be exempt by paying $300 to the Sec of War. Lincoln is invested with Dictatorial powers in all save the name; they have allowed him to suspend the Act of Habeas Corpus, an exercise of power which on the part of the British Parliament would shake Victoria's throne. The people I suppose will submit. The Frankfort Convention has been dispersed by a file of soldiers yet we hear no news of a revolt in Kentucky. A negro Regt is in service under Milroy at Winchester Va. Ah! that Stonewall Jackson could bring him to his bearings! Baton Rouge is garrisoned by them & their conduct is reported as infamous. In Northen Ala one Abolition hero has immortalized himself by confiscating all *agricultural & even garden tools*, has issued an order to the effect that not a *seed* shall be put into the ground & ordering the arrest of all farmers found in the pursuit of their avocations. We do not yet know his name but I will get it & the Order. Senator Wilson,[52] a hypocrite, after prating all his political life about the "Equality of the Negro," has introduced a bill in the Abolition Congress providing that "No white man shall be put under the orders of any one of African descent." There is consistency for you! They are to be equal *here* with us but not with the *blue blood* (blue from poverty) of the Yankee's! Vice President Hamlin has gone to Maine to raise a Brigade of Negroes. He as the highest in rank of the children of Ham, ought to be made Brigadier & let the gradations in command be determined by the Anglo Saxon Blood in their veins until it descends to the full blooded African private. Wait until a Brigade of Cuffies sees one of their Regts annihilated by their Southern Masters. The rest will be hard to catch.

A very pleasant letter from Margaret urging me to come up & see her and get well, but I am so much better that I think I do not need a change, and this is no time for visiting. We find by a recent reconnoisance that there is no material change in the Army before Fredericksburg as we had supposed. Fighting Joe is still "waiting for the roads to harden." We hear that Tom Jones has been sent to Savannah & George Miller[53] is now with his Regt in Charleston, so I have two nephews engaged in the defence of that place. And Amo Coffin, too, will be called out when the attack is made, three stakes in the field!

MARCH 9, 1863

Went on Thursday to Hascosea for the first time in some weeks. Marked the places for Allen to plant my fruit trees as I could not stay long, nor am I

---

[52]Henry Wilson (1812-1875), a lawyer, newspaper editor, and state politician, adamantly opposed slavery. A United States senator from Massachusetts from 1855 until 1872, Wilson used his position to urge emancipation as a war measure and sought the freedom of slaves in the border states. In 1872 he was elected vice-president under Grant and served until his death. *Concise Dictionary of American Biography*, 1221.

[53]George Devereux Miller, the son of Henry Watkins and Frances Devereux Miller, was a private in Co. D, Thirty-first North Carolina Regiment. On November 7, 1863, he transferred as a private to Co. K, Fourteenth North Carolina Regiment. Manarin and Jordan, *North Carolina Troops*, V, 489. See Introduction.

well enough to do it my self. The enemy made a third attack on Fort Mc Allister without serious result on either side. The Iron Clads after a night & days bombardment drew off without any apparent damage, they having in that time demolished one gun carriage & slightly wounded two men, which is all the loss on our side. The Yankee prints claim to have passed Vicksburg through their boasted canal, but as it is not confirmed by our accounts, we take the liberty of disbeleiving it. Their Congress passed a bill before its adjournment making Treasury notes a legal tender. So Lincoln is now absolute, as he has the power of the purse & the sword, besides which the authority to suspend the act of Habeas Corpus at his discretion makes him despotic. How true are Elwood Fisher's words published thirteen years ago. He said the epitaph of the Northern nation could be written in few words thus— "Here lies a nation who lost their own liberty in a vain endeavour to give freedom to the Negro."[54]

MARCH 23, 1863

Came home today from a fortnight's visit to father's. Have enjoyed the society of Father, Mama, & Sue greatly. Played innumerable games of Chess with Father & return to my home duties and home pleasures in much better health & more fitted in every way both to fulfil the first & enjoy the last than when I left. We have watched the mails, Ah! how anxiously for news from our Army, but as yet there has been but little done—before Charleston absolutely nothing. The Abolition fleet of Iron Clads is massing itself at Port Royal, but since the bombardment of Fort McAlister, which they say was undertaken to test their invulnerability, they have remained entirely inactive. Burnside it is rumoured is to take command, but that is not authentic. The canard about their fleet having passed through the canal opposite Vicksburg was got up for the benefit of the European news, the English steamers having sailed at the time of its promulgation. Banks has advanced with his Gunboats & the U S frigate Mississippi & attacked our batteries at Port Hudson. They were repulsed with heavy loss on their side. The frigate Mississippi was burned. The Richmond (Banks Flagship) driven back disabled. Two gunboats in a crippled condition succeeded in running past, but as the Indianola & Queen of the West are in fighting trim, *they*, we hope will soon settle accounts with them. The expedition down Yazoo Pass, after encountering almost unheard of difficulties in the swamps & from the trees that over hang those crooked Rivers the Cold Water & Tallahatchie, reached Fort Pemberton where the latter river joins the Yazoo. We maintain that we repulsed them & at our last news they were landing for a land attack. Per contra they assert that they have

[54]The quotation reads: "Here were a people who disputed about the capacity of the African for liberty and civilization, and did not themselves possess the capacity to preserve their own." Elwood Fisher, *Lecture on the North and the South, Delivered before the Young Men's Mercantile Literary Association of Cincinnati, Ohio, January 16, 1848* (Wilmington, N.C.: Buell and Blanchard, 1849), 30.

been successful, have captured 25 steamers & command the Yazoo. We wait further developments. The object of the expedition was to gain possession of the country in the rear of Vicksburg & cut off our supplies and thus force us to surrender. Van Dorn has made a most masterly escape from three or more Brigades which surrounded him & hoped gradually to close upon him & take him as it were in a net. By a forced night march, he out manoevred them & made good his escape. At Tullahoma, below Murfresboro, a battle with Rosencrans is considered imminent. Let us hope that Gen Johnston & not Bragg will be in command. Gen Hooker dispatched 3,000, some say more, men on a reconnoisance in force it is supposed. They crossed the Rappahanock at Kelly's Ford, but Fitz Hugh Lee with his Cavalry falling upon them after an obstinate engagement put them to flight with heavy loss, their hospital and guns falling into our hands. This brilliant exploit it is thought checked the advance of the army at that point & will give "fighting Joe" something to think of. Our loss 250 killed & wounded; theirs much heavier. In this state Gen Hill has not been idle but his movements are wrapped in so much doubt that I will not chronicle them until I hear further. Suffice it that his expedition was undertaken mainly to procure supplies of corn & forage from the Eastern Counties in which attempt he has we hear been eminently successful. Daniel's brigade, in which James is, is in the advance & are said to be below New Berne tearing up the R R from Morehead to that place. So far rumour gives to Pettigrew the post of honour. His brigade it is said captured Newberne but owing to the bursting of their large gun could not maintain themselves against the Gunboats & were consequently forced to evacuate it— but this is not authentic.

A most fiendish expedition left Port Royal a short time since, destination unknown, supposed Florida, with the open and avowed object of inciting the Negroes to revolt! The Northen papers actually glory in it & gloat over the sweet morsel of revenge in store for them with a savage ferocity. God avert their infamous acts! They declare that they are in correspondance with the slaves throughout a large & populous portion of the Confederacy, who only wait their arrival to rise against their masters & strike a blow for the *Union*— the *Union*, bosh and balderdash!—what does Cuffee know or care for it? I do not beleive the negroes will rise at their bidding, but that does not lessen the malignity of their black hearted wishes and attempts.

I have been much worried by personal matters latterly—at one time so much so as to make me really unhappy. I refer to our property & pecuniary matters. Father in consequence of the War & expected high taxes and the depreciation of the currency thinks he had better make an entire change in the tenure by which we hold this property. Last June's freshet has diminished the value and certainty of the Estate so much that he wishes to make other arrangements. Now all change is greivous whilst it is going on, particularly so when one lives in such happiness & contentment as we now do, so I must, I know, make up my mind to a season of suspense & anxiety—a *change* which perhaps will at first gall; but I will strive for cheerful contentment with my lot, be it what it may, & a firm reliance upon God who will give us all things needful for us. Father most kindly wishes to free Patrick from the debt which the present ownership of this property entails. The only fear I have is that it will weaken his interest in & enjoyment of the plans for improvement which he is now continually carrying on, but I will hope for the best. The farm at Hascosea is to be enlarged & that is to be ours without encumbrance of any sort. It has given us so much care, thought, & anxiety, but I have striven to cast it all on One who knows what is for our best & having food & raiment to endeavour therewith to be content; but it is hard to change our plans & hopes after so many years indulging them & the struggle is at times no slight one, but courage, all will yet be right! Courage—& keep a cheerful heart.

March 26, 1863

First Swallow came! They are a little later than usual, but this is a backward Spring. We had snow & sleet on the 20th & 21st in Va the heaviest fall of snow of the season. Hooker's Army is at a stand-still in consequence. We have another freshet in the River & the Lowgrounds again full of water; no getting to father's but by canoe. Patrick has gone out to attend to the re-packing of the cotton at Hascosea, a Legacy of trouble & anxiety left us by the Christian Burnside & the foolish orders issued to move it last Feb a year ago. Well, I hope this is the last of it, and the ownership will I trust soon be upon the broad shoulders of the Government who can bear it better than we can. Am busy getting three boxes ready to send to our nephews in Charleston. We have not much to send, but poor fellows, anything will be welcome to them, for it is hard living at best & everything is so high that their purses cannot accomplish many dainties.

March 28, 1863

River very high and still rising. Went out yesterday with Patrick in the canoe, the water as smooth as a lake. He shot several partridges and Musk Rats. The chase was most exciting, for *chase* it was, paddling through the thickets between bushes, now entangled in a vine, now floating with the current so as not to alarm the prey & then pursuing it with all the strength of Mr E's muscles, aiding Ned's. Ned showed himself as keen as a pointer dog in finding & pointing at the partridges. No public news. The papers say it is the lull which precedes the storm, a lull which will soon be fearfully broken. God defend the right!

MARCH 30, 1863

We have destroyed two of the enemies gunboats which attempted to run past our batteries at Vicksburg, sunk one & the other lies on the opposite shore a wreck. Gen Loring at Fort Pemberton has repulsed the expedition which came down Yazoo Pass destroying a Gunboat the Sciota & some transports. The enemy are re-inforcing & we, it is said, are doing the same in the Sunflower. Col Ferguson has repulsed the expedi[tion] sent down that River to join the one down the Yazoo Pass & thinks he can maintain himself & destroy it. Rosencrans is retreating towards Nashville, supposed to join Grant & march down the Mississippi Valley to ensure the fall of Vicksburg. So far all is good & hopeful for the future. The River is falling. Well for us that it is, for the Hunter Trunk Dam has been in great danger from the side current from the break above. Walked there with Patrick this afternoon. Its escape was a narrow one. As it is, half the base is gone. Busy all the morning making a model of an obstruction to navigation which Patrick thinks may be used with advantage in the Harbour of Charleston. It is a Scotch invention patented just before the war & perhaps Gen Beauregard has not seen it. So Mr E has concluded to send him both drawings & a model of it. My harmless little cardboard affair requires a great stretch of imagination before it can be magnified into a barrier to oppose the passage of an iron clad with torpedoes bearing death & destruction moored at intervals along it. I hope that Gen B will use it, as it will be a delightful thought to Patrick should he be enabled to contribute even a mite to the defence of his native city.

This morning whilst stooping down admiring the beauty of my Hyacinths, my ear in consequence close to the ground, suddenly I heard the unmistakable "boom" of a heavy gun in Southerly direction. Never since the war began have I heard one so plainly. Throwing off my bonnet I listened & distinctly heard two more in quick succession in the same direction, probably a Gunboat in the Chowan, & that report heard by me in such tranquil repose may carry agony to the heart of some of our poor neighbors on that River! The enemy have been very busy in the inglorious task of destroying seines & fisheries there latterly & it is most likely that they are shelling some defenceless village like Winton or some isolated house such as Mr Etheridges at Coleraine—feats which their valour has accomplished once before.

APRIL 1, 1863

News of the success of our Cavalry in the west under Forrest, Wheeler, & Morgan, capturing prisoners, 800 in no., arms & equipments, burning Commissary stores & destroying a R R Bridge on the Nashville road at Brentwood—thus annoying Rosencrans to whom they have (the Abolitionists) given the sobriquet of "Old Holdfast." They claim to have received from New Orleans tidings of a complete victory at Port Hudson & that all their vessels with the exception of the Mississippi, which they declare they burned because she was aground, were safely past our batteries, but that is for Europe as a Steamer sailed last week. O! universal Yankee nation how you do lie! Your moral sense is perverted, you see no shame in it. We suffer from aprehensions that our army in Va will be forced to "*fall back.*" Sec Stanton has a rumour to the effect that we are removing our machinery and munitions of war to a less exposed place than Richmond. Numbers of troops have, we know, left Gen Lee—some to So Ca, some to the Blackwater—& the country is filled with reports of the intentions of Government & the need of food, which are very painful, tho I do not credit the whole of them. Prices are fearfully high even for depreciated currency, which fact, however, loth & slow I have been to admit, is indisputable—Lard 1.25, Bacon 6.00 & upward, Flour $30 per barrel, Tea $7 per lb, sugar $1.12 ½ to 1.25 per lb, boots $50 a pr, Long cloth $2. to 2 25 a yard, Cotton Cards $30 for two pair, I think, Salt considered cheap at $25 per bu, butter $2 per lb—& every thing else in proportion. The country has been clamouring for a Tax—a high Tax & they have got one now. At least the House has passed it & there is little doubt but that the Senate will follow suit. It is enormous! Sidney Smith's taxed Englishman was a favoured individual to what a taxed Confederate will soon be. I fear me that the vice of lying and false swearing will be amazingly increased. The temptation to under estimate one's property will be great.[55] When it is published as a law I will enumerate some portions & mention the amount we pay.

Last week the Battery constructed above us was taken in tow by a steamer to be carried down to a landing below us to be ironed. From some mismanagement they allowed her to drag the boat then under headway of steam past the landing & attempting to turn she ran afoul of the boat crashing her wheel & damaging her greatly. Shameful conduct some where & conduct which will be felt in the Army, for this is one of two Steamers upon which we depend to carry our supplies to Weldon. One boat was lost from the drunkenness of the person in charge last summer—now this from incapacity! It is too bad and we have had a part of a cargo ready bagged for *three* weeks waiting for her to come & take it and yet all the time is the out cry—"*send on your corn*"! They put a negligent ignoramus in charge because forsooth he has interest enough to get the appointment which keeps him from the Conscript Camp & then the nation & army suffer! Ah! patriotism, these stupid worthless officials try you sadly! Our gun at Rainbow Gen Beauregard wished for at Charleston & instead of sending the order to some man of sense who knew the country & that

---

[55]The *Raleigh Register*, April 4, 1863, reported on a bill entitled "An act to lay taxes for the common defence, and carry out the government of the Confederate States" which had passed the House but was pending in the Senate. This tax, finally passed April 24, 1863, incorporated a graduated income tax, license tax, a tax-in-kind amounting to one tenth of each farm's agricultural produce, and an internal revenue duty on enumerated items. The income collected by this measure was of benefit to the Confederacy, but the act was extremely unpopular in North Carolina. Randall and Donald, *Civil War and Reconstruction*, 256-258.

the best, in short the only practical, way of getting it there was to send it back by steamer to Halifax & there put it on the R R, some num-skull of a commissioned officer ordered it to be hauled 25 miles across the country to Tarrboro to the R R there. The consequence was that after dismounting & with great labour moving it about 300 yds it stuck hopelessly in the mud & there it lies useless to every one waiting, like fighting Joe, for the "roads to harden."

We have had terrible weather latterly which has I fear played havoc with our Peach crop. "George the 4th" is the only one that I have examined which gives promise of fruit. "Miss Timmons" is deceitful. "Old Mixon" a cheat & "President," "Ravenel's favorite," "Grape Mignon," "Newington," & "Early York"—blackhearted! Hard names to give my friends. The Apples will I hope escape, as they are very backward. My two hens in the house yard, Mrs Marllow & Katrine Von Tassel, laid in 75 days 118 eggs between them. Pretty well, considering one was a pullet!

Sue is gone to Raleigh to attend the Communion & Kate Miller's wedding which latter is to take place on the 15th. I must try to make a wedding Cake, tho the war has diminished my stores sadly. Mr E read me this morning an extract, "The best way to see Divine Light is to put out thine own candle." What a world of wisdom, of faith, and of trust in God & humility does it contain! "Put out thine own candle," vain man, that the Sun of Righteousness may enlighten you.

APRIL 5, 1863

Sunday—Came home in a canoe from father's where we have been for two days, Mr E having business with him. Weather uncomonly cold & cloudy for some days, anything but farming weather. No news. It is supposed the enemy delay their advance on Charleston until the Connecticut election which takes place tomorrow & is the first open issue of Peace or War presented to the people. Seymour[56] takes the ground that the war is iniquitous, unjust, cruel, unconstitutional, & suicidal. Peace on any terms. Let the South go, but Peace for the North. We shall see how many agree with him. Mr E quite sick, threatened with rheumatism, with considerable fever.

APRIL 8, 1863

Went yesterday to Hascosea. Very imprudent in Mr E, as he is covered with a thick eruption which I hope, however, is only nettle rash & fever with it. Quite cold; the only evidence of Spring as you drive up is the Peach blossoms but for them it looks like Jan. Country much excited about the

---

[56]Thomas Hart Seymour (1807-1868) served as a United States congressman from Connecticut from 1843 until 1845, as governor of Connecticut from 1850 until 1853, and as the United States minister to Russia from 1854 until 1858. He also led the Connecticut peace Democrats during the Civil War. *Concise Dictionary of American Biography*, 942.

Taxes now being assessed. They are enormous. Met neighbors who all stopped & talked them over. Prices too are ruinous. I do not see how salaried men can live. I preserve in the 2d vol. of this book a slip cut from a Richmond Paper as reference for the future: $5 in gold brought $21 a few days since in Chatham County & a lot of negroes average $1800. One man, a miller, $4,400—so much has our currency depreciated.

Seward entertained the Hatien minister at dinner the other day. Think of that! The Caricatures put forth against the Abolition party in its first rise & which were the amusement of our childhood actually realized. I mark the slip A no 2.[57] The country has been filled with rumours of the taking of Washington in this State, all of which are untrue. Gen Hill is down in that part of the country, has issued a circular recommending the farmers to commence their spring work & promising them so far as he can afford it protection from the enemy. A dispatch from Gen R Taylor dated Berwick's bay to Gen Cooper tells us of the capture of the Federal Steamer Diana, mounts five heavy Guns but little injured. Abolition loss 150—killed, wounded, & prisoners.

Our Army has been reduced to ¼ lb of Pork a day, only one third the full ration. We are discussing the propriety of reducing our negro allowance in the face of it & sending the surplus to the Qr Master. It seems hard that Cuffee should not feel somewhat of what his masters & betters endure. Sent off a box to Tom & Frank Jones containing 2 hams, 2 sausages, half a side of Bacon, 2 bottles Red Pepper, 2 do black, 4 bottles of Tomato Catsup, some white beans, a quantity of butter, & a lot of Tobacco. A box to Amo with a ham, half a side of bacon, some butter, a sausage, a bottle of black and one of Red Pepper, some Tobacco, & a pair of Epaulettes & some things for his Mother, stockings, sugar plums, & pop corn for the children. Mr E sent a bu of Beans to Sister F. She writes that are worth ten dollars in Raleigh. A can of Lard to Jessie & some seed corn for Mr Gantt. I hope they will go safely!

Correspondance, demanded by Parliament, between Mr Mason & Lord Russel is published in our papers. It is most humiliating & insulting to us & I earnestly hope that the President will at once withdraw Mr M & no longer keep him standing hat in hand, a target for Lord Russel's petty malice & mean selfishness to vent itself upon. The great negro expedition sent out from Port Royal which was to carry sorrow & woe to our hearts & our hearths by corrupting our negroes, making them affiliate with their armed brethren, has returned in shame & confusion of face. They landed at Jacksonville, Florida, committed all kinds of horrible & brutal excess, plundered, burned, & stole, but a handful of white men drove them pell mell back to their boats and the Yankees could do nothing with them, so they put back to their friend and sympathizer Gen Hunter.[58]

---

[57]This newspaper clipping appears on page 30 of the second volume of the diary.

[58]The First South Carolina Regiment of Colored Troops (Union), commanded by Col. Thomas Wentworth Higginson of Massachusetts, together with the Eighth Maine and part of the Sixth Connect-

April 10, 1863

Went up to Conneconara on the afternoon of the 8th, Mr E. intending to go to Halifax with father on the 9th about the assessment for our taxes, but in this he was disappointed for he felt so unwell & was so covered with the eruption which was inflamed and angry that he thought it best to decline the expedition. About twelve o'clock, the day being pleasant, we thought it best to come home as he had every symptom of a severe illness. We were forced to come on horseback on account of the late freshet & the ride was most distressing to him as his fever was very high and his headache severe. Sent at once for the Dr who, however, has not reached us yet. In the meantime he has continued very unwell & his fever unabated.

There is no evil though without a corresponding blessing we are told & this sickness keeps him from going off at once to Charleston to assist in the defense of his native state, for we hear that the long expected attack has at last commenced. The Captain of the Steamer brought father a paper on the morning of the 9th which told us that the enemies fleet had safely crossed the Bar and that our boats had gone down to the Forts to meet them. This did not tend to soothe the irritation under which Mr E was already suffering & he actually chafed at the restraint which kept him at home. With the mail came a note from father telling us that there was only undefined rumours of severe fighting at Charleston. "The reliable Gentleman" had seen on the bulletin boards at Richmond on the evening of the 8th that we had sunk one and disabled four Iron clads, but there was no paper of later date than the one we had in the morning, so we must wait for another mail with what patience we may. A letter from James dated "Tafts store" tells us that General Hill has the town of Washington completely invested, that there has been a good deal of Artillery fighting which is still going on, does not know the General's plans. Father writes that he has driven off re-inforcements by water from Newberne, that he had sent in a Flag of Truce demanding the surrender of the place or the removal of non combattants, both which were refused, which seems infamous.

James goes on to personal matters which concern me so nearly that I had as well transcribe that part of his letter. "I saw General Robertson of the Cavalry today. He says that he had an interview with Gen Hill the other day about the appointment of field officers for the 41st Regt. (Baker's Cavalry) & asked him if he had any reccomendations to make. At first Hill said 'No.' Afterwards he said the two Edmondston's. This was very satisfactory to Robertson & we have been reccommended for the officers—you Lt Col & I Major. Robertson asked me to accept if appointed, which I agreed to cheerfully, such a good chance to get out of the Qr masters Depart. Robertson

---

icut regiments, quietly occupied Jacksonville and successfully fought several skirmishes in the vicinity of the city. On March 28, 1863, the Federals evacuated the city after destroying much of it. *Official Records (Navy)*, Series I, XIII, 738, 745, 794; Boatner, *Civil War Dictionary*, 433.

asked me if you would accept. Told him I did not know." Neither do I, for it is the very same post that Gen French offered him whilst he held in his hand Hill's reccommendation (his superior officer's) for the Colonelcy of the same Regt! & which he at once declined. In fact I think it was insulting in French but when Robertson offers it under different circumstances the case is different, tho how he will like to serve under Baker, a junior both in years & original Rank & confessedly ignorant & incompetent & inefficient, is more than I can say. He is too sick just now to be worried about it, & after all it is as well not to take trouble by the forelock, as the appointment may not come.

The Northern papers say that Hooker is preparing for an advance but *that* we have heard every few weeks since the battle of Fredericksburg. The expedition down Yazoo Pass has returned a complete failure. We learn this from their own admission as also that that down the Sunflower is alike fruitless & that the canal from Lake Providence has submerged an enormous tract of country & produced only a feeling of undying & bitter hate from the inhabitants, whose property is thus destroyed & injured, to the U S Government. The water not being deep enough for their purposes, they also admit in addition a repulse at Port Hudson & are under serious aprehension that the two vessels which succeeded in running past may be captured by the Queen of the West & the Indianola. Their hope now is to starve us out. They think we are suffering, ignore the fact of the depreciation of our currency, & quote the high price of provisions to prove it, are jubilant over some mobs & riots which they call "bread riots." We call them mobs for plunder & beleive that they were instigated by the Yankees. They are composed of low foreigners, Irish, Dutch, & Yankee and in place of wanting bread they threw Rice, flour, etc., in the street & mobbed dry goods & shoe stores! This in Richmond; that at Salisbury was exaggerated.[59] It was a small affair for plunder alone. The war exercises our ingenuity. I have just finished an excellent & really handsome & useful pair of gloves for Mr E, knit of Rabbit fur & wool, equal proportions spun together. They are warmer than wool & not too coarse for horseback & now I am making a set of table mats of *corn shucks*. They promise to be pretty.

The season very backward. Hard frost the last three mornings which I fear ends all hope of peaches & Pears. My dwarf pears are in beautiful bloom & it

---

[59]The Salisbury mob, composed chiefly of soldiers' wives and some men, congregated at a storehouse owned by Michael Brown. Angered by a food shortage, the crowd chopped down the front door of the storehouse to get the flour they needed and earlier had been refused. Brown then agreed to deliver ten barrels of flour, and the crowd dispersed. The Richmond riot also was triggered by speculators who hoarded staples. One paper in Virginia attributed the riot to "prostitutes, professional thieves, Irish and Yankee hags, gallow birds from all lands but our own." In actuality, the rioters were mainly women, the wives of laborers and poorer members of the working class, who began by seizing food and clothing but soon began to take anything available. The breakdown in law and order grew throughout the South as goods became increasingly scarce and money grew increasingly worthless. *Daily Sentinel*, March 25, 1863; *Register* (Petersburg, Virginia), April 8, 1863; Barrett, *Civil War in North Carolina*, 188; Mary Elizabeth Massey, *Ersatz in the Confederacy* (Columbia: University of South Carolina Press, 1952), 166.

is a severe disappointment to *lose* the *fruit* of our labour for another year. The 1st Asparagus shoot made its appearance on the 1st of April & as yet it is the only one. Redbud in blossom. On the 8th are beginning to have a few shad & Rock, which is a releif to my housekeeping cares.

APRIL 11, 1863

For once the "reliable gentleman" was correct! We have sunk an Iron Clad & disabled more, to what extent we cannot tell; however, as the news is Telegraphic only, but signed "G. T. Beauregard." We are very anxious for fuller accounts. The attack commenced about 2 on the afternoon of Tuesday the 7th and lasted until ½ past five when the fleet drew off. No further attack has since been made. The Connecticut Election has gone against the Democrats by 3,000 majority. It is said that the New York Herald gained the Election for the Administration by publishing an extra in flaming Capitals, "Charleston in the possession of the Union Army"; "The Star Spangled Banner floats triumphantly over Fort Sumpter"; "The Rebellion crushed"; "The fountain head of Secession destroyed," etc.! Can any cause prosper which requires such lies to bolster it up? We have taken & destroyed a Gun boat in the Coosaw River. This river separates Port Royal from the main land, so we are circumscribing their bounds.

Mr Edmondston quite sick in bed all day. The anxiety he is in about Charleston I think increases his fever. He suffers much from fever & the irritation of this eruption. The Dr tells us it is an epidemic accompanied in most cases with sore throat. This he is spared.

APRIL 12, 1863

Further but still meager details of the attack on Charleston. We have lost one paper which is annoying. The attack was opened on Tuesday. On Monday Eight Monitors, the Ironsides, & 65 vessels of various sizes were seen lying off the Bar. Thirty five vessels entered the Stono & they landed a force of six thousand men on Coles & Battery Islands. Between two & three o'clock on Tuesday afternoon five Monitors & the Ironsides were seen rounding the point of Morris Island, the Keokuk, a double turreted Monitor, in the advance. At three P M the action opened. Fort Moultrie firing the first gun. Sumter opened with a broadside on the Keokuk ten minutes later. The fleet formed in line of battle off the Fort at the distance of about two thousand yards. Battery Bee, Forts Wagner & Beauregard & the battery at Cummins Point opened firing by Battery. The fleet replied with great rapidity. The Forts & Batteries replied with spirit & accuracy. The Ironsides took position to the left of Fort Sumter & directed her attention exclusively to the Fort, throwing shells only. Fort Sumter acknoledged the compliment by pouring the contents of her biggest guns into the sides of that pride of the Abolition Navy. In about forty five minutes steam was seen issuing in dense volumes from her & she withdrew from the action & remained to the South of Fort Sumter a silent spectator of the rest of the battle.

Almost all the smoke stacks of the fleet were struck several times & as the engagement proceeded the firing from our side became more & more accurate. The Iron Clads now concentrated their fire on the Fort. The Keokuk occupied the post of honour, which was of course the post of danger. She paid severely for it, being struck several times. At five o'clock she followed the example of the Ironsides & drew off evidently seriously crippled. The other monitors continued the fight for about half an hour when they steamed off & came to anchor off Morris Island.

The casualties on our side were a drummer boy killed & five men wounded in Fort Sumter. The fort was struck thirty four times & had a shot through her flag but received no damage. In Fort Moultrie one man was killed by the falling of the Flag Staff. No casualties at Cummin's Point. The other Batteries have not been heard from. This from the Charleston papers of Thursday the 9th. On that day Beauregard telegraphed to General Cooper that an Iron Clad supposed to be the Keokuk had sunk off Morris Island, her smoke stack visible above the water. The wreck was visited by a Confederate officer (so it is said) and her turret found to be pierced through & through with a ball. She was said by the Yankees to be plated with iron of *eleven inch* thickness but I cannot credit it! On the 9th, our last accounts, the fleet still lay off the Bar but gave no evidence of an intention to renew the attack.

The sinking of the Keokuk is a blow to the prestige of the "Turretted Monsters" which will tell as much in our favour as against them. God be praised that he has so far brought out so signal a deliverance to us. We must wait now with what patience we can until Monday night for more news. Monday the 13th is the second aniversary of the surrender of Fort Sumter to our arms. We think the attack was timed in the hope, on their part, to commemorate it by raising the U S. flag again in the place from which it was taken. God avert such a disaster from us & give them a signal disappointment. Mr E a little better but very weak & much reduced.

APRIL 12, 1863

Sunday—Came brother to see us. He tells us that the riot in Richmond was more serious than we supposed, 20,000 persons being assembled in the streets. The President & the Gov of Va were both out & the mob was dispersed only by threats of firing upon them. But I do not see that they attacked the right places for food. Shoe stores & dry goods establishments will not satisfy the cravings of hunger & I am not disposed to beleive that it was a bread riot. The ring leaders were hucksters in the market, one of whom had bought two Veal the day before for $100 & sold them for $250, two hundred and fifty dollars. She could not have been hungry. The news from Washington brought by a courier to Tarrboro is that Gen Hill had, in addition to driving back re-inforcements by water, defeated a land force sent for the same purpose. He placed his men in ambush & as they came on suddenly fired upon and put them to utter confusion and rout. Large quantities of grain & provisions have been brought out from the adjoining counties, which is a great releif to us.

Father leaves in the morning for Raleigh to attend Kate Miller's wedding.[60] Will be back in a week. Mr E very unwell. It makes me sad to see him suffer so.

APRIL 16, 1863

Mr Edmondston has been very sick these last three days. His sufferings from this terrible Rheumatism have been severe. I fear he is no better today but just now he sleeps. News from Charleston to the 15th. No further attack upon our forts. Most of the vessels engaged in that of Tuesday were supposed to be injured, as workmen could be seen in numbers busily repairing them. They left on the 13th, the Monitors three going North & four South, perhaps to hide their defeat by an attack on Wilmington or Savannah. The Ironsides was towed off, tho she has two engines of her own. There were two lines of battle formed instead of one. The Passaic led the first, the Keokuk the second. The Keokuk approached nearer than the others by three hundred yards. She fought at nine hundred yds distance, the others 1200 and 1400. One gun in Sumter, a Columbiad, burst during the engagement. Happily, however, no one was injured by it. This gave rise to the impression that a gun has been dismounted, altho it was in Moultrie that rumour located the accident. The damage inflicted on us was so trifling that it may be set down at nothing. A negro hid himself behind the fort on the outside, but Cuffee's discretion proved equal to his valour, for he was killed by a fragment of a shell. So ends the long threatened bombardment of the "*Hive of Secession*." Our thanks are due to that God in whose hands are the issues of battle!

In this state Hill has Washington almost in his power. He demanded, as I before said, that the women & children should be sent out, which order being refused he returned answer that if in the attack a single one of them was injured that he should refuse quarter & kill every prisoner he took. This had the desired effect & they allowed our defenceless non combattants, whom they desired to keep only as a shield to their manly breasts, to leave. What cowards! Wise has driven the enemy out of Williamsburg, which he now holds. A rumour not yet authenticated has it that Longstreet has taken Suffolk with one million lbs of Bacon. There has been skirmishing there certainly

---

[60]Kate D. Miller and Capt. George B. Baker were married on April 15, 1863, at Christ Church in Raleigh by the Reverend R. S. Mason. Marriage Bond of George B. Baker and Kate D. Miller, Wake County Marriage Bonds, April 13, 1863, State Archives.

& fighting we suppose, as heavy guns were heard here a few days, but we cannot yet credit such results. In the West Forrest, Morgan, & Wheeler annoy Rosencrans, cutting off & destroying R R. and waggon trains. He (Rosencrans) seems to be making an entirely new disposition of his troops. What his plans are remain to be developed. The attempts on Port Hudson & Vicksburg, both abandoned by the enemy, we are left in undisturbed possession of both points.

A letter from James last night tells us that provisions are plenty & that the Army is subsisting on supplies drawn from within the enemy's lines, thus husbanding the stock (a large one) which we have already accumulated from there. Mr Seddon's *"five weeks"* are gone so I suppose provisions must have come in faster as there are no indications of a "falling back" of our Army in Va. Wheat Harvest will now soon commence in Ala & Georgia & we have received a lesson in Economy which I hope will not soon be forgotten. A letter from Captain Haxall tells Patrick that James is "considered a redeeming feature about" the Qr Master's Dept., being one of the few officers in that Department in the service who can claim any familiarity with his duties.

APRIL 22, 1863

Bad news from Vicksburg. Five of the enemy's Gunboats have suceeded in passing our batteries. Eight made the attempt but three were destroyed by our guns. An attack is deemed iminent there. A new battery mounting Parrot Guns has opened on our fortifications. So their late abandonment of their canal & their post opposite us was it seems only a ruse. A "reterer pour sauter" in the hope of finding us off our guard. They pretend now that their late advance on Charleston was a "reconnoisance in force" to get the range of our guns. Why then were so many transports needed & so many troops landed on Cole's & Folly Island? Why, too, were bets so freely offered & refused by Army officers in Washington as to their success? Another peice of Emersonian philosophy which does not blind us. Truly they are apt scholars of their teacher & readily discard the *"monstrous corpse of their memory"* & have no "fear lest they contradict themselves." I have found it necessary to read a little of Emerson latterly in order to be able to talk with a young neice[61] whose Mother has unfortunately allowed her to dabble in his poluted stream & I know not which disgusts me most, his utter want of principle or his depth of folly. Such a tissue of imitative nonsense! Such a very weak tincture of Carlyleism, emboding doctrines & practises, however, that strike at the root of every precept of morality both Divine & Human, in his senile injunctions to "lead a true life," not to "spill your soul." He exhorts his readers to—"speak out—everything they think—out upon guarded lips," bids them

---

[61] The substance of Mrs. Edmondston's quotations were taken from Emerson's essay "Self-Reliance." Rachel Jones was probably the young niece dabbling in Emerson's "poluted stream."

to "reverence the Divinity within them," tells them that "to be great is to be misunderstood." "Suppose you do contradict yourself, What then? If you would be *a man* speak today what you think if it be in words as hard as canon balls & let tomorrow speak what it thinks in hard words again though it contradict every thing you say today." "*Consistency is to be gazetted henceforth.*" "It is the hobgoblin of weak minds." Truly the Yankee nation seem to have followed his teachings, for they lie today, & tomorrow replace the first by a second as false as the first whose only merit is that it contradicts its predecessor. They clamor for Peace, for War!—deify or debase their leaders, Lincoln & Seward, just as the whim seizes them.

Emerson & such men as he are, to use one of their own expression, their "Representative men." His mind is the Key which unlocks the enigma of their conduct. One word more of his wicked nonsense and I have done with him— his definition of "genius." "To beleive your own heart, to beleive what is true for you is true for all men, that is genius." What a pragmatical, insufferable, detestable, set of young folks we should have were his teachings carried out! What quarrelsome, defiant, selfish mortals we should all be! Mr Emerson one greater than you, has told us that the "heart is deceitful & desperately wicked," "that the tongue is a fire, a world of iniquity," but you alas! reject His teachings, degrade your Redeemer to a level with Socrates & Galilleo, say that "prayer is abject"! You deliberately trample underfoot the "children's bread" provided in "their father's house," feed them on *husks*, husks of your own choosing. You reject "Divine light," walk then by the feeble "light of your own candle."

Mr Edmondston has been quite sick the whole week past suffering with pain & fever. I hope he is decidedly better, tho he still has a little fever & is much reduced & very feeble. This is the eighteenth day of his sickness with continuous fever the whole time. How he would suffer were he now in Camp! Such contradictory reports about Hill & Longstreet before Washington and Suffolk that I will not mention them. The enemy, however, are alarmed about Norfolk, have ordered the disarming of the citizens, & threaten to burn the place should we advance upon it. Ah! what a blunder, to give it up! Hooker's movements seem to indicate "a change of base" & that he is to make his advance by McClellan's old route, via the Peninsula between York & James Rivers across the Pamunky & into the swamps of the Chickahominy. May he meet with the same reception & like fate!

April 28, 1863

Bad news again from Vicksburg! I fear our gunners there are getting remiss, as they have allowed more gunboats & transports to pass their batteries. True they sunk some and disabled others, yet some ran by, it is feared, intact. The Yankees claim to have forced us to destroy the Queen of the West in Grand Gulf & to have sunk the Diana there, but we do not credit it. Hill has certainly fallen back from Washington in this State, why we know not. He has succeeded in getting a quantity of provisions from within the enemy's lines, however, & has written the *coarsest personal* letter I ever saw from the pen of a gentleman to Edward Stanley, the so-called Military Gov of N C. Perfectly unneccessary & entirely unmilitary, the document would disgrace an underbred school boy. Stanly's reply is equally coarse & personal, with the aditional merit of being untrue. Hill did one of the finest things of the war at Boonsboro in Maryland where he held the whole of McClellan's Army at bay a whole day & ensured to us the fall of Harper's Ferry & allowed Jackson & Lee to unite for the battle of Sharpsburg. It is a pity to see him destroy with his pen the reputation he has won with his sword. I knit him a pr of nice gloves last winter which were not sent, however, for the want of his address. I am half glad of it now. His letter is *so* ungentlemanly and unneccessary.[62] A letter from James, however, tells us that we must not judge harshly of his falling back. People at a distance should suspend their censure. His R R communications were threatened & it was best in all respects for him to do as he has done. He, James, confirms the account of the supplies he has gained. I am sorry to say that he has been quite sick, confined to his bed for four days. I wish he could get a furlough and come here for a short time and recover perfectly. About Suffolk, matters continue uncertain. Longstreet at one time had cut off the water communication destroying one & disabling two gunboats by his Batteries. This the Yankees admit, but they claim to have reopened the navigation of the Nansemond. They are disarming the inhabitants of Norfolk & threaten if Suffolk is taken & an advance made upon them there to burn the town! Hooker has been repulsed in another so called *reconnoissance* and driven back across the Rappahanock with heavy loss.

In Tennessee nothing but Cavalry expeditions with varying success, generally in our favour, however, as we destroy their R R communication, burn the bridges, & capture their waggon trains. Forrest, Morgan, & Wheeler are thorns in the side of Rosencrans.

Walking in the garden this morning I espied the first Rose of the season. True it was only a common Bouisault, but then it was *a Rose,* an unmistakeable Rose, none the less welcome for being rather late in making its appearance!

The Committee on the Seal for the C S A have, I see, adopted the design suggested by Mr Edmondston last summer through the columns of the Examiner, viz., the figure of Washington on Horseback, the design taken from the Equestrian Statue of that noble patriot in the Capitol Square in

---

[62]Hill's letter was dated March 24, 1863. Stanly replied in kind, and the *Raleigh Register* published the correspondence on April 22, 1863.

Richmond.[63] I am glad of it, for it is simple, majestic, and appropriate. Ah! would that such an one [were] now at the head of our Armies as he was at once soldier & statesman, untainted with party spirit, unwarped by personal predelictions.

Went to Hascosea on Sat the 25 and commenced planting my Dahlias. Intended to return on Monday & finish but the River has prevented me. I put them in in rather quieter times than I took them from the ground. Then Foster was reported as advancing upon us. I remember my labours of housing them were unduly interrupted by the tidings that he was in force at Williamston.

MAY 1, 1863

Dined yesterday at Father's. Found all well & pleased to see me again after so long an absence. Heard from Sue & Rachel all the particulars of Kate Miller's wedding. Her Aunt Sophia entertained & gave them their wedding feast, nice bride's cake she sent me, but the *Raison* cake was really a clever substitute for the genuine article, being made of dried cherries and whortleberries. The eye was well deceived, but to the taste it was rather sour tho' not more so than cake made from old raisins often is. "*Confederate Raisins*" are dried Peaches clipped to bits with scissors, & quite nice puddings do they make. Puddings! what a reminiscence! It seems ages since I dabbled in eggs & sugar, currants, maccaroni, & sage. "What shall I have for dessert?" seems a question of medieval times, so long it is since the question perplexed me. Kate's wedding outfit, that is her underclothing, is a fit one for war & for a soldiers wife, who perforce must practice economy & management. Her Chemises are made of her Aunt Sophia's fine linen sheets & her drawers, which I had made for her, were cut from some of her Grandmother's fine cotton ones—think of that!

No public news except that more gunboats & transports have passed Vicksburg. The country, I am glad to see, begins to clamor at it, so I hope it will be stopped. The enemy slowly & from a great distance shell our works there, tho with little damage.

Sometime since in a skirmish at [———] between some of Van Dorn's Cavalry & the enemy they captured part of a Battery commanded by Capt Freeman, taking him & some of his officers and men prisoner. We heard that they had wantonly shot him, but the particulars which now reach us outrage every feeling of decency, civilization and humanity. It seems that Van Dorn ordered a charge, determined at all hazzards to retake the guns (in which by

---

[63]Edmondston's suggestion appeared in a letter signed "Sigillum," published in the *Richmond Enquirer*, October 1, 1862, with other design proposals for the Confederate seal. His plan called for: "A horse fully caparisoned, with a figure of General Washington either standing beside him as in Stuart's great picture, or bestride him, as may be thought best, with the words above 'Seal of the Confederate States' and between the motto 'Justice, Mercy, Truth.' " There is no evidence that Edmondston's suggestion was given any particular weight by the committee that finally adopted the design for the seal.

the way he was successful), when the Yankees seeing the Cavalry forming for the purpose ordered Capt Freeman to take command of his Guns & to point them at his comrades & mow them down as they came up, which of course he refused, when, horrible to relate, they instantly & in cold blood shot him.[64] In retaliation, we *took no prisoners* that day, but we retook the guns & the slaughter was terrific.

There are rumours of war between the U S & England, but we do not beleive them & in fact have lost all interest in England. We feel almost as indifferent to her as we do to Austria or Turkey. If the U S were to let us alone, England & herself might re-enact the "Killkenny Cats" for ought we care.

Father has written a fine letter on the food and farming question to Gov Vance, which I preserve marked A. No. 3.[65] The Gov has published it. We go out this afternoon for a couple of days at Hascosea; I on gardening, Mr E on farming, bent.

No news from Suffolk. We lost a Battery there last week by Gen French's mismanagement. He exposed & failed to support it. He is a Jersey man, low bred & vulgar. His heart cannot be in his business. I wonder why President Davis ever made him a Major Gen'?

May 4, 1863

Went on the 1st to Hascosea, planted Dahlia & Tube Rose Roots and gardened generally. Ochra crop put in & forced Cucumbers set out from the Hot bed. Came back on Sunday. Met an invitation to dine at father's on the road which it was too late to accept & beside James Edmondston's servant was awaiting us with his baggage & I had his wardrobe to over look & some supplies to see after for him. So I was up bright and early on Monday morning, set my handmaidens to repair the damages of a Campaign on wearing apparel & Mrs Capstick like "*walked around*" his buttons myself & got ready a box of stores for him—2 bottles Pepper, Butter, Honey, Pickles, &—strange sight—"A Reminiscence of the Past," as a witty grocer advertises it, a box of Sardines! This with some Loaves of bread, bottles of Vinegar, Blackberry cordial, some Wedding Cake for him to dream on, a box of yeast powders, some Tobacco & a pouch sent him by father & a bag of Hominy, 2 bottles of Pepper for Col Leventhorpe, 2 do. for Capt Haxall & some butter, a jar of pickles, and a bottle of Vinegar for him filled a good sized box. Dainties are fast disappearing from my household stores & bacon & Hams we hear he has in plenty.

News met us of an advance of the Yankee Army on the Rappahannock. Hooker crossed, it is supposed with Lee's connivance, about fifteen miles

---

[64]According to Confederate newspapers, Capt. Samuel L. Freeman, commander of Co. B, Harding's Tennessee Artillery, was assassinated by Federal officials while being held prisoner. *Raleigh Register*, April 23, 1863, quoting the *Chattanooga Rebel* of April 14, 1863.

[65]This letter appeared in the *North Carolina Standard* on April 28, 1863. It was not included in Mrs. Edmondston's diary.

above Fredericksburg. It is thought he hopes to outflank us & cut off our communications with Richmond. We have every confidence in Gen Lee, still whilst a battle is imminent we cannot but feel anxious. The situation is a grave one & should Lee not be prepared the result may be sad indeed to us. Our strong position at Fredericksburg is thus rendered useless to us, as the battle will in all probability be fought on what is now our left Flank.

As for the news from the West, I cannot understand it. There is so confused a jumble of odd names of places, contradicting & duplicate Telegrams that it would puzzle an Oedipus to make sense of them. Price has taken the field in Missouri & matters are looking up there. More transports have passed Vicksburg, but through an ordeal of fire, as few escape uninjured.

MAY 5, 1863

News last night principally rumours. The enemy under General Stoneman have made a dash into our lines and emulous of Stuart have penetrated into the heart of Va, cutting Telegraph wires, tearing up R R tracks, but as I do not know whether the particulars are authentic I will wait until they are confirmed. Rumour has it that we fought on Sunday the 3d & repulsed the enemy at every point save one & took five thousand prisoners. Stonewall Jackson and A P Hill both wounded, the first slightly, the latter severely, but we do not know whether it be true or not; in fact we do not know that there has been a fight—not even a Telegram. Matters in the West more confused than ever. I cannot keep up with them—a skirmish here at some unpronounceable unheard of before name in which we are successful & another there at some equally unknown place from which we retire. Morgan, Van Dorn, and Forrest destroy R R Bridges & tear up tracks until one would think there were none left to be destroyed. They capture one waggon train only to make room for another, but our eyes are bent now on Fredericksburg & Gen Lee. God grant him the victory. Rachel Jones came to make us a visit last night.

MAY 6, 1863

News of a Victory at Fredericksburg! Hooker is repulsed & is in retreat. More than that we cannot tell, but that fills our hearts with grateful praise. Lee telegraphs that by "the blessing of God we have gained a great Victory"—10,000 prisoners are captured, no details of our loss in either killed or Wounded. The Cavalry expedition sent out to beat up our quarters carry dismay and surprise to an unexpectant country. They have torn up the R R track between Gordonsville & Richmond, stolen horses, & captured an old engine. Beyond that they have effected nothing, but the insult is great & a burning shame which must be wiped out in blood ere it can be atoned. One of the Col's, one Davis, boasts that he is a Virginian, is familiar with the country over which he has often fox hunted! More shame to him a traitor & a renegade! Their movements are wrapped in obscurity, & they have cut the

Telegraph wires so that our intercourse with the Army is destroyed for the present. The next news we hear of them will, I hope, be that they are all in the Libby Prison,[66] but it is the most daring thing the Yankees have as yet attempted & should put us on our guard against despising our enemy.

Where is Stuart? "One blast upon his bugle horn were worth ten thousand men."[67] Where is he that he allows the Abolitionists thus to career through our lines & pluck his Laurels unwithered from his brow?

May 7, 1863

News from the Rappahanock! A victory, tho dearly bought! The Abolitionists crossed, as I before stated, about 15 miles above Fredericksburg after making a feint at that point. He strongly entrenched that wing of his army which rested upon the River, but Jackson making a rapid march got into his rear beyond Chancellorsville whilst Lee made an attack in point at that point. Thus pressed, his left Flank was doubled up upon his right which lay on the River (the Rapid Ann) which he crossed in great confusion, the slaughter being terrific. In the mean time Early who had been left in command of Fredericksburg & the intrenchments there was attacked by over whelming odds under Gen Sedgwick (I wonder if he is any kin of mine)[68] & driven from the post, Sedgwick even gaining Marye's Hill. But let me tell the rest in Lee's own words—"At the close of the battle of Chancellorsville on Sunday the enemy was reported as advancing from Fredericksburg in our rear. General McLaws was sent back to arrest his progress & repulsed him handsomly that afternoon. Learning that this corps consisted of his corps under General Sedgwick I determined to attack it & marched back yesterday with General Anderson & uniting with McLaws & Early in the afternoon, succeeded by the blessing of Heaven in driving Gen Sedgewick over the River. We have reoccupied Fredericksburg, & no enemy remains south of the Rappahanock in its vicinity." Dated May 5th.

Hooker is on the South bank of the Rappahanock, reported as entrenching & receiving reinforcements, but he is a beaten man. His prestige is gone and to God are our praises due. "With His own right hand and His holy arm hath

---

[66]Libby Prison, located on the James River in Richmond, housed Union officers and became notorious for its harsh conditions. Stoneman's Raid, during the Chancellorsville campaign, was led by Gen. George Stoneman (1822-1894), commander of the Cavalry Corps, Union Army of the Potomac. The purpose of the raid was to disrupt Lee's lines of communication before Hooker's major advance against the Confederate forces. Boatner, *Civil War Dictionary*, 482, 673, 803. For information on Stoneman's Raid in North Carolina, see the four-part article, Ina W. Van Noppen, "The Significance of Stoneman's Last Raid," *North Carolina Historical Review*, XXXVIII (January, April, July, October, 1961), 19-44, 149-172, 341-361, 500-526.

[67]Scott, *Lady of the Lake*, canto 6, stanza 18, lines 481-482.

[68]Mrs. Edmondston was related to some of the New England Sedgwicks through the Dwights who, like herself, descended from Jonathan Edwards. Gen. John Sedgwick of Connecticut, however, does not seem to have been one of this group.

He gotten Himself the victory."[69] Fill our hearts with grateful praise, and may we as a nation ascribe unto God the praise due unto His name.

Jackson's wound was in this wise. At midnight on Saturday night, his troops being drawn up in line of battle, a body of men were seen a short distance in advance of our line. It being doubtful whether they were friends or enemies, Gen Jackson & staff rode forward to reconnoitre. Whilst thus engaged, his own men being unaware of his movements, mistook himself & staff for enemies & fired a volley into them instantly killing one & severely wounding Gen Jackson & Major Crutchfield.[70] One ball struck his left arm below the elbow & ranging upwards shattered the bone near the shoulder. Another passed through his right hand. He instantly fell to the ground. His brother in Law[71] laid down by his side to ascertain what were his wounds. In a moment the unknown troops in front who proved to be the enemy advancing captured two of his staff who were standing over him without, however, perceiving him. A stretcher was procured & four of his men were bearing him to the rear when they were all shot down. His arm has been amputated above the elbow, and the injury to his right hand is severe, one of the bones having been shot away, but it is beleived that he will recover the use of it. He is reported as doing well & Mrs Jackson—who was in Richmond has joined him. He is a heavy loss to us & the Yankees will think their defeat cheaply purchased with his life. Of course they will say that his men did it purposely & that they were demoralized—but who will beleive them?

The Cavalry raid in the vicinity of Richmond is most annoying & insulting, but they have done but little real damage besides destroying a span of the R R Bridge over the Chickahominy & delaying our communication with Fredericksburg. The damage will soon be repaired, but the additional suffering to our wounded is a serious consideration. They captured an ambulance train, destroyed the engine & paroled the wounded. A young lady having heard of their advance informed Col Duke[72] of Wise's Legion who was, with a small detachment of men—infantry, fortunately within reach. He placed his men on the train & reached Tunstall's at the very moment that they did. Taking them thus by surprise, he killed several & captured fifteen of the

---

[69]Psalms 98:1b.

[70]Col. Stapleton Crutchfield, chief of artillery in Jackson's Second Corps, lost a leg at Chancellorsville. Gen. Robert E. Lee's report, September 21, 1863, stated that "Captain [J. K.] Boswell, chief engineer of the corps, and several others were killed and a number wounded." General Stuart, arriving shortly afterward, directed Jackson's command during the remainder of the battle. *Official Records (Army)*, Series I, XXV, Part I, 795, 798-799, 803, 809.

[71]Mrs. Edmondston evidently thought she was referring to Daniel Harvey Hill. However, Ambrose Powell Hill stood over the wounded Jackson at Chancellorsville. Jackson and D. H. Hill married Mary Anna and Isabella Morrison respectively, daughters of Robert Hall Morrison. Freeman, *Lee's Lieutenants*, II, 568-569; III, 814; Ashe, *Biographical History*, VII, 138.

[72]Col. R. T. W. Duke commanded the Forty-sixth Virginia Infantry. *Official Records (Army)*, Series I, XVIII, 920.

marauders. They came within two miles of Richmond, stealing Mr John Young's horse from before his door in his sight. He, poor man, offered no resistance thinking Gen Lee was beaten and that this was the advance of Hooker's army. He had no time for "an abstraction" then, fond as he used to be of them.

MAY 8, 1863

Dined at Father's with Rachel. A letter from Thomas J. tells us that he hopes to bring his bride out from the enemy's lines & spend a short furlough he has with his Grandfather. The panic in Richmond at the Cavalry raid was fearful. One body of them went west towards Columbia & attempted to blow up the Aqueduct of the James River Canal, in which attempt, however, they failed. They have stolen horses & alarmed the country, but beyond the insult have done us but little damage. Gen Fitz Hugh Lee encountered them, captured 30, & killed several, but his horses were too much jaded to pursue them. Rumour puts their no down at from ten to twenty thousand. This must be an exageration, as they could not subsist in the country where they now are. Two Regts of them are making their way across the country towards West Point or Williamsburg. This detachment it is which burnt the Chickahominy bridge and paroled the wounded prisoners; they also burned a train of eighty waggons with a quantity of grain at Ayletts, a village in Prince William. They took the teams leaving eighty or ninety of their own exhausted horses in their stead.

A marauding party sent out through Alabama towards Rome, Georgia, where the Gov has important works, was not so fortunate as their brethren in Va. Forrest pursued them, skirmishing from day to day, & before they reached their destination captured the whole command. Men, horses, & equipment 1700 strong—they were marched as prisoners into the place they came to destroy. The excesses, the robery, the wanton destruction of property, committed by them almost exceeds beleive, was it not eclipsed by another band sent into Mississippi from their head quarters in Louisianna. So far this last has escaped punishment, there being no Confederate troops in that region. With the romantic element left out, their conduct is more like a body of half civilized marauding caterans of the 16th Century than Christian warriors of the enlightened nineteenth. Yet we have the most Christian Burnsides word for it that they are *Christians*.

MAY 9, 1863

Gen Lee's dispatch to the President dated Chancellorsville May 7th tells us that "After driving Sedgewick across the Rappahanock on the night of the 4th I (he) returned on the 5th to Chancellorsville. The march was delayed by a storm which continued all night and the following day. In placing the troops in position on the morning of the 6th to attack Gen Hooker, it was ascertained that he had abandoned his fortified position. The line of skirmishers was pressed forward until they came in range of the enemies batteries planted on the north of the Rappahanock which from the configuration of the ground completely commanded this side. His army, therefore, escaped with the loss of a few additional prisoners." Signed R E Lee, General. So he is gone, driven back, beaten ignominiously by a far inferior force, for we had but 80,000 (eighty thousand) men all told, whilst he has 158,000 (one hundred and fifty eight). Our loss is stated on the best authority now attainable at nine hundred killed & six thousand wounded many of them slightly so. We lost some prisoners, but all told killed, wounded, prisoners, and missing—eight thousand covers it. Theirs is estimated at thirty thousand. We have nine thousand prisoners! We took fifty three canon & lost five on Marye's Hill, belonging to the Washington Artillery. The no of muskets captured & picked up on the battlefield is enormous. Were Lee now to advance, a large part of Hooker's Army could not fight for want of a weapon. They are piled by the side of the R R track—a wonder to the beholder. The enemies loss in generals is heavy, including the infamous Sickles. Six are enumerated, but they are not of consequence enough to interest me. We lose one—Gen Paxton—in command of the old Stonewall Brigade. We have lost several Colonels, but as yet the details are not published. Stoneman is reported as encamped in heavy force near Gordonsville. Ah that we could capture him! No news of importance from the West. Van Dorn is dead, but how we hear not. Forrest, Wheeler, & Morgan continue to annoy Rosencrans & capture his marauding parties. In Louisianna we have had a repulse. At Grand Gulf Gen Taylor was forced to retreat, which he did fighting, after two days battle. He had 3000, the enemy 20,000 men, yet he came off in good order, bringing guns & stores. One waggon (whose mule gave out) only was captured. Our loss not heavy. All quiet before Vicksburg.

MAY 10, 1863

Came brother & his son John to dinner—full of our Victory, which all admit to be a glorious one, throwing that of Fredericksburg in the shade. Hooker is terribly beaten & that too by a force one half his own. Off with his head & let him too take a house in N Y & join the clique of beaten Generals—"*Beaten Row*"or "*Vanquished Square*" or "*Conquered Place*" and call it as their taste may be. Jackson reported as doing well.

MAY 11, 1863

Went out Hascosea after dinner with Mr E on horseback. Everything is terribly backward there. The garden wants work & the flowers resent the neglect by refusing to bloom. A little girl ran out from the house of one of our neighbours & stopped us to ask for some flowers for their May party next Friday. Promised to send them, much to her gratification. Ah! me what happiness have May Queen's conferred on me in times gone by & what a contrast to the times does a Queen of May now present.

The mail came in after tea & heavy news it brought us. A chill went through my heart as Mr Edmondston unfolded the paper & I saw that it was in mourning. I felt that Jackson was dead! & so it proved! He died of pneumonia on Sunday the 10th, eight days after the amputation of his arm, died in the fulness of his reputation, the brightness of his glory, a Christian patriot, unselfish, untiring, with no thought but for his country, no aim but for her advancement. I have no heart to write more, tho the paper is full of news. I care for nothing but him. It is as tho a Divine voice has said again "Little children keep yourselves from idols." [73] He was the nation's idol, not a breath even from a foe has ever been breathed against his fame. His very enemies reverenced him. God has taken him from us that we may lean more upon *Him*, feel that He can raise up to Himself instruments to work His Divine Will.

MAY 12, 1863

Woke up this morning with a sense of a heavy misfortune. Asked myself what had happened & remembered that Jackson was dead! Omitted to write yesterday that my nephew Thomas Jones had brought his wife to fathers. We go up to see her this morning. I shall offer her a home until the war is ended—for she cannot return into the lines of the hated enemy & since Hill's repulse at Washington, they have grown more stringent & oppressive. The papers are full of McClellan's & Burnside testimony respecting the command & conduct [of] the Army of the Potomac. I take little interest in any of them, or anything they say. They only offer an additional proof, if proof were wanting, that neither Lincoln, Halleck, Stanton, McClellan, Burnside, or Hooker understand the first principles of a gentleman. Deficient alike in self respect & respect for each other, they know not what is due themselves from their subordinates, or their subordinates from their own hands. Faugh! they disgust me, a set of cold blooded quill drivers. They have neither the instincts or the impulses of gentlemen.

MAY 14, 1863

Came Tom Jones & his bride to spend a few days with us, we having dined with them at father's yesterday. She seems a pleasant tempered sensible affectionate young person. Rachel, Sue, & Lieut Elliot[74] dined with us. Concluded

---

[73] I John 5:21.

[74] Charles Gilbert Elliott (1843-1895), adjutant of the Seventeenth North Carolina (Second Organization) Regiment, was an engineer and inventor from Elizabeth City. He contracted with the Confederate Navy Department to build an "iron-clad gun-boat, intended, if ever completed, to operate on the waters

not to separate the young folks, to go out to Hascosea & entertain them there where our means for making them comfortable are more ample. Lieut Elliot is superintending the construction of a Gun boat at Edwards Ferry within two miles of us. He feels uneasy for the want of a guard. A bold Yankee commander could make a dash & burn it without meeting the slightest opposition, so denuded is our county of both men & arms.

MAY 23, 1863

Some days since I opened you O my Journal, but I have been busy and preoccupied. On Friday the 15th went to Hascosea, taking the young folks all with us. They had a merry time until Sunday the 17th when they all left. Thomas returns to his Regiment & his wife to her home in Perquimans, for we could not persuade her to remain with us & leave her mother in the enemies lines alone. She gave us a terrible account of the want of faith, the entire disregard of the most solemn oaths, & protestations which our Christian enemies exhibit towards the defenceless inhabitants within their power—tales of murder & outrage at which the heart sickens & the blood revolts. How long O! Lord?—how long will thou permit them thus to lord it over any portion of our country? But Thy will be done!

Patrick & I remained alone at Hascosea on Gardening & farming bent until Wednesday, the 20th when we returned to the plantation & sent for Rachel to come back & finish her visit to us. As we sat in the piazza just at dusk who should come riding up but James Edmondston! His command is ordered to Va & he waits only to load his waggons with corn & see them fairly on the road when he follows. We had a most pleasant & only too short a visit from him. He is in good spirits & quite well again & as usual most affectionate & delighted to see his brother & myself. He speaks most enthusiastically of Gen D H Hill, says that no matter how much one personally may dislike him, yet in action & under fire he commands the admiration & respect of every one. Says he is not to blame for the bad fortune of his campaign around Washington, that he not only was outnumbered but that he was deficient in Artillery of heavy enough calibre to cope with Gen Foster. He blames & regrets as much as we do his unfortunate correspondance with Stanley & Foster in which he is both coarse & weak & laments the idiosyncrasy which makes him thus rush into print. James left us on Saturday at sunrise for Lee's Army at Fredericksburg, which it is reported is to advance upon Hooker. Troops are being pressed on to him & with the exception of the forces at Wilmington there are but three Brigades left in this State!

---

of Albemarle and Pamlico Sounds." This ram, the C.S.S. *Albemarle*, was constructed at Edward's Ferry in Halifax County. Elliott married Lucy Ann Hill of Halifax County following the Civil War, and practiced law in Norfolk, Virginia; St. Louis, Missouri; and in New York. Barrett, *Civil War in North Carolina*, 214; Clark, *Histories of the North Carolina Regiments*, V, 315-323; Marriage Bond of Gilbert Elliott to Lucy Ann Hill, Halifax County Marriage Bonds, April 10, 1865, State Archives; Manarin and Jordan, *North Carolina Troops*, VI, 204.

Affairs in the South West now engage all our attention. Grant with a column of 100,000 infantry & a large force of cavalry has crossed the Mississippi at Grand Gulf below Vicksburg. He was met by a Confederate force which being too weak to encounter him fell back fighting towards Jackson, Grant pressing on him. We were forced to evacuate the place, at least Gen Pemberton did so, tho some persons contend that it was unnecessary. Of this we cannot judge, but Grant occupied it in force, burned the Government & State property, the State House, the Court House, & committed the most shocking excesses, robbing, stealing, & destroying private property of all kinds. After two days occupation of Jackson, Grant in his turn evacuated it & fell back to Edwards Depot between Vicksburg & Jackson where Pemberton, Loring, & others of our Generals met & repulsed him; but being reinforced from Jackson, we were outnumbered and fell further back to the R R Bride over the Big Black. Loring with a Confederate force was cut off but finally cut his way through with heavy loss to Crystal Spring. In some of these engagements, as yet we know not which, Gen Tilghman was killed. Pemberton entrenched at the Bridge & a battle was expected there at the last advices.

Gen Johnston is collecting an Army, we hope rapidly, to fall on Grant's rear, but we get only meager Telegraphic Dispatches, & the only thing we certainly know is that Vicksburg is seriously threatened by a heavy force in the rear. They hope to cut off all supplies & invest it both by the River & Land, but Gen Joe Johnston is in there & he is a Tower of Strength. Grant must be a master of strategy to out manovre him. We wait with eager suspense for news.

At the North Lincoln has entered into a trial of strength with "Free Speech" as personified by Vallandigham. He has been arrested & tried by a Court Martial for a public speech he made at Dayton in which he animadverted against the War & the Government. The sentence of the Court is to a confinement for two years in one of the Government Forts & Burnside, the Christian under whose auspices the Court was held, has named Fort Warren as the place of his imprisonment. The North seems in a ferment, but they talk so much—*brag, bluster, & submit,* that I suppose it will all effervesce in talk & Mr Lincoln will be allowed to be as despotic as he chooses. What a nation they are! They give up the dearest rights of freemen without a struggle! We must have been as "salt" to them heretofore & that they have preserved a shadow even of independance or liberty is owing to Southern spirit—Southern resistance to tyranny.

To our pleasure we hear that the Abolitionists are blockading the River just above Plymouth, in order to keep the Gun boat which we are building at Edwards Ferry from attacking them. I hope that their barricade will be effectual against themselves also. Yesterday a company of Infantry passed here on their way to the Ferry, with orders to guard it and to picket the River from

Norfleet's to Pollock's Ferry, so we will be under guard. Heard last night that Lieut Wiggins[75] of the Scotland Neck Riflemen had been killed whilst gallantly heading a charge of his Company on the Blackwater. He was a fine young man, brave, impetuous, impulsive, and high spirited. Patrick thought more highly of him than he did of most of the young men under his command & he commanded my regard essentially for he refused and did [his] utmost to induce others to refuse to sign the request for Mr E to resign when the company, wanting to get rid of Lieut Smith, could think of no other way than to get a new election of all the officers. I feel deeply for his parents who were proud, & justly so, of him.

MAY 24, 1863

Sad news from our Army in the South West. Pemberton was forced back to the R R bridge on the Big Black which being a strong position he was resolved to hold, but Grant instead of attacking crossed the River higher up & thus outflanked him. So Pemberton destroyed the bridge (a heavy work about a mile in length) & retreated to Vicksburg 12 miles off. Grant followed & now closely invests Vicksburg on the land side. Vicksburg is said to be strongly entrenched & supplied with provisions & ammunition for a five month's seige. Gen Joe Johnson is at Jackson collecting an army with which to fall on Grant's rear & the next news we hear may be that the place is releived by a battle and a glorious Victory! God grant it!

After James left yesterday, I went up on horseback to dine at father's & brought Rachel back with me, she having gone up with Sue the day before. Vicksburg was in every heart & on every tongue. The President who is familiar with the localities is reported to be in good spirits about it, says that Grant is in a trap & too far from his base of supplies & that Gen Johnston in his rear can cut them off & harrass him terribly. Vicksburg will be exposed to a terrific bombardment from front & rear. Ah! that it may with stand it.

Whilst at father's came an order from Lieut Orrel[76] in command of the picket station at Edwards Ferry ordering the removal of all canoes from the River—a wise precaution but one which I doubt me originated with Lieut Col Edmondston, for those young inexperienced (I was almost ready to say *boys*) never thought of it. Lieut O's order proved him both young & ignorant, for he "assumes the command of the River from Pollock's to Norfleet's Ferry" & does not vouchsafe to tell us by whose orders or by what authority! His Col or his Brigadier should teach him a lesson.

---

[75]Alfred S. Wiggins, second lieutenant in Co. G, Forty-first North Carolina (Third Cavalry) Regiment, was encamped at Franklin, Virginia. In pursuit of Federal cavalry moving toward Suffolk, Wiggins was killed on May 17, 1863, when his horse bolted past the retreating Federal column. Clark, *Histories of the North Carolina Regiments*, II, 785; Manarin and Jordan, *North Carolina Troops*, II, 228.

[76]A Lt. W. C. Orrell was a member of Co. E, Twenty-second North Carolina Regiment. Clark, *Histories of the North Carolina Regiments*, II, 178.

I forgot to mention in its place that the cavalry, Baker's, about which Gen French behaved so unhandsomly to Patrick has got itself into terrible trouble. The officers, always discontented with Baker, who has proved himself ignorant & inefficient, at length in a body signed a request for him to resign, for which he very properly placed them under arrest & they are all suspended from command and are to be Court Martialed. In the mean time they have, we hear, preferred charges against him, which they should have done before, & their superior in authority, the redoubtable Gen French himself, has demanded a Court of Inquiry as to his conduct in losing a Battery before Suffolk, for which he had the pleasure of hearing himself called a _____ fool by Gen Longstreet, who, however, did not know that French was the responsible person when he said so. Longstreet's expression, when he heard of the circumstances of its capture, was "Well so soon as he is exchanged I will have that Captain[77] shot for sending away his horses & exposing his battery thus." An Aid interposed with, "Perhaps Gen, he is not responsible. I hear he acted under orders after remonstrance." "Well then I will Court martial the _____ fool who gave the orders." French standing by! After the newspapers made an outcry as to the folly and injustice of the act the Maj Gen demanded a court of Inquiry to white wash himself with all.

A gallant thing has been done in the Chesapeake & Albemarle Canal by a company of Partizan Rangers under Capt Elliot. He captured two boats the Arrow and the [Emily] with all on board & a large mail. Steamed through the Canal past Elizabeth [City] & Edenton under the Guns of two Gunboats & brought his prizes safe up the Chowan to Franklin & delivered them and his prisoners to the officers in command there without the loss of a man—a gallant act & skillfully executed.

May 26, 1863

Good news from Vicksburg! The enemy assaulted our works from the land side & were repulsed with terrible loss to him but with a slight one to us. One estimate, which must be over the mark, makes it "10,000." "His dead strew the ground in front of our works." An official dispatch from Gen Johnston tells us that an assault on the Yazoo road upon Pemberton's entrenchments has failed; one on the Jackson road has been made, & still another—in all of which we repulsed them, but at which with such success does not appear. Johnston is in Grant's rear constantly receiving re-inforcements. When he is strong enough I suppose he will fall upon him, so after all our anxiety he may

---

[77]The captain of this battery, Robert M. Stribling, was ordered by Longstreet and French to defend Fort Huger near Suffolk. The captain placed five guns in the fort, which commanded the Nansemond River, but no garrison was ever sent to him to help support the position and it fell to Federal raiders on April 19, 1863. The "capture of Stribling's battery," as this affair was referred to in the Confederate army, created a tremendous stir and aroused sharp resentment on the part of those concerned, many of the officers seeking to evade responsibility for the capture. Freeman, *Lee's Lieutenants*, II, 485-490.

be crushed as between two millstones, Vicksburg & Johnston, & our stronghold saved to us! God grant it! Hooker has issued an order to his army, congratulating them on the battle of Chancellorsville, which for cool effrontery, unblushing lying, actually pales those of his cheif Major Liar Gen Halleck. It is astounding to what a depth of infamy can poor human nature sink! Apt disciple of Emerson, you do not indeed cumber yourself with the "monstrous" corpse of your dead memory! How can he henceforth look a gentleman in the face is a question for the curious.

Price is bestirring himself in Arkansas. It is rumoured that he has taken Helena, but we do not know this. Negro Regiments are being mustered into the service of the U S throughout the country. A glorious cause that requires Cuffey's arm, Cuffey's valour, to sustain it! I never mentioned half that Patty (my new neice) told me of the Yankee villainy & oppression in the North Eastern counties—paper would fail me. They lie, steal, & murder unblushingly. They came to her mother's house in search of her brother Lieut Skinner, who was at home wounded after the battle of Sharpsburgh & voluntarily pledged their word to the old Lady that not a single one of the _____ blackskins should go on board of their boats. She, being still distrustful, went out & ordered the negroes to their houses. They obeyed, when the Commander came up & told her "not to distress herself, that he was the Commander of the expedition, that he gave her his word that though they might go down to the River that not a _____ black skin should put a foot on board; that he hated them," etc. Then re: itering the words & oaths of his subordinate she accordingly went in & would you beleive it, Journal, they took every *negro man* & some of the women that they owned & they are wealthy people and had a large force! They even stole the old lady's spectacles! Of course taking all the poultry & what sheep & hogs & beef they wanted.

They went to Mr Tom Newby's, my brother in-law's uncle, an old man & feeble, shot down his son in cold blood at his father's hearth as he was rising from his chair with the inquiry, "who's there?" on hearing their footsteps! He fell dead on the hearth & *they would not suffer his father to remove the body from the fire whilst they remained*! They dragged him, the old man, about with them from place to place demanding where this article & where that was which they wanted & took every thing they fancied, rumaged his papers, took his son's clothes, & actually stationed themselves in his wife's bed chamber, she being sick in bed & an old lady, & mimicked her distress & her calls to her servant to come and get her, her gown! They took every article of clothing from her neice's wardrobe, a child of twelve or thirteen, & before her face gave them to a negro child & when they went off drove every negro he owned, some of them at the point of the bayonette, & all his horses and mules before them. The negroes they sent on board their boats to Roanoke Island, & the only reason for their peculiar barbarity that could be found was that he had had a son, not the one they killed, formerly in the Service. Mr Newby is a man between seventy & eighty & they beat & abused him, even pricking him with their bayonettes! Think of that! His son's corpse was badly burned on his own hearth stone, in his sight. Are they fiends or men? Yet we are told they are "*Christians.*"

May 27, 1863

Not one word from Vicksburg, not even an editorial allusion in yesterday's paper, which makes us a little uneasy, but we hope that "no news will prove good news" & so try to be content. Mr Vallandighan has been taken from Cincinnatti in a Gunboat & is en route, it is said, but with secresy it would appear, to Fort Warren in Boston Harbour. If the North *bear this*, then indeed are they enslaved and Lincoln can declare himself "Perpetual Dictator" when he likes. I preserve the proceedings of the Court Martial which sentenced him marked A no 4,[78] for it will not be beleived that proceedings so arbitrary can be countenanced in a Government which was until recently free. How true is Elwood Fisher's epitaph on the U S Government, "Here lies a nation which lost," but I remember I recently quoted them so Journal I forbear.

May 31, 1863

At Hascosea. Came out on Friday the 29th to Hascosea for the Summer and am as usual on such occasions up to the eyes in household matters. Every inch of woodwork in the house to be washed, every carpet & mat shaken or spunged, every peice of furniture rubbed (tho this year it goes without its usual polish tho for the want of Linseed Oil), and worse than all every article taken out of the store room & it scrubbed and cleaned, & old Harry looking not unlike an old grey Rat himself, busy, stopping his confrere's holes for days to come for aught I know. Mean always hereafter to eschew tame Rabbits! To them do I owe the eruption worse than Goth or Vandal which has swooped down upon me. Then Aaron has two rooms given up to disorder & dust for an indefinite time whilst he mends the plaster. Which will it be, his "*back*" or his never failing "*chills*" which will keep him in an excuse this time? The first I expect momentarily to hear is "*give out*" & should that refuse "*to fail him*" a timely chill will kindly, "tek" him before his job is finished.

Bad news from below Kinston—two, some say *one*, Regt of our Infantry allowed themselves to be surprised & surrounded whilst on Picket; 150 were captured whilst the rest ignominiously scattered & ran! Cols Faison & Rutledge[79] and Gen Ransom bear the brunt of the blame, but Hill says it is a "disgraceful affair."

---

[78]No newspaper clipping pertaining to the Vallandigham sentence was found in Mrs. Edmondston's diary.

[79]Henry M. Rutledge was colonel of the Twenty-fifth North Carolina Regiment in Ransom's Brigade. Paul F. Faison was serving as colonel of the Fifty-sixth North Carolina Regiment. The skirmish referred to

Continued fighting before Vicksburg. Grant has made six desperate assaults & been driven back each time with terrible slaughter. Before one series of redoubts he lost 5,000 men! Our soldiers continue cool & resolute, reserving their fire until the enemy is within range. Our loss is small. Johnston threw in 10,000 reinforcements, Porter has command of the Yazoo. Haines Bluff is in their hands, & we have destroyed the Navy Yard at Yazoo City to prevent its falling into their possession, together with two half finished gunboats. Our hopes of a Navy seem doomed to be crushed!

Mr Lincoln has commuted Vallandigham's sentence of imprisonment into banishment to the Confederate States whilst the war continues, & he has accordingly been brought under a Flag of Truce to our lines. He announced himself "a citizen of the U. S. with whom you are at war" & said "I claim to be treated as a prisoner of War." He has no right to any such claim, much as we sympathize with him. The only *right* he has is that of the unfortunate & we should receive him kindly & give him at once a passage to a neutral country, say the West Indies or Canada, & let him go where he lists. Here his own self respect forbids him to stay. Policy demands that he leave us. We ought to make no demonstration over him but let him go, so soon as he can, out of our borders. He is not banished for being friendly to us but for hostility to the U S Government. If he acts with prudence & discretion I should not wonder if this arbitrary act of Lincoln would eventually make him Pres. of the U S, but little do I care who fills that seat!

JUNE 3, 1863

Went to the Plantation with Mr. E and Rachel. Met Father who gave us our mail. Good news from Vicksburg. Grant has fallen back from the immediate front of the works & has commenced entrenching. His loss has been fearful, ours slight. Vicksburg is completely surrounded, but we have full rations for ninety days & a strong position I hope ammunition enough. We hear nothing of Johnston, but no one is uneasy on that account. He is reinforcing & at the right time will *ACT*. Two Gunboats were sunk by the water batteries, but Porter's command of the Yazoo is a tower of strength to Grant. He is no longer dependant upon waggon trains for his subsistance. We get most meagre accounts of the garrison, owing to the investiture cutting off couriers. It is rumoured that Beauregard has gone to join Johnston with 20,000 men & that a detachment has left Bragg's army for the same destination. If so, Grant will be crushed and Vicksburg saved. Pemberton is in command within, *a*

---

occurred at Gum Swamp on May 22, 1863. The Twenty-fifth and Fifty-sixth regiments, guarding the Atlantic and North Carolina Railroad eight miles below Kinston, were attacked by Union troops from New Bern. The Confederate troops retreated when they were attacked from the rear by a second Federal column which had earlier crossed the swamp along an unfrequented path. The Fifty-sixth lost 165 men captured, and a court of inquiry was called about Faison's conduct. Faison was acquitted of all blame for the fiasco, however. Clark, *Histories of the North Carolina Regiments*, II, 291, 294; III, 318-319, 324-328; Barrett, *Civil War in North Carolina*, 162-164.

Yankee, & therefore I do not trust him tho he did marry my old schoolmate Martha Thompson of Norfolk. Our own blood should command us now, especially in a post of such danger & importance as Vicksburg.

JUNE 9, 1863

News from Vicksburg still good. Grant has fallen back five miles & is entrenching. Pemberton holds his own. Grant gave him three days to consider of a surrender. He replied "that he did not want a quarter of an hour—that his men would die in the trenches"! The loss of the enemy is fearful. They admit 20,000. We claim more. Our loss as yet slight, one General (Tilghman) on our side against six on theirs. They claim to have captured 5,000 men. We do not beleive it, but our means of information are meagre. Rumours that Johnston has beaten Grant reached us on Sat, but the papers were silent & yesterday there was no mail. Kirby Smith has succeeded in crossing the Mississippi at Port Hudson in the teeth of Banks. The seige of that city is said to be raised by his defeat of Banks in an action in which Banks lost an arm, but this needs confirmation. Our batteries there sunk a transport & drowned 700 men, reinforcements to Banks or Grant. The next news will be stirring.

The President has revoked the exequater of Mr George Moore, British Consul at Richmond, for contempt of our Government in refusing to exhibit his authority for exercising consulor power in the State of Mississippi when he was accreditted to the State of Va. As this is likely to grow into importance, I preserve the paper marked A no 5. Hunter commanding in S C has addressed so remarkable a letter to President Davis that I preserve that also.[80] He is surely crazy, first to write to Mr Davis at all contrary to all military rule or etiquette. Beauregard is the person he should communicate with & then to pen such a letter! A monimaniac alone could have penned it. Burnside has signified to Gen Bragg that if he retaliates for the hanging of two Confederate officers as spies that he, Gen Burnside, will put to death every Confederate officer he holds as prisoner. They have stopped the exchange of officers by Flag of Truce & enlisted men only return—a preliminary I suppose to the hanging threatened by the Christian General. The cruelies, practised upon citizens increase instead of lessen. Recently the General in command at New Orleans arrested two steamboat loads of the inhabitants, allowed them if married $1000, if single $200 of their own property, confiscated the rest, & landed them upon the seashore in a desolate swampy region betwen N O & Mobile without food or shelter or the possibility of obtaining it. Most of them were women & helpless children, many infants, & yet these are the people whom the "best government the world ever saw" claims as its subjects & entitled to its protection. The children could scarcely have forfeited their right to it if their

---

[80]These newspaper accounts are preserved on page 27 of the second volume of the diary.

mothers had. The same thing has occurred at St Louis, Memphis, & New Berne in this state.

James described the situation of eighty or more whom he saw left at the terminus of the R R by their Yankee tyrants in the woods, without the ability to get further. Still within the enemies lines, our teams could not assist them & the private means of transportation have all long been stolen. Gen Daniel, on hearing it, sent down a Flag & obtained permission to send for them, & James accordingly went with his waggons. He described their situation as pitable in the extreme, of all ages from six weeks to eighty five! We claim that it is a virtual recognition of the fact that their authority no longer extends over the whole South—this sending persons whom they regard as criminals out of their jurisdiction. Mr Vallandigham's is a noted case of tacit recognition. The want of food for the army, forage particularly, is great. Waggons constantly come from the Blackwater—*60* miles for corn. Patrick being absent I on Sat delivered 5 barrels to a Gov Agent for Jenkins Brigade—for which he paid $15 per barrel. I was ashamed to take the money, but it is the Government's own doing. They have depreciated their own paper until $15 is worth only $5. Prices are very high, but money is plentiful & becoming more so.

On Monday came Mr Hill & brought Mr E the charges of the officers against Col Baker. They are very serious & if proved his character, not only as an officer but as a gentleman and a man of honour, is gone! The theiving of the Yankees passes beleif—furniture, clothing, books, nothing is sacred. They stole all General Buckner's furniture & in a recent raid up the Combahee in S C what they could not carry off they burned. Mr W H Heyward our old neighbor in Charleston lost every thing on his plantation, negroes & all. They are arming & drilling the negroes and have several Brigades of them in the field already. Grant in one of his assaults on Vicksburg placed them in the front & pushed them on at the Bayonette point. The slaughter of the poor creatures was terrible. Grant left his dead & wounded uncared for for five days in front of our lines. Their sufferings were fearful & at last, by their own admission, we it was who cared for & suggested to him to send a flag of Truce & bring them in!

JUNE 10, 1863

Today came Sue on horseback to see Rachel who left this afternoon for Raleigh with her Uncle John. She brought news received through one of her husband's relatives of my sister Nora, about whom we have long been anxious, living as she does within the Federal lines, & so near to that den of oppression—Memphis. She has suffered severely for the Tories came to her house whilst she was sick in bed, ransacked it from top to bottom, took her silver, such of her clothes as they wished, her husband's instruments & horses & carried him off a prisoner & threw him into Jail. After some little time, however, they released him & he was again at home. She says that as yet they have food sufficient, but know not how long it will be the case, for there are neither mules nor horses in the country & in consequence no crop has been planted & they are exposed to depredations, thefts, & seizures at any moment. Poor child, brought up as she has been in the lap of luxury, what will become of her and her four little children? I weep when I think of her! Ah! that she could get here where bread at least is certain.

The news still good from Vicksburg; our troops hold out & we are assured that both provisions & ammunition are abundant. Pemberton can stand a long seige. Johnston is organizing a force for his releif, but his movements are wrapped in secresy. The Yankee accounts of their own loss is terrible. They admit that their "fire did not injure us much," that "we took it cooly, whilst the slaughter on their side was terrific"! On Sat their troops "refused to be again led up to a slaughter pen," when, will he nil he, Grant was forced to commence throwing up paralels & "spades were trumps" once more! The news of a victory at Port Hudson confirmed. Kirby Smith, however, was not there, tho it is supposed some of his troops were crossed from the west Bank to Gardner's (who commands the garrison) assistance. *He* it was, *Gardner*, who defeated Banks. The slaughter here was terrible also! They again put the negro Regiments in the front & at the first charge six hundred out of a Regiment which they call the Louisiana were killed. Sherman was severely wounded by a minie ball & carried to New Orleans, from whence we hear that he is since dead, but that lacks confirmation.

The seige of Port Hudson is for the present raised. Farragut with the Richmond and other war steamers took part in the action but with out effect. Within a few weeks three thousand persons have been banished from N O & landed in the swamps beyond Pascagoula & told to shift for themselves! Every thing they leave is immediately seized upon by the harpies of the U S Government & confiscated, whether for public or private use does not appear. Milroy & Stahl at Winchester are emulating them. Waggon trains of women & children are left at night in the woods within a short distance of our lines, with $100 in Yankee Treasury notes only & told not to return under pain of death. This is not the worst, for in many cases families are separated, mothers ordered to go & leave their children. Neither age nor sex are respected. Young girls accused of secession proclivities are sent without protector across the lines or dragged to Camp Chase, torn from their homes & exposed to the insults of an Abolition prison. My blood boils as I write it!

I lead so different a life, so calm, so quiet, so peaceful that my heart overflows with thankfulness & praise to the Giver of all my good gifts who hath made me to differ?!

My house is now in perfect order. Every one of my possessions, every book, paper, peice of cloth, Linen, China, & Glass has been inspected & compared with the muster roll of my little possessions. The Store Room, the Pantry, the bed chambers, all have been routed out & put to rights again. I beleive it only remains for me to examine the Kitchen ware & take an account of stock. When I have done & can tell all about every thing I own & when I compare the quiet, the repose, the happiness which results from a well ordered home with the anxiety, the distress, the heart crushing misery, which those under the Federal rule endure—I feel almost ashamed that I suffer so little for the Cause, the glorious Cause of our Country's freedom! Something I may do for my distressed country women & that I will set about speedily. Nora has lost all her servants & has no one to do anything for her four little ones.

I preserve an account of the departure of a negro Regiment from Boston, which I think in deliberate fiendishness equals any thing I have yet seen. No! a Debate in the Senate of the State of Penn surpasses it. One cannot beleive a Christian of the 19th Century wrote it. It is more like the vindictive ravings of a Feegie or New Zealand savage! Next to the account of the Mass Regt I place a bit of the antecedents of its Col Shaw.[81] What can we expect of men in whose veins runs such debased, such ditch water blood, but think of a city applauding it. Are there ten righteous men left in Sodom?

Forty physicians in New Orleans, registered enemies of the U S they call all who refuse the oath, applied for leave to quit the city. Will it be beleived that, tho they were sending off boat loads every day against their will, their application was *refused* on the ground that they should need their services in case of an Epidemic this summer. What oppression!

June 12, 1863

News! still glorious news from the South West! Vicksburg holds out! Port Hudson is releived, Sherman dead, & Kirby Smith has taken & holds Milliken's Bend which commands the Mississippi above the Yazoo & can consequently prevent Grant from receiving supplies or reinforcements from Memphis, which is, since the capture of Haines Bluff by Admiral Porter, his base line. Glorious news if true & there seems no reason to doubt it. Grant has sent to Hurlbut at Memphis to have 30,000 beds ready for the wounded & to send him the same no., *thirty thousand*, re-inforcements. Hurlbut says he has not the troops, but a large detachment, some say an Army Corps, has left Rosencrans & is en route for Vicksburg. I hope Kirby Smith will demand their passes at Milliken's Bend! But thirty thousand wounded! We estimated Grant's loss, killed, wounded, & prisoners at 40,000, that is, the letter writer's did, but one & all we considered it exagerated. A comparison of their own data, however, the no at which they themselves have arrived makes it 50,000! Good God what slaughter! No wonder they refused to march up to the "slaughter pen" again. No wonder that they hailed "*spades*" as they did! Grant is advancing regularly by paralels, the first being five hundred yards

---

[81] These newspaper articles are on page 26 of the second volume of the diary.

from our outer works. A cavalry force under one Jackson has cut its way into Vicksburg, which must be a great encouragement to the garrison. God be with & strengthen them! How many hopes and fears hang now on those gallant men! If Pemberton holds out I shall be almost inclined to forgive him his Abolition birth.

On the Potomac, after a pause since the battle of Chancellorsville, Hooker seems to be bestirring himself. Unusual activity has been observed amongst his army for some days, fortifying the upper fords to prevent Gen Lee from crossing on his aggressive movement, but until Tuesday last no news of an advance on his side.

On that day, however, the papers announced that he had thrown a Brigade over at Deep Run below Hamilton. Crossing, they advanced upon our troops stationed there, but at the first shout as our men rose from their ambush, they fled precipitately, not even coming within musket shot of us, where upon they commenced entrenching & are still at it, tho' why Gen Lee allows it, he knows best. He must have some most excellent reason, a reason which in the end we will all admit.

Wednesday's paper contained to our surprise a dispatch from Gen Lee to the War Department—as follows—"The enemy crossed the Rappahanock this morning at five A. M. at the various fords from Beverly's to Kelly's with a large force of cavalry accompanied by infantry & artillery. After a severe contest until five P M General Stuart drove them across the River"—signed R E Lee. Further news of the next day, Thursday the 11th, tells us that to our mortification it was at first a surprise, in which the enemy got the best of it, but our men rallying on the re-inforcements recovered everything but the prisoners & horses which were immediately hurried over the river.

The enemy numbered about 10,000 Cavalry besides infantry & artillery. They surprized two of our Regiments at breakfast, the horses grazing, the men unarmed. Three companies of the third & one of the first Virginia were captured & about 600 horses and some horse artillery. They then fell on Jones Brigade which was in the act of forming, guns & pistols not loaded. Taking them thus at an advantage our line was peirced, & broken & they pushed on to Brandy station where was Gen Stuart's headquarters. This & the station they captured. Our men recovering came forward & threw themselves sabre in hand on the enemy & they in turn were driven back with the loss of many prisoners & a battery, we recapturing our guns but not our prisoners. The fight fluctuated through the day & was the severest Cavalry engagement of the war & one where sabres were more freely used than ever before. We lost many men from their sharpshooters posted in the woods. Our killed & wounded number several hundred it is feared & we lose about two hundred taken prisoner. We, however, have now in Richmond three hundred & two of their men whilst more are known to be on the road. Of their dead & wounded we can form no estimate as they were carried across the River. Victory, however, finally settled decisively in our favor & they were driven back to the Rappahanock which they recrossed.

Amongst the killed is Lieut Col Hampton[82]—of South Carolina, a *gentleman and a gallant officer*, one drop of whose blood is worth a regiment of our opponents. Of Revolutionary descent, polished manners, high education, refined, & elegant in his tastes, his loss is one which his country will long feel. He has occupied a high post in the world of fashion also, & the news of his death will send a thrill of triumph through many a Northern breast whom he has out shown in the drawing room but who never dreamed of measuring swords with him on the field—& this man died by the hand of a vile *mercenary*! The ways of Providence are indeed inscrutable.

Col Sol Williams[83] of the 2d North Carolina Cavalry is also killed & his body is now in Richmond. This is the Regiment which at one time it was thought that the Gov would place under Patrick's command & which brother said was not given to him, tho his name was mentioned in high terms to the Gov in connection with it, because of his want of political influence. I remember I was a little disappointed & how blind and short sighted I am! What anguish, what misery, has my heavenly Father spared me! When will I learn to trust all to Him who knows what is for my best, to repine at nothing which comes from His Almighty hand? God forgive me & *increase my faith*.

Col Butler of S C had his foot shot off and Gen W. H. F. Lee received a severe sabre cut in the thigh. He is a son of the Comdg General. We had three Brigades engaged—Hampton's, Lee's, & Jones. The battle is known as that at Brandy Station. The enemy seem to be improving in their Cavalry management. I suppose they are learning how to ride, a pity for us, for all our best horses are exhaused, victims to bad management & no forage. I wish that the spirits of all those who have perished through Maj Gen French's dunder headed ignorance, folly, & indifference could come back & *neigh* out their complaints around him. With Macbeth he would "*Sleep no more*"![84]

Was very busy all day yesterday copying Receipts. Such nice ones! "Chocolate puddings," "Soup a la Reine," "French Ratafia," etc., etc., which I have been years in collecting but never found it convenient to put in my book until now. I was not at all like a man I have read of somewhere who when he had a poor dinner took a Recipt Book & read to his assembled family the most tempting and appetizing Receipts which he could find until in a

---

[82]Lt. Col. Frank Hampton of the Second South Carolina Cavalry Regiment was mortally wounded at Brandy Station. He was a brother of Gen. Wade Hampton. *Official Records (Army)*, Series I, XXVII, Part II, 729; Freeman, *Lee's Lieutenants*, III, 15; Chesnut, *Diary from Dixie*, 305.

[83]Col. Solomon Williams, of Nash County, commanded the Nineteenth North Carolina (Second Cavalry) Regiment. He was killed at Brandy Station, June 9, 1863. Clark, *Histories of the North Carolina Regiments*, II, 79, 83, 92; Manarin and Jordan, *North Carolina Troops*, II, 100-101, 104; V, 114.

[84]Shakespeare, *Macbeth*, act 2, sc. 2, line 36.

short time, so strong was his imagination that he convinced not only himself but them that they had dined sumptuously! I was not all so, for I longed for sugar, oranges, almonds, & what not to realize for Mr E & myself some of the dainties of which I wrote.

Patrick has been reading me the new poem Tanhauser[85] & even the magic of his reading, the modulation of his voice, cannot yet convince me that it is "good." There are fine lines in fine thoughts & well turned, but it does not to me rise above the mediocre. One feels ready to exclaim with old Seldon, "Tis ridiculous for a Lord to print verses—tis well enough to make them to please himself but to make them public is foolish. If a man in a private chamber twirls his Band strings or play with a rush to please himself 'tis well enough; but if he should go into Fleet St & sit upon a stall & twirl a Band string or play with a Rush—then all the boys in the Street would laugh at him."[86] And so it is with these two Lordlings young Bulwer & Julian Fane son of the Earl of Westmoreland. Their Poem is pure, refined, & has some beautiful & graceful lines in it, but it lacks *power*. The true Promethean spark is wanting & were it not for the position they will hold both in the world of fashion & letters (for a corner of Bulwer's mantle must descend upon his son) I do not think that five years hence it would be remembered.

Ah! Mrs Edmondston, Mrs Edmondston, sour grapes! sour grapes! You feel that it is better than you can do. Yes! but I do not "twirl a rush—or play with my band strings" in Fleet St. They do & I am at liberty to laugh. I am trying, too, to read Victor Hugo's "Fantine," the first part of Les Miserables,[87] but it is uphill work—Coarse, radical, & unprincipled—all the faults & sins of human nature are put on the head of an impersonal scapegoat called "*Society*" who bears them to all appearance with as much sang froid as the veritable scapegoat of the Israelites of yore did the sins of the congregation.

Were it not that Mr Hill has been at some trouble to get it & has paid me the compliment of lending it to me for a first reading & will of course ask me for my opinion of it, I should throw it aside in disgust. With all its other faults, it is not even natural, over drawn & dramatic. I cannot interest myself in the adventures of an ignorant convict & a Parisian grisette who, one sees at a glance, will soon fall lower yet. "The Surpries," where the three lovers desert their mistresses is coarse, brutal, & worse than all—vulgar. Vulgar!—am I wrong to recoil so from that? I fear vulgarity revolts me more than wickedness & that I know is not right. Wickedness I can pity & pray for, but vulgarity!

---

[85]"Tannhäuser, or the Battle of the Bards" was a poem written in 1861 by Edward Robert Bulwer-Lytton in conjunction with Julian Fane. Bulwer-Lytton (1831-1891) was the first earl of Lytton, and the son of Edward George Lytton Earle Bulwer-Lytton, the first Baron Lytton. See footnote 31, 1860, and footnote 44, 1863. Benét, *Reader's Encyclopedia*, 714; *Dictionary of National Biography*, XVIII, 178.

[86]Selden, *Table Talk*, 116.

[87]*Les Misérables*, a historical novel by Victor Hugo (1802-1885), was published in 1862. Benét, *Reader's Encyclopedia*, 524, 728.

faugh! After thinking even of Fantine my mind flies back with pleasure, as to a verdant spot, to Tanhauser. That is pure, refined, & the work of a *gentleman*. He does not deify impurity & excuse it because it is the fault of *Society* & yet I warrant that he would be as gentle with the repentant sinner & do more to reform her than ever the sentimental apologist who wrote Fantine from a pair of moral stilts would do. Eugene Sue[88] is a Radical, a Red Republican, an admirer of the French Revolution & had his impossible theories full sways, Heaven would blush at the spectacle presented to it. But it is time to stop & yet I have something more to say, but I will for once deny myself the pleasure of chatting with you O Journal.

JUNE 15, 1863

Went to the Plantation with Mr E and came back worn out with fatigue. I beleive it is the dry weather which affects one thus. It has not rained to speak of since the 6th day of May & vegetation is in consequence parched up. Tomorrow the moon changes however & we look with hope to that as a period to our sufferings.

News yesterday to the effect that Vicksburg still holds out. Grant is hauling water eight miles to a portion of his command. He is advancing by regular paralels. His men have had enough of *assults*. The papers are filled with the sufferings of our compatriots driven from the lines of the enemy. Their object undoubtedly is to replace them with Yankee Abolitionists & then claim the country by *vote of the inhabitants when Peace is made*, a flimsy veil but one which I hope our rulers will tear off. The enemy are begining to understand our weak points & are sending Cavalry expeditions into the heart of our land which carry fire & sword with them & strike dismay into the hearts of our scattered population. God keep us from one, for we are entirely defenceless.

The more we hear of the battle at Brandy Station, the more disgraceful is the surprise & the more glorious the courage our men displayed tho' thus taken at advantage. The official statement of our loss is killed 50, wounded 280, missing 153. The enemy admit a much greater loss under all three heads. Amongst their killed is Col Davis who boasted that he was a kinsman of our President & had foxhunted over every inch of ground between Hanover & Richmond, & the wounded shows the name of the English mercenary, Sir Percy Wyndham,[89] who bears too good a name to be associated thus with such scoundrels. An extract from a Northern paper, giving an account of their foray into Prince William, boasts that they destroyed everything, barns, provisions, & cattle & that the "farmers were compelled to stand quietly by &

---

[88]Eugène Sue (1804-1859), originally an army doctor who began to write stories based on personal experiences, developed into a novelist best known for popular romances, such as *Les Mystères de Paris* (1843) and *The Wandering Jew* (1849). Benét, *Reader's Encyclopedia*, 1081-1082.

[89]Percy Wyndham was the colonel of the First New Jersey Cavalry. *Official Records (Army)*, Series I, XII, Part I, 168.

see the destruction of their farming implements." Where is the Christianity which Burnside boasts of? All centred in his Christian bosom, whence it shows itself by "Death Penalties," muzzling the Press, & driving defenceless women & children from their homes at the bayonette's point!—faugh!

Came Edie, Mama's maid, with her baggage saying that Father & herself will be out tomorrow for the summer.

June 17, 1863

Moon changed & no prospect of rain. The drought is getting alarming. The corn does not grow. The potatoes cannot be set out & the garden vegetables are burning up, but it is our Father who withholds it. He will send it in His own good time. Have been busy with my Honey today. The yeild is but poor & the comb dark. That terror of Bee keepers, the "webb," i.e. "the moth" of Books is reported as in possession & last year the hives were not robbed on account of Mr E's sickness. So the combs are dark & uninviting. Must change the Hives & try to do better another year. Making Walnut Catsup & Walnut Pickles. I have not made the first since '56 and my stock is now all gone—so must make a double portion.

I like housekeeping & housewifery cares, tho today they sit uneasily on me as I am far from well. My old enemy my liver is I fear in the wrong & I am suffering under one of Hannah Moore's[90] two ills of life—"*bile*." Her other foe was "*sin*" & tho I am never free from that still I fear my conscience is not delicate enough to cause me constant compunction for it. I fear I am too easily contented with a confession of it without that godly sorrow which worketh amendment.

The 17th of June. Two years today since Patrick marched to Wilmington & what a life time has been compressed into it! What a sorrowful heavy hearted woman I was today two years ago & how God has blessed me since then! He is at home, well, & we are as yet undisturbed. Make me thankful O God. Today two years since Papa was buried, buried from a world of sorrow & distress, for how many pangs has merciful Death spared him! How he would mourn over the sufferings of our country men exposed to Abolition tyranny! God alleviate them & give them strength to bear what Thou layest upon them.

That wretch Milroy it is reported has been forced by Jenkins to evacuate Winchester where he has ruled with a rod of iron. I hope it is true but particulars are wanting. Vicksburg still triumphant, tho the Northern papers have it that it is surrendered, yet our dates are later than theirs. Nothing more on our side from Kirby Smith and Milliken's Bend, but from the North we

---

[90]Hannah More (1745-1833), an English author and philanthropist, suffered successive illnesses of a bilious nature which she often referred to in her letters. William Roberts (ed.), *Memoirs of the Life and Correspondence of Mrs. Hannah More* (New York: Harper and Brothers, 2 volumes, 1834), I, 67; II, 215, 289.

hear that the slaughter there was great. They say we refused to give quarter to negroes & killed them even after they were wounded & that Cuffee behaved better than his white officers. This is only a ruse to get negro officers appointed & so to releive the Anglo Saxon from the retaliation threatened by our President & sanctioned by our Congress which I preserve marked A no 9.[91]

The seige of Port Hudson is renewed by land & River, but as yet it holds out. Rosencrans is reported as re-inforcing Grant, & Joe Johnston is said to have 40,000 men in his rear. So stirring news may be hourly looked for. Grant pretends to have dispatches from Pemberton, delivered to him by the treachery of the Courier, one Douglas, an Illinois man, with doleful tales of Pemberton's distress, but we do not beleive one word of it. Yankee as he himself is, he would surely have selected a Southron for such a post at such time.

On the Rappahanock the force thrown over by Hooker at Deep Run has quietly withdrawn after mounting seige guns of heavy calibre. A little shelling, ineffectual on both sides, was all that took place on either side. It is supposed to be a ruse of Fighting Joe's & that he either wished Lee to attack him or, as some prisoners we took aver—it was intended to withdraw our attention from Falmouth opposite Fredericksburg whilst he removed his stores. The Depot there has been burned & many fires observed on his line, so it is thought he intends to evacuate Stafford & try some other "On to Richmond route." A demonstration was made upon the Chickahominy a few days since, but it was a demonstration only, as the troops have withdrawn to their gunboats without accomplishing anything. The coast of Georgia is threatened with invasion by a party of raiders up Turtle River. Grierson in Louisiana has been driven back from another threatened foray by a timely advance of ours, for which God be thanked.

Ah! what bad generalship to deliver New Orleans to the enemy as Lovel did. I am happy to say we now never hear of him. May he long rest in obscurity. The *"mistake"* in drawing him thence amounted to a *"crime."*

JUNE 17, 1863

As was predicted Hooker has evacuated his camp opposite Fredericksburg. Our pickets have entered Falmouth which they find deserted & the bridges between that place and Acquia Creek and Dumfries are all reported burned. Our cavalry hang on the rear of the enemy & cut off stragglers. Hooker's headquarters are at Dumfries or at Manassas but when his next advance will be attempted it is impossible to say. The South side of the James is the only route that they have not yet tried. We wonder at Lee's allowing those two Brigades that crossed at Deep Run to get off so easily, but he knows better than we & we have no right to criticise one who has acted with the success

---

[91]This newspaper article is not in the diary.

and judgment shown by him heretofore. Such men as Lovel, Pemberton, Loring, Bragg, who have so often failed, command no respect, for our faith is lacking. They have committed so many blunders that their prestige is gone, but with Lee, Johnston, & Beauregard the case is widely different.

The news from the Chickahominy is disgraceful to some one, probably the General in command of the Department for the Gunboats reported in the Chickahominy have landed about one thousand men who have orders to make their way to Williamsburg, burning, pillaging, & destroying as they go, and well do they execute their infamous orders. From a prominent point on the South side of the James their line can be traced by the smoke of the burning houses & barns in their rear. Women & children turned out houseless to starve in the midst of a deserted wilderness. Cattle & hogs butchered wantonly on the ground lie as they were shot, & our government allows this! Two hundred determined men could put them to flight, or a dignified protest from Mr Davis & more than a *threat* at retaliation would stop it. That portion of our population, whose defence in civilized warfare is their weakness, their inability to molest the invaders, is, in this brutal war, made to suffer more than any other the horrors incident to it.

The family of Mr Buffington of Florida, three young girls & a little boy, were ordered to leave the enemies lines & carried to Port Royal S C to be sent into ours by a Flag of Truce. When there they requested an interview with their father, then a prisoner at that fort in Abolition hands, and will it be beleived, it was denied them, altho the eldest stated that they knew no one to apply to for assistance, that they had but little money, & knew not where to go nor whom to go to. Gen Hunter rudely refused it, & sent them unfriended & unprotected into our lines. With the party was the venerable mother of Gen Kirby Smith,[92] infirm & over seventy years of age, whose only crime & for which she was driven from her home was that her son was a General in the Confederate service. Nay, with a refinement of cruelty, Mr D H Lilly of Randolph, Beverly County, Va, who was imprisoned at Wheeling under Pierponts[93] beneficent rule was allowed to see his wife and three children, but all communication denied him & the bare fact that they had been arrested for giving a meal to two Confederate soldiers imparted to him & when at length he was released all information respecting them was refused him. He was conducted out of the lines & at this moment knows nothing of them. In the hope that they, too, may have been sent within the Confederate lines he advertises for news of them in the Richmond papers. They were brought into the same

---

[92]There are references to this episode in the Edmund Kirby-Smith Papers in the Southern Historical Collection.

[93]Francis Harrison Pierpont (1814-1899), a lawyer and Virginia Unionist, aided in the organization of West Virginia, where he served as provisional governor from 1861 through 1863. He also served as governor of the Virginia counties under Federal control but not included in West Virginia. *Concise Dictionary of American Biography,* 798.

prison where he was confined & put in the room next him, but so soon as they learned the relationship between them, they were removed where they refused to tell him.

Today came Father, Mama, & Sue to spend the summer with us, Mama, I am sorry to say, quite sick. Ewell, Jackson's successor with the Stonewall Brigade, is reported as having taken Winchester & cut off that stain on humanity, Milroy's retreat. I hope it is true; for he will be hanged without mercy so soon as he falls into our hands & thus a stop may be put to the atrocities which are now with impunity practised upon our unfortunate women & children. I preserve an extract from a Philadelphia paper which passes in review some of their most notorious generals to show what some of the best of the nation think of their own agents. What must be the state of public opinion which keeps in place & countenances wretches such as these? From their tender mercies good God deliver us! I place, also, by it an order of the renegade Hurlbut issued at Memphis. Nora, poor thing, is within 20 miles of this brute's headquarters & even now may be suffer[ing] from his tyranny.

Col Sol Williams of the 2d North Carolina Cavalry, killed at Brandy station, was married only three weeks before his death to Miss Pegram of Petersburg. Poor thing—henceforth how dark is her future life to her!

June 19, 1863

God be thanked for the glorious news which reached us last night. I give it in General Lee's own words.

> To His Excellency President Davis—
> God has again crowned the valour of our troops with success. Early's division stormed the enemy's entrenchments at Winchester, capturing their artillery, etc.
> June 15th 1863—   R E Lee

Later news tells us that Ewell surrounded the place on Saturday night. On Sunday he summoned it to surrender. Milroy refused, saying that if an attempt was made to storm the position he would fire every house in the place. Ewell replied that he would carry it by assault & that if a single house was fired he would refuse quarter & hang every Yankee he captured. Soon after this parley the assault was made, the outer works captured, & in two hours the Abolitionists capitulated. Ewell on taking possession found that Milroy, whilst the fighting was going on, had at the head of six hundred cavalry cut his way through a weak part of our lines & escaped. Ewell leaving Early to take charge of the prisoners, stores, etc., at once pushed on towards Martinsburg. They made no attempt to fire their stores which fell into our hands. We took six thousand prisoners, much ammunition, stores enough to supply our army for two months, a large number of waggons & fine horses. Our loss in killed & wounded does not exceed 50, which seems almost incredible. So much authentic. Now for rumours which are: that Ewell has crossed the Potomac & taken possession of Maryland Heights opposite Harpers Ferry, whilst another body advancing on that place by the direct road from Charleston captured it & with it immense stores which Milroy had recently sent thither from Winchester; also that Johnson's Division had captured at Berryville two thousand men en route to re-inforce Milroy. It is thought that he (Milroy) will not be able to make his escape, as the whole country from Winchester to the Potomac swarms with our troops & Jenkins with a large force of Cavalry is hovering along the border. Great news, which stirs every fibre of our hearts & bodies with thankfulness. God has indeed blessed us.

From the Rappahanock the news is that Hooker's army has disappeared. It is supposed to be concentrating near Alexandria. A P Hill hangs on his rear & from the heavy firing it is thought has engaged his rear guard. Hooker is in Washington & will doubtless pursue the same course that McClellan took last fall to cut off our advance into Maryland & Penn. The latter State, Penn, is represented as in a blaze of excitement, the militia called out, Gov Curtin[94] in Washington demanding protection and tendering the State force, & the whole border in a state of wild alarm. No news from Maryland, she being so crushed by the "despot's heel" that she exhibits no feeling whatever. The last act of infamy was perpetrated by the City Council of Baltimore in a unanimous vote approving of the Vallandigham's banishment! Think of that! Where is the blood of Carrol of Carrolton?[95]

JUNE 20, 1863

Another dispatch from General Lee to the effect that General Rhodes has captured Martinsburg with 200 prisoners, a large amount of grain & ammunition, & a number of guns. Our loss, *one* killed! A rumour has it that Mrs Milroy the wife of the rapacious General, with her plunder, was also taken. She has rendered herself even more obnoxious than her husband, personally insulting Ladies of respectability & position, using the grossest & vituperative language. She herself ordered Mrs Logan & family to leave their house & the lines for the matter of that & went in person to attend to the removal & to see that not more than $100 worth of property was taken with her. She then installed herself into the house & appropriated all Mrs Logan's & daughters furniture, plate, & wearing apparel to her own use. Such wholesale stealing &

---

[94]Andrew Gregg Curtin (ca. 1815-1894) was the wartime governor of Pennsylvania. Curtin raised double his state's quota of troops and received authority from the legislature to equip and maintain this extra force, the Pennsylvania Reserve Corps, at state expense. He also received funds from the state for the support and schooling of war orphans. After the war he served as minister to Russia under Grant and as a Democratic congressman from Pennsylvania from 1880 until 1887. *Dictionary of American Biography*, IV, 606.

[95]Charles Carroll (1737-1832) of Carrollton Manor in Frederick County, Maryland, was a politician and wealthy landowner during the Revolutionary period. He served on committees of correspondence and safety, as a member of the Continental Congress, signed the Declaration of Independence, and later became a United States senator from Maryland. *Concise Dictionary of American Biography*, 146.

plundering as she has carried on beats even her country men, skilled as they are in such acts! She came to Winchester with one small trunk & goes out with *nine* large ones, all stolen. Milroy was a boatman on the Ohio river previous to the war, some of the scum which this commotion in society has thrown to the top of the Northern society.

Ewell, the commander of this expedition, commenced the war under rather laughable circumstances. In the early part of the invasion of Va it will be remembered that the Yankees dashed into Fairfax Court House & attacked Capt Mar's Company, killing him & dispersing his men before sunrise in the morning. A gentleman was observed in the street unarmed rallying Mar's men, calling to the citizens to stand firm, showering down a torrent of imprecation on the Yankee heads, & by his personal exertions making a stand with both citizens & soldiers which in a short time repulsed the enemy & drove them from the town. He was entirely unarmed & in fact had but a single garment on, but regardless of either fact he stood where the bullets flew thickest & after the repulse of the invaders went calmly back to bed![96] The next we hear of him was at the first battle of Manassas where, however, he was put in action. We then find him in the Stonewall Brigade as Jackson's second in command. He distinguished himself in all the engagements of that celebrated corps until the second Manassas where he lost a leg. He had just reported for duty when Jackson died & he in his last moments expressed the desire that Ewell his right hand might succeed him. Mr Davis promptly acceeded to his wishes, sent him a Lieut Gen's Commission, & Lee ordered him into the advance on Winchester & ably has he vindicated the correctness of Jackson's estimate of him. Tho' he has but one leg, he has acheived a feat of which his great cheif even might have been proud. We will watch his future career with great interest.

We have found out the reason that the Abolitionists lose so *few men in* their engagements with us, whence comes the discrepancy between their account & ours. They count only as *dead* the *native born Americans*. The Irish, Germans, & negroes, of whom their army is mainly exposed, go for nothing. They do not even swell the list of the wounded! At any rate they are consistent for they care for none of them & it is nothing to them how many foreigners we kill. But what a nation!

JUNE 21, 1863

Last night came brother in "*doleful dumps*" about the rain. So gloomy was he that even the news from Winchester could not cheer him, but this morning a passing shower put a new face on everything.

---

[96]Ewell described this incident in his report from Fairfax Court House, dated June 1, 1861. Federal cavalry passed through Fairfax firing at the windows and doors of the hotel, whereupon Ewell positioned Captain Marr's light infantry company, the "Warrenton Rifles," to intercept their return. On returning, the Federal troops were repulsed by Marr's company, but Marr was killed. In the final attack Ewell received a flesh wound. *Official Records (Army)*, Series I, II, 63-64.

Gen Lee will now annihilate Hooker & Pemberton continue to hold
Vicksburg. It is [———] days since we have had rain enough to more than
commence to drip from the eves and this shower is a timely releif to parched
vegetation. "Then God sendest a gracious rain on thine inheritance &
refreshed it when it was weary." No news from Vicksburg either yesterday or
today. Father thinks it a good sign but the suspense is painful. Not one word
of Gen Johnston, yet our confidence in him does not flag. From Port Hudson
we hear that the enemy have been repulsed in *twenty seven* different assaults,
every time with great loss to them but little to us. Gen Bragg has issued an order, which I append, refusing the privilege of a flag of Truce to the escort of
those unfortunate citizens whom Yankee barbarity exile into our lines &
another giving aid & comfort to those unfortunates whom they bring, the first
instance in which Governmental protection has been accorded them. So I
preserve it.

As to Gen Lee's movements, or where are his head quarters, we are in
profound ignorance. We anticipate an advance into Maryland & rumour has
it that our advance guard has crossed the Potomac, but officially or even
authoritatively we know nothing. We look for great things, a redemption of
the last campaign, a success at Sharpsburg. Lincoln is in a state of great
alarm & is calling for 150,000 volunteers to defend the Capitol & the borders
of Penn. Gov Curtin has called out the militia of the latter state and the panic
is wide spread. They begin to feel something of what a war of invasion is, tho
God forbid that we should ever press on them the cup which they have compelled us to drink of. I hope an enlightened, a sublime Christianity will make
us retaliate only so far as to ensure our future protection. Hooker's army is
massed about Alexandria. Lee's, it is reported, is on the upper Potomac, but
we know nothing of it.

I omitted to mention a gallant thing performed by some of our officers
because it came through an Abolition channel & we thought it a ruse to
justify them in their future harsh treatment of their prisoners. The Steamer
Maple Leaf sailed from Fortress Monroe with a number of Confederate
prisoners—officers. These rose on their guard when outside the Capes, overpowering them, & in turn making prisoners of them. They then headed the
vessel to the shore & landed on Virginia soil some where in Chesapeake Bay,
when 200 of them left, first paroling the Captain & crew & binding them by a
solemn promise to proceed on their voyage & not give the alarm. They
refrained from burning the vessel on account of some of our wounded who
were on board & for whom there was no shelter & secrecy was necessary as
they were still in the enemies lines. Forty-six gentlemen refused to leave, the
terms of their parole forbidding them to accept rescue. Some of the others
have arrived in Richmond & from their account I write.[97] I am sorry to add,

[97]The official report of this incident noted that the U.S.S. *Maple Leaf* was bound for Fort Delaware, June
10, 1863, with ninety-seven captured Confederate officers aboard. They overpowered the guard, leaving on

that the example in good faith set them by Southern gentlemen had no effect on their Yankee captors, for not only did they violate their solemn engagement & put about for Fortress Monroe but gave every information which could help to recapture the fugitives. Cretan faith, truly, but what should we expect? They carry not about with them the monstrous "corpse of their memories."

Gov Vance has ordered out the Militia,[98] 3000 thousand for six months. If enough do not volunteer by the 17th day of July, then a draft will be made & they ordered at once into camp. All between 40 and 45 are subject to it. Patrick is 44 today! Would that it had been deferred for one year! God grant him many more happy & peaceful birthdays & may we spend them *together*.

Vallandigham has sailed for Nassau from Wilmington, so much for the boasted *Blockade*. He was requested by some exponent of bad taste to make a speech at Goldsboro. A gentleman who heard him decline told it to Brother. The individual in question promised him full time as they "could detain the cars for a ¼ an hour." Mr V. answered "that there were two excellent reasons which forbad it—first the *other passengers might object to the detention*—& secondly, that as he was traveling through the country by the consent of the Confederate Government it would be he thought necessary *first to telegraph to Richmond & get permission* before he could with propriety do so." The gentleman *ought to have wilted*, but brass such as his is Corinthian in its toughness!

JUNE 24, 1863

Our Army is certainly "over the border," tho where Lee's headquarters are, neither friend or foe can tell. The Northern papers are full of accounts about the "conduct of the rebels," how they pay for everything, leave private property unmolested, are *"quite civil & orderly."* They fear that this is only in Maryland & that once in Penn a different tale will be told. Penn is in a state of the wildest alarm. The public Records are being hurried from Harrisburg, the match ready to be applied to Carlyle Barracks.[99] Horses & cattle being driven in haste to the mountains, & valuables, plate, books, etc., are in process of removal. Conscience it is that thus makes cowards of them. They remember their conduct at Jackson where they mutilated & burned what State papers they could find; how every Court House in their march has been sacked and

board thirty of the officers who refused to participate, and landed at Cape Henry to escape into the interior. *Official Records (Army)*, Series I, XXVII, Part II, 786.

[98]Vance's proclamation, reported in the *North Carolina Standard* on June 24, 1863, established the state's Home Guard, which replaced the militia. The militia law, covering male conscripts between eighteen and forty-five years of age, had been overruled by the intensive Confederate conscription acts. Vance's new state defense rested upon men between eighteen and fifty years of age who were exempt from Confederate army service because of their age or positions. Clark, *Histories of the North Carolina Regiments*, IV, 645-646, 649.

[99]These were cavalry barracks located at Carlisle, Pennsylvania, near Harrisburg, the state capital. Boatner, *Civil War Dictionary*, 123.

the County Records, titles to Land, deeds, wills, & the papers necessary to the proper management of the country in peace, wilfully and needlessly, nay say wantonly and brutally, destroyed. Women & children driven from their homes, their property stolen, their houses burned, their food, that food necessary to their daily subsistence, taken from them. Cattle & Hogs slaughtered and left to rot where they fell, forage & grain burned in the field, agricultural implements destroyed, fences torn down & stock pastured on the growing crops; their wearing apparel taken from Ladies & given in their sight to the vilest of Camp followers; how works of art, books, pictures, pianos, handsome furniture, old family relics—such as carved chairs, plate, China—have been packed up by U S officers & sent North to their wives; servants incited to rebellion; horses in some instances the only horse, the only means that a poor woman had to send to mill for bread for her little ones, taken by these brutes in human form. Our fellow countrymen in Grant's Lines are actually starving for food, he having stolen everything in the way of subsistence, nay the very paper which brings us the account of the humane moderation of our men contains an official account of the proceedings of a Court Martial which actually condemned a man [———] of Maryland to be hanged for feeding & sheltering two Confederate soldiers! Lincoln the despot kindly steps in & commutes the death penalty to imprisonment during the war in Fort Delaware. Grant me patience whilst I write! Well may they tremble for fear that a just retribution will be meeted out to them, but they have to deal with gentlemen & Christians who profess not the mere lip Christianity of Burnside but the exalted Christianity of their great exemplar. They remember that "Vengeance is mine saith the Lord—I will repay"![100]

JUNE 25, 1863

Great news, news from the North & South! Grant impelled, it is supposed, by the fear that the occupancy by us of Milliken's Bend (of which we have official news) will cut off his supplies, has made another desperate attack on the fortifications at Vicksburg and has again been repulsed with terrible loss. His dead strew the ground in front of our works. One of our scouts, who has returned from their Camp, says they estimate their loss at 10,000 and say they are much dejected & begin to fear lest Johnston should fall on them. Gen Taylor holds Millikens Bend. Kirby Smith is at Shreveport. All the Yankee forces have left the interior of Lou. New Orleans, of course, is still held by them, but the Teche, the Tensas, [illegible] Donaldsonville, etc., all evacuated. Bayou Sara they completely destroyed, scarcely a house left! An attack was made by a portion of Rosencrans command upon Knoxville & after two hours hard fighting driven back with heavy loss.

---

[100]Romans 12:19.

Our little Navy has carried dismay & destruction into the heart of Abolition Commerce. Five vessels have been captured off the mouth of the Chesapeake & another reported off Delaware Bay. Thirty U S vessels have gone out in pursuit of her. Fifteen Captains arrived in New York, all of whose vessels had been destroyed by the Ala or the Florida. Marine Insurance is at a fabulous rate in New York & importers, China & Whale traders, tremble for their profits. Oil & Tea have gone up & seamen's wages increased one half. Thirteen new vessels have recently been destroyed by Capt Semmes & a new vessel has just raised her colours, making a [———] Confederate War steamer afloat. Success & prize money to her!

From Maryland the news continues good. A P Hill's division is the last one that has crossed. Head Quarters still a secret from the public. A Cavalry fight has taken place in Loudon between the enemy & Robinson's & Fitz Hugh Lee's commands, but the accounts are so diverse that I will omit details for the present. Capt Haxall is Robinson's aid & in his brigade are all the troops raised for Edmondston's Battalion & there would he be, were he now in the service. What misery & unhappiness, what torturing suspense, has a Good God spared me! Be with those less blessed than I am O Lord! Calm their aching hearts & give them Thy peace! Ah! with what pride will they welcome their loved ones home once more! What honest exultation in the thought that they have fought for their Country!

Prisoners from Winchester are crowding into Richmond. The stores & ammunition captured there are immense. It is thought they portend that an advance in force down the Valley was intended, nipped now, however, in the bud. The Yankees are lost in wonder at our forbearance. A wild cry goes up from them for troops. Gov Seymour[101] has called McClellan to his help to organize the New York Regiments. The infamous seventh Regt, Col Lefferts,[102] is again in the field & will again, I hope, show their heels to their late Southern hosts whom they would "rather *die* than fight." Again may they be entertained in Richmond.

Lincoln has seized the pen & under his own signature defends Mr Vallandigham's arrest & banishment. Did ever ruler make so egregious a blunder in the art of King-craft? Job's wish "Oh! that mine enemy had written a book"[103] comes home to us now. Our enemy has written a book & covered

---

[101]Horatio Seymour (1810-1886), a political moderate but a strong Unionist, served as governor of New York from 1853 until 1855 and again from 1863 until 1865. As the war governor he ably met the state's army quotas but opposed the extra-constitutional powers Lincoln adopted during the war. After the war Seymour ran as the Democratic candidate for the presidency in 1868 but was defeated. He continued to exert extensive political influence, however, and helped defeat the Tweed Ring in New York. *Concise Dictionary of American Biography*, 941.

[102]Col. Marshall Lefferts commanded the Seventh Regiment, New York State Militia. He later worked as an engineer and became president of the Gold and Stock Telegraph Company in 1871. *Official Records (Army)*, Series I, II, 582; *Concise Dictionary of American Biography*, 558.

[103]Job 31:35b.

himself with ridicule. It is hard to say which is worst his grammer or his Logic! He annihilates one Anglo Saxon prerogative—freedom of speech. What thanks the Yankee nation owe us for having kept them free for so long! Left to themselves they are the prey to every 'ism that stalks. Abolitionism & military despotism now rule their country.

JUNE 27, 1863

I do not think negroes possess natural feeling. I see so many instances of neglect & insensibility to each other amongst them that I seriously doubt it. For example, Vinyard's child Morgan I accidentally discovered to be ailing & puny looking. I found it out from hearing the poor thing cry & tho I was assured nothing was the matter with it went to the nursery to see myself. Its changed appearance shocked me, but thinking it was its teeth, gave it some simple physic only & then went daily to the nursery to see it. Still it dwined & what was strange its gums were but little swollen. At last it had high fever & was really ill & wishing to see for myself how much it would eat, told her to nurse it before me, when to my horror I heard that she had weaned it! Weaned it full three weeks ago! So the mystery was solved. No extra care, no extra provision had been made for it. The meat & bread at the nursery upon which the others throve was deemed sufficient for him. No tea, no milk, no sugar, no gruel, no hominy, no pap,—meat & bread alone—& it without a tooth in its head. Regularly, four times a day, had she left her work & gone to it under pretence to me of suckling it & yet not one drop did the poor thing get! The only reason that I can give for such conduct is that in dividing straw-berries amongst the servants I had omitted her because her eating them had given the baby colic & as fruit season was coming she feared to lose her share, so she weaned it; nay, so secret did she keep it whilst she was doing it that she acquiesced in the propriety of my not giving her *plums*, altho there was no earthly reason against it as the poor child was not allowed to suck. So soon as I discovered it, suitable provision was made for him & a bottle and quill provided for him to suck. It was really touching to see his delight when I had at length succeeded in coaxing him to suck it by putting a peice of ham fat on the end of the quill. Already he cries after his bottle and knows it as well as his nurse does. But think of his mother's insensibility. I can scarcely bear to look at her since & yet when he was sick one would have thought her in the depths of affliction whilst I kept her at her sewing. The large tears rolled down on her work in a manner touching to behold; yet when the sight of them molified me & I sent her out to stay with it, I never could find her in the nursery on any of my visits there. The woman Hopey who nursed it always had the baby in charge, whilst she idled about the kitchen & premises. Seeing this I sent her back to her work, when the sluices were opened again & a flood of tears followed, but I was obdurate and they soon dried. Now how is such a woman to be managed? The more the child is removed from her, the more callous she will become, & yet left to her it will not long be in the land of the living.

Another instance I preserve in my book, marked A no 18,[104] in a letter from a gentleman describing the late raid of the Abolitionists up the Combahee when all the negroes on a plantation left with them, leaving behind an aged & bed ridden woman *stripped naked*, her children having stolen her clothes & bed clothes before they left.

The papers have no news in them, filled only with accounts of Yankee outrages upon defenceless citizens, houses burned, agricultural implements destroyed, and attempts made to *burn* the standing wheat in the fields. This has been done in numerous instances in Eastern Va, amongst others on the Brandon Estate on James River owned by the Harrisons, relatives of my step Mother Mrs Devereux. The family were at home & witnessed it. Piles of brush were gathered & set fire to in the wheat, but fortunately it was too green to burn. They threw the fences down but as McClellan had previously stolen all the stock there was nothing to molest it. They left saying they would come again in a fortnight when it would be drier. Grant in his official report to his Government says, "I have destroyed every thing useful for thirty miles around Vicksburg." This confirms the accounts we have had of the suffering of our people within the Abolition lines. Is it not incredible that a nation calling itself enlightened & Christian can tolerate such conduct in its agents? Yet they exult in it & hound them on.

July 1, 1863

A letter last night from James dated Williamsport Md. June 17th. So he is quite in the advance, for we see that he is in Rhodes Division. He tells me that he has been in the impressing business lately & expects to do nothing else, that they "have carried everything before them, Milroy's whole force captured, all his stores, etc. We will now advance." He sends me "two pr of garter boots & a lot of I cant tell whether it is 'Union' or 'hair pins' which I did'nt pay for, but *took* so you need have no compunctions of conscience about using them." Good news & releives us greatly as we have been uneasy about him. The Yankee marauders who have been wasting the country north of Richmond seem to have it their own way. They have burned the bridge over the South Anna after overpowering the guard but not without a gallant defence on their part, but what could fifty men do against a thousand?; ravaged the country, burning large quantities of wheat just housed, barns, houses, churches, even attempting to set fire to the shocks of wheat in the field, stolen negroes & horses, & taken many private citizens prisoner. At Mr Williams Wickham's house in Hanover they found Gen Fitz Hugh Lee severely wounded in the fight at Brandy station. They ordered out Mr Wickham's carriage &

---

[104]This letter is preserved on page 21 of the second volume of the diary.

putting him in, despite the fact that he was in no state to be moved & was suffering severely, they carried him off with them.[105] Was ever such barbarity? Imperilling his life to allow them to indulge in the Luxury of a lie, for they will now announce to the world that they have taken our Comdg. Gen. R E Lee.

The Northern papers loudly threaten that Gen Dix will march on from Fortress Monroe & take Richmond, but we do not feel uneasy as to that. What we mind is the insult, the spoiling our citizens under the very eyes of the Government, & the impunity with which they make their escape after committing such excesses. The news from the army meagre but still good. Our men are forbidden to take anything without paying for it & conduct themselves in a quiet and orderly manner. We impress supplies & horses for the use of the army, nothing more. Our advance has entered Carlyle, Penn, meeting no resistance. It is reported but lacks confirmation that a battle has been fought at Harrisburg in which we were victorious and now hold the town. This is Northern news, however. Our last advices were from York. The R R bridge across the Susquehannah is reported as destroyed. No troops as yet confront us. Gen Knipe with 10,000 mostly raw recruits fell back as we threatened Carlyle. We have seized all the mills but as yet destroyed but little property. The roads through Penn are crowded with refugees & run-a-way negroes & they seem in terrible panic. Hooker's whereabouts unknown— supposed north of Washington. Imboden's Cavalry have destroyed the Baltimore & Ohio R R for seventy miles; not a bridge, scarcely a culvert, left & the magnificent tunnel through the Mountains a complete wreck. Two years steady work with a large force will not repair the damage inflicted by us upon this main artery of Washington & Baltimore.

July 3, 1863

Yesterday came Capt Cook[106] & Lt Elliot, & father & Patrick both being out, I invited them to remain to dinner, so that they might not be disappointed in the object of their visit. Capt Cook is in the regular Naval service & has seen life in many different countries whilst under the old government. He seems a plain sensible unaffected man. He has suffered terribly by this war,

---

[105]Mrs. Edmondston's reference to Gen. Fitzhugh Lee, a nephew of Robert E. Lee and one of his best cavalry commanders, is misleading. The cavalry officer wounded at Brandy Station was Gen. William Henry Fitzhugh Lee (1837-1891), Robert E. Lee's second eldest son. While convalescing at Hickory Hill in Hanover County, the home of William F. Wickham, he was captured on June 26, 1863, during a Federal raid and was held until March, 1864. His wife, Charlotte Wickham Lee, died in December, 1863, while he was imprisoned. After his release Lee continued to fight until the surrender at Appomattox. He returned to farming and served as the Democratic congressman from Virginia from 1887 until 1891. Boatner, *Civil War Dictionary*, 475, 477-478; *Concise Dictionary of American Biography*, 558; *Official Records (Army)*, Series I, XVII, Part II, 683.

[106]James W. Cooke of Beaufort was sent to Edward's Ferry to aid in the construction of the *Albemarle*, which he later commanded during the bombardment and capture of Plymouth in April, 1864. *Richmond Enquirer*, May 7, 1864; Clark, *Histories of the North Carolina Regiments*, II, 616, 618-619; III, 8-9; V, 192, 318-321.

having been driven from a delightful farm he owned in Fairfax not far from Washington City. He had an orchard of five hundred of the choicest peaches which he tells me he hears have been cut down by the enemy. An acquaintance passing his house took notes of the state of affairs so as to inform him & one item alone was that his pianna stood in the yard, the keys, etc. torn out & the frame used as a horse trough. He gave me a receipt for preparing the "very best Cayenne pepper," but I cannot see the advantage it posseses over the pepper itself. Make a strong decoction, a pepper tea, mix fine meal with it, make into thin cakes, dry brown in the oven & pound. I brought out my own domestic Cayenne & he was forced to admit its superiority, tho the other may serve as a substitute when unable to dry & pound it carefully as I do.

Mrs & Miss Smith & Miss Hines calling. Miss H told me an anecdote of Gen Viele and Negrodom that is worth preserving. The neice of our friend Dr Charles E Johnson[107] of Raleigh, Mrs Tunis of Norfolk, lost all her servants by the blandishments of their Yankee confreres. One of her women left her two children, one an infant in arms, the other just able to walk behind her. Mrs. T, having the whole care of her own children did not choose to be burdened with two piccaninnies, so taking one in her arms & the other by the hand, she went to Headquarters & desired to see Gen Viele. The sight of a Southern lady carrying a negro baby gained her immediate admittance. When she thus addressed him—"As these children, Gen Viele, have been deprived of their mother by your act I come here to surrender them to you," at the same time making a motion to give him the infant.

"Good God! Madam," said he springing to his feet, "you do not mean to leave these children here with me?" "That sir is my intention," and suiting the action to the word she deposited the baby upon his table in the midst of his papers & calmly saying "Good Morning sir," walked out & left them both behind her! What a subject for Punch![108] A negro baby sprawling amongst official papers, "morning reports," "proceedings of Courts martial," "General orders," & clutching as reason for being there, Lincoln's "Emancipation Proclamation."

Capt Cook gave us the Key to the loss of the Atlanta, viz., Mr Mallory's[109]

[107]Gen. Egbert L. Viele (1825-1902), a West Point graduate and civil engineer from New York, commanded Viele's Brigade during the attack on Norfolk and later became the military governor of that city from 1862 through August, 1863. After the war he returned to civil engineering, served as commissioner of parks from 1883 until 1884, and was a United States congressman from 1885 until 1887. Boatner, *Civil War Dictionary*, 877; *Concise Dictionary of American Biography*, 1116. Dr. Charles E. Johnson of Raleigh was appointed surgeon general of the North Carolina medical corps in May, 1861, with the rank of colonel. He served in this capacity until the Confederate government took over all military hospitals in May, 1862. In addition to organizing the medical corps of North Carolina, Dr. Johnson aided in establishing and equipping three North Carolina hospitals, two in Petersburg and one in Richmond, Virginia. Clark, *Histories of the North Carolina Regiments*, IV, 623-624, 628.

[108]*Punch*, the satirical weekly paper in England, was first published on July 17, 1841. Benét, *Reader's Encyclopedia*, 892.

[109]Stephen Russell Mallory (ca. 1813-1873) was a Florida lawyer who had served in the United States Senate prior to the war. He participated in congressional naval reform while a senator, and when Florida

stupid wrong headedness. It seems that *three* of the best officers in the navy, Tatnall, Page, and Sinclair, examined her & the Sound through which she was to
pass on her way to the sea. Each one, at different times & in succession, having been placed by him in command. One of them said he would take her out
only in obedience to orders & under protest. All united in saying that she
drew too much water to get out with her full armament in the face of an
enemy, that there were two mud flats which she must cross at high tide, that
before she reached the second the tide would be on the turn & she must lie
between the two exposed to heavy fire or get aground by going on. Mr
Mallory, however, with a sublime contempt for common sense confided her to
a Lieut of the name of Webb,[110] whom he promoted Commander on his volunteering to do what those better informed than himself refused to attempt. He
went out & the disgraceful scene ensued which dyes every cheek with shame.
The Yankees say he fainted on the Quarter Deck after surrendering, but that
we do not beleive. Suffice it, she fired nine shots, none of which struck her an-
tagonists, got aground & fell into the enemy's hands fully equipped and ready
for sea, Brook guns, Torpedos, two magazines filled with ammunition, provisions, water, everything intact, her pilot House alone having been shot away.
What an imbecile! Another desperate assault on Port Hudson in which two
Wisconsan Regts who volunteered to head it were, the Yankees say, annihilated. Our loss slight! God be thanked! From Vicksburg the news continues good, the garrison in good spirits, the North in a terrible panic at the
advance of our army & the shipping interest in despair at the destruction
wrought by the Alabama!

July 4, 1863

Came Mr Hill, his daughter, & Miss Norwood to make a call. Mr H told us
that he heard on the R R train yesterday that Hooker had been deprived of
command & one Meade, a Brigadier only, had been placed at the head of the
Abolition army. Fighting Joe we are sorry to part with you! Your fighting
propensities did us no harm whilst your blunders, Joe, were of immense service to us. Maj Meade fill your shoes, O, deposed enemy as successfully as you
have stood in those of Burnside & McClellan! Unfortunately for you, your antecedents are such that you cannot take a house in "Beaten Row" & form

---

seceded in 1861, he was appointed secretary of the Confederate navy, a post he held throughout the war.
His contributions to the Confederacy were remarkable considering there was no navy when the Con-
federacy was formed. Mallory never succeeded in building a large fleet of the highly prized ironclads,
however. After the war Mallory returned to his law practice in Florida. *Concise Dictionary of American
Biography*, 633. For a complete discussion of Mallory, see Joseph T. Durkin, *Stephen R. Mallory: Confederate
Navy Chief* (Chapel Hill: University of North Carolina Press, 1954).

[110]The C.S.S. *Atlanta*, a powerful ram under the command of William A. Webb, went aground in Warsaw
Sound while attempting to attack Union blockaders on June 17, 1863. Webb succeeded in getting his ship
afloat again, but she "repeatedly failed to obey her helm." It was this failure and the ship's lack of
maneuverability which forced Webb to surrender. *Official Records (Navy)*, Series I, XIV, 287, 692, 697;
Civil War Naval Chronology, III, 94-95.

another of that clique of vanquished Generals. But I forget, Yankee memories are short & Yankee honour when wounded, like the wounded air, "soon close! where past the shaft no trace is found." McClellan will forgive your strictures & Burnside forget how you displaced him, & as for the populace they cry "Le roi est mort, Vive le roi!" in the same breath!

JULY 5, 1863

At Church but no service, Mr Cheshire being sick. Mrs Halsey's last child was buried today. Poor thing, what desolation! A wife, the mother of two children, a widow & childless within three short years. Heard that Col Peter Evans had been wounded in the fight near Aldie & is a prisoner in the enemy's hands. His wound is serious. What sorrow for his wife. Father brought Capt Cook home with him.

JULY 6, 1863

Heard a rumour which has made me not a little uneasy, tho father says it is very foolish to be so. I accept the imputation; am both uneasy & anxious— ergo foolish. The Yankees, it is said, have made a raid upon the Wilmington & Weldon R R, tearing up the track and cutting the wires. Every one says that we have troops there so I try to be incredulous.

JULY 7, 1863

Today came Lieuts Elliot & Treadwell[111] & the latter confirms the rumour of yesterday. A force of about one hundred men came up through Onslow & destroyed the road for three miles not far from Magnolia. Lieut T was at Wilson & there being no train in consequence was forced to hire a vehicle in which to come over. Gen Martin is at Kinston & the enemy have thus again outwitted him. Rumours of a fight in Maryland in which we have gained a signal victory reach us, but where or how we are left to count the hours for the mail to come in to learn.

Magruder too is said to be within five miles of N O, but rumours are as plenty as Blackberries, so I will not fill you O! my Journal today with what I may have to contradict tomorrow. I wander about the house, try to sew, play chess, & make blunders from preoccupation & at last take refuge in my own room & try to bury thought in Wilkie Collins "No Name"—in which for a time I am successful as I find it deeply interesting, far superior to *"Great*

---

[111]Adam Tredwell, formerly the acting paymaster of the North Carolina navy attached to Commo. William T. Muse, was promoted to assistant paymaster in the Confederate navy in 1862. He was then attached to the staff of Commo. W. F. Lynch and Commo. R. F. Pinckney, with headquarters at Wilmington, and eventually obtained the rank of captain. Clark, *Histories of the North Carolina Regiments*, V, 299, 313.

Expectations," which should rather be "Great Disappointments," for *disappointed* I am, little as I now expect from Dickens.[112]

Capt Cook tells me an instance of Yankee barbarity which he says came to him from an officer, C S N, who had it from a Yankee officer in the Albemarle Sound. Whilst up one of our rivers (which he did not learn) a boat came on board one of their Gun boats with twelve negroes on board. She steamed on her way & when in the Sound found that they (the Run-a-way negroes) had Smallpox amongst them, when the Captain made them all jump overboard at the point of the bayonette. Of course all were drowned. This passes the conduct of the pickets on the Rappahanock who attracted the attention of our sentries by shouts of "Here's your Nigger."—Take him back! we do not want him!" to a negro whom they were forcing down the bank into the water, he making what resistance he could. On being forced into the water he struck out for the Southern side & when he came near enough for them to see him to their horror they saw that he was covered thickly with Smallpox pustules. The poor creature's strength failed before he could reach this side & the current swept him down the river—murdered by Yankee philanthropy!

Capt Cook still with us, a gentlemanly, well informed, & eminently practical man. I hope he will construct such a boat as will *deter the* Yankees from an advance up our River.

July 8, 1863

News! News! News!—so much of it that I do not know how to begin to tell it! There has been a battle, a terrible battle at Gettysburg in Penn. We get Yankee accounts alone of it, but from their gasconade, bluster, & boasting, we pick the grain of wheat & are sure that the modest telegram which announces to us that Meade is falling back to Baltimore & Lee pursuing him is true. We lose three Brigadier's, Garnett, Barksdale, & Kemper killed—Pender & Scales wounded. I know none of the Col's so do not enumerate them. On their side the loss is heavier, including Reynolds, said to be the best General they have. He commanded the 3d army corps. Sickles, the infamous, loses his leg, so he will assassinate no more men because the world had discovered what he had long known & winked at. They have taken 2,000 (two thousand), we twelve thousand prisoners! The slaughter terrific both sides admit. The bridge over the Susquehanna at Wrightsville has been destroyed, whether by us or them I cannot understand. Gen Lee has issued orders for the government of his army in the enemy's country so widely different from those

---

[112]William Wilkie Collins's (1824-1889) *No Name* was published in 1862; Charles Dickens's *Great Expectations* in 1860. These two authors later collaborated in the novel *No Thoroughfare*, published in 1867. Benét, *Reader's Encyclopedia*, 227, 456; *Webster's Biographical Dictionary*, 333; *Dictionary of National Biography, Supplement*, II, 46-48.

that emanate from the pens of their Generals that I preserve it for contrast. Read it & then turn to Pope's and Steinwehr's! A no 20.[113]

These twelve thousand prisoners of ours refuse their parole, in order I suppose to embarras us & weaken Lee by the guard which they will force him to send with them. They deserve to be shot but we are, fortunately for them, too much under the law of Knightly honour & chivalry to give them their deserts.

The Yankee papers report that Johnson has cut Grant to peices & that Vicksburg is releived, but it does not elate us in the least, for we do not beleive it. The accounts from Louisiana are very fine but too good & a little contradictory. Brashear city has been taken by Gen. Dick Taylor. Magruder threatens New Orleans. Banks has fallen back from Port Hudson with only five thousand men & more to the same effect. It does not affect us much. We know not how much to beleive & Gettysburg eclipses all else. The news from Tennessee & Bragg is bad, *very* bad. He has fallen back from Tallahoma & virtually abandoned Tenn and part of North Ala, but we must not yet blame him. He may have been weakened by reinforcing Johnson in order to rescue Vicksburg. Let us wait before we condemn him. The damage done to the R R at Magnolia is slight, but a handful of miscreants have scoured the country burning & destroying everything before them, under Gen Martins very nose too! Murad the Unlucky I call him.

Went with Father and Mama to call on Mrs Clark & Miss Hines. Mrs James Smith poor thing did not make her appearance, being too much distressed about her brother, Col Evans, of whose fate they are yet in ignorance. How I pity those poor people who have friends at Gettysburg! What agony they must endure. From Mr Smith we learned that the enemy under the German Gen Weitzel had advanced to Williamston which they occupied & burned a few more houses. Col Martin[114] holds Rainbow Banks where he is strongly entrenched. Brisk firing has been heard there today. The Yankees may intend only a diversion or they may be coming up to destroy the Gunboat now building. A few hours will determine. Gettysburg, however, absorbs every thought, so that we almost forget our own fate in that of our Army.

July 9, 1863

Glorious news, too good to be true! We hear unofficially that the fight was renewed on Sunday. Gen Hill made a feint of falling back. Meade pressed on when the two wings commanded by Ewell & Longstreet swept round & enclosed the entire Yankee Army; 40,000 men laid down their arms. Now this

---

[113]Newspaper clippings containing these orders appear on page 22 of the second volume of the diary.

[114]William F. Martin, a lawyer from Pasquotank County, initially served as captain of Co. L, Seventeenth North Carolina (First Organization) Regiment. He subsequently was elected colonel of this regiment and remained there until it was disbanded in March, 1862. Martin was next commissioned colonel of the Seventeenth North Carolina (Second Organization) Regiment on May 16, 1862. Manarin and Jordan, *North Carolina Troops*, VI, 119, 192, 204.

cannot be true. So large a number of men would not surrender in an open plain & in their own country. The Telegraph has played pranks with its message. I will not transcribe the flying rumours, the reports brought by "reliable gentlemen" & "wounded officers." There has been a fight & victory seems to incline to our side. We *hope* but we dare not beleive as yet.

Came brother yesterday afternoon, like "Widrington" in *"doleful dumps,"* beleives a wild rumour gotten up I fancy by speculation to the effect that Vicksburg has capitulated. We laugh at it in spite of what we hear Com Barron says about its want of provisions & Johnston's weakness. Mr E & himself armed themselves & went down to the store with the intention if need was of keeping on & volunteering under Col Martin at Rainbow but met the good news on the road that we had ambushed the enemy at Gardner's bridge[115] & that they had retired leaving ten of their number dead on the field, for which God be praised! Ah! for news from Penn! God keep Gen Lee. Give him wisdom & to his men endurance, obedience, & moderation.

July 10, 1863

Grant me patience with the news! I know not what to beleive! I hate to fill my Journal with rumours & yet it will be no truthful expositor of our lives if I fail to relate the state into which these uncertain Telegrams have brought us. One tells us that the fight was not renewed on Sunday, consequently the 40,000 men whom it reported as refusing parole were *not* captured & Lee is not pressing Meade who is not falling back to Baltimore, but per contra *Lee* it is who is falling back to Hagerstown. Now which is true? But our perplexities do not end here. A Dispatch which freezes the marrow in our bones, signed, too, Joseph E Johnston, tells Mr Seddon that Vicksburg has capitulated, that the garrison march out with the honours of war, officers wearing their side arms. This no one seems to beleive tho it is countersigned by one of Johnson's staff. The impression is that the wires have been tampered with by sugar speculators.

The news from the North Via Fortress Monroe inform us that Grant is retiring, that Vicksburg is releived, that Banks has been driven from Port Hudson, cries aloud for succour for N O & says Louisiana is slipping from the grasp. Then, too, another telegram from Loring dated Jackson tells us of his successes on the 'Big Black,' news of Dick Taylor's & Magruder's victories, one at Port Hudson the other in the Teche, whilst another has it that they have joined forces. I take refuge in utter unbeleif. I wish I could convince myself that the war is a myth, a hideous dream, but alaas! it presses too heavily to be thrown off like an incubus. There is but one comfort left—that

---

[115]Union forces in North Carolina raided the Wilmington and Weldon Railroad on July 5, 1863. The troops, led by Lt. Col. George W. Lewis, destroyed over two miles of track at Warsaw, North Carolina, besides burning and capturing many Confederate stores. Barrett, *Civil War in North Carolina*, 164; *Official Records (Army)*, Series I, XXVII, Part II, 859-860.

our *Government* unlike the Yankee despotism does not lie. Its official Dispatches are all true, for they come from Gentlemen & through Gentlemen's hands do they pass until they reach us. So when we see 'R E Lee' signed to a dispatch we can rely on it, as there is no Telegraph to be tampered with by unprincipled speculators, as we hope and beleive is the case with Johnston's reported Dispatch. Vicksburg cannot have fallen! Not ten days ago they drove 300 mules out of the city. Surely, Yankee tho he is, Pemberton is not a traitor! He must have been able to inform Johnston of his situation. I cannot beleive it. As for the news from Penn, I never expected so much as they gave us, so am not depressed when they take the surplusage away. Give me the bare fact of a *Victory* & I am content without a *"rout."* I have been so occupied with public that I have omitted all mention of private matters.

Last week we had a freshet in the River, a heavy one which drowned a large portion of our corn. We hoped, however, to save much of it, as the water remained up but a short time. These hopes, however, are all crushed, for a second rise higher & slower than the first is now in progress. The crop is all re-submerged & much that escaped last week is destroyed this It is a heavy blow. The loss to Father and Mr Edmondston is heavy, heavier to Father than to Patrick, for the Low grounds proper at Looking Glass are not in cultivation this year. But God has sent it. We must not repine.

I have been very unwell for some days & the suspense about public matters, the wearing anxiety about Vicksburg, & the uneasiness about the river do not help to make me better. Hannah More's ill *"bile"*—oppresses me. I leave our killed & wounded until they are authenticated. I hope they are exagerated. Petigru again wounded!

July 11, 1863

I have no heart to write. Vicksburg has fallen! It is all true. No lying speculator has imposed upon us. Pemberton has surrendered! As yet it is all dark. We are told that they were reduced to the verge of starvation & yet 200 mounted men of the garrison have been paroled & have reached Jackson, the officers allowed to march out with their side arms, retain their *horses* & private property. Now who ever heard of a beleagured city starving with horses & mules in it? Pemberton drove 500 mules out of his lines not ten days since & now lo, he is starving. The garrison surrendered on the 4th of July. I would have waited until the 5th & not have sullied our national anniversary with such an act. My doubts of Pemberton return. He is a Pennsylvanian & his heart cannot be in the cause as ours is. Can he be a traitor? I am not willing to trust him. I could have born the disaster better had it come to us through a Southern hand.

Ah! Mr Davis, Mr Davis, have we not suffered enough from Northern Generals. Remember Lovel & New Orleans & now comes Pemberton &

Vicksburg to crown that first disaster! Just at the moment of triumph too. Banks driven from Port Hudson and Johnston nearly ready to fall on Grant. We remember Pemberton's blunders before he was shut up in Vicksburg, blunders which his defence of it had almost made us forget, & then his bluster about holding out whilst there was a "pound of Mule's flesh" left. Think of Londonderry, think of Antwerp,[116] & then think of marching out with 200 mounted men besides officers, horses & citizen's "stock," which now they are "in haste to remove." We remember all this I say, & thoughts too bitter for words rise in our hearts against *this Northerner, this Pemberton*! The truth will never be known, smothered in a court of Inquiry, as was Lovels conduct at New Orleans. Grant me patience O Lord! grant me patience. Let me see Thy hand in it & make me cease to repine at the instruments Thou hast chosen to chastise us with!

From Lee's army we get only Northern accounts through lying newspapers in Yankee pay & tho they are depressing enough, we do not credit them. They have it that Lee is beaten & in full retreat, demoralized & scattered & that Meade's victorious army presses on him whilst French & Milroy's late command & a host of other generals in Buckram bar his retreat across the Potomac. They will "fight him eight hours" by "Shrewsbury clock"[117] no doubt. We know from our operator at Martinsburg that he is at Hagerstown, a retreat certainly but rendered necessary on account of his wounded & thirteen Thousand prisoners with whom he is encumbered. The Yankees say he left his wounded on the field, not one word of which we beleive. In the face of their victory Keyes & his marauders are ordered immediately to Washington. Eastern Va is deserted by them & if Lee had been beaten surely they are not such fools as not to reinforce him & send him before he recover from the shock in a triumphant "On to Richmond" march. I have not said so much of Keyes as I ought perhaps. Latterly, he has long since ceased to give us uneasiness & has merely been ravaging the country, burning & destroying with the usual Yankee wickedness, barbarity, and wantonness.

D H Hill has been more than a match for him & he is now gone back to his master Lincoln. I do not tell all the Yankees say of our pretended defeat. I shall have the truth soon from our own side. We are sad enough today without their lies to madden us in addition. What with the loss of Vicksburg & our crop, well may we say—"The King does not dine today." At present prices we lose $30,000 worth of corn by this rise (Father, brother, & Patrick I mean), a heavy blow, but we are in God's hands. We see Him in it & do not murmur,

---

[116]Londonderry, a major port in the county of Londonderry, Ireland, was besieged by James II for 105 days beginning in April, 1689. Antwerp, in present-day Belgium, resisted invading Spanish troops in 1584 for fourteen months before surrendering. William Bridgwater and Elizabeth J. Sherwood (eds.), *The Columbia Encyclopedia* (Morningside Heights, N. Y.: Columbia University Press, Second Edition, 1950, supplement of illustrations and record of events, 1950-1956), 82, 1154.

[117]Shakespeare, *King Henry IV*, part 1, act 5, sc. 4, lines 151-152.

but when a human instrument like Pemberton peirces us, we feel it deeply & keenly, tho' it is God still who allows it. We should remember that.

Suffolk has been evacuated, not a Yankee left in it after thirteen months occupation. An order was issued to burn it, but before it could be carried into execution Lee was over the border & fearing retaliation, Dix countermanded his barbarous edict.[118] So, we go. Grant's army is marching on Jackson, "burning every dwelling that they come to on their route," women & helpless children turned without food or shelter into the woods & fields. How long O Lord? how long?

JULY 12, 1863

Sunday—No mail last night, a note only from Mr McMahon telling us that Lee had fallen back in good order six miles, cause unknown, that it was reported that fighting had been going on all day yesterday at Charleston. The enemy were landing troops on Morris Island. We were re-inforcing as rapidly as possible, two trains having just passed, having on board part of Colquitt's Brigade bound there. This is the same Brigade which last thursday week was hurried from Kinston to Richmond to meet Dix & Keyes. They having decamped, it can be spared to Beauregard. Pray God it be not too late! We are in great suspense, the river, too, still rising, but the damage to the crop is already done. At the most all we have left to lose is some work on the dams. This freshet is worse for us than the terrible one of June 62. Then we were enabled to replant & tho the corn was not merchantable still it saved much that was, which would otherwise have been fed to the stock, but it is now too late. God's will be done! Father has just come out having remained on the River last night. He reports it as falling, having reached the height of 23 ft 2 in on his staff, 10 in less than last June's freshet.

JULY 13, 1863

Over at Mr Hill's this morning. Lee's situation on every lip, in every heart! Every one has some near & dear friend with him about whom they feel anxious—I a brother in law, whom I love as tho he were my own, & a nephew. Another nephew fighting today perhaps in Charleston harbour.

The news from our Army which we gather from Northern accounts more cheering. "Rogues" are "falling out" & "honest men" are getting "their due." One newspapers accuses another, the "Baltimore American," of

---

[118]Maj. Gen. John A. Dix concluded that Suffolk was no longer a strategic place for making friends of secessionists because the people in the surrounding country were "bitter and implacable." He considered the security of the inland connection at Suffolk with North Carolina through the Dismal Swamp Canal an insufficient justification for holding Suffolk when other lines of defense were as strategic and more easily defended. *Official Records (Army)*, Series I, XVIII, 711-712, 718.

"*hideous Munchausons*"[119] about the battle of Gettysburg, says they captured no guns & as to the "acres of waggons" upon the capture of which it "congratulated its readers, *it is* "*a lie*"! It states also that it is false that Lee's retreat is cut off. His pontoon bridges are not destroyed. The force sent to do it was too weak & did not attempt it. "*The Rebels are not demoralized.* Lee is in a strong position & can deliver battle or retreat, yes maintain himself where he is at his option." This we beleived before, but it is pleasant to be assured that our enemy lies. Pray God for good news from his own pen.

Sad accounts from Jackson. Grant is advancing. Our pickets have been driven in. We know not whether or not Johnston has a force sufficient to face him, whether he will defend the town or retreat. "A wounded officer," those irresponsible circulators of wild reports, brings the news to Mobile that Gen Dick Taylor has taken New Orleans & that Magruder is advancing on Fort St Philip now garrisoned by negroes. *Much of it do we beleive*, even tho the officer's name is as is not customary given. Lt Col Scott, call him "John Doe" or "Richard Roe" at once! Men of straw all. The Telegraph re-affirms that Magruder has captured seven thousand negroes at Brashear City, with the addition that he has sent them to Texas. I wonder if he has ever left Texas himself? I doubt it. We ought to have sworn Telegraph operators, who should give heavy bond, to transmit no-lying Dispatches. Much anxiety would be thus saved us.

An official correspondance is published by Mr Davis which shows the Yankee Government in a worse light than ever & proves it discourteous & cruel & regardless of the lives of its own 'subjects,' I had better call them.

Mr Stevens, the Vice President, went down to Fortress Monroe in a Gun boat disarmed for the purpose, authorized by Mr Davis to proceed to Washington & endeavor to have the war carried on in a more Christian & humane manner & to demand the evidence on which Burnside the Christian hung two of our officers whom he found recruiting in Kentucky, in order if possible to obviate the neccessity he is under of executing two Abolition Captains upon whom the lot has fallen to suffer the death penalty in retaliation for their murder. He was also to arrange some other & more speedy mode of exchange & to remove some difficulties which have arisen about exchanges & which have put a stop for the present to all exchanges of officers. Will it be beleived that after keeping him waiting in Hampton Roads for two days, whilst the Commandant of the Fort telegraphed to Washington for instructions, the request for an interview was discourteously refused as "inadmissible" & he was told that the "customary agents & channels are adequate for all needful military communications & conference between the U S. forces &

---

[119]Baron Münchausen, a character in a collection of satirical stories by Rudolf Erich Raspe (1737-1794), generally stood for any traveler who encountered exciting adventures. Benét, *Reader's Encyclopedia*, 749, 908.

the insurgents" & that in the face of the virtual suspension of the Cartel so far as officers are concerned & notices of retaliation which have been given on both sides & whilst the lives of two of their Commissioned officers hung in the balance, men whom the laws of War give us a right to put to death, humanity alone making us pause and endeavor to save their lives. President Davis has suspended the execution until the wife and child of one of them can come on & pay him a last visit. I preserve the correspondance as it does honour to Mr. Davis head and heart. A no 21.[120] He has been quite sick but is recovering. Thank God for it, for tho' he is culpable in putting Pemberton in command, no one else would have made so few mistakes or acted with such moderation, humanity, & clear sightedness as he has done. He commands the respect & admiration of the world as a wise ruler and a Christian gentleman.

JULY 14, 1863

No news from any point last night but Charleston & that not of a nature to cheer the gloom into which the loss of Vicksburg has thrown us. From the Proclamations of the Mayor conscripting all free blacks between 18 & 60 & impressing all able bodied slaves to work on the defences, the appeals to the citizens, the meagre accounts of the battle, the reproaches which the papers heap on those who failed to comply with the requisition for negroes & instead paid the fine when called on by Mr Shannon to send them to work on the for-tifications, it would appear that they are taken unawares & unprepared. God grant it be not so, but the prospect seems gloomy enough now. I trust and beleive that the attack is only a feint to draw troops from Lee or perhaps to test the mettle of the two new Yankee Commanders, Dahlgren & Gilmore, & satisfy the North that their Government is not carrying on a mere defensive warfare. They commenced the attack on Thursday morning by unmasking several heavy Batteries on Folly Island, which speedily forced our men to abandon theirs opposed to them on Morris Island. A force was then landed on Morris & the attack commenced, the enemy aided by the Monitors which kept up a heavy fire upon our men. In spite of it, however, (Col Graham[121] Comdg) our troops repulsed the advance & drove them back to Folly. Mr E fears that we have accounts of only one landing place. They may have been more successful at other points. Up to Friday night the Forts had not been at-tacked; 11 Iron clads & thirty other vessels were off the Bar. We wait in eager & feverish anxiety for further news.

---

[120]This correspondence is preserved on page 22 of the second volume of the diary.

[121]Robert F. Graham was colonel of the Twenty-first South Carolina Volunteers. Graham, commanding the troops on Morris Island and the garrisons at Forts Wagner and Gregg, was relieved of command in July, 1863, by Gen. William B. Taliaferro, who was determined to stop Federal soldiers from gaining any further holds against the Charleston defenses. Johnson and Buel, *Battles and Leaders*, Volume IV: *The Way to Appomattox*, 13-14, 18, 75, hereinafter cited as Johnson and Buel, *Battles and Leaders*, IV; *Official Records (Army)*, Series I, XXVIII, Part I, 416.

Today father finished McCauley's last volume,[122] revised & edited by his sister—two years and more since it was published & it awaiting our perusal all this time! Who would have thought it ten years since when the first vols were published? But so it is. We have lost all interest in anything save the war, even McCauley palls on us. We live but in the *present*.

JULY 15, 1863

More encouraging news from *Lee*. The *papers* say that he has written the President telling him that he has been victorious in every attack he has made on the enemy, that he evacuated the heights at Gettysburg because he found that they were commanded by higher points still & he did not think their possession worth the human life it would cost to occupy them. He fell back to Hagerstown to secure the vast baggage train collected by his cavalry & on account of his wounded & prisoners. The Yankees abate somewhat of their claims for a magnificent victory, admit that they have no guns & lessen the number of their prisoners. They complain terribly of their loss particularly in officers—60 field officers are dead or mortally wounded whilst the number of subalterns mounts up to 250 already known. Their wounded 15,000. Of their *dead* they make no mention. No battle as yet at Jackson tho Johnston is prepared to defend the place.

Desperate fighting on Morris Island on Sat the 11th; the enemy protected by the Monitors made several assaults. The last news, dated 13th, says no more fighting since, but they seem preparing to throw up entrenchments for long range Guns about the centre of Morris Island. Batteries Wagner & Gregg are the points of attack. We have no account of one day, Sunday's, work. It would appear that they made a lodgment then. Colquitt's Brigade must have reached there on Sunday. They & the other reinforcements will, I hope, tell a different tale.

We were inexpressibly shocked last night by news of the death of our neighbor Mr John Whitaker. He was killed in a skirmish near Fairfax Court House. Poor fellow he had just received the prospect of promotion by the intended promotion of his Col & Lieut Col. He received his promotion to the Majority a little more than a year since when Crumpler[123] was killed before Richmond. His poor wife, she has lost four children within a few months & now her husband! His death, too, in a pecuniary point of view is a heavy blow to his family, as he had purchased a large estate from father, none of which

---

[122]Thomas Babington Macaulay's *History of England*, Volume V, was only partially finished at the time of his death. It was edited and revised by his sister Hannah More Macaulay, Lady Trevelyan, and published in 1861. *Webster's Biographical Dictionary*, 935.

[123]Thomas Newton Crumpler, a lawyer and state legislator from Ashe County, initially served in the Ninth North Carolina (First Cavalry) Regiment as captain of Co. A, and later as major of the regiment. Crumpler died of wounds on July 11, 1862. Clark, *Histories of the North Carolina Regiments*, I, 418, 420, 483, 485; V, 11; Manarin and Jordan, *North Carolina Troops*, II, 7, 10.

The Confederates decided to invade the North, hoping to force the Federals to withdraw troops from Vicksburg and Chattanooga. The culmination of this plan was the Battle of Gettysburg, July 1-4. Lee's Confederates won the first two days but lost the third; by the fourth day, when heavy rains prevented pursuit by the Federals, Lee began his retreat. Though figures vary as to the losses on both sides, both Confederates and Federals sustained heavy casualties. Among those killed at Gettysburg was Col. Henry King (Harry) Burgwyn. Mrs. Edmondston mentions his death in her July 15 entry. The painting of John R. Lane, Burgwyn, and Zebulon B. Vance, left to right, three colonels of the Twenty-sixth North Carolina Regiment, was done by W. G. Randall. Burgwyn was elected colonel after Vance resigned at the time he became governor-elect of North Carolina. The original painting is in the North Carolina Museum of History.

was paid for. He hoped to be able to work it out & thus leave his family wealthy, but those hopes will all be crushed—for who can manage it for her & it must, I suppose, again be sold. Mr Ouseby, Capt Carey Whitaker, & Col Harry Burgwyn are all reported dead.[124] Gens Pender, Scales, Hood, & Kemper & Hampton wounded. Armistead, Barksdale, Garnett & one other dead.

[124]William C. Ousby, captain of Co. F, Forty-third North Carolina Regiment, was killed at Gettysburg. Cary Whitaker, originally a lieutenant in the Enfield Blues of the Bethel Regiment who later became captain of Co. D, Forty-third North Carolina Regiment, was cited by Gen. Junius Daniel for his "bravery and

Lincoln calls loudly for 300,000 more troops, which it is thought he will get by draft. Port Hudson reported as surrendered. This we were prepared for. The bitterness of that cup we drained in the surrender of Vicksburg.

JULY 16, 1863

No news from Lee, that is, no official news. Rumours plenty but who heeds them? At Charleston things remain as they were. The enemy mounting heavy guns at long range at the south end of Morris Island; Fort Sumter shelling them steadily, but it would seem ineffectually. Pray God that Beauregarde's reinforcements arrive & he drive them back with the bayonette before they effect a permanent lodgment. No news from the Southwest. Pemberton is, I hope, ashamed to report. The Yankees say he announced to Grant that he could hold out for an indefinite period but that he surrendered to save the destruction of human life. I cannot yet beleive that of him, for he knew releif must arrive before an "indefinite time had passed over his head." Admit that and he is a traitor!

JULY 17, 1863

News that Lee has recrossed the Potomac in safety & unmolested. For that God be praised, tho it is a sore disappointment to us that he was forced to do so. We have official news to that effect—nothing more. Fighting at long range about Jackson. News from Charleston gloomy—enemy entrenching on Morris Island. Amo sent me a sketch of the harbour & defences. We have but a tiny portion of the island left on which to manevre our troops. If Battery Wagner falls, the despondant ones predict that the loss of Sumter is but a question of time, but I am more hopeful. What will Sumter be about if it allows itself to be invested by paralels? Can she not shell them out?

Came Miss Susan Hines to make us a visit. She brings news of the death of three of our young acquaintance at Gettysburg—Capt Hyer Baker of Florida; a brother of our neighbor, Mr Hall, in command of a Regt from this his native State; Major Ive Saunders, who has escaped unscathed through all the great battles of Va & Maryland beginning with Bethel; & Capt Campbell Iredell,[125] whose wife is a daught of our old friend Dr Johnson. All young men in the bloom of life, they make up the number *of eleven* young men of our acquaintance killed in this advance of our Army. The no. of those wounded we cannot

---

coolness" at Gettysburg but was not killed there. Henry King (Harry) Burgwyn, Jr., who succeeded Vance as colonel of the Twenty-sixth North Carolina Regiment, was killed at Gettysburg on July 1, 1863. Clark, *Histories of the North Carolina Regiments*, II, 334-335, 352, 358, 374; III, 2; *Official Records (Army)*, Series I, XVII, Part II, 563, 570, 573, 643.

[125]Campbell T. Iredell, captain of Co. C, Forty-seventh North Carolina Regiment, was mortally wounded at Gettysburg on July 1, 1863. He had married Mary Johnson on November 1, 1859. *Raleigh Register*, November 16, 1859; Clark, *Histories of the North Carolina Regiments*, III, 84, 103, 106-107; Moore, *Roster of North Carolina Troops*, III, 332.

even estimate. My God it is terrible! Eleven young men of family, education, & position slaughtered in this horrible manner. God help their families!

JULY 19, 1863

Johnston will, it is said, fall back from Jackson so as to draw Grant from his base of supplies, so we may hear of the abandonment of Jackson at any day. Had Vicksburg held out two days more, Johnston would have attacked Grant, with what success who can tell? Hope fills the cup with a tempting draught which disappointment turns to [illegible] in our grasp! Ah Pemberton! Pemberton!—why did not you remain in Penn with your own blood & ruin your own nation instead of ours. We have found out, that is the papers have, that Bragg falling back was "a masterly movement." It looks to us uninitiated folks like "a *change of base—a la McClellan*," but we were not born Brigadiers General!

Commander Cook came up from the River yesterday afternoon & brought us the cheering news that Clingman's Brigade had attacked & driven the enemy back from Morris island, but as this was not confirmed by the papers we know not what to think of it. Passengers by R R brought the rumour, adding that the Brigade was terribly cut up in the assault. We have a nephew, George Miller, a private in the 31st Regt in that brigade, so we are uneasy on his account. From Lee's army we hear nothing, but that he has crossed the river safely, the Yankees attacking his rear guard, but were repulsed without much loss to us. Gen Pettigrew, who had been wounded in the wrist at Gettysburg but who has not left the field being severly wounded & at Winchester, per contra the enemy says that they captured 2000 men, killed Gen Pettigrew, & have possession of his body. God pity his friends exposed to the torture of statements so opposite. Time only will show the truth.

Yesterday was published the President's Proclamation calling out the men between 40 & 45—a sad thing but it is necessary in the face of the draft of 300 000 ordered by Mr Lincoln. Mr Edmondston has just passed his 44 birthday. I know not whether or not his Major's Commission will exempt him. If not, God's will be done! Brother is not yet 44 & with the large business which rests on his shoulders & his numerous little children, I cannot see how he can be spared.

We have news of a terrible riot in New York[126] caused by the enforcement of the draft. Eighteen or twenty persons lost their lives, many houses were torn down, several negroes killed, the Mayor's house sacked, the Tribune office attacked & saved only by the desperate efforts of the police. A man bearing the

---

[126]Draft riots in New York City, from July 13 to 16, 1863, caused great concern in the North. Buildings were demolished, more than a dozen citizens were killed, and $1.5 million worth of property was destroyed. Federal troops finally restored order there and in other cities, killing and wounding over 1,000 people; and the draft was postponed until August 19, 1863. Rioters in Boston and Philadelphia were forcibly dispersed, and altercations occurred in Vermont, New Hampshire, New Jersey, Connecticut, and Ohio. *Official Records (Army)*, Series I, XXVII, Part II, 875-940; Boatner, *Civil War Dictionary*, 245-246.

unfortunate likeness to Greely was severely beaten by the mob & left for dead. Would that the punishment had fallen on the right head! The tumult was appeased only by the assurance of Gov Seymour, on authority from Washington, that the draft should be discontinued and the action of the Common Council pledging themselves to make up the quota of exemption money for each man drafted from New York City, $300 per capita, & as 16,000 men are liable to military duty in that modern Sodom, their municipal taxes alone will be no light sum. If the other Northern cities follow suite, Mr Lincoln will be disappointed in his army but I have little hope of that. He will strengthen the military & Police force & make another & a successful effort.

The Northern papers claim that the war is ended, that *Peace* has smiled on them, Lee's army annihilated, Johnston's cut to peices, Charleston in their hands, the navigation of the Mississippi opened, and many more such lies. My paper would blush were I to record them all, but just as all these bright incidents dawned on them the Rebels incited this riot in New York to cloud their happiness! How weak must be their cause to need such props to bolster it up! We will show them that "there is life in the old land yet" and that they have much to do ere they conquer a "*Peace.*"

July 21, 1863

Mr Edmondston at the Plantation all day. He came home in the afternoon & interrupted Father & I in a peaceful game of Chess with the tidings that the storm of war was threatening to sweep over us & convert our mimic into actual warfare. The enemy have made a sudden advance via Greenville to Tarboro, which they occupy, burning the bridge to prevent Gen Martin from advancing upon them & cutting off their rear. One column then advanced towards Rocky Mount, which it is rumoured they occupy & are tearing up the R R track. This was at first announced to us as fact with the addition that the Factory at the Falls of Tar River known as "Battles" had been burned, but later news induces us to hope that the tidings are premature.[127] The other column threatens us, their object being, it is said, to destroy the Gunboat and Battery now being built at Edwards Ferry.

Off went Mr Edmondston hot haste to Capt Bishop the Militia Captain of this district to induce him to call out the men & endeavor to stop them by ambuscades, tearing up bridges, & "bush whacking" as they call it generally, but alaas, so thorough is the Conscript that but few men are subject to Capt

---

[127]Federal forces in New Bern raided Greenville, Tarboro, and Rocky Mount during a six-day period from July 19 through July 24, 1863. They destroyed large quantities of private and commercial property and burned the bridge over the Tar River at Greenville. At Rocky Mount they burned a six-story cotton mill, the railroad bridge, and Confederate supplies and destroyed the naval works, railroad cars, and supplies in Tarboro. The attack reached Sparta but was met with organized Confederate resistance and the Federal raiders began their retreat. The raid successfully disrupted railroad transportation for a short time and netted the Union forces 100 prisoners, 300 slaves, and 300 horses and mules. *Official Records (Army)*, Series I, XXVII, Part II, 963, 976; Barrett, *Civil War In North Carolina*, 164-166.

Bishop's orders. So an address was hastily written & signed by Capt B & himself, calling on every one old & young to rally for the defence of their firesides & all night were they sent from house to house for signatures. This morning early he was off to Clarksville to complete the organization.

Before breakfast came Mr Hill bent on doing something, so he is resolved to tear up the bridges all through the neighborhood. He was deaf to my suggestions that some of them not being longer than from six to ten feet their absence would impose no barrier worth mentioning to a resolute force of two hundred men, as he intends leaving the sleepers, the first fence would supply rails enough for an extempore floor, & that he would only annoy and embarras the neighbors, that he had better go up to Beech Swamp ten miles up the road where an otherwise impassible swamp is crossed by thirteen bridges connected by causeways. The destruction of those would be an object & neither artillery or Cavalry could cross for days if it was properly done. He went off without heeding me & I suppose added to the panic & distress of the more isolated part of the community by cutting off their communication with the more thickly populated part of the neighborhood.

Mr E came back to dinner & gave us the agreeable information that Lieut Col Lamb of the 17th N C Troops with part of his Regt had had an engagement in which he had killed, wounded, or made prisoners of twenty seven of the marauders & that their advance was supposed to be checked. No news of the Rocky Mount column. He is out again this afternoon with the rest of the neighborhood to complete the organization & if need be to picket the roads & "bush whack" them should they advance. The men from the Gunboat, with a single field peice which they have there, are to join the raw troops & if Col Lamb be forced to retire form a corps of reserves upon which he can fall back. But we are entirely defenceless. The handful of elderly men left to us are unable to do much towards protecting their homes & the want of organization tells sadly against them. I must remove my silver & at least save *that* from their mercenary hands. I think I will send it to Sophia to take care of for me. No trains to Halifax from either North or South & the Telegraph below Enfield is silent which looks ominous.

Capt Smith came from Weldon and brought a paper by which we learn that Johnston Pettigrew is indeed dead, died of wounds received in the passage of the Potomac, he commanding the rear guard. He escaped barely with his life before Richmond; severely wounded, he languished in prison for months; exchanged, he was in the field before his wounds were healed. Wounded in the wrist at Gettysburg, he refused to leave his command &, disabled as he was, continued at the head of his Brigade to fall in the fulness of his usefulness & vigor at Shepardstown.

Brigadier Gen Pender is also dead of wounds received at Gettysburg, another able & gallant officer. Thirteen young men, children of our acquaintance, are already dead & every few days another is added to the list.

On July 21 Mrs. Edmondston wrote: "I must remove my silver & at least save *that* from their mercenary hands." The silver tray pictured above is engraved on the back with the names of the Catherines and Katherines to whom it has belonged. Catherine Ann Johnson gave it to her daughter, Catherine Ann Devereux (Mrs. Edmondston), in 1836; she, in turn, passed it on to her niece Katherine Johnson Devereux in 1875. (The name is misspelled on the tray.) The last name engraved on the tray is the present owner, Katherine Devereux Jones Stone of Buffalo, New York. The tray measures 13⅞ inches in width and 1⅛ inches in height at the highest point of the scallop. (Photograph courtesy of Mrs. S. H. Millender, Mebane, N.C.)

Lees Army reported in fine condition. The enemy admit that he brought off all his baggage, provisions, & guns—nothing of all he "*plundered,*" they say, was retaken. They admit a repulse and loss of seventeen prisoners at Shephardstown. What has become of the 2,000 prisoners they claimed to have captured there with Pettigrew's body? Were they in "Buckam" too.?

July 22, 1863

Last night came home Mr Edmondston, wet, wearied, & disgusted! No head, no organization, nothing done, but fruitless riding about all day listening to rumours & "reliable accounts" which the next comer contradicted. One thing only is certain, that the enemy have retreated from both Rocky Mount & Tarrboro. They burned both factories at the former place, destroyed the Telegraph station, the R R bridge, the Depot, & some other houses. An engagement is supposed to have taken place at Sparta in which our troops commanded by Major Kenedy[128] repulsed them, but this is not certain.

---

[128]John Thomas Kennedy, initially captain of Co. B, Sixty-second Georgia Regiment, and later the major and lieutenant colonel of the same regiment, was assigned guard and picket duty with a portion of his regiment in eastern North Carolina during 1863. Kennedy's command, which contained three North Carolina

Lieut Col Lamb's engagement is accounted a myth, so I had better record no more news until it has stood the test of time. Our people seem to be learning the vice of lying as cleverly as the Yankees—vide Vicksburg & the enormous deception practised on us there! The only comfort we have is that we do not lie officially a la Seward, Stanton, & Halleck. Were our Government inclined to remodel the dispatches of our generals, it would find that gentlemen like Lee, Johnston, & Beauregard would not bear it as meekly as McClellan, Pope, & Hooker have done. Even Meade either lies himself or allows the General in Chief to lie in his name. Witness his dispatch from Shepardstown. But the spark of *honour* is extinct in the bosom of a nation who has Lincoln for head, Seward for Premier & *Butler* for its model General! No mail last night. Ransom's Brigade reported at Weldon, but the bird has flown, the Yankees all gone, leaving only ruin & desolation behind them.

JULY 23, 1863

Yesterday came Lieut Elliot & Mr Peter Smith with bad news for our future comfort. Two Yankees, originally deserters from them to us, have redeserted and returned to their former friends. One was a workman; the other an enlisted soldier employed at Edwards Ferry; one to construct, the other to guard the boat and battery now in process of building there. The soldier gained the confidence of his officers by shooting a Yankee prisoner who attempted to escape from the prison at Salisbury, he being on guard at the time. The workman came with papers from the Sec of War & Gen Winder & was accordingly put to work on his fiat. They surveyed all the approaches to the boat, we now find, some days since & were noted amongst their companions as being remarkably inquisitive. They left in a canoe under pretence of getting chickens. On their absence being known an express was sent to Rainbow with orders to have them arrested as they passed. The sentries were doubled & the River picketed on both sides by Col Martin & yet his sentinel allowed them to pass even after hailing & making them come ashore! The dunderhead allowed himself to be deceived into the beleif that they were neighborhood people! My mind misgives me that they will yet work us mischeif as they are remarkably intelligent & are possessed of full information as to the forces available for the protection of the boat, the roads leading to, & the work done upon it.

When will we learn to distrust Yankees? The enemy carried off in their late foray into Edgecombe about 500 negroes & a number of horses. They destroyed every vestige of a Gun boat being built at Tarrboro, even burning a quantity of timber in the ship yard there. They set the county bridge over the

---

companies, successfully defended a position outside Tarboro during the July, 1863, raid by Federal cavalry. It captured several prisoners, killed two men, and chased the Federal troops back to Tarboro, where the burning river bridge delayed its progress. Manarin and Jordan, *North Carolina Troops*, II, 623, 655-656; Clark, *Histories of the North Carolina Regiments*, IV, 71-74, 77-78.

Tar on fire in five places, but our troops were fortunately in time to extinguish it before much damage was done. We were not so fortunate with the R R bridge over the same River at Rocky Mount, which was entirely consumed. Our gratitude is due to Major Kennedy of Griffin's Rangers & to Lieut Col Lamb, 17th N C Troops, who, in two separate engagements on different sides of the river, repulsed them & hastened their retreat. They were compelled to disgorge a large quantity of their plunder, so severe was the onset made upon them by our troops.

July 25, 1863

Yesterday came a letter from Sister F. giving us a rumour that James had been wounded at Gettysburg. Mr E does not credit it as he is sure he would have heard it from some authentic source by this time but it makes me uneasy & unhappy.

Gen Lee's army said to be in fine condition—in Va Meade crossing the Potomac in *"pursuit,"* the North much exasperated against him for *"allowing Lee to escape."* He in consequence tendered his resignation which, however, Lincoln refused to accept, but the attention of both Government & people is directed from him & his shortcomings by the *"Draft Riot"* in New York. It has continued for a week & 280 people are *known* to have been killed. More *than half these are negroes.* The poor creatures have been dreadfully persecuted, the populace charging them with the war, & punishing them indiscriminately, hanging them to Lamp posts is of frequent occurrence, their houses sacked, they terribly beaten & left for dead, and all the cruelties which an enraged mob can perpetrate carried out to the full. The excitement is extending to other cities, and Messrs Seward & Lincoln will from present appearances have their hands full in recruiting their army.

Johnston has evacuated Jackson & fallen back to the line of Strong River considerably to the South where he will made a stand. We expected this & so are not dejected. Came last night particulars of the fall of Port Hudson. Their defence was gallant in the extreme and Gardner did not sully his fame by a surrender when "he could hold out an indefinite time" as Pemberton says he did. In the veins of one flows our own blood, in those of the other that of our enemies. There lies the difference.

As yet we are successful before Charleston, keeping the enemy under cover of his Gun boats & Batteries on Folly Island. A desperate assault was made on Sat last on Fort Wagner in which God blessed us with a signal victory. The enemy admit a loss of 2,000 whilst ours is not fifty!

Major David Ramsay[129] of Charleston, grandson of the Historian, a slow spoken formal gentleman whom I remember once meeting at the Va Sprs,

---

[129]David Ramsay (1749-1815), a physician, Revolutionary War veteran, South Carolina legislator, and a noted historian, wrote numerous works on South Carolina history. His grandson, Maj. David Ramsay of

performed a most gallant act, raising our flag which had been shot away in the face of a tremendus fire both from Gun boats & sharp shooters. He was afterwards severely wounded by the negro Regt under command of Shaw, the Massachusetts Regt to which the infamous Gov Andrews[130] pins his name. Shaw was killed. I had a List of his antecedents which I intended to preserve in my repertory but unfortunately lost it. Suffice it that his Grandfather Shaw was bribed to marry his Grandmother, Miss Parkman (he being her father's porter) in consequence of the ladys having given birth to a mulatto baby who was shipped off to St Domingo. Col Shaw, her descendant, comes naturally by his negro proclivities.

We killed many negroes & took twenty prisoners, the disposition of whom exercises our government greatly. If we recognise them as prisoners of War, we give up a principle. If we hang them, as they deserve, we fear retaliation upon our officers, one of whom is worth the whole of them either taken or to be taken. Mrs Sawyer[131] wife of one of the Yankee officers, upon whom fell the lot to suffer in retaliation for the execution by Burside the Christian of two of ours for recruiting in Kentucky has arrived but, sad to say, our government refuse to allow her to come to R. I think them in the wrong. The Lincoln Government, it is said, has given ours notice that if they are put to death it will again retaliate by the execution of Gen Fitz Hugh Lee, son of our General, & Capt Winder, now in their hands & they have accordingly been confined in a case mate underground in Fortress Monroe.[132] Gen Lee, it will be remembered, was taken by that theiving villain Kilpatrick from his uncle-in-laws house whilst wounded & moved at the risk of his life; we misgave them then lest they had some sinister design in his capture. What that was now plainly appears. How I pity Mr Davis, thus called upon to sacrifice feeling to principle! God give him strength to stand by the right & enlighten him as to what the "*right*" is.

---

the Charleston Battery, was on Morris Island under heavy bombardment when "the flag halyards were cut and the Confederate flag blew over into the fort. Instantly Major Ramsay . . . sprang forward and replaced it on the ramparts. . . ." Ramsay was later wounded in the engagement. *Official Records (Army)*, Series I, XXVIII, Part I, 416-420; *Concise Dictionary of American Biography*, 838.

[130]John Albion Andrew (1818-1867), lawyer, state legislator, and a leader of antislavery opinion, was the wartime governor of Massachusetts, serving from 1860 until 1866. Andrew strongly advocated the formation of Negro regiments in the Union army for use during the war. *Concise Dictionary of American Biography*, 23.

[131]Mrs. Sawyer was the wife of Capt. Henry Washington Sawyer of New Jersey who, with Capt. John M. Flinn of Indiana, was selected as a hostage to be executed in retaliation for Burnside's execution of two Confederate officers in Kentucky. *Official Records (Army)*, Series II, VI, 82, 87.

[132]Gen. William Henry Fitzhugh Lee and Capt. R. H. Tyler of Virginia were selected as hostages by the Federal government to counter Jefferson Davis's threats of retaliation against Union prisoners for depredations committed by Federal troops in the field. An erroneous impression occurred, possibly because of a similarity in sound, that a "Captain Winder," presumably the son of the Confederate prison commander Gen. John H. Winder, had been chosen as the co-hostage with General Lee. William Best Hesseltine, *Civil War Prisons: A Study in War Psychology* (Columbus, Ohio: Ohio State University Press, 1930), 56-57, 96-97, hereinafter cited as Hesseltine, *Civil War Prisons*.

Morgan with his Cavalry has been carrying dismay into the hearts of the Ohioans by a foray into their midst. He is now reported as surrounded near 'Galipolis,' but it causes us little uneasiness as it is "*Yankee* news."

JULY 27, 1863

What a life is ours, kept on the tenter hooks of anxiety by these miserable Yankees. Scarce do we recover from one raid before we are threatened with another. Mr Edmondston left home this morning for Dawson's X Roads to attend the enrolment of the Militia & Father & Mama for Conneconara. Scarce were they gone when a note from Mr Hill informed us that a Dispatch from Col Martin had been received telling us that the Yankees had left Plymouth with a force of 3000 infantry, 6 peices of Artillery, & 1 company of Cavalry en route it was supposed for Weldon Via the Gunboat. The militia meeting is just in time for them so I hope an organized force will be ready to oppose the marauders. Pray God that Ransoms Brigade have not left Weldon & that the messenger sent there may be in time so that they may be here & drive them back. This I fear is the work of the deserters that left here 9 days since. We are in God's hands & He will do what seemeth to Him good. Sent the note to father so that he be not taken by surprise.

Full accounts of the assault on Fort Wagner. It was a desperate one, the ground in front of our works strewed with dead & dying. Our loss, thanks be to God, slight. The negro Regts. terribly cut up. We still hold Fort Wagner under a continuous shelling from Gun & Mortar boats. The enemy reinforcing. We must do the same if we would continue to hold out. No authentic news from Lee. We know not what a day may bring forth. God be with him & his brave soldiers!

At night—Whilst at dinner came Mr Edmondston from Dawson X roads. The news of the advance of the enemy came upon the assembled multitude before the new organization of the militia had been made. Their motions were hastened in consequence & much to his surprise he was, unsolicited by him, elected Captain. This does not interfere with his commission as Major which by Legislative enactment is in abeyance whilst this new call for the Militia is made because so many of the old are in the army that the former organizations are postponed.

He immediately gave all neccessary orders, telegraphed to Gens Whiting & Martin (Capt Cook had already notified Richmond), & ordered out the Company, 90 men, to meet at nine tonight to obstruct the roads—each man to bring three days rations with him. He accordingly has been busy looking up Ammunition, getting Buck shot & accoutrements generally in order to give them a warm reception. Axe work I rely upon more than Gunpowder from the hands of these raw, undisciplined, & many of them feeble men. Obstruct the roads so that their artillery cannot pass & reinforcements may arrive in time.

Ransoms Brigade left Weldon on Friday last! Too bad this game of "move house" played on so gigantic a scale!

At night Patrick left for his new scene of labours. Anything to be useful to ones country if it is to be a leader of Militia! Pray God he may infuse some of his own spirit within them! God be with & protect him & bring him back safe to my arms. Just going to bed came a note from Capt Cook who left us on Friday with some directions about his papers which he left here. He tells me that the enemy are advancing from Plymouth, Washington, & Murfresboro via this place, four or five thousand strong in each column. Now this I do not credit. There must be an overestimate of their number. They have not so many troops in N C. I do not beleive there is half that number.

July 29, 1863

This is a terrible state to live in. Expectation & anxiety unsettle and destroy one's peace of mind to that degree that we are ready for anything. We sit here at home in a calm of *desperation*, I fear tho perhaps it may be *resignation*, unable to do anything but determined to meet the fate in store for us as becomes christians & patriots—something analagous, I suppose, to the resignation & calmness with which most persons meet death when it is inevitable— struggles, murmurs, & repining are alike useless & the human mind takes refuge in that sublime repose which is the admiration of all who witness even the violent death of men of high spirit.

Mama came out on Monday night, Father remaining on the River. Herself, Sue, & I compose the household & we even wait for news with a calmness that surprises me. Can it be *Faith* or do we indeed realize the promise "as thy days so shall thy strength be"? Was up early yesterday & my first work was indicative. I made a number of Rifle Cartridges & sent them with a Canteen of Tea to Mr Edmondston. I received messages constantly yesterday from him all telling the same tale, viz., a steady advance of the enemy in heavy force from Plymouth. The last courier reported them across Gardner's Creek the bridge over which had been rebuilt by them. The 24th N C, Col Clark, is at Jackson to repel a column advancing from Murfresboro; a few troops in Halifax & aid promised from Weldon. Pray God Col Martin hold out until it reaches him. Put in a place of safety some valuables & some meat, but it is but little that we can save. I look at our books, friends which we have been years in collecting, with a sigh to think that a few days may see them desecrated by theivish hands, torn, mutilated, & cast out, perhaps burned, & ourselves wanderers without a home or a roof to shelter our heads! Gods will be done! As I write, a messenger comes in from Mr Edmondston. No news he tells us, not one word from below. Can the courier be captured? Is it guns or thunder which I hear in the distance all this morning? God be with and grant us Peace!

Morgan's command, 2500 men, is we fear cut off, surrounded, & made prisoners of in Ohio, he with a squad of men only making his escape, but I will wait for news until it comes from our own side. These *Cretan* accounts take up paper to no purpose. An official report, for instance, of an attack on Drewry's Bluff has appeared in the Northern papers, whereas we *know* that the Gunboats did not ascend so high & that not a gun was fired! Gen Lee officially contradicts, in a Dispatch to Gen Cooper, Meades late official dispatch to his Government of the capture of a Brigade of men & many guns at Falling Waters. Gen Lee says that he only notices it because of its official character, that Meade captured only a few stragglers, men wearied & footsore who on account of the heaviness of the roads could not keep up. Two Guns were abandoned because of the failing of their team the jaded horses could not be replaced with others until the head of the column was so far in advance that it was thought a needless risk to return for them & they were therefore abandoned. He officially gives Meade the lie. Which General will the world beleive? Pope, Halleck, & McClellan, even if Meade be innocent, your sins will be visited on his head, but Gen Meade had you the honour of a preux chevalier[133] you would not allow your Government thus to tamper with your fair fame! You were said to be a gentleman, but "it is hard to touch pitch without being defiled."[134] No mail last night.

July 30, 1863

Yesterday afternoon came Mr E home, the militia all having been disbanded. The last Dispatch from Col Martin at Rainbow being to the effect that the Yankees had all returned to Plymouth. Father came & with him Tom Devereux. The news they brought from Northampton was that a force several thousand Cavalry had pressed through the Country, repulsing a small force of outposts at Dr Godwin Moores, passed through Jackson but at Crump's Mill coming upon six companies of the 24th N C were driven back after a short engagement & our men being reinforced the pursuit was continued. Later came Capt Cook & Mr Elliot confirming father's news with the addition that Jenkins Brigade it was who had re-inforced the 24th N C & that all serious cause for uneasiness was over. They brought a message from Com Lynch requesting Mr Edmondston to come & see him, so the carriage was ordered & he went immediately to see the Dead Sea Explorer. It was late when he got home. The business Com Lynch wanted him on was what he had no authority to perform as it rests with the Governor to detail or call out the Militia. So with grateful hearts for our deliverance we went to bed thanking God that the foot of the enemy had not come nigh us.

---

[133]French, "brave knight."

[134]Shakespeare, *Much Ado About Nothing*, act 3, sc. 3, line 61.

This Morning came Dennis full of four Yankee deserters whom he yesterday met on the road when he went to the P O & who he saw deliver themselves up to our pickets. I asked how he "knew them to be Yankees so soon as he saw them." "Why Miss Kate! I knowed em—they was four coarse looking Irishmen."

Went to the plantation this morning where soon came Mr Williams, the nephew of our neighbor Mr Higgs. He overthrew our peace of mind most signally with the tidings that on being repulsed at Crump's the enemy retreated to an almost impregnable position at Gatlins Mill on Potacasey, that heavy reinforcements of infantry had arrived to them in the night, & that they were busy intrenching. They were piloted by the infamous Foster,[135] who at one time declared himself elected Gov of N C.

Ransoms and Jenkins Brigade are in or near Weldon & the Militia through the country generally are out—so perhaps we may hold them in check. Their conduct in Jackson was as usual marked by theiving & plundering of all kinds coupled with the most wanton destruction. They tore up Mrs Calverts wearing apparel, tore her children's clothes into shreds, & tossed them into the street, took all the provisions & horses and drank all the Liquor in the town. The negroes with the exception of two belonging to Mr Calvert ran into the woods. These two they took & tied & took them off with them, but the first night they succeeded in escaping and returned home. Our neighbor Mr Jacobs being there on business was seized and robbed of everything about him even to his Hat & then left on foot on the road, they taking his buggy & horse.

Came home from Looking Glass to dinner & found a Courier awaiting Mr E with a dispatch from Col Martin to the effect that his pickets had been driven in, enemy landing from Gunboats, etc., etc., so we were plunged into a sea of anxiety once more. So here we are again on tenter hooks!

AUGUST 1, 1863

Life is scarcely worth purchasing at the price of such anxiety as we live in. For three weeks now we have led lives that our worst enemies need not envy us. Late at night of the 30th came another Dispatch from Col Martin telling us that the enemy had retired. The Militia had been ordered out again, & there was no time to countermand the order. A thousand rumours flew on the wings of the wind as to the doings of the enemy in Northampton—now they

---

[135]Charles Henry Foster (1830-1882), a native of Maine living at the outbreak of the war in Murfreesboro, North Carolina, adopted the Union cause and claimed that most North Carolinians were Unionists who feared the retaliation of Confederate authorities if they admitted their loyalty to the Union. Foster soon engineered an election on Hatteras Island which sent him to the United States Congress, but Congress refused to seat him. Marble Nash Taylor, the Methodist pastor to the Cape Hatteras Mission and a political cohort of Foster, was the claimant to the provisional governorship of North Carolina, not Foster. Norman C. Delaney, "Charles Henry Foster and the Unionists of Eastern North Carolina," *North Carolina Historical Review*, XXXVII (July, 1960), 348-366.

were fighting, now retreating, & anon stealing. Was it best to disband the Militia or march them to the Gun boat? Who knew? We lived in a state of suspence cruel to behold.

I rode down to the boat in question with Capt Cooke & Thomas to see the object of so much care & anxiety, found a negro force busily employed throwing up entrenchments & preparing to mount a couple of small cannon which the Department have sent here to defend it. The boat is much larger than I had supposed & seems a strong & substantial peice of work. Heard of nothing but the Yankees & their violent & outrageous proceedings. They did us one service by robbing our neighbor Mr Lewter's negro, who had been sent to Northampton by his master, of every thing he had about him, even his hat and pocket knife and neck handkercheif. This has excited such horror and indignation in the minds of our servants that the Yankees will find them deaf to their blandishments, "charm they never so wisely." As we sat quietly at tea came a dispatch to Capt Cook from Lieut Elliot telling him that the enemy were at Rich Square in force and inquiring for the Gunboat. Instantly he was off, Rich Square being scarcly five miles from it, but fortunately for us the height of the River will for the present prevent their bringing their guns near enough to the bank to do it much damage.

Patrick off, too, to Clarksville to meet his Company & the rest of us went to bed in a very unquiet frame of mind. After midnight came Patrick home, no dispatch having come needing the Halifax Co which is also under his orders & in view of the height of the River, all promising a quiet night, he sent them home. Just as he was going to bed we found father had been suddenly taken sick, the result, I fear, of sleeping on the River & anxiety and unsettlement of mind. Mama & I waited on and got what we could to releive him, and long after "the wee sma hours agont the twal" we at last got to bed.

This morning Sue & Thomas left for Raleigh; Sue, I fear, for the rest of the summer. Patrick went to Clarksville to see about this Militia Company & shortly after came Capt Cooke worn & wearied out having been up all night. The advance to Rich Square was from a third body of troops. They came up from Murfresboro or Winton in force, when within a short distance they halted and suddenly wheeling retreated rapidly down the same road by which they came. It is supposed that they were met by the information that their friends at Gatlin's Mill were retreating & fearful of being cut off & surrounded, made what haste they could to rejoin them, but long after came Col. Bell[136] from Halifax and confirmed the news of the retreat of the force at Gatlin's Mills, so now God help us. When will it all end? I had written thus far when a knock on the floor overhead apprised me that father was awake & on going up

---

[136]David Barnes Bell, a Halifax County resident, served as the captain of Co. I, First North Carolina (Six Months, 1861) Regiment until his resignation on August 31, 1861. Clark, *Histories of the North Carolina Regiments*, I, 78, 113, 125; Manarin and Jordan, *North Carolina Troops*, III, 46.

to see him I found that he was willing to take some tea & whilst I was preparing it came Mingo with the news that the Yankees, *one million in number*, were at Mr Bowden's four miles from Montrose! Their train he represents as "9 miles long." This of course is a terrible exageration but his story is a straight one. A ray of hope lies in the fact, however, that a soldier is trying to impress horses at the plantation & to make his task easier I think he must have coined this terrible raw-head-&-bloody-bones story & I mention it here only to show what a state of anxiety we live in, the prey of every idle rumour, a continual weighing of facts, & balancing of probabilities. God deliver us from them! & give us repose! Father quite sick in bed all day, & this anxiety does not make him any better.

AUGUST 3, 1863

As I thought! the negroes had been duped by an unprincipled Militia man who wanting a horse took that means to get one. It does seem indeed that truth, honour, & honesty have left the world! & tho our reason told us on Sat that the story was a false one, still *our feelings* made us most uncomfortable. Mr E went down to the River that afternoon to reassure & calm the fears of the negroes & to look after any more irresponsible persons who might desire to get horses by any means in their power &, being belated, remained all night. About one o'clock came brother & awakened me by calling me at my window in the back piazza. I soon let him in & we sat down in the dim passage lighted by one tallow candle and he gave me the news & his views of the war, our situation, the state of the country, etc., etc., & really they were so gloomy that I went back to bed depressed & miserable & when I awoke in the morning it was with a sense of a heavy misfortune having befallen me. All day I felt the weight of an undefined sorrow upon me & even now his doleful predictions are sounding in my ears. What a misfortune to look on the dark side of things as he does. Life would be a burden to me viewed through such sombre glasses. Father's state makes me uneasy. His head trouble[s] him more than a mere billious attack warrants, I fear. He came near falling from dizziness twice.

No news from Gen Lee except that he is falling back to the line of the Rappahanock. Longstreet's corps occupy the heights below Fredericksburg again, just where he started from. Morgan we fear is captured in Ohio, his Command certainly dispersed, & many of them prisoners. We are loth to beleive the Yankee accounts & do not yet give up hope. Papers filled with discussions about the battle of Gettysburg, pros and cons as to Anderson's Division & Heth's under Pettigrew's command, but I will not fill you O! my Journal with discussions so profitless. Suffice it that we did not gain the battle. Both sides retreated, so we must call it a drawn one, but our loss in both men & officers is terrible. Sharpsburg was a bloody memory for North Carolina, but Gettysburg exceeds it in honor. The best blood in our state cries from the ground.

Pennsylvania soil is drunk with it. God be with the widows & children of these poor men who have thus died in defence of their country. Grant is falling back after destroying Jackson. Want of water prevents his advance at this season. His men are going up the river by boat loads, whether to Rosencrans, Meade, or home we know not. The Draft has been quietly effected in Phila & the Mayor of N Y has vetoed the ordinance of the Common Council paying the quota for all drafted from the city, on the ground that it was truckling to the mob, so I suppose it will go on there also.

Vallandigham has reached Canada & is out in an address to the people of Ohio whose candidate for Gov he is. He is for Peace, says they can never conquer us & I think his faith in re-construction is a little shaken. Before Charleston a continuous shelling & throwing up of Batteries on both sides is going on—no assault since the bloody one of July the 18th. The Croakers predict its fall, but I am more hopeful. I do not beleive the U S flag will ever again wave over Fort Sumter. The Ironsides & the Monitors take part in the shelling but not much damage done. I hope & beleive they will yet abandon the attack.

Was up early this morning to give four soldiers of Griffins Regt[137] their breakfast who poor fellows came foot sore & wearied last night begging a nights lodging. How my heart melts at sight of a soldier! These are from Georgia, have been sick below Hamilton, & are now en route to rejoin their Regt. Am so sleepy that I am ashamed of myself. How many hours do I daily waste in bed in the morning? N'importe *I do not think it healthy to get up early!*

August 12, 1863

A long period of hot weather since I last opened this book during which God be thanked our army seems to have been inactive tho we get the most slender accounts of Lee & his whereabouts. A slight skirmish at Brandy's station in which both sides claim the victory but in which every Colonel we had on the field was wounded & an advance of Gun boats up James River & their repulse with one crippled by our field batteries below Drurys Bluff are the most important military movements. The two armies seem to be massing on either side of the Rappahannock & a fight may soon be expected but not I hope until the intense heat moderates. Such weather as we have had must increase the suffering & mortality amongst the wounded tenfold.

August 16, 1863

No news in the papers. Military operations seem brought to a sudden stand by the intense heat; Cavalry skirmishes & capturing an occasional outpost is

---

[137]Joel R. Griffin was colonel of the Sixty-second Georgia Regiment, organized at Garysburg, North Carolina. The regiment was composed of seven Georgia and three North Carolina companies. Clark, *Histories of the North Carolina Regiments*, IV, 72-74.

all we hear of. The Yankee Cavalry seems to have improved in both dash & daring latterly & I am sorry to say ours do not seem to keep pace with them, but our horses need forage & our facilities for transporting it are far behind those of our enemy. A letter from Mr Haigh to father tells him that his son Charles, Sergeant Major of Evans Regt, writes him that Robertson's Brigade in which he is was reduced during the Penn Campaign to 200 horses. I can scarce credit it! Hood of Texas has been made Lieut Gen & placed in command of all the Cavalry of Northern Va. I am glad that is not Stuart. His head is said to be deficient. He can *execute* but not *plan* a movement.

A court of Inquiry called to investigate matters in the South West particularly the surrender of Vicksburg. I have not much hope from it as Gen R Ransom is at the head of it. Why cannot Mr Davis employ *gentlemen*? A open mouthed swearing braggart like Robert Ransom is no fit judge in any case, a mean bully such as he is cannot be impartial. His brother Gen Mat Ransom seems to have half the newspapers in his pay to glorify his conduct during the late advance of the Yankees into Northampton, yet he will, nevertheless, find it hard to make us at home beleive that the reason he did not follow and crush them, as he *says* he could have done, was that "he had orders from the Sec of War not to press them." We prefer beleiving that a man who has had his face slapped for cheating at cards & took it tamely was recreant to his duty, slow, or *even showed the white feather again*, to the other horn of the dilemma, viz., that we have so infamous a government that it suffers its citizens to be plundered with impunity when it has the power to punish. But I consume time & paper upon them, only I cannot help reiterating that I cannot see why the President puts such people with such antecedents & such parentage, & who have done so little to redeem either the one or the other, in offices of trust—but then Mrs Edmondston they are Democrats!

Gen Taylor has captured thirty four New York cotton planters who had settled themselves down in La & sent them for safe keeping to Texas—too good treatment for thieves and "*squatters*."

Our matters seem looking up in the trans Mississippi. Texas is a stir, the Gov[138] having taken the field with 10,000 State troops. Morgan & most of his command, sad to say, is undoubtedly captured. The high water in the Ohio prevented his crossing, but 'ere they succeeded in surrounding him he had traversed two States, carried fear & dismay into the hearts of the Abolitionists themselves, broken up & destroyed many lines of R R communication, & burnt large quantities of Commissary stores.

---

[138]Francis Richard Lubbock (1815-1905), born in South Carolina, moved to Texas in 1836, where he served as clerk of the Texas congress, comptroller of the Texas Republic, lieutenant governor of the state, and as governor of Texas from 1861 until 1863. He refused renomination in 1863 and joined the Confederate army with a commission as lieutenant colonel. In 1864 he was promoted to full colonel and served on Davis's staff in Richmond until the collapse of the Confederacy in 1865. After the war Lubbock continued to live in Texas and served as the state treasurer from 1878 until 1891. Boatner, *Civil War Dictionary*, 495-496; *Concise Dictionary of American Biography*, 592.

The hot weather does not seem to cool the animosity of the Yankees against non combattants. Witness the orders issued by Meade against the residents along the Alexandria & Orange R R, which I append marked B.11.[139] Some accounts of outrages upon women I delay recording, for they are so shocking that I cannot credit them. I wait for proof. Mrs Sanderson of Natchez is said to have been hung, Mrs Fort of Canton, Miss, whipped to death, & Mrs Hall of Weitzel Co Va exposed in a manner too shocking to write unless proved to be the truth.

Before Charleston matters continue as they were, an occasional bombardment of Battery Wagner only breaks the monotony of the seige—if we may call it so. We have thrown up heavy works which flank Wagner & another attempt to take it by assault would be even more bloody than that of the 18th of July. The enemy admit that they cannot damage it by shells & now pretend that they will be able to breach Sumter with their long range guns which they have mounted in a battery on Morris Island, but we know that is all gas & bluster & to make capital with the masses at home.

Lincoln's draft seems to give him much uneasiness. He has ordered 13,000 New England & Indiana troops to New York to overawe the mob during the drafting & ordering out of the conscripts. Gov Seymour is in the midst of a sharp correspondence with him respecting the method in which the enrolment has been carried out. He draws his attention to the fact that in 9 nine Democratic Distcts the quota of men called for by the draft is nearly as great as in 19 nineteen Republican Dists where the population is *far greater than in the Democratic*, remonstrates upon the injustice of such unequal demands, & requests that the draft may be suspended until another enrolment has been made. Mr Lincoln in reply refuses to postpone the draft & gives as a reason that "the Rebels are driving every man into the Army like cattle in a slaughter pen." Seymour admits the fact but reminds his Excellency that *where every* man is driven it is easier to be borne than when injustice & partiality drive some & favour others, & that too for political opinions. So there are the elements of a nice little quarrel between them.

AUGUST 17, 1863

Mr E and father at Halifax Court. Two lads, one just under the other just over sixteen, soldiers in Faison's Regt came begging something to eat. It made me almost weep to look at them, so young & undergoing such hardships. They seemed scarcely able to stagger under the weight of their Knapsacks, Cartridge boxes, & Enfield muskets. They were unable to keep up with the Regt in the long hot march of yesterday, missed the camping ground, & were forced to pay 50 cts each for a supper & have been all the morning without breakfast, marching on the traces of their Comrades, missed the road, & were

---

[139]The order, issued by Halleck rather than Meade, is in the second volume of the diary on page 19.

well nigh exhausted by twelve o'clock when they reached here. They have been 16 months in service. Truly as President Davis said, "it is grinding our seed corn." How long will it last? It was touching to see them eat & when I filled their haversacks with a supper for tonight; child like I think their gratitude was more excited by the peaches & apples than by the ham & bread with which I crammed them.

Since I last wrote we have heard from James. He is safe & well. The accounts he gives us of the crossing of the Potomac have been anticipated by the newspapers, but they are terrific! He says he worked seven days & nights at Williamsport, most of the time up to his waist in water, crossing our wounded and our wagon trains. He was in the "teamster's fight" when our extra duty men & teamsters repulsed the flower of the Yankee cavalry at Williamsport & saved the whole transportation of the Army congregated at that point & secured the line of "retreat for the Army." The trains were guarded by a few only of Imboden's Cavalry. The accounts of the loss at Gettysburg which he gives me is heartrending. "Petigrew's Brigade went into the fight on the second under the command of a Major! Iverson's Brigade nearly demolished & our Brigade (Daniels') lost nearly 900 killed & wounded, only two field officers remain unhurt." The letter has been so long delayed that there is no news in it; otherwise I would copy it. It was most welcome to us however as it gave us an *assurance* of his safety.

AUGUST 18, 1863

Fine cool bracing day, for which I am glad on account of our poor soldiers who must suffer terribly this weather. News by the papers of a terrific bombardment of Battery Wagner. Indications, too, of a desperate conflict there soon. What they are they do not tell us, but Ransom's Brigade is ordered in hot haste to Charleston, which was the reason of Faison's Regt making such a march yesterday & the day before. My two young friends to whom I yesterday gave a dinner will have a stirring time before many days pass over their heads. Father & Mr E at Halifax Court.

AUGUST 20, 1863

Dined yesterday at the plantation with Mr E, the first time I have done so this summer. Enjoyed myself greatly but *life* itself is an enjoyment to me. Lord make me more thankful for the blessings & the happiness which thou hast sent me.

The bombardment of Fort Sumter continues incessantly day & night! It is said to be terrific but as yet with slight damage to us. The loss of life *very* small in consideration of the number of shot & shells thrown. Battery Wagner has been repaired at night heretofore, new sand bags being placed where others had been displaced & mounds of Sand heaped in the furrows left by shot &

shell. In order to prevent this & also to wear out the garrison the enemy have lighted a brilliant Calcium Light which illuminates the shore, the forts, the fleet, & the adjacent Islands. Many persons are despondant as to the future fate of the city, but so am not I. I cannot beleive that it will fall. The fire from the Monitors is said to be *incessant*, one releiving the other. They contend that it is possible for them to breach Sumter at long range. We think they will find themselves mistaken. We are told that sand bags to the depth of 20 ft have been placed on the outside of the wall. I know not how it is managed, for I know the *sea did* wash at least two faces of it, but that may have been altered. One thing I do not like, however. She replies as yet only with her barbette guns. This to me looks ominous. She should show all her teeth.

Meade's army has fallen back from the line of the Rappahanock, it is said, to a stronger position to await reinforcements. Why is it, our army neither needs or gets half so many reinforcements as does the Yankee. We must either fight better or they must desert more than we do.

The Mrs Fort whipped to death by the Yankees in Mississippi was born and brought up here in this neighborhood within a mile of Conneconara Church![140] She was a Miss Ricks & years ago, before my day, the Ricks & Forts moved from this State to Mississippi & there some of them, her brother Ben Ricks in particular, made a very large fortune. Two Yankee officers, names unfortunately not given, went to her house about two o'clock at night & demanded that she should tell them where her money was secreted and get it for them. This she was either unable (having secreted none) or refused to do, my informant knew not which. They then commenced whipping her & at sunrise she died under the torture of their lash! For four hours they persisted—until nature gave way & she fell a victim to their more than Haynau like barbarity. Think of it! My blood tingles as I write. I have written for information particularly as to the names of the miscreants & it shall not be my fault if the civilized world does not ring with the infamous outrage.

The papers too confirm the hanging of Mrs Sanderson at Natchez. A Federal officer & a squad of men went to her house and demanded "the where-a-bouts of her husband." She asked "what they wished with him?," to which they replied "that was their business not hers" & reiterated their demand. When she refused to tell them, whereupon the officer *took off his scarf* & hung *her with it in her own house* & departed leaving her *hanging* there. Her neighbors came in & cut her down, but it was too late. Life was extinct. The outrage on Mrs Hall of Weitzel I leave the second vol of this book to relate as I preserve it there marked B 6.[141]

[140]The Conneconara Church was located about nine miles south of Halifax and one mile east of Crowell's Crossroads.

[141]The clipping is in the second volume of the diary on page 27. It describes an alleged outrage committed by Federal soldiers against the wife of L. H. Hall, member of the state legislature from Wetzel County, West Virginia.

O! that a just God would look down & punish such wretches! They abuse the gift of life which he grants them by the perpetration of such deeds. I preserve also the facts of a case of judicial murder which they are about perpetrating on the person of Dr Wright of Norfolk, marked A 23.[142] I had formerly a slight acquaintance with Dr Wright. He then lived in Edenton in this state & so far from finding him the bloodthirsty wretch that they describe I thought him gentlemanly & courteous in his deportment. O Peace! Peace! How long will my defenceless countrymen be called on to suffer such wrongs?

AUGUST 21, 1863

Today is the Fast proclaimed by President Davis, when he request[s] the nation "to unite in prayer & humble submission under His chastening Hand & to beseech His favour on our suffering country." I append the proclamation, together with that of Gen Lee enjoining the observance of the day upon the Army.[143] O that God would be entreated, that He would give us a place & a name amongst the nations of the Earth, & that he would grant us Peace— Peace & a happy deliverance from the hand of our enemies!

AUGUST 22, 1863

The bombardment of Sumter the telegraph tells us still continues, mostly from their Parrot guns on Morris Island. Sad to relate it adds, "Their fire begins to tell on Sumter which replies only at long intervals" & then goes on with the usual balderdash about "the defence of the harbour not depending on Sumter," a preparation I fear for the news of its fall, for it is a way our papers have that so soon as we lose a thing or a place—Hey—presto! it becomes valueless. Did we beleive some of them, the Yankee nation has actually conferred a favour upon the South by their capture of Vicksburg. "They have caught an Elephant" & much more nonsense to the same purpose. The fact I recorded of Maj Gen Hood's having been created a Lieut Gen & placed in command of the Cavalry of the Army of Va is a mistake, an announcement made I suppose by some one who wished it to be true.

The draft at the North so far is proceeding quietly tho Mr Lincoln has receded from his demands greatly in the face of his declaration that he would not do so. Not more than half the men at first demanded are now called for. Have been very busy the past few days in a contest with my old enemy, the Peach tree borer. Find my labours of last Aug. and March have resulted in

---

[142]The newspaper article is in volume two of the diary on page 19. Dr. David Minton Wright, living in Norfolk but formerly of Edenton, shot and killed Second Lt. A. L. Sanborn, commander of the First Regiment, United States Colored Volunteers, on July 11, 1863. He was tried by court-martial and sentenced to be executed. In response to numerous requests and protests claiming that Wright was insane, Lincoln reviewed the matter but concluded that the accused was guilty and approved the sentence of the military court. *Official Records (Army)*, Series II, VI, 157, 170, 188, 216-218, 360-361.

[143]This proclamation and the orders of General Lee appear on page 25 of the second volume of the diary.

some good, as we have had more sound fruit this year than usual in spite of the wet, but as yet the dimunition of their numbers is scarcely perceptible. Broke both my knives this morning which at this time is a heavy loss, for I can scarcly replace them.

AUGUST 23, 1863

The bombardment of Sumter still continues terrific. The Parrot Guns from the land batteries had up to Thursday night struck Sumter two thousand five hundred times! The missiles are 200 lb balls, eight in in diameter & two ft long with a flat head of chilled iron. The shells are of the same dimensions. The southern face of Sumter is crumbling under this iron hail even tho the battery is distant 4620 yds—or two & five eights of a mile. It seems almost increadiblle, yet so it is. The Ironclads keep at a respectful distance from the fort. On Monday they withdrew with their flags at half mast, supposed for the death of some officer of high rank. Would that it was Dalgren himself! All noncombattants have been ordered to leave Charleston & it is determined to defend the place inch by inch & if neccessary destroy it rather than suffer it to fall in the hands of so barbarous a foe.

The French in Mexico are emulating the Yankees and Austrians in whipping women. A lady of the name of Rubio received 200 lashes for refusing to receive French officers into her house. Her husband offered her weight in silver to the French General to save her from it, but Gen Forey insisted on making an example of her. I warrant his nation will have self respect enough and decency to repudiate the act.[144] It seems there are more Haynau's than one in the world!

Father had a letter today from his sister Mrs Polk. The accounts she gives of the sufferings witnessed by an acquaintance of hers (a Mrs Butler—who went through the Yankee lines under a pass from Grant) of the negroes about Vicksburg are heart rending. She says for miles & miles the road was lined with them. The locks of the fences had been converted by means of boughs into rude shelters under which they lay on the ground dead & dying by scores. As she passed she was met by entreaties from the poor creatures that she would tell their masters to come & take them. One poor creature rushed in front of the horses, threw up his arms, and begged her for God's sake to stop and listen to her. She did so and a tale of horror it was. Two of her children were dead & two more were dying on the ground in a corner of the fence! She begged that her master might be told of it. Why did you leave him?

---

[144]Élie Fredéric Forey (1804-1872) commanded the French forces in Mexico in 1862 and 1863. Forey later became a marshal of France. *Webster's Biographical Dictionary*, 540. The *State Journal* (Raleigh), August 24 and 26, 1863, carried items on the situation in Mexico. French troops were imprisoning and shooting those who refused to take the oath of allegiance to the empire. The Mexicans, on the other hand, were accused of taking no prisoners and urging a war of extermination.

Why are you here? asked Mrs B. "O, Missis we didn't leave! They drove us before them like hogs"!

A pestilence has been bred in Vicksburg & the whites are dying there at the rate of 300 a day. Negroes they take no account of. Starvation & death are emancipating them rapidly enough to suit that proto Abolitionist Wilberforce himself. What ignorance that man showed! He proves the wrong which can be done by a tender conscience when uninlightened. The negro race have philanthropy such as his to thank for an amount of suffering such as the world rarely showed before. A Puritanic desire to make all men conform to their Procrustian bed, see what it leads to. I preserve Mr Carlyle's American Iliad in a Nut on the next page. There is keen satire in it.[145]

AUGUST 25, 1863

The South face of Sumter is a crumbling ruin, & the North too begins to show signs of falling. The Parrot guns have made a complete breach through & through it. Col Rhett[146] the Commander is slightly wounded by a shell. We should not have hard thoughts of him, for he has done his duty, yet our sympathy would be greater did we not remember Mr Ransom Calhoun's death & how he met it in a duel with this same Rhett, his inferior in command, who without outward compunction stepped into his shoes.

Last week arrived at Wilmington from Europe two 500 lb. guns intended for Charleston. It was necessary to unship two Engines apeice to get them to their destination & their progress was necessarily slow. We had hoped that they would arrive in time to be mounted in Sumter & they would soon silence the 200 pounders of the enemy & send many a Monitor to the bottom of the sea, but I fear we are doomed to disappointment, tho' Sumter has been ordered to be held to the last extremity even as a 'forlorn hope' & the garrison is said to be brave & determined.

A notice without signature was sent by a flag of Truce to Gen Beauregard announcing the intention of Gen Gilmore to shell the city in a few hours. Beauregard's Cheif of Staff returned it for signature & shortly after its redelivery five shells were thrown into the city from a Morris Island battery. Beauregard remonstrated as contrary to the usages of civilized warfare, there not having been notice sufficient given for the removal of non combatants. Accordingly, Gilmore graciously postponed a renewal of his shelling until the

---

[145]An unidentified newspaper clipping, quoting the article "The American Illiad in a Nutshell" from "the August number of Macmillan's (London) Magazine," was pasted in the diary under the August 25, 1863, entry.

[146]Col. Alfred Rhett of the First South Carolina Artillery, commanding Fort Sumter, was wounded by a shell that burst above the messroom where he and others were eating dinner. Rhett, the son of Robert Barnwell Rhett, had previously killed his commanding officer in a duel at Fort Sumter. *Official Records (Army)*, Series I, XXVIII, Part I, 608, 615; Laura A. White, *Robert Barnwell Rhett: Father of Secession* (1931; reprint ed., Gloucester, Mass.: Peter Smith, 1965), 226.

next day, short enough time for a city of such size to be evacuated. Gov Bonham[147] & Gen Beauregard some days ago ordered all noncombattants to remove but, of course, many are forced to postpone their departure to the last moment. To all it is a cruel alternative & many persons know not the place to go to. Our papers contend that Gregg & Wagner can make a fierce defence & that they may yet find Charleston impregnable, even tho Sumter is leveled. God grant it be so! The shells are thrown from a distance of five miles, so we hope the damage will be inconsiderable.

AUGUST 26, 1863

The enemy's fire upon Sumter slackened throughout the 24th (our last date), the fleet not participating at all. At 12 oclock at night they opened fire upon the city with eight inch Parrott shells as yet without damage to us. This seems mere blind rage & spite, for it does not advance their Military manovres in the slightest.

Received last night the sad news of the death of poor little Mary Edwards, Isabella['s] eldest child, a sad blow to her poor Mother. She was a child of uncommon promise, of very decided character, & of great beauty. She was too just of an age to begin to repay her Mother for her care & nurture, being nearly twelve years of age. We were very fond of her & looked forward with great pleasure to a visit from her at no distant day. The ways of Providence are past finding out!

Letters from James give us good news of the condition and spirits of the Army. He says the despondancy now abroad amongst our people does not extend to it. It was never in better fighting trim or with more enthusiasm than at present, for which God be thanked. He says also that the desertions, now alaas so common, are in nine cases out of ten owing to low spirited despondant letters from home! Fie!

AUGUST 29, 1863

Not one word from Charleston since I last wrote. We know not whether to think it a good or a bad omen but hope for the best. A long letter from Amo giving a minute account of a visit he paid Fort Sumter. He alas confirms the news of the damage inflicted upon it. The Southern face is completely demolished & but for a strong "Ramp of sandbags & a Reinforce wall" which had been built in anticipation of the effect of the bombardment, I suppose the Fort would be untenable as the parapet is leveled to the terrepleine. Every gun upon the Southern, western, & Northwestern faces dismounted, the Northwestern wall breached, the Northern & eastern faces still stand, one

---

[147]Milledge Luke Bonham (1813-1890), a brigadier general in the Confederate army (1861-1862) and a Confederate congressman from South Carolina, served as governor of South Carolina from 1862 through 1864. He returned to active service in the army in 1865 and fought with Johnston until his surrender. Boatner, *Civil War Dictionary*, 72-73; *Concise Dictionary of American Biography*, 88.

Gun only having been dismounted—in short, he says Sumter will have to be abandoned, as only twelve guns are serviceable. Commissary & ordnance store were being sent off in large quantities & efforts were making to throw the guns over into the water so that they could be floated off & used elsewhere, but in spite of this there is no need to despond. Wagner, Gregg, & our other batteries are as strong & as defiant as ever. He is indignant at the barbarity of shelling the city at the dead hour of the night & well he may be. I preserve the account of the bombardment published in the Courier, as well as Gen Beauregard's correspondance with Gen Gilmore to which I have already referred, marked B no 1 and some accounts of Yankee barbarity & some of their general orders which speak for themselves, marked respectively B no 1, 2, 3, 4, 5, 6, 7, 8, 9, 10, 11, 12.[148]

Yesterday came James' Servant William from Orange Court House bringing good news of him. He sent his Quarter Master's vouchers for his brother to take care of for him. To me he sent a quantity of Stationary, paper, envelopes, pens, holder, pencils, etc., captured from the enemy—the triumph of possessing them should sharpen my wits, season you, O Journal, with Attic salt—& what I consider as a present indeed four papers of English pins! I told him if he dared to send me Yankee pins I would make a cushion of him & I see he has heeded. Never do I desire to see aught from that country again save it be a legitimate capture, a prize of war. My Stationary was taken from the field of Gettysburg, so I use it with pleasure. He sent his brother a hat, a fine Parisien one such as now commands $60 in Halifax & to Amo a fine undress officer's coat with a photograph of the owner in the pocket, also from the field of Gettysburg. It made me shudder to look at! It seemed as tho stained with blood.

I have been busy today rumaging up what stores I had to send him tomorrow, but I am low down in delicacies now, yet a jar of Mixed Pickles, one of Pickled pepper, one of butter, a can of Lard, 2 bottles of Walnut Catsup, a ½ Gallon of Honey, a bottle of Cayenne Pepper, ½ bu of Hominy, do of Meal, a bu of potatoes, Green Corn, Green Pepper & Tomatoes, 2 Hams, a side of Bacon, 5 Watermelons, & a coop of chickens are things not to be despised in Camp where naught is seen but Beef & Flour, for William tells me that is the whole Commissariat.

We have had a success in the Rappahanock in the capture by Lieut J Taylor Wood[149] of two Gun boats, the Reliance & the Satelite, followed the next day by the taking of a supply boat loaded with Coal, the Currituck. I fear the only good that will result to us will be the prestige, for as we have no navy

---

[148]These newspaper clippings are in the second volume of the diary on pages 14-27.

[149]Lt. John Taylor Wood, a Confederate naval officer, led a Confederate boat expedition in capturing the U.S.S. *Reliance* and the U.S.S. *Satellite* off Windmill Point on the Rappahannock River, August 23-24, 1863. *Civil War Naval Chronology*, III, 78, 132-133; VI, 292, 298.

to support them, they will perforce ere long have to be destroyed, but it was a gallant act & shows that our Navy "*still lives.*"

The Kentucky Election has under the auspices of the Christian Burnside of course gone for the U. S., as the first act which his impartial Christianity dictated to him was to declare the State under martial law & forbid any but "Loyal" citizens approaching the polls. The draft in N Y goes on under what auspices I record by a slip from one of their own city papers, marked B no 13. Also the manner in which their boasted "free navigation of the Mississippi" is carried on in another slip, marked B no 14.[150]

Another Raid is I see in preparation for N C; from New Berne they announce it, tho none can tell where it will fall.

The Standard newspaper does its best to induce them to penetrate the heart of N C by its advocacy of reconstruction, its abuse of Mr Davis, its insisting that the masses in the country are sick of the war, & ready for peace on any terms, complaining, grumbling, and abusing everything & everybody generally in the Southern Confederacy. I wish the people of Raleigh would fling the types and press into the streets & take Holden the Editor, Mr Bat More[151] his supporter, able Lawyer tho he be, & send them into the enemy's lines where their proper place is.

Holden, a miserable illegitimate son of a worthless woman, to presume to dictate laws or public opinion to the gentlemen of North Carolina. Such assurance! He is for anything that will advance him, W H Holden! He advocated Secession, was elected to the Convention, declared that the bonds which united N C to the Federal Government were forever broken, that she had resumed her own sovereignty, etc., etc., all in the hope that he would be a leader, would perhaps be Governor, but when he found that the people of N C rejected him, sought a worthier, a more honourable exponent than himself, hey presto, such a whining as he sets up about the war, its miseries, the neccessity of reconstruction, the alternative before us as was never before heard. Had he been made Governor the whole State might have starved, but as he is not our sufferings are intolerable. Bad as he is tho' the Yankees make him out worse than the reality, for they forge articles which they pretend to copy from his paper to blind the masses at the North & in Europe as to the state of public sentiment amongst us. May they carry their deception further than to poor mean little Holden.

---

[150]These accounts are on page 16 of the second volume of the diary.

[151]William Woods Holden (1818-1892), the editor of the *North Carolina Standard*, was a leading advocate of the peace movement in North Carolina, beginning in 1863. Holden developed into a hostile critic of the Confederate administration in Richmond and of the Democratic leaders in North Carolina. Bartholomew Figures Moore (1801-1878) was a prominent lawyer, former state legislator and attorney general, and an unwavering Unionist. He refused to recognize the right of secession, declined to take the oath of allegiance to the Confederacy, and opposed the war. Moore did not wholeheartedly support Holden, however, and later opposed Holden's governorship during Congressional Reconstruction. *State Journal*, May 2, 13, 27, 1863; Ashe, *Biographical History*, III, 193-207; V, 275-286; *Concise Dictionary of American Biography*, 444, 691.

They write the most extraordinary articles advocating white slavery, selling Irish & Germans & poor "white trash," & credit them to the leading papers amongst us, the Richmond Enquirer for instance (which they will call Mr Davis organ, which it is not for it is edited by that vulgar red Republican Irishman—T F Meagher),[152] & some others merely for effect in England. Nor are they without success as a M P stated in his place latterly that he would have voted & spoken in behalf of the Southern Confederacy but for that very article, not one line of which the Southern Confederacy ever saw. But Truth like Pan is dead & such absurd lies as some of them are! They gravely assert that there is a guard kept around Mr Davis' house in Richmond to prevent his escape. His escape from whom & who orders the guard? The people, the Government, or the Army? Can people be gulled with such monstrous inventions? Time & paper would fail me to relate more of them!

SEPTEMBER 4, 1863

In my own room at night. It would need no prophet to tell you, O Journal, that Mr Edmondston is from home. When he is here I keep better hours & never think of touching you after tea; still less of actually retiring to my room with you & chatting after the rest of the family are in bed. But so it is. When he is away I take strange liberties.

By order of Gov. Vance the Senior Captain of the Home Guards in Halifax was ordered to rendezvous the Home Guards at Halifax in the shortest possible time, "with such guns & axes as could be procured & three days rations. Should the enemy advance, trees will be felled across the roads & bridges torn up or burned." So runs the order. It fell like a thunder clap upon us last night, as we had heard rumours only of an intended advance from New Berne & that Raleigh was in a panic, thinking the Yankees were coming there to look after the "Union feeling" of which the Standard speaks so lovingly, but we thought it rumours only, the Yankees being supposed to have their hands full before Charleston. The order was dated Aug 29th but reached here Sept 3d only, time enough to have done with all need for the services of the gallant Home Guard, but there was nothing for it but to obey. So cooking a Ham & biscuit & getting his Camp fixtures in order for him Mr E was off today for that delectable place Halifax! When will this upturning & unsettling cease & we be left in *Peace* to enjoy the blessings with a bountiful Providence has vouchasafed to us? What would Lord Falkland have said had fate cast his time in our

---

[152]Thomas Francis Meagher (1823-1867), an Irish nationalist who fled to the United States in 1852 to escape English persecution, served as a brigadier general in the Union army. His command, the Irish Brigade, operated in Virginia until May, 1863. Mrs. Edmondston evidently confused Meagher with John Mitchel, another Irish nationalist residing in the United States who supported the Confederacy and served as editor of the *Richmond Enquirer* and of the *Richmond Examiner* (1862-1865). Mitchel returned to Ireland in 1875. Boatner, *Civil War Dictionary*, 540; *Concise Dictionary of American Biography*, 662, 683.

rather than in his own times! The Clarendon tells us he engeminated the word *"Peace! Peace!"* His groans now would be terrific.

But little public news. The enemy captured our rifle pits in front of Wagner by a surprise a few nights since & we seem to have allowed them to rest in quiet possession of them, even suffering them to approach within a few hundred yds of the Fort. I have often to remind you, however, Mrs Edmondston that you were not born a Brigadier Gen, so do not criticise the action or inaction of those who perhaps were.

The fire upon Sumter is slackened & we have Yankee reports of great exhaustion of both officers & men on board the iron clads, & with a glass the workmen seem busy on the sides of the monsters, whether to repair damages or to give additional strength for a final onslaught we know not. It is now thought that an attempt to run past our batteries & get into the Harbour will soon be made at night. May the 'bottom' be the resting place of many a one when they do try it. *"Drunken Dick,"* the shoal upon which we on our Bridal journey were so nearly wrecked will, I hope, give a good account of himself & thump many of them to peices on his stalwart back!

On fast day, whilst the whole town were at Church the Yankees suddenly opened fire upon Chattanooga without one word of warning, altho it is to their knoledge filled with Hospitals and refugees from Mississippi. Rosencrans is taking a leaf from the Christian Burnside's book. He inaugurated that policy in this State & Gilmore & Rosencrans improve on his teachings.

I prefix marked, B no 15, the Retaliation order of Gen Halleck, threatening Gen Fitz Lee & another officer with death by hanging should he execute Captains Flinn & Sawyer as retaliation for the murder of two of our officers by the said distinguished Christian Gen Burnside; also an English view of the manner in which the war is carried on, marked B no 16 and B no 17. Grant's order respecting the hiring of the negroes by which it appears that that monstrous cheat the Abolition Government has resolved itself in reality but not in name to a stupendous Slave owner, hiring out the "unbleached Americans" as, they call them, for their food and clothing & one twentieth of the proceeds of their labour, an account also of how they drove the negroes to slaughter at Port Hudson, B no. 18. A bill of fare found in Camp at Vicksburg, B no 19. An Appeal to the British Public, B no 23. A beautiful letter from the Mother of Gen Wharton declining in her son's name a nomination to Congress (B no 20) a Defence of the President from some charges preferred by the press against him (B 21) & several Prices Current B. no 22,[153] but it is time to go to bed, so Journal good night.

"Stolen waters are sweet"[154] and I have enjoyed my contraband chat greatly and written myself sleepy!

---

[153]These newspaper clippings are in the second volume of the diary on pages 12-13, 16-18, and 24.
[154]Proverbs 9:17a.

SEPTEMBER 6, 1863

Yesterday afternoon came home Mr Edmondston, the Home Guards being no longer needed. This calling them out without consideration at a time like this when every man is needed in the Fodder field is much to be deprecated. They may like the boy in the Fable "cry Wolf" once too often. No news by the papers. The attack on Charleston flags, the Bombardment is not kept up with the spirit it was & from some intercepted letters of the enemy they appear to be losing their confident hopes of taking the city.

After two nights shelling sleeping women & children, the battery of our gallant and brave foe became suddenly silent, it is said, from the bursting of their only gun of sufficiently long range to reach the city, so no thanks to them. I was out yesterday morning visiting &, sad to say, death had been before me in eight households! Three of the ladies had lost a brother each & one her husband, all killed in the recent advance in Penn; one a brother of Camp fever; one had one son lying in the house severely wounded (& probably disabled for life on the field of Gettysburg), having last week buried another son; the seventh mourned the loss of a husband & two children. One of the ladies, Mrs Whitaker, whose husband was killed at Middleburg, has also lost of Diptheria, within a few months, four children! How sorrowful it seems & out of all these sufferers one only there was who did not trace her sorrow to this unnatural war. Even the children lost by Mrs Whitaker would probably now be alive had they not been forced from home, for the disease Diptheria has not prevailed here. The eighth lady wore mourning for her brother who died of disease contracted in Camp, having been discharged a hopeless invalid. All this misery lies at the doors of Messrs Seward, Lincoln, & Buchanon, a bloody record!

SEPTEMBER 8, 1863

Yesterday at the plantation all day, Mr E busy in the construction of a mill to grind our crop of sorgho Sucre & thus to furnish our negroes with almost a neccessity to them—*Molasses*. It annoys & frets me to see the importance attached to the opinions of that fly on the chariot wheel, Holden. The feeling against him is intense & bitter. Our Army have held meetings repudiating his doctrines & today I preserve an address published by them, at once manly, dignified, & temperate. As part of the Hist of the times it deserves a place in my repertory—B 28. A letter from the infamous Hovey (for whose orders see the last of the 1st vol of my Journal), B 25, endorsed by the Yankees as "patriotic" (we call it savage) & tending from their own stand point to prolong the war. B 26 & 27 speak for themselves & tell the same tale as B 29— where armed men revenge themselves for acts of open & legitimate warfare upon defenceless women & children. Gen Stuart answers well. Would that our Government would *act* & carry out some of its Retaliatory threats. Tho scarcely worth the room, I insert a recent letter of Mr Lincoln's, B 30,[155] as a marvel of elegant rhetorical composition—a model *"fleet"* that which "wherever the ground was a little damp *they* have been & made their tracks" & wonderful English which jumbles up nouns personified in the singular with plural pronouns. I should like to hear him parse it. Lindley Murray[156] would turn in his grave.

But Journal, I am getting too discursive. I fear that you will prove that I "have dwelt" too "long in the alms basket of words" & that like Paroles I have apparently been at "a great feast of the languages & stolen the scraps."[157] I shall sign your death warrant if I go on! & yet in the isolated life, I lead it is a pleasure to me to *write myself out* as it were.

Did I tell you that Brother John had been appointed by the President "Tithing man" for N C[158] & that, to my sorrow, he had declined the office preferring that of State Qr Master? After the commotion made over Maj Bradford's appointment & its rescinding by Mr Davis to gratify the people of N C, it seems to me that 'noblesse oblige' that the native born appointee should accept it, but Patrick says I am too high strung & have not divested myself of my "loyal" feelings to the President.

Capt Cook was off yesterday. At short notice he received orders to report to Gov Vance for the reception of his orders respecting a cargo of cotton which the State of N C wishes shipped to Nassau. Commander Cook, CSN, is to command the vessel. We gave him a few commissions, some shoes, Tea, etc., but thank God our wants are not many. It is two years since I bought a shoe & I have still a good stock on hand & for the reason that having no good cobbler near us for the past few years I have, when my shoes needed mending, laid them up in ordinary as it were. Now Abraham's work is quite good enough for me & he repairs an old pair occasionally & I think myself blest!

The Bombardment of the forts below Charleston has been renewed with great energy & vigor. They wish a harbour for their Iron clads before the September gales. May they have a "Snug Harbour" and that *below* right speedilie!

---

[155]The newspaper clippings numbered B25-B30 are on pages 7-11 and page 18 of the second volume of the diary.

[156]Lindley Murray (1745-1826) was a Scottish-American grammarian known as the "Father of English Grammar." *Webster's Biographical Dictionary*, 1076.

[157]Shakespeare, *Love's Labour Lost*, act 5, sc. 1, lines 39-43. These lines were spoken by Costard and Moth, not by Parolles, who was a character in *All's Well That Ends Well*.

[158]The *North Carolina Standard*, in reporting John Devereux's appointment as chief "Tithing-man" for the Confederacy in the state, in place of Major Bradford, stated that "Mr. Devereux is a native of the State—a gentleman of intelligence and business habits, and will no doubt perform the duties of the office as acceptably as anyone who could be appointed." The *Sentinel*'s report added, "We question if a better selection could have been made." Devereux declined the office and H. A. Badham was appointed in his stead. The *Standard*'s comment was, "Mr. Badham is a native of the State and will no doubt make an efficient officer." *North Carolina Standard*, August 12, 19, and September 9, 1863; *Sentinel*, August 13, 1863.

SEPTEMBER 9, 1863

Sorrow on sorrow. The Telegraph last night tells us that we have evacuated Morris Island, actually given up Wagner which was after the destruction of Sumter our point d'affair. What it means God only knows, but from a sentence in one of brother's letters I fear me it is a want of Gunpowder, which would also explain Lee's mysterious inactivity. He says we "shoot away more in one day than we make in two." God help us if it be true. Then Charleston is lost! May that hated enemy find it only a heap of ruins!

More sorrow still, domestic sorrow of the most bitter kind, came too in the mail, sorrow which I have no heart to write, sorrow which I would gladly forget, for it can never be a *sanctified sorrow*, a sorrow which time mellows & dignifies as it touches.

Father had letters, too, from Nora, poor thing, from whom we have not been able to hear in months. She is well and as usual cheerful, but she has endured & is enduring every thing from the hands of these "loathed Yankees."

Nora's Letter—dated Aug 18 1863. She says "you may form some idea of the life we lead—when I tell you that our house has been searched *twelve times* by the *Kansas Jayhawkers*, besides by divers other troops at different times. Almost every day our lot is visited by some band of Yankees; they have taken off every saddle & bridle & even the waggon & sulky harness besides *six* horses, so that Robert has to give up his practice. We have managed so far to live comfortably &, tho needing many things, have suffered for nothing, but the prospect gets darker & darker & how we are to *live* through this winter *God knows, for I do not*!! I turn sick when I look forward to what we must go through. It is impossible to get supplies even if we had the money, Greenbacks, & that is getting very scarce with us, for Robert can do nothing but a little practice around town & for that I do not expect he will get a cent. . . . We have been more fortunate than some of the country people round, whose houses have been burned, but we do not know at what moment we may be left without a roof to cover us. We expect it so constantly that I keep our clothes all packed up & the trunks standing by the windows, so that if neccessary I can, myself, throw them out & thus have something to wear.

All of our negroes have left together with two of Sister Mats & seventeen of Williams, indeed negro property is worse than useless for they do no work unless they choose & the owners dare not correct them else off they go and report at Moscow & then he (the master) may look out the next raid that is made. I wish sometimes that there was not a negro left in the country, for they keep the Federals informed of everything & they (the Federals) are always ready to beleive & act on what the negroes tell them. And as to the idea of a *faithful servant, it is all a fiction*. I have seen the favourite & most petted negroes the first to leave in every instance. So disgusted have I become with the whole race that I often wish I had never seen *one* & tho the learning to do our own work would be hard, I beleive we would all be happier & healthier. When our first left us in the Spring we could not hire others, so Robert worked in the garden, fed the cows, & pigs (we do *not own a horse*), whilst I cooked, milked, & scoured, and we both thrived & fattened on it. My health was never so good. My children are all pictures of health and of this, the greatest of blessings, our enemies cannot deprive us.

I cannot begin to tell you what we had to submit to from the Jay Hawkers. They came about daylight & took Robert off down town. I was very sick & he told me to stay in bed as he supposed they only wanted to make him take the oath of allegiance & that they would not come into my room, but after they carried him off they came back & commenced searching the house. I then got up & dressed *with one of them standing in the open door. Five* of them then dashed in shaking their fists & pistols in my face, cursing me, & calling me all kinds of names, as "Liar," "She" devil, etc., etc., jumping *into* the beds & tramping all over them to see if any thing was hidden in them, throwing all of our clothes on the floor & wiping their wet muddy feet on my nicest dresses, breaking open locks before they could be opened & taking everything they fancied, Bedclothes, wearing apparel, Jewelry, silver, provisions, tobacco, *any and everything*. After they had stripped the house they went to Robert's office & scattered his papers out in the street, threw his books in the mud, tearing & trampling on them & took his case of Amputating Instruments & every other instrument he had except one or two lancets which he had in his vest pocket. Our losses in that raid amounted to twenty five hundred dollars and many of the things which they took cannot be replaced in the present state of the country.

One thing which has ruined this country is that many men, some of high standing, have taken the oath of allegiance to save their property & those who refuse to take it are not allowed to bring out anything from Memphis & are marked for spoiliation. I have got Robert to say that he will take this oath to avoid being thrown into a prison (as has often been done), but he will never take it to save the last dollar he has in the world, nor would I wish him to do it except as an alternative of being taken from us & thrown into prison, leaving our children with no one to protect or provide for them except myself.

The Yankees will come to the house & ask "if he has taken the oath." On being told he has not they will say, "*Well then, you will have 50 lbs of bread baked by sunrise tomorrow*" & this too when flour is $20 per barrel & lard 21 cts a lb, so if a poor body has a supply of neccessaries they soon go in feeding the Yankees.

You cannot conceive how I want to see you all. I feel as if I would give all I have in the world & undergo any fatigue just to get to you all once more. I wish I could get there. You would soon see me & the children even if Robert could not come. I cannot get one tenth of the letters sent me & those I get are so long on the way that I do not know what may have happened since they were written. . . . I received a letter from Sue for instance about two weeks ago written in Feb. . . . last news before this being a note from you written in Oct. It is all a chance whether you get any of mine. They are sent by persons who run through the Yankee lines into Miss & if there is any danger of their being taken—all letters are destroyed." Then some messages & "oceans of love" to all. She signs her name "N" only. In a PS she tells that she may possibly get letters if we send them to "Gen Polk & ask him to send them by some discharged soldier of the 6th, 9th, 13th, or 154th Tenn. Regts., as those Regts are all from this neighborhood & some of them come home sick or discharged every few weeks."

Sorrow enough for one day, you will say my friend sorrow enough. This & the other greif which I do not confide to you makes me sad & heavyhearted indeed.

SEPTEMBER 11, 1863

The most cowardly thing that the Yankee Government has yet done in its home administration, & the greatest confession of weakness that it has made, is the postponement of the draft in Ohio until after the election. They fear Vallandigham and his party too much to incur the odium of it now.

Longstreet's Division is we hear now en route from Va to Tennessee, Lee being strong enough to face Meade without him. The move is carried on with great secresy. Rumour tells us that Longstreet is to assume command, but I know not how that can be, as Bragg is a full Gen & Longstreet a Lieut Gen.

An official Telegram from Beauregard to Cooper tells us that during the night of the 8th the enemy in thirty Launches attacked Fort Sumter. Their coming having been expected, at a preconcerted signal all the Batteries bearing on Sumter, assisted by a Gunboat Ram, opened upon them & completely repulsed them, taking one hundred & fifteen prisoners (and thirteen officer[s] amongst them) & three colours! Good news & shows that their is life in the old ruin yet!

The associated press telegram gives a fuller account & from it we learn that they succeeded in making landing a portion of their force, but after 15 minutes contest in which the Charleston Battalion fought principally with brickbats & hand grenades they were driven back in disorder with the loss above mentioned. We captured four or five barges & what is most excellent, the original Flag which was hauled down from Sumter when Maj Anderson surrendered & which with Yankee bravado they boasted that they would again hoist upon the Flag staff. The loss of the enemy in their crowded boats is supposed to be terrible. We have, however, no means of ascertaining. We are, God be praised, without a casualty on our side, which seems wonderful. A flag of truce was reported as coming up, which Beauregard refused to receive until explanations had been made by them of their firing upon one which we sent to them a few days since.

Sad news of desertions from our Army.[159] Ten men were shot in front of Lee's army last week & what is humiliation indeed they were all from a N C Regt! the 3d Cavalry, Baker's about which so much injustice & favouriteism has been practiced. I omitted to mention that after being for weeks under arrest & in their turn preferring charges of the gravest nature against their Col, the officers were ordered to resume their commands without trial & without investigation of the cause of their complaint against their commanding officer. They have done so under protest & this is, I suppose, one of the first fruits of such injustice.

Two Regts have been sent from Lee's Army to arrest deserters in the Western part of this State. Raleigh rumour has it that they are an organized body, have elected officers, & entrenched themselves in a Camp in Wilkes County—not one word of which do I beleive, for where are they to get powder & provisions in quantity sufficient to support a Brigade or even a Regt? They must be mere predatory bands, outlaws subsisting by theft & pillage, who will disperse or be taken prisoners at the first determined onslaught made upon them. But the existence even of such bands is most serious & depressing, due I suppose in great part to the teachings of the Standard & to the encouragement held out by Holden to discontent & disaffection in the Army, by assurances of sympathy & like feeling at home. How wise the injunction of the Bible to "respect the powers that be—for they are ordained of God"[160] & what misery and anarchy does an infringment of it entail upon a nation! The Standard commenced by inveighing against President Davis. It has culminated in dishonor and treason!

SEPTEMBER 16, 1863

Mr Lincoln has, we hear, receded from his determination to exchange no officers if we continue to refuse exchange to the officers of negro Regts. Our Government is firm, so Cuffee's Commanders will find themselves on a different footing from their bretheren with Anglo Saxon followers.

On Monday father left for the Salt Sulphur Spr but on coming from the plantation yesterday who should we meet on the road but brother—just from our house. He told us that when he met father in Halifax he had nearly persuaded him in view of the difficulties of traveling, which are great & of which

---

[159]Lee reported desertions from Alfred Moore Scales's North Carolina brigade on July 30, 1863. Col. William L. J. Lowrance, reporting from Scales's headquarters to Joseph A. Engelhard in the adjutant general's office, blamed desertions on "that disgraceful 'Peace' sentiment spoken of by the Standard." The desertion rate among North Carolina troops, however, estimated at 20 percent, was no higher than that of other states in the North and South during the war. *Official Records (Army)*, Series I, XXVII, Part III, 1052; Barrett, *Civil War in North Carolina*, 171; Lefler and Newsome, *North Carolina*, 457.

[160]Romans 13:1. "For there is no power but of God: the powers that be are ordained of God."

a detention of some hours in Halifax had already given him a foretaste, to return, when a dispatch from Gen Ransom to the Commander at Rainbow to be on the alert, for a Yankee Raid was expected, arriving at the very moment when he hesitated, decided the matter at once & he retraced his steps, having determined to remain at home. Brother gave us sad news of the deserters in the West, but I must beleive them exagerated. He says they have defeated the militia in Wilkes & have an entrenched Camp, but if we have such difficulty in getting powder, where under the sun do they find it? Besides I cannot beleive there are so many fools in one state as their reported number would imply.

Last week a Regt of Benning's Brigade, Georgian, passing through Raleigh threw Holden's types etc all into the street but did not materially injure anything in the office, dispersing in an orderly manner on the Governor's remonstrating with them & representing the consequences of their conduct. Next morning Holdens friends proceeded to the Journal office & literally sacked & gutted it, demolishing presses, forms, mixing type, & even attempting to fire the building.[161]

This is purely a private quarrel. The two papers have been an embodiment of the Kilkenny cats in their threats of what they would do to each other. The editors have fought personally, shooting at each other & coming to fisticuffs. Public affairs have nothing to do with the retaliation of the foolish citizens. It is a revenge taken on Spelman[162] Holden's friends & yet the impudent Englishman Spelman attempts to wear the martyr's crown & says in a card which he publishes that it is "*the Cause*" for which he suffers. "*Cause,*" a pretty cause, his own unbridled license of tongue & low vulgarity. If it was the "Cause" why was not the Register office mobbed. That is good only by comparison. Decent is not the term to apply even to it. Less indecent than the Standard is the utmost we can say for it. It rouses my indignation to see the fair fame of N Carolina compromised & herself abused for the petty personal squabbles of two low born vulgar penny a liners! Holden's office was mobbed by the soldiers because he insulted them by an advocacy of reconstruction. Spelman's because Holden friends could not bear to see him get the advantage of their cheif, especially as some of his employees aided the soldiers.

---

[161]Soldiers in Henry Lewis Benning's Georgia brigade, passing through Raleigh en route to Virginia, mobbed the *Standard* office on September 9, 1863, destroying furniture and the printer's type. Governor Vance remonstrated with the crowd and the soldiers soon departed. The next day a crowd of Holden's supporters attacked the office of the *State Journal* (Raleigh), the voice of the Confederate administration. Vance again confronted the agitators and succeeded in dispersing the mob. *Sentinel*, September 11 and October 8, 28, 1863; Barrett, *Civil War in North Carolina*, 195.

[162]John Spelman, a native of England, published the *State Journal* from 1860 until 1882. Mary Wescott and Allene Ramage, *A Checklist of United States Newspapers (And Weeklies Before 1900)*, Part IV, *North Carolina* (Durham: Duke University, 1936), 643, 645-646, hereinafter cited as Wescott and Ramage, *A Checklist of United States Newspapers*.

Faugh! I am sick of such a storm in a tea kettle! What is of far more importance to us, our large gun, "the Peacemaker,"[163] bought at such expense from England burst at the first fire! Fortunately no one was hurt, but our hopes are sadly crushed by the disaster. It was mounted at White Point. Ah! me what pleasant hours in times now long past have I spent there!

From Lee's Army we hear of slight skirmishes, marchings & countermarchings almost daily. Meade "is ready in line of battle," then "he retreats," "reconnisance in force," etc., etc. Manoevres which two years ago would have been chronicled as "most important" are passed almost without comment, such proportions has the war assumed. The same can be said of Bragg's army. Rosencrans & Burnside are effecting a junction & matters assume importance there which increases every hour. Our whole R R transportation is taxed to the utmost to press reinforcements from Lee's army to that of Bragg. Since the evacuation of Morris Island the enemy have done little but strengthen himself & enlarge and repair Battery Wagner. Sorrowful indeed that they have it in their power thus to approach us under cover of defences which have cost us so dear. Three Monitors have been withdrawn from the conflict. As they were towed away we infer that they are disabled. The Yankee Army, God be praised, suffers as much from desertion as does ours; not only their drafted men but their *veterans* desert by companies.

September 22, 1863

On Friday night in a pouring rain came James home on a thirty days furlough. He is looking remarkably well & is in fine spirits. Says Lee's Army wants for nothing & that tho appearances to outsiders seem to favour the notion yet to those informed of the meaning of the manoevres now going on there is no immediate prospect of a battle. Meade is making reconnoisance in force only. On Sat came Capt Graves & Dr Watkins[164] to make Patrick a little visit and for releif from the weariness of Camp life. No army news whatever. The enemy before Charleston strengthning their position, annoyed only by our batteries. Chattanooga has been abandoned & Bragg is falling back, in which strategy all military men uphold him. It is a "*retirer pour sauter*"[165] but we

---

[163]The "Peacemaker," a Blakely rifled gun manufactured in England, was set up on White Point at the juncture of the Ashley and Cooper rivers in Charleston and was fired as a mortar for coastal defense. The manufacturers of the gun in England contended that any large gun would burst when fired that way. *Sentinel*, November 14, 1863, quoting the London *News*; Boatner, *Civil War Dictionary*, 68-69.

[164]B. S. Watkins was an assistant surgeon of the Twenty-fifth North Carolina Regiment. The "Capt Graves" Mrs. Edmondston referred to possibly was William W. Graves of Transylvania County, captain of Co. E, Twenty-fifth North Carolina Regiment. The reference could also have been to William G. Graves of Caswell County, captain of Co. H, Fifty-sixth North Carolina Regiment. He temporarily commanded Companies E and H of his regiment while they guarded the construction work on the ram *Albemarle* at Edward's Ferry. Clark, *Histories of the North Carolina Regiments*, II, 292, 297; III, 316, 319, 331, 351; IV, 635; Manarin and Jordan, *North Carolina Troops*, V, 290.

[165]French, "withdrawal instead of advance."

domestic "militarists" think it "esprit de corps" on their part and have no faith in Bragg. Longstreets Corps is re-inforcing him. On Sunday came an order to Mr E as Capt of the Home Guards to arrest all deserters & recusant Conscripts in his Dist. Today he has the pleasure to report that there are none of the first & one doubtful case only of the second class in his command. Miss Lee writes my neice Annie Devereux that her younger brother[166] has made a formal tender of himself to the Yankee Government in the place of his brother Fitz Hugh Lee now held by them under sentence of death by hanging. Should we retaliate for Burnside's murder by shooting Capts Flinn & Sawyer? An instance of self devotion the paralel to which must be looked for in ancient & more chivalric days than ours! He gives as a reason that his brother has a wife & child whilst he is unmarried. Noble young man! Worthy son of such a sire! If there is a spark only of justice left in the Yankee nation, such an instance of generous self devotion ought to fan it into flame & Gen F. H Lee & Capt Winder be at once released. The injustice of holding them hostage to prevent punishment for the crime of the Christian Burnside is too palpable to admit of argument.

SEPTEMBER 23, 1863

Today came a dispatch from Bragg dated "Chicamauga River" Sept 20th to the effect that after two days hard fighting he had driven the enemy from "several positions and now hold the field but he still confronts us; losses on both sides heavy especially in officers. We have taken over twenty peices of artillery and some twenty five hundred prisoners." We hold our breath with anxiety & remembering Murfreesboro & Perryville are afraid to rejoice. "*He still confronts us*" & Rosencrans force is at rallying. God be with them! Give them *endurance* & to the nation a splendid victory! I went to the plantation yesterday on horseback. A delightful day. We had a slight frost in the morning which made it more like Oct than Sep. I hope, however, that premature as it is it has done but little harm. We never before had so early an intimation of the approach of winter.

SEPTEMBER 27, 1863

Sunday—Have been all the week looking & hoping for details of Bragg's recent victory which come in but slowly. Rosencrans has fallen back to Chattanooga where he is fortifying, rumours of our having cut him off to the contrary notwithstanding. Our loss in officers is heavy. Hood of Texas, our best Cavalry general, has lost a leg, but is doing well. Our loss *estimated* at 5000 killed & wounded. Bragg's official Telegram tells us [we have] taken seven

---

[166]The Lee referred to probably was George Washington Custis Lee, an aid to Jefferson Davis. It is impossible to determine which of the Lee sisters wrote the letter in question. Robert W. Winston, *Robert E. Lee: A Biography* (New York: William Morrow & Company, 1934), 272-273, 326; Chesnut, *Diary From Dixie*, 303.

thousand prisoners, of whom two thousand are wounded, twenty five stands of colours & guidons and 36 peices of artillery & have already collected 15,000 small arms over and above those left by our killed & wounded and more a coming in. Rosencrans sent in two flags to ask a cessation of hostilities in order to bury his dead & to attend to the wounded, but Bragg returned for answer that he had prisoners enough to do the one & Yankee surgeons sufficient to releive the other & so should press on. Rosencranz has been reinforced by Burnside the Christian, so he may make a desperate stand yet, spite of the fact which we take from their own papers that two Divisions of his army were seized with a frightful panic & ran riot, 10,000 of them & they with difficulty being again rallied. Victory may be plucked from our grasp yet. Rosencranz is strong in a dogged obstinate resistance—"Old Holdfast" as his troops call him. "Bragg is a good dog, but Holdfast is a better" said an old proverb of our childish days. We may yet live to see it re-exemplified. God grant that we may not! How true it is that Bragg does not possess the *heart*, the *confidence* of the country. We fear to rejoice, fear to pluck the fruit lest it turn to ashes in our grasp!

On the Rapid Ann Lee's & Meade's armies confront each the other. A series of skirmishes mostly cavalry occur almost daily with varying success. They drove us back on Wednesday or Thursday & on Friday we ambushed a Brigade & captured 700 of them together with their officers.

The shooting of ten deserters which I recorded as having taken place in the 3d Cavalry is a mistake of the Reporters. He should have put it 13th Infantry. I have censured Baker wrongly for that but from no fault of mine.

There is but little doubt now of a fact which I deferred mentioning, viz., that Semmes has sunk the Vanderbilt. Altho not official, the story has reached us in too many ways to be longer doubted. That pride of the Yankee Navy lies midst the Coral Caves off the coast of Florida, sent there by the Confederate Cruiser, the Alabama. Capt Maffit has been received at Brest in the Imperial Navy Yard with orders to supply her with everything she wishes save munitions of war.[167] We must build no hopes of speedy recognition on that fact, however, as it is but a return of courtesy on the part of the Emperor for assistance rendered by us to a French man of War ashore on our coast two years since. We rescued the crew & gave them free passage to Norfolk then in our possession, tho we were unable to save the vessel, the Yankees in the meantime not content with "passing by on the other side" but actually shelling our boats whilst engaged in the humane task!

---

[167]Mrs. Edmondston was in error as to the C.S.S. *Alabama* which, together with the U.S.S. *Vanderbilt*, was operating in the vicinity of South Africa during this period. John Newland Maffitt (1819-1886), a Confederate naval captain, commanded the C.S.S. *Florida*, anchored in Brest, France, for repairs since August, 1863. Boatner, *Civil War Dictionary*, 500; *Civil War Naval Chronology*, III, 106, 121, 125-126, 134, 151, 153.

And this reminds me that I have too long lost sight of the progress of the French in Mexico. As yet it has had no bearing upon our condition & therefore I have taken but little interest in it, but as that cannot long continue, I ought to mention it in time so that when it comes you, O Journal, will not be found entirely ignorant of matters there. The French, under pretence of a redress for commercial injuries, have conquered the whole of Mexico, so that the pliant Junta have under Marshal Forey's[168] influence offered an imperial crown to Maximillian, second brother of the Emperor of Austria.[169] He wavers about accepting it whilst Lord Clarendon[170] on the part of England has been ordered to make a solemn representation in his name of the dangers which envision it—to lift the gilded bauble for a moment as it were & to show the real crown of thorns hidden underneath it. The U S throws itself into a ferment of indignation at this breach of the "Monroe Doctrine," blusters & threatens to annihilate France, pretends to beleive that she is in league with the Southern Confederacy & that Mr Davis has already or soon will cede to her all our territory west of the Mississippi, & exhausts herself in threats and declarations of his determination to allow no foreign domination on this continent. We sit passive but by no means uninterested spectators of the contest. Something must "turn up" to our advantage in it but as yet we see not what it is to be. The story of Marshal Forey's having ordered 300 lashes to be given Mad Rubio for refusing to admit French officers into her house is a vile Yankee fabrication, trumped up by them to throw their own infamous conduct to the women of the South into the shade. None but Yankees or Russians could be guilty of such outrages on humanity & manhood.

Father left us for Raleigh on Thursday the 24th. When he returns he will bring Susan with him.

---

[168]By July, 1863, the French forces in Mexico had conquered Mexico City and were prepared to subdue the remnants of opposition from the followers of Benito Juarez, the deposed president of Mexico. Napoleon III, eager for rich conquests and the chance to stop Anglo-Saxon expansion in the New World, sought to impose a French empire in Mexico under the immediate control of a puppet emperor. The United States opposed this breach of the Monroe Doctrine, but Confederate authorities were prepared to recognize Napoleon's Mexican state if it would win French recognition of the Confederacy. Randall and Donald, *Civil War and Reconstruction*, 510-513.

[169]Ferdinand Maximilian Joseph (1832-1867), archduke of Austria and brother of Franz Joseph, emperor of Austria, accepted the proffered Mexican throne on April 10, 1864, and reached Mexico the following June. One of the major inducements for his acceptance was the promise of French military aid in subduing the remaining rebel Mexican forces. After vigorous diplomatic pressure from the United States, however, France withdrew the last of its army in February, 1867. Juarez launched a successful campaign which forced Maximilian's surrender in May, 1867, and Maximilian was executed on June 19, 1867. *Webster's Biographical Dictionary*, 993; Randall and Donald, *Civil War and Reconstruction*, 511, 649.

[170]George William Frederick Villiers (1800-1870), the fourth earl of Clarendon, was a distinguished British diplomat who began his career in 1820. In 1853 he first became head of the British foreign office, and he continued his affiliation with the foreign office the rest of his life. From 1856 until 1864 Villiers served as the British ambassador to France, but in 1865 he again assumed control of the foreign office. *Dictionary of National Biography*, LVIII, 347-350.

September 29, 1863

Went yesterday with Mama to see Samantha. Found her husband quite sick. Poor thing, she is a bad manager & has a hard time. I am very sorry for her but there is little I can do to help her.

Passed some hunters "on a stand" for Deer. What a thrill of old associations the sight of them awakened! Remembrances of dreamy October days, of woods one flush of gorgeous couloring, of repose deep, untroubled, & serene, of quiet broken only by the steady chirp of the autumn cricket chirping, as he only does after the first frost, of dropping nuts & falling acorns, of plenty and prosperity, corn fields with bended heads awaiting the gatherers hand, of, to sum it all in one word, Peace. And then I looked within. Saw my own mind torn & harrassed by anxiety with wearying care for the future, distressed for my war lost country, for my wounded & dying countrymen, sympathizing with the anguish of lonely hearts, with the cares of mothers for the daily bread of their children, with the sorrow & heaviness which oppress the manly bosoms of our soldiers separated from their loved ones & forced to live in "idleness or peril" & my own heart melted within me! & with Lord Falkland I engeminated the word "*Peace! Peace!*"

Found every one busy with cards & spinning wheels. My own homespun dress was much admired & queries made as to whether I had spun it myself. I was sorry to be forced to answer in the negative, for I have never been forced to lay my hand to the distaff. Perhaps I had better learn, for who knows what my future is to be? I should be proud indeed had I made such an overcoat for my husband & Mrs Brinkley[171] has for her son—a matter, too, of just pride!

From Georgia we hear but little. I cannot honestly think Bragg has won "a great Victory" whilst Rosencranz remains upon this side the Tennessee. Longstreet holds Lookout Mountain from whence those learned in military matters say he can at pleasure shell Rosencranz out of Chattanooga. If so, why, does he not do it at once? Why wait for Burnside et al to re-inforce him. The papers maintain that our Cavalry are upon the north bank of the Tenn cutting off the enemy's supplies. I only *hope* it is true!

Before Charleston the quiet is interrupted only by our batteries on Sullivan's island shelling the working parties on Morris Island. The Yankees are enlarging & strengthning our legacy to them (Fort Wagner) & mounting heavy guns at Fort Gregg. The northern papers tell us that by Mr Lincoln's own order a cargo of shells charged with what they call "Greek Fire"[172] has been shipped to Gilmore—with which he is to destroy the city of Charleston.

---

[171]Spencer Brinkley, a farm overseer aged forty-two who owned three slaves, and his wife Martha are listed in the Halifax County census for 1860. Eighth Census, 1860, Population Schedule, Halifax County, 81; Slave Schedule, 53.

[172]The Raleigh *Sentinel*, probably the source of Mrs. Edmondston's information, described Greek fire as "a peculiar compound of bitumen, naptha, and pitch of a most offensive odor, and possessing the property of burning either on the surface or under the water." *Sentinel*, September 1, 1863.

Yankee barbarity & Yankee assumption, calling their villainous mixture of tar and sulphur by the name of the Classic compound so long lost to the civilized world! I preserve, Marked B 31,[173] the description of the poisoned balls now being made at the U S Arsenal. The use of such weapons should deprive the combattants of all claim to be considered as civilized & our Generals should issue orders to refuse quarter to all troops using them.

Before Lee's army all continues quiet. Predictions of an early battle so rife last week have not been verified. Cavalry skirmishes & picket shooting are the only things going on to break the monotony of Camp life.

OCTOBER 1, 1863

Today came Father & Susan back from Raleigh. They traveled with a number of the Chickamauga prisoners en route for Richmond, mostly Irish & Dutch, vile mercenaries! Father saw two of our Confederate soldiers just exchanged from David's Island.[174] They told him that they had been well treated & had but a single instance of shabbiness to complain of & that was so indicative of Yankee meanness that I record it. A donation was made by some kind hearted persons of good clothing to the Confederate prisoners, but the Col in command of the post before issuing it had all the skirts of the coats & the buttons cut off. He should be known as "Col Curtail" henceforth! They showed the garments to him & he saw that it was true. The Charleston papers suggests that the skirts were sold to make caps, vests, etc., so *"Col Curtail"* has a Yankee eye for the *"main chance."* I preserve the remarks of the Charleston Editor on it, marked B 32.[175]

Sue told me so laughable an instance of the detestation of Yankees in even little children that I cannot let it pass. Little Laura, the youngest but one of brother's children, a saucy little four years old, being out of temper generally & desiring to make an exhibition of it, began thus

"I loves *Rats*, I does! I loves spiders, I does!" No notice being taken of her ill humour, she rose higher in the scale of antipathies—"I loves Thousands (ie. thousand legs—centipedes) I does! I say, I loves lizzards I does! I loves snakes too, I does!" Then another pause, but being still treated with distinguished neglect, she capped the climax with, "I say I loves *Yankees*, I does! Sister Nan do you hear me? I say, I loves *Yankees*, I does," which was as far as she could go! Talk of reunion with a nation classed in the minds of little ones such as this with *"Rats, Thousand Legs, & Snakes."*

OCTOBER 7, 1863

On Sunday night after I had retired came James on his way back to his post in Gen Lee's army. He left all in S C well & reports a most wholesome state of

---

[173]This newspaper article is not in the diary.

[174]David's Island was a military hospital near New York City. Clark, *Histories of the North Carolina Regiments*, IV, 703.

[175]These remarks are in the second volume of the diary on page 7.

feeling as regards the safety of Charleston as prevalent there; says the people are hopeful & the soldiers are defiant & confident.

On Monday Sue & I escorted by him went down to see the Gunboat launched, but like most of her sex she was uncertain & disappointing & beyond seeing all our neighbors assembled we had our ride for nothing. She, however, took her future element without accident we heard at three o'clock the next morning, her builders being forced to wait for the moon to rise ere they could persuade the coy maiden to venture upon the slippery *"ways"* that lead to the water.

On Tuesday I was busy getting together a store of good things for James to take back to Camp with him & succeeded beyond my most sanguine expectations. Managed to rig up some flannel drawers for him too, low as my stock of dry goods is. Copied a long letter on finance from Father to the Hon Mr Boyce[176]—sound, sensible, & judicious. Would that Mr Meminger[177] and Congress were both imbued with the spirit & letter of it.

Had, too, a severe fall which was neither sensible, judicious, or graceful in me & a most narrow escape from serious injury. As it is I suffer still from its effects. James left this morning in good spirits.

We have found out that the letters "A D" affixed to the name of a Regt in the U S service mean *"African Descent."* 1st S C. A D, Mass A D, Maryland A D—are all Cuffies! What next? Confusing, as it might mean "Anglo Saxon" or "American Descent," but Cuffee has the precedence.

The Yankee cheif of the Medical Department[178] has been discharged for allowing it to transpire from his office that their losses in the Penn campaign amounted to *54,000.* Good God! Think of it! 54,000 souls on one side in a little more than a fortnight. Our loss is not officially known. It was heavy but nothing like that!

---

[176]Mrs. Edmondston was probably referring to William Waters Boyce (1818-1890), a former United States congressman from South Carolina, a state legislator, and a member of the Confederate Congress from South Carolina from 1862 until 1864. After the war Boyce moved to Washington, D. C., where he practiced law until his retirement. *Biographical Directory of Congress*, 582; *Who Was Who in America, Historical Volume, 1607-1896* (Chicago: Marquis Who's Who, Inc., Revised Edition, 1967), 136.

[177]Christopher G. Memminger (1803-1888) served as secretary of the treasury from 1861 until June 15, 1864. Memminger was blamed for the collapse of Confederate credit and finally resigned his position in disgust. Although not forceful in winning acceptance for his own fiscal policy, Memminger recognized the need for an adequate taxation program in the Confederacy. The Confederate Congress rejected his proposals, however, in favor of the expedient of paper money. Memminger's requests for suitable taxation and loans to finance the war eventually were accepted, but the damage to the southern economy had already been done. *Concise Dictionary of American Biography*, 668; Randall and Donald, *Civil War and Reconstruction*, 256-261.

[178]William Alexander Hammond (1828-1900), a neurologist who served as an army surgeon from 1849 until 1859, was a native of Annapolis, Maryland. He was a graduate of the University of the City of New York. Appointed surgeon general in 1862, he initiated many reforms before he was dismissed in 1864 after clashing with Secretary of War Stanton. *Concise Dictionary of American Biography*, 394.

From Chattanooga we learn that Rosencrans is completing a third line of defences. We wait, it is said, for Wheeler & Forrest to break up his communications & summon thus General Starvation to our aid. Before Charleston Gilmore has suddenly renewed the Bombardment of Sumter from the same long range battery which threw the upper walls down. It is said now to be impregnable to all save an assault hand to hand.

As part of the history of the times I preserve, B-33, an account of the treatment Mayor Monroe met with at the hands of the Yankees. None other than a Russian or a savage could have been guilty of it. Also B 34, the method in which they intend partitioning N C; B 35, slight mention of their thefts; B 36, the system to which they have reduced counterfeiting; B 37, the outrages committed by their negro soldiers; & B 38, a sketch of Seward as a Historian from the Examiner, which I think clever; & lastly B 39,[179] Gen Lee's official report of the Penn Campaign. He is reticent, does not tell us much, but what he does say can be relied on & implicitly beleived, which is more than can be said of the reports of Yankee Generals. "To lie *like a slave*" has been proverbial; henceforth we should say, "*Lie like a Yankee*"!

OCTOBER 8, 1863

As a proof of the benefits derived by the Yankee Nation from the boasted opening of the navigation of the Mississippi, the Insurance Officers refuse to insure boats upon the Father of Waters, so insecure do them deem it. They complain loudly that scarce a boat arrives that has not been damaged or some of her crew killed by guerrillas who swarm on the banks, appear suddenly, discharge their peices, pick off the men on deck, & before the guns of the boat can be brought to bear on them disappear as suddenly as they appeared. The very Boat which Grant sent up with the glad tidings that the "*Mississippi was free*" was *sunk* before she reached St Louis, & yet a Proclamation has gone forth to the world that that mighty river was again under the jurisdiction of the U S!

A terrible thing, shocking to the last degree, took place at the battle of Chickamauga. The shells of the enemy set fire to the woods in the battle field—ground over which the battle had raged with fury & from whence we had driven them & which was still covered with their wounded & horrible to relate the maimed & disabled men unable to escape perished in the flames! Many of them were rescued by us severely burned, but numbers of charred corpses of men evidently burned to death were found when the tide of Battle allowed us to attend to the wants of our enemies wounded. We hope our wounded had all been removed, but who can tell; in such a wide extent of thick brushwood what scenes of suffering were witnessed by God's eye alone? Lieut Gen Polk has we see been ordered to leave his command and report to

---

[179]These newspaper clippings are in the second volume of the diary on pages 2-6.

——and there await further orders. This is based upon some disagreement it is said between the two Generals as to the conduct of Gen P upon the battle field of Chickamauga. Gen P is confident of acquitting himself before the proper tribunal of all blame in the premises. Gen Hindman is in a similar predicament. We know not what the charges are & tho I never thought he ought to have been made Gen or left his Bishopric for the army, am exceedingly sorry that he should be placed in so unpleasant a position.

I preserve, B 40, several prices current and B 41,[180] a heartrending account of the sufferings of our wounded after the battle of Gettysburg. Can such things be? No news of importance from Chatanooga. We have Rosecrans surrounded on this side of the River. Our lines extending for six miles in a crescent around the town, but his rear is still open & his communications uninterrupted. Longstreet, it is pretended, can at any moment shell him out of the place from his position on Lookout mountain with perfect impunity. If so, why does he not do it & why does an able general like Rosecranz remain to be shelled? Very like "Dicky! Dicky! come & be killed," I think. Faugh! Our papers are learning the Yankee vice!

Mr E & Father much occupied with their Syrup making. "From morn until dewey eve"[181] I never see Peter. Mill making & syrup boiling absorb him completely & all to feed the down trodden much oppressed Cuffee with "*sweeties.*" Are Abolitionists really blind, or is it all a Wilberforcian sham?

I still suffer severely from the effects of my ungraceful fall. My poor *boot heels* bear the brunt of the blame & the family are eloquent upon the dangers which encompass them whilst obstinate I maintain per contra that it was my own carelessness & am as much wedded to "*heels*" as ever (there is a spice of contradiction in you I fear Mrs E!).

Let who will make the laws provided you let me make the songs of a people—said in substance some wise man or other, Lord Bacon,[182] I beleive; but as an instance of its truth I copy an anecdote from a Yankee paper. Some Yankee officers being at a house in Northern Va noticed a bright sprightly little girl of three or four years old & one of them asked her to sing for him. "What shall I sing," she said; "O! anything you like, sing me the song you like best," when without further prelude "the little rebel" began,

> "Jeff Davis rides a white horse—
> "Lincoln rides a mule!
> "Jeff Davis is a gentleman!
> "And Lincoln is a fool!"

---

[180]These newspaper articles are in the second volume of the diary on the front inside cover, and on pages 1 and 4.

[181]John Milton, *Paradise Lost*, bk. 1, line 742.

[182]Andrew Fletcher of Saltoun (1655-1716), *Conversation Concerning a Right Regulation of Governments for the Common Good of Mankind*, published in 1704. "If a man were permitted to make all the ballads, he need not care who should make the laws of a nation." Bartlett, *Familiar Quotations*, 384.

to an old nursery tune, much to the surprise & chagrin of the Yankee, for, hastily putting her down, he exclaimed "What folly to think we can conquer a nation when the very children think & sing thus."

One peice of good news I have to tell you, O Journal, & I have done so. Mr Mason, our minister to England, has been ordered by the President to withdraw & join Mr Slidell in France. We have been long suffering & patient enough under the slights of that little great man Lord John Russel & our government will no longer bear them. Good news I say, for tho I used to love, admire & revere England, yet now her selfishness & narrow mindedness have disgusted me. She too worships the "Almighty Dollar" as much as the Yankees & not with so farsighted an eye. She too winks at injustice in those she *thinks* strong & oppresses the weak who cannot retaliate. *The Law of Nations*! a humbug & a sham, a veil too flimsy to delude any people now that England has worn it threadbare.

OCTOBER 10, 1863

All day yesterday with Mr E at the plantation. Left home just after sunrise. The whole earth seeming clothed in a garment of diamond & rubies. How much not only of time but beauty do you daily lose by your practice of getting up late Mrs E? (Yes but what I lose I gain in health & in the capacity to enjoy both beauty & time!) Looked at the mill grinding the cane & at the witches over the cauldron boiling the juice. "Dawdled" about generally with Mr E. Knit a whole stocking & read half at least of the "Bachelor of the Albany." Yes, Mrs E., because you exercised the accomplishment learned in your youth from your mother of reading & knitting at the same time, & came home in the twilight to the delightful news that Bragg was shelling Chattanooga, that the Tennessee was rising, & that Rosecranz had lost in consequence his pontoon bridge, that Forrest had captured & burned 500 of his waggon trains loaded with supplies, that Norfolk was evacuated, Meade falling back, that six steamers at different points had been burned on the Mississippi, that a long Yankee Ammunition train had been exploded at Bridgeport by an irate Cuffee throwing a loaded shell at his companion; that collisions, in anticipation of the election on Monday next, were occurring in Ohio between the military & the civilians, and lastly that an expedition sent out at night from Charleston had succeeded in damaging the Ironsides with a torpedo. Enough good news for once, so I retired thankful & hopeful to bed after beating father three games, & had one drawn one, at chess. Rosy dreams ought to have attended me but, instead, I had what is better a—dreamless night & awoke this morning so happy & buouyant that I scarcely know how to comport myself.

OCTOBER 15, 1863

All day yesterday Mr E busy grinding & boiling his Sorghum Sucre, out here a troublesome job, something like "preserving" on a huge scale & in the end "great cry & little wool," as it takes gals of juice to make *one* of syrup. Was up betimes this morning with the intention of going to a wedding in Halifax, but the morning was so unpromising that we feared to venture, dressed as we would be like "*wedding guests*," in the buggy, the carriages having both been sent to Weldon for Sophia & her four children & Mrs Jones & Rachel. I am now momentarily expecting them. We will have a house full when they come!

We have had a fight in Va & claim to have driven a part of Meade's army across the Rappahanock, captured 400 prisoners & killed & wounded many more—our loss slight. Nothing new from Chattanooga, tho rumour has it that Joe Johnson is in Rosecranz' rear. I preserve Gen Polk's farewell to his corps. He will now, I suppose, having sheathed the sword, resume the Surplice— pity tis that he doffed it! The President has gone out to the south western army to accommodate the differences between his Generals.[183] Sad to relate he takes *Gen Pemberton* with him!—ominous of disaster.

The victory at Sabine Pass proves a most brilliant one. Forty eight men repulsed twelve thousand (12,000), took 385 prisoners without loss to themselves, with 6 (six) guns they captured 385 men & drove back 12,000, captured two Gunboats & disabled two more. This is authentic. We can scarce credit it.

Before Charleston there is the usual shelling without much effect on either side. The enemy now seen turning their attention to Fort Johnston on James Island, ignoring Sullivan Island & its defences. I hope its *offensive* power will not allow itself to be forgotten but keep them well posted as to its efficiency.

Rumours as pregnant as Lord Burleigh's nod[184] reach us from the New York Herald of peace propositions being discussed between Richmond & Washington. Much do we beleive of it! Wool to be pulled over the eyes of the Ohio Electors! "Keep us in good people." "Keep us in a little longer, we are making a beautiful Peace for you, which shall neither compromise the North or degrade the South."

OCTOBER 19, 1863

Rumours only from Va. Lee still pressing Meade, part of our force said to be in his rear. A series of skirmishes mostly Cavalry have been of daily occurrence for a week past. Skirmishes do I say? They would be called "*battles*" in any other war than this gigantic one—1,000 prisoners & 7000 horses & mules

---

[183]President Davis visited Bragg's headquarters shortly after the battle at Chickamauga. It was reported at the time that Davis sought to reconcile a serious difference between Bragg and Longstreet over military strategy. Johnson and Buel, *Battles and Leaders*, III, 608, 639-640, 709.

[184]In Richard Sheridan's play *The Critic* (1779), the character Puff writes a play entitled *The Spanish Armada* in which a Lord Burleigh speaks no lines but restricts himself to a memorable nod. Benét, *Reader's Encyclopedia*, 890, 1023; Clayton Hamilton (ed.), *Plays of Richard Brinsley Sheridan* (New York: Macmillan Company, 1926), 279-339.

have arrived at Gordonsville en route for Richmond. A whole division of the enemy was yesterday reported as captured, but we wait for Lee's official Dispatch *with* a calmness and confidence doubly striking when it is contrasted with the impatience and distrusts with which we view Braggs inaction. Rosecranz is in an almost impregnable position, we now hear, in spite of the ability which we boasted of possessing of "shelling him out" at pleasure. Bragg's is equally so & the two generals stand with bristled feathers like two game cocks, each waiting & wishing for the other to attack. We annoy & cut off the supplies in his rear & "Personne"[185] says that if Bragg is content to wait without risking the gage of battle, Rosecranz will fall into his hands. *may–be–so*! When the sky falls "Bragg will catch larks."

The Alabama is again at work, capturing and destroying Yankee shipping. The Florida too has been distinguishing herself, as the Yankee rates of Marine Insurance testify. Have been reading a pleasant account of our Penn Campaign from the pen of an English Officer published in Blackwood.[186] His sympathies are decidedly with us & the admiration he expresses for Lee and Longstreet is peculiarly grateful coming from an English source. He ridicules the jubilant feeling of the North—says they are grateful not for Victory which they did not get but because the Army of the Potomac was not so badly whipped as before. He compliments the behavior of our troops in not retaliating on the enemy the horrors which we had undergone in the highest manner; says it was wonderful that our discipline admirable, etc., etc.

In this connection I must relate an anecdote which the narrator had from the lips of the officer. When in Penn he stopped at a farm house by which our whole army passed thrice & the woman told him that with one exception our troops had been most civil & polite to her. He expressed regret that any of our men should have forgotten themselves & asked how it was? when she answered that seeing a soldier in her Cherry tree, she went out & asked him to content himself with eating the cherries to which he was welcome but not to break the branches as he was doing, when he answered her & told her to go back in the house & that if she did not let him alone that he would tell General Lee on her!

The officer replied "Well madam if you can give me his name or that of his corps perhaps he will find that some one will tell General Lee on him." When she said that she did not know his name or to what Regt he belonged—that it was a *coloured gentleman who spoke* thus to her & she never asked his name! Think of it! The only person in that vast army which thronged past her door

---

[185]"Personne" was the pseudonym of Felix Gregory De Fontaine, army correspondent of the *Charleston Courier*. Charles N. Baxter and James M. Dearborn (comps.), *Confederate Literature: A List of Books and Newspapers, Maps, Music, and Miscellaneous Matter Printed in the South During the Confederacy, Now in the Boston Athenaeum* (Boston: Boston Athenaeum, 1917), 93.

[186]"An English Officer" [Garnet Joseph Wolseley], "A Month's Visit to the Confederate Headquarters," *Blackwood's Magazine*, XCIII (January, 1863), 1-29.

who was rude to her was a saucy negro who had a white southern man been by would in all probability have been thrashed for it with one of the limbs of the tree he had broken! It speaks volumes for our soldiers.

My sisters are with me so that I have now a large family, no less than 9 white souls besides ourselves in number. Was yesterday at the funeral of Mr Peter Smith's second child, a little girl 7 or 8 years of age.[187] She died most suddenly and sadly of Diptheria after great suffering. With death so rampant throughout the country, when young men in the bloom & promise of life are cut off by scores, it seems wrong to mourn for a child; but parents I suppose do not reason *thus*; they only *feel* & ask the old question "is their any sorrow like to my sorrow"?[188]

October 21, 1863

Yesterday came news of the battle of Bristow Station in which Cooke's and Kirkland's N C Brigades lost one 500 the other 650 killed & wounded. Shameful mismanagement somewhere which permitted a retreating army to ambush & cut up thus two Brigades & thus to capture 5 peices of cannon. Cooke says his support was a mile in the rear & he in the meantime was exposed to a heavy front & flank fire from men posted behind a R R embankment & on the skirt of a pine thicket. The lagging supporters coming up at length the Yankees were driven off to their main body, we re-capturing one of the guns we had lost.

In this engagement I greive to say that my nephew Capt Thos D Jones 27 N C was wounded in the side. His mother got a letter from him last night telling her that he was in the officer's Hospital in Richmond, severely but not dangerously wounded, that he had telegraphed to his wife to come to him, that he did not know where she would carry him, to her brother in law's in Oxford[189] or here, & that he was comfortable & well cared for, and urging her not to be uneasy about him. All say well, but Ah! the cruel anxiety that lies beneath it! What fear of Erysipels, of Hospital Gangrene, of ill effects from his long journey, and other misfortunes, the dread of which can be averted only by a firm and unwavering Faith! We sent off Owen this morning with both letters & Telegrams, urging him so soon as he could be moved to come at once to us & in a few days we hope to welcome him. Meade is retreating in great confusion, say the papers. This affair at Bristow does not, however, look much like it. We have captured many prisoners but as yet no stores or munitions of

---

[187]Peter Smith's daughter, Susan Evans Smith, died on October 17, 1863. She was six or seven years old. Smith and Smith, *History of Trinity Parish*, 86, 101.

[188]Lamentations 1:12a.

[189]Martha Ann (Pattie) Skinner Jones's sister, Catherine Leigh Skinner, married Robert Lassiter and resided in Oxford. Because her home in Perquimans County was behind enemy lines, Pattie often stayed with the Lassiters in Oxford. Information from records supplied by Francis E. Winslow of Rocky Mount, hereinafter cited as Francis E. Winslow Records.

war. The papers claim that we will annihilate Meade before he reaches Washington but nous verrons.

Father & Mama left us this morning for their home on the river. We shall ere long, God willing, follow them & be settled I hope for the winter.

OCTOBER 24, 1863

Anxiously looking for news from Tom Jones which, however, has not yet reached us. The usual shelling only before Charleston, principally on our side, annoying the enemy's working parties. An ominous silence from Chattanooga & a cessation on our part of the boasting & threats of what Bragg could at pleasure do to Rosecrans, which to my disgust has filled our papers latterly. They are beginning to find out that "Holdfast" is a "better" "Dog" than "Bragg." "*A little more grape—Captain* Bragg."[190] How much harm has that reputed speech of old Taylor's (for both Bragg & himself deny that he made it) done us! It made Bragg's reputation, gave him a wife, and to the nation an incompetent general. How many lives hung on those idle words, "A little more grape, Captain Bragg"! The affair at Bristow Station was more serious than at first supposed. Two of our Brigades, Cooke's & Kirkland's, blundered upon two whole Army Corps of Meades & were in consequence sadly cut up. Cook, Kirkland, & Posey—all Brigadiers—are wounded. Cooke badly—our loss heavy. The Yankees a[re] jubilant over Meade's retreat in which they claim to have outwitted Lee. He has certainly escaped, but Lee has 1500, he 400 prisoners. Lee cannot follow further on account of the wasted state of the country, a wilderness & a desert with food for neither man or beast, & his lines of communication are too long to be kept up at this season with such roads as we shall soon have, whilst Meade's rear rests on his Depot at Washington. Strange, however, for an invading Army to exult thus over a mere *escape*. Their joy at that makes them forget that they promised themselves "*to winter in Richmond.*"

The Ohio & Penn elections have gone for the Republicans, Vallandigham beated by 50,000 majority. True that both bribery & the bayonette were used freely to effect it, but those are weapons which Lincoln will have at his command next fall as fully as now & by their influence he will occupy his seat for another four years.

Our trust is only in our God & our own right arm. I never hoped anything from Northern sentiment, so I am neither despondant or disappointed now that we have not got it. The Yankee will make Peace when he is compelled. Then "Ah! my brother, how I have & do love you! Give me your trade as before! You are welcome to my notions."

---

[190]Shakespeare, *Henry V*, act 2, sc. 3, line 55. "And hold-fast is the only dog, my duck." The order requesting "a little more grape" has been attributed to Gen. Zachary Taylor (1784-1850). Bartlett, *Familiar Quotations*, 552.

Yesterday came Capt Cooke, Capt Graves, & Lieut Elliot to dine. They told us that the Gunboat had been towed up to Halifax to be finished at a heavy expense to government, but that little great man Com Lynch could not get a house large enough for his dignity short of the town & that bag of wind, Sec Mallory, listened to him in preference to men of sense & capacity; but he is so stuffed with conceit, so utterly empty headed himself, that I suppose he cannot distinguish good counsel from bad. I have seen this Sec Mallory, seen & heard him, & he is just the man to be blinded by a dose of flattery skilfully administered. He is emphatically as I said before "a bag of wind." The boat is to be named the "*Albemarle.*" God grant that she may free her namesake Albemarle Sound from Yankee sway!

OCTOBER 26, 1863

News yesterday from Tom Jones. He is not so well as he had hoped. His wife is with him & he will be here so soon as he can travel. Heard of another wounded soldier, brother of one of our neighbors, just at home from the Army in Tennessee, very poor & destitute of every comfort. Sent what I could to him & Patrick will go himself & see what we can do for him.

Yesterday, God be praised, my husband was preserved from injury altho for a few moments in great danger. He was driving James' horse in the buggy when he became frightened, misbehaved, & attempted to run; but being checked in his desire, he reared upright & losing his balance fell heavily to the earth. The shafts of the buggy breaking at an opportune moment threw his weight to the side & instead of his falling backward upon Mr E, as every one thought he must do, he fell on his side making a complete wreck of the vehicle. God make me thankful for this renewed instance of His Kind Providence. A Telegram signed R E Lee tells us that Gen Imboden has captured the garrison at Charlestown taking possession of the place. Prisoners number 430 besides arms & munitions of war. The Mississippi is anything but a free highway to Yankee transports; not one has yet reached New Orleans in safety. Their Insurance Offices still refuse to Insure at any payable rate. So much for their manifesto! Habeus Corpus has been suspended throughout the entire North. Seward may now "touch his little bill" and arrest who he likes with impunity. Matters in statuo quo before Charleston & no news whatever from Chatanooga.

Sue left us yesterday. She is a fine sensible girl & I shall miss her society greatly. The tithe Law[191] divides with the much vexed "Currency question" every ones thoughts & conversation. The former is a source of never failing

---

[191]The tithe tax, a tax-in-kind, required farmers to reserve one tenth of their yield from certain crops for the use of the Confederacy. The enumerated crops included wheat, corn, oats, rye, buckwheat or rice, potatoes, sugar, molasses, cured hay and fodder, cotton, wool, tobacco, peas, and other produce of a similar nature. Randall and Donald, *Civil War and Reconstruction,* 257-258.

mystery & annoyance to Cuffee. Anything so impersonal as the Government they cannot understand, so Henry makes it of the masculine gender. He "does not begrudge" *him* some of the corn & fodder because he is doing all he can to keep the Yankees away from here. *He* shall have some, etc. Rather more liberal than another negro of whom I recently heard who was charged by his master to put aside every *tenth* load of oats for the Government & on being asked if he had done so replied with great exultation, "No! he aint got none from here. Dere aint no ten loads cause I cram 'em all in the nine loads! Dere aint no ten loads left for him"!

OCTOBER 28, 1863

News today that Rosecranz has been superceded & "two fools," as the Examiner calls them, put in his place—i.e., Thomas in his immediate command & Grant over the whole department of the South West. Grant was successful before Vicksburg, so we should say "Great may I call him for he conquered me," but we, none of us, consider him equal to "Old Holdfast" (Rosecranz) & rejoice that the Yankees do not know when they have a good General! Long may they rest in ignorance!

A thrilling escape of Stuarts is given in today's papers. During Meade's late retreat, he with two thousand men was on reconnoisance between Warrenton & Catlett's Station. On reaching the latter place on Tuesday they found heavy bodies of the enemy's infantry moving along the R R to Manassas. They accordingly wheeled & attempted to retrace their steps to Warrenton, but on reaching a road which crossed their route leading from Manassas to Warrenton they found this road also occupied with heavy columns of the enemy. Night came on as they reached this road, & hearing the heavy tramp of the enemy's infantry & the rumble of their artillery in front of them, Gen Stuart withdrew his command into a thicket of old field pines, hoping that they would pass him by unnoticed & leave the road clear to Warrenton. They passed so near that the word of command & even ordinary conversation could be distinctly heard by our men. Any accidental sound, the discharge of a pistol for instance, would have been fatal to them so much were they outnumbered.

A council of War was hastily called & it was determined to abandon the Artillery, to divide the cavalry into six columns, & with the edge of their swords to cut their way through the enemy's ranks & to rejoin Gen Lee. But on reflection Stuart resolved not to desert his nine peices of Horse Artillery, but calling for Volunteers determined to abide where he was & to send to Lee for re-inforcements. Three men stepped forth at his call, their names not given, & disguising them with infantry Knapsacks he directed them to fall into the enemy's column, to cross it, & make their way to Warrenton & tell General Lee "to send some of his people to help him out." They obeyed orders & reached Warrenton in safety.

In the meantime the last Division of the enemy halted & bivouacked opposite Stuart, within one hundred and fifty yds of his position, so close indeed that they could hear the Yankees pouring out oats to feed their horses. During the night two of Meade's officers straggled into our line & were taken prisoners. One of them said—"All right Gen, we sup with you tonight; tomorrow you dine with us," so sure was he that Stuart would be captured! At daylight Stuart was informed by the cracking of our skirmishers rifles that Lee had received his message & was sending "some of his people" to his assistance. So as Lee's advancing columns attracted the enemy's attention in front he opened upon them in the rear with Grape & Canister & in the confusion consequent upon so unexpected an attack he limbered up his artillery & giving the word "Charge," dashed through the enemy's lines & rejoined Lee in safety, leaving one hundred & eighty of the enemy dead on the field.

An escape so narrow has not been recorded since the war began & vexed indeed will that Yankee commander be when he learns near what strange bedfellows he slept that night! I have mentioned Stuart's victory over Kilpatrick on the 19th, therefore do not now allude to it again. In this retreat & pursuit we lost 1,000 men killed, wounded, & prisoners & in our turn taken *two thousand* prisoners. Of their killed & wounded we have no means of judging & their late Surgeon Gen Hammond has received too severe a lesson recently to permit his successor to fall into his error & permit it to leak out from his office. I preserve a correspondence between our Commissioners for the Exchange of prisoners on the treatmen Morgan & his men met with, which speaks for itself and tells the same old tale of Yankee meaness and Yankee lying—B.[192] What a nation!

Yesterday Mr E went out Deer Hunting & the party was so fortunate that he brought me home a fine fat haunch as his portion of the spoils—"finer or fatter ne'er ranged in a forest or smoked in a platter"!

Besides the romance of the thing, the reminiscences of Robin Hood & Friar Tuck it awakens, the addition to my larder is a consideration with beef at 50 cts and turkey's $10 a peice, & we with *nine* in family!

October 31, 1863

Lincoln has, we see, called for an additional 300,000 Volunteers to keep up the "Union Army" & to preserve the "glorious Union." Yankee Volunteers will, however, be like Glendower's "spirits from the vasty deep" and we may well ask him Hotspur's pertinent question, "but will they come when you do call for them"?[193]

---

[192]This correspondence was not located in the diary.

[193]Shakespeare, *King Henry IV*, part 1, act 3, sc. 1, lines 53, 55.

The cartel for the exchange of prisoners is virtually suspended by the double dealing & duplicity of the Yankees. Stanton, it appears, is opposed to any exchange whatever, thinking to "deplete" our armies by retaining the prisoners they take. We have, however, the advantage in point of number just now, however, & the question how to feed them is beginning to be a serious one to us. There are four thousand in the City of Richmond & five thousand at Belle Isle & still they come.

Our country is full of rumours of a Yankee advance. Some have it by way of the Roanoke, others by Tarrboro. Whichever it may be, the military are on the alert troops moving in hot haste to Tarrboro & Greenville. Capt Graves & his command are, to our sorrow, ordered to the latter place—there being no immediate prospect of the Gunboat's being finished. Com Lynch, that little great man, is ordered to Wilmington & has interest enough to get the iron intended for the 'Albemarle' transferred along with him to that point to be put on a gunboat in process of construction there. It was originally brought from Wilmington so that the freight on it going & coming & the expenses incident to so many handlings will make it mount up to $5 per lb. before it is finally fixed in its place! But what can we expect of a pudding headed bag of wind like Sec Mallory & a man who has weakened the little judgment he originally possessed by opium eating, as Com Lynch has done, when they meet in conjunction. "Woe worth the fate!—Woe' worth the day"! [194]

No news from Chattanooga. Yankee like, our press is hugging the fond conceit that Rosecranz will soon be "*starved out.*" The boasts of our ability to shell him out at pleasure have grown "small by degrees & beautifully less." Now we will soon *starve him* into submission. We shall see! But I forget *Rosecranz* is gone. *Thomas* it is who is to perish or surrender. The enemy before Charleston have resumed the offensive. A furious cannonade has been opened from the Monitors, Gregg and Wagner, upon the sea face of Sumter without, however, a single casualty on our side. They have renewed, too, their attempt to bombard Charleston. The "Swamp Angel," as they called their gun which burst after the fifth shot, having been replaced by another, a round shot was thrown into the city which struck the *Union* Bank without, however, injuring any one. Ominous that, that the only *Union* thing in Charleston should receive the first fire! This gun is, too, reported as having burst, being unable to stand the charge of powder required to send a ball such a distance. England has filled the measure of her partiality and injustice by issuing an order stopping the egress of five Rams which were being built in her Dock Yards on our account. She says nothing of the munitions of war, the guns, powder, etc., so freely shipped to our enemies; but when aid to us is the question her eyes, which were so resolutely closed before, are suddenly wide open & she sees with

---

[194]Scott, *Lady of the Lake*, canto 1, stanza 9, line 166. "Woe worth the chase, woe worth the day. . . ."

horror the slightest stain on her neutrality. *Neutrality*! Heaven save the mark! Faugh! Lord Russel's shameless duplicity disgusts me! God forbid that ever he or his inherit Woburn![195]

Sad news from Norfolk. Dr Wright has been executed for the unproven offence of shooting a Yankee officer who was insulting the women and children of Norfolk. Even could they have proved the deed *Justifiable Homicide* is the only verdict which an unpacked Jury could have found, but Lincoln and his officials do not do such things by halves. Like Mr Kirkpatrick they "mak sicker" & consumate their bloody work. But we are told that "The blood of the martyrs is the seed of the Church"[196] & if so, every drop of the blood thus inhumanly shed by our enemies will rise up against them, spring up Cadmus–like in armed men who will drive them from the soil they thus desecrate. This judicial murder has excited a deep feeling amongst us & if any thing was needed to intensify our hatred & bitterness to the "loathed Yankee" this has done it. Open war we can stand but this mockery of justice eats like a canker worm into our hearts & poisons our whole blood against them. They attempt now in their pursuits to villify & ridicule their victim. They but bind us the closer to him!

I have received through our County man, Mr Nicholson, who was in Jackson Miss when it occurred, a full & authentic account of the whipping of Mrs Ford by a Yankee officer, with the horrible addition that she was also under their auspices whipped by two of her own servants. She was left by them one mass of gore & blood & tho still alive when Mr N left her life was despaired of by her physician & friends. God be thanked the citizens of the county succeeded in taking the two negroes & Mr N saw them hung in Jackson. Would that I could get the name of the officer, but it was a Dutch name & Mr Nicholson could not recall it. I hope yet to do so! *Every* nerve & fibre of my frame tingles as I think of it! Increase my *faith* O God! Increase my faith! Thou seest this wickedness & in thine own good time Thou wilt punish it! Let me not murmer because I see not the end. Let me repeat *Deo Vindice*, the motto on our national seal—"Deo Vindice"! In Thy sight let all the earth keep silence!

Rev Mr Walkup, chaplain to a Va Regt, who was here a short time since told me a peice of their petty theivery which before such outrages as that pales to nothing, but I will record it as an instance of Yankee meanness only. He vouched for the story, having it from the lips of the lady whom he knew well as

---

[195]Lord John Russell (1792-1878), first earl of Kingston Russell, was the third son of the Duke of Bedford whose chief family seat was Woburn in Bedfordshire. The house had descended in the family from the first Earl of Bedford, John Russell (ca. 1486-1555), who had received the earldom in recognition of his services to the Tudor family. The earldom became a dukedom in 1694. *Webster's Biographical Dictionary*, 1292-1293, 1294.

[196]Quintus Septimius Tertullian (ca. 155-225), *Apologeticus*, 50. Bartlett, *Familiar Quotations*, 143.

a person of high & upright conduct & great probity. She resided near Alexandria, Va & when the war broke out was travelling in Europe. On her return she was detained some time in New York owing to the impossibility of getting transportation or a passport through the enemies lines. She had heard that her house had been sacked & plundered by the high minded Yankees & one day meeting in society a lady with a dress on that looked very familliar to her, she ventured to ask her "where she had got it."

"Oh!," said she "where did I get this?" "*This*," taking hold of it, "is one of our *Southern trophies*! _____ sent it to me from Va." A few more questions sufficed to convince her that *the ladies* friend had been one of the party who pillaged her house & that the dress in question *was her own*, which she had left in her wardrobe at home when she sailed for Europe. Just *think of that*! I see by the way that Lincoln has rewarded the piano theif Gen Rufus King with a mission to Rome. As he is fond of music perhaps he wishes to hear the "Miserere."[197]

Mr E. has been to see the wounded soldier I spoke of & finds him in want of everything. He was wounded at Chickamauga & his Mother being in Tenn in the enemies lines he came here to a sister whom he has not seen since he was seven years of age. She, poor woman, is a widow with several little children to support and has as much as she can do to effect it. They are literally without a comfort & he with a hole in his thigh into which one can almost get his fist. Please God he shall want henceforth for nothing that we can give him. All else should be provided her. God make me thankful that my lines are cast in such pleasant places & that I want for nothing.

NOVEMBER 13, 1863

Nearly a fortnight since I have opened this book & what a fortnight of sorrow and distress! On Sat the 31st of Oct as Rachel & I were walking in the garden came Sister Betsy after us reading a letter from Pattie containing good news from her son Thomas. Whilst we were listening to it my little maid servant Betsy came to say that Master wanted me directly. I stayed but the conclusion of the letter & with a heart full of thankfulness & gratitude retraced my steps to the house. One glance at Mr E was sufficient! I saw "bad news" stamped on every feature & even attitude. He placed in my hands a letter to him, also from Pattie, urging him to come on to her directly, that the Surgeons had pronounced Tom in a hopeless state, the ball having passed through the Kidneys. This letter was one day later than the first. Our preparations were soon made & in half an hour we were in the carriage on our way to the R R. We were fortunate enough to catch the train & after a most anxious and fatiguing journey reached Richmond about sunrise on Sunday,

---

[197]The *Miserere*, the fifty-first Psalm, is so called because of the beginning words "Have mercy upon me, O God." Benét, *Reader's Encyclopedia*, 728.

the 1st of Nov. We drove at once to the Officer's Hospital, No 4—10th St & to our inexpressible releif found Thomas still living, tho in a state of the last degree of exhaustion after a night of incessant hemorrhage. He had bled to the verge of sinking & the Surgeons could not give one drop of either stimulant or tonic for fear of exciting arterial action. They told us plainly that his chance for life was but small, that the first point was to reduce the pulse which, weak as it was, beat at 200!! A recurrence of hemorrhage *was certainly fatal*. He *might* survive otherwise—had he vitallity enough left to rally after so great a loss of blood, but he was young & in God's hands. So passed Sunday.

That night his sufferings were intense from obstructions in the bladder. Every ten or fifteen minutes they would recur but I never heard him murmur or complain. On Monday he was to the astonishment of all better & his hopes were high of a recovery. Under the influence of Verraltria(?) his pulse sank & tho weak his surgeons were more hopeful about him. On Tuesday night he was so evidently sinking that Mr Edmondston considered it his duty to tell him that he might die at any moment. His calmness & self possession did not for one moment forsake him. He said he did not know he was so ill, thanked his Uncle, said he did not wish to be deceived & asked if he was then dying. His Uncle told him "No," but that he was so weak that he knew not at what moment he might sink and that if he had any wishes to express he had better not leave it until he became weaker. Accordingly he disposed of his worldly affairs, leaving all that he had to his wife Patty, in the hearing of us all, mentioned some little matters that he wished attended to, & in the handsomest manner gave to Lieut Skinner[198] (his brother-in-law—and first Lieut) his promotion, telling him that since he had been in Richmond he had bought a pr of Shoulder Straps, which he wished him to take, that he had rather he should have them than any one else. His calmness & self possession never for one moment forsook him & with a deep humility of soul, relying only on the merits & mediation of his Saviour did he turn to God, confessing his sins & imploring his mercy. The next day the Surgeons pronounced him no worse & as there was no recurrence of hemorrhage our hopes rose & he became sanguine of recovery.

But why dwell upon the events of that sad week? We fluctuated between hope & fear until midnight of Thursday when he was evidently dying. His brother in Law was forced to leave him on Friday morning, dying tho he was, having already stretched his leave to the last moment. This day he took a last farewell of us all separately. To us he spoke of the affection he had always entertained for us, commended his young wife to our care & protection, & requested her to return home with us to remain at least until such time as her Mother could come out of the enemy's lines.

---

[198]Benjamin S. Skinner of Perquimans County was a captain in Co. F, Twenty-seventh North Carolina Regiment. Moore, *Roster of North Carolina Troops*, II, 420.

To her he had previously spoken (during the night of that dreadful hemorrhage—before our arrival). He had told her that her Mother was old, her brother in the Army, and unable to help her, that he had known his uncle (Mr E) from childhood, that he had never failed or even disappointed him, & that to him he wished her to look for advice and assistance when he should be gone. We promised him always to befriend her & assured him that so long as we had a home she should, when she desired to, share it with us.

His parting with his sister Rachel was particularly affecting. That with his young wife is too sacred for me to touch on! During the morning I prayed with him, commending his soul to God, & telling him that he was so weak that I feared to tire him & should not again pray but at his request. He thanked me & from that time so long as he could speak he was constantly asking his Uncle or I to read a Psalm, a hymn, or to pray. His Uncle read him the Hymn "Just as I am," when he joined in the last line—"O Lamb of God I come! I come!"—of every verse—& again the same thing in the hymn "Thy will be done." These two, with "Rock of Ages," he frequently asked for.

About midnight on Friday night it was evident he could live but for a few moments when suddenly a fine band of music struck up as it seemed, in the silence of the night, immediately under the window. It was, however, a serenade in honor of the Presidents return to Richmond we were told. At first it shocked and revolted us terribly, but as we noted its effect on him our feelings under went a change. So long as the music lasted he lay quietly peacefully breathing his last. When it, however, ceased his struggles recommenced, to be again soothed by the music! It was a scene never to be forgotten. The dying man emaciated to the last degree beyond speech but evidently not of hearing quietly breathing his life out, we hanging, as it were, on his every breath & the whole room filled with the strains of that rich music! At last to all appearance all was over, his last sigh drawn, when his wife in an agony of greif called on him "to stay just for one *moment. Tom, my Tom! Just for one moment!*" When to the surprise of all he opened his eyes, fixed them on her, & attempted to speak & died with his last glance upon *her!*

Poor young thing, her greif was heart rending. I have often heard of the eloquence of greif, but never did I realize it untill then. She recounted how little she had seen of him, how long life would be without him, & dwelt on her sorrow in a strain of deep pathos which melted every heart. Poor young creatures! Married the 1st of last Jan., separated by the rude fortune of war five days after, to meet again & only for a few days in May & again for a few more in Oct, & then for the third & last time when she was summoned to attend on his death bed & to receive his last farewell in an Hospital. Their whole married life spent in each other's society could be compressed into three weeks!

His wishes with regard to his burial were that when Peace came he should be laid beside his father in Perquimmans &, with the sole exception of not being in the mean time buried in Richmond, he left all to his wife's direction. She preferred our bringing the body home with us, where we could watch over & attend to his grave. So making all our preparations we left Richmond with it on Sat afternoon & reached home on Sunday the eighth, & on Monday we consigned it to the Grave in our little Country Church Yard, there to remain until Peace once more smiles on our land when his last wishes will be religiously carried out.

His wife, mother, & sister are still with us, so we are a sorrow stricken family. The calls upon our sympathy have been so great that I feel almost worn out mentally & bodily, for during the week we were in Richmond we never undressed save for a change of clothing nor slept more than two consecutive hours. I cannot close this account of my poor nephew without a tribute to the Hospital & to the kindness he received whilst there. He was in the Officer's Hospital No 4—10th St under the supervision of Mrs Lewis Webb & the Surgical direction of Dr Reid.[199]

Mrs Webb is a lady in every sense of the word, of rare beauty, & of delightful manners which at once command respect & excite affection. She has given her voluntary services to the Hospitals since the commencement of the War, first at a private's Hospital, and now to the officers. Thomas had every attention & kindness shown him & in view of the medical attendance he received & the services of an experienced nurse, one accustomed to gun shot wounds, I do not hesitate to say that he was better off than he would have been at home. When the no of patients admit it, the friends of the sufferer are allowed to remain with him day & night. His wife & Mother, accordingly, never left him but took their meals in the house, paying for the privilege only $3 per diem, whilst the patients are charged but $2. Mr E, Rachel, and myself had rooms & took our meals at the Powhattan Hotel close by. We occupied the rooms but in name as we did not sleep there for a single night, using them only to dress in. The charge there was $10 per diem but in view of the errand on which we came & the little use we made of the house, when Mr E came to settle our bill, the proprietor insisted on charging us half price only, so instead of $244 we paid but $122 for one weeks board.

But to return to the Hospital & its arrangements, Mrs Webb was every thing that woman or friend could be to us & the tenderness & kindness of her manner added tenfold to the obligation she conferred upon us. Mr Crisswell, the Ward Nurse, was indefatigable; day and night it was the same thing, ever cheerful & attentive. The wonder was to us when he slept, particularly when we remembered that Thomas was but one out of numerous patients under his

---

[199]Mrs. Edmondston was probably referring to Dr. James B. Read of Savannah, Georgia, who was a Confederate surgeon on duty in Richmond in 1863. Horace H. Cunningham, *Doctors in Gray: The Confederate Medical Service* (Baton Rouge: Louisiana State University Press, 1958), 225, 232, 236.

charge, three of whom were desperately ill, one actually dying whilst we were in the Hospital! His name was Russel from Alabama & he was without friend or associate with him & his disease, Typhoid Pneumonia, requiring the closest care. Another, Lieut Bridgers,[200] from this State had two wounds, one of which had paralyzed him & the other had passed through his side, & he lay with a Minie ball *actually in his lungs*. It was impossible to extract it & the wonder was that he lived at all & yet his sister assured me that Mr Crisswell was as attentive to him as he could be.

Thomas sense of his kindness was such that he desired a handsome bequest to be given him after his death, saying he would have died long before & suffered trebly but for him and accordingly Mr E, after consulting with his wife & Mother gave him in Capt & Mrs Jones name $200, accompanying with a note in which he expressed their & our gratitude.

Mrs Wilkerson, the Ward Matron, was also most kind & attentive & even the servants testified their sympathy. The Hospital is kept beautifully clean, scouring & dry rubbing apparently going on all day, and the fare of the patients & guests is as good as the market affords. Mrs Webb told me that she rarely received donations from any one, the general impression being that "it being an Officer's Hospital stood in need of none, that the Officers were rich, they could pay for what they wanted whilst the poor privates, who could not, got everything given them. This she assured me was a great mistake; that when in charge of the private's Hospital she frequently returned to the Government $5000 per month from the commutation money allowed by it for the sick soldier whilst now she had always the greatest difficulty & was sometimes unable to make both ends meet for the same time. The Government furnishes the building, the Surgical assistance, & the attendants who are detailed from the army. Every other expense has to be met by the per diem, including Lights, fuel, & provisions besides bedding & in short everything else. We promised to do what we could for her & she will send an Agent out in a short time with transportation to buy & to receive contributions. So noble an institution should not be allowed to fall through.

On Tuesday Mr E was quite sick & on Wednesday kept his bed with a severe cold with bilious & rheumatic symptoms, but today I am happy to say he is releved & up again. We went on Tuesday to Ringwood to bring a relative & friend of Mrs Jones jr to her—a Miss Hoskins[201]—with whom she had been educated and brought up. She arrived on Wednesday & her presence is already a great comfort & alleviation to her. She also remained with us to assist in cheering up Rachel & she does much to assist me in soothing her.

---

[200]Sidney H. Bridgers, a second lieutenant in Co. A, Forty-seventh North Carolina Regiment, died November 15, 1863, from wounds received at Bristoe Station. Clark, *Histories of the North Carolina Regiments*, III, 84; Moore, *Roster of North Carolina Troops*, III, 326.

[201]Ringwood is a community in the southwest portion of Halifax County, west of Enfield. Sallie Hoskins of Perquimans County was a niece of Baker Hoskins. See footnote 215, 1863. William S. Powell, *The North Carolina Gazetteer* (Chapel Hill: University of North Carolina Press, 1968), 415.

And now for a little public news. From Chattanooga our accounts are most gloomy. Every mind seems prepared to hear that, spite of all the loud boastings of what he could at pleasure do, that Bragg will soon be "*falling back.*" Thomas has been heavily re-inforced & commands Lookout Valley & is shelling the mountain of that name. He has reopened his communication & instead of being annihilated threatens to advance on Bragg. The country rings with curses loud & deep both of Bragg & Mr Davis for keeping him in command. The pressure brought to bear upon the President in order to induce him to remove him is prodigious, yet nevertheless he resists it & obstinately persists, in the face of evidence of incompetency which is, to say the least, *overwhelming*, in risking the Cause & the *Country* even in the hands of a General who has already cost us rivers of the best blood in our land which is "as water spilled upon the ground." God sees the end & He only can bring success out of so discordant & jarring elements! Generals at variance with their Commander, soldiers who have lost confidence in his abilities & even his courage (for D H. Hill has openly charged him with a *personal want of it*), Division Commanders petitioning to be removed & threatening to throw up their Commissions, & even (as is the case with Lieut Gen Polk) refusing to serve under him, a country loudly clamoring against his incapacity & want of Generalship—such are some of the obstacles in the way of our success. Mr Davis is in fact his only friend!

Before Charleston the enemy have been unusually active, having recommenced the Bombardment of Sumter with greater fury than ever & with a signal failure to accomplish more than the entire destruction of the upper works. The casemates protected by sand mounds & bags remain intact & we are assured that the stern old Fort can resist it indefinitely.

We have had a serious disaster in Northern Va. Two Brigades—Hoke's N C & Hays' Lou—being on picket on the North bank of the Rappahanock were surprised by a sudden motion of the enemy, surrounded by an entire Army Corps (Sedgwicks), & after a desperate resistance & being almost cut to peices in the encounter, were the greater portion of them captured, 600 only escaping out of both Brigades. Our entire loss, killed, wounded, & prisoners, mounts up to 1500 (fifteen hundred). This coming as it does on the sad affair at Bristow Station has been a severe blow to us & makes us if possible more deeply lament the loss of Jackson, who was never surprised or taken at unawares. But God's will be done! He saw fit to take him; we should not murmur.

NOVEMBER 16, 1863

Yesterday Sister Betsy & Rachel left us for father. I very busy today getting ready for our semi annual move to the River. Letters from J N E tell us that the late "surprise was complete," our loss 1500. He says "we have returned to our old line on the Rapid Ann after a most precipitous retreat from the Rappahanock." The letter is dated at "Orange Court House," a sad commencement for a winter campaign, but—Courage!—Courage!

NOVEMBER 24, 1863

On Friday the 20th just as we were in the hustle & confusion of moving from Hascosea to Looking Glass who should come in on us but Frank Jones, his Mother, Sister & Aunt Susan accompanying him. He had succeeded in obtaining a short furlough & came on to see Pattie and his Mother. Poor fellow! Tom's death is a deep distress to him & he seems sorely cast down by it. The young folks stayed to dinner & then shutting up the house for the winter we came down to Looking Glass, they escorting us. Scarce were we here when up came Mr Peter Smith & Capt Cook, the former bringing a large Hen Hawk which he had shot at our gate. Acknoledging my debt of a Chicken Pie to serve the time honored demand which the shooter of a Hawk has a right to make upon the nearest House, I had also to thank him for the promptness with which he mended my spectacles for me, at a time too when they were much needed by me.

On Sat came Frank & Rachel to stay all night with Pattie, so what with a houseful & the urgent necessity of getting settled a little before Sunday, I had my hands full also, besides being far from well; but a stout heart & cheerful servants who were both mindful and heedful helped on wonderfully. No news of any interest from either the army in Northern Va or that before Chattanooga. Rumours are rife that Longstreet occupies Knoxville, but we know not whether or not to trust them. The Yankee Secretary of War has issued an order so in accordance with right & justice that we stand amazed as we read it! He upon proof that a Bronze Equestrian Statue stolen from Fredericksburg was the private property of Mr Douglas Gordon of that place orders it to be restored to his sister Mrs [————]. We know not what this portends! So strange is it that we think it must be a harbinger of Peace! The Yankee Government awakening to a sense of justice or paying any regard to the rights of those whose land they have invaded must betoken the advent of the Millenium.

Our Government has been guilty of a foul wrong to our prisoners now in the enemies hands. It has allowed the admission of 40,000 Rations for the Yankee prisoners now in Richmond. This is not only unjust but shortsighted—40,000 Rations will not feed 12,000 prisoners for four days, & yet at that cheap rate does it suffer the Yankee nation to purchase a character ill deserved by it for generosity & magnaminity & admit the pretext on its part to refuse to feed our poor men now exposed to their tender mercies. Rather should Mr Commissioner Ould[202] have said to them in answer to their application to be allowed to send them "No! Gentleman. Exchange we will & gladly, give two of your men for one of ours. Retain your rations & issue them to your returned and exchanged prisoners." But when will we learn dignity or prudence?

The previous bombardment of Sumter still continues. Since the present attack commenced 15,000 shot & shell have been thrown at her, 5,000 of which missed. The whole number including the former attack amounts to 23,000 & still it resists & seems to have the power to hold out. On Friday the 20th an attack was made with launches which met with so warm a reception that they retreated. Three attempts were made in this way all of which failed. Baffled at Sumter the enemy, as in a rage, opened upon the city with 100 parrot guns, but here again their efforts were futile, as the only effect was the killing of a harmless negro woman & slightly injuring a white person. They boast in their Yankee prints that they took St Michel's Spire as a target! The sacralegious Vandals! If the sanctity of the venerable structure could not induce you to spare it, where O ye disciples of Ralph Emerson & Margaret Fuller,[203] where is your sixth, your *aesthetic* sense, the worship of the beautiful? Could not its beauty, rising as it does in simple Majesty, protect it? No! for in their eyes nothing is sacred, not even a church spared by the British in the Revolutionary War, but *that* was a *christian* warfare, our foes were not Yankee.

Made a cap yesterday for Mr Edmondston, quite a triumph in its way, light, warm, & becoming. He said it would not disgrace Parisian hands. O! Mrs Edmondston! busy planting hyacinth roots, getting settled, & knitting gloves for Mrs Webb.

Pattie, poor thing, much distressed. Her outbursts of greif are heart rending. God comfort her! Her cousin Miss Hoskins is a great assistance to me & a most valuable and pleasant addition to our circle, cheerful, high spirited, & unselfish. Her whole aim seems to be to render herself useful & her whole thought for others. They have it under discussion to return to their homes in the North Eastern Counties, now under Butler's rule, but we hope to dissuade them from it.

I forgot to mention that Butler, "the beast," Butler of New Orleans & of Bethel memory has been placed in command of the Yankee department of Va

[202]Robert Ould, a lawyer and acting judge advocate of the Confederate armies prior to 1862, was the Confederate agent for the exchange of prisoners. The arrangement mentioned here is described in Hesseltine, *Civil War Prisons*, 69, 120-123. Hesseltine gives the number of rations as 24,000.

[203]Sarah Margaret Fuller (1810-1850), a native of Massachusetts, was one of America's foremost critics and writers. A strong social reformer and transcendentalist, Fuller taught school, edited the *Dial* with Emerson and George Ripley, wrote critical reviews for the *New York Tribune*, and advocated the equality of men and women. She moved to Rome, Italy, in 1847 where she married Angelo Ossoli and joined him in the 1848 revolution there. After the collapse of the Roman Republic in 1849, she and her husband fled to Florence where they lived for a year before sailing for New York. The Ossolis were drowned at sea when their ship sank off New York in 1850. *Concise Dictionary of American Biography*, 320-321.

& N C with Head Quarters at Fortress Monroe. So we may look for some signal act of barbarity soon, something characteristic, at once *mean*, *cowardly*, & *cruel*.

NOVEMBER 29, 1863

I do try to obey the Psalmist injunction & "not exercise myself in great matters which are too high for me,"[204] but this General, this *Bragg*, & Mr Davis' pertinacity in keeping him in command in spite of his repeated failures try my humility sorely! On the 24th he telegraphs to Gen Cooper, "We have had a prolonged struggle for Lookout Mountain today & sustained considerable loss in one Division. Elsewhere the enemy has only manoevred for position," which is, as the Examiner say, merely an announcement that Thomas is *flanking him*! Next day he tells the whole of his bad fortune, but as I announced his barren Victories in his own words, let me use the same medium to record his pregnant defeats. "*Chickamauga.*" So, mon General, you have fallen back from Chattanooga, concluded not to shell the Yankees out at pleasure. But to go on, "Chickamauga Nov 25, 1863.
Gen S Cooper A, & I Gen [———] "After several unsuccessful assaults upon our line today, the enemy carried the left centre about four o'clock. The whole left soon gave way in considerable disorder. The right maintained its ground repelling every assault. I *am withdrawing all to this point.*" signed—"Braxton Bragg."[205] That is to say, Gen Bragg, you are defeated & instead of shelling have been shelled. "Let not him that putteth on his armour boast as he who putteth it off"![206]

This is a heavy blow to us, one under which the Confederacy staggers to the centre. Yet let us not be discouraged. "Tis of the wave and not the rock." No other official news since, tho Telegrams from Atlanta tell us that the slaughter was terrific & what fills us with the saddest forebodings, that none of the wounded *have as yet been brought in*. Can it be that they were deserted? captured? God in his mercy forbid. We have been cruelly anxious since Thursday when we received the news, but since then (& it is now Sunday) our unfortunate Gen distinguishes himself like the little man in the Spectator "*by a profound silence.*"[207] Nor are our anxieties confined to the South West, for Meade is

---

[204]Psalms 131:1b.

[205]Bragg's report was sent to Gen. Samuel Cooper (1798-1876), the adjutant and inspector general of the Confederacy and the highest ranking officer in the Confederate army. Cooper replied to Bragg on November 30, 1863, and stated that Bragg's "request to be relieved has been submitted to the President, who, upon your representation, directs me to notify you that you are relieved from your command, which you will transfer to Lieutenant-General Hardee, the officer next in rank and now present for duty." *Official Records (Army)*, Series I, XXXI, Part II, 682; Boatner, *Civil War Dictionary*, 175.

[206]Henry Wadsworth Longfellow, *Morituri Salutamus*, stanza 10.

"Let him not boast who puts his armor on
As he who puts it off, the battle done."

[207]*Spectator*, No. 1 (March 1, 1711).

again advancing, apparently with the design of giving battle. Our army occupies the old battlefield of Chancellorsville, saddened to us by the loss of Stonewall Jackson, & is said to be in fine trim & discipline. Heavy canonading was heard by the last accounts at Ely's & Germanna fords, and it was supposed that Meade was endeavoring to cross. *God defend the Right!*

My nephew Thomas Devereux,[208] my brother's eldest son, joined the army last week just in time to flash his maiden sword. God shield and protect him! He was *eighteen* only the middle of this month. Ah! my country! how long will you thus be drained of thy best blood! thy future glory and strength!? Where are our men of education & science, our enlightened Statesmen, our wise Rulers to come from when our youths of eighteen are snatched from their studies, their minds but half disciplined, their intellectual development but half completed, their memories but half stored & thrown into the turmoil of a Camp & left to encounter "idleness or peril"? But courage! courage & faith! God, out of the humblest means, the most discordant elements, can bring forth the most glorious end, the most delightful harmony, & tho my young countrymen may not be so skilled in the learning of Greece & Rome, tho the quadrature of the circle & the Mysteries of the Conic Sections may be a sealed book to them, let us trust that they will bring back from the battle field a *knoledge of men*, of the *secret springs* of the human heart, & that fitted, as they will be by having learned *obedience*, to *govern*, the future of our country in their hands will be both glorious & prosperous; and that *War* whilst she strips from them many a modern refinement & even the wisdom of the schools will gild them with her own barbaric virtues, a lofty contempt of danger and a chivalric devotion to woman as the type of all that is gentle & pure—a spirit of self sacrafice which will make them spring to the defence of the weak, a devotion to their country & her cause which shall haunt them like a passion, a love of honour, and a contempt of all that is mean, which shall be their guiding star through life!

Sally Hoskins left us on Friday the 27th, having paid what was to us a most pleasant visit. Have been very busy since she left knitting her a pr of gloves which Pattie will take to her on Tuesday, for she then leaves us & together do these two demoiselles encounter the perils of brute Butler's savage reign, returning to their homes within the lines, sorely against our wishes and advice, but young folks "maun hae their way," and I hope the change will be of service to Pattie & cheer up her drooping spirits.

---

[208]Thomas P. Devereux, Jr., a student at the Virginia Military Institute, joined the Daniel-Grimes Brigade in 1863 as courier. James Edmondston was the assistant quartermaster for this brigade. Clark, *Histories of the North Carolina Regiments*, IV, 513, 517, 519. Copies of the letters written by Devereux to his family during this time are preserved in the Devereux Papers and in his letterbook in the State Archives.

NOVEMBER 30, 1863

My cousin Fanny Polk,[209] daughter of the Lieut Gen, has been paying a visit to her Uncle (Father), & as she spent some time both in New Orleans when under Butler's rule & also has been frequently at Bragg's head quarters when visiting her father, the reminiscences she brings with her of both places are highly entertaining. Butler actually issued an order in N O making *knitting needles* "Contraband of War," because the ladies occupied themselves knitting socks for the Confederate Soldiers. Knitting needles—contraband of war! What a storm in a Tea Kettle! Her Mother, my Aunt, was forced to go in person to his head quarters to obtain a permit to leave the city. With her went an elderly lady who also wanted a pass who, poor thing, was not only a little deaf but exceedingly sensitive regarding the fact that she was forced to use an ear trumpet & by means of a Fan, P K H F, etc., attempted to conceal it using it only to listen to general conversation. She announced the fact of her deafness & Butler accordingly took a seat close to her so that he could speak in her ear. During the conversation he unfortunately spied the end of the trumpet peeping from under some of its coverings when, in a transport of fear, he started to his feet & in an accent of horror exclaimed, "Good God! Madam" what is that! a Pistol?," putting at the same time several feet between himself & the innocent trumpet. His confusion, or rather the confusion of any other than himself, can be better imagined than described when he discovered the harmless nature of the object of his terror.

Mrs Phillips who was imprisoned for nearly three months on Ship Island was by his orders never left more than *five minutes* at a time without the presence of a *sentinel in her chamber.* Her release was obtained by her husband & friends representing the fact to him that she was *enceint.*[210] When after much influence had been brought to bear on him he magnanimously declared that "the innocent should not suffer with the guilty" & signed an order for her release with the proviso that she be removed from N O. Her treatment had been such, however, that before it came the unfortunate lady had lost the cause of his unwonted clemency, which fact, however, was concealed from him lest he should rescind the order. She had been imprisoned, when residing in Washington, for illuminating her house in honor of the first battle of Manassas. She had during her imprisonment in N O saved her candle ends for the purpose & fortunately hearing of the second battle of Manassas, which took place during her confinement, she at once lighted every one of them, sticking them all about the room & when asked by the sentinel why she did so, she calmly told him it was "the only evidence she could give of her joy at the defeat of the Yankees."

---

[209]Frances Polk (1835-1884) was the daughter of Leonidas and Frances Devereux Polk. She later married Peyton H. Skipworth. See Introduction.

[210]French, "pregnant."

Butler's infamous order no [————] was issued at the instance of & by the *instigation of his wife* in revenge for the contempt with which the Southern women treated her, the only female in N O who called upon her being a noted woman of the town & that at the instigation of some wild young men. Mrs B was in her carriage to return the visit, under the escort of an Aid of her husband's, when he stepping to the public room of the Hotel in which she then lodged to obtain some information as to the way to the address which the woman had left behind her learned the character of the house to which Madame was bound & thus unveiled the trick—hence her ferocity against the real ladies of New Orleans!

Gen B afterwards took possession of the finest private house in the city, driving up with Mrs B to inspect it without warning or notice of any kind to the Mistress of it, the Master being absent. Whilst he was telling the lady down stairs that his occupation of it was a "military neccessity," Mrs Butler went upstairs & rumaged the bed chambers & came into the parlour & announced that she was "surprised to find everything so nice, it really was quite neat, considering, & turning to the lady ordered her "to *remove nothing*," & accordingly in half an hour during which she (Mrs B) remained on the premises. The unfortunate lady of the house was ejected from it with a very *small* portion of her own & her children's wardrobe, Mrs Butler falling heir to all the rest."—& yet Butler *left New Orleans alive!* The men of honour & spirit must all have been in the Army! How long will he live after Peace?

Forrest, Fanny tells us is illiterate & vulgar, a negro trader in his antecedents. He makes no pretension to anything, not even military skill, does not desire a large command, says he can do more with a small one. He told her that his men had taken a vow to spare no Yankee prisoner who was found with anything belonging to a woman upon him. No matter what it was, if it was stolen from a woman, that man never reached head quarters; he was "*lost*" on the way.

"What do you call them thar things you ladies have hanging round your frocks?" he said to her, "them thar things sowed round the bottom like ruffles?" "Flounces do you mean Gen Forrest?" "Yes, Flounces, I beleive you call them. Well my men took a lot of Yankees once & they all had ladies clothes, dresses, shawls, & I do not know what not & my men took the dresses & tore the flounces off & hung the Yankees with 'em instead of with ropes & left them hanging there, too! I tell you when my men are about, the Yankees let the women alone."

Andrew Polk,[211] the youngest brother of the Bishop & an old playfellow of my own, now a gentleman of large fortune in Tenn, had a quantity of silver

---

[211]Andrew Jackson Polk, the son of William and Sarah Hawkins Polk and the brother of Leonidas Polk, resided in Maury County, Tennessee. Joseph H. Parks, *General Leonidas Polk C.S.A.: The Fighting Bishop* (Baton Rouge: Louisiana State University Press, 1962), 14, 68-69.

ware & plate which he with the assistance of a faithful servant secreted on the occupation of the country. The Yankees, coming to the house for plunder & getting wind of the silver, demanded of the negro where his master had hidden it. He refused to tell them. Seizing his little child about four years old, they held it over the well & threatened to drop it in unless he told. Still he refused. They asked him again, repeating the threat. He still persisted in his refusal. They then warned him that *this* was the last time & if he did not *this* time tell, in the child should go; but he steadily refused to answer when, horrible to relate, they dropped it & in the agony of the moment the unfortunate father gratified their cupidity! One of the number caught the child, it is true, after it had fallen out of the father's sight in the well curb, but the effect on him was the same as tho they had killed it.

Whilst I am on the subject of Yankee outrages, I may as well mention here what Pattie & Sally told me occurred within their knoledge in our North Eastern Counties. At the battle of Gettysburg Lee took some Penn Militia with arms in their hands prisoners. Immediately an order was issued for retaliation. So accordingly a squad of armed men came suddenly to Mr Charles Wood's,[212] Pattie's brother-in-law, and at whose house she happened to be staying & ordered him to put on his old militia uniform & come with them. Now Mr Wood was an old U S militiaman, had never borne arms for the Confederate States, but was living peaceably at home. His wife had been confined five days before, & yet these barbarians, in spite, too, of a promise they gave Mrs W not to enter her room, broke it & went up to her bed & gazed in her face! When taxed by Mr W with bad faith he cooly admitted it, saying he wished to see whether it was really a woman. The Monthly nurse who was present, taking the baby out of the cradle held it to him saying "if that was your object, Sir, why not ask me & I could have showed you the baby—I hope now you are convinced"! They ransacked the house, taking Mr W.'s saddle, bridle, & every horse & mule on the premises & mounting themselves made the owner walk, dressed as he was in his U S Militia Uniform, through all the streets in Hertford. Pattie protested against it & fearlessly taxed them with cowardice & urged her brother-in-law not to put on the Uniform, when they answered if he did not they would put it on for him & out of consideration for his wife's condition he yeilded.

The same scene was enacted on the same day at the house of Mr Granberry,[213] another old Militia officer, his wife too having just been confined. The fright she underwent threw her in such a condition that for days her life was despaired of. They took the two gentlemen & sent them prisoners

[212]Charles Wingfield Wood (1829-1906) of Perquimans County was the husband of Mary Elizabeth Skinner (1835-1907), Pattie's sister. Francis E. Winslow Records.

[213]Joseph Gordon Granberry (1822-1889) of Perquimans County was married to Isa Benedict Gordon. Granberry Tucker Records.

to Point Lookout, since when they have been removed to Washington City, & that is all their friends know of them!

In Elizabeth City one Addison White[214] proposed to join a band of Guerrillas & arming himself went at night to a rendezvous where he expected to meet them. The Yankee's had, however, been before him and he found a band of them there who arrested him. After keeping him prisoner for some weeks, threatening daily to shoot him if he did not take the oath, one night about sundown without trial or orders of any kind, a squad of them took him down to the wharf & putting him up as a target, one by one they shot at him until they killed him & refusing to allow his body to be moved, would let no one come near it.

His wife had been in the habit of sending his meals to him by her brother, a lad of twelve years of age, & accordingly next morning prepared & sent his breakfast. On the way the boy met a cart drawn by a negro with the body in it. He ran back home & explained, "O! Sister! sister! Brother Ad! Brother Ad!" Whilst the poor woman was vainly endeavouring to get him to answer her coherently, the cart with her husband's body drove into the yard. That Pattie tells *me she knows to be true*. In the same prison was confined her brother in law, Mr Baker Hoskins,[215] Sally's Uncle. Daily did these fiends offer him the oath & on his refusing it say to him, "Very well! be ready tomorrow at twelve o'clock and we will shoot you as we did Addison White." For three long weeks he lived expecting each day was to be his last when, without known cause, they released him as they had arrested him.

Pattie's brother, Mr James Skinner,[216] was also arrested & that night a party of negroes headed by his foreman, who sometime before had gone to the Yankees, came to his dwelling & suddenly burst open the doors & the first thing Mrs Skinner knew of their presence was their firing pistols through the house. A waiting maid, child of the foreman, slept in a room adjoining her mistress & being frightened ran into the bed chamber from whence she was summoned by the father telling her to get her things & take what she wanted & come with him. Mrs S, on hearing the firing, opened her door & thinking they were Yankees called out to them to behave themselves, that there was no one to make resistance to them, & that such conduct was as useless as it was improper," when one of the negroes answered, "if she did not take he[r] d— head in that door they would blow he[r] d— brains out!" They afterwards learned that Mr S. was arrested at the instance of the negro foreman, who feared & wanted him out of the way. This was the same night on which they went to Mr Newby's house, of which I have before spoken. Mr Newby, poor

[214]Addison White, a twenty-eight-year-old farmer, and Althea, his twenty-year-old wife, resided in Pasquotank County. Eighth Census, 1860, Population Schedule, Pasquotank County, 110.

[215]Baker Hoskins, a cousin of Pattie Skinner Jones, was also her brother-in-law, having married her sister Alethea Skinner (1837-1911). Francis E. Winslow Records.

[216]James Leigh Skinner was the oldest brother of Pattie Skinner Jones. Francis E. Winslow Records.

old gentleman, was dreadfully beaten by them & has since died! How long will our people be called to suffer such wrongs? How long, O Lord, how long?

Mr E was off early this morning in consequence of a message from his 1st Lieut to the effect that they had arrested three Yankees. He found when he got to Clarksville that it had occurred in Mr Mongomery Whitaker's Disct adjoining & that they had been properly disposed of, sent whence they came, which was Danville, being escaped Yankee prisoners. They had walked the length of our land without molestation having their Uniforms covered with a blanket. They made the mistake of killing one of Mongomery Whitaker's hogs & confiding in the Hog feeder, they told him he was free, that they were Yankees come to free all the negroes, & that they could help themselves to what they liked; but the negro, holding fortunately for us, a different system of ethics informed his master of their proceeding—hence their arrest! & whilst I am on the subject of Yankee prisoners, I may as well record the infamous lies with which the whole North rings respecting our treatment of them. They accuse us of *starving* them whilst the fact is that they have the same rations as our men in the field! Their papers are filled with accounts of "Rebel barbarity," but it is only a pretext of Messrs Seward et als to keep up the enthusiasm of the multitude for the war by exciting their hatred against us. They preach a Crusade whose object is to deliver the starving Union prisoners in Richmond, hoping thus to get recruits. If the truth were told, it is our cow gored by their Bull; our unfortunates in their hands are the real sufferers!

DECEMBER 1, 1863

The first day of winter! A winter how full of suffering & anguish to our bleeding country! Today Pattie left us for her home in Perquimans. I have been very busy knitting a pr of gloves with which to surprise Sally & finishing off a pr for Pattie. Glove making is getting to be my trade, as I have now ready to send by today's mail a beautiful pr to Mrs Webb at the Hospital in Richmond.

Went to Father's to dinner & read Gen Lee's dispatch dated Nov 29th in which he says that a "rain storm prevailed yesterday—no movements of any importance by either army. This morning the enemy is deploying in line of battle in our front." So we may at any moment look for news of another battle on the classic field of Chancellorsville. The heavy rain of Sunday must have prevented all offensive movement & the freshets to which the Rapid Ann is peculiarly subject may embarras Meade's calculations, but a battle cannot be far distant. No news from Longstreet & that from Bragg is meagre & dismal in the extreme. The savages before Charleston take St Michel's Spire as a target & Amo writes "prove themselves *good artillerists*." The sacralegious wretches! The bombardment of Sumter flags, the "Swamp Angel," as they call their marsh guns, turning his attention on Charleston. Came home on horseback with Mr E, the first evening we have spent alone together since last April! So we return to our normal condition.

DECEMBER 3, 1863

Very busy dying warp for Mr E's & my own clothes. So we have come to it & are to wear our own homespun! In fact I find that almost all articles of prime neccessity except salt, iron, & paper can be produced at home by us. This ink, for instance, is of my own manufacture & I do not see why it is not as good as the "*boughten*" article. Am turning one of my dresses &, tell it not in Gath, one of Mr E's coats. I shall soon rival Mrs Marrowsmith in the Bachelor of the Albany who we are told "outdid Ovid's Metamorphoses with an old coat or a tarnished curtain."

Heavy news from Bragg again. He is in full retreat towards Dalton. He lost the finest park of Artillery that we have at Lookout Mountain—the Washington. Indeed the Yankees claim to have captured forty peices there, & not content with that he has now lost Fergusson's Battery & most of the waggons belonging to one Division of his Army. He was pursued in force to Ringgold where the enemy attacked his rear, inflicting this damage upon him. The enemy was at length repulsed & he continued his retreat pursued by ten thousand mounted infantry. The country people, God help them, are leaving their homes & retreating with our army, and the roads are nearly impassable. So much for an incapable general & an obstinate President!

The breach of the Cartel is exciting great attention in the newspapers of both countries. I preserve an extract from a New York paper showing that they admit whose the fault is. As to the closing sentence about our treatment of their prisoners, *that* is mere balderdash, written for *effect. They know it to be false.* Per contra I place by it the testimony of Dr Wilson, surgeon of 1st Va Cavalry, recently returned by Flag of Truce, containing his experience of a *Yankee* prison. News from Lee up to the 30th says "no movement of importance by either army yesterday. The enemy is in line on the east side of Mine Run. This army is in position on the West side"—signed R E Lee General. The Examiner tells us that Meade is between Lee & Fredericksburg and that both armies are equidistant from Richmond. On Friday a sharp engagement took place in which we gained a decided advantage, taking a number of prisoners & capturing & destroying an ordnance train of a hundred waggons & much valuable property beside. Johnson's Division of Ewell's Corps was alone engaged & we lost about five hundred killed & wounded, whilst that of the enemy was much more heavy, estimated at three to one. We took many & lost no prisoners. During the fight Rosser's Cavalry Brigade made a dash in their rear capturing & destroying the ordnance train mentioned above. Would that we could have brought if off, as our losses in that line by Blockade Runners captured off Wilmington have recently been heavy. I preserve a copy of a ticket to a Yankee fete—recently given in New Orleans.[217] To what has the Crescent City fallen! Mosby is doing as good service in Meade's rear, capturing waggon trains & picking up prisoners, tho the last is questionable in view of the Yankee refusal to stand to their engagements & fulfil the provisions of the Cartel. Mr Ould, our Commissioner, told them truly when he closed his letter to Meredith,[218] the Yankee one, with the remark that the reason of their conduct was patent: they esteemed our prisoners as more than double the value of their own, a right estimate, for theirs are foreign mercenaries & mean Yankees—the off scouring of their cities.

DECEMBER 4, 1863

No fighting as yet on the Rapid Ann, Meade is it is said fortifying. An Artillery duel took place on the 30th with some slight infantry skirmishing, our loss slight, one officer, Capt Raines,[219] only of the Artillery killed, none hurt. An impression prevails that Meade does not mean to fight unless attacked, his object being only to occupy Lee and prevent reinforcements being sent to Georgia where Bragg, the unlucky or the incapable, still continues to retreat *sternly*, as the Yankees say, pursued by the mounted infantry. We learn that at his own request he was on last Monday releived from command & the command tendered to Lieut Gen Hardee who with great modesty declined it but consented to retain it until another appointment can be made. Who Murad the Unlucky's final successor will be does not yet appear, but whoever he is, he will have a difficult post to fill. To remedy all Bragg's blunders & releive his disasters will take much military ability & a keen insight into *men*. *There* it appears that Mr Davis is deficient.

Fears are now expressed for Longstreet, but not one word have we from him beyond the fact that Knoxville was invested. Sherman has been sent to reinforce Burnside the Christian, so our fears are not without basis. But *Faith*! faith! & courage—by God's help tho all seems dark around us we will yet prevail! God keep us true to ourselves and our *cause*. The Northern papers report the loss by guerrillas of seventeen fine boats on the Mississippi within the last four months valued at seven million, together with sixty lives. "*Free navigation*" that! The Father of Waters is opened with a vengeance! Mrs Winder of Baltimore, mother of Gen Winder, age *85* has been imprisoned in her house in Baltimore under Military surveillance upon charge of corresponding with the South. What next?

---

[217]A copy of the ticket described by Mrs. Edmondston was not located in the diary.

[218]Gen. S. A. Meredith (1816-1874) served as the United States commissioner for the exchange of prisoners from 1863 until 1864, when he returned to active service in St. Louis, Missouri. Boatner, *Civil War Dictionary*, 543.

[219]Capt. Charles I. Raines of the Andrews Artillery Battalion was "killed by a solid shot while fearlessly and ably discharging his duty." *Official Records (Army)*, Series I, XXIX, Part I, 848, 895.

DECEMBER 5, 1863

Saturday—Mr E. at Dawson's X Roads drilling his Company. I & my handmaids busy all day making "auld clarthes look amaist as weel as new"[220] & am wearied to death stitching & fitting! Ah! for the days of dress makers & Tailors!—days I hope not far in the future!

Better news from Georgia, & the mental thermometer has gone up in consequence, so am gay & bouyant once more! Cleburne's Division engaged Osterhause this side of Ringgold driving him back with a loss of 1500 killed, 320 prisoners, & four stand of colours. On their retreat they burned a portion of Ringgold & destroyed the bridge and R R track at Chickamauga. Kelly's Cavalry defeated them, inflicting heavy loss on them at Cleaveland on Wednesday. News reliable but not official that Longstreet has forced Burnside to capitulate. Now for the barber to shave that Christian head as he had Morgan's shaved & a cell for him in a Confederate Penitentiary! Justice is a heaven born virtue, Mrs E, see that you do not allow it to degenerate into vindictiveness!

A new Military department has suddenly sprung up for us like an oasis in the Desert, that of "*West Tennessee.*" Col Richardson commencing with a single Cav Regt has increased it to a Brigade and four Battalions, all mounted & equipped at Abolition expense besides turning over to the Confed Gov. $600,000 worth of arms, clothing, & stores, all captured! He is a thorn in the Yankee side, cutting off R R communication, capturing waggon trains, & keeping a large force fully occupied in looking after him. Walker keeps the Mississippi closed to all but iron clads. The Yankees admit that the ravages of the guerrillas are "quite troublesome." Meade is falling back. The mail which has this moment come in brings us Gen Lee's Dispatch dated Orange Court House Dec 2d which tells us that "The enemy retreated during the night. Pursuit was made but he had recrossed the Rapid Ann before we reached it. A few prisoners were captured. Signed R E Lee"

The paper of the day before told us that our Cavalry had penetrated to Meade's rear in the neighborhood of Fredericksburg, surprised & captured a train of one hundred waggons & a number of prisoners, all of which were brought off safely. So the "alarums as of a battle joined" have all ended in smoke. For a time at least, thank God, the blood shed has been stayed! Official telegram from Bragg confirm the retreat of the Abolitionists across the Chickamauga "destroying everything in their route." Their loss heavy in their attack on our rear guard under Gen Cleburne." So there is a lull there too in the storm of battle. Our interest now all centers on Longstreet, of whose capture of Knoxville we have still only rumours, nothing official which seems strange. The N Y Herald announces the escape of Gen John Morgan & six

---

[220]Robert Burns, *The Cotter's Saturday Night*, stanza 5.

other Confederate Officers from the Ohio Penetentiary & of Morgan's arrival at Toronto. God grant it be true![221]

"*One blast* upon his bugle horn" is "worth ten thousand men."[222] Perhaps he may reach home in time to see his Christian enemy shaved, for be assured he will not "tarry at Jerico until his head be grown."[223] Revenge will be the best hair oil that can be applied to him.

DECEMBER 7, 1863

Very uncomfortable reports of Longstreet's having raised the seige of Knoxville & being in full retreat to Virginia reaches us from Dalton, the head quarters of the Army of Georgia. Yankee papers affirm it positively. As yet nothing from him, so *Hope* is not quite dead. One Telegram has it that he was still there on the 4th. Nous verrons. I fear he is shelling Burnside in the same way we claimed he would shell Grant from Lookout Mountain, Mr E fears another Suffolk affair. I still hope.

DECEMBER 11, 1863

A fortunate thing it is for us in this Confederacy that it is not 'de rigueur' to testify greif on the receipt of bad news by rending one's clothes! Did that ancient custom prevail the frequency with which one misfortune follows another would tell sadly upon our slender wardrobes! Perhaps, however, the ancients mingled economy in their sorrow and rent their clothes at the seams only. Even that, with thread at 1.75 cts per spool, which I this day paid for one in Clarksville, would be rather hard on us. But to go back to the bad news which has metaphorically rent all the clothes in the country within the past few days. Official dispatches have been received from Gen Longstreet from a point thirty miles from Knoxville in full retreat from that place to Virginia. What he has accomplished the Examiner says may be summed up in a few words—*nothing*. Gild the pill as ye may, Mr Davis, it is a bitter one to swallow. I say Mr Davis for he is, we are told, who detached Longstreet from Bragg's command before the late battle. By his orders, too, was the army of Northern Geo reorganized in the face of the foe & to this cause is the late disaster at Lookout ascribed. Brigades were recast, divisions remoddled, & when the shock of battle came men were led into action by generals who had never led them before. Regiments had lost their old & tried supporters, their fellow

---

[221]Gen. John Morgan and six other Confederate officers escaped from their prison in Columbus, Ohio, on November 27, 1863, by cutting through the pavement of their cells and burrowing under the sewer walls immediately below. A reward of $5,000 was offered for Morgan's apprehension. Although two escapees were captured near Louisville and returned to prison, they refused to give any information about Morgan. Morgan subsequently commanded the Department of Southwest Virginia in 1864. *Official Records (Army)*, Series II, VI, 588, 632, 649, 665-667, 671; *Concise Dictionary of American Biography*, 698.

[222]Scott, *Lady of the Lake*, canto 6, stanza 18, lines 81-82.

[223]II Samuel 10:5b. "Tarry at Jericho until your beards be grown. . . ."

regiments in their Brigades, & had to rely on men whom they had never seen before & upon whose support they could not with confidence, *which experience* gives, rely. *Hence* our defeat & hence the small loss we endured, for some Regiments gave way without waiting to see how their new comrades fought. A want of sense it appears to us to reorganize thus in the face of the foe. Mr Davis Message came last night, an able document especially in reference to our *foreign relations*. Lord John Russel, her Majesty's Secretary for foreign affairs, is shown in his true light, petty & deceitful, under the mask of neutrality, claiming credit with the U S. for favouring it. Faugh! If he be a diplomat—I'll none of them! His lies have not the merit of plausibility!

The President's summary of Home affairs is rather gloomy. The currency & the soldiers whose term of enlistment is to expire in the spring are knotty points, but God has led us heretofore & He will lead us still. It is sad to myself to realize how my admiration has lessened for Mr Davis, lessened since the loss of Vicksburg, a calamity brought on us by his obstinacy in retaining Pemberton in command, & now still further diminished by his indomitable pride of opinion in upholding Bragg.

The Examiner says, "It is some comfort we grant to have a President who does not disgrace us by Hoosier English but it is a comfort which is dearly bought at the price of a Memminger & a Bragg." His favourites have cost us much: Mallory, a Navy; Memminger has flooded the land with useless Treasury notes, sapped the fountain head of our prosperity; Huger cost us Roanoke Island & in consequence Norfolk. (He also let McClellan escape at [———]; Lovel, New Orleans; Pemberton, Vicksburg and the two together the greater part of the Mississippi Valley. Bragg lost us first Kentucky and then Tennessee. His obstinacy in refusing to give Price the command lost Missouri & now the incapable Holmes, also his favourite, is clinching the loss and letting Arkansas slip away likewise. Truly I fear that to him is not given the first element of a ruler—"the discerning of Spirits." He upheld Sidney Johnston when unjustly assailed, however. "No general have I, if indeed great Johnston be not one." Here let us do him justice, but to give such a man as [———] a Lieut Gen'ship for "auld acquaintance sake" only seems trifling with the interests of the country. But let me "not speak" too much "evil of dignities." Mr Davis whilst he has made many mistakes has presided over our fortunes with dignity & Christian forbearance. Toward a man so harrassed with care as he is, & with such heavy responsibilities resting upon him as he has, requires that we should judge him kindly. Who would have done better if placed in his seat?

Sue, Rachel, & Col Clark dined with us today. Col C gives a melancholly picture of the country late in his command—below Hamilton. The Yankees have destroyed everything & burnt upon a large scale, many plantations being left without a house upon them. They misinterpret our forbearance in

Penn last summer, think we abstained from devastating the country through fear, & this is the return they make us. Have been riding on horse back every afternoon latterly & enjoy my rides with Mr E greatly.

DECEMBER 12, 1863

Patrick in Halifax today to attend a Battalion Drill, humbug, for the company has never yet been drilled in the school of the Company & the Major in command knows as much of handling a Battalion secundum artem[224] as my dog Picket does—Hey Picket! I my dying and sewing. No public news.

Quantrell, the Missouri guerrilla, has killed his pursuer Gen Blunt who went out promising to bring in his head. Out of Blunts whole command twelve men only escaped. It seems bloody, but then this Blunt was one of the instruments employed by the U S to lay waste and destroy two and a half counties in Missouri. Not a dwelling is said to have escaped. Delicate women and children turned homeless upon the world at the commencement of a Missouri winter, but Blunt has met his reward.

DECEMBER 14, 1863

Prices are almost fabulous now & yet we hear of but little distress & tho' when I was in Richmond Corn meal was $18 a bu. yet we did not see a street beggar. Work is scarce, money plenty, prices high, & almost all those who wish can make a livelihood. Men of fixed salaries, clerks, clergymen, etc., & invalids are the sufferers. Miss Myers told me that she paid in Danville $750 for a barrel of Sugar & moveover feared to have it all brought down to Richmond, such was her fear of Burglars! Mr E got me last week a pr of fine French boots in Clarksville for which he paid $60, but I consoled myself for the seeming extravagance by resolving to send 12 or 14 lbs of butter to Petersburg where it is from 4 to 5 per lb. With cotton at 12½ the boots would have cost in good times 48 lbs of cotton. Now with the staple at $1.00 in Halifax they cost only 12 more, viz., 60. The box of supplies which we sent Amo last month (for a list of which see ante) was valued by the insurer at $100! But the most ludicrous instance of high prices is the value put by the Express Agent on my night gown & cap and 1 lb of Hyco smoking tobacco left by us in our room at the hotel in Richmond & sent after us—viz., $40—& bear in mind that the gown, tho a neat one, was made before the war—three years since. I view my wardrobe with more respect since. I preserve several prices current marked [———].[225]

I have always forgotten to give Lt Gen Polks command. Altho solicited by the President in person he persisted in refusing to serve under Gen Bragg & was therefore transferred to the Department of Mississippi under Gen Joe

---

[224]Latin, "according to art."

[225]Several price lists appear in the front inside cover of the second volume of the diary.

Johnson where he now is, Hardee taking his command and he Hardee's. All uphold him in condemning Bragg, tho the clerical Gen has not a great military reputation in the Army himself. I know not how it is. We hear so much in praise or in derogation of almost every officer in the service that it is hard to form an unbiassed opinion. Each subaltern has his favourite & all the rest are incapables!

DECEMBER 20, 1863

Have been all the week busy collecting supplies for the Officer's Hospital, Mrs Webb having sent an Agent, Mr Wilkinson, & requested us to assist him. We have succeeded beyond our most sanguine expectations, Mr W having left with as much as he could carry on the R R at one trip, having expended $8 eight alone since he has been here. But little public news. The enemy under Gen Averill in the west of Va have made a swoop upon Salem, Roanoke County, burning & destroying, & unfortunately succeeding in getting off safely. Their main object to annoy Longstreets rear & cut off his communication. I know not to what extent they succeeded. Battalion of cavalry captured in Charles City. No pickets out & the sentinel's asleep, the Commanding Officer absent in Richmond, the papers say. The greatest loss we have sustained is in *the horses*. Shelling as usual before Charleston, no damage as yet. Whenever the barbarians open on the City our Batteries open on them with such severity as to drive the gunners from their post. I pase opposite a sketch of Fort Sumter as it appears through a glass from Sullivan's Island, done by Amo & sent us to give us a correct idea of its power of resistance.[226] He says "The channel face is still good & strong as you may see & the guns that look through the embrasures are not Quakers. If the fleet attempt to come in they will find a formidable antagonist still in the old ruin."

Mr Lincoln's Message is out & a proposition for submission offered us so ridiculously absurd that imagination loses itself in wondering why it is offered. He has risen in his offers of pardon. Two years ago it was all below the rank of Captain. He has now risen to the Colonels whom he includes in his amnesty. The oath he tenders us is both unconstitutional & illegal, both of which facts he admits. We think it meant only for Europe, for he must know that we will not listen to it. He announces a most anti-democratic doctrine when he declares that the vote of *one tenth* of the population shall be sufficient to send members to Congress & in Yankee eyes decide the status of the State—by no means "*vox populi.*" He creates an upper tendom, to use one of Willis[227] is affectations at once. A dominant race. We are free it appears to live

---

[226] The space for this sketch is blank in the original diary.

[227] Mrs. Edmondston is referring to "the upper ten thousand," a phrase used in 1860 by Nathaniel Parker Willis (1806-1867), an American poet, dramatist, and journalist, to describe the wealthier or more aristocratic people of a large community. The phrase was also used by James Fenimore Cooper in *Ways of the Hour*, published in 1850, and in 1843 by Thomas C. Haliburton in *Sam Slick in England*. Burton Steven-

on an equality with the negro! The only thing required of Southern freemen & gentlemen is to give up their own rights & swear to protect the negro in those given him by Mr Lincoln in his Proclamations, take him around the neck & from a slave make a master of him at Yankee bidding. He offers us pardon! Pardon for what? Forgiveness for what? Forgive us for having himself invaded our land, ravaged & desolated our homes? Forgive us for his own sin! for having deluged our country with the blood of our brothers & sons, slain on their own soil & in defence of that soil? Pardon to us, for having himself attempted to incite our slaves to revolt? Forgive us for the horrors he attempted to inaugurate? Forgive us for Butler's outrages & for the atrocities he himself, Abraham Lincoln, has countenanced & sanctioned in his Satraps! He claims our allegiance forsooth! *He*, elected for four years by a partial vote of fanatics & knaves, mouths it like a King, assumes the "pure divino" & offers us pardon. Better learn State craft, Mr Lincoln, before you attempt to practise *"King craft."*

DECEMBER 29, 1863

Just at home from Father's where we went to spend our Christmas. Came home on horseback with Father & Mr E. Had a fine view of a large Buck which ran across the field from swamp to swamp in full sight of us for more than a mile. Very free & independant and full of life he looked, an embodiment of liberty, but I fear the uppermost feeling in the hearts of all three was regret at his being so far out of range of Mr E's gun. How sordid! The River has been up again & left the roads anything but pleasant—a sad drawback to the pleasures of locomotion.

Averill, to our disgrace be it recorded, made good his escape from under the very noses of our troops. The devastation & destruction he committed was great, but as usual the Abolitionists, true to their instincts, omitted no petty details. They took possession of a College at Salem & after robbing the boys (for they are all under eighteen) of all their clothing & treating them personally with great indignity, they fed their horses from the trunks of the students from mere wantonness, tearing open the hinges & using them as troughs! But immagination shrinks in horror from the detail of the outrages committed about the 11th of the month by a party sent out from Norfolk by that wretch Butler upon the unfortunate inhabitants of our North Eastern counties, within in fifty miles of us too.

In Camden county they went to the house of a Mrs Wright & entering her dairy against her will drank all her milk. That night two of the wretches were taken violently ill & died, when they returned to the house & accusing Mrs W. of having poisoned the milk seized, *tied*, & threw her in a cart & sent

son, *The Home Book of Quotations, Classical and Modern* (New York: Dodd, Mead and Company, Tenth Edition, 1967), 1859.

her to Norfolk for trial. In vain she protested that she was innocent, that the negroes (for the band was composed of them under white officers) had been eating fish, oysters, & every thing else that the country afforded & then drinking quantities of milk it produced its usual effect in inducing cholera morbus. They would listen to no reason, but sent her as she was to Butler's tender mercies. They did not escape unscathed, however, more than a hundred having been shot by the citizens & Guerrillas in their mad progress through the country. A detachment of men under Lieut Munden[228] having taken some of the negroes prisoner, they went to his house &, without warning of any sort, seized Mrs Munden, tied her, & took her to the Elizabeth City jail where she was confined in a cell with two black sentinels constantly in her room for some days, they sending him word that whatever was done to the negro prisoners would instantly be visited in like manner on her. My God, is it not horrible! Can such things be? The result my informant Mr Leary had not heard, he having left the county during the raid.

Mrs Charles Wood, the sister of my neice Mrs Jones, was surprised by the sudden entrance of her maid servant who had ran off from her to the Yankees some time before. She walked in—& said, "Well Mary (Mrs W's name), how is Charles? (her master). I have brought some things for your children, for tho' I do not like you, I am fond of them, but as I see you have moved my things which I left here I shall not give them to them! But never mind, I know where to help myself." & suiting the action to the word she ascended the stairs, went to Mrs W's closets & threw from the window what she chose, bed linen, blankets, Counterpanes, clothes, etc., to about fifty armed negro men who surrounded the house. Could I have survived it? "As thy days, so shall thy Strength be."

One brilliant exploit of our sailors will worthily close the record of *this* year's War & I thank God that I am able thus to bring it to an end. A party of nineteen determined men took passage at different times in the Steamer Chesapeake, bound from New York to Portland, & having on board a most valuable cargo of such things as we most need. When a few days out, at the dead hours of the night, they arose & mastering the crew put the Captain in irons & heading the vessel's head to land, when in sight of it put the whole of them into boats & then steamed quickly out of sight. The engineer of the boat was wounded; with that exception it was accomplished without blood shed. They were acting under Confederate orders and were to report to the Command of the [———] at [———] without loss of time.

Before Charleston the shelling flags & there are signs of abandoning the attack, but whether intended as a feint to throw us off our guard or not we cannot tell. The shells thrown into the city do but little damage. Two women, one

---

[228]William J. Munden was a lieutenant in Co. A, Sixty-eighth North Carolina Regiment. Clark, *Histories of the North Carolina Regiments*, III, 713.

white the other an aged black, are as yet the only wounded & the injury to the buildings is but slight. Contrary to my intention of never writing another line of poetry, I copy on the next page a Prayer for Peace with which I last week amused myself. Its great merit is its sincerity & truthfulness at right. Well for me that I left this vacant space, as it is now my sad fate to record the recapture of the Steamer Chesapeake, so exultingly mentioned above. Want of coal seems to have occasioned it. She was lying near Halifax, N S in Sambro Harbor, waiting for coal when the entrance was blocked by three Abolition Gunboats. The comfort in the disappointment is that the prisoners on being landed at Halifax were immediately seized by a boat's crew in the slip & hurried off by the crowd in attendance on the wharf. Upon Government officers attempting to arrest them they were seized & held by prominent citizens of Halifax & were thus rendered unable to execute their office. The prisoners all were finally hurried down the Bay &, snatched from Yankee clutches, are at large in Nova Scotia. John Bull must settle with the Yankee as he can & will doubtless make Seward beg pardon for carrying them there at all or demand thanks for having rescued them, all of which Seward will with grace perform.[229]

A Prayer for Peace

O Thou who hatest nothing that Thou hast made and who dost not willingly greive or afflict the children of men, look down, behold, visit, and releive this land & in Thine own good time grant us Peace.

By our streams whose purple flood
Bathe our plains, now drunk with blood
Where the War Horse' iron heel
Stamps the Earth with War's red seal
By our fields—unploughed—unsown
By our roof trees bare and lone
By the homes which through our land
Ravaged, desolated stand
Smouldering ruins, blood bedrenched
House hold fires forever quenched
House hold joys forever fled
House hold hopes forever dead
                    Grant us Peace!

---

[229]The seizure of the U.S.S. *Chesapeake*, conducted by seventeen Confederate sympathizers under the direction of John C. Braine and Vernon G. Locke (alias Capt. John Parker), was carried out on December 7, 1863. The United States Navy quickly hunted the *Chesapeake* down and recaptured her on December 17, although most of the Confederates escaped. *Official Records (Navy)*, Series I, II, 513, 524, 539-541; *Civil War Naval Chronology*, III, 162-163.

Where Thy sacred Peace once smiled
See our Altars War defiled!
Hear our chimes once sacred note
Thunder forth from War's red throat!
By our father's graves which stand
Desecrate throughout our land
By the foot of stranger spurned
By our cities sacked and burned
Into charnel houses turned
      Grant us Peace!

By our sundered household ties
Widow's wail and children's cries
By the boding care and fears
Stretching into future years
By the loneliness of greif
Greif and tears without releif
By the sorrow & distress
Of the wife's last fond caress
By the husband's bursting heart
Wrung with agony to part
Clasped in embrace of speechless woe
Clasped closer still yet bid to go
By the tears our Mother's shed
Sorrowing o'er their noble dead
Bending o'er the bloodstained bier
In an agony of fear
Lest another hope as dear
Cold and stark and murdered lie
Breathing out life's parting sigh
In defiant battle cry
      Grant us Peace!

By our hopes—forever crushed
By the tones forever hushed
By the blood which from the ground
Cries to Thee with vengeful sound
By that time of utter horror
Which from hope no ray can borrow
Days of hunger, cold and sorrow
By our captive comrades passed
Into Northern dungeons cast
By the vengeance deep and strong
Vengeance for unuttered wrong
Which to womanhood belong
      Grant us Peace!

In our ancient Freedom's might
Fight we now for Freeman's right
Stand we where our Father's stood
Fight we as their children should
By the love of wife and child
By our Honour undefiled
By our Country's sacred name
By the patriot's deathless fame
By that Charter writ in blood
Written in a crimson flood
Of our father's sacred blood!
And on many a hard fought field
By our brother's signed & sealed
Charter we will never yield
                          Grant us Peace!

Went out on horseback with Mr Edmondston to Hascosea on the 30th to attend to the putting up of the year's provision of pork there—a beautiful day, the air soft & balmy, making the very inhalation of it a cordial. He finished his labours in time to take me [on] a long walk, a real tramp over the farm, showing me his improvements both accomplished & intended. Slept in the room off the piazza, the 'Work Room' as it is called, thinking the atmosphere of the house which has been so long closed would be damp. Proposed an early start so as to wind up the year at Looking Glass, but "L'homme propose," for we were awakened at daylight with heavy rain, rain which continued incessantly the whole day. I have rarely seen more inclement weather. It seemed as tho the year was going out in tears for the sorrow and misery which he had brought us and at night it was fearful. Nevertheless we had our Egg Nog as usual & wished each other & the servants, and were wished by them in turn, "A Happy New Year" amidst the howling of the wind & the roaring of the tempest.

So died 1863!—a year of calamity & distress the like of which God grant may never fall to our lot either as individuals or members of the community to see again. We look back to it as to a time of horror, but nevertheless God has sustained us through it all & in its fulness have we tasted the fulfilment of His promise "*As thy days, so shall thy strength be.*"

1864

JANUARY 2, 1864

Woke up on the morning of the 1st at Hascosea to a bright sun & had the pleasure of seeing the clouds which had overcast the sky roll gradually away under his influence. May they indeed be typical of those which now "o'er cast our fate" & may the disasters and sorrows of 1863 be "in the deep bosom of the ocean buried." Came down on horse back with Mr E, but at the Mill we got a foretaste of the flood which awaited us, as we were forced at the high water to cross with some risk to the horses upon the pier head. Mr E found ample employment awaiting him—no less than 70 hogs slaughtered & ready for salting. Dined at home & then went up on horseback to Father's to see my sister Mrs Miller, who is down for a short visit only, Mr E following after dark. He, poor fellow, was forced to leave very early in the morning to return to his duties at home & sent Owen after me about 10 to tell me to come home at once as the road would be impassable from the river water, & altho I made all expedition, riding as fast as the frozen roads & the ice would allow me (for it was bitterly cold), when I reached the Beaver Dam I found a torrent surging before me! Mr E had provided that Dick & a canoe should be in attendance for fear that the water should be so deep as to wet my feet. Expecting Owen to lead my horse over, but as that was impossible I sent them back to take a circuit of some miles through the woods & crossing in the canoe, walked home. Found him very busy & full of anxiety about my being out in such severe weather, but thank God I am in excellent health and can bear exposure. He made me a New Year's gift—nothing less than this handsome & valuable blank book in which to write my Journal! He had it made for his own use some years ago & I am the more touched by it as I know he prized it highly, as it was ruled according to order and marked with his name.

No public news of much interest except the paroling of five hundred of our men by the Abolition Government & the like number of theirs by ours. Gen Butler of New Orleans memory has been appointed agent for the exchange of prisoners, but as he has been outlawed by Proclamation of Mr Davis, we very properly refuse to treat with him. His appointment was intended only to throw additional difficulties in the way of the resumption of the Cartel and at the same time to insult us. The manner in which he is treating the unfortunate inhabitants of Norfolk & Portsmouth adds, if possible, additional blackness to his conduct & stamps him deeper with the stain of infamy! I preserve his orders (B)[1] relative to taking the oath & to show the wantonness of his tyranny. He visited a Camp of our prisoners at Point Lookout a few days since accompanied by his body guard & Staff & was I am thankful to say received with such hisses & scorn that tho he attempted to speak to them he could not make

---

[1]This clipping was not preserved in the diary.

himself heard. The Lousianians called out to him to "pay them the money he stole from them in N O." He was asked by others why he did not come to see them on the battlefield & "if he still made war upon women"? & many other such home thrusts were made him until at last he turned rein & galloped out of hearing, accompanied by a storm of hisses from many thousand men.

JANUARY 7, 1864

Terribly startled this morning by a heavy &, for some moments, continuous cannonading. So heavy was it that in our sitting-rooms, with doors & windows closed, it was distinctly audible, the windows even jarring at the sound. What can it be? We lose ourselves in conjecture & the gloomy thoughts it awakens are intensified by the sad tidings that we yesterday received of the death in action of two of our young neighbors, members of the Scotland Neck Rifles. They were ambuscaded below Greenville & these two, Mr Frank Ferrall & Mr David Camp, killed, whilst Mr. John Baker was wounded & in the hands of the enemy. Their bodies were brought home for burial yesterday. Scarce three weeks have passed since we heard of the death of another, the widow Whitehead's son & stay, killed at Kelly's Ford in Northern Va.[2] Truly this War will be a bloody memorial to us all!

The enemy before Charleston celebrated Christmas Day by a continuous & unprecedented shelling of the city. For hours they kept it up with, however, but slight damage to either life or property; an old man of eighty five & his sister-in-law were seriously wounded & have since died, whilst sitting by their own fire side—a shell bursting between them! Gen Joe Johnston has assumed command of the Army of Northern Georgia. All quiet there. Grant's movements are wrapped in mystery, as he is retreating on Nashville, leaving Chattanooga strongly garrisoned, however. Have been very busy for the past two days packing boxes for friends in Camp & Major James E, still in Hospital at Richmond, however, Thomas Devereux, & Lieut Skinner, James & Lieut Skinner's servant being here to take them on. Mr E also sent a box of country fare to his friend Gen Gatlin, Adjt Gen of the State, "a trifle to commence housekeeping," which he did on the 1st at Raleigh. Finished 2 pr of gloves for Mr & Mrs Haigh of Fayetteville & sent them off by mail today. Quite proud am I of Mrs H's, knit of Shetland wool with fancy cuffs.

JANUARY 9, 1864

Yesterday came Col Clarke to dinner on his way to Father's, his Regt having been again relieved from duty below us & being now on the march to

---

[2]Pvt. Frank (Francis B.) Ferrall and Lt. David C. Camp, members of Co. G, Forty-first North Carolina (Third Cavalry) Regiment, were killed during a skirmish with the First North Carolina (Union) Volunteers near Greenville. First Sgt. John L. Baker was a member of the same company. "The widow Whitehead's son" was probably James F. Whitehead, a member of Co. D, Forty-third North Carolina Regiment. Clark, *Histories of the North Carolina Regiments*, II, 785; Manarin and Jordan, *North Carolina Troops*, II, 228, 229, 230.

Weldon. He tells us that the canonading we heard yesterday before was only the usual practice of the gunners on Thursday, the sound being conveyed to us with such distinctness by the River which is out of its banks, the Low-grounds between us & Rainbow being in fact a lake. This added to the frosti-ness of the atmosphere, snow on the ground & every thing fast locked in ice & sleet, made the reverberation terrific! The reports sounded as tho' scarce five miles off, jarring, as I said before the windows. It was a great releif to know our fears were groundless, for our forebodings had been most painful.

The papers tell us that there is every indication of a land & sea attack soon being made upon Wilmington. Butler is massing forces they affirm at Wash-ington for the purpose, whilst Iron Clads are rendezvous-ing at Beaufort for the naval expedition. Wilmington is now of great consequence to us, being the only port open north of Mobile in the Confederacy. Beauregard telegraphs from Charleston to the War Department under date of Jan 4th that the enemy has been reconnoitering & sounding in the vicinity of Dewees Inlet indicating a possible movement in that direction. His encampments on Cole's Island have been increased. It is thought it will be necessary for Gen B to cover Charleston on the land side with his whole force. This, added to the indispen-sable necessity of defending the Charleston & Savannah R R, increases his difficulties greatly. The attack on Wilmington is designed, say the papers, to take Charleston in the rear by preventing our throwing in reinforcements & supplies.

Longstreet still holds a post which threatens East Tenn & Kentucky & obliges Grant to detach a strong portion of his force to guard him. In West Tenn the inhabitants are flocking by scores to Forrest & Richardson's com-mands, Regt after Regt coming out for arms. So deprived of all resource are the poor inhabitants, so crushed by oppression & tyranny that they leave their homes gladly. I append, marked D-1, 2, 3, details of the ferocity & brutality of Abolition rule both in Missouri & this State.

After much discussin Congress has repealed the Substitution Act & places all the principals in the field without, however, releasing the Substitutes! By some it is urged that this is a breach of Faith by the Government whilst others contend that it is merely the resumption of a privilege granted for no definite time, that those who have furnished substitutes ought to be thankful for the immunity so long granted them and not grumble at being now called on to "*shoulder arms*." That wise body is now exercising itself about the Exemp-tion's. Truly this weak body is a mill stone around the neck of our young Con-federacy. It neither knows its own mind, nor will it give the people theirs. At every session it argues & re-argues the same fact, goes over the same ground, & makes the same speeches to Buncombe i.e., "*the Army*." There is the weak point of our legislators, all wish to stand well with "*the Army*," and "what will the army think of it"? has greater weight with them than "what is for the good of the country"? A sorrowful fact, but it is true; our gloomiest anticipations arise from the conduct of our law givers.

JANUARY 17, 1864

Last Sunday, a week ago today, as we walked on the snow by the sheet of ice left by the freshet & amused ourselves with the pleasant tinkling sound & seemingly endless gliding motion of peices of ice which Patrick threw upon it, to our great surprise we saw a buggy with a dashing looking officer in it approaching the Flume. As he had "*pressed*" a cart as pilot, we gave ourselves no great uneasiness as to his fate which in the end we thought would be to turn back & spend the night at Conneconara, but we were mistaken. Under the friendly guidance of "Hatch" & the Cart he got over safely, when who should the stranger prove to be but *Major James*! Tired of Hospital life, the intrusion of a Typhoid Fever patient into his room fairly routed him & he decamped at once, changing his base with a rapidity which McClellan might envy & came to us to complete his convalescence. He has now been with us a week & tho still far from well seems both in spirits & health to have improved.

No public news whatever, papers filled with the ovature paid in Richmond to Gen Morgan & details of the outrages committed by Wild in Eastern N C Vide D & D. Private letters tell us that the half is not told. Armed negroes, originally run-aways from their owners to the Yankees, now disgusted with their new rulers, fugitives in turn from the Yankee army, demoralized & lost to all restraint or sense of dependance, their Masters mostly absent, rove through the country & seize from the defenceless inhabitants what they list. God help them & keep us from a like fate. The tender mercies of Abolitionism! Butler has been made by their nation a Jailor on a huge scale, no less than the custodian of all the prisoners in their hands. Certainly they know his capabilities best. Unfitted to cope with armed men or to manoevre an army in the field, his sphere is to triumph over the defenceless, insult innocent women, and to add hardship to an already severe lot. Our refusal to treat with him was it seems anticipated by them & he was selected as the Agent of Exchange only to enable them to throw the onus of the suspension of the Cartel upon us. *What a nation!*

JANUARY 24, 1864

All day yesterday at Hascosea. Had a "*set too*" with all hands against my enemy the Peach tree borer. Now that I have learned his habits, I have him, I hope, at a disadvantage. Set out a young orchard of seedling peaches to the South of the house; that is, I began it for I had but fourteen trees large enough to transplant. Commenced trimming my Grape Vines, but my ignorance makes me timid. I fear the free use of the knife according to theory. I dined at H the day before having gone out with Mr E on horseback. Two delightful days! Not many such fall to us in Jan. James left on Thursday for a jaunt up the country. All quiet along our lines. Whilst setting out my trees, however, the heavy boom of cannon reverberating through the pine forest startled me not a little. It came in sad contrast to my peaceful occupation. It came from the direction of Weldon & was without doubt a Confederate Gun fired for practice, but it was a stern reminder of War & I sighed as I thought of the many sad hearts within its sound even. Apropos of guns, those we heard on the 7th were Yankee guns fired at Plymouth! We Confederates can make no such free use of powder as to practice regularly. That is a privilege of our enemies.

JANUARY 31, 1864

Such weather as we have had for the past ten days! Maderia could not surpass it. I have been much out of doors, transplanting, pruning, & getting ready for Spring work. Have been frequently to Hascosea & to father's & had Sue & Father here with me.

All continues quiet along our lines. Gilmore keeps up his barbarous shelling of Charleston without inflicting much damage on ought save the character of his country, but that is lost beyond redemption. Troops are being massed at Goldsboro & Kinston under secret orders. What it portends we know not. Rumour has it we are to attack New Berne to forestall the Yankee attack on Wilmington. Per contra, another says that the Yankees are collecting a heavy force there, that Meade is in command, & that N C is to be the seat of the War & that the Summer Campaign opens here. God avert it. A party of Yankees came up to Windsor in Bertie last Thursday & committed the usual excesses, taking off with them the Episcopal Clergyman, the Cashier of the Bank, and a leading merchant, all non combattants.[3] This is not War but sheer barbarity. When will it end? A band of Yankees from Butler's command came up the James & destroyed every out house, the crops, & provisions on the Brandon estate owned by Mrs Devereux's relatives.[4] This seems the more wanton as it was spared by McClellan in his famous "change of base," as well as by the British in the Revolution, and there seems no reason for it now beyond the fact that Butler is in command. Seven members of the Signal Corps were there captured.

This afternoon came brother in better spirits than usual. He is on his way to Harrell'sville to look after a lot of Bacon left there by the carelessness of *somebody*. The Yankees came up & set fire to it, but fortunately for us the flames skimmed over on the surface only & almost the whole amount has been

---

[3]Cyrus Waters, rector of St. Thomas Episcopal Church in Windsor from 1860 until 1865, was the clergyman referred to. Lorenzo S. Webb and Dr. Turner Wilson were also taken by the Yankees. All were subsequently released. *Richmond Enquirer*, February 10, 1864; Barrett, *Civil War in North Carolina*, 202.

[4]Ann Mary Maitland, Thomas P. Devereux's second wife, was related to the Harrisons, owners of Brandon, through her mother Susannah Harrison of Prince George County.

saved in good condition. The Advance[5] is again in safely with a valuable cargo, run in in the teeth of the Blockaders. This is our N C vessel & Capt Crossan deserves well of the State for his boldness & skill in so often bearding the Yankee Lion successfully.

Letters from my neice, Mrs T. D. Jones, give me an account of what herself, mother, & sisters underwent from the hands of the Yankees & their allies, armed negroes—make my blood boil in my veins. On leaving us on the 1st of Dec she went at once to her Sister Mrs Wood's house where her Mother & Brother were, the latter at home on a sick furlough with a wounded foot.

"Early the next morning," I quote her own words, "Ma, Sallie, & I were awakened about daylight by men's voices talking loudly in the house. . . . Soon one of the little servants came up & told us that the house was full of Yankees & that they were looking for Joshua.[6] You may be sure we were quickly up and then, Aunt Kate, before we could get any of our clothing on we heard the report of a gun & a shout of 'we've got him! we've got him!' Mama & I rushed out just as we were, in our night dresses & bare feet, expecting to see our poor J killed. Oh! Aunt Kate, I cannot tell you the horror of that moment! When we got out on the piazza we saw J running across a field which was just over the road from the house & two Yankees in hot pursuit. They fired on him four times but the brave little fellow never halted until compelled to do so by his lame foot & the rapid gaining on him of his yelling pursuers. They treated him very roughly after his surrender; & allowed him but five minutes to get ready to go with them.

They were the roughest, most brutal looking set of men I ever saw: It seems that they came to Hertford in the night . . . there they found one of sister Mary's servants who told them about J being a ranger & who gladly piloted [them] out to Sister Mary's. . . . J was asleep when one of the negro girls ran in & told him the yard was full of Yankees. He sprang up & dressed as quickly as possible taking his gun with him & attempted to escape, but as he reached back, they burst open the front door of the house. They saw & halted him but he did not stop; they ran after him but he slipped under the house & they lost sight of him. They looked around for him a while & then rushed into Sister Mary's room where she was all undressed & told her that she had a Guerilla hid in her house & if she did not tell them where he was they would burn the house down. She had not seen him that morning and of course could not tell them. Whilst they were in the house poor J thought it would be a good time to try & get off, for he knew that the negroes all saw him go under there

[5]The *Advance* was an English sidewheel steamer previously named the *Lord Clyde*. Capt. Thomas M. Crossan, formerly an officer in the United States Navy, was the first commander of the state-owned blockade-runner. Hill, *Bethel to Sharpsburg*, I, 220, 335-337.

[6]Joshua Skinner (1845-1911), youngest brother of Pattie Skinner Jones and a student at the Virginia Military Institute, fought with the cadets at New Market. He was captured and imprisoned at Point Lookout. Francis E. Winslow Records.

& was afraid that they would inform on him, as they doubtless would have done, so he crept out & was just climbing the fence into the field when one of the wretches saw & fired at him. He fell over into the field & they thought he was killed, but he had only stumbled & he soon sprang up & ran. Then began the chase & at last the ungracious surrender. He hated it so bad, Aunt Kate, & I was so proud of him! I wish you could have seen how nobly he acted after his surrender. I know you would have admired him....

J & his hateful captors were hardly out of sight before a whole troop of armed negroes came up, the most impudent set that you can imagine, Aunt Kate. Sister Mary's nurse who left her a year ago came up with them. She was dressed very finely & was exceedingly insolent & abusive. She went into the house followed by a guard of armed men (negroes) & told Sister M that she left a bed & some clothing when she went away & that she intended to have others in the place of them. She then went to Sister M's bed & commenced rolling it up, sheets, blankets, & all. Sister M stopped her & told her that she must not take that bed. She dropped it & ran up stairs, tore one of the beds there off the stead, tied it up in a quilt, & gave it to two of her escort who carried it down stairs & put it in a cart ready for moving. She then went to the wardrobe where the bed linen was kept, helped herself to two prs of blankets, 2 prs of sheets, 2 white Marseilles quilts, two bed quilts, napkins, pillow cases, etc. She also took Ma's cloak & shawl, sister M's shawl, two easy chairs, in short everything she could possibly carry off. In the meantime the negroes belonging to the farm were packing up & getting ready to go with them and as a matter of course stealing everything they could find. They were very abusive, *cursing us*, & *calling* us by our *names*. They called Mr Wood *"Charles"* whenever they spoke of him. The house was filled with armed negroes from early in the morning until two o'clock in the afternoon & they were like wild things, Aunt Kate, running about & peeping into every crack & corner & cursing most dreadfully whenever they could not find things to steal. One of the wretches told me that he knew me, that I was Pattie Skinner, & that he was coming back to marry me soon! I said the wicked . . . then, Aunt Kate, it was more than I could stand! When they left, every negro on the land went with them & Sister M was left entirely without help save what we could do for her. Nearly every negro in Hertford left also.

One of my Cousins, Sally Harvey,[7] was slapped in the face by one of their own servants because she tried to keep her from taking her dresses! The print of the negroe's hand was on my cousin's face for several days!

Poor Mr Snowden,[8] our clergyman, was robbed of a bed & nearly all his bed clothing. They did not leave him enough to cover comfortably with. His

---

[7]Sallie Harvey, daughter of Thomas and Emily Creecy Harvey, was a distant cousin of Pattie Skinner Jones. Francis E. Winslow Records.

[8]William E. Snowden, Episcopal minister and a native of New Jersey, moved to North Carolina and married Harriet A. Skinner in 1842. In 1848 Snowden was appointed missionary in Hertford, Perquimans

daughter's clothes, dresses, & underclothing were nearly all taken & if he dared to say a word he was cursed. All that from his own servants, Aunt Kate! Just before the Yankees left Hertford the Rangers attacked them & drove them to their boats. They shelled the town but did very little injury. A lighter containing about fifty negroes got aground & the Yankees were in such a hurry to get off that they could not wait for it. So of course they were captured by the Rangers & the lighter burned. Two of Sister M's women with their children were on board; they were immediately sent over the lines. . . . We have not heard from Joshua since his capture. We hear he has been sent to New Berne. We are very anxious about him."

FEBRUARY 2, 1864

Last night about bed time came James, much improved by his jaunt. He was reduced to traveling in a cart, having missed Owen whom we had sent for him. He brings no news beyond the fact of the massing of troops at Goldsboro & Kinston & that we have a Pontoon train coming up from Wilmington, which looks like an advance on our part. Maj Gen Picket is in command. He has left his wife[9] at Gen Ransom's house & she is in such depths of greif at his departure that the wise ones argue from it that she knows there is something more than usual in prospective. The papers are as silent as the grave on the whole matter. Father & Mr E very busy surveying in order to find the Level of the cut in the Dam where Father proposes to put in a flume in order to releive the dams from all pressure save that below eighteen feet by flooding the Low Grounds when the river reaches that height. A troublesome & expensive job & to my mind of doubtful utility, but I exercise myself in things too high for me so I had better *seek my level*.

All day yesterday at Hascosea transplanting & pruning. Met some officers' of Ferrabee's Regiment, which had been ordered here from Northern Va to recruit their horses. They give a heart breaking account of the desolation wrought in that whole country. The Quarter Master[10] rode up to the Flower Garden where I was at work & told me that the sight of it & my employment was a refreshment to him, that there was not a fence or an enclosure in the whole country where he had been! He came to order the tax-in-kind to be

County, and was the first rector of the Holy Trinity Parish, formed later in 1848. He held this post until 1867, when he resigned the rectorate and went to St. Paul's Episcopal Church in Beaufort, Carteret County. Raymond A. Winslow, Jr., *History of the Church of the Holy Trinity, Hertford, North Carolina* (N.p.: N.p., 1969), 11-12, 18, 37.

[9]The second wife of George Edward Pickett was the young and beautiful La Salle Corbell of Chuckatuck, Virginia, whom he married on September 15, 1863. Niles, *The James*, 235, 254, 259; Freeman, *Lee's Lieutenants*, II, 491.

[10]Dennis Dozier Ferebee, a lawyer who resided in Camden County, was colonel of the Fifty-ninth North Carolina (Fourth Cavalry) Regiment. He resigned his commission March 24, 1865, and later served on Vance's staff. The quartermaster referred to was probably Capt. William D. Holloman, assistant quartermaster of the regiment. Clark, *Histories of the North Carolina Regiments*, III, 456; Manarin and Jordan, *North Carolina Troops*, II, 263, 266.

paid to him, orders having been issued to that effect & requested that the corn might be unshelled & the Hay not baled & that he would haul it, for all of which we should be much obliged to the Government.

On the road home met Mr Peter Smith & some other of our neighbors on their way from Halifax Court. They told me that the rumour was that we had taken New Berne & that Col Shaw of the [———] N C was certainly killed, his body having passed on the train the night before. Poor fellow! he is the officer who was so severely & as most persons now beleive unjustly censured for the fall of Roanoke Island. He was called a Yankee, a traitor, & I know not what, but his only fault seems now to have been a want of capacity for the situation in which he found himself & for that the blame should rest on the shoulders of those who placed him there. A simple Colonel of no military ability, he was unable to cope with the difficulties which surrounded him, difficulties which required a man of the first order & a far *stronger force* & *heavier canon* to meet successfully. The country has long ago acquitted him of all blame in the matter & to Sec Benjamin & Maj. Gen Huger, as principals, do we look for the liquidation of the debt of responsibility, the misery, the bloodshed & the loss which have followed in the train of that most unfortunate event! If Col Shaw was a Yankee he came to N C under six months of age & even that is denied by his friends. He was a Southern man by education & instinct but *weak* & an aspirant for political honours, which gained him many enemies, but he has expiated his faults real & imaginary now & has died a soldier's death in his country's cause. May he rest in Peace! God be with his family! Sent off yesterday to Mrs Webb for the Hospital thirty eight dozen eggs, for which, sad to say, I had to pay $1.00 per doz! Twenty five dollars of the money was sent me by our neighbours to be expended as I thought best for the Hospital. The rest was our contribution.

FEBRUARY 6, 1864

Busy with my Garden seeds, dividing them with friends who are not so fortunate or so provident as I was last summer. I have a fine stock, as times go, but it seems meager to what I once thought a necessity for a good garden. Last evening came Mary & Sue on horse back. Sad rumous they bring us, but they are but rumours, to the effect that we have failed in our attack on New Berne & have fallen back, Barton's Brigade being the scapegoat this time. Gen Martin has stormed & taken Morehead City and Dame Rumour says holds it. The newspapers "distinguish themselves" like the little man in the Spectator "by a profound silence" on the whole subject, so Mad Rumour's reign is undisturbed. We have had some success of minor importance, capturing a wagon train of eighty wagons in Hardy County, burning a Gunboat, the Smith Briggs, & capturing her crew and a detachment of 130 men sent out to destroy a Factory & Mill in Isle of Wight County. The prisoners boast that they were in the foray which destroyed Brandon. Col Griffin[11] also repulsed the enemy & drove them to their boats at Windsor, killing ten of them.

FEBRUARY 8, 1864

Sad to say it is true that we have fallen back from New Berne! Gen Picket made a *reconnoissance*, as he now calls it, "within a mile & a half of New Berne. . . . Met the enemy in force at Batchelor's Creek, killed, & wounded about one hundred in all; captured thirteen officer's & two hundred & eighty prisoners, fourteen negroes, two Rifled peices & caissons, three hundred stand of small arms, four ambulances, three wagons, fifty five animals (of what sort Gen Picket?), a quantity of clothing, camp & garrison equipage, and two flags. Commander Wood (C S) captured & destroyed the U S gunboat Underwriter"—signed G E Picket Maj Gen Comdg. He dates his dispatch from Kinston, so the Examiner's hopes of a great battle the next day would not have been so sanguine, had he been acquainted with the geography of the country! Gen Whiting reports from Wilmington that "Gen Martin . . . broke the R R at Shepherdsville, driving the enemy from their works at Newport barracks & across Newport river," so I suppose expectation which has been on tip toe for days past can now rest comfortably on the sole of her foot again. It is mortifying truly! James left us today to return to duty. His health is much better & the rest has been of service to him.

FEBRUARY 9, 1864

On Saturday evening the enemy in heavy force crossed the Rapid Anne at three fords, Morton's, Raccoon, & Barnet's, the last three miles only from Orange Court House. At two they were repulsed, but at Barnets heavy firing on Sunday morning denoted some action, so says the Examiner. This movement of Meade's, he goes on to say, is supposed to be intended merely to engage Lee's attention & to cover movements on the Peninsula. Information given by a deserter has warned the authorities that an advance on Richmond from that quarter was in anticipation & accordingly at nine o'clock on Saturday night a demonstration in heavy force was made and our pickets at Bottom's Bridge driven in. The alarm was given in Richmond and all the available force marched out to meet them. The second class militia was ordered out & a thousand rumours flew wildly through the streets. A large force of the enemy consisting of three Brigades of infantry, four Regiments of

---

[11]Col. Joel R. Griffin, commanding the Sixty-second Georgia Cavalry, reported on January 31, 1864, that his force of 200 men repulsed 1,200 of the enemy, driving them from Windsor into their boats. Lt. Cmdr. Charles Flusser of the United States Navy, however, reported that he occupied the town with a force of 350 soldiers, held it for several hours, and returned to his boats on the Roanoke River "without a single shot from the enemy." *Civil War Naval Chronology*, IV, 12; Clark, *Histories of the North Carolina Regiments*, IV, 73; *Official Records (Navy)*, Series I, IX, 423-424.

Cavalry, & twelve peices of Artillery are massed at Barhamsville & advancing in the direction of Talleysville. Gen Wade Hampton at Hamilton's Crossing telegraphs "that the enemy are advancing." Everything indicates a renewal of McClellan's attack through the swamps of the Chickahominy.

FEBRUARY 10, 1864

Was interrupted whilst writing by the forage master of Ferrabee's Regt in search of corn & fodder for his horses. He remained all night & his heart seemed quite won by the present of a bottle of Red Pepper & a peice of transparent soap! He has been in Va under Gen Lee's command for months & speaks in the warmest terms of affection & confidence of him. He says "*Marse Robert*," as the men all call him, can carry them anywhere. They think him as pure a patriot as Washington and a more able General. They speak of him amongst themselves universally as "Marse Robert" & use it as a term of endearment & affection. God bless & keep him! He telegraphs to Gen Cooper that "the force of the enemy which crossed at Morton's ford have been driven to the cover of their guns. . . . During the night they recrossed to the North Bank. . . . This morning they have disappeared. They left seventeen dead & forty six prisoners in our hands. Our loss four killed & twenty wounded. The guard at the Bridge, a Lieut and twenty five men, while bravely resisting the passage of the enemy were captured." From Talleyville the last accounts represent the Yankees as retiring in the direction of New Kent Court House. Their movements would seem to indicate an extension of their lines over a belt of country some twenty or thirty miles wide & would put them this much nearer Richmond. Good news from West Tennessee. The line of the Memphis & Charleston R R is free from the enemy & Forest holds the whole country. They are concentrating in force, however, in Florida. Eighteen Gunboats & transports are landing troops at Jacksonville.

FEBRUARY 14, 1864

Have been for several days out at Hascosea gardening. Such weather as we have is almost unprecedented, fine bracing white frosts and a succession of them whilst the middle of the day is mild & serene & so it has been for some weeks past. On cutting the Scuppernong Grape Vine it bled as in the latter part of March! I congratulate myself on not having delayed my pruning. It is now too late for it. Am today dressed in my homespun dress, warp & filling spun & then woven on the plantation. Very comfortable & neat it is & does Becky and Cap credit. They are the manufacturers.

Congress has been distinguishing itself by another foolish bill. Another do I say? Their name is Legion! This one, however, forbids the exportation of Cotton, Tobacco, Rice, or any of our staples & the importation of what they term Luxuries, Brandies, Engraving, Statuary, Laces, Silks, Cotton or Linen fabrics, and even Dolls! Women & childrens finery are strictly prohibited, but *masculine* adornments, "galloon braid," gold stars, gold wings, and every-thing pertaining to fine Uniforms are by all means to enter! That Congress is an "unco squad"!

Not much public news. The shelling of Charleston continues. No change in the Fleet & no other active movements. The incapables at Richmond have allowed one hundred & nine Yankee officers to burrow under their noses out of the Libby Prison. One hundred & nine!—Colonels, the infamous Streight at their head, Majors, Captains, Lieutenants, Prisoners bought with the blood aye the lives of our soldiers in the field & held as hostages for the well being of our unfortunate comrades immured in Northern Dungeons, wearing their lives away in hopeless captivity, are allowed thus to hood wink sleepy sentinels aye perchance to bribe greedy officials. It is too bad! Twentytwo have been re-captured but what are they amongst so many. Turner[12] is the name of the Commandant; Turn out he has proved himself; turnedout I hope he will find himself. Re-enlistments for the War are going on rapidly & uni-versally through the whole army. Congress stands hat in hand & bows to every Regiment, nay, in some cases even to Battalions & Companies. A vote of thanks is tendered to all. A "cute" Yankee by studying the proceedings of the Confederate Congress could give a pretty accurate "guess" as to the strength of our Army. Gold is quoted at 200 percent (two hundred) in New York, higher than it has yet been and the sixth sense of the Yankee nation which lies in its pocket throbs keenly in consequence.

FEBRUARY 16, 1864

Just at home from Father's where we went on Sunday afternoon. On Mon-day Sue & I accompanied Father and Mr E to Halifax & for the first time we saw the interior of a Court of Justice. Our business there was to prove Thomas Jones Will, but the lawyer, Mr Bat Moore, deciding that this county possessed no jurisdiction over it, we had our ride for our pains. I think him mistaken (I will talk of War before Hanibal himself, it appears) as my impres-sion is that the Legislature allowed the Will of a citizen of a County within the enemy's lines to be admitted to probate in any County in the State, but the man learned in the Law thinks it must be an *adjoining* County to the Yankee lines. I wish Father had placed the business in the hands of some other lawyer than that Unionist Bat Moore! I felt indignant when I saw the paper en-dorsed in poor Thomas' hand "To be opened if I never return" in his posses-sion & remember what was his opinion of the *Cause* in which that young life was offered up.

---

[12]Maj. Thomas P. Turner was the commandant of Libby Prison. This escape, which occurred February 9, 1864, was a factor in hastening the transfer of prisoners from Richmond to the newly established prison at Andersonville, Georgia. Richmond papers reported the capture of twenty-five of the 109 escapees within 20 miles of Richmond, although forty-eight prisoners were eventually recaptured. *Official Records (Army)*, Series I, XXXIII, 559-561, 565-566; Series II, VI, 966; Hesseltine, *Civil War Prisons*, 131-132, 195.

Whilst the Lawyers were deciding upon the course to be pursued, Sue & I amused ourselves looking around upon the novel scene. The swearing in of the Grand Jury which was going on struck us with particular amusement. I had imagined the administering an oath a solemn thing but I found it instead simply ludicrous—five or six unconcerned indifferent looking men grasped simultaneously the sides & corners of a greasy looking leather bound book whilst a spruce looking clerk gabbled over something the only audible words of which were "so help you God," & the book then passed from lip to lip & they were sworn jurors; & in place of the solemn silence I had presumed prevailed, everybody was attending to their own business, talking & laughing as they listed. Mr Smith took my affidavit to a conversation I had held in May 1861 with Mrs Van Courtlandt respecting her sentiments toward the North & her intention of making the South her residence, to be used in her behalf in a suit brought by the Confederate States to Confiscate some property she has here as an Alien Enemy. I hope it will be of use to her, for poor Lady, it will be a cruel mortification to her as well as a great injustice should she thus be recorded.

Went to see the Navy Yard and the Gunboat "Albemarle," our old acquaintance upon whom we waited until dark last summer at Edwards Ferry to see her take her proper element. She is now nearly completed, Engines & Propeller in & will, if the Department at Richmond send on the iron to complete her armour, steam down the river next month. Captain Cook is in command of the station & his energy & decision in getting so much accomplished in so short a time is surprising. We saw some of the famous Brooke Guns, much smaller in the bore than I had supposed. Susy & I made a call on Mrs M'Guire & Mrs Torney & came home in a cold rain which at times seemed determined to become sleet. In the Felton plantation we were met by Tom the Foreman with the news that another of Father's young negroes had left his work & gone off (I omitted to mention that two had gone off the night before) & that there were two white men with guns hiding in a neighboring Pine thicket. So soon as Mr E reached fathers he made all necessary dispositions for arresting them, dispositions which would have been successful but for the treachery of the foreman Jesse Bartly who, in spite of postive orders to the contrary (whilst Mr E was coming home for his arms), put them across the river, giving as a reason his fear lest "young Master should tell them (the negroes) to fall on the men & take them & that some of them would get shot." A villain! I hope father will sell him, for he is unworthy of the position of trust he holds.

About dinner time came Col Clarke having walked from Halifax! Mary should be complimented by such an instance of devotion. We had the happiness on Monday to receive a letter from Nora. She is quite well but gives a terrible picture of the state of the country & the oppression under which they live. Band after band of Yankee marauders succeed each other & rob at their

The C.S.S. *Albemarle* was a Confederate ram built on the Roanoke River. Mrs. Edmondston refers to its being "nearly completed" when she wrote in her journal on February 16, 1864. The photograph shown here was made at the Norfolk Navy Yard after the ram was salvaged, about 1865. (Photograph from Naval Photographic Center, Department of the Navy, Washington, D.C.

pleasure. Their Col, one P—says that "he has a right to take what he pleases, that he is ordered to burn the Mills, destroy provisions, in short make Fayette county a wilderness," & takes credit to himself for what he has left undone! They enter houses at night & actually strip the covering from the beds in which women & children are lying! It is terrible to think of, the insult & outrage to which she and her children are exposed. As yet, thank God, they have suffered for nothing and are able to hire servants.

Congress has most ungraciously prohibited the importation of Carpets. After begging and beseeching us to take the carpets from our floors & bestow them on the poor soldiers in place of blankets, now to prohibit us from replacing them seems a most ungenerous return for our sacrifice. Tea & Coffee are likewise interdicted. I suppose they wish to reduce us to Spartan simplicity & I shall not be surprised if their much talked "of Currency Bill" should make nails a legal tender in imitation of Lycurgus' Iron money.[13] President Davis

---

[13]Lycurgus, lawgiver of Sparta, supposedly prohibited the use or importation of gold and silver as money and substituted iron for the legal currency. Clough, *Plutarch Lives*, 55.

should order a Thanksgiving upon the 22d of Feb, for then the nation is releieved of this wretched incubus. If we heed them we shall all dine on Black Broth, that is, all but Congress men & Government officials, for they leave the door open for themselves to dress sumptuously and "to fare daintily every day."

FEBRUARY 19, 1864

Our Wedding day! Our one great anniversary of the year! Came home last night tho bitterly cold to keep it alone at home. Early on the morning of the 17th came a message to Mr E from Father requesting him to go down upon the Chowan & bring Lewis home, he having been arrested by our Pickets there. He accordingly went & Father sending the carriage for me, in the afternoon I went up to Conneconara to remain during his absence. It was intensely cold & Mr E had a terrible two days journey of it. It seems that Lewis and Hilliard the run-aways went up to a man whom they took to be a Quaker & asked his aid. He pretended that he was such & under the pretence of sheltering them took them to the house of a Mr Lassiter where he was staying & secured them. He himself was a soldier on leave. During the night they succeeded in getting apart (he had fastened them together), but Hilliard could not get the chain from his neck. Getting to the door they ran off & the soldier seizing his musket fired in the direction where he heard the chain rattle & Lewis says struck Hilliard. In the darkness they got off but soon became separated in their flight. Lewis ran on until he came to a picket station of Col Griffin's Regt.

Taking them to be Yankees he rushed up to them with "How d'ye! Mr Yankee, How d'ye! I am so glad to see you. We have been looking a long time for you." They humoured the joke & in a short time he cursed "the Rebels" soundly. Seeing the roof of a shed under the cliff he asked "if that was the Gunboat?," to which they answered in the affirmative when he said all right I feel safe now. When they told him to take a gun & come with them, they were going to fight immediately, he objected & on their insisting said "it was not fair—they ought to drill him first." I mention all this to show how he had been tampered with, for a more innocent, ignorant, inoffensive negroe than himself does not exist. He stammers so as to be almost dumb & how he found tongue to say all this is a marvel to those who know him. They amused themselves with him for some time threatening to hang & to shoot him & frightened him so that when his young master came he welcomed him most heartily as a deliverer & made a full & free confession, telling Mr E that it was through the persuasions of the Ferryman Jesse Bartley who was worked on by a free man Henry Cumbo who traveled regularly through our lines to the Yankees, that himself and many others of father's young negroes had been induced to consent to go off. On Thursday afternoon Mr E brought him home to Connecorara and a more penitent, distressed and, as the negroes say "*convinced*" individual has rarely been seen. His disclosures implicating several others, Father made his arrangements to sell them & we came home late on Thursday the 18th to aid him in carrying his wishes out & sent for Mr Whetmore to take the negroes to Richmond. He came here today to dinner & is off for Connecorara where we follow in a short time. No public affair worth recording.

Congress expired yesterday, for which God be praised! I would gladly join in a Jubilate or a Te Deum over its dissolution. Weather bitterly cold. Hands all day filling the Ice House & if we can judge from present prospects it will keep well. But half a wedding day. Mr Whetmore & this tiresome business of the negroes having absorbed one half.

FEBRUARY 22, 1864

Just at home from fathers where Mr E says he has been leading the life of an Old Bailey Lawyer. I hope the worst is now over. Jesse Bartley (near sixty years of age) seems to be the prime mover. He, by the inducement of a fine suit of clothes & a pr of boots, has persuaded several of fathers prime hands to agree to desert and run off to the Yankees. Lewis & Hillard seem to have been the pioneers, but Dow, Elzey, Rimmon, & Joe Spier are so deeply criminated that today they go off to Richmond. Joe Axe, the husband of my maid Fanny, & many others are by no means free from suspicion, but it has been determined on account of their youth to deal more mildly with them. Hoody Manuel, a hoary headed old traitor, it has been decided to keep & by his aid to arrest the arch apostate "*Cumbo.*" The Yankees give him $200 for every ablebodied negro he brings in to them & out of this sum he bribes his middlemen Jesse & Manuel who unsuspected work on the victims.

Whilst at Fathers we received the parting sting of our weak & imbecile Congress—the suspension of the Act of Habeas Corpus (or what is the same, delegating the power to suspend to the President), the Military, the Currency, and the Tax Bills. The first puts our liberties in the grasp of a simple man; the second resolves us with a Military despotism by putting all men between seventeen & fifty five into the service, allowing the President to *detail* whom he sees fit for domestic police, raising food for the Army, etc.; the third repudiates one third of the currency now in circulation, if not funded in four per cent bonds before the 1st of April; & the fourth taxes us so heavily that after Government has taken what it wants it leaves us little else to live on. Those who have their property out at interest are taxed 5 per cent leaving them one per cent for themselves, whilst the owners of slaves & whose money is invested in farming are so heavily mulcted that it almost amounts to an abolition of Slavery entirely so far as the profits are concerned. Well may we sing "Jubilate" over the death of such a body. I preserve the acts in my repertory marked severally B[14] . . . monuments of weakness on the part of Congress & of Ulysses like endurance on the part of the people.

In Kanawa we have captured & destroyed a gunboat & brought Gen Scammon & Staff prisoners to Richmond—to tunnel themselves out I suppose a-la-Streight & his 108 comrades. In Florida and on Johns Island Beauregard telegraphs that we have repulsed the enemy. In Missippi a column has advanced upon & taken possession of Jackson which was evacuated by us on their approach. Gen Polk, the Comdg Gen, has retired from Meridian & thrown himself between the enemy and Mobile. An attack from three points simultaneously is meditated upon that place: One from the Sea, another from Grant's Pass on the coast from N O, & a third from Jackson, Sherman in command. Bishop Polk's force is said to be feeble & his policy is to keep Sherman in play & detach him from his supports, draw him further from his base, & then suddenly to turn and fall upon him. Sixty five of the escaped Yankee officers have been recaptured, leaving forty four still at large. I hear of nothing being done to Turner, the Comdt of the Prison. We ought to call him "the Ration Saver."

The Alabama is again striking terror into the Yankee Pocket by the destruction she makes in their East India Shipping. When last heard from she was off Sumatra, having burnt one & bonded another A No 1 Clipper Ship.

February 24, 1864

Went today to Nettie Spruill's[15] funeral, poor thing! I remember her so lively & pleasant a child, the idol of her family, but her suffering has been so long that even her mother, whose heart strings are wrapped up in her, is resigned to her loss. For months she has been cut off from companionship of any save her nurses, her disease Consumption, causing her not only the last degree of prostration but acute suffering & yet I hear she was patient & resigned, aye even longed to die and be at rest. Poor Rebecca, my early friend! Death has spared you this pang! Thou hast gone before! Saw Mrs Spruill & her daughters in sight of my life long friendship. Poor woman, she reminded me of my mother's death & said that her child had died as she had done. Deep in my debt of gratitude for her kindness to me then, a debt I can never repay.

Dined at Hascosea & came home about sundown. Mr E off immediately to Conneconara in search of information against Cumbo whom he hopes with Hoody Manuel's aid (now turned States Evidence) to capture. It is near bed time & he is yet absent. Sent off yesterday a box to Amo & Charlie of such substantials as are left us. Mr McMahon values it at $200. The Dahlia &

---

[14]These newspaper articles are at the beginning of the second volume of the diary.

[15]Nettie Spruill was the daughter of Mr. and Mrs. George Evans Spruill. Montgomery, *Sketches of Old Warrenton*, 378-379.

Tube Rose Roots with which it is packed "for damage," as Papa used to say, going for nothing I suppose. Sent also some supplies to Col Clarke now stationed at Twilight station.

FEBRUARY 26, 1864

Have just seen a most sorrowful sight, the ruins or rather the ashes of our neighbor—Mr Whitmel Hill's house. It took fire from a spark on the roof and was in a short time entirely consumed. My friend Nannie evinced the utmost coolness & presence of mind & by her own exertions & the directions which she gave the servants, who all rendered the most efficient aid, much of the furniture, all the groceries & clothing of the family were saved. Mr Edmondston hapened to be passing on his way to Hascosea but too late to enter the building as the roof had just fallen in & the only thing he could do was to take charge of what had been rescued & see that it was put in a place of safety. He gave Nannie the keys of our Hascosea house & begged her to induce her father when he should come home to consider it as his own & remove at once there. Poor Mrs Tom Hill, owing to the inefficiency of her maid, lost all her jewelry, her childs & most of her own clothing, five new dresses for summer wear &, sad to say, all her infant clothes for which she will soon have use. Mr E carried me out in the buggy to tender what aid we could but found them on the eve of leaving for her sister's, Mrs Peter Smith's, where they will remain for the present. Sue & her cousins Sarah & Mattie Dunlop have just left us, having been interrupted in a visit they were making us by the arrival at Father's of Nannie Devereux & her Cousin Miss Myers.[16] It is pleasant to have young faces in the house.

FEBRUARY 28, 1864

Have just read in the Examiner General Orders No 23, by which "General Braxton Bragg is assigned to duty at the seat of Government & under the direction of the President is charged with the conduct of military operations in the Armies of the Confederacy," by order signed S Cooper Adj & Ins. Gen. So the deed is done! What we last week laughed at as idle & wild, a foolish rumour which no one heeded, is "un fait accompli." Gen Bragg, Bragg the incapable, the Unfortunate, is Commander in Chief! Unhappy man, unhappy in his birth, for he is, I beleive, the son of his parents who was born in jail where his Mother was imprisoned on a charge of murder & the murder, too, of a negro,[17] & now doubly unhappy in being elevated to a post for which he is

---

[16]Sarah Harrison Dunlop and Isabella Matoaca Dunlop were children of James and Isabella Lenox Maitland Dunlop of Petersburg, Virginia. Nannie (Annie Lane) Devereux's cousin "Miss Myers" was probably a daughter of Ellen Kennon Mordecai, a step-sister of Nannie Devereux's grandfather Moses Mordecai. Ellen K. Mordecai married Samuel Hays Myers of Richmond, Virginia. "Kennon Letters," *Virginia Magazine of History and Biography*, XXXI (July, 1923), 187.

[17]This story has been variously repeated, though usually with regard to one or the other of General Bragg's brothers: Thomas (1810-1872), North Carolina governor (1855-1859), United States senator

unfit over the head of a man too who has won the confidence of the country. The object of execration to the greater part of the nation, he will be viewed with suspicion & dislike and will ere long have cause to rue the blind unreasoning friendship with which Mr Davis regards him. Pray God the Army may submit & that this insult to their Idol Gen Lee be patiently borne by it.

Every mouth filled with criticism of the Currency & the Tax Bills. I have not heard one voice raised in their favour. We draw comfort from an odd source, the Richmond Examiner, who says . . . "therefore in spite of maladministration or perverseness or imbecility there is a healthier confidence that the people will bring all things right in the end. We are to have a splendid army in the field this spring & one way or another it will be fed. That is enough & with that nothing can fatally hurt us. *We can bear even Gen Bragg*, for he is not to command any Army in action, & he will surely scarce order Lee to fall back or Johnston's troops to hunt the duck in Mississippi or Beauregard to evacuate Charleston or Polk & Maury to raise the white flag on the Forts of Mobile! . . . This Confederate people is going to carry our Cause through & the whole Government along with it. . . . No incubus or Old Man of the Sea will weigh a feather. By Heaven's blessing we will carry them all on our shoulders, will pull through the very Quartermasters & even if that be possible the Commissaries themselves. There will be a heavy drag indeed. Yes Heaven's blessing alone can aid us. Whilst Mr Davis makes such a toy, such a play thing of a nation's love, reverence, & admiration, casts it away idly & lightly as a thing of naught, to indulge a personal predilection, what can we expect? The preamble of the act repealing Habeas Corpus recites that it is in accordance with his wishes. That sentence has cost him thousands of hearts & Bragg's elevation will cost many more. Shades of the Barons of Runemede who bequeathed to us that Charter which secures our birthright of freemen, weep over the degeneracy of your children."

Sherman is reported as falling back towards Vicksburg. We have had a cavalry engagement in which we were victorious. The cause of the retrograde now is unknown, supposed to be the impossibility of obtaining supplies. No further advance from Grant's Pass. Polk's force, my Aunt writes, is small, so our thanks are due to Sherman for not pressing him. Another success in Florida. A letter from Amo containing drafts of the Yankee missiles thrown into the city. Up to Feb 23d the number thrown amounted to between six & seven thousand & the damage done so slight as scarcely to be appreciable. Butler as brutal as ever in Norfolk, vide the order of his Satrap Wild, & his treatment of Miss Roan B. & [———].

(1859-1861), and the Confederate attorney general until 1862; or John (1806-1878), a member of Congress from Alabama. Margaret Crossland Bragg, Bragg's mother, was an "energetic and intelligent" woman. No substantiation of the rumor Mrs. Edmondston recorded was located by the editors. Don C. Seitz, *Braxton Bragg: General of the Confederacy* (Columbia: State Company, 1924), 1, 2; *Concise Dictionary of American Biography*, 102.

Busy yesterday cutting out shirts for Mr E out of some sheets & Valences. Fortunately I have linen for the bosoms as it is $15. Saw last week in Halifax a peice of gray confederate Uniform cloth, imported, which was held at $175 per yd! Sugar in Petersburg on the 22d, $12.50; flour, $300 to 325 per bll; Sorghum Sucre Syrup, $35 per gal; Sausage meat, $6 per lb; Bacon, $5 do; Corn & Meal, $10 per bu; Peas & Beans, $25 to 30 do; vide the price current. B

March 5, 1864

Saturday—Have had a busy week, having been since Tuesday out at Hascosea gardening. I have used the scissors & prunning knife so much that my hand is actually sore & so disfigured with scratches that it makes me laugh to look at it. Went on Friday to attend to poor Tom's grave. I had a rustic cross of cedar made for the head stone which will I hope before the summer is over be covered with ivy and had the grave itself covered with ivy, thinking that better than turf. I carried some evergreens but found that they would interfere with the general plan of the Cemetery, so gave them to Mrs Smith to be used at her discretion. I found her there superintending some workmen engaged in preparing the earth for placing a fine collection of evergreens which Mr Cheshire was to bring in the afternoon. Went to see Mrs Spruill, poor woman, & had a rapid canter home & found Mr E engaged in plans for the capture of Cumbo, Hoody Manuel, & some white men who are lurking about Mr. Johnston's & father's plantation. Today he had quite a levee in the dining room at Hascosea & came home to Looking Glass "a toute bride"[18] to meet some other (Northampton) men here & tonight he is off posting guards & looking about for them.

We missed several mails whilst out at Hascosea & stirring times indeed has the Confederacy passed through. On the 29th Gen Lee telegraphed from Orange Court House that the enemy's Cavalry were moving on both his flanks, that one column had gone in the direction of Fredericks' Hall on the Central Road & the other in that of Charlottsville. On this all the defences available were brought into action. The Richmond Clerks (Government) were called out & measures taken to intercept the marauders, for such only are they to be termed, for their object seemed to be only negroes and horses, their errand to burn & to steal. They divided themselves into several parties, each seeming to vie with the other, Kilpatrick in command, he the prince of theives! But I beg Gen Butler's pardon! No one can out rank him in that line. One division pursued almost the same route as that taken by the Raiders last summer, through Goochland, past Hanover, & thence across the Pamunky. They burned Mr Morson's house, barn, & outhouse, sacking & plundering as

---

[18]French, "at full speed."

they listed & then going to his neighbor and brother in law Sec Seddon's,[19] they burned his barns and provisions, only leaving the residence. One troop came within 2½ miles of Richmond, to the house of Mr John Young, & ordered dinner & there remained for two or three hours, making their band (a fine one) play for them. They were, contrary to the usual custom very polite & did no damage but made fine speeches to the ladies, & apologized for taking the mules & horses Mr Y being from home, fortunately for him, at the time.

This, (Kilpatrick's) Division, came down to Battery no 9 of the Richmond Defences & threw several shells at long range at it, but none of them came close enough to do any damage save to Mother Earth who received them in [her] bosom—Iron seed which I hope will be repaid with interest by her children! At night Gen Hampton with the 1st N C Cav & a portion of another Regt surprised & drove them from their camp in great confusion; he was too weak to follow, they having 3500 men. This was at Atlee's Station. Gen H took many prisoners & horses. During Tuesday night one hundred & thirty eight prisoners were brought in representing twelve Regts of Cav. They had beside two Brigades of light Artillery, but it were long to follow the track of each party, the same tale is stamped in the pathway of all. Col Bradley Johnson repulsed them at Hanover. Maj Beckham[20] with his Horse Artillery drove them back when within two miles of Charlottesville.

The account sums up on our side *The Insult!!* several Mills burned, many negroes, mules, & horses captured, private dwellings burned, provisions destroyed, women & children frightened, Capt Ellery[21] of the Richmond Bat killed, & several men slightly wounded; on theirs—*their failure to take Richmond!!* between three & four hundred men captured including several officers from Lieut Col down, two or three hundred killed, & many severely wounded & left at houses on the way, several peices of field artillery, many mules & horses, eighty or a hundred horse accoutrements, McClellan saddles, etc., captured, their horses thoroughly jaded & broken down so that they

---

[19]James A. Seddon (1815-1880) was a prominent Virginia lawyer and politician. He served in the United States Congress (1845-1847, 1849-1851), the first Confederate Congress, and as the Confederate secretary of war. Seddon and his brother-in-law, James M. Morson, were cousins; each was married to a daughter of James Bruce of Woodburn in Halifax County, Virginia. *Concise Dictionary of American Biography*, 930-931; "Bruce Genealogy," *Virginia Magazine of History and Biography*, XII (April, 1905), 452. See also footnote 287, 1862.

[20]Maj. R. F. Beckham (1837-1864), the son of John G. and Mary C. Beckham, served in the Stuart Horse Artillery (Virginia) Battalion. He was killed near Franklin, Tennessee, during an advance of Hood's army. James Madison Beckham, *Genealogy of the Beckham Family in Virginia* (Richmond: O. E. Flanhart Printing Company, 1910), 47.

[21]Capt. Albert Ellery, chief clerk in the second auditor's office and a member of the Departmental Battalion, was killed in the fighting around Richmond, March 2, 1864. *Richmond Examiner*, March 3, 1864. The Departmental Battalion, also known as the Richmond City Battalion, was a part of the "local defenses, special service" organization composed of about 1,300 men from the War, Treasury, Navy, and Postmaster General's departments and of battalions formed by men in the quartermaster's office, the arsenal, armory, and Tredegar ironworks. *Official Records (Army)*, Series I, XXXIII, 1301.

are unfit for service, & their men (mostly Dutch) demoralized & dispersed. So say Journal, on whose side is the balance?

Gen Finnegans' victory in Florida appears much more important than we had supposed. It seems it was intended by the Yankees to take possession of the State or such portion of it as should enable them to claim that it cast its vote for them in the Presidential Election. They landed at Jacksonville & came on unmolested to Ocean Ponds (on old maps called Alligator) where Finnegan met them with a small body of Georgians & Floridians, about one third their own number. They put two Regts of Black troops in their van, driving them on at the point of the bayonette. They were met by the 19th Georg. & the slaughter was terrific; carnage such as even this bloody war has rarely witnessed. As we advanced they retreated & for miles the earth was strewed with dead negroes. Then came the whites—& spite of their immense odds—10,000 to 3,500—so dreadful was the onslaught that they broke & fled. There was more *dead on the field than Confederates in action.* We lost *sixty* only killed & between six and seven hundred wounded mostly, however, slightly so, the negroes shooting wild & the Yankees occupied hiding behind & driving them on. At the last accounts the scattered remnants of the Yankee force was running to their "Gun Boats." Sherman's late advance upon Polk's lines seems to have been intended as a ruse to draw troops from Johnston. A heavy advance has been made from Chattanooga upon Dalton & from all that we can learn from prisoners & Yankee papers Johnston was expected to "fall back," but he did not come up to their expectations, when Grant not wishing to bring on a general engagement "fell back"—disappointed himself. Longstreet is making some movements in West Tennessee which the papers grow eloquent in entreating us not to despond at. "It all means well, tho he seems to retire," may-be-so, but we will wait until we learn more. The seige of Charleston flags & the Yankee Press is sick of it & says it ought to be abandoned "Le jeu ne vaut pas la chandelle."[22] They now pronounce their famous "Greek Fire" a humbug, "attended with more danger to the projectors than to the projected against." No wisdom like that gained by experience, O most sapient Yankee nation.

Mosby has performed a brilliant exploit; promotion, it seems, has not spoiled him. He attacked a body of the enemy one hundred & eighty strong, routed them, killing fifteen, wounding many more, capturing seventy with horses, arms, equipments, etc., with a loss to himself of one killed, 4 slightly wounded; & on the 26th near Upperville with 60 men he attacked 250 of the enemy's Cavalry who retreated before him leaving six (one Captain) dead on the field and one Lieut & seven Privates in Mosby's hands. The number of their wounded was so great that they impressed waggons to carry them & the

---

[22]French, "The game is not worth the candle."

road was strewn with equipments, arms, Haversacks, etc. His own loss, two wounded. but I preserve Gen Stuarts official dispatch D.[23]

Whilst in the garden at Hascosea clipping & prunning on Tuesday or Wednesday, suddenly came through the still air the boom of cannon. Conjectures were vain, but in due course of time came the tidings that we were attacking a Gunboat on the Chowan & that after disabling we were proceeding to take possession when three more came to the rescue & tho we kept up the action injuring more of them, yet were eventually forced to retire.[24] Ransom's Brigade it was in action. Col Clarke was I suppose there.

Today March the 5th the first Peach bloom (the Honey Peach) expanded at Hascosea & driving home I found the Plums also struggling into blossom. Am quite excited by a new method of sticking evergreen cuttings, given me by Mrs Smith yesterday, i.e., in Peat, black wet sour looking stuff. I should think it would need all the lime in the Confederacy to make it available for the purposes of vegetation, but she showed me the results & I came home with a handful of rare & choice cuttings which she gave me & put them down according to her instructions, choosing a Northern exposure & building a shelter of Pine bushes over them & next fall 'nous verrons.' Chatted with Mr E of my Arboretum which, when the war is over and nails are cheap so that I can enclose it, I am going to have. I do not think I will admit a deciduous tree & but few shrubs. Tho Mad de Stael does call Evergreen the "devil de la nature," I like them. Have had the girls to dine with me twice, once here on Monday & again on Wednesday at Hascosea, and am as busy as these thorn pricked fingers will let me be netting them some fancy nets for their hair. Nannie is well informed, pleasant & lady like, has a good address & does her parents much credit. But I am sleepy, near twelve o'clock & no Mr E. I wish the Yankees had old Hoody Manuel, & Cumbo, too, for that matter.

MARCH 8, 1864

News last night which makes the blood of all true hearted Confederates boil in their veins at this new instance of Yankee wickedness & meanness. Lieut Pollard Comdg Company H of the 9th Va Cavelry, aided by some Home guards & a small detachment from Lieut Col Robbin's Command, followed a large party of the Yankee Cavalry, harrassing their rear all day Wednesday, crossing the Mattapony after them. The Enemy under Col Dahlgreen's command took the fork of the road leading to Walkertown when Lieut Pollard, hastily dividing his force, left a small body in pursuit & taking the other fork

---

[23]The dispatch was not preserved in the diary.

[24]The Federal gunboat *Bombshell*, combing the Chowan River for refugees, deserters, and Negroes, was fired upon by Confederate batteries which came close to capturing her on March 1-2, 1864. She escaped under the covering fire of the U.S.S. *Southfield* and *Whitehead*, both under the direction of Lt. Cmdr. Charles Flusser. *Civil War Naval Chronology,* IV, 26; Barrett, *Civil War in North Carolina,* 212.

succeeding in a circuit, & having been joined by the forces above named, appeared on their front about eleven at night; Dahlgren ordered a charge—& in the act was shot through the head. A fight then ensued in which he took 90 prisoners, 35 negroes, & 150 horses & the rest of the enemy dispersed in the darkness in wild flight through the woods. On Col Dahlgren's person was found memoranda & orders disclosing a most diabolical plan in which, God be praised, he was defeated.[25] He was to cross to the South side of the James about thirty miles above Richmond with one Squadron, keeping the other on the North side, signalling each other as they went. That on the South side was to seize the bridges at Richmond, release the prisoners on Belle Isle, arming them from waggons which they carried loaded with small arms for the purpose & supplying them with oakum balls soaked in tar with which they were all well provided for the purpose of destroying the city by fire.

The North side party was to destroy the Arsenal etc. at Bellona & the two Squadrons making a junction in the city were to seize Mr Davis & his Cabinet, *hang them* immediately, join the prisoners in setting the city on fire, & by daybreak be across the Pamunky in full retreat, leaving murder, rapine, & a city in ashes behind them. But God ordained otherwise. A negroe whom they seized for a guide brought them, doubtless in good faith to them, to a point on the James where he told them they could cross; but the River being higher than he was aware of, when they reached the place, they were unable to do so, whereupon they instantly hanged him. This, however, disconcerted their plans and meeting with a stouter resistance than they thought, they were forced to retreat without so much as entering Richmond. Are our enemies civilized? Do they even *profess* the doctrines of Christ? What sort of a return is this for the way our troops acted towards them in their last summer's campaign into Penn? We respected all private rights, horses only excepted, & not *one* private dwelling in ashes marked the footsteps of our army. One only was molested & that by three men, Mississippians, who had all of them had their own houses burned by the enemy & their wives & children driven out homeless. They dared not *burn* it in retaliation, for they feared the smoke would betray them & that Gen Lee in stern justice would visit on them the penalty of a violated Order, so they only hacked & hewed the furniture to peices, & tell me how many thousand of our Southern homes have been thus and worse treated? Blood thirsty tho it appears, our Government ought to adopt a different course with men captured on such an expedition. It is not regular warfare & they are not entitled to the privileges of prisoners of war. It is mockery

[25]Lt. James Pollard of the Ninth Virginia Cavalry and Lt. Col. William T. Robins of the Twenty-fourth Virginia Cavalry conducted the Confederate attack on Col. Ulric Dahlgren's command. Dahlgren (1842-1864) was the son of Rear Adm. John Adolphus Bernard Dahlgren of the United States Navy. The authenticity of the papers allegedly found on Dahlgren's body has been the subject of considerable controversy. The possibility of forgery exists although recent study of the documents has produced evidence supporting their authenticity. Virgil Carrington Jones, *Eight Hours Before Richmond* (New York: Henry Holt and Company, 1957), 92-93, 100-103, 123-129, 136-141, 143-148, 168, 174; Boatner, *Civil War Dictionary*, 218-219.

to insist that they are. Dahlgren is the son of the Commodore now in command before Charleston. The one aids in the infamous attempt to destroy a whole city & to hurry thousands of non-combattants incapable of resistance to a dreadful death. The other is even worse; at the head of a gang of picked ruffians armed with fire balls, his deliberate purpose is to turn loose upon innocent women a mixed multitude, a mob of prisoners, without even the show of an authority to command them, with orders to pillage, burn, destroy, murder; in short, do all that their evil passions prompt them, whilst he himself a commissioned officer of the U S hangs without trial the heads of a Government whose meanest soldier his Government has admitted to the rights of a belligerent. Talk of Punic Faith no more! hence forth let it be "Yankee faith." Like father like son. Dahlgren and Kilpatrick's paths are marked with desolation, vide some of the particulars marked D.[26]

MARCH 10, 1864

Eighteen years today since we first commenced housekeeping, since I first took my seat opposite Mr E at the breakfast table! Eighteen years that I have been "premier officer de la bouche"[27] to him, eighteen years of great happiness & contentment, for which my God I thank thee. My happiness apart from Mr E has arisen—but what am I saying? I have no happiness apart from him. The enjoyment I take in life & its cares would be small indeed without him to share them.

New disclosures of the villainy intended by the enemy in their late raid. The Yankee press is diabolical in its glee as it recites the enormities expected to be perpetrated by Kilpatrick, Dahlgreen, & their crew of scoundrels, but a merciful God has brought them all to naught & instead of triumphant cruelty are many bloody graves & four hundred dejected prisoners before whom the gallows looms in the distance. Gen Ransom has marched through our North Eastern counties destroying the Locks of the Dismal Swamp Canal & threatens Suffolk. We have no particulars, telegrams only. Sherman is in full retreat, terribly harrassed by Forrest and his Cavalry. His advance was no feint to draw off troops from Johnston but a move on Mobile or Selma & terribly in earnest. Our Cavalry cut off his supplies & reduced him to the third of a ration. The poor inhabitants on his route suffer for it, for he has deprived them of everything in the shape of food & almost lodging, for his course is marked by naked chimneys standing in a heap of ashes which shows where once there was a home. Brownlow[28] the infamous is dead.* Some wag,

*a mistake or rather a *Yankee lie*

---

[26]These clippings are not in the diary.

[27]French, "first cook."

[28]William Gannaway Brownlow (1805-1877) was a leading Tennessee Unionist and Reconstruction governor of that state. An itinerant preacher, writer, and editor of the *Knoxville Whig*, he had predicted in

more witty than reverent, says that is the reason it is so hot; his Master gives him so warm a reception below that we feel it here.

MARCH 12, 1864

Mr E drilling the Home Guards. Father very busy putting down his long projected Flume. To me it seems but the beginning of sorrows. He was unfortunate in having rain after so long a spell of fine weather to begin it in & today all hands are driven from the work by a sudden & rapid rise in the river. He dined here today & yesterday but left hurriedly for fear of being cut off by the water in the Beaver Dam. Sarah Dunlop & her sister & their escort home, Mr Corbin Carr, also dined with us. Set two Dorking Hens on 24 eggs & 4 Bremen Geese on forty eight today. Ah! Mrs Edmondston you were born methinks "to love pigs & chickens."

Gen Ransom has seized & holds Suffolk & has beaten up Butler's quarters within five miles of Norfolk. Well done General Mat! I ought to quote to myself the adage "A prophet is not without honour,"[29] etc., for certainly I never expected it of him but was prepared for failure when I heard he was in command. The victory in Florida most decisive. The Yankee press are bitter over the fact that 2500 lives were lost in an attempt to secure an Electoral vote for Mr Lincoln. How does the dear people like that? Bombardment of the forts below Mobile has commenced. I wonder whether in earnest or not? But time will show.

MARCH 20, 1864

All Father's work at the new flume thrown away, for on Sunday last the foundation of it was washed up & started on a rapid voyage over the Low grounds in the direction of Conneconara, doubtless to pay its respects to him! It all has to be done over again. Walked with Mr E there this morning & through the breach in the dam to the river's brink. The earth is washed out deeply & the different strata formed by successive freshets are very perceptible. I did not realize the rapid increase of the deposite until we noticed the young growth which had been cut down & ere the stumps had begun to show marks of decay, they were buried at least three ft in the earth & trees of a larger size in vigorous growth upon them.

As is universally in all newly opened spots on the river bank, we found quantities of Indian pottery but of an unusual manufacture. All that I have hitherto seen being simply baked clay & of a small size, but these had sand &

1832 that slavery would shake the United States to its foundations. Until it was suppressed in October, 1861, his paper continued to publish Unionist arguments and support Lincoln; and Brownlow was charged with treason for the content of his final editorial. After the war and his two terms as governor, Brownlow served in the United States Senate for one term; then he returned to Tennessee where he rebought and edited the *Knoxville Whig. Dictionary of American Biography*, III, 177-178.

[29]Matthew 13:57.

gravel as large as a pea worked up in them & the peices seemed to indicate that they had composed a vessel of considerable diameter. Perhaps the utensil formed part of the "abbattrie de cuisine"[30] of some Cheif or they may have composed some Sacred vessel & may have been as precious in the eyes of their possessor as the "Shards of the Luck of Edenhall."[31] One thing is certain, from the vast quantity of these peices of pottery & the area over which they are thickly distributed, this country must in former days have supported a dense Indian population. Would that one could speak & relate to us its history & tell us how many years have rolled by since it last saw the light! The only perfect pot I have ever seen is in my possession at Hascosea & was dug out by the negroes whilst excavating earth for the dams at Polenta. It was found sitting on some charcoal & half burned sticks at some depth in the earth, just as the Indian Squaw who last used it may have left it! It may be older than Columbus!

Have been amusing myself this last week compiling what I term "a book of Contemporaries" begining at the Creation & coming regularly down, collecting in groups the distinguished men & acts of past time. I have nearly finished the form, the skeleton so to speak, and indicated the more remarkable and well known points. The rest the *flesh* is to be the product of my future reading; when I meet an important factor or character, date him & preserve him for future reference. It differs some what from a Chronological table in its form & constitutes a book of leaves. Have been re-reading Neibuhr,[32] having finished Plutarch, & relish my pabulum so much that I propose to review Gillie & even Gibbon,[33] so much for getting interested in a thing.

I met an anecdote in Tatler recently which amused & struck me as so apropos to something which happened to me recently (i.e., an Authoress reading her own verses to me & putting my politeness & sincerity to a severe test by asking my candid opinion) that I must record it here. Philoxemus, it is said, being invited to dine with Dionysius[34] (tyrant of Syracuse) and to hear him recite some poetical composition, was the only one of the guests who took the liberty of censuring it. He was condemned to the mines, but being soon after set at liberty and invited to hear another recitation, he held his peace when

---

[30]French, "set of kitchen dishes."

[31]Traditionally the luck of the Musgrave family of Edenhall, in England, supposedly depended on a goblet left by the "little folk" at St. Cuthbert's well. Benét, *Reader's Encyclopedia*, 332.

[32]Barthold Georg Niebuhr (1776-1831) was a German historian, statesman, and philologist. His primary work was the *History of Rome* (three volumes, 1811-1832). *Webster's Biographical Dictionary*, 1100.

[33]John Gillies (1747-1836) was a Scottish historian and classical scholar. Edward Gibbon (1737-1794) was a prominent English historian and member of Parliament. His major historical work was *The History of the Decline and Fall of the Roman Empire*, published in five volumes between 1776 and 1778. *Webster's Biographical Dictionary*, 595, 591.

[34]Philoxenos of Leucadia was an ancient Greek epicure described in Aristotle's *Ethics*. Benét, *Reader's Encyclopedia*, 849. The Dionysius mentioned in the text probably referred to Dionysius the Elder (ca. 430-367 B.C.), a political despot who ruled Syracuse, held extensive influence in Greece, and promoted writing and drama. *Webster's Biographical Dictionary*, 42.

it came to his turn to give his opinion. "What," said Dionysius, "have you nothing to say on this occasion?" "Carry me back to the mines," said Philoxenus. Dionysius, we are told, was not displeased with the answer. I shall often think of that dry terse answer, "Carry me back to the Mines."

We have had some sharp cold weather. The peaches are I hope, however, only thinned out by it as they are not in full bloom. On the 17th, St Patrick's, we had ice of some thickness, & I bid adieu, alas, to the full glory of my hyacinth bed, as some of my handsomest flowers were frozen transparent & fell hopelessly down & now lie black & blasted amongst their hardier brethren. But for public news—matters of general interest journal; bear in mind that *that* is your sheet anchor, your hold on life, for even now I have some times fears lest I be compelled to sacrifice you to the manes of the Time spent (shall I say lost) in your compilation.

Rummors which no longer excite or interest us of a recognition by France. The time is gone by when we would have prized it & I feel very much as Dr Johnson did towards Ld Chesterfield.[35] What is more to the purpose we have sunk two of the best vessels in the Yankee Navy, one the Housatonic off Charleston by a torpedo exploded under her bows by our submarine boat the Hunley.[36] She sank in eight minutes with her twelve guns & 300 men many of whom were drowned, but sad to relate the brave crew of the Hunley are supposed also to have perished as nothing has been heard of either men or craft since! Sad indeed! I have not heard their names as the fact is kept a secret to increase the panic felt on board the other Yankee blockaders. The second boat, or rather vessel, for she was a first class Man of War, the Peterhoff, ventured too near our Batteries at Fort Holmes at the mouth of Cape Fear, when bang, a double headed shot struck her full in the quarter! & before she could turn, a second went through her smoke stack, a third disabled her, & she lay at our mercy. Father Neptune soon embraced the tyranical vessel & put an end to her stopping ships on the high seas.[37]

---

[35]This reference is to Dr. Samuel Johnson's famous letter of rebuke to Lord Chesterfield, February 7, 1755. Chesterfield wrote two articles praising Johnson's *Dictionary* and proposed becoming Johnson's patron. Johnson, angry that Chesterfield had waited until all the hard work was done before offering his support, wrote the letter in which he expressed his resentment and defended literary independence over the patronage system. Chesterfield amiably accepted the rebuff. *Dictionary of National Biography*, LIV, 32.

[36]The *H. L. Hunley*, built at Mobile in 1863, was a submarine with a speed of four miles an hour in "smooth water and light current." Commanded by Lt. George E. Dixon, the *H. L. Hunley* successfully torpedoed the U.S.S. *Housatonic* off Charleston on February 17, 1864. The loss of life on board the *Housatonic* was limited to five men, but the entire crew of the *H. L. Hunley* perished when the submarine sank. A theory was advanced that "the torpedoes being placed at the bow of the boat she went into the hole made in the *Housatonic* by explosion of torpedoes and did not have sufficient power to back out, consequently sunk with her." *Official Records (Navy)*, Series I, XVI, 427; *Civil War Naval Chronology*, IV, 21. The important aspect of the engagement was that a submarine had sunk an enemy ship with torpedoes for the first time in naval history.

[37]On March 6, 1864, the U.S.S. *Peterhoff* was accidentally rammed by the U.S.S. *Monticello*, another blockader, off New Inlet, North Carolina. On March 7, the U.S.S. *Mount Vernon* destroyed the submerged *Peterhoff* to prevent the Confederates from salvaging her. *Civil War Naval Chronology*, IV, 29.

Sherman has retreated to Vicksburg whilst our cavalry followed close on his heels, dashed into Yazoo city, burnt a lot of Yankee cotton (stolen) awaiting shipment, commissary & qr Master stores, killed a number of the enemy, & were out with a loss of seventy on our side killed & wounded. Grant is in Washington enjoying a ovation & the title of Lieut Gen & Com in Cheif, assisting too at a Council of War which the Yankee papers tell us determine on a new "On to Richmond," this time with three columns each of 100,000 men in buckram? Hey Mr Bluster? They mourn the failure of Kilpatrick's incendiary raid upon which Dahlgreen had the hardihood to "ask God's blessing" & promised his crew of cutthroats that if successful they would write their names on the hearts of their countrymen & winds up with a flourish about the braves who swept through Richmond & their "holy cause." Has God given them over to a strong delusion that they should beleive a lie or is this all bosh & balderdash—a hypocritical flying in the face of the Almighty? The Exchange of prisoners has been resumed for which thank God! The Enemy receded from their demands that Butler should be the agent of exchange & quietly dropped back to Maj Mulford[38] with whom Mr Ould, our Commissioner, formerly treated. Two boat loads of our unfortunate men have arrived & the details they give of the horrors of a Northern Prison House, particularly those whom the Christian Burnside sent to the Ohio Penitentiary, freeze ones blood with horror one moment & the next makes it boil in our veins with indignation.

Mr Wilkinson, the Agent of the Hospital, has been here for supplies. His trip was almost unsuccessful, for besides some Potatoes which Mr E had bought for him, some Lard which we could ill spare from the plantation but felt forced to sell him, & some Peas which Mr E gave him squeezed from the seed peas & the few household things I could contribute (very few indeed) & some eggs, 27 doz, which we bought from the negroes, he went back as he came. No one else had anything to spare, so swept is our country by Gov Agents & Commissaries. Mrs Webb wrote me that the "Major was again with them with a very badly burned foot." Mr Wilkinson tells that is very *severely* burned & that it will be three or four months before he is fit for duty, does not know how the accident occurred & James has not written himself.

Sunday evening—have just come in from a long walk with Mr E; went to look at his secret drains finished & in progress. One which will be covered tomorrow runs through a ridge, 'the Holly Ridge,' & is such a marvel of a skilfully cut ditch that I must record its dimension—8 ft 9 in in depth & only two ft wide at top & narrower at bottom & this for some twenty or more yds

[38]Maj. John Elmer Mulford was an assistant to Gen. S. A. Meredith, United States commissioner for the exchange of prisoners. Mulford later returned to active duty in the army and was brevetted brigadier general in July, 1864. Boatner, *Civil War Dictionary*, 543, 574; Hesseltine, *Civil War Prisons*, 102.

when it gradually falls off to a less Brobdignag[39] depth! It is what is called a debouchere, to draw the water from one level to another paralel to it but lower & thus save its running back a half mile or more around the head of the Ridge. Patrick is an excellent farmer, scientific & practical, & uses his knoledge to the best purpose. I enjoy my walks & rides with him. They are at once pleasant & improving. I thank Thee O God that Thou has cast my lines in so pleasant places, that Thou makest me to taste the blessing which I read in yesterday's Lesson—promised the Israelites "Ye shall rejoice in all that ye put your hand unto, ye and your households" Deut. 12th-7th.

MARCH 21, 1864

Today came Father to lay again the foundation of his Flume. Inauspicious weather for it commenced snowing briskly after breakfast & continued all day. He proposed to me to go with him to call upon Mr & Mrs Urquehart of Va now on a visit to their relatives here. So with the soft fleecy flakes of snow falling around us we started but at the Mill met Mr U & Mr Hill who told us that the ladies were out, so we returned home. Father & Mr Urquehart are secret ditchers con armore, & it was most amusing to see their recounter. Each opened his budget and "Sir, did you ever try this?" & "Yes sir, I dug a drain." "My pipes." "I have a low flat marshey peice of land, and sir, I have a secret drain 1500 yds long." Sometimes they talked both together, Mr U standing at the carriage door powdered with snow flakes, illustrating his "crooked pipes" with father's cane—altogether as pleasant a sight as one often sees, two white headed venerable men "rejoicing in what they put their hands to"!

MARCH 22, 1864

Snowing fast & furiously all day & today, which was not the case yesterday, the snow lies where it falls, & the earth is wrapped in a winding sheet. My Hyacinths peep out from their white envelope & make one sad to look at them. They remind me of fair young girls who have just taken the White Veil & are not yet dead to all of Earth's enjoyments. The brilliant yellow of Forsythia now in magnificent bloom shows in sickly contrast to the pallor of all around it. White does not bring out its beauty as strongly as does a green carpet. Ah! for the Peaches! We breath a sigh over, I fear now extinct, hopes of a harvest. No dawdling through the "fragrant orchard" this summer, no flitting from tree to tree in search of new beauties, and, fie, Mrs Edmondston, for so sublunary a thought, no luscious desserts which cost the pleasure only of gathering.

---

[39]Brobdingnag was the land of giants in Jonathan Swift's *Gulliver's Travels* (1726). Benét, *Reader's Encyclopedia*, 144.

Father dined with us again & contrary to our entreaties left in the snow and sleet for home, mama being alone. Patrick had so amusing an instance of the effect of the snow upon Cuffey that I must record it. Being at Father's Flume endeavouring to pursuade him to come in & let him superintend it for him he saw Kenny who with Joe Exum (two stout stalwart men) had stopped work "*to warm*," holding his *hand spike* to the fire to warm it also before he resumed his labor of lifting & carrying timber, a fact which he frankly admitted. Think of that, ye hard worked navvies of England, ye poor labourers of Ireland, who in storm & sleet are forced to toil still for the daily bread which ye need in hard even more than in good weather. A southern negro when forced by a pressing & unusual neccessity to work in a soft falling fleecy snow stops to warm himself and his handspike. The sleet commenced after dinner—& ere that Cuffy was snugly housed for the night.

March 23, 1864

The deepest snow we have had for years. On a level where there was no possibility of a drift it, this morning, was 7 inches deep & when we remember that for twenty-four hours it melted as it fell & accumulated only after the earth was chilled, we may well be amazed at the quantity which has fallen. Mr E came in from riding & called me out this afternoon to look at the traces of worms, or what seemed to us to be such traces, all over the surface of the snow. It was most singular, as tho myriads of earth worms had been thrown down & left each an impression of his tortuous figure on the soft white substance. Not a worm, however, could we find, nor even a place where he had seemingly wriggled into the bosom of his mother Earth. They seem to have come there to make their impressions in intaglio and then to have vanished. On going in I turned to Gilbert White's Nat Hist of Selbourne[40] & there found in a note to that delightful book that such a thing as the snow having been covered with Earth worms had occurred in the knoledge of the Editor, but he was more fortunate than we were, for he saw the worms themselves & in such numbers as to attract his attention from the window, whilst we saw only the impression left by the unhappy wretches struggling in their icy bed. The weather described precedent to the fall of snow then & that before this fall correspond exactly. Father dined with us again. His Flume goes on bravely.

Mr & Mrs Lincoln have given a practical evidence of their approval of amalgamation by receiving with "marked attention" two negroes at their late Levee, two coloured surgeons of a negro Regiment now stationed at Washington. Think how society must have changed in Washington within the last three years! What would Gen & Mrs Washington have thought of such guests at a Presidential Levee? It is enough to make Mr Jefferson (author tho he is of

---

[40]Gilbert White (1720-1793) was an English naturalist and curate who wrote *A Natural History and Antiquities of Selborne* (1789). Benét, *Reader's Encyclopedia*, 1205.

many of the defects of government which led to our present unhappy state) turn in his grave!

April 4, 1864

Went to Hascosea via Conneconara on the 30th, bent on accomplishing much garden & Horticultural work, but the "clerk of the weather" played us an April Fool on a grand scale, for it rained incessantly—& being on horseback—& knowing that we could not cross at Hill's Mill (for we left the river rising), we were weather bound until Sunday, when we came down to the Mill, & sending our horses back, crossed in a canoe & found Dick & a mule cart with plenty of clean straw for mistress' equipage, whilst Ananias held a horse for Master. So through ploughed fields, our bridgeless ditches, across furrows & hedgerows, with many a thump & jolt, I came at last safe home. I was repaid for my ride across "the untrodden ways," however, by a full sight of a Doe & fawn which started up a few ft only in front of us. I had a view of them in the open field for more than a mile as they ran, startled, to their court. The dam stopped often apparently to allow the fawn to rest & if the eye was once removed from them, when quiet, it was impossible for me to distinguish them again until they recommenced their flight, so exactly correspondant were they in colour to the stubble and dry grass with which the field was covered. In a lane near Hascosea we saw the first martin looking wearied & worn out, with his plumage ruffled as tho just off a long journey! They are late this year, as they generally arrive about the 25th of March. Today a solitary individual made his appearance here, but he looked too much tired & disgusted with the weather which greeted him (a dull cold rain & keen east wind, seemingly laden with Pneumonias, Pleurisys, and all other ills that lungs are heir to) even to chirrup!

The newspapers are dull which is a good sign for us. Grant is to head another "On to Richmond," which is to start about the 15th of this month. Pray God that Bragg may have nothing to do with the campaign against him. He has been beaten too often by him already. The financial crisis is for the present over. Funding in 4 per ct Bonds having ceased on the first, all notes over the $5 have now lost 33 1/3 per cent out of every dollar. There is great gratulation & glorification made by some persons over the reduction of the Currency, but I cannot see what permanent good is to result from it so long as that body—Mr Meminger has power to stamp and sign more by the millions. I wish his parents had never thought of emigrating from Germany to this country. He would now in all likelihood be vine dressing, eating black bread & sour Krout instead of faring "sumptuously every day" & coining money as fast as the good genius in a Fairy tale! The analogy holds good in more points than one. Those fairy gifts had a way of becoming useless, turning to gingerbread, dry leaves, nuts & medlars, at the most inconvenient time, even as his

Treasury notes are now little but waste paper. I wish Gov Bennett[41] had left him alone in the Orphan House & that he might have filled an humbler sphere with equal happiness to himself & less damage to his adopted country.

To our surprise Forrest is reported at Paducah! "O where was Morgan then?" That is his field & without disparagement to Gen Forrest, *it is where Morgan ought to be*; but there is a screw loose between him and the Government. I will not accept the Examiner's account of it, but there is something which we do not see into. I append Gen Johnston's report of Pemberton and his disobedience of orders with respect to the defence of Vicksburg. The instinct of the country was right in placing the blame where it did. *Mr Davis is a firm friend.* I preserve also a speech made in the Yankee Congress by a Mr Allen respecting the Yankee hero *"Ben Butler."* We do not paint him much blacker. Also some strictures on Burnside the Christian.[42] Ah! mon General! it is easier to "stand like a sea God," distinguished only by your "yellow belt," than to face such an attack as that. You think it too personal, hey my Christian hero?—but you must remember that deeds such as yours, arresting men in the dead of night because they claim freedom of speech, sending soldiers & gentlemen to a Penitentiary & confining them in cells too narrow to turn in, burning houses, stealing carriages & pianos, have two points of view—one, that taken by flatterers & theives who make a convenience of you & the other, that of honest men & patriots who have a rude habit of calling things by their right names.

APRIL 18, 1864

We have had since the first of this month a succession of heavy rains & consequent freshets in the river. So cold, wet, & backward a Spring has rarely been known. Corn planting which should be over is but fairly begun & the Low grounds are a Lake, with the prospect of continuing so for some time to come. Since the Snow Storm of the 22d of March there has been five distinct freshets, one 21 ft 1 in, another 21 ft 7 in, so there has been but little dry land to be seen. We have made three trips to Hascosea & three times has the weather disappointed us & delayed our work there. We came back from one nearly fruitless one on Sat. We succeeded, however, in bedding Potatoes & I in planting my Dahlia & Tube Rose Roots. Sad to say I found on opening my "bank" of the former that I have lost more than half of my ample stock. This would not be so much a subject of regret did I not fear that some of my finest varieties have perished altogether. The prospect for Pears is good & that for

---

[41]Thomas Bennett, governor of South Carolina in 1820, took the eleven-year-old Memminger from the Charleston Orphan House and raised him. Memminger, born in 1803 in the Duchy of Württemberg, Germany, had accompanied his mother to Charleston after his father's death. His mother died shortly after arriving in South Carolina, and Memminger was placed in the orphanage at the age of four. *Dictionary of American Biography*, XII, 527-528.

[42]These newspaper articles are not in the diary.

Peaches, spite of our fears, fair. The crop is much thinned out, but if we escape future late frosts we will have an abundance. Sowed my Flower seed but was forced to entrust my Ochre & Corn to Allen's superintendance.

Whilst at Hascosea soldiers were constantly passing & from some Georgians belonging to a Battery, which was en route from Hamilton to Weldon, we learned that an attack was considered iminent there, the Yankees having thrown a Pontoon bridge over the Chowan at Murfreesboro & a cavalry advance in force is expected across the county of Northampton in the tract of that taken by Onderdonk & his plunderers last summer. The men we entertained were intelligent, & most grateful for the little kindness we had it in our power to show them; they confirmed the account we had previously heard of the repulse of a Regt of Negro Cavalry at Suffolk by a charge of Artillery. anomalous as it appears! It is a fact they ran too fast for the infantry to keep up or even to get in range when "*a Charge*" by sections of two Batteries was ordered. They said it was ludicrous in the extreme—Field pieces thundering down upon the ranks of the cavalry!—no need to stop to unlimber, pursuit was the word! & Cuffee scattered right & left. They *took no prisoners & never intending taking any.* A beautiful field peice was captured from them & tied to it was a prisoner, one of our men, who understood that he was to be hanged! One other was liberated in Suffolk, who had been informed that such was to be his fate the next day!

Preparations are going on at the North for an overwhelming advance on Richmond. Grant is in command. Gen Baldy Smith is to approach up the Peninsula. Spear is to attack Weldon whilst Burnside tries his old route from New Berne to Goldsboro. Grant himself is to manage Lee. All his corps commanders have been changed & the Yankee Nation is, as usual, jubilant & defiant & as to the result—confident. The Herald (excuse me, my dear Journal, from copying anything from its polluted pages into yours—but I take it second hand, expurgated as it were by the Editor of the Examiner), but the Herald with its usual vanity says "Upon Gen Grant there now concentrates the deepest interest with which *The World* ever watched the actions of any single soldier. We are now, therefore, at that point which must be reached in all great Wars before the war can go forward with irresistable force to the accomplishment of its purpose. We have found our hero!" This is the seventh *Hero* that the Yankees have found! I suppose they think "there is luck in odd numbers." Poor "little Napoleon," unfortunate "fighting Joe," Burnside the Christian, Pope the despiser of his "rear," McDowell, Meade—where are you all now? The North has found a *hero*! "Sound drums & trumpets blare"! The North has found a Hero! Borardo I think set the church bells ringing when he found a name for his hero "Rodomonte,"[43] but the North is more fortunate

---

[43]Rodomont, king of Sarza (Algiers), was a Moorish military hero in Matteo Marie Boiardo's epic *Orlando Innamorato* who fought in the Saracen army against Charlemagne. Benét, *Reader's Encyclopedia*, 938, 125.

still. It has found a hero with name and all complete, "Ulysses S Grant," the triumphant Hero of their yet unwritten Epic! Yet unwritten, but soon to stand forth traced in characters of Blood, blood alaas, of Southern freemen as well as of Northern mercenaries!

Forrest is still successful in Western Kentucky & Tenn; has captured immense quantities of arms & provisions, burned Steamers, & now holds himself at Mayfield, a thorn in the Yankee side. Rumours of a victory gained by us near Shrevesport, La by Kirby Smith over Banks, but they are rumours only for the truth of which we as yet only pray. Farragut after some days shelling the Forts below Mobile has drawn off saying the place must be taken by land—impregnable by sea. The seige of Charleston still continues. The Swamp Angel slowly shells the city. Three unsexed women were seen the other day to visit the batteries & to pull the strings which discharged a shell into the city. With it I suppose went a prayer from their polluted lips that it might destroy some happy home, kill some mother or helpless babe in that "hive of Secession." Can we wonder at the *men* when the women set such an example! They it is, the Northern papers say, who are the principle advocates & practicers of "Miscegenation." Faugh!

To the astonishment of the Yankees a little Steamer rushed down James River the other day & exploded a Torpedo under the Bows of the Minnesota & was off before they could fire upon her & lost in the darkness. They say, which I am sorry to hear, that no damage was done. We must hope for better luck next time, for it was a gallant & daring act.

Suffolk is again occupied in force & another Regt of negro cavalry awaits the charge of a Battery of Southerners. Recently in Miss we attacked a Regt of mounted Cuffies & not one was left to tell the tale! The negroes have a hard time in the Yankee service. Put by their new masters in the front, they bear the brunt of the day & do not receive from their old masters the quarter or the mercy shown by them to prisoners of war, but are shot down without hesitation, not allowed even to surrender. We desire to have no complications on the subject of negro exchanges.

April 19, 1864

In my ride with Mr E yesterday afternoon, after visiting the usual objects of plantation interest, the corn planting, the ditches, the cattle, etc., he took a by path through the "forest primeval" called in negro dialect the "High Woods" & known on the map of the plantation as the "Brown Woods." Very intricate indeed was our path, tracing the mazes of the "Saw Scaffold Bottom" & even with the help of the "blazes" on the trees would I often have been at fault, but Mr E followed it with the sagacity of an old hunter, he being a Master of Wood Craft. I can understand & enter into the old Plantagenet[44] love of Veal

[44]Plantagenet was the surname assumed by Geoffrey, Count of Anjou, as a symbol of humility. His son, Henry II, founded the House of Plantagenet that reigned in England from 1154 until 1399. Benét, *Reader's Encyclopedia*, 859.

& Venison, for a right of seignory over so extensive & unbroken a peice of woodland is pleasant even here in this wooded country where a forest is no novelty & deer are to be had for the "driving." What it must be then in such a land as England where woodland can be held by but few even of the wealthy, and where game has to be strictly preserved. It becomes then an apanage of power and as such has a double zest. Our road lay through a thicket of Crab apples & a vast extent of Dogwood, neither yet in bloom. I could not enjoy the beauty of the former as I wished from the necessity of bending to my saddle bow to protect my eyes & my new riding hat with its pretty "Coq's" plume from the overhanging branches. Mean to ask Mr E to take me there again a fortnight hence when both trees will be in blossom to enjoy the beauty & to inhale the perfume of the flowers & to be sure to wear my old hat with neither plume or veil. Mr Edmondston & Father are both a little "tete montee"[45] on the subject of secret ditches. He told me whilst riding over them today that he had this winter put down ten thousand yards of it!

APRIL 22, 1864

Went on the 20th to fathers & found my neice Miss Jones there on her way to our house. She came home with me in the afternoon and was much amused when we reached the Flume and were forced to adopt the, to her, novel mode of locomotion in a Canoe! Stirring news from the West. Forrest has "attacked Fort Pillow on the 12th with part of Bell's & McCulloch's Brigades under Gen Chalmers. After a short fight we drove the enemy, 700 strong, into the fort under cover of their Gunboats & demanded a surrender which was denied by Maj L W Booth Comdg U S Forces. I stormed the Fort & after a contest of thirty minutes, captured the entire garrison killing five hundred & taking one hundred horses & a large amount of qr master's stores. The officers in the Fort were all killed, including Maj Booth. I sustained a loss of twenty killed & sixty wounded. Among the latter is the gallant Lieut Col Wm M Reid whilst leading the 5th Miss. Over one hundred citizens who had fled to the Fort from conscription ran into the river & were drowned. The Confederate Flag now floats over the Fort." signed A. B Forest Maj Gen.

The Northern papers confirm the above in every particular & add that soon after the attack Forest sent in a Flag of Truce, demanding a surrender which was refused & the fighting was resumed. Soon after a second flag came in which was also refused, when the rebels came in swarms compelling a surrender. ". . . The incarnate fiends commenced an indiscriminate butchery of whites & blacks . . . The coloured soldiers becoming demoralized rushed to the rear, their white officers having thrown down their arms, both whites & blacks were then bayonetted, shot, or sabred. Out of a garrison of six hundred, two hundred alone were left." Very likely it is all *true* & I hope it is. If

---

[45]French, "excited."

they will steal our slaves & lead them on to murder & rapine, they must take the consequences!

We have Northern news of the immediate attack of Fort Halleck at Columbus Kentucky upon the capture of Fort Pillow—as yet we hear nothing of it, tho a Yankee steamer reports the U S Flag as "*down*" when it passed. We have again possession of Paducah & had summoned the Fort there to surrender. Fighting was going on on the 15th. This is Yankee news. The victory at Cane Creek near Shreveport is admitted by the enemy who say the expedition will have to be abandoned & that the Teche country & La Fourche will again fall into quiet possession of the rebels. As yet we have no particulars of the battle. We have captured one of Banks' Courier from whose dispatches we learn that the Red River had suddenly fallen & that forty transports & gunboats were caught above the Rapids & that they could not get out until the river rises. Ere that I hope Gen Smith or Dick Taylor will have paid their respects to them. The advance on Suffolk seems to be a feint only, as all the troops have fallen back & from present indications intend an advance by the Peninsula. Burnside the Christian's movements are still veiled in mystery. Grant is reported as falling back to Centreville, but the Northern press maintains an ominous silence as to his motions. The Gold market is furious in the North. On the 14th it rose to 189 but subsequently fell to 174. Sterling Exchange 205. They say, "Where are we to look for releif? Congress might help us, but Congress seems to be past all hope. We look then to Gen Grant & his gallant armies for a rescue. With his successes we shall have better times, but should the Washington Directory or the accidents of War entangle him so as to bring on him misfortune instead of success, why then we may look for the Deluge"!

Mr Edmondston has just come in & brought us news of a gallant & glorious success of our arms here in our own borders. On Sat *our* Gunboat the Albemarle under command of Capt Cooke steamed down the River to Plymouth whilst Hoke's & Ransoms brigades under command of Hoke advanced by land. The boat passed one Battery in the night & attacked the other altho four Gunboats lay there. Running her sharp prow into one she became entangled. When the Yankee Commodore Flusser called to him to surrender he refused, and drawing his pistol responded to a shot! Dividing his men into two squads, one to load the other to fire, he assembled them on the upper deck & kept up so steady & raking a fire that the Yankees could not board her until the action of the Engine & the current freed his vessel. His opponent sunk instantly, when Flusser steamed up, cut his hauser, & retreated followed by a parting shot from Capt Cooke. He sunk another boat & the fourth followed in Flusser's wake. On shore Hoke was not idle. He stormed the battery after having refused the terms proposed by Weitzel who was in command in response to his demand for a surrender & took the whole of the force, 2500 men prisoners, officers & men. We lost from 2 to 500 killed &

wounded. The enemy's loss was smaller, being protected by their fort. Amongs the killed & prisoners were numbers of negroes who had run off from their masters living here in this community. Some of the young men which brother lost last winter were among the number. Many of Mr. Ed Hill's were killed. The steamer with our dead and wounded passed here on Tuesday. Little did I know when I heard her laboured puff of what her freight was composed! We captured one million lbs of Bacon, large quantities of Beef & of Beef Cattle, ten Batteries, sunk two boats, which can be raised & made available, it is thought, 2500 prisoners many of them officers, quantities of dry goods & groceries, amunition, small arms, & all the et ceteras of a garrison, & what is better, with the aid of the Gunboat we can hold the post. This is supposed to be the cause of the sudden abandonment of Suffolk, as it gives the ability to flank any force there or in the N E counties. The prisoners are en route to Richmond, negroes & all. How thankful we should be to God for this signal triumph! Plymouth has been a thorn in our side & the garrison there a perpetual uneasiness to us. Its loss may compel a change in Grant's programme, especialy if the Gunboats in the Neuse succeed in joining the Albemarle, as we may then attack Hatteras & flank Norfolk & open the most magnificent trade in Blockade Running yet seen.

APRIL 26, 1864

More good news from Plymouth. The Yankee Commodore Flusser who cut the hauser & retired so suddenly had good reason for his precipitancy, for he was able only to reach Edenton where his vessel sunk, having nine shot through her hull & he himself died from his wounds. So Capt Cooke sunk three Gunboats & captured a small steamer. Well done for the Albemarle. Beauregard has taken command here in our State. Last week his headquarters were at Weldon. Today they are at Goldsboro, rumour says to superintend an advance on Newberne.

Polk's Corps we hear is to occupy Richmond to be in readiness to ward off an attack from the Peninsula. Some persons think that the real advance of the Campaign is to be made into Georgia, that this openness of the Yankees about their advance on Richmond is but a feint, & that when we weaken Polk & Johnson, they will mass suddenly & advance with a crushing force from Chattanooga. Nous verrons! Longstreet was by the last accounts at Charlottsville Va to reinforce Lee & the two are, it is said, suddenly to fall on Grant & prevent his advance. All travel save that of soldiers & all transportation except for the army has been stopped on our R R. Permits are refused to citizens, be their business never so urgent! This order is by no means a dead letter but is rigidly enforced & much private inconvenience results therefrom. Our victory at Shrevesport, or rather Cane Creek near that town, is confirmed. Banks is driven back so severely handled that a reorganization is necessary ere he can advance again. The Yankee's are loud in their complaints & threats of indiscriminate slaughter. Should the accounts of the bloodshed at Fort Pillow prove true, Lincoln has again distinguished himself by a speech remarkable only for platitudes & indisputable truisms. But I have no room for his nonsense.

Dined yesterday at Mr Peter Smith's to meet a party invited in compliment to Mrs Cook. Mr Edmondston, poor man, the only representative of the masculine gender amongst *nine* feminines! I felt for him. Father & Mama dined with us on Saturday.

APRIL 30, 1864

Came home from Hascosea where we went on the 28th to spend 24 hours only, but the River rising suddenly we were kept for three days. Had a galop up to Conneconara to see Sophia who, poor thing, is in feeble health & has come home to recruit. Not much public news. All stand expectant waiting the issue of the impending battle. The Abolitionists are doing their best to blind us as to their real plans, now occupying Suffolk in force, suddenly evacuating it, & landing troops from Ocean steamers at Yorktown. A whole army corps was there last week, when presto, they vanish to appear again at Barhamville thirty miles from Richmond, having reached that point via the York River, McClellans old route. We are preparing for the coming shock, one of the most uncomfortable evidences being the prohibition of all travel save military on the R R to & from Richmond. No matter how urgent the private necessities may be, the fiat is inexorable. No passports are issued. Susan is thus detained in Petersburg far beyond the time allotted for her visit. Gen Grant seems to hold Joe Hooker of fighting memory in no high estimation, vide the endorsement on his report of the battle of Lookout Mountain. Gen Joe, how do you relish such aspersions on your veracity? But you are a Yankee & your point of honour is not easily assailable. Gen Beauregard has his head quarters at Weldon to watch, it is said, any advance by the Southside or through our North eastern Counties. Will send him a basket of supplies, for, poor man, he must mourn for the flesh pots of Egypt in that terrible place. Dreadful in "piping times of peace," what must it be now when successive detachments of troops have swept the whole county in search of supplies?

Have read an article on "*Miscegnation*" from a late New York paper that disgusts & revolts my whole nature. What a people, to desire a mixture of African blood to "to energize" and "revivfy their own." They think the superiority of the Southron arises from the "magnetic" influence of their "dusky attendants." Faugh! it sickens me!

MAY 1, 1864

The news from Plymouth has reached New York & a howl has gone up in consequence. What is of more importance to us Gold has accompanied it & is quoted at 184, higher than it has yet been. Yankee accounts from Louisiana are so confused & muddled that I can make nothing of them. Shreveport, Cane Creek, Grand Ecore, & Pleasant Hill are commingled so that it seems as tho they won brilliant victories at the three last & were in a few miles of their goal, the first, but alas, for their consistency. After a flourish of trumpets they wind up with "General Banks having fallen back to Grand Ecore, 35 miles from Pleasant Hill, 55 from Mansfield (Cane Crk?), & 95 from Shreveport, will advance again as soon as he is reinforced & adequate supplies received." The Confederates claim to have *driven* him back from Cane Creek when within a few miles of Shreveport will he nil he, & that too with terrible slaughter, as the papers say. "Oh! Yankee! Yankee!"

MAY 5, 1864

Burnside is on the move from Anapolis *certainly*. I have said nothing of the Christian warrior, as his plans & movements have been so uncertain that one rumour contradicted the last. Now, however, he has dismissed his transports & declining to "stand like a sea god distinguished by his yellow belt" again, he marches over land to Alexandria, leaves his negro Brigade along the Orange & Alex R R, & brings his White troops to reinforce Grant. Some change in the Yankee programme has evidently taken place & the key to it is to be found in order of Meade's announcing to his troops whose term of enlistment expires this month that the date of their mustering into service is not when they were sworn in & signed their enlistment papers but when they left the respective States in which they were levied. This has caused great discontent amongst the "*Veterans*." He urges them to comport themselves well & not to sully their Laurels by insubordination & hints plainly enough at Military Law & its bloody enforcement should they neglect his admonition. The Penn Legislature has taken the matter in hand & petition Congress that the rights of her citizens in the army be not disregarded.

Rumours are rife that on Monday last an expedition under Hoke went down to attack New berne, but a profound silence is maintained on the subject by all the papers. Heavy cannonading heard in the direction of Washington. In the extreme west all goes well for us. The Yankees admit a second defeat at [———] & claim to have killed Kirby Smith & Stirling Price. We have heard naught of it & have no uneasiness as regards our gallant Generals. Our Victory at Cane Creek was decisive. The Abolitionists themselves admit that "Banks army is demoralized" & fearfully cut up. More than thirty transports & some Gunboats are caught above a Raft in the Red River by a sudden fall in the water & the crews are blowing them up burning them to prevent their falling into our hands. Great activity prevails in our army in Northern Va, but we know nothing save that a battle is imminent & even now may be raging. God defend the right!

Sophia & her infant are with us this week. She is quite weak but a few days of careful observation of her has lessened my anxiety on her account. Her baby is the best I almost ever saw.

MAY 7, 1864

No mail today, which is hard on poor Pattie whose brother, whom she almost idolizes, may be in the midst of a bloody battle. Rumours by this train tell us that the battle commenced on the 6th & that Lee is getting the advantage of Grant. Train after train of troops pass Halifax going Northward. Hoke is said to have been ordered to 'face about,' leave New Berne, & concentrate at Petersburg. On his approach the Yankees evacuated Washington which fell with hands without a fight & retired into their retrenchments at New Berne. Hoke was following when he received the order above mentioned. We do not understand what it means, for, thank God, our leaders are singularly reticent & we are content to wait trusting in their wisdom.

President Davis has met with a heavy misfortune in which he has the sympathy of the country. One of his children, a bright little boy of four years of age, fell from the piazza of his father's mansion into the paved court yard below, fracturing his skull & sustaining such other injuries that he died within an hour. God comfort the poor parents. On Mr Davis the blow falls at a most trying period when every energy & nerve is strained in the service of his country. God bless & keep him!

MAY 8, 1864

Sunday—Today came one of our missing mails & we can but conjecture what tidings we have lost. I scarcely know where to begin—but—place to "Marse Robert." He telegraphs under date of May 5th 1864 that "the enemy crossed the Rapid Ann at Ely's & Germanna fords. Two corps of this army moved to oppose him, Ewell's and Hill's. They arrived this morning in close proximity to the enemy's line of march. A strong attack was made on Ewell who repulsed it capturing many prisoners & four peices of artillery. The enemy subsequently concentrated upon Hill who with Heth's & Wilcox's divisions unsuccessfully repelled the desperate assault. A large force of cavalry & artillery on our right was driven back by Rosser's Brigade. By the blessing of God we maintained our position until night when the contest closed. We have to mourn the loss of many brave officers & men. The gallant Gen J M Jones was killed & Brg Gen Stafford, I fear, was mortally wounded whilst leading his command with conspicuous valour." Signed R E Lee. Then the Telegraph flashes wild reports of "Longstreet's hurling his 30,000 veterans against Grant with the fury of a thunderbolt," but as they are not official we doubt them. On the 6th we are told that "fighting between Lee & Grant was resumed, news from the front cheering, 2,000 pris taken in the battle of yesterday," etc., where, presto, our intelligence is stopped & we learn by a letter from Mrs Dunlop at Petersburg that a fleet of Gunboats have come up James River, landed at City Point, & made a sudden attack on the Richmond & Petersburg R R at Port Walthal Junction & that no train had arrived from Richmond on Sat. Buckner with 7000 men was within a few miles of Port Walthal Junction on Friday covering Richmond from the marauders. The transports were supposed to contain troops for the Peninsula & he felt no uneasiness as to the force on the R R. Cavalry were said to be advancing from Ivor upon Petersburg & a thousand rumours prevailed as to the force & its destination.

A letter from Mr McMahon in Halifax complicates the matter terribly. He tells us that the Bridge over Stoney Crk between Petersburg & Weldon is down, that Beauregard has left Weldon & expects to fight his way through to Petersburg, & that if successful will "bring" (carry?) with him a train with 150,000 lbs of Bacon on board, that Hoke is en route with a large force for the same point, every train being engaged in carrying troops. We have missed so many mails that we have not heard of this advance & it takes us completely by surprise. I do not see how we can hear today, as with the Telegraph if not the R R cut at Pt Walthal Junction & the Stony Crk Bridge down, there is but little possibility of a mail's coming through, and in the mean time what may not have transpired on the Rapid Ann! Lee & Longstreet may have driven Grant to the wall. I hope our force is strong enough to outnumber any James River or South side advances & must beleive the attack is planned simultaneously with the battle on the Rapid Ann in order to distract & annoy us & thus prevent our pushing fresh troops on to re-inforce Lee. Our suspense is cruel & poor Patty seems to suffer intensely. All day long her moans & cries sound in my ears. Poor thing, it is tearing open her wounds afresh, just as she began to feel the healing influence of time. My heart bleeds for her. The weather is intensely hot & this must add to the sufferings of our wounded ten fold. The thermometer at ½ past six yesterday afternoon stood at °87!

From Northern Georgia we hear that the enemy are advancing on Johnston, repairing both R R as they advance. A battle seems imminent there also, but northern Va concentrates our interest so entirely that we almost forget how important a point Dalton is & what an army of our compatriots are there exposed. From the Trans Mississippi we now get a confirmation of our second Victory. Price met Steele & completely routed him, capturing his whole waggon train—no particulars. In Mississippi the enemy are again advancing in spite of Sherman's late fruitless foray, fruitless of all save plunder & misery. McArthur with 10,000 infantry, two batteries of Artillery, & 250 cavalry are approaching Yazoo City. The last news from the Abolitionists in James River is that one of their Gunboats had been blown up by a torpedo & from their movements it was supposed they intended taking Drewry's Bluff in the rear. I hope we are prepared to give them a warm reception.

Our Ram, "*The Albemarle*," is carrying everything before her in the sound. She last week captured a small Steamer, a Schooner, 2 barges, & 300 bar. of corn. She has gone into Pamlico & her appearance it was which caused the rapid evacuation of Washington. Fishing is being resumed in those waters & a large supply of food thus ensured to our army. We have two more, one in the Neuse & the other in the Tar, waiting a rise of water to join her. The Bomb Shell, the Yankee gunboat, sunk at Plymouth has been raised & now acts as a tender to her. Ah for news! Glorious news from Va! God be with our poor wounded! The seige of Charleston has been abandoned, says the Herald. A firing is still kept up at intervals on the city, but active operations have ceased.

MAY 9, 1864

No mail again today. Rumours only of skirmishing at Jarrats Depot on the Petersburg R R. It is hard on all of us but especially so on poor Pattie. Her anxiety is intense.

MAY 10, 1864

Tuesday—At Church today to hear the Bishop.[46] Heard more rumours than I can record of the enemy's doings on the Petersburg R R, but as they are rumours only will not credit them. One thing only is certain our communication with Richmond is interrupted by them. Capt Cooke has had a severe fight with Yankee Gunboats in Albemarle Sound. His Smoke Stack was so riddled with shot that he could not burn coal & but for a supply of Lard & Bacon he would have been taken. He kept up his fires with these, however. Sunk two steamers & fought his way back to Plymouth with one gun disabled & her smoke stack with holes in it through which a man might creep. He lost his new tender, the Bombshell. She was sunk & her crew captured. Ten men were killed on the deck of the Albemarle. She engaged eleven boats at once & escaped them all. They threw a net made of Rope over her but the ropes which held it to the steamers parting, it fell harmless off her sides into the water. For her preservation God be thanked. Heard today for the first time in my life the prayer in the Prayer book appointed to be read in time of Dearth & Famine, a signal instance of God['s] past goodness to us as a nation. May we not be ungrateful for the blessings we have enjoyed and in Thy goodness continue them to us O Lord!

MAY 14, 1864

Strange to say the first news we have had from Northern Va in more than a week came on the 12th in the Charleston paper, having been flashed along the wires in the interior of this state Via Danville, Greensboro, Charlotte, &

---

[46]Thomas Atkinson (1807-1881) served as the Episcopal bishop of North Carolina from 1853 until 1881. Gaines M. Foster, "Bishop Cheshire and Black Participation in the Episcopal Church: The Limitations of Religious Paternalism," *North Carolina Historical Review*, LIV (January, 1977), 53.

Capt. James W. Cooke, commander of the *Albemarle*, was a North Carolinian. Mrs. Edmondston commented on his efficiency in her discussion of the building of the *Albemarle*. (Photograph from Naval Photographic Center, Department of the Navy, Washington, D.C.)

Columbia. An official dispatch of Gen Lee's under date of May 6th tell us that "Early this morning as the Divisions of Gen Hill engaged yesterday were being releived, the enemy advanced & created some confusion. The ground lost was recovered as soon as fresh troops got into position & the enemy driven back to his original line. . . . Afterwards we turned the left of his fresh line & drove it from the field, leaving a large number of dead & wounded in our hands, among them Gen Wadsworth. A subsequent attack forced the enemy into his entrenched lines on the Brook Road. Every advance on his part thanks to Almighty God has been repulsed. I greive to announce Gen Longstreet severely wounded & Gen Jenkins killed. General Pegram badly wounded yesterday." Signed R E Lee.

Additional accounts tell us that the fighting was very severe, principally with musketry, the ground being unsuited for artillery. They attempted to turn our right & to get between Lee & Richmond. The North Carolina troop behaved most gallantly. "Cooks Brigade fought well & loses heavily." This announcement has added to poor Patty's anxiety, for the 27th is in that organization. Longstreet had turned the enemy's left & was pressing them back steadily when he was severely wounded in the shoulder by Mahone's Brigade. Think what a blunder! To be shot by the enemy is not enough it appears. Our generals must fall by our own hands too![47] The same unfortunate Brigade also wounded Gen Jenkins of So Ca mortally. He has since died of his wounds. We hear that this is the *third* time that that Brigade has fired on our own troops, never before, however, at so shinning a mark. God grant that

---

[47] Confederate Generals Micah Jenkins and James Longstreet were shot by Confederate soldiers while commanding brigades at the Wilderness, May 6, 1864. Both incidents were similar to the circumstances surrounding the death of Stonewall Jackson. Jenkins was killed; Longstreet, disabled from action for five months, returned to his command on October 9, 1864. Boatner, *Civil War Dictionary*, 435, 490-491.

Longstreet may recover. He is Lee's right hand! The battle field is about twenty five miles below Orange Court House, in the Wilderness above Chancellorsville, & will be called the battle of the Wilderness.

The enemy are retreating towards Chancellorsville & Fredericksburg. On the 8th Lee again telegraphs to the Sec of War, "General Gordon turned the enemy's extreme right yesterday evening & drove him from his rifle pits. . . . Gens Seymour & Shaller captured. The enemy has abandoned the Germanna Ford road & removed his pontoons toward Ely's. . . ." R E Lee. A second dispatch of the same date from Spottsylvania Court House also to Mr Seddon says, "After a sharp encounter with the fifth Army Corps & Warren's and Torbert's division of Cavalry Gen R H Anderson with the advance of the army repulsed the enemy with heavy slaughter & took possession of the Court House. I am the more grateful to the Giver of all victories that our loss is small." R E Lee. On the 9th he again telegraphs, "After repulsing the enemy from Spottsylvania Court House that morning they received reinforcements & renewed the attack on our position but were again handsomely driven back." R E Lee. On the 10th a further official dispatch dated Spottsylvania Court House, May 10th, says Grant has entrenched near that place, frequent skirmishing along our line resulting favorably to us, our casualties small, among the wounded Brig Gen Hayes & H H Walker. This is all official intelligence so that it can be relied on, but it is a mere skeleton & affords little comfort to those anxious hearts who have friends in the front of the battle.

A telegram from brother tells us that up to Sat night the 8th his son Thomas was unhurt, for which God be thanked. We hear of the death of some of our young friends—W H Heywood, jr., Mr Walker Anderson,[48]—& that Mr Wm Saunders[49] is again wounded in the face. Bad for a bridegroom, as he is. Messrs Heywood & Anderson are the second members of their respective

---

[48]William H. Haywood, second lieutenant of Co. K, Seventh Regiment North Carolina State Troops, was mortally wounded at Wilderness, Virginia, on May 5, 1864. He was a son of former United States Senator William H. Haywood and brother of Lt. Duncan C. Haywood, Co. E, Seventh Regiment North Carolina State Troops, killed at Gaines's Mill, Virginia, on June 27, 1862. Lt. Robert Walker Anderson, formerly aide-de-camp to his brother Gen. George Burgwyn Anderson who died from wounds received at Sharpsburg in 1862, served as ordnance officer to Gen. John R. Cooke's brigade and also was killed at Wilderness, Virginia. Manarin and Jordan, *North Carolina Troops*, I, 444; IV, 9, 453, 457, 503; Ashe, *Biographical History*, IV, 28-31; VI, 302-303; Clark, *Histories of the North Carolina Regiments*, I, 368, 383; IV, 506-507.

[49]William Laurence Saunders (1835-1891) saw active service throughout the war with the Forty-sixth North Carolina Regiment, which he eventually commanded as colonel. He was twice wounded, at Fredericksburg and Wilderness, Virginia, and the second wound was initially thought to be fatal. After the war Saunders served as clerk of the North Carolina Senate, coedited the *Wilmington Journal* with Joseph A. Engelhard, and helped to establish the Raleigh *Observer*. Saunders also directed the activities of the Invisible Empire (Ku Klux Klan) in North Carolina. He later served as secretary of state (1879-1891) and compiled the state's colonial records. Ashe, *Biographical History*, IV, 381-389; Clark, *Histories of the North Carolina Regiments*, II, 439; III, 64-65, 70, 75-76, 79; *Concise Dictionary of American Biography*, 913; Wescott and Ramage, *A Checklist of United States Newspapers*, Part IV: *North Carolina*, 627, 686; J. G. de Roulhac Hamilton, *Reconstruction in North Carolina* (1914; reprint ed., Gloucester, Mass.: Peter Smith, 1964), 461, 575.

families who have been killed in this bloody war, Mr Duncan Heywood having died on the field before Richmond & Gen Anderson fell mortally wounded at Sharpsburg. The news from the enemy in James River is meager. On the 9th they shelled our works at Drury's Bluff but without effect. On the 8th they were repulsed with a loss of one thousand killed & wounded from Chester, a point on the R R between Petersburg & Richmond. On the 10th they renewed the attack & were again repulsed. Smith & Gilmore are in command & even Butler, it is said, has adventured his precious person to the dangers of War, but this I doubt even tho four of our pickets report that he narrowly escaped them at City Point. From the Weldon and Petersburg R R we have but rumours & they are to the effect that the raiders have retired with heavy loss after destroying the bridge over Stoney Creek.

From Louisianna we hear that Banks has retreated to Alexandria. The Yankee Gunboat Eastport has been blown up & two transport's captured. The remainder of the fleet is above the Rapids with no chance of escaping. Taylor had captured four thousand prisoners. Price's success was complete. Marmaduke had captured Steele's white waggon train. Steele was surrounded. Price demanded his surrender. He acceeded on condition that the negroes be treated as prisoners of war. Price refused & the terms were referred to Kirby Smith who replied "that the negroes should be sent to their owners." Steele refused to capitulate. Smith was reinforcing Price & it was thought Steele would soon be glad to accept the rejected terms as he was surrounded & without supplies. We have retaken Fort De Russy & Cheneville. The enemy made a stand at Markham but were defeated with heavy loss. Their reinforcements by the river were driven back at Fort de Russy, four gunboats were burned above the falls, & Walker had crossed Red River & was marching South in pursuit of the retreating army. The destruction of property has been immense. Our forces burned the cotton, in anticipation of the enemy's advance, & the Yankees destroyed private property, dwellings, barns, Gins, Churches—everything in short which could be burned in revenge. The course of their army is a blackened desert, women & children turned out homeless & desolate to perish by the wayside!

In N C Gen Hoke invested New Berne & delayed his attack for the arrival of the Albemarle when heavy firing told him she was engaged on her own element & in the mean time came "the necessity for him to move off," which we interpret to mean orders to leave New Berne & concentrate in Va, which he has now done. Before marching he tried a coup de main[50] & summoned the garrison to surrender. They demanded four hours to consider it but unfortunately discovered before the time had expired that we were preparing to move off and so refused and Hoke had not time to make them, or in the words

[50]French, "bold stroke, sudden attack."

of the Courier to give them another "*Hoke ache*" (*hoe cake*). He cut their communications with Morehead City & but for the attack on the Albemarle in all probability New Berne would have been in our hands before he was ordered to Richmond as their force is but a small one. Amongst the prisoners captured at Plymouth was the brother of Mrs. Hamilton Polk—Beach[51] of Hartford the second in command. A comentary on this war truly—Brother seems against Brother, tho in this instance it is against brother-in-Law.

Flusser was not, it appears, the immaculate man of honour the Yankees represented him. It admits of proof that with his own commissioned hand he stole Miss Russel's watch & the inside, the works & jewels, of her sister Mrs Griffin's from the watch maker's in Hertford where they had been sent for repair. The jeweler secreted the case of Mrs G's watch, he having the interior in his work bench in the act of repairing it when Lieut Commander Flusser USN came into his shop & took it. Miss Russel is now residing temporarily in Scotland Neck with my neighbor Mrs Whitaker & her exclamation on hearing of his death was "well now I hope he will have to answer for stealing my watch"! Pattie tells me that he has been seen to chase chickens through the streets of Hertford in full uniform—actually to sully his commissin by chicken stealing! He met his death whilst attempting to drop a bombshell down the smoke stack of the Albermarle! Whilst lighting a slow match the shell exploded in his hand and he was blown into peices.

The official Dispatch of Capt Cooke's late fight tells us that he encountered nine of the enemy's Gunboats, two of them very large, from the blockading Squadron. He sunk the largest, disabled two others without serious injury to the Albemarle, but lost his tender. We heard of seven gunboats & four small steamers, but it seems he has done better. The iron clad built at Wilmington, "*the Raleigh,*"[52] bearing the broad person of Com Lynch steamed out of Cape Fear & dispersed the blockading squadron there, much to the astonishment of the Yankees. She thinks she disabled one as a shot struck her fairly. She was out for hours & not a Yankee came in sight after their flight until she was back in the river again.

---

[51]Francis Beach served as colonel of the Sixteenth Connecticut Volunteers. *Official Records (Navy)*, Series I, IX, 652. Alexander Hamilton Polk, son of Gen. Leonidas Polk, married Emily Beach in 1854. William H. Polk, *Polk Family and Kinsmen* (Louisville, Ky.: Bradley and Gilbert, 1921), 286, hereinafter cited as Polk, *Polk Family and Kinsmen*.

[52]The C.S.S. *Raleigh*, a powerful ram commanded by Flag Officer William F. Lynch, steamed out of New Inlet, North Carolina, on May 6, 1864, to engage and distract Union blockaders while a Confederate blockade-runner slipped through the Union lines. The *Raleigh* successfully routed two Union ships on the first day of battle but was forced to withdraw herself the next day when she was attacked by four Union ships. While attempting to enter the mouth of the Cape Fear River, the *Raleigh* was damaged when she ran aground; and Lynch ordered the ship destroyed to prevent the Union navy from salvaging her. *Civil War Naval Chronology*, IV, 56-57.

MAY 18, 1864

The state of suspense in which we live is fearful. This is now the thirteenth day since we have had a mail from Richmond & constant fighting has been going on. A couple of letters from Sue containing a resume of the news & rumours about Petersburg & some strips cut from the Petersburg Express brought by a train hand is the nearest approach to direct information we have had. The Raleigh Confederate[53] gives a few telegrams, some of them only official, which reach it via Danville.

So far as our information extends, every road leading to Richmond has been cut by bands of marauders. Spears Cavalry have been operating between Weldon & Petersburg, the bridge over Stoney Creek destroyed by fire, & that over Nottaway by artillery. We saved the most important one, however, over the Meherin. Severe fighting has been going on in Chesterfield between the Appomattox & the James, but we know nothing of the details. A rumour reaches Halifax of the death of Col Clarke, which is not, however, authentic. The Weldon people are flying in dismay & the countryside is alive with wild & improbable stories, which no one can contradict for the want of authentic information. The Danville Road has been cut by a band of marauders sent out by Butler. Another & a large body threatens Richmond from Hanover. They approached within a mile of the Richmond fortifications & were repulsed on Mr Stuart's farm. Fitz Lee & Stuart are in pursuit of them & Stuart telegraphs that he will intercept them at the Yellow Tavern. This on the 15th.

Another dispatch in the same paper says "Gen Stuart died on Wednesday from wounds received on Thursday." We know not what to beleive, but are at sea in a midst of wild sensational rumours, each more alarming than the last. Nothing more from Lee. Reports only that he has had another engagement near Spottsylvania Court House, the enemy repulsed with fearful slaughter & preparing to cross the Rappahanock at Fredericksburg, dispirited & demoralized, but who can tell if that be true? We get no Richmond papers & passengers and "reliable gentlemen" have it all their own way. God be with those who have friends on the battlefield. Their brains must well nigh reel with the suspense & anxiety. Heavy skirmishing about Dalton in which as yet Gen Joe Johnson gains the advantage. A battle may take place there at any moment. Steele's surrender to Price confirmed & we hear that Banks is shut up in Alexandria, the Confederates holding the River below, & that his supplies being cut off, Kirby Smith demands his surrender, but this is rumour.

---

[53]The *Daily Confederate* (Raleigh) was published by A. M. Gorman and D. K. McRae from 1864 through 1865. Wescott and Ramage, *A Checklist of United States Newspapers*, Part IV: *North Carolina*, 598.

MAY 18, 1864

At Father's to dinner & the whole of us greatly dejected by the message we got from Halifax—"no mail—no news"; no rumours—so to bed with what patience we can until tomorrow.

MAY 19, 1864

Rode out to Hascosea to while away the time until the mail should come in. Met a soldier & stopped him to ask the news. He told us that a mail arrived in Halifax from Richmond late last night, that Gen Dearing had captured Spears Cavalry, 1000 strong, somewhere between the Danville & Petersburg roads, that Lee had captured fifty Yankee Generals, & that Gen Daniel was dead!

Went on to Hascosea & transplanted Dahlia cuttings & set out sprouted Tea nuts until near dinner time when we came home just escaping a heavy shower—which it would have been bad for Pattie & I to have been caught in as we were heated & excited, having performed the last part of our journey on foot, one of our carriage horses having given out entirely, so we deserted him & took to "Shanks mare."

We found the mail awaiting us &, thanks again to Susan's fore thought & kindness, we were releived of a crushing load of anxiety. Besides her letters containing all the information she could gather, she sent us slips from the Petersburg papers &, wonderful to tell, a Petersburg paper of yesterday morning. It contained the greatest solace we could have under the losses & anxiety we have sufferd. A congratulatory order of Gen Lee to his troops under date of the 16th—what a blessing that we can trust implicitly everything which comes from his hand! He tells them that "the heroic valour of this army with the blessing of Almighty God has thus far checked the advance of the principle army of the enemy & inflicted upon it heavy loss . . . assures them that it is in their power under God to defeat the last great efforts of the enemy, to acheive the independance of your native land & earn the lasting love and gratitude of your country men & the admiration of mankind." Signed R E Lee. Words such as these mean something coming from him. His last official dispatch to the President tells him under date Sunday the 15th "that the enemy has retired his right & extended his left towards Massapona Church & occupies the line of the river, his right being east of the stream."

We have no further details of our dead beyond a confirmation of what the soldiers told us of Gen Junius Daniel. He died on Sat of wounds received on Thursday. His body had arrived in Richmond. My nephew Thomas Devereux is his courier & a part of his military family & attached particularly to his person, so that our anxiety is cruel as regards his safety. God be with him & help his poor parents to bear the load of sorrow which now oppresses them.

Yankee papers captured from Butler's command claim a victory, say that Lee is falling back to Richmond, but with strange inconsistency admit a loss of thirty one General Officers & forty five thousand men! By loss I mean killed, wounded, & captured. Fredericksburg, from their own account, is a vast hospital, and a Squadron of Cavalry could not deploy through the streets so thickly were they strewn with wounded men! No details on either side. They claim to have captured our Maj Gen Edward Johnson, but they are such Cretans that until we hear it from our own side it does not concern us. Coming south in Hanover within six miles of Richmond their cavalry under [———] have been turned aside with a heavy loss by Fitz Hugh Lee & Stuart. Here at the Yellow tavern Stuart, sad to say, has lost his life. His funeral together with that of Col H Clay Pate[54] took place in Richmond.

I well remember dining at the same table with Col Pate & his wife at the Ballard House for several days consecutively a little more than two years since. Mr E and himself were in Richmond on the same business, each raising a Battalion of Cavalry. How can I be thankful enough to Almighty God for having ordained them different lots in life. Butler, with even more than usual mendacity, telegraphs to his Gov the very day on which he sustained so signal a repulse at Pt Walthall Junction that he had obtained a great victory, had cut Beauregards forces in two, had destroyed the bridge over Swift Creek between Richmond & Petersburg, beaten Hill, & would soon whip out Beauregard & advance on Richmond, whereas the truth is he is confined in the narrow point of land between the Appomattox & the James. After repeated skirmishes which we would once have called battles, he can advance no further. He has attacked Drury's Bluff & been repulsed, has lost three, if not four, of his gunboats, and has now no prospect of success. His troops commit the most terrible excesses, rob, murder, & insult defenceless citizens with impunity. Numbers have been killed & our own loss has been heavy, but no permanent advantage has accrued to the Yankee arms from his buckling on his harness.

Our uneasiness about Col Clark is happily ended, as Sue's letter is of a later date than the attack on Drury's Bluff in which he was reported killed. At the Stoney Creek bridge, just as it had been repaired, back came Spear's & his Cavalry but a few troops stationed there & some citizens, hastily collected, held them at bay for half an hour. When the thunder of Gen Dearing's detachment of cavalry was heard approaching, when they left at double quick, with the loss of many men. Gen D was in pursuit, but whether with the result announced by my soldier friend does not yet appear.

In the Valley of Va Gen Breckenridge has defeated Sigel at New Market with heavy loss & sent him back to Winchester. The corps of Cadets at the Va

---

[54]Henry Clay Pate, colonel of the Fifth Virginia Cavalry in Brig. Gen. Lunsford L. Lomax's brigade, was killed at Yellow Tavern on May 11, 1864. *Official Records (Army)*, Series I, XXXVI, Part I, 778, 780, 818, 835, 1027.

Military Institute were out on this occasion & suffered severely, losing five killed & fifteen wounded. We have long ceased to wonder at our boys' fighting. Our *Cause* animates them & makes men of them ere their "beards be grown." Averill & his horde of marauders is again repulsed near Augusta Court House, I beleive, but the accounts refers to some news we have lost so it is not clear to my mind where, but they are in retreat. From Dalton we have additional accounts of heavy skirmishing, but they are telegrams only & only leave on us the impression of a battle being imminent, both armies as yet manoevring in the course of which they sometimes clash. From Lousianna we have Gen Taylor's congratulatory address to his troops in which he sums up their victories, Mansfield, Pleasant Hill, and Blair's Landing & mourns the loss of Gens Green & Mouton. Steele's surrender subsequent to the address is confirmed, but as yet nothing authorative from Banks at Alexandria. I cannot keep the record of all the gunboats we destroy there or those that they set fire to, to prevent their falling into our hands; they seem to be Legion, but I had better wait for official accounts.

One anecdote of the Army of Northern Va which has reached us I must record. During one of the recent battles Gen Lee placed himself at the head of a Texas Brigade in order to lead them into battle—when—as one man—they halted & cried out *"We will not advance unless you go back"*! Was ever a nobler tribute paid by men to a Commander? So far we have the names of fifteen of our Generals killed & wounded including Johnson, whom the Yankees claim to have captured, viz., five killed, 9 wounded, & 1 prisoner against twenty two Yankees whose fate we know, viz., ten killed, eight wounded, & three prisoners. Stuart & Ransom on our side & Heckman on theirs are included, tho neither of them were in Northern Va, these last being around Richmond. Every where so far have our arms been successful. God make us thankful. He it is who giveth us the victory & in His own good time He will grant us Peace! Peace & a name and place amongst the kingdoms of the earth.

May 20, 1864

Sunday—Up at Fathers on horseback with Pattie on Friday to see Sue who on that day got back from Petersburg. She is full of the stirring times & the excitement through which she has just past. She tells us that there is no question of the fact that Gen Bragg ordered the evacuation of the town of Petersburg to take effect on 2 o'clock of the last Sunday, today week, but that Beauregard interfered & said "No! No! a thousand times No! it was suicidal to think of it, if they took it it must be through oceans of blood, he would defend it to the last at all extremities." An Aid with more tongue than discretion told her informant that he had seen the Order countermanding it. Just like Bragg! Mr E says that if we are saved, with Bragg to direct & Robt Ransom to execute, it will be by a miracle. Fighting is of daily, almost hourly, occurrence around Petersburg. Beauregard presses Butler whose headquarters are said to be on the deck of the Greyhound (one of the swiftest steamers the Yankees have) with a full head of steam on. From thence he witnessed the attack on Drury Bluff on Monday, when they endeavoured to take the fortifications in the rear and were so signally repulsed and with so heavy loss by us. In this fight it was that Col Clarke was wounded in the shoulder by a fragment of shell. Numbers of the Yankee wounded were left in our hands & have been brought to Petersburg & cared for in a Hospital there. One of them called out to a negroe attendant, "Kill me, kill me at once, and put me out of pain! I am suffering so horribly. Kill me!" To which the negro gravely answered "I cant do it for you myself, Marster, I am sorry but I can't do it myself but just let some o dese Souf Callinians know it sah and dey will do it in a minute for you wid pleasure sah"!

Yesterday Sophia & Sue dined with us, but no more news from General Lee & nothing worth recording except a singular discrepancy between our own & the Yankee accounts of the recent military operations. Gen Lee says that he "has repulsed the enemy in every advance." Grant claims to have driven Lee to his last entrenchment, says he is in full retreat towards Richmond, issues a congratulatory order to his troops, & assumes the Laurel crown with great complacency. Breckenridge claims to have beaten Sigel & to have driven him back to Winchester. The Washington government announce that Sigel it is who has beaten Breckenridge. Morgan reports himself as having repulsed Averill, driven him with severe loss across the New River, with a severe wound in his own marauding head, whilst Washington shouts a paen over the fact of Averill's actually advancing on Lynchburg. The same is true of Sheridan & his horde, with great loss to ourselves it is true, but still we have done it. We have turned him aside from his "On to Richmond" & made him rejoin his commander, but Washington says he has been successful in his enterprise. Speare was driven pell mell through the country inflicting vast private suffering & destroying two R R Bridges, pursued so closely that he could not pillage as he listed, but he too, Washington tells us, has gained a signal triumph; whilst to crown the whole, Beauregard has Butler hemmed in—in a point of land between the Appomatox and the James which Gilmore is endeavouring to hold at the point of the Spade—when, hey presto! a Yankee paper picked up in one of their abandoned Camps tells the Yankee Nation in an official Dispatch from Maj Gen Butler that he has occupied Petersburg. Was ever the like before known? The Father of Lies has had ample employment for the past fortnight at any rate.

MAY 25, 1864

Out at Hascosea where we came for a few days. A tremendus battle was, we hear, joined between Beauregard and Butler on Sunday night of which we have as yet no particulars save that Beauregard directed his men to fall back seemingly in confusion to a point where he had sixty guns concentrated. The manoevre was executed with perfect success. At one discharge fifteen hundred Yankees were put hors du combat! Mr Hill tells us that the want of cooperation on Monday of which we have had hints in the papers & which caused Beauregard's "well laid scheme" to go-a-gley lies at the doors of Whiting, Barton, & Martin. Ransom (Matt) had cut them off from the James & Whiting, Barton, & Martin were to advance from the Appomatox, but they failed to come up. I will not say what Rumour has it that Beauregard has done in the premises until it is confirmed, as it affects the character of the delinquents.

Lee has changed his front to meet Grant who has swung his whole army to Lee's right, has abandoned "his base" at Fredericksburg, & seems making for York River. Lincoln calls for 200,000 more troops, admits (that is Washington papers do) a loss of 70,000 men, orders a thanksgiving for Victory, & the Bishop of New York has actually had a solemn Te Deum sung in Trinity Church for the success of the Union arms. One would think that their hymns of victory would be drowned by the groans of their wounded. To the wail of their mourners who sound the Coronache over their dead they turn a deaf ear.

Colonel Clarke's wound is more serious than we at first heard. His shoulder "is crushed" and peices of bone are already being discharged from it. Poor man, disabled I fear for life! Mr E has written & urged him to come to our house so soon as he can travel, offering to go for him, but it will be some time ere he can leave the Surgeon's hands I fear. He is at a friend's house in Richmond. My journal is becoming a mere chronicle of battles, bloodshed, & death. I think I must curtail my account of military matters & mention only the most important.

More of our young friends have sealed their devotion to the cause with their blood. Mrs Iredell has lost another son, James, Major of the 53d N C killed and Cadwallader her youngest wounded; Mrs Haywood another son, William, killed; Mrs Sasser a son Phil, "missing"; Mrs Saunders—another son, Col Wm, wounded in the face. Her son Joe wounded in the same place has been in the hands of the enemy since Gettysburg. These are all the hope & stay of widowed mothers. Mr Smedes has lost another son killed. Chas Haigh, son of our old friend, reported killed.[55] These are but a part. Time fails me to

---

[55]Maj. James Johnston Iredell, transferred to the field and staff of the Second Battalion, North Carolina Infantry, from the Fifty-third North Carolina Regiment, was killed at Spotsylvania, May 12, 1864. Capt. Cadwallader Jones Iredell of Co. E, Ninth North Carolina (First Cavalry) Regiment, was wounded on May 11, 1864. Philemon H. Sasser, a second lieutenant in Co. A, Thirty-third North Carolina Regiment, also was wounded. Lt. Col. Joseph Hubbard Saunders of the Thirty-third North Carolina Regiment was wounded at Gettysburg and imprisoned at Johnson's Island. His brother was Col. William L. Saunders (see footnote 49, 1864). Edward S. Smedes, a second lieutenant in Co. I, Fifth Regiment North Carolina State Troops, was killed at Spotsylvania, May 12, 1864. A Charles T. Haigh, listed in Clark as first lieutenant in Co. B, Thirty-seventh North Carolina Regiment, was reported killed at Spotsylvania while leading a charge. Manarin and Jordan, however, list another Charles T. Haigh, of Cumberland County, in the Sixty-third North Carolina (Fifth Cavalry) Regiment, present and accounted for through December,

tell of all our acquaintances who have fallen. Mr E's cousin Dana Colchetre[56] was severely wounded in the wrist in one of the fights before Petersburg. We have sent for him and if he is in a state to be moved hope to have him here where we can attend to his wants.

How long can this continue? Our country is drained of her best & bravest, our mothers are bereaved, our wives widowed, & still the tale of blood goes on! Ah that Lincoln & Seward could but be made to feel the weight of human suffering which their wickedness has occasioned! What a reverse picture does our peaceful home exhibit! But I cannot enjoy it! I walk in my garden where one hundred & twelve varieties of Rose all in splendid bloom salute me at once & think how many of my noble young countrymen have closed their eyes forever on all scenes of earthly beauty & enjoyment. How the sight of such a blaze of splendour would fall cold & dead on the hearts of thousands of my country women who weep—friends lost to them forever. At this moment perhaps, whilst I linger along these fragrant walks enjoying the delicious perfume & letting my eye rest admiringly in the sight of beauty around me, the sword of the enemy may drink the blood of thousands of my fellow country men. I think on the anguish of anxiety, the horror of uncertainty which now pervade the hearts & homes of so many & I turn sickened from the sight and long to be able to do something to show my devotion to my country in this her hour of need, something to alleviate the suffering of her wounded soldiers who lie bleeding to preserve her honour intact. But what can I do? Remote from the scene of strife, too far from the R R & a surgeon to take charge of a severely wounded man whilst the slightly wounded are eager to press to their own homes, I feel powerless to do aught. Even the few comforts I could send them I have not transportation for, so entirely is the R R usurped by the pressing calls of military necessity.

MAY 26, 1864

No papers later than Monday morning, so we are still without news of Beauregard's last battle. A Yankee Diary picked up on the battlefield tells us of Butler's narrow escape from our Pickets to whom he rode up by mistake. He says, "He ran so fast that we could have played a game of Yuchre (Yankee mode of spelling Euchre) on his coat tails!"—complains of the officers reserving all the plunder to themselves but says they picked up many valuables "at Howletts." They sacked Mrs Friend's house & in fact have done so to every residence & farm within their reach, shot defenceless citizens, insulted women, & stole & plundered everything they saw. A dispatch from Gen

---

1864. Clark, *Histories of the North Carolina Regiments*, 118, 289, 486; II, 537-538, 567, 592, 667; III, 258; IV, 258, 473, 711; V, 155, 519; Manarin and Jordan, *North Carolina Troops*, II, 44, 373, 377; III, 264; IV, 185, 234; Ashe, *Biographical History*, IV, 382; Battle, *History of the University of North Carolina*, I, 285, 813.

[56]Sgt. W. D. Cotchett, who served in Co. A, Twenty-fifth South Carolina Volunteers, was wounded in action at Port Walthall Junction, May 7-8, 1864. *Charleston Courier*, May 16, 1864.

Beauregard tells Gen Cooper that Gen Walker rode by mistake into the entrenchments of the enemy & requested to surrender but was fired upon, his horse killed & he wounded in the foot so badly that amputation had to take place.[57] This he learned by Flag of Truce. Patty suggest[s] that we ought by way of retaliation take Gen Heckman of Butler's command & cut off his foot also to teach the Yankees how to treat a tender for surrender.

MAY 27, 1864

Set out yesterday for Looking Glass but was compelled to return by high water on all the roads. In consequence of the heavy, almost unprecedented, rain of Wednesday afternoon all the bridges are washed up. The "terrific battle" of Sunday night of which Mr Hill told us & in which Beauregard displayed such remarkable strategy has not even a place in the newspaper. On the contrary everything along our lines is reported as "more quiet than it has been for days." I beleive I will never again mention a rumour or record a single item of news until I see it either in an official form or from a source from whence sensation dispatches never issue. Mr Hill heard it as a matter of fact & as such repeated when, in fact, there was no fight at all on that evening. One thing, however, we can take comfort it: if we are deceived it is by wild reports which fly from mouth to mouth & like a rolling snow ball gathers as it goes. Our Generals & our Government do not deliberately deceive us as the Yankee Generals & Government do their credulous people. Butler telegraphs that he has Fort Drewry invested, that by a sortie of the garrison Gen Heckman & staff narrowly escaped capture, when the facts are—a signal repulse for him ere he reached the fortifications of Drewry's Bluff & the actual lodging of Heckman, his staff, & a part of his command in the prisons appointed for the Abolition prisoners in Richmond. On the 9th "information was received in Washington of the sinking in Albemarle Sound of the rebel Ram Albemarle by the U S steamer Sassacus."[58] Have they no shame that they thus persist in telling such lies. Mr E thinks it is done in order to secure Lincoln's nomination by the political convention which meets on the 7th of June, but they are short sighted if they think so flimsy a tissue of falsehoods will last until then. Even now the truth begins to peep out.

They have been forced to admit Sigel's defeat by Beckenridge but insist it has no bearing on the great Cause. Kautz's party has rejoined Butler, they now say, but without effecting the object he proposed. Kautz's & Speare's seems to be identical commands. Speares is the second &, to us it seems, the

---

[57]Gen. William S. Walker, on May 20, 1864, accidentally rode into the Federal lines near Petersburg. He was shot in the ankle when he refused to surrender. The wound later resulted in the amputation of his foot, and he was discharged that year. Boatner, *Civil War Dictionary*, 886-887.

[58]The *Sassacus*, commanded by Francis A. Roe, was one of seven well-armed gunboats ordered by the United States Navy, late in April, 1864, to "take care of" the C.S.S. *Albemarle*. In an engagement between the two, on May 5, 1864, the *Albemarle* disabled the *Sassacus* with a shot through her starboard boiler. *Civil War Naval Chronology*, IV, 54, 55; Clark, *Histories of the North Carolina Regiments*, V, 321-322.

most prominent of the two. Grant has swung his army along the arc of a circle occupied by Lee as a defensive line, no longer attacking the upper part of it. Lee withdraws his army to face him anew. "Gen Lee without abandoning his defensive line has responded to Gen Grant's movement by occupying the south bank of the North Anna river & offers to the enemy a free crossing of the Mattaponi," says an editorial in one of our papers.

Letters last night from Mr Haigh tells us that it is his grandson, Chas T. Haigh, who is killed. His son is still safe. This young man is barely nineteen; he is the son of Mr John & Caroline Haigh. Ah! well do I remember a happy time in June 1844 when I went to his Father's house to meet him, a happy bridegroom bringing his wife home. A merry *"in-fair"* we had, but they have seen much sorrow since then.

There has been heavy fighting in Northern Georgia in which we claim the victory but as yet nothing is decided—no general engagement. Kilpatrick the theif is reported wounded at the recent engagement at Resaca. Virginia will wear no weeds for him, a theif & a Robber.

May 30, 1864

Grant continues his attempt to flank Lee. Lee still continues to frustrate him. Grant appears to have receded from his determination as expressed to his government "to fight it out on this line if it takes all the summer." Summer is not quite here & he has changed his base of supplies *twice* already & circumstances seem to indicate a third, to the White House & York River. Skirmishing goes on constantly, endeavours on Grant's part "to feel our lines." Lee has offered battle, but the gage has been declined. Grant is now moving down the Pamunky towards the Peninsula, his army massed on Totopotamoy Creek & shows no dispositions to move further South. The suspense is most painful. Our fate hangs in the balance. May a merciful God shorten our period of probation & give us Peace!

News from the Army of Northern Georgia, cheering. Gen Joe Johnson has inflicted heavy loss upon Sherman, tho as yet there is no general engagement which cannot, however, be long delayed. We have captured many prisoners, a Brigade Commander, & immense numbers of small arms. Cleburn's Division on the 28th engaged the 4t Army corps under Howard; took 200 prisoners exclusive of the wounded which fell into our hands, killed one thousand, with a loss to us of five hundred men, Maj Gen Howard Johnson & Brig Gen King, the piano stealer, wounded.

The New York World & the Journal of Commerce were suspended by his highness A Lincoln for publishing immediately after the battle of the Wilderness a proclamation appointing a day of fasting & prayer & calling into military service by volunteering & draft 400,000 men, which proclamation proved to be a forgery. Seward & Lincoln accordingly let loose the phials of their wrath upon the unfortunate Editors, ordered their arrest & imprisonment in Fort Lafayette & a military occupation of their premises. When their highnesses were at length appeased & allowed the delinquents again to resume their avocations, the Editor of the World comes out in an address to him which proves old Hudibras to have been a keen observer of human nature. He says, "No Rogue ere felt the halter draw/With good opinion of the Law."[59] And so Mr "Manton Marble,"[60] for so is he yclept, after applauding His Excellency in every step he has hitherto taken in trampling on the Constitution now endeavours to shelter himself behind its broad Aegis! Rob, steal, murder, seize presses, Churches, Slaves, horses, yes the land itself in the South, put your foot down firmly, crush out these Southern Aristocrats, you are a *hero & a patriot*, but touch *me, me Manton Marble* & Abraham Lincoln, you are a wretch too vile to enjoy the light of day. Thus does he now discourse, now that he has felt "the halter draw." Pity Mr Lincoln, that whilst you were about it you had not tightened & ended Mr Manton Marble's commendations & Phillipics at one stroke. A rascal! But if I dwell on the behaviour of my Yankee bretheren, I shall be in a fair way to emulate Mama's condition. She said with great earnestness a few days since, "I declare! if this war continues much longer I shall lose the little Christianity I have got!"

So it is with me. The bounds where Christian charity ends & I can "be angry and sin not" are very ill defined in my mind when I read either of the outrages or the meannesses of the Yankee. I rejoice when I hear of their slaughter by thousands, which is all right, for by their death the lives & liberties of my fellow countrymen are preserved. I never stop as Mrs McPheeters did to resolve "that I will be wicked for this once." When I hear of any of their Generals sharing the fate of that infamous Lyons, it is all good news to me.

This reminds me that I never copied the list of the Generals lost during the last few weeks in the Virginia Campaign. I do it now, premising that I have kept no record of the Louisianna or Georgia enemies Generals. These are Lee's, Beauregard's, and Morgan's alone. Confederates killed Maj. Gen Stuart, Brig Gens Jones, Stafford, Jenkins, Daniel, Gordon, Perrin, & Jenkins again—8; Wounded, Lieut Gen Longstreet, Brig Gens Pegram, Hayes, Walker, Benning, Ransom, Ramseur, McGowan, R. D. Johnson, Walker again—10; Prisoners, Maj Gen Edward Johnson, Brig Gen Stewart —2. Of the Yankees so far as known to us, killed, Maj Gens Wadsworth & Sedgwick—2; Brig Gens Hayes, Carr, Webb, Taylor, Owens, Stephenson,

---

[59]John Trumbull (1750-1831), *McFingal*, canto 3, line 489. Stevenson, *Home Book of Quotations*, 1083.

[60]Manton Malone Marble (1835-1917), a newspaper reporter and editor, owned and published the New York *World* from 1862 through 1876. During the Civil War Marble opposed the expansion in power of the federal government and clashed with many of Lincoln's war policies. In 1864 the *World* and other New York papers innocently published a forged document written in Lincoln's name which called for 400,000 more troops and a national day of fasting and prayer. Lincoln immediately ordered Marble's arrest, and a military guard occupied the *World*'s offices for three days. Marble was quickly released but angrily assailed Lincoln in an editorial published May 23, 1864. *Dictionary of American Biography*, XII, 267.

Rice, Baglie & Ames—11; Wounded, Brig Gens Warren, Stephens, Robinson, Morris, Getty, Talbot, Baxter, Wright, Smith, & Averil, & two whose names I have lost belonging to Butler's Command—12; Prisoners Seymour, Shaller, Neil, & Heckman—4; 20 Confederates, 27 Yankees. The Yankee papers admitted a loss of 31, independant of Heckman & the two whose names I have lost, making their loss 34, but we had no account of their names. We have lost two Jenkins &—what is a little odd—we have now three Gens *Walker* all wounded in the foot!

Speaking of wounded Generals, I must tell an anecdote of a little girl who had just begun to read the papers for herself. She looked up from her paper & said "Bad news, sister, bad news, Gen Wheeler is dead"! "How do you know my dear?" "Because I see that Gen Johnston has just reviewed his *corpse* (corps)"!

JUNE 1, 1864

No mail. A note only from Mr McMahon telling us that "all the trains are pressed for military necessities by Gen Beauregard. Butler has moved to the North side; only negro troops remain on this side. Rumours of great success & much favour to our side; rumours, however, not as reliable as might be. Rumour says fighting yesterday the 31st." It is hard to wait, but military necessity makes all bend to it. Pattie very unhappy about her brother. Suspense is agony.

JUNE 5, 1864

Talk who will of the seed of noble blood having run out, that we have degenerated from the spirit & hardihood of our ancestors, I have just read a letter which gives them all the lie. It is from Captain Skinner to his sister, my neice Mrs Jones. It is dated "Front line of Entrenchments Near Old Church, May 31st." He says in it—

Pattie we have had a dreadful time & a hard time & all is not yet over but I hope the worst is passed. Grant has been taught such a severe lesson by Lee & his ragged rebels that he is the most cautious man to be found. Battle has been offered him a half a dozen times since leaving Spottsylvania C H but he has not accepted. This army is in fine condition & overflowing spirits, notwithstanding that we have lost heavily & suffered untold hardships. Until the 29th we lived on 4 crackers & a ¼ lb of meat per day, but now our rations have been doubled & all are jubilant, tho before that happy event there was not a murmur to be heard & yet men in my company were whole days at a time without a morsel. We are all dirty & if you will pardon the expression— *Lousy*, having been 25 days without a change of clothing. During this time we have marched, counter-marched, fought, etc., without intermission. We have passed but three nights since May the 4th that we have not been in line of battle, required to keep on not only all our clothing but our accoutrements. We are worn & dirty but a[re] cheerful & confidant relying on our God for the Victory. Don't be distressed. I am perfectly contented and if I can hear from you & our mother occasionally, I am really happy. Don't imagine that because a battle is impending that we are long faced & miserable. On the contrary we are cheerful, in a word we are all right! I fear you suffer more than I. Our poor old company (yours & mine) has suffered greatly. We were in the engagements of the 5th, 6th, 10th, 12th, & 23d. I had but thirty men to carry into action in the begining. Of these I lost 4 killed & 18 wounded, one of the latter mortally. . . . A few who were wounded on the 5th have returned and are ready to try it again. . . . By the mercy of God I escaped. I firmly beleive that I will pass through unharmed. . . . If you love me, dont be troubled but trust all to God & pray for your dear brother Ben.

How can such men ever be conquered? The manly & bold spirit, the cheerful endurance of hardship, the firm reliance upon God that breathes in every line can never be crushed & the tender solicitude he shows for her anxiety goes straight to the heart, so bold, so frank, so hearty & so unselfish. Elsewhere he speaks in most simple earnest tones of his faith & trust in Gen Lee. He closes his letter saying that they "are ordered to march he knows not where," but Gen Lee has ordered it, & whatever he orders is right. On the 1st "Marse Robert" telegraphs to the Sec of War, "There has been skirmishing along the lines today" & after some particulars says "A force of infantry is reported to have arrived at Tunstal's Station from the White House. . . . They state that they belong to Butler's forces." If so, & I scarce beleive it a ruse de guerre,[61] Butler has gone by water around the Peninsula in stead of crossing through the Swamps of Chickahominy made famous by McClellan's retreat. All of his forces have not, however, left Bermuda Hundred, as we have an official telegram from Beauregard saying that he had "captured his rifle pits near Ware Bottom Church," dated June 2d. The details of the skirmishing of Lee's army are all favourable to us. I use the word skirmishing but it does not express what really took place. In comparison to the grand attack it is a skirmish but whole army corps are engaged on both sides. For instance,

about six wednesday night the enemy made another desperate attack on our right. They massed their forces in six lines & hurled them on our position with great rapidity. Our men no sooner recovered from the shock than they assailed them in turn & drove them back. . . . During the engagement 4 companies of a Wisconsin Regt volunteerd to take a battery by assault. When they arrived within 200 yds of the Battery it opened upon them. . . . When within 50 yds from our breastworks in front of the Battery, our infantry opened a galling fire upon them which mingled with that of the Battery annihilated the whole Battalion—not one was seen to escape. . . .

Two car loads of wounded were sent to Richmond & they reported that not a single man of the four companies got back! That is "skirmishing" with a vengeance. We take many prisoners. For instance, in this account alone, Ewell flanks them on the Mechanicsville pike & takes 500, Wilcox's skirmishers

---

[61]French, "stratagem of war."

bring in 100, Hampton at Ashland 75 & 300 horses. We rush on them "whilst at dinner, capture many prisoners, & all the dinner," which to men living on ¼ lb of meat & 4 crackers a day must have been the most welcome of the two! Ewell took three lines of breastworks with but slight loss to himself, but amongst the killed is the brave Gen Doles of Geo. Thus it goes. Time fails me to tell you all. I preserve in my repertory 2 letters from an Englishman, correspondant of the London Herald, giving an account of the battles of the Wilderness & Spotsylvania C H.[62] They stir the blood like the sound of a trumpet & are said by those who ought to know that they are as true in detail as they are spirited & graphic in description. Lee's army now lies in Hanover county covering Richmond. "Cold Harbour," "Atlee's," "Hanover Old Church," "Storr's Farm," "Ashland," names familiar as household words two years since in McClellan's advance, are now all occupied by our forces. Breckenridge has joined Lee & Whiting is ordered there, & speaking of Whiting, the rumour of which Mr Hill told us respecting himself & Martin we are told on newspaper authority is false. He, it seems, is still in command as is also Gen James Martin. As for Barton, Gen Robt Ransom says he has suspended him—but magnanimously "gives him the benefit of an investigation." As to the "coup de theatre."[63] about breaking his sword on the field, we hear nothing of it, but from that lying jade Rumour who at the same time deposes Martin & Whiting—& do not beleive that Beauregard ordered any such thing. To be suspended by that foul mouthed, ill governed tempered man Robert Ransom jr is prima facie no disgrace. Barton had he his deserts is doubtless the better man & the better soldier of the two.

From Gen Johnston we hear officially under date of June 1st, "This army is in a healthy condition. In partial engagements it has had great advantage & the sum of all the combats amounts to a battle." Signed J E Johnston. He also reports reinforcements from the 17 army corps to be on their way to reinforce Gen Sherman—bad news for us, for I fear we are already out numbered there, but the victory is not always to the strong.

JUNE 7, 1864

Our last news from Richmond, Sat June 4th, told us that our army was standing in line of battle; Fighting on our whole line, 7 miles long, at intervals all day Thursday and Friday & with success on our side at every point. The last official intelligence from Gen Lee is dated Thursday night & states that on that "afternoon the enemy made an attack on our right with unimportant results. In the evening Gen Early attacked the right of the enemy & drove him from his intrenchments. . . . & pursued them until dark. . . . A P Hill dislodged the enemy from Turkey Hill on our extreme right." What cheers our very

---

[62]These letters were not found in the diary.

[63]French, "unexpected stage effect."

heart of hearts is that the slaughter on our side is slight; that of the enemy is reported at 10,000. The fighting is along the line of the Chickahominy, upon fields made sacred by the blood of our compatriots shed two years since when they drove McClellan back from the very gates of Richmond. Grant throws column after column upon Turkey Ridge which commands the site of the two famous bridges over the Chickahominy, "Grape Vine" & "McClellan" over which the young Napoleon threw his beaten army in his memorable "change of base" when he retired to James River. Grant wishes them to shorten his line of transportation as well as to advance upon Richmond. Transports in the James would be a material aid to him now. I beleive it is "Grape Vine Bridge" over which Maj Gen Huger allowed McClellan to pass in the night, thus enabling him to escape & claim that "masterly strategy" which excited our ridicule so much in 62. The mail has just come in & with it a dispatch from Gen Lee of June 3d. After some details of the points of attack & their results, he winds up with, "Our loss today has been small and our success under the blessing of God all that could expect."

June 8, 1864

One almost feels in reading the accounts of the battles now in progress around Richmond as tho the tide of time had gone *backward* & we were living over again the stirring scenes of two years ago when McClellan made his grand attempt on our Capitol. The names of the battlefields are all repeated but alas, many well known names, names of men who were active then in driving back the invader & spoiler from our land, are now missed from the record of living honour. Gaines Mill, Chickahominy, Bethesda Church, Hanover Old Church, & Seven Pines, Cold Harbour recall the thrill with [which] we first became familiar with their names.

The paper of the 7th tells us that "Yesterday was a quiet day along the Chickahominy. The enemy had abandoned our left & part of our centre apparently in great haste. Early pursued them for two miles capturing sixty prisoners who stated that Grant was retiring to the White House because his men would not fight." No one, however, beleives that, but the impression which generally prevails is that he is making for James River & will cross to the South Side. Bad news from the valley & Stanton, but as it is a very *bitter* pill I prefer waiting until I am forced to swallow it ere doing so. I fear, however, that delay will not "sugarcoat" it & that Stanton is really in Yankee possession, but I live in hope that it is not so bad as that, tho the War Office does not, tho without official intelligence of the fact.

June 11, 1864

Have been reading my account of the battles around Richmond in 1862 & am very much disgusted with them. They are bald, meagre, & flat to an unaccountable degree. I knew everything that was going on so well myself & was so familiar with the name of each skirmish that I suppose I thought it useless to particularize them, but in order to remedy in some measure my own defects in the narrative of now passing events I preserve another spirited letter from an English correspondant describing the battle of Spotsylvania C H, as his first did that of the Wilderness.[64]

Grant & Lee still confront each other, their lines of battle being but three or four hundred yds apart, but all is quiet, not a gun fired along the whole line! Grant sends in a Flag & requests an interval for the purpose of burying the dead & caring for the wounded, to which Lee replies that "none of his dead lie between the lines & that his wounded are all cared for." Rather late in the day for Gen Grant to assume the humane. He left thousands of bloated corpses festering in the sun at Spotsylvania C H & marched off with seeming indifference as to whether they were buried or not. His proposal now is considered merely a ruse de guerre to gain time for some new change of base. All things seem to point to a crossing of the James River on his part & an assumption of Butler's late route. An immense pontoon bridge has been floated up the James & now lies below Berkeley. Were he to attack Petersburg in force, Lee could, I think, get there & confront him on his arrival. The fortifications there are enormous, but as yet have no guns mounted upon them. There is even more than the usual amount of lying in the Yankee papers as to their successes. Lee has been driven routed from Cold Harbour, which place they now hold. Butler has defeated Beauregard so signally that the "wily Creole" has fled. Our gunboats in the James are annihilated. Grant is in the entrenchments around Richmond & many other novel inventions of their fertile imaginations dazzle the minds of the reading northern public. Do they beleive it? Or have they a peep behind the scenes and pretend to do so, so as to aid in bolstering up the Stock Market & the price of Gold? The New York World, however, illustrates the truth of the old maxim "sweet are the uses of adversity,"[65] as since its suspension it tries to tear the veil from the eyes of its countrymen, asks "what is the use of such deceit?" & gravely announces "that here after we for one are resolved to speak the truth as regards military successes or reverses."

Lee tells us in a dispatch of the 8th that the enemy have been unusually quiet today & on the whole extended his line. "Two divisions of his cavalry under Gen Sheridan are reported to have crossed the Pamunky yesterday at New Castle Ferry." Signed R E Lee. So Sheridan is out on other raid— probably to prevent reinforcements being sent to Imboden in the Valley & prevent Hunter from being driven from Staunton. For bitter tho' the pill is, we have been forced to swallow it without gilding, with the added bitterness too of the death of Gen William E Jones, a gallant & able officer, who fell at the

---

[64]This letter was not located.

[65]Shakespeare, *As You Like It*, act 2, sc. 1, line 12.

head of his command whilst barring the advance of that bloodthirsty theif Gen Hunter down the Valley.

On the 9th a body of Kautz's Cavalry, about four thousand strong, made a sudden dash upon Petersburg by way of the Jerusalem plank road. They were met by a body of citizens militia who manned the works & repulsed them manfully & with heavy loss in two charges, reserving their fire until the Yankee cavalry were within forty paces. This changed their tactics & as we had but 170 (one hundred & seventy) men all told, it was an easy maer for them to flank breastworks & trenches of more than a mile in extent, so the gallant band of civilians were ordered to retreat. On came the enemy in double column, sabres drawn. Thundering down to the very outskirts of the City, they planted a cannon on a hill opposite the Water Works & prepared to shell the city. Their advance column already were across the bridge at the foot of the hill when a new feature was put on the whole affair by the opportune arrival of Graham's Battery which reached Reservoir Hill, unlimbered, & with remarkable precision & rapidity threw a shower of shell into their midst. They paused, when suddenly, Dearing's Cavalry Brigade, dismounted, charged them with a yell down the hill. This was more than they expected, for as yet they had seen none but militia. So wheeling, they started back up the Water work hill in confusion. Here they paused but seeing a part of their forces, with whom they expected to unite, retreating from the direction of Blandford Church road before Sturdevant's Battery, they incontinently fled abandoning a handsome cannon & six horses on Jackson['s] old field about a mile from the Church. The gallant militia lost nine killed & many wounded, but inflicted a heavier loss on the enemy.

We took a few prisoners who say that the object of the expedition was the capture of Petersburg. We opine, in which God grant we may be mistaken, that it was a pioneer company sent out by Grant to feel the way for him, tho the troops were from Butler's command. Grant, "butcher Grant" as his men call him, succeeded so well by swinging around from his base & infesting Vicksburg, cutting off its communications, that we think it more than likely that foiled as he has now been on the North side of the James, he will try the same tactics on the South side of the Appomatox, having Bermuda Hundred, the place at which Kautz's party crossed as a base. Could Lee reach Petersburg in time to confront him? To do so certainly he ought to have a pontoon bridge or bridges at Drewry's Bluff. O that we had peace! This constant anxiety & watching must tell on our men! How does Gen Lee support it? God's blessing only & God's strength enables him to bear up under. What a position does he occupy—the idol, the point of trust, of confidence & repose of thousands! How nobly has he won the confidence, the admiration of the nation, for I remember that when Gen Joe Johnston was wounded at Seven Pines & Lee in consequence took the head of the army himself, many persons both doubted his ability in the field & deplored his removal from the Cabinet. An excellent one to plan to lay out a campaign but with too little energy to carry it out, they even called him *"old-stick-in-the-mud"* & quoted the mishaps of the Western Va campaign against him! Should any one now dare to remember or to apply that soubriquet to him their heads would to a certainty be broken, if not by one of his men by a civilian. Such is [the] confidence & affectionate trust we all repose in him. "Marse Robert" can do any & all things. God grant that he may long be spared to us. He nullifies Bragg, Ransom, & a host of other incapables. Bragg is blamed for the loss of Staunton. Justly I dare say, he has lost us so much elsewhere that it would not be "Bragg, the Unlucky" were he now to fail. Let us hope that his evil genius may exhaust itself in that last 'coup' & that he may have no heavier misfortune in store for us.

JUNE 16, 1864

Hascosea—Came out from Looking Glass for the summer on Monday 13th (later by some days than we have been in some years) & The Lares & Penates of our household fled for days, affrighted from the onslaut made on them by dust brooms & scrubbing brushes! Now that Peace is in some measure restored & we can once more move about the house without encountering a scouring tub, they have returned & sit pluming their ruffled feathers & enjoying the atmosphere of comfort around them. On Sunday the 12th saw in the Looking Glass Garden the first corn tassel, so summer is here in real earnest.

The news from the Valley is discouraging. Staunton is seized & as yet held by Hunter, who has assembled around himself all the predatory bands which have hitherto infested the out skirts of that beautiful section, ravening like wolves & ready to pounce upon their prey whenever the shepherd should relax his vigilance. Bragg having drawn off all the protectors of the fold, Averil, Crook & [———] can work their own sweet will at leisure. They have accordingly thrown themselves into Lexington and menace Lynchburg & Charlottsville, but Breckenridge has been ordered back to his late field again & the next news we hear will, I hope, be that Hunter is flying in the traces & after the manner of Sigel. We have but few particulars. Communication is cut off & the Telegraph wires are down. From Cold Harbour we learn that after days of inaction behind his paralels Grant is once more in motion, "still moving on our right." He repulsed a body of our Cavalry at Bottom's Bridge & threw a portion of his forces across the Chickahominy & is moving down both banks of that stream. Conjectures are idle as to his plans & future movements, tho' all things point to an attack on the South Side with Bermuda Hundred's as base. Transports are landing supplies below Malvern Hill, to which point part of his forces seem moving. Hampton has signally defeated Sheridan, sent him flying in great disorder across the Pamunky towards the White House with the loss of a large portion of his command, dead on the field & 500 captured & on their way to

Richmond. His loss in officers is very heavy. Hampton's loss small, for which God be praised.

JUNE 17, 1864

Inexpressibly shocked last night by the news by Telegraph of Uncle Polk's death! He was killed instantly by a cannon ball. Gens Johnston, Hardee, & Hood were with him when he fell. My poor Aunt! God be with & comfort her! Contrary to many anticipations, Gen Polk has proved himself an excellent officer, "a good fighting General," handling his men well & commanding the confidence as well as the affection of his men. He leaves children none of whom, however, are of tender age. He had a daughter Lilly,[66] married scarce a month since to Lieut Huger, formerly of his Staff, but who losing a leg on the bloody field of Murfresboro, has since been assigned to Bureau duty. Poor girl! it is sad to exchange the orange blossom for the Cypress so soon! What a life of contrast has Bishop Polk's been! How little could one foresee that his Lawn Robes would be exchanged for the Uniform of a Lieut Gen, or that the soldier of the Cross would eventually die the Soldier of his Country!

Official dispatches from Gen Lee confirm Hampton's defeat of Sheridan in all its particulars, says that "the enemy retreated in confusion apparently by the route he came leaving his dead & wounded on the field." The fight occurred at Trevillian's not far from Louisa C H. He says also, "At daylight this morning it was discovered that the army of Gen Grant had left our front," so it would appear that Gen Ulysses stole a march literally upon "Marse Robert," tho how it was possible I cannot understand as the lines of the two armies were in some places only 50 yds apart and in none more than 150. He was reported as still moving but no fighting as yet. He is now going from Richmond, 'a retirer pour sauter,' but Lee will be ready for him.

Lincoln & Andy Johnson of Tenn are the nominees of the great Republican Convention which last week met in Baltimore, a nomination secured by lying, but as there are to be three Richmond's in the field,[67] we can sit afar & watch who out lies & out Generals the other & amuse ourselves with their strategems.

Congress has adjourned after issuing a Manifesto, at once weak, whining, & useless, which I do not think it necessary to preserve. Capt Cooke has at his own request, in consequence of his health, been removed from the command of the Albemarle & Capt Maffit of the Florida memory assigned to the duty. Poor gentleman, I pity him! How he will chafe cooped up in this narrow

---

[66]Elizabeth D. Polk married W. E. Huger on April 27, 1864.

[67]The "three Richmonds" running for the presidency in 1864 included two Republican and one Democratic candidates. Abraham Lincoln, the official nominee of the Republican party, was opposed by John C. Frémont, the candidate of Radical Republicans dissatisfied with Lincoln. Gen. George B. McClellan was the Democratic party's nominee. Randall and Donald, *Civil War and Reconstruction*, 467-475.

crooked river after roaming at will the broad bosom of the sea in search of Yankee commerce.

At the Plantation today called to see Mrs George Pope[68] in quest of a home for the girl Catherine Jackson. I fear we are doomed to much trouble on her account. She came to me a fortnight since, barefooted with her clothes in her hand, to say that she had not a shelter for her head. Provided for her temporarily & have been ever since looking out for a permanent employment for her but as yet unsuccessfully. She left Samantha some months since & there is so little about her to attract or interest one in her behalf & she is so ignorant, boorish, & disagreeable in her ways that few are willing to receive her as an inmate. Mrs Pope consents to keep her for four weeks only to do some spinning.

Morgan is again at work in Kentucky & Forest has gained signal successes in North Alabama, cutting up & scattering Sherman's reinforcements & supplies, but we are without particulars.

JUNE 18, 1864

Last night came a note from Susan telling us that she was in receipt of a letter from her cousin Miss Dunlop of Petersburg written at Weldon, saying that her Mother, Sisters, & self had been driven from their homes by sudden advance of the Yankees upon the city. Without warning or note of their intention, they advanced in force & commenced an indiscriminate shelling of the town. The Hospital flag was instantly raised upon the S C Hospital but to no purpose. They actually shelled it with the flag flying![69] Richmond papers of the 16th say that nothing definite is known of Grant's motions. He is supposed to be crossing the James & making a junction with Butler with the intention of advancing upon Petersburg on both sides of the Appomattox as a prelude to a new attack on Richmond. Prisoners say that he has been drunk since the battle of Spotsylvania C H & that there is a vast amount of disaffection and discontent in the Yankee Camp, but it does not do to credit all that they say. Beauregard will, I hope, be able to keep the enemy in check at least until Lee comes up & then together they will be able to drive him to his Gunboats.

JUNE 19, 1864

Yesterday came Sister Betsy & Rachel to make us a visit. There was no mail but the news they brought from Petersburg, derived from passengers, is exciting in the extreme. The cars were crowded with women & children flying from the brutal shelling of their Christian brethren! Several ladies have been

---

[68]The 1860 Halifax County census listed George H. Pope, a thirty-three-year-old farmer, as the husband of Martha Pope and as the father of two children. Eighth Census, 1860, Population Schedule, Halifax County, 73.

[69]The *Sentinel*, June 22, 1864, mentioned an account in the *Express* which reported the shelling of hospitals in Petersburg and recalled that Grant was guilty of the same barbarity in Vicksburg.

killed. They had taken all our batteries & at one time turned our own guns upon us, but we retook battery no—,[70] the Key of the position, & were able to command the others & it was hoped they would soon be forced to evacuate them. This is Refugee news, however, & as they leave in a panic they always exagerate the danger—so I omit many details which they gave us—enough, however, to fill our hearts with deep anxiety. We have no news of Gen Lee but are sure that he is in the right place & will at the right time *act*. Should Grant invest Petersburg on the South side of the Appomattox, succeed in cutting off Lee's Southern communication, it will be a most serious thing for us as a community, as we would be exposed without protection to predatory bands sent off from the main army in search of plunder; but beyond that, thanks to the farseeing of our head, Mr Davis, it would scarce effect the well being of Lee's army, as the Danville road is safe & by it supplies could be forwarded. The Danville junction with the N C R R[71] is now finished & open for travel. Its inception & execution we owe to Mr Davis suggestion and energy. God bless him!

About Sundown came a note from Mr McMahon telling us that additional news from Petersburg had been received; brought, however, by a passenger, so we know not how much to credit. He says that at one time the Yankees had taken all our fortifications & were rushing into the town when by an opportune arrival they were met by a body of our "grey backs" supposed to be Lieut Gen Longstreet's Corp, who drove them in a hand to hand struggle, with tremendous slaughter, back & repossessed the fortifications & that the city was now considered "safe." God grant it. Should they, however, succeed in investing the city on the South side of the Appomattox & maintain themselves there, it would, as I said before, be a terrible thing for us, but God's will be done! Our times are in His hands!

JUNE 20, 1864

At the plantation with Mr E. We had sent for the girl Catherine Jackson. I tried to set forth, to her, her shortcomings & deficiencies in a firm yet kind light, particularly her utter want of veracity, her idleness, & her horrid unwomanly practice of chewing tobacco & her fancy for straying about the country alone. We have provided her with a home for more than a fortnight during

---

[70]The defenses around Petersburg, similar to those around Richmond, were strengthened with artillery batteries or redans established at consecutively numbered intervals. From June 15 through June 18, the Union forces under Grant managed to capture several of these points (3, 4, 7, 8, 12, 13, and 14) but failed to break through the Confederate line. This forced Grant to besiege Petersburg instead of taking it by direct assault. *Sentinel*, June 18, 22, 1864; Boatner, *Civil War Dictionary*, 644-646.

[71]The potential military usefulness anticipated by an extension of the Richmond and Danville Railroad to Greensboro caused the North Carolina General Assembly to pass a resolution in 1861 urging its immediate construction. The line was begun during the war, and President Davis publicly sanctioned its construction in 1862; but the Greensboro-Danville connection was not completed until late in the war. Charles W. Turner, "The Virginia Southwestern Railroad System at War, 1861-1865," *North Carolina Historical Review*, XXIV (October, 1947), 468, 473-474.

which time she has barely spun a lb of cotton. Sent her to Mrs George Pope with an admonition that she would not please unless she was more industrious.

News but meagre from Petersburg but all good. Gen Lee telegraphs that we have retaken the entrenchments at Howlets, from whence we conclude that he is South of the James. Confirmation of the repulse of the enemy before Petersburg, which is now considered safe from their attacks. The slaughter was terrific on their side, ours slight. Not much news from the Valley & that not encouraging. They have taken & burned all the important buildings in Lexington & menace Lynchburg, but Breckenridge will, I hope, frustrate their designs. They have no supplies, no waggons, & live off the country, pillaging, robbing, & committing the most horrible outrages. Johnson still holds Sherman at bay. He dare not attack altho invited to do so. Morgan, we hear from the North, holding his own in Kentucky.

June 22, 1864

Gen Lee is certainly in Petersburg. Mr Dunlop writes that he has seen him riding with Beauregard. The damage done by the shelling of the town is inconsiderable. There is no news of importance, as since their repulse the enemy contents himself with firing at Long range, shelling & skirmishing. News from the North tells us that "Grant has command of the new campaign against Richmond on the South side of James River with his headquarters at Bermuda Landing," which is a tacit admission of failure in the Spotsylvania C H "line" by which the hero was to take R. if he "fought on it all the summer." A new "on to Richmond"! Hunter's forces are retreating from the vicinity of Lynchburg; 4 peices of artillery & 200 prisoners have been captured, but we have nothing official or definite, but we hope that they have done their worst. For a horrible outrage see my repertory, and this is not a single instant of such brutality! Yesterday came Mama's maid Edie as her avant courier & today we are expecting Father, Sue, & herself to spend the rest of the summer and fall with us. How thankful I am to Almighty God that we have so peaceful & quiet a home to offer them.

June 23, 1864

Yesterday came Father, Mama, & Sue to spend the summer with us. No news. Yankee accounts of the repulse of Morgan in Kentucky—which we bear most philosophically, as not crediting the source from whence they come. One peice of good news for us—an augury of better times for the future. Mr Meminger, that German incubus on our finances, has actually resigned! The Examiner says we cannot be worsted in his successor, be he who he may.

Butler is sending out parties from Suffolk with orders to seize all the horses & destroy all the agriculturial implements in the country. Our North Eastern counties be at his mercy. God help the wretched inhabitants!

JUNE 26, 1864

A most anxious week! No mails from Richmond for days. Rumours only of fighting around Petersburg in which we are victorious & Forays & raids of the enemy cutting our R Rs & Telegraphs, with which I will not fill you my Journal. Suffice it that we are in a most uncertain & harrassed state of mind. Mr McMahon sent us a telegram just received by him telling us that we had signally repulsed the enemy, captured many prisoners, & held two lines of his breastworks, but I know not from whom it came. The Weldon & Petersburg R R is certainly cut & heavy fighting has been going on there, at least heavy guns have been fired, and that is all we know certainly. Of the latter fact we have the testimony of our own ears.

Pattie today received a letter from her sister, Mrs Wood, now unfortunately in the enemies lines. She confirms the account given in the papers of Butler's savage order mentioned above. Her house has been recently visited by a party of Yankees who took off her horses, mules, carriage, buggy, every spade, plough, hoe, & even plough lines & gear on the plantation, leaving her with a growing crop (which she had hired free negroes to cultivate for her own & children's support) & no means whatever of tending it. She went herself to the commander of the expedition & represented her condition—her husband a prisoner in their hands & who had never been in arms against them, her little children, & her total inability to support them without her team, but for sole answer he replied that "the mules were just such animals as he wished & that they were too valuable to be returned." The Lieut in command of the Gunboat on which the marauders came up, it almost seems in mockery, told her that "the Captain was acting without orders, as private property was to be respected." Yet he nevertheless admitted the plunder on board of his boat, thus aiding & abetting in the theft, mocking her with deceitful promises that he "would report him & that her property should be returned." Insult to injury—for he had the power then & there to make the Captain do his duty by refusing to receive the ill gotten goods on his boat. The weather for the last few days has been intensely hot. How our poor soldiers must suffer in the trenches & on their dusty marches & ah! how fearfully it will add to the mortality amongst our wounded!

JUNE 27, 1864

News today from Petersburg brought by a Maj Shepperd, who left that place on horse back & came to Stony Crk where he took the cars, to the effect that "Petersburg is now considered safe." The wires were last night working between Weldon & Petersburg, but as the enemy were entrenched 8000 strong within 3/8th of a mile of the R R, it was not considered safe to allow cars to pass. The Danville Road has been torn up at Keysville, a short distance from Clarksville, so no more news of Lee or Breckenridge can reach us for a time.

Was startled today by a messenger riding up & putting into my hands a note from Col Bell to Mr E enclosing an official dispatch from Gen Whiting to Gen L S Baker to which Mr E was *requested to forward with all speed* & telling him that a raid had been made upon the Wilmington R R below Goldsboro. Gen Baker was kind enough to write by the servant who "sped on the fiery cross" that it was a "threatened" raid which he did not beleive the enemy had force to make. There is in the papers a most disgraceful account of an advance of the enemy below Kinston, in which tho they were but 300 strong they defeated the 6th Cavalry, Folks, &, part at least of the 67th infantry, killed several of them & took 60 prisoners, losing themselves "but one man & he drowned by falling into Cobb's mill tail"! Disgraceful truly! The papers call it "botched on our side." They were piloted by a deserter from Nethercutts Bat named Taylor Waters, & to his shame be it said, from Lenoir County.[72]

Have been much interested latterly curing & drying my own tea! Tea from my own plants & very fine indeed it is. Good judges pronounce it an excellent article! My stock of either time or patience does not admit of my rolling it "a la Chinoise," tho I tried it partially. I simply dry the leaves slowly on a chafing dish over the fire taking care to bruise them as they become hot & being careful not to burn or scorch them. I have fifty or more young plants from last year's nuts which in a few years, if they yeild in the ratio that my present number of old plants (eight) have done, will supply me amply—something of an object when tea is, as now, $50 per lb in Petersburg and $25 in Charleston. So much for our late wise Congress tampering with the law of imports. Our present august body is but little better, as it has left the evil unremedied. I have been also busy plaiting straw for Mr E's hat. Wheat straw is softer than Rye, but the blanched part of the rye is so much longer that one is tempted to forego beauty for ease of manufacture. It is pleasant to feel that we have the ability at least to be independant of these vile Yankees, that in spite of their boasted blockade, kept up with such expenditure of both men & money by them, we are not forced to forego our usual comforts or luxuries. The excesses the wretches commit are almost incredible.

JUNE 30, 1864

This state of suspense & entire ignorance of the motions of our army is very wearing & yet such is our confidence in Gen Lee & his veterans that I have known more suffering & anxiety occasioned by a stoppage of the mail when the crisis was not near so alarming or important. No one seems to fear for the

[72]Maj. John H. Nethercutt's Eighth Battalion, North Carolina Partisan Rangers, merged with Maj. Clement G. Wright's Thirteenth Battalion North Carolina Infantry on October 2, 1863, to form the Sixty-sixth North Carolina Regiment. Since "Nethercutt's Battalion" ceased to exist on that date, Mrs. Edmondston's reference to it meant either that the deserter formerly had served in the battalion or that he came from the Sixty-sixth Regiment. In either case, the "Taylor Waters" mentioned was not listed in Moore's *Roster*, nor in Manarin and Jordan's account of the Eighth Battalion, North Carolina Partisan Rangers. Manarin and Jordan, *North Carolina Troops*, II, 382, 584-585; V, 247; Clark, *Histories of the North Carolina Regiments*, III, 689.

final result. A scarcity of supplies is the only dread we entertain from this interruption of the trains. Capt Cooke sent us a dispatch yesterday telling us that the Danville road was torn up for *nearly thirty miles*, that Gen Lee had detached two Brigades after the raiders under Gen Fitz Lee, that he came up with them at Stanton Bridge, defeated & put them to flight, leaving behind them their dead & wounded & many prisoners, that they were reported to have crossed the Weldon & Petersburg R R on the night of the 29th. We have absolutely *no* other news from Va & are as completely in the dark as regards news from Richmond or the Valley as tho an ocean rolled between us. Hunter, Averil, & Crook were at the last accounts flying before Breckenridge by way of Liberty, a 'total change of base' on his part. Then Early's division has marched north, one rumour has it to attack Washington, another is positive that he is at Charlottsville, whilst a third locates him in Lynchburg! The enemy have detached Warren's corps to defend Washington against him. So his secret move has at any rate had one good effect.

In Georgia Gen Johnston keeps Sherman at bay with the most marked ability, with far too small a force to risk a general battle, he yet continues to force Sherman to fight him to such disadvantage that he gains signal successes with but small loss to himself. One such battle, that of the Kenesaw, has just been fought. Johnston['s] loss, such was his admirable disposition, was almost nothing, whilst an army corps of Sherman's was cut to peices. Johnston *says little* but *does* much. Long life to him!

JULY 2, 1864

Still without direct news from Richmond or Petersburg. The severe battle reported to have taken place last Friday a week ago was undecisive, yet we lost, sad to say, 400 prisoners. Gen Fitz Lee has driven Kautz from the Danville road & is said to be in pursuit of him. Hampton has had "adoe,"[73] as the Morte d'Arthur has it, with a party of raiders, whether the same or not we cannot tell at Stoney Crk—& repulsed them. The Scotland Neck Rifles were engaged, lost some, killed, wounded, & captured. Amongst the two last is Dr Hugh Davis,[74] a man whom Mr E liked & trusted & in the last category is the Col of the Regt, Col John Baker,[75] he on whose account Gen French behaved so unhandsomely to Mr E. Ah! Mrs E! I fear me you glorify yourself with the thought that had your husband been there he would not have been captured!

---

[73]"Adoe" is an obsolete variant of "Ado," meaning a stir or flight.

[74]Hugh J. Davis, a private in Co. G, Forty-first North Carolina (Third Cavalry) Regiment, was wounded and taken prisoner near Petersburg on June 21, 1864. He died in a Union hospital on July 7, 1864. Manarin and Jordan, *North Carolina Troops*, II, 230.

[75]Col. John A. Baker, captured near Petersburg on June 21, 1864, was confined in several federal prisons until his release from Fort Pulaski, Georgia, after taking the Oath of Allegiance on March 6, 1865. Manarin and Jordan, *North Carolina Troops*, II, 180.

True Madam, but then he might have been killed! So instead of self-exultation, be thankful that God has spared you the suffering & anxiety now endured by Mrs Baker.

Hunter is retreating as fast as whip & spur can aid him before Early. No time now for foraging & "living off the country." Sauve qui peut & the Devil take the hindmost is the order of the day. He was overhauled near Salem & lost besides killed & wounded 200 prisoners. The road is strewed with his dead horses & cast off equipments—arms, caissons, & even cannon. He finds the road by Liberty "*a hard one to travel.*" "All quiet around Petersburg & plenty of prisoners" is our last account from there, but all our news comes from passengers who walk to Stoney Crk, so that it is both old & uncertain when it reaches us, & news like a egg should be *fresh* to make it valuable. Grant boasted that he would eat his 4th of July dinner in Richmond. God grant he may do so & in "the Hotel de Libby" to boot with attendants a plenty in the shape of Confederate soldiers to see that he wants for nothing of the privileges usually accorded to a prisoner of war! Hunter with usual Yankee barbarity shelled the town of Lexington without notice & on entering sent a squad of men to Ex Gov Letcher's[76] house & summoning Mrs L, gave her ten minutes to remove such things as she wished to preserve from the house & occupied five minutes of the ten telling her what things she was to leave untouched. So that *five minutes* was all three Ladies had to save wardrobe, provisions, & bedding. The savages, they cannot understand & are incapable of being made to appreciate the sublime lesson taught them last summer by Gen Lee in his march through Penn!—a spectacle, however, at which one day the civilized world will stand in amazed admiration, amazed that an army burning under the sense of such wrongs & outrages on their own homes could yet leave unmolested the homes of their enemies when in their power, & *this*, & deeds worse than this, is the return we get for it!

July 5, 1864

Still no mail!—meagre & unsatisfactory dispatches only which serve but to stimulate our interest by hints of great deeds & stirring scenes enacted by our army but of which all details are denied us. Early on Sunday morning came news from Mr Hill that we had captured 2800 of the raiders about Belfield. No confirmation of it was, however, brought by the mail & we lived in hope until today when Gen Holmes (now stationed at Weldon) is reported to have

---

[76]Maj. Gen. David Hunter burned the Virginia Military Institute, the homes of its professors, and the home of former Virginia governor John Letcher on June 12, 1864, in retaliation for the cadets' participation in the war and for "a violent and inflamatory proclamation" he found written by Letcher which allegedly directed the people in the area "to rise and wage guerilla warfare" against Union troops. The order to burn the institute excited considerable comment at the time of the incident and later led to a retribution claim by the institute against the United States government. *Official Records (Army)*, Series I, XXXVII, Part I, 96-97; Jennings C. Wise, *The Military History of the Virginia Military Institute From 1839 to 1865* (Lynchburg, Va.: J. P. Bell Co., Inc., 1915), 362-372.

confirmed it with the additional pleasing intelligence that we had retaken 2000 captured negroes & all their other plunder. Through the Scotland Neck Riflemen we also get the same intelligence, they saying "that it was the last of the Yankee Cavalry" which, however, we know to be a mistake. Charleston is again threatened, but we beleive it only a feint to weaken Lee. The troops in this state have been ordered there & their places here filled by the young reserves—lads between seventeen & eighteen, jocularly known as the "*new Issue*"; but the boys gave so capital an answer to that sarcasm recently that I must record it. A body of them being marched past some veteran soldiers, the cry was playfully raised by the veterans—"Room, room for the new Issue." "Yes, stand back," retorted the boys, "stand back you old fives! Stand back!—there is no discount about us," which effectually turned the laugh on their elders!

Rumours yesterday and today reach us that Grant is abandoning the South Side and re-crossing the James. God grant it be true, but we fear to trust it. "Marse Robert," God bless him, has we hear given orders that the Petersburg and Weldon road be instantly repaired. This seems to verify the good news & it will not be long ere we are blessed with a sight of his official Dispatches, which we can always trust to the letter.

The Yankees with but a handful of men in Wagner & at their "Swamp Angel" (anglice Devil) keep up their barbarous shelling of the City of Charleston in defiance of every rule of civilized warfare & our Government has therefore given them official notice that hereafter their own prisoners shall be confined in barracks in that part of the city most exposed to their fire & that if they hereafter keep up the inhuman practice of shelling a city which they have not strength sufficient to leaguer it will be at the expense of the lives of their own men there confined. So we wait to see what action they will take in these pleasant premises. The Yankee women, who amuse themselves pulling the string that discharges a shell upon the homes of Southern women & children can now intensify the excitement & show their devotion to the "old Flag" by sacrificing their own compatriots, their own husbands, brothers, & sons, it may be, upon the altar of their fanaticism.

Morgan has returned in safety from his expedition into Kentucky after destroying the R R tracks & capturing quantities of provisions on their way, we hope, to Sherman. By the way he (Sherman) was to have dined yesterday (July the 4th) in Atlanta. But Gen Joe Johnston has changed his "table de hote"[77] in the same manner that Lee has disappointed Grant. Gentlemen the Southern Confederacy wishes you both a "good digestion"! Their Generals have, it is true, given you a hard nut to crack but "kernals" are not to be had for big words, so Courage! We get no news from the North, so know not what to make of a telegram which has accidentally reached one of our Southern

---

[77]French, "host's table."

papers to the effect that "Vallandigham has returned to Ohio & that the Chicago Democratic Convention have pledged themselves to protect him." We hope it means a fire in Mr. Lincoln's rear, but as yet we are in the dark.

JULY 11, 1864

On Friday as we were sitting down to dinner came Major Smith, now of the Commissary Depart, formerly our commission merchant in Norfolk. Commission merchant! Ah! what a reminiscence of Peace! of "Bills of Lading," "Accounts of sales," of the *"shipment of goods as per invoice"*—when we had something to sell & were able to spend our income as we listed. Now how changed! His occupation gone, he now caters for the necessaries of life for soldiers instead of supplying civilians with the superfluities. But God's will be done! He brought news of a furious bombardment of Petersburg which will in all probability result in the destruction of the place. Two Iron foundries have been already destroyed & many private dwellings injured. Early's corps occupy Winchester & Harper's Ferry & Lincoln has recalled Burnside to the defence of Washington. Grant has contracted his lines, withdrawn his left further from the Weldon R R, either in consequence of his weakened force or the signal defeat of Kautz & his army of theives. They, I am happy to say, are completely demoralized & dispersed with the loss of 3000 horses captured by us (whilst their march is marked by the carcases of others shot by them to prevent their falling into our hands); a train of Army Wagons laden with plunder, 20 peices of elegant light artillery, amunition, baggage, and small arms too tedious to mention. Our prisoners amount already to more than 2000, whilst squads of them a[re] being daily brought in by our cavalry & the citizens along their route. The excesses committed by them exceeds beleif.

The Examiner, in an article urging our authorities to treat them as felons & proving that they are not entitled to the privileges of prisoners of War, says "For the present we only speak of the comparatively paltry affair of merely stealing or destroying property. But we all know that there is far blacker crime than this calling aloud for vengeance on the miscreants. From many a fair & once peaceful county of our State rises one long wild wail—the shrieks of violated women gone crazy with despair & shame seem to load the air, & to demand of earth & heaven the base blood of their ravishers. Grey haired old men & women driven insane by rage & terror have died with maniac yells or idiot drivellings." The details are horrible—too much so to be even thought on, far less expressed, & yet men captured in the commission of such enormities claim the immunity due to prisoners of war. The paper goes on to say "In short the matter is not capable of argument: marauding or pillage & outrage inflicted on noncombattants is not war & those who practice it cannot be considered prisoners of war, but enemies of the human race to be extirpated without delay."

If we have any delicate squeamishness on this point our enemies have none, as Gen Morgan knows to his cost. When he went raiding last year in Ohio (tho not as they are now doing in Va) they treated him as a horse stealer & penitentiary convict. . . . Morgan's men destroyed only public property & took such horses & forage as were needful to his progress but never insulted women nor pillaged houses of plate & money. Recently in Kentucky Gen Burbridge refused to receive a Flag of Truce from Morgan, seized two officers who bore it, & sent the captured & paroled Yankee Gen Hobson, who accompanied them, back to his command & all because he was not engaged as Burbridge maintained in legitimate warfare! All of the scoundrels, officers & privates, recently captured had stolen silver about them & there were waggon loads of Ladies clothing, elegant chemises, dresses, & female paraphanalia of all kinds. Their wounds were all bandaged with female underclothing torn into strips. A train of carriages a mile long & more the 2000 negroes were also taken. I preserve accounts of their outrages—both in Va and Northern Georgia in my repertory.[78]

The sufferings of our fellow citizens exceed beleif. Maj Smith told us that when recently in Georgia he saw a shed 100 ft long knocked up with rough boards & divided into compartments like oxstalls inhabited by Missippians driven from their homes by Sherman, the infamous. He told me, too, that an old school mate of mine, Mrs Bonsal of Norfolk, had taken refuge near Williamsburg from the severity of Yankee rule in Norfolk, that such was the closeness with which she was watched by the theives intent only on plunder that she was forced to secrete a peice of Bacon & some meal in her bed, cook it by stealth, conceal it about her person, & take her children aside privately and give it to them; otherwise it would be snatched from their hands by these brutes in human shape. One of her children died & with her own hands she made its coffin & buried it. Mr Carter of Shirley was forced to do the same thing a few weeks since when he had the misfortune to loose his wife. He has since been sent off a prisoner to some Northern pest house. The amount of misery endured by private citizens—noncombattants, who in all civilized warfare are exposed only to the unavoidable hardships incident to an upturned and unsettled country, exceeds beleif. The Yankee nation can never wipe out the stigma which this war has left upon them. It is indelible. Chase, their Secretary of State, has resigned. Apparently he has no desire "to be in at the death."

In Northern Georgia Gen Johnston has fallen back from Kenesaw Mt to avoid a flank movement of Sherman's & the enemy have occupied Marietta, which we have evacuated. Our movement was skillfully executed & we lost nothing but the ground. As yet we hope to retain Atlanta, but Gen Johnston is weak. He, however, handles the few men he has with masterly ability, keeps at

---

[78]These accounts were not found in the diary.

bay a largely superior force, & inflicts terrible damage upon Sherman, whilst Forest harrasses his rear, cuts off supplies, & throws trains off the track in a manner which proves him a master of that style of warfare.

JULY 14, 1864

Today came the first mail which we have had from Richmond for three weeks & a day! The mail bag was "a sight for sair 'een" with its late lean sides puffed out with the accumulated issues of three dailies & several weekly newspapers besides letters and pamphlets. The assembled family sat down & such reading, talking, comparing of notes, & "did you see this?" "listen here," "could you beleive it," & "well! we *have* been out of the world, just think of this, & we never to have heard it." Sometime two reading at the same time made a pleasant Bable which will not soon be forgotten. In the midst of it who should come in but Mr Dunlop of Petersburg! & the budget of news brought by him added to the overwhelming accumulations of the past three weeks have well nigh bewildered me.

In the first place Early is in Maryland! He has gained a signal victory at Monocacy Crk, cut the communication between Washington & Baltimore & thrown both cities into a panic. Hagerstown in flames behind him. He has orders to spare *nothing* which can sustain or support our army & it is hoped that permission to *retaliate* some little of the horrors endured by us has been given him. Lincoln clamours for more troops; 100 days men are being rapidly pressed on from New York & New England. Yankee accounts say that Early captured supplies at Martinsburg sufficient for a campaign. Sigel is reported killed, but that is, too, bad news for us. Rather let him live to blunder a little longer. New York is in a ferment—a quarrel between the civil and Military authorities. It seems that the suppression of the Journal of Commerce & the World mentioned sometime ago was by order of Gen Dix, whereupon a civil process was entered upon by the proprietors of the papers & Maj Gen Dix summoned into Court, which summons he refused to obey, alleging his responsibility to a Military court alone, whereon Gov Seymour declared that the supremacy of the Law should & would be asserted & called out 200,000 militia to compel the recreant Gen to admit the jurisdiction of the Civil Arm. There the matter stands.

Vallandigham remains unmolested at Dayton, makes speeches as he lists, & openly defies Mr Lincoln to meddle with him. But the saddest part of the news to us is the treatment our people in Va have met with from the hands of these bands of scoundrels under Sheridan, Kautz, Wilson, & Hunter. Butler sent out a foraging party into the Northern Neck, Negroes under a white officer. Details of the outrage of *twenty five* ladies by that band alone have been filed in Richmond! One was!—but my pen shrinks from the recital. Many are *dead* & some with a far less happy fate live shreiking maniacs or sunk in hopeless misery. Hunter's men were, if any, only a little behind in the commission of such deeds. From the Valley & about Lynchburg the recital of his brutalities would make a fiend blush. The papers are filled with letters from women of refinement & education detailing treatment which they have received themselves & hinting at conduct to others, in their knoledge, too dreadful to be written. Robbery, murder, & plunder is so common that it almost ceases to excite remark. The papers are filled with advertisements of stolen property, negroes, books, silver, & clothing recaptured by Hampton & Fitz Hugh Lee from the infamous wretches. The names & marks on a quantity of silver taken in Wilson's own private ambulance are given, & the owners requested to come forward & claim it, & notices of coupons, certificates of stock, registered Bonds, notes, evidences of indebtednesses, etc., stolen by them are so common that we scarcely notice them. Whilst one reads the catalogue of horrors it seems more like a recital of the conduct of the Sepoys in India than that of a nation nominally at least Christian!

Sad to relate the Alabama, our pride & our hope has been sunk off Cherburgh by the Kearseage, a Yankee sloop of War. The A. was just in from a long cruise, was not in fighting trim, & it seems an excess of gallantry in her to go out & attack her well appointed adversary, but there are intimations that she was only allowed three days provision by the hospitable French & I suppose Semmes knew that a battle was inevitable, so he put on all steam & tho far inferior to the Yankee both in the power of his machinery and the calibre of his guns, entered with spirit into the unequal contest. His men fought until the water ran into the muzzles of their guns! & even after all hope was over refused to allow the Flag to be struck, determining to go down rather than be captured & Capt Semmes was forced to draw his Revolver & insist on his order to lower the flag being obeyed. The gallant Yankee fired five times upon her whilst the White flag was waving at her peak! As she went down her men sprang overboard & were rescued by the boats of the Kerseage & those of an English yatch, the Deer Hound, belonging to Mr John Lancaster who on seeing the Alabama steam out of Port followed her to see the engagement. Semmes was picked up by one of her boats, concealed underneath some sails in the bottom of the boat, & with eleven other officers & some of the men safely landed at Southampton. Not a vestige of the Alabama fell into the hands of the Victors! Everything went down & she has left only her fame behind her. Not a vestige did I say? I mistake. She has left an ugly remembrance in the shape of an unexploded five inch shell which passed through the stern posts of the Kerseage & lies a sleeping Lion amongst her timbers not to be disturbed [illegible] great risk of destroying his bed. So we may yet hear of the revenge of the Alabama. Like Sampson she may yet crush her enemy. Semmes is already taking steps to get a new & better vessel in England & we may soon hear of him as a further scourge to Yankee commerce.

Our prisoners have all been removed from Pt Lookout to Elmira in the State of N Y. Fort Delware, that seat of misery & oppression, is also being rapidly depopulated. Mr Dunlop gave us the Key to this movement in the information that two ships were being fitted out at Wilmington well officered & manned & carry 20,000 stand of arms whose destination was Pt Lookout with the mission to release the prisoners there confined. Unhappily for us, someone betrayed the secret—a traitor—and the Yankee government put an end to the expedition by removing the prize. He tells us that day & night the shelling of Petersburg goes on with, however, comparatively little damage. The inhabitants have almost all left & those that remain are hopeful & cheerful. Mrs D and two of her daughters have returned to the city despite the fury of the fire, & we are in daily expectation of seeing the rest of the children here, having written for them so soon as we heard of their unpleasant situation in Chapel Hill. They will be with us until it is safe to return to their father's roof.

He gave us many interesting incidents of the seige of Petersburg & of the state of unpreparedness in which we were when Butler made his first advance. A Lady living near Bermuda Hundred, having sure information of the approach of the enemy, sent a verbal message (being afraid to trust it to paper) by her confidential servant to the Commandant at Petersburg, telling him that Fort Clifton was menaced & that there were not troops enough there to defend it. This message the boy, recreant to his trust, carried to the Yankees who advanced confident of success thinking to obtain an easy victory; but, thanks to a Kind Providence, in the mean time a detachment of S C troops had arrived and but a short time before Butler's attack manned the works and gave him that terrible repulse which saved both Richmond and Petersburg. Beleiving themselves to have been deceived by the negro, they gave him what he deserved for his treachery to us—viz—a *hanging*.

The poor market men captured by them on their attack on Petersburg itself were asked "what troops were then in the town?" They answered in good faith, "none," & accordingly on came Kautz—was held at bay by the militia men & on their being flanked & forced to retire was, as I related, entering the town when they were met by a shell from Graham's Battery & retired precipitately on sight of Dearing's Cavalry.

One of the market men seeing how matters had turned out said to the other, "Come we had better get out of the way. The soldiers are there—tho we did not know it, & these Yankees will think we deceived them." "No," said the other. "I told the truth & I shall go home—there is nothing to fear," & accordingly did so: but short shrift had he! for a party of the Cavalry followed his little cart & hung him at his own door whilst his more crafty companion made his escape. Had they been as wise as serpents they would have refused to answer the questions & would thus have done their duty to their country & escaped the fury of the irate Yankees.

Grant has detached more than an Army Corps for the defence of Washington, which makes us uneasy on Early's account. Would that he could knock the White House about Mr Lincoln's ears & retreat safely into Va again.

There has been considerable activity before Charleston—a renewal of the shelling & an advance on James Island. Gen Sam Jones, Patrick's old friend is now in command of our forces there. He has repulsed the enemy in several slight skirmishes with heavy loss both in killed & prisoners. A night attack on Fort Johnson was signally driven back by us with the loss of several barges. The shelling of Sumter has been again resumed but without effect. Fighting both on John's & James' Island & from papers captured in one of the engagements we learn that the whole of the available Yankee force on the Atlantic coast is there engaged.

We were terribly startled by a rumour brought by our mail boy from Halifax a few days since to the effect that Gen Bragg with 1500 men had gone South. We feared Charleston was doomed, but as we have not yet heard of a disaster there & there is no intimation of a "falling back." We hope that "Murad the Unlucky" has carried his ill omened visage elsewhere. Mr Davis ought not thus to trifle with even the *prejudices* of a people who have so much at stake & who have reposed such implicit confidence in him, who have done all that lay in their power to strengthen his hands with such self denying alacrity, & who have borne the miseries inflicted on them with the most uncomplaining fortitude.

Mr Dunlop told us that he had been applied to by the Confederate Generals for guides for a night attack which they proposed making on a portion of the enemies lines some distance from Petersburg. The Rev Mr Miller & Dr Osborne came to him & recommended some men for whom they could answer as "*steady, upright, pious,* men, religious and trustworthy." "No! No!" was his answer. "Those are not the sort! your steady, pious, religious men do not go 'possum hunting!' I want some hearty frolicksome fellows who spend half the night in the woods." An odd way of putting it, but there is much practical good sense in it.

Prices are higher than ever in spite of Mr Meminger's sagacious schemes of finance. Vide the list of Government Prices in the Schedule marked D.[79] I last week pd $3 per doz for some as inferior horn buttons as I ever saw. Flour with the new crop coming in sells by retail at our County mills at $150 per lb! Mr E last week paid $50 for a half ream of paper & Tea is 35 per lb in Charleston! Famine prices and in the teeth of New Issues & New Crops! What is to become of us? Sister B & R were charged $25 a peice for a night's lodging in Halifax!

---

[79]Numerous clippings giving prices and commercial reports are on page 1, volume 3, of the diary.

JULY 16, 1864

I do not seem to be idle yet I accomplish very little daily—true I spend several hours at Chess with Father & that breaks my time into fragments, but I must manage better & read more. My employments all hang until I am ashamed of them. Mr E came home from Clarksville the other day & told me that he had discovered why he had never liked [———]. He did "not like Poetry, could not bear it, said he only read Shakspeare, Milton, Byron, & our greatest modern Poets because it was incumbent upon a man of polite education not to be entirely ignorant of them"! As he came home he rode with our neighbor Mr J H Davis, a man of no cultivation & but little education, who had been present at the conversation & commenting on it he expressed his surprise that a man such as [———] should entertain such a sentiment, when Mr D said suddenly "not like Poetry, sir! not like Poetry! why Poetry is the Voice of Nature!" Now that was an original idea with the man who expressed it. It is by no means likely that he ever heard it & had he tried for years he could have said nothing better. It far surpasses Leigh Hunt, Burke, Robertson, or any of the great minds of the cultivated of this Earth who have endeavoured to define it. In terseness, comprehensiveness, & truth, it stands alone. Mr Davis has more in him than I ever suspected, tho "the spoils of Time"[80] have never been unfolded to him.

JULY 18, 1864

Such good news from Early yesterday that we fear to trust it. I scarcely know where to begin. In the first place the victory over Gen Lew Wallace at Monocacy is confirmed, together with the capture of immense stores at Martinsburg, amongst other thing 100,000 bu of shelled Oats! Gunpowder Bridge is destroyed & the communication thus cut between Phila & Baltimore. We hold Anapolis Junction & the Relay House & are within six miles of Baltimore. Gov Bradford's magnificent mansion on the [———] road 7 miles from Baltimore has been *burned in retaliation* for the burning of Gov Letcher's residence in Lexington by Hunter's theives. A righteous retribution! Best of all "the Rebels are reported in force on Frank Blair's Silver Spring farm seven miles from Washington and are actually shelling the city itself, having possession of some heights which command the Yankee Capital! Shells are flying in *Washington City*!" Think how the tables are turned. Lincoln is in a ferment of fright. Shouts "Free men to the Rescue!," which cry is taken up by Gov's Bradford & Curtin[81] who beg that the people "will come at once. What ever

---

[80]Thomas Gray, "Elegy Written in a Country Churchyard," stanza 13. Stevenson, *Home Book of Verse*, 3533.

[81]Augustus W. Bradford (1806-1881), a prominent Baltimore lawyer, served as the wartime governor of Maryland. His house was burned in 1864 by Confederate raiders in retaliation for the destruction of John Letcher's home. Andrew Gregg Curtin (ca. 1815-1894), a lawyer and state politician, was governor of

you do come quickly!" but the Freemen are tired of rallying to the cry of "the Capitol in danger" & come very slowly & with manifest reluctance. They are tired of taking "Blue Pills" from the hand of the Rebels, think they have paid enough, & sent men enough for the defence of the National Capitol, & prefer resting at home. The Yankee papers are eloquent in their appeals, hold up the example of Petersburg, conjure their readers to emulate the conduct of that handful of Rebel militia who kept the picked troops of the army of the Potomac at bay for hours & prevented the occupation of the city, but so far the dear people refuse to listen to the voice of the charmer, charm he never so wisely. Fifteen thousand Marylanders are reported to have joined us, but that we cannot beleive. The "despot's heel" has crushed "Maryland! my Maryland" too thoroughly for that evidence of spirit.

July 21, 1864

The anniversary of the battle of Manassas. In what mercy is the gift of fore knoledge denied us. What a check would have been put upon our joy on that occasion could we have foreseen that three years hence we should still be engaged in the same bitter life & death struggle! The attack on Charleston is over. The enemy have been repulsed at all points, driven to their original lines, & now content themselves with their usual shelling of Fort Sumter & the city. One year has now elapsed since the city was first beseiged, during which time the "Swamp Angel" has thrown seven thousand nine hundred shells into a place occupied only by women & children. Amo writes his Uncle that in the night attack on Fort Johnston there were but *fourteen* men on duty in the fort. They held [———] hundred at bay & on being hastily reinforced by [———] that handful repulsed [———] Yankees and took [———] prisoners. It seems almost incredible that the Key to the City of Charleston, to retain which blood has been poured out like water, should have been left thus weakly defended. Had Fort Johnson fallen, Sumter, Moultrie, & the city itself must have followed. Think of the fate of Charleston resting on fourteen men only! Criminal carelessness somewhere!

We were electrified yesterday by the announcement that Gen Joe Johnson had been releived of the command of the Army in Northern Geo & that Gen Hood had been assigned to duty there. We cannot understand it. To us who are not born Brigadiers Gen it has appeared that Johnston with comparatively but a handful of men has been keeping a host at bay, retiring so slowly as to exhaust and weary Sherman out, & we confidently expect that he will wait combinations in Sherman's rear, combinations which we do not understand but in which Kirby Smith plays a distinguished part, & then turn like a Lion

Pennsylvania from 1861 through 1867. After the war he served as minister to Russia under Grant but switched to the Democratic party in 1873 and served as the Democratic congressman from Pennsylvania from 1881 until 1887. *Dictionary of American Biography*, II, 553-555; IV, 606-608.

at bay, deliver battle in front of Atlanta, & rescue the prize from the very grasp of his antagonist. But we must be in the dark as to something in his plans or conduct, for Mr Davis would not be guilty of the injustice of thus snatching his Laurel's from him at the moment of Victory unless something serious had occurred! A wild rumour runs through the country that he is insane, but we cannot credit it. There has been too much method in his madness. We must wait 'ere we decide for further developments & have no right even to form an opinion. Despite partizan newspapers & their wholesale & rash denunciation, the whole country *knows* that Mr Davis has the welfare & honour of the country as much at heart as any one in it & the assertion that he would do aught to embarras & perplex one of his generals is so monstrous as to be unworthy of the slightest credence. He has his faults but, God knows, a want of patriotism is not amongst them, & tho he makes mistakes, they are honest ones. Joe Johnston has possessed our confidence, a confidence that will not lightly be withdrawn, but when two such men as Mr Davis & himself are at issue, for the sake of Justice and sweet Truth let us withhold our condemnation of either party until the facts are known.

Preparations for the abandonment of Atlanta are already made, stores, pontoon bridges, etc., all removed. Should such a step be taken it would indeed be a heavy blow to us, as four R R centre there & we have immense work shops & foundries, the loss of which we cannot supply.

Our Army is retreating from Maryland, bringing off with them vast quantities of provisions & forage. Washington has been so heavily reinforced that we could not hope to effect anything there. The 'morale' of throwing shells into the city is all we have reaped. Canby's corps which left New Orleans to reinforce Grant arrived at Fortress Monroe just in time to respond to Mr Lincoln's frantic appeals for help & without disembarking steamed up the Potomac & saved Washington. Two other Army Corps have followed, so Gen's Early & Breckenridge "return over the border." Gen B exhibited his fine feelings at national expence by sparing Mr Frank Blair's[82] house & effects. He had no right to do so. He was sent to *retaliate* for the outrages committed in Va & to those unfortunate people who may hereafter be exposed to Yankee barbarity, barbarity from which a different line of conduct on the part of our troops may protect them. It matters little that "Gen Breckenridge was once hospitaly entertained for some days at Silver Spring" & therefore spared the mansion of his entertainer. Justice before generosity!

---

[82]Francis Preston Blair (1821-1875), a staunch abolitionist and influential politician from Missouri, served as a major general in the Union army until 1864, when he was elected to the United States Congress. He agreed with Lincoln's views on Reconstruction and opposed Radical Republicanism after the war. This clash with the Republican party led Blair back to the Democratic party in the late 1860s, and from 1871 until 1873 Blair served as a Missouri Democratic senator in Washington. *Concise Dictionary of American Biography*, 80.

July 24, 1864

Sunday—Today came most unexpectedly brother in good health & spirits. His little boy John is out of danger. We have had fine rains & the prospect for a crop is good & to crown all his happiness he brought news of a victory of Hood over Sherman in front of Atlanta! We had taken 2000 prisoners, 28 peices of cannon, 4 stand of colour, whilst the dispatch went on to say that Hardee was in their rear & fighting still going on. A telegram only gives us the news, but still it is official & signed by Gen Hood. Bragg has made his appearance out there which, I fear, bodes us no good, but we must hope for the best.

Brother gave us a most interesting account given him by an eye witness of an interview between Edward Stanley & an old negro of his fathers when he came to N C as her Military Governor. The negro it seems was sick & in consequence Mr Stanley went to see him. Abram, for such was his name, turned his face to the wall as his young master entered the cabin. When Stanley holding out his hand addressed him thus, "Well Uncle Abram I am sorry to see you laid up thus. I know you must have been sick or you would have been to see me." To which the negro replied, "God knows Marse Ned that I never thought to live to see the day when I should have to say I was sorry to see you. But what are you doing here? Go! over Marse Ned, go over and stand along side of your own folks. Take a glass of water & a crust of bread with them, but stand by them, & if you wont do that go back, Marse Ned, where you come from! go back! & never let it be said that your father's son turned against his own folks."

Time fails me to tell how his brother Alfred,[83] then a prisoner on parole, met him & what he said to him of the desecration of the grave yard & the oppression of the people. He gave Burnside a parole for a year & on the expiration of it, he, tho an old man between sixty and seventy, has often been known to leave home on foot at night, walk through the swamps & woods for miles to the nearest Picket station, & give information to them when any movement was projected by the enemy. He has, & it is on record, brought into our pickets between thirty & forty Yankee horses & equipment, the riders of which, to use a slang phrase, he had lost in the woods. He has now a post under the Confederate Gov, within our lines, or it would not do even to tell such a fact, but as I record the infamy of one brother, justice demands that the patriotism of the other should not be passed over. All honour to Alfred Stanly!

July 27, 1864

Our retiring troops have had an engagement with a body of Yankees sent after them at Snicker's Gap in which the pursuers were repulsed with heavy

---

[83]Alfred Stanly, Edward Stanly's brother, was arrested by Gen. John G. Foster because of his secessionist sympathies. *Sentinel*, September 22, 1863.

slaughter & 300 men captured. The Yankee papers claim to have recaptured many of our waggons containing our Maryland spoils, but our people deny it.

Sue said today at breakfast that "old Lincoln had demoralized her sense of numbers; that he had so often called for 500,000 men that she had got to view it as a small affair, a mere drop in the bucket." Just now he is clamouring for that number & likewise proclaiming a fast & threatening a draught in fifty days if the quota be not filled up by volunteering within that time. Posts have been opened in all of the Southern States in Yankee power for the recruiting of negroes in order to fill up the quota of the different northern States. State agents are sent out & the stolen negroes accredited to the state who steals them, by authority of the Yankee Sec of War. This is raising an army with a vengeance—poor Cuffee!

July 30, 1864

On the 27th came Mr Dunlop of Petersburg bringing his daughter Mattie to remain with us whilst the city is undergoing so furious a bombardment. Poor man, he has cause for deep anxiety, his own home beleaguered & liable at any moment to be blown up, his wife and two daughters persisting in remaining there—rather than endure the miseries of refuge-ism, the rest of his family scattered, one son severely wounded, others in the army, whilst his eldest daughter, a married woman, lives in Atlanta & is exposed to all the horrors of a city in a state of seige, shells flying about her hourly. His cup seems full without the addition of the immense cost of the merest necessaries of life. The expense to which he is now put merely to *live* would, if long continued, seriously embarras a princely fortune. What blessings we enjoy! Grant O heavenly Father that they fall not on unthankful hearts! May our lives be a hymn of Praise to Thee for Thy goodness to us!

All as usual before Petersburg. Grant is not dead as reported by deserters but still lives to burrow under our earth works & shell a city occupied only by women & children & filled with Hospitals! In the valley Gen Ramseur has met with a reverse which has nipped his growing promotion in the bud. It is a muddled affair, but it seems he led a division sent out to reconnoitre, threw out neither scouts or skirmishers, & walked open eyed into an ambuscade in which he lost heavily both in guns & prisoners. He is much blamed, but where is an unfortunate general who is not? Next day, however, Early repaired his mishap. On the now classic ground of Kernstown he fell upon Hunter & put him to the most ignominious rout. The panic equaled that of the first Manassas. We recaptured guns & prisoners, taking scores of Yankees by way of reprisal, drove him pell mell into & out of Martinsburg which we reoccupy, and our army now stands at Harper's Ferry in attitude of advance, but whether again on Washington or into Penn we outsiders cannot tell, but advance it will.

Grant has recalled the troops he detached to defend Washington, needing more than he can get, & under Hunter has collected all the available force left in Maryland. These are now but a routed & disorganized & disjointed mass, so Early & Breckenridge can repair the blunders made in their late attack & let us reap more substantial fruits of victory than forage & horses. Peace seems to be sending its shadow ahead, as recently two southern Gentlemen & that political adventurer Geo N Saunders associated themselves together & addressed a letter to Greely demanding a safe conduct to Washington to discuss the preliminaries of Peace. It is needless for me to enter into all the detail of their correspondance. Suffice it that Messrs Clay of Ala, Holcombe of Va, & Saunders of Dixie met with a most decided rebuff at the hands of Mr Lincoln, he telling them in a paper addressed with Machievelli-like craft "To all whom it may concern," that the safe conduct should be granted if the Confederate States were willing to renounce slavery, return to the allegiance of the U S, lay down arms, in short give up all we are fighting for & submit ourselves to his royal clemency.[84] Balderdash!

Simultaneously with the debut of these self constituted Commissioners, two Yankees, one a Rev Col, the other an Abolition penny-a-liner, make their appearance in Richmond, are entertained at the Spotswood House, have two interviews with Pres Davis, and leave as they entered.[85] To whom they were accredited does not appear, but certainly to some one less impersonal than "To All whom it may concern," or they would never have seen Mr Davis. We get only Northern accounts of their interview and as I do not beleive what the Yankees say I will not record them. I cannot avoid saying, however, that I think the self styled "Southern commissioners" might have found a more worthy channel through which to attempt to open negotiations than that wretch Greely! "Can a man touch pitch and not be defiled?" Peace itself would be sullied in passing through his hands.

---

[84] A group of Confederate sympathizers, Clement C. Clay, Jacob Thompson, James P. Holcombe, and George N. Sanders, gathered in Canada in 1864 to agitate for the end of the war on southern terms and to harass the Lincoln government during the election year. Greeley learned of the commissioners' presence in Canada through an intermediary but was wrongly informed that they were authorized by the Confederate government to negotiate for peace. Greeley contacted Lincoln who agreed to meet with the men if they were official representatives of the Confederacy. Greeley met with the men at Niagara in July and learned they held no official standing and that their interest in peace was dubious. Lincoln, informed of their real purpose in Canada, then issued a proclamation stating his terms for a peace settlement: restoration of the Union and the abolition of slavery. These terms were completely unacceptable to the South. Harlan Hoyt Horner, *Lincoln and Greeley* (Urbana, Ill.: University of Illinois Press, 1953), 301-317; Randall and Donald, *Civil War and Reconstruction,* 470-472.

[85] James F. Jaquess, a preacher, Methodist college president, and colonel of a Union volunteer regiment during the war, together with James R. Gilmore, a writer and friend of Greeley who used the pseudonym Edmund Kirke, met with Davis in Richmond on July 17, 1864, as the unofficial representatives of the Lincoln administration. They expressed the North's interest in peace, but negotiations broke down because of Confederate insistence on complete political separation from the Union. Randall and Donald, *Civil War and Reconstruction,* 472; *Concise Dictionary of American Biography,* 490, 344.

Matters before Atlanta cause us grave anxiety. Sherman is shelling the place. Hood has again repulsed him & Forrest has broken up his communications, but he seems not to flag in consequence. McPherson, said to be the ablest man in the Yankee service, was killed in the recent battle, which seems now to have been more bloody than we had thought. The Yankees admit a loss of 15,000 & say we lost 7000. I know not how it is. McPherson's Laurels, it is said, are worn by Maj Gen Grant. To him is due all the credit of the advance & attack on Vicksburg. If so I hope Sherman will feel his loss.

July 31, 1864

Sunday—At Church & intensely hot! God pity our soldiers in the trenches! Rumours of great doings at Petersburg. Grant has burrowed to some purpose underneath our lines. He has sprung a mine which has blown up 150 yds of our entrenchments & sad to relate two Companies of S C troops. This brought on an engagement in which we defeated him signally with immense slaughter, killing a vast number of negroes. This by train. We must wait some days for the mail, & I will not record all the sensation rumours I hear. I have said but little of the State Elections now in immediate prospect, because I have felt but little anxiety as to their result & I verily beleive most of the agitation we see in the papers is caused by the laziness of the Editors. Not content with the war, they must have their little petty party politics to squabble over & so fill their papers with little trouble to themselves. They have made a Collossus of Holden, & the storm that has been raging in their teapot over him is terrific. The event goes far to justify my opinion, for in the election which has taken place in the army he has been beaten so far by Vance that his votes are not even counted. Vance now has 17,000 majority. I could never beleive that North Carolina was in any danger of electing a man like him for its head—the illegitimate son of a wicked woman, devoid alike of the instincts & breeding of a gentleman, a mere agitator for his own selfish ends. Never was more noise made over a more contemptible individual. I hope never to hear of him again!

August 1, 1864

Today Mr Dunlop left for his home leaving little Mattie with us. Poor homesick little child, from my heart I am sorry for you! He sends us another batch of rumours from the R R modifying & correcting those of yesterday, but I will wait for Marse Robert's official dispatch ere I record the results. Grant is throwing troops to the North bank of the James & Gen S D Lee has joined Hood with 10,000 reinforcements, so Atlanta may yet be saved. No news, and it is too hot to do anything but keep cool.

August 3, 1864

No mail today which creates a vague uneasiness. Visions of Raiders, burnt bridges, & torn up tracks fill our minds. We learn officially from Petersburg

that at 5 A M on Sat. the enemy sprung a mine under one of our salients &
immediately opened his batteries upon one whole line & on the city. In the
confusion he obtained possession of the salient but in half an hour was driven
out with immense slaughter, we capturing 12 stand of Colours, 74 officers, including Brig Gen Bartlett, & 855 men. It is supposed that 118 of our men were
in the salient at the time it was blown up. The negro troops immediately after
the explosion rushed into our lines shouting out "No Quarter! Remember
Fort Pillow," where they were met with such determination by their old
masters & granted to the full what they so earnestly clamoured for that in
spite of the Yankee bayonetts behind them they turned & ran incontinently.
One of them recognizing in a Mississippi Co his young master, rushed up to
him in the thickest of the fight & throwing his arm around him cried out,
"You shall not hurt my young Master," when a ball struck & wounded them
both, happily not mortally! His return to his allegiance probably saved his
life, for but few of his companions were left to tell the tale of their encounter.

The scene in the pit made by the explosion after the battle was over & our
line re-established, it is said, beggars description. It was ghastly! On our side,
sad to say, we lost Gen Elliot of S C mortally wounded. We fear it is Gen
Stephen E the gallant defender of Ft Sumter, a man whom we can ill spare.

Grant had thrown heavy bodies of his troops over to the north bank of the
James. The night of the explosion he recrossed them with great rapidity. It
now appears that he intended the movement as a blind to mislead Gen Lee,
hoping that he would so weaken himself before Petersburg so that when he
sprung his grand mine the city would be at his mercy, but Gen Lee is to old a
bird to be caught with chaff. He threw men enough over the river to confront
Grant at Deep Bottom & give him the repulse I mentioned on Monday & yet
maintained himself intact in his trenches. The labour Grant has been at is
enormous. The explosion has revealed his burrows. I do not trust the
newspaper dimensions of the excavation, so refrain giving them, but it must
without exaggeration have been a stupendous work. Most of it was, we learn,
performed by negroes, our own stolen negroes working at the point of the
bayonette against us. Poor deluded oppressed people!

The U S have distinguished themselves by a solemn act of banishment of
two British subjects, Mr & Mrs Christie, sometime resident in a boarding
house in Baltimore, for the heinous crime of throwing away a small U S flag.
On 4th of July last Mrs C took from the window of a room occupied by an U S
officer a small U S flag & threw it away. Her husband is charged with being
an accessory to the action of his wife upon which a tempest arises in the U S
teapot & they are banished! Where! O where has liberty fled?

Early is, it is beleived, over the border again. At any rate Lincoln thinks so,
as he clamours for loyal citizens to rush to the defence of the Capitol. This
time we think his destination is Penn, and we hope 'ere his return that he will

set the Coal mines on fire & let those Dutch Yankees understand feelingly what *Retaliation* means.

AUGUST 5, 1864

Good news from Georgia! Stoneman the Raider, who has written his name in blood & tears upon the hearts of the women & children in Virginia, has with five hundred of his fellow theives been forced to surrender to Gen Iverson after having had his command cut to peices & dispersed by the Geo militia & Reserves in front of Macon. His rout is entire & for the present the Geo R R is safe from Sherman's nefarious designs. Fighting at Atlanta where, however, Hood still holds his own & occasionally inflicts heavy loss on his opponent. We tremble when we think of Atlanta. The loss of Vicksburg rises as a sad memory forbidding us to trust too much in the safety of any place beleaguered as it is, whilst the thought of Richmond & how long & gallantly it has been defended bids hope rise in our bosoms.

West of the Mississippi we are everywhere triumphant. Not a Yankee raises his head in Texas, Louisiana, or Arkansas, whilst Missouri swarms with Guerrillas. Two Regts sent out against them by Gen [———] instead of opposing joined them & bid defiance to the authority of the U S. Kentucky is under strict martial law, Habeas Corpus suspended, & her citizens exposed defenceless to the tyranny and insults of U S soldiers. So much for their attempted *neutrality*, the neutrality of the dollar! The loss on both sides before Petersburg in the affair inaugurated by the springing of the mine in Mahone's front much heavier than at first supposed. Yankee prisoners say theirs mount up to 5000 killed & wounded. We lost 200 by the mine alone. Amongst the Yankee dead within our lines was found the renegade & traitor Gen Thomas, a base son of Va. Meet was it that her soil should drink his blood when he turned against her & led to the conquest of his native land a band of negro assassins which he had organized! He it was who has been most strenuous for the employment of negro troops, making himself their Champion & exponent. The mill of the gods grind slowly, it is true, but none the less surely for its delay. Rumours reach us that we also are mining & that Beauregard will ere long teach Grant that that is a game at which two can play!

Sister Betsy & Rachel left us this morning. I am sorry for it, for I shall miss R greatly; she is a most unselfish, self denying, & excellent young woman, & I have a strong affection & great respect & esteem for her.

AUGUST 6, 1864

From Northern accounts we learn that Early has thrown a body of men over the Potomac, who advanced rapidly across the State of Maryland into Penn, appeared suddenly before Chambersburg, & demanded $500,000, threatening if their demand was refused to burn the town instantly. During the conference, however, on the subject the town was fired in several places &

reduced almost to ashes, the rebels retiring no one knows where, but Averill the ubiquotous followed, "whipped them handsomly," when they retreated across the Potomac. Nothing from Early himself, so we take the liberty of doubting all the latter part of the Yankee news. Their own newspapers cannot heartily condemn the act, say that it was in retaliation for outrages committed by their army at the South & clamour loudly that the war be henceforth conducted on the principles of enlightened Christianity & civilization. They say that a large body of the Northern people condemned the barbarity of burning Alexandria, La, Washington, N C, Bluffton S C, & many other places, but the act having been *committed at such a distance* from them *they did not feel the enormity of it—as they now do—when brought to their own doors.* What unblushing impudence! I am glad that Mr Davis has at last brought these followers of the Golden Rule to a realing sense of its importance.

AUGUST 16, 1864

Ten hot days since I last wrote in my Journal, during which I have been quite unwell—and sick servants & much company. Grant & Staff were reported at Harpers Ferry by the Northern papers, when instantly the rumour ran like wild fire that Lee had followed & confronted him with his whole army in the Valley, leaving Beauregard to defend Petersburg against the remains of Grants beaten force. A few days, however, showed the falsity of the Madam Rumour's assertions, for Lee is at Deep Bottom & an engagement eminent between Grant & himself, the Yankee hero having returned to as rapidly as he left his dispirited army. Beauregard's mine has been exploded & effected all it aimed at—a counter mine to a new Yankee work which it effectually nipped in the bud.

I omitted to mention that a few days after the burning of Gov Bradford's house in return for the distruction of Gov Letcher's, Hunter issued a "Retaliatory Order" & sent out a squad of men to burn the residences of Gen Hunter (said to be his relative) and Hon Mr Boteler.[86] This they executed with the usual Yankee barbarity, when Early ordered McCausland & Bradley Johnson to show them what a losing game we could make them have of it by burning Chambersburg. This we are assured is the true history of the burning of that dutch Yankee place. Not to be outdone in ferocity, Butler sends a fleet of gunboats up the Rappahanock with orders to burn the residence of Mrs Seddon, the widoed sister-in-law of our Sec of War & to inform her that he did it because Early had burn Hon Montgomery Blair's[87]

---

[86]The homes of Alexander Hunter, a state senator, Col. Edmund Lee, and Alexander R. Boteler, a former member of the Confederate Congress and a colonel in the Confederate army, were burned to the ground near Shepherdstown, West Virginia, by Federal troops in July, 1864. Freeman, *Lee's Lieutenants*, I, 128, 413; III, 571.

[87]Montgomery Blair (1813-1883), the brother of Francis P. Blair, Jr., was a prominent lawyer and judge who served as postmaster general under Lincoln. A moderate, he was forced out of office by Radical

country house near Washington. Mrs Seddon & her children were turned out of house & home at a few minutes notice & left destitute. Her husband died before the War. She suffers for being the Widow of the brother of our Sec!

We have had a great disaster before Mobile. Farragut steamed past Fort Morgan with a fleet of [———] Gunboats mounting more than 200 guns & has almost annihilated our little squadron lying in the Bay! Worse than all, the best Ram we own, the Tennessee, Admiral Buchanan's flag ship, fell into their hands after a desperate engagement.[88] Admiral B lost a leg & with his crew are prisoners. I do not mention the other boats by name but the Morgan only escaped. Next day Fort Gaines, altho victualed and armed for a six month seige unexpectedly surrendered—to the astonishment of every one. General Page, the superior in command, went over at night to see how things were progressing when he found Johnson the commander of the post on board the Yankee fleet arranging terms of capitulation. He left preemtory orders that he *should not* surrender, superceeding him from command at the same time, & returned to his own post. In the morning the Yankee flag was seen waving from the Ramparts. This is all we know & I refrain from all comments until we hear more. It seems incredible!

No news from Early. Yankee accounts of a Victory over McCausland & Johnson. We hope it was by men in buckram. Peace rumours are rife & intimations that the North West is going to divide the U S anew by seceeding & making terms with us to secure to them the navigation of the Miss, but little do we heed them. Peace must be carved out by the points of our swords!— naught else do we trust in. The barbarities of the Yankees & especially Hunter's late conduct have embittered the war to that degree that Peace seems scarcely possible; I preserve particulars, marked [———]. The future of the Yankee nation one could say with Horace, "Posterity thinned by their father's crimes/Shall read with greif the story of their times!"[89] for they are surely laying up a heritage of shame for their descendants.

AUGUST 20, 1864

Since we can no longer get news we resort to old Blackwood's for our light Literature & find them most entertaining & instructive. Mr E read me a few days since from one of Aug 1849 a no of "Christopher under Canvass" (Prof

---

Republicans in 1864 and eventually joined the Democratic party. *Concise Dictionary of American Biography*, 80-81.

[88]Adm. Franklin Buchanan, commanding the ram C.S.S. *Tennessee* and the Confederate fleet in Mobile Bay, was defeated by Rear Adm. David Glasgow Farragut's fleet on August 5, 1864. Comdr. James D. Johnston assumed command of the *Tennessee* after Buchanan was badly injured in the battle. See Johnston's account of this episode in Johnson and Buel, *Battles and Leaders*, IV, 401-406; *Civil War Naval Chronology*, IV, 95-97; VI, 312.

[89]Horace, *Odes*, book 1, ode 2, lines 21-22.

Wilson),[90] & I was greatly struck by a sentiment which seems applicable to our Northern neighbours. "Good manners give a vital efficacy to good Laws. These few words comprise the needful constituents of national happiness & prosperity. . . . *Good laws without good manners are empty breath.*" They have proved the truth of it! Good Laws they had & an abundance of them, but they lacked the essential *good manners.* Good manners would have kept them from intermedling with their neighbour's concerns, would have frowned down John Brown Raids, & have silenced the teachings of all laws *"higher"* than that of good breeding & of the Golden Rule. Want of manners it is which has broken up the Government & deluged the country with a sea of blood. Want of manners on the part of our Northern brethren has carried mourning into thousands of Southern homes & threatens in their own country to break up the foundations of their society & to bring ruin upon their national prosperity. Want of manners, want of nice observance of the point of honour, without which neither nations or individuals can long flourish, has brought all these evils upon them. I am wearied with war & bloodshed, with accounts of skirmishes & advances, or retrograde movements & barren victories which seem to have no end. Lee advances to meet Grant, who has thrown a strong force over the James. They skirmish, we repulse, when presto, they make demonstrations on the Southside with the like result. Change the name of the places & generals & the same accounts might stand for the movements of Hood & Sherman before Atlanta. I am worn out with them & deeply indeed do I feel for our soldiers whose lives are thus passed "in idleness or peril." God grant them stout hearts & willing minds & grant O grant us Peace!

The enemy have been looking for a scapegoat on whose head to lay the failure of their memorable "fiasco" of the 30th of July & the lot seems to have fallen on the Christian Burnside, who has been relieved from the command of the Army Corps & ordered to report at Washington. He bore the brunt of his failure before Fredericksburg with such distinguished meekness & so humbly risked the rod with which Mr Stanton chastised him that he has doubtless been selected as the victim to sacrifice to Lieut Gen Grant's popularity on account of his *Christian virtues!* Ah *pluck!* How it does dignify a man! What a respect it excites even in a vanquished enemy! Who wants a "sucking dove" for an opponent? Yet I am sorry for the fall of Burnside's meek bald head. We shall miss his blunders. Meade as a man, a general, & gentleman has commanded more respect from us than any general the Yankee nation has yet put forth. Grant is a mere butcher. Take away his brute force, his numerical

---

[90]John Wilson (1785-1854), Scottish essayist, professor of moral philosophy at the University of Edinburgh, and novelist, was one of the principal contributors to *Blackwood's Magazine,* in which he used the pseudonym Christopher North. *Dictionary of National Biography,* LXII, 107-111; Benét, *Reader's Encyclopedia,* 1216. The article mentioned was one of the chapters of *Die Borealis; or Christopher under Canvas,* which appeared first in *Blackwood's Magazine,* June-September, 1849, and April-May, 1850.

superiority, & he is nothing. As for Hunter & Butler, they are as weak as they are cruel & *that speaks volumes*. I will not sully my page with a mention of them!

No news from Mobile, save that the loss of Forts Powel and Gaines does not imply a surrender of the town. Gen Maury now Lieut Gen claims that he will make it a second Charleston. God grant it. Peace meetings at the North & popular offers of reconstruction, but it falls on deaf ears. They say a financial crisis is upon them, but little do we heed them. A new Confederate Steamer, the "Tallahassee," commanded by John Taylor Wood a nephew by marriage of our President has suddenly made its appearance in Northern Waters. She swept into New York harbour & bearding the lion in his den captured several vessels & Pilot boats inside of Sandy Hook. New York is in a blaze allegorically. Would it were so literally.

Had company to dinner on Wednesday, Mr & Mrs Ed Hill and their guest Miss Berkely Botts of Va (neice of John Minor B[91] the infamous), Dr & Mrs Wood, & Mrs Whitaker. I do not think we see Company enough. I get out of the way of entertaining them & I fear I was unable to make my guests forget the heat as I would have liked to have done. When *we have Peace* I will do better.

AUGUST 22, 1864

No mail since the 18th & yesterday came tidings of the cause of the failure which has perplexed us not a little. The enemy have again cut the Petersburg & Weldon R R at Reams' Station 9 miles from Petersburg. Rumours of a similar disaster to both the Southside & the Danville Road, but we know not how to credit them. God knows how this state of uncertainty & ignorance distresses us! The cutting of the R R is always a preliminary to an advance on Grant's part. He has been unusually active crossing & recrossing the James as a feint to throw dust into Gen Lee's eyes, so as to conceal the point of his real attack, & like the cuttle fish muddy the water so as to make good his escape; so the next news (when we get it) will be stirring.

I have fallen into sad idle ways this summer, & in order to correct them take a hint from the Spectator & faithfully record the doings of one day and see how little—how absolutely little, do I effect. The first thing on leaving my chamber on Sat morning was the usual family prayers. Then seizing a stocking I darned a few runs whilst Mr E read the regular no of the Spectator with which we occupy ourselves whilst breakfast is brought in. Breakfast. Peeled a muskmelon & prepared it for pickling, dawdled about, put up a few seeds, & read a sermon on the death of Moses to Patty. Went to the Storeroom with Dolly & ordered dinner & had 2 barrels of flour packed. Darned a little more

---

[91]John Minor Botts (1802-1869), a former Virginia legislator, United States congressman, and a staunch Whig, remained a Unionist after the war began and was imprisoned by Confederate authorities in 1862. He was later released but was restricted in his travels. After the war he adopted a radical view and lost the support of the conservative Virginia Unionists. *Concise Dictionary of American Biography*, 92.

on Mr E's stockings. At ½ past 9 father called me to chess—played until 12. Got the Luncheon & cut some water melons for the girls. As it was overcast & pleasant went into the garden, gathered the Musk melons, walked around the Flower Garden, peeped at my grapes, wound up my stroll at the "soltaire" where I had directed Fanny to bring my tea. Read the lessons for the day & did some other little devotional reading. Drank my tea, wrote my Journal, went to the house, arranged the fruit for Dessert, dressed for dinner, dined, talked to Mr E whilst he smoked his cigarrito, chatted with Patty, took up the interminable stocking, darned a little, when father proposed chess. Played for an hour & a half at least, seized the stocking again, put it down to commence Mattie's straw Hat for her & to teach her how to sew the straw, & as a shower prevented my usual afternoon walk, at the stocking again until near dark. Arranged the waiters for tea with the girls assistance, lit the candles, & superintended the tea table. Ordered breakfast, finished the inevitable pr of socks, darned two pr for myself, went to my room & closed the day with a warm bath & the evening lessons.

Now what a little did I accomplish. True I had more of the servants work to superintend & execute myself on account of its being the midsummer Holidays & I had allowed Betsy & Fanny to go to the dinner at the Plantation & Madame Vinyard's Confinement threw the stocking darning on me, but what did I that would entitle me to the sensation that "something accomplished—something done had earned a night's repose"? I must do better for the future.

Vinyard made her appearance in the house today, her child Frances being four weeks old on Sat, so that my labours as a stocking darner are happily at an end. Will I substitute anything as useful in its place? One thing I must arm myself with—a double stock of patience, for Vinyard always a trial will be a double one after her months idleness.

The mail has just come in with details of the engagement of Tuesday at Deep Bottom. At one time the enemy had possession of a mile of our entrenchments, Grant having encassed 40,000 men on one point, but by slowly retreating & keeping a bold front we prevented their further advance until, reinforcements coming up, we drove them from our lines in confusion & with great slaughter. Sad to say we lost Maj Gen Girardy & Brig Gen Chambliss killed, which was not I fear compensated by the loss of their dancing Master Gen Ferero, who cut his last caper at Deep Bottom. Ferero's death was a gain to them & a corresponding loss to us. Girardy & Chambliss were fine young officers & both leave wives & families of small children to mourn for them.

I referred above to the "Soltaire." I have never described it. We have had a small house in the garden known to the rest of the world as a tool or root House privately fitted up, as a with drawing room. A couch, two chairs, a table for writing, an ink stand, a portfolio, a vase of flowers, a shelf, a few books, & *a broom* constitute its whole furniture. Here Mr E & myself retire when we wish to be absolutely *alone*. When I find him in it before me I enter

only on suffrance. It is a private place of whose very existence no one but ourselves know of & when we are wearied, out of sorts, or have some thing to do
which demands quiet & seclusion we retire there & shut out family cares &
with them all the rest of the world. It is so arranged that we can see out
without being seen in turn & here have I taken my bible, prayer book, & Journal & with the perfume of sweet flowers around me I can daily read & lift up
my heart in gratitude, better I fancy than I can in the house. Here, too, we
make little appointments to meet at a certain hour & chat & spend the time at
our ease. I come in & find some little evidence that he has been before me, a
peach or a pear or a book left open at the page he has been reading, & I go out
& leave a memento for him—a Rose, a vase of fresh flowers, a half written letter, & the air of secresy & seclusion with which we invest the time spent there
gives it a double zest. It is like "Stolen fruit or bread eaten in secret."

AUGUST 28, 1864

The past week we have fully exemplified in our daily life the beauty &
value of *faith*! *Faith*! Is it in God? In our cause? Or in Gen Lee and his army?
Or, as I hope and beleive, is it in all three? On Monday came news that we
had recovered possession of the Petersburg & Weldon R R, that Heth had
advanced, & after flanking had driven back the enemy, taking 3,000 (three
thousand) prisoners, that in another fight 800 more were captured, & that
the road would soon be in running order. All this occurred on Thursday and
Friday 18 and 19th. Then an ominous silence until Thursday. No mail, no
rumours even; yet, tho uneasy, we were not depressed. Congratulated ourselves that the Danville road was uncut & hoped each day for papers. They
came at last & with them bad news. After his repulse on Friday Grant on
Sunday advanced in heavy force, again seized the R R & driving our men
back hastily & strongly entrenched himself, his centre holding the Weldon
R R whilst his left flank stretched westward for more than a mile to the
Vaughn waggon road. We attacked with great fury, carried his outer works,
but retired from the inner which were found to be too strong for us & at going
to press we had been unable to dislodge him. Then came the triumph, the
comfort of our Faith. Serious tho our position was, terrible as would be the
result to us nationally & personally should Grant be enabled to maintain
himself, interposing as it were his whole body between us & Lee & allowing
forage parties to range at will through our whole country which would be in
his rear, yet not a despondant thought, not a doubt arose in our minds, but
we rested in the calm conviction that Gen Lee would in some manner out
general Grant & regain possession of the R R before he could inflict much
damage upon us. Some feared as the intrenchments "which had sprung up
like magic" were so strong that a great loss of life would ensue, whilst others
more confident in Lee's strategy trusted in his skill to manoevre the Yankees
from their post; & true enough the next day brought news by letter from Mr

R. Dunlop, now at Weldon, that the train from Stony Crk had come in & reported that two severe fights had taken place, that Lee had dislodged Grant, & then held the whole line of the road & that our prisoners were estimated at from 3 to 7000 & that he had captured 16 peices of Artillery. As yet no particulars and this is but passenger news, yet we trust & beleive it implicitly!

No official accounts of the capture of Memphis by Forrest, a complete surprise, the Yankee Gen Washburne* with his whole staff & 500 prisoners falling into our hands. Forrest was unable to hold it but retreated with his prisoners & immense booty. An offset to this triumph on our part we, however, find in the loss of Fort Morgan below Mobile which has fallen into the enemies hands, whether by surrender or assault we do not yet understand. Fort Gaines fall has never yet been explained; so, as in that case, we must also reserve our judgment until the facts are before us. Hood holds his own before Atlanta. Wheeler is in Sherman's rear cutting off his waggon trains, destroying bridges, & interrupting his communications generally. He, at the last account, menaces Dalton where Sherman has collected immense supplies. Pray God he may succeed in destroying them! Northern news that Mr Lincoln has consented to receive *Peace Commissioners* at Baltimore. His famous bulletin addressed "To all whom it may concern" has brought him into such disfavour with the Yankee Peace party that he trembles for his reelection. He now wishes to patch up matters with them before the Chicago Convention nominates his successor—hence this "Canard." He hopes with its feeble Quack to drown the voice of the "Peace Democrats," who accuse him of a desire to prolong the War. Mr Lincoln, we thank you & we see clearly through your shallow designs. Your Olive branch is not large enough to hide the drawn sword with which you still menace us.

News but meagre from the Valley. Sheridan has fallen back from before Early (who is still at Strasburg) the Yankees say to a more defensive position on the Potomac. We say Early drove him to it! Early has received the cognomen of the "Great Harvester" from the fact that he captured many hundred Reaping machines on the B & Ohio R R &, dividing them amongst his men, he has been for weeks quietly thrashing & sending South the Wheat Crop of that fertile section & that under the very nose of the Yankee Gen! Below Wilmington Yankee War Steamers are shelling the woods along the Coast at Masonborough Sound & Rumour has it are preparing to land troops for an overland attack on Wilmington. "Nous verrons"! The Yankee prisoners in our hands are increasing to that extent that we are almost in the condition of "the man who caught the Elephant." We know not what to do with them.

*A mistake—Washburne escaped *in his shirt*! Forrest captured & eventually exchanged his whole wardrobe for a suit of Confederate Grey which Washburne sent in by a flag of truce, receiving his own clothes in return

AUGUST 29, 1864

What a prey we are to rumours of all kinds! We were summoned from the "soltaire" yesterday by the announcement that Mr Hill was in the house. Patrick lay on the couch reading at his ease whilst I amused myself with my journal, the conviction that Gen Lee held the R R adding greatly to our Sabbath peace & quiet. Mr Hill somewhat dashed our comfort by the news he had from "a soldier just from the battle field" to the effect that Lee had not taken the line of R R tho he had defeated the Yankees, but nevertheless such is our *Faith* that we went to bed with a calm conviction that tho it might be true that he had not yet taken it he soon would do so & that Grant could "work us no annoy." Today brought Gen Lee's official dispatch of Thursdays fight about which, as there is some discussion amongst us, I will transcribe.

Headquarters A N V, Aug 26, 1864. Hon J A Seddon—Gen A P Hill attacked the enemy in his entrenchments at Ream's Station yesterday evening & on the second assault carried his whole entire line. Cooks & McRae's N C Brigades under Heth's & Lane's N C Brigade & Wilcox's Division under Connor with Pegram's Artillery composed the assaulting column.[92] One line of breastworks was carried by the cavalry under Hampton with great gallantry which contributed largely to our success. Seven stands of colours, 2000 prisoners, & nine peices of Artillery are in our possession. Loss of the enemy in killed & wounded is reported heavy, ours relatively small. Our profound gratitude is due to the Giver of all victories & our thanks to the brave men & officers engaged. Signed R E Lee, General.

Some of us think that he captured the R R, others not, whilst others again suppose that by a flank movement A P Hill got into the rear of Grant's centre which was represented as holding the R R within three miles of Petersburg & made the attack at Ream's nine miles from that place & that Grant is, as it were, enclosed between two divisions of our army. We wait the issue not as usual with "feverish impatience" but with a calm confidence that all will be right. Pattie, poor thing, is in great distress & anxiety as her brother is in Cook's Brigade & was therefore in the assault. Pray God we may soon hear of his safety.

Busy all morning purifying salt for table use, making pickles & Vinegar, Chess, straw sewing, etc., & in the afternoon commenced reading Woodstock to Patty. Last week read Aurora Floyd[93] & like it.

---

[92]Gen. William McRae and Gen. John R. Cooke each commanded brigades attached to Gen. Henry Heth's division. Gen. James H. Lane, commanding the First Brigade of North Carolina Troops, attached to Gen. Cadmus M. Wilcox's division, was temporarily placed under the command of Gen. James Conner of South Carolina during the Reams's Station battle and other skirmishes around Petersburg. Pegram's Battery, an outstanding Virginia artillery unit, was commanded by Col. William Johnson Pegram. Boatner, *Civil War Dictionary*, 171, 471, 630; Manarin and Jordan, *North Carolina Troops*, IV, 398-399, 403-404; V, 5; Clark, *Histories of the North Carolina Regiments*, II, 168, 170, 172; III, 30, 388; V, 212; Freeman, *Lee's Lieutenants*, III, xliv, 632, 673-674.

[93]*Woodstock* (1826) was a novel by Sir Walter Scott about the various disguises and escapes of Charles II from England during the Commonwealth. Benét, *Reader's Encyclopedia*, 1224. *Aurora Floyd*, a novel by Mary

AUGUST 31, 1864

It is as we suppose, A P Hill has flanked Grant on the left & holds the R R at Ream's Station whilst Grant still occupies his entrenchments on it before Petersburg. The Examiner tells us that Grant is in a situation of great difficulty. God grant it! Before Atlanta Sherman is on the move, has abandoned one line of entrenchments which we hold. Some think it a feint to draw Hood out; others that Wheeler's exploits in his rear have put him on short commons. If the telegrams speak truth (they are not official) our captures of supplies there are enormous. One item is seven thousand beeves!

We get some good stories of our common people from Yankee correspondants & which bear the stamp of truth. One old Lady near Atlanta said to a Yankee officer who rode up to her house immediately after the attempted flanking of Joe Johnson by Sherman "you'uns don't fight we'uns fair! Mr *Hooker now he went round*!" Good soul, to her notions of military strategy were comprised in a fair stand up give & take fight!

Another was accosted by a party of Yankees "Well how goes it old Lady. You're Secesh too I suppose?" "No! honey *that I aint*!" "Why hows that? You're Union then?" "No, thank the Lord I aint that neither." "Well what in the name of wonder then are you?" "I'me a Baptist, honey, a Baptist! For forty years I've been a hard shell Baptist and please the Lord I'll die one too!"

As I am in an anecdotical vein this morning; I cannot do better than give one of Cuffee which is excellent. The negro baker of the Va Military Institute belonged to the Institution & during Hunter's late brutal foray through the Valley, when he destroyed it & plundered the citizens of Lexington, Abram lost everything he had, clothes, money, everything stolen by the Yankees. After their retreat, relating his losses to some sympathizing friend he was asked, "Did you tell them that you belonged to the State of Virginia?" "No! No! sir that I did'nt if I had they'd have burnt me up along with the rest of the State property!"

In the Enquirer of yesterday is published an official Circular from Mr Benjamin giving an account of the late visit of Mr Lincoln's Peace commissoners to Richmond. Comment is unnecessary. See the paper itself marked [———][94] O Yankee, Yankee, when will you learn fair dealings? Mr B's statement shows conclusively that Mr Lincoln's move for Peace is but a political trick to blind the Peace party.

SEPTEMBER 3, 1864

Who can tell what a day will bring forth? The affliction into which poor Pattie was in one moment plunged sends a pang through every heart & makes

---

Elizabeth Braddon Maxwell (1837-1915), was published in 1863. *Webster's Biographical Dictionary*, 183; H. W. C. Davis and J. R. H. Weaver (eds.), *Dictionary of National Biography, 1912-1921* (London: Oxford University Press, 1927), 377-378.

[94]This paper was not found in the diary.

all tremble for the future. On the first, the day before yesterday, she received a letter from her sister, Mrs Gilliam, telling her that her brother Capt Skinner (whom she idolized more than any other human being) had been instantly killed whilst gallantly leading a charge at the battle of Ream's Station. He had just shouted to his men, "Forward boys! Forward once more & we have got them!!" when he was struck by a Minnie ball in the left temple & fell. His men pressed on, carried the Yankee works, & returned to find him cold & stiff in death. His cousin Willie Mallory[95] (a member of his company) & another of his men buried him on the field of battle & wrote his sister an account of his death. Poor Pattie! Her grief is fearful! Her wounds are torn open afresh & the "low beginnings of content" which God in his mercy had granted her are broken up from the foundation. In the most heartrending accents she would call on her husband, on her brother, exclaim that they were her all, her all, Aunt Kate, Aunt Kate my all, my all! until ones heart & brain almost reeled at the presence of such sorrow. Ah! How much more heavy is the pressure of greif when there is nothing to be done but to look the dreadful fact steadily in the face, than when there is a need for *action*, for exertion, for thought of some kind.

Her sisters entertain hopes of recovering the body & burying for the present in Oxford & I have sent a man on to the battle field to make the attempt. Mr Edmondston accordingly took her yesterday to that place in the hope of being in time for the funeral. Poor thing, my heart bleeds for her! He was indeed her "all," her stay, her support, & her comfort & to him alone she looked for what of happiness the future had in store for her. I cannot trust myself to speak of his death. It seems to have brought the war even nearer to me than the death of my own nephew did. Perhaps on account of its suddenness! But if there is one fate in the future, one punishment for the damned more terrible than another, it will surely be those who have inaugerated and carried on this dreadful war, who have sown the country broadcast with blood & misery. Mr Lincoln! Mr Lincoln! We call you to the bar of Judgment, you and your arch tool Seward! On you two falls the weight of the heaviest retribution which man was ever yet called to suffer.

Capt Benjamin Skinner was an uncommonly fine young man of parts more solid than brilliant. He had made himself beloved by his associates & idolized by his family for a kindness of disposition, an unselfishness of character, which showed itself in constant acts of self denial for their sakes. Firm, upright, & just in his dealings with all men, he was distinguished for modesty of disposition, a cheerful evenness of temper, a kindly playfulness of manner as rare as it is valuable, a good soldier,—gallant, brave, and uncomplaining even amids

---

[95]W. S. Mallong of Perquimans County was a first sergeant in Co. F, Twenty-seventh North Carolina Regiment, which Benjamin Skinner had commanded as captain. Moore, *Roster of North Carolina Troops*, II, 420; Claiborne T. Smith, Jr., Papers, Southern Historical Collection.

the greatest of hardships. He was almost worshiped by his men and he commanded in no small degree the respect and admiration of his superior officers. As the head of his family his death will long be felt by them; for to him, young as he was, they all looked up as to a common centre. To his Mother & Pattie his loss is irreparable & to his youngest brother now immured in a Northern Prison the want of his example & influence is incalculable. He was but a type of thousands of other young men who daily lose their lives on the altar of Southern independance. "Independance" my God! how dearly bought! Hasten the time O Lord when we shall be free! free from the ravages of this Northern Minos[96] who thus devours the flower of our youth!

All day yesterday I wandered about worn out in body & mind, unable to do anything or even to think of any thing save Pattie & her sorrow's. Mr E & herself left early in the morning & he cannot get back at earliest before twelve o'clock tomorrow. I think I shall scarce know rest until he comes. A tiny note from him this morning dated Weldon gives us the ill omened news that in spite of the blood shed at Ream's the Yankees still hold the R R at that point. No explanation of the heavy firing on the 1st, so we are forced to think it must have been further down the road. He tells me also that McClellan & Wood are the nominees for the Chicago Convention for Pres & Vice Pres of the U S. Little do I care whom they place in that seat; be it the arch Enemy himself, he would suit his subjects rarely. I do not beleive in their Peace humbugs & Restoration of the Unions—canards "Peace," "Reconstruction," & "Union" are party cries all alike empty. Give them but the *power* & we will see what kind of *Peace* they will give us. Peace lies in our own good swords & unerring aim.

September 4, 1864

Disappointed today in my hope of seeing Mr Edmondston. The carriage came back from Weldon empty. Why is it that I am so uneasy? I am ashamed of myself for apprehensions which I can neither define or conquer, & it being Sunday I am debarred from active employment which would help to dispel them. Father heard at Church from some one more fortunate than we in getting papers that a battle, with as yet doubtful results, was in progress between Hood & Sherman. I do not like such "*doubts.*" With Kirkpatrick I like to "*mak siccar.*"[97]

---

[96]According to Greek mythology Minos, king of Crete and husband of Pasiphaë, conquered Athens and exacted a tribute of seven young men and women yearly. These prisoners were fed to the Minotaur, the offspring of Pasiphaë and a bull sent by Poseidon to Minos. Athens was delivered from this tribute when Theseus killed the Minotaur. Benét, *Reader's Encyclopedia*, 726; "Minos," *Encyclopedia Americana*, XIX, 211.

[97]"I will mak siccar," meaning to make certain. Sir Walter Scott, *Tales of a Grandfather: Being Stories Taken from Scottish History*, Volume I of *The Prose Works of Sir Walter Scott with His Last Additions and Notes* (Philadelphia: Carey & Hart, 3 volumes, 1841?).

SEPTEMBER 5, 1864

After midnight last night to my infinite surprise & pleasure I heard Mr E's step on the back step—& in a moment after his tap & voice at my window. I needed no light to find my way to the door to let him in when he told me that brother & Mr Wm Smith were with him, having come in the Sunday's train from Raleigh. Mr S brought him down from Halifax in his buggy. I soon had beds ready for our tired guests & could scarce beleive that already my gloomy presentments were at an end & heartily ashamed was I of having, I can't say, indulged for I struggled womanfully against them but having had them. He had been detained in Oxford by a heavy rain & as his throat was already sore preferred losing a train to riding 24 hours in his wet clothes. Pattie bore the journey well & the presence of her sister seemed to compose & comfort her. God be with this poor young thing! Bad news today from Atlanta. A telegram tells us that it has fallen, tho how or why remains to be seen. Brother is despondant & a gloom is cast over the family in which, however sad as the news is, I cannot share. My thankfulness for Patrick's return counterbalances all this depression.

SEPTEMBER 6, 1864

Official accounts today of our loss in the battle of Reams' Station. A P Hill has "the honour to report the correct list of the results of the fight at Ream's Station on the 25th. We captured 12 stands of colours, 9 peices of Artillery, 10 caissons, 2150 prisoners, 3100 stand of arms, & 32 horses. My own loss in cavalry, artillery, & infantry is 720 men (seven hundred & twenty) killed, wounded, & missing." The charge of the N C troops on the breastworks was magnificent, gallant almost beyond record even in this war of gallant deeds! Pegram turned the enemy's own guns on them with terrible effect. He fired "second fuses" on the retreating mass doing great execution.

Atlanta has certainly fallen but I am recovering from the shock, which brother intensified, by suppositions at once crushing & heart breaking. That Hood's "army was cut to peices, demoralized, & melting like a summer dew" was with him a foregone conclusion. Grant was to do something to Lee, I do not think it was to defeat him, which was to cause *his* army also to melt away! Peace with reconstruction was to stare us in the face, but why record gloomy & despondant doubts & anticipation from which I have already recovered. I never held them, but they oppressed me like a weight, a "peine forte et dure." Thank God for my elasticity, the best personal boon he has given me!

SEPTEMBER 8, 1864

Yesterday came Mr E's sister Jessie with her two children, Amo & Lizzie, to make us a visit. We have long looked forward to this pleasure & enjoy it now to the very full. We are very fond of them & intend making the most of their society. Interchange of opinion, long confidential talks, family news, going over the time which has passed since we met, have occupied us so entirely that I almost forget our disappointment in the loss of Atlanta & the bad news from Hood.

It seems from his official statement that "on the evening of the 30th the enemy made a lodgment across Flint river near Jonesboro. We attacked them there on the evening of the 31st with 2 corps but failed to dislodge them. This made it necessary to abandon Atlanta which was done of the night of the 1st. On the evening of the 1st that portion of our lines held by Hardee's corps near Jonesboro was assaulted by a superior force of the enemy & being out flanked was compelled to withdraw during the night with the loss of eight peices of artillery. Prisoners taken report the enemy's loss to have been very severe." Press dispatches assure us that our loss did not exceed 600 & that Hood left nothing but blood stained mines in Atlanta, blowing up his amunition & removing supplies. We hope so! Heavy news in a telegram from Bristol, east Tenn. Morgan, Morgan the dauntless, the brave, the unreproached, is dead, shot through the head by a Yankee bullet, his Staff all surprised & captured. Our sorrow is great, for we expected great things of his future, but God sees not as we see. He will make it good to us. Let us trust in Him for the day of our deliverance. The Peace Convention at Chicago fails to interest or amuse us. It is but a move on the political Chess board! They all mean to destroy us if they can. Their impotence is our only safe guard. McClellan & Pendleton are their nominees. I knew Pendleton's wife[98] in days gone by, but it seems as long ago as when "Adam was a baby." She is the daughter of Francis Key author of the "Star spangled Banner."

September 16, 1864

On Tuesday last whilst sitting reading my Bible alone in the "Soltaire," I was suddenly aroused by a heavy report, a *boom* as tho an explosion had taken place. So loud was it that I convinced myself that it was distant thunder & stepped out into the garden to see the cloud from whence it came, but the sky was "without speck or spot or stain." "The blue Vault" was as clear as crystal. I called to the servants to know what it was, but they as much overcome with surprise as myself. They had also heard it & accepted the fact that it was thunder without examination. In the afternoon & all the next day a heavy canonade was heard by many, Mr E amongst the number, but my ears were not so sharp, *deafened I said by the first report.* Anxiously did we look for news on Wednesday and on Thursday and again today, Friday, but alaas! we

---

[98]George Hunt Pendleton (1825-1889) was a prominent state legislator of Ohio, a United States congressman, senator, and minister to Germany under Pres. Grover Cleveland. Pendleton, a leader of the peace Democrats during the Civil War and the vice-presidential nominee on the McClellan ticket of 1864, was married to Alice Key, the daughter of Francis Scott Key and the niece of Roger B. Taney. *Dictionary of American Biography,* XIV, 419-420.

have been doomed to disappointment! No mail! not even a Raleigh paper which would give us a Telegram, meagre it is true, yet still something on which to found conjecture. Every neighbor who comes in is full of eager questions, for the report or explosion was heard through a circuit of fifteen miles, but no one can throw the least light upon it. Pray God it be another Yankee Magazine blown up & with even more damage than that at City Point some weeks since. This want of news tho keeps us cruelly anxious.

Our loss before Atlanta was heavier than the Press Reports, but as we have no official statements it is idle to enumerate them. Hood fell back in good order, Sherman following. Very soon, however, Sherman gave up that game & fell back himself to Atlanta & commenced fortifying. He there promulgated an Order so infamous that a Russian example must be sought if we would find a paralel amongs civilized nations. He finds it for the interest of the U S that *every inhabitant* should be banished from Atlanta & its vicinity and accordingly directs that those who wish to go North shall be allowed to do so whilst those who prefer remaining at the South shall be sent through his lines into Hoods and proposes to Hood an armistice for ten days in which to execute his barbarious intentions. Hood accepts in order to spare the unfortunates any additional suffering but comments most severely upon the inhumanity of the Order.[99] It seems to us so short sighted a peice of conduct that we can but hail it as an evidence that the Devil is forsaking his own, leaving him now in the lurch. What can he expect but resistance to the death from every Southern man, woman, & child in the future?

McClellan is out in his acceptance of the nomination of the Chicago Convention in a string of balderdash about this "glorious Union" which is almost too absurd to provoke Laughter. "The Union" & "the Constitution," *two corpses*, murdered by Northern fanatics. It is more than Northern demagogues can now do to galvanize them. They sit in dumb, dead silence, grimly staring at their murderers.

Amo left us on Tuesday the 13th for a visit to Raleigh. In the meantime we are enjoying Jessie's society in full. It is long since we have seen her & she is Mr E's favourite sister, the one nearest his own age, & she it was who was the companion of all his childish pranks, the confidant & friend of his mature years.

---

[99]Sherman, unable to capture Hood's army but determined to retain possession of Atlanta, evacuated the city's civilian population in order to turn the city into an armed camp. Sherman offered transportation and food to the citizens who elected to go north and transportation as far as Rough and Ready, Georgia, for those who wished to go south. Those fleeing his lines were also allowed to remove furniture, clothing, and those slaves who voluntarily wished to go with them. To Hood's protests over this "unprecedented measure," Sherman pointed out that Johnston removed families from Dalton and that Hood himself rendered fifty houses uninhabitable because they stood in his way. He also questioned Hood's accusation of cruelty, noting that "God will judge us in due time, and He will pronounce whether it be more humane to fight with a town full of women, and the families of 'a brave people' at our back, or to remove them in time to places of safety among their own friends and people." *Official Records (Army)*, Series I, XXXIX, Part II, 414-422; Boatner, *Civil War Dictionary*, 34.

SEPTEMBER 17, 1864

Last night when Mr E came home from the plantation he brought us the Key to the terrific explosion which so startled me on Tuesday & has been ever since a matter of grave conjecture with the whole community. It appears that one of our big guns at Weldon, "Long Tom" or "Laughing Charley," had been so long loaded that it was thought expedient to fire it off. The charge happened to be a [———] inch shell, one of the largest size made. From some unknown cause, the explosion of the shell was almost simultaneous with the report of the gun, hence the prolonged & booming sound which caused us such uneasiness. We were greatly releived as the want of a mail made us fear that it came from some device of Grant's, which would "work us some annoy." The heavy cannonading heard that day & the next was along the lines & a furious shelling of the city which was kept up for some hours with but little damage.

News from Thomas Devereux up to the 6th—he was well but on the 5th had his horse killed under him. He lost his saddle & bridle and is I suppose poor fellow a foot. Thanks to a merciful God for his preservation!

Details of poor Morgan's death. He died by *treachery* & the treachery, too, of a woman! but as statements vary as to what the name of the infamous wretch is, I will wait for authentic accounts. Himself & staff stopped for the night at the house of a Mrs Williams. When they were asleep a *woman*, whose name should be associated with that of Arnold, mounted her horse & eluding our pickets rode to the Yankee headquarters & returned with a body of Yankee Cavalry whom she guided to the house in which Morgan slept. He was aroused by his hostess, who endeavoured to aid his escape, but another woman, a *Yankee*, Mrs Fry told his pursuers which way he went.[100] After a desperate struggle in which he discharged every load in his pistols, killing several of his opponents, he received a shot through the heart & expired instantly! In consequence of the brutal treatment he met with when a prisoner in the hands of the Christian Burnside, he had determined never again to be taken alive & too well did he keep his vow. We are much cast down by his sad fate & Father, in vain, attempts to console us by repeating those lines from Chevy Chase, [———] but I do not like the sentiment contained in them, it is too "*French.*" "*Le Roi est mort*"! "Vive le Roi."[101] They compliment the living at the expense of the dead.

---

[100]Morgan was surprised and killed in Greeneville, Tennessee, on September 4, 1864, while attempting to escape through the garden of a house where he had been sleeping. Whether his death was due to betrayal by Lucy B. Williams has been the subject of some controversy. See Cecil F. Holland, *Morgan and His Raiders* (New York: Macmillan Company, 1942), 339-340, 345-348, and Howard Swiggett, *The Rebel Raider: A Life of John Hunt Morgan* (Indianapolis: Bobbs-Merrill Company, 1934), 263-264, 273-295.

[101]French, "The King is dead! Long live the King."

SEPTEMBER 19, 1864

Came Amo back from Raleigh on Sat jaded & worn out. He brought good accounts of Hood's army from an intelligent officer with whom he "fore gathered" in his journey. The army is in fine spirits, well disiplined, & defiant, but long for Johnston to be again at their head. They do not under-value Hood & he possesses their confidence & affection but in a less degree than Joe Johnston whom they all look upon not only as unequaled in strategy but as martyr to personal ill will, either of the President or some one high in his influence. Rumour whispers that Mrs Davis has much to do with it, that Mrs Johnston and herself do not visit whilst Mrs Bragg is her warm personal friend. I must beleive, however, that Mr Davis is superior to such influences. He is not a man to be led by a "Commercia Major" & has the good of the country too much at heart to sacrifice it to personal pique. If he makes mis-takes, & who that is mortal does not?, they are honest ones!

Patrick sent Amo some Turnip seed sometime since with directions to sell them & divide the proceeds for his trouble. He brought us on our portion in the shape of Sugar [———] lbs of the seed buying [———] lbs of Sugar—the one being sold for $[———] and the other bought at $6, so ten lbs of sugar standing normally at $60 cost us only [———] lbs of turnip seed, for which we have no use & which we never before sold! Indeed barter has be-come the order of the day. We pay for our weaving in Lard! Two lbs of Lard pays for the weaving of 2 yds of coarse cloth & recently two of our neighbors, Mrs Peter & Mrs Ben Smith,[102] desiring to carry their children for change of air to the up country could get board only on promising to pay for it in Bacon & Lard, and part of their baggage actually consisted of bags of bacon and kegs of lard! Spartan simplicity. The Yankees are endeavouring to force our authorities into a special exchange of prisoners by placing our officers in a Stockade on Morris island outside of Gregg & Wagner & exposed to our fire. They want their *officers* but not their *men* & tho we have expressed a desire & have done all that in us lay to effect a general exchange of all prisoners they refuse to accede to it, raising innumerable difficulties & now demanding that we shall surrender our own slaves, captured from them, in return for our free white citizens captured by them. Our government refuses to admit the status of negroes to be equal to that of whites & claim that when we recapture slaves they are ours & return at once to their normal state. Butler has written a letter on the subject, distinguished only for bad Logic & impertinence, which I hope Mr Ould will treat with the contempt it deserves.

---

[102]Benjamin Gordon Smith was a twenty-two-year-old Halifax County farmer. His wife, Louisa Catherine Hill, was named for Mrs. Edmondston. Claiborne Thweatt Smith, Jr., *Smith of Scotland Neck: Planters on the Roanoke* (Baltimore: Gateway Press, Inc., 1976), 114.

SEPTEMBER 20, 1864

Letter from Frank Jones telling us that 900 Yankee officers have been placed in a stockade on Sullivan's Island in retaliation for a number of ours confined in like manner by the enemy on Morris Island.[103] In the mean time Yellow fever has made its appearance in the city, a danger more deadly to the unaclimated Yankee than bullet or ball, & there are many confined there. I hope it will precipitate a general exchange. Sherman, however, takes the position that the men in our hands whose term of service has expired are not entitled to Exchange for our enlisted men in theirs & this want of faith to its subjects, I had better call them at once, is the treatment the best Government under the Sun gives its own & its adopted sons! Stepmother like conduct, which none but a Yankee would have the face to perpetuate; but as Mrs Hines says, "they have forgotten if they ever knew how to blush."

A Dispatch from Gen Lee tells us that Hampton succeeded in getting in Grant's rear, capturing 2500 fat beeves, 300 prisoners, a no. of waggons, mules, & horses & returned safely with the loss of fifty men only. In Albemarle Sound, too, we have had a success—16 men of the Steamer Albemarle went out in small boats, boarded & burnt the steamer Fawn, a boat running through the Dismal Swamp Canal from Norfolk to Yankee head quarters in the North Eastern Counties, with the crew, several commissioned officers in transit to their commands, and 25,000 in gold. As a set off, however, the enemy claims to have captured our N C steamer the Advance with a load of Cotton & 28,000 in specie off Hatteras.[104] We fear it is true, but she has made a vast sum for the state besides enabling her to provide well for her troops in the way of clothing and shoes and I hope her loss will soon be replaced.

SEPTEMBER 22, 1864

Dined yesterday at the plantation with Jessie, Amo, and Mr E. A merry day but somewhat oppressed by the uneasiness we felt as to the cause of a terrific

---

[103]Gen. Samuel Jones requested that Bragg send him fifty Federal prisoners for detention in Charleston in order to discourage Union forces from shelling portions of the city occupied by noncombatants. Gen. J. G. Foster of the United States Army replied that Charleston citizens had received ample opportunity to leave the city. Foster also contended that the city was being bombarded because it supplied munitions of war to the Confederacy, and that the Confederate attempt to defeat this objective by placing unarmed and helpless prisoners under fire was reprehensible. Foster subsequently requested permission to use an equal number of Confederate prisoners in the same manner. On October 31 Foster acknowledged a letter from Gen. W. J. Hardee, commanding Confederate forces in South Carolina, Georgia, and Florida, who informed him that Union prisoners had been removed to a place of safety. Foster accordingly moved his Confederate prisoners to a safe place as well. *Official Records (Army)*, Series I, XXXV, Part II, 131-132, 134-135, 138-139, 141, 143-145, 147-148, 150-151, 163-164; Series II, VII, 185, 608, 625, 768, 773, 826-827, 1073.

[104]The mail steamer *Fawn* was burned by members of the *Albemarle* crew during the night of September 9, 1864, on the Albemarle and Chesapeake Canal. The *Advance* successfully completed over twenty voyages for the state before her capture. Her loss was another blow to the state's efforts to bring supplies into the Confederacy from abroad. *Civil War Naval Chronology*, IV, 111; VI, 189, 337; Clark, *Histories of the North Carolina Regiments*, V, 337-339.

canonading which took place from daybreak to nine o'clock in the direction of Petersburg. Grant is reported as extending his lines to the left & is now three miles to the west of the Weldon R R. Lee's policy, the wise ones say, is to allow him thus to weaken by extending his line & suddenly to hurl himself upon & break through it, thus dividing his army. It may be so, but I am not a Brigadier either by birth or brevet.

SEPTEMBER 23, 1864

The cannonade on the 21st proves to have been only a rather more than usually vigorous shelling on Grant's part, from which no damage resulted, God be thanked. News of an engagement near Winchester in which I fear we were not successful, as the bringing off of our guns & waggon trains is mentioned as a cause of gratulation. Early telegraphs that "the loss on both sides was heavy." We compelled the enemy to retire, but at night fall we also did the same thing, falling back to Fisher's Hill, Sheridan being too much worsted to pursue. Sad, sad to relate, we lost Maj Gen Rodes, one of the best Generals of Division we have & Brig Gen Godwin, a gallant & good officer. Rodes tho from Alabama commanded N C troops almost exclusively & Godwin's Brigade were all from this state. Mourning is sown broadcast throughout our land I fear by this sad battle. Thomas Devereux is in Rodes Division. How long will it be ere we are at rest? Godwin was at one time Provost Marshal of Richmond & we saw him frequently there in the spring of 62.

SEPTEMBER 26, 1864

On Sat 24th came James to make a flying visit & see his sister Mrs Coffin. He is well & in good spirits but saddened me by confirming the estimate I have so often heard given of Gen Lee's & Beauregard's armies. Together, he says, they have not more than 40,000 men fit for duty! Yet he is hopeful & says if Grant will only extend his lines & attempt to take in the Southside R R, Lee will annihilate him! James is now "Inspector of Field Transportation" & holds the cheif power of Impressment in this State—disagreeable and hard duty & too much power to be in the hands of any one man. Pray God he use it descreetly & justly, "without fear, favour, or affection." He left for his Head qts at Greensboro today.

OCTOBER 2, 1864

Have been quite sick for the last few days. Went on Tuesday the 27th to the plantation with the young folks on a party of pleasure, but mine was marred by a chill which took me before I reached there. So spent a miserable day with headache & fever & was glad to get home in the afternoon to my bed in which I remained doing my devoirs to Calomel & Quinine all the next day. Am still much out of sorts.

From the Valley meagre but heavy news. Early has continued to fall back before an overpowering force of the enemy until he has reached the *neighborhood of Stanton*, pursued by Sheridan whom he has occasionally repulsed. We hear that he made a stand at Weir's Cave but with what result we as yet cannot learn. His loss since the battle of Winchester is small, which is a great blessing. Our Cavalry behaved badly, we fear, in that battle, but our details are so slight that as yet we ought not to condemn them. Sheriden has been heavily and suddenly reinforced & out numbers Early five to one, but the retreat is not yet over. A tiger at bay is a formidable antagonist & Sheridan may yet learn what it is to drive Confederate soldiers to the wall. So Courage, Courage, & patience! Hood has thrown himself into Sherman's rear. The papers are Delphic in their oracular predictions of a great success soon to attend our arms there, so we wait in hopeful expectation to see what the future will bring forth.

Our household has again been saddened for the Angel of Death has brought sorrow to one of its inmates. Poor little Mattie heard on Thursday that her brother Mr Colin Dunlop[105] serving in Hood's army, had been killed on the 1st at Jonesboro. On the very day on which she sympathized so deeply with Pattie in the loss of her brother a like affliction fell upon herself! Mr Dunlop was a fine young man, useful & high spirited. His family will feel his loss greatly & his country has need of all such men now. He served in a Texas Regt, was captured at Arkansas Post, & when exchanged by the enemy was so reduced & emaciated from the effect of the sufferings endured by him when a prisoner that his father passed him by without recognizing him, altho he was at the Flag of Truce boat in search of him. For days after his arrival at home he knew none of his brothers or sisters & the most devoted nursing only restored him to comparative health. He returned to his command to die at length by a Yankee bullet. The ways of Providence are inscrutable.

Forrest reports officially that he has taken Athens Ala, 1300 prisoners, 500 horses & mules, provisions, RR cars, etc., in abundance. One more blow to Sherman's rear. O! for one crushing one! News from Tom Devereux. He has again had a narrow escape, a bullet lodging in his saddle so close to his leg as to bruise it. Neither himself or horse hurt. This at the battle of Winchester. God only knows what his fate may have been on this disastrous retreat of Early's! Early & Grimes both had their horses shot under them as did Tom's friend & fellow courier Sherwood Badger. He is now even with Tom.

OCTOBER 5, 1864

Heavy fighting on the north bank of James River on the 30th, in which, however, we remained victorious. The enemy seized fort Harrison, a salient of Chaffin's Bluff temporarily abandoned by us, & as yet have not been driven out. The Examiner seems to think we can do so at pleasure. Gen Dunnivant of

---

[105]Colin McKenzie Dunlop (1836-1864) was the son of James and Isabella Lenox Maitland Dunlop.

S C was killed. Our loss slight; that of the Yankees heavy. Cuffee as usual suffered much more than his philanthropic brethren. Two of our lines of defence around Richmond were penetrated but the enemy were finally driven back with great slaughter. Skirmishing before Petersburg up to the same date, & appearances seemed to point to an extension of Grant's lines westwardly. This from newspapers, the 2d being our last news. The train of the 3d brought news that on that day a heavy fight was in progress between Lee & Grant & that Lee was getting the best of it. A "Cantabitur urbe" has it that on that day the 3d Grant received a tremendus drubbing at Lee's hands on the Southside R R which he attempted to take. God grant it be true! Official reports from Early tell us that he holds Staunton, that the enemy is massed about Harrisonburg. No more fighting. It is supposed that Early's retreat is over & hoped that he is out of the region of Monongahela Whisky & Apply Brandy! "John Barleycorn" is said to have had as much to do with our reverses in the lower Valley as the Yankees, overwhelming as were their members. It is a shame! No news from Hood.

The President has been out to Georgia & made a most remarkable speech at Macon. I do not beleive it has been correctly reported. I can only say of it that it sounds more like one of Lincoln's purelities than one of Mr Davis' statesman like & dignified utterances. Beauregard, it is said, is to take command of the Armies of Geo & Ala with authority to combine & concentrate the troops as he shall judge best. Forrest continues to annoy Sherman's rear, tearing up RR & burning cars until one would think his communications were entirely cut off. But it seems as tho the RRs grow like an Earthworm, the better for being cut!

How we do change. Capt Cooke sent me last week a present of captured tin wire, pans, plates, funnels, etc., & I declare I feel as tho I had had a present of Plate! My borders seem increased!

The shelling of Charleston has been heavier than ever & that whilst the enemy know that the Yellow Fever is prevalent there & consequently no troops are in the city proper. Noncombattants prostrated with disease are the subjects they wreak their vengeance on. Their Gun, their famous "Swamp Angel," has exploded under the constant use they have latterly put it to. Hood & Sherman have had a special Exchange of the prisoners captured on each side in the last Campaign & amongst the Exchanged is Stoneman the Raider! The Yankee successes in the Valley have stilled all their late clamours for *Peace* & shown even better than we knew before of what stuff their so called "*Peace party*" is composed. I beleive I prefer Lincoln to McClellan for my part—if I have any choice between them.

OCTOBER 10, 1864

To our sorrow we woke up this morning to a "killing frost." The potatoes, peas, & Dahlias bear dismal evidence of its severity; they look as tho' they were scalded. I fear the Sorghum crop will be seriously cut short by it & the potatoes have lost a fortnight's growth by it.

Yesterday came two more of the Misses Dunlop, refugees from Petersburg, & others of their family are soon to follow. A beleaguered city, altho it is on but one side, is, Gen Lee says, no place for women & children. The difficulty, nay impossibility, of getting fuel will drive many families out—to say nothing of the price of provisions which, owing to the transportation being all absorbed by the army, is fearful. Every soldier we see, however, comforts & cheers us with the assurance that Grant can never drive Gen Lee from it, that it will never be given up, that Lee's army is invincible. The military situation remains the same. The capture from us of Fort Harrison on the North side of the James & ft. McRae on, Grant's extreme left, by him are the only changes. The quid nuncs say, but how they find it out I cannot tell, that Gen Lee had no objection to Grant's taking possession of the latter point, as he desires his line to be extended so that by a sudden blow he can pierce it, but I doubt whether Gen Lee desires any closer approach to the South Side road at which Grant is aiming. Since Sheridan's repulse at New Market he has been quiet, no longer pressing on Early. The northern papers say that having gained his point, effected all that Lieut Gen Grant desires, he will now rest a while on his Laurels. A short time ago the points at which he aimed were Lynchburg, the Central & the Tennessee RR & the canal! O! Yankee! Yankee! Hood is well in Sherman's rear having possession we hear of the [———] RR at Marietta. A battle is thought imminent between them. Forrest is also operating on Shermans rear, cutting lines of communication, capturing supplies & blockhouses, until their number seems to be Legion!

One third of the Guard for Home Defence in this State has been ordered to take the field; the men to be determined by draft on Wednesday next.[106] The officers to accompany them are to be assigned, so I am quite at sea as to Mr E's destination. He may leave me at a moment's warning. Yellow Fever raging at New Berne, making steady progress at Charleston where it has appeared amongst the Yankee prisoners. Their blood be on Lincoln's head! He it is who has power to exchange them & for a peice of petty policy refuses to do so. He is out in (to the North) a most humiliating confession. He says that if McClellan's platform, the abrogation of negro soldiers in the Yankee army, is put into execution that it will be impossible for the North ever to conquer The

---

[106]General Order No. 24, October 4, 1864, issued by the adjutant general's department, instructed commanding officers of the Home Guard in the counties of Surry, Yadkin, Rowan, Cabarrus, Mecklenburg, Lincoln, Gaston, and Cleveland, and all the counties east of these, to assemble the men under their commands without delay. Once assembled, the men were divided into three classes, determined by lot or draft, which rotated duty shifts unless all units were required for defense. The battalion officers were required to arm and equip the men and to report to Gen. Collett Leventhorpe in Goldsboro for organization into regiments. Adjutant General's Department, Military Board, *Minutes, May 16-August 11, 1861. Executive Department. General and Special Orders, August 18, 1863-April 11, 1865*, 478-479, State Archives, hereinafter cited as *General and Special Orders*, Adjutant General's Department Papers.

South. He has 200,000 of them now under arms. Remove them from the Union armies & their cause is lost. The South will be triumphant. Pleasant that for the Anglo Saxons & the Anti miscegenation-ist at the North to hear! Their boasted "*Union*" depends upon poor Cuffee's black arm!

OCTOBER 12, 1864

Jessie & her children left us this morning after an early dinner for their home in S C. We have had a pleasant visit from them & Jessie has much improved in health. Some time when Peace smiles on us I hope they will repeat it. Mr Edmondston in Halifax all day attending to this miserable business of drafting one third of the Home Guard for immediate & active service. I will not know until late tonight what my fate is to be, so can settle to nothing. I wander from the potato field to the Apple gatherers & back again in a demoralized state conducive to anything but happiness. God's will be done & grant Faith to bear cheerfully what is before me! We gained great successes on the North side of the James on Friday the 7th, but as details are meagre & our mails irregular, I will wait for further news.

OCTOBER 13, 1864

Late last night came Mr E home from Halifax & gave me the pleasant news that he had not been assigned to the duty of commanding the Co of Home Guards sent from the county of Goldsboro. Maj Pearson, disliking the onus of naming the officers, determined to decide the matter by lot & the duty fell on Captain Ponton.[107] We are told "the lot is of the Lord," so should be content.

This morning father called me up into his room & surprised me with a present to us of $10,000 in Certificates of Indebtedness from the Confederate Government! He gives the same to each of his daughters. It is part of the proceeds of a recent sale of cotton he has recently made. He warned me that there was every probability of its depreciation, the sum being too large to be fairly realized from the cotton he sold. At any rate it secures us $600 per annum exempt from taxation for some years to come & tho we may fear future repudiation, all we have to do is to enjoy the present & feel grateful to him for his generous & unselfish liberality. Many fathers would retain the money in their own hands in order that their children might feel & acknoledge their dependance upon him. Not so with him; he realizes "the glorious privilege of being Independant"!

OCTOBER 18, 1864

On Sunday the 16th Father & Mama left us for their own home, the early frost having rendered such a step safe a full month earlier than usual. I all day

---

[107]Maj. W. A. Pearson and Captain Ponton of Halifax County were members of the Second Regiment in the Home Guard, as organized in the spring of 1865. Clark, *Histories of the North Carolina Regiments*, IV, 653.

yesterday with Mr E at the plantation; his molasses mills being out of order he was kept busy all day. Have just gathered my tea nuts, nearly a peck of them & clipped my Tea plants a second time. How I wish we had plants enough to supply us; we would laugh at Yankee Blockaders.

The war news is good. We repulsed a heavy attack on the North side of the James on the Darby town road on Tuesday the 11th. Our loss small; that of the enemy heavy. In the Valley our cavalry have met with a repulse from pressing too far ahead of their infantry supports annoying Sheridan's rear. We lost five guns & many prisoners, but Early coming up, Sheridan continued to fall back. Grant has issued an order which, for barbarity, equals anything yet done in this most barbarous of all wars. He directs the Valley of Va to be laid entirely waste, everything which can support life to be destroyed and all the stock of all kind to be driven off or killed. His Lieutenants are carrying it out to the letter! In one day Sheridan reports he burned [———] Mills, [———] Barns filled to the roof with wheat, oats, & corn enough to maintain Early for three months, all the farming implements, the seed wheat, has fed 3000 sheep to his army & driven off stock & horses in such quantity that there has been as yet no account taken of them! Grant tells him "to leave the Valley such a waste that next year a crow flying across will have to carry his own rations with him." What a monster! Fit associate for Butler & Sherman! He is a disgrace to humanity! His cheif engineer was killed by a band of guerrillas & as retaliation he ordered every dwelling within an area of five miles to be burnt! I preserve Grants order & Sheridans report, both official, & such conduct is tolerated by a nation who *calls itself Christian*!

From Georgia we get but little news, the War Depart surpressing all details for fear of giving information to the enemy. Hood is well in Sherman's rear & has possession of the RR. We beleive we were victorious at Alatoona & that we captured 3000 Yankees altho Stanton reports officially that we were beaten with heavy loss. Rome is in our hands, but Stanton publishes a dispatch from that point. Atlanta we beleive to be evacuated but of that have no confirmation, mere rumours. One thing is certain, Stanton & Lincoln are terribly alarmed & lie more than ever to hide their fears & to prevent their reverses having an unfavourable effect on the coming election. By their falsities they have influenced in their favor the Penn & Ohio State Elections & if they can continue keep the public mind in the dark until the 8th of next month, it may be well for them. Grant us overwhelming victories at all points ere then! But why should I wish to disappoint them? Lincolns election, if there is a choice, is better for us than McClellan's, because he is the greater fool. I honestly beleive McClellan will be a better President for the Yankees & a more formidable antagonist to us than Lincoln; so therefore, Hurrah for Lincoln, the greatest and most corrupt fool of the age! He has attempted to buy off McClellan from the Presidential contest by an offer of the command of the army, flattering him with the assurance that a man of his patriotism will, he is sure, choose that post in which he can render the greatest service to his country & that his (McClellan's) military are greater than his diplomatic talents, but little Mac is "too old a bird to be caught by such chaff."

OCTOBER 19, 1864

Today Susan & the three Dunlops left us, so Mr E and I are once more in our normal state, alone in the house for the first time in more than six months—quite a contrast to this day week when we were twelve in family. All our fighting latterly has been on the North side of the James about Ft Harrison an outwork of Chaffin's Bluff, which the enemy is strengthening greatly; we undervalue the post now that we have lost it according to our invariable Southern custom. If it is of no use, why do we try so hard to retake it? On the 7th there was a heavy fight on the North bank in which we lost Gen Gregg of Texas killed & some prisoners but took more & repulsed the advance of the enemy with heavy loss. On the 11th the same scene on almost the same ground was reenacted with greater loss to Grant & less to us & every preparation is being made for a desperate attack upon us so soon as Butler has finished his famous canal across Dutch Gap, which the Yankees think is to work wonders in their behalf. The battle is to be waged on the river & on the land simultaneously. God grant us the Victory! We expect it just before their election leaving time enough only for them to lie if unsuccessful, to claim a victory even in the face of a defeat, & if successful, sound drums & "trumpets blare." Mr Lincoln will be floated triumphantly into the Presidential Chair amids the acclamations of the populace. "The Rebellion is crushed!" "The Union saved!" "The South conquered!" & so on ad nauseum." Query—do not the Yankee masses like to be deceived? & is not he amongst them the greatest man who can oftenest gull them? It seems so to us. Deliver us from such a people!

OCTOBER 22, 1864

There certainly must be a Yankee operator somewhere in our Telegraph offices in the Southwest. He lies so unmitigatably & unblushingly. Last week he flashed over the wires the news of a great victory at Alatoona, assured us that we had captured 300 prisoners & held the place & that Rome also was in our possession. It now proves to be all a falsehood & we cannot be too thankful to the Government for refusing its sanction to any such tissue of lies. The fact is that Maj Gen French, our old French of Cotton burning memory, attacked Alatoona, captured two lines of breastworks, & fell back from before the third, leaving his wounded & dead in the hands of the enemy & "rejoined his Corps with precipitation." I wonder if any thing better is expected from him. They lean on a broken reed who do. Rome is still in Yankee hands, but we are entrenched at Kenesaw & have completely destroyed all of Sherman's RR communication. He is cut off from his army by the interposition of ours between it & him, he having gone North to enjoy his laurels after taking Atlanta.

Mosby has been doing us yeomen service in Sheridan's rear. Some days since he defeated a party sent out to rebuild the Manassas Gap RR, taking the most of them prisoners, & securing a train of waggons & a large quantity of RR iron. Now he has made a sudden swoop upon the B & Ohio RR, destroyed a train, captured many officers & two paymasters with $200,000 in Green backs. Gen Lee has complimented him in Gen Orders & given an enumeration of the spoil he has taken & the loss he has inflicted on the enemy. This was previous to these last exploits; now the list is longer. The capture of the Manassass Gap party receives significance & importance from Sheridan's subsequent movements. He proceeded down the Valley, obeying Grant, the Monster, orders literally, leaving a desolation behind him until he reached Chester Gap when suddenly turning to the right he threw his corps across the Blue Ridge, intending to march in the direction of Alexandria & thence to reinforce Grant or else to ravage the Peidmont country & threaten Charlottsville & Gordonsville leaving one corps under Crook to amuse Early in the Valley. But Early was too wise to be thus caught. He threw himself through Thornton's Gap & fell suddenly on Sheridan's flank, defeated him with great loss, & drove him pell mell back through Chester Gap into the Valley & then suddenly falling upon Crook routed him & sent him "a toute bride" through Strasburg. This is not official news, but no doubt is entertained of the authenticity in Richmond. As yet no details are received. God be thanked, for this must seriously disconcert Grant, the butcher's, plans. It will strain Lincoln & Stanton's power of lying to the utmost, too, to conceal it until after the election. They deliberately falsified the Votes of both Penn & Maryland in claiming them for the Republicans. Their own organs now admit a large Democratic gain in the home votes of Penn & announce that Maryland has rejected the new Abolition constitution. The army vote of both States is to be heard from. The spirit of lies is certainly abroad.

Before Richmond & Petersburg all remains quiet, Grant digging & Butler busy with his Canal. He has put some of our prisoners, commissioned officers too, to work on it in retaliation, as he calls it, of our delivery of captured slaves into the hands of their own masters. What Yankee impudence! George the 4th might well say "that he had heard of 'Corinthian Brass,'[108] but he thought the American (i.e. Yankee) surpassed it."

Finished two knitted undershirts for Jessie today. I commenced them for myself but her want seeming greater than mine gave them to her, very soft, fine, & comfortable they are, and I hope they will be of use in re establishing her health.

October 25, 1864

What a life of uncertainty is ours! Came Mr Hill last night on his way from Court & told us that it was true that Early's victory had resulted in defeat. He

---

[108]The term Corinthian brass was used colloquially to denote excessive impudence or assurance.

urged pursuit too far, when the enemy turning recovered all & more than all he had lost. Nothing more of the circumstantial account but by passengers of his double victory on both sides of the Blue Ridge, so we are forced to the conclusion that it is a fabrication. God help our country! I fear me they are learning the Yankee vice of lying. Rumours brt by Mr G. Smith of a land attack on Wilmington, but he is proverbially unreliable & a sensation maker, so defer uneasiness even until something more definite. Bragg, I am sorry to say, has been sent there—a bad augury for us! Murad the Unlucky's fate will follow him. Mr H cheered us with the assurance that Lee had 25,000 reinforcements & was ready for Grant's grand attack. Nothing from Geo. Hood has forbidden dispatches being sent from his army & tho the papers are filled with conjectures, his very where-a-bouts is unknown. The papers publish a private letter of the Yankee Gen Custer so utterly repulsive, so shocking to all sense of decency or modesty or refinement, that I will not soil my repertory with it & wish I could wipe it from my memory as an injury done to my refinement by the knoledge even that such things are done in the world & this, "Fannie," to whom this shocking letter was written, is an associate of Mrs McClellan & moves in good Northern society. To what an abyss of corruption are they fallen! All day today at the plantation with Mr E. All hands there digging potatoes, a fine crop. Would that we could send of our abundance to our soldiers, but *transportation*—there is the difficulty. We are so deficient in *that* & the Yankees know it & therefore aim their blows at our RR's. Yesterday took up & housed my Dahlia roots & now for planting my hyacinths. So we go! A round of pleasures!

October 29, 1864

Afternoon—Just at home from the plantation where I dined with Mr E, a lovely day, the perfection of a dreamy autumn day! Every thing so still that you could almost hear the graceful fall of the many tinted leaves as they wavered down. The solitary chirp of the grasshopper, that note so associated with the fall & which he never uses until September, alone broke the intense silence. It is as tho nature is hushed into repose. Before closing her eyes for her winter's sleep she prepares for it by a season of meditation and prayer. Her ripened fruits, her matured grain stand forth a silent thank offering of Praise to Almighty God. One can scarcely beleive on such a day as this that a bloody and cruel war devastates our land, that men's pride & passion are making a ruin, yea a hell, of a land so calm, so quiet, so beautiful, but yet so it is.

Sheridan in the Valley has destroyed every thing before him. Blood & carnage, smoking ruins, the cries of houseless women & children alone mark his track. Our arms met with a serious disgrace on the 19th inst. Early attacked Sheridan, routed him, drove him before him for miles, capturing his waggon train, 15 peices of Artillery, his stores, ammunition, & transportation, but suddenly—one account says whilst our men were engaged in the pillage of a rich camp—a small body of cavalry appeared before our men flushed with victory. Then arose a wild cry of "We are flanked, we are flanked," & a general "sauve qui peut" commenced! Our own cavalry dashed in wild confusion through the town of Strasburg, alarming the artillery horses which became unmanageable & in the confusion the Yankees recaptured all they had lost, their guns & camp equipage. Sad to say [————] of our guns. Order being restored, the enemy retired too weak to press their advantage & night closed on the disgraceful scene. The Examiner says Apple Brandy did it all!

Another account says that Early defeated two army corps but came on the third securely entrenched, made three assaults upon it but being repulsed each time retired when the enemy following, cut up, defeated him, and recapturing all they had lost. But this is a lame story. But the divers accounts of the same battle which have found their way into print teach us one thing, at what value to rate all unofficial contemporary history. Our Generals & our Government, thank God, do not lie! Unlike the Yankee official statements, our can always be relied on. When Maj Gen Early makes his report we may depend upon getting the result truly. Sheridans' bombastic dispatch gives itself the lie. It is written only to glorify "Maj Gen Sheridan Comdg U S forces in the of Va."

All quiet before Richmond & Petersburg. The Darbytown defeat rises in importance as we get Northern accounts of it. One of their best Division Commanders—Birney, who led the attack, is dead; we say of wounds received there, they say of malarious fever contracted on the James. No authentic news from Hood. He hides himself as effectually as a cuttle fish. All we know is that the Yankees lie terribly about him & bluster over Sherman's position so that we beleive they lie about him also. I think, Mrs Edmondston, you had better stop, for you have given "the Lie" almost as often as Sir W Raleigh in his famous poem "Goe soul the body's guest."[109]

October 31, 1864

At church yesterday where heavy news met us. The Albemarle was sunk on Thursday morning by a Yankee Torpedo boat! She lies now at the wharf at Plymouth submerged but her guns out of water. Lieut Warley's[110] dispatch is of the breifest. We learn from it that she went down under heavy fire, that we

---

[109]This line of poetry, from *The Lie*, stanza 1, is usually attributed to Sir Walter Raleigh and was first published in 1608. *Chambers's Cyclopaedia of English Literature*, I, 308.

[110]Lt. Alexander F. Warley, commanding the *Albemarle*, reported from Plymouth on October 27, 1864: "At or about 3 o'clock a.m. on the 27th, the officer of the deck discovered a small steamer in the river, hailed her, received an unsatisfactory answer, rang the alarm bell, and opened fire. . . . The boat running obliquely, struck us under the port bow, running over the boom, exploded a torpedo, and smashed a large hole in us just under the water line. . . . The boat surrendered and I sent Lieutenant Roberts to take charge of her. . . . The water gained on us so fast that all our exertions were fruitless, and the vessel went down in a few moments, merely leaving her shield and smokestack out." The officer in charge of the Union torpedo launch, Lt. William B. Cushing, managed to escape by swimming to shore after his launch began to sink. Hiding until morning, he stole a skiff and rowed the eight miles back to Albemarle Sound and the Union navy. *Official Records (Navy)*, Series I, X, 624; *Civil War Naval Chronology*, IV, 124-126.

The *Albemarle* played an important role in the war before she was sunk on October 27 by Lt. William B. Cushing and fourteen men in a small launch. They sank her with a torpedo attached to a spar. Mrs. Edmondston commented on the *Albemarle* in several entries during the months the ram was in active service. (Photograph from Naval Photographic Center, Department of the Navy, Washington, D.C.)

Lieutenant Cushing, left, and Edward J. Houghton were the only survivors of the fifteen men who went on the successful expedition to sink the C.S.S. *Albemarle*. (Photograph from Naval Photographic Center, Department of the Navy, Washington, D.C.)

captured all of the crew of the Torpedo boat with the exception of the Captain, who was killed. No lives lost on our side. We hear unofficially that our young neighbor James Hill was slightly wounded in the ancle. Unless we can succeed in raising her before the Yankees attack us again it will go hard with us. She is our safe guard & the only assurance we have of holding Plymouth. If a Torpedo boat can come up & sink her in spite of our land batteries, of what effect will they be against Iron clad gunboats! All now depends on the skill and briskness of our engineers. Tonight came the first fruit of the uneasiness & anxiety which her loss will occasion us. As Mr E & I sat at our Tea after a day spent at the Plantation, a day of disappointments, too, for I went down in my riding dress expecting to spend the morning in a ride on horseback with him over the farm, but was prevented by visitors whom we met on the way & who returned & dined with us there—but to go back from this digression to what happened whilst Mr E & I sat at Tea. There came a peaceable enough looking letter from Mr John Davis which, on being opened, was found to be dated at Raleigh, Oct 31st, today & contained an order signed by Gen Gatlin, Adgt Gen, for Mr E to take his company at once to Plymouth & there report to Gen Baker.

It being suspiciously unofficial in appearance & wording & being directed originally to Capt 'Edmonds,' & erased by pencil marks & 'Edmondston' written in a different hand—containing no orders for the other companies in this Battalion ('tho the Battalion in Maj Pearson's absence is under Mr E's command), being dated at Raleigh *today*, & no evidence whatever about it to show that it was an Express Dispatch, no date at "Weldon Office of Express Co" etc., that Mr E. knows not what to think of it, but ordered his horse & went at once to Mr Davis' three miles through the woods—& the night pitchy dark—to ascertain where he got it & whose were the endorsements on the back & other little queries as to its antecedents, which he deems neccessary before he orders the remnant of a Co—which the late draught has left him— to rendez vous at Plymouth. The force there must be weak indeed if these Home Guards now here are needed, undrilled, old, feeble, & undisciplined as they are. So I being left alone sent Neptune to the Soltaire where my journal has spent the summer & confide my cares, anxieties, & sorrows to its faithful bosom!

Details of our late disaster in the Valley make us blush deeper & deeper over the unaccountable panic which seized our troops. Can it be beleived that twenty five Yankee Cavalry recaptured eighteen of their own guns & took twenty three additional ones of ours?! & yet so it is! We defeated & routed them shamefully, took three camps & all their artillery & waggon train, stopped for five hours, dispersed to plunder & feast on the good things in the Yankee commissariat, when a small Yankee force reformed & advanced, it is now thought to reconnoitre, when hey! presto, a wild panic set in & abandoning everything our frightened men rushed pell mell down the road in utter confusion. The Yankees were so astonished that they stood utterly dumbfounded & looked on the rout! Twenty five cavalry spurred on the artillery train, sabred a few drivers, broke down a small bridge in its front, & quietly turned the horses heads & marched them off the scene! Early sent for five hundred men to retake them & was told that not a Maj Gen on the field had so many under his command. Next morning, however, they reorganized themselves and were all in rank again. Our loss is but slight. In the Victory 1000 will cover it all; in the defeat 500 prisoners & a few only killed. Maj Gen Ramseur was wounded & fell into the hands of the enemy, whether in the victory or the defeat I cannot gather. He died the next morning—a sad fate. Just married, after long opposition; a good officer & an excellent young man. God be with his poor young wife!

Letters from my nephew Tom Devereux give a most graphic account of the scene. He says "I reckon one half our army was in the rear plundering the enemy's camps which they had abandoned," but his letter only confirms amusingly what I have written above, so I will not repeat it. He gives a sad picture of the desolation Sheridan has wrought. He tells us that "you people at home do not know what war is. Just look at this Valley. There are but five mills from Stanton to Strasburg—seventy miles. In the same space they have burned 2000 two thousand barns & I do not know how many dwelling houses. They burnt every barn that had wheat in it & drove off every cow, hog, or sheep that they could lay their hands on." I have preserved Sheridans official account of his own barbarities. "Out of his own mouth" we "judge" him.

The shelling of Charleston has got to be such a regular every day peice of barbarity that it ceases to make much impression on anyone. The damage to life & limb is slight & where the damage done to property is at once repaired, that is slight also; but if the breaches in roof or walls are neglected & the weather adds its influences to the injury already sustained, the work of destruction goes on rapidly. Some gentlemen absentees have carpenters & stone masons engaged by contract to visit their houses every day and repair the damage instantly. The shells have a range of about five miles; 200 lb Parrot Guns are their favorite engines.

All Hallow'een! What a night of merriment in days gone by! What a contrast to my present, sitting alone watching for my husband who is abroad on an errand of War, for Owen has just come in with a message from him to the effect that he had gone to Mr Shields, his 1st Lieut, I suppose to order out the company—so the missive was authentic.

NOVEMBER 2, 1864

What a life of excitement, anxiety, & distress is that led by a people exposed as we are to the viscissitudes of War! Got Mr E ready to take the field yesterday, got provisions for some days, packed his carpet satchel, over hauled all his military accoutrements, & resolutely kept down all the sad forebodings which in spite of me would sometimes rise in my heart & almost choke me. He absent all the morning getting his Company ready. At dinner he came in & electrified me with the tidings that Lieut Warley, the Commandant of the Albemarle, had blown her up! As we feared the Yankee gun boats made an immediate advance & shelled the town.[111] Rumour had it that we repulsed them, sending one boat off in a sinking condition; but that can scarcely be so, for subsequently we hear that the Yankees got a position in Little River, from whence they could not be dislodged because Gen Martin in his wisdom having leveled an earthwork known as Ft Warren in which was a battery, which commanded the position.

This act of Lieut Warley's cannot be sufficiently condemned. It is premature to say the least of it, for until the Yankees actually entered the place, or the terms of capitulation were about to be discussed, it was his duty to stand by his ship & resolutely defend her. She lay in water so shallow that her guns were not submerged & ten days work would have set her afloat again. But no! the fashion set by Com Tatnall, when he blew up the Virginia, must be followed by every other numbskull in the Confederate navy who, like him, gets drunk and neglects his duty. The explosion covers up all. He goes off in a blaze of false glory and nonsensical heroism but takes excellent care that his own person shall not suffer. The subsequent event proves how wrong, how wickedly foolish, it was thus to destroy her; for tho we had a strong force there, 4 Regts & 2 batteries, no sooner did they hear the explosion which destroyed one of the main objects of their defence than they became demoralized & rumour says "*ran!*" but this last needs confirmation.

Suffice it to say, in the words of Capt Cook in a hasty letter he wrote Mr E this morning . . .

Plymouth is in possession of the Yankees. All our artillery captured & all the guns & horses of the Montgomery Blues captured except two guns & a few of the horses. I am having all the guns I have at Halifax brt down to mount at Ft Branch. All of our forces have fallen back to that point, three Regts & Nelson's Artillery & the two guns of the Montgomery Blues.

And so goes all our security & the delightful sense of freedom from the personal presence of our hated enemies. So it all goes & we are once more

---

[111]With the destruction of the *Albemarle*, Comdr. W. H. Macomb of the Union navy, in charge of the District of the Sounds, North Atlantic Squadron, determined to attack the batteries at Plymouth. The squadron found the Roanoke River below Plymouth blocked by sunken ships opposite the batteries and was forced to ascend Middle River and enter the Roanoke above Plymouth to carry out the attack. Heavy firing ensued and one Union ship was heavily damaged before the explosion of a Confederate magazine forced the Confederates to evacuate Fort Williams and Plymouth. The Federal forces captured thirty-seven prisoners, twenty-two cannon, a large quantity of ordnance stores, and the sunken remains of the *Albemarle*, which was not destroyed as Mrs. Edmondston reported. *Official Records (Navy)*, Series I, XI, 12-15; *Civil War Naval Chronology*, IV, 127.

plunged into the sea of doubt & anxiety which was our position before the for-tification of Rainbow Banks, for be it known to you O, Journal, that some Confederate Gen,—Beauregard it is whispered, ordered that strong point to be dismantled, saying that the possession of Plymouth rendered it unnec-cessary. Yes, but he never dreamed that that strong point would be in such hands as those of Lieut Warley & Gen Lawrence Baker. Gen Baker has known & has spoken of the insufficient guard kept there by one drunken Col Wortham[112] & yet he having the power to remedy it has passively let it go on until the result is seen in drunken worthless pickets who let the Torpedo boat come up and sink what was better than five thousand men to us & open the door to Lieut Warley's hasty act. The best commentary on the defence is the fact that we lost *three* only killed & fifty prisoners who, being new conscripts from that part of the country, gave themselves up in hope of being released but the Yankees handcuffed every man of them. Perhaps, however, that was for ef-fect. From all we learn now it was a disgraceful peice of business. Plymouth was conquered by Apple Brandy (drunk by whom, I hope a Court Martial will declare). This is the verdict of the neighborhood. How true it is, it is for others to decide. Today came a Telegram which should have been received yesterday countermanding the order for Mr E to take his compan*ies* (plural this time) to Plymouth, so once more but for how long we know not we are allowed to remain at home.

"Turn we the picture" from demoralization & defeat to triumph & victory. Gen Lee has had a brilliant success. He has repulsed three assaults on our right, centre, and left signally. We have over his own official signature (and when did that ever deceive us?) an assurance that on the North side on which two attacks were made he was repulsed with the loss of several hundred prisoners and 4 stands of colours, "our loss slight." This on Oct 27th. On the 28th he tells us that in Heth's attack the day before, Mahone captured 400 pris, 3 stands of colours, and 8 peices of artillery, which however "could not be brt off, the enemy holding the bridge. In the attack subsequently made by the enemy, Mahone broke through 3 lines of breastworks & during the night the enemy retreated from the Boydton road leaving his wounded & more than 250 dead in the field. About nine a small force assaulted & took possession of our works on the Baxter road but were soon driven out. On the Williamsburg road Gen Field captured upwards of 400 pris & 7 stands of colours. The enemy left a number of dead & wounded in our front & today retreated to his former position."

That occupation of our lines on the Baxter road was effected by a Yankee trick. After night a no of them came up to our picket line professing to be deserters, having short carbines concealed under their clothes, & as Gen

---

[112]George W. Wortham (1828-1883), of Granville County, was colonel of the Fiftieth North Carolina Regiment. Clark, *Histories of the North Carolina Regiments*, III, 161, 198, 202.

Cooper has ordered all such to be hospitably received & entertained they were allowed to enter, but their sheeps clothing having fallen off, they were soon driven out with much loss to themselves.

Grant has since remained sulkily within his lines waiting for his Lieuts to gain laurels for him from such posts as Plymouth & such men as Early. Poor old Jubal! He became so jubilant over the victory which Gordon won for him that he did not stop to secure it & let 25 Yankee horseman snatch it from his grasp. He has issued an address to his troops censuring them severely & if it is true that he was drunk himself, he must be made of Corinthian Brass to be able to pen it.

November 3, 1864

Not one word from Hood & the Yankees are equally ignorant about Sherman. For the first time since the invention of the Telegraph, says the Examiner, "two large armies have disappeared wholy from sight." The capture of Plymouth hangs like a pall on our spirits. God's will be done. He exalts & He depresses! Grant us faith to see His hand in it & to know & confess that that state in which He places us is the one in which it is best for us to be. The weather is just into the Yankee's hands for it has rained incessantly since yesterday morning, the very thing for them, for it will raise the river & enable their boats to run up. The river is now & has been for months very low in consequence of unusual dry weather. God knows what is for our best! Knitting steadily on father's undershirts all day. Mr E read to me, a now unusual treat, "Martin or the Memoirs of a Statesman." Very interesting & suggestive it is. History reproduces itself. Would that we could learn the lesson it teaches us.

November 4, 1864

Yesterday knit 14,600 stitches on Father's undershirt besides reading & house keeping. It (the shirt) begins to look immense!

November 7, 1864

At the plantation getting my hyacinths in the ground. Set with my own hand 608 (six hundred & eight) splendid blossoming bulbs (Owen dug the holes) & my store of smaller bulbs which need a year's growth to perfect them is to large to count. Was interrupted by rain & came home to Hascosea in a drizzle, my little nephew John Devereux accompanying us.

November 15, 1864

Have been busy this last week either going to the plantation with Mr E or gardening. Have planted two squares in my garden with tea, one from plants raised this summer, the other with roots of the current year, so we shall in a few years be independant of the blockade. Have also done what I ought to have done years ago i.e., made a large Fig Plantation. Some of these days I will rival Smyrna in my own dried figs. Who knows?

All quiet along our lines. Now that their election is over the Yankees confess they never beat Price in Missouri & that their recent heavy demonstrations along our lines, which they then called a "reconnoisance in force" and said their loss was slight, was intended to be a general assault & advance but that they were repulsed with heavy loss. Some of their papers even state it at 7000!

There is little doubt that Mr Lincoln is re elected President of the U S. I wish that Gen Lee would order a shotted salute along our whole line in honour of the event, receive him with defiance as well as exultation, for there is little doubt he is our best antagonist; the weaker the man, the weaker the Government, & to use his own classic words, "a precious mess" he has "got into."

No news of Hood but that he has crossed the Tennessee & is going to conduct his campaign in middle Tennessee where there are abundant supplies of all kinds. Forrest has had a signal success at Johnsonville—sunk gun boats and transports, destroyed immense army supplies. The enemy had in addition to what was in their transports a space covering ten acres of forage, supplies, & army munition, all of which Forrest destroyed by fire. Mr E in Halifax all day attending to the second class HD who are ordered to the front, the first Class having served the time for which they were called out.

NOVEMBER 17, 1864

Mr E again all day at Halifax & I have had a hard days work all alone. I yesterday went to see father & for the first time in my life driving myself in the buggy! I was not well enough to go on horseback & as our faithful old carriage horse "Jim," who has carried me about for ten years at least, died this summer, the buggy is my only conveyance, so with my little maid Betsy by my side & Dick for a Courier, I held the reins & let old Grachus take his own way up to Conneconara. Found Father quite unwell with cold & chills & so much delighted with his new undershirt which I carried him & so confident that it was all he wanted to cure him that I told him he could put it on immediately, as I would undertake to have another one done 'ere he wanted a change. So came home & went to work from tea to 11 o'clock knit as rapidly as I could & a good record my fingers left of themselves, for I knit 10,880 stitches.

This morning put up Jessie's 2 shirts to go by Express. Mr McMahon[113] (Express Agent) valued one of them at *$75* (seventy five dollars)! Wrote her a letter, put up Mr E's dinner, & a loaf of bread for Captain Cook, who I am sorry to say is in very bad health, gave Mr Walker, a soldier, his breakfast and hunted up a blanket for him, put up an undershirt which I had mended up for

---

[113]M. McMahon was a twenty-seven-year-old merchant born in Ireland. Eighth Census, 1860, Population Schedule, Halifax County, 83.

another soldier who has been separated from his baggage & caught in this severe weather with neither overcoat or Flannel & he a feeble man detailed on light duty—one Mr Holmes. Weighed my butter & sent up to Halifax the first instalment of a payment in it for a block of cotton for my own wear & then set to work, & tho interrupted by my Vinegar manufacture & some trouble about a tight barrel, by constantly plying my fingers I finished the body of the second undershirt, got it washed & strained out on the table to dry & by four o'clock was ready for a walk over to Mr John Lawrence's[114] to call on Miss Ida Whitton, my maid Fanny attending me. I knit 5776 stitches & it took 140 pins, the positions of all of which had to be altered & tightened once & some of them twice before the shirt was properly strained to its full dimensions, so as it is not yet 7 o'clock I do not think I have been idle today. As I abuse myself soundly for indolence, sometimes I think I am excusable in occasionally enumerating my acts when I am the reverse. I am now just listening for Mr E's footstep, when tea, a nice chat, the newspapers, a little more knitting, and to bed. Mr E is in command of the Battalion, the 46th Bat N C H D, & this week he has been kept busy enough ordering out the 2d class.

Looking over some old papers a few days since I found some lines on "Twilight" written when I was quite a young girl. I have slightly altered the phraseology only in one or two lines but have not touched or changed one of the ideas & preserve them here as a kind of memory of what I was when I wrote them. I well remember the evening. They are dated Charleston Feb 18th 1845.

Twilight—

Now tis the hour when like a timid bride the Earth
Drops her soft silvery veil, to hide her blushes from her Bride-
    groom's gaze,
Hush! in its inmost essence let thy wrapt spirit drink in the in-
    tense silence.
Thou may'st hear! nay—thou may'st feel! the great heart of Nature
    beat!—
Through her whole being throbs one vast pulsation! & our human
    hearts
Catching the inspiration, beat with it in melodious unison!

Is there one so dull—so wrapt in earthly care
That at the approach of Twilight, he doth not feel his worldiness
    dissolve,
And as a heavy vapour rolling off—leave behind it naught but high
    & deep & holy affections.

---

[114]In 1860 John T. Lawrence, a thirty-eight-year-old farmer born in Northampton County, lived in Halifax County with his wife, five children, and an overseer, E. M. Whitehead. Eighth Census, 1860, Population Schedule, Halifax County, 51.

Tis then that purified from Earthly dross & free, the Soul, leaving
    its tenements
Hovers o'er all it holds most dear; contemning time & space it
    trembling flies
Mingling its essence with a dear one's thoughts!

            Leaving Earth 'tis free to soar at will
And stand on high, full in the presence of its God! shrinking it
    stands,!
And trembling holds commune with Holiness.
Then O' then it is that rising full in view its vileness, & its
    guilt, refuse concealment
And o'erwhelmed with its own nothingness—the fainting heart—
    feels in its

              force—the Atonement!—

                    Charleston Feb. 18th 1845—

I wish I had kept more of my youthful effusions. It in a way rejuvenates me to read them & I seem to take up an old train of thought & feeling in a manner unexpressibly pleasant to me. It is as tho I am the same & yet not the same person all at once. I can correct crudities & awkwardnesses but somehow amidst any criticisms comes a vein of the freshness of youth which enchants & disarms me. I remember so well what I thought & felt when I wrote the above lines. It was just one year before my marriage. Ah Time! What a gilder thou art!

November 20, 1864

All ready (in fact partly moved, my wardrobe being gone) to move to the Plantation for the winter but kept here by bad weather for two days. Finished Father's second undershirt last night & I find that there are only 66,064 stitches in each, much fewer if my memory serves me correctly than in the last I knit for him, but these are stouter. As yet all quiet before Petersburg & Richmond but the Yankees have recalled all furloughs & ordered every man to report to his command by the 14th inst, so as the Dutch Gap Canal is nearly finished, their grand 'coup' will not be long delayed. We uninitiated have just learned why they dig that canal, for they hold certainly one bank of the river all around the bend, but it seems that fearing that our iron clads would come down & attack them, they some time in the summer sunk obstructions to prevent it. In the meantime we constructed batteries which commanded these same obstructions & when they wished to take them up, they found themselves unable to do so under the heavy fire which it was in our power to concentrate on them, hence the necessity for their famous canal! They outwitted themselves in that instance.

Gen Beauregard telegraphs to Gen Cooper that Forrest (at Johnsonville) destroyed four gunboats, eight guns each, fourteen steamers, & twenty barges & between seventy five & one hundred thousand tons of Commissary & Qr. Master's stores on the landing & in warehouses. The movements of Hood & Sherman are still wrapped in mystery. Hood is in Central Tenn. The Yankees say that Sherman has abandoned his fruitless search after him & has returned to Atlanta & that at the head of a movable column he intends to hurl himself at Augusta, Savannah, & Charleston & that the nation is soon to be electrified by the tidings which they will hear from him. Some amongst us contend that he will march South through the Cotton States & take Mobile in the rear, but very few attach any importance to any such threats, regarding it as a mere canard to throw us off our guard & that his real object is to fall on Hood's flank, whilst Thomas is to confront him before Nashville. Pray God that Beauregard divine & defeat his designs and O! may he have faithful scouts & the best of Cavalry which will indeed be to him as "eyes to an army," which good Cavalry always are.

The enemy came up to Jamesville a few days since from Plymouth but were repulsed. We even have rumours of the burning and evacuation of Plymouth itself but no one credits them. If in this comparatively quiet part of the country it is impossible to obtain authentic information of what goes on within fifty miles of us, what difficulties must beset Beauregard & Hood in that war tost country where they are? How much depends on a faithful scout and what a hazardous service it is they render us!

Mosby is rivaling the fame of a Paladin of Romance. The loss he inflicts on the enemy is absolutely amazing & his hair breadth escapes & gallant deeds of daring would fill a volume. He has made the Yankees abandon the Manassas Gap R R & is by stern retaliation forcing them to treat him & his captured men according to the usages of war. Seven of his men were hung under the plea that theirs was not regular war fare. It is even reported that they were tortured for hours, as is the manner of savages, before being put to death; but bad as they are I cannot credit that without proof. But a night or two after Mosby, in sight of the Yankee camp (had it been day), hung four & shot three of his prisoners & left the bodies with placards affixed saying by whom and for what they were killed.

Sometime since a proposition was made in some of the papers to conscript & arm as soldiers a body of negroes & thus reinforce our army, holding out as incentives to faithful service in the field the promise of freedom after the war was over. I considered it so wild & ill considered a scheme that I never once mentioned it, but Mr E. thinking it best to combat the begining of evil, in an able paper over the signature of "South" in the Richmond Enquirer, reviewed the whole ground & pointed out the inevitable result of such a measure in a manner at once forcible & convincing. His article has excited great attention

& commendation in some quarters, whilst others have attempted to refute it but in a manner so feeble as to show that they do not grasp the subject in its full bearings.

The President in his late Message suggests the propriety of taking 40,000 slaves & making pioneer labourers & engineers of them, hinting at the promise of ultimate freedom & pointing plainly to the fact that should we find it necessary to arm our slaves this 40,000 trained & disciplined body would be the nucleus of the organization. Upon this hint some wise Congressman has introduced a bill for the enrollment, & I beleive impressment, of I know not how many negroes for active service in the field next spring! Can one credit it? That a Southern man, one who knows the evils of free negro-ism, can be found willing to inflict such a curse on his country? I am sorry to say I fear Mr Davis was but speaking for effect and rather to the *Yankee nation* than to his *own*. I am sorry, I say, for I consider such conduct undignified & unworthy of Mr Davis, for that he really advocates the measure I cannot & will not beleive, but that that silly Congress should consume their own time & our money in a grave discussion over the best means of destroying the country is a depth of folly deeper than I can fathom!

November 23, 1864

Came down yesterday from Hascosea for the winter having been detained by bad weather for four days. It was quite time, for one could almost fancy themselves in "the Cave of the Winds." Outside a continual drip! drip! drip!, inside a howling & humming as tho every door & window had resolved themselves into an Eolian Harp & were tuned to Concert pitch. It is far more pleasant here in our little snuggery in cold or wet weather than in that large empty Hascosea House. It does not do for two people to cower over the fire in a space meant for twelve. One feels one's own finitude too keenly! Suffered an infliction for two mortal hours this morning (three would be nearer the mark) in the shape of a visitation from one of our neighbors at home on furlough. The minuteness with which he related his adventures, how the Yankees ran him, how "nigh they come to hitting of him," & the quantity of tobacco he spit on the andirons so wearied & disgusted me that I got quite nervous & was essentially releived when he stated his business, viz., (to get Mr E to have his saddle bags mended) & departed. One naive confession he made to the effect that he would not go into another such a battle as he escaped from "no not for $50,000," & yet the man is no coward. Thus is it to be, I fear, for some years to come. Every man of small calibre has come home a hero with a string of adventures as long as a three volume novel which "against the stomach of your sense" he insists on pouring into your ear. Well poor fellows! Perhaps it is their meed & I ought not to grudge them the little gratification of a harmless vanity, but it is a terrible bore nevertheless.

November 25, 1864

Dined at Father's yesterday. All well but himself. Sister B & Rachel there, so there is a houseful. Shermans move the engrossing subject. Where is he going? He has sent out detachments in so many directions who have carried fire & sword with them that it is hard to discover the situation of his main body. He leaves a waste behind him, but as his intentions cannot long be veiled, speculation here is useless; but my heart bleeds for the poor people not only along his route but on his various threatened routes. What terrible suffering do one & what heart sickening suspense do the others endure! God be with them & give them the fruition of His promise, "As thy days are so shall thy strength be." Out this morning with Mr E on horseback riding all over the crop, a delightful day & I enjoyed the resumption of my old habits greatly. The crop shows the drought & also the triumph of his secret ditches. Some land which never made *anything* before has a fair crop upon it and other peices are much improved. So much for enlightened husbandry!

Mrs. Edmondston refers to her father-in-law's love of Scotland in her November 30, 1864, entry. The Edmondston ancestral home, Hascosea, in Lerwick, Shetland Islands, Scotland, is pictured above. (Photograph from files of Beth Crabtree.)

NOVEMBER 30, 1864

St Andrew's—How this day reminds me of Papa! What an anniversary it was to him & how he enjoyed the annual meeting of the St Andrew's Society. He was the centre & heart of the Scotchmen in Charleston & the widow's and daughters of many of his deceased countrymen looked to him as their protector & nearest friend. For years was he President of the Society & the interest he took in the dispersing the funds of that noble charity ceased but with his death.

Georgia is the all engrossing point now. All eyes and hearts are fixed there. For days have we been kept in the most cruel suspense, one rumour contradicting another before we had fairly taken in the first one. Whether Milledgeville is burned or not, time only will disclose to us. Atlanta I think we can now beleive is evacuated, but even that is not certain, such are the consequences of a destruction of all R Rs & Telegraphs. Gen Wayne (Adjt Gen of Georgia) we are told holds the bridge over the Oconee, but Sherman may flank that militia force & get to Savannah, if that is his destination, without a fight. Beauregard is out in a stirring proclamation to the Georgians telling them he will soon be with them. Bragg, I am sorry to say, has gone there. It seems an augury of success to Sherman, but it is worse than useless to mention all the reports and rumours we hear. Whilst on horseback with Mr E yesterday, heard heavy firing towards Petersburg, but we get our mails so irregularly that it may be days ere we learn the result. Ah! for peace!

DECEMBER 3, 1864

A terrible rumour which makes the very core of my heart ache has reached us today. They say that the enemy have taken Stoney Crk Station & 300 negroes. Nothing else, no account of fighting or loss of any other kind. Stoney Crk is ten miles or more south of Ream's Station & should they be able to maintain themselves there, God help this section of country!

DECEMBER 4, 1864

Had my faith been stronger I might have saved myself yesterday's heartache, for we learned at night that the attack on Stoney Crk was a predatory raid only, the Depot & some few Commissary stores & forage captured and burned, when on the approach of Fitz Hugh Lee the enemy retreated rapidly carrying off however some 100 or 200 prisoners. No news of Sherman.

DECEMBER 9, 1864

Have been for the last week on such a qui vive of expectation, expectation each day disappointed & hope deferred until the next, that I have not cared to write until I had something definite to say of Sherman & even now all I can say is that he is still in Georgia, devastating & burning as he goes. Our troops have concentrated there & the papers bid us be of good cheer & assure us that the War Depart has cheering news which for the present it is best not to publish. So I hope on, tho this is now the 27th day since he evacuated Atlanta when we expected & by authority, too, to hear of his annihilation or surrender. Beauregard is there, however, and he may nulify Braggs unfortunate presence.

Foster made a demonstration up Broad River with transports, Gunboat, & Monitors, landed at Pocotaligo & marched inland it was supposed to create a diversion in Sherman's favour, but at Grahamville he was met by a body of our troops & held in check until reinforcements arriving he was driven back to his boats. The engagement on our side was a most handsome & spirited affair, for we were far inferior in numbers. It reflects great credit on the officers in command (Gen Gustavus Smith and his troops were for the most part raw Georgia Militia for the first time under fire) tho who the superior was I cannot learn for we have lost so many papers latterly that we are behind the times.

The Yankees tell us that Thomas has beaten Hood signally. They lost 500, we 7,000 men, but as Thomas immediately fell back from Franklin to a point within three miles of Nashville, & Hood's cavalry crossed Duck River on their flank whilst his army "continued to press on," their paper victory does not distress us in the least. The Yankees are great financers and understand the pulse of the Gold market exactly.

Father, Dr and Mrs Osborne, & Sister Betsy dined with us today, Mama being too unwell to come down. Had a pleasant day, some what saddened by the news rec'd from Halifax that a column of the enemy 20,000 strong were advancing on Belfield, their supposed objective point being Weldon. I remember my panic last week over Stoney Crk & endeavour to possess my soul in quietness, but it is hard to do. Gen Lee has his troops well in hand & I cannot think he will allow one of his main lines of communication to be thus cut with impunity. State troops are hastening to Weldon & trains pass laden with soldiers, so we must hope for the best. We miss Hampton now. Had not the necessities of the service called him to Georgia, this would never have happened. He is sending back a good account of himself there, however. He has defeated Kilpatrick, more than Wheeler has yet been able to say for himself.

It has pleased the Yankee Nation to resume one of the practices of civilized warfare and to consent to an exchange of prisoners. The cartel has accordingly been resumed and several thousand of our unfortunate men delivered at Savannah. Their condition almost beggars description; sick, ragged, & emaciated, their own mothers would scarcely know them. The deaths that occurred in the passage alone fill a long column of closely printed newspaper. The names are printed consecutively two or more on a line in small print and yet to that length does the death roll extend! Comment is useless. The Exchange is to continue & Charleston is now selected as the point at which it is to be effected, so for the present the shelling of the city ceases. The seige has now been continued five hundred and fourteen days.

DECEMBER 13, 1864

"The enemy repulsed at Bellfield," is the cheering Telegram which reaches us from Halifax. "Reported however as advancing on Kinston & troops are being rushed back to that point," so in their desire to create a division in Sherman's favour they keep us on the qui vive. As for him "Sherman the Desolater" we hear of him within twenty five miles of Savannah, we skirmishing with him as he goes. Foster is making another attempt on the R R near Poctaligo, in which I hope the Geo militia will repeat the lesson they gave him at Grahamville a few days since. The battle is known as that at Honey Hill & Gen Gustavus Smith commanded. Georgia militia almost exclusively fought it though they were near the close reinforced by some Confederate troops. All honour to them. No news from Hood or Nashville, save through Yankee medium & they are too false to be recorded.

Brother dined with us today. Looks well and does not seem so *very* despondant, tho he says Sherman will get through & Lee's evacuation of Petersburg and Richmond is "but a question of time." Lee will fall back by the South Side R R to Danville & the upper Roanoke & leave this country to be pillaged at leisure by Yankee marauders! This is in the future? I cannot beleive it & will not weaken myself or dim my faith by contemplating it. Our times are in His hands who knows what is for our best & He has promised that "as our days so shall our strength be." He told us of an instance of oppression hideous to contemplate. Mr Lucius Polk,[115] brother of the late Gen Polk & father of Brigadier Lucius Polk, remarked of Sherman's letter published last spring, in which he set forth his notions as to the best manner to deal with the South, that it was *infamous*. For this he was arrested, carried to Nashville, thrown into prison, & after a time tried by court martial & sentenced to be banished to South America. Some influential friends interposing, however, the sentence was commuted to the payment of $50,000 and an imprisonment. Has the North lost all memory of Freedom? A free speech & free press were once their boast. Where have they gone?

Very busy over the Dye Pot. We wear homespun only & every step needs my close supervision. War is certainly teaching us to live economically & within ourselves. Dr Osborne dined with us. He tells us that a certain cure for an old sore is to bathe it constantly in Glauber salts, i.e., in water in which Glauber Salts is dissolved, a cold application used as a constant lotion. We

---

[115]Lucius Junius Polk (1802-1869) of Maury County, Tennessee, a brother of Leonidas Polk, was not the father of Brig. Gen. Lucius Eugene Polk (1833-1892). Lucius E. Polk was the son of Dr. William Julius Polk, a half brother of Leonidas and Lucius Junius Polk. Polk, *Leonidas Polk: Bishop and General*, I, 48, 146; Ashe, *Biographical History*, II, 365.

have a most inveterate case, Nelson, for whom he prescribes it. If it cures
him—no one need despond.

DECEMBER 14, 1864

No mail last night but such a number of rumours that we are at no loss for
speculations. In the first place Hood has beaten Thomas, captured 7000
prisoners, & killed I forget how many. Knoxville & Chattanooga are
evacuated & in our possession. The force at Belfield has been beaten & driven
back. Beauregard has beaten Sherman & the Yankees have captured Ft
Branch, Col Hinton[116] & all his men, so the "reliable gentleman" &
"passengers" tell us. O! I forgot heavy fighting all along Lee's lines, particularly between Howlett's & Chaffin's Bluff & a fight in progress at
Kinston, food enough for thought. Today however Mr E learned at the Gunboat that Ft Branch was not taken, neither were Hinton's men, Hinton himself being the only capture and that the enemy had retreated to Plymouth
again. The mail tonight brought us but little satisfaction, all our papers being
old, so we must wait in suspense another 24 hours.

Letters from Aiken, however, give us an account of a fight at Tulafinny
Bridge about five miles below Pocotaligo, another desperate attempt by
Foster to cut the Charleston & Savannah R R in which God be thanked he
was again foiled. In this battle Amo was severely (tho not dangerously, thank
God) wounded in the head. His escape has been a narrow one, his sister says
"the sixteenth part of an inch above the temple." His mother writes, "I send
you an account of the late fight at Coosawatchie in which our boy Amo was
severely, tho thank God not dangerously, wounded in the forehead. You will
observe the names of five others (Cadets), one of them Jos. W. Barnwell, a
younger son of the Rev W H Barnwell, whom you remember. He was shot in
the knee and dropped instantly. Amo and one of the Cadets immediately
rushed forward to pick him up, when Allen Green fell shot in the cheek. Amo
snatched Green's gun, took deliberate aim & saw the Yankee who had shot
Green drop. He then carried Joe Barnwell to the rear & turning his head to
pass an order (he acting as adjutant to the corps) received this ball, it striking
him in a slanting direction in the forehead & glancing over the left temple. He
fell without knowing anything more. Charles E was just in the act of firing his
gun, when one of the Cadets called out "Lieut Coffin's killed!" Shot in the
head! Charlie says he felt as tho he was shot & his eyes felt blinded & he
knows he missed his aim. He did not look in the direction in which his brother

---

[116]James W. Hinton, a lawyer residing in Pasquotank County at the time of his enlistment, had served as
lieutenant colonel of the Eighth Regiment North Carolina State Troops until his promotion in 1863 as
colonel of the Sixty-eighth North Carolina Regiment. This regiment was detailed for duty within the state,
although under Confederate authority. Colonel Hinton was captured during a skirmish near Hamilton on
December 13, 1864. Moore, *Roster of North Carolina Troops*, I, 273; IV, 147; Manarin and Jordan, *North
Carolina Troops*, IV, 521, 523; Clark, *Histories of the North Carolina Regiments*, III, 713, 721-722.

was until someone called out "Coffin go pick up your brother," when he ran
to him and found one of the Cadets assisting him to rise. . . . Charlie carried
him to the rear where the wound was examined and dressed by Dr R W
Gibbs. . . . Charlie was detailed for the purpose of carrying the wounded
home. . . . We were not aware that the boys had left the Citadel. . . . You can
imagine then, my dear Kate, my shock on having my two boys come home on
Friday, Amo very pale from loss of blood with his head bound up & Charlie
excited and weary. . . . Amo is quite cheerful and sends much love to yourself
and Uncle. . . . Lizzie tells me that when Amo shot the Yankee who wounded
Green, that Green thanked him most heartily & told him "*it made him feel so
much better.*" Characteristic! It is a week today since he was wounded; we shall
feel seriously uneasy & unhappy until we hear again. God be with him, watch
over, & restore him to health speedily.

DECEMBER 20, 1864

The news from Sherman so old & meagre that it is not worth recording—
rumours of fights whose results never reach us, threats of "cutting him off"
which seem doomed never to be executed. He has burned the trestle work of
the R R Bridge across the Savannah, holds a portion of the Gulf R Road, &
has made several assaults on our lines all of which have been repulsed. We
now hear he has carried by assault Ft McAllister on the Ogeechee. If so, he
must be in communication with the gun boats, for this is the point which
made so desperate a defense against them months ago. I fear me Savannah
will fall if it be true. Beauregard left there in the last train which went over the
Charleston & Savannah Road & passed through a terrific shelling at
Pocotaligo, but God preserved him to us & turned aside the missiles of death
from his path. It showed true moral courage in him thus to leave a
beleaguered city, for his command extends over Tenn, Geo, & Kentucky, and
who can tell what the loss to the *Cause* would be were he to be captured? The
plans of a campaign are in his head & neither his life or his fate are his own.

We have Hood's official dispatch concerning the battle of Franklin. We
gained a victory but a dearly bought one. We drove the enemy

from the centre lines of their temporary works into their inner lines, which they
evacuated in the night, leaving their dead & wounded in our possession & retired on
Nashville closely pursued by our cavalry. . . . We have to lament the loss of many
gallant officers & brave men, *Major Gen Cleburne*, Brig Gens John Williams, Wirt
Adams, Gist, Strahl and Granberry killed; Major Gen John Brown, Brig Gens Carter, Manigault, Quarles, Cockrell, and Scot wounded, & Brig Gen Gordon captured.

A sad list. Cleburne was the soul of the army. He it was who retrieved our fortunes in a measure after the disastrous battle of Lookout Mountain, covering
our rear & inflicting heavy loss on the pursuers. An Irishman by birth, he rose
from the ranks by dint of merit and merit alone. A strict disiplinarian he was

the idol of his command. So proud was his of him that the desire to serve in his command drew hosts of his country men from the ranks of the enemy. His loss will be felt in the Army of the Tennessee. Wirt Adams & Gist had a high reputation. The others are unknown to me but none the less lamented on that account.

At night father dined with us today, whilst at dinner came a Courier to Mr E. bringing a note from a Lt Col Beaseley[117] wishing to see him without delay at Clarksville "to consult" with him. The messenger told us that the enemy in heavy force were advancing both by river & land from Plymouth. Report has them 10,000 strong but that two Gunboats had been blown up by our torpedos, of both which items we may beleive as much as we will. Their object is supposed to be the destruction of the gunboats now building within two miles of us—pleasant neighbours those.[118] Since the wanton destruction of the Albemarle, I have not the enthusiasm I once had in the construction of Gunboats. It seems but time & labour lost.

Patrick was off at once & I am alone with my anxiety & uncertainty, and sadder than all comes a rumour which Owen brt me from Halifax tonight. He heard one gentleman tell another that a dispatch had just been received saying that Mr. Davis, our President, Mr Davis, was dead! I cannot & will not beleive it. God has not sent such a bitter draught for us to drink. It cannot be true. Mr Davis has had his faults & we have felt them keenly, but who would not have had more? He is but human and liable to err, but his failing all lean to Virture's side & where he errs once another man would have erred a thousand times. He is obstinate, but how much better is that than to be vaccillating and given to change? He persists in giving us Bragg & depriving us of Joe Johnston, but what would we do were he like the Yankee exponent, & changed Lee and Beauregarde for a whim or for a reputed failure? He is an upright Christian gentleman who has conferred honors on his position, dignified, statesmanlike, an ardent patriot, a firm, humane, and judicious ruler. The few mistakes he has made are those only of a kind, noble, & generous disposition. God preserve him to us! He is the embodiment of our Southern character abroad & at home, the object of love and reverence. I know no greater blow than his death would be to us. God avert it from us!

---

[117]Lt. Col. W. F. Beasley belonged to the Seventy-first North Carolina Regiment, Second Junior Reserves. Beasley, a cadet at the Hillsboro Military Academy before the war, previously had served as a lieutenant in the Forty-eighth North Carolina Regiment and as major in Anderson's Battalion. Clark, *Histories of the North Carolina Regiments,* IV, 25, 27-28; V, 640.

[118]The vessels under construction included a gunboat at Halifax, for service on the sounds, and another gunboat being built at Edward's Ferry for operation on the Roanoke River. The construction of a new ironclad was also contemplated to attack the Union ships in Albemarle Sound. *Official Records (Navy),* Series I, XI, 755.

DECEMBER 21, 1864

Whilst I was writing last night in came Mr Edmondston with the gratifying news that the Yankees were not on this side of the River but in Bertie in the Indian Woods, committing, however, fearful ravages. When last heard from they were at Mr Joe Pugh's[119] destroying everything. Gen Leventhorpe was at Hamilton with a strong force, sufficient he thought to manage them, their destination supposed to be Edwards Ferry & the destruction of the Gun Boats there their object.

DECEMBER 22, 1864

News of an attack on Wilmington. My God when will this cease? The Raiders in Bertie are supposed to have retired as we hear naught from them. No mail. Troops flocking to Wilmington. Have suffered severely today in fact for a fortnight past I have been in pain, first with toothache, then from an ineffectual attempt last Sunday to extract the offending member. The attempt & the state the tooth was left in put me almost beside myself until yesterday when we sent for Dr Hall, who had it out in a trice giving me little pain, but its loss has failed to releive me. In fact every tooth and place where a tooth has been in that side of my face pains me excessively. Dolly says "your teeth are like Bees when you interrup (anglice, distress) one, they all angers," & comforts me with a minute & graphic relation of her own sufferings on a similar occasion.

DECEMBER 23, 1864

Mr E went up to father's today & gave Rachel such an account of the pain I was in (& it was & is severe) that she came down to remain with me. She has been quite unwell herself & I am but poor company.

News from Savannah of fighting, but Sherman is in communication with his fleet, so he can escape if hard pushed & at any rate supply himself with amunition. My disappointment is intense. God grant Savannah itself fall not into his hands, but my fears are grave. No news from Wilmington.

DECEMBER 25, 1864

Came Mr E. home yesterday from Clarksville (where he had been to order out the 1st class Home Guards) bringing with him a Proclamation of Gov Vance calling on every man "who can handle a musket or stand behind a breast work" to rally at Wilmington for its defence. A levy en masse of the whole State is ordered, so this morning we packed a few things in a Satchel for him & taking his "blanket" as the Gov orders he is off to report to Gen Leventhorpe for duty.

---

[119]In 1860 Joseph I. Pugh was a thirty-six-year-old farmer living in Halifax County. Eighth Census, 1860, Population Schedule, Halifax County, 62.

A sad Christmass! In place of Santa Claus bringing me anything—he takes my husband from me for an indefinite time. When will we see a "Merry" one? "Merry Christmas," it seems a mockery thus to salute one in this war torn country. How can we be "merry" with our best & dearest gone, exposed to Yankee bullets, to danger & to sudden death! We sit quiet spectators of this gigantic game of War, a game where all we hold dear is at stake, when the next turn of the wheel may behold us houseless exiles, wanderers on the face of the Earth! Grant us Faith, good Lord, faith in thy merciful Providence, an humble resignation of ourselves into Thy hands, & an earnest conviction that whatever befall us, Thou hast ordained it & that therefore it is right. Thou hast said "As thy days so shall thy strength be"! Thou hast given us "Thy Son to take our nature upon Him & as at this time to be born of a pure virgin." Thou wilt not leave us comfortless. Increase our Faith.[120]

December 27, 1864

Last night came tidings of the fall of Savannah! The Telegram tells us that it was "successfully evacuated" on Tuesday the 20th, nothing more. So fall all our hopes, all our boasts of "crushing" Sherman. How empty they now seem! We know nothing of the state of affairs, nothing of the force we had, nothing of our casualties, so form no judgment even or opinion of the event. It stands before us in sorrow only, a sad fact which has others sadder in its train. We have Yankee news of a great Victory by Thomas over Hood, but we try not to allow it to discourage or cast us down. We remember their Cretan character and know how to estimate their paper victories, but coming as it does on the fall of Savannah, it instills another drop of bitterness into our cup!

This morning came Mr E home from Hamilton on his way to Wilmington. He found Gen Leventhorpe gone, having repulsed a fleet of the enemy's gunboats. He sunk six & crippled some others. Three were blown up by Torpedos, one got aground & was blown up, & two were sunk by our Batteries, when the rest retreated to Plymouth. Gen L left a good force at Ft Branch & hurried off to a new scene of fighting at Goldsboro. Mr E is to be off again tomorrow. He would go today but his buggy is broken & his horse tired out & I must prepare rations for a long absence from home for him. God make us thankful for this gleam of sunshine on our path. If He fight for us, vain is the rage of our enemies! The engagement took place at Poplar Point below Rainbow Bend. In all probability it has saved us from being ravaged & desolated. Ah! for Peace!

December 28, 1864

Yesterday the meagre dispatch brt us from Halifax was "No mail & no news, communication cut off," so we are left to chew the cud of doubt & anxiety for another 24 hours. Mr E was off today to take the train for Wilmington

---

[120]From the Collect for Christmas Day in the Episcopal *Book of Common Prayer*.

in obedience to Gov Vance's Proclamation. He gave me minute directions about his business & the management of the Plantation during his absence, so I hope I will be able to carry it on as it should be done whilst he is gone. Rachel has promised to remain with me, for which I am very thankful, but Ah! me we both miss him sadly.

DECEMBER 29, 1864

As R & I sat at our knitting last night about 9 o'clock came a man's step in the piazza. With many misgivings & timid queries as to "who was there"? I at length opened the door, when there stood Mr E himself on his own threshold nearly denied admittance! There was no train nor has there been one for days further than Rocky Mount, so what are we to think of our Gov calling out every one able to fire a musket or stand behind a breastwork to defend their native soil & providing no means whatever for their reaching the point assailed? Mr E came home as it was idle to wait in Halifax, but this morning he was off again on the chance of communication's being resumed, when he would again make the attempt. If that failed he thought he would go at once to Headquarters at Raleigh & there get an assignment to duty. He brt news of an attack & a repulse of the enemy below ft Fisher. A small work known as Ft Anderson* was allowed to fall into the enemie's hands, our forces being directed to retire in seeming confusion, when another body of our men fell suddenly on their flank & rear & the seeming fugitives rallying, we drove them pell mell before us "up to their necks" in the sea & recovered Ft Anderson. We killed about 1000 & what loss the sea covered will never be known. Ft Fisher was attacked & firing steadily & with deliberation inflicted damage on the fleet, but to what extent cannot be told. In consists of 250 vessels all told, Monitors, War Steamers & transports. Butler is reported as landing a strong force at Ft. Macon for an advance via New Berne & Washington. The same troops who recently left Hamilton are being hurried back to Tarrboro, whether to repel a new advance up this River or one from Washington is not known. Mr E was in a sad state of uncertainty as to what step he had best take. This deficiency of information & uncertainty as to transportation is a great drawback to decision. No news, no particulars that is, of the evacuation of Savannah. We have lost our papers & know only the bare event itself but that is humiliation enough!

Sherman has effected a brilliant "coup," to march through the whole State of Geo, take its principal city & seaport in spite of our utmost endeavour, nay in our very teeth, to effect a communication with the fleet, with an army too which we proclaimed jaded and foot sore (but of whom he gives a very different account). It does indeed entitle him to pride & exultation. Well may we

* A mistake Ft Anderson was taken against our wishes.

hang our heads & say "The King does not dine today." Would that we had boasted less!

Bad accounts of Amo. The temporal Artery has twice spouted out bleeding, which however, his father being near, was soon stopped, but Erysipilus has intervened. His head is fearfully swollen. He is unable to open his eyes or to swallow aught save fluids & that in small quantities. His sufferings are very great and we feel seriously uneasy about him. Ah! War! War! who can describe thy horrors?

Papers last night tell us that our President Mr Davis has been very ill & is even now still prostrated, but thank God he is recovering! The sensation excited through the whole country by the rumour of his death is an earnest of how we value him. Even his opponents were appalled at the probable consequences of losing him! May God long preserve him to us & may our speedy rise as a nation to Independance & Peace be monument to his vigor, ability, & patriotism.

DECEMBER 30, 1864

At sundown yesterday to our great releif & pleasure came Mr Edmondston. When near Halifax who should he meet but brother who gave him the gratifying intelligence that the enemy's fleet had all disappeared from off Wilmington. The attack is (as Mr E has always thought it) now considered but a feint designed to draw our attention off from some other point, Charleston or Savannah. It came near being successful however, but for the terrific blow on the night, Thursday last, I think it was, when they first hove in sight & then but for the indecision & slow movements of the Commander, supposed *Butler*, in delaying the attack, Wilmington would have fallen an easy prey into their hands. Ft Anderson was taken not by stratagem but because we could not help it & they were driven from it by the desperate fighting of the Reserves, mainly the Juniors. The boys fought most nobly and regained the port. At one time Ft Fisher itself was cut off. There were not troops enough to man the defences of the town; neither provisions, *powder*, or indeed arms for the men Gov Vance called out were there—in fact there was not provisions for the Confederate troops for two days! Had a determined advance been made at once, Wilmington must have fallen & what a blow would that have been, but God be thanked the enemy did not know our weakness & He raised up that great wind in which was our salvation.

Brother gave Mr E some sad statistics on the food & Powder supply, but he is ever gloomy & looks on the dark side. God will not give us over a prey into the hands of our rapacious enemies. He will yet help & deliver us. One of the saddest results of our situation that I have yet seen is a letter from Gen Lee to Mr Miles,[121] Chairman of the Military Committee in Congress, advising the

---

[121]Lee's letter to William Porcher Miles was written in reply to a letter from Miles on October 24, 1864, soliciting Lee's opinion on this subject. Copies of Miles's letter of October 21, and a second letter of

conscription, emancipation, & arming of 200,000 slaves immediately. It proves to me that Gen Lee knows more of getting an army in the field than he does of Cuffee, that he is a better military strategist than Statesman, that he understands more of a state of War than he does of a time of Peace! Should we take his advice, we but recruit for the Yankee army & destroy at one blow the highest jewel in the crown of Peace! Our Country is ruined if he adopt his suggestions. We give up a principle when we offer emancipation as a boon or reward, for we have hitherto contended that Slavery was Cuffee's normal condition, the very best position he could occupy, the one of all others in which he was the happiest, & to take him from that & give him what we think misery in the place of it, is to put ourselves in the wrong essentially. No! freedom for whites, slavery for negroes, God has so ordained it!

November 3, 1864, thanking Lee for his reply, are in the William Porcher Miles Papers, Southern Historical Collection. The question of using slaves as Confederate troops surfaced as the number of whites available to fight declined to a critical level. Davis believed the use of Negro troops was preferable to defeat. Lee publicly agreed in several letters to Confederate authorities and also urged the immediate emancipation of Negro soldiers after enlistment. The Confederate House of Representatives, on February 20, 1865, passed a regulation authorizing the conscription of troops regardless of race. The war ended, however, before many slaves were drafted by the South, although evidence exists that some blacks were used in combat by the South. Randall and Donald, *Civil War and Reconstruction*, 522. For a full discussion of this issue see Robert F. Durden, *The Gray and the Black: The Confederate Debate on Emancipation* (Baton Rouge: Louisiana State University Press, 1972), and James H. Brewer, *The Confederate Negro: Virginia's Craftsmen and Military Laborers, 1861-1865* (Durham: Duke University Press, 1969), 102-103, hereinafter cited as Brewer, *Confederate Negro*.

1865

January 9, 1865

"Out of the abundance of the heart the mouth speaketh,"[1] but the hand writeth not. Never were we more absorbed in outward matters, never have we looked on them so anxiously as now, & yet it is days since I have written aught of them. This negro question, this vexed negro question, will if much longer discussed do us more injury than the loss of a battle. Gen Lee advises the Conscription & ultimate Emancipation of 200,000 Slaves to be used as soldiers. One or two rabid partizan papers, Democratic, I might almost say Agrarian to the core, seize on the proposal, hold it up to the people, to the army, in the most attractive lights. They promise the white soldier that if the negro is put in the army, for every negro soldier fifteen white ones will be allowed to return home. They use it as an engine to inflame the passions of one class against another, tell the poor man that the War is but for his rich neighbor's slaves, that his blood is poured out to secure additional riches to the rich, etc., etc., nay one paper, to its shame be it said, the Richmond Enquirer, openly advocates a general Emancipation! as the price for fancied benefits to be obtained by an alliance with England & France. Actually it offers to sell the birthright of the South, not for a mess of pottage, but only for the hope of obtaining one. The Traitor, recreant to principle, lost to every sense of national honour, & blind to what constitutes a true national prosperity—the wonder is that he finds anyone either to read or think seriously of his monstrous proposition. But so it is. Coming as it does on the evacuation of Savannah when we are almost ready to sink under the accumulation of Yankee lies & Yankee bragg, over their boasted Victory over Hood, our money depreciated & depreciating daily more & more, deafened on one side by loud mouthed politicians who advocate "Reconstruction to save Annihilation," "Reconstruction as a choice of Evils," & on the other by the opponents of the Government who expatiate with alass too much truth upon the mismanagement, the waste, the oppression which, cast our eyes which way we will we see around us, threatened again with a new suspension of Habeas Corpus, the Constitution daily trampled under foot by Impressment Laws & Government Schedules, what wonder that many unthinking people catch at this straw as at hope of salvation & delivery from present misery without pausing to ask themselves what will be their condition when they have accepted it. But sounder & better councils will prevail. This beaten and crushed Abolitionist, the Enquirer, will find that the body of the people are against him, that the foxes who have lost their tails are too few in number to

---

[1] Matthew 12:34b.

govern those who still retain theirs. Slaveholders on principle, & those who hope one day to become slaveholders in their time, will not tacitly yeild their property & their hopes & allow a degraded race to be placed at one stroke on a level with them. But these discussions & these thoughts have occupied us for the past fortnight & such a deluge of gloomy forebodings have been penned out upon us that I almost hailed the frequent mail failures as a blessing.

The tide now seems turning. God has blessed us with a signal victory over the Yankee fleet. God's blessing & God's hand alone it is, for we had but little to do with it. Yankee accounts of the doings of their great Armada have reached us, which make our hearts rise in gratitude to Him who exalteth & who casteth down. In the first place there was no cooperation between the land & naval forces. Then came the gale which drove them out to sea, then the bombardment of Ft Fisher, when the bursting of six six-hundred-pound Parrot Guns on six different Vessels destroyed the confidence of the men who saw their comrades torn, mangled, & bleeding amongst the ruins of their own offensive engines. Then a barge with two hundred & *fifteen tons* of Powder was floated to within a short distance of Ft Fisher & exploded without the slightest result. "The Rebels were not even paralized by it," but why continue the tale of their disaster? Suffice it that God's hand is apparent in it all & the fleet has returned to Hampton Roads discomforted, defeated, dejected, & out of repair & quarrelling miserably amongst themselves. To God alone be the Glory.

Better news but still not authentic reaches us from Tenn. We hear that in a second battle we regained some of the prestige lost before Nashville, of which however we have still only Yankee accounts, but I will refrain all but passing mention of them until'they are confirmed. Still they influence our spirits wonderfully. What cheers our very hearts is an intimation that Mr Davis has reinstated Gen Joe Johnston in command. The whole nation hails it with acclamation. Gen D H Hill too is ordered to report to Gen Beauregard, so our old dogs of War are unleashed again.

Sherman is reposing himself in Savannah after his leisurely saunter through Geo & bloodless conquest of that city. He makes a magnificent Christmas gift to Mr Lincoln of the City of Savannah with arms, munitions of war, cotton, Rice, seige guns, etc., too tedious for me to enumerate. He even includes the 25,000 inhabitants in his munificent donation; so, as other autocrats do, he has now only to enslave & deport them. God help them! The evacuation took them entirely by surprise we hear. Few of them escaped & they with the loss of all their effects. Sherman has a right to his self glorification. Let him indulge it whilst we cherish the hope that Beauregard will yet pluck the Laurel crown from his brow & trample it in the dust. His programme, as announced, is the capture of Branchville and advance along the lines of R R into Va. Nous verrons! No news from Petersburg or Richmond for days. All quiet since the defeat of the demonstration on Gordonsville.

As for ourselves, since the negroes holiday at Christmas, for Christmas shone no holiday to any but them, we have been engaged with our year's supply of meat. Frying up Lard, squeezing out cracklins, & all the, to me, disagreeable et ceteras of "a hog killing" are I beleive a perfect happiness to Cuffee! The excitement & interest over the weight of their favorites, the feasting on chitterlings & haslets, the dabbling in grease, seems to constitute a negro paradise, whilst the possession of a "bladder to blow" or better still a hog tail is all a negro child needs of earth's enjoyments. Well we "killed Hogs" here, then we went to Hascosea & did the same thing there.

As usual we were weatherbound & detained 24 hours longer than we intended to remain. Mr E ordered a large box of books, principally farming periodicals (which we had bound the winter before the commencement of the war & which came home whilst we were in great excitement about Ft Sumter & which we have since refrained from opening on account of our unsettled state & the determination we from time to time take to pack up all our books) to be opened, & we passed the time most pleasantly & profitable, rubbing up our old knoledge, forming new plans, agricultural, horticultural, & domestic which this spring & summer we hope to put in execution. I lent an especial eye to the Poultry yard—am armed with several infalible receipts to cure & to prevent "the gapes," all of which I shall try on my spring chickens. In Vinegar receipts too I have come home quite learned & I now sigh for a peice of genuine Vinegar plant! I have some very fine Vinegar made from the skimmings of last year's Sorghhum, but alas, it is too little for my many uses. I used to be famous for Pickles, but my cunning has departed, as the price of whisky and Apple Brandy has risen, for on them did I rely to give my Vinegar body. I am now making yeast by the pailful and even contemplate malting some corn to supply the deficiency. This war is teaching us many things. Dying, spinning, and weaving are no longer unknown mysteries to me. I think of making a compilation of all my practical knoledge on the subject and I intend for the future Peace or war to let *homespun* be my ordinary dress. The object of my ambition is to have a black watered silk trimmed with black thread lace. Think of it! How shall I feel when I pull off my russet yarn spun & woven on the Plantation & bedeck myself in that style! It seems so long since I wore a silk dress that I begin to doubt if I ever owned one.

I have been reading Motley's "United Netherlands"[2] & have derived great comfort from it. We are not so divided, lean not so much on foreign aid, & are not reduced near so low as they were, & yet by perseverance they triumphed. Their advantage lay in a command of the Sea, however, an ability to export

---

[2]John Lothrop Motley (1814-1877) was an American historian and diplomat who wrote extensively on the history of the Netherlands. *A History of the United Netherlands*, four volumes published in New York and London between 1860 and 1868, was his second major work dealing with the Netherlands. During the Civil War Motley served as the United States minister to Austria (1861-1867) and briefly as the minister to Great Britain (1869-1870). *Concise Dictionary of American Biography*, 709.

and import as they liked, an assistance we too would have did foreign nations uphold their own international Law on the subject of Blockades! International Law, a humbug & a sham, designed only by the strong as a police code to keep order amongst themselves but ignored & forgotten when a weak power suffers from its infringement. This it is which has changed our once strong love to England into Gall! this & the manner in which her boasted *Neutrality* is maintained. Her *Neutrality*, heaven save the mark, is only another word for *deceit*, for mean low petty trickery, for cringing to the U S, saying to us "Am I not in Peace my brother" & stabbing as Joab-like under the fifth rib. Neutrality, faugh! I am reading, too, Ld Bacon's Essays[3] regularly through, one every day, & what a mine of thought they are! The foundation, nay the superstructure, of almost all modern moral Essays is found in them. It is sorrowful in the extreme to see how the human mind but reproduces itself, how the same gem appears generation after generation, modified only in the setting. Sometimes I come on a thought or an idea that I fancied I had thought out of myself, which I had hugged to my heart as my own, when hey presto! I recognize it again stamped by the hand of a master in a form at once so terse, so complete, so chisled, & so chaste that tho two hundred years old, it stands forth as clear, sharp, & distinct as tho just from the mint; & with a sigh I relinquish my proprietorship and take refuge with Solomon in the declaration that "there is nothing new under the sun."[4]

JANUARY 19, 1865

I have for days been so occupied that I have not thought of my journal, but now for a resumé of the events of the past fortnight. On Tuesday the 10th we had heavy rain, high wind, thunder & lightening all day & at night the river was reported as rising again, having just commenced falling from the rain of the previous Friday. Higher & higher it rose all Wednesday & on Thursday the new dam just above our line was reported as "giving way." Father & Mr E with all hands went to work & remained there until the water rising on both sides drove them away. On Friday the 13th, the whole Low grounds being under water & the river still rising, Mr E "paddled" up to father's to see how he was faring, when a terrible & heartrending scene met his eyes! The water was pouring *over* the dam for almost its whole length. A terrible break had taken place above the house & the river was rushing in with tremendus fury carrying everything before it. The stable was gone, not a vestige of it being left. Father with his own hands released the horses about midnight! The bank had slipped behind the kitchen & it was expected every moment that it,

---

[3]Francis Bacon (1561-1626) became a prominent English philosopher and author while serving in various political capacities under Elizabeth I and her successors. Bacon's *Essays*, published between 1597 and 1625, remain one of his most significant contributions. *Webster's Biographical Dictionary*, 85.

[4]Ecclesiastes 1:9. ". . . there is no new thing under the sun."

too, would go & the house itself stood in a strong current, the water being within two inches of the sills! & seemed in imminent danger of settling.

Mr E at once urged the necessity of abandoning it & insisted that the whole family should take canoes & come at once down to us. To this father at once assented in favour of all but himself, but Mama absolutely refused to leave, having great fear both of water in the abstract & canoes in particular, but the rest of the family consisting of Dr & Mrs Osborne, Mrs Jones & Rachel, Susan, Sarah, Belle, Mattie, & Katie Dunlop at once embarked, & by God's favour passed safely through the currents & reached the Looking Glass hill in time for dinner. Mr E having convoyed them safely, returned immediately to Conneconara for father & Mama. He found two of the supports to the house on the River side gone, washed away, whilst others were in a strong current & might go at any moment, whilst the water had risen during his absence a half inch or more. This decided the matter, so embarking with him both father & Mama soon joined their family here & with them were made as comfortable as the curcumstances would admit of. Looking Glass was stretched to its utmost capacity, we opened the Overseer's house & colonized the young folks and Mrs Jones there. Dr & Mrs Osborne had the spare room & Father & Mama occupied ours, whilst for the nonce we took the extension sofa in the

When the floodwaters made it necessary to evacuate Conneconara, the family took canoes and went to Looking Glass. Nine people in addition to Mrs. Edmondston's parents had to be cared for, and the overseer's house was opened and the "young folks" and Mrs. Jones were "colonized" there. Shown above is a side view of this house. For a front view, see page 2. (Photograph courtesy of Dr. Claiborne T. Smith of Philadelphia.)

sitting room. Early hours were involved in this arrangement but we got on famously in spite of our close packing.

On Sunday Father, Mama, Dr & Mrs Osborne left us the water having fallen from underneath the house. The damage done by this freshet is very great. The dams are torn to peices; there are *eighteen* breaks on the Conneconara plantation alone, one new one here only but the old ones much enlarged. The River barns all had water in them which necessitated the removal & handling of the corn which is a heavy job. The Flume is much injured, but in fact the damage is so great that in all probability the dams will never be replaced & the flume will henceforth be useless.

Two or three spans of the Weldon R R Bridge have been carried away & what is worse than that the Bridge on the Danville road, Lee's main Artery, has also been destroyed.

On Monday Mr E went up again to Conneconara & found there Dr Kellum, a friend of Dr and Mrs Osborne. He invited him to dine with us on Tuesday, which he did. He seems a man of the world, well bred & traveled. On Wednesday the girls went home, leaving Mrs Jones & Rachel only with us. On Tuesday we heard that the Yankee fleet had returned & recommenced a furious assault on Fort Fisher. Bragg telegraphs that "there is no cause for alarm, that all goes on well, Whiting in command," that he has repulsed a vigorous assault, etc., etc., but adds a P S by which we learn that Fort Fisher has fallen. It was taken by superior numbers. Altho Wilmington was swarming with troops & they had ample warning, there were not men enough in the garrison to resist the onslaught upon them. So will it ever be where Bragg commands. Bragg the Unlucky is a Millstone which Mr Davis persist in tying around our necks! Whiting & Lamb are both captured, "desperately," one account says, "slightly," another, wounded. We since hear that Ft Caswell has been blown up & abandoned, the fall of Fisher having made it unteneble. So we fear it will soon be with Wilmington, tho now troops are hurried & a determination "to hold it at all hazzards." Too late in the day I fear. Ft Fisher was the Key & that has been thrown away. What renders it more disastrous is the fact that it was preconcerted by the enemy as an adjunct to Sherman's advance upon Branchville that has been delayed by the freshets in all the Rivers, Roanoke not being the only unruly & rebellious stream. Could we have repulsed the attack on Fisher a new combination would have been needed, but God disposed otherwise. We leaned on a broken reed which has peirced our hand. Out on Bragg the unlucky & out on Mr Davis for maintaining him in command!

On Tuesday Mr E received orders to proceed at once to Goldsboro with his command. It was impossible to get out of the plantation on account of high water yesterday but today he is off probably for some time. I looked well after his Commissariat, as it is almost impossible to get anything to eat & then not without paying a fabulous price for it. There is much sickness on the plantation, severe colds with pleuretic tendencies being almost an epidemic. King, poor fellow, is dying, his chronic disease having fallen on a vital part. Mr E told me before he left that a College of Physicians could do him no good.

JANUARY 22, 1865

God certainly blesses me in a most signal manner! Mr E went off on Thursday expecting to be gone for some time. He gave me minute directions as to the management of the farm in his absence, but for the sickness he could leave no programme for me to go by, & had he been detained these past two days I should have been at my wits end. He got to Halifax on Thursday & there found written orders awaiting him from Maj Pearson telling him to send off the men & to return home himself & take command of the county during his (Pearson's) absence & to await further orders. So, most unexpectedly to us, he came in to dinner on Friday. Well was it for me that he did so, for never before in our lives have we had so many cases of sickness on the plantation at once.

The weather was wretched yesterday, such as to keep me within doors, yet had he not been at home I should have been obliged to go out & in my ignorance prescribe. Happily the cases are all similar & should they not have yeilded at once to treatment I could have sent for the Dr, but then it is often days before he can come so great is the distance & so constant the calls upon him. King was buried in the rain yesterday & this morning there are *nine* quite sick patients on the plantation to say nothing of those only ailing. There are *seven* people with blisters drawn or drawing on them at this moment, so I may well say I should have been at my wits end!

No public news. Dr Kellum tells us that two of Longstreets divisions, Kershaws and another, have gone to S C to meet Sherman. He, however, is detained by high water, no bridges & heavy roads which last have not been improved by the past two days weather. Our River is rising again furiously. I forgot to mention the height of the last freshet—25 ft 2 in on father's staff— ours was washed down—higher by more than a foot than it was ever known to be before. Ah! that Ft Fisher had stood! The elements on our side, we might have struck a signal blow.

The discontent with the Government increases. Revolution, the deposition of Mr Davis, is openly talked of! Who can tell how it all will end? Vain are our conjectures. We wait with folded hands what is in store for us. God grant that it be neither Emancipation or Subjugation; be it what it will, may we see His hand in it all.

JANUARY 26, 1865

What a condition is ours! Compelled to a ceaseless vigilance, exposed to evils from which the imagination shrinks in horror, the moments of repose we enjoy are so few that we scarcely enter into the enjoyment of them ere they are fled. There is now in progress a Yankee raid in Northampton, the adjoining county to ours, its object is said to be destruction of the Gun boat building within a half a mile of us. Last night came Mrs Whitaker's negroes here for safety. The advance of the enemy will be through her plantation & the attack made from her side of the river, so her manager has in a measure broken up & sent the negroes to this side for shelter. We feel seriously uneasy about brother who left here on Sunday for Murfresboro. I hope he has not fallen into the hands of these raiders. Much & serious sickness amongst our negroes. How thankful I am that Mr E is at home! I would not know what to do for them.

JANUARY 27, 1865

Yesterday came Mr E home from the Gunboat where he went to see if he could do aught in its defence & brought us the gratifying news that the Yankees were retreating. Two Companies of Cavalry crossed the river on the night of the 26th in pursuit of them. Father's flat was brt down from the Ferry to set them across. Capt Cooke & General Baker with a good force were there, but will it be beleived that Gen B left the post when the Yankees were hourly expected & when applied to by a Col in the junior Reserves for "orders" when about to mount his horse, turned & said "Orders, Sir? What orders have I to give? Why if the Yankees come fight them! That is what they used to say to me when I was a Colonel"! & rode off to a relative's house in Scotland Neck & spent the night at his ease!

Now is that man fit to command? Is he fit for the post to which he has been elevated? I trow not! What cared he if the news which reached him in the morning was that the boat had been burned? Had he been alive to his responsibilities he would not have left everything to a young Colonel entirely without experience or military knoledge.

Patrick also brought us news that an armistice for thirty days had been agreed on between Lee & Grant, but for the details & how far it extends we must wait the slow course of the mails, rendered in our case still slower by the cutting off of our communication with father—too much water for horseback & too little for convenient canoe navigation. Involving a long walk as it does even that is now denied us, for the ice formed so thick in the shallow bottoms yesterday and last night that it is impossible for any one to get there today. Mr E saw brother at the Navy Yard—for which God be thanked. He was near the enemy but saw nothing of them. Thirteen seriously sick negroes reported this morning, some of them Typhoid cases.

JANUARY 29, 1865

Sunday—Mr Edmondston left home this morning, having been ordered to Goldsboro with the whole Home Guard of the state. They are to be reorganized, how I know not; but the Legislature in its wisdom has so ordained it. I have been so much blessed in having Mr E at home with me for so long that I have neither right nor inclination to repine at his absence. If he only had strong health & was able to face the hardships of Camp life, not one word would I say, but ah! me, knowing as I do his unfitness for active service & the risk he runs from exposure, it is hard to see him go.

We get so little public news now-a-days that my journal stands a chance of being barren of plumbs—a real "mile-stone pudding." Father endorsed on the back of a letter yesterday that "Blair had returned to Richmond, Gen Lee had been made Commander in Cheif, Pocotaligo abandoned, & a line taken up on the Saltkehatchie, Mahone's Division at Weldon en route for S C. As for Blair's return, so little hope have I of any definite results from any Yankee negotiations whilst they are as now triumphant that I beleive I omitted to notice the fact that he was in Richmond with propositions for Peace! Peace with them means just now subjugation & Abolition of Slavery, neither of which are we ready to submit to, so it will all end in smoke, if indeed it be not a "*cute*" Yankee trick intended to throw dust in our eyes.

As for Gen Lee's Commander ship I should have rejoiced in it more than I now do had he not sanctioned the suicidal scheme of conscribing & emancipating an indefinite number of negroes & their families. Pray God his authority be strictly limited to our military & that he meddle not with our civil affairs! Johnston has not been put in command. At the last accounts Gov MaGrath[5] of S C was consulting in a non-official way with him. Perhaps this accounts for the "falling back" from Pocotaligo, for he is a master of the Fabian policy! God bless him. Sec Seddon with the Ass Sec of War have resigned, but as yet the President has not accepted their resignation.

The discontent with Government & Mr Davis is getting to be extreme; open accusations of a want of faith, of oppression, & of a disregard to the prosperity & happiness of the people meet one everywhere. I fear we are entering into the first stages of "sedition and tumult" so ably described by Ld Bacon.

I was rendered more downhearted than I have yet been by a remark of one of the boys in a Regt of Junior Reserves now stationed near us. On my asking if the shoes he had on (which were very inferior) were issued him by Govt, he answered in the affirmative & went on to say that government did no more for them than it could help & never gave them anything they could possibly get for themselves. It seemed to sap at once the foundation of his faith, his reverence, & his affection. How can he be a good soldier who has no love for

---

[5]Andrew Gordon Magrath (1813-1893), a prominent lawyer and judge in South Carolina prior to the war, served as South Carolina's secretary of state on Governor Pickens's executive council (1860-1861), as judge of the Confederate district court in the state (1861-1864), and as governor of South Carolina (1864-1865). Briefly imprisoned after the war, Magrath resumed his law practice in Charleston. *Dictionary of American Biography*, XII, 203-204.

the power to whom he owes allegiance. The sight of these boys, none of them over eighteen, went to my heart, & the knoledge that in this bitter weather they are exposed without shelter (& without sufficient food if their accounts be true) gives me many a pang. I cannot enjoy the comforts God has vouch safed me for thinking of the contrast between my & their condition. Surely it would have been wise, to say nothing of humane & fatherly, to have sent them home in Nov. & there allowed them to stay until April. They have neither the firmness of frame or the strength of constitution to endure such exposure. It is as Pres Davis characterized it the early part of the War, "Grinding our seed Corn" to use them thus.

JANUARY 30, 1865

Mr E to my pleasure got home last night. When he reached Halifax he found that the Home Guard had been for the time disbanded & were on their return from Goldsboro. So one unintentional service was done us by Maj Pearson entrusting his orders to a private hand instead of the mail. It was so long en route that it was countermanded ere it reached his hands! Thank God for this new blessing. At all events he misses the severe weather we now have.

FEBRUARY 5, 1865

On Tuesday the 31st as we came home from Hascosea we met one of our neighbors who delighted us with the announcement that in a late Richmond paper he had seen that Vice President Stevens, R M T Hunter, & Judge Campbell[6] had been sent on by our Government to Washington as Commissioners to effect a treaty of Peace & this joyful news was confirmed when we reached home by James Edmondston whom we found awaiting us. The Commissioners, as named, have certainly gone & as we are told under Mr Lincoln's assurance that a fitting reception would be accorded them. That Mr Hunter is one of them gives us the liveliest satisfaction. He is not a man who will be "trifled" with or who will allow our dignity as a nation to suffer the slightest infringement. He "knows our rights & knowing dare maintain them." Of Judge Campbell we know less, but my aunt Mrs Polk tells us he is a true & stern Southern patriot. As for that body, Vice President Stevens, the less we say of him the better. He is a make weight, I suppose, a sop to the Peace-on-any-terms men unfortunately amongst us.

---

[6]The peace conference held at Hampton Roads on February 3, 1865, between Lincoln and Seward on behalf of the United States, and Alexander Hamilton Stephens, Robert Mercer Taliaferro Hunter, and John Archibald Campbell for the Confederacy, resulted in a stalemate. The southern commissioners, eager to bring an end to hostilities but unable to sacrifice southern independence to achieve it, hoped to establish an armistice or ceasefire for an indefinite period. Lincoln, however, insisted on reunion and the abolition of slavery before any suspension of hostilities. These differences ended the discussion but convinced Stephens that southern independence was impossible as the military strength of the Union was overwhelming. Randall and Donald, *Civil War and Reconstruction*, 524-525; *Concise Dictionary of American Biography*, 140, 470, 1000-1001.

On Thursday at father's to call on my Aunt & Cousins Mrs & the Misses Sally & Susan Polk[7] with Mr E and James. I can scarcly find words to express the pleasant impression made on me by my young cousins whom I have not seen since their infancy. Both are charming, but Susan! if I was a man I could go wild over her. Such a sweet gentle face, a true Devereux in every line. I hope I shall see much of her as I am sure I shall become attached to her. Aunt Fanny is much changed since I have seen her & poor thing looks deeply dejected. The loss of her husband & the uncertainty she is in about her second son, Mecklenburg,[8] from whom she has not heard since Hood's advance into Tenn, are enough to depress her.

Yesterday Mr E came from Scotland Neck with the rumour that a vessel had landed on our coast below the mouth of Cape Fear bringing the news that England & France had recognized us as a separate nationality. The day is passed for gratitude to them for it even if true—it is now only a concession wrung from them by a sense of their own interest which forbids them to allow the U S to subjugate us & be once more an undivided power. We care but little for this tardy concession of our rights. We have lost our Ports & a paper Blockade, break it as they will, is effective to us now. Had Bragg held Ft Fisher & the mouth of Cape Fear it would have been of immediate & substantial benefit to us; as it is we must wait in the hope that the chances of War will bring about a collision between the Great powers of the Earth & the U S. When rogues fall out etc., but the news even is problematical. It may all be a delusion. God help us! We know not whom to beleive nor who to trust.

James says it is a vile slander to say that Gen Early drinks or that the campaign in Maryland was lost through either his or Breckenridge's fault. Gen Early is sober & his disasters in the Valley were attributable to his want of men. The wonder is that he did so much. If this be true I have done a gallant officer great injustice in this journal, but the blame lies not at my door. I but re echoed the voices of the press & the community at large. I am not a Court Martial & can only mention things as I read them or as I hear them from apparently unprejudiced people. How heartily can we endorse Sir Robt Walpole's "Read no History to me my daughter, Read no History to me! I know how it is made." James tells us that a gentleman who knows him well & in whom he has great confidence, one Calhoun Benhan,[9] I forget his title, has

---

[7]Sarah H. and Susan R. Polk were the daughters of Leonidas and Frances Devereux Polk. Sarah (Sally) married a Blake of South Carolina, and Susan married Dr. Joseph Jones. Zella Armstrong (comp.), *Notable Southern Families* (Chattanooga: Lookout Publishing Co., 4 volumes, 1918), I, 178.

[8]William Mecklenburg Polk (1844-1918), son of Leonidas and Frances D. Polk, served in the Confederate army as a captain on his father's staff. After the war he received a medical license to practice gynecology and served as dean of the Cornell Medical School from 1898 until his death. *Concise Dictionary of American Biography*, 809; Johnson and Buel, *Battles and Leaders*, III, 662-663.

[9]Calhoun Benham, United States district attorney for California, left that state in October, 1861, en route for New York in the company of two other men. Suspected of treasonable sympathy for the South, the three

given him a sketch of Bragg's character & he finds the key to his failures in the fact that even in the conception of grand & magnificent schemes he is bent upon finding a scapegoat upon whom to lay the blame should failure ensue. He sees clearly, plans deliberately, but in the last moment, when (say I) had he the fire of true genius he would so far from hesitating embrace the responsibility. He looks around & says to himself "Now all this *may* fail and if so where shall I cast the odium?" This "t'was you—t'wasnt me" disposition cost us the fruits of the situation at McLemore's Cove. He worded his order to Hindman, "Gen Hindman *may* attack at day break" & waited with feverish impatience until 10 o'clock for Hindman's Guns. Hindman not being equal to the situation did not attack & so the enemy escaped. Had he used "*will*" instead of "*may*"—the Yankee army would have been at our mercy & he then had the want of generosity bitterly to reproach Hindman & charge upon him the failure and that by disobedience of orders. Hindman's reply was "I was not ordered to attack. I was left my discretion & used it. I knew nothing of the state of the whole field." True enough! Bragg had couriers from every part of it & ought to have made himself the governing principle.

There is now a terrible war of criminations & recriminating going on about the fall of Ft Fisher, but I am sickened by it & have neither room nor interest to record it. He ordered Whiting to come to him eight miles off for consultation on the eve of the attack & on Whiting's sending him word that he could not then leave his post, for an immediate attack was about to ensue, sent back the messenger with the order to Whiting to consider himself under arrest. The messenger reached the fort & found a desperate hand to hand conflict going on & delivered his message after Whiting had twice with his own hand torn down the enemy's flag! Comment is unnecessary. Whiting was taken prisoner, desperately wounded, defending a post which Gen Bragg ought to have seen better manned & fully reinforced, especially when he had the men to do both. Gen B, the *martinett*, arrests him for not deserting it at the critical moment. Had Whiting obeyed him & had the fort fallen during his absence, what a magnificent scapegoat he would have made of himself to cover Gen Braggs faults with all! Who then so open mouthed in condemnation as Gen Bragg would have been?

FEBRUARY 8, 1865

James, Mrs Jones, and Rachel all left today, so Mr E & I are in our normal condition once more. Rumours of the return of our Peace Commissioners too soon to have effected much.

---

were arrested before reaching New York and imprisoned at Fort Lafayette before being paroled in December, 1861. Benham maintained his innocence throughout the ordeal and eventually was pardoned by Lincoln. A Calhoun Benham was later listed as serving under Gen. Patrick R. Cleburne of the Army of Tennessee as assistant adjutant general with the rank of major. *Official Records (Army)*, Series I, XXX, Part II, 153, 156; Series II, II, 1009-1020.

February 9, 1865

At Father's to dinner. Had a long talk with my Aunt & Cousins with whom I am much delighted. They are all pleasant companions & the girls are charming & very attractive. Had too a chat with Susan about some of her own matters, with which no one else has any concern, so my friend check your curiosity. Our Commissioners have indeed returned, having been met at Fortress Monroe by Mr Lincoln & his wily Secretary, Mr Seward. The interview took place on board of a Steam boat, our Commissioners not being allowed to land. Rumour whispers that they were not allowed to go to Washington for fear of the populace making too strong demonstrations in their favor. Mr Lincoln utterly refuses to treat with our authorities, as it would be a recognition of them. The terms he informally offers us are 1st *submission*, entirely, utterly, & abject to the U. S., then an adoption of the new & remarkable Constitution of their country just passed by the Federal Congress, one clause of which is the Abolition of Slavery, in consideration of which he promises so far as depends upon himself a liberal & lenient construction of the pains & penalties incurred by the leaders of the Rebellion. That is I beleive all. Mr Lincoln related a few anecdotes. Was reminded "of a man in Illinois" once or twice, shook hands with our Commission. Seward, the hypocrite, wished them God's blessing, drank a bottle of Champagne with them, when up steam & ho for Richmond!

Now what Yankee trick was in hand when by means of their decoy duck Blair they tolled our three Commissioners from Richmond to Fortress Monroe on their way to Washington & contrary to expectation met them half way & then sent them back with a declaration which could have been given as effectively by Blair? What astounding peice of deceit & State craft are we to see arise from such a proceedure? Time I suppose will show. Both Lincoln & Seward admitted in conversation that they expected embroilments with foreign powers in consequence of their maintanance of the War but professed their beleif that they "would manage the rebellion" before they came on. Mr Davis tells us in his message to Congress covering the official report of the Commission "that he had a written notification" of the willingness of the U S Government to treat with unofficial agents on the subject of Peace, so we cannot be accused of hasty precipitate or undignified action in the premises. I preserve the Message & Report, marked [———].[10]

Fighting again before Petersburg. Grant is attempting an extension of his lines on our right towards Hatcher's Run. Our loss 500 killed, amongst whom is Maj Gen Pegram, a gallant officer poor fellow, just one fortnight after his marriage![11] Gen Sorrell of Geo wounded in the Lungs. In S C Sherman has

---

[10]These reports were not found in the diary.

[11]Gen. John Pegram (1832-1865), commanding a cavalry division in the Army of Northern Virginia, had married Hetty Cary of Baltimore on January 19, 1865. Boatner, *Civil War Dictionary*, 629-630; Freeman, *Lee's Lieutenants*, III, 629.

manoevered our men from their defences on the Saltkehahlie by making his troops march up to their waist in mud & water through the swamp & across the river at two points, one above & another below our entrenched position, thus flanking us on two sides with a heavy force. We consequently fell back behind the Edisto on Branchville. It is rumoured that he has cut the S C R R at Midway on the Augusta side of Branchville & we do not doubt it. Thus we are cut off from our friends in Aiken, but I hope not for long. In this state an Army corps is landing at New Berne and the R R to Goldsboro is being relaid by the enemy & every thing indicates an immediate & heavy advance into our interior. For days past members of Dickson's Battery[12] have been passing & repassing us, with orders to report both up and down the River. They have eaten every thing in my larder & the squad at dinner yesterday told us that the enemy were advancing in their gunboats & their object an immediate advance up the River.

FEBRUARY 12, 1865

Got home last night from Hascosea where we spent the last two days. Dickson's Battery out there also making a forced march to Hamilton to meet the enemy. Before we had a fire lighted they were upon us. Poor fellows, foot sore, cold, & hungry. Got them warmed & fed & Mr E ordered a waggon to take them some miles on their way in order to rest & releive them. My heart bleeds for them. Some of the men we have entertained are gentlemen born & bred, tho they are marching on foot as private soldiers over our muddy half frozen almost impassable roads. One of them was a son of the Rev Mr Curtis of Hillsboro, & his mother is a De Rosset of Wilmington,[13] & yet he was no better off than the worst of them. God help them & hasten the time when they can honourably return to their own homes & resume the garb & occupations (the manners they have never laid aside) of gentlemen!

FEBRUARY 14, 1865

Father here to dinner today much depressed & despondant. This terrible up turning & overthrowing of all his plans made by the late freshet bears hard

---

[12]Dickson's Battery, originally Second Co. G, Fortieth North Carolina (Third Artillery) Regiment, was redesignated Co. E, Thirteenth Battalion North Carolina Light Artillery in November, 1863. Henry Dickson, formerly a first lieutenant in the company, was elected captain of the battery in April, 1863. The battery served in eastern North Carolina through most of the war and was stationed at Hamilton during the first three weeks of February, 1865. Clark, *Histories of the North Carolina Regiments*, IV, 353-354; Manarin and Jordan, *North Carolina Troops*, I, 443-444, 585.

[13]Moses Ashley Curtis (1808-1872), married to Mary de Rosset of Wilmington in 1834, was a prominent botanist and an Episcopal minister in Hillsborough for several years. His son, John Henry Curtis, served as a private in Co. E, Thirteenth Battalion North Carolina Light Artillery until his death during the battle at Bentonville on March 20, 1865. Clark, *Histories of the North Carolina Regiments*, IV, 341; V, 640-641; Manarin and Jordan, *North Carolina Troops*, IV, 446, 587; *Concise Dictionary of American Biography*, 207; Gary S. Dunbar, "Silas McDowell and the Early Botanical Exploration of Western North Carolina," *North Carolina Historical Review*, XLI (October, 1964), 428-433.

on him. He struggles manfully & takes it apparently with great equanimity & resignation, but it cannot be borne by one at his time of life as it can by younger people. The employment, the policy of a life, is gone & it is hard to have to remodel one's system of farming & management at his age, but the resolution, the Christian spirit, with which he makes the endeavour excite our tenderness & admiration in the highest degree.

FEBRUARY 15, 1865

Rumours that Sherman has possession of Kingsville, but I do not beleive it. Surely we have not again been flanked & forced to evacuate Branchville! The situation of our friends in Aiken gives us the keenest anxiety & the total inability to hear aught of them increases it still more.

FEBRUARY 16, 1865

My Aunt & Cousins dined with us today. Such nice girls, so pretty & engaging, so intelligent & straight forward. There is something deeply touching in my Aunt's appearance & manner. When one thinks of the changes she has seen, of her widowed estate, of the partial loss of her eyesight, of the fortune to which she was born, & of the enjoyment of which she is now deprived (let us hope but temporarily) & see how cheerful and pleasant she is & what an interest she manifests in what goes on around her, one cannot but wonder at & admire her.

Sad news of the capture of my brother in law, Col Clarke. He has recently been (in consequence of disability for active service from the wound received last summer) assigned to duty as Commandant of the Post at Raleigh & when captured was on his way in an Ambulance with another officer to Petersburg. At Dinwiddie C H they were overhauled by the enemy in a manner most unexpected to them both & hurried off to Yankee instead of Confederate Head Quarters. I fear the confinement will go hard with him, for his health is delicate & his wound still open & from its position on the shoulder blade he needs the services of an attendant to dress it. I am deeply sorry for poor Mary. Her distress must be very great.

FEBRUARY 17, 1865

At Hascosea all day. Mr E has had the Grape Arbour raised & the arbour all thoroughly repaired & enlarged & a great improvement it is. I busy enlarging my Asparagus beds. Not one word from the South, not even a rumour. I know not what to think of it. Gov Vance out in a Proclamation announcing to us how the Peace negotiations have failed & calling on us to be of good cheer & to stand by one another & vigorously to prosecute the war & assuring us of ultimate success. All right & true. We *will* succeed! God will not desert & deliver us over to the enemy this goodly land which He has given us! We will yet leave a fair inheritance free & independant to our children.

Butler, the Yankee Representative man, having been by them deprived of command in consequence of his failure below Wilmington, the agency for Exchange of Prisoners devolves on Gen Grant. The Cartel will therefore now be resumed we are told & the Exchange is to go on regularly man for man till all be exchanged. Good news to our poor soldiers languishing in Northern Pest houses, but pray God the enemy really intend it & do not show us some unworthy Yankee trick & again refuse to execute their solemn engagements.

FEBRUARY 18, 1865

At Father's on horseback this afternoon to see Mama, who has a cold & sore throat. Found her better. Sad news from the South. Frank Jones writes that he will soon be here on a furlough, for Charleston is to be evacuated! Letters from Richmond or rather from Longstreet's Headquarters tell us that the President has ordered the evacuation of *Charleston, Augusta, & Wilmington,* so that Hardee can have a strong force wherewith to meet Sherman. The papers tell us that a battle is imminent before Columbia. Sherman avoided Branchville, crossed the Edisto higher up, cut the Columbia Road below Orangeburgh, & rumour says was at last accounts 20 miles from Columbia. Another account say he is advancing by the Lexington road & has crossed the Congaree & yet we are also told that Beauregard has telegraphed that he intends to hold the line of the Congaree; but I did not see the Dispatch, & many persons do not beleive that Beauregard is there! The papers are singularly reticent & we know next to nothing of the situation. My faith is strong. Sherman cannot long go on thus in his conquering course, but if Wilmington, Charleston and Agusta be indeed evacuated & with their strong defences held against us by the enemy the blow he inflicts on us is fearful. God Help us and fight for us in this extremity. Be Thou our defence, our Sheild & Buckler, & vain will be the rage of our enemies!

We have a notice of a fight between Wheeler & Kilpatrick on the 11th near Aiken in which "Wheeler enticed Kilpatrick from his entrenched Camp, defeated & drove him five miles," so we fear the enemy has been in the village & can only pray that they have left our old mother & our sister & helpless little ones unmolested. God be with them and grant them a deliverance out of all their troubles.

It is sad to see father, usually so sanguin, thus cast down. I look forward, indeed I beleive we all do, to the 4th of March with a sort of undefined sense that it will bring us releif, tho' of what kind I cannot myself tell. Recognition by the European powers will do us but little good without Intervention also & of that we have no hope. Lincoln can no longer after the 4th of March claim to be our President by anything but the right of conquest. Hitherto his claim to be our Constitutional Head has been allowed. That expires on the 4th & it remains to be seen whether or not the various foreign Consuls will present their credentials to Mr Davis. Without a single seaport, however, I do not see how they can do it. The power that *is* will be the one they recognize & so the loss of Charleston may cost us the glittering bauble (which, however, we so much covet) Recognition!

Negroe Soldiers in the Army is since Lincoln ultimatum again brt forward in Congress, but as yet thank God, voted down.[14] A most unwise and unjust system of taxation is proposed in that august body. I do not wince at its *heaviness*, but I confess I do at its *injustice*, but I do not understand "Currency." When I meddle with it I feel I am touching "things too high for me." So Mrs Edmondston, leave finance & the Currency and that vexed subject "the taxes" to wiser heads.

One thing, however, deeply pains me, i.e., the growing distrust with which all men view "the Government." It is getting to be considered an instrument of oppression & tyrrany because it does not keep faith with its citizens. The Conscript Act was a huge breach of promise, the act diminishing the value of the money was another, and now this last fatal step of refusing to take its own bonds in discharge of its own demands will I fear breed still more mischeif. It takes ones whole surplus at its own price & for sole equivalent gives you a peice of yellow paper, an I O U, refuses point blank to give you a circulating medium & immediately after comes another agent, demands I know not what per cent of tax on your property & absolutely refuses even to look at your demand on Government which you received from his brother Agent not long before. In private life that would be called *Swindling*, & shall a nation of gentlemen be less careful of their national honour than is a Jew broker of his good name and jems?

February 19, 1865

Mr E was at Clarksville yesterday & contrary to his usual custom was detained until quite late so that I was getting quite uncomfortable about him. When he came in however he had a sad state of things to relate to me. Our neighbor the Messrs Smith's negroes have either taken a panic—lest they be put into the army or have become completely demoralized & have commenced going off by tens & twenties to the Yankee's. On Friday night Mr R. Smith lost twenty, Mr James Smith 14, & others in different proportions to the number of fifty five, all prime hands, just what the Yankees want to recruit their army. An order was issued last week calling on the planters to give a descriptive list of all their negroes between 18 & 50. An indiscreet agent, a Captain of Milita, went about pencil & book in hand and applied to many

---

[14]The Goldsboro *State Journal*, February 18, 1865, reported on the progress of the bill in the Confederate Congress providing for the use of Negro troops. The bill passed by a vote of 38 for and 35 against. The *Richmond Enquirer*, March 22 and 23, 1865, carried items about a company of sixty-five Negroes raised by Capt. J. R. Chambliss at Camp Winder in Richmond. A combat troop of Negro soldiers formed from hospital personnel in Richmond also existed and engaged in the fight to defend Richmond in March, 1865. Brewer, *The Confederate Negro*, 102-103, 186. See footnote 121, 1864.

negroes for their ages, etc. This coupled with the intimation which they have had from the free discussion of the expediency of putting them into the Army, which many of them have heard from their masters whilst waiting at table, others from illiterate persons who *spell* out the papers and know not the difference between offering a Resolution or introducing a Bill & its final passage, & so have asserted that Congress had actually placed them in Army, has so excited & frightened the whole negro population that some of them went off without a moment's preparation, making a Hegira more sudden than that of the Israelites from Egypt. The order came to Mr E & I strongly urged him to take no notice of it. Whether it was issued by Confederate or State authority I considered it equally intrusive and offensive. The tax list gives them the no & that should be information sufficient for them. He thought differently however & gave it. We see no effect of the panic amongst our people. Probably the extreme isolation in which we keep them has prevented their being affected by it.

Came Mr Brinkley[15] to dinner & to unburden his mind and get Mr E's opinion as to the state of our affairs. He seems downhearted enough, but has heard from his son, who I mentioned was wounded & captured in that sad affair of Ft Fisher. He is recovering & when heard from was just being removed from Smithville to N Y. Had our pudding in honour of the day, the 19th of Feb, & in the afternoon Mr E insisted on opening one of our few remaining bottles of wine which I have been hoarding for an emergenc. The taste of the fine dry old sherry with its rich bouquet & nutty flavour carried us back to Peace & to the blessings we then enjoyed, brought back visions of after dinner merriment, of a long polished Mahogany table, of cut glass decanters circulating in their silver coasters through a wilderness of beautiful fruit & fine nuts, of hearty & innocent mirth, of laughter & song &, as we smiled over the reminiscence came the memory of many who once joined us, the merriest of the merry, whose voices we shall hear no more, of dear friends many of whom now, alas, fill bloody graves, of disappointed hopes & young lives cut short by the hand of a ruthless & relentless foe, & we sighed in the midst of our happiness, and O, how heartily did we both re-echo the toast "to our next Wedding Day! may we celebrate it in Peace!" God grant it!

FEBRUARY 20, 1865

At the Gunboat with Mr E. I had no idea how rapidly the work had gone on nor of what a fine large boat it is! Messrs Smith and Elliot, the contractors, deserve the greatest credit for the energetic manner in which they have carried

---

[15]Spencer Brinkley's son, William H. Brinkley, served as a private in Co. F, Thirty-sixth North Carolina (Second Artillery) Regiment until the battle at Fort Fisher. Wounded on January 13, 1865, Brinkley was sent to a hospital in Smithville where he was captured by Union troops and later confined at Point Lookout, Maryland. He was released upon taking the Oath of Allegiance on June 3, 1865. Manarin and Jordan, *North Carolina Troops*, 1, 259.

it so near to completion. Heard more bad news of the state of feeling amongst the negroes. Mr Peter Smith told us that he had lost every negro man he had but one, an old hog feeder the night before (last night). Mr J N Smith had but four left! Out of a large plantation his father lost most of his men and some women who, will it be beleived, left young children behind them. All of our neighbours have suffered. Mr Bishop & Mr Shields our nearest neighbours at Hascosea have each lost four. Nearly a hundred crossed the river last night & went into Bertie on their way to the Yankee lines. So much method do they seem to observe & so well are they piloted that the idea of its being a panic seems to lose ground & yet the ones to whom the Militia Capt spoke are those to go off. But they go not alone, for as I said before women & old men accompany them. Pray God they meet hard lines & come back with an "evil report" of their new found friends. Our time seems not to have come as yet, but who can tell how many hours it may be delayed?

Heard bad news from the South, but hope it prove rumour only. Columbia is said to have fallen! I cannot credit it. A Yankee force has been at Tarrboro & burned the Commissary stores there. It is not known how strong they were or whether they have yet retreated. A heavy force is also said to be advancing on Kinston. God help us! The wolf is at our throats! What next is in store for us? The Yankee presence amongst us cannot long be delayed, for these negroes will carry an account of our defenceless condition & of our plentiful land & abundant crops. There is grain enough here to feed Lee's army for months, could he but get it. Transportation is what we want.

The River looked beautifully this evening & as the canoe floated over its calm still bosom my heart rose in Gratitude to God the Giver for all His blessings. Long may it be ere that placid water be vexed with the presence of Yankee Gunboats!

February 21, 1865

At the Gunboat again with all the young folks. Met there Captain & Mrs Cooke & a young party from Scotland Neck. Our young people at home to dine with us. I do not think young folks enjoy themselves as they used. Is it the war? The demoralization amongst our neighbours negroes continues. Mr Peter Smith lost all the males at his house last night. Many females too have gone. To use the expression of one of the gentleman, "it spreads like a revival at a Camp Meeting." Ours are as usual and show no signs of disaffection.

February 22, 1865

At Hascosea with Mr E, the natal day of our Government. Matters seems gloomy but even at the worst they may turn. Hear that Charleston is evacuated, that Sherman has taken possession of Columbia after a battle in which some of our Western troops behaved badly tho' they were led by Beauregard in person, but I hope these are but mere rumours.

FEBRUARY 24, 1865

Mr E at Halifax yesterday in compliance with the order to reorganize the Home Guard, a most senseless peice of business, for if they wish a change of officers in the hope of getting a better set, they hope against hope. That is all I have to say. One of the newly elected Lieuts was so drunk that he knew not how to comport himself & the Captain is by no means a sober man. Mr E was, as we knew he would be, thrown out. He would not *"treat"* or drink Apple Brandy with the men to be made Com in Cheif, far less Captain of the Home Guard. What he will do now I know not. That remains to be seen. Had he gone before a surgeon he would have been placed in the class who are to remain in the county, & as the men who compose it are mostly from his own district would no doubt have been their Captain, but he did not do so, so I wait in simple faith, trusting that he will not be separated from me. Independantly of his health, he is of vast use here at home, particularly now whilst the negro population is so excited. God will direct & may I see that what He ordains is for the best.

Wilmington certainly evacuated & the enemy advancing up the R R. At the last accounts they had seized the bridge over the North Eastern Branch of the Cape Fear. Home Guard all ordered to Raleigh on Monday, that being the point now threatened. No newspapers & no authentic news. Our uncertainty is cruel. Prisoners rapidly exchanged. Congress adjourns tomorrow, for which God be praised. Our only hope is that they do not pass the Negro Conscript Bill. That would be the climax of our fate. The absurdities of our Legislators are fearful. When we succeed it will be in spite of them.

Came Mr Dunlop to dinner, is hopeful & says that the Military circles are sure of Sherman's speedy defeat, laughs at the idea of an abandonment of Petersburg or Richmond. He comes for his family; if the step, however, should be taken he intends taking them to England. Assures us that there is complication between the U S & France. The "Ides of March" are near & they will I hope show something of it. Upon God alone do we trust. Rachel spent the night with me but went back with Mr D.

Soldiers of the 3d Ala here collecting forage. They dined with us & told us that they had heard from home but once since the 1st of Nov when Sherman cut the Geo roads. Poor fellows! How could I bear that! God would support me. "As thy days so shall thy strength be."

FEBRUARY 25, 1865

A miserable day, mist & rain until the earth is like a soaked sponge & smokes like a seething cauldron. Mr E at Enfield to see Surgeon Branch. I hard at work alone all day turning one of his thick overcoats! *Think* of it! One more debt I owe the Yankees! Did I ever think in former days that I would come *to sewing* on or he to *wearing* a *turned* coat! However, it looks very nice and

I am thankful that it is worth the labour & also for my ability to do it. So we go!

FEBRUARY 26, 1865

Late last night came Mr E home from Enfield miserably wet & tired, having been detained by the breaking in of a bridge at—Beech Swamp—& then in the darkness—driving into the creek at the Mill not knowing that the river had risen rapidly during his breif absence. The first intimation he had of it was the water runing into the buggy, even the cushions were soaked! Kuhlborn seized all the light articles he had with him. His dinner basket, flask, sheepskin, etc., are in the grasp of the water spirit! The Surgeon at Enfield, a stranger to him, not only gave him the Certificate of disability for active service but expressed the greatest surprise how a man in his condition could for one moment think of incurring the hardships of the service, even as a commissioned officer. He told him that as a private he could not serve for a week, but would be entirely disabled by the fatigues & exposure of a soldiers life before that time had elapsed! Nevertheless it is necessary for him to go before some board at Raleigh 'ere he can be finally discharged, so he leaves tomorrow. This has been a painful necessity to Mr E, one he has shrunk from so long as he held a post the duties of which it was possible for him to discharge, but he had no alternative. Even as an officer I doubt his ability to discharge his duty. Quiet & a regular life & strict regimen are indispensible for his very existence, leaving comfort entirely out of the question.

He brt sad news of inefficiency & bad management on Bragg's part in the evacuation of Wilmington. We were pressed so closely that part of Clingman's Brigade was cut off & captured (would that Bragg had been with them) & some of our forces so scattered & separated that they are entirely inefficient. The Garrison of Ft Anderson were happily gotten out and have gone to Fayetteville. Hoke's Division has fallen back to Warsaw, the enemy at Burgaw—Sherman still pressing on, we since the battle at Columbia falling back. The last news placed Sherman within 45 miles of Charlotte. It is thought we will make another stand in front of that place. Lee has certainly gone on to take command in person. Who fills his place before Petersburg we know not. Pray God he be competent & vigilant.

Home Guard all ordered to Raleigh to resist Terry's advance from Wilmington. Foster it is reported organizing an expedition up the Roanoke in conjunction with him. The Yankees are certainly bent on doing *something* before the 4th of March. They have some great object in view to produce the extraordinary activity. God grant we defeat it. Breckenridge has been made Sec of War. I am sorry to lose him from the field. He has always been successful & "*prestige*" is a great element in military affairs. Napoleon beleived in *Luck* & Breckenridge is not only able but *lucky*.

Mr E brt me a paper of needles from Enfield, for which he paid $10, & two skeins of blk silk $5 each. He brt me from Halifax a peice of long cloth to look at and buy it if I wished it at $45 per yd for the peice, $50 for part of it! I decided that we could not afford it. I was not willing to wear the price of three barrels of corn in one chemise. I prefer Rockfish[16] or even domestic home-spun rather than commit such an extravagance. Think of $1800 for a peice of long cloth.

FEBRUARY 27, 1865

Mr E off this morning for Raleigh. His departure was much saddened by tidings brt by Mr Brinkley before breakfast to the effect that "Charlotte was in Sherman's hands and that we had evacuated Goldsboro." This was the rumour which lengthened the faces of the "quid nuncs" at Clarksville last night; it shall not lengthen mine for I do not beleive it. The River steadily rising. I am on an island, a kind of 'Anglo Saxon Robinson Crusoe' with Ethiopian's only for companionship. Think of it! I sit here the only white soul for miles and they cut off from me by an angry sea & have not a single tremour! Indeed I beleive I rather like the isolation produced by the water, for it prevents any but our own negroes having access to me & I would not relish having to entertain wandering soldiers whilst I am entirely alone. Am interrupted by my paddle man with the mail, old newspapers only, but father writes me that his advices from Halifax are to the effect that there is "no news," so I did well not to be long faced this morning!

The papers are filled with rumours as to what happened before the occupation of Columbia, but I will not fill you, O my Journal, with them. We evacuated Columbia after a heavy skirmish (so we are told) because we had not troops to hold it. If that be so I know not where others are to come from with which to enable us to make a stand anywhere. From present accounts Beauregard has made foot cavalry of his soldiers & Sherman emulating him comes galloping after! We draw comfort from the fact that the "race is not to the swift—or the battle to the strong." So Beauregard, fleet as he is will be overtaken by Sherman, & then beware Gen Sherman! Your turn will come, for strong as you are you will lose "the battle." Does not such badinage at such a crisis, Mrs Edmondston, strike you as like the "crackling of thorns under a pot"?[17] I will not offend you by carrying the simile further & asking whose "laughter" the "crackling thorns" reminded Solomon of! Charleston is certainly evacuated. My heart bleeds for it and it stirs every fibre of my frame to think that the Yankee flag again floats over Sumter. One comfort only

---

[16]Mrs. Edmondston apparently was referring to the cotton cloth produced by the Rockfish Company located near Fayetteville. During the war John Haigh served as president of the company. Elizabeth Yates Webb, "Cotton Manufacturing and State Regulation in North Carolina, 1861-'65," *North Carolina Historical Review*, IX (April, 1932), 130.

[17]Ecclesiastes 7:6a.

remains to us—*They could not take it by direct attack.* The blood stained bricks, drunk with the best blood of the South, seem to cry out at the pressure of a Yankee foot.

MARCH 2, 1865

Yesterday came Father to take me back home with him to remain during Mr E's absence, but I gave him such good reasons for my remaining here that he at once acquiesced in their propriety and agreed to stay and dine with me. So we had a good bout at chess, a long talk, & our dinner, when I walked with him to his canoe & saw him take ship & paddle off & came back to my maids and their work. Such shaping & hemming, such making of new clothes, and remaking of old as I have had since Mr E left, Arachne is a joke to me. Suddenly, however, my work was put to a stop by Fanny's exclaiming "*Here Master—he self now.*" So down everything went and I welcomed the wanderer home once more. He found when on the cars that his presence in Raleigh was not needed, that the matter could be arranged by forwarding his papers, so he did so and took the return train.

He brought but little news of Sherman's where-a-bouts. Nothing definite is known. Gen Johnston has been placed in command of the Army of the Tenn & of the states of S C, Geo, and Florida. In his orders assuming command he says he has been placed there by the Gen-in-Cheif, so that would seem to imply a collision between Gen Lee & the President, but we outsiders know nothing. We watch the game of War from afar, powerless but deeply interested spectators. One thing is certain Sherman has not attacked Charlotte & rumour now points to Fayetteville in this State as his next stage. There it is thought he will unite with Terry from Wilmington whilst Schofield from New Berne marches on Goldsboro & the three together will simultaneously advance on Raleigh. Let us hope that we may be able to frustrate their designs.

Mr E brought further sad accounts of mismanagement in the evacuation of Wilmington, which I suppose is also to be laid to Bragg's account; 50,000 lbs of Bacon were burnt & boxes on boxes of shoes tumbled into the water, whilst our barefooted troops marched out hungry & without rations before the face of the victorious enemy. The want of discipline and even mutuny in Hoke's Division is fearful & the daily desertions appalling. These tidings he had from Mr McMahon who was domiciled with the army for days, endeavouring to get 250 bales of Cotton which he had in Wilmington brt out. In this he was successful thus showing that if a private citizen could get transportation to save his own property, the Gen Commanding could surely have secured the Government property, possessing as he does absolute power over all Railway officials. The mismanagement in the navy was astounding. Pinckney[18] the officer in command, *left*, positively *left*, & threw the whole duty on an agent, one

---

[18]Commo. Robert F. Pinkney, under the command of Gen. R. F. Hoke, was ordered "to organize all the naval forces in his department and those from Charleston into one command under his charge, and assign

Walker. Our seamen lost everything but what they had on, nay worse the entire cargo of a Blockade Runner which had succeded in running in, comprising everything that was needed to complete the Gunboat now building below us was destroyed! & that as we have seen from no want of transportation. The Yankees are now at Burgaw Station & Hoke about seven miles in advance of them. A truce for seven days for the exchange of prisoners has been agreed on between the two forces & our Agent for exchange, Col Hatch,[19] is there conducting it as rapidly as possible. The sufferings of the Yankee prisoners on their backward route are represented as very great, but we were not to blame for it & it was not in our power to alleviate it. They had been collected to the number of several thousand there for Exchange when Terry refused to receive them & it became necessary to remove them rapidly to prevent their falling into his hands. Such a step had not been contemplated & consequently no provision had been made for them; hence their suffering. On the heads of their own Government & countrymen be it! Our hands are clean! The Yankees are relaying the track of the Wilmington & Manchester road & intend soon running trains through from Charleston. We have given Sherman a base, a stick which he will now use to break our own heads. News from Frank Jones at Fayetteville says before the evacuation of Charleston everything belonging to the Navy was destroyed & also the greater part of the city. For that God be thanked! Would that the Yankee found it only a heap of ruins!

MARCH 3, 1865

Out on horseback with Mr E on my new horse, for he has exchanged my little filley the Queen of May for one which he thinks more suitable to me. She is older but promises well. The earth like a sponge, so wet has it been. Came Owen back from Weldon where we sent him with an invitation to Capt & Mrs Langdon to come down and visit us. Mrs L is the daughter of an old Camden friend, who has recently married & her husband is now stationed in Weldon as Ass. Qt Master.[20] They will be with us next week.

No News. The House has passed the Negro Enlistment Bill, making it, however, voluntary with the Masters whether they send their slaves or not, deprecates any action which interferes with the rights of the owner, authorizes

---

them to duty at the batteries at the obstructions . . ." along the coastal and inland waters of North Carolina. *Civil War Naval Chronology*, IV, 50; VI, 198; *Official Records (Navy)*, Series I, XII, 188; Clark, *Histories of the North Carolina Regiments*, V, 313.

[19]Col. William Henry Hatch (1833-1896), a lawyer and United States congressman from Missouri after the war, served as the assistant agent of exchange of the Confederate army. *Concise Dictionary of American Biography*, 411-412; Clark, *Histories of the North Carolina Regiments*, V, 624.

[20]Capt. Richard F. Langdon, of New Hanover County, initially acted as lieutenant in Co. E, First Regiment North Carolina State Troops before his assignment as assistant quartermaster of the Third Regiment North Carolina State Troops. On September 15, 1864, Langdon was reassigned to the command of the ordnance train for Gen. Robert E. Rodes's division. He retained this post until the end of the war. Manarin and Jordan, *North Carolina Troops*, III, 191, 485, 488; Clark, *Histories of the North Carolina Regiments*, I, 137.

the President to *ask* for the slaves only & makes no change in his status toward his master or society. Should the owners refuse to comply the States are to be called on to furnish each its respective quota, an attempt on the part of our wise Congress "to run with the hare & hunt with the hounds," an attempt which will end in utter failure to do either. It will unsettle the negroes & add nothing to the efficiency of our army. Our Legislation during the war has truly been only a series of Millstones hung needlessly around our necks! Some day I will enumerate them & show what weight we as a people have submitted to be saddled with. A new tax bill, but as I do not understand taxes I shrink from endeavouring to fathom this. One thing only I know & that is that our "Tax in kind"[21] is increased from a tenth to a fifth (afterwards reconsidered). That touches a farmer so nearly and palpably that I need no instructor to explain it to me.

March 5, 1865

Sherman advancing on Cheraw, skirmishing within a few miles of that place. What force we have to confront him with, Johnston, Lee, and Beauregard only know.

March 12, 1865

Have been all the week at Hascosea, I gardening when the weather would permit, Mr E busy with his potatoes. Unfortunately for us we found that the recent warm damp weather had rotted more than five hundred bushels of them, so to prevent their being an entire loss he has been pounding, pounding, & pressing them preparatory for distillation.

On the 10th the Congressional Fast Day we heard the pleasant news that we had repulsed Schofield below Kinston, taking 1600 prisoners. D H Hill was in front, Hoke in their rear, but our joy is damped by the fact that Bragg is Com in Cheif. Some contre temps will be sure to happen & some how or other we will lose the fruit of a victory gained by him.

Letters from Capt Langdon deferring his visit to better weather & roads, so we remained at Hascosea until Sat afternoon when we had a canter home through the high woods, the river still being too high to admit of crossing at Hill's mill. The season being backward, that silly Honey Peach, however, looks as tho it was trying to bloom. Even Vegetables learn by experience, but this one seems inapt. I preserve a correspondence between Sherman & Hampton in which the gentleman gets the better of the Yankee.[22] By it we see

---

[21]The tax reforms passed on March 11 and 17, 1865, were adopted in an effort to bolster and extend the tax schedules of 1863. The earlier bill had been weakened by allowing taxes to be paid in depreciated currency, and by granting rebates. The 1865 revisions sought to increase the revenues collected by taxing goods and hard money. Randall and Donald, *Civil War and Reconstruction*, 257-258.

[22]This correspondence, dated February 24 and 27, 1865, dealt with the military practice and ethics of executing prisoners in retaliation for crimes committed by foragers in pillaging and burning civilian properties. Hampton claimed the right of defending the land against marauders, while Sherman insisted foraging

that Columbia has been burned! God help the poor women & children, for it is on them that the magnanimous Yankee nation makes war.

MARCH 14, 1865

As I feared, Bragg's evil genius is in the ascendant! The victory at Kinston has done us no good, for we hear from Halifax that it is occupied by the enemy & that we have evacuated Goldsboro. The rumour runs that Weldon is also to be given up & that all our troops are ordered to Raleigh to meet Sherman there. This, however, I cannot beleive, for our armies in the field cannot afford to lose the grain crop still in this section; even the Tithe has not yet been collected & there is food enough here to feed Lee for weeks, so I hear. Should Weldon be given up, God help us. We would be delivered over utterly defenseless, a rich prize for greedy Yankee marauders. The state of mind into which this news has thrown us is pitiable. Such terrible uncertainty! The desire to rescue a few necessaries in case of being overrun, & the utter inability to find a place of safety for them, taxes our faith & patience to the utmost. God help and sustain us!

Particulars of the occupation and burning of Columbia reached us last night. They are horrible. Five thousand people left homeless in a few hours. The Yankee demons rushed infuriated through the streets yelling & with savage imprecations & brandishing blazing torches with which they fired the town. The work of pillage went on until even those cutthroat theives were satiated. Sherman, with an utter want of all noblesse, or chivalric feeling which would have made him protect the property & family of his opponent, occupied Gen Hampton's house as his head quarters! What would Bayard, Du Guesclin, or the Black Prince[23] have thought of such a breach of the courtesies of War? How thankful we should be that there was nothing in Charleston left for them to triumph over! Our own hands destroyed it & save the seige guns & the soil itself, little fell into their avaricious hands. The Yankee flag was raised in Columbia in two places simultaneously by two negroes. We are unable to understand the effect intended to be produced by

---

was a necessary component of war. He added that, although excesses possibly occurred, he could not "permit an enemy to judge or punish with wholesale murder." *Official Records (Army)*, Series I, XLVII, Part II, 546, 596-597.

[23]Edward of Woodstock (1330-1376), Prince of Wales (Black Prince), famed for his army career fighting the French during the 100 Years' War, engaged French forces over the disposition of the throne of Castile. Peter the Cruel, the legitimate ruler, was deposed by his brother and the French army commanded by Bertrand Du Guesclin (1320?-1380). Edward subsequently defeated the French in 1367, restored Peter to the throne, and took Du Guesclin prisoner. Du Guesclin eventually paid a large ransom for his freedom and again fought Peter the Cruel, this time displacing him permanently from the throne. The generosity of Edward toward other military leaders and nobility was well known, but he also was noted for acts of extreme cruelty toward peasants and the poorer classes. *Webster's Biographical Dictionary*, 155, 447, 469; J. R. Tanner and others. *Decline of Empire and Papacy*, Volume VII of *The Cambridge Medieval History*, by J. R. Tanner and others (New York: Macmillan Company, 8 volumes, 1911-1936), 361, 363-365.

this coup de theatre, but doubtless the Yankee nation is not so dull as we are on this point.

A letter from Amo mailed at Charlotte giving us an account of the terrific march that battalion of State Cadets, mere boys, underwent. The S C senior reserves broke down under it & had to be disbanded. How the boys stood it is a wonder. The retreat was from Columbia to Wadesboro in this state; nowhere were we strong enough to make head against our insolent foe. He has no news from Aiken save that a severe Cavalry fight took place in the streets of the town, in which we repulsed Kilpatrick but afterwards fell back, and it is now in the enemies lines. God be with our friends there!

March 15, 1865

At father's with Mr E in a canoe yesterday afternoon, by father's request, as he wished to discuss our situation with Mr E, but found there a note from Mr McMahon telling us "that the powers that be had reconsidered the matter & decided to hold Weldon at all hazards and this portion of the R R." This gives us temporary releif. Bragg has fallen back towards Raleigh, but as yet the enemy have not occupied Goldsboro. A great battle is thought to be imminent somewhere between Raleigh & Fayetteville, but no one knows either Johnston or Sherman's position & in consequence our suspense is cruel. Mr McMahon tells us that he learns, & officially, that Gen Hampton fell in with Kilpatrick's Cavalry, took some seventeen hundred prisoners, 1000 horses, 15 peices of artillery, & his whole wagon train, a complete surprise, & caused himself to leave his *coat, pants,* & *boots* behind. So Kilpatrick has lost his spurs! What a ridiculous figure he must have cut, running off "sans culotte."[24]

Congress has passed a vote of thanks to Gen Hampton for his "manly" letter to Sherman & pledging themselves to his support in carrying out his intentions as expressed therein of retaliation on Sherman two to one for every man Sherman "murders" (as he himself expresses it) "for shooting his (Sherman's) foragers" when found burning private houses. Sherman says it has been officially reported to him that his "foragers are murdered" after being captured and that he has ordered a similar no of prisoners in his hands to be "disposed of in like manner" i.e., "*murdered.*" Hampton's letter is a masterpiece. This morning came an Agent from a Committee of citizens organized according to Gov Vance's suggestion to collect voluntary subscriptions of meat, meal, & flour for the army. These supplies are to be over and above

---

[24]Confederate cavalry under Gen. M. C. Butler, of Hampton's command, surprised Kilpatrick's headquarters during a dawn raid on March 10, 1865. Kilpatrick and his officers were forced to abandon the camp in their nightclothes, but they managed to reach their men before the Confederates consolidated their victory. Kilpatrick escaped capture and managed to retake his headquarters and the female companion he abandoned during the hasty retreat. The story of his morning flight attracted considerable attention and was dubbed "Kilpatrick's Shirt-tail Skedaddle" by the Federal infantry. Barrett, *Civil War in North Carolina,* 305-309.

every man's *surplus* that the Government already has. It must be from his own stock of provisions, *what he denies himself for the sake of the army.* We on consultation together had determined last week to deprive ourselves of meat at one meal per diem & to give what we thus save to the army, but so pressing is the need that we go beyond that & give 500 lbs of meat which we had intended for our own table & will live on bread & vegetables instead. Mr E gave 500 lbs of Meat & 1500 lbs of meal, promising if the necessity continues to do yet more, so I must bestir myself & make every inch of my garden do its whole duty. There will be many days this summer when we cannot taste meat, but what of that if our army is fed.

Yesterday Mr E received a full exemption from all "military service on account of physical disability" from the authorized Board of Medical Examiners. I am most thankful for this, for he will now be able, being untrameled, to do much more voluntarily than he otherwise could. He can judge his own strength & ability & when he finds it overtaxed immediately retire and come home to recuperate. He will thus be of more service than he would be if under orders all the time. If another had the right of judging of his condition & strength I know that a Hospital would soon be his lot & once broken down it would be long if ever ere he recovered again.

MARCH 19, 1865

On the 17th St Patrick's came Mr Brinkley for the tithe & announced to us "that the Yankees had burnt *Fadesville*[25] sure, but that Picket and one other general had whipped Sheridan *good*, whipped him good for certain," but as the papers said nothing of either event, we hoped that that part of his intelligence which destroyed Fayetville is incorrect, but yesterday's news made us tremble for the unfortunate town. Sherman entered it on Sunday, our troops with the exception of Gen's Hampton & Hardee with about 100 cavalry having fallen back, Hampton charged the Yankee cavalry, 200 in number, through the streets, driving them back, killing numbers, and taking many prisoner. With his own hand he killed several, indeed his exploits sound more like those of a Paladin of Romance than of a General in the 19th century! At the head of five of his men he drove the Yankee's through the streets of the town & ere the advancing column came up was off in safety with his prisoners! Sherman came up during the day & since then we have had no account of his proceeding. Mrs Williams (Isabella Huske) was robbed & treated with great personal indignity, her wedding ring torn from her fingers, & the earrings from her ears, & a pistol placed at her head she was forced to show

---

[25]Fayetteville, which Sherman occupied on March 11, 1865, was not burned but considerable property was deliberately destroyed. The former United States Arsenal, railroad property, factories, town shops, and every mill in the vicinity but one were razed. Many private homes on the outskirts of the town were burned, and most residential dwellings in Fayetteville were thoroughly plundered. Barrett, *Civil War in North Carolina*, 311-317.

the wretches where she had concealed her silver. When she left her house they were preparing to fire it. She made good her escape & is now at my sister Mrs Miller's. God help me & keep me from ever being placed in a like situation, but I hope that if I am, my blood will rise superior to fear & enable me to defy the base ignoble cowards! My after life would be embittered by the reflection that I had yeilded to them. But no one knows what they will do until they are tried. God deliver me from the trial!

All the public buildings & even the Churches in Raleigh have been seized for Hospitals. We even hear that a private house has been impressed, but that I doubt. Mrs Miller writes that she has cooking done for 280 patients in the Episcopal Church. These men were wounded in the battle below Kinston. What will become of the unfortunates from the now impending battlefield? God be with them! The last news from Sherman report him as seeming avoiding a battle & turning to the north East, seemingly to effect a junction with Schofield & Terry, but our news is exceedingly vague & unsatisfactory in the last degree. God grant us a speedy & a glorious Victory & enable us "to drive the invader & spoiler from our land!"

The President has, I am sorry to say, sent a Message to Congress in which he tells us that Richmond is in greater danger than it has been since the commencement of the War. (We may thank him for it, for had he not releived Joe Johnston & sent Hood off at a tangent into Tenn, Sherman would now be entangled in the mountains of Geo). He expresses his satisfaction that the negro conscription bill has been passed, demands more men, more money, & more power, says the silver in the Confederacy must be coined to pay the army, Habeas Corpus suspended & a huge Militia bill passed. Ah! had our civil affairs been managed half so well as our Military, in what a different situation would we now find ourselves!

I have been much entertained latterly with the Life of Bertrand Du Guesclin by Gen Jamison of S C & this has led me back to the fountain head—Froissart[26]—& I have read it again for the third or fourth time with I beleive greater zest than I ever did before. So much struck was I yesterday with a prayer of the Black Prince before the battle of Navarretta that I transcribe it here as more suitable to our situation (with a slight alteration in the last clause) than aught I can write. Would that Joe Johnston or Gen Lee *had* a copy of it. How apt would it be from their lips?

God of Truth, the Father of Jesus Christ who hast made & fashioned me, condescend through Thy benign Grace that the success of the battle of this day may be for

---

[26]David Flavel Jamison (1810-1864), a South Carolina lawyer, state representative, and president of the secession convention, temporarily withdrew from public service between 1861 and 1862 to finish his two-volume *Life and Times of Bertrand Du Guesclin*, published in London and Charleston in 1864. *Dictionary of American Biography*, IX, 604-605. Jean Froissart (1333?-1400?) was a French chronicler. His classic work was *Chronique de France, d'Angleterre, d'Ecosse et d'Espagne*, covering history between 1325 and approximately 1400. *Webster's Biographical Dictionary*, 563.

me and my Army; for Thou knowest that in truth I have been solely emboldened to undertake it in the support of justice & reason to reinstate this King on his throne who has been disinherited and driven from it as well as from his country.

Froissart is a wonderful book & one which should be almost a 'vade mecum' in a boy's education. The nice sense of honour, the high chivalric tone, the admiration of personal courage which it inculcates must go far to form a standard of true manly excellence in the mind of a high spirited youth. What a contrast does it present to the conduct of that blood thirsty selfish buccaneer, Walker![27] I have just read his War in Niccargua & close the book in dusgust at his miserable selfishness, asking myself the question is he a hypocrite? or has God given him over "to strong delusion that he should beleive a lie" when he talks so cooly of his rights in Niccaragua? *Rights*! A strong cord and a short shift is all he was entitled to! His murder (execution he calls it) of Corral was a deliberate cold blooded, brutal, & infamous one & as to his trial, it was a mockery & a sham.

Speaking of Central America brings me to Mexico. England has recognized Maximillian as Emperor of that former Republic & Queen Victoria has written an autograph letter to his wife in which she styles her her "well beloved sister Charlotte." By what logic is it save that of the strong arm that England has convinced herself that it is her duty *to* recognize the puppet set up by the Emperor Napoleon, a foreigner & at this moment at war with his coveted subjects & his duty *not* to recognize the Southern Confederacy? Query—had we adopted a monarchial instead of a Republican Government, made Mr Davis King instead of President, would he not now have been my well beloved "brother Jefferson" instead of the so called President of the Confederate States?

MARCH 21, 1865

On Sunday the 19th the news from Halifax was to the effect that Goldsboro was to be reoccupied & held at all hazards; Sherman at Averysboro between Raleigh & Fayetteville & seemed to be trying to effect a junction with Schofield; Joe Johnston at Smithfield. Mr E heard heavy & continuous firing

[27]William Walker (1824-1860), an American lawyer, journalist, and filibusterer, invaded Nicaragua in 1855 to aid rebel forces in overthrowing the local government. Walker and his followers quickly defeated government forces under Gen. Ponciano Corral, and Walker became commander-in-chief of the army. In July, 1856, Walker became president of Nicaragua, and the United States recognized his regime. Walker lost control of the country during a brief war with four neighboring republics in 1857 and was forced to flee to the United States. In an attempt to retake Nicaragua in 1860, Walker landed in Honduras, one of the enemy republics, and was captured and executed for illegally entering the country. The book referred to, Walker's *The War in Nicaragua*, published in New York and Mobile a few months before his last expedition, described Walker's seizure of the Nicaraguan government in 1855 and his execution of Corral in the same year for treason against the Walker regime. *Dictionary of American Biography*, XIX, 363-365; *The National Cyclopaedia of American Biography, Being the History of the United States* (New York: James T. White & Company, 50 volumes, 1898-1972), XI, 24.

the whole afternoon, but tho I stood by his side with my hand in his, my attention strained to the utmost & listened as closely as I could, I was unable to distinguish a sound, altho he gave my hand a pressure at every gun he heard. Last night's mail, however, brought tidings "of a battle joined." For two days has the fight been progressing & still is it undecided. The exact locality we know not, but how much trembles in the balance!

Brother writes from Raleigh that Sherman effected a junction with Schofield at Elizabethtown in Bladen county, that on Friday there was a sharp fight at Black River (which divides Sampson from Cumberland) without decisive result. He is most despondant as to the result, says Johnston can only with the force he has *delay Sherman*, that in a few days Raleigh will be occupied! He will be forced to leave as otherwise he would be a prisoner in the hands of the enemy, but his family will remain & run the risk of the treatment they will receive from these murderous scoundrels. I hope for better things. Johnston will *defeat* Sherman, perhaps kill him or shoot off his other leg & compel him to retreat & we will be saved the miseries of having our whole country overrun by these bloodthirsty harpies. Johnston I am confident will be victorious, yet, nevertheless, we live in a state of anxious excitement pitiable to witness.

News of Gen Whiting's death at Governor's island from wounds received in the defence of Ft Fisher. What kind of humanity is that which forces a sorely wounded man to take such a journey? Was aught else but death expected from it? Whiting cost us dear last spring before Petersburg when in consequence of having drunk too much he failed to obey orders & thus disconcerted Beauregard's plan for the capture of Butler & his army. A plan, too, which was sure to have succeeded, for it was laid in accordance with information received from Butler's private secretary who had deserted to us the night before with his master's papers. The sequel proved that had Whiting performed his part of the programme, Butler's whole army must have surrendered, for he escaped through the gap which Whiting should have filled, but his conduct at Ft Fisher was gallant in the extreme & its loss lies at the door of no one but those of Gen Braxton Bragg! Whiting was an able & gallant officer. His greatest faults are unregulated thirst which he indulged at improper times, but he has laid down his life in the service of his adopted country (for he was by birth a Yankee). I see by his obituary that he was born of Mass. parents in Mississippi where his father, an officer in the U S A, was stationed, but his education & association as well as his parentage were all Massachuset. He married a lady of N C when in the old army he was stationed at Smithville[28] & we should forget his defects.

---

[28]Gen. William H. C. Whiting married Kate Davis Walker, daughter of Maj. John Walker of Smithville and Wilmington on April 22, 1857. Marriage Bond of William Whiting and Kate Davis Walker, State Archives.

The enemy has executed by hanging a Capt Beale,[29] whom they charge with carrying on an irregular warfare. I know nothing of the facts of the case or who Capt Beale is, but one thing I do know & that is that in such a war for the defence of ones own soil, ones own home & fireside, no warfare can be called illegal or irregular & that it is the duty of our Government to *retaliate*. Had it done so for the execution of Dr Wright of Norfolk, murdered in cold blood for resisting an encroachment on his rights as a private citizen, the Lincoln Government would have found it necessary to maintain stronger garrisons in our captured towns & our citizens in their lines would have suffered far less from their oppressive tyranny. The time to begin was when Mumford was hung in N O. Some kind of negro soldier bill has passed both houses of Congress, but we get no Richmond papers & are ignorant of its provisions. It seems a sort of 'coup de grace' which Congress is giving us after torturing us with bad legislation for four years. Our ills spring not from the Yankees but from bad Government which has crippled our resources & thus allowed them to gain an ascendancy over us. When we gain our Independance it will be in spite of our rulers!

MARCH 23, 1865

No news as yet. Rumours & sensational reports only calculated to harrow us up. At one time we hear "the enemy advancing on Weldon from all points," then "fighting at Smithfield yesterday between Johnston & Sherman," "Schofield holds Goldsboro," & so on. The cars ran off the track on the 21st, so no mail has arrived at Halifax since that day & we are left to the exercise of our own judgment as to what we beleive & what reject. Our state of anxiety is pitiable.

High & furious winds both today & yesterday. It is sorrowful to see how the peach blossoms are buffeted about. The air is filled with them together with those of the plumb & elm. I see I neglected to record the date of their expansion as I usually do. They were straggling into bloom on the 14th but pinched by the wind. On the 15th George the 4th & Honey & a few volunteer's could be called "in bloom." On the seventeeth (St Patrick's) riding with Mr E. on the River bank I saw the first plum blossoms & on the 18th we had our first shad. The River has been high since the 25th of Feb with but a short intermission. One day only have I been able to cross the Flume on horseback. On

---

[29]John Yates Beall of Jefferson County, Virginia (later West Virginia), an "acting master in the Confederate navy" placed on trial before a military commission at Fort Lafayette, New York, was accused of being a spy in Ohio and New York and of "carrying on irregular or guerrilla warfare against the United States. . . ." The commission convicted Beall of unlawfully seizing a steamboat and of sinking another and of attempting to derail a passenger train in New York. Beall was hanged on February 24, 1865, and the Confederate House of Representatives requested an investigation into Beall's execution. Commissioner of Exchange Ould reported that the case was not brought to his attention before the execution and that the northern papers did not publish the case until a few days before the sentence was carried out. *Official Records (Army)*, Series II, VIII, 279-281, 398, 400.

Monday Mr E had a canoe waiting for the girls & they left the carriage on the other side. The weather has been unusually warm, some days we have even been without fire in our chamber & vegetation has advanced with giant strides. Would that Peace followed its example!

Later in the Day

God be thanked. We have news of a victory! On the 20th Lee telegraphs to the Sec of War that on the 19th Gen Johnston "attacked the enemy near Bentonville, routing him & capturing three guns, a mile in the rear he rallied on fresh troops but was forced back slowly until six P M, when receiving more troops he apparently assumed the offensive which was resisted without difficulty until dark. This morning they are entrenched. Our loss small. The troops behaved admirably. A dense thicket prevented rapid operations." signed R E Lee. This was the battle on Sunday the guns of which Mr E heard so distinctly, for it was just at the hour when we stood in the yard, he pressing my hand at every report.

MARCH 24, 1865

Came my Aunt, Mrs Polk, with my cousins to make us a visit. The anxiety we all suffer prevents our full enjoyment of each other's society, yet it seems to bind us closer together. The arrival of the mail, however, has thrown us into the deepest dejection. Rumour after rumour of the most conflicting character reaches us. "Raleigh is to be evacuated says one," "Johnston is falling back on Hillsboro," says another. Sherman ditto on Fayetteville. A heavy raid in the direction of Wilson. Grant moving on Stoney Crk. "Weldon heavily threatened"—& so on. My aunt has determined if the next mail does not bring news of the evacuation of Raleigh to leave & return to her children in Asheville fearing that if she delays she will be unable to reach them. She has consented to leave her two daughters here for the summer, so we shall have them with us at Hascosea, which will be a great pleasure to us. Came Rachel & Frank Jones & sister Betsy to dinner. The young people remembering the engagement they had at the "Refugee House" (as they call the overseer's house) during the freshet determined to remain & occupy their old quarters, so we try to be a merry party.

MARCH 25, 1865

Came rumours of another victory, but we fear to rejoice. What is more substantial is the fact that Johnston still remains at Smithfield & the idea of an evacuation of Raleigh seems, from the reports & conduct of those who ought to know, to be abandoned. We hear that Sherman has lost heavily. We have had three engagements with him, in all of which we have been successful. He is reported falling back both to Fayetteville & Goldsboro now held (thanks to Bragg) by Schofield, but which is true, we have not the means of knowing. We hear sad accounts of the suffering in Fayetteville. Sherman robbers stripped the town of every thing in the way of food & the inhabitants are literally living on *parched corn*. God help them.

A letter from Amo today gives us heart felt pleasure. He has heard from Aiken & the enemy have never had possession of the place, & our friends there are living unmolested & secure. After the cavalry skirmish of which we heard & in which they were worsted they never returned, & the wave of War sweeping by them, left them at Peace. Amo gives a terrible account of the devastation committed by Sherman in his march. He says "Everything has been swept away by the remorseless enemy, families reduced in a moment from affluence to beggery, rich & poor alike robbed of their last grain of corn, negroes rendered desperate by hunger in a state of insurrection, & hundreds who never before knew want destitute of clothing, food, & shelter. Columbia is a pile of smoking ashes," etc.

The mail is just in, directs my thoughts from all but the news it brings. Brother writes from Raleigh, "We are very busy evacuating, indeed are nearly through. . . . Present appearances indicate that Sherman is going to move up the Weldon road & I would advise you strongly to prepare for him." Mr McMahon writes that "we have news to the effect that Gen Lee attacked Battery No 5 & captured it," but was compelled to leave it by the enfilading fire of Grant's other batteries. Losses heavy on both sides. We captured 800 prisoners, one Brigadier & Staff, & killed Gen Warren. Heavy fighting on the North of the James. No particulars, but we are reported successful. My Aunt & her daughters left us, she having determined to return to Ashville.

MARCH 26, 1865

Sunday. Just at home from father's where Mr E & I went to bid my Aunt goodbye. I have had such a rapid gallop that my hand is scarce steady enough to write, but I must add a line to say that it is the *State* government only which is evacuating *Raleigh*. The archives, State military stores, etc., are all as a matter of precaution being sent west. As yet there are no indications of the Confederacy following its example. Officers assure citizens "that the storm of War has swept past them."

MARCH 28, 1865

Our anxiety about my nephew Thomas Devereux is very great. A letter received from him last week tells us that he had just been moved from the extreme right to the centre. He says as long as "we stay here we are out of the War," so little chance does he think there is of an attack by Grant. He little dreampt that Lee would so soon hurl himself Grant & [illegible] Battery no 5! Poor fellow, would that we could hear of his safety, for he is in the very front of the fight.

The Senate Committee have just published an answer to the President's last Message to Congress in which it must be confessed they get the better of his Excellency, but it is greatly to be deplored that they have thought it best thus to make public our family dissensions. It must give aid and comfort to our enemies. If Mr Davis scolds his Congress & they defend themselves, why cannot they do it in secret session? But thus to proclaim that they have mutual causes of complaint each against the other seems to me at this juncture to be neither wise or prudent. The perusal of the papers reminds one of the quarrels between Charles 1st[30] & his Parliament, so rare is it in modern times, too, for the Executive & the Legislative branches of a Government seriously to disagree.

The negro bill is out. It disclaims all interferance with the master's rights, but the agents are doing all they can to nulify that clause in its provisions. Amongst other vile deceptions they make use of is promising all who will come forward & volunteer "freedom & a home of their own amongst their own people." They will get none of ours. I consider it a point of patriotism to keep them at home.

MARCH 31, 1865

No news but that of Thomas Devereux's safety in the late fight before Petersburg. Lee tells us our losses are small, so we can smile at Stanton's gasconading bulletin giving his countrymen the particulars of a paper Victory. Warren's loss is one that they will feel greatly, for he was one of their best Generals. Johnston's lines reach from Louisburg to Tarrboro. The line of the Tar is to be defended, so we are now told. Should he continue to fall back the Roanoke is the next defensible point. We should then be in the storm of War & suffer as our Southern compatriots have done. In Fayetteville the actual pangs of hunger have been felt by the whole population. For days have they subsisted on parched corn & a little rice. From their fate Good Lord Deliver us! On the 29th came Captain and Mrs Langdon to make us a visit. Today Captain L left, Mrs Langdon remaining with us. Sherman is said to be at Goldsboro refitting & getting his men shod & his waggons repaired, when he will proceed to make mince meat of the remains of the so called Southern Confederacy. So say our Northern brethren.

APRIL 2, 1865

Yesterday the 1st came the first swallow. The sight of him made me heartsick with hope deferred. I have so often hailed him as the harbinger of Peace

---

[30]Charles I (1600-1649) of the House of Stuart served as king of Great Britain from 1625 until 1649. His continual disagreements with Parliament over money, state policy, and constitutional procedure led to the dismissal of three Parliaments in four years and to a period of eleven years when Charles ruled without convening Parliament. The friction between royal prerogative and parliamentary control eventually led to civil war between royalists and parliamentarians, and Charles I was beheaded. *Webster's Biographical Dictionary*, 284.

& been disappointed. Dined at Father's with Mrs Langdon & Mr E. Came home hurriedly through a rapidly rising water, the current across the road in several places being already strong. Mr E took advantage of the day (1st of April) to address Susan a humourous letter signed "Mr Hairbald," announcing himself as agent for an association of ladies engaged in collecting the hair of the Southern women which it was thought they would sacrifice for the benefit of the cause & calling on her and her young friends to sacrifice their fair tresses on the altar of their country. A ship is to be loaded with these contributions & to return freighted with provisions in exchange. The girls replied in an equally humourous spirit, telling Mr Hairbald that emulating the example of the women of Carthage they responded to his appeal & as an earnest sent him a package containing their braids of (false) hair! He gravely pocketed the parcel & to their dismay brt it home & has had me busy today fabricating for each of them a braid of *Horse hair* & cowtails which he is to send them with a letter of thanks from the Ladies of the Association, acknoledging the receipt of the hair through Mr Hairbald & in their name presenting each a braid of native growth to be kept as a *"hair* loom" & as an evidence to posterity of their noble devotion and signing himself *"James Mohair,"* Sec of the Association. The girls will be some time without their outward adornments, for he will tease them well ere he gives them up. Well it is for all of us that we can enter into a jest just now!

Our news depends on the disposition of the person from whom we get it. Bro writes that "Sherman can go anywhere, for Johnston is too weak to oppose him," whilst Maj Gale[31] assures us that the army is in fine spirits & wants for nothing. He thanks God devoutly that *"that Man"* (as he calls Bragg) "has been removed from amongst us; his very presence is an injury to the army." Bragg has been assigned to some bureau duty or other, which, however, we know will be mismanaged, & his presence felt. Maj G thinks that Richmond will be evacuated this spring, in which I hope he will be mistaken. Mr E. has heard heavy and continuous firing all the morning. I listen but can distinguish nothing. He was right about Bentonville. This cannonade is, however, in a Northerly direction some where on Lee's lines.

April 3, 1865

Today came father in a canoe & spent the day with us. We had a regular Chess seance, playing steadily for *six hours*, & a game of chess with him is no child's play but takes deep thought & study. News that Grant has captured the Boydtown Plank Road & that his Cavalry have cut the South side road at Ford's Station; bad for us & explains the firing Patrick heard on Sunday. God grant us strength to endure what he has in store for us.

---

[31]Seaton E. Gales, a lawyer from Wake County, served as adjutant of the Fourteenth North Carolina Regiment until 1862. He later served as assistant adjutant general on the staff of Brig. Gen. Stephen D. Ramseur. Manarin and Jordan, *North Carolina Troops*, V, 394, 482.

April 4, 1865

News tonight of a raid through Northampton County towards Weldon. We hear that Jackson a small town about 12 miles from us was burned in the night without giving the inhabitants warning or allowing them to save anything. This is negro news but is considered reliable. What fiends in human shape are our enemies! No news from Va.

April 5, 1865

Whilst at dinner today enter Fanny with—"Master, Bro Robin say Daddy tell him to come here & tell you that the Yankees are comin & that they are burning Mr Jacob's[32] house now." Appetizing news that! Mr Jacob's house is just four miles from us on the other side of the river & the Gunboat their probable objective point, only a mile from us on this side. Mrs Langdon & I summoned our maids & had our wardrobes put into our trunks in the hope of being able to save them should they treat us as Robin says is Mr Jacob's fate. Our valuables, silver, jewelry, etc., have long ago, since Burnside's days, been sent out of their reach, so now we sit in momentary expectation of hearing the report of cannon or the hissing of a shell, to announce that the attack on the boat has commenced. What may be our fate ere another morning? However, I will go & take our usual afternoon walk. God is our refuge & help & I hope when the time of trial comes that I shall not "*greatly* fear."

April 6, 1865

Came news last night, news that I cannot realize; it falls on my outward ear, but I do not beleive that it fully enters into my inner sense or I could not be thus calm. Lee after four days heavy fighting in which the slaughter on both sides has been terrific has evacuated Petersburg certainly & [illegible] persons add Richmond also. His Army is said to be at Burkeville at the junction of the South side & Danville R R s. Mrs Davis has left Richmond & gone to Charlotte, but she left once before, so it may be again only a cry of "Wolf," & the Government may not intend to follow & Richmond may be safe. Capt Langdon writes his wife that Weldon is certainly to be held, that he has been ordered to bring all the supplies on the Seaboard & on the Petersburg Roads to that point.

No particulars of Lee's fight except a rumour through Capt L that Grant attacked Lee's Right. Lee massed his troops to defend it when Grant swooped down on the defences of Petersburg, his object having been to make Lee weaken them by a feint attack. This I cannot credit. Lee is master of the art of

---

[32]There are several Jacobs families listed in Halifax and Northampton county population schedules of the 1860 census.

strategy & if he is overpowered it must have been through sheer force of numbers. Weakened as he has been by desertion he was unable to cope with the fresh crowds of foreign mercenaries under Grant. We may thank the Government for much of the desertion. Their attempt to coerce a *free* people by their oppressive Conscript Act, their appointment of incompetent officers who were careless of the comfort & discipline of their men, & their own excessive & ill judged leniency to the crime of desertion in the first years of the war & the ease with which a pardon was obtained, all invited it; & the continued announcements to the offenders that this was the last opportunity for them to come in and return to their allegiance has brought the service into contempt. Now see the result! A noble cause & a free people well nigh sacrificed upon the altars of *Bad Government* & *Bad Faith with the people.* Who can tell the end?

I sit stunned & am unable to look forward to a single day, to a single consequence in the future. I do not feel even the enormities practised by the enemy on our neighbors in Northampton! The fact that they were reported as in retreat last night failed to animate me. Jacob's house was not burned, but his neighbour Norwood's[33] cotton was, which accounts for the smoke & smell which filled the soft spring air last night. Mr Smallwood was robbed of everything and had several shots fired at him but succeeded in making his escape. Dr Moore's horses every one taken.[34] In short the country swept of horses and provisions and utterly sacked. A force was in advance upon the gunboat on this side, so we hear, but were deceived by false news & the cavalry in retreating came upon their own infantry & had a smart skirmish when both fell back.

I know not whether or not to credit this, but Lee's disaster absorbs all else. If with the defences of Petersburg & Richmond, which are as perfect as human skill can make them, he cannot confront Grant, where can it be done? God help us. We are in the crisis of our fate as a nation. I almost cease to regret our want of mails. They come fraught only with disaster & death. It will be days & perhaps weeks ere we hear of Tom Devereux's fate. God support his parents!

Had a heavy disappointment last night. My Aunt Mrs Polk has shrunk from the separation from her daughters for so long a time in the unsettled state of the country & has got Capt Spotswood to come down and take them to her in Raleigh, so we shall lose the pleasure of their society this summer. I am sorry, for I was begining to become much attached to them. Sally is a girl of uncommon character & energy & Sue is most attractive. Life is made up of disappointments!

---

[33]Littleton Norwood, a forty-four-year-old farmer from Northampton County, lived with his wife Falina and six children. Eighth Census, 1860, Population Schedule, Northampton County, 4.

[34]The 1860 census listed M. W. Smallwood as a sixty-year-old farmer, and C. G. C. Moore as a forty-one-year-old physician. Eighth Census, 1860, Population Schedule, Northampton County, 65, 72.

APRIL 11, 1865

Hascosea. What a life has been ours the past few days! I have but a few moments in which to record the events through which we have passed & then farewell my beloved Journal for a time, may it be but a breif one.

On the 7th came a squad of pickets to Looking Glass with tidings that the enemy were approaching from Northampton, it was thought, to burn the gunboat & advised me to conceal my valuables as speedily as I could. Got Mr E to secrete a jar containing our own & Mr Langdon's money & our title deeds & his Confederate Commission & waited as best we could. Just at dark the whole hemsphere was suddenly lighted up with lurid flames whose origin none could be blind to. It was the gunboat! Silently & solemnly it burned on, whilst we stood an excited group & listened for some sound indicating the presence of the enemy, but none came.[35] When reassured we went into our tea, when a sudden heavy footstep on the piazza sent all the blood to my heart, but it proved to be only Capt Cooke, who after ordering the firing of the boat came over to bid us adieu, as orders are out for the evacuation of this whole country!

He reported the enemy at Potacassy bridge plundering & devastating every thing in their reach. He showed us also a copy of an order from Gen Johnston commanding that the bridges over the Roanoke at Weldon & at Gaston be burned at 12 o'clock that same day in order to protect his rear against Sheridan's Cavalry, now engaged on a raid on the north side of the River. We had on receipt of the pickets news, sent our own and Mrs Langdon's wardrobe's to Hascosea as being for the nonce safer than Looking Glass, so we concluded that as the burning of the Gunboat gave us a little respite that we would go out there ourselves the next day & by burning & concealing our valuable papers try and prepare for this irruption of irresponsible vandals upon us.

Capt Cooke told us that Sherman had reinforced Grant by water & that Richmond and Petersburg had been lost by the fact that Lee was overwhelmed by sheer numbers. The enemy came upon him nine columns deep. We repulsed eight, but the ninth over-lapped & completely enfiladed and flanked us. The slaughter was terrific! The Yankees compute their loss at 30,000. No particulars of the fall of Richmond itself, nor did he know whether or not the Archives of Government had been saved. On Sat the 8th we came out here bringing a few provisions & some other of our valuables which we thought it advisable to carry about with us & have been ever since destroying our private papers & making what preparations we can for the future. On

---

[35]Comdr. W. H. Macomb reported from Plymouth on April 13, 1865, that the Confederate troops at Weldon had burned the bridge, evacuated the town, and destroyed the ram at Edward's Ferry. The battery at Rainbow Bluff was dismembered as well, and the guns were thrown into the Roanoke. He added that, with the exception of torpedoes, the river was clear for navigation. *Civil War Naval Chronology*, V, 86.

Sunday came Capt Langdon & brt the joyful news that on Friday Lee had repulsed Grant with tremendus slaughter at Jetersville a few miles from Burkeville where he has his headquarters.[36] Grant pushed on confident of victory but was sent reeling back with the assurance that, tho outnumbered, the Army of N V was not yet beaten.

Mr Davis is out in a stirring Proclamation assuring us that we are not and will not be subjugated, exhorting us to stand firm, and assuring us of ultimate success. God Grant it! Capt L assures us that all the Con Archives save those of the 2d Auditor, Treasury were saved, which is good news. Nothing authentic from Richmond. Weldon is to be evacuated so soon as the stores in & arround it can be removed & F Branch as the picket guard tells us is also to be given up in a few days. Johnston's Headquarters are at Ridgeway on the R & G R R & his Left wing now resting on Tarrboro is being gradually with drawn towards that point with the supposed intention of joining Lee by Clarksville & Danville, so that in a few days we shall be within the enemy's lines & exposed to the fate of our unfortunate compatriots. God give us grace to bear it!

Yesterday came the Impressing officers with orders from Gen Johnston to *take all the best of our team*, to leave us only the worthless & the inferior. The order runs, "take all that will be of service to the enemy." The feeling against it is intense throughout the country. We think that as the Government confessedly is too weak to protect us, that at least it ought not thus to deprive us of the means of making a support—say to us, "*take care of yourselves*" & let us do the best we can; but no, this morning the two best mules we have here were taken & as I write I see six of the pick of the team at Looking Glass & Mr E's new blooded Filly, for which he gave $5000 not two months since, coming up—a sad procession to join those already impressed. Our premises are used as a temporary depot for them & there are now 50 mules & horses, the very best in the whole country, wandering up and down there, coupled by twos together, in a most disconsolate forlorn & homesick manner. I would think less of it were I not sure it is impossible in the Government to feed them for one month. In a few weeks their bones will whiten the red clay hills of Warren & Granville through which Johnston returns and we shall not have even the poor satisfaction of knowing that they aided the cause for that short period.

Upon the heels of the horse impressers is to come another gang with direction to take all our meat save three months supply! The Yankees themselves

---

[36]The engagement at Jetersville (Amelia Springs) occurred on April 5, 1865, during Lee's retreat from Richmond in order to join Johnston's forces in North Carolina. The Federal cavalry under Sheridan, in several rearguard skirmishes, harried the retreat and finally, at Jetersville, managed to place themselves between Lee and his destination. The Union cavalry also captured Lee's wagon train, filled with the supplies Lee needed to continue field operations. Lee's troops were forced to forage along their march for subsistence and this greatly slowed the Confederate army's movements. This contributed to Lee's surrender at Appomattox four days later on April 9, 1865. Boatner, *Civil War Dictionary*, 10-11, 22; Johnson and Buel, *Battles and Leaders*, IV, 719, 724; *Official Records (Army)*, Series I, XLVI, Part I, 1107, 1265-1266.

could hardly do worse. We have given & freely given all we could spare & were we asked to give more and live on vegetables, would do it cheerfully & willingly for the sake of *the Cause*, but this forced patriotism is not the thing, is not the way to treat a free & generous people, & ere long hearts will be alienated from the Government & system that thus tramples on our rights, our feelings, & our sacred honour. What is to become of our eighty five negroes thus deprived of food & employment? The Government says make them work with *hoes*, but suppose we have no hoes & no ability to get them, what then?

And now, old friend, you my Journal, for a time good bye! You are too bulky to be kept out, exposed to prying Yankee eyes and theivish Yankee fingers. You go for a season to darkness & solitude & my record must henceforth be kept on scraps of paper, backs of letters, or old memorandum books which I can secrete. Think how Sheridan's bumming officers would seize upon the "Journal of a Secesh Lady—a complete record of a daily life spent in the Southern Confederacy from July 1860 to April 65" & how I would feel thus dragged from the recesses of private life & for aught I know published for the amusement of a censorious, curious, and critical public?

No, old friend, we must part. I trust you to Owen's fidelity, hoping the time may yet come when I can withdraw you from your retreat & finish you with a triumphant announcement of Peace & Independance! So once more, Good bye!

OCTOBER 4, 1865

Commenced this morning copying into my book—the Journal I have kept on odds & ends of paper since last April. Some of my notes were lost during my sickness, so where they are not complete I have destroyed them.

Journal——Copy
APRIL 12, 1865

Aniversary of the taking of Ft Sumter four years ago & it seems as tho a life time were crowded into them. How bitter the Yankee Jubilantee over its repossession makes us feel.

Today came Capt Nichols, James' second in command, to take away the mules & horses collected by his agents, stock impressed from us unfortunates who see our means of livelihood thus taken from us without a hope even that they will ever do the country or the Cause one particle of good. It is neither kind or fatherly in our government, when forced to desert us, to rob us at the same moment. "Tom," father's foreman, expresses it more forcibly than elegantly when he says, "*The Gov—ner*" (African for *Government*) "ought to tell us I cant scuffle for you no longer. Now you scuffle for yourselves. Instead of that, young Missus, he leaves us & take all away wi' him"!

Capt N told us that James' servant had been robbed of his whole wardrobe by a "Galvanized Yankee," i.e., a Yankee prisoner who has been allowed to take the oath of allegiance to the Confederacy & to serve in the army, so I sent him a supply of underclothing, some pickles, & provisions & a carpet blanket which fortunately he had left here, to which his brother added his own camp chest & furniture all complete.

Very busy all day & am tonight worn out with company, anxiety, fatigue, & excitement. Just at night came one of Capt Langdon's clerks, a Mr O Neale, with a letter from Mrs L. to Mr E. asking him to send the buggy & a baggage waggon immediately to Weldon for her. Poor thing, she has had a bitter bitter disappointment. She had her luggage all packed on a special car chartered to go through to Augusta & sat with her Hat & shawl on—waiting the moment of starting, when a train came in with the tidings that the N C R R had been cut in two places by the enemy, once between Hillsboro & Greensboro & again near Salisbury. Weldon is to be immediately evacuated, the Cars & Engines destroyed, & the bridge burned, & all Government property there which cannot be removed is to be immediately destroyed. So in this terrible emergency she, poor woman, knows not where to go & has appealed to us for a temporary home. She shall have it with much pleasure & glad am I that we have it to offer.

The R R Bridge over Quankey Crk at Halifax was burning when Mr O' N passed, so hence forward we are without a mail either way & for news must depend on reports & rumours brought by irresponsible persons. The Yankee's will be the heralds of their own advance, but please God, I shall not fear them. My times are in His hands & He will be my sheild and buckler. Suppose they do destroy my pleasant & luxurious home, what then? God will provide for me & I shall not want!

APRIL 13, 1865

Rarely has it been my lot to pass a more wretched night. I could not sleep for excitement & anxiety & well it was for the safety of our horses that I was wakeful, for some theif, embolden by the successful attempt made at Clarksville the night before to steal horses from the corral of impressed horses there, followed them here in order to repeat the trick, but finding them gone endeavored to remunerate themselves for their trouble by taking some of ours; but fortunately I heard some unusual noises & raising the window demanded, "who was there," and getting no answer, called for the man servants & aroused poor, tired, and nearly worn out Mr E. He was promptly on the spot & found the horses out & the stable empty, but the theif was gone. So all hands being thoroughly aroused he concluded to make a midnight start for Mrs Langdon. News that Hardee is evacuating Raleigh & pressing West.[37]

---

[37]Confederate troops evacuated Raleigh on April 12, 1865, except for Gen. Joe Wheeler's cavalry which remained behind to destroy supplies and the railroad station. The stragglers in Wheeler's cavalry finished

God help Margaret & her helpless girls. Tom was safe up to Monday, the 3d, the day after that fearful battle before Petersburg.

APRIL 14, 1865

Last night came Capt & Mrs Langdon, utterly exhausted with fatigue & excitement. The scenes they have passed through beggar all description. The wholesale plunder & the petty theft almost exceed beleif. Capt L was enabled to secure some sacks of Gov Salt for Mr E by giving a memorandum of the quantity taken to the officer in charge so that at some future day they can be paid for. Their possession is a great releif to Mr E, for the want of it is a fearful question in the future.

Capt L brt some additional particulars of the battle before Petersburg & the evacuation of Richmond. The carnage was fearful. Our men were completely outnumbered, in fact almost surrounded by the enemy. A P Hill was killed in the streets of Petersburg, but as yet no list of our losses can be made out. It is a fearful blow to us, but not death. Only let us be true to ourselves & we will yet outride the storm. If we but stand by our President & our Army and present a stubborn dogged resistance, we will yet conquer.

APRIL 16, 1865

How can I write it? How find words to tell what has befallen us? *Gen Lee has surrendered*! Surrendered the remnant of his noble Army to an overwhelming horde of mercenary Yankee knaves & foreigners. On Sat as Mr E & I sat at what has been for the past few days our constant employment, i.e., burning our private papers, came a note from Mr McMahon telling us that the news had been brought by a Courier in search of that drunken Gen Baker & was in a dispatch to him from his Adj Gen now at Ridgeway waiting until his cheif should be sober enough to evacuate the region entrusted to him by a too confiding country. We could not credit it & were enabled to dine as usual, having convinced ourselves that it was a Yankee canard, but in the afternoon came Mr Richard Smith jr & Jimmie Hale, who had left home to join the army but on getting some miles north of Halifax met crowds of paroled soldiers who told them that there was no army & no Headquarters to report to, that Lee had surrendered when he had but 11,000 muskets all told under his command & was completely surrounded by Grant and Thomas' combined armies. It appears (so were they told) that Sherman whilst apparently lying still at Goldsboro actually reinforced Grant heavily by way of New Berne & Fortress Monroe & that all the Sailors & marines released by the evacuation of our

their withdrawal the following day as Kilpatrick's cavalry marched into the city. Governor Vance had sent a delegation to Sherman on April 12 offering to surrender the city peacefully and requesting Sherman to guarantee the safety of its citizens and property. Mrs. Edmondston's brother, Maj. John Devereux, accompanied the delegation as a member of Vance's staff. Barrett, *Civil War in North Carolina*, 373-377; *Official Records (Army)*, Series I, XLVII, Part III, 191.

seaports, 50,000 in number, were formed into a corp which also joined him, so that he was thus enabled to enfilade & nearly surround Lee's works before Petersburg & drive him from them. Lee, as we have seen, fell back along the line of the South Side R R, Grant pressing him closely. Again & again that noble old man with his band of heroes paused & delivered battle, each time with fearful loss to their prisoners, but at length utterly exhaused by fatigue, privation, & incessant fighting, fighting for the last three days continuous, near Appomatox Court House he found his rear molested by Thomas with the Army of Tennessee. Utterly unable to cope with this new enemy, his troops already thinned by exhaustion, wounds, death, & sad to say desertion, he took the only course left to him & *surrendered*! Some of the Cavalry, thank God, escaped & were furloughed by the Sec of War Breckenridge & ordered to report at Charlotte or to the nearest Confederate Headquarters within 20 days.

Fitz Lee escaped up the valley with a portion of his command, but sad to say Fitz Hugh Lee, the gallant son of our commander, is said to have been killed, Good God! We stand appalled at our disaster! What have we done to be thus visited? The *Lee*, Lee upon whom hung the hopes of the whole country, should be a prisoner seems too dreadful to be realized! Grant, it is said, issued a special order enjoining his troops to spare his life & to offer him no indignity & at the surrender refused to accept his sword, saying he was not worthy to receive it, & released him on his simple parole. But he is lost to us, lost to the *Cause* in future. Endeared as he is to our hearts & proud as we are of him, yet his word has been plighted & well we know that the Yankee will never release him—they have not knighthood enough for that. Noble old man, we almost forget our own loss in sympathy with you. He has been neither out manoevred or out generaled but *crushed*, crushed by mere *brute force*, force he could no more resist than he could the fall of an avalanche! We but love him the more for his misfortunes. Where Gen Johnston now is, or the President, none know. We hear, however, that they have gone South, leaving Hardee in command. Sherman's troops entered Raleigh on Wednesday the 12th & rumour has it that they committed no excesses. I fear me, however, that as usual she is but a lying jade, so little faith have I in his wolves.

Since we heard of our disaster I seem as tho' in a dream. I go about in a kind of "*drowsy dream*." I sleep, sleep, sleep endlessly; if I sit in my chair for ten minutes, I doze. I think of it, but I cannot grasp it or its future consequences. I sit benumbed. It is to me like the idea of eternity. I beleive it, yes I assent to it, but with a simple mental assent without once comprehending or even feeling it. I sit & hear the young folks & Mrs Langdon talk of books, of poetry, & they seem to me to be talking of what *was* long, long ago. I read books, I liked poetry, when was it? Where are they all gone? I seem to grope after my own ideas, my own identity, & in the vain attempt to grasp it I fall asleep. I am not dejected, am not cast down. Seemingly the loss of New Orleans & of

Vicksburg affected me much more. What is it that sustains me? Not faith in the Army! That is gone, that band of heroes has melted away. Not faith in Mr Davis. I have not felt that since he removed Gen Johnston, but I beleive it is faith in the *country*. Faith in the *Cause*, an earnest beleif that eventually we will yet conquer! We cannot be defeated. That it is which I beleive sustains and I pray God I may never lose it!

It is an odd state to which I have reduced myself, to an utterly paperless condition. I am entirely without a record of my life up to July 60 & what I reserved, my Journal, since then is secreted where perhaps I may never see it again. As I said before, I am utterly paperless. Every letter I possessed, letters which I had cherished as my heart's blood, mementos of those I had loved & lost years ago, literary memoranda, excerpts, abstracts, records of my own private self examinations, poetry—all, all destroyed & as I look at my empty cabinets & desks & feel the void that their emptiness causes within my heart, a hatred more bitter than ever rises within me as I think of the "*loathed Yankee*" whose vulgar curiosity & unbounded barbarity has rendered the destruction of these private papers a matter of self preservation. I never thought to shed such tears as the burning of Mr Edmondston's letters to me, letters written both before & since our marriage, wrung from my eyes. As the packet consumed scarce could I refrain from snatching it from the flames & at least keeping *one*, one of those precious sheets which seemed to me transcripts of our young hearts & young love; but the thought of seeing them in Yankee hands, of hearing them read in vile Yankee drawl amidst peals of vulgar Yankee laughter, or worse still, of knowing them heralded abroad in Yankee sensational newspapers, restrained me! This has been the fate of thousands of my fellow countrywomen, for the Northern journals teem with private papers stolen from Southern Households & published to a vulgar curious world as specimens of Southern thought, Southern feeling, & Southern composition. When I thought of all this, I say, I restrained my hands, but turning to Mr Edmondston, I buried my face in his lap and fairly wept aloud!

April 17, 1865

Mr E up & off early this morning to Enfield in the hope of recovering some of our own & of father's mules impressed last Tuesday. The officers were unable to reach Johnston's Headquarters & attempted to return but hundreds of the animals escaped & now, we hear, stray throughout the roads and fields on the upper part of the county. Mr O Neale coming down from Weldon to Capt Langdon yesterday met a soldier who presented him with four which he had taken up & knew not what to do with, having naught to give them to eat & no money to buy it with. Mr O. N. took but one, as he had no halter, & left the others for some more fortunate traveler who might be better provided. Had a hurra and a hunt for the valuation of the mules & horses (eight of one & two of the other) taken from us. Mr E was sure he had given me the paper. I remembered naught of it, but fortunately for my consistency attempted no denial of the fact but feared I had hidden it with my Journal & other valuables. Finally, much to his annoyance, Mr E left without it, when, conceive my mortification, having occasion to empty my pocket not long after he left of the various & miscellaneous articles which had accumulated there during the past week of confusion, I found it there. Off I sent Owen instantly with it after him, but my character as Secretary is gone forever. Henceforward I shall have to bear the brunt of every mislaid paper & what renders it the more provoking is that heretofore my character in that respect has been irreproachable.

Some time since I took up my pen to write to James, but an unconquerable fit of nothing-to-say came over me, so instead of doing what I ought & finding something I yeilded to the dolce par niente feeling & wrote some lines, which I indulge myself in copying as a reward for having burnt so much of my own composition poetry & prose, last Friday and Sat, trusting that the small size & insignificant look of this little old account book will enable me to conceal them from all prying and inquisitive Yankee eyes.

"Man's Noblest Poem is Man's Bravest Deed"
                                        Bulwer

Say not we have no Poetry!
The nation's daily life struggling 'gainst adverse fate is in itself
                a grand unwritten Epic!
See yon long line of fresh lipped boys forth with their Mothers'
                prayers & blessings on their heads—
Forth they wish to meet in their green youth, the stern o'erwhelming
                shock of furious War!
Hear their defiant shout as thro' their ranks crashes with deadly
                force the hissing shell!
They rush to Death as to a Carnival! Cheap their lives when laid
                upon their country's Altar!
See the scarred Veteran drowning the thought of home, of wife,
                of child, of household joys,
In the stern sense of patriotic Duty! What to him the Camp's dis-
                comforts? Midst the pelting storm,
Beneath the burning Sun—Aye, pinched with cold & starved,
                unflinching he performs it.
Hark to the trumpet call—"To Arms"! See the long ranks of
                bristling steel, rank after rank,
Seeming in endless lines, the foemen furious come. Calm he awaits
                them, Till at the word,
Sudden a lurid light breaks like the lightening's flash along his
                serried lines.

Then like a hound unleashed, with yell & cheer, whilst yet the
                    shifting smoke
Eddies upon the morning breeze. See! see! him charge the unbroken
                    steel!
                              Find ye no Poem here?

Enter with gentle step the darkened Hospital. Bend o'er each couch
                    of pain—it holds a Wounded hero!
Hearst thou one murmur, one regret, for having thus in the full
                    flush of manhood given their *all*
To sheild their country from the tyrant's sway? No! but from
                    fevered lips rises the wish
To be once more in the full front of battle. Eyeing his maimed
                    limb the wounded veteran
Sighs that n'eer again in the stern crash of arms can he confront
                    his hated foe!
See that noble matron smiling altho her heart strings burst
                    the while
She bids her loved one go. Calmly she arms him for the fight
                    & with a firm endurance
Bears the unwonted weight of wearing care brought on by his
                    prolonged absence.
And tho at times faint, weary, almost heart sick, & well nigh
                    crushed beneath the unwelcome burden,
Not one murmur, one complaint, escapes her.
                              Cheerly she writes him,
Lest some sad thought of her, or of his loved ones in his distant
                    home,
Weaken his arm when he confronts his country's foes.
See yon lone mourner, of husband & of child bereft. She
                    wears her greif as tho' it were a robe of honour.
Looking up from out the depth of her resigned woe she buries
                    in daily care for others
That great sorrow which else would eat & gnaw into her very
                    being.
She simply says "I gave them to my country" & passing on
                    wears out her life
In ministring to those thrown by the chance of War upon
                    a bed of pain.
                              Call ye not that true Poetry?

'Tis not in times like these when what we hold most dear,
                    most sacred, our hopes, our passions, & our joys

Die in the full vigor of our manly strength, crushed by the
                    Juggernaut of War!
When 'een our daily lives, by suffering made sublime, rise by
                    self sacrafice to sacramental power.
Tis not *now* that men *write* poetry. Our lives are Poems
                    & in the record of brave deeds,
Of calm endurance, of patient fortitude, the legacy of Blood
                    we leave behind us,
Our children yet shall find their noblest Poem!

CAE—Looking Glass—March 23d, 1865

APRIL 19, 1865

Heard on Sunday last a rumour which seems so incredible, so much on the sensation order, that I did not record it, but it has since come to us in so many shapes & from such different sources that there must be some foundation in fact for it. Mr O'Neal brt us the news fresh from Weldon, viz., that hostilities had broken out between the French & Yankees & that a naval engagement had taken place between them off Matamoras & the next day some paroled prisoners from Lee's army en route for their homes assured us that they had read a Proclamation from the Pres. of the U S calling on all the men in Va between the ages of 18 & 40 to volunteer under the U S flag to fight their country's foes, the French, & threatening in case of their failure to do so to conscribe them & to send them to Mexico! This we thought mere gas, but yesterday came Mr Hyman & some of Lee's Battery, 10 N C,[38] on their way home from the Surrender who assured us that the Yankees were offering a bounty of $150 in gold to all & any Southern soldiers who would enlist in their army, assured us that they beleived the rumours, and moreover added that a French fleet was off Norfolk & that an engagement had taken place between it & the Yankee fleet there in which Bro Johnathan[39] was "*terribly smashed.*"

A fortnight since we heard that France had recognized us, but so often have we been deceived by false hopes that we none of us gave it a second thought, & now comes flying on Mercury's heels the announcement that the French had entered Norfolk! This is too much! Vast as is our credulity, this we cannot swallow! I can only earnestly hope that Johnny Crapeau[40] & Bro Johnathan have in fact fallen out in Mexico & that in the struggle we shall

---

[38]William R. Hyman of Martin County and R. W. S. Hyman of Washington County served as privates in Co. H, Tenth Regiment North Carolina State Troops (First Artillery). Lee's Battery was not a part of the Tenth North Carolina but was an Alabama company, also known as the Montgomery Blues, which fought in conjunction with North Carolina troops on several occasions. Clark, *Histories of the North Carolina Regiments*, V, 175; Manarin and Jordan, *North Carolina Troops*, I, 131.

[39]"Brother Jonathan" is a generic name for a New Englander or Yankee. Benét, *Reader's Encyclopedia*, 147.

[40]The expression "Johnny Crapaud" denotes a Frenchman. Benét, *Reader's Encyclopedia*, 252.

regain our own again. O that it only be true! We will soon set another army in the field, but cut off as we are from all mail facilities, we can only hope and long, knowing nothing of what really transpires.

In the whole of Lee's army we hear there was only one man found mean enough to join the enemy & this was an eastern Va, who volunteered to drive a wagon for them in preference to walking home, but this is wayfarers news.

Rosser & Fitz Lee burned 6000 of the enemy's wagons before they knew of the Surrender, they having succeeded in getting out before it took place. Sherman has left Raleigh, leaving a garrison of 3000 men as guard to his newly appointed military Gov of N C.[41]

A pleasant procession has just entered the yard midst the shouts & laughter of the negroes, who show all their ivory at thus welcoming home their youthful compeers the mules. Eight long eared gentlemen & Mr. E's grey filly are once more in their own stalls, but where is the tenth, James' bonnie gray steed? Very lean & lank do the wanderers look as tho they had missed their master's crib for the past week, but Cuffy will soon make up their lost meals to them. Mr E went to Enfield for them again today and as it seems with better success than on Monday.

April 20, 1865

It seems that the return of our impressed horses is due not to the wisdom of the Impressing Officers, but to the energy of our fellow citizens who knowing the impossibility of their getting thro the Yankee lines, followed them & forced them at the pistol's point to surrender them, but not before they had made way with & lost large numbers of them. They actually swapped one animal off for some whisky or rather Apple Brandy, for that is the country drink now. Capt Nichols, their lieu., left & not being heard of for three days, his subordinates yeilded, stipulating for some of the best animals for themselves. The horses they mounted & drove the mules off, whilst our neighbours returned peaceably with theirs & our property. Mr E's filly was of the number reserved by the impressing gentlemen for their own use but was saved to us by the sagacity & promptness of our little neighbour Dempsey Higgs,[42] a lad of 12 years of age, who hearing the reservation in her favour privately ordered his servant to mount & ride her off out of sight! So when she was called

---

[41]On April 29, 1865, Gen. John McAllister Schofield (1831-1906) assumed military control of the state as commander of the Union Department of North Carolina. Prior to Johnston's surrender to Sherman, Schofield commanded the eastern division of the North Carolina department, which included Fort Anderson, Wilmington, Kinston, and Goldsboro. Schofield held his post as chief military commander of the state until June 27, 1865, when he resigned to pursue his military career. Boatner, *Civil War Dictionary*, 726-727; *Concise Dictionary of American Biography*, 920; Barrett, *Civil War in North Carolina*, 388-389; Lefler and Newsome, *North Carolina*, 461, 482.

[42]Dempsey P. Higgs, listed as being nine years old in 1860, was the son of Jacob Higgs. Eighth Census, 1860, Population Schedule, Halifax County, 72.

for she was not to be found & time pressed too closely to make search for her. The officers have behaved most oppressively & unjustly and brought unnecessary odium on the Government by their unjustifiable conduct.

Gen Baker has been running about the country in search of some one to surrender to & has actually issued an address to his command beseeching them not to desert him & assuring them "he would expose them to no danger but that he would surrender to the first force large enough for him to do so to with propriety." Whether or not he has been successful in his search we know not, but we have *seen* several soldiers whom he has *discharged* from Confederate service.[43] He has thus discharged the whole of the Montgomery Blues, an Artillery Co. The men give as a reason for this extraordinary conduct is that for a wonder he was *sober for once* and actually knew not how to comport himself in so unusual a condition!

We are told that A P Hill is not dead & what gives us all the most sincere pleasure is the news that Gen Fitz Hugh Lee was not killed as reported but was surrendered with his father. Gen Gordon made the actual surrender of the Army of Northern Va to Gen Grant & when Gen Lee tendered his sword to the Commander of the Northern Army, he refused to accept it, saying that "he was not worthy to receive it." A magnanimous speech & one which I confess I did not expect from the Yankee hero! The Yankee's have no reason for exultation over their prowess in conquering Lee's veterans, for they had by their own admission more than 150,000 men & innumerable cannon, whilst he was reduced to a handful—11,000 men & but two Guns! Even Yankee bragg cannot bluster over that!

Tom Devereux we hear from a soldier who saw & knew him is safe & was paroled with the rest of his command, so our minds are releived about him. Hardee is safe over the Haw River. Where Sherman and Grant are no one knows. Pray God that Hardee with the remnant of our hopes keep out of their clutches. Captain Langdon left us yesterday to endeavour to make his way to Johnston's head quarters. Mrs L remains with us until quieter times.

It is odd to be utterly without a mail, neither to expect or to be able to send a letter off, yet such is ours. Epistolay by correspondance is at end & not a newspaper can we hope to see, so if like the Atheniens we seem constantly to hear or to tell some new thing we must be pardoned!

A soldier of Mr E's old command who stayed here last night told me that one of his comrades in whom he had confidence told him that he had taken a

---

[43]Brig. Gen. Laurence S. Baker wrote Sherman on April 18, 1865, stating that since General Johnston had surrendered his army, of which Baker's command formed a part, he also wished to surrender; and Baker requested the same terms as those given Johnston's army. Sherman replied on April 19 that Johnston had not made a formal surrender but had agreed on general terms which, if approved in Washington, would terminate the war and apply to all armies of the Confederacy. He suggested that Baker either accept the terms offered Lee at Appomattox or wait a few days for more general arrangements between Johnston and himself. *Official Records (Army)*, Series I, XLVII, Part III, 246, 249-250.

N Y Herald of the 5th from a Yankee prisoner & that it contained the recognition of the French Emperor of the Confederacy. I can scarce credit it. Surely we must have heard of it sooner.

April 23, 1865

Looking Glass. Came down from Hascosea on the 21st Friday & on the 22d came father on his way home from Scotland Neck to dine with us & brought such a budget of news that I stand aghast and in my bewilderment know not what to credit & what to reject. First—Mosby, the gallant, has dashed into Richmond, taken it, & put the negro garrison there to the sword & vanished, leaving a note to the Yankee Com in Cheif to the effect that he does not consider himself as included in the Surrender & that ere long he will return when he hopes to be able to hold the city.[44] (Mem that last intimation more than doubtful, it is so very impolitic!). Next—Lincoln, Lincoln the oppressor is dead! actually dead, killed in the Theatre by Booth the actor! Seward the Arch Villian badly cut in the breast & throat. Lincoln's & Mr Chase sons badly wounded whilst Seward's son & a man named Davis are badly wounded & Raymond, the little villian is killed. In short, such wide spread destruction affected as could only have been produced by the explosion of an Infernal machine.

We sift the news & vainly endeavour to separate the chaff from the wheat. Lincoln's death seems the only certain item & that is affirmed by the Petersburg Intelligencer, now published by a Yankee intruder, & it has made its appearance in mourning to the head of the Yankee nation. "Exult not over thine Adversary," but if Booth intended to turn assassin why, O why, did he delay it for so long? Andy Johnson, the Vulgar renegade, now Pres of the U S has incontinently fled, actually run a way from Washington City in mortal terror lest the fate of his cheif also befall him. Pah! Lincoln the rail splitter was bad enough, but Johnson, the renegade tailor, is worse.

In the afternoon came Dr Langdon CSA, the Captain's brother, in search of him. He is one of Lee's paroled soldiers and our sympathies are such with those of that noble band who remained true to their colours and their cheif that any of them are welcome to our house & we consider it a privilege to do all we can for them. He confirms the fact of Lincoln's death and of the wounding of Seward, but had heard naught of the wholesale blood shed amongst the dignitaries of Washington City with which Rumour had electrified our ears. Lincoln was shot in his box at the theatre & Seward stabbed &

---

[44] The Raleigh *Daily Standard*, April 22, 1865, reported that the commander of the Union forces at Fairfax Station received a message from Mosby stating he did not care about Lee's surrender and was determined to fight it out as long as he had a man left. Instead, rather than surrender, Mosby disbanded his Rangers on April 20, 1865, quietly returned to civilian life, and resumed his law practice. Boatner, *Civil War Dictionary*, 571; Charles Wells Russell (ed.), *The Memoirs of Colonel John S. Mosby* (Bloomington: Indiana University Press, 1959), 360-361.

left for dead in his own house by an unknown man who had insisted on seeing him & despite the efforts of his servants and family forced himself into his sick chamber. He now lies in a most critical situation & the next news may be of his death. This news came from a lady in Weldon who assured Dr L that she had seen a copy of the Petersburg Intelligencer containing it, so as this is the fourth time & from four different quarters it has reached us, I think we may credit it. What effect it will have on us, on our *Cause*, remains to be seen. Lincoln was not, it is true, the Government of the U S, but Seward was its main spring & his sudden death, should it occur, and the exaltation of Johnson may cause a revolution at the North in which we may once more regain our rights.

APRIL 24, 1865

Yesterday came news from Halifax which indeed took us all by surprise. Who can tell what a day may bring forth? Mr McMahon sent us a copy of the Articles of Capitulation agreed upon by Gen Joe Johnston on the part of the Confederate States & by Gen Sherman on that of the U S, articles so strange in their character, so diametrically opposite to all that we have heard of Gen Johnston, that we may well pause & ask ourselves if they are not a Yankee canard, a trick played by them in order to dispirit us & to keep us quiet under their hateful rule, whilst they fasten the links of their chain tighter around us. Gen Johnston is essentially a *soldier* & he has hitherto especially eschewed all interferance with or even expression of opinion of aught that concerned the Civil Arm of the government & yet here we find him assuming to treat of matters which belong solely to the Executive & to Congress. The paper bears date, "State of N C—Durham's Station, the 18th day of April A D 1865," & purports to be a "Memorandum of the basis of an Agreement between Gen Joseph E Johnston—Comdg. Confederate Army & Maj Gen W E Sherman Comdg Army of the U S, but as the paper may be Historic, I give a synopsis of each Article:

Art. 1st

The Armies in the field are to retain their status quo until notice is given, say forty eight hours allowed.

Art 2d

The Confederate Armies now in existence to be disbanded & conducted to their several State Capitols, there to deposit their Arms & public property in the several State Arsenals, the officers & men to file an agreement to cease from acts of War & to abide the action of the State & Federal authorities. The number of Arms & Munitions of War to be reported to the Cheif of Ordnance in Washington City subject to the future action of the U S Congress & in the mean time to be used solely to maintain peace & order within the States respectively.

Art 3d

The recognition by the Executive of the U S of the several State Governments on their Officers & Legislatures taking the Oath prescribed by the Constitution of the U S & where conflicting State Governments have resulted from the War, the legitimacy of all such shall be determined by the Supreme Court of the U S.

Art 4th

The re-establishment of all the Federal Courts in the several States with powers as defined by the Constitution & Laws of Congress.

Art 5

The people & inhabitants of all the States are to be guaranteed, so far as the Executive can their political rights & franchises, as well as their rights of person & property as defined by the Constitution of the U S & States respectively.

Art 6th

The Executive authority of the U S not to disturb any of the people by reason of the late War as long as they remain in peace & quiet & abstain from acts of armed hostility & obey the laws in existence in the places of their residence.

Art 7th

In general terms the War to cease, a general Amnesty so far as the Executive of the U S can command—on condition of the disbandment of the Confederate Armies, the deposition of Arms & resumption of peaceful pursuits by the officers & men composing such Armies.

Not being fully empowered by our respective Principals to fulfil these terms, we individually and officially pledge ourselves to promptly obtain the necessary authority and to carry out the above programme.

Signed

W T Sherman	J E Johnston
Maj Gen Comdg U S forces	Gen Comdg C S Army
in N C	in N C

Contrary to my intention I have copied the above articles in extenso, but I do not I confess credit them. Such an assumption of authority on the part of Gen Johnson seems unparaleled. He has no more right to treat of the resumption of Courts, the Sovreignty of the States, etc., than has Gen Baker to disband & release from Confederate service the men under his command. Not one word of the President, of the Congress of the Con State; not even a reference to them, the very Government under whom Gen Johnston holds his Commission entirely ignored, *our armies* disbanded forsooth, the Yankee held intact within our very borders, we delivered up like sheep to their Imperial will on the bare guarantee, too, of their honour, faugh! Lee our Com in Cheif restricted himself when he capitulated to the army actually under his command. Johnston surely will not venture more. It is a vile Yankee trick meant to juggle us into an admission of their sovreignty over us, a snare into which they wish us to fall, so that hereafter they can tighten the noose around our necks. Who is to judge of what is "Peace & quiet"? & what are acts of armed hostility? Who but they the muddiers of the water which we the poor sheep are compelled to drink? Suppose a Yankee should enter a gentleman's house & be insolent & get kicked out. That forsooth is an act of "armed hostility" to the U S Government & to be resented accordingly? I do not think the famous treaty ever saw the light west of Raleigh. The Yankees can print what they like for it is beyond the power of our rulers to enlighten us or even to deny it![45]

Pray God we compromise not ourselves in our ignorance. Mr M tells us that the death of Lincoln & wounding of Seward is again reaffirmed, but not one word of the errant tailor. Dr Langdon assures us that he knows A P Hill was killed whilst gallantly fighting his way out of Petersburg but that all the Lees are safe. Sad to say Gens Picket Bushrod Johnson, and R Anderson were releived from command a few days before the Surrender, for having been absent from their commands during the fight on the day previous (previous to their releif I mean). In fact they were all drunk! What a sorrowful thing that men who had won their reputation at the edge of the sword should in a moment of weakness peril it by a gratification of an appetite. I give this on Dr Langdon's authority.

APRIL 27, 1865

Yesterday came Capt Langdon back from Warren County, Johnston's capitulation, which sad to say is too true, having put an end to his efforts to join him. Johnston's *surrender is true*, & the long heads amongst us say that we should be thankful for the terms he has secured. Good God! I cannot write!

APRIL 28, 1865

Capt Langdon has seen a N Y Herald giving the particulars of Lincoln's death & of the attempt on Seward's life. The terrible scene which was reported to us so minutely, of how the cry "Sic Semper Tyrannis" was raised in the

---

[45]The broadly worded terms of surrender originally drawn up between Sherman and Johnston were rejected by Andrew Johnson. Sherman, interested in complying with what he understood to be Lincoln's Reconstruction policy, offered generous military terms and also incorporated political Reconstruction for the South in his terms, guaranteeing property rights which, in southern eyes, included slaves. These terms disallowed, Sherman proffered terms of capitulation similar to those given Lee at Appomattox. *Official Records (Army)*, Series I, XLVII, Part III, 206-207, 294; Randall and Donald, *Civil War and Reconstruction*, 528-529.

Theatre & one hundred & forty pistols discharged at once into Lincoln's box, the immediate extinguishment of the lights & the escape of the conspirators, exists but in imagination. No such coup de Theatre was enacted.

The deed was committed by Booth & Booth alone. He made his preparations deliberately & secretly, by barring the door which led from the box to the passage, the proscenium I beleive it is called, & taking off the lock of the box and having bored a gimlet hole in the door, watched his opportunity & about the middle of the play entered the box noiselessly & shot Mr Lincoln in the back of the head! Mrs L, Miss Clara Harris, & Maj Rathbun[46] being in the box with him, Maj Rathbun instanly seized him & called for help, but Booth stabbing him & shaking him off, jumped to the front of the box & leaped to the stage & shouting "*Freedom*" made good his escape! The attempt on Seward was substantially as we heard it. He was in bed with a broken jaw bone. The unknown man stabbed him & his attendants & Sewards life is due to the bandages and splints with which his neck was surrounded protecting his throat. His assailant too also made his escape.

Capt L. was at Dr Hawkins's[47] (Pres of the R and G R R) house when he returned from Raleigh from a conference with Sherman to which he had been summonded to report the transportation with which he could furnish him. He told Dr H the names of his engines & even knew which had been destroyed at Weldon, so we have traitors amongst us. Sherman was most grandiloquent & boastful, not only of what he had done but of what he could & would do! It sickens me to think of his manner, so as humiliation is not a pleasant vale to dwell in I will pass it over. He expressed a hope of being soon able to take his army home (God grant it), "that is should his Government acceede to the terms he had offered Johnston. Failing that he intended "to gobble" (such was his elegant expression) "Johnston up," & from the style of his conversation it seemed as tho the whole Confederacy would be but a bonne touch to his Lordship!

The route that he proposes to follow lies thro' Oxford, Danville, & Lynchburg & then down the undevastated portion of Va (if he can find it!) to Alexandria. Says he will sweep a path of from 50 to 75 miles wide perfectly bare of *all* forage & will take such provisions & animals as he will need. Professes an unwillingness to rob the people & hypocritically whines over the suffering he

---

[46]Clara Harris, the daughter of United States Senator Ira Harris of New York, and her fiancé Maj. Henry Reed Rathbone, attended the play at Ford's Theater with the Lincolns on the night of Lincoln's assassination. Sandburg, *Abraham Lincoln: The War Years*, IV, 272, 281.

[47]William Joseph Hawkins (1819-1894), a practicing physician in Ridgeway, North Carolina, was elected president of the Raleigh and Gaston Railroad in 1855, a post he held almost continuously until October, 1875. Sherman wrote Hawkins on April 20, 1865, that a Federal construction party was unemployed and could repair the Cedar Creek bridge. Sherman further stated he had no objections to restoration of the railroad to Hawkins, but that he would like to borrow or rent some locomotives and cars. *Official Records (Army)*, Series I, XLVII, Part III, 258; *Cyclopedia of Eminent and Representative Men of the Carolinas of the Nineteenth Century* (Madison, Wis.: Brant & Fuller, 2 volumes, 1892), II, 329-330.

must cause, but gives the lie to his scruples by not shipping his army from New Berne, Wilmington, & Petersburg, all ports within easy reach of him. It needs no seer to divine his object in his cruel & murderous act. It is to disable and cripple us so much the more & to make us dependant upon the North for our very existence. Would that the women & children who will be starved & die by his cruelty could haunt every moment sleeping or waking of his future life. He runs ten trains per day between Morehead City & Raleigh & sends out numbers of forage parties daily, three hundred waggons in a party, who forage the country for 50 miles to find food for his army. He most graciously promises to repair the damage of Cedar Creek (burnt he says by that fool Baker) & to leave the same for the benefit of the R R, but I doubt me but he will find his advantage in his generosity in the facilities it will give him for foraging in this section and the collection of a Depot of supplies at Oxford.

Dr H saw brothers grounds, his grove, his yard, and whole premises one camp ground for Yankee soldiers—tents as far as the eye could reach. God help his helpless family! Sherman has 200,000 men in & around Raleigh & for 10 miles around the country seems one vast camp. He saw, too, numbers of negroes, men, women, & children, dressed in their master's & mistress's clothes hurrying from all quarters into Raleigh as to a carnival. Guion's Hotel[48] had been assigned them as Quarters & was packed to overflowing with them. Sherman when asked what was to become of them said that he should take all "the able bodied men as teamsters, the rest he should leave to us. There was ample employment for the strong at the North—none for the feeble."

Andy Johnson has been quietly inaugurated President & made a speech, & such a speech, maudlin drunk. He said amongst other things that "Treason was a crime to be punished, not forgiven," & wound up with the announcement that his "heart was too full" (of Whisky?) to say more—the vulgar old sinner!

Mobile, Montgomery, Selma, and Augusta are all in the occupancy of the enemy. God watch over & keep Mr Davis. We had hoped that he was well en route for the trans Mississippi, but I fear that these blood hounds will intercept him; $100,000 in gold is offered for his capture. Sherman says that if taken the general sentiment of the North will be to hang him. God forbid!

APRIL 29, 1865

Yesterday Father on his way to Hascosea met Mr Hill who told him that a soldier from Johnston's army had told him that his Mightiness Andy Johnson

---

[48]The Guion Hotel stood on the corner of Halifax and Edenton streets; it was later known as the National Hotel. The building was purchased by the state and demolished in 1922 to make room for the Agriculture Building. Elizabeth Culbertson Waugh and others, *North Carolina's Capital, Raleigh* (Raleigh: Junior League of Raleigh, Inc., and the Raleigh Historic Sites Commission, Inc., 1967), 37.

had refused to sanction the terms agreed on by Sherman & that in consequence Johnston had disbanded his army. Instead of surrendering they broke
their arms & dispersed. How true this is none can tell for we are entirely mail-
less. Ah, that I knew of Mr Davis' safety, that I could do something for him.
Despite his mistakes (& mistakes he made but honest ones) he is still our exemplar & our head & as such I reverence him. True by his removal of
Johnston he brought us into our present humiliating condition, but this was
an error of judgment for which we should pardon him. Gen Lee has committed many blunders—none, however, fraught with such misery to the nation
because he was not its Head, but who now remembers or visits one of them
upon him? Let the same robe of charity & oblivion cover Pres Davis mistakes
and let us now remember that he is our chosen Head & is unfortunate.

MAY 7, 1865

What use is there in my writing this record? What profit, what pleasure, do
I find in it? None! none! yet altho it is an actual pain to me I continue it from
mere force of habit. We are *crushed!* subjugated! and I fear, O how I fear,
conquered, & what is to me the saddest part, our people do not feel it as they
ought—like men who have lost their Liberty. The cup has not to them the full
bitterness which a once free people ought to find in the draught held to them
by a Victor's hand. They accept the situation tacitly, fold their hands, & say
"resistance is vain," "we have done all that men could do," we are out numbered, over-run, & have not the where withal to set an army in the field. Their
once high spirit, their stern resolve, seems dead within them! "The War is
over" & that fact seems to console them. O My God, can the very spirit of
Freedom die out thus & leave not a trace behind it? Are the lives laid down in
its defence to be but as water spilled on the ground? Is the very memory of one
dead to vanish from our midst? One would think so from the conduct of those
around us. On Thursday, on our way out to Hascosea, we met crowds of people, almost the whole neighborhood it seemed to me, on their way to a Pic Nic
at Hills Mill. The usual preparations for dancing had been made & there they
spent the day feasting, dancing, fishing, & merry making in their old familiar
way. It seems almost like dancing over their husband's, brothers, & sons
graves. Do they realize what they do, or are they stupefied by the calamity
which has befallen them & say "let us eat & drink for tomorrow we die." O
my Country, my Country, I look forward to the future with bitter forebodings
when I see your children thus forgetful of your and their own *honour*, of their
own *blood!*

Rumours innumerable of the Yankee plans, the Yankee intentions towards
us. One is that they have deposed our Governor Vance & ordered a new election to fill his Chair; another that Schofield (now in command in Raleigh,
Sherman having gone to Charleston) has issued an Edict of Emancipation to
our Slaves & the oath of Allegiance to the U S is shortly to be enforced upon

every one of us—men, women, & children. Every one is discussing it—& sad to say I have not heard a dissentient voice, or rather a resistant voice. All proclaim it illegal, cruel, & tyrannous but say that they are not free agents & cannot help themselves.

Came home from Hascosea last night & found a note from Father telling us that negroes with Yankee papers were circulating amongst ours, that Lorenzo Dow whom he sold more than a year since for intending to run off to the enemy, had returned, that most of the Burgwyn negroes had gone to the Yankees, & what was good news, he was in immediate expectation of seeing Brother, having heard of him at Mr Long's the night before. He sent us a New York Herald, so intensely Yankee, so full of bragg, bluster, & triumph that it made me sick to glance over it. Read it I did not. The only interest it possessed for me was to see if there was aught of our President in it & what fate their clemency meets to our unhappy country, but naught met my eyes but low, bombastic threats against us. England, France, & I beleive the rest of the habitable globe, so inflated are they with their victory!

MAY 8, 1865

Yesterday came Sue & Rachel with the astounding news that brother had arrived & had gone to Montrose with the intention of freeing his negroes & soon after came Messrs Gilliam & W Smith & announced that he had done so & that father was to follow suit this afternoon. I could not understand it. It seemed inexplicable to me & suicidal in the last degree. Schofield has, it is true, issued such an order, but so has his cheif, Lincoln, three years ago & if Lincoln's Edict has not the force of Law, I do not see how Schofield's can. Passed a most anxious afternoon & night, Mr E and I discussing the fact & viewing it in every point of view, as it bears upon our future life, upon our plans, & our property & talking over our fears for the terrible days which seem to be coming upon us, our Country, Mr Davis, & all manner of sorrowful & harrowing subjects.

This morning came father & told us to our releif that both the girls & the gentlemen were mistaken, that brother & himself had merely announced to their negroes that *Mr Schofield said* they were free, but that they (their masters) did not beleive they were, but that if any of them wished to go away and try their freedom to go *now*—at once & to stay away, that their places could be supplied, but that in the fall when their own rights & those of the negroes were defined & settled there would be ample time to talk of it & that if they were then free that they should be paid for their labour out of this year's crop. In this last clause I think they made a mistake. Make no promises, so as to have none to break, is a good rule in dealing with both children and negroes & negroes are but ignorant children at best, but I feel vastly releived that they have not endorsed Messrs Lincoln & Schofield Edict &, as Hope springs eternal in the human breast, begin to think I have taken a large share of suffering causelessly & uselessly. The Lord reigneth! & out of this seeming terrible ill, good may yet result, good of which we at present dream not.

Brother brings a vivid picture of the Yankee power & the Yankee brutality. Details of Sherman's march through S C reach us through themselves that are heart sickening. The system of "bumming," for with Sherman it is a system, is brought as near the perfection of villainy as the human mind can come. Sherman the theif, Sherman the Prince of Bummers, is a title to which he may well lay claim. *Columbia was burned by his orders*, so his officers admit, altho he attempts to deny the direct order saying only that he ordered Slocoms devils to the advance, well knowing that they would do their duty & need no orders!

The rule they keep over Cuffee astonishes him vastly. The whip with which the Yankee Vice Provost has armed himself is one which no Southern Over-seer ever dare even owned. Public opinion if not the owners' orders would soon have banished it. The only instrument of correction ever used on our negroes was a switch cut from some neighbouring bush & these new punish-ments, Bull whips, Hanging up by the Thumbs, & Bucking, astonish them not a little. Except stealage & threats of burning his house down when the family were not as complaisant as the Yankee soldiers expected in lending them chairs, crockery, etc., brother's family have faired pretty well. Every particle of their fences destroyed & the garden deprdated upon was what they expected, but they had a guard & a Gen's Head quarters in their yard, so they fared better than we feared. He now has a Yankee Lieut Col *actually boarding* at his house. He came & requested quarters & as his presence insured protec-tion against his men encamped around the house, they were granted him. He behaves well for a Yankee with the exception of occasionally getting drunk, but he is not then intrusive but confines his tramping to his own room. His name is Noble of the [———] Maine.[49]

Howard's corps has gone North, but 130,000 men are still encamped in and around Raleigh. The suffering of some of the people in the country has been terrible, robbed of everything & driven out without a shelter to their heads. Mrs Hinton (Jane Miller),[50] without a moment's warning was surrounded by a gang of theives who tore off her doors & windows & reduced her house to a ruin to build themselves quarters, robbed her of everything & forced her to seek shelter in the town. She had to walk for three miles through their camp with her children, & lost every thing she had in the world.

Most of brothers servants remained true to him. His nurse Adelaide is a noted instance. She would go to her Mistress & young mistresses & beg them to excuse her & then beseech them to bear all and to keep their tongues in "their heads before these devils" if they wanted a shingle left over them. "I

---

[49]The Noble referred to was probably Lt. Col. Joseph Noble of the Ninth Maine Regiment, then stationed in North Carolina. *Official Records (Army)*, Series I, XLVII, Part I, 57.

[50]Laurens Hinton of Wake County married Jane C. Miller on September 24, 1851. Marriage Bond of Laurens Hinton and Jane C. Miller, State Archives.

hears 'em, honey, I hears what they say & I knows what they will do if you give them any excuse. Be civil to them." But so far was she from taking her own advice that her vituperation of them became a subject of merriment to the wretches who gave her the soubriquet of the "Major Gen." She told them on more than one occasion "that a country that had such mean men in it as they was ought to keep its own meanness at home and not harry other folks with it."

Have just read a letter from my neice Nannie which does *one's* heart good so intensely bitter is it. Such hate as it expresses one does not often read of, but unfortunately for me I am beginning to feel it. She says that at Guion's, the negro head quarters, they have nightly balls & that the *Yankee Officers* dance with *the negro women*!

May 13, 1865

Such a week as the past has been, I hope never to see again. Excitement & anxiety have ruled each day, until at last I became heartsick & weary & longed for rest, rest, come how it would, only rest. As we had feared, father's negroes either misunderstood or pretended to misunderstand father's & brother's talk with them. On Monday several of them were absent from work & one man kept his wife at home contrary to plantation discipline. A firm & resolute hand checked all disobedience at home, however, and a visit to Weldon satisfied some of the absentees, who have almost all returned, professing to have found out that they were better off as they were. We have lost none here. The poor creatures seem as usual, only terribly dejected, & are much more tender & affectionate in their manner to us than ever before. It is a terrible cruelty to them, this unexpected, unsolicited gift of freedom, & they are at their wits ends. Their old moorings are rudely & suddenly cut loose, & they drift without a rudder into the unknown sea of freedom. God help such philanthropy.

At Hascosea—Hope getting into some trouble about her work, having stolen some of her cotton & getting what the negroes call "crowded" about it, concluded that as father's carpenters told her she was free, that she & her family would taste some of the sweets offered them. So on Wednesday their house was found vacant. They "toted" off their best clothes & some of their provisions, leaving the rest behind them. Whither they went no one knows. If to Weldon we will have them back ere long, for the Yankee commandant there makes all who come to him a short oration to the effect that they are *free*, that they belong to no one, but enjoins them to go back to their Masters & work for their living, if they get only 50 cts a month to spend on Brandy. He selects such as he wishes for the Army, the young, strong, & able bodied, and drives the rest from his presence, telling them that freedom does not mean freedom from work and that he has nothing to give them to eat.

Father & brother went up to see him & found him sitting in his office without any stockings on, doing business as tho he was in full dinner costume. Think of that refined gentleman giving the Law to us! He sent for Mr Tillery who had lost 20 of his hands to make some arrangements with him for their return home & told him when they came back if they would not work to send to him & he would send a file of men down to the plantation to *thrash* them until they would be glad to do so. What a nation! This nominal freedom is only to keep up appearances in Europe, to annoy us, & to deprive us of our property—all at one stroke. They have no love for the negro, no desire for his happiness or welfare. He is only a stick where with all to beat us.

Yesterday most unexpectedly came James & his friend Mr Adam Milliken,[51] & a most terrible account had they to give us of their adventures & what they had undergone. James was ordered before Johnston's surrender to report to Qr Master Gen Lawton &, having left, was not included in his paroled men. He was well on his way South with a wagon, four mules, the Qt M Gen's horse (a magnificent animal), a quantity of stores for his journey, meat, flour, tea, coffee, etc., & with a party of gentlemen had nearly reached the S C line in Anson Co when his camp was suddenly surrounded by a band of armed men who robbed them of every article they possessed. Seeing they were soldiers from Lee's army, he pleaded Orders but was answered by an insolent laugh & "Orders, Major, orders are played out." They took every thing, even his pistol, & turned the party adrift with a horse apeice only & a few clothes. Mr Milliken & himself made their way with some difficulty to Greensboro, where they were forced to take a parole & after many adventures & delays at length reached here with only the clothes in which they stood.

June 26, 1865

Hascosea—In the Solitare—More than a month since I wrote a line in my Journal, but what of that? I have only missed the enumeration of a series of petty annoyances, of humiliating orders from our Yankee masters. Conquerers they are not, for our Conquerers are our own "familiar friends," our own Congress, our public men, our own President & his imbecile Cabinet. They it is who have beaten us. This Journal is now but a pain and greif to me. It is a transcript of disappointed hopes, of crushed expectations, which have all the bitterness of death without the lively hope of a Resurection. A few words will give my life since Johnston's Surrender, a few words, but containing the sorrows and cares of a life time.

The Negro Emancipation has been accomplished. The unfortunates have been thrust blindfold upon the ills of a state of which they know nothing. They enter with confidence & pleasure, expecting that freedom from care

---

[51]This reference is probably to A. W. Milliken, a corporal in Co. F, Forty-third North Carolina Regiment. Moore, *Roster of North Carolina Troops*, III, 212.

which they have hitherto enjoyed & which a state of dependance guarantees them, together with an entire immunity from all work or all necessity for self provision, but on the threshold of their new life a cruel disappointment awaits them. The Yankees tell them that "freedom does not mean freedom from work," but freedom from the Whip & from the degredation of being sold. Now as but a few of them have ever felt the first to any noticeable degree, none of them in the manner in which the Yankees assure them they have, & as the second always secured them a comfortable home & an assured subsistence, they prefer a degredation which they cannot understand to being turned adrift & told to shift for themselves when they have taxed their master's patience beyond human endurance. They occupy themselves ceaselessly trying their new chains, seeing how little work they can accomplish & yet be fed and endeavouring to be both slave & free at the same moment—a slave on the food, shelter, & clothing question but free where labour is concerned. Accordingly they are in continual difficulty & make our lives anything but beds of Roses. I with an unusually large family, *nine* persons, not strong health & miserably spirits, for I am becoming dejected and gloomy and a great deal of sewing on hand, for I cannot get my seamstresses to sew, O no, they only hold their needles & sleep, for are they now free, having any thing but an easy or comfortable time.

At one blow we have lost a large portion of our property. Father's is diminished by $350,000 or $400,000 & what is sadder still, his liabilities remain the same, whilst his ability to meet them is lessened ten fold! The future stands before us dark, forbidding, & stern, whilst the happy past smiles back at us with the lustre of a vanished summer sunset, & we have to repeat again & again to ourselves, "Shall I receive good at the hands of the Lord and shall I not also receive evil?"[52]

At present all is as gloomy as can well be, at home present domestic discomfort & dismal anticipations of still greater evils to come, whilst abroad the Vulgar Yankee nation exults over our misfortunes, places its foot upon our necks, & extols its own prowess in conquering us. *Conquering* us, for sooth. They have already forgotten how many of their own dead our soil covers & every defeat which we inflicted upon them and over which they set up so terrific a howl of *the nation* in danger at the time is now a glorious victory, for which Te Deums should at once be sung. Their hated troops are now stationed at all points amongst us. They command all the R Roads & other routes of travel & they have the ability to force their detested oath down the throat of every man amongst us. Our President is in their power actually manacled to an iron bar, loaded with a weight of iron which his feeble frame can scarcely sustain, whilst every vile crime which their fertile imaginations suggest to them (assassination, robery, murder, & treason being amongst the

---

[52]Job 2:10.

slightest) is laid to his charge. Their sensation newspapers meantime vie with each other in the attempt to ridicule & vilify him & the Yankee nation at large pour out their petty spite & venom upon him, clamuring for his blood, because he has committed Treason against their sovreign majesty. Treason! faugh! Our State Governments are all set at naught, they affecting to treat us as Territories, we, Sovreign States, Sovreign in our own right, who withdrew from a compact entered into voluntarily with them, but by the grace of foreign mercenaries forsooth we are now but appendages to their mightiness.

Here in N C they have taken the lowest, most abject, & degraded man they could find amongst us, one Holden, & exalted him to the post of provisional Governor,[53] a base born bastard with neither the breeding or the instincts of a gentleman is placed over us & in utter defiance of the fact that six months since we utterly repudiated & almost to a man rejected him as not fit to be our exponent & head, we are now told "Lo! he is your own, born amongst you, your own native Statesman. What more can you ask?" When Secession was triumphant, when it was the gaining side, who so warm a Secessionist as Holden? He pledged "the last man & the last dollar in N C" to fight the Yankee, but when the Cause of the South failed, when to be a patriot involved loss & perhaps danger, who so quick to forget the appeals he had made to his fellow citizens to unite as one man against their foes? Where can these same foes find a readier tool or a more subservient instrument to oppress & call to account those who *if in* error but followed his teachings!

Sorrow on sorrow! No one is well, no one is happy! Anger, indignant anger, fills every heart & no man swallows that hated oath without becoming tenfold more bitter than he was before. A sense of personal humiliation is forced upon him & he resents it by infusing a double portion of hate in the sentiment with which he regards those who have degraded him. No one can buy or sell aught without first perjuring himself. He can practice no trade or profession, can neither get married or have a physician to prescribe for him should he be sick. The only thing which his Yankee masters leave him free to do is to *die*. Death is free to all. Death comes to set him free. Few of us but with Tristam would "meet him cheerily as thy true friend"!

July 2, 1865

The horrors of Yankee rule seem beginning to culminate. On Friday last a lady of this community heard her brothers servant regretting to one of his fellows "that their drill had been so badly attended the night before & hoping that the next night they would do better." She informed her brother & husband of the speech & they accordingly with their neighbours armed themselves & unobserved kept their eyes upon the two negroes.

---

[53]William W. Holden was appointed provisional governor of North Carolina by Andrew Johnson on May 22, 1865, to replace the military department commanded by Schofield. Lefler and Newsome, *North Carolina*, 483-484.

They were followed about midnight to a rendezvous in the woods, where they found about sixty men & boys awaiting them. It appeared that they had what to them was a complete Military organization, the servant who had first been overheard being their Brigadier with a full general's staff under him, all the rest being either Colonels or Captains, privates only being wanted to make it an army! Measures were taken for their arrest, but unfortunately it was so badly managed that seventeen only were taken, whilst but two were slightly wounded & unfortunately none were killed. Unfortunately I say, for a sharp, stern, & bloody retribution falling on their heads in the beginning of their mad career would not only spare many valuable lives but prevent many of the misguided wretches themselves from meeting hereafter a worse fate.

Upon being questioned they admitted that their intention was to drill & exercise themselves until Christmass, when they intended to seize the land & drive out the white people. They said, moreover, that they were disappointed & dissatisfied with the freedom which the Yankees gave them. The Yankees had promised them four years ago that so soon as the war was over they should have not only their freedom but the houses & land of their masters, that this promise had not been kept, for they were worse off now than they were before the war. Not only had they to work all the same but they had now to support their old parents, their wives, & their children. That the Yankee soldiers told them that they would never get the White folks property until they rose & helped themselves—& that they intended to do.[54]

They uttered much other such Red Republicanism which it is useless to waste my time in recording. Suffice it the whole seventeen were sent up to Maj Taylor & his adjunct of the Freedman's Bureau, Captain Turner, today, but there is little hope that aught will be done with them. Maj Taylor will call them "*his sons*," tell them of rights of their Masters, enjoin them to work, say that Freedom does not mean freedom from work, and dismiss them. As for Capt Turner, he is such a ninny head that there is no telling what absurdity he will fall into. If we would have Justice or Protection, it must be taken into our own hands, for we have no Civil Law & the Military is but a hideous engine of oppression; but it is a terrible alternative for a high minded law abiding people to be forced it—Let the guilt lie on the heads of those who

---

[54]Mrs. Edmondston's reference to a possible attack upon whites by the emancipated blacks in her neighborhood, timed to coincide with the Christmas holidays, occurred during the opening months of an insurrection scare which swept through the South during the summer and fall of 1865. Dan T. Carter, in his study of this panic, concluded that the actions and reactions of the white community during this period indicated their gullibility and susceptibility to mass hysteria. Rumors and distorted accounts of alleged conspiracies ignited the South into a frenzy of vigilante activity and fear, although substantive proof of an organized plot never appeared. Mrs. Edmondston's description of a military organization among the neighborhood blacks during the last week of June, however, predates Carter's earliest evidence of white agitation, and this possibly indicates that there was some fire behind the smoke at this locality. Dan T. Carter, "The Anatomy of Fear: The Christmas Day Insurrection Scare of 1865," *Journal of Southern History*, XLII (August, 1976), 345-364.

forced it upon us, on theirs be the blood shed in this desperate attempt for self protection. Amen!

JULY 28, 1865

Wednesday—Quite sick! Indeed I have no heart to be well! My bed is I beleive the best place for me. Since Monday a new element of bitterness has been infused into our daily lives. On that day Father & Mr Edmondston were forced in order to protect themselves against Yankee & negro insolence & to preserve the remnant of our property, to go to Halifax & to take the hated oath of Allegiance to that loathed Yankee Government!

We feel a deep & abiding resentment towards a nation who thus debases our sense of personal honour & weakens the heretofore sacred obligation of an oath taken in the name of Almighty God. Who considers it binding? No one. Not one person whom I have heard speak of it but laughs at and repudiates every obligation it imposes. It binds one no more than a promise at the pistols point to a highwayman! & is it not in fact made to a nation of theives who say to us, "Your property, your very existence, nay protection to your person, to your honour, to that of your wives & children or this hated oath." Were it a simple question of life, many would not hesitate: but this oath—or see yourself plundered alike by Yankees & negroes; this oath—& or perhaps daily insult & outrage; this oath, or turn out of your house & loved home & see them possessed by the very offscouring of the world; this oath—or a life of exile & dependance. Rather than this, welcome the oath. I swear everything & anything, both possible & impossible, say light is darkness, heat is cold, Andy Johnson is a gentleman, Seward is truthful, Yankees are honest—what you will. I assent to it all. Yes & hate you whilst I do it and determine but to bide my time, to fling it to the winds when I can do so with safety. Yes Yankee nation, "*cute*" as you are, you cannot fathom the depth of hate, contempt, & rage with which you have filled the breast of every true Southron. You have lowered our standard of morality. You have sullied the purity of our integrity. You have made us say with the lip what we did not intend to fulfil with our *acts*, made us promise what we will not pay, & for all this we hate you!

Brother has asked & received pardon at the hand of his high mightiness Andy Johnson for the crime of being worth more than $20,000. Well may he count it a crime when he remembers that his Uncle & protector, old Jesse Johnson, was bribed to sobriety by the promise of a cow by the father of the man he now outlaws for the crime of wealth. This Andy was then one of the family. Had he obtained his present elevation by the weight either of intellect or character, this would but add to his honour, but no, a miserable drunken demagogue, an Agrarian & Red Republican, he has risen only by pandering to the worst vices of the populace. He has exalted himself by pulling others down. In a seething cauldron the thickest scum ever rises to the surface.

At the Plantation all day yesterday with Mr E but was to unwell & too unhappy to enjoy myself as of yore. Gathered my tea leaves & laid down & felt miserable the rest of the day. My God, enable me to look beyond the human instrument to Thy Hand which chastises us!

OCTOBER 1, 1865

Three months since I wrote a line in this book, and *three what months*! In the first place sorrow, anger, anxiety, & distress to such an extent as were endured by me during the months of May, June, & part of July bore their usual fruit & after some weeks of indisposition my health at last gave way & for five weeks I was seriously ill. My Liver became thoroughly disordered & I suffered all the horrors incident upon such a condition. Added to this I had a severe attack of Pleurisy which gradually slided into Yellow Jaundice & reduced me so that I was unable to walk across my room. Even now I have not recovered my strength & vigor.

Mr E heard of the death of his eldest brother in Charleston more than 6 weeks after its occurrence so completely were we shut off from communication with the rest of the world by the stoppage of our mails, & at the same time he received tidings that his Mother was so much affected by the event & so much annoyed by the change in her domestic affairs that she had given up housekeeping & had started for the Shetland Island intending to spend the remnant of her days with her son Thomas in Scotland. She wrote appointing a rendezvous in Philadelphia, to which place she urged Patrick to come & take his last leave of her. So accordingly as soon as it was deemed safe for him to leave me he hurried on & fortunately found her with her daughter Mrs. Zogbaum. Her experience of the voyage from Savannah to Phila had convinced her that a longer one was impossible to her with safety, so happily for her children on this side of the water she has given it up we hope forever. My state was such that he allowed himself but twenty four hours in the city & then in despite of poor James inclinations—posted back & found me scarce able to turn in bed, but thanks to a merciful God, I have now recovered & am able once more to enjoy *Life*. Grant that a sense of His mercies may henceforth follow me & that hereafter my daily life may show forth His praise!

During the whole of my sickness I was nursed in a most devoted & affectionate manner by my maid Fanny. Her faithfulness was a subject of remark by every one who saw her. At times she actually wept over me & with the most earnest & tender solicitude she constantly cared for me & yet when I was scarce able to walk without assistance she left me without provocation or warning, left me in the night, and that too without the slightest notice. Poor thing, I hear now that her husband, Joe, one of Father's Carpenters has been trying to entice her off since the Proclamation of Freedom & that now taking advantage of a temporary indisposition of her child, he has promised that if she would go with him she should do naught but tend it whilst he would support her in idleness. She has at length succombed and has gone off into the unknown future with only him to depend on. She actually left without bidding me good bye, altho she knew I neither would or could detain her.

For a fortnight her compeer Vinyard filled her place most efficiently & cheerfully, but getting weary of well doing she announced that she was sick & retired from the house, her disease being cheifly intense "*Laziness.*" Her husband made the most unreasonable complaints on her behalf, one of which was to the effect that "carrying the server had made a hole in her stomach into which he could put his fist." Now as the said formidable server can only hold three medium dishes & she has not lifted it for six weeks, Owen having brought it in from the Kitchen & Dolly carrying it out, I fear his fellow servants are right when they say his desire is to provoke his master by sauciness so that he will discharge him, thinking he will in that case get his money, but I fear that "the woman thou gavest me" is at the bottom of his discontent. I shall welcome Christmas, for it will rid me of her. Such idleness, neglect, & wilful carelessness, I never conceived of as she exhibits. With the ability to govern her firmly & consistently I have lost a very fair servant. No one could put up with her now.

The Freedman's Bureau, facetiously known as the "Free Nigger's Christ" is the source of the most unmitigated annoyance to our whole country. The very old Fiend himself could scarce have devised a more effectual method of irritation or a more perfect system of perpetual worry. No sooner are the negroes seemingly contented & begining to work steadily than some Major, Capt, or Lieut in the Free negro service with more time than brains announces a Speech to the Freedmen in Halifax, when "down goes the shovel & the hoe" and presto away they all start to drink some new draught from the "Free Spring," & they come home with their heads so filled with their fancied rights, so puffed up with what the "New Orders" to be issued at Christmass are to give them, that discipline & order are at an end for days.

These Janus faced & double tongued Yankees, these agents of the "Freedman's Bureau," talk one way in public & another in private to them, so the poor negro knows not what to beleive. If the negroes are contented & quiet, their occupation and their *pay* is gone. So they must foster discontent & this is done by holding out false hopes to the poor deluded creatures & telling them that it is their Master's fault that they are not all realized. The better sort amongst them are begining to see that they have been duped &, disappointed in their expectations of houses & Land & team & implements of labour, are becoming soured & discontented to a degree not at all surprising. When both sides of the question are viewed a feeling of animosity & antagonism towards their masters is sedulously cultivated by the Bureau. Ere long I fear it will culminate in rapine & murder on their part & in stern retribution on that of the Whites.

Our foreman Henry, one of the most intelligent of his class, is much changed & in place of an affectionate cheerful simplicity of manner & speech he has become discontented & moody. Thinks he ought to have Land because his forefathers cleared it and he has worked it, cant beleive "Mr Governer," i.e.—the Government—is going to give him his bare freedom with nothing to maintain it, & many such Agrarian notions, which he says the Major says ought to be.

There is no Civil Law in the Country, no Habeus Corpus. The Freedman's Bureau reigns triumphant. Our petit maitre here in Halifax, one Pennyman, on coming into office had a regular "Jail Delivery," after the manner of Sovereigns on coming to the Throne, & actually released every criminal confined there without even the form of trial!

In Northampton a respectable farmer of the name of Ray gave a negro woman a moderate & proper whipping for striking her mistress, his wife. The cheif of the Bureau in that county told him with admirable consistency "that had he knocked her down & beaten & even all but killed her he would have been fully justified from the facts before him," but that O terrible! O shocking! he had presumed "to whip her," whip a free woman, altho she had not a mark of it on her. So accordingly he arrested & sent him up under guard to Raleigh to be judged by the cheif oppressor there, one Elisha Whittlesay,[55] a full blooded Yankee & there the poor man still is, six weeks after the commission of the offence, imprisoned without trial for resenting what the sub Lieut acknoledges cause for "half killing."

Can we long stand this? They tell the negroes that they are our equals, but to do them justice, as a general rule, the poor creatures are slow in learning the lesson of Red Republicanism thus set them. Those that I have come in contact with are still respectful & even subservient, but O! how utterly worthless and Lazy!

OCTOBER 4, 1865

Nothing but more oppressions, & exactions & the most impertinent & officious meddling with one's own private concerns. Were I to write them all this would be but a tiresome repetition of the same story, to wit, a preference of the Negro to the white man, a deliberate attempt to debase the latter in a vain endeavour to elevate the former. A desperate effort is being made to awaken in the Ethiopian mind a desire for the right of suffrage & to secure an admission to them as evidence in a Court of Justice, but as yet Cuffee is dull as

---

[55]Col. Eliphalet Whittlesey of the Forty-sixth United States Colored Infantry, a native of Connecticut, served as the assistant commissioner of the Freedmen's Bureau in North Carolina from 1865 through 1866. Boatner, *Civil War Dictionary*, 917; Hamilton and Williams, *Graham Papers*, VI, 339n.

regards mere abstractions (for such they are to him) & prefers a right to be idle & a free admission into his master's smoke House. As to the right of suffrage, if Northern fanaticism ever force that from the South, I hope that the Anglo Saxon blood will for a time hold in abeyance their rights on that point & give the controul of the ballot box entirely to the negro & help them send the blackest, most stupid, & most ignorant field hand to be found to sit by their white brethren in the Halls of the now debased Congress. But it will scarce come to that. Even they have not yet sunk as a majority to that depth of folly.

Commenced today copying into my book the scraps of paper, old memorandum books, etc., on which I have kept my Journal since I secreted it on the 11th of last April. Fortunately my task is not a heavy one. My sickness & the utter despair I was in all last summer having curtailed my record sadly. What an emptiness it all is!

Mr Davis is still kept imprisoned at Fortress Monroe, exposed to all kinds of petty tyrrany, his fate still undecided. Vile personal abuse, threats of hanging him, of trying him by a Military Court, of bringing him to the bar of a civil tribunal on a charge of Treason, etc., etc., fill the Northern Journals, whilst the Government evinces a wickedness in regard to him controuled only by its weakness & fears.

Gov Vance is still on parole in Washington City. Some Yankee politician asked him in general society a short time since "why he was detained there?," with a view of embarrassing him, when he promptly answered "that he was detained there as security for one W W Holden who having pledged the last man & the last dollar in N C to support the war—& failing in his promise— he Vance, as Gov of the State, was detained there as security on the Bond." The Politician after that left him alone.

The Amnesty, or as generally spoken of the "d—m nasty," oath has been generally taken by the South at large, but still Mr Johnson withholds his d— nasty Proclamation of pardon. Let him keep it! Who cares?

November 15, 1865

Walking with Mr Edmondston in an unfrequented path a few days since— we picked up first some peices of Confederate notes of the value of $10 & further on some N C Treasury notes, thrown there in all probability by some negro who had learned their worthlessness. It gave me a pang, thus to see "Mine honour in the Dust," a pang all the keener as regarded the N C notes, for they were defiled by their own *familiar friend*. North Carolina's own sons in Convention assembled had cast the first slur on her by Repudiation! Went to Church last week for the first time since the Surrender & heard of course the Pres of the U S prayed for. How I longed to tear the leaf out of the book! O!

that the Southern Bishops stand staunch & refuse to strike hands with the bloody ones of the North! Where then will be Bishop Atkinson's place.[56]

DECEMBER 16, 1865

Our Representatives in Congress have been refused admission into that body & sent home in the face of their election having been in accordance with orders from the U S Government issued through its mouth peices, the provisional governors. They design to debase us still lower, it appears, before they allow us an entrance into their glorious Union. At the same time that they refuse to let us "come in" they declare that we were "never out." The N C Convention[57] has prostrated the State so low that I doubt if she can find more dust to lick up. Their declaration that the Ordinance of Secession was null & void & their Repudiation of the War debt is I should think abject enough to please even a Yankee Conquerer!

One lesson we ought to learn from the negroes, i.e., simple faith. They exemplify it in their conduct to a striking degree. Firm in their expectation of "New Orders" at Christmass, which *are* to make all things straight, they refuse to enter into any Contracts for the coming year. The fears of an emeute—which were entertained by some—are dying out. They are orderly & subordinate but incorrigibly lazy. Occasional acts of insubordination by the returned negro soldiers occurs here & there, but in this neighbourhood we are exempt from all the ills of Emancipation save those which spring from Laziness & Theft. These vices share the immunity enjoyed against taxation enjoyed by "lying."

Mr Davis still sighing in uncertainty at Fortress Monroe. Some time since he had his hair cut, when his jailor, a Col in the Yankee army, took his hair from the barber for the purpose of selling it. A few days since it needed cutting again, when he had it gathered up & took it with him to his quarters. Scarce had he entered them when an orderly came post haste with an order from the Commandant of the fort, the same Col, requiring that it be delivered to him, but Mr Davis had been too quick for him. He had already destroyed it! In his narrow walk on the Esplanade of the Fort which his jailors have been obliged to grant him to save his life, which was in danger from confinement, he was

---

[56]Bishop Thomas Atkinson of the Episcopal Diocese of North Carolina appeared as a delegate at the General Triennial Convention of the Episcopal church held in Philadelphia during October, 1865. He was instrumental in effecting a reunion between the northern and southern branches of the church which had separated as a result of the war. Marshall DeLancey Haywood, *Lives of the Bishops of North Carolina* (Raleigh: Alfred Williams and Company, 1910), 173; Ashe, *History of North Carolina*, II, 1038-1039. See also Hugh T. Lefler, "Thomas Atkinson, Third Bishop of North Carolina," *Historical Magazine of the Protestant Episcopal Church*, XVII (December, 1948). See also footnote 46, 1864.

[57]The North Carolina Convention, convened October 2, 1865, met to implement the presidential plan of Reconstruction in order to restore North Carolina to the Union. The delegates repealed the Ordinance of Secession, declared slavery was abolished, provided machinery for the election of a governor, legislators, and representatives to the United States Congress, and repudiated the state war debt. Connor, *North Carolina*, II, 268-271; Lefler and Newsome, *North Carolina*, 484-485.

one day much annoyed by a squad of Yankee women, friends & visitors of the keeper of the Bastile, who planted themselves in his way in order to stare at him. Seeing this he seated himself on a gun carriage & lighting his segar began to smoke, gazing the while out to seaward. Next day came an order prohibiting him from having segars in future. These are but samples of the petty tyrrany with *which a great and magnanimous Government* treats its conquered opponent.

DECEMBER 29, 1865

Christmass has come & gone without disturbance of any kind. We dined with father & found that he was in the same unsettled condition as regards labour for the coming year as ourselves. Two of his people & one of ours have since Christmass signed a contract for '66, but all the rest exhibit the force of inertia in a most striking degree. They admit that they do not know what is to become of them or where they are to go next year & yet they will not agree to work so as to secure their future from want. Mr E told them three months since that in consequence of the abandonment of the Low grounds that the farm could not support them all & offered to designate who he should part with so as to enable them to obtain other homes in time. He has even told them that the last ration has been issued from the Smoke House to those who are to go, but he is still met with the same absolute overwhelming indifference. They will do nothing but sleep & get wood for themselves, & even tho living under his roof, eating his bread, & burning his wood, with but two exceptions they refuse to do the daily necessary plantation labour, the care of the stock—& here ere the year closes I must pause to record the *only* instance of faithfulness which out of so large a number has fallen under my immediate notice. These are our servants Owen & Dolly. Ever since the Surrender, when to use the Negro expression "Free sistence (system) just broke out," they have been unwaveringly true, faithful, cheerful, industrious, & grateful. They both turn with scorn & abhorrence from even the mention of wages. They desire only to live & to be treated for the future as they have hitherto lived & been treated. Not only have they been faithful themselves but they have earnestly endeavoured to make others follow their example. The little comfort we have enjoyed this summer is due to them alone. Fanny would, I now hear, have left long ere she did but for Owen's influence & the little that Vinyard did do was in defference to their representations. Amongst so many opposing causes they deserve especial commendation for their steady adherance to us in spite of opposing causes, temptation, & even threats. They have never swerved from their duty. For some time they have been our only servants (if I except a plantation woman who milks & makes the beds) and more faithful, cheerful, or affectionate ones it would be hard to find.

In direct contrast to them stands Henry, our foreman & for fifteen years Mr E's right hand man. He has enjoyed his master's favour & confidence in no small degree, confided in & confiding, he has been trusted with everything, & up to the Emancipation showed himself worthy of—honest affection, etc., and faithful. His perquisites of office have been large. Exempt from hard work, he was more like a manager than a field hand. His allowances & privileges were—

1st	A house with 4 rooms & 2 fire places
2d	Garden & half acre of ground
3d	A double allowance of cloth—both winter and summer
4h	double allowance of Meat [———] lbs
6	do meal 52 bu
7	Wife & children fed & clothed as the other women & children were
8h	Wife, tho able bodied, allowed to stay in the house & work so as to cook for him
9h	A blanket, a hat, & 2 prs of shoes every year.
10	Occasionally boots extr & Over Coat extra
11h	A boy to haul & cut his wood for him
12h	Unlimited Chickens, Ducks, Bees, etc—(liberty to raise)
13	A horse when he asked it to ride off on Sundays & holidays—
14	From $25 to $50 at Christmass regulated by the amt of the crop.

Such were some of Henry's privileges, & I do not think I have enumerated them all. Some, such as Duck, Chickens, & Bees, he enjoyed in common with the rest of the people; the others are just double what they got & yet in spite of all this, nay whilst in actual enjoyment of them, no sooner did the Yankee poison begin to work in his brain than he became moody, disappointed, & grasping, thought he had a right to land, team, & every thing on the plantation, & what he could he helped himself to with no sparing hand. Actually had the face to say that he ought to have the "House field" & the best mule in the stable & "then he would ask no man any odds." The "House field" is the best & largest field on the plantation. Even whilst enjoying his perquisites as foreman he became negligent and utterly careless of his master's interest, refused "to keep the time" of the people, & has been & is the head & front of all the discontent and grumbling on the plantation. Singularly intelligent for a negro, he professes to be unable to understand his rights or his position, makes the most exhorbitant demands for the one and is dissatisfied with the other. He broke his contract in Nov about his child, my favorite little handmaiden Betsy, by demanding her immediate delivery to him, altho he had agreed to let her remain until Christmass, & when he found that his master would not be so imposed upon & that if he persisted he would be forced to leave himself, he became overwhelmed with contrition & begged in the most abject manner that she & him be allowed to remain and besought his Master that he would let it be as it had between them in years gone by. He claimed her, however, at Christmass when she was of course resigned to him, altho he knew I had a large family & only Owen & Dolly to wait on us, & she has accordingly spent this week in idleness under the paternal roof. Poor simpleton! He has a slight knoledge of tools & the constant measurement of himself by himself, & contrasting his fancied knoledge with the ignorance of his fellows, has turned his head, & as he fancies himself an architect when he is in fact a mere Jack Leg & could not earn his salt at what he calls "*his trade.*"

We have had a houseful of young folks this fall, neices, nephews, & their young friends in constant succession, but now even James, the Major, has deserted us; & reduced to Sister Betsy & Rachel, we feel quite shorn of our fair proportions.

December 31, 1865

Sunday—A miserable unsettled annoying day to us all but especially so to poor Mr E, who has been busy with the negroes, settling accounts & discharging those he does not wish to keep. Amongst the number is Henry, poor fellow, made worthless by emancipation!

Some of our discharged people have provided themselves with homes & have had the most specious promises of fabulous wages & almost unlimited "leave to lie up" made them. We have lost but few, if any, we wished to keep & their places Mr E hopes to supply with other & better ones. Some of them, altho a week of utter & entire idleness has passed over their heads, have no homes & do not seem to care to seek one.

"The Nigger Man" in Halifax, i.e., the agent of the Bureau, is much to blame for this state of things. He gets $1 for every contract signed under his auspicies & of course he has an interest in preventing the negro from settling himself for the year without his aid. In order to facilitate his plans he has postponed making his promised speech from day to day, but now he announces his last appearance, positively his last, on the 1st of Jan. By that day homes for the year ought to be secured & work commenced, but such is the anxiety to hear him utter "new orders" which by rights should have been issued on Christmass that not a negro (& he knows it) will contract until after their announcement. So his harvest will be a rich one. It is unprincipled on the part of Mr Pennyman, but what care he so that his $1 per contract is secured.

The negroes this past summer have been paid in a ratio according to the crop, but Mr E finds it a most annoying and unsatisfactory business and will never employ them in that manner again but pay them a stipulated sum and have settlements at short intervals.

So ends this terrible year of 1865! Thank God it is over! It has brought us untold misery, unhappiness, care, & anxiety, but God has mercifully preserved us through it all & spared us much that others of our unfortunate country men have suffered. Praised be His name for the blessing He has left us & may we be enabled to see His hand in all His future dealings with us! So now to our egg nog and brighter hopes for 1866!

1866

JANUARY 1, 1866

Made a most active beginning of the New Year, for the first tidings which greeted us this morning was that every negro man except Owen on the plantation was up & off before daylight to hear "the Major" i.e., 3d Lieut Pennyman, "Speak," leaving the whole plantation, stock, Horses, Hogs, & Cattle, unfed & uncared for. It has been up hill work to get it done after a fashion since Christmass. Indeed Mr Higgs (the overseer) & Owen have done much of it themselves, but this morning there was no pretence to anything. All were up & off, so Master, Mr Higgs, & Owen had to feed & water about 40 horses & mules, 250 hogs, besides sheep & horned cattle & yet these creatures had an extra ration furnished them, are living at our expense under our roofs. But why should I wonder at negro gratitude? It is but the effect of Yankee teaching. But if ever there was moral courage exhibited on earth it has been done by Owen today. The sole one of his race, despite popular opinion, he has stood to his duty and resisted the temptation & the example of the multitude! "Faithful amongst many."

If the U S Government desire us Confederates ever to "harmonize," as Bill Arp has it, the first step should be to release Mr Davis! True, as a nation we know & admit that his errors of judgment, especially his removal of Gen Johnston, contributed greatly to our defeat, yet still he is our *Head*, & to punish him thus by a cruel & hopeless imprisonment rankles deep in our hearts. If he is guilty, we are doubly so, for we exalted & encouraged him & this imprisonment without even a hope of trial makes us loathe the very name of Yankee justice.

The murder of Wirtz, one of the underlings in command of the prison post at Andersonville,[1] on pretext that he was responsible for the sufferings of the Yankee prisoners there was a base & wicked pandering to the worst passions of the Northern people, besides being a cowardly & abortive attempt to hide from the world that the Yankee Government alone was responsible for the suffering of its own children by its steady & resolute adherence to the selfish policy which led it to refuse an exchange of prisoners, altho often urged by us to the step. The cruelties & enormities practised in their open "Black Holes" upon our men in their hands should wipe out what they allege against us on

---

[1]Henry Wirz, commandant of the notorious Confederate prison at Andersonville, Georgia, was tried, condemned, and executed by order of a military commission on November 10, 1865, for permitting the reprehensible conditions that prevailed in the prison to persist. The military commission, which tried Wirz for murder, abrogated traditional trial procedures and legal guarantees, however, and prosecuted Wirz in an emotional and vindictive manner. The defense for Wirz maintained that the conditions at Andersonville were no worse than those which existed in some of the northern military prisons, and that these circumstances resulted from the war and not from deliberate cruelty. The defense also insisted that Wirz's arrest following his parole, granted at the time of Johnston's surrender, violated the terms of his parole and that the trial was a miscarriage of justice. *Official Records (Army)*, Series II, VIII, 773-781, 784-794; Randall and Donald, *Civil War and Reconstruction*, 643-644.

that score. At any rate a higher victim than poor Wirz should be sought. On their own heads be the Vendetta thus inaugurted by them. "Deo Vindice."

When Mr Johnson gets into "Delirium Tremens" (no extraordinary occurrence if his own people are to be beleived) he cries out that Mrs Surratt[2] haunts him, that she gives him no peace, he cannot stay alone, etc. Mrs Surratt is an innocent victim whom "he did to death" by approving the finding of a corrupt military Commission who condemned her, pledged by their regard for their own popularity to sacrifice some one for the assassination of Mr Lincoln. Would that Wirz would join her and together cry out "doth murder sleep" until he find the Presidential pillow any thing but one of Roses.

January 4, 1866

We went to bed last night congratulating ourselves that at length we had begun to taste some of the immunities of Free negroism. The negro contracts were all signed by them & witnessed & they seemed not only contented but *thankful* for them. Such of the people as Mr E did not wish, or who did not wish themselves to remain, were moving or had moved off goods & chattles & we had a feeling as tho' some of our cares were at an end. At least we had no longer negro children or babies to be responsible to God for; that was shifted to the shoulders of the Yankees and their parents, Yankees first, for taking them from good & competent attention. Nay, Mr E need no longer trouble himself to make a parcel of lazy women support themselves. That care was henceforth their husbands. Their idleness was no charge to him. All seemed merry as a marriage bell, but presto, scarcly was breakfast dispatched when up came every negro man on the plantation, H F Solomon alone excepted, to announce that they were discontented with their contracts, wished higher wages, more privileges & only ten hours work and to say that their bargain must be changed because they had heard that some body somewhere was going to "*do better.*" This Mr E. steadily refused, set forth the folly of signing an agreement one day & drawing back the next for some idle rumour or for some unprincipled emissaries sent forth to tamper with them & by promises & word of mouth bargains which it cost nothing to break, showed them that their arch tempter, one Smallwood, did not give them so much as he did, that he hauled them no wood & would charge them for the pasturage of their hogs, etc., etc., but no.

The Demon of change & discontent was abroad, so with sullen looks & unwilling footsteps they went off discontentedly to begin the year's labour. Two

---

[2]Mary E. Surratt was executed by the United States government for alleged participation in the conspiracy to assassinate Lincoln. Mrs. Surratt, who owned the boardinghouse in Washington, D.C., where Booth and his fellow conspirators planned the assassination, was accused of providing "aid, counsel, abet, comfort, and support" to the conspirators, one of whom was her youngest son, John Surratt. She was found guilty and hanged along with three other of the convicted assassins on July 7, 1865. Subsequent investigation proved that her arrest and execution were a gross miscarriage of justice. *Official Records (Army)*, Series II, VIII, 696-700; *Concise Dictionary of American Biography*, 555; Boatner, *Civil War Dictionary*, 821.

of them, Hatch & little Aaron, went off to Halifax to lay their complaints before the "master man" there, as Hatch calls the Freedman's Bureau agent, this Pennyman. Mr E. sent Mr Higgs (his overseer) off with a copy of the contract & a letter to Lieut Pennyman, in which he reminded him of the pledge he had given that he would compel the negroes to keep their contracts when made & a request that he now return Hatch & Aaron to their homes. So we will now see whether this thorn in our sides acts according to the Law or not.

Terrible weather for ten days back. Incessant rain & mist. Cuffee ought to echo amen to the prayer, "pray ye that your flight be not in the winter." Smallwood, the enticer of our poor negroes from their comfortable homes, has not yet hauled their things from the rivers bank altho he promised to do so some days since. He has no houses for them, expects them to build them themselves & that at this time of the year & the trees yet growing of which they are to be made. He promises unlimited credit at his store and whisky is to flow like water around them. Assures them that he will.

[End of Volume IV, Original Manuscript Journal]

EPILOGUE

by

Mary Moulton Barden

[*Editor's Note*: In 1869 Kate Edmondston's sister Mary Bayard Clarke, with money earned by her writings, purchased one of the oldest homes in New Bern. She named it the Louisiana House because of its double-porch style of architecture. She and her husband, Col. William J. Clarke, lived there until they died in 1886; their daughter Mary inherited the house. Mary and her second husband, George Moulton, lived in the house; and she willed it to her five children to be used as a home so long as one of them survived. The surviving child, Mrs. Celia Moulton Lively, died in December, 1975. Following her death, a large number of Devereux, Clarke, and Moulton letters and pictures were found in the attic of the house, which for over a century had been a depository for family keepsakes and papers.

Mrs. Barden, a niece of Mrs. Lively, used the family papers mentioned above in writing this epilogue. Letters from members of the Devereux, Clarke, and Edmondston families give information on events in the lives of family members after Mrs. Edmondston terminated her journal in 1866. Most of the letters pertaining to Hascosea were written to William (Willie) Edwards Clarke, second son of William and Mary Bayard Clarke, by his aunt Nora Cannon and her oldest daughter Katie.]

Nora Cannon, a sister of Catherine Ann Edmondston, was the only one of the Devereux children to suffer severe personal hardship during the Civil War. She and her husband were both harassed by the Union troops occupying their town of Somerville, Tennessee. Dr. Cannon's horse, wagon, and medical instruments were confiscated, and without them he could not practice medicine. Soon after his death, which occurred about 1867, Nora and her small daughters returned to her family in North Carolina where she paid extended visits to each of her sisters. By 1868 she considered her home to be with Kate and Patrick Edmondston at Hascosea. Mrs. Edmondston, by her own admission not overly fond of children, probably found having her family circle suddenly increased by four lively children to be a real trial. Mary Bayard and William Clarke, her sister and brother-in-law, often took "refuge in the garret" to escape the "pandemonium" of Nora's visits.

Katie Cannon wrote to her cousin Willie from Hascosea in June, 1868, giving glimpses of their life there. There was much work to do, because "there are no servants here except Owen." She and James Edmondston amused themselves playing cards while her Aunt Kate and "Uncle E." went to Philadelphia "to bring his Mother here to live with him." In December of that year she wrote Willie about her sixteenth birthday present from Aunt Kate, "a splendid Topaz breast-pin, the largest Topaz I ever saw."

Mrs. Edmondston's father, Thomas P. Devereux, died on March 7, 1869. Ten months earlier, with debts exceeding $290,000, he had declared bankruptcy and had authorized settlement of his estate with distribution of the proceeds to his creditors. Following his death a lawsuit against the estate was renewed by his nieces Lillie Blake and Georgina Townsend, who were daughters of his brother George. They argued that their share of their grandmother's estate had never been properly settled. Ten years passed before the suit was decided in favor of the estate by the North Carolina Supreme Court, but the United States Supreme Court later overturned this decision. These financial problems together with the deep personal grief resulting from her father's death added to Kate's burdens.

In the fall of 1869, following her grandfather's death, Katie Cannon enrolled at St. Mary's School in Raleigh. She wrote to Willie, "Mama is going to come up to Raleigh the first of Dec. and stay until Feb. She will be here on my birthday which is the 4th of Dec. and I am going to leave School the 3rd for I have always said that I would not go to school after I was seventeen. Mama is going to carry me home as a young lady in Feb. and you cannot imagine how happy I am whenever I think of it." Her dreams of happiness were not fulfilled, however, for Nora wrote the following March that Katie had not had a single visitor and found Hascosea very dull after "the gaieties of Raleigh and Hillsboro." Katie was bored, but her mother stayed busy with housework and nursing the Edmondstons, who fell ill at the same time. Nora wrote to Willie, "Your Uncle and aunt Kate *both* got sick on my hands—here was work to do; housekeeping, nursing, ordering the farm work, and teaching school!!"

Patrick Edmondston maintained his role as a community leader. He was vice-president and member of the Executive Committee of the Scotland Neck Agricultural Society. In that capacity he attended the Agricultural Congress in Augusta, Georgia, in November, 1870, accompanied by his wife. Nora was left in charge of the plantation, encountering many problems during their absence. She again wrote to Willie:

Just after they left a most fearful religious excitement broke out among the poor ignorant negroes. There were two grand rascals who were at the head of it declaring that Christ had entered into their bodies and that they only uttered the words of the Lord and did his work; they refused to work and ordered the other hands to quit the fields and go to the woods and pray and some times the cotton baskets would be left in the row for an hour or two while the negroes were scattered around in the woods praying. At last I lost all patience and ordered the two ring leaders either to go to their work or to leave the plantation and not come on it again till Mr. E. came home, enforcing my command by telling them that my commands must be obeyed whether the Lord's "were or no" and "if they were seen on the place they should have a quick trip to the next world for I should shoot them down as if they were mad dogs."

After this she had less trouble, but she could not sleep at night for fear the gin house, which was full of cotton, would be set on fire. Three other gins in the neighborhood were burned during the Edmondstons' absence. When

Kate and Patrick returned two weeks later, they both became ill. Nora sat up "three whole nights & three more I dozed and slept by the fire" to keep a watch on Kate.

Poor health continued to plague Mrs. Edmondston. In February, 1871, she wrote to Mary Bayard Clarke from Looking Glass, saying she had had a "heavy cold" and had been uncomfortable for days. She went on to say that they had had a grand hunt to wind up the hunting season and she would have a nice dinner in addition to what she could expect from "hunter's luck." Though she had only a substitute cook, she was managing both at Looking Glass and Hascosea. It developed that the hunt could not be held because the "Roanoke River put an embargo by stopping the 'King's highway' or Looking Glass Creek," and the dinner had to be saved for a later time.

Nora looked forward with much pleasure to her frequent visits in New Bern. In March, 1871, she wrote Willie about a concert given there to raise money for the rebuilding of Christ Episcopal Church which had recently burned. "Oh it was a treat to me for I do love music and I hear so little—that is one of my *little trials*. . . . The three things I miss most in that country home are *Church, Doctor,* and *Music.*"

In the heat of July she described to Willie the uneventful routine at Hascosea where dinner was the "event of the day." She added, "This monotonous existence has been somewhat varied lately by the advent of your Aunt Betsey and Rachel but they as you know are so quiet that their presence caused only a slight ripple and they have fallen into our quiet life as naturally as if they had always formed a part of the family circle at Hascosea."

Life continued in this pattern until August 19, 1871, when Patrick died unexpectedly. Kate was devastated by her sudden grief and in a letter to her nephew, wrote:

Hascosea Sept. 10, 1871

My dear Willie—

Greif is a great leveller—so do not think that anything you can say to me is unbefitting in point of age—I am so weak in mind—almost as powerless as a little child! I am utterly uncapable of any extended process of thought for every power & energy of my intellectual being seems numbed. So do not hesitate to write me freely & to direct me as you did O how tenderly! & kindly in your letter to the Source where alone is to be found comfort. You young people have a great deal in your power that you can do for me. . . . You can preserve in me a remnant at least of my youth.

You can prevent the crust of age & isolation thickening around & over me until I become self absorbed—self contained—hateful to myself & to all with whom I come in contact. I have hitherto been absorbed in one object only—*your Uncle*—if he was pleased—if he was satisfied—I was content—& my absorption was so complete that other objects were shut out from my vision.

It requires one to be a widow & childless—who has hitherto enjoyed the elasticity of youth—& who has leaned on one person alone—to feel the utter desolation which

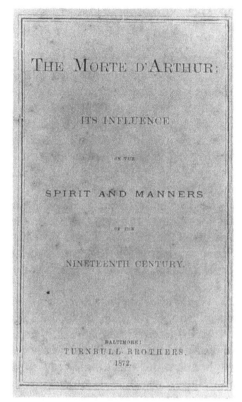

Mrs. Edmondston published *The Morte d'Arthur* anonymously in 1872. Much of its contents was taken from her journal. (Booklet was photographed from copy owned by Mrs. Graham A. Barden, Jr., of New Bern.)

seizes on her when that object is suddenly taken from her & with it the brightness of life—the visions of youth depart. I feel as tho age has sprung like an armed man on me during the last three weeks. It is for you young people to keep alive a memory at least of youth & happiness. I feel as one who has hitherto been a keen enjoyer of nature sights—were he suddenly afflicted with color blindness. The things are there—the earth—the sky—the clouds—the flowers. But where is their brightness? But I should not dim you with a realization of my sorrow—God avert such greif from your forehead.

Write me often and beleive me ever your affectionate

Aunt Kate

Following the death of Patrick, Mrs. Edmondston's health deteriorated steadily. Again writing to Willie, on July 30, 1872, she referred to having been sick for a week and then being unable to write for days because "letters of business & affection flew up at me every time I went to my desk and imperatively commanded my attention. . . ." She also referred to the death of

Patrick's mother, whom she called Mama, which necessitated additional letters, and to still another illness. She added that "My habits of life and
thoughts are all shattered and I do very little as I formerly did it. . . ."

In the same letter, however, Mrs. Edmondston sounded like her old self
when she advised Willie on his future career, referring to his "treading the formal walks of Law—a walk in which routine and study run almost an even
race with genius and intellect. I am glad of it for I should think you would
make a good lawyer—take care however—lest in your admiration of your
Lecturers who make 'everything so plain' that you do not lose the habit of
thinking for yourself & of your own self making your deductions & mastering
your conclusions!"

In the spring of 1872 Kate achieved an old ambition of seeing her words in
print when she had a small forty-page pamphlet entitled *The Morte d'Arthur;
Its Influence on the Spirit and Manners of the Nineteenth Century* printed by Turnbull
Brothers of Baltimore. It was published anonymously, but upon receiving a
copy her sister Mary Bayard Clarke immediately guessed the identity of the
author. The publication bitterly denounced the "barbaric conduct" of the
Union army and generals during the Civil War and compared it to the
"Chivalry and Good Manners" of the Southern army. Mrs. Edmondston
dedicated the book to her aunt, Frances Devereux Polk, as follows:

Dedication.

TO MRS. POLK,

WIDOW OF THE RIGHT REV. LEONIDAS POLK,

WHO, WHETHER AS A SOLDIER OF THE CROSS WHEN BISHOP OF LOUISIANA, OR
AS A SOLDIER OF THE SOUTHERN CONFEDERACY WHEN LIEUT. GEN. POLK,
C. S. A., EXEMPLIFIED IN HIS LIFE AND CHARACTER THE SPIRIT
OF ANCIENT CHIVALRY AS HANDED DOWN TO US IN THE
MORTE D'ARTHUR, THIS TREATISE ON MODERN CHIV-
ALRY IS AFFECTIONATELY DEDICATED BY ONE
WHO HAS KNOWN AND REVERED HER
FROM YOUTH, IN ADMIRATION OF
HER MANY VIRTUES.

Much of the content was taken from her journal. In the booklet Mrs. Edmondston denounced the Freedmen's Bureau as "that worst engine of
tyranny which far-sighted malice ever imposed on a conquered people. . . ."
Throughout its pages she spoke of the harsh treatment of women and children
by Union generals such as Butler and Sherman; in contrast, General Lee was
extolled as a "Christian Gentleman." Mrs. Edmondston quoted Lee's

General Orders to his troops when they invaded Pennsylvania, exhorting them "to abstain with most scrupulous care from unnecessary or wanton injury to private property. . . ." Kate's pamphlet clearly revealed that she had not forgiven any grievance against the North.

On January 3, 1875, Catherine Ann Devereux Edmondston died, probably of consumption, at the Raleigh home of her sister, Frances Miller. She was fifty-one years old, the first of her generation of Devereuxs to die. Kate was buried beside Patrick in the yard of Trinity Episcopal Church in Scotland Neck.

Mrs. Edmondston's sister Frances had turned her home into a boarding house after her husband's death and continued to support herself in this manner after the war, drawing on an elite clientele. As the oldest of the sisters, Frances became a "mother figure" for the others in the family. She was outraged when the "free thinking" Mary Bayard refused to conform to her dictates. This attitude, plus the Republican sentiments held by Mary Bayard's husband, caused bitterness in the family which never completely dissipated. Frances was sixty-five years old when she died of paralysis in 1881. She had two sons, George and Henry; her daughter Kate, one of Mrs. Edmondston's favorite nieces, married Capt. George Baker and lived in Fayetteville after the war. He died in 1872 and four years later she married T. M. Argo. She died in Raleigh in 1886.

Elizabeth Jones, often referred to as Sister Betsey, went with her children Rachel and Frank to Baltimore to make her home. Her oldest daughter Bettie and her husband, whom Mrs. Jones considered "a good Southerner at heart,"

The Edmondstons were buried in the cemetery at Trinity Episcopal Church in Scotland Neck. Patrick's middle name is misspelled as is Catherine's first name. She was often called Kate, a fact which may have led to the spelling of the name with a "K." (Photographs from files of Beth Crabtree.)

continued to live in Owego, New York, because they did not want to leave the graves of their three children who had died of scarlet fever in 1870. Elizabeth, barely subsisting, wrote Mary Bayard in January, 1879, "I am dependent on my daughter's daily labor for my food and lodging. I don't say *clothing* for we neither of us buy any—simply *cannot*." She died unexpectedly of pneumonia a few months later. Rachel, who never married, continued to live and teach in Baltimore until her death. Pattie Skinner Jones, the young widow of Sister Betsey's son Thomas, returned to her family in Perquimans County. She never remarried and died in 1885 at the age of forty-three.

Mattie Dunlop of Petersburg, Mrs. Thomas P. Devereux's homesick niece who spent the last months of the war as a refugee with the Edmondstons, apparently committed suicide. Mary Clarke wrote her brother Willie on March 30, 1873, saying that Mattie had died but nobody would say how. "From all I can learn she took something that killed her but whether on purpose or not we can't find out." She was about nineteen years old at the time.

Mrs. Edmondston's sister Sophia Turner was plunged into the political turmoil of the times. Her husband Josiah so enraged the Republican administration of Gov. William W. Holden with his mocking editorials in the Raleigh *Sentinel*, that Holden had Turner arrested and briefly imprisoned during the Kirk-Holden War of 1870. He continued to fight the Radicals through his newspaper until 1872 when the presses of the *Sentinel* were destroyed by his enemies.

Sophia developed an addiction to morphine which by 1871 caused Josiah to tell her, in a letter, of the "deep felt mortification which weighs upon me morning, noon, and night." In 1877 Turner wrote Sophia's brother, John Devereux, that his house had been made a place of "torture and torment" and that he "must find some place for Sophia other than my house." Consequently, Sophia was committed to an insane asylum in Raleigh for treatment, leaving her four boys and young daughter Margaret without adequate care. Sister Betsey wrote Mary Bayard in January, 1879, that the doctor had allowed Sophia to go home for a month's visit to make better arrangements for her daughter's care. "Mr. T.'s conduct is simply *atrocious*—to have left that poor little girl all these months alone with not even a faithful servant woman to attend to her! This at least is what has been told me; she has been there with only those boys, even *he* being away a great deal of the time. . . . I don't see how Sophia poor child has stood it so long. . . . What a dreadful fate hers has been." She felt however, that Sophia was much better off in the hospital than at home where she had to work so hard.

Sophia Turner left behind a small booklet of poems that she wrote while a patient in the asylum. They are autobiographical and reveal her intense loneliness and fears. The first one, entitled "Insanity," dated March, 1878, begins:

Oh say! is there grief any greater
    Than to feel that your mind's giving way,
Or can there be Cross any heavier
    Than for Reason to yield up her Sway?

To feel that your thoughts are all floating
    Away from your grasp one-by-one
Never stopping a Prayer to mutter
    Not *even* "Thy will be done."

To feel that your friends are all thinking
    T'were better for you to have died
Before this dark cloud came upon you
    And *Reason* resigned *Her Pride.*

Another poem dated September 27, 1878, gives her first impression of the asylum when she thought she had "got to a Hell upon Earth," but it later tells of the kindness and help she received from the people there. Josiah Turner evidently abandoned his wife after her commitment for many of the poems tell of her longings to see his face or to receive "a word, a glance, a smile." She also wrote of her fears of death and the comfort she received from her religion. Sophia Chester Devereux Turner died September 25, 1880, and was buried in the Turner family plot at St. Matthew's Episcopal Church in Hillsborough.

In the meantime, Mary Bayard Clarke had continued writing and in 1870 published a long narrative poem in book form. Patrick wrote to her on December 27 to say that he had finished reading *Clytie & Zenobia*, and he congratulated her "on the happy & charming rendering of the classic legend. You have succeeded in making a pretty & graceful Poem of smooth and polished verse. . . ."

Neither he nor .Mary Bayard was able to attend the January 11, 1871, wedding of Nora Cannon's daughter Katie to John Primrose of Raleigh, held at Sophia Turner's Hillsborough home. Patrick explained that he would be unable to attend because his "business is in a tangle from my trip to Georgia & So Car⁰ & from the dilatory character of some work upon my cotton gin." Mary Bayard did not attend because of ill feelings in the family engendered when her husband joined the Republican party in 1868. His acceptance of a commission as colonel in the North Carolina State Troops resulted in a feud with her sisters Sophia Turner and Frances Miller and with her brother John Devereux. Sophia's husband Josiah Turner, through editorials in the *Sentinel*, launched vicious personal attacks on Clarke and other Republicans. The differences in political views also strained relations between Kate Edmondston and the Clarkes.

Mary Bayard and William Clarke moved to New Bern when William became headmaster of the New Bern Academy in 1869. In 1870 he was appointed Republican judge of the Third District Superior Court of North Carolina, in which capacity he served until 1874. Their son Willie graduated from Columbia Law School and joined his father in practicing law. In December, 1879, William J. Clarke began editing a Republican newspaper, the *Signal*, in Raleigh; this, however, was a financial failure in spite of help from Mary Bayard and Willie.

By early 1871 the strained relationship between Kate and Mary Bayard had somewhat abated, as was shown by their correspondence. The oldest son of the Clarkes, Francis Devereux, sent "marriage cards" to Mrs. Edmondston in October, 1873. She expressed pleasure in receiving the cards and extended good wishes for his future, inviting him to bring his wife to visit, though "Hascosea is very dull I know but you will bring your own sunshine with you so you will not mind that."

Francis (Frank) Devereux Clarke taught at the Deaf and Dumb Institute of New York and was later superintendent of the Michigan School for the Deaf in Flint. His innovative methods of teaching the deaf received national acclaim. The Clarke's youngest son, Thomas Pollock Devereux Clarke, joined Frank in working with the deaf and became head of the Washington State School for the Deaf in Vancouver. Willie continued to practice law in New Bern and was a leader in the Republican party; he served in the state House of Representatives, 1876-1880, and in the state Senate, 1881-1883. In 1889 he became postmaster of New Bern. Willie Clarke, two of his small children, and a neighbor's child drowned in 1901 when their small boat sank on the Neuse River a short distance from his home.

Nora Cannon had visited the Clarkes in New Bern in 1885, and the next January, following the death of William J. Clarke, had written Mary Bayard from Tennessee that "as Death lessens the number of our family, those who are left behind should cling closer together. You and I and Susy are the only sisters left now of the family—and tho separated by distance let us be near in love & keep each other posted as to our affairs."

On November 23, 1873, Mrs. Edmondston wrote to Mary Bayard to explain why she had not been able to attend the wedding of the Clarkes' daughter Mary to Rufus Morgan of Franklin. She had had pleurisy and was still far from well, but she longed for news of the wedding, adding, "It will seem like a play from the outer world to me shut up in this dull sounding house." In 1880 Mary Clarke Morgan was widowed when her husband died suddenly from eating poisoned mushrooms. He had gone to California hoping to make a fortune raising bees and selling honey and had planned to send for his family in a few weeks. His widow, left with no means of support for herself and two small children, learned taxidermy and, with the help of her brothers Willie and Tom, established a small business.

Mary Bayard continued to write poems, plays, hymns, short stories, newspaper articles, and book reviews and to correspond with other writers of the
day. Often the income she received was the sole support of the family as her
husband and son had great difficulty in collecting their legal fees. With her
health failing and no money to hire a servant, Mary Bayard was physically
unable to cope with household cares, however. In November, 1883, she was
partially paralyzed but was able to continue her literary work on a limited
basis. William J. Clarke died on January 23, 1886, and on March 10 she suffered a severe stroke. Three days later her daughter Mary was married at her
bedside to George Moulton of Hampton Falls, New Hampshire. Mary Bayard
Clarke died March 30, 1886, and was buried in the family plot in the Cedar
Grove Cemetery in New Bern.

In 1872 Nora Cannon was teaching at St. Mary's School in Raleigh where
she and her daughters, Nonie, Sadie, and Mattie, shared her third-floor room
in the main building. She was delighted to be near her new granddaughter,
Eliza, born to Katie and John Primrose November 19, 1871. Nora was proud
of the fact that she supported herself and her children without assistance from
any of her relatives except for a small gift from William J. Clarke. In a letter to
Willie she also referred to $50.00 granted each of the girls, which was paid to
the president of the school by a society in Baltimore. She wrote, "You should

The Pollock-Devereux plot in Raleigh's City Cemetery contains the graves of several members of the
family including George Pollock and John and Frances Devereux.

have heard the tone of voice in which I told sister Kate of the fact that except for the $20.00 given me by your Father I had made all we lived on & when she asked 'how' it was as good as a play. 'By my sewing machine. I often sewed til 12 o'clock at night.'"

Nora continued teaching until she returned with her girls to Tennessee about 1875. There, in 1881, she was elected superintendent of the schools in Fayette County and served for two years. The first woman elected to public office in Tennessee, she proved a capable administrator and was reelected to the post in 1886; she served until her death in August, 1888.

Nora's daughter Katie and her husband John Primrose had two daughters and continued to live in Raleigh. A letter to the Clarkes, dated April 7, 1874, told of his "melancholy death." He was bankrupt and died of "Mania a potu," or delirium tremens. His widow later married Frederick R. Olds, a newspaperman of Raleigh who was well known for his collection of documents and artifacts which formed the nucleus of the present-day North Carolina Museum of History.

Another daughter, Sarah Beaumont (Sadie) Cannon married Walker Kennedy. They were coeditors of the *Memphis Commercial Appeal*, one of the South's largest newspapers. Sadie wrote four novels, a children's book, and a book of poems.

Kate Edmondston's brother John Devereux was unable to free his father's estate from debt as Thomas P. Devereux's will had directed. Economic conditions worsened, the plantations were lost, and he entered a small insurance business in Raleigh. He and his family continued to live at Wills Forest. In 1893 he died following a long illness, and there was insufficient money to pay his debts. Wills Forest was sold and Margaret made her home with one of her daughters until she died in 1910 at the age of eighty-six.

The Devereuxs had eight children. According to family sources, their two sons were "no comfort to them." Thomas Pollock Devereux, Jr., a lawyer, "disgraced the family by becoming a Republican." He often entertained his numerous nieces and nephews, who did not share the feelings of the older generation, with stories of plantation days. He died in 1912, having never married. The younger son, John, a brilliant man, "broke his father's heart with his dissipations," married a woman his family considered beneath him, and severed his family ties. Only his sister Margaret Mordecai (Meta) Devereux heard from him after he moved to Oklahoma and became a federal judge. In 1921 John was found dead under suspicious circumstances; though murder was suspected, it was never proved. The oldest daughter, Annie Lane, never married and made her home with her mother in Raleigh. Katherine Johnson Devereux married Joseph J. Mackay and lived for many years in Asheville, Durham, and Raleigh. Ellen (Nell) Devereux married Col. John W. Hinsdale of Fayetteville and lived in Raleigh where many of their descendants live today. Meta and her husband, Samuel T. Ashe, made their home in Wilmington. Laura, who did not marry, was killed in a fall in the mountains in 1904. Mary Livingston Devereux, the youngest daughter, married Arthur Winslow and lived in Boston.

Susan Harrison Devereux, called Sue in the journal, was the youngest of the sisters and the only child of Thomas P. Devereux and his second wife, Ann Mary Maitland. She lived with her mother's relatives in Petersburg where she probably taught school. In her later years she lived at the Louise Home in Washington, D.C., which was established by W. W. Corcoran as a home for "gentlewomen of the South." She was extremely deaf and used an ear phone which consisted of two horns connected by a long tube. A visitor would yell into one horn while Aunt Sue placed the other over her ear. She entered into conversations spiritedly though her remarks were often inappropriate.

Aunt Sue never wavered in her loyalty to the Confederacy. During World War I she was visited by a young relative who was an Annapolis midshipman. She turned to him and said, "I see you are wearing the uniform of a traitor to your country! There is a lot of waving of the flag now-a-days, but there is always only *one Flag* for me!" With that she threw open the door to her room and pointed to a Confederate flag which stretched from floor to ceiling. She died in 1931 at the age of ninety-two. She was the last to be buried in the family plot in Raleigh's City Cemetery.

MILITARY LEADERS

ANDERSON, JOSEPH REID (1813-1892) was born near Fincastle, Virginia; he graduated from West Point in 1836 and resigned from the army the following year. In 1843 he leased the Tredegar Iron Company in Richmond and became its owner in 1848. The company became a leading producer of locomotives, munitions, and naval machinery, and Anderson, a secessionist, supplied cannon and ammunition to the southern states. He entered the Confederate army and was commissioned a brigadier general in 1861. From 1861 to 1863 the Tredegar Works was the sole Confederate source of heavy guns; it was also the laboratory for Confederate ordnance experiments as well as producer of ironclad plates, railroad rolling stock, and furnace machinery. *Concise Dictionary of American Biography*, 22.

ANDERSON, RICHARD HERON (1821-1879) was born in Statesburg, South Carolina; he graduated from West Point in 1842 and served in the Mexican War. Commissioned a brigadier general in the Confederate army in 1861, he rose to major general in 1862. His service record included the second battle of Bull Run, Antietam (where he was wounded), Chancellorsville, Gettysburg, the Wilderness, and Spotsylvania. *Concise Dictionary of American Biography*, 22.

ANDERSON, ROBERT (1805-1871) was born near Louisville, Kentucky. Graduating from West Point in 1825, he taught artillery tactics at the military academy and fought in the Seminole War before being severely wounded in the Mexican War. He was in command of the defenses at Charleston, South Carolina, in 1860 and sustained the opening salvo of the Civil War at Fort Sumter in 1861. Promoted to brigadier general the same year, he commanded the Departments of Kentucky and Cumberland before retiring because of disabilities in 1863. Brevetted major general in 1865, he was present for the reraising of the United States flag at Fort Sumter, April 14, 1865. Boatner, *Civil War Dictionary*, 15.

ANDREWS, ALEXANDER BOYD (1841-1915) was born near Franklinton, North Carolina. After graduating from Henderson Male Academy, he went to work for his uncle, P. B. Hawkins, who had a contract to build part of the Old Blue Ridge Railroad. When the war broke out, Andrews joined the First North Carolina Cavalry and served under Jeb Stuart. He was severely wounded at Jack's Shop in Virginia in 1863 and was never able to resume active service. After the war he returned to the railroading business and became one of the leading economic figures in the New South and first vice-president of the Southern Railway in 1895. *Concise Dictionary of American Biography*, 23; Ashe, *Biographical History*, I, 45-59.

ARMISTEAD, LEWIS ADDISON (1817-1863) was born in New Bern, North Carolina. He attended West Point and won two brevets in the Mexican War. Rising to the rank of brigadier general in the Confederate army, he led the Fifty-seventh Virginia Brigade from the Peninsular campaign to Gettysburg, where he died on July 3, 1863, in Pickett's charge. *Concise Dictionary of American Biography*, 27; Boatner, *Civil War Dictionary*, 26.

ASHBY, TURNER (1828-1862) was a planter, grain dealer, and local politician of wealth and influence in the Shenandoah Valley when he led a voluntary cavalry company to Harpers Ferry in response to John Brown's raid in 1859. A cavalry officer under Stuart and Jackson, he rose to the rank of brigadier general and served at the first battle of Bull Run and as commander of the Seventh Virginia Cavalry during the Shenandoah Valley campaign. He was killed June 6, 1862, in a rearguard action near Harrisonburg, Virginia. Boatner, *Civil War Dictionary*, 28.

AVERELL, WILLIAM WOODS (1832-1900) was a native New Yorker who graduated from West Point in 1855. After service in the Indian wars, where he was wounded, he commanded the Third Pennsylvania Cavalry and the brigade protecting Washington's defenses, 1861-1862. Twice relieved of command during the war, first by Hooker and then by Sheridan, he still attained the rank of major general (USV) before resigning in May, 1865. In 1866 he was named United States consul general of Canada, a post he held for three years. Boatner, *Civil War Dictionary*, 35.

AVERY, CLARK MOULTON (ca. 1820-1864), of Burke County, North Carolina, enlisted in the First North Carolina in 1861. He later served in the Thirty-third North Carolina before being killed at Spotsylvania in May, 1864. Manarin and Jordan, *North Carolina Troops*, III, 36; Clark, *Histories of the North Carolina Regiments*, IV, 191.

BAKER, EDWARD DICKINSON (1811-1861) was born in England. Serving in the Illinois legislature and Congress, he resigned in 1846 to assume command of a brigade in the Mexican War. A close friend of Lincoln, he moved to the west coast where he was elected United States senator from Oregon. He twice declined commissions as a general in the Union army and chose instead to accept a commission as colonel of the Seventy-first Pennsylvania (dubbed the "First California" in his honor). He was killed at the battle of Balls Bluff on October 21, 1861. Boatner, *Civil War Dictionary*, 39.

BAKER, LAURENCE SIMMONS (1830-1907) was born in North Carolina and graduated from West Point in 1851. After frontier duty in Indian scouting and fighting, he was appointed lieutenant colonel of the First North Carolina Cavalry in 1861, though he personally opposed secession. He fought under Lee from the Peninsula to Appomattox and rose to the rank of brigadier general. He saw action at Antietam, Fredericksburg, and Gettysburg and was given territorial command of North Carolina with his headquarters at Goldsboro in 1864. Wounded twice during the war, he led a brigade of reserves to meet Sherman in South Carolina before an old wound forced him to step aside. Commanding a brigade at Bentonville, he tried to join Johnston in 1865 but was cut off by Union troops. He was paroled at Raleigh, May 8, 1865. Boatner, *Civil War Dictionary*, 40.

BANKS, NATHANIEL PRENTISS (1816-1894), of Massachusetts, was commissioned major general (USV) in May, 1861. A former congressman and governor of Massachusetts (1858-1861), he headed the Departments of Annapolis and the Shenandoah. Defeated by Jackson at Cedar Mountain, he assumed command of the

Department of the Gulf and led the Red River campaign of 1863. His taking of Port Hudson, the last obstruction to the free navigation of the Mississippi, won him the "thanks of Congress." He was mustered out in August, 1865. Boatner, *Civil War Dictionary*, 42.

BARKSDALE, WILLIAM (1821-1863) was born in Tennessee, attended the University of Nashville, studied law, and ran a proslavery newspaper during the Mexican War. He resigned his congressional seat from Mississippi when the state seceded and later entered the Confederate army as colonel of the Thirteenth Mississippi. He led his regiment during the first battle of Bull Run and the Peninsular campaign. Appointed brigadier general in August, 1862, he saw action at Antietam, Fredericksburg, Chancellorsville, and Gettysburg, dying of wounds on July 3, 1863, after his capture in the Peach Orchard. Boatner, *Civil War Dictionary*, 43-44.

BARRON, SAMUEL (1809-1888) was born in Hampton, Virginia. After a distinguished career in the United States Navy, he resigned to join the Confederate navy in 1861. He commanded Fort Hatteras and was imprisoned after its capture. Upon his release he commanded naval forces in Virginia, 1862-1863, and went to England to secure delivery of two ironclad rams. He served as commander of Confederate naval forces in Europe and supervised the raiders *Stonewall* and *Georgia*, 1863-1865. *Who Was Who in America*, 111.

BARTLETT, WILLIAM FRANCIS (1840-1876), of Massachusetts, was a student at Harvard who enlisted as a private in the Fourth Battalion of Massachusetts Volunteers at the beginning of the war. Commissioned captain of the Twentieth Massachusetts, he lost a leg at Yorktown, was mustered out, but then organized the Forty-ninth Massachusetts and was elected colonel in November, 1862. Twice wounded at Port Hudson, he organized the Fifty-seventh Massachusetts, a Negro unit, in 1864 and was wounded while leading it in the battle of the Wilderness. He was wounded and captured at Petersburg before being mustered out in 1866 as major general (USV). Boatner, *Civil War Dictionary*, 48.

BARTON, SETH MAXWELL (1829-1900), of Virginia, graduated from West Point in 1849 and saw garrison and frontier duty before joining the Confederate army in 1861. Appointed brigadier general in 1862, he led a brigade under Kirby Smith until December, 1862, when he went to Vicksburg. Captured and paroled after the siege of Vicksburg, he took his brigade to New Bern in January, 1864, fought at the Wilderness, and defended Richmond. He was captured at Sayler's Creek and released from Fort Warren, July, 1865. Boatner, *Civil War Dictionary*, 48-49.

BAXTER, HENRY (1821-1873), of New York, was commissioned captain of the Seventh Michigan in 1861 and led the assault crossing at Fredericksburg, where he was wounded in the lung. Promoted to brigadier general (USV) in 1863, he suffered two other wounds during the war and was brevetted major general (USV) in 1865. After the war he was minister to Honduras, 1866-1869. Boatner, *Civil War Dictionary*, 51.

BAYARD, GEORGE DASHIELL (1835-1862), of New York, graduated from West Point in 1856 and fought in the Indian wars. He was cavalry instructor at West Point when given a leave of absence to command the First Pennsylvania Cavalry in 1861. Named brigadier general (USV), he fought against Jackson and led the advance to Cedar Mountain before being mortally wounded at Fredericksburg. Boatner, *Civil War Dictionary*, 52.

BEALL, JOHN YATES (1835-1865), of Virginia, attended the University of Virginia and studied law. Joining the Confederate navy in 1862, he sabotaged Union ships in the Chesapeake Bay area and captured several Federal vessels including the *Alliance*. In 1864, from a base in Canada, he attempted to capture a Union warship on Lake Erie, but the plan failed because of a mutiny. Arrested for attempting to derail trains in New York, he was convicted of espionage and executed despite pleas for clemency from the governor of Massachusetts and Radical Republican Thaddeus Stevens. *Who Was Who in America*, 115.

BEAUREGARD, PIERRE GUSTAVE TOUTANT (1818-1893), of Louisiana, graduated from West Point in 1838, served as engineer on Winfield Scott's staff in the Mexican War, and briefly served as superintendent of West Point, 1861, before his native state seceded. He commanded Confederate forces at Charleston during the attack on Fort Sumter. At first Bull Run he commanded the line while J. E. Johnston brought reinforcements forward. Promoted to general in the Confederate army, he was second-in-command to A. S. Johnston at Shiloh. Later he headed the defenses of the Carolina and Georgia coasts, defeated Butler at Drewry's Bluff, repelled the Petersburg assaults, and returned as second-in-command to J. E. Johnston in the Carolinas campaign. After the war he supervised the drawings for the Louisiana lottery and published several works on military subjects. Boatner, *Civil War Dictionary*, 54-55.

BENNING, HENRY LEWIS (1814-1875), nicknamed "Rock," was a native Georgian who graduated from the University of Georgia. He practiced law and served as a justice of the Georgia Supreme Court (1853-1859) where he ruled that the state supreme court was not bound by the United States Supreme Court on constitutional questions. Commissioned colonel of the Seventeenth Georgia in 1861, he fought at Malvern Hill and the second battle of Bull Run. Promoted to brigadier general in 1863, he fought at Gettysburg, Knoxville, Chickamauga, and the Wilderness, where he was severely wounded. Fort Benning is named for him. Boatner, *Civil War Dictionary*, 59-60; *Concise Dictionary of American Biography*, 68.

BERRY, HIRAM GREGORY (1824-1863), of Maine, began the war as colonel of the Fourth Maine but rose to the rank of major general (USV) in November, 1862. A former state legislator and mayor of Rockland, he fought at the first Bull Run and in a number of other Virginia battles. He was killed leading a bayonet attack at Chancellorsville. Boatner, *Civil War Dictionary*, 61-62.

BIRNEY, DAVID BELL (1825-1864), of Alabama, was commissioned colonel of the Twenty-third Pennsylvania in 1861 and rose to brigadier general (USV) the next year. The son of abolitionist James G. Birney, he was educated at Andover and studied law at Cincinnati before practicing in Philadelphia. He took part in the Peninsular campaign, second Bull Run, and Gettysburg and attained the rank of major general (USV). He died of malaria in October, 1864. Boatner, *Civil War Dictionary*, 64-65.

BLUNT, JAMES GILPATRICK (1826-1881), of Maine, graduated from an Ohio medical school and practiced medicine there before becoming engaged in Kansas politics. With John Brown he helped escaped slaves reach Canada. Named lieutenant colonel of the Third Kansas in 1861, he was promoted to brigadier general (USV) in 1862 and took command of the Department of Kansas. He saw action in the western theater, was promoted to major general (USV), and successfully opposed Price's raid in Missouri in 1864. He was mustered out in July, 1865. Boatner, *Civil War Dictionary*, 71.

BOOTH, LIONEL F. was the Union major in command of Fort Pillow, Tennessee, with 262 black troops and 295 white troops in his charge. Confederate forces under Brig. Gen. James R. Chalmers attacked the fort on April 12, 1864, and Nathan B. Forrest arrived a short time later. Forrest demanded the fort's surrender from Maj. William F. Bradford since Booth had been killed by a sniper. What happened after Bradford's refusal is still a matter of dispute. The North claimed that a massacre followed, whereas the South maintained that the Federals refused to surrender in the face of certain annihilation. Federal losses included approximately 231 killed, 100 seriously wounded, 168 whites and 58 Negroes captured. Alleged atrocities included murdering most of the garrison after it had surrendered; burying black soldiers alive; and setting fire to tents filled with wounded Federals. Boatner, *Civil War Dictionary*, 295-296.

BRAGG, BRAXTON (1817-1876) was born in Warrenton, North Carolina, and graduated from West Point in 1837. He served with distinction in the Mexican War but resigned from the army in 1856 to operate his Louisiana plantation, during which time he designed a drainage and levee system for the state. Appointed brigadier general in the Confederate army in 1861, he commanded the coast between Pensacola and Mobile and was soon promoted to major general. He saw action at Shiloh in 1862 and soon thereafter became full general, relieving Beauregard as commander of the Army of Tennessee. His withdrawals at Perryville and Stones River brought him considerable criticism, but his victory at Chickamauga in 1863 temporarily stilled dissatisfaction. He attacked the Federals at Chattanooga but soon retreated into Georgia. In 1864 he served in Richmond, nominally as commander in chief. Boatner, *Civil War Dictionary*, 78-79; *Concise Dictionary of American Biography*, 102.

BRANCH, LAWRENCE O'BRYAN (1820-1862) sprang from a prominent and wealthy North Carolina family; he was reared by his uncle, Gov. John Branch. He attended the University of North Carolina at Chapel Hill and graduated from Princeton. A moderate Democratic congressman, he resigned his seat at the outbreak of the war and was commissioned brigadier general in the Confederate army in 1861. After commanding the forces around New Bern, he joined Jackson to fight at second Bull Run, Fairfax Courthouse, and Antietam, where he was killed. Boatner, *Civil War Dictionary*, 80.

BRECKINRIDGE, JOHN CABELL (1821-1875), of Kentucky, graduated from Centre College and fought in the Mexican War. A prominent Democrat before the Civil War, he was elected to Congress in 1851 and again in 1853 before being elected vice-president under Buchanan in 1856. He was the southern fire-eaters' candidate for president in 1860 and won seventy-two electoral votes. Forced to flee Kentucky in 1861, he was appointed brigadier general in the Confederate army and served under A. S. Johnston. Though inexperienced, he served ably at Shiloh, Vicksburg, Port Hudson, and Murfreesboro and rose to the rank of major general. Davis named him secretary of war in February, 1865, and he fled south with the rest of the Confederate cabinet after Appomattox. He was J. E. Johnston's adviser during surrender negotiations. Boatner, *Civil War Dictionary*, 82-83; *Concise Dictionary of American Biography*, 104-105.

BRIDGERS, JOHN LUTHER, of Edgecombe County, North Carolina, enlisted in the First North Carolina in 1861 at the age of forty-one. Originally commissioned captain, he was appointed lieutenant colonel of the North Carolina Artillery in August, 1861. After seeing action at Bethel, he briefly commanded Fort Macon before being relieved at his own request and retiring. Manarin and Jordan, *North Carolina Troops*, III, 4; Clark, *Histories of the North Carolina Regiments*, I, 77, 90, 500, 515.

BROWN, HARVEY (1796-1874), of New Jersey, graduated from West Point in 1818 and fought in the Seminole and Mexican wars. He commanded Fort Pickens, Florida, 1861-1862, and was brevetted brigadier general in the regular service. He then took command of the defenses of New York harbor and the city itself. While stationed there he helped quell the draft riots of July, 1863. He retired from active service the following month. Boatner, *Civil War Dictionary*, 90.

BROWN, JOHN CALVIN (1827-1889), of Tennessee, a lawyer, returned from Europe at the outbreak of the war to enlist as a private. Quickly commissioned colonel of the Third Tennessee, he was captured at Fort Donelson. He was appointed brigadier general in the Confederate army soon after his release and fought in Kentucky and Tennessee and then Georgia. He rose to the rank of major general. After the war he was a legislator and Democratic governor of Tennessee, 1870-1874. Boatner, *Civil War Dictionary*, 91.

BUCHANAN, FRANKLIN (1800-1874) was born in Baltimore, Maryland. He joined the navy in 1815 and became Bancroft's chief adviser in the planning of the Naval Academy at Annapolis, of which Buchanan was the first superintendent (1845-1847). After service in the Mexican War he commanded the flagship in Perry's expedition to China and Japan (1852-1855). He commanded the Washington Navy Yard, 1859-1861, but resigned to join the Confederate navy in 1861. He commanded the *Merrimac* on its initial appearance in Hampton Roads, 1862, and he opposed

Farragut at Mobile Bay. He was taken prisoner of war in 1864 and released in 1865. Boatner, *Civil War Dictionary*, 94; *Who Was Who in America*, 150.

BUCKNER, SIMON BOLIVAR (1823-1914) was born in Munfordville, Kentucky; he graduated from West Point in 1844, taught philosophy there, and fought in the Mexican War. He resigned from the army in 1855. Offered general officer commissions by both the North and the South, he remained neutral until Kentucky was invaded by the Federals. He joined the Confederate army as a brigadier general and surrendered to Grant at Fort Donelson in 1862. He ultimately rose to the rank of lieutenant general, fought at Chickamauga, and commanded the District of Louisiana. He was elected Democratic governor of Kentucky, 1887-1892. A lifelong friend of Grant, whom he had known since West Point, he was a pallbearer at Grant's funeral. Boatner, *Civil War Dictionary*, 95-96; *Concise Dictionary of American Biography*, 121.

BUELL, DON CARLOS (1818-1898) was born in Marietta, Ohio. He graduated from West Point in 1841 and served in the Mexican War. Appointed brigadier general (USV) in 1861, he helped organize the Army of the Potomac and provided important support to Grant at Shiloh. In 1862 he was promoted to major general (USV) and opposed Bragg at Perryville. He was criticized for not pursuing Bragg's retreating forces. He was mustered out of the volunteer service in May, 1864, and he resigned from the regular service the following month. Grant vainly made several attempts to have the government restore him to military service. Boatner, *Civil War Dictionary*, 96-97; *Concise Dictionary of American Biography*, 121.

BURBRIDGE, STEPHEN GANO (1831-1894) was a Georgetown, D.C., businessman and Kentucky plantation owner who was commissioned colonel of the Twenty-sixth Kentucky in 1861. He distinguished himself at Shiloh and was commissioned brigadier general (USV) in 1862. He saw action throughout the Ohio and Mississippi valleys and was brevetted major general (USV) for repulsing Morgan's Ohio raid in 1864. He resigned in December, 1865. Boatner, *Civil War Dictionary*, 106.

BURNSIDE, AMBROSE EVERETT (1824-1881), of Indiana, graduated from West Point in 1847 and served in the Mexican War. He resigned from the army in 1853 to manufacture firearms, including a breech-loading rifle he invented in 1856. He entered the Civil War as colonel of the First Rhode Island Volunteers and commanded the unit at the first battle of Bull Run. Promoted to brigadier general, he led a successful assault on the coastal installations of North Carolina and attained the rank of major general. He twice refused command of the Army of the Potomac, finally accepted, and then was relieved of it after Fredericksburg. He later fought at the Wilderness and Spotsylvania before being relieved of command for ineptitude in the Petersburg mine assault. After the war he was elected to three terms as governor of Rhode Island before serving as United States senator from that state until his death. Boatner, *Civil War Dictionary*, 107-108.

BUTLER, BENJAMIN FRANKLIN (1818-1893), of New Hampshire, was a shrewd criminal lawyer and politician before the war. Named major general (USV) in 1861, he took command of the District of Annapolis before capturing Forts Hatteras and Clark in North Carolina. In 1862 he occupied New Orleans and served as a capable but controversial military governor. He hanged William Mumford for pulling down the Union flag and issued his notorious "woman order" that instructed his troops to treat hostile and insulting women as common prostitutes. He was nicknamed "Silverspoon" for allegedly stealing southerners' silverware. In 1863 he assumed command of the Department of Virginia and North Carolina but was sent to New York City in 1864 to handle anticipated election riots. His incompetence at Fort Fisher led Grant to relieve him of command. After the war he was a Republican and then Greenbacker congressman from Massachusetts, save one term, between 1866 and 1879, a leader in the impeachment of Johnson, and governor of Massachusetts (1882). Boatner, *Civil War Dictionary*, 109-110, 945-946; *Concise Dictionary of American Biography*, 130-131.

BUTLER, MATTHEW CALBRAITH (1836-1909) graduated from South Carolina College, studied law, and married the daughter of Governor Pickens. He resigned from the legislature to join Hampton's Legion as a captain and fought in the first battle of Bull Run; he lost his right foot at Brandy Station in 1863. On his return to active duty he was appointed brigadier general in the Confederate army and commanded his brigade in the defense of Richmond. He was promoted to major general in 1864 and joined Johnston to oppose Sherman in the Carolinas. After the war he was a lawyer, legislator, Democratic senator, and major general of volunteers by appointment of President McKinley during the Spanish-American War. Boatner, *Civil War Dictionary*, 110.

CANBY, EDWARD RICHARD SPRIGG (1817-1873), of Kentucky, graduated from West Point in 1839. He fought in the Seminole War and Mexican War. Commanding the Department of New Mexico at the outbreak of the Civil War, he prevented a Confederate invasion of California by holding that territory for the Union. Appointed brigadier general (USV) in 1862, he commanded troops in New York City after the draft riots. He later was promoted to major general (USV), saw action west of the Mississippi, and received the surrender of Taylor and Kirby Smith. As brigadier general in the regular service, he commanded the Department of Columbia in 1866. He was killed on a peace mission to the Modoc Indians of northern California in 1873. Boatner, *Civil War Dictionary*, 118; *Concise Dictionary of American Biography*, 141.

CARTER, JOHN C. (? -1864) was commissioned captain of the Thirty-eighth Tennessee in 1861 and fought at Shiloh. He commanded the regiment at Chickamauga and Chattanooga before being appointed brigadier general in the Confederate army in 1864. He was mortally wounded at the battle of Franklin, Tennessee. Boatner, *Civil War Dictionary*, 130.

CHALMERS, JAMES RONALD (1831-1898), of Virginia, graduated from South Carolina College in 1851 and was admitted to the bar in Mississippi two years later. Appointed brigadier general in the Confederate army in 1862, he fought at Shiloh and Stones River, where he was wounded. He was with Forrest at Fort Pillow, and he fought in the Franklin and Nashville campaigns. After the war he served in the

Mississippi legislature and was a Democratic congressman from the same state, 1877-1883, and an Independent congressman, 1884-1885. Boatner, *Civil War Dictionary*, 135; *Who Was Who in America*, 168.

CHAMBLISS, JOHN RANDOLPH, JR. (1833-1864), of Virginia, graduated from West Point in 1853 but resigned from the service the following year to become a planter. He was aide-de-camp to the governor of Virginia, 1856-1861. Commissioned colonel of the Thirteenth Virginia Cavalry in 1861, he served under Stuart. He commanded the Fifth Virginia Cavalry at Chancellorsville and fought at Gettysburg. He was named brigadier general in the Confederate army in December, 1863; he commanded brigades at the Wilderness and around Petersburg before dying at Deep Bottom in August, 1864. Boatner, *Civil War Dictionary*, 136.

CLARK, DAVID (1820-1882) was born in Littleton, North Carolina. One of the most prominent and wealthiest planters in the state, he was commissioned brigadier general of the state militia in January, 1862, and assigned the command of the defenses of the Roanoke River with the militia of seven contiguous counties under his orders. He assembled the militia at Plymouth when Roanoke Island fell but subsequently retreated to Williamston, where he was relieved of command in April, 1862. His son Walter became a noted state supreme court justice and historian. Ashe, *Biographical History*, VII, 67-68.

CLEBURNE, PATRICK RONAYNE (1828-1864) was born in Ireland. After serving in the army there, he migrated to America and became a druggist and lawyer; he organized the Yell Rifles when the war began. After seizing the Little Rock Arsenal, he was made colonel of the First Arkansas and then appointed brigadier general in the Confederate army in 1862. He fought at Shiloh before rising to major general. During the Atlanta campaign he signed a statement with thirteen other officers that the slaves should be freed and used as soldiers. Called the "Stonewall Jackson of the West," he was killed at Franklin, Tennessee. Boatner, *Civil War Dictionary*, 158-159.

CLINGMAN, THOMAS LANIER (1812-1897) was born in Huntersville, North Carolina, and graduated first in his class at the University of North Carolina at Chapel Hill. He studied law, entered politics as a Whig, but later joined the Democrats because of the slavery issue. He served in the state legislature, United States Congress, and Confederate Congress. Appointed brigadier general in the Confederate army in 1862, he participated in the defense of Goldsboro and New Bern, commanded a brigade at the Wilderness, was wounded at Cold Harbor and severely wounded at Weldon Railroad. He rejoined his command only a few days before the surrender of Greensboro. Boatner, *Civil War Dictionary*, 159; *Concise Dictionary of American Biography*, 174.

COBB, THOMAS READE ROOTES (1823-1862) was a graduate of the University of Georgia, lawyer, and author of numerous books on slavery as well as newspaper and magazine articles. He was a leading influence in the secession movement in Georgia, and after a stint in the Confederate Congress he was commissioned colonel of Cobb's Legion in 1861. He led the unit in the battles of Seven Days', second Bull Run, and Antietam before being named brigadier general in the Confederate army, November, 1862. He was killed at Fredericksburg the following month. His brother was the prominent Georgian politician and Confederate general Howell Cobb. Boatner, *Civil War Dictionary*, 160.

COCKRELL, FRANCIS MARION (1834-1915), of Missouri, graduated from Chapel Hill College in 1853, studied law, and was admitted to the Missouri bar in 1855. He fought from Carthage to Vicksburg and was commissioned brigadier general in the Confederate army in 1863. He led a brigade in the Atlanta campaign. Five times wounded and three times captured during the war, he was a Democratic senator from Missouri, 1875-1905, when Roosevelt appointed him to the Interstate Commerce Commission. Boatner, *Civil War Dictionary*, 161; *Biographical Directory of Congress*, 715.

COLQUITT, ALFRED HOLT (1824-1894), of Georgia, graduated from Princeton, studied law, fought in the Mexican War, and entered politics as a fire-eating states' rights Democrat. He served in the state legislature and Congress. Rising to the rank of brigadier general in the Confederate army, he saw action in the Peninsular campaign, Antietam, Fredericksburg, Chancellorsville, North Carolina, Florida, the Wilderness, Spotsylvania, and Petersburg. A licensed Methodist preacher, he advocated temperance and was elected Democratic governor of Georgia, 1876-1882, and United States senator, 1883-1894. Boatner, *Civil War Dictionary*, 166; *Concise Dictionary of American Biography*, 182.

CONNER, JAMES (1829-1883) studied at South Carolina College, practiced law, and became an ardent secessionist. Rising from captain of the local militia company at Fort Sumter to brigadier general in the Confederate army, he participated in many key battles and led the Twenty-second North Carolina at Chancellorsville and Gettysburg. Twice wounded in the same leg, he continued in command in the field although the leg had to be amputated in October, 1864. After the war he became attorney general of South Carolina (1876). Boatner, *Civil War Dictionary*, 171.

COOKE, JOHN R. (1833-1891), of Missouri, graduated from Harvard and joined the army in 1855 as an engineer. After fighting at first Bull Run, he was named chief of artillery for the Department of North Carolina and was then promoted to colonel of the Twenty-seventh North Carolina. Wounded at Seven Pines, he was commissioned brigadier general in the Confederate army in 1862 and assumed command of a North Carolina brigade. At Fredericksburg his unit held the famous stone wall, and he was wounded again. His father was a Union general (see following sketch), and he was a brother-in-law of Jeb Stuart. Boatner, *Civil War Dictionary*, 173-174.

COOKE, PHILIP ST. GEORGE (1809-1895), of Virginia, graduated from West Point in 1827 and served in the Mexican War. Promoted to brigadier general in the regular service in November, 1861, he did not follow the rest of his family into the Confederacy but fought for the Union. He retired as a major general in 1873. His son-in-law was Jeb Stuart. Boatner, *Civil War Dictionary*, 174.

COOPER, SAMUEL (1798-1876) was born in Hackensack, New Jersey, but became the highest ranking officer in the Confederate army. Appointed a full general from Virginia in 1861, he served throughout the war in Richmond as adjutant and inspector general. One of a minority of West Pointers of northern origin who sided with the South, Cooper had known Jefferson Davis when the latter was secretary of war in the 1850s. At war's end he fled with Davis from Richmond. Boatner, *Civil War Dictionary*, 175.

CROOK, GEORGE (1829-1890), of Ohio, graduated from West Point in 1852 and saw service as an Indian fighter in the Pacific Northwest, where he was wounded by a poisoned arrow. Named colonel of the Thirty-sixth Ohio in 1861, he participated in operations in West Virginia before being promoted to brigadier general (USV) in September, 1862. In 1864 he became commander of the Department of West Virginia and fought in Sheridan's Shenandoah campaign. Rising to major general (USV) in October, 1864, he was captured in February, 1865, at Cumberland, Maryland. After the war he earned a reputation as the army's best Indian fighter. Boatner, *Civil War Dictionary*, 209.

CURTIS, SAMUEL RYAN (1805-1866) was a native New Yorker, West Point graduate (1831), engineer, lawyer, and congressman from Iowa when he resigned in 1861 to become colonel of the Second Iowa. Rising to the rank of major general (USV), he led a series of successful operations in Missouri and Arkansas and commanded the Departments of Kansas and the Northwest. Boatner, *Civil War Dictionary*, 215.

CUSTER, GEORGE ARMSTRONG (1839-1876), of Ohio, graduated from West Point at the bottom of his class in 1861. Because of his brilliance as a cavalry leader, he was commissioned brigadier general (USV) in 1863 at the age of twenty-three. In 1865 he was promoted to major general (USV). From the first Bull Run until Lee's surrender he participated in every battle fought by the Army of the Potomac, save one. He was brevetted for gallant and meritorious services at Gettysburg, Yellow Tavern, Winchester, Fishers Hill, and Five Forks. He is best remembered for his legendary defeat at the Little Big Horn in 1876. Boatner, *Civil War Dictionary*, 216.

DAHLGREN, JOHN ADOLPHUS BERNARD (1809-1870) was born in Philadelphia. Son of the Swedish consul there, he was appointed midshipman in the United States Navy in 1826. He invented the Dahlgren gun, a rifled cannon, and took command of the Washington Naval Yard in April, 1861. Promoted to rear admiral in 1863, he commanded the South Atlantic blockading squadron until the end of the war. Boatner, *Civil War Dictionary*, 218; *Concise Dictionary of American Biography*, 211-212.

DAHLGREN, ULRIC (1842-1864), of Pennsylvania, was the son of Admiral Dahlgren. He was Burnside's aide-de-camp and then served on the staffs of Hooker and Meade at Chancellorsville and Gettysburg respectively. On the retreat from the latter battle he was badly wounded and lost his leg. He was killed during a spectacular raid on Richmond in 1864 in an attempt to free Federal prisoners. Boatner, *Civil War Dictionary*, 218, 460-461.

DANIEL, JUNIUS (1828-1864), of North Carolina, graduated from West Point in 1851 and served on the frontier before resigning to manage his father's Louisiana plantation. Commissioned colonel of the Fourteenth North Carolina in 1861, he fought in the Seven Days' battles and at Malvern Hill. After being appointed brigadier general in the Confederate army in 1862, he was sent to North Carolina. He later fought at Gettysburg and was killed in the Wilderness campaign of 1864. Boatner, *Civil War Dictionary*, 222.

DAVIS, BENJAMIN FRANKLIN (1832-1863), of Alabama, graduated from West Point in 1854. Despite his southern background, he remained with the Union army at the outbreak of the war. Commissioned colonel of the Eighth New York Cavalry in 1862, he led his unit in the famous escape from Harpers Ferry during the Antietam campaign before being killed at Beverly Ford (Brandy Station). Boatner, *Civil War Dictionary*, 224.

DEARING, JAMES (1840-1865), of Virginia, was a cadet at West Point who resigned when his native state seceded. He commanded the Virginia battery in Pickett's command during the Peninsular campaign. He also fought at Fredericksburg, Chancellorsville, and Gettysburg and commanded Pickett's cavalry in the winter of 1863-1864 in the District of North Carolina. Later he was given a cavalry brigade in the New Bern expedition and was appointed brigadier general in the Confederate army. He died from wounds suffered at the battle of High Bridge. Boatner, *Civil War Dictionary*, 228.

DEVENS, CHARLES (1820-1891), of Massachusetts, graduated from Harvard in 1838 and served in the state legislature. A brigadier general in the Massachusetts state militia at the beginning of the war, he was commissioned brigadier general (USV) after being wounded at Balls Bluff. He briefly commanded the Department of Virginia and North Carolina and served most of the war in Virginia. After the war he became justice of the Massachusetts Supreme Court (1873-1877) and then attorney general for President Hayes (1877-1881) before returning to the state supreme court. Boatner, *Civil War Dictionary*, 238; *Concise Dictionary of American Biography*, 231.

DIX, JOHN ADAMS (1798-1879) was a native of New Hampshire who fought in the War of 1812 at the age of fourteen. A good friend of John C. Calhoun, he studied law with the South Carolinian before resigning from the army to enter Democratic politics in New York. He became United States senator from that state (1845-1850) and secretary of the treasury in 1861. Lincoln appointed him major general (USV) in 1861, and he commanded the Department of Annapolis. His subsequent commands included the Departments of Pennsylvania and Virginia. He was later minister to France and governor of New York (1872-1874). Boatner, *Civil War Dictionary*, 241-242.

DOLES, GEORGE PIERCE (1830-1864), a Milledgeville, Georgia, businessman, was commissioned colonel of the Fourth Georgia in 1861. He fought at Antietam and was appointed brigadier general in the Confederate army in November, 1862. He was killed on June 2, 1864, at Bethesda Church after having commanded his unit at Fredericksburg, Chancellorsville, and Gettysburg. Boatner, *Civil War Dictionary*, 243.

DUNOVANT, JOHN (1825-1864) served as major of the state troops at Fort Sumter before being commissioned colonel of the First South Carolina in 1862. Dispatched to Virginia in 1864, he led the Fifth South Carolina at Drewry's Bluff and Cold Harbor. Appointed brigadier general of the Confederate army in August, 1864, he was killed in October at Fort Harrison, Virginia. Boatner, *Civil War Dictionary*, 252.

DU PONT, SAMUEL FRANCIS (1803-1865), of New Jersey, was named midshipman in 1815 and became a career naval officer. Placed in command of the Philadelphia Navy Yard (1855-1860), he presided over the board convened in Washington in June, 1861, to plan the war's naval operations. He commanded the fleet that sailed to Port Royal and was promoted to rear admiral with the thanks of Congress in 1862. Defeated at Charleston in 1863 after obeying orders with which he disagreed, he left his command that same year. He died on active duty in June, 1865. He was the nephew of E. I. Du Pont, founder of the chemical and munitions company. Boatner, *Civil War Dictionary*, 252.

EARLY, JUBAL ANDERSON (1816-1894), of Virginia, was a graduate of West Point (1837). He fought in the Seminole and Mexican wars, served as a lawyer and Whig legislator, and voted against Virginia's secession. Nevertheless, he was commissioned colonel of the Twenty-fourth Virginia and commanded the Sixth Brigade at the first Bull Run before being appointed brigadier general of the Confederate army in July, 1861. He fought in the Peninsular campaign until wounded at Williamsburg, saw action at the second Bull Run, Antietam, and Fredericksburg. Promoted to major general in 1863, he led his unit at Chancellorsville, Gettysburg, the Wilderness, and Spotsylvania. Defeated by Sheridan in the Shenandoah Valley, he started west in disguise to join Kirby Smith, but the war ended before he could reach him. He then fled to Mexico and Canada but later returned to Lynchburg to practice law. President of the Southern Historical Society, he wrote his memoirs of the war and commented frequently on the Gettysburg controversy. Boatner, *Civil War Dictionary*, 254-255.

ELLIOTT, STEPHEN, JR. (1832-1866), of South Carolina, was the son of an Episcopal bishop and ran his father's plantation until Fort Sumter when he acted as captain of the Beaufort battery. After various assignments in South Carolina, he was sent to Petersburg in May, 1864, and rose to the rank of brigadier general in the Confederate army. During the siege of Petersburg he was mortally wounded at the Crater. Sent home to Beaufort, he died on March 21, 1866. Boatner, *Civil War Dictionary*, 262-263.

ELLSWORTH, EPHRAIM ELMER (1837-1861), of New York, achieved fame before the war as the organizer of the Chicago Zouaves, a drill outfit. The group performed at the White House in 1860. Raising the Eleventh New York, he arrived in Washington in May, 1861. He was killed by James T. Jackson, proprietor of the

Marshall House Tavern in Alexandria, on May 24 when he removed a Confederate flag from the roof. Jackson was immediately killed by Francis E. Brownwell, and a correspondent of the New York *Tribune* who witnessed the episode sensationalized it in the northern press. Boatner, *Civil War Dictionary*, 263-264.

EVANS, NATHAN GEORGE (1824-1868), of South Carolina, attended Randolph-Macon College and graduated from West Point in 1848. He became major adjutant general of South Carolina forces during the bombardment of Fort Sumter before being commissioned captain in the Confederate cavalry. He played a distinguished part in the southern victory at first Bull Run and was promoted to colonel. His exploits at Balls Bluff resulted in his elevation to brigadier general. He commanded the so-called "tramp brigade" that was usually in the Carolinas but was often sent on temporary duty elsewhere. In 1863, however, he was tried and acquitted twice: the first time for drunkenness and the second for disobedience. Stripped of his command by Beauregard, who considered him inept, he briefly returned to the field in 1864 before suffering an injury from a fall from his horse. Boatner, *Civil War Dictionary*, 268.

EWELL, RICHARD STODDERT (1817-1872), was born in Georgetown, D.C., and graduated from West Point in 1840. Serving in the Mexican War and Indian wars, he was commissioned colonel in the Confederate army in 1861 and rose to lieutenant general by 1863. He saw action at both battles of Bull Run, Gettysburg, and the Wilderness and lost his leg. He was captured several days before Appomattox. Boatner, *Civil War Dictionary*, 268-269; *Who Was Who in America*, 243.

FARRAGUT, DAVID GLASGOW (1801-1870) was born in Tennessee and entered the navy as a midshipman in 1810. He saw action in the War of 1812 and the Mexican War. At the outbreak of the Civil War he left Norfolk and moved north. He commanded the New Orleans expedition in 1861 and was promoted to rear admiral in 1862 for his success in opening up the Mississippi River as far as Vicksburg. The highlight of his career was the capture of Mobile in 1864 at which he is alleged to have barked his famous order, "Damn the torpedoes." Promoted to admiral in 1866, he was the first in the United States Navy to hold that rank. Boatner, *Civil War Dictionary*, 275-276, 558-559.

FERGUSON, SAMUEL WRAGG (1835-1917), of South Carolina, graduated from West Point in 1857 and served on the Utah expedition. He was commissioned brigadier general in the Confederate army in 1863 and fought in the Atlanta campaign. Boatner, *Civil War Dictionary*, 277.

FERRERO, EDWARD (1831-1899) was born in Spain and, as his father before him, taught dancing in New York City. Active in the state militia, he was commissioned colonel of the Fifty-first New York and led the regiment, 1861-1862, at Roanoke Island and New Bern. After fighting in Virginia, he was promoted to brigadier general (USV) in late 1862, but his commission expired the following March. Transferred to the West, he participated in the Vicksburg campaign and was reappointed brigadier general (USV). He is best known for his action in the Petersburg mine explosion of

July, 1864. Burnside selected Ferrero's command, a Negro division, to lead the assault on the Crater. Despite the cancellation of the orders, the attack took place while Ferrero swigged a jug of rum and let his subordinates direct the fight. Though blamed for his part in the debacle, he was brevetted major general (USV) for his role in the Petersburg and Richmond campaigns. Boatner, *Civil War Dictionary*, 277.

FIELD, CHARLES WILLIAM (1828-1892), of Kentucky, graduated from West Point in 1849. After service on the frontier and as cavalry instructor at the military academy, he joined the Confederate army and served under Jeb Stuart. He was named brigadier general in 1862 and fought at Fredericksburg, the Seven Days' battles, and second Bull Run, where he was wounded in the hips. He later saw action at Cold Harbor and the siege of Petersburg. After the war he served as doorkeeper in the United States House of Representatives, 1878-1881. Boatner, *Civil War Dictionary*, 279.

FINEGAN, JOSEPH (1814-1885), a Florida lawyer, was appointed brigadier general in the Confederate army in 1862. After commanding the Department of Middle and Eastern Florida, he was sent to Virginia in 1864 where he fought at Cold Harbor and Petersburg. Boatner, *Civil War Dictionary*, 279.

FLOYD, JOHN BUCHANAN (1806-1863), of Virginia, graduated from South Carolina College and became a lawyer and cotton planter in Arkansas. Elected governor of Virginia in 1849, he served as Buchanan's secretary of war (1857-1860). Northerners accused him of stockpiling guns in the southern arsenals in anticipation of their capture by Confederate forces. Appointed brigadier general in the Confederate army in 1861, he served in West Virginia and at Fort Donelson before being relieved of his command by Davis. In poor health he died in August, 1863. Boatner, *Civil War Dictionary*, 286; *Who Was Who in America*, 254.

FORREST, NATHAN BEDFORD (1821-1877), of Tennessee, enlisted in the Confederate army as a private after rising from poverty to affluence through cotton, real estate, livestock, and slaves. He raised and equipped a battalion at his own expense and in October, 1861, was commissioned lieutenant colonel. He fought at Fort Donelson and Shiloh before being named brigadier general in the Confederate army; he later rose to the rank of lieutenant general. He earned a fearsome reputation as a fighter and raider. Sherman once asserted that Forrest had to be "hunted down and killed if it costs ten thousand lives and bankrupts the Federal treasury." After the war he helped organize the Ku Klux Klan. Asked to name the war's best soldier, J. E. Johnston chose Forrest, "who, had he had the advantages of a thorough military education and training, would have been the great central figure of the Civil War." Boatner, *Civil War Dictionary*, 288-289.

FOSTER, JOHN GRAY (1823-1874), of New Hampshire, graduated from West Point in 1846. After serving in the Mexican War, he taught engineering at the military academy and was at Fort Sumter during the bombardment. Appointed brigadier general (USV) in 1861, he commanded the First Brigade, North Carolina Expedition, at Roanoke Island, New Bern, and Fort Macon. Named major general

(USV), he commanded the Department of North Carolina, 1862-1863. He later headed the Department of the South, 1864-1865, and continued in the regular service as a lieutenant colonel of engineers after the war. Boatner, *Civil War Dictionary*, 301-302.

FRANKLIN, WILLIAM BUEL (1823-1903), of Pennsylvania, graduated from West Point in 1843, first in his class. After surveying expeditions to the Rocky Mountains, service in the Mexican War, and supervision of harbor improvements, he was named brigadier general in the regular service in 1861. He saw action at first Bull Run, the siege of Yorktown, and Antietam. He was named major general (USV) in 1862 and later participated in the Red River expedition. For his war service he was made major general in the regular army but resigned in 1866 to become vice-president of Colt's Fire Arms Manufacturing Company. Boatner, *Civil War Dictionary*, 303-304.

FRÉMONT, JOHN CHARLES (1813-1890), of Georgia, taught mathematics in the navy before joining the army's topographical engineers in 1838. He became known as "The Pathfinder" for his explorations of the Rockies, and he helped secure California for the United States in 1846. Court-martialed and forced to resign from the army for insubordination and mutiny, he continued his explorations in California and served as United States senator, 1850-1851. He was the Republican nominee for president in 1856. Appointed brigadier general (USV) in 1861, his Civil War career was marred by incompetence, first as commander of the Western Department, and then as head of the Mountain Department when he opposed unsuccessfully Jackson's Shenandoah Valley campaign. Relieved of command in 1862, he spent the rest of the war in New York awaiting orders. Lincoln was also forced to revoke Frémont's emancipation proclamation in Missouri in 1861. Financial irregularities in a proposed transcontinental railroad resulted in his being convicted and fined in 1873, but he served as governor of Arizona, 1878-1881. Boatner, *Civil War Dictionary*, 314-315; *Concise Dictionary of American Biography*, 315-316.

FRENCH, SAMUEL GIBBS (1818-1910) was a native of New Jersey and graduate of West Point (1843). He served in the Mexican War and on quartermaster duty in Washington before resigning in 1856 to take over a plantation near Vicksburg. Appointed brigadier general in the Confederate army in 1861, he was sent to New Bern in 1862 where he took command of the Department of Southern Virginia and North Carolina. Rising to the rank of major general, he participated in the Vicksburg and Atlanta campaigns. Boatner, *Civil War Dictionary*, 315-316.

FRENCH, WILLIAM HENRY (1815-1881), of Maryland, graduated from West Point in 1837. Serving in the Seminole and Mexican wars, he was aide-de-camp to Franklin Pierce in the latter. When Texas seceded, he marched his garrison to the Gulf of Mexico and sailed to Key West. He was named brigadier general (USV) in 1861. He saw action at Antietam, Fredericksburg, and Chancellorsville and was promoted to major general (USV) in 1862. He continued in the regular army until his retirement in 1880. Boatner, *Civil War Dictionary*, 316.

GARDNER, FRANKLIN (1823-1873) was a native of New York who was appointed to West Point from Iowa. After graduating from the military academy in 1843, he fought in the Mexican War and saw frontier duty. Commissioned lieutenant colonel in the Confederate army in 1861, he served in Tennessee and Mississippi before commanding a cavalry unit at Shiloh. Named major general in 1862, he took command of Port Hudson and was captured there in 1863. Later exchanged, he served the remainder of the war in Mississippi. Boatner, *Civil War Dictionary*, 323.

GARNETT, RICHARD BROOKE (ca. 1817-1863), of Virginia, graduated from West Point in 1841 and fought in the Seminole and Mexican wars. After serving on the Utah expedition, he was appointed brigadier general in the Confederate army and assumed command of the Stonewall Brigade. After fighting in the Shenandoah Valley in 1862, he was arrested by Jackson for withdrawing the brigade at Kernstown. Released when Jackson hurried to Cedar Mountain, he was sent to Tarboro, North Carolina, in 1863. He was killed in Pickett's charge at Gettysburg. Boatner, *Civil War Dictionary*, 324.

GARNETT, ROBERT SELDEN (ca. 1819-1861), of Virginia, graduated from West Point in 1841, taught at the military academy, and fought in the Mexican War. Serving as commandant of West Point before the Civil War, he was in Europe when the conflict began but returned to become adjutant general of the Virginia state troops. Appointed brigadier general in the Confederate army in June, 1861, he was killed at Carrick's Ford, Virginia, the following month. Boatner, *Civil War Dictionary*, 324-325.

GATLIN, RICHARD CASWELL (1809-1896) was a native North Carolinian and graduate of West Point (1832). He served in the Black Hawk, Seminole, and Mexican wars. In 1861 he was named brigadier general in the Confederate army and prepared the defense of New Bern before becoming seriously ill and resigning in 1862. He then served as adjutant and inspector general for North Carolina. Boatner, *Civil War Dictionary*, 327.

GILLMORE, QUINCY ADAMS (1825-1888), of Ohio, graduated from West Point in 1849, first in his class. After supervising the construction of harbor fortifications, teaching engineering, and serving as quartermaster at West Point, he was named chief engineer on the Port Royal expedition of 1861. Promoted to brigadier general (USV) in 1862, he rose to major general the following year and commanded the Department of the South. He fought at Drewry's Bluff and elsewhere and was severely injured by a fall from his horse while pursuing Early. The author of numerous professional books and treatises, he continued on active service after the war with the rank of colonel. Boatner, *Civil War Dictionary*, 343.

GIRARDEY, VICTOR J. B. (? -1864), of Georgia, was commissioned lieutenant with the Third Georgia in 1861. He fought in the Peninsular campaign, at Chancellorsville, and at Gettysburg. For his performance in the Petersburg mine assault Lee appointed him brigadier general "on the spot" in 1864. However, he was killed at Deep Bottom two weeks later. Boatner, *Civil War Dictionary*, 344.

GIST, STATES RIGHTS (1831-1864), of South Carolina, attended South Carolina College and Harvard Law School. After seeing action at Fort Sumter and first Bull Run, he was commissioned brigadier general in the Confederate army in 1862. He served at Vicksburg, Chickamauga, Missionary Ridge, and in the Atlanta campaign before being killed at Franklin, Tennessee, while leading a charge. Boatner, *Civil War Dictionary*, 344-345.

GODWIN, ARCHIBALD CAMPBELL (? -1864), of Virginia, was commissioned colonel of the Fifty-seventh North Carolina. Serving in the Maryland campaign, the battle of Fredericksburg, and Gettysburg, he was captured at Rappahannock Station. After his exchange he was named brigadier general. He was killed at Winchester in September, 1864. Boatner, *Civil War Dictionary*, 346.

GORDON, GEORGE WASHINGTON (1836-1911), of Tennessee, was named drillmaster of the Eleventh Tennessee at the war's outbreak. Serving mostly in Tennessee, he was promoted to brigadier general in the Confederate army in 1864, wounded, and captured at Franklin. After the war he was Democratic congressman from Tennessee, 1907-1911. Boatner, *Civil War Dictionary*, 348; *Concise Dictionary of American Biography*, 354.

GORDON, JOHN BROWN (1832-1904), of Georgia, graduated from the University of Georgia, became a lawyer, and managed a coal mine in Alabama. At the outbreak of the war he was the captain of a volunteer group of mountaineers, but he was quickly named colonel of the Sixth Alabama and fought in the Peninsular campaign. Wounded at Antietam, he was promoted to brigadier general in the Confederate army in 1862. He commanded his Georgia brigade at Chancellorsville, Gettysburg, the Wilderness, and Spotsylvania. He rose to the rank of major general in 1864 and led the assault on Fort Stedman at Petersburg. His wife accompanied him during the war, much to the annoyance of Jubal Early, who once wished aloud that the Federals would capture her. After the war Gordon was a Democratic senator from Georgia (1873-1880; 1891-1897) and governor of the same state (1886-1890). Boatner, *Civil War Dictionary*, 348-349; *Concise Dictionary of American Biography*, 354-355.

GRANBURY, HIRAM BRONSON (1831-1864) was named captain of the Seventh Texas in 1861 and sent to Kentucky. He commanded the unit at Chickamauga and Missionary Ridge before being appointed brigadier general in the Confederate army in 1864. He was killed in a charge at Franklin, Tennessee. Boatner, *Civil War Dictionary*, 351.

GRANT, ULYSSES SIMPSON (1822-1885), of Ohio, graduated from West Point in 1843 and distinguished himself in the Mexican War. However, the grind of frontier military duty on the west coast and loneliness for his family caused Grant to begin drinking. He resigned in 1854 to avoid a court-martial. Unsuccessful as a businessman, he found a new opportunity in the war with his appointment to brigadier general in 1861. He won national attention in 1862 and 1863 for his operations at Forts Henry and Donelson, Shiloh, and Vicksburg. After his victories around Chattanooga in 1864, he was promoted to lieutenant general and made general in chief of the armies. His relentless pursuit of Lee through a costly strategy of attrition finally ended the war. Grant's two terms as president (1869-1877) were besmirched by corruption and bad management despite his honesty and good intentions. He failed in an effort to win the Republican nomination for president for a third time in 1880. Financially ruined in 1884, Grant, fatally ill with throat cancer, spent the last months of his life writing his autobiography, considered one of the greatest in the English language. Its sale of 300,000 copies earned $450,000 for his widow. Boatner, *Civil War Dictionary*, 352-353.

GREEN, THOMAS (1814-1864), of Virginia, fought Indians in Texas and later served in the Mexican War under Zachary Taylor. He was clerk of the Texas Supreme Court when commissioned colonel of the Fifth Texas Mounted Rifles in 1861. He attained the rank of brigadier general and served mostly in Texas and New Mexico during the war. He was killed in 1864 at Blair's Landing while leading a cavalry attack on Federal gunboats. Boatner, *Civil War Dictionary*, 355.

GREGG, MAXCY (1814-1862) was a South Carolina lawyer and leader of the states' rights faction. A veteran of the Mexican War, he was commissioned colonel of the First South Carolina before being promoted to brigadier general in the Confederate army in late 1861. He fought in the Peninsular campaign, second Bull Run, Antietam, and Fredericksburg, where he was mortally wounded. Boatner, *Civil War Dictionary*, 358.

GRIERSON, BENJAMIN HENRY (1826-1911), of Pennsylvania, was commissioned major of the Sixth Illinois Cavalry in 1861. Promoted to colonel in 1862, he led a number of raids in western Tennessee and northern Mississippi. Serving in the western theater of the war, he reached the rank of major general in the regular service in 1865. After the war he continued in the army as a career officer until his retirement in 1890. Boatner, *Civil War Dictionary*, 359.

HALLECK, HENRY WAGER (1815-1872) was a native New Yorker who graduated from West Point in 1839. As the author of *Elements of Military Art and Science* (1846) and the translator of Jomini's *Vie de Napoléon*, he earned the reputation of an intellect and the nickname "Old Brains." He spent most of the war as Lincoln's military adviser and general in chief. Appointed major general in 1861, he proved an able administrator of the Departments of Missouri, Ohio, Kansas, Kentucky, and Tennessee, but an incompetent field commander. He was ordered to Washington in 1862 where his administrative abilities proved valuable, but his lack of strategic aptitude was a constant source of consternation to Federal commanders in the field. When Grant became supreme commander in 1864, Halleck was demoted to chief of staff. Cantankerous and crafty, he had a reputation for being the most unpopular man in Washington. Boatner, *Civil War Dictionary*, 367.

HAMMOND, WILLIAM A. (1828-1900), a native of Annapolis, Maryland, received an M.D. from the University of the City of New York in 1848 and entered the army as a surgeon. He resigned in 1860 to teach at the University of Maryland but rejoined the army in 1861. In 1862 he was appointed surgeon general with the rank of brigadier general in the regular service. Court-martialed for irregularities in liquor contracts, he was dismissed from the service in 1864, but that decision was overturned in 1879. The founder and editor of several medical journals, he was a pioneer in the treatment of mental and nervous disorders. His *Treatise on Diseases of the Nervous System* (1871) was described as the first such textbook written in English. Boatner, *Civil War Dictionary*, 370; *Concise Dictionary of American Biography*, 394.

HAMPTON, WADE (1818-1902), scion of a prominent South Carolina family, graduated from South Carolina College in 1836. As a wealthy planter and state legislator, he held conservative views in regard to southern policy but did not favor secession. He raised the Hampton Legion and led the unit at the first Bull Run. Promoted to brigadier general in 1862, he was second-in-command to Jeb Stuart and saw action at Antietam and Gettysburg, where he was wounded. When Stuart died, he became the Confederate commander of the cavalry corps; he was promoted to lieutenant general in 1865. His election as governor of South Carolina in 1876 ended Reconstruction in that state. Reelected in 1878, he shortly thereafter was chosen United States senator, a post he held until 1891. Hampton's grip on South Carolina politics (1876-1890) epitomized the Bourbon South. Boatner, *Civil War Dictionary*, 370-371; *Concise Dictionary of American Biography*, 394.

HARDEE, WILLIAM JOSEPH (1815-1873), of Georgia, graduated from West Point in 1838, studied in France, and fought in the Seminole and Mexican wars. Later he became commandant of cadets at West Point. Commissioned brigadier general in the Confederate army in 1861, he organized the Arkansas Brigade and transferred to Kentucky. He rose to lieutenant general by 1862 and saw action at Shiloh, Stones River, and in the Atlanta campaign. He commanded the Department of South Carolina, Georgia, and Florida during Sherman's march to the sea. Boatner, *Civil War Dictionary*, 374.

HAYS, HARRY THOMPSON (1820-1876), of Mississippi, was a New Orleans lawyer who fought in the Mexican War and was active in Whig politics. As colonel of the Seventh Louisiana, he fought at the first Bull Run and was named brigadier general in the Confederate army shortly before Antietam. He commanded the Louisiana Brigade at Chancellorsville, Gettysburg, and Spotsylvania, where he was seriously wounded. Kirby Smith promoted him to major general in the last days of the war. Boatner, *Civil War Dictionary*, 390.

HAYS, WILLIAM (1819-1875), of Virginia, graduated from West Point in 1840 and fought in the Seminole and Mexican wars. He commanded a brigade of flying artillery at Antietam and was promoted to brigadier general (USV) in November, 1862. He was wounded and captured at Chancellorsville but returned in time to fight at Gettysburg. He continued in the regular service after the war. Boatner, *Civil War Dictionary*, 390.

HECKMAN, CHARLES ADAM (1822-1896), of Pennsylvania, served in the Mexican War and was appointed lieutenant colonel of the Ninth New Jersey in October, 1861. He served with Burnside during the North Carolina expedition and was wounded at New Bern in 1862. Named brigadier general (USV) later that year, he served in North Carolina and Virginia until his capture at Drewry's Bluff in 1864. Imprisoned at Charleston where he came under the bombardment of Union guns, he was later released and saw further action at the close of the war. He resigned in May, 1865. Boatner, *Civil War Dictionary*, 391-392.

HETH, HENRY (1825-1899), of Virginia, graduated from West Point in 1847, served in the Mexican War, and saw action on the frontier against the Indians. He resigned from the army to join Confederate forces in 1861 and was appointed brigadier general in 1862. After duty in Kentucky and Tennessee, he was transferred to the Army of Northern Virginia at Lee's request and fought at Chancellorsville and Gettysburg, where he was wounded. Reaching the rank of major general, he fought at the Wilderness, Spotsylvania, and Petersburg and was on the retreat to Appomattox. Boatner, *Civil War Dictionary*, 398.

HILL, AMBROSE POWELL (1825-1865), of Virginia, graduated from West Point in 1847 and served in the Mexican War. Commissioned colonel of the Thirteenth Virginia in 1861, he served in West Virginia and northern Virginia before being named brigadier general in the Confederate army in 1862. He rose to lieutenant general in 1863 and succeeded Jackson when the latter was killed. He led the newly created Third Corps in the Gettysburg and Wilderness campaigns. He was killed at Petersburg in April, 1865. Boatner, *Civil War Dictionary*, 400.

HILL, DANIEL HARVEY (1821-1889), of South Carolina, graduated from West Point in 1842, fought in the Mexican War, and taught mathematics at Washington College in Lexington, Virginia, and then at Davidson College. He became superintendent of the North Carolina Military Institute in 1859 and fought at Big Bethel before being appointed brigadier general in the Confederate army in 1861. Rising to major general by 1862, he led his unit in the Peninsular campaign and defended Richmond during the Gettysburg campaign. When he went to Chickamauga in 1863 and recommended the removal of Bragg for incompetence, Davis instead relieved him and blocked his promotion to lieutenant general. Hill surrendered with Johnston in North Carolina in 1865. After the war he ran a newspaper and magazine in North Carolina and became president of the University of Arkansas, 1877-1884, and then of the forerunner of the Georgia Military Academy, 1885-1889. Boatner, *Civil War Dictionary*, 401.

HINDMAN, THOMAS CARMICHAEL (1828-1868), of Tennessee, attended school in New Jersey, fought in Mexico, became an attorney, and served in Congress. An ardent secessionist, he was appointed brigadier general from Arkansas in the Confederate army in 1861 and led a division at Shiloh. After service in the Trans-Mississippi Department, he fought at Chickamauga and Chattanooga. He attained the rank of major general before an eye injury in the Atlanta campaign disqualified him for further field service. Boatner, *Civil War Dictionary*, 402.

HOBSON, EDWARD HENRY (1825-1901), of Kentucky, fought in the Mexican War but was a banker and businessman. Appointed colonel of the Thirteenth Kentucky in 1862, he fought at Shiloh, where he was wounded and promoted to brigadier general (USV). In 1863 his command pursued Morgan's raiders for 900 miles and twenty-five days through Kentucky, Ohio, and Indiana. Later he was appointed Burnside's chief of cavalry but ill health prevented him from accepting it. He was mustered out in 1865. Boatner, *Civil War Dictionary*, 403.

HOKE, ROBERT FREDERICK (1837-1912), of North Carolina, graduated from the Kentucky Military Institute. He joined the North Carolina forces in 1861 and was appointed brigadier general in the Confederate army in 1863. Wounded at Chancellorsville, he returned to active duty in the Carolinas to squelch banditry in the Piedmont before being sent to the Tidewater section to check Union movements. He was promoted to major general for his stunning capture of Plymouth in April, 1864. After fighting at Bentonville, he surrendered with Johnston. Boatner, *Civil War Dictionary*, 404.

HOLLINS, GEORGE NICHOLS (1799-1878), of Maryland, served in the navy in the War of 1812, was captured at Bermuda, and participated in the bombardment of Nicaragua in 1854. He joined the Confederate navy in 1861 and was named commander. He commanded the naval station at New Orleans that same year before being promoted to commodore and organizing the naval forces on the upper Mississippi. He returned to New Orleans in 1862 when Farragut threatened and after the city's capture spent the remainder of the war on various boards. Boatner, *Civil War Dictionary*, 405.

HOLMES, THEOPHILUS HUNTER (1804-1880), a native North Carolinian, graduated from West Point in 1829. A veteran of the Seminole and Mexican wars, he returned to North Carolina in 1861 to organize and command the Southern Department of Coastal Defense. His West Point classmate Jefferson Davis appointed him brigadier general in the Confederate army; he rose to lieutenant general in 1862, fought at Malvern Hill, and commanded the Trans-Mississippi Department. In 1864 he returned to North Carolina to assume command of the state's reserves. Boatner, *Civil War Dictionary*, 406.

HOOD, JOHN BELL (1831-1879), of Kentucky, graduated from West Point in 1853. Wounded in Indian fighting on the frontier, he resigned from the army to join Confederate forces in 1861. Appointed brigadier general in 1862, his "Texas Brigade" fought at the second Bull Run and Antietam. He was wounded at Gettysburg and lost his right leg at Chickamauga. Promoted to lieutenant general in 1864, he eventually commanded the Army of Tennessee during the Atlanta campaign. At the end of the war he tried to reach Kirby Smith but surrendered at Natchez in May, 1865. Hood's gallant offensives ended in disaster, but his brigade retained a reputation for being among the best combat troops of the Confederacy. Boatner, *Civil War Dictionary*, 407-408.

HOOKER, JOSEPH (1814-1879), of Massachusetts, graduated from West Point in 1837. After service in the Seminole and Mexican wars, he resigned from the army in 1853 but offered his services to the Union when war came in 1861. After serving in numerous battles and rising to the rank of brigadier general in the regular army, Lincoln appointed him commander of the Army of the Potomac in January, 1863. Defeated at Chancellorsville soon thereafter, he was relieved of his command but later served in the Tennessee and Atlanta campaigns. He retired from the regular service in 1868 after suffering a paralytic stroke. He was dubbed "Fighting Joe" by the Associated Press during the Seven Days' battles, a nickname he detested. To reciprocate he ordered—an innovation in American journalism—that all news dispatches sent from the Army of the Potomac be signed to assure responsible reporting. Boatner, *Civil War Dictionary*, 409-410.

HOVEY, ALVIN PETERSON (1821-1891), of Indiana, served in the Mexican War and became an associate justice of the state supreme court in 1854. He switched from the Democratic to Republican party and was named colonel of the Twenty-fourth Indiana in 1861. For gallantry at Shiloh he was promoted to brigadier general (USV). He participated in the Vicksburg campaign and was credited by Grant with the victory at Champion's Hill, where his brigade lost a third of its strength to casualties. In 1864 he recruited 10,000 unmarried men who became known as "Hovey's Babies." After the war he was minister to Peru (1865-1870), congressman (1887-1889), and governor of Indiana (1889-1891), dying in office. Boatner, *Civil War Dictionary*, 412; *Who Was Who in America*, 331.

HOWARD, OLIVER OTIS (1830-1909), of Maine, graduated from West Point in 1854, served on the frontier, and taught mathematics at the military academy. He fought at Bull Run and was promoted to brigadier general (USV) in 1861. He lost his right arm at Fair Oaks the following year and saw action at Antietam and Fredericksburg. Promoted to major general, he fought at Chancellorsville, Gettysburg, Lookout Mountain, Missionary Ridge, and Atlanta. During Sherman's march to the sea he saw action at Fayetteville, Bentonville, and Goldsboro. He attained the rank of major general in the regular service and received the thanks of Congress; in 1893 he received the Medal of Honor. At the end of the war he was named commissioner of the Freedmen's Bureau. He founded Howard University for Negroes in Washington and served as its president, 1869-1874. He later became peace commissioner to the Apaches and commanded the Departments of the Columbia and the Platte before his retirement in 1894. Boatner, *Civil War Dictionary*, 413-414.

HOYT, HENRY MARTYN (1830-1892), of Pennsylvania, served with his state's volunteer troops and rose to the rank of brigadier general before being mustered out in 1864. He was captured during the assault on Fort Johnson at Morris Island, South Carolina. After the war he was elected governor of Pennsylvania, 1878-1883. Boatner, *Civil War Dictionary*, 415.

HUGER, BENJAMIN (1805-1877), of South Carolina, graduated from West Point in 1825. He was Scott's chief of ordnance in Mexico. He resigned from the army to join

Confederate forces in 1861 and was appointed brigadier general with command of the Department of Norfolk. Later elevated to major general, he led his division without distinction at Seven Pines and Malvern Hill. An investigation by the Confederate Congress held him responsible for the loss of Roanoke Island in February, 1862, and he was relieved of his command and transferred to the western theater. After the war he farmed in Virginia and North Carolina. Boatner, *Civil War Dictionary*, 416.

HUNTER, DAVID (1802-1886), of Illinois, graduated from West Point in 1822. He served on the frontier and in the Mexican War and was stationed in Kansas in 1860 where he corresponded with Lincoln about secession rumors. Appointed brigadier general (USV) in 1861, he was severely wounded at Bull Run. Promoted to major general, he assumed command of the Western Department. After capturing Fort Pulaski in Georgia in April, 1862, he issued an order emancipating all slaves in Union hands, but Lincoln annulled the order. Hunter also authorized the first Negro regiment (First South Carolina) and was upheld by Congress. The Confederacy termed him a "felon to be executed if captured." After the war he accompanied Lincoln's body to Springfield and returned to Washington to head the commission that tried the assassins. He attained the rank of major general in the regular service and retired in 1866. Boatner, *Civil War Dictionary*, 418-419.

HURLBUT, STEPHEN AUGUSTUS (1815-1882) was born in Charleston, South Carolina, and was admitted to the bar of that state in 1837. After serving as adjutant to the South Carolina Regiment in the Seminole War, he moved to Illinois and was elected to the legislature as a Republican. Appointed brigadier general (USV) in 1861, he fought at Shiloh. Later promoted to major general, he participated in the Vicksburg campaign. While commanding the Department of the Gulf, he was charged with corruption but was honorably mustered out in 1865. As a Republican leader in Illinois after the war he was again accused of corruption and drunkenness but was elected to the legislature, named first commander in chief of the Grand Army of the Republic (1866-1868), appointed minister to Colombia (1869-1872), elected to Congress (1873-1877), and once again appointed minister to Peru (1881-1882). His altercation with Judson Kilpatrick, minister to Chile during the Peru-Chile War, embarrassed the United States. Boatner, *Civil War Dictionary*, 420; *Who Was Who in America*, 339.

IMBODEN, JOHN DANIEL (1823-1895), of Virginia, graduated from Washington College and became a lawyer and legislator. He fought at the first Bull Run and was promoted to colonel in 1862. He attained the rank of brigadier general and led a raid into West Virginia in 1863. Felled by typhoid fever in 1864, he spent the remainder of the war on prison duty at Aiken, South Carolina. Boatner, *Civil War Dictionary*, 423.

IVERSON, ALFRED (1829-1911), of Georgia, left military school to fight in the Mexican War. He entered the regular army in 1855 and served on the frontier, in the Kansas border disturbances, and on the Utah expedition. When Georgia seceded, he joined the Confederate army and was stationed at Wilmington, where he fought along the Cape Fear River. He was commissioned colonel of the Twentieth North Carolina in 1861. Appointed brigadier general in the Confederate army in 1862, he fought at Fredericksburg, Chancellorsville, and Gettysburg. He later fought Stoneman near Macon, Georgia, and captured him at Sunshine Church. Boatner, *Civil War Dictionary*, 429.

JACKSON, HENRY ROOTES (1820-1898), of Georgia, graduated from Yale, practiced law, and was a United States diplomat to Austria in the 1850s. Appointed brigadier general in the Confederate army in 1861, he served in West Virginia but resigned to become major general of the Georgia state troops and a supporter of Gov. Joseph Brown. After the fall of Atlanta, he was reappointed brigadier general in the Confederate army and commanded a brigade at Nashville, where he was captured. He later served as minister to Mexico, 1885-1886. Boatner, *Civil War Dictionary*, 430-431; *Who Was Who in America*, 344.

JACKSON, THOMAS JONATHAN (1824-1863), of Virginia, graduated from West Point in 1846 and served with distinction in the Mexican War. A staunch Presbyterian, nonsmoker, and teetotaler, he taught at the Virginia Military Institute before the war and commanded a company of cadets at John Brown's hanging in 1859. Commissioned brigadier general in the Confederate army in 1861, he and his brigade won acclaim at the first Bull Run, and he earned the appellation "Stonewall." Promoted to major general, he conducted a brilliant campaign through the Shenandoah Valley but inexplicably proved feckless after rejoining Lee on the Peninsula. However, his military genius manifested itself again at the second Bull Run and Antietam. Rising to lieutenant general in October, 1862, he performed masterfully at Fredericksburg and Chancellorsville but was mortally wounded accidentally by his own men at the latter battle. Said Lee: "I know not how to replace him." Boatner, *Civil War Dictionary*, 432.

JACKSON, WILLIAM HICKS (1835-1903), of Tennessee, graduated from West Point in 1856. After service on the frontier and in Indian fighting, he joined Confederate forces in 1861 and was named brigadier general in 1862. He fought in the Vicksburg and Atlanta campaigns and assumed command of all Tennessee cavalry in 1865. At the end of the war he was a Confederate commissioner for the parole of troops in Alabama and Mississippi. Boatner, *Civil War Dictionary*, 433.

JENKINS, ALBERT GALLATIN (1830-1864), of Virginia, graduated from Harvard Law School in 1850, served two terms in Congress, and resigned his seat in 1861 to join the Confederacy. As colonel of the Eighth Virginia he engaged in several raids throughout the mountain counties until elected to the Confederate Congress in February, 1862. He returned to military duty as a brigadier general in August, 1862, and led a 500-mile raid through West Virginia and into Ohio. He was wounded at Gettysburg and again at Cloyd's Mountain, Virginia, where he was captured. He died shortly thereafter. Boatner, *Civil War Dictionary*, 435; *Who Was Who in America*, 348.

JENKINS, MICAH (1835-1864), scion of an aristocratic plantation family, graduated from the South Carolina Military Academy at the head of his class and helped organize other military schools in the state. Commissioned colonel of the Fifth South Carolina, he led the unit at the first Bull Run. He was named brigadier general in 1862 and was severely wounded at the second battle of Bull Run. At the battle of the Wilderness he was fatally shot by a Confederate soldier in a manner reminiscent of Stonewall Jackson's death. Boatner, *Civil War Dictionary*, 435.

JOHNSON, BRADLEY TYLER (1829-1903), of Maryland, attended Princeton, practiced law, and entered Democratic politics. Commissioned major of the First Maryland, he fought at Bull Run and led his regiment at Winchester and Harrison-burg. He subsequently fought at the second Bull Run, Antietam, and the Wilderness. Appointed brigadier general in 1864, he executed Early's orders to burn Chambersburg, Pennsylvania. Later that year he was sent to Salisbury as commandant of prisons. After the war he wrote extensively on state finances, law, and history. Boatner, *Civil War Dictionary*, 437.

JOHNSON, BUSHROD RUST (1817-1880), of Ohio, graduated from West Point in 1840 and served in the Seminole and Mexican wars before teaching in Kentucky and at the University of Nashville. Commissioned brigadier general in the Confederate army in 1862, he commanded Fort Donelson before its surrender and led a brigade at Shiloh. After promotion to major general in 1864, he saw action around Petersburg and at the Wilderness. After the war he returned to the University of Nashville as chancellor. Boatner, *Civil War Dictionary*, 437.

JOHNSON, EDWARD (1816-1873), of Kentucky, graduated from West Point in 1838 and fought in the Seminole and Mexican wars. In 1861 he was commissioned brigadier general in the Confederate army and commanded Jackson's old division at Gettysburg after being promoted to major general in February, 1863. He was captured at Spotsylvania, exchanged, and captured again at Nashville. Boatner, *Civil War Dictionary*, 437-438.

JOHNSON, RICHARD W. (1827-1897), of Kentucky, graduated from West Point in 1849. After service on the frontier and in Indian fighting, he was promoted to brigadier general (USV) in 1861. He participated in the Tennessee campaign and was badly wounded at New Hope Church. He rose to the rank of major general in the regular service. Later he taught military science at the universities of Missouri and Minnesota and became active in Democratic politics. His writings included manuals for the Sharps rifle and the Colt revolver and a memoir of Gen. George H. Thomas (1881). Boatner, *Civil War Dictionary*, 438-439.

JOHNSTON, ALBERT SIDNEY (1803-1862), of Kentucky, graduated from West Point in 1826. He served in the Black Hawk War but resigned from the service because of his wife's poor health. He enlisted in the Texas army in 1836 and became secretary of war for the Republic of Texas. After rejoining the United States army for service in the Mexican War, he commanded the Department of Texas (1856) and led the Utah expedition (1858-1860). In 1861 the Federal government offered him a commission as second in command to Scott, but he accepted a generalship in the Confederate army instead. At Shiloh he was hit in the leg and bled to death before the gravity of the wound was recognized. Leaders both North and South evidently agreed in 1861 that Johnston was the ablest soldier on the continent. Boatner, *Civil War Dictionary*, 440.

JOHNSTON, JOSEPH EGGLESTON (1807-1891), of Virginia, graduated from West Point in 1829. He served on the Black Hawk expedition and in the Seminole War, where he was aide-de-camp to Scott. During the Mexican War he was wounded five times and led the storming column at Chapultepec. During the 1850s he served on the frontier and in the Kansas border disturbances as well as on the Utah expedition. In 1861 he joined Confederate forces as a brigadier general and was in command at the first Bull Run. Fourth in seniority behind Cooper, A. S. Johnston, and Lee after being made general of the Department of the Potomac, he became embroiled in a feud with Davis and demanded a higher status. Twice wounded at Seven Pines, he was relieved of command by Lee in 1862. He was placed in command of the Department of the West and subsequently took command of the Army of Tennessee during the Atlanta campaign in which he maneuvered skillfully before Sherman's overwhelming strength. He led the same unit in the Carolinas campaign and surrendered to Sherman in April, 1865, outside of Durham, North Carolina. After the war he was a Virginia congressman (1879-1881) and wrote a number of books and articles about the war. Boatner, *Civil War Dictionary*, 441; *Concise Dictionary of American Biography*, 506.

JONES, JOHN MARSHALL (1821-1864), of Virginia, graduated from West Point in 1841, served on the frontier, taught tactics at the military academy, and went on the Utah expedition. He became a brigadier general in the Confederate army in 1863, having seen action at Winchester, the Seven Days' battles, and second Bull Run. He fought at Gettysburg before being killed at the Wilderness in 1864 leading the Stonewall Brigade. Boatner, *Civil War Dictionary*, 442.

JONES, WILLIAM EDMONSON (1824-1864) was a native Virginian and graduate of West Point (1848). He commanded the Seventh Virginia Cavalry, 1861-1862, and was promoted to brigadier general in the latter year. He fought with Stuart in the Gettysburg campaign and was killed on June 5, 1864, at Piedmont, Virginia. Boatner, *Civil War Dictionary*, 444.

KAUTZ, AUGUST VALENTINE (1828-1895), a native of Germany, graduated from West Point in 1852. At the outbreak of the war he served in Ohio and Kentucky and later commanded a cavalry unit in Virginia and North Carolina. He rose to the rank of major general in the regular army and was a member of the military commission trying Lincoln's assassins. He retired from the service in 1892. Boatner, *Civil War Dictionary*, 449.

KEARNY, PHILIP (1814-1862), a native New Yorker, entered the army in 1837 after graduating from Columbia and studying law. He observed the French cavalry in the Algerian war of 1840, distinguished himself in the Mexican War, and lost his left arm in the capture of Mexico City. He resigned in 1851 and fought for the French in Italy. Appointed brigadier general (USV) in 1861, he performed brilliantly at

Williamsburg, Seven Pines, and second Bull Run before being killed when he accidentally rode into the enemy's lines at Chantilly on September 1, 1862. He had just recently been promoted to major general (USV). Kearny, New Jersey, is named after him. Boatner, *Civil War Dictionary*, 449.

KEIFER, JOSEPH WARREN (1836-1932), of Ohio, graduated from Antioch College and practiced law before the Civil War. Rising from major to colonel of the 110th Ohio by 1862, he fought in the various Virginia campaigns and was brevetted brigadier general (USV) in 1864 and then major general (USV) in 1865. After the war he was active in the Grand Army of the Republic and served four terms in Congress (1877-1885), including speaker of the house for the Forty-seventh Congress. Boatner, *Civil War Dictionary*, 450; *Biographical Directory of Congress*, 1148.

KEMPER, JAMES LAWSON (1823-1895), of Virginia, attended Washington College and the Virginia Military Institute before practicing law and fighting in the Mexican War. Active in the Virginia legislature, including a stint as speaker of the house, he commanded the Seventh Virginia from the first Bull Run to Williamsburg. Appointed brigadier general in the Confederate army in 1862, he served in Virginia and North Carolina before going to Gettysburg, where he was seriously wounded and captured. He saw no further field service but was promoted to major general in 1864. He was Democratic governor of Virginia, 1874-1877. Boatner, *Civil War Dictionary*, 452; *Concise Dictionary of American Biography*, 520.

KERSHAW, JOSEPH BREVARD (1822-1894), son of a prominent South Carolina family, was a lawyer, legislator, and veteran of the Mexican War. He attended the state secession convention in 1860 and was commissioned colonel of the Second South Carolina in 1861. Named brigadier general in the Confederate army in 1862, he fought at second Bull Run, Chancellorsville, and Gettysburg. He became a major general in 1864 and saw action at the Wilderness, Spotsylvania, and Cold Harbor. Captured by Federal forces, he spent several months in a Boston prison before returning to South Carolina as a legislator and jurist. Boatner, *Civil War Dictionary*, 457.

KEYES, ERASMUS DARWIN (1810-1895), of Massachusetts, graduated from West Point in 1832. He was twice Scott's aide-de-camp and taught cavalry and artillery at West Point. Appointed brigadier general (USV) in 1861, he fought at the first battle of Bull Run, in the Peninsular campaign, and in the diversionary maneuvers around Richmond during the Gettysburg campaign. He rose to the rank of major general but became embroiled in a dispute with Gen. John A. Dix and resigned in 1864. Boatner, *Civil War Dictionary*, 458.

KILPATRICK, HUGH JUDSON (1836-1881), of New Jersey, graduated from West Point in 1861 and was commissioned captain of the Fifth New York. Wounded at Big Bethel, he was promoted to lieutenant colonel of the Second New York Cavalry; he served in the defense of Washington and participated in numerous raids and skirmishes. After promotion to brigadier general (USV) in 1863, he fought at Gettysburg and then was transferred to the western theater. Severely wounded in the Atlanta campaign, he commanded Sherman's cavalry in the march to the sea. He attained the rank of major general in the regular service before his resignation in 1865. Active in Republican politics, he was minister to Chile in the 1860s and again in 1881. A controversial man noted for his "notorious immoralities and . . . dare-devil recklessness," he earned the sobriquet "Kill Cavalry." Boatner, *Civil War Dictionary*, 459-460.

KING, JOHN HASKELL (1818-1888), of Michigan, entered the army in 1837 and saw action in the Mexican War. Major of the Fifteenth United States Infantry, he led his unit at Shiloh, Corinth, and Murfreesboro, where he was wounded. Promoted to brigadier general (USV) in 1862, he fought at Chickamauga and in the Atlanta campaign. For his war service he reached the rank of major general in the regular army. He retired from the service in 1882. Boatner, *Civil War Dictionary*, 463.

KING, RUFUS (1814-1876), of New York, was attorney general of that state under William Seward, 1839-1843. When the war broke out, he organized the "Iron Brigade" in Wisconsin and was appointed brigadier general (USV). He served mostly in Virginia and opposed Jackson at Groveton. After serving on the commission that tried Fitz-John Porter, he resigned because of ill health in 1863. Appointed minister to the Vatican, he helped apprehend John H. Surratt, who had fled to Italy following Lincoln's assassination. Boatner, *Civil War Dictionary*, 463.

KIRKLAND, WILLIAM W. (1833-1915) was commissioned colonel of the Eleventh North Carolina and fought at the first Bull Run. After service at Winchester (where he was wounded) and Gettysburg, he was promoted to brigadier general in 1863. He later saw action in the Wilderness campaign and at Fort Fisher, Wise's Fork, and Bentonville; he surrendered at Greensboro. Boatner, *Civil War Dictionary*, 465; Hamilton and Williams, *Graham Papers*, VI, 49n.

KNIPE, JOSEPH FARMER (1823-1901), of Pennsylvania, enlisted in the Mexican War and later became a prominent merchant. He was commissioned colonel of the Forty-sixth Pennsylvania in 1861 and was promoted to brigadier general (USV) in 1862. He suffered wounds in the Atlanta campaign and at Winchester and Cedar Mountain. After being mustered out in 1865, he became superintendent of the federal penitentiary at Fort Leavenworth, Kansas. Boatner, *Civil War Dictionary*, 466.

LAWTON, ALEXANDER ROBERT (1818-1896), of South Carolina, graduated from West Point in 1839 but resigned to attend Harvard Law School, from which he graduated in 1842. He practiced law in Savannah and was a leading proponent of secession in the Georgia legislature. Before Georgia seceded, he seized Fort Pulaski on the orders of the governor. Appointed brigadier general, he commanded the Georgia coast before fighting at second Bull Run and Antietam, where he was badly wounded. Despite his protests, he was appointed quartermaster general in 1864 and performed well in a difficult job. After the war he was active in Democratic politics, president of the American Bar Association (1882), and minister to Austria (1887-1889). Boatner, *Civil War Dictionary*, 473.

LEE, FITZHUGH (1835-1903), nephew of Robert E. Lee and James M. Mason, barely escaped dismissal from West Point while his uncle was superintendent, but he managed to graduate in 1856. Severely wounded in Indian fighting, he was a tactical officer at the military academy when he resigned to join the Confederate army. He served with J. E. Johnston and Jeb Stuart before being promoted to brigadier general in 1862. He fought at Antietam, Chancellorsville, and Gettysburg and was promoted to major general in August, 1863. Seriously wounded at Winchester in 1864 after having three horses shot from under him, he did not return to action until January, 1865. He surrendered two days after Appomattox. He was elected Democratic governor of Virginia (1885-1889) and was consul general to Havanna (1896-1898) when he entered the army as major general (USV) for the Spanish-American War. He wrote *General Lee* in 1894. Boatner, *Civil War Dictionary*, 475.

LEE, ROBERT EDWARD (1807-1870), of Virginia, graduated second in his class at West Point (1829). He emerged from the Mexican War with a brilliant reputation and served as superintendent of West Point, 1852-1855. When John Brown raided Harpers Ferry, Lee was sent to quell the insurrection. Lincoln offered Lee command of the Federal armies in April, 1861, but the Virginian instead chose to join the Confederacy. Military adviser to Davis until June, 1862, he succeeded J. E. Johnston as commander of the force that then became known as the Army of Northern Virginia. An aggressive and pugnacious general, Lee thwarted Federal attempts to capture Richmond for three years and undertook two invasions of the North. His military prowess emanated from an ability to gauge his enemy's strength and disposition, calculate its movements, and maintain the initiative. Despite inferior numbers and resources Lee executed his audacious plans with a skill that ranks him among the greatest generals in military history. Already a legend in his own time, he accepted the presidency of Washington College after the war. The college's name was later changed to Washington and Lee. Boatner, *Civil War Dictionary*, 476-477.

LEE, STEPHEN DILL (1833-1908), of South Carolina, graduated from West Point in 1854. After service on the frontier, he joined the Confederate army as aide-de-camp to Beauregard during the attack on Fort Sumter. He saw action at the second Bull Run and Antietam before being appointed brigadier general in 1862. He was captured at Vicksburg, exchanged, and eventually promoted to lieutenant general. After the war he was a planter, legislator, and president of Mississippi Agricultural and Mechanical College, 1880-1899. He was no kin to the Lees of Virginia. Boatner, *Civil War Dictionary*, 477.

LEE, WILLIAM HENRY FITZHUGH (1837-1891) was R. E. Lee's second eldest son. A graduate of Harvard where he was a classmate of Henry Adams and Theodore Lyman, he joined the regular army and went on the Utah expedition. A cavalry officer for the Confederate army, he served with Stuart before being appointed brigadier general in 1862. He was severely wounded at Brandy Station and then captured by Federal troops while convalescing. Held until March, 1864, he returned to Confederate service and was promoted to major general. After the war he was a Democratic congressman from Virginia, 1887-1891. Boatner, *Civil War Dictionary*, 477-478; *Concise Dictionary of American Biography*, 558.

LEVENTHORPE, COLLETT (1815-1889) was born in England and served in the British army before settling in North Carolina. Commissioned colonel of the Thirty-fourth North Carolina in 1861, he later commanded the District of Wilmington. He was captured at Gettysburg and held for nine months. On his release he was promoted to brigadier general of North Carolina state troops; he led them at Petersburg, and defended the Weldon Railroad before surrendering with Johnston. Boatner, *Civil War Dictionary*, 481.

LONGSTREET, JAMES (1821-1904), of South Carolina, was a graduate of West Point (1842) who served in the Mexican War and on the frontier before joining the Confederacy as a brigadier general in 1861. He rose to the rank of lieutenant general after fighting well at Antietam; his earlier blunders had caused failures at Fair Oaks and Seven Pines as well as at second Bull Run. After performing with distinction at Fredericksburg, he was made commander of the Department of North Carolina and Southern Virginia, but he showed little aptitude for independent command. He partially disagreed with Lee's plans for the Gettysburg campaign, and his misunderstanding of them contributed to the Confederacy's defeat there, though Lee never blamed Longstreet for it. After serving in the western theater, he returned to Lee for the Wilderness campaign and was seriously wounded in 1864. After the war he joined the Republican party, which, coupled with the growing realization that Gettysburg had been the turning point of the war, led to his social ostracism. Increasingly he had to depend on political appointments for a living. Boatner, *Civil War Dictionary*, 490-491.

LORING, WILLIAM WING (1818-1886), a native North Carolinian, fought in the Seminole War as a boy before graduating from Georgetown College. He became a lawyer and legislator but entered the Mexican War where he lost his arm at Chapultepec. Joining the regular army, he served in the far West before accepting a brigadier generalship in the Confederate army in 1861. Promoted to major general in 1862, he fought in the Vicksburg campaign and later surrendered with Johnston's army in North Carolina. In 1869 he entered the service of the Khedive of Egypt, commanded the defenses of Alexandria and the Egyptian coast, and was made a pasha before returning to America in 1879. Boatner, *Civil War Dictionary*, 492.

LOVELL, MANSFIELD (1822-1884), of Maryland, graduated from West Point in 1842 and served in the Mexican War before resigning in 1849. A municipal officer in New York City, he was appointed major general of the Confederate army in 1861. He fought at New Orleans and in Mississippi before being relieved of his command under mounting political pressure. Given no further command assignments, he was a volunteer staff officer for J. E. Johnston in 1864. Boatner, *Civil War Dictionary*, 494.

LUBBOCK, FRANCIS RICHARD (1815-1905), of South Carolina, moved to New Orleans and then Texas by 1836 where he was lieutenant governor from 1857 to 1859. Governor of Texas, 1861-1863, he declined renomination and entered the Confederate army as a lieutenant colonel. Appointed to Davis's staff, he was captured with the Confederate president in 1865. After the war he was state treasurer of Texas from

1878 to 1891. Boatner, *Civil War Dictionary*, 495-496; *Concise Dictionary of American Biography*, 592.

LYON, NATHANIEL (1818-1861), of Connecticut, graduated from West Point in 1841 and saw duty in the Mexican War and on the frontier, including "Bleeding Kansas." A strong advocate of Lincoln and the Republican party, he safeguarded Union property and interests by holding the St. Louis Arsenal at the outbreak of the war. Soon thereafter appointed brigadier general of the Missouri volunteers, he died at Wilson's Creek, thereby becoming the North's first military hero. Boatner, *Civil War Dictionary*, 497-498.

McARTHUR, JOHN (1826-1906), a native of Scotland, was a blacksmith who immigrated to Chicago in 1849 and became a partner in the Excelsior Iron Works. A colonel with the Twelfth Illinois, he was promoted to brigadier general (USV) in 1862 and major general (USV) in 1864. He fought at Fort Donelson and Shiloh as well as Vicksburg. His attack against Hood's left wing at Nashville in December, 1864, turned the battle into a Confederate rout. Boatner, *Civil War Dictionary*, 522; *Concise Dictionary of American Biography*, 599.

McCALL, GEORGE ARCHIBALD (1802-1868), of Pennsylvania, graduated from West Point in 1822. He served in the Seminole and Mexican wars before resigning in 1853. Appointed brigadier general (USV) in 1861, he resigned in 1863. In the summer of 1862 he was captured at New Market Cross Roads and sent to Libby Prison. Boatner, *Civil War Dictionary*, 522-523.

McCLELLAN, GEORGE BRINTON (1826-1885), of Pennsylvania, graduated from West Point second in his class (1846). He earned a distinguished military reputation for his part in the Mexican War and for a report he wrote on military methods in Europe, but he resigned in 1857 to become vice-president of the Illinois Central Railroad. When the war began, he served as major general of the Ohio volunteers but was soon made major general in the regular service. Given command of the armies around Washington, he later succeeded Scott as commander in chief of the Federal forces. He proved a brilliant organizer and administrator in training the Union army, but his lack of initiative and aggressiveness on the battlefield finally prompted Lincoln to relieve him when he failed to pursue Lee after Antietam. McClellan was the Democratic candidate for president in 1864. After the war he was elected governor of New Jersey, 1878-1881. Boatner, *Civil War Dictionary*, 524.

McCLERNAND, JOHN ALEXANDER (1812-1900), of Kentucky, was a lawyer who fought in the Black Hawk War and served in the Illinois legislature and Congress (1843-1851; 1859-1861). He resigned his seat to accept a brigadier generalship (USV). Tactless and independent-minded, he hated abolitionists, disliked West Pointers, and criticized Grant in letters to Lincoln and Halleck. Grant, displeased with his attitude and fighting ability at Vicksburg, ordered him to Illinois. Ill health forced McClernand to resign his commission in 1864. Boatner, *Civil War Dictionary*, 525; *Concise Dictionary of American Biography*, 603.

McCOOK, ALEXANDER McDOWELL (1831-1903), of Ohio, graduated from West Point in 1852, taught at the military academy, and served on the frontier. Commissioned brigadier general (USV) in 1861, he fought at the first Bull Run, Shiloh, and Chickamauga, where he was blamed for the Union fiasco but was later exonerated by a court of inquiry. After the war he served as aide-de-camp to Sherman and retired from the regular service with the rank of major general in 1894. Boatner, *Civil War Dictionary*, 526-527.

McCOOK, ROBERT LATIMER (1827-1862), of Ohio, began the war as colonel of the Ninth Ohio. Promoted to brigadier general (USV) in 1862, he fought in West Virginia and Kentucky. At the battle of Mill Springs, Kentucky, he was wounded in the leg and forced to direct his command from an ambulance. Confederate guerrillas overturned his car and killed him in cold blood near Decherd, Tennessee. In reprisal his regiment ransacked a number of homes in the area and hanged several of the culprits. Boatner, *Civil War Dictionary*, 528-529.

McCOWN, JOHN PORTER (1815-1879), of Tennessee, graduated from West Point in 1840 and served in the Mexican War and on the Utah expedition. Appointed brigadier general in the Confederate army in 1861, he was named major general the following year and given command of the Army of the West. He subsequently served under Kirby Smith. Boatner, *Civil War Dictionary*, 529.

McCULLOCH, BEN (1811-1862), of Tennessee, followed his neighbor Davy Crockett to Texas where he distinguished himself at San Jacinto. He fought with the Texas Rangers in the Mexican War and later joined the gold rush to California before returning to Texas. A brigadier general in the Confederate army, he was killed at Pea Ridge by sharpshooters. Boatner, *Civil War Dictionary*, 530.

McDOWELL, IRVIN (1818-1885), of Ohio, attended college in France before graduating from West Point in 1838. After service in the Mexican War and staff duty, he was appointed brigadier general in the regular army in 1861 and given command of Union troops south of the Potomac. He was defeated at the first battle of Bull Run and succeeded by McClellan. His failure at the second Bull Run led to a court of inquiry which exonerated him, but he was never afterwards employed in the field. He retired from the regular army as a major general in 1882. Boatner, *Civil War Dictionary*, 531; *Concise Dictionary of American Biography*, 610.

McGOWAN, SAMUEL (1819-1897), of South Carolina, graduated from South Carolina College, practiced law, and served in the state legislature. He was a major general in the South Carolina militia and fought in the Mexican War. After participating in the bombardment of Fort Sumter, he served at the first Bull Run. Commissioned colonel of the Fourteenth South Carolina in 1862, he saw action in the Peninsular campaign, second Bull Run, and Antietam. Suffering four wounds during the war, he was appointed brigadier general in the Confederate army in 1863 and led his brigade at the Wilderness and Spotsylvania. After the war he was a legislator and associate justice of the South Carolina Supreme Court. Boatner, *Civil War Dictionary*, 533.

McLAWS, LAFAYETTE (1821-1897), of Georgia, graduated from West Point in 1842 and served in the Mexican War and on the Utah expedition. Appointed brigadier general in the Confederate army in 1861, he fought at Yorktown before being promoted to major general in 1862. He saw action at Antietam, Fredericksburg, Chancellorsville, and Gettysburg. A disagreement with Longstreet resulted in his vindication by Davis. After the Carolinas campaign he surrendered with Johnston's army. Boatner, *Civil War Dictionary*, 536.

McPHERSON, JAMES BIRDSEYE (1828-1864), of Ohio, graduated first in his class at West Point (1853) and taught engineering there. When the war erupted, he became Halleck's aide-de-camp in the Department of Missouri and then Grant's chief engineer at Forts Henry and Donelson and at Shiloh. Rising to major general (USV), he continued to serve with Grant in the Vicksburg campaign before assuming command of the Army of the Tennessee. He was killed at Atlanta. Boatner, *Civil War Dictionary*, 538.

MAFFITT, JOHN NEWLAND (1819-1886) was born at sea and entered the navy as a midshipman in 1832. He joined the Confederate navy in 1861 and the following year took a cargo of cotton to England. Given command of the *Florida*, he ran the blockade at Mobile Bay and ultimately captured about fifty-five Federal and merchant ships during the war. He retired to Wilmington, North Carolina. Boatner, *Civil War Dictionary*, 500; *Concise Dictionary of American Biography*, 630.

MAGRUDER, JOHN BANKHEAD (1810-1871), of Virginia, graduated from West Point in 1830 and served in the Seminole and Mexican wars. He was nicknamed "Prince John" because of his courtly manner and reputation for lavish entertainment. He won immediate notoriety with his victory at Big Bethel in 1861. Appointed major general in the Confederate army that same year, he proved capable but cautious in several battles. He captured Galveston in 1863 and opposed Banks's Red River campaign. At the end of the war he refused a parole and became a major general under Maximilian in Mexico. Boatner, *Civil War Dictionary*, 501.

MAHONE, WILLIAM (1826-1895), of Virginia, graduated from the Virginia Military Institute in 1847. Originally quartermaster general for Virginia after secession, he was appointed brigadier general in the Confederate army in November, 1861. Wounded at second Bull Run, he fought at Gettysburg and the Wilderness before being named major general in 1864 by Lee for his performance at the Petersburg Crater. At the end of the war his division constituted the best shock troops in the army. After the war he became president of a railroad, headed the Republican party in Virginia, and led the Readjuster movement that temporarily overturned Bourbon Democratic rule. Advocating the reduction of Virginia's debt, protection of Negro rights, and social and economic legislation, the Readjusters helped elect Mahone to the United States Senate, 1881-1887. Boatner, *Civil War Dictionary*, 502; *Who Was Who in America*, 400.

MALLORY, STEPHEN RUSSELL (1813-1873) was born in Trinidad but grew up in Florida. He studied law, became a judge, and fought in the Seminole War. A

Democratic senator from Florida (1851-1861), he resigned to become secretary of the navy for the Confederacy. Boatner, *Civil War Dictionary*, 503-504; *Who Was Who in America*, 400-401.

MANIGAULT, ARTHUR MIDDLETON (1824-1886), of South Carolina, was a rice planter and veteran of the Mexican War. He served on Beauregard's staff early in the Civil War before being promoted to brigadier general in the Confederate army in 1863. He led his brigade at Chickamauga, Chattanooga, and in the Atlanta campaign. He received a serious wound at Nashville. Boatner, *Civil War Dictionary*, 507.

MARMADUKE, JOHN SAPPINGTON (1833-1887), of Missouri, attended Yale and Harvard before graduating from West Point in 1857. He went on the Utah expedition and chose to join the Confederacy when secession came, though his father, a former governor of Missouri, was a Unionist. As colonel of the Third Missouri, he fought at Shiloh and was appointed brigadier general in November, 1862. He served mainly in Missouri throughout the war and rose to the rank of major general before being captured. He was elected Democratic governor of Missouri, 1884-1887. Boatner, *Civil War Dictionary*, 513; *Who Was Who in America*, 403.

MARTIN, JAMES GREEN (1819-1878) was born in Elizabeth City, North Carolina, and graduated from West Point in 1840. He lost his right arm in the Mexican War, served on the frontier, and was named adjutant general of North Carolina troops in 1861. Soon appointed major general of the militia, he prepared all state troops for service in the Confederate forces and supervised the defense of the state. Appointed brigadier general in the Confederate army in 1862, he commanded the district of North Carolina, distinguished himself at Howlett's House in Virginia, and surrendered at Waynesville in 1865. Boatner, *Civil War Dictionary*, 514; *Concise Dictionary of American Biography*, 646-647.

MAURY, DABNEY HERNDON (1822-1900), of Virginia, graduated from West Point in 1846 after having graduated from the University of Virginia. After fighting in the Mexican War, he taught at the military academy for five years. Joining Confederate forces in 1861, he served in the Trans-Mississippi Department and was promoted to brigadier general in 1862. Placed in command of the Department of the Gulf in 1863, he held that post for the remainder of the war. After the war he organized the Southern Historical Society and wrote a number of histories. He was minister to Colombia, 1885-1889. Boatner, *Civil War Dictionary*, 519-520; *Concise Dictionary of American Biography*, 655.

MEADE, GEORGE GORDON (1815-1872) was born in Spain of American parents. He graduated from West Point in 1835 and served in the Mexican War. Beginning the Civil War as a brigadier general of volunteers, he rose steadily in rank and assumed command of the Army of the Potomac—a post he held until the end of the war—just two days before Gettysburg. His failure to pursue Lee after that battle marked him as an ordinary general. Moreover, his cantankerous disposition made him very unpopular with his subordinates. Said Grant in his memoirs: "General Meade was an officer of great merit, with drawbacks to his usefulness that were beyond his control." After the war he commanded the Reconstruction military district that comprised Alabama, Georgia, and Florida. Boatner, *Civil War Dictionary*, 539-540.

MEREDITH, SULLIVAN AMORY (1816-1874), of Pennsylvania, supervised the drilling, equipping, and forwarding of 30,000 Pennsylvania troops at the beginning of the war. He later organized the Fifty-sixth Pennsylvania and joined McDowell's forces at the second Bull Run, where he was severely wounded. He became commissioner for the exchange of prisoners and served under Rosecrans in St. Louis, 1864-1865. Boatner, *Civil War Dictionary*, 543.

MILROY, ROBERT HUSTON (1816-1890), of Indiana, graduated from Norwich University, fought in the Mexican War, and took a law degree at Indiana University in 1850. Appointed brigadier general (USV) in 1861, he rose to major general (USV) the next year, served in Virginia, and commanded the defenses of the Nashville and Chattanooga Railroad. So vigorous was his suppression of guerrillas in West Virginia that the Confederates put a price on his head. Boatner, *Civil War Dictionary*, 552; *Who Was Who in America*, 429.

MITCHEL, ORMSBY McKNIGHT (1810-1862), of Kentucky, graduated from West Point in 1829, taught mathematics there, and resigned in 1832 to teach at Cincinnati College. He also practiced law and wrote several books on astronomy. Named brigadier general (USV) in 1861, he commanded the Department of the Ohio and assumed command of the Department of the South in 1862 after his promotion to major general (USV). He died of yellow fever at Beaufort. Boatner, *Civil War Dictionary*, 557.

MORGAN, JOHN HUNT (1825-1864), of Alabama, fought in the Mexican War and entered business in Lexington, Kentucky. Commissioned captain in 1861 and given a squadron of cavalry for scouting, he engineered the famous Morgan raids. After seeing action at Shiloh, he was promoted to brigadier general in the Confederate army and was captured near New Lisbon, Ohio, in 1863. He subsequently escaped from the Ohio State Penitentiary and commanded the Department of Southwest Virginia. He was killed by Federal troops at Greeneville, Tennessee, in 1864. Boatner, *Civil War Dictionary*, 566.

MOSBY, JOHN SINGLETON (1833-1916), of Virginia, was a lawyer who rose to prominence during the war as the leader of partisan rangers. Attaining the rank of colonel, he operated in Virginia and Maryland and once seized $168,000 in Federal greenbacks which he divided among his men for uniforms and equipment. During the last winter of the war his rangers controlled much of eastern Virginia, an area which became known as "Mosby's Confederacy." After the war he became a Republican and supporter of Grant's presidency. He was United States consul at Hong Kong, 1878-1885, and assistant attorney for the Department of Justice, 1904-1910. Boatner, *Civil War Dictionary*, 571-572; *Concise Dictionary of American Biography*, 708.

MOTT, GERSHOM (1822-1884), of New Jersey, fought in the Mexican War before being commissioned lieutenant colonel of the Fifth New Jersey in 1861. Wounded at second Bull Run, he was appointed brigadier general (USV) in 1862 and fought at Chancellorsville, where he was again wounded. He later fought at the Wilderness, Petersburg, and Richmond, and attained the rank of major general (USV). Boatner, *Civil War Dictionary*, 572.

MOUTON, ALFRED (1829-1864), of Louisiana, graduated from West Point in 1850. He was brigadier general of the Louisiana militia (1850-1861) before being commissioned colonel of the Eighteenth Louisiana. Wounded severely at Shiloh, he was promoted to brigadier general in the Confederate army in 1862 but died two years later at Mansfield. Boatner, *Civil War Dictionary*, 572-573.

MULLIGAN, JAMES ADELBERT (1830-1864) was colonel of the Twenty-third Illinois, the so-called "Irish Brigade" which he raised. Promoted to brigadier general (USV) in 1864, he was wounded at Winchester. As his men were removing him from the battlefield, he observed that the colors were about to be captured and ordered his men to leave him and save the flag. As a result, he was captured; he died of his wounds three days later. Boatner, *Civil War Dictionary*, 574.

OSTERHAUS, PETER JOSEPH (1823-1917) was born in Prussia and graduated from military school in Berlin. He immigrated to America in 1848 and settled in Missouri as a merchant. During the war he served in Missouri and Tennessee, participated in the Vicksburg campaign, and rose to the rank of major general (USV). From 1866 to 1877 he was United States consul to France and later saw diplomatic service in Mannheim, Germany, 1898-1900. Boatner, *Civil War Dictionary*, 613.

PAGE, RICHARD LUCIAN (1807-1901), of Virginia, was a nephew of Robert E. Lee. He served in the navy until the Civil War. Named aide-de-camp to Virginia's Governor Letcher, he supervised fortifications at the mouth of the James River before being appointed commander in the Confederate navy. Later he commanded the depot at Charlotte, North Carolina, for two years and was listed as a brigadier general in the Confederate army in 1864. In that capacity he organized the outer defenses at Mobile Bay and was captured at Fort Morgan in August, 1864. Boatner, *Civil War Dictionary*, 615.

PATTERSON, ROBERT (1792-1881) was born in Ireland. He served in the War of 1812 and the Mexican War. A successful grocery merchant in Philadelphia, he invested in the Louisiana sugar industry and owned thirty cotton mills in Pennsylvania. Named major general (USV) in 1861 and given command of the Pennsylvania troops, he failed to prevent J. E. Johnston from reinforcing Beauregard at Bull Run and under heavy criticism was mustered out in July, 1861. Boatner, *Civil War Dictionary*, 623; *Concise Dictionary of American Biography*, 771-772.

PAXTON, ELISHA FRANKLIN (1828-1863), of Virginia, attended Washington College and Yale before graduating at the head of his law class at the University of Virginia. He fought at the first Bull Run before joining Jackson as adjutant general and chief of staff. Promoted to brigadier general in 1862, he died at Chancellorsville. Boatner, *Civil War Dictionary*, 624.

PEGRAM, JOHN (1832-1865), of Virginia, graduated from West Point in 1854, taught at the military academy, and served in the Utah expedition. Commissioned lieutenant colonel in the Confederate army, he surrendered to McClellan during the West Virginia campaign of 1861. Appointed brigadier general in 1862, he served under Kirby Smith and then with the Army of Northern Virginia. He was wounded at the Wilderness. He was killed in February, 1865, in the battles around Petersburg. Boatner, *Civil War Dictionary*, 629-630.

PEMBERTON, JOHN CLIFFORD (1814-1881), of Pennsylvania Quaker stock, nonetheless graduated from West Point in 1837. He served in the Seminole and Mexican wars and on the Utah expedition before being commissioned lieutenant colonel in the Confederate army in 1861; he had refused a colonelcy in the Federal army. He rose to the rank of major general by 1862 and commanded the Department of Mississippi, Tennessee, and East Louisiana during the Vicksburg campaign. His defeat by Grant led to suspicions of treason, but his mediocre generalship, not disloyalty, accounted for Vicksburg's fall. After being exchanged, he resigned in May, 1864, and served the remainder of the war as colonel and inspector of artillery. Boatner, *Civil War Dictionary*, 631.

PENDER, WILLIAM DORSEY (1834-1863), a native North Carolinian, graduated from West Point in 1854. Joining the Confederate forces in 1861, he was elected colonel of the Third North Carolina, later transferring to the Sixth North Carolina. Promoted to brigadier general in 1862, he commanded a North Carolina brigade at the Seven Days' battles and fought under Jackson at second Bull Run. He was wounded three times at Chancellorsville but did not leave the field. Promoted to major general he was severely wounded on the second day of the battle of Gettysburg and died shortly thereafter. Boatner, *Civil War Dictionary*, 631.

PETTIGREW, JAMES JOHNSTON (1828-1863), of North Carolina, graduated from the University of North Carolina at Chapel Hill and worked at the Naval Observatory. He studied Roman law in Germany and became a strong opponent of the resumption of the slave trade. After seeing action at Fort Sumter, he enlisted in Hampton's Legion, became colonel of the Twelfth North Carolina and then brigadier general in the Confederate army in 1862. He was wounded, bayoneted, and captured at Seven Pines. Later exchanged, he fought at Gettysburg and led his division in Pickett's charge. Though wounded in the hand there, he took part in a rearguard action that resulted in a fatal wound at Falling Waters two weeks after Gettysburg. Boatner, *Civil War Dictionary*, 649.

PICKETT, GEORGE EDWARD (1825-1875), of Virginia, graduated from West Point in 1846 at the bottom of his class. After service in the Mexican War and Indian fighting on the frontier, he entered Confederate forces in 1861 and rose to brigadier general the following year. He was severely wounded in the shoulder at Gaines's Mill and promoted to major general. He formed the troops at Gettysburg for one of the most famous charges in military history, though he did not lead it. Sent to recuperate after that shattering battle, he commanded the Department of Virginia and North Carolina. His attack on New Bern in 1864 was poorly planned and poorly executed. He later took part in the Petersburg and Appomattox campaigns. Boatner, *Civil War Dictionary*, 651-652.

PILLOW, GIDEON JOHNSON (1806-1878), of Tennessee, graduated from the University of Nashville, practiced law, and was a partner of James K. Polk and a considerable power in the Democratic party. He fought in the Mexican War and sustained two wounds. Becoming a Douglas Democrat, he favored a moderate course of conciliation rather than secession but was appointed major general of the Tennessee state troops when war came. Later appointed brigadier general in the Confederate army, he was second in command at Fort Donelson, which he abandoned shortly before its surrender to Grant. Reprimanded and suspended, he never held another important command. Boatner, *Civil War Dictionary*, 653-654.

PLEASANTON, ALFRED (1824-1897), born in Washington, D.C., graduated from West Point in 1844. After service in the Mexican War, in Indian fighting, and in the Kansas border disturbances, he transferred to the Second United States Cavalry in 1861. The following year he was commissioned brigadier general (USV) and fought at Antietam, Fredericksburg, and Chancellorsville. Appointed major general (USV) in 1863, he saw action at Gettysburg before commanding the Districts of Central Missouri and St. Louis. He retired from the regular service in 1868. Boatner, *Civil War Dictionary*, 655-656; *Concise Dictionary of American Biography*, 805.

POLK, LEONIDAS (1806-1864), of North Carolina, graduated from West Point in 1827 after having briefly attended the University of North Carolina at Chapel Hill. Kin to Pres. James K. Polk, he studied for the Episcopal ministry and was ordained a deacon in 1830. First missionary bishop of the southwest in 1838 and then bishop of Louisiana in 1841, he helped establish the University of the South in 1860. His friend and classmate Jefferson Davis prevailed upon him to accept a commission as major general in 1861, and Polk defeated Grant at Belmont, Missouri. Commanding the Confederate right at Shiloh, he personally led four charges. In 1862 he was promoted to lieutenant general. Bragg tried to court-martial him after Chickamauga for failing to attack when ordered, but Davis reinstated him. Polk was killed at Pine Mountain during the Atlanta campaign. Boatner, *Civil War Dictionary*, 657-658.

POPE, JOHN (1822-1892), of Kentucky, graduated from West Point in 1842 and saw service in the Mexican War. Appointed brigadier general (USV) in 1861, he commanded forces in Missouri and Mississippi before being promoted to major general (USV) and being made head of the Army of Virginia by Lincoln. He earned Lee's personal animosity by prescribing harsh treatment of southern sympathizers in occupied areas of Virginia. Soundly defeated by Lee and Jackson at second Bull Run, he was relieved of command by McClellan. He retired from the regular army in 1886 as a major general. Boatner, *Civil War Dictionary*, 658-659.

PORTER, DAVID DIXON (1813-1891), of Pennsylvania, sailed with his father, Commo. David Porter, as a youth and joined the United States Navy in 1829. In 1861 he was named commander and with Farragut captured New Orleans. In cooperation with Sherman he captured Arkansas Post in 1863 and was present at the surrender of Vicksburg. After participation in the Red River campaign, he fought at Fort Fisher, for which he received his fourth "thanks of Congress" of the war. Promoted to vice-admiral in 1866, he was superintendent of the Naval Academy. In 1870 he was promoted to admiral of the navy. Boatner, *Civil War Dictionary*, 661.

PORTER, FITZ-JOHN (1822-1901), of New Hampshire, graduated from West Point in 1845, became artillery and cavalry instructor there, and took part in the Utah expedition. Appointed brigadier general (USV) in 1861, he directed the Yorktown siege and later became major general (USV) in 1862. At the second battle of Bull Run Pope relieved him for "disobedience, disloyalty, and misconduct in the face of the enemy." Forced out of the service in 1863, Porter spent the following decades trying to clear his name. The Schofield Board in 1887, after a year's investigation, concluded that he had been given an impossible order "based on conditions which were essentially erroneous and upon expectations which could not possibly be realized." Scholars, however, still disagree on Porter's actions at second Bull Run. Boatner, *Civil War Dictionary*, 661-663.

POSEY, CARNOT (1813-1863), of Mississippi, was a captain in Jeff Davis's Mississippi Rifles in Mexico, where he was wounded at Buena Vista. As colonel of the Sixteenth Mississippi, he saw action at Bull Run, Balls Bluff, the Seven Days' battles, and Antietam. Commissioned brigadier general in the Confederate army in November, 1862, he led his own brigade at Fredericksburg, Chancellorsville, and Gettysburg. Severely wounded in the left thigh at Bristoe Station, he died in November, 1863. Boatner, *Civil War Dictionary*, 663.

PRICE, STERLING (1809-1867), of Virginia, was a legislator, lawyer, and Missouri farmer as well as congressman (1845-1846) before serving as a brigadier general in the Mexican War and governor of Missouri (1853-1857). Disgusted by the aggressive policies of Unionists at St. Louis, he recruited 5,000 men who, along with the state guard which he commanded, fought at Wilson's Creek and Lexington, Kentucky. Officially joining the Confederacy in 1862, he was named major general and led an unsuccessful raid into Missouri in 1864. He escaped to Texas and then Mexico where his personal plans collapsed with the government of Maximilian. Boatner, *Civil War Dictionary*, 669; *Who Was Who in America*, 495-496.

PRINCE, HENRY (1811-1892), of Maine, graduated from West Point in 1835 and served in the Seminole War, Mexican War, and on the Utah expedition. As brigadier general (USV), he was captured at Cedar Mountain in 1862. After commanding Federal troops in North Carolina, he later fought in Virginia and Tennessee. He retired from the regular army in 1879. Boatner, *Civil War Dictionary*, 671.

PRYOR, ROGER ATKINSON (1828-1919), of Virginia, graduated from Hampden-Sydney College in 1845 as valedictorian and studied law at the University of Virginia.

A Virginia congressman, 1859-1861, he resigned his seat, joined the Confederate army, and urged the bombardment of Fort Sumter but declined the opportunity to fire the first shot. After serving in the Confederate Congress, he was commissioned brigadier general in 1862 and led his brigade at Williamsburg and Seven Pines. In 1863 he resigned since he had no brigade to command and enlisted in Fitzhugh Lee's cavalry. Captured at Petersburg in 1864, he was exchanged shortly before Appomattox by Lincoln's personal order. After the war he went to New York and became a prominent newspaper writer and lawyer. Regarded at one time as the "most effective secessionist speaker in Virginia," he was appointed associate justice of the New York Supreme Court, 1896-1899. Boatner, *Civil War Dictionary*, 674; *Concise Dictionary of American Biography*, 828.

QUANTRILL, WILLIAM CLARKE (1837-1865), of Ohio, spent several years on the frontier as a gambler and petty thief before becoming entangled in the border disturbances between Kansas and Missouri. After fighting at Wilson's Creek, he undertook guerrilla operations in Missouri and four days after his capture of Independence was commissioned captain in the Confederate army. In 1862 he went to Richmond and received a commission as colonel though he had hoped for more. Rejoining his men in early 1863, he burned and plundered Lawrence, Kansas, where some 150 men and boys were killed. Late in the war he raided Kentucky, where he was fatally wounded near Taylorsville by Federal troops. Boatner, *Civil War Dictionary*, 675; *Concise Dictionary of American Biography*, 833.

QUARLES, WILLIAM A. (?-1893) was commissioned colonel of the Forty-second Tennessee in 1861 and served under A. S. Johnston. After surrendering at Fort Donelson, he consolidated a brigade at Port Hudson, joined J. E. Johnston, and rose to brigadier general in 1863. He was seriously wounded and captured at Franklin, Tennessee, in 1864. Boatner, *Civil War Dictionary*, 675.

RAINS, JAMES EDWARD (1833-1862), of Tennessee, graduated from Yale, practiced law, and accepted a commission as colonel of the Eleventh Tennessee in 1861. He was killed at Stones River on December 31, 1862, after having been promoted to brigadier general in the Confederate army the month before. He had served mostly in eastern Tennessee. Boatner, *Civil War Dictionary*, 677.

RAMSEUR, STEPHEN DODSON (1837-1864) was born in Lincolnton, North Carolina, and graduated from West Point in 1860. Commissioned captain of a North Carolina battery, he served at Yorktown. As colonel of the Twenty-ninth North Carolina, he led the unit at the Seven Days' battles and Malvern Hill, where he was seriously wounded. Appointed brigadier general in the Confederate army in 1862, he commanded a brigade at Chancellorsville, Gettysburg, the Wilderness, and Spotsylvania. He was named major general in 1864 before suffering a mortal wound at Cedar Creek and dying at Sheridan's headquarters in Winchester. Boatner, *Civil War Dictionary*, 677; *Concise Dictionary of American Biography*, 839.

RANSOM, MATTHEW WHITAKER (1826-1904), a native of Warren County, North Carolina, graduated from the University of North Carolina at Chapel Hill, practiced law, and served in the state legislature. Originally opposed to secession, he joined the First North Carolina as a private when Lincoln called for troops. He saw action at Seven Pines and Malvern Hill, and as colonel of the Thirty-fifth North Carolina led his unit at Antietam. Appointed brigadier general in the Confederate army in 1863, he fought at Drewry's Bluff, Fort Stedman, Five Forks, and Appomattox. A Whig before the war, he became a Democratic senator from North Carolina, 1872-1895, during which time he was a leader in the Compromise of 1877 after the disputed presidential election and a prime mover behind the defeat of the Lodge "Force Bill" in 1890. Turned out of office by Republican-Populist fusionists, he became minister to Mexico, 1895-1897. Boatner, *Civil War Dictionary*, 679; *Concise Dictionary of American Biography*, 843.

RANSOM, ROBERT, JR. (1828-1892), a native of Warren County, North Carolina, was the younger brother of Gen. Matt Ransom and a graduate of West Point (1850). After service on the frontier in Indian fighting and in the Kansas border disturbances, he joined Confederate forces in 1861 and was appointed colonel of the First North Carolina. He rose to the rank of major general and commanded the post of Richmond until 1863 when he became ill. Bad health curtailed his activities thereafter, though he served in eastern Tennessee and Virginia. He surrendered at Warrenton in May, 1865. Boatner, *Civil War Dictionary*, 679.

RENO, JESSE LEE (1823-1862), of Virginia, graduated from West Point in 1846, fought in the Mexican War, and taught at the military academy. He served as chief ordnance officer on the Utah expedition. Named brigadier general (USV) in 1861, he took part in Burnside's North Carolina expedition and rose to the rank of major general (USV) before the second battle of Bull Run. He was killed at South Mountain. Reno, Nevada, is named for him. Boatner, *Civil War Dictionary*, 691.

REYNOLDS, JOHN FULTON (1820-1863), of Pennsylvania, graduated from West Point in 1841. After service in the Mexican War, Indian fighting, and the Utah expedition, he was commandant of cadets at West Point when the war began. Named brigadier general (USV) in 1861, he took part in the defense of Washington, became military governor of Fredericksburg, and was captured at Glendale. Promoted to major general (USV) in late 1862, he was killed by a sharpshooter at Gettysburg. Boatner, *Civil War Dictionary*, 694.

RICHARDSON, ROBERT V. is believed to have been appointed to a generalship in the Confederate army in December, 1863, but his nomination was returned to Davis by the Senate in February, 1864. Boatner, *Civil War Dictionary*, 697.

RICKETTS, JAMES BREWERTON (1817-1887), of New York, graduated from West Point in 1839. He served in the Seminole and Mexican wars and was commanding a battery at the first Bull Run when wounded and captured. Promoted to brigadier general, he fought at the second Bull Run and Cedar Mountain as well as Antietam, where he was wounded. He received six wounds during the war and rose to the rank of major general (USV). After the war he continued in the regular service as a brigadier general until his retirement in 1867. Boatner, *Civil War Dictionary*, 699-700.

ROBERTSON, BEVERLY HOLCOMBE (1826-1910), of Virginia, graduated from West Point in 1849. He served in cavalry operations in Virginia, 1861-1862, before being appointed brigadier general in the Confederate army in June, 1862. After Cedar Mountain and the second Bull Run, he was sent to North Carolina. Returning to Virginia in 1863, he fought under Jeb Stuart at Gettysburg and was named commander of the Second District of South Carolina under Beauregard. He was relieved of his command "owing to mutinous remarks to his brigade," and he later surrendered with Johnston in 1865. Boatner, *Civil War Dictionary*, 702.

RODES, ROBERT EMMETT (1829-1864), of Virginia, graduated from the Virginia Military Institute and taught there before the war. Named colonel of the Fifth Alabama, he fought at the first battle of Bull Run and was appointed brigadier general that same year (1861). He was severely wounded at Fair Oaks and again in the Antietam campaign. Promoted to major general in 1863, he led his division at Gettysburg, the Wilderness, and Spotsylvania. He was killed at Winchester in September, 1864. Boatner, *Civil War Dictionary*, 706-707.

RODGERS, JOHN (1812-1882), of Maryland, was appointed midshipman in 1828 and served on the expedition exploring and surveying the North Pacific, 1852-1856. His Civil War service began with the purchase of three small steamships at Cincinnati which became the nucleus of the Mississippi flotilla. He became captain of the monitor *Weehawken* and distinguished himself in the attack on Fort Sumter in 1863 and later against the Confederate ironclad *Atlanta*. *Concise Dictionary of American Biography*, 878-879.

ROSECRANS, WILLIAM STARKE (1819-1898), of Ohio, graduated from West Point in 1842. Before the war he supervised construction in New England and taught at the military academy before resigning in 1854 to enter business. In 1861 he was appointed brigadier general (USV) and commanded the Army of Occupation in West Virginia. In 1862 he was promoted to major general (USV) and led the Army of the Cumberland until his defeat at Chickamauga. He later commanded the Department of Missouri and received the thanks of Congress for the battle of Stones River. Resigning from the army in 1867, he was appointed minister to Mexico, 1868-1869, and elected to Congress from California, 1881-1885. Boatner, *Civil War Dictionary*, 708; *Who Was Who in America*, 525-526.

ROSSER, THOMAS LAFAYETTE (1836-1910), of Virginia, resigned from West Point in 1861 and fought at the first Bull Run. As colonel of the Fifth Virginia Cavalry, he led his regiment at second Bull Run, Chancellorsville, and Gettysburg before being appointed brigadier general in 1863. At Buckland Mills he defeated his former friend and classmate, George A. Custer, and the two became bitter rivals, clashing again in the Shenandoah Valley and in the retreat from Petersburg to Appomattox. At the latter battle Rosser led his command on a raid through Union lines and was not captured until May 2, 1865. After the war he became involved in railroading and was chief engineer in the Indian territory where Custer was stationed; they again became good friends. Boatner, *Civil War Dictionary*, 709-710.

SCALES, ALFRED MOORE (1827-1892), born in Reidsville, North Carolina, studied at Caldwell Institute and the University of North Carolina at Chapel Hill before practicing law. An ambitious Democratic politician before the war, he served in the state legislature and was elected to Congress, 1857-1859. When the war came, he joined the North Carolina volunteers and was elected colonel of the Thirteenth Regiment. He took part in the battle at Yorktown and was promoted to brigadier general in 1862. He suffered wounds at Chancellorsville and Gettysburg. After the war he again served in the state legislature and was elected to Congress, 1875-1884. He was elected governor of North Carolina in 1884. *Who Was Who in America*, 537; Beth G. Crabtree, *North Carolina Governors, 1585-1974: Brief Sketches* (Raleigh: Department of Cultural Resources, 1974), 104-105.

SCAMMON, ELIAKIM PARKER (1816-1894), of Maine, graduated from West Point in 1837 and remained there to teach mathematics. During the Mexican War he was aide-de-camp to Scott but was dismissed in 1856 for "disobedience of orders." Becoming president of Cincinnati College as well as a professor, he was commissioned colonel of the Twenty-third Ohio in 1862. He saw service in West Virginia and was promoted to brigadier general (USV) before being captured and sent to Libby Prison. He was recaptured during the siege of Charleston. After the war he was United States consul on Prince Edward Island and a mathematics professor at Seton Hall College. Boatner, *Civil War Dictionary*, 724-725.

SCHOFIELD, JOHN McALLISTER (1831-1906), of New York, graduated from West Point in 1853 and taught there and at Washington University in St. Louis until the outbreak of the war. Appointed brigadier general (USV) in 1861, he saw service in Missouri and Tennessee and rose to the rank of major general (USV) before taking part in the Carolinas campaign. He commanded the Department of North Carolina in 1865 and received the Medal of Honor in 1892. He was a secret envoy to France, 1865-1866, and served as secretary of war during Johnson's impeachment (1868). He became superintendent of West Point, 1876-1881, and was commanding general of the army, 1888-1895, before retiring as a lieutenant general. Boatner, *Civil War Dictionary*, 726-727; *Concise Dictionary of American Biography*, 920.

SCOTT, THOMAS M. (? -1864), was commissioned colonel of the Twelfth Louisiana at the beginning of the war and fought at Port Hudson and the siege of Vicksburg. During the Atlanta campaign he was commissioned brigadier general in the Confederate army and distinguished himself at Peach Tree Creek. He was mortally wounded at Franklin, Tennessee, 1864. Boatner, *Civil War Dictionary*, 728.

SCOTT, WINFIELD (1786-1866), of Virginia, had been general in chief of the army for twenty years when the Civil War began. A War of 1812 and Mexican War veteran, he was the Whig candidate for president against Franklin Pierce in 1852. He pleaded with President Buchanan to reinforce Federal forts and armories in the South in 1860 and personally commanded Lincoln's bodyguard at the inauguration.

Too old and sick for active duty, he was succeeded by McClellan in November, 1861. Nicknamed "Fuss and Feathers," he was the only non-West Pointer of southern origin in the regular army to remain loyal to the Union, according to Boatner. Boatner, *Civil War Dictionary*, 728-729; *Concise Dictionary of American Biography*, 926-927.

SEDGWICK, JOHN (1813-1864), of Connecticut, graduated from West Point in 1837, fought in the Seminole and Mexican wars, and served on the frontier in the Kansas border disturbances and Utah expedition. Promoted to brigadier general (USV) in 1861, he participated in the defense of Washington and the Peninsular campaign, suffering wounds at Glendale and Antietam. Later he was named major general (USV) and saw action at Chancellorsville and Gettysburg before being killed by a sharpshooter. Reputedly he was one of the best-loved higher officers of the entire army, and statues to him stand at Gettysburg and West Point. Boatner, *Civil War Dictionary*, 730-731.

SEYMOUR, TRUMAN (1824-1891), of Vermont, graduated from West Point in 1846, fought in the Mexican War, and taught at the military academy. He was at the bombardment of Fort Sumter before being promoted to brigadier general (USV) in 1862. He saw extensive service in Virginia and South Carolina during the war and attained the rank of major general in the regular service before retiring in 1876. Boatner, *Civil War Dictionary*, 733-734.

SHALER, ALEXANDER (1827-1911), of Connecticut, was commissioned lieutenant colonel of the Sixty-fifth New York in 1861 and was promoted to brigadier general (USV) in 1863. He commanded the military prison on Johnson's Island, Ohio, 1863-1864, and was later captured and placed under the guns during the bombardment of Charleston. Brevetted major general (USV) in 1865, he received the Medal of Honor in 1893. He wrote *Manual for Light Infantry Using the Rifle Musket* (1861). Boatner, *Civil War Dictionary*, 734; *Encyclopedia Americana*, XXIV, 654.

SHAW, HENRY MARCHMORE (1819-1864), of Rhode Island, graduated from the medical school at the University of Pennsylvania in 1838 and practiced medicine. Moving to Camden County, North Carolina, he was elected Democratic congressman, 1853-1855, and 1857-1859. A colonel in the Confederate forces, he was killed near New Bern in 1864. *Who Was Who in America*, 549.

SHAW, ROBERT GOULD (1837-1863), of Massachusetts, studied at Harvard and entered business in New York City. As lieutenant in the Second Massachusetts, he was captured in 1862. After his release he was named colonel of the Fifth Massachusetts, the first Negro unit from the free states. He was killed and buried with his men in an assault on Fort Wagner at Charleston, South Carolina. *Who Was Who in America*, 549.

SHERIDAN, PHILIP (1831-1888), of New York, graduated from West Point in 1853. After an undistinguished early military career that included discipline problems and court-martial charges, he assumed command of the Second Michigan Cavalry in 1862. He quickly distinguished himself at battles in Kentucky and Tennessee and won two stars. In 1864 he undertook his brilliant Shenandoah Valley campaign that destroyed Early's army at the decisive battles of Winchester, Fishers Hill, and Cedar Creek. He climaxed his Civil War career by blocking Lee's withdrawal beyond Appomattox. During Reconstruction he was military governor of Texas and Louisiana, but his regime was so harsh that he was recalled. Rising to the rank of full general, he succeeded Sherman as commander in chief of the army in 1884. Boatner, *Civil War Dictionary*, 747-748.

SHERMAN, THOMAS WEST (1813-1879), of Rhode Island, graduated from West Point in 1836 and fought in the Mexican War. Commissioned brigadier general (USV) in 1861, he commanded the Port Royal expedition. He lost his right leg at Port Hudson and continued in the regular service until 1870 when he retired as a major general. An officer of high ability, he was not particularly suited to handling volunteers unused to military discipline. Boatner, *Civil War Dictionary*, 750.

SHERMAN, WILLIAM TECUMSEH (1820-1891), of Ohio, graduated from West Point in 1840 and was stationed in California during the Mexican War. After a career in banking, law, and as head of what is now Louisiana State University, he volunteered for the Federal army at the outbreak of the war. Appointed brigadier general (USV) in 1861, he feuded with the administration over strategic policies and with the press, which called him insane. Wounded at Shiloh, Sherman seemed to thrive under Grant and convinced his superior not to resign despite ill treatment by Halleck. After the Vicksburg and Chattanooga campaigns, Sherman assumed direction of the main military operations in the West. The Atlanta campaign, march to the sea, and Carolinas campaign demonstrated his superior military talent, and he is considered by some historians the best Union commander of the war. Promoted to lieutenant general in 1866 and full general in 1869, he succeeded Grant as commander in chief of the army, a post he held for fourteen years. Boatner, *Civil War Dictionary*, 750-751.

SICKLES, DANIEL EDGAR (1825-1914), of New York, was a Democratic senator (1857-1861) who gained notoriety in 1859 for pleading temporary insanity for the first time in legal history after slaying Philip Barton Key, son of Francis Scott Key and his wife's paramour. Named brigadier general (USV) in 1862 after the Senate had rejected an earlier nomination, he fought in numerous battles in Virginia and lost his leg at Gettysburg. After the war he was made military governor of the Carolinas, but his vigorous execution of Reconstruction policies forced Johnson to relieve him in 1867. Two years later he retired from the regular service with the rank of major general. He was minister to Spain, 1869-1873, and chairman of the New York State Monuments Commission, 1886-1912, before being relieved for mishandling of funds. His interest and political know-how contributed in large measure to the preservation of Gettysburg battlefield as a national park. Boatner, *Civil War Dictionary*, 760.

SIGEL, FRANZ (1824-1902), a native of Germany, graduated from the German Military Academy in 1847 but was forced to flee the country after the 1848 revolutions. He taught school in New York City before becoming head of the schools at St. Louis. When the war began, he rallied the Germans to the Union cause. Appointed brigadier general (USV) in 1861, he rose to major general (USV) the following year and fought in Missouri and Virginia. Though considered an inept general, his mobilization of German support proved important. "I fights mit Sigel" became the Germans' slogan. Boatner, *Civil War Dictionary*, 761.

SILL, JOSHUA WOODROW (1831-1862), of Ohio, graduated from West Point in 1853 and taught there before resigning in 1861 to join the faculty of a Brooklyn college. Commissioned colonel of the Thirty-third Ohio in 1861, he fought in the West Virginia campaign and was killed at Stones River in 1862. His classmate Sheridan named Fort Sill, Oklahoma, after him in 1869. Boatner, *Civil War Dictionary*, 762.

SLOCUM, HENRY WARNER (1827-1894), of New York, graduated from West Point in 1852 but resigned from the army in 1856 to practice law. After being severely wounded at the first Bull Run, he was named brigadier general (USV) and then major general and fought at Antietam, Fredericksburg, Chancellorsville, and Gettysburg. Later he served in Tennessee, commanded the post at Vicksburg, and took over the Army of Georgia for the march to the sea. He saw action at Averasboro, Bentonville, Goldsboro, Raleigh, and was present at Johnston's surrender. After the war he was a Democratic congressman from New York, 1869-1873, and 1883-1885. Boatner, *Civil War Dictionary*, 765; *Concise Dictionary of American Biography*, 965.

SMITH, EDMUND KIRBY (1824-1893), of Florida, graduated from West Point in 1845, served in the Mexican War, and taught mathematics at the military academy. Appointed brigadier general in the Confederate army in 1861, he was severely wounded at the first Bull Run. After service in Tennessee and Kentucky he rose to lieutenant general in 1862 and was later sent to the Trans-Mississippi Department. When Vicksburg fell, he was cut off from Richmond and essentially had an independent command. Promoted to the rank of full general in 1864, he thwarted Banks's Red River campaign. His was the last Confederate force to surrender—June 2, 1865, at Galveston. After the war he was president of the University of Nashville, 1870-1875, and taught at the University of the South for eighteen years. Boatner, *Civil War Dictionary*, 769-771.

SMITH, GUSTAVUS WOODSON (1822-1896), of Kentucky, graduated from West Point in 1842, taught engineering there, and supervised harbor construction in New England; he also fought in the Mexican War. After a misunderstanding with Federal authorities over alleged disloyalty, he offered his services to the Confederacy in September, 1861, and was appointed major general. Illness and a feud with Davis forced Lee to relieve him of his command in 1862. He resigned from the Confederate army the following year when six general officers were promoted over his head to become lieutenant generals. In the last stages of the war he was major general of the Georgia militia, and he opposed Sherman's march to the sea before surrendering at Macon in

April, 1865. Among his writings were *Confederate War Papers* (1884) and *Battle of Seven Pines* (1891). Boatner, *Civil War Dictionary*, 771-772.

SMITH, WILLIAM FARRAR (1824-1903), of Vermont, graduated from West Point in 1845. As colonel of the Third Vermont, he fought at the first Bull Run and was commissioned brigadier general (USV). He saw extensive action in Virginia and Maryland and in a letter to Lincoln sharply criticized the Federal army's leadership at Fredericksburg. Lincoln, who agreed, had to head off an attempt by Congress to relieve Smith of his command. Transferred to the West in 1863, he performed with distinction in the Chattanooga campaign and was promoted to major general (USV). He later fought at Cold Harbor and Petersburg before retiring from the regular service in 1867. Considered several times for command of an army, he too often obscured his great military ability with contentiousness and the propensity for criticizing the plans of other generals. Boatner, *Civil War Dictionary*, 775-776.

SORREL, GILBERT MOXLEY (1838-1901), of Georgia, was Longstreet's volunteer aide-de-camp at first Bull Run before being named acting adjutant general. He continued to serve with Longstreet through Antietam and fought at Gettysburg and Chickamauga. He led four brigades in a successful envelopment of the Federal left flank at the Wilderness and was commissioned brigadier general in late 1864. Commanding a brigade of Georgia troops, he suffered a severe chest wound at Hatcher's Run in February, 1865. His memoir, *Recollections of a Confederate Staff Officer*, is considered among the best of that genre. Boatner, *Civil War Dictionary*, 778.

SPEAR, SAMUEL PERKINS (1815-1875), of Massachusetts, served as an enlisted man in the Seminole and Mexican wars. Appointed lieutenant colonel of the Eleventh Pennsylvania in 1861, he was brevetted brigadier general (USV) for great personal bravery at Darbytown near Richmond. He later commanded brigades in Virginia and North Carolina and was wounded at Five Forks. Boatner, *Civil War Dictionary*, 781.

STAFFORD, LEROY (? -1864), of Louisiana, accompanied Richard Taylor to Virginia as lieutenant colonel of the Ninth Louisiana and succeeded him as colonel. He fought at second Bull Run, Antietam, Chancellorsville, and Gettysburg before his promotion to brigadier general in October, 1863. He was fatally wounded at the Wilderness. Boatner, *Civil War Dictionary*, 790.

STARKE, WILLIAM E. (? -1862) served under Floyd at Lewisburg as colonel of the Sixtieth Virginia. He was sent to Goldsboro, North Carolina, before fighting in the Seven Days' battles. Appointed brigadier general in 1862, he fought at the second Bull Run and was killed at Antietam. Boatner, *Civil War Dictionary*, 792-793.

STEELE, FREDERICK (1819-1868), of New York, graduated from West Point in 1843 and fought in the Mexican War. Rising to brigadier general (USV) by 1862, he commanded the District of Southeast Missouri and spent most of the war fighting west of the Mississippi. He participated in the Vicksburg, Arkansas, and Mobile campaigns and attained the rank of major general in the regular service. Boatner, *Civil War Dictionary*, 794-795.

STONE, CHARLES POMEROY (1824-1887), of Massachusetts, graduated from West Point in 1845 and fought in the Mexican War. Named brigadier general (USV) in 1861, he led the force that captured Alexandria. However, after the Federal fiasco at Balls Bluff, he was arrested and imprisoned for 189 days. Though no charges were ever brought against him, he was suspected of treason in connection with the battle. Finally released, he was kept under surveillance, though Banks, Hooker, and Grant all recommended him for responsible posts. In 1864, no longer able to bear the suspicions about him, he resigned. After the war he became chief of staff for the Khedive of Egypt. Boatner, *Civil War Dictionary*, 800.

STONEMAN, GEORGE (1822-1894), of New York, graduated from West Point in 1846, fought in the Mexican War, and served in the Southwest until the outbreak of the war. Appointed brigadier general (USV) in 1861, he was a cavalry commander and led numerous forays, notably at Chancellorsville and during the Atlanta campaign when his poor judgment led to his capture with 700 of his men. Released several months later, he raided southwestern Virginia and then North Carolina (1865) in support of Sherman's Carolinas campaign. He attained the rank of major general in the regular service. He was elected Democratic governor of California, 1883-1887. Boatner, *Civil War Dictionary*, 801.

STRAHL, OTHO FRENCH (? -1864), of Ohio, was a lawyer in Tennessee when the war broke out. Serving as captain and then lieutenant colonel of the Fourth Tennessee, he was promoted to brigadier general in the Confederate army in 1863 and led his brigade at Chickamauga, Chattanooga, and in the Atlanta campaign. He was killed at Franklin, Tennessee. Boatner, *Civil War Dictionary*, 811.

STREIGHT, ABEL D. (? -1892), of New York, was colonel of the Fifty-first Indiana before being brevetted brigadier general. He resigned in March, 1865. Boatner, *Civil War Dictionary*, 811.

STRINGHAM, SILAS HORTON (1798-1876), of New York, entered the navy as a midshipman in 1809 and fought in the War of 1812. Given command of the North Atlantic blockade at the beginning of the Civil War, he devised an innovative bombardment technique during the successful expedition at Hatteras Inlet. Because of his age, he was retired as commodore in December, 1861, but later served as commandant of the Boston Navy Yard until 1865. Boatner, *Civil War Dictionary*, 811.

STUART, JAMES EWELL BROWN (1833-1864), of Virginia, graduated from West Point in 1854 and served on the frontier (where he sustained a serious wound in Indian fighting) and in the Kansas border disturbances. He was Lee's volunteer aide-de-camp at Harpers Ferry in 1859. Appointed brigadier general in the Confederate army in 1861, he fought in the Peninsular campaign before being promoted to major general and given command of the cavalry of the Army of Northern Virginia in 1862. His cavalry raids and skirmishes have made him a legend though he exhibited poor judgment in his Gettysburg raid. He was mortally wounded at Yellow Tavern. Personal bravery, good humor, swagger, and flamboyance made him an ideal cavalry officer. Boatner, *Civil War Dictionary*, 812-813.

SUMNER, EDWIN VOSE (1797-1863), of Massachusetts, joined the army in 1819 and fought in the Black Hawk and Mexican wars and later served on the frontier. Appointed brigadier general (USV) in 1861, he fought in the Peninsular campaign, Antietam, and Fredericksburg. Promoted to major general (USV) in 1862, he died in New York on the way to a new command in Missouri. Boatner, *Civil War Dictionary*, 818.

TATTNALL, JOSIAH (1795-1871), of Georgia, was educated in England before joining the navy in 1812 as a midshipman. He fought in the war with Algiers and the Mexican War. Named captain in the Confederate navy in 1861, he took command of coastal defenses in Georgia and South Carolina. When the Confederates abandoned the Peninsula in 1862, he destroyed the *Merrimac* to prevent her capture. Censured for his action, he demanded a court-martial which ultimately acquitted him. During the remainder of the war he attacked the Union blockade and defended the Savannah River. Boatner, *Civil War Dictionary*, 826.

TAYLOR, RICHARD (1826-1879), of Kentucky, was the son of Zachary Taylor. He studied in Europe and at Harvard and Yale before becoming a Louisiana plantation owner. Originally a Whig like his father, he became a Democrat and voted for secession at the Louisiana convention. Appointed brigadier general in the Confederate army in 1861, he fought under Jackson in the Virginia campaigns before being promoted to major general and transferred to command the District of Western Louisiana. He stopped Banks's Red River campaign in 1864 and was advanced to lieutenant general despite a clash with Kirby Smith, his superior officer. He surrendered in Alabama in May, 1865. Because of his family background and personal friendships with Presidents Johnson and Grant, he was able to plead the South's case during Reconstruction. His memoir, *Destruction and Reconstruction* (1879), ranks among the best books of its kind. Boatner, *Civil War Dictionary*, 827-828.

TERRY, ALFRED HOWE (1827-1890), of Connecticut, attended Yale and practiced law until commissioned colonel of the Second Connecticut in 1861. He led the Seventh Connecticut in the Port Royal expedition and was named brigadier general (USV) in 1862. He held commands in Virginia and North Carolina and won the thanks of Congress for his service at Fort Fisher. After the war he remained in the regular service (retiring as a major general in 1888) and was Custer's superior officer during the Little Big Horn debacle. Boatner, *Civil War Dictionary*, 831.

THOMAS, GEORGE HENRY (1816-1870), of Virginia, graduated from West Point in 1840, fought in the Seminole and Mexican wars, taught at the military academy, and served as major in the Second United States Cavalry under A. S. Johnston and R. E. Lee before being given a leave of absence in 1860 for suffering a severe facial wound from an arrow. Named brigadier general (USV) in 1861, he fought in Kentucky and Tennessee, was promoted to brigadier general in the regular army in 1863, and took command of the Army of the Cumberland. He led the army at Lookout Mountain, Missionary Ridge, and in the Atlanta Campaign and was dubbed the "Rock of Chickamauga" for holding the left wing against tremendous odds. For his service at Nashville, he was advanced to major general in the regular service (1864). Boatner, *Civil War Dictionary*, 836.

THOMPSON, M. JEFF, a native Virginian, was mayor of St. Joseph, Missouri, in 1860. When the Civil War began, he became a Confederate partisan and raised a battalion known as Thompson's "Swamp Rats." When Frémont issued his emancipation proclamation in August, 1861, Thompson announced a counter-proclamation and launched a series of raids. Serving west of the Mississippi, he finally surrendered in May, 1865. Boatner, *Civil War Dictionary*, 837-838.

TILGHMAN, LLOYD (1816-1863), of Maryland, graduated from West Point in 1836, fought in the Mexican War, and worked with the Panamanian Railroad until the Civil War. Named brigadier general in the Confederate army in 1861, he was inspector at Forts Henry and Donelson and surrendered with the former. Subsequently released, he fought with the Army of the West and was killed in May, 1863, at Champion's Hill. Boatner, *Civil War Dictionary*, 839-840.

TORBERT, ALFRED THOMAS ARCHIMEDES (1833-1880), of Delaware, graduated from West Point in 1855 and participated in the Utah expedition. As colonel of the First New Jersey, he led his unit in the Peninsular campaign and fought at second Bull Run, South Mountain, and Antietam. After promotion to brigadier general (USV) in 1862, he fought at Gettysburg and in the various Virginia campaigns. He rose to major general in the regular service before resigning in 1866. After the war he held diplomatic posts in Central America (1869-1871), Havanna (1871-1873), and Paris (1873-1878). Boatner, *Civil War Dictionary*, 842.

VAN DORN, EARL (1820-1863), of Mississippi, graduated from West Point in 1842, fought in the Seminole and Mexican wars, and saw extensive duty in the Indian campaigns on the frontier. At the outbreak of the war he succeeded Davis as major general of Mississippi troops and quickly rose to major general in the Confederate army. In 1862 he assumed command of the Trans-Mississippi Department, fought at Pea Ridge, and then took command of the Army of the West. His loss to Rosecrans at Corinth led to his transfer to a cavalry command. He was killed in May, 1863, in a bizarre episode in which a private citizen—perhaps a personal enemy—shot him for allegedly violating the sanctity of his home. Boatner, *Civil War Dictionary*, 867.

VANCE, ZEBULON BAIRD (1830-1894) was born in Buncombe County, North Carolina, and attended the University of North Carolina at Chapel Hill. After studying law, he entered politics as a Whig, but when that party disintegrated he became a Know-Nothing. While in Congress, 1858-1861, he supported Union measures and opposed secession. However, when his state seceded he volunteered for the Confederate army and became colonel of the Twenty-sixth North Carolina. He fought in the Seven Days' battles and at New Bern. Elected governor in 1862, he frequently opposed the Davis administration in Richmond, especially on the question of conscription. He was reelected Democratic governor in 1876 and entered the United States Senate in 1879, where he served until his death. Vance remains one of the most popular figures in Tar

Heel history. Boatner, *Civil War Dictionary*, 866; *Concise Dictionary of American Biography*, 1101.

VIELE, EGBERT LUDOVICKUS (1825-1902), of New York, graduated from West Point in 1847 and fought in the Mexican War. He resigned to become a civil engineer and drafted plans for Central Park in New York, though they subsequently were not used. Commissioned brigadier general (USV) in 1861, he became military commander of Norfolk in 1862, superintended the draft in northern Ohio, and resigned in 1863. After the war he was commissioner of parks for New York City and a Democratic congressman, 1885-1887. Boatner, *Civil War Dictionary*, 877.

WADDELL, ALFRED MOORE (1834-1912) was born in Hillsborough, North Carolina, and graduated from the University of North Carolina at Chapel Hill. A lawyer before the war, he became colonel of the Third North Carolina Cavalry, 1862-1864. After the war he was a Democratic congressman, 1871-1879. During the 1898 white-supremacy campaign, he led the coup d'etat that overturned Republican control of municipal government in Wilmington and that resulted in his serving as mayor until 1905. *Who Was Who in America* (Chicago: A. N. Marquis Co., Fifth Printing, 1962), I, 1283.

WADSWORTH, JAMES SAMUEL (1807-1864), of New York, studied at Yale and Harvard and read law with Daniel Webster. A Free Soiler who became a Republican, he was a delegate to the Washington Peace Conference in 1861. Commissioned brigadier general (USV) in 1861, he became military governor of Washington the following year. An unsuccessful gubernatorial candidate in New York in the fall of 1862, he returned to the war and fought at Chancellorsville and Gettysburg. He was mortally wounded at the Wilderness. Boatner, *Civil War Dictionary*, 882-883.

WAINWRIGHT, JONATHAN MAYHEW (1821-1863), of New York, was appointed midshipman in the navy in 1837. At the outbreak of the Civil War he served with the Atlantic blockading squadron. Commanding the *Harriet Lane*, he played a decisive part in the taking of New Orleans and the lower Mississippi by Union forces. He was killed while defending his ship against boarders at Galveston. *Concise Dictionary of American Biography*, 1122-1123.

WALKER, HENRY HARRISON (1833-1912), of Virginia, graduated from West Point in 1853 and served as aide-de-camp to the Kansas governor during the border disturbances. Made colonel of the Fortieth Virginia, he was wounded during the Seven Days' battles and commanded the defenses of Richmond. Appointed brigadier general in the Confederate army in 1863, he fought at the Wilderness and Spotsylvania, where he was again wounded. He announced the surrender of the Army of Northern Virginia to Davis at Danville on April 13, 1865. Boatner, *Civil War Dictionary*, 884.

WALKER, WILLIAM HENRY TALBOT (1816-1864), of Georgia, graduated from West Point in 1837, fought in the Seminole and Mexican wars, and became commandant of cadets at West Point. Despite poor health, he was appointed brigadier general in the Confederate army in 1861 and fought in Florida and Virginia. He resigned his commission to accept an appointment as major general of Georgia troops and joined Governor Brown in the anti-Davis faction. Reappointed brigadier general in the Confederate forces in 1863, he performed so well that J. E. Johnston's praise to Davis resulted in Walker's promotion to major general. He was killed in the battle of Atlanta. Boatner, *Civil War Dictionary*, 886.

WALKER, WILLIAM S. (? -1899) fought in the Mexican War as a midshipman. Commissioned colonel in the Confederate army in 1862, he commanded the forces at the battle of Pocotaligo, South Carolina, and was promoted to brigadier general. In 1864 he commanded the post at Kinston, North Carolina. At Petersburg he accidentally rode into the Federal lines and was shot and captured. After his release, he was put in command at Weldon. Boatner, *Civil War Dictionary*, 886-887.

WALLACE, LEWIS (1827-1905), of Indiana, was a newspaper reporter, legislator, and veteran of the Mexican War before being named brigadier general (USV) in 1861. The following year he rose to major general (USV) and served at Fort Donelson. Disputes with Halleck led to the loss of his command twice, but he was restored both times by Lincoln and Grant respectively. He served on the court-martial of Lincoln's assassins and presided over the court-martial that convicted Henry Wirz, commandant of Andersonville Prison. After the war he became governor of New Mexico (1878-1881) and minister to Turkey (1881-1885). He is best remembered for his novel *Ben Hur*, written at the governor's residence in Santa Fe and published in 1880. Boatner, *Civil War Dictionary*, 887.

WARREN, GOUVERNEUR KEMBLE (1830-1882), of New York, graduated from West Point in 1850, second in his class. Before the war he taught mathematics at the military academy, surveyed the Mississippi delta, and participated in the Pacific Railroad expedition. Named colonel of the Fifth New York in 1861, he fought at Yorktown, Malvern Hill, second Bull Run, Antietam, and Fredericksburg. Appointed brigadier general (USV), he was named chief topographical engineer for the Army of the Potomac and was wounded at Gettysburg, where he distinguished himself. Fighting in Virginia in the last stages of the war, he was summarily relieved of command by Sheridan at Five Forks. Though later exonerated by a court of inquiry, he was professionally ruined. He remained a career officer. Boatner, *Civil War Dictionary*, 891.

WASHBURN, CADWALLADER COLDER (1818-1882), of Maine, was a teacher, lawyer, land speculator, and Republican congressman from Wisconsin (1855-1861; 1867-1871). He served as a delegate to the Washington Peace Conference in 1861 and rose to major general (USV) during the war. He saw action in the western theater. After the war he was elected governor of Wisconsin (1872-1873). Boatner, *Civil War Dictionary*, 892; *Concise Dictionary of American Biography*, 1147.

WAYNE, HENRY CONSTANTINE (1815-1883), of Georgia, graduated from West Point in 1838, taught there, and fought in the Mexican War. In 1855 he participated in the war department's camel experiment in Texas. He was appointed brigadier general in the Confederate army in 1861 but declined it in early 1862. Boatner, *Civil War Dictionary*, 897.

WEITZEL, GODFREY (1835-1884), of Ohio, graduated second in his class at West Point (1855). An engineer, he constructed harbor fortifications and was stationed at Fort Pickens, Florida, Cincinnati, and Washington, where he was chief engineer of defenses. Promoted to brigadier general (USV) in 1862, he served on expeditions to Port Hudson, LaFourche, and Sabine Pass. During the latter part of the war he was stationed in the Department of Virginia and North Carolina and attained the rank of major general in the regular service, in which he continued after the war. Boatner, *Civil War Dictionary*, 899-900.

WHARTON, JOHN A. (? -1865), of Texas, was a lawyer before the war. He joined B. F. Terry's Texas Ranger regiment and fought in Kentucky before being named colonel of the unit. He led it at Shiloh. Appointed brigadier general in the Confederate army in 1862, he fought at Stones River and Chickamauga and was promoted to major general in 1863. He commanded the cavalry in the Red River campaign of 1864. A private feud resulted in his death in April, 1865. Boatner, *Civil War Dictionary*, 909.

WHEELER, JOSEPH (1836-1906), of Georgia, graduated from West Point in 1859. Named colonel of the Nineteenth Alabama, he fought at Shiloh and was promoted to brigadier general in 1862 and major general in 1863. He fought during the Knoxville siege, the Atlanta campaign, and the march to the sea through the Carolinas. He surrendered in Atlanta after Johnston's surrender. Nicknamed "Fightin' Joe," he was known for his dogged aggressiveness. Lee ranked him with Jeb Stuart as one of his two best cavalry officers. After the war Wheeler became Democratic congressman from Alabama, 1881-1883, and 1885-1900, during which time he was the ranking Democrat on the ways and means committee and a sturdy advocate of reconciliation between the North and South. Boatner, *Civil War Dictionary*, 910; *Concise Dictionary of American Biography*, 1181.

WHIPPLE, AMIEL WEEKS (1816-1863), of Massachusetts, graduated from West Point in 1841 and served on the frontier before the war. After serving on McDowell's staff, he was named brigadier general (USV) in 1862 and commanded a brigade in the defense of Washington. He was mortally wounded at Chancellorsville. Boatner, *Civil War Dictionary*, 912.

WHITING, WILLIAM HENRY CHASE (1824-1865), of Mississippi, graduated from Georgetown (D.C.) College with the highest ranking attained up to that time. He then graduated from West Point first in his class (1841). Joining the Confederate army, he planned the defenses of Charleston harbor and served as J. E. Johnston's chief engineer for the Army of the Shenandoah. After being appointed brigadier general in August, 1861, he reinforced Jackson in June, 1862, and returned to the Peninsular campaign. He was military commander of Wilmington, 1862-1864, and then took command of Petersburg. Having been promoted to major general in 1863, he returned to North Carolina near the end of the war and was mortally wounded at Fort Fisher. Boatner, *Civil War Dictionary*, 916.

WILCOX, CADMUS MARCELLUS (1824-1890), a native of Wayne County, North Carolina, graduated from West Point in 1846 after attending the University of Nashville. He served in the Mexican War and was a groomsman at Grant's wedding in 1848. As colonel of the Ninth Alabama, he fought at first Bull Run. He rose to the rank of major general in the Confederate army and participated in such battles as Chancellorsville, Gettysburg, Spotsylvania, and Petersburg before surrendering at Appomattox. Considered one of the best subordinate officers of the South, he wrote *Rifles and Rifle Practice* (1859), the first American textbook on the subject. Boatner, *Civil War Dictionary*, 918-919; *Concise Dictionary of American Biography*, 1203.

WILD, EDWARD AUGUSTUS (1825-1891), of Massachusetts, studied medicine at Harvard and in Paris and became a medical officer in the Turkish army during the Crimean War. Wounded at Fair Oaks in 1862, he was mustered out, but he helped raise black troops and assumed command of them as brigadier general (USV) in 1863. He led an expedition of the Second African Brigade through eastern North Carolina, 1863-1864, and was arrested in June of the latter year for refusing to obey orders to replace his brigade quartermaster. The finding of his court-martial was set aside, and he later served in the Georgia Freedmen's Bureau. Boatner, *Civil War Dictionary*, 919.

WILKES, CHARLES (1798-1877), of New York, entered the navy as a midshipman in 1818 and had a distinguished career. In 1838 he commanded an expedition to Antarctica, where an area is named Wilkes Land. He became a Union hero when he arrested Mason and Slidell, Confederate commissioners on their way to England, in 1861 by removing them from a British mail steamer. The *Trent* Affair created tensions between the United States and England and generated English sympathy for the southern cause. Boatner, *Civil War Dictionary*, 847, 925.

WILLIAMS, JOHN STUART (1820-1898), of Kentucky, was a graduate of Miami University of Ohio, lawyer, and veteran of the Mexican War. Appointed brigadier general in the Confederate army in 1862, he operated in eastern Tennessee and opposed Burnside's advance to Knoxville. He later served in the Atlanta campaign and surrendered with Johnston. Boatner, *Civil War Dictionary*, 927.

WILLICH, AUGUST (1810-1878) was born in Germany, the son of a Napoleonic veteran. Given a military education, he was an officer in the Prussian army forced to flee after the 1848 revolutions. Settling in the United States, he worked as a carpenter in the Brooklyn Navy Yard. Joining the Ninth Ohio in 1861, he gained popular acclaim for routing Terry's Texas Rangers and was named brigadier general (USV) in 1862. He rose to major general (USV) and served in the Army of Ohio and Army of the Cumberland. During the Franco-Prussian War he offered his services to his homeland but was refused. Karl Marx described him as "a spiritual communist and Knight of a noble conviction." Boatner, *Civil War Dictionary*, 929-930.

WINDER, CHARLES SIDNEY (1829-1862), of Maryland, graduated from West Point in 1850. A veteran of Indian fighting on the frontier, he was present at the bombardment of Fort Sumter and commanded the South Carolina Arsenal. Commissioned brigadier general in the Confederate army in 1862, he commanded the Stonewall Brigade during the Shenandoah Valley campaign but was killed by artillery at Cedar Mountain. Both Jackson and Lee considered him an officer of great potential. Boatner, *Civil War Dictionary*, 940.

WINDER, JOHN HENRY (1800-1865), of Maryland, graduated from West Point in 1820 and fought in the Seminole and Mexican wars. Appointed brigadier general in the Confederate army in 1861, he commanded the Libby and Belle Isle prisons in Richmond. In May, 1864, he assumed a post at Goldsboro in the North Carolina and southern Virginia district before being placed in charge of Andersonville Prison with supervision of all prisoners in Alabama and Georgia. Toward the end of the war he had responsibility for all prisoners east of the Mississippi. He died of fatigue and strain in February, 1865. His alleged cruelty to prisoners when weighed against inadequate supplies of clothing, food, and medicine has long been the subject of controversy. Boatner, *Civil War Dictionary*, 940-941.

WINTHROP, THEODORE (1828-1861), of Connecticut, graduated from Yale in 1848 and traveled extensively in Europe, Central America, and the western plains. He enlisted in the Seventh New York at the war's outbreak and died leading the advance in a skirmish in June, 1861. A number of his books, all published posthumously, enjoyed great popularity, including *Cecil Dreeme* (1861) and *John Brent* (1862). *Concise Dictionary of American Biography*, 1236-1237.

WISE, HENRY ALEXANDER (1806-1876), of Virginia, was a graduate of Washington College in Pennsylvania; he also studied law under St. George Tucker. Elected to Congress as a Jacksonian Democrat, 1833-1844, he broke with Jackson on the bank issue and became a close friend and adviser to President Tyler, who appointed him minister to Brazil, 1844-1847. He returned to become a power in the Democratic party and serve as governor, 1856-1860. Appointed brigadier general in the Confederate army in 1861, he raised troops in western Virginia and fought at Roanoke Island. During the remainder of the war he was stationed at coastal defenses in South Carolina before serving in the battles around Richmond and Petersburg. Boatner, *Civil War Dictionary*, 944; *Concise Dictionary of American Biography*, 1237-1238.

WOOD, JOHN TAYLOR (1830-1904) was the grandson of Zachary Taylor and a graduate of the Naval Academy (1853). When the war broke out, he joined the Confederate navy and served aboard the *Virginia*. In 1863 he became naval aide to Davis and distinguished himself in a series of raids on Union ships in the Chesapeake. Commanding the steam sloop *Tallahassee* on a raiding expedition from Wilmington, North Carolina, to Halifax, Nova Scotia, in 1864, he captured or destroyed more than sixty vessels. Promoted to captain in 1865, he accompanied Davis on the retreat from Richmond, escaped to Cuba, and entered business in Canada. *Concise Dictionary of American Biography*, 1245.

WOOL, JOHN ELLIS (1789-1869), of New York, was a veteran of the War of 1812 and the Mexican War. When the Civil War broke out, he succeeded in keeping Fort Monroe from falling into Confederate hands. He occupied Norfolk and Portsmouth, Virginia, in 1862 and was promoted to major general in the regular service, making him the fourth ranking general in the Federal army. He retired in July, 1863. Boatner, *Civil War Dictionary*, 948.

WORDEN, JOHN LORIMER (1818-1897), of New York, entered the navy as a midshipman in 1835. Captured at the beginning of the war and released, he supervised John Ericsson's *Monitor*. Commanding the ironclad, he met the *Merrimac* in March, 1862. During the battle he was blinded by an explosion, and his second in command had to take over. Promoted to captain in 1863, he commanded the *Montauk* in the South Atlantic blockading squadron. He was superintendent of the Naval Academy, 1869-1874, and retired as a rear admiral in 1886. Boatner, *Civil War Dictionary*, 948-949; *Concise Dictionary of American Biography*, 1253.

WRIGHT, AMBROSE RANSOM (1826-1872) was a Georgia lawyer and Democrat who remained neutral until Lincoln's election, at which time he called for secession. He served as a state commissioner to Maryland in an attempt to persuade that state to secede. Named colonel of the Third Georgia, he went to Roanoke Island and then South Mills before being promoted to brigadier general in the Confederate army in 1862. He fought at second Bull Run, Antietam, Gettysburg, and the Wilderness and advanced to major general in 1864. Boatner, *Civil War Dictionary*, 949.

INDEX

A

Abolitionists: discussed, 273

Adams, John Quincy: denounced, 266

Adams, Wirt: 645

Adams, Zachariah T.: identified, 310n

Advance: capture of, 618; reference to, 519, 519n; runs blockade, 519; successes of, 618, 618n

Agnew, Richard: 353n

Agriculture: affected by floods, 190; cotton crop, 279, 287, 309; crops grown, 14, 19, 20, 42, 45, 46, 50, 54, 97, 140, 143, 144, 186, 215, 268, 368, 408, 461, 623, 627; mentioned, 19, 140, 143, 144, 546, 548; methods of, 19, 20, 23, 34n, 41, 45, 46, 49, 97, 127, 140, 143, 144, 215, 312, 314; periodicals concerning, discussed, 654; problems of, 34, 44, 45, 49, 50, 97, 127, 144, 190, 191, 232, 239-240, 307, 361, 368, 372, 373, 408, 427, 428, 429, 461, 621-622, 624

Aiken, S.C.: book about, 33n; cavalry fight there, 678; Edmondstons visit, 32; is home of Charles Edmondston, xv; kaolin deposits there, 30n; mentioned, 27n, 28n, 78, 90; news from, 267, 685; no news from, 264, 265; situation there gives anxiety, 665, 666; war preparations there, 29-30; wedding anniversary observed there, 23

Alabama: after war, 707; secedes, 36, 37; war in, 390, 538, 539, 548, 608, 620

Alabama, C.S.S.: destroys shipping, 530; mentioned, 357, 417, 422, 470, 470n, 479; sinks *Hatteras*, 351, 351n; sunk, 590; victories of, 283, 335-336, 347

Albemarle, C.S.S.: burns mail steamer, 618; Catherine Edmondston visits, 446; commanded by A. F. Warley, 628n; constructed, 125n, 392n-393n; described, 526; destruction of, 628, 628n, 629, 632, 646; disables *Sassacus*, 568n; entrenchments protect, 446; in action, 550, 551, 556, 559, 560, 568, 618, 618n; iron for removed, 485; James W. Cooke helps construct, 420n; launched, 474; new captain of, 578; pictured, 527, 629; spies scout, 439; threatened, 425, 436, 442; towed to Halifax, 482; troops guarding, 468n; troops removed from, 485

Albemarle and Chesapeake Canal: 618n

Albemarle Sound: gunboats in, 536; naval victory there, 91; vulnerability of, 115

Aldie, Va.: Confederate hospital there, 252

Alice, C.S.S.: captured, 177

Altoona Conference: discussed, 269, 269n

Amelia Springs: engagement at, 691n

Ames, Adelbert: 571

Amnesty: accepted, 720; Lincoln offers limited form of, 508-509. *See also* Oath

Anderson, Eliza Clinch: identified, 47n

Anderson, Fort: attacked, 649, 650; garrison escapes from, 672; mentioned, 700n

Anderson, George: Union officer apologizes, 293

Anderson, George Burgwin: killed at Wilderness, 558n

Anderson, Joseph Reid: sketch of, 741

Anderson, Richard Heron: mentioned, 183, 388, 447, 558, 705; sketch of, 741

Anderson, Robert: at Fort Sumter, 29, 37, 47, 48, 49, 78, 465; sketch of, 741

Anderson, Robert Walker: identified, 558n; killed, 558, 558n

Andersonville Prison: commander at, 726, 726n; reference to, 525n

Andrew, John Albion: advocates Negro regiments, 441, 441n; identified, 441n

Andrews, Alexander Boyd: commands Ninth N.C. Regiment, 210n; identified, 144n; sketch of, 741

Andrews, Garnett: 259n

Andrews, W. S. G.: at Hatteras, 90n

Anecdotes: related, 560, 564, 568, 571, 588, 596, 610, 664, 687

Animals: are found, 700; hopes of recovering, 696; taken for war use, 691

Anthony, Charity Barnes: 208n

Anthony, John Hill: identified, 208n; killed, 208

Anthony, Lucy T. (Mrs. John Hill): identified, 232n; loses cotton, 232

Anthony, Whitmel Hill: 208n

Antietam Campaign: casualties, 267, 268; described, 261-263; details of, 264-265; discussed, 257

Antwerp (Belgium): siege of, 428, 428n

Ariel: captured by *Alabama*, 335n

Arizona: victory there, 84

Arkansas: losses in, mentioned, 506; war in, 346, 397, 601

Arkansas, C.S.S.: at Vicksburg, 218: destroyed, 233n; rams Union ships, 218;

C

632; reports on Federal raiders, 446; requests relief from command, 578; sends gifts, 621; visits Edmondstons, 420, 435, 482, 493; visits Thomas P. Devereux, 423; warns of Federal raid, 442

Cooke, Mrs. James W.: 670

Cooke, John R.: identified, 609n; mentioned, 480, 481, 557, 557n, 558n; sketch of, 750; wounded, 320, 481

Cooke, Philip St. George: rumored killed, 318; sketch of, 750

Cooper, Samuel: identified, 495n; mentioned, 524, 531, 568, 634, 638; quoted, 495n; sketch of, 751

Corinth, Miss.: battle of, 163; evacuated, 195; mentioned, 256, 274, 275; skirmishes, 185. *See also* Mississippi

Cornish, John Hamilton: at wedding anniversary, 28, 29; identified, 28; mentioned, 28, 29

Cotchett, W. D.: identified, 567n; wounded, 567

Cotton: bought as security for loans, 311n; burning of, 232, 303, 309, 311, 311n, 319; confiscated, 118; crops reduced, 144; damage to, 232, 239-240; grown by Edmondstons, 14; losses of, suffered, 232; problems with, 372; speculation in, 309, 311; weighing of in Halifax, 320

Cotton cards: cost and manufacture of, 121, 121n

Cotton cloth: manufactured, 673n

Cotton fleet: 341

Cotton Plant: capture of, discussed, 289, 290; is steamer, xxxviii

Cowles, W. H. H.: identified, 211n; repulses Federals at Winton, 211-212

Craven County: gunboat captured in, 311, 311n

Crisswell, Mr.: receives bequest, 491; ward nurse in Richmond, 490, 491

Cristie, Mr. and Mrs.: banished, 600

Crittenden, John Jordan: criticized, 42; identified, 42n; mentioned, 53

Crittenden Compromise: 36n, 42n

Cromwell, Oliver: his bones disinterred, 225, 225n

Crook, George: mentioned, 577, 584; sketch of, 751

Crossan, Thomas M.: captain of *Advance*, 519, 519n

Crumpler, Thomas Newton: identified, 432n; killed, 432, 432n

Crump's Mill: Federal troops at, 444

Crutchfield, Stapleton: wounded at Chan-

cellorsville, 389, 389n

Cumbo, Henry: his role in escape of slaves, 528; mentioned, 529, 530, 533, 536

Curles Neck: Federal troops retreat to, 207; location of, 205n

Curlew: captures ship, 91

Currency: depreciation of, 376, 378, 378n, 401, 668, 720; inflation of, 507; reduction of, 545; treasury notes as legal tender, 370. *See also* Money

Currency Bill: criticisms of, 532

Currie, John: reports Federal raid, 292

Currie, Samantha: Catherine Edmondston visits, 261; hires Catherine Jackson, 282; mentioned, 91, 231, 277, 278, 300, 317, 472, 579

Curtin, Andrew Gregg: calls out militia, 414; identified, 412n, 539n; quoted, 593; seeks protection for Penn., 412

Curtis, John Henry: identified, 665n

Curtis, Mosley Ashley: identified, 665n; reference to, 665

Curtis, Samuel Ryan: sketch of, 751

Cushing, William B.: pictured, 629; sinks *Albemarle*, 628-630, 628n

Custer, George Armstrong: criticized, 627; sketch of, 751

D

Dahlgren, John Adolphus Bernard: mentioned, 431, 454, 537n, 538; sketch of, 751

Dahlgren, Ulric: identified, 537n; killed, 537, 537n; mentioned, 536, 538, 542; sketch of, 751

Dahlgren Papers: reference to, 537n

Daily Confederate (Raleigh): publishers of, 561n; quotes telegrams, 561

Daily Journal (Wilmington): editor of, 558n

Daily Standard (Raleigh): cited, 702n

Dam No. 5: cut, 99n; location of, 99

Daniel, Junius: aids refugees, 401; at Kinston, 319; brigade of, 371, 451; cites Cary Whitaker for bravery, 433n; killed, 562, 570; mentioned, 318; sketch of, 752

Daniel-Grimes Brigade: 496n

Darling, Fort: location of, 178n

Daughtrey, George L.: is Conneconara overseer, 124n; mentioned, 124, 296

Daughtry, George: death of, 295, 296; reports attack on Hamilton, 210

Daves, Elizabeth Batchelor Graham: wife of John Pugh Daves, 173n

W

CPSIA information can be obtained
at www.ICGtesting.com
Printed in the USA
LVHW061627210723
753015LV00007B/541